PRENTICE HALL
WORLD HISTORY

CONNECTIONS TO TODAY
THE MODERN ERA

Elisabeth Gaynor Ellis
Anthony Esler

With Senior Consultant
Burton F. Beers

PEARSON
Prentice Hall

Upper Saddle River, New Jersey
Needham, Massachusetts

Acknowledgments and illustration credits begin on page 774, which constitutes an extension of this copyright page.

ISBN 0-13-181759-0

2 3 4 5 6 7 8 9 10   08 07 06 05 04

Authors

Elisabeth Gaynor Ellis

Elisabeth Gaynor Ellis is a historian and writer. She is a co-author of *World Cultures: A Global Mosaic.* Ms. Ellis, a former social studies teacher and school administrator, has taught world cultures, Russian studies, and European history. She holds a B.A. from Smith College and an M.A. and M.S. from Columbia University.

Anthony Esler

Anthony Esler is Professor of History at the College of William and Mary. He received his Ph.D. from Duke University and received Fulbright Fellowships to study at the University of London and to travel to Ivory Coast and Tanzania. Dr. Esler's books include *The Human Venture: A World History* and *The Western World: A History,* as well as several historical novels.

Senior Consultant
Burton F. Beers

Burton F. Beers is a retired Professor of History from North Carolina State University. He taught European history, Asian history, and American history. Dr. Beers has published numerous articles in historical journals and several books, including *The Far East: A History of Western Impacts and Eastern Responses,* with Paul H. Clyde, and *World History: Patterns of Civilization.*

PROGRAM REVIEWERS

ACADEMIC CONSULTANTS
Africa
Abraham Kuranga
Department of History
Cincinnati State, Technical
  and Community College
Cincinnati, Ohio

Ancient World
Maud Gleason
Department of Classics
Stanford University
Palo Alto, California

Chicano/a Studies
Shirlene Soto
California State University
Northridge, California

East Asia
Burton F. Beers
Department of History (retired)
North Carolina State University
Raleigh, North Carolina

Economics
Richard Roehl
Department of Economics
University of Michigan
Dearborn, Michigan

Richard Sylla
Department of Economics
Stern School of Business
New York University
New York, New York

Medieval Europe
Kathryn Reyerson
Department of History
University of Minnesota
Minneapolis, Minnesota

Modern Europe
Douglas Skopp
Distinguished University Teaching
  Professor of History
State University of New York
Plattsburgh, New York

Religion
William L. Pitts, Jr.
Department of Religion
Baylor University
Waco, Texas

Benjamin Ravid
Department of Near Eastern
  and Judaic Studies
Brandeis University
Waltham, Massachusetts

Michael Sells
Department of Religion
Haverford College
Haverford, Pennsylvania

Thomas Smith
Department of Religious Studies
Loyola University New Orleans
New Orleans, Louisiana

South Asia
David Gilmartin
Department of History
North Carolina State University
Raleigh, North Carolina

Susan Wadley
Department of Anthropology
Syracuse University
Syracuse, New York

Southwest Asia
Linda T. Darling
Department of History
University of Arizona
Tucson, Arizona

Women's History
Lyn Reese
Women in World History Curriculum
Berkeley, California

CONTENT REVIEWERS
David Beaulieu
Former State Human Rights Commissioner
St. Paul, Minnesota

Samuel Chu
Department of History
The Ohio State University
Columbus, Ohio

Susan Douglass
Educational Consultant
Falls Church, Virginia

Shabbir Mansuri
Founding Director, Council on Islamic
  Education
Fountain Valley, California

José Morales
Chair and Assistant Professor, Latin
  American, Caribbean, and Latino
  Studies Program
New Jersey City University
Jersey City, New Jersey

Mark Peterson
Coordinator of Asian Studies
Brigham Young University
Provo, Utah

Charlotte Stokes
Supervisor of Social Studies, K–12
Prince Georges County Public Schools
Prince Georges County, Maryland

Part I   **Early Civilizations.** **2**
    1 Toward Civilization (Prehistory–3000 B.C.) 2
    2 First Civilizations: Africa and Asia (3200 B.C.–500 B.C.) 4
    3 Early Civilizations in India and China (2500 B.C.–256 B.C.) . . . 6

Part II   **Empires of the Ancient World.** **8**
    1 Empires of India and China (600 B.C.–A.D. 550) 8
    2 Ancient Greece (1750 B.C.–133 B.C.) 10
    3 Ancient Rome and the Rise of Christianity
      (509 B.C.–A.D. 476) 12
    4 Civilizations of the Americas (1400 B.C.–A.D. 1570) 14

Part III   **Regional Civilizations.** **16**
    1 The Rise of Europe (500–1300). 16
    2 The High Middle Ages (1050–1450) 18
    3 The Byzantine Empire and Russia (330–1613). 20
    4 The Muslim World (622–1629) 22
    5 Kingdoms and Trading States of Africa
      (750 B.C.–A.D. 1586) 24
    6 Spread of Civilizations in East Asia (500–1650) 26

Stone Age cave painting

Indian statue

Start Smart

Before you start your study of World History, check out these special pages.

▶ **Focus on Themes** xxviii
Use themes to organize your understanding
of world history.

▶ **Skills Handbook** xxix
Build, practice, and apply key social studies skills.

Stained-glass window

PREPARE TO READ **30**

Chapter 1 **The Renaissance and Reformation** (1300–1650) . . . **32**
1 The Renaissance in Italy 34
2 The Renaissance Moves North 40
 Exploring the Human Drama: Shakespeare's World
 of Drama 42
3 The Protestant Reformation 44
 Assessing Your Skills: What Is the Goal of Education? 47
4 Reformation Ideas Spread 49
5 The Scientific Revolution 54

Chapter 2 **The First Global Age: Europe and Asia**
(1415–1796) **60**
1 The Search for Spices 62
2 Diverse Traditions of Southeast Asia 67
3 European Footholds in Southeast Asia and India . . . 71
 Exploring the Human Drama: Cyclone Rips
 Through Calcutta 73
4 Encounters in East Asia 75
 Assessing Your Skills: Letter From the Celestial Emperor
 to the "Barbarian" King 77

Chapter 3 **The First Global Age: Europe, the Americas,
and Africa** (1492–1750) **82**
1 Conquest in the Americas 84
2 Spanish and Portuguese Colonies in the Americas 87
 Exploring the Human Drama: Southwestern Architecture:
 A Blending of Cultures 90
3 Struggle for North America 92
4 Turbulent Centuries in Africa 96
5 Changes in Europe 101
 Assessing Your Skills: The Commercial Revolution 103

Chapter 4 **The Age of Absolutism** (1550–1800) **108**
1 Extending Spanish Power 110
2 France Under Louis XIV 114
 Exploring the Human Drama: Living at Versailles 117
3 Triumph of Parliament in England 119
 Assessing Your Skills: The Struggle Between King
 and Parliament 123
4 Rise of Austria and Prussia 125
5 Absolute Monarchy in Russia 129

Test Preparation **136**

*Italian artist
Leonardo da Vinci*

Ocean-going ship

*Catherine the Great,
empress of Russia*

Unit 2 ENLIGHTENMENT AND REVOLUTION 138
1707–1850

PREPARE TO READ 140

Chapter 5 The Enlightenment and the American Revolution (1707–1800) **142**
  1 Philosophy in the Age of Reason 144
    Assessing Your Skills: What Limits Should There Be on Freedom of Speech? 146
  2 Enlightenment Ideas Spread 149
    Exploring the Human Drama: The Great Mozart 152
  3 Britain at Mid-Century 154
  4 Birth of the American Republic 158

*American statesman
Benjamin Franklin*

Chapter 6 The French Revolution and Napoleon (1789–1815) **164**
  1 On the Eve of Revolution 166
  2 Creating a New France 171
  3 Radical Days 176
    Assessing Your Skills: Execution of a King 177
  4 The Age of Napoleon Begins 182
  5 The End of an Era 186
    Exploring the Human Drama: Napoleon's Retreat From Moscow 189

Early steam engine

Chapter 7 The Industrial Revolution Begins (1750–1850) . . . **194**
  1 Dawn of the Industrial Age 196
  2 Britain Leads the Way 199
    Assessing Your Skills: Impact of the Railroad 201
  3 Hardships of Early Industrial Life 203
    Exploring the Human Drama: Spinning Thread in a Textile Mill 205
  4 New Ways of Thinking 208

Chapter 8 Revolutions in Europe and Latin America (1790–1848) **214**
  1 An Age of Ideologies 216
  2 Revolutions of 1830 and 1848 219
    Exploring the Human Drama: Art and Revolution 221
  3 Latin American Wars of Independence 225
    Assessing Your Skills: Toussaint L'Ouverture on Slavery 227

Test Preparation **234**

*South American liberator
Símon Bolívar*

Unit 3 INDUSTRIALISM AND A NEW GLOBAL AGE 1800–1914 236

PREPARE TO READ 238

Paris, France, in 1900

Chapter 9 Life in the Industrial Age (1800–1914) **240**
  1 The Industrial Revolution Spreads 242
    Assessing Your Skills: Is Technology a Blessing
    or a Curse? 245
  2 The World of Cities 249
  3 Changing Attitudes and Values 253
    Exploring the Human Drama: Sipping Tea
    in a Victorian Parlor. 255
  4 A New Culture 260

Chapter 10 Nationalism Triumphs in Europe (1800–1914) . . . **266**
  1 Building a German Nation. 268
    Assessing Your Skills: Crowning the German Emperor. . . . 270
  2 Strengthening Germany 272
  3 Unifying Italy 275
  4 Nationalism Threatens Old Empires 279
  5 Russia: Reform and Reaction 282
    Exploring the Human Drama: Russian Ballet. 285

German laborer

Chapter 11 Growth of Western Democracies
  (1815–1914) **290**
  1 Britain Becomes More Democratic 292
  2 A Century of Reform. 295
    Exploring the Human Drama: Famine Devastates
    Ireland. 299
  3 Division and Democracy in France. 301
  4 Expansion of the United States 306
    Assessing Your Skills: The Growth
    of American Suffrage 308

Chapter 12 The New Imperialism (1800–1914) **314**
   1 A Western-Dominated World 316
   2 The Partition of Africa 319
      ☑ **Assessing Your Skills: A Schoolroom in East Africa** 323
   3 European Challenges to the Muslim World 325
   4 The British Take Over India 329
   5 China and the New Imperialism 333
      ◈ **Exploring the Human Drama: Meeting the Emperor** 335

West African throne

Chapter 13 New Global Patterns (1800–1914) **340**
   1 Japan Modernizes 342
      ☑ **Assessing Your Skills: Industrialization in Japan** 344
   2 Southeast Asia and the Pacific 348
   3 Self-Rule for Canada, Australia, and New Zealand 351
   4 Economic Imperialism in Latin America 356
   5 Impact of Imperialism 361
      ◈ **Exploring the Human Drama: The Influence
      of African Art on Picasso** 364

Test Preparation **368**

Japanese textile workers

Unit 4 WORLD WARS AND REVOLUTIONS 370
1910–1955

PREPARE TO READ 372

Chapter 14 World War I and Its Aftermath (1914–1919) 374
1 The Stage Is Set. 376
   Assessing Your Skills: Is War Ever Justified? 377
2 The Guns of August 380
3 A New Kind of Conflict 383
   Exploring the Human Drama: Caring for the Wounded . . . 384
4 Winning the War 388
5 Making the Peace 392

Soldier in World War I

Chapter 15 Revolution in Russia (1917–1939) 398
1 Two Revolutions in Russia. 400
2 From Lenin to Stalin. 405
   Assessing Your Skills: Collectivization 409
3 Life in a Totalitarian State 411
   Exploring the Human Drama: A Revolution
   in Filmmaking 414

Chapter 16 Nationalism and Revolution Around
the World (1910–1939) 418
1 Struggle for Change in Latin America 420
   Assessing Your Skills: Remembering the Revolution 421
2 Nationalist Movements in Africa and the Middle East. . . . 424
3 India Seeks Self-Rule. 429
4 Upheavals in China. 432
5 Empire of the Rising Sun. 436
   Exploring the Human Drama: The Tokyo Earthquake
   of 1923 438

Mexican mural by Diego Rivera

Chapter 17 Crisis of Democracy in the West (1919–1939) **. . . 442**

   1 The Western Democracies 444

   2 A Culture in Conflict 450

        🌐 *Exploring the Human Drama: Jazz!* 453

   3 Fascism in Italy. 455

        ✅ *Assessing Your Skills: Totalitarianism* 457

   4 Hitler and the Rise of Nazi Germany 459

Chapter 18 World War II and Its Aftermath (1931–1955) **. . . 466**

   1 Aggression, Appeasement, and War 468

   2 The Global Conflict: Axis Advances 473

        🌐 *Exploring the Human Drama: Surviving the Blitz* 475

   3 The Global Conflict: Allied Successes. 479

        ✅ *Assessing Your Skills: The Holocaust* 481

   4 Toward Victory 485

   5 From World War to Cold War 489

Test Preparation **496**

1920s "flapper"

World War II battlefield

Unit 5 THE WORLD TODAY 498
1945–Present

PREPARE TO READ 500

Chapter 19 The World Since 1945: An Overview (1945–Present) 502
  1 The Changing Political Climate 504
  2 Global Economic Trends 510
    Assessing Your Skills: What Is the Relationship
    Between People and the Environment? 514
  3 Changing Patterns of Life 516
    Exploring the Human Drama: Computers and the Arts . . 519

Chapter 20 Europe and North America (1945–Present) 524
  1 The Western World: An Overview 526
    Assessing Your Skills: The European Union 529
  2 The Western European Democracies 532
  3 North American Prosperity 537
  4 The Soviet Union: Rise and Fall of a Superpower 541
    Exploring the Human Drama: Meltdown at Chernobyl . . . 543
  5 A New Era in Eastern Europe 547

Chapter 21 East Asia and Southeast Asia (1945–Present) 554
  1 Japan Becomes an Economic Superpower 556
  2 From Revolution to Reform in China 560
    Exploring the Human Drama: Helping Protesters
    in Tiananmen Square 564
  3 The Asian Tigers 566
    Assessing Your Skills: War Refugees in Korea 569
  4 Southeast Asia and the Pacific Rim 571

Chapter 22 South Asia and the Middle East (1945–Present) . . 578
  1 Nations of South Asia 580
  2 Forces Shaping the Modern Middle East 586
    Assessing Your Skills: Water Scarcity
    in the Middle East 589
  3 Nation Building in the Middle East: Three Case Studies . . . 592
    Exploring the Human Drama:
    Naguib Mahfouz: Views of Egypt 595
  4 The Middle East and the World 597

First moon landing

Fall of the Berlin Wall

Chapter 23 Africa (1945–Present) **604**
   1 Achieving Independence 606
       🔘 *Assessing Your Skills: Ghana Wins Independence* 608
   2 Programs for Development 612
   3 Three Nations: A Closer Look 618
   4 Struggles in Southern Africa 622
       🔊 *Exploring the Human Drama: Reporting on*
       the Election in South Africa 625

Chapter 24 Latin America (1945–Present) **630**
   1 Forces Shaping Modern Latin America 632
   2 Latin America, the United States, and the World 638
   3 Mexico, Central America, and the Caribbean 642
       🔊 *Exploring the Human Drama: Hurricane Strikes!* 645
   4 Focus on Argentina and Brazil 648
       🔘 *Assessing Your Skills: Helping the Street Children*
       of Brazil 652

Namibian independence celebration

Test Preparation **656**

Unit 6 Case Studies on Contemporary Issues
   Case Study Project Overview **660**
   1 Russia and Germany: After Communism 666
   2 Ukraine and Yugoslavia: The Resurgence of Nationalism . . . 670
   3 Japan and Mexico: The Path to Prosperity 674
   4 Argentina and South Africa: The Road to Democracy 678
   5 The Czech Republic and South Korea: Democracy and
      Economic Development 682
   6 Women in National Development: Bangladesh
      and Norway 686
   7 Civil Participation: Australia and the United States 690

REFERENCE SECTION **694**

Primary Sources and Literature **695**

World Atlas **722**

Glossary **734**

Spanish Glossary **742**

Index **751**

Credits **774**

SPECIAL FEATURES

Assessing Your Skills

 Synthesizing Information

Gather clues from different sources to understand key ideas.

The Commercial Revolution 103
The Struggle Between King
   and Parliament 123
Impact of the Railroad 201
The Growth of American
   Suffrage 308
Industrialization in Japan 344
Collectivization 409
Totalitarianism 457
The European Union 529
Water Scarcity in the Middle East . . .589

 Comparing Viewpoints

Explore issues by analyzing opinions across time and place.

What Is the Goal of Education? 47
What Limits Should There Be on
   Freedom of Speech? 146
Is Technology a Blessing
   or a Curse? .245
Is War Ever Justified? 377
What Is the Relationship Between
   People and the Environment? 514

 Analyzing Primary Sources

Gain insights by examining documents and photographs.

Letter From the Celestial Emperor
   to the "Barbarian" King 77
Execution of a King 177
Toussaint L'Ouverture on Slavery 227
Crowning the German Emperor 270
A Schoolroom in East Africa 323
Remembering the Revolution 421
The Holocaust 481
War Refugees in Korea 569
Ghana Wins Independence 608
Helping the Street Children of Brazil .652

Exploring the Human Drama

 Humanities Link

Experience great literature and arts from around the world.

Shakespeare's World of Drama 42
Southwestern Architecture:
   A Blending of Cultures 90
The Great Mozart 152
Art and Revolution 221
Russian Ballet 285
The Influence of African Art
   on Picasso .364
A Revolution in Filmmaking 414
Jazz! 453
Computers and the Arts 519
Naguib Mahfouz: Views of Egypt 595

 Disaster!

See how major disasters affected people's lives.

Cyclone Rips Through Calcutta 73
Napoleon's Retreat From Moscow . . .189
Famine Devastates Ireland 298
The Tokyo Earthquake of 1923 438
Meltdown at Chernobyl 543
Hurricane Strikes! 645

 You Are There . . .

Travel back in time to become an eyewitness to history.

Living at Versailles 117
Spinning Thread in a Textile Mill 205
Sipping Tea in a Victorian Parlor 255
Meeting the Emperor 335
Caring for the Wounded 384
Surviving the Blitz 475
Helping Protesters
   in Tiananmen Square 564
Reporting on the Election
   in South Africa 625

Taos Pueblo, New Mexico

Virtual Field Trip

Start an Internet activity by visiting sites around the world.

A Masterpiece by Michelangelo 38
Khmer Temple 68
Conquistadors in Mexico 85
A Victory for Parliament 121
Enlightenment Painters 151
The Tennis Court Oath 169
Forging the Anchor 204
San Martín Crossing the Andes 230
Impressionism 262
The Hapsburg Empire 280
New Immigrants to the United States 310
Livingstone and Victoria Falls 320

A Railway in Japan 346
Allied Push Toward Victory 390
Socialist Realism 413
Defying British Law 431
A Masterpiece of Modern Art 451
Pearl Harbor 478
The Space Age 520
Fall of the Berlin Wall 535
Indonesian Textiles 575
A Diverse City 587
Freedom for Namibia 626
Central American Street Scene 646

San Martín and O'Higgins cross the Andes, 1817

SPECIAL FEATURES

Biography

Meet fascinating history makers.

Indira Gandhi

Martin Luther 46
Elizabeth I 50
Henry the Navigator 63
Trung Sisters 70
Samuel de Champlain . . .92

King Affonso 98
Cardinal Armand
   Richelieu 115
Maria Theresa 127
Montesquieu 145
George Washington . . .161
Maximilien Robespierre 178
Napoleon 186
Prince Clemens von
   Metternich 191
James Watt 198
Adam Smith 208
Louis Kossuth 223
Florence Nightingale . . .250
Ludwig van
   Beethoven 260
Otto von Bismarck 273

Peter Stolypin 287
Emmeline Pankhurst . . .298
Abraham Lincoln 309
Menelik II 324
Sun Yixian 337
José Rizal 350
Cecil Rhodes 362
Kaiser William II 379
Edith Cavell 389
V. I. Lenin 402
Joseph Stalin 406
Mohandas K. Gandhi . . .430
Hirohito 436
Marie Curie 450
Adolf Hitler 460
Haile Selassie 468
Erwin Rommel 486

Jacques Cousteau 515
Youssou N'Dour 521
Tony Blair 532
Dr. Martin Luther
   King, Jr. 539
Mikhail Gorbachev 544
Mao Zedong 561
Aung San Suu Kyi 574
Indira Gandhi 583
Gamal Abdel Nasser . . .594
Jomo Kenyatta 609
Bishop Desmond Tutu . .624
Fidel Castro 638
Jean-Bertrand
   Aristide 647

Geography and History

Investigate the connection between history and geography.

Piracy on the Seas 91
Being "Sent to
   Siberia" 131
The Battle of
   Waterloo 188
Europe's Canal Boom . .202
A Deadly, Microscopic
   Enemy 226
A "Living Laboratory" . .258

Russia's Long
   Iron Road 286
Conserving the
   Wilderness 311
British Railroads and
   Indian Nationalism . . .332
French Failure
   in Panama 360
Getting "Over There" . .391

A Land of Many
   Nations 400
Building New
   Settlements 428
The Maginot Line 448
Working on a Deadly
   Railroad 480
The Coldest Place
   on Earth 505

Offshore Oil Rigs 528
The Threat of Disease . .565
Afghan Refugees 584
Preserving Africa's
   Wildlife 614

Connections to Today

Explore links between historical events and your world today.

A Revolution in Communication . . .43
Guangzhou's International Trade . .76
The Banana Wars 104
Our Puritan Heritage 122
Virtual Salons 150
Knowing Left From Right 175
Day Care .210
Mexican Independence Day 229
When the Lights Go Out 244
A Van Gogh at Auction 263

Vatican City 278
Your Senior Years: Is Your
   Future Secure? 297
The Power of Oil 328
A Quandary for Quebec 351
A New Balkan Powder Keg? 380
The Russian Orthodox Church 412
Rekindling Hope in
   South Africa 425
Going to the Movies 452

Rationing and New Products 474
The Last Shreds of an Empire 504
Social Security 538
Taiwan: Rebel Province or
   Independent State? 566
A People Without a Nation 586
A New Name for a Nation 620
The China-Panama Connection . .644

SPECIAL FEATURES/PRIMARY SOURCES

Global *Connections*

See connections between events in different parts of the world.

Witch Hunt in Salem 52
The Jesuits in Asia 79
Europe's Sweet Tooth . .101
Cartloads of Silver
  and Gold 110
American *Philosophe* . .149
American Revolution and

French Revolution 172
Freedom for Enslaved
  Americans 284
Aid for Ireland 300
"Thank God for Tea!" . .329
The Russo-Japanese
  War 347

The Monroe Doctrine
  in Action 359
Authoritarian Rule
  in Eastern Europe 458
Fighting and Writing
  in Spain 470
Endangered Languages 516

The Enduring Impact of
  Pope John Paul II 548
The Scars of War 627
Cutting Down Lives? . . .640

Did You Know?

Find out something new or unusual about history.

A Renaissance Body
  Snatcher 57
The Death of the
  Dodo 72
A High-Maintenance
  King 116

The Real Robinson
  Crusoe 153
The Origin of
  Madame Tussaud's
  Wax Museum 176
How Banquets Helped

Spark a Revolution . . .220
The Proper Victorians . .254
Mutiny on the *Bounty* . .355
The Christmas Truce . . .383
A Hard Man to Kill 401
Mussolini's Plaster

Rome 456
The Berlin Airlift 493
The People's Car 534
Life in Singapore 567
Israel's Citizen Army . . .597
Escape From Cuba 639

Primary Source

Relive history through eyewitness accounts, literature, and documents.

Giorgio Vasari, *Lives of the Most Eminent
  Italian Painters, Sculptors, and Architects* 37
John Calvin, *On the Christian Life* 48
Journal of Antonio Pigafetta 66
*The Commentaries of the Great
  Afonso de Albuquerque* 71
Bartolomé de las Casas, *Short Description
  of the Destruction of the Indies* 88
William Bradford, *Of Plymouth Plantation:
  1620–1647* 93
Thomas Hobbes, *Leviathan* 120
Catherine the Great, *Memoirs* 133
Diderot, *Encyclopedia, or Classified Dictionary
  of the Sciences, Arts, and Occupations* 147
Declaration of Independence 159
O. Browning, *Dispatches from Paris* 168
"La Marseillaise" 181
Isabella Beeton, *Beeton's Book of Household
  Management* 207
Karl Marx and Friedrich Engels, *The Communist
  Manifesto* 211
George Gordon, Lord Byron,
  "On This Day I Complete My Thirty-Sixth Year" 218
Guglielmo Marconi, quoted in
  Scrapbook, 1900–1914 247
Elizabeth Cady Stanton, "The Solitude of Self" 256
Helmuth von Moltke, quoted in *Readings
  in European History* 271
Giuseppe Mazzini, *Life and Writings* 275
Thomas Paine, *Rights of Man* 292
Archibald Forbes, *Daily News* (London),
  May 26, 1871 303
Rudyard Kipling, "The White Man's Burden" 317

Kwangsi Bandit Group, quoted in *Chinese
  Civilization and Society* 334
John Standfield, quoted in *The Fatal Shore* 353
Gilbert Amado, *História da Minha Infância* 357
British soldier at Gallipoli 387
Harold Nicolson, *Peacemaking, 1919* 393
English eyewitness, *Russia Under the
  Bolshevik Regime* 404
Jomo Kenyatta, quoted in *A History
  of the African People* 424
Gao Xingzu, Wu Shimin, Hu Yungong, Cha Ruizhen,
  *Japanese Imperialism and the Massacre
  in Nanjing* 435
George Orwell, *The Road to Wigan Pier* 446
Sophie Yaari, quoted in *To Save a Life: Stories of
  Holocaust Rescue* 463
Werner Pluskat, quoted in *Nothing Less
  Than Victory* 484
Winston Churchill, speech of March 5, 1946 491
Charter of the United Nations 507
P. Houston, *Third World Women Speak Out* 518
Claudia Goldin, quoted in the *New York Times
  Magazine*, May 16, 1999 531
Robert G. Kaiser, *Russia From the Inside* 542
"The Art and Practice of Japanese Management" . .557
Vietnamese Declaration of Independence 571
Jawaharlal Nehru, "Tryst With Destiny" speech 580
David Grossman, *The Yellow Wind* 598
Kenneth Kaunda, speech, March 18, 1966 613
Ken Saro-Wiwa, unpublished remarks 619
Dom Hélder Câmara, *Revolution Through Peace* 637
Octavio Paz, *One Earth, Four or Five Worlds:
  Reflections on Contemporary History* 642

PRIMARY SOURCES

▶ Primary Sources and Literature

Niccolò Machiavelli, *Discourses* 696
Bernal Díaz, *The True History of the
  Conquest of New Spain* 697
King Affonso I, *Letter to King John of Portugal* 698
Miguel de Cervantes, *Don Quixote* 699
The English Bill of Rights 700
John Locke, *Two Treatises on Government* 701
Jean-Jacques Rousseau, *The Social Contract* 702
Declaration of the Rights of Man and the Citizen 703
Miguel Hidalgo, *Decree of Hidalgo* 704
Simón Bolívar, *Address to the
  Congress of Venezuela* 705
Charles Dickens, *Hard Times* 706
Fukuzawa Yukichi, *Autobiography* 707
Erich Maria Remarque, *All Quiet
  on the Western Front* 708
Mohandas Gandhi, *Hind Swaraj* 709
Franklin D. Roosevelt, *The Four Freedoms* 710
The Universal Declaration of Human Rights 711
Mao Zedong, *The People's Democratic Dictatorship* .712
Chinua Achebe, *Things Fall Apart* 713
Kwame Nkrumah, *Autobiography* 714
Lech Walesa, *Nobel Peace Prize Lecture* 715
Mikhail Gorbachev, *Perestroika* 716
Vaclav Havel, *New Year's Address* 717
Mario Vargas Llosa, *Latin America,
  the Democratic Option* 718
Aung San Suu Kyi, *Freedom From Fear* 719
Nelson Mandela, *Glory and Hope* 720
Harry Wu, *The Outlook for China, Human Rights* 721

PRIMARY SOURCES: In Text

Michelangelo, *Poems* 38
Niccolò Machiavelli, *The Prince* 39
Martin Luther, Speech Before the Diet of Worms 45
Alexander Pope, *Epitaphs* .56
Canons and Decrees of the Holy Council of Trent 59
The Glass Palace Chronicle of the Kings of Burma . . .67
Pak Chi-won, "The Story of Ho" 78
The Log of Christopher Columbus 81
Portuguese settler, quoted in *Latin America:
  A Concise Interpretive History* 91
Mayflower Compact 93
Olaudah Equiano, *The Life of Gustavus Vassa* 98
Olaudah Equiano, *The Life of Gustavus Vassa* 107
Louis XIV, quoted in *From Absolutism to Revolution* . .115
John Evelyn, *Diary* 122
Jacob von Grimmelshausen, *Simplicissimus* 126
Frederick William, quoted in
  The Heritage of World Civilizations 128
Alexander Pushkin, *The Bronze Horseman* 131
Archbishop François de Fénelon, *Letters* 135
Alexander Pope, *Essay on Man* 144
Thomas Paine, *Common Sense* 158
Voltaire, *Philosophical Dictionary* 163
Arthur Young, *Travels in France During the Years
  1787–1789* 168
*Proclamation of the National Convention,
  August 23, 1793* 178
Maximilien Robespierre, quoted in
  Pageant of Europe 179
Memoirs of Philippe Paul de Ségur 188

(continued)

Middle Eastern market

(continued)

Captain J. Kincaid, *Adventures in the Rifle Brigade* . .193

J. P. Kay, quoted in *Mill Life at Styal* 203

William Godwin, "Political Justice" 210

"A Working Day," in *Labour and the Poor
in England and Wales, 1849–1851* 213

Memoirs of Prince Metternich 216

Simón Bolívar, "Letter From Jamaica" 233

J. H. Bridge, *History of the Carnegie Steel
Company* 242

Émile Zola, *Germinal* 247

Times (London), quoted in
Crises in English History, 1066–1945 251

Anna Mazzoni, *La Liberazione della Donna* 253

William Wordsworth, "It Is a Beauteous Evening,
Calm and Free" 260

Charles Dickens, *Oliver Twist* 262

John Hollingshead, "London Poor" 265

Otto von Bismarck, quoted in *Modern
and Contemporary European History* 268

Otto von Bismarck, quoted in *Economic
Development of Europe* 273

Kaiser William II, quoted in *Europe Since 1815* 274

W. B. Brooke, quoted in *Garibaldi:
Great Lives Observed* 277

Peter Kropotkin, *Memoirs of a Revolutionist* 282

Father George Gapon, quoted in *Revolution
From 1789 to 1906* 289

Benjamin Disraeli, *Sybil* 292

Constance Lytton, *Prisons and Prisoners* 295

Letter to the *Times* (London), December 24, 1846 . . .300

Georges Clemenceau, quoted in
Clemenceau and the Third Republic 301

Emma Lazarus, "The New Colossus" 306

Émile Zola, *Aurore,* January 13, 1898 313

Lord Lugard, *The Rise of Our East African Empire* . . .316

Chief Machemba, Letter to Herman von Wissman . . .319

Thomas Macaulay, quoted in *Sources
of Indian Tradition* 332

Liang Ch'i-ch'ao, *On the Harm of Not Reforming* 339

Ii Naosuke, quoted in *Selected Documents
on Japanese Foreign Policy* 342

Matthew Everingham, quoted in
"Children of the First Fleet," *National Geographic* . .354

Rudyard Kipling, "The Ballad of East and West" 361

Benito Juárez, *Notes for My Children* 367

Barbara Tuchman, *The Guns of August* 382

Richard H. Davis, *With the French in France
and Salonika* 383

William Pressey, quoted in *People at War
1914–1918* 386

Siegfried Sassoon, "Suicide in the Trenches" 388

Ernst Lissauer, "Hymn of Hate" 389

Sergyei N. Kurnakov, *Savage Squadrons* 397

V. I. Lenin, quoted in *The Russian Revolution, 1917* . .402

Maxim Gorky, "Days With Lenin" 404

Soviet army officer, quoted in *Stalin:
A Political Biography* 408

Anna Akhmatova, "Requiem" 415

Eugene Lyons, *Assignment in Utopia* 417

Arab pledge, quoted in *Arab Nationalism:
An Anthology* 427

Mao Zedong, "On the Tactics of Fighting
Japanese Imperialism" 435

The Way of Subjects, quoted in *Human Record:
Sources of Global History* 439

*Manifesto of the Second Pan-African
Congress* 441

Erich Maria Remarque, *All Quiet
on the Western Front* 444

William Butler Yeats, "The Second Coming" 450

"Go, wondrous creature! mount where Science guides;
Go, measure earth, weight air, and state the tides;
Instruct the planets in what orbs to run,
Correct old Time, and regulate the sun."
—Alexander Pope, *Essay on Man*

Adolf Hitler, *My New Order* .462

Martin Niemoller, quoted in *Time* magazine 462

Gaetano Salvemini, *The Fascist Dictatorship
in Italy* 465

W. H. Auden, "In Memory of W. B. Yeats" 472

Winston Churchill, radio address, June 4, 1940 474

British World War II song 482

Douglas Williams, "Dunkirk: May 28–June 4, 1940" . .495

Julius K. Nyerere, *Freedom and Development* 504

Nguyen Sa, "No Time" 523

Simone de Beauvoir, *The Second Sex* 531

New York Herald Tribune, May 3, 1945 534

John F. Kennedy, Inaugural Address 537

"Liberal Leaders Warn Yeltsin to Protect His
People," Reuters Information Service 553

Lu Ting-yi, speech delivered May 26, 1956 561

Haing Ngor, *A Cambodian Odyssey* 573

*Voices From the Whirlwind: An Oral History
of the Chinese Revolution* .577

Indian National Constitution .580

Declarations of the Ayatollah Khomeini 592

First Book of Maccabees 597

The Palestinian National Charter, Article 1 597

Zade Teherani, quoted in *Inside Iran* 603

Ngugi wa Thiong'o, *A Grain of Wheat* 606

John Pepper Clark, "The Casualties" 618

Catherine Bertini, speech delivered
February 19, 1998 629

Carolina Maria de Jesus, *Child of the Dark* 632

Pope John Paul II in Nicaragua, Reuters
Information Service 655

MAPS

CHAPTER MAPS

Artists of the Renaissance 33
Renaissance Italy, 1505 35
Major European Religions About 1600 51
Trade Between Europe, Africa, and Asia About 1700 ..61
Early Voyages of European Exploration, 1487–1609 ...64
Empires and Kingdoms of Southeast Asia 69
Land Claims in the Americas and Africa, 1675 83
Land Claims in the Americas About 1700 94
Triangular Trade 99
European Nation-States, 1700 109
The Wars of Philip II, 1571–1588 112
Europe After the Thirty Years' War 126
Expansion of Russia, 1689–1796 130
Partitions of Poland, 1701–1795 135
North America, 1783 143
United Kingdom of Great Britain 155
The American Revolution in the East 160
Revolutionary France at War, 1793 165
Napoleon's Power in Europe, 1812 184
Europe After the Congress of Vienna, 1815 190
Major Centers of Industry in Great Britain, 1825 195
British Cotton Trade About 1850 200
Railways in Great Britain 201
Revolutions in Europe, 1815–1829 215
Revolutions in Europe, 1830 and 1848 222
Independent Nations of Latin America About 1844 ...228
Latin America About 1790 228
Industrial Growth, 1800–1900 241
Centers of Industry, 1871 243
United States 243
Unification in Europe, 1873 267
Unification of Germany, 1865–1871 269
Unification of Italy, 1858–1870 277
The Balkans, 1878 281
Western Democracies, 1900 291
The Siege of Paris, 1870 302
Expansion of the United States, 1783–1898 307
Imports From Africa and Asia About 1870 315
Imperialism in Africa to 1914 321
European Colonies in Africa About 1850 321
The Suez Canal, 1869 327
Imperialism in India to 1858 330
Imperialism in China to 1914 336
Imperialism in Asia, the Pacific,
  and the Americas, 1900 341
Imperialism in Southeast Asia and
  the Pacific, 1900 349
Canada, 1867–1914 352
Geography of Australia and New Zealand 354
Imperialism in the Caribbean and South America,
  1898–1917 358

The World at War, 1914–1918 375
European Alliances, 1914 378
Europe at War, 1914–1918 385
Europe, 1914 394
Europe, 1920 394
Russian Revolution and Civil War, 1917–1922 399
Soviet Union, 1917–1938 407
Major Nationalist Movements, 1910–1939 419
The Middle East, 1920s 427
Civil War in China, 1925–1935 434
Japan's Expanding Empire to 1934 437
Rise of Dictatorships in Europe, 1917–1939 443
Major Battles of World War II, 1939–1945 467
Aggression in Europe to 1939 471
World War II in Europe and North Africa 483
World War II in the Pacific 487
Cold War in Europe 492
Divided Germany, 1945 492
The World Economy 503
The Great Liberation and the Cold War, 1945–1990 ..506
Political Map of Europe 525
European Union, 1957–2004 529
Migration to Western Europe 530
Radiation Levels 543
New Nations in Eastern Europe 550
Nations of the Pacific Rim 555
Korean War, 1950–1953 568
Vietnam War, 1968–1975 572
Independence in South Asia and the Middle East ...579
Partition of India, 1947 581
Water Resources in the Middle East 589
Arab-Israeli Conflict, 1948–2003 599
Ethnoreligious Groups in Iraq 600
African Independence 605
Desertification in Africa 615
Population Density of Latin America 631
Economic Activity in Argentina 649

REFERENCE SECTION MAPS

The World: Political 722
Africa: Political 724
Africa: Physical 725
Asia: Political 726
Asia: Physical 727
Europe: Political 728
Europe: Physical 729
North and South America: Political 730
North and South America: Physical 731
Australia and Oceania: Political-Physical 732
Map Projections: Robinson, Mercator, Interrupted ...733

CHARTS AND GRAPHS/SKILLS HANDBOOK

CHARTS AND GRAPHS

The Scientific Method .... .55
Tools of Ocean Navigation .... .65
Destinations of Enslaved Africans, 1500–1870 .... .99
First Five Voyages of the English East India Company 103
The Columbian Exchange .... .107
Land Ownership in Ireland .... .155
Separation of Powers .... .163
Population and Land Ownership in France, 1789 ..... .167
Reforms of the National Assembly .... .174
Napoleon's Troops in Russia .... .189
Travel Times to London .... .201
British Output of Coal, 1820–1850 .... .213
British Exports of Coal, 1820–1850 .... .213
Steel Production, 1880–1910 .... .265
Expansion of Suffrage in the United States .... .308
Sailing Distances to London .... .327
Investments by Industry in Meiji Japan .... .344
Standing Armies in Europe, 1914 .... .378
World War I Technology .... .386
Turning Points in Russia, 1914–1921 .... .403
Soviet Agricultural Output, 1928 and 1932 .... .409
Unemployment, 1928–1938 .... .465
Health Statistics of Selected Countries .... .513
Votes in the European Union Council .... .529
Women Working Outside the Home .... .553
Japanese Motor Vehicle Exports .... .558
World Crude Oil Production .... .588
Population Pyramids .... .629
Ethnic Diversity in Latin America .... .632
The Impact of Hurricane Mitch .... .645
Urbanization in Brazil .... .650

CAUSE AND EFFECT

Protestant Reformation .... .53
Columbian Exchange .... .105
The French Revolution .... .185
Independence Movements in Latin America .... .231
Industrial Revolution .... .252
New Imperialism .... .367
World War I .... .395
Worldwide Economic Depression .... .449
Collapse of the Soviet Union .... .546
Partition of India .... .585

THE COLUMBIAN EXCHANGE

From the Americas to Europe, Africa, and Asia

maize
potato
sweet potato
beans
peanut
squash
pumpkin
peppers
pineapple
tomato
cocoa

From Europe, Africa, and Asia to the Americas

wheat
sugar
banana
rice
grape (wine)
olive oil
dandelion
horse
pig
cow
goat
chicken
smallpox
typhus

FACT FINDER

Native American Population of Central Mexico ..... .86
The Rise of Napoleon .... .182
Average Life Expectancy in Selected Industrial
    Areas, 1850–1910 .... .249
Casualties of World War I .... .392
Effects of the Five-Year Plans .... .408
Casualties of World War II .... .490
Welfare-State Spending in Britain, 1975–1980 ...... .527
Soviet Domination of Eastern Europe .... .547

UNIT TIME LINES

Unit 1, 1300–1800 .... .30
Unit 2, 1725–1850 .... .140
Unit 3, 1800–1925 .... .238
Unit 4, 1910–1960 .... .372
Unit 5, 1940–2015 .... .500

SKILLS HANDBOOK

Contents xxix
Learning From Maps xxx
Understanding Charts and Graphs xxxii
Interpreting Visuals xxxiv
Analyzing Primary Sources xxxvi
Comparing Viewpoints xxxviii
Synthesizing Information xl
Analyzing Cause and Effect xlii
Asking Questions xliv
Problem Solving and Decision Making xlvi
Using the Internet xlviii

Use This Book to Succeed in World History

You can use this book as a tool to master world history. Spend a few minutes to become familiar with the structure of the book and see how you can unlock the secrets of world history.

Reading Focus	Vocabul
■ How did Napoleon rise to power?	plebiscite
■ How were revolutionary reforms changed under Napoleon?	annex
■ How did Napoleon build an empire in Europe?	blockade

Napoleon's Rise to Power

Napoleon Bonaparte was born in Corsica, a French-ruled island in the Mediterranean. His family were minor nobles, but had little money. At age nine, he was sent to France to be trained for a military career. When the revolution broke out, he was an ambitious 20-year-old lieutenant, eager to make a name for himself.

Napoleon favored the Jacobins and republican rule. However, he found the conflicting ideas and personalities of the revolution confusing. He wrote his brother in 1793: "Since one must take sides, one might as well choose the side that is victorious, the side which devastates, loots, and

Find What Is Important

This book makes it easy to figure out what you really need to know about world history. Each section starts with Reading Focus questions that point out the most important ideas in that section. As you read, notice that the content is organized into several parts with red headings. As you read the paragraphs under the red headings, you can learn the answers to the Reading Focus questions. Later, you will find that the Section Assessment reviews each of these important ideas.

Learn in Many Ways

Don't depend just on the main text. Discover world history through all parts of this book—from primary sources to pictures, from charts to activities. Preview each chapter by looking at photographs, a map, and a time line. See connections between main ideas and illustrations. Be transported back through time by reading primary sources. Read stories about real people who have changed the world. Witness grave disasters and relive great moments. Research exciting topics. Act out human dramas. Use all of your senses to explore world history.

Primary Source

The Genius of Leonardo
Italian artist and architect Giorgio Vasari is best known for his engaging book of biographies of Italian artists including Leonardo da Vinci (pictured above):

"Leonardo practiced not one art but all of those that are dependent upon design, and he had great talent for geometry besides being very musical, playing the lute with great ability and being excellent in the art of improvisation. . . . In entertaining, Leonardo was so pleasant that he won everyone's [heart]. . . . though he may well be [said] he owned nothing and to [work]ed little, he always kept [servant]s as well as horses."

—Giorgio Vasari, *Lives of the [Most] Eminent Italian Painters, [Sculptors, and Architects]*

[A]ssessment

[Primary] Source What [d]etails did Vasari include [about Leon]ardo da Vinci?

Disaster!

EXPLORING HUMAN DRAMA

CYCLONE RIPS THROUGH CALCUTTA

The storm surge—walls of water pushed by powerful winds—is the deadliest part of a cyclone. Waves start small, but as the

Violent winds and rain struck Calcutta. Breaking waves caused a deafening roar. Then, a monstrous 40-foot wave crashed down on the shore. According to some reports, as many as 300,000 people died and 20,000 boats sank.

Native American Population of Central Mexico

Source: Nicolás Sánchez-Albornoz, *The Population of Latin America*

Palace of Versailles

Portfolio Assessment

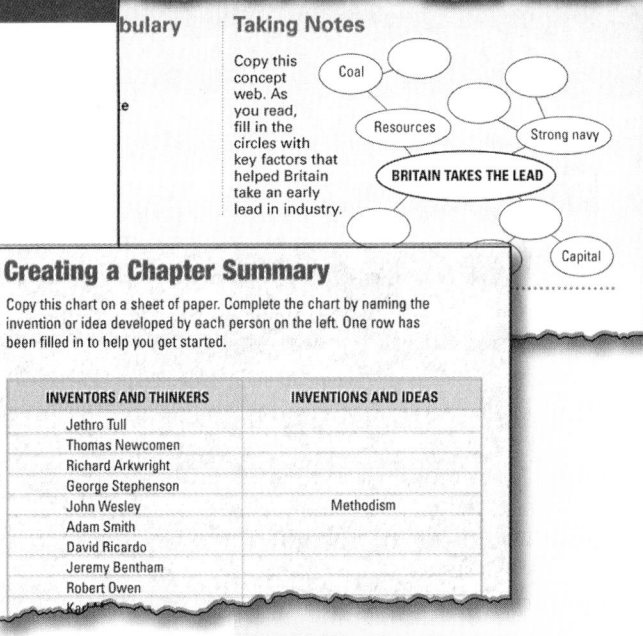

Organize Your Reading

Does so much world history content seem overwhelming? This book has ways to help you organize it. Use the Taking Notes exercise at the beginning of each section to help you take notes as you read. Then, at the end of the chapter, complete the Creating a Chapter Summary graphic organizer. This will help you capture the main ideas of the chapter in a visual way.

Develop Your Skills

Success in world history requires you to master social studies skills. Learn these skills in the Skills Handbook. Practice them by answering questions on maps, pictures, primary sources, charts, and graphs. In each chapter, you can also find an Assessing Your Skills feature, which focuses on analyzing primary sources, synthesizing information, or comparing viewpoints. Then, review your skills by completing the Skills Assessment activities at the end of every chapter.

Go online at PHSchool.com and discover a high-tech world of Internet resources. You can travel the globe on virtual field trips, learn through Internet activities, or prepare for exams with online self-tests. The resource center has primary sources, biographies, Web site links, and more. For news, data, and maps, link to Prentice Hall NewsTracker, *DK World Desk Reference*, or Infoplease.® And don't forget the interactive online textbook, where you will find animations, videos, and help with reading, homework, and tests.

For Internet activities, primary sources, current events, maps, and more, use **Web Code mmk-1000.**

Reading Informational Texts

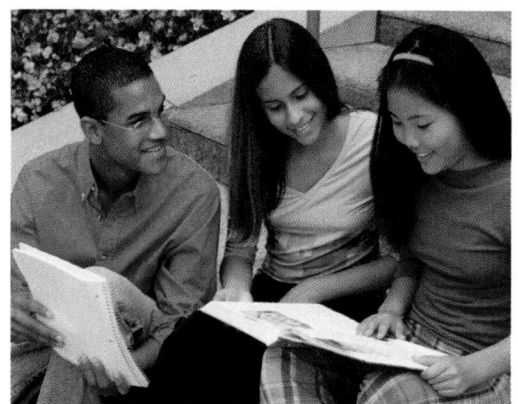

Reading and understanding the material in a textbook is not the same as reading a novel or magazine article for pleasure. The purpose of reading a textbook is to acquire information. You can use various strategies before, while, and after you read to increase your comprehension of the information in your textbook and other informational materials.

Previewing

Before you read, preview the text to get an idea of what you will be reading about. Previewing will give you an overview of the chapter or section, help you consider what you already know, and give you some idea of the author's purpose and point of view.

- Read the chapter or section title.
- Read introductory material such as focus questions, vocabulary, and main ideas.
- Scan the headings and subheadings.
- Look at photos, maps, and charts.
- Check highlighted words and definitions.
- Read the final paragraph or summary.
- Read the questions at the end of the section or chapter.

Reading Actively

As you read, actively interact with the author's words to determine the meanings of words, the main ideas, and the details that support the main ideas. Active readers become involved with the material that they are reading by thinking, questioning, challenging, and sometimes disagreeing with the author's ideas.

- Take notes as you read.
- Turn headings into questions and look for the answers.
- Recall related information that you have previously learned.
- Use context clues and word structure to determine word meanings.
- Distinguish between facts and opinions.
- Identify main ideas.
- Stop every so often and ask yourself, "Do I understand what I have read?"
- Reread difficult passages. If you still have questions about the content, get clarification from your teacher or a classmate.

Determining Organizational Patterns

While you are reading, notice how the text structure highlights connections and relationships among ideas. Here are some common organizational patterns and strategies that work well with them.

Classification The author divides a topic into parts according to common or shared characteristics. **Strategy:** Use a concept web such as the one below.

Sequence of Events The author organizes information in chronological order, or the order in which the events occur in time. **Strategy:** Use a flowchart or time line such as the one below.

Cause and Effect The author describes the relationship between events that have happened (effects) and the reasons they happened (causes). **Strategy:** Use a cause-and-effect chart such as the one below.

Compare and Contrast The author describes the similarities and differences between people, places, things, events, or ideas. **Strategy:** If more than two items are compared, use a matrix or table. If two items are compared, use a Venn diagram such as the one below.

Reviewing and Analyzing

After you finish reading, it is time to review, summarize, and think critically about what you have read.

- Review the headings and subheadings.
- Review the notes you took.
- Summarize the author's main ideas.

- Recognize the strengths and weaknesses of the author's logic and arguments.

Writing for Social Studies

Research shows that writing about what you read actually helps you learn and remember new content. Good writing skills are also important for doing well on tests. Here are some tips to guide you through your social studies writing assignments.

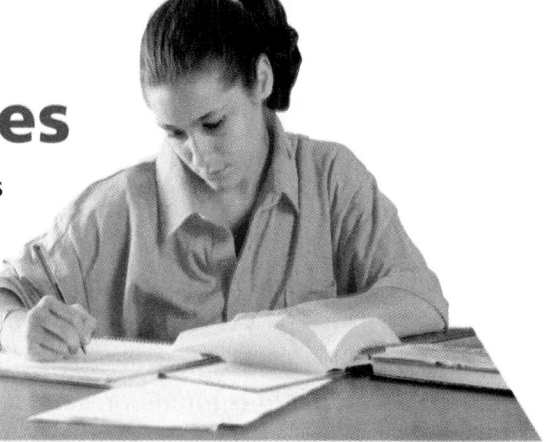

Expository Essays

An expository essay is one in which you explain something in detail.

Step 1: Identify and Narrow Your Topic
Your essay might focus on causes and effects or on problems and solutions.

Step 2: Gather and Organize Evidence
Jot down your ideas and supporting details. Then organize them in an outline or graphic organizer.

Step 3: Write a First Draft
Write a strong topic sentence, and then organize the body of your essay around your similarities and differences, causes and effects, or problems and solutions. Be sure to include details, facts, and examples.

Main idea —— Migration from Mexican farming villages is causing the population of Mexico City to grow. This is happening because the popula-

Details —— tion of Mexico is growing at one of the highest rates in the world. In rural villages there are not enough farming jobs for everyone.

Conclusion —— As a result, many rural families are moving from the countryside to live in Mexico City.

Step 4: Revise and Proof
Check spelling, sentence structure, and the logical flow of ideas. Be sure you've included transition words between sentences and paragraphs.

Persuasive Essays

A persuasive essay addresses a topic on which there are differing opinions or viewpoints.

Step 1: Select and Narrow Your Topic
Choose a topic that provokes disagreement. Decide on your point of view.

Step 2: Gather and Organize Evidence
Create a graphic organizer that states your position at the top and lists the arguments.

Step 3: Write a First Draft
Clearly state your position. Present arguments in favor of your position, and refute opposing arguments that could be used against your position.

Step 4: Revise and Proof
Check to make sure you have made a logical argument and that you have not oversimplified the argument.

Main idea —— It is vital to vote in elections. Voters have

Argument for —— a say in government by electing officials to run the government. Not every cam-

Argument against, refuted —— paign promise is kept, but most politicians do their best to follow the will of

Conclusion —— the majority. Therefore, every vote counts.

Writing Short Answers on Tests

On some tests, you may be given a choice of writing prompts, or assignments.

Step 1: Select a Writing Prompt and Budget Time

Choose a topic that interests you and that you know about. To budget time, allow about one quarter of your time to prepare to write, one half of your time to write a first draft, and the last quarter of your time to revise and edit.

Step 2: Analyze the Question or Assignment

Pay special attention to key words that indicate exactly what you are supposed to do. Examples of such words are *explain, compare, describe, argue,* and *summarize.*

Step 3: Gather and Organize Ideas

Divide your topic into subtopics. Jot down main ideas and supporting facts and details. Then organize them in an outline or graphic organizer.

Step 4: Write a First Draft

Write a strong topic sentence introducing your main ideas. Include specific and detailed information that reflects the wording of the question. Develop each main idea in its own paragraph. Support each idea with pertinent facts and details.

Step 5: Revise and Proof

Make sure you have responded adequately to the test question. Check spelling, sentence structure, and the logical flow of ideas. Be sure that you've included enough evidence in support of each of your ideas.

Writing for Research Assignments

Sometimes, you are given an assignment that requires you to conduct research and write an essay or paper reflecting your research.

Step 1: Identify and Narrow Your Topic

Choose something you're interested in and make sure that it's not too broad. For example, instead of writing a report about Panama, write about the construction of the Panama Canal.

Step 2: Acquire Information

Locate several sources of information about the topic from the library or Internet. Create a source index card for each resource. For each detail or subtopic, record notes on an index card. Also, record the source. Use quotation marks when you copy the exact words from a source.

Step 3: Make an Outline

Use an outline to decide how to organize your report. Sort your index cards into the same order.

```
Building the Panama Canal
Outline
    I. Introduction
    II. Why the Canal Was Built
    III. How the Canal Was Built
        A. Physical Challenges
        B. Medical Challenges
    IV. Conclusion
```

Step 4: Write a First Draft

Write an introduction, a body, and a conclusion. Leave plenty of space between lines so you can go back and add details that you may have left out.

Step 5: Revise and Proof

In addition to the usual checks, make sure that you have not plagiarized by using the words of an author without quotation marks.

Step 6: Create a Bibliography

At the end of your research paper, use your source cards to compile a bibliography.

Human History Is Fascinating and Complex

To make world history easier for you to grasp, this textbook emphasizes nine themes. They can help you focus on the key features of each society and event you read about.

Theme: Continuity and Change

History is the story of change. Some changes can be as quick as a revolution. Others, such as the spread of democratic ideas or the shifting roles of men and women in many nations, may take decades or even centuries. Although change is always taking place, enduring traditions and concerns link people across time and space.

Theme: Geography and History

Geography influences where people settle, how they live, and how goods and ideas travel. Since ancient times, people have dug irrigation canals to water farmlands, and control of waterways or mountain passes has determined the outcome of wars. Today, environmental issues often stir heated debate.

Theme: Political and Social Systems

Monarchs, presidents, dictators, tribal councils—each society has a form of government to ensure order and guard against outside threats. Societies around the world have also developed other important institutions to ensure order, including legal systems, social classes, and the most basic unit of all—the family.

Theme: Religions and Value Systems

Today, as in the past, religion exerts a powerful impact on the world. Belief in one God guided the histories of Jews, Christians, and Muslims. Buddhism and Hinduism shaped many Asian cultures. Nonreligious values, such as Greek ideals of beauty and individuality, have also had a wide influence.

The first moon landing, 1969

Theme: Economics and Technology

Who controls vital resources? How are goods exchanged? What work do people do and how are they paid for that work? Economic questions such as these are often closely linked to technology. From Stone Age farming tools to the printing press to the steam engine to the computer, technology has transformed the world again and again.

Theme: Diversity

The vast diversity of the world's cultures is reflected in many ways, including language, ethnic background, customs, beliefs, and clothing. Such diversity has enriched the human experience. Yet, at the same time, cultural or ethnic differences often lead to bitter conflict.

Theme: Global Interaction

Different parts of the world may interact in many ways—through migration, trade, warfare, or the exchange of ideas. When people traveled by oxcart or sailing ship, interaction was a slow process. Today, communications networks can link all parts of the globe instantly.

Theme: Impact of the Individual

Everyone who ever lived is part of the human story. Yet some people have such an impact on events that we remember them long after they die. For good or ill, individuals such as Confucius, Christopher Columbus, Marie Curie, Stalin, and Mohandas Gandhi have had a lasting influence on our world.

Theme: Art and Literature

Since the days of Stone Age cave paintings, people have created art and literature to express their lives and values. In the Middle Ages, Europeans built soaring cathedrals to the glory of God. Today, novelists and filmmakers from Nigeria to Brazil vividly depict the challenges of modern life.

SKILLS HANDBOOK

CONTENTS

Learning From Maps xxx

Understanding Charts and Graphs xxxii

Interpreting Visuals xxxiv

Analyzing Primary Sources xxxvi

Comparing Viewpoints xxxviii

Synthesizing Information xl

Analyzing Cause and Effect xlii

Asking Questions xliv

Problem Solving and Decision Making xlvi

Using the Internet xlviii

Learning From Maps

How Will I Use This Skill? **Maps are not just for textbooks. They can help you find your way on a bus or in a car. They can help you understand about events in other parts of the world. You can even use them to learn about tomorrow's weather.**

Learning the Skill

To learn from a map, you have to look closely at the map's features. Use the map and the information below to learn about the various parts of a map.

Civilizations of the Ancient Middle East

Black Sea
CAUCASUS MTS.
Caspian Sea
ARMENIAN PLATEAU
ASIA MINOR
TAURUS MTS.
MESOPOTAMIA
Euphrates R.
Tigris R.
ZAGROS MTS.
Mediterranean Sea
SYRIAN DESERT
Babylon Kish
Erech
Ur
Persian Gulf
ARABIAN DESERT
Sinai Pen.
Nile R.
Red Sea
EGYPT

Azimuthal Equal Area Projection
0   150   300 Miles
0   150   300 Kilometers

Fertile Crescent
Akkad
Sumer
Babylonian empire

30°E   40°E   50°E
40°N
30°N

N W E S

1. **Read the title** The title gives a clue to the main topic of the map. **What is the title of this map?**

2. **Use the scale** You can use the scale of miles and kilometers to calculate the distance between two points. A short distance on a map represents a larger distance on the Earth. For example, one inch may represent 100 miles. **How far is it from Ur to Kish?**

3. **Observe the locator map** The locator map shows which part of the whole Earth is shown on this map. **How does the locator indicate the area shown on the main map?**

4. **Check the compass** The compass shows which direction is north on the map. You can also find the other directions—south, east, and west. Some compasses also show intermediate directions, for example northeast, which is the direction between north and east. **In which direction would you travel to get from the Sinai Peninsula to the Caspian Sea?**

5. **Notice the latitude and longitude lines and numbers** Latitude lines indicate the distance north or south of the equator. Longitude lines show distance east or west from the Prime Meridian, an imaginary line that runs through Greenwich, England. Latitude and longitude are measured in degrees (°). **What desert is located around 30° N latitude?**

6. **Identify bodies of water and other physical features** Maps often show oceans, rivers, mountains, and other physical features. Sometimes, color or shading is used to identify different features. Water, for example, is usually blue. Mountains are indicated by gray shading called relief. **Name three bodies of water shown on this map. Which mountain range is farther north—the Taurus Mountains or the Zagros Mountains?**

7. **Use the key** The key explains colors or symbols used on the map. Here, purple shows Sumer. **How is the Babylonian empire shown?**

8. **Identify political areas** Political areas, such as countries, empires, or cities, can be shown with borders, colors, or other symbols. They may be labeled on the map or in the key. **Describe the location of Mesopotamia.**

Practicing the Skill

Practice learning from maps by recalling the steps you just learned and by answering the following questions based on the map below.

1. What is the title of the map?
2. About how far would you travel to get from Beirut to Riyadh?
3. Study the locator map. What region of Africa is part of the Middle East? What region of Asia is part of the Middle East?
4. In what direction would you travel to get from Ankara to Tehran?
5. Use latitude and longitude to tell the location of the Strait of Hormuz.
6. **(a)** What are three important rivers in the Middle East? **(b)** What body of water separates Egypt from Saudi Arabia?
7. **(a)** A desalinization plant removes the salt from salt water to make it suitable for drinking and watering crops. How are desalinization plants shown on the map? **(b)** Where are most of them located?
8. **(a)** Through what countries does the Tigris River flow? **(b)** Through what countries does the Euphrates River flow? **(c)** Why do you think leaders from these countries meet to discuss water resources?

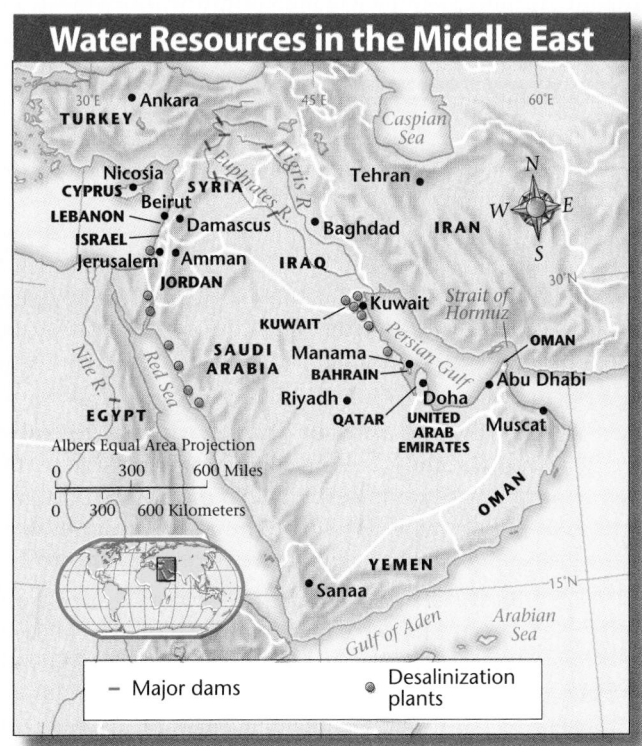

Applying the Skill

Choose a map in your textbook. Based on the skill lesson on these pages, write a series of questions that test understanding of how to read and use the map. Trade with a partner and answer each other's questions. Then, check your partner's answers.

Understanding Charts and Graphs

How Will I Use This Skill? A graph shows numerical facts in picture form. Bar graphs and line graphs allow you to compare things at different times or in different places. You often see this type of graph in newspapers, where it might show a change such as the increase in student enrollment at your school or the average temperature over the last month. Circle graphs, or pie charts, show how a whole thing is divided into parts. The segments in a circle graph represent percentages of the whole, helping you better compare the parts.

Learning the Skill

To interpret a graph, you have to look closely at its features. Use the graphs and the information below to learn how to use various types of graphs.

Bar graph

Travel Times to London

Source: E. J. Hobsbaum, *Industry and Empire*

Circle graph

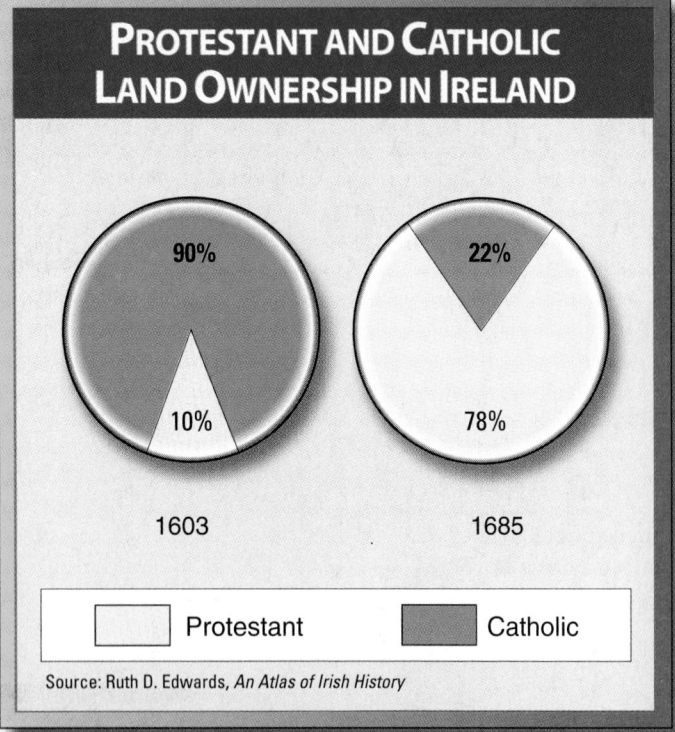

PROTESTANT AND CATHOLIC LAND OWNERSHIP IN IRELAND

Source: Ruth D. Edwards, *An Atlas of Irish History*

1. **Read the title** The title of any kind of graph tells you the main topic of the graph. **What is the title of the bar graph?**

2. **On line and bar graphs, identify the labels** Notice the labels on the bottom and side of the graph. For example, on the bar graph, the bottom, or horizontal axis, refers to hours. **What does the side, or vertical axis, of the bar graph refer to?**

3. **Determine what the bars or lines represent** Graphs use labels or a key to make clearer what the graph is about. On the line graph, for example, the red line represents the amount of steel produced in Germany. **On the bar graph, how are travel times in 1830 shown?**

4. **On circle graphs, identify the parts into which the circle is divided** A circle graph may have labels on the parts to tell you how the circle is divided. Sometimes, however, the graph includes a key to explain the use of color on the graph. For example, on the circle graph, Protestant land ownership in Ireland is shown in beige. **What color is used to show Catholic land ownership?**

5. **Read the graph** Use the title, labels, and colors to understand the meaning of the graph. You can learn from the circle graph that in 1603 Protestants owned 10 percent of the land in Ireland. **What percentage did Protestants own in 1685?**

6. **Interpret the graph** Often, graphs show trends, or tendencies in a given direction. The line graph shows steel production from 1880 to 1910 in three different countries. **(a) Which country had the greatest rise in steel production during this time? (b) Do you think this rise benefited other segments of the nation's economy? Why or why not?**

Line graph

STEEL PRODUCTION, 1880–1910

Sources: *European Historical Statistics, 1750–1970,* and *Historical Statistics of the United States*

Practicing the Skill

Interpret the graph at right by recalling the steps you just learned and by answering the questions that follow.

1. What is the topic of the graph? How can you tell?
2. What percentage of enslaved Africans was shipped to Portuguese Brazil? To Europe and Asia?
3. To what other parts of the world were enslaved Africans shipped?
4. Can you learn from this graph how many slaves were shipped to North America in 1875? Why or why not?
5. Can you tell from this graph what percentage of enslaved Africans was shipped to the Caribbean? Why or why not?
6. Could this information be presented on a line graph instead of a circle graph? Explain.

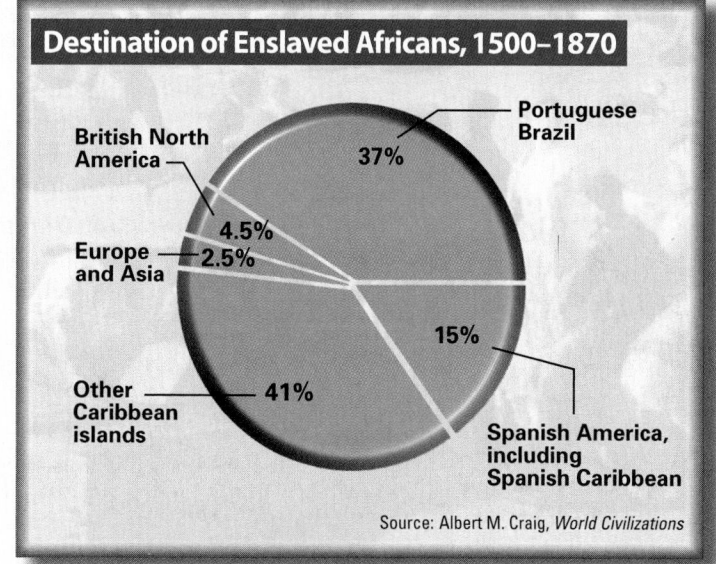

Destination of Enslaved Africans, 1500–1870

Source: Albert M. Craig, *World Civilizations*

Applying the Skill

Conduct a simple poll among your classmates about a topic related to school, such as the number of hours per day each student spends doing homework or the material used by each student to cover his or her textbooks. Then, create an appropriate graph to display the results of your poll. Be prepared to explain your graph to the class.

Interpreting Visuals

How Will I Use This Skill? **In today's fast-paced "information age," we are bombarded with visuals of all kinds. Television, film, the Internet, and print media all carry images that are designed to convey information or influence attitudes. People use drawings, art, photographs, and computer graphics to communicate facts and ideas. Today, literacy means not only the ability to read and write but also the ability to understand and interpret visuals.**

Learning the Skill

Use this black-and-white photograph and the following steps to learn some of the methods involved in interpreting visuals.

In the 1950s, children in Europe and other parts of the world were taught they could survive a nuclear attack. This 1954 image was used to advertise a bogus "radiation-resistant" blanket.

1. **Identify the content of the visual** The content of a visual includes all the individual images that make up the larger visual. Be careful to look at both the foreground and background. Note which images seem to have the main importance in the visual. **What are the three main images in this photograph?**

2. **Note the emotional elements** An artist or photographer often tries to convey attitudes and emotions in a visual. **What feelings are conveyed by the boy's position and facial expression?**

3. **Read any text that accompanies the visual** A visual often has a title, caption, or other accompanying text that helps you to interpret it. **When was this photograph produced?**

4. **Determine the purpose of the visual** A visual may be intended to provide information, to persuade, or to entertain. A good starting point for determining the purpose of a visual is to consider the individual or group that produced it. **Who produced this visual? What do you think was its purpose?**

5. **Learn more about the visual or its creator** Sometimes, it is helpful to do some research to better understand the visual or its creator. If you did research on this photograph, you would learn that in the 1950s, the United States and the Soviet Union were engaged in a dangerous rivalry, including a race to build weapons. This rivalry was called the Cold War. Many people feared that a terrible nuclear conflict might erupt at any time. **Does this information refute or confirm your understanding of the picture? Explain.**

6. **React to the visual** React to the visual based on its apparent or intended purpose. If the visual was meant to inform, decide how well it conveys information to you. If it was meant to persuade, consider how effective it might be at influencing the attitudes of those who view it. If it was meant to be entertaining, react to it in those terms. **Do you think this photograph was an effective commercial advertisement that had an influence on people in the 1950s? Why or why not?**

Practicing the Skill

Interpret the visual below by recalling the steps you have just learned and by answering the questions that follow.

Honduran Street Scene
In this colorful folk art painting by Jorge Ferman, one can learn much about the culture of the Central American country of Honduras.

1. **(a)** What are some of the main images in the painting? **(b)** What images provide the background?
2. Do you think the painter portrays village life in Honduras in a favorable or unfavorable way? Explain.
3. How does the painting suggest that Honduras has a tropical climate?
4. What do you think is the purpose of this painting?
5. If you did some research about rural life in Honduras, you would learn that more than 50 percent of the population works in agriculture. Common crops among small farmers are corn, beans, and squash. On large plantations, people grow such cash crops as coffee and cotton. Based on this information, does the painting seem to convey an accurate or inaccurate vision of life in a Honduran village? Explain.
6. **(a)** What emotions does the painting cause you to feel? **(b)** Based on the painting, would you like to visit Honduras? Why or why not?

Applying the Skill

Select a visual in a current newspaper or magazine that appears in print or online. Print out, cut out, or reproduce a copy of the visual and any accompanying text. Use the steps that you have learned in this skill lesson to write an interpretation of the visual.

Analyzing Primary Sources

How Will I Use This Skill? Primary sources include official documents, as well as firsthand accounts of events. They may also include visual evidence, such as a news photograph, a painting by an eyewitness, or a political cartoon. They are a valuable source of information about the past. Historians often use primary sources to prepare their narratives, which are secondary sources. You use primary sources when you watch an interview on television or listen to a friend tell you about something that happened at school.

Learning the Skill

Use the excerpt, the cartoon, and the steps that follow to learn about analyzing primary sources.

The following excerpt comes from *The Satires,* a series of poems written by Juvenal about life in Rome in the first century A.D. In this excerpt, Juvenal recounts a friend's reasons for moving away from Rome.

66 Since at Rome there is no place for honest pursuits, no profit to be got by honest toil—my fortune is less today than it was yesterday. . . .

What shall I do at Rome? I cannot lie; if a book is bad, I cannot praise it and beg a copy. I know not the motions of the stars . . . no one shall be a thief by my cooperation. . . .

Who, nowadays, is beloved except the confidant of crime? 99
— Juvenal, *The Satires* (tr. Lewis Evans)

This cartoon by Arcadio Esquivel from Costa Rica shows the world being bulldozed. Costa Rica has been more successful than many other countries in balancing the need for development with the need to preserve the environment.

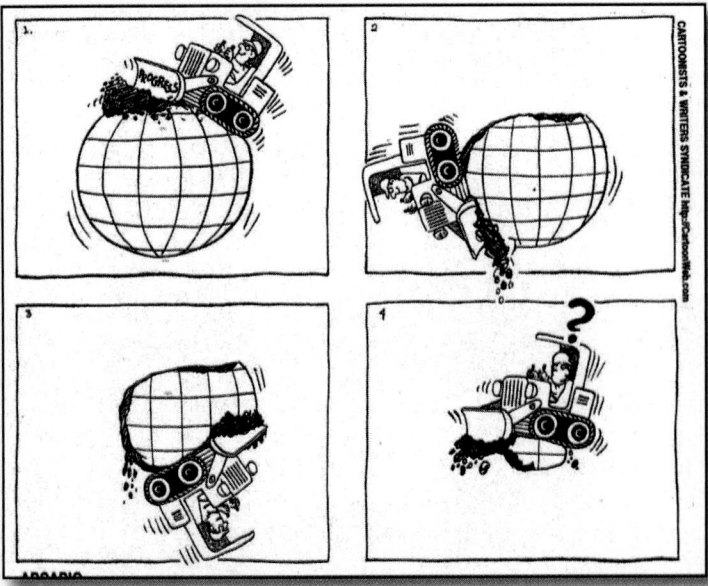

1. **Read the headnote or caption** Often, primary sources are presented with a short introduction about the writer or the document. The headnote with the excerpt above, for example, explains that the excerpt was written by Juvenal. **According to the headnote, when was this primary source written? Why was it written?**

2. **Read the primary source** As you read the primary source, identify unfamiliar words and try to gather the general meaning of the source. **In this excerpt, what is the writer's main point?**

3. **Identify facts and opinions in the written source** A fact can be proved true. An opinion, on the other hand, cannot be proved. Often, you can identify opinion statements by introductory words like "I think"or by strongly positive or negative words, like "gorgeous" or "despicable." Another clue is a statement that exaggerates. **Identify an opinion statement in the excerpt.**

4. **Read the source line** You can often get additional information about an excerpt by reading the source line. In this case, for example, you can learn that the excerpt is a translation. **Who translated Juvenal's words?**

5. **Identify bias and evaluate reliability** You have seen that primary sources include both facts and opinions. They may also reveal the bias of the author. These factors affect the reliability of the source. Other factors that affect reliability are the time that may have passed between an event and the author's writing about it and the author's own earlier experiences. Suppose you knew that Juvenal had served in the army, hoping to make his way into government service, but in the end, had not received the promotion he hoped for. **How might that fact affect Juvenal's reliability as a commentator on Roman society?**

6. **Learn from political cartoons** Political cartoons can also be primary sources. They reflect the observations of one artist about events of the time. They often use symbols to represent other things. **(a) In the cartoon on the opposite page, what does the bulldozer represent?** Cartoons also use exaggeration to make their point. **(b) What is exaggerated in this cartoon? (c) Explain the point of view expressed in the cartoon.**

Practicing the Skill

Analyze the primary source below by recalling the steps you have just learned and by answering the questions that follow.

In 1947, India gained independence after hundreds of years as a colony of Great Britain. India's new leader, Jawaharlal Nehru, had worked to bring about independence. He addressed the nation on its first independence day.

66 We are a free and sovereign people today, and we have rid ourselves of the burden of the past. We look at the world with clear and friendly eyes, and at the future with faith and confidence. . . .

Our first and immediate objective must be to put an end to all internal strife and violence, which disfigure and degrade us and injure the cause of freedom. They come in the way of consideration of the great economic problems of the masses of the people which so urgently demand attention.

. . . Production today is the first priority, and every attempt to hamper or lessen production is injuring the nation, and more especially harmful to our laboring masses. . . . 99
—Jawaharlal Nehru, Independence Day speech, August 15, 1947

1. **(a)** Who wrote this document? **(b)** Under what circumstances?
2. **(a)** Identify one fact in Nehru's speech. **(b)** Identify one opinion statement.
3. **(a)** What was Nehru's purpose in giving this speech? **(b)** Do you think his purpose affected the words he spoke? **(c)** Do you think he achieved his purpose?
4. **(a)** Is the speech a reliable source for understanding Nehru's goal for his country? **(b)** Why or why not?

Applying the Skill

Use Internet or library sources to find a primary source that interests you. Remember that it can be either written or visual. Follow the steps outlined on these pages and then write a paragraph analzying the primary source.

Comparing Viewpoints

How Will I Use This Skill? **When people describe an idea or event, they usually provide some facts and their own personal viewpoints. A person's viewpoint is shaped by subjective influences such as feelings, prejudices, and past experiences. You often encounter divergent viewpoints, as when two of your friends describe the same event differently, when two politicians recommend different policies, or when two newspapers analyze a news event in different ways. By analyzing and comparing viewpoints, you will be able to better understand issues and form your own viewpoint.**

Learning the Skill

Throughout history, people have tried to educate their children. But they have not always agreed on the goals of education. Read the excerpts below and compare the two viewpoints by using the steps that follow.

Henri Christophe, king of Haiti, set up schools for outstanding students of his nation. He believed these schools would help Haiti maintain the freedom it had won fewer than 15 years earlier. In 1817, he wrote:

66 To form good citizens we must educate our children. From our national institutions will proceed a race of men capable of defending by their knowledge and talents those rights so long denied by tyrants. It is from these sources that light will be diffused among the whole mass of the population.99
—King Henri Christophe, 1817

Leo Tolstoy, a Russian aristocrat of the late 1800s, became a famous novelist as a young man. Later, he turned his attention to social issues. In 1902, he wrote:

66 You can take a puppy and feed him, and teach him to carry something, and enjoy the sight of him; but it is not enough to rear and bring up a man, and teach him Greek; he has to be taught to live, that is, to take less from others, and give more.99
—Leo Tolstoy, 1902

1. **Identify the authors** It is important always to identify the writer or speaker. **Who are the authors of these two documents, and where and when did they live?**

2. **Make sure that you understand the arguments being made** Try to identify the main idea and supporting arguments made by each author. **(a) According to Christophe, what is the goal of education? (b) Why does Tolstoy compare raising a puppy to teaching a person Greek?**

3. **Consider the authors' backgrounds** A person's attitudes, beliefs, and past experiences affect that person's viewpoint. By knowing the author's background, you can make judgments about the viewpoint. **How might the backgrounds of Christophe and Tolstoy affect their viewpoints?**

4. **Find common information** If two viewpoints are on the same topic, there should be some points that they agree on. Often, these will be basic facts. **According to both viewpoints, what is true about education?**

5. **Find opinions** Differentiate the opinions from the facts. The opinions represent the author's viewpoint. **Name two words used by Christophe that signal opinions.**

6. **Evaluate the validity of each viewpoint** Evaluate viewpoints by recalling the authors' background and determining if their opinions are based on facts or reasonable arguments. **Are the viewpoints of Christophe and Tolstoy based on reasonable arguments? Explain.**

7. **Draw conclusions** After following the above steps, you are ready to draw conclusions about the viewpoints and the topic that they deal with. **(a) Do you think Tolstoy's view was typical of Russian aristocrats? (b) Why might the king of Haiti have been so concerned about maintaining the freedom of his nation?**

Practicing the Skill

The document and poster below reflect different viewpoints on industry and labor in the Soviet Union during the early 1900s. Compare the two viewpoints by answering the following questions:

1. Who are the authors of the letter?
2. Based on both documents, what was one goal of the Soviet Union?
3. **(a)** According to the poster, what was the general attitude of Soviet workers? **(b)** According to the letter, were most people in the camp treated justly? Explain.
4. Which viewpoint seems more trustworthy to you? Explain.
5. What methods did the Soviet Union use to increase economic production?

This letter protesting prison conditions was written to government leaders of the Soviet Union by former prisoners.

❝ We are prisoners who are returning from the Solovetsky concentration camp because of our poor health. We went there full of energy and good health, and now we are returning as invalids, broken and crippled emotionally and physically. . . . It is difficult for a human being even to imagine such terror, tyranny, violence, and lawlessness. . . . The Unified State Political Directorate [OGPU] without oversight and due process sends workers and peasants there who are by and large innocent. . . .

They die a slow and painful death . . . from hunger, cold, and backbreaking 14–16 hour days. . . . We . . . are asking you to improve the pathetic, tortured existence of those who are there who languish under the yoke of the OGPU's tyranny. . . . To this we subscribe: G. Zheleznov, Vinogradov, F. Belinskii. ❞

—Letter to the Presidium of the Central Executive
Committee of the Communist Party,
December 14, 1926

Poster produced by the Soviet government, 1930s.

Applying the Skill

Use the Internet or library resources to find two documents expressing different viewpoints on a major turning point in world history. Some examples are the fall of the Roman empire, the Crusades, the Reformation, and World War I. Make copies of the documents. Then, use the steps that you have learned to write a paragraph comparing the viewpoints.

Synthesizing Information

How Will I Use This Skill? **If you want to know whether a movie is worth seeing, you can read a review, watch a television commercial, view a film clip on the Internet, and talk to people who have seen the movie. You can combine the different pieces of evidence to develop a more complete impression of the movie. This process of combining pieces of evidence is called synthesizing. Today and in the future, synthesizing information will help you to become better informed and to make better decisions.**

Learning the Skill

Study the three different pieces of information on this page about some developments in the 1400s and early 1500s. Then, follow the steps to learn how to synthesize information.

The caravel, shown above, helped Europeans sail across and into the wind.

Improved Technology Several improvements in technology helped Europeans conquer the vast oceans of the world. Cartographers, or mapmakers, created more accurate maps and sea charts. European sailors also learned to use the astrolabe, an instrument developed by the ancient Greeks and perfected by the Arabs, to determine their latitude at sea.

Along with more reliable navigational tools, Europeans designed larger and better ships. The Portuguese developed the caravel, which combined the square sails of European ships with Arab lateen, or triangular, sails. Caravels also adapted the sternpost rudder and numerous masts of Chinese ships. The new rigging made it easier to sail across or even into the wind. Finally, European ships added more weaponry, including sturdier cannons.

Hardships on the Uncharted Sea

In his journal, Italian sailor Antonio Pigafetta detailed the desperate conditions Magellan's sailors faced as they crossed the Pacific Ocean:

"We remained 3 months and 20 days without taking in provisions or other refreshments and ate only old biscuit reduced to powder, full of grubs and stinking from the dirt which rats had made on it. We drank water that was yellow and stinking. We also ate the ox hides from under the mainyard which we softened by soaking in seawater for several days."

—Journal of Antonio Pigafetta

1. **Focus on a topic** It is usually not very fruitful to synthesize bits of information that have little or nothing in common. The different pieces of information should be on some common topic. **To what common topic do all three bits of information relate?**

2. **Analyze each piece of information** The purpose of synthesizing is to gather evidence on a topic from more than one source. Before you can synthesize, you need to make sure that you understand the main idea and supporting details found in each source. **(a) What is the main idea of the Improved Technology paragraphs? (b) What was the benefit of the caravel? (c) What is the main idea of Pigafetta's firsthand account?**

3. **Look for similarities** Information is more complete and reliable if more than one source provides the same or similar information. Noting and analyzing the similarities will help you reach a more complete understanding of the topic. **Which two sources support the idea that European sailors became better equipped to sail the seas?**

4. **Look for differences** It is also important to look for inconsistent information or other perspectives. **Which sources convey the idea that European sailors still faced hardships at sea?**

5. **Draw conclusions** Our knowledge of a topic becomes more complete when we draw conclusions based on information synthesized from a variety of sources. **Was ocean travel easy or difficult for Europeans in the early 1500s? Explain.**

Practicing the Skill

Study the different pieces of information on this page about developments that occurred between the 1500s and 1700s. Then, answer the following questions:

1. With what general topic do all three pieces of evidence deal?
2. **(a)** What does Las Casas complain about? **(b)** How does the painting show social change in the Americas? **(c)** What is the main idea of the graph?
3. Which two sources emphasize negative effects on Native Americans?
4. Do you think all Europeans were cruel to Native Americans? Explain.
5. Based on the evidence, were the early encounters between Native Americans and Europeans generally harmful or beneficial to the Native Americans? Explain.

Portrait of a Spanish man in the Americas, his wife of Native American ancestry, and their daughter.

A Brutal System

Bartolomé de las Casas, a conquistador turned priest, spoke out against the encomienda system and the treatment of Native Americans:

"It is impossible to recount the burdens with which their owners loaded them [75 to 100 pounds], making them walk [hundreds of miles]. . . . They had wounds on their shoulders and backs, like animals. . . . To tell likewise of the whip-lashings, the beatings, the cuffs, the blows, the curses, and a thousand other kinds of torments to which their masters treated them, while in truth they were working hard, would take much time and much paper; and would be something to amaze mankind."

—Bartolomé de las Casas,
Short Description of the Destruction of the Indies

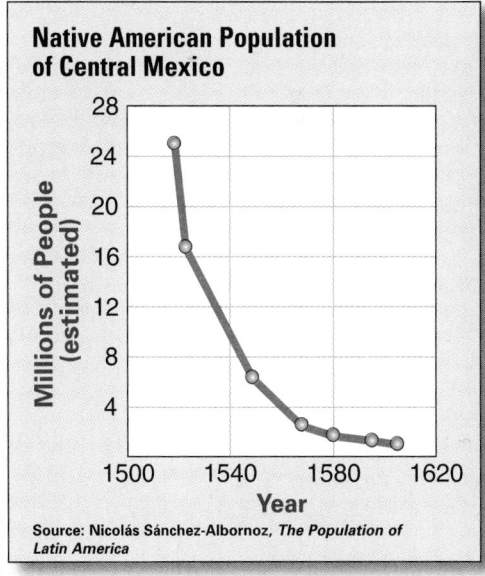

Native American Population of Central Mexico

Source: Nicolás Sánchez-Albornoz, *The Population of Latin America*

This graph shows the impact of diseases from Europe and of fighting against Europeans.

Applying the Skill

Select a current economics topic, such as e-commerce, international trade, or stock market trends. Find three different pieces of information on the topic, including at least one visual. Write questions to analyze and synthesize the information. Trade papers with a partner and answer each other's questions.

Analyzing Cause and Effect

How Will I Use This Skill? People often try to figure out the causes and effects of things. For example, government officials always conduct an investigation after an airplane accident. Their goals are to identify the causes of the mishap and to then use that knowledge to prevent future accidents. By analyzing causes and effects and by taking appropriate action based on what is learned, you can gain greater control over events and conditions that affect your life.

Learning the Skill

Read the passage below about a school soccer team. Then, follow the steps to learn how to analyze causes and effects.

> A high school soccer team has won the division championship. The team's coach was named coach of the year. The team's colors were blue and gold. All the team members attended practice regularly. Because they passed all their classes, no team members were dropped from the team. As a result of winning the division title, the soccer team competed in the state tournament. The championship game was seen by college coaches on cable television. Several weeks later, a few of those coaches invited some of the players to apply for admission to their colleges and play soccer for them.

1. **Identify the central event** Identify the central condition or event whose causes or effects you wish to study. In the introductory paragraph at the top of this page, for example, the central event was airplane accidents. **What is the central event in the soccer story?**

2. **Disregard irrelevant information** Disregard information that has little or nothing to do with the central event. **What information in the story is neither a cause nor an effect of the team's performance?**

3. **Identify possible causes** Causes precede the central event. They are the reasons that the central event or development occurred. In a reading passage, key words that can help you identify causes include *because* and *due to*. **What are the causes of the central event in the soccer story?**

4. **Identify possible effects** Effects come after the central event. They occur as a result of the central event. In a reading passage, key words that indicate effects include *therefore* and *as a result*. **What are the effects of the central event in the soccer story?**

5. **Make generalizations** After investigators find the causes of an accident, they do not think about one plane only. They generalize and consider how the same conditions might cause an accident for other planes. For example, faulty electrical wiring can cause a fire in all planes, not just the one under investigation. **Make a generalization based on the soccer story.**

6. **Make recommendations** By understanding causes and effects, you can recommend actions or make predictions based on what you have learned. **How can any school sports team improve its chances for success?**

Practicing the Skill

By A.D. 1000, East African port cities, such as Mogadishu, Kilwa, and Sofala, were thriving centers of trade. Study the facts below, which are listed in random order, and copy the blank cause-and-effect chart at right. Then, answer the questions below and fill in the chart. (As you work, you may want to consult the world map in the Atlas at the back of this book.)

- Muslim merchants from Arabia and other lands settled in East Africa.
- Africa had gold, ivory, and other valuable resources.
- East African trading cities thrived.
- Mansa Musa ruled an empire in West Africa.
- Favorable winds aided travel between Asia and Africa.
- There were natural harbors along the East African coast.
- Arabic words became part of the Swahili language in East Africa.
- Muslim merchants introduced their religion to East Africa.

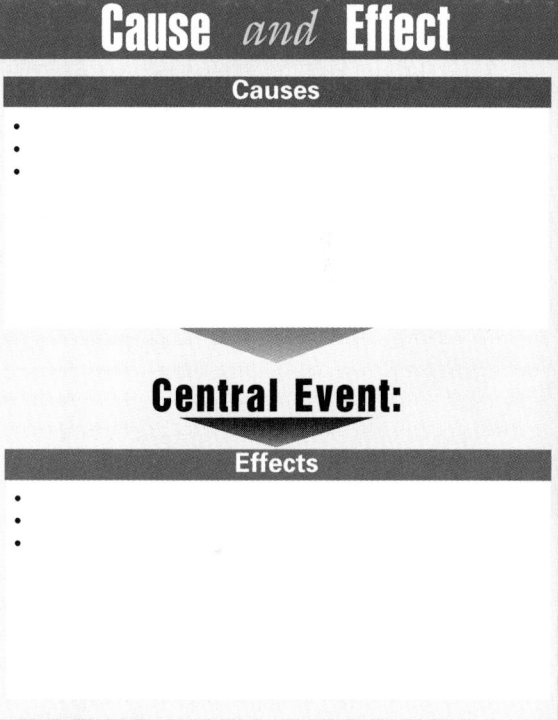

Cause *and* **Effect**

Causes
- •
- •

Central Event:

Effects
- •
- •
- •

1. Which of the facts above is the central event whose causes and effects can be determined? Write the central event in the appropriate place on the chart.
2. Which one fact is most probably neither a cause nor an effect of the central event?
3. What three facts were most probably causes of the central event? Write them in the appropriate place on the chart.
4. What three facts about Africa were most probably effects of the central event? Write the three facts in the appropriate place on the chart.
5. In general, what is often a common effect of thriving trade between different lands?
6. In general, if a government wanted to build a profitable center for overseas trade, what do you think would be a good geographic location for the trade center?

Applying the Skill

Suppose that your dentist tells you that you have two cavities. Create a chart identifying probable causes and effects of the cavities. Then, based on the chart, write two generalizations and two recommendations.

Asking Questions

How Will I Use This Skill? Asking questions is a key part of the critical-thinking process. By asking questions, you become an active thinker and learner rather than a passive observer. Using this skill will help you get the most out of any information that is presented to you.

Learning the Skill

Study the chart below and the biography on the left. Then, follow the steps to learn some of the techniques involved in asking useful questions.

Biography

Elizabeth I 1533–1603

"She takes great pleasure in dancing and music," noted an English observer of Queen Elizabeth I. The normally thrifty queen employed some 50 singers, 40 musicians, and several songwriters to stage concerts for her.

Elizabeth I also loved plays. She especially enjoyed the works of William Shakespeare, whom she helped to promote. The queen provided financial support and prestige for major acting groups, which led to a flowering of English theater.

Elizabeth's 45-year reign inspired other writers of the day. Poet Edmund Spenser dedicated *The Faerie Queene* to Elizabeth I.

Four Categories of Questions			
Comprehension	**Analysis**	**Evaluation**	**Prediction**
Who?	How?	Is it beneficial or harmful?	If this occurs, then what might happen?
What?	Why?	Is it ethical or unethical?	If this does not occur, then what might happen?
Where?	What are the different points of view?	Is it logical or illogical?	If this had or had not happened, then what might be different?
When?	What are the causes and effects?	Is it relevant or irrelevant?	If this solution is implemented, how might the problem be affected?
How much?	What is the similarity or difference between this and that?	What are some advantages and disadvantages?	
What are the examples?	What is the problem?	What is the best solution?	
	What are some possible solutions?	What is my opinion?	
	What evidence supports the ideas?	What evidence supports my opinion?	

1. **Ask basic comprehension questions** Comprehension questions will help you to summarize or define the basic contents of what you are reading, seeing, or hearing. You might ask, "Who is discussed in the biography?" or "Where did she live?" **Ask and answer two more comprehension questions.**

2. **Ask analytical questions** Sample analytical questions are in the second column of the chart. Unlike comprehension questions, these questions involve some higher-level critical thinking. You might ask, "How do Elizabeth's accomplishments still have an impact on our lives today?" **What other analytical question could you ask?**

3. **Ask questions that evaluate** Examples of these questions are in the third column of the chart. In this step, you make judgments and form opinions based on evidence. An evaluation question might be "Based on the biography, do you think Elizabeth's spending habits were beneficial or harmful to the English people?" **Ask another evaluation question.**

4. **Ask hypothetical questions** These questions usually involve the word *if*, as do the questions in the fourth column of the chart. At this stage of critical thinking, you ask yourself questions that lead to a hypothesis or theory about what *might happen* or what *might have happened*. **Ask and answer a hypothetical question.**

Practicing the Skill

Review the chart on the preceding page once again and study the three maps at right. Then, follow the steps below to practice the skill of asking questions.

1. Write a basic comprehension question about the main idea of the three maps.
2. Write an analytical question about what happened to Poland. (Clue: Note how the borders of the countries around Poland changed over the years.)
3. Write a question that evaluates some aspect of what happened to Poland.
4. Based on what the maps show about international relations in Europe in the 1700s, write a question that leads one to make a prediction about Europe in the 1800s.

Partitions of Poland, 1701–1795

Applying the Skill

Videotape a short segment from a national news report on television or cut out an article from the national news section of a newspaper. Write a series of questions on the news story. Include one or more questions for each of the following four categories: **(a)** comprehension, **(b)** analysis, **(c)** evaluation, **(d)** prediction. Write an answer to each of the questions.

Problem Solving and Decision Making

How Will I Use This Skill? **Throughout your life, problems will arise. Today, a problem may be a dispute with a friend or a tough math test. Later, as a citizen and voter, you will be asked to make decisions about problems affecting the community, nation, or world. If you handle problems fearfully or haphazardly, they may overwhelm you. You will be more likely to find solutions if you make decisions in a logical, systematic way.**

Learning the Skill

We will use a case study to learn the skills of problem solving and decision making. Study the situation described below and copy the incomplete chart. Then, follow the steps and answer the questions.

A Problem for Japan and China

In the 1800s, Japan and China faced a problem. Industrialized nations had developed machinery and weapons that were superior to what the Japanese and Chinese had. Some industrialized nations used their new power to demand special trading privileges in Asia.

Options for Japan and China		
Option	**Advantages**	**Disadvantages**
1. Give in to demands of the industrialized powers.	• Avoid conflict. •	• Native merchants lose profits to foreigners. •
2. Give in to demands, but also build modern machines and weapons.	• •	• •
3. Refuse the demands and reject much of the new technology.	• •	• •

The Decisions
- The Japanese government decided to follow option 2.
- The Chinese government decided to follow option 3.

Effects of the Decisions
- Japan quickly became a modern industrial and military power. After suffering defeat in World War II, Japan demilitarized. Today, it remains one of the world's leading industrial powers.
- China was defeated in several wars, first by Great Britain, and then by Japan. Foreign nations gained special privileges in China. Today, China is still struggling to become a leading industrial power.

1. **Identify the problem** It is almost impossible to solve a problem without examining it and having a clear understanding of its roots. **Why were foreign powers able to make demands on Japan and China?**

2. **Gather information and identify options** There is always more than one way to cope with a problem. Never follow the first option you think of. Instead, identify as many options as possible. **Describe an option, other than those in the chart, that Japan or China could have chosen.**

3. **Consider advantages and disadvantages** Analyze each option by predicting the benefits and drawbacks of choosing that option. **On the chart that you copied, fill in advantages and disadvantages for each of the options that Japan and China had.**

4. **Make a decision and implement the solution** Choose the option that seems to offer the best advantages and the least significant disadvantages. **Why do you think China decided on option 3?**

5. **Evaluate the decision** After a while, study the effects of the option that was implemented. If the problem has been solved, then stay with the decision. If the problem persists, has worsened, or has given rise to new problems, then start the process again and choose another option. **Do you think China should have chosen another option after evaluating its decision? Explain.**

Practicing the Skill

Consider this situation. A friend of yours works at a restaurant. Each month, your friend spends more than he or she earns. The money is spent on food, clothing, movies, computer software, video games, and other items. To pay for all the expenses, your friend borrows money from other friends. The result is that your friend owes more and more money each month.

1. **(a)** What problem does your friend have? **(b)** What are the underlying causes of the problem?
2. What options does your friend have? List and describe as many options as you can think of. Do not weigh the advantages and disadvantages yet. Do not reject any options yet.
3. Make a chart similar to the one on the preceding page. In the chart, describe possible advantages and disadvantages for each option.
4. Study your finished chart. Which option seems to provide the most valuable advantages and the least harmful disadvantages? Write a paragraph identifying the decision that you think would be best for your friend. Include a brief explanation as to why you think that decision is best.
5. Ask a classmate to study the options, advantages, and disadvantages on your chart and to evaluate your decision. Does your classmate agree or disagree with your decision? Explain.

Applying the Skill

Think of a problem that is affecting your school or community today. Work with several of your classmates to try to solve the problem. Remember to follow each of the problem-solving and decision-making steps that you have learned in this lesson. When you have finished your work, consider submitting a proposal to a leader in your school or community.

Using the Internet

How Will I Use This Skill? By "surfing the Net," you can link to millions of computer sites sponsored by businesses, governments, schools, museums, and individuals all over the world. The Internet provides many services, including information, e-mail, and online shopping. As a student, you may often use the Internet as a valuable research tool.

Learning the Skill

Use the steps below and the computer screen images to help you learn how to use the Internet. For this lesson, assume that you are searching for information on the Crusades, which were a series of holy wars between Christians and Muslims that began in the late 1000s.

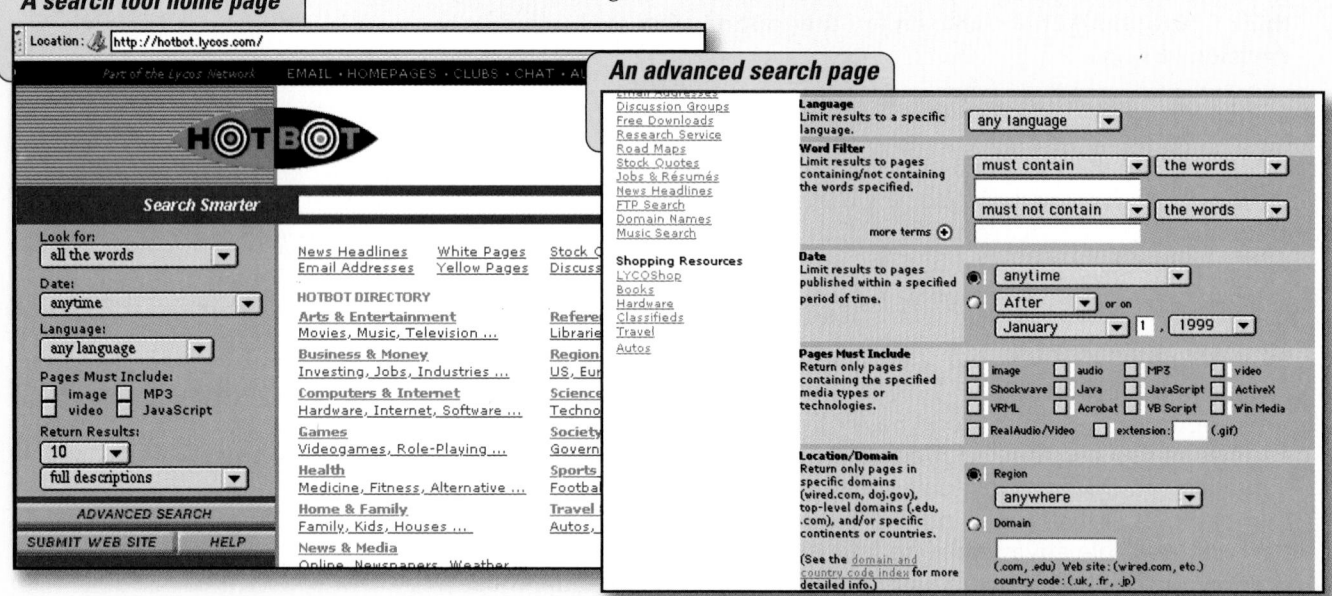

A search tool home page

An advanced search page

1. **Begin a search** Sometimes you know the Internet site you want and its URL, or Uniform Resource Locator. At other times, you must use search tools, such as AltaVista, HotBot, and NorthernLight, which are Internet sites that help you find other Internet sites. Some search tools are directories that list sites by category. For example, see the category called "Health" on the home page above. Other search tools are search engines that look for sites based on keywords that you choose and input yourself. Still others provide both a directory and an engine. **What does the search tool shown above provide?**

2. **Click on a help button** Search tools provide instructions on how to conduct a search. **Where is the help button on the above home page?**

3. **When you use a search engine, type in keywords** The keywords should briefly summarize your topic of choice. Usually, you should not input entire phrases or sentences like "When did the Crusades begin?" Instead, type in the word "Crusades" only. Then, click the search button. **Where is the box in the samples for typing keywords?**

4. **Use Boolean language** Two common Boolean terms are *AND* and *OR*. Use *AND* between two words when you want documents that contain both words. Use *OR* when you want documents that contain either of the words. **If you typed in "Crusades" and "Holy Wars," should you use *AND* or *OR* between them?**

5. **Try an advanced search** After clicking on the advanced search button, you can refine and limit your search. For example, you can specify documents produced only after a certain date or documents only from the **.edu** domain. Limiting the domain in this way will provide sites produced only by schools or other educational sites. The **.org** domain contains only sites produced by organizations. Another common domain is **.gov** which is used by government sites. **To what other domain could you limit your search?**

6. **Evaluate the quality of sites** When the search results page comes up, read the summaries and open those sites that seem to best match your topic. Note when each site was last updated. Note the sponsor or author, too. Universities, museums, libraries, and government agencies are usually the most useful and reliable for social studies research. **Who is the sponsor of the first site on the Crusades in the sample results page?**

7. **Explore, revise, and ask for help** Explore a variety of sites and compare them so you can select the one best suited to your needs. If the results are unsatisfactory, revise your search by typing in new keywords or by using another search tool. Seek guidance from teachers, librarians, and your parents. **What are two other keywords you could try in your search about the Crusades?**

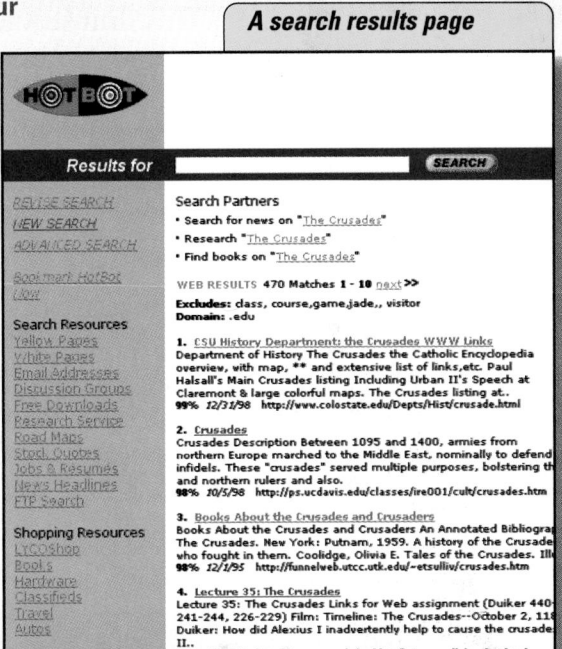

A search results page

Practicing the Skill

Use the Internet to do research on the Mongol empire, especially the Yuan dynasty that the Mongols established in China in 1279. Answer the following questions as you conduct your search:

1. What search tool do you choose? Why?
2. Describe one useful instruction that this search tool provides to users who click on the help button.
3. What keywords and/or Boolean language do you use in your search? Why?
4. How can an advanced search help you?
5. Which site provides the most useful and complete information about the Mongols and the Yuan dynasty? Explain.
6. Revise your search by inputting "Kublai Khan." How are your search results different from those of your earlier search?

Applying the Skill

Use the Internet to search for museum sites that have Native American art and artifacts. You may wish to limit your search to a particular Native American people. You could also limit your search to a particular type of art such as pottery or weaving. Print out your search result pages and circle the descriptions of those sites that you would recommend because they are the most appropriate. For each recommended site, identify the author or sponsor and explain why you recommend it.

CONNECTING WITH PAST LEARNINGS
Prehistory to Early Modern Times

Coffin of an Egyptian king

To understand modern world history requires familiarity with the history of ancient and medieval times. Events, concepts, and relationships that began thousands of years ago continue to have an impact on contemporary times.

This unit serves as a review of key developments from prehistory to early modern times. It focuses on major trends and revolutionary ideas of earlier eras—trends and ideas that transformed people and their cultures in new ways. Highlights include the emergence of river valley civilizations, the cultures of Greece and Rome, and the growth of empires and regional civilizations.

Part I   Early Civilizations

1 Toward Civilization (Prehistory–3000 B.C.) 2
2 First Civilizations: Africa and Asia (3200 B.C.–500 B.C.) 4
3 Early Civilizations in India and China (2500 B.C.–256 B.C.) 6

Stone Age cave painting

The Acropolis

Part II Empires of the Ancient World

1 Empires of India and China (600 B.C.–A.D. 550) 8
2 Ancient Greece (1750 B.C.–133 B.C.) 10
3 Ancient Rome and the Rise of Christianity
(509 B.C.–A.D. 476). 12
4 Civilizations of the Americas (1400 B.C.–A.D. 1570) 14

Part III Regional Civilizations

1 The Rise of Europe (500–1300) 16
2 The High Middle Ages (1050–1450) 18
3 The Byzantine Empire and Russia (330–1613) 20
4 The Muslim World (622–1629). 22
5 Kingdoms and Trading States of Africa (750 B.C.–A.D. 1586) 24
6 Spread of Civilizations in East Asia (500–1650). 26

The Church of Hagia Sophia

A Tang woman

1

Part I — Early Civilizations

1 TOWARD CIVILIZATION (PREHISTORY–3000 B.C.)

Key Facts

- About 12,000 years ago, during the Neolithic period, or New Stone Age, people learned to farm.
- By about 5,000 years ago, the advances made by early farming communities led to the rise of civilizations.
- Historians define eight basic features common to most early civilizations: cities, well-organized central governments, complex religions, job specialization, social classes, arts and architecture, public works, and writing.

Historians call the earliest period of human history the Old Stone Age, or the Paleolithic age. This long period dates from the time of the first stone toolmakers to about 10,000 B.C. Paleolithic people were nomads, moving from place to place to follow game animals and search for edible plants. They lived in small hunting and food-gathering bands of about 20 to 30 people.

Stone Age people learned to adapt to their environment for survival. Men and women made simple tools and weapons such as digging sticks, spears, and axes. They developed spoken language, which let them cooperate as they worked. During the ice ages, people invented clothing made of animal skins and learned to build fires.

The Growth of Farming

About 11,000 years ago, nomadic bands made a dramatic breakthrough. They learned to farm. By producing their own food, they could remain in one place. This change from nomadic to settled farming life ushered in the New Stone Age, or Neolithic age. Neolithic farmers settled in permanent villages and developed new skills and tools.

People also learned to tame some of the animals they once-hunted. Rather than wait for migrating animals to return each year, the new city dwellers rounded them up and herded the animals or penned them in enclosures. This practice enabled people to have meat, and eventually animal labor, without leaving villages and farms.

Because people could now settle in one place, agriculture led to a growth in population. This growth in population led, in turn, to increased interaction among human communities.

Village life also reshaped the roles of women and men. Heads of families formed a council of elders to make important decisions. Often, a village chief emerged. During times of want, warfare increased. Success in battle enabled some men to gain status as warriors. These warriors had power over both women and other men. The status of women declined, though they did not lose all their influence or rights.

About 5,000 years ago, the advances made by early farming communities led people to a new stage of development—the emergence of civilizations.

	3000 B.C.	2500 B.C.	2000 B.C.
AFRICA	3100 B.C. Menes unites Egypt	2550 Great Pyramid and Sphinx at Giza	2050 Middle Kingdom of Egypt begins
THE AMERICAS	3200 Cultivation of maize and cotton	2400 Temple platforms in Peru	2000 Permanent towns in Valley of Mexico
ASIA AND OCEANIA	3000 Sumerian city-states thrive	2500 Indus Valley civilization	2000 Development of Chinese writing
EUROPE	3100 Skara Brae settlement		2000 Bronze Age in Europe

Beginnings of Civilization

Historians define eight basic features common to most early civilizations: (1) cities, (2) well-organized central governments, (3) complex religions, (4) job specialization, (5) social classes, (6) arts and architecture, (7) public works, and (8) writing.

In Africa and Asia, the first cities emerged after farmers began raising crops in fertile lands along river valleys. The nutrient-rich soils and a reliable source of water allowed farmers to produce surplus, or extra, crops. These surpluses provided more food and helped populations to expand. As populations increased, some villages grew into cities.

Organized Governments

The challenge of farming in a river valley contributed to the development of city governments. To control flooding and channel waters to fields, early farmers worked together. Through cooperation, they built dikes, dug canals, and carved out irrigation ditches.

Such projects required leadership and well-organized governments. Some city governments grew powerful and complex. Over time, government bureaucracies grew. A bureaucracy is a system of managing government through specialized departments run by appointed officials.

Social Classes

Social organization also became more complex. People were ranked in social classes according to their jobs. Priests and nobles were usually at the top. Next came wealthy merchants, followed by artisans, or skilled craft workers. Below them stood the vast majority of people, peasant farmers. Slaves were at the lowest social level.

A critical new skill emerged—writing. Priests probably developed writing in order to record the amount of grain collected or other information. Early writing was made up of pictograms, or simple drawings showing the ideas represented. As writing grew more complex, specially trained people called scribes learned to read and write.

The First Empires

As ancient rulers gained more and more power, they conquered territories beyond the boundaries of their cities. Some were able to conquer many cities and villages, creating empires. An empire is a group of states, territories, and peoples ruled by one person. While empire building brought painful defeat for conquered peoples, it also helped end war and establish connections between neighboring communities.

Review

1. **Identify:** **(a)** Old Stone Age, **(b)** New Stone Age.
2. **Define:** **(a)** nomad, **(b)** bureaucracy, **(c)** artisan, **(d)** pictogram, **(e)** empire.
3. What dramatic breakthrough allowed nomadic bands to settle in villages for the first time?

1600
Nubian kingdom established

1290–1224
Reign of Ramses II

750–650
Nubian rule over Egypt

1400
Rise of Olmec civilization

850
Chavín culture in Peru

500
Adena mounds in Ohio

1650
Shang dynasty in China

1100
Assyrians expanded power

539
Persian empire created

1700
Height of Minoan civilization

750
Greeks colonize the Mediterranean

Key Facts

- A rich civilization emerged in the valley of the Nile River in Egypt.
- Independent Sumerian city-states developed in Mesopotamia, an area of fertile land between the Tigris and Euphrates rivers.
- The Hebrews developed Judaism, a monotheistic religion based on the worship of one God.

The first civilizations took shape in the river valleys of North Africa, the Middle East, India, and China. Though they grew in isolation across a widely scattered area, they developed complex ways of life and beliefs that continue to affect our world today.

Ancient Kingdoms of the Nile

More than 5,000 years ago, a rich farming civilization grew in the valley of the Nile River in Egypt. To control the Nile's annual floods, village people learned to cooperate. They built dikes, reservoirs, and irrigation ditches to channel the river and store water for the dry season. Eventually, these villages joined together into two kingdoms. About 3100 B.C., King Menes united these kingdoms, creating along the Nile the world's first unified state.

After Menes' reign, the history of ancient Egypt can be divided into three main periods: the Old Kingdom (about 2700 B.C.–2200 B.C.), the Middle Kingdom (about 2050 B.C.–1800 B.C.), and the New Kingdom (about 1550 B.C.–1100 B.C.).

During the Old Kingdom, pharaohs (FAIR ohz), or the Egyptian rulers, organized a strong central state. They built majestic pyramids to serve as tombs. During the Middle and New Kingdoms, trade and warfare brought Egypt into contact with other civilizations. New

ideas, customs, and technologies spread from one people to another in a process called cultural diffusion. Powerful New Kingdom pharaohs such as Queen Hatshepsut and Ramses II established a large empire that eventually reached the Euphrates River. After Ramses II, Egyptian power slowly declined.

A Queen of Egypt
Queen Nefertiti, wife of an Egyptian pharaoh

Egyptian Civilization

Egyptians worshipped many gods and goddesses. They also built tombs to preserve their bodies for the afterlife and they filled them with items that they would need in their new lives.

Egyptian society was organized into classes. The pharaoh, who was considered both a god and a king, ruled at the top.

Next came the nobles, who fought the pharaoh's wars. A tiny class of merchants and artisans developed. Farmers and slaves were at the bottom of society.

City-States of Ancient Sumer

To the northeast of the Nile lies the Fertile Crescent, an arc of soil-rich land. More than 5,000 years ago, the independent city-states of Sumer grew along the Tigris and Euphrates rivers in a part of the Fertile Crescent called Mesopotamia. A city-state is a political unit made up of a city and the surrounding lands.

Floods and Irrigation Control of the Tigris and Euphrates rivers was the key to the development of a civilization in the Sumerian city-states. Villagers built dikes and irrigation ditches. Using clay bricks, Sumerians built ziggurats, or soaring pyramid-temples.

The city-states of Sumer often fought for control of land and water. War leaders gained importance and eventually became hereditary rulers. A social hierarchy (HI uh rahr kee), or system of ranks, emerged. The highest rank included the ruling family, leading officials, and high priests.

Advances in Learning By 3200 B.C., Sumerians had invented the earliest form of writing, called cuneiform (kyoo NEE uh form). Scribes, or the specially trained people who knew how to read and write, maintained records for the kingdom.

Invaders, Traders, and Empire Builders

Mesopotamia's location at a geographical crossroads made

it tempting to invaders, some of whom built great empires. Sargon, the ruler of Akkad, conquered the city-states of Sumer about 2300 B.C. He built the first empire known to history.

About 1790 B.C., Hammurabi (hah moo RAH bee), king of Babylon, brought much of Mesopotamia under his control. He published a remarkable set of laws, the Code of Hammurabi. This code was the first major collection of laws in history. In 539 B.C., Persian armies overthrew Babylon.

Warfare and trade in Mesopotamia spread ideas and technology around the Mediterranean world. Knowledge of iron-working became common throughout the region. An Assyrian king founded one of the first libraries. The Phoenicians, famous as sailors and traders, created an alphabet. The Persians improved trade by encouraging the use of coins among merchants.

The Roots of Judaism

Among the many peoples who occupied the Fertile Crescent were the Hebrews. According to the Torah, the Hebrews' most sacred text, they once lived in Mesopotamia. About 2000 B.C., they migrated into a region known as Canaan.

The early Hebrews developed Judaism, a monotheistic religion (based on the belief in one true God). They recorded events and laws, such as the Ten Commandments, in the Torah. Prophets, or spiritual leaders, urged the Hebrews to obey God's law. These prophets preached a strong code of ethics, or moral standards of behavior. They urged both personal morality and social justice, calling on the rich and powerful to protect the poor and weak.

Civilizations of the Ancient Middle East

Geography and History

Like the Nile River in Egypt, the Tigris and Euphrates rivers gave rise to early civilizations.

By 1000 B.C., the Hebrews established the kingdom of Israel. A famous ruler, King Solomon, built a splendid temple dedicated to God, at Jerusalem. Eventually the kingdom split into two parts. A series of invading armies captured the Hebrew kingdoms.

During their captivity, the Hebrews became known as Jews. They lived under foreign rulers until about 2,000 years ago, when many were forced to leave their homeland. This diaspora (di AS puhr uh), or scattering of people, sent Jews to different parts of the world. Wherever they settled, they built close-knit communities and kept their traditions. Today, Judaism is considered one of the world's major religions for its unique contribution to religious thought.

Review

1. **Identify:** **(a)** Nile River, **(b)** Fertile Crescent, **(c)** Mesopotamia, **(d)** Hebrews.
2. **Define:** **(a)** pharoah, **(b)** cultural diffusion, **(c)** city-state, **(d)** ziggurat, **(e)** hierarchy, **(f)** cuneiform, **(g)** scribe, **(h)** monotheistic, **(i)** prophet, **(j)** ethics, **(k)** diaspora.
3. Name two geographic locations where early civilizations developed.

3 EARLY CIVILIZATIONS IN INDIA AND CHINA (2500 B.C.–256 B.C.)

Key Facts

- India's first civilization grew in the Indus River valley.
- The Aryans moved into the Indus Valley and built a new civilization along the Ganges River.
- During the Shang and Zhou Dynasties, the ancient Chinese made significant achievements in many areas.

As civilizations took shape in the Nile Valley and Fertile Crescent, people in India and China carved out their own civilizations. These grew along the fertile river valleys of Asia.

Cities of the Indus Valley

India's first civilization emerged in the Indus River valley about 2500 B.C. The people of the Indus flourished there for 1,000 years, building a civilization that covered the largest area of any in ancient times. Its two main cities, Mohenjo-Daro and Harappa, were both carefully planned. Each city was laid out in a grid pattern, with blocks larger than modern city blocks. Houses had complex plumbing systems, with baths, drains, and water chutes that led to underground sewers.

Most Indus people were farmers. Powerful leaders, perhaps priest-kings, made sure the cities had a reliable supply of grain. Merchants and traders sailed with cargoes of cotton cloth, grain, copper, and pearls all the way to the cities of Sumer.

By 1750 B.C., the quality of life in Indus Valley cities was declining. Scholars think the final blow fell about 1500 B.C. with the arrival of nomadic people from the north. The newcomers were Aryans. With their horse-drawn chariots and superior weapons, they overran the cities and towns of the Indus region.

Kingdoms of the Ganges

The Aryans were Indo-European people who migrated across Europe and Asia seeking water and pasture for their horses and cattle. Over several centuries, waves of Aryan groups moved through the mountain passes into northwestern India. In time, Aryans spread eastward to the forests of the Ganges River basin. They made tools of iron and built walled cities. By 500 B.C., a new Indian civilization had emerged. It consisted of many rival kingdoms, though people shared a common culture.

Most of what we know about the Aryans comes from the Vedas, a collection of prayers, hymns, and other religious teachings. Aryan priests memorized and recited the Vedas for a thousand years before they were written down.

Indus Valley Civilization

Indus Valley civilization, 2500 B.C.–1500 B.C.

HINDU KUSH
Khyber Pass
Bolan Pass
ASIA
Indus R.
30°N
Harappa
Mohenjo-Daro
THAR DESERT
Brahmaputra R.
HIMALAYA MTS.
NORTHERN PLAIN
Ganges R.
VINDHYA MTS.
Narmada R.
INDIA
Arabian Sea
WESTERN GHATS
DECCAN PLATEAU
EASTERN GHATS
Bay of Bengal
15°N
N W E S
Mercator Projection
0   250   500 Miles
0   250   500 Kilometers
75°E
90°E
INDIAN OCEAN

Geography and History

As in Egypt and Mesopotamia, the Indus Valley civilization grew up in a fertile river valley. Indus people built great cities and carried on farming and trade.

Chinese Craftmanship
Zhou dynasty dragon head of bronze and gold

Society The Aryans divided people into social classes by occupation. The three basic groups were the priests; the warriors; and the herders, farmers, artisans, and merchants. Eventually, the Aryans added a fourth group—non-Aryans whom they had conquered. This group was at the lowest level of society. It included farm workers, servants, and other laborers. Over time, these divisions gave way to a more complex system of castes. Castes are social groups into which people are born and which they cannot leave.

Religious Beliefs Aryans were polytheistic. That is, they believed in many gods. As society developed and changed, people moved toward the notion of a single spiritual power beyond the many gods of the Vedas. They called this power brahman and believed it lived in all things. Some Aryans became mystics, or individuals who devote their lives to seeking spiritual truth.

Early Civilizations in China

Long distances and physical barriers separated China from Egypt, the Middle East, and India. This isolation contributed to the Chinese belief that China was the center of the Earth and the sole source of civilization. This led the ancient Chinese to call their land the Middle Kingdom.

Geography Great barriers blocked the easy movement of the Chinese to the outside world. High mountains, brutal deserts, thick jungles, and the vast Pacific Ocean lay between China and the rest of the world. Still, the people of China found ways to trade with neighboring peoples. In time, Chinese products reached the Middle East and beyond.

Chinese history began in the Huang He valley, where Neolithic people learned to farm. As in other places, the need to control the river through large water projects probably led to the rise of a strong central government.

The Shang and Zhou Dynasties About 1650 B.C., a Chinese people called the Shang came to power in northern China. In 1027 B.C., the Zhou (JOH) people overthrew the Shang. The Zhou dynasty lasted until 256 B.C. A dynasty is a ruling family. To justify their rebellion against the Shang, the Zhou dynasty promoted the idea of the Mandate of Heaven, or the divine right to rule. Later, this idea expanded to explain the dynastic cycle, or the rise and fall of dynasties. If rulers became corrupt, the Chinese believed that Heaven withdrew its support, or mandate, and the dynasty fell.

Religion By Shang times, the Chinese had developed complex religious beliefs. They prayed to many gods and nature spirits. Over time, Chinese religious practices came to center on respect for ancestors. The Chinese called on the spirits of their ancestors to bring good fortune to the family. The Chinese also believed that the universe reflected a balance between two forces, yin and yang. Yin was linked to the Earth and female forces, while yang stood for Heaven and male forces.

Science and Technology During the Shang and Zhou periods, the Chinese studied the movement of the planets, recorded eclipses, and created an accurate calendar. They developed the technology of bronzemaking and silkmaking. Under the Zhou dynasty, the Chinese made the first books. They bound strips of wood or bamboo together, and drew characters on the flat surfaces. By 256 B.C., China was a large, wealthy, and highly developed center of civilization.

Review

1. **Identify:** (a) Monhenjo-Daro, (b) Aryans, (c) Vedas, (d) Zhou dynasty.
2. **Define:** (a) caste, (b) polytheistic, (c) brahman, (d) mystic, (e) dynasty, (f) dynastic cycle.
3. Name the four basic groups, or castes, into which the Aryans divided people.
4. What were some of the religious beliefs of the Chinese during the Shang dynasty?

Part II — Empires of the Ancient World

1 EMPIRES OF INDIA AND CHINA (600 B.C.–A.D 550)

Key Facts

- In ancient India, two major religions developed—Hinduism and Buddhism.
- Under the Maurya and Gupta empires, India grew into a center of trade.
- Shi Huangdi united all of China. Under the Han rulers who followed Shi Huangi, Chinese civilization made huge advances.

Between 600 B.C. and A.D. 550, strong, unified empires emerged in India and China. These civilizations set patterns in government, religion, and philosophy that influenced later cultures.

Hinduism and Buddhism

Two major religions, Hinduism and Buddhism, grew in ancient India. Hinduism has no single founder and no single sacred text. It grew from the beliefs of the different groups who settled in India. Even so, all Hindus share certain basic beliefs. They believe that everything is part of the unchanging, all-powerful spiritual force called brahman. The most important Hindu gods represent aspects of brahman. The goal of life for Hindus is to achieve union with

brahman. Reincarnation is the rebirth of the soul in another bodily form. Reincarnation allows people to work toward union with brahman through several lifetimes.

Another major religion, Buddhism, emerged in the 500s B.C. While it shared many Hindu traditions, Buddhism differed from Hinduism. It urged people to seek enlightenment through meditation, rather than through the priests, formal rituals, and many gods of Hinduism.

Buddhism's founder was Siddhartha Gautama. He was known as the Buddha, which means the "Enlightened One." The Buddha taught that desire causes suffering. To overcome suffering, people should rid themselves of desire.

Buddhism's final goal was to achieve nirvana, or union with the universe and release from the cycle of rebirth.

Powerful Empires of India

For centuries, northern India was a battleground. Then, in 321 B.C., Chandragupta Maurya (chun druh GUP tuh MOW uhr yuh) forged the first great Indian empire. The Maurya dynasty eventually conquered much of India.

The most honored Maurya emperor was Chandragupta's grandson, Asoka. Turning his back on violent conquest, Asoka converted to Buddhism. He ruled by moral example. His policies brought peace and wealth. Asoka also paved the way for the spread of Buddhism throughout Asia.

After Asoka's death, rivals battled for power. Despite unrest, India developed into a center of world trade. It established contact with civilizations in Africa, the Middle East, and Central and Southeast Asia. Then, about 500

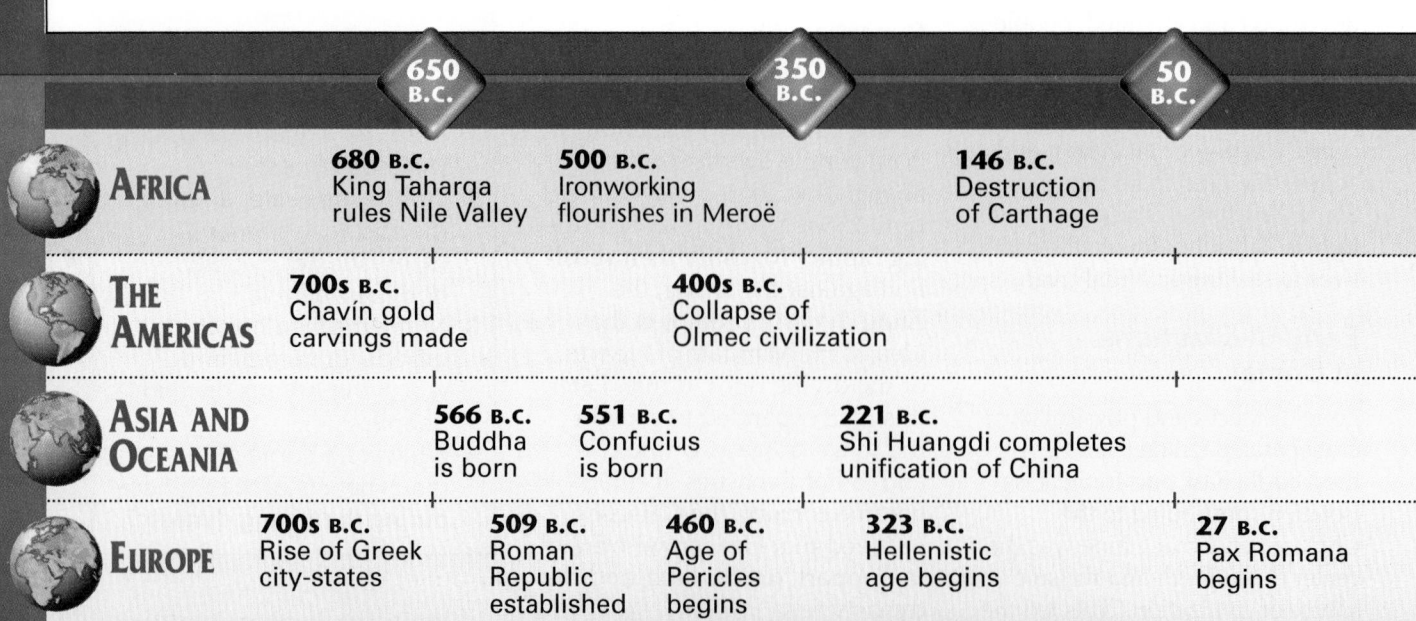

	650 B.C.	350 B.C.		50 B.C.
AFRICA	**680 B.C.** King Taharqa rules Nile Valley	**500 B.C.** Ironworking flourishes in Meroë	**146 B.C.** Destruction of Carthage	
THE AMERICAS	**700s B.C.** Chavín gold carvings made	**400s B.C.** Collapse of Olmec civilization		
ASIA AND OCEANIA	**566 B.C.** Buddha is born **551 B.C.** Confucius is born	**221 B.C.** Shi Huangdi completes unification of China		
EUROPE	**700s B.C.** Rise of Greek city-states **509 B.C.** Roman Republic established	**460 B.C.** Age of Pericles begins	**323 B.C.** Hellenistic age begins	**27 B.C.** Pax Romana begins

years after the Mauryas, the Gupta dynasty united much of India. Under the Guptas, who ruled from A.D. 320 to about A.D. 550, India enjoyed a golden age of peace and achievement.

Pillars of Indian Life Most Indians of that period were village peasants. Then, as today, the village and the family maintained order in daily life. The caste system also greatly influenced Indian society. Caste rules governed every part of life—including where people lived and how they earned a living. Despite its inequalities, caste created a stable social order.

Philosophy and Religion in China

China's most influential philosopher, Confucius, was born in 551 B.C. A brilliant scholar, Confucius took little interest in religious matters. He was concerned with social order and good government. He taught that harmony resulted when people accepted their place in society. He put filial piety, or respect for parents, above all

other duties. Confucius' ideas came to influence every area of Chinese life and eventually spread to neighboring countries.

Another Chinese philosopher, Hanfeizi, introduced ideas that differed sharply from the ideas of Confucius. He insisted that the only way to achieve order in society was to pass strict laws and to impose harsh punishments. Hanfeizi's teachings came to be known as Legalism. Many feudal rulers, including the Qin emperor who united China in 221 B.C., believed Legalism was the most effective way to maintain order.

A third philosophy, Daoism, arose around the same time. Daoists sought to live in harmony with nature, rather than to bring order to human affairs. They viewed government as unnatural and therefore the cause of many problems.

Strong Rulers Unite China

When the Zhou dynasty weakened, a powerful new ruler, Shi Huangdi, rose to unify all of China. He spent 20 years conquering the

warring states. He built a strong government and set the stage for China's classical age. His most remarkable and costly achievement was the building of the Great Wall.

After Shi Huangdi died, a new dynasty, the Han, was founded. It lasted from 206 B.C. to A.D. 220. Under Han rulers, the Chinese made huge advances in trade, government, technology, and the arts. The Silk Road, which eventually stretched 4,000 miles, linked China to the Fertile Crescent. The Han empire brought 400 years of unity to China.

Review

1. **Identify:** **(a)** Siddhartha Gautama, **(b)** Confucius, **(c)** Shi Huangdi, **(d)** the Han Dynasty.
2. **Define:** **(a)** reincarnation, **(b)** nirvana, **(c)** filial piety.
3. What are two basic teachings of Hinduism?

50 B.C. **A.D 250** **A.D 550**

23 B.C.
Roman attack on Nubia fails

A.D. 350
Axum converts to Christianity

A.D. 100s
Mochican civilization rises

A.D. 200s
Hopewell culture flourishes

A.D. 500s
Height of Mayan civilization

A.D. 100
Paper invented in Han China

A.D. 320
Gupta golden age begins

A.D. 135
Jewish diaspora begins

A.D. 476
Western Roman empire falls

Key Facts

- Through trading contacts, Minoan and Mycenaean cultures borrowed many ideas from older civilizations.
- After the Persian Wars, democracy flourished in Athens.
- Guided by a belief in reason, Greek artists, writers, and philosophers used their genius to seek order in the universe.

Unlike many other civilizations, Greek civilization did not rise in a fertile river valley. Instead, it grew in a rugged corner of southeastern Europe. Over time, independent Greek city-states created a civilization that set a standard of excellence for later civilizations. Greek ideas about the universe, the individual, and government still live on in the world today.

Early People of the Aegean

The island of Crete in the Aegean Sea was home to the Minoan people, the earliest civilization in the region. The Minoans were traders who set up outposts throughout the Aegean world and on the Greek mainland. Through contact with Egypt and Mesopotamia, this early people gained ideas and technology that they adapted to their own culture. Minoan civilization reached its height between about 1750 B.C. and 1500 B.C. By about 1400 B.C., Minoan civilization had vanished. A natural disaster may have helped destroy these island people.

The Mycenaeans, another civilization of sea traders, soon dominated the Greek mainland and Crete. They flourished between about 1400 B.C. and 1200 B.C. The Mycenaeans, too, absorbed both Egyptian and Mesopotamian ideas, which they passed on to later Greeks. They are best remembered for

the Trojan War. The poet Homer described the conflict in his two epic poems, the *Iliad* and the *Odyssey*. These poems reveal much about the values and religion of the ancient Greeks. The heroes display honor and courage. Such ideals greatly influenced Greek culture. Three thousand years later, the epics

of Homer and the ideals of the ancient Greeks continue to inspire us.

The Rise of Greek City-States

When Mycenaean civilization declined, the Greeks seemed to step backward. For centuries, Greeks lived in small, isolated farming villages. Eventually, they began to build many small city-states. However, they frequently warred among themselves. Despite their differences, Greeks shared a common culture, including their language, religion, and festivals. They became skilled sailors and

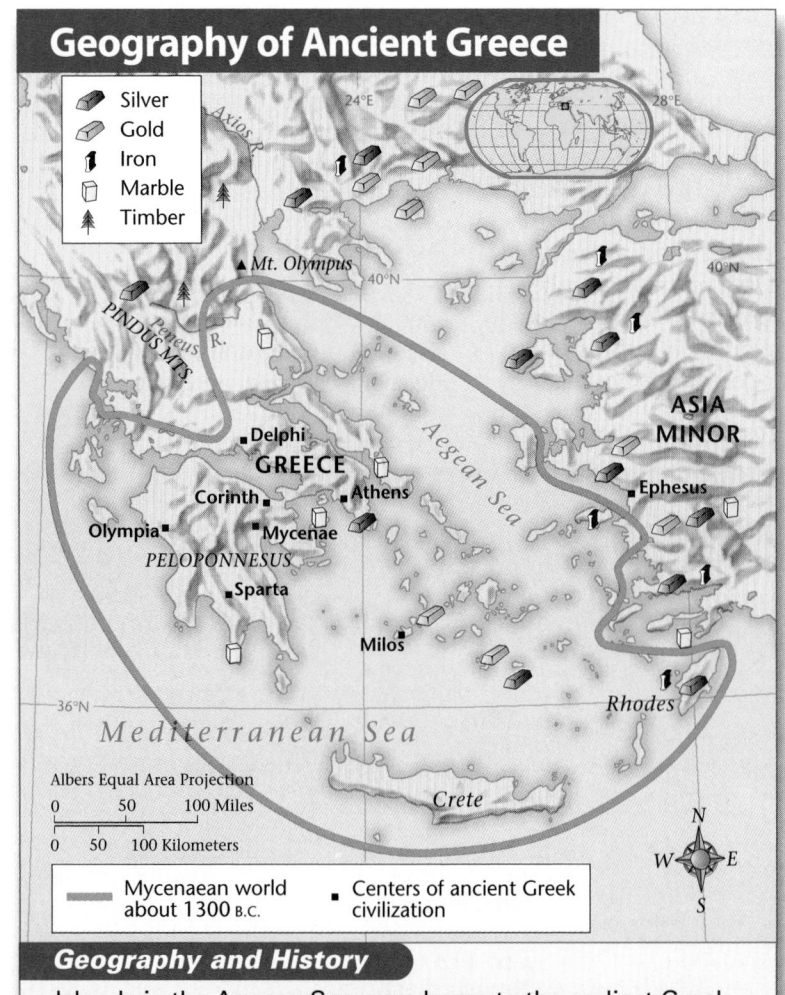

Geography of Ancient Greece

Silver
Gold
Iron
Marble
Timber

Mt. Olympus

PINDUS MTS.

Peneus R.

Delphi
GREECE
Corinth   Athens
Olympia   Mycenae
PELOPONNESUS
Sparta

Aegean Sea

ASIA MINOR

Ephesus

Milos

Rhodes

Mediterranean Sea

Crete

Albers Equal Area Projection

0   50   100 Miles

0   50   100 Kilometers

—— Mycenaean world about 1300 B.C.
• Centers of ancient Greek civilization

Geography and History

Islands in the Aegean Sea were home to the earliest Greek civilizations. Later, independent Greek city-states arose on the Greek mainland.

traders. Eventually, Greek colonies took root all around the Mediterranean. Greek ideas and culture spread.

As their world expanded after 750 B.C., the Greeks evolved a unique version of the city-state, called the polis. Typically, Greeks built cities on two levels. On a hilltop stood the acropolis (uh KRAHP uh lihs), or hilltop city. There, the Greeks dedicated temples to the gods and goddesses. On flatter ground below lay the walled main city with its marketplace, theater, public buildings, and homes.

Governing the City-States At first, the ruler of the polis was a king. A government in which a king or queen exercises central power is a monarchy. Slowly, power shifted to a class of noble landowners. The result was an aristocracy, or rule by a land-holding elite. As trade expanded, a new middle class of wealthy merchants, farmers, and artisans formed in some cities. They challenged the land-owning nobles for power and came to rule some city-states. The result was a form of government called an oligarchy. An oligarchy is government by a small, powerful elite, usually from the business class.

Sparta and Athens In the Greek city-state of Sparta, a warrior society took root. Spartan boys trained for military service. Girls exercised regularly. Because men were occupied with war, some women gained responsibilities such as running the family's estates. In contrast, the city-state of Athens evolved into a democracy, or government by the people. By modern standards, Athenian democracy was quite limited. Only male citizens participated.

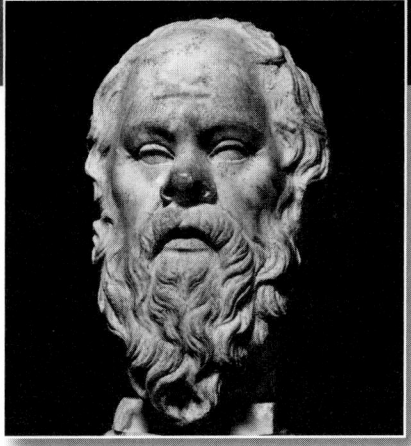

Greek Wisdom
Socrates, an Athenian philosopher

Victory and Defeat in the Greek World When the Persians threatened the Greeks, the city-states briefly joined together to defend themselves. After the Persian Wars, Athens thrived. Under the leadership of Pericles, a Greek statesman from 460 B.C. to 429 B.C., democracy and culture flourished. Athens developed a direct democracy. Under this system, a large number of male citizens took part in the day-to-day affairs of government. Athenian power and influence increased.

The Glory That Was Greece

Greeks had great confidence in the power of the human mind. Many Greek artists, writers, and philosophers denied that events were caused by the gods. Instead they used observation and reason to find causes for what happened. Philosophers and teachers like Socrates, Plato, and Aristotle developed new ideas about truth, reason, justice, and government. People developed new styles of architecture, sculpture, and painting that reflected those ideas. Philosophers, poets, and dramatists set the standard for what later Europeans called the classic style.

Alexander and the Hellenistic Age

While the Greek city-states warred among themselves, King Philip of neighboring Macedonia built a superb army. Eventually, Philip controlled all of Greece. When he died, his 20-year-old son Alexander took the throne. Over the next 12 years, this confident young man earned the title Alexander the Great. His conquests spread Greek civilization through the Mediterranean world and across the Middle East to the outskirts of India.

Alexander's conquests linked a vast area. He and his generals founded new cities. Greek culture blended with Persian, Egyptian, and Indian cultures to create the Hellenistic civilization. Art, science, mathematics, and philosophy flourished. The city of Alexandria became a center of learning. Even as Greek political power waned, Greek ideas came to dominate the Mediterranean world. This legacy later influenced the civilizations of Rome and Western Europe.

Review

1. **Identify:** (a) Homer, (b) Pericles, (c) Alexander.
2. **Define:** (a) polis, (b) acropolis, (c) monarchy, (d) aristocracy, (e) oligarchy, (f) democracy, (g) direct democracy.
3. What cultural ties united the Greek world?
4. How were Greek city-states governed?
5. Why did many Greek philosphers and writers reject the belief that events were caused by the whims of the gods?

Key Facts

● Conquest and diplomacy helped the Romans spread their rule from Spain to Egypt.

● During the Pax Romana, Roman emperors brought peace, order, and prosperity to the lands they controlled.

● Christianity, which began in Roman-held lands in the Middle East, spread throughout the Roman empire.

Rome expanded across the Mediterranean and grew into a huge, diverse empire. Rome's 1,000-year history had many lasting effects. Probably none was more important than the spread of key parts of the civilizations of Greece, Egypt, and the Fertile Crescent westward into Europe.

The Roman World Takes Shape

Rome began as a small city-state in Italy. The Romans were an Indo-European people who settled along the Tiber River in small villages. Their neighbors, the Etruscans, ruled much of central Italy, including Rome. After the Romans threw out the hated Etruscan king in 509 B.C., they resolved never to be ruled by a monarch again. Instead, they set up a republic, a government in which officials are chosen by the people. At first, the most powerful people in government were patricians, or members of the landholding upper class. Eventually, commoners, or plebeians, also gained the right to be elected to the Roman senate.

As Rome's political system changed, its armies expanded Roman power across Italy. By about 270 B.C., Rome occupied all of Italy. Rome's success was due partly to skillful diplomacy and partly to its efficient, well-disciplined army. Furthermore, Rome generally treated its

defeated enemies with mercy. By 133 B.C., Roman power reached from Spain to Egypt.

From Republic to Empire

Military victories put the Romans in control of busy trade routes. Incredible riches flooded into Rome from conquered lands. This new wealth, however, had disturbing consequences. Increased corruption and self-interest replaced virtues such as simplicity, hard work, and devotion to duty. Attempts to reform the system led to a backlash. For 100 years, Rome faced a series of civil wars.

Eventually, a powerful Roman general named Octavian restored order. Although he

was not called a king, he exercised absolute power. Taking the name Augustus, he ruled from 31 B.C. to A.D. 14, and brought the 500-year-old republic to an end. A new age dawned—the age of the Roman empire.

As Rome's first emperor, Augustus helped the empire recover from the long period of unrest. He laid the foundation for a stable government and undertook economic reforms. The 200-year span that began with Augustus ended with emperor Marcus Aurelius. It is known as the Pax Romana, or "Roman Peace." During this time, Roman emperors brought peace, order, unity, and prosperity to the lands under their control.

The Roman Achievement

Through war and conquest, Rome spread its civilization to distant lands. Yet, the civilization that developed was not simply Roman. Rather, Rome acted as a bridge between the east and the west by borrowing and transforming Greek and

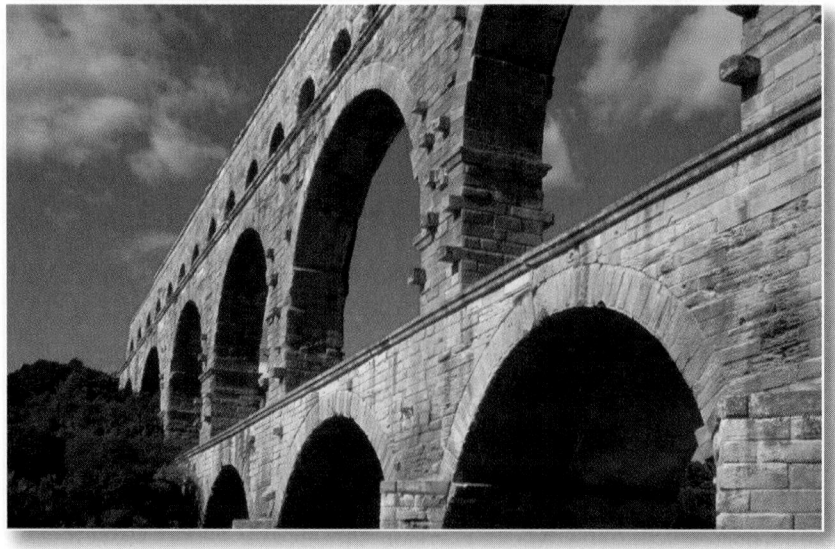

A Roman Aqueduct
Roman engineers built this aqueduct across the Gardon River in present-day France.

Jesus Healing a Woman
This Roman mural depicts Jesus miraculously healing an afflicted woman.

Hellenistic achievements. This blend of cultures became known as Greco-Roman civilization.

The Romans greatly admired Greek culture. They took Greek ideas and adapted them to their own ways. Roman sculptors, for instance, used the Greek idea of realism to reveal an individual's character in each stone portrait. Roman architects improved on design elements such as the arch and the dome. Above all, Romans excelled as engineers. They built roads, bridges, aqueducts, and harbors throughout the empire. Many of these remained standing long after Rome fell.

Probably the greatest legacy of Rome was its commitment to the rule of law and to justice. These ideas still shape western civilization today. The rule of law fostered unity and stability. Roman law would become the basis for legal systems in Europe and Latin America.

The Rise of Christianity

Early in the Pax Romana, a new religion, Christianity, sprang up in Roman-held lands in the Middle East. Its founder was a Jew named Jesus. Jesus was born around 4 B.C. in Bethlehem. He was prophesied to be the messiah, or savior sent by God to lead the Jews to freedom. The teachings of Jesus were firmly rooted in the Jewish religion. He believed in one God and accepted the Ten Commandments, a collection of laws that Jews believed God gave them.

At the same time, Jesus preached new beliefs. He called himself the Son of God and taught that his mission was to bring salvation and eternal life to all of God's children—anyone who would believe in him. He extended the Jewish ideas of mercy and sympathy for the poor and helpless to include forgiveness and love for enemies.

To some Jews and Romans, Jesus was a dangerous troublemaker. Eventually, he was executed. But his disciples, or followers, believed that Jesus had risen from the dead, talked with them, and then ascended into heaven. Slowly, a few Jews accepted the teaching that Jesus was the messiah, or the Christ, from the Greek for "the anointed one." These people became the first Christians.

For a while, Christianity remained a sect, or small group, within Judaism. Then Paul, a Jew from Asia Minor, set to work to spread the new faith to non-Jews. At first, Rome persecuted Christians. Nevertheless, Christians organized into a church and grew in strength. Eventually, Christianity reshaped Roman beliefs.

The Long Decline

After the death of the emperor Marcus Aurelius in A.D. 180, turmoil rocked the Roman empire. Eventually, the empire split into two parts, east and west, each with its own ruler. In the west, a corrupt government, poverty and unemployment, and declining moral values contributed to the decline. Germanic peoples along the northern borders began to claim territory from the weakened empire. Then foreign invaders marched into Italy and, in 476, took over Rome itself.

But the Roman empire did not disappear from the map. The eastern Roman empire continued to prosper under the emperor Constantine and other emperors. In time, the eastern Roman empire would become known as the Byzantine empire. It would endure for another 1,000 years.

Review

1. **Identify:** **(a)** Augustus, **(b)** Pax Romana, **(c)** Jesus.
2. **Define:** **(a)** republic **(b)** patrician, **(c)** plebeian, **(d)** messiah, **(e)** sect.
3. Why did Rome change from a republic to an empire ruled by an emperor?
4. Give an example of a Roman achievement that continues to influence western civilization today.
5. Describe the relationship between Christianity and Judaism.

4 CIVILIZATIONS OF THE AMERICAS (1400 B.C.–A.D. 1570)

Key Facts

- Between A.D. 300 and A.D. 900, Mayan civilization flourished from southern Mexico through Central America. In the 1400s, the Aztecs conquered most of Mexico and built a highly developed civilization.
- By the 1500s, the Incas established a centralized government in Peru.
- Eight culture groups developed in North America. Their diverse ways of life were strongly influenced by geography.

The first American civilization, the Olmecs, began in the tropical forest along the Mexican Gulf Coast. Olmec society lasted from about 1400 B.C. to 500 B.C. Later, other advanced civilizations developed in Middle and South America, including those of the Mayas, Aztecs, and Incas. Diverse groups of people lived in North America.

Civilizations of Middle America

The first settlers in the Americas were nomadic hunters who probably migrated across a land bridge between Siberia and Alaska. Gradually, they populated two vast continents. These early people adapted to a variety of climates and resources. Between 8500 B.C. and 2000 B.C., Neolithic people in Mexico, or perhaps farther south, began to raise a variety of crops, including corn, beans, and squash. They also learned to tame animals.

The Mayas Although the Olmec civilization was the first in the Americas, more is known about the Mayan city-states of Central America. Mayan farmers cleared the rain forests to produce maize, or corn, to feed their cities. Mayan society was divided into social classes. Each city-state had its own ruling chief. Priests held great power. Pyramid temples and palaces served as altars and burial places. The Mayas developed a

hieroglyphic writing system and an accurate calendar. Today, millions of people in Central America speak Mayan languages.

The Aztecs Several hundred years after the decline of Mayan civilization, the Aztecs conquered most of Mexico. By 1500, the Aztec empire numbered about 30 million people. War brought immense wealth as well as power to the Aztecs. Tribute, or payment from conquered peoples, helped the Aztecs turn their capital into a magnificent city.

The Aztecs developed a complex social structure with

North American Culture Areas About 1450

Arctic/Subarctic

Northwest Coast

California/Great Basin/Plateau

Southwest

Great Plains

Eastern Woodlands

Southeast

Azimuthal Equal Area Projection

0   500   1000 Miles

0   500   1000 Kilometers

Geography and History

As Native Americans spread out to populate North America, they developed varied cultures. The map shows culture areas in which tribes shared similar ways of life.

a single ruler or emperor at the top. A large class of priests performed the various rituals and sacrifices needed to please the many Aztec gods. Conquered peoples often supplied both tribute and human sacrifices for Aztec religious rituals. As a result, the conquered peoples were unhappy and they often rebelled. When armies from Spain later arrived, they found allies among the peoples who were ruled by the Aztecs.

The World of the Incas

In South America for more than 2,000 years, civilizations rose and fell. Then in the 1400s, the Incas came down from the Andes mountains of Peru. Led by Pachacuti, a skilled warrior and leader, they rapidly conquered an empire that stretched 2,500 miles down the Andes and along the Pacific coast. By the 1500s, the Incas of South America had established a centralized government in Peru, ruled by a god-king and a powerful class of priests.

Incan Government The emperor had absolute power over the Incan empire. He claimed to be divine and lived in splendor. From the capital at Cuzco, he ran an efficient government. His chain of command reached to every village. Specially trained officials kept records on quipus, collections of knotted colored strings, which probably noted dates and events as well as statistics.

Incan Achievements The Incas worked to unite their conquered peoples. They imposed their own language, Quechua (KEHCH wuh), and religion on the people. They also created one of the great road systems in history. It was even more extensive than the roads that united the Roman empire. The Incan

Mayan Society in Art
Mayan potters fashioned clay figurines depicting people at all levels of society. Here, an aristocrat poses in his formal robes of state.

roads wound more than 12,000 miles through mountains and deserts. In the 1500s, civil war broke out in the Incan empire. The fighting weakened the empire at the moment that Spanish invaders were about to arrive.

Peoples of North America

Before 1500, many groups of Native Americans with diverse ways of life lived in North America. Culture groups included societies in the Arctic, Northwest Coast, California, Great Basin, Southwest, Great Plains, Southeast, and Eastern Woodlands. These societies were strongly influenced by geography.

The Anasazi The best-known society of the desert southwest is that of the Anasazi. These resourceful people built large villages, later called *pueblos* by the Spanish, of stone and adobe brick. At the center of their village life was the kiva. A kiva is a large underground chamber used for religious rituals. In the late 1100s, the Anasazi began to build housing complexes in the

shadow of canyon walls. Cliffs offered protection from raiders. By the late 1200s, drought forced the Anasazi to abandon their cliff dwellings. Their traditions survive today among the Hopi and other Pueblo Indians.

The Mound Builders Far to the east of the Anasazi, in the Mississippi and Ohio river valleys, other farming cultures emerged as early as 700 B.C. The Hopewell people left behind giant earthen mounds in many different shapes. Objects found in Hopewell mounds suggest that trade networks stretched from the Gulf of Mexico to the Great Lakes. By about A.D. 800, this culture was replaced by the Mississippians, who grew corn and other crops. They built large towns and ceremonial centers. Their greatest center, Cahokia in present-day Illinois, housed as many as 40,000 people by about 1200. Variations in climate and resources encouraged the development of different cultures. In the far north, the Inuits adapted to frozen terrain. Along the Northwest Coast, rich food sources encouraged wealthy societies. In the Eastern Woodlands, warring farming villages eventually settled their differences and formed the Iroquois League.

Review

1. **Identify:** **(a)** Olmecs, **(b)** Mayas, **(c)** Aztecs, **(d)** Incas, **(e)** Anasazi, **(f)** Mississippians.
2. **Define:** **(a)** tribute, **(b)** kiva.
3. Who ruled the Mayan city-states?
4. Describe two steps the Incas took to unite their empire.

Regional Civilizations

1 THE RISE OF EUROPE (500–1300)

Key Facts

- In the 800s, a ruler named Charlemagne temporarily reunited much of Europe. He revived learning and furthered the blending of German, Roman, and Christian traditions.

- Feudalism, the manor economy, and the Roman Catholic Church were dominant forces during the Middle Ages.

When Germanic peoples ended Roman rule in the West, they began to create a new civilization. Their culture differed greatly from that of the Romans. They had no cities and no written laws. Instead, they lived in small communities, ruled by elected kings whose chief role was to lead them in war. Europe became a fragmented, largely isolated region.

The Early Middle Ages

Between 400 and 700, Germanic invaders carved Europe into small kingdoms. Then around 800, Western Europe had a moment of unity when Charlemagne (SHAHR luh mayn), or Charles the Great, built an empire reaching across France, Germany, and part of Italy.

He revived learning, extended Christian civilization into northern Europe, and furthered the blending of German, Roman, and Christian traditions. He also set up a strong, efficient government.

After Charlemagne died in 814, his empire crumbled. The resultant power struggle, which lasted almost 30 years, came to an end in 843 when Charlemagne's grandsons divided his empire into three regions. A new wave of raiders overran Europe, plundering and looting. Muslims, Magyars, and Vikings all attacked the fragmented territories held by Charlemagne's heirs. Kings and emperors proved too weak to maintain law and order. People needed to defend their homes and lands. In response to that basic need for protection,

a new system, called feudalism, evolved. The rise of feudalism led to new networks linking all levels of European society.

Feudalism and the Manor Economy

Under the system of feudalism, powerful local lords divided their large landholdings among the lesser lords. In exchange for land and protection, these lesser lords, or vassals, pledged service and loyalty to the greater lord. A lord granted his vassal a fief (FEEF), or estate. It included the peasants who worked the land. Feudalism gave a strict order to medieval society.

Feudal lords battled constantly for power. Many nobles trained from boyhood for a future occupation as a knight, or mounted warrior. In the later medieval period, knights adopted a code of conduct called chivalry. Chivalry required knights to be brave, loyal, and true to their word. In warfare, knights had to fight fairly and be generous to their enemies. Since warfare often meant seizing lands, lords fortified

	500	750	1000
AFRICA		**600s** Islam spreads to North Africa	**800s** Ghana controls gold-salt trade	
THE AMERICAS		**600** Mayan civilization thrives	**800s** Mississippian civilization flourishes	
ASIA AND OCEANIA	**500s** Buddhism introduced to Japan	**622** Muhammad's hijra from Mecca to Medina		**960** Song dynasty in China
EUROPE	**500s** Byzantine empire reaches height		**800** Charlemagne crowned emperor by pope	

their homes to withstand attack. Medieval strongholds gradually became sprawling stone castles.

The heart of the medieval economy was the manor, or lord's estate. Most manors included one or more villages and surrounding lands. Most of the peasants on a manor were serfs, who were bound to the land. Peasants could not be purchased and sold like enslaved people, but they spent their lives working for the lord of the manor. In return, the lord gave them the right to farm some land for themselves, as well as protection from invaders.

The Medieval Church After the fall of Rome, the Christian Church split into an eastern and a western church. The western church, headed by the pope, became known as the Roman Catholic Church. As the Church grew stronger and wealthier, it became the most powerful secular, or worldly, force in medieval Europe. Some Church leaders, including the pope, ruled over their own territories, like feudal lords. Additionally, Church officials were often appointed to

high government positions by the ruling nobility because they were the only educated people. Eventually, the pope claimed to have authority over all secular rulers.

The Church also controlled the spiritual lives of Christians throughout Europe. Christians believed that all people were sinners and that many were doomed to eternal suffering. The only way to avoid hell was to believe in Christ and participate in the sacraments. Because the medieval Church administered the sacraments, it had absolute power in religious matters and significant control over European society.

Economic Expansion and Change By the 1000s, advances in agriculture and commerce spurred economic revival throughout Europe. People used new iron plows to improve farming, and windmills to grind grain into flour. The adoption of the three-field system enabled peasants to leave only a third of their land unplanted, and thus expanded crop production. New trade routes and goods also

increased wealth. Traders and their customers first did business at local trade fairs. Later, as these markets closed down during the winter, merchants settled in local towns and attracted artisans who made goods for them to sell. Soon, towns became trade and manufacturing centers. Merchant guilds, or associations, came to dominate life in medieval towns. By 1300, Western Europe's economic revival was making momentous changes in medieval life.

Review

1. **Identify:** (a) Germanic tribes, (b) Charlemagne, (c) Roman Catholic Church.
2. **Define:** (a) feudalism, (b) vassal, (c) fief, (d) knight, (e) chivalry, (f) manor, (g) serf, (h) secular, (i) guild.
3. What effect did Charlemagne's rule have on Europe?
4. How was medieval society organized under feudalism?

1000	1250	1500
1000 East African trading cities prosper	**1250** Empire of Mali reaches height	**1500** Kongo kingdom flourishes
1000 Anasazi build pueblo towns	**1438** Incan empire founded	**1500** Aztec empire reaches height
1206 Delhi Sultanate founded	**1368** Ming dynasty ends Mongol rule	**1520** Reign of Suleiman begins
1066 Normans conquer England	**1215** English Magna Carta signed	**1389** Ottomans defeat Serbs at Kosovo	**1462** Reign of Ivan the Great begins

2 THE HIGH MIDDLE AGES (1050–1450)

Key Facts

- During the High Middle Ages, feudal monarchs began to build a framework for the modern nation-state.
- European contacts with the Middle East during the Crusades revived interest in trade and exploration.
- Beginning in the 1300s, famine, plague, and war marked the decline of medieval Europe.

During the early Middle Ages, hundreds of feudal nobles ruled over territories of varying size. Most were loyal to a king or other overlord, but royal rulers had little power. During the High Middle Ages, feudal monarchs started to increase their power. Over many centuries, they built the framework for what would become the European nations of today.

Growth of Royal Power in England

When William the Conqueror took the throne of England in 1066, he helped unify England and strengthen the monarchy. William's successors built a system of tax collecting. They also strengthened finances and law. Other English kings broadened the system of royal justice and developed the basis for English common law, or law that is common—the same—for all people, regardless of rank. An early jury system also developed. A jury, or group of men sworn to speak the truth, determined which cases should be brought to trial.

Evolving Traditions As the English kings strengthened the throne, they conflicted with nobles and the Church. Out of those struggles came traditions of government that would influence the modern world. In the early 1200s, a group of nobles

checked the growing power of the English kings. They forced King John to sign the Magna Carta, or great charter.

The Magna Carta The Magna Carta contained two basic ideas that in the long run would shape government traditions in England. First, it said that the nobles had certain rights. Over time, the rights that originally had been granted to nobles applied to all English citizens. Second, the Magna Carta made clear that the monarch, like his or her subjects, must obey the law. This included respecting the legal rights of the people. The king also agreed not to raise new taxes without first consulting his Great Council of lords and clergy. Eventually, the Great Council became the Parliament.

Imperial Crown
Holy Roman emperors first wore this jewel-encrusted gold crown around the late 900s.

English Monarch and Parliament
In this scene, the king of England presides over Parliament. On either side of him are his vassals.

The Holy Roman Empire and the Church

The Holy Roman Empire arose from the patchwork of many Germanic states that formed after the death of Charlemagne. When a single ruler united the separate kingdoms, the pope crowned him "emperor." His successors took the title Holy Roman emperor.

During the early Middle Ages, the Church had spread its influence across Europe. By the High Middle Ages, both popes and monarchs were extending their authority. Explosive conflicts erupted. Popes clashed with the Holy Roman emperors who ruled lands from Germany to Italy. Some conflicts arose over who would control appointments to high Church offices. Eventually, some popes claimed the right to remove kings and emperors from the throne. Refusal to obey the Church could result in excommunication. Excommunication was a harsh penalty. It meant that someone could not receive the sacraments, or sacred rituals of the Church.

The Cathedral of Notre Dame
About 1140, Medieval architects developed the Gothic style of architecture, exemplified by this cathedral in Paris.

In the 1200s, the Roman Catholic Church reached its peak of power. However, after a French king engineered the election of a French pope, the papacy entered a period of decline.

Europeans Look Outward

In 1050, Western Europe was barely emerging from isolation. However, several civilizations in the Middle East and Asia had long been thriving political and economic powers. Muslims, as believers in the Islamic faith are called, had built a great empire and created a major civilization. It reached from Spain across North Africa and the Middle East to India.

The Crusades Begin In the eastern Mediterranean, Byzantine civilization was a rival to Islam. The Byzantines were Christians. Then Muslim Turks invaded the Byzantine empire. They also attacked Christian pilgrims to the Holy Land, or Palestine, in the Middle East. The Byzantine emperor asked the pope in Rome for help. Soon, thousands of Christian knights from Europe, as well as armies of ordinary men and women, left for the Holy Land to fight the Muslims. They fought a series of crusades, or holy wars.

Effects of the Crusades For 200 years, crusaders marched and fought. For a time, they held parts of Palestine. The Crusades failed in their chief goal—the conquest of the Holy Land. Instead, they left a bitter legacy of religious hatred behind them. However, the Crusades increased European

trade, heightened papal power, and increased the power of feudal monarchs. Contacts with the Muslim world also introduced Christians to regions they had never known existed.

Learning, Literature, and the Arts

As economic and political conditions improved in the High Middle Ages, a revival of learning took place. The Church wanted better-educated clergy. Royal rulers needed literate officials for their growing bureaucracies. Schools sprang up around the great cathedrals, eventually becoming the first universities. Ideas and texts that had originated in ancient Greece reached the universities through the works of Muslim scholars. New writings began to be produced in the vernacular, or everyday languages of ordinary people. Spain's great epic, *Poem of the Cid*, told of conflict with Islam. Famed Italian poet Dante Alighieri (DAHN tay al lee GYEH ree) wrote the *Divine Comedy*, an imaginary journey into hell and purgatory.

A Time of Crisis

In the late Middle Ages, a serie of disasters struck. Bubonic

plague, a disease spread by fleas on rats, raged throughout the world and eventually throughout Europe. Unsanitary conditions aided the spread of the disease, which was called the Black Death. Approximately one in three people died, more than in any war in history.

The plague brought social upheaval and plunged the European economy to a low ebb. Unable to provide sufficient comfort to people, the Church faced opposition and reform efforts. Famine and war added to the turmoil of the period. Western Europe would not fully recover from the effects of the Black Death for 100 years.

Review

1. **Identify:** **(a)** Magna Carta, **(b)** Holy Roman Empire, **(c)** Black Death.
2. **Define:** **(a)** common law, **(b)** jury, **(c)** excommunication, **(d)** sacrament, **(e)** crusade, **(f)** vernacular.
3. What principles were established in the Magna Carta?
4. What were the results of the Crusades?

3 THE BYZANTINE EMPIRE AND RUSSIA (330–1613)

Key Facts

- After the fall of Rome, Greco-Roman heritage survived in the Byzantine empire.
- Traders and missionaries brought Byzantine culture and Eastern Orthodox Christianity to Russia and Eastern Europe.
- Invasions and migrations created a mix of ethnic and religious groups in Eastern Europe.

The fall of Rome left Europe divided. To the west, medieval civilization began to grow. To the east, the Roman empire survived as the Byzantine empire. Byzantine civilization later influenced Eastern Europe and Russia, bringing Greek culture as well as Eastern Orthodox Christianity to the Slavic people.

The Byzantine Empire

As German invaders pounded the Roman empire in the west, emperors moved their base to the eastern Mediterranean. By 330, the emperor Constantine had rebuilt the Greek city of Byzantium. He renamed it Constantinople. In time, the eastern Roman empire became known as the Byzantine empire. During the Middle Ages, Constantinople thrived, controlling key trade routes that linked Europe and Asia. The Byzantine empire also protected Western Europe from invaders from the east.

Justinian's Code The most famous Byzantine emperor was Justinian, who ruled from 527 to 565. He was aided by his wife Theodora. Justinian set up a commission to collect and organize the laws of ancient Rome. The result was known as Justinian's Code. By the 1100s, Justinian's Code had reached Western Europe, influencing the laws and principles of the Roman Catholic Church as well as medieval monarchs. The

An Influential Empress
Theodora, seen in this mosaic carrying a church offering, encouraged her husband, Justinian, to protect women's rights.

code thus preserved and spread the heritage of Roman law.

Byzantine Christianity As in Western Europe, Christianity was important in the Byzantine empire. But a division grew between Byzantine Christians and Roman Catholics. In the Byzantine empire, the emperor controlled Church affairs, rejecting the pope's claim to

authority over all Christians. Further, Byzantine clergy retained the right to marry. By 1054, a number of such controversies caused a **schism,** or permanent split, between the Eastern (Greek) Orthodox and Roman Catholic churches.

By the time of the schism, the Byzantine empire was declining. In 1453, Constantinople fell to the Ottoman empire. The ancient Christian city, renamed Istanbul, eventually became a great center of Muslim culture.

Byzantine Heritage For 1,000 years, Byzantine civilization had thrived, blending Christian beliefs with Greek science, philosophy, arts, and literature. The Byzantines also expanded upon Roman achievements in engineering and law. When the empire fell in the 1400s, Greek scholars left Constantinople to teach at Italian universities. They took valuable Greek manuscripts to the West. They also took their knowledge of Greek and Byzantine culture. The work of these scholars contributed to the European cultural flowering known as the Renaissance.

The Rise of Russia

The early history of Russia began in the fertile area of present-day Ukraine. During Roman times, a people called the Slavs moved into southern Russia. Then, in the 700s and 800s, the Vikings began to travel on Russian rivers, trading and collecting tribute from the Slavs. The Vikings also traded with Constantinople. Eventually, the city of Kiev in the Ukraine became the center of the first Russian state. Kiev served as a vital trade center.

Trade brought Kiev into the Byzantine sphere of influence. Constantinople eventually sent missionaries to convert the Slavs to Christianity. About 863, two Greek monks adapted the Greek alphabet so they could translate the Bible into Slavic languages. This alphabet became the written script still used in Russia and Ukraine. With the adoption of Byzantine Christianity, Russians acquired a written language. A class of educated Russian priests grew. Russians adapted Byzantine art, music, and architecture.

The Mongol Conquest In the early 1200s, the Mongols of central Asia overran land from China to Eastern Europe. Though they were fierce conquerors, the Mongols were generally tolerant rulers. But the absolute power of the Mongols served as a model for later Russian rulers. Mongol rule also cut Russia off from Western Europe at a time when Europeans were making rapid advances in the arts and sciences.

Rise of Moscow Eventually, the princes of Moscow gained power and defeated the Mongols. Between 1462 and 1505, Ivan III, known as Ivan the Great, brought much of northern Russia under his rule. He and his successors took the title czar, the Russian word for Caesar. Ivan III built the framework for absolute rule. His grandson, Ivan IV, further centralized royal power. He undercut the privileges of the nobles and bound the serfs to the land. Ivan IV introduced Russia to a tradition of extreme absolute power that earned him the title "Ivan the Terrible."

Shaping Eastern Europe

In Eastern Europe, no single ethnic group dominated the region. An ethnic group is a large group

Growth of Russia, 1330–1584

☐	Extent of Mongol conquest, 1300
☐	Moscow, 1300
★	Battle site
☐	Land added, 1330–1462
☐	Land added, 1462–1533
☐	Land added, 1533–1584

Geography and History

Between 1300 and 1584, Russia grew from a small area around Moscow to a large territory.

of people who share the same language and cultural heritage. Over time, many groups settled in Eastern Europe. In the early Middle Ages, the Slavs came from Russia. Waves of Asian peoples moved into the area, among them the Huns, Avars, Bulgars, Khazars, and Magyars. Germanic people added to the mix.

Later, Byzantine missionaries carried Eastern Orthodox Christianity, as well as Byzantine culture, throughout the Balkans. At the same time, German knights and missionaries spread Roman Catholic Christianity to the area. In the late Middle Ages, Eastern Europe was a refuge for many Jewish settlers when Western European Christians persecuted them.

Many kingdoms and small states arose in Eastern Europe. Poland often had to battle

Germans, Russians, and Mongols to survive. The Magyars of Hungary controlled parts of present-day Slovakia and Romania. By the late 1100s, the Serbs built a kingdom in the Balkan peninsula. By the 1500s, however, the Ottoman Turks ruled over much of southeastern Europe.

Review

1. **Identify:** (a) Constantinople, (b) Justinian, (c) Kiev, (d) Ivan III.
2. **Define:** (a) schism, (b) czar, (c) ethnic group.
3. Describe the legacy of Byzantine civilization.
4. What element of Mongol rule continued to influence the Russian czars, even after they ousted the Mongols from Russia?

4 THE MUSLIM WORLD (622–1629)

Key Facts

- The religion of Islam emerged on the Arabian peninsula in the 600s.
- Muslim civilization eventually created cultural ties among diverse peoples across three continents.
- By the 1500s, the Mughals, Ottomans, and Safavids dominated the Muslim world.

In the 600s, a major religion, Islam, emerged in Arabia. Within a few years, Arabs spread Islam across a huge empire. The Arab empire eventually broke apart. Still, Islam continued to spread, creating shared traditions among diverse peoples. Islamic civilization opened routes for the transfer of goods, ideas, and technologies.

Rise of Islam

Muhammad, the prophet of Islam, was born in Mecca in western Arabia about 570. According to Muslim belief, when Muhammad was about 40, he was called in a vision to become the messenger of God. He spent the rest of his life spreading Islam. Eventually, thousands of Arabs embraced the new religion.

Like Judaism and Christianity, Islam is monotheistic. Muslims believe in one all-powerful, compassionate God. All Muslims accept five basic duties, known as the Five Pillars of Islam. They include belief in one God, daily prayer, charity to the poor, fasting, and the hajj, or pilgrimage to Mecca. Muslims also hold that the Quran contains the sacred word of God and is the final authority on all matters. Over time, Muslim scholars have applied the teachings of the Quran to every aspect of daily life. In this way, Islam is both a religion and a way of life.

Islam Spreads

When Muhammad died in 632, Abu Bakr was elected to be the first caliph, or successor to Muhammad. He launched a breathtaking military campaign to conquer territory across the Byzantine and Persian empires. A key reason for the Arabs' swift and wide-ranging conquests was their belief in the holiness of their faith and certainty of paradise for those who fell in battle.

A series of rulers led the conquests that carried Islam from the Atlantic to the Indus Valley. Eventually, the Abbassid dynasty moved the capital of Islam to Baghdad and ruled until 1258. Under the Abbassids, Baghdad exceeded Constantinople in size and wealth. But as the 1200s drew to a close, the Arab empire had fragmented and fallen. Independent Muslim caliphates and states were scattered across North Africa and Iberian peninsula in Europe, while Mongol converts to Islam ruled the Muslim Middle East.

Golden Age of Muslim Civilization

The advancing Muslim empire united people from diverse cultures, blending the cultures of Arabs, Persians, Egyptians and other Africans, and Europeans. Muslim society was more open than that of medieval Europe. People could advance in society, especially through religious, scholarly, or military achievements. Muslim leaders imposed a tax on non-Muslims but allowed Christians, Jews, and others to practice their own faiths. Many non-Muslims converted to Islam. In later centuries, Turkish and Mongol converts helped spread Islam far across Asia.

Between 750 and 1350, Muslim merchants established a vast trading network. Islamic ideas, products, and technology spread across the Muslim world and beyond. Muslims

Open-Air Marketplace
Muslim bazaars sold local goods as well as a variety of imports made available by a vast trading network.

pioneered the study of algebra and made contributions in the fields of astronomy, philosophy, and literature. Muslims also made advances in medicine and surgery. Islamic art reached new heights. Artisans developed elaborate mosaics of abstract and geometric patterns. In the field of architecture, domed mosques, or houses of worship, came to dominate Muslim cities. Baghdad became a great Muslim center of learning.

Muslims in India

About 1000, Turkish converts to Islam began making raids into India. Then, in the late 1100s, a Muslim sultan, or ruler, defeated Hindu armies. He set up a capital in Delhi. His successors founded the Delhi sultanate, which lasted from 1206 to 1526.

Muslims and Hindus Muslim rule brought changes to India. Widespread destruction of Buddhist monasteries contributed to the decline of Buddhism as a major religion in India. Many Hindus were killed. Some converted to Islam. Eventually, Muslim rulers grew more tolerant and Indian Muslims absorbed elements of Hindu culture.

Akbar the Great
As ruler of the Mughal empire, Akbar tried to promote harmony among the diverse peoples of India.

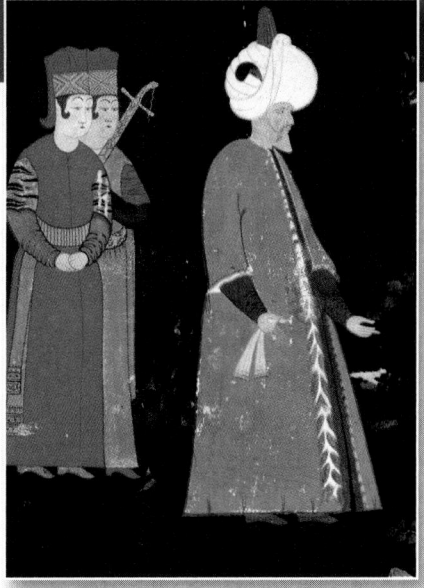

A Magnificent Sultan
Europeans dubbed Suleiman "the Magnificent" because of the splendor of his court. But they also admired his virtues as a ruler.

Mughal India In 1526, Turkish and Mongol invaders again poured into India. At their head rode Babur. He swept away the remnants of the Delhi sultanate and set up the Mughal dynasty, which ruled from 1526 to 1857. In the late 1600s, economic hardship sparked rebellions against the Mughal dynasty. Eventually, European traders began to work against the once-powerful Mughal empire.

The Ottoman and Safavid Empires

While the Mughals ruled India, two other dynasties, the Ottomans and the Safavids dominated the Middle East and parts of Eastern Europe. All three empires owed much of their success to new weapons, including cannons and muskets.

The Ottoman Empire The Ottomans were Turkish-speaking nomadic people who had migrated from Central Asia. In the 1300s, they moved across Asia Minor and into the Balkans. In 1453, they captured Constantinople and renamed it Istanbul. The Ottoman empire

was a powerful force for 500 years. Under the sultan Suleiman (SOO lay mahn), who ruled from 1520 to 1566, the Ottoman empire enjoyed its golden age. Ottoman poets adapted Persian and Arab models to produce works in the Turkish language. Painters produced detailed miniatures and illuminated manuscripts. Architects designed hundreds of mosques and palaces. At its height, the empire stretched from Hungary to Arabia and Mesopotamia and across North Africa. By the 1700s, European advances in commerce and military technology left the Ottomans behind.

The Safavid Empire By the 1500s, the Safavids (sah FAH weedz), a Turkish-speaking Muslim dynasty, had united a strong empire in present-day Iran. Pressed between the Ottomans and the Mughals of India, the Safavids fought many wars. The outstanding Safavid ruler, Shah Abbas the Great, ruled from 1588 to 1629. Abbas revived the glory of ancient Persia. His capital became a center for the international silk trade. In the late 1700s, a new dynasty, the Qajars (kah JAHRZ) won control of Iran. They ruled until 1925.

Review

1. **Identify: (a)** Muhammad, **(b)** Baghdad, **(c)** Mughal dynasty, **(d)** Ottoman empire.
2. **Define: (a)** hajj, **(b)** caliph, **(c)** mosque, **(d)** sultan.
3. What are some of the teachings of Islam?
4. How did Islam spread far beyond Arabia so quickly?

5 KINGDOMS AND TRADING STATES OF AFRICA (750 B.C.–A.D. 1586)

Key Facts

- Between 800 and 1600, a series of powerful West African kingdoms controlled the rich Sahara trade route.
- Indian Ocean trade routes led to the growth of wealthy city-states along the East African coast.

Vast migrations of people have contributed to the rich diversity of African cultures. One such series of migrations, called the Bantu migrations, probably occurred because of changes in the environment. Over a period of a thousand years, Bantu peoples from West Africa moved south and east to populate most of southern Africa. Today, as many as one third of Africans speak a language in the Bantu family.

Early Civilizations of Africa

Long before the Bantu migrations, important civilizations rose and flourished in Africa. While ancient Egyptian civilization developed in Northern Africa, another Nile civilization—called Nubia or Kush—took shape to the south.

The Kingdom of Nubia For 4,000 years, powerful kings and queens reigned over Nubia. From time to time, the Egyptians to the north conquered the land, but Nubians always regained their independence. As a result of conquest and trade, Nubian rulers used many Egyptian traditions. By 500 B.C., Nubian rulers moved their capital to Meroë (MEHR uh wee), a thriving trade center. Meroë produced iron for tools and weapons. The city may have spread iron technology across the savanna lands into West Africa through its extensive trade networks. Finally,

about A.D. 350, invading armies from the neighboring African kingdom of Axum overran Nubia.

North Africa Unlike Nubia, North Africa and Egypt were ruled, for a time, by the Greeks and then the Romans. Under Roman rule, Christianity spread to the cities of North Africa. Islam eventually replaced Christianity as the main religion of the region. North Africa benefited from the blossoming of Muslim civilization. Linked into a global trade network, North African ports did a busy trade in grain, wine, ivory, and gold.

Kingdoms of West Africa

By A.D. 100, settled farming villages on the western savannas of Africa were expanding. Soon trade networks linked the savanna to forest lands in the south and then sent goods across the Sahara.

West African Treasure
This gold scorpion may have been used as a weight.

By A.D. 200, camels, brought to North Africa from Asia, had revolutionized trade across the Sahara. Camel caravans created new, profitable trade networks. Gold and salt were the major products. Gold was plentiful in present-day Ghana, Nigeria, and Senegal. North Africans sought gold to trade in exchange for European goods. West Africans traded gold to North Africans in exchange for an equally valuable item, salt. People need salt in their diet to stay healthy, especially in hot, tropical areas.

The Kingdom of Ghana By A.D. 800, the rulers of the Soninke people had united many farming villages to form Ghana. The king controlled gold-salt trade routes across West Africa. So great was the flow of gold that Arab writers called Ghana "land of gold." Over time, Muslim merchants established Islam in Ghana. Muslim art, technology, and philosophy were influential as well. When the empire of Ghana declined in the late 1100s, it was swallowed up by a new rising power, the kingdom of Mali.

The Kingdom of Mali Mali emerged by 1250. It controlled both the gold-mining regions to the south and the salt supplies of the Sahara. The greatest emperor of Mali was Mansa Musa (MAHN sah MOO sah), who came to the throne in 1312. Musa expanded Mali's borders. A convert to Islam, Musa journeyed to Mecca in 1324 to fulfill the hajj. Musa's pilgrimage forged new ties with Muslim states and brought scholars and artists to Mali.

The Kingdom of Songhai As Mali weakened in the 1400s, a new West African kingdom,

Songhai (SAWNG hī), arose. Songhai forged the largest state that had ever existed in West Africa. The kingdom controlled trade routes and wealthy cities like Timbuktu, a leading center of learning. Songhai prospered until about 1586. At that time, civil war and invasion weakened and splintered the empire.

Trade Routes of East Africa

By the time the kingdom of Axum conquered Nubia about A.D. 330, Axum had long been an important trading center. Located southeast of Nubia, Axum linked trade routes between Africa, India, and the Mediterranean world. A powerful Axum king converted to Christianity in the 300s. At first, Christianity strengthened ties to the Mediterranean world. However, in the 600s, Islam came to dominate North Africa, leaving Axum an isolated island of Christianity. Axum slowly declined, but its legacy survived in present-day Ethiopia.

As Axum declined, a string of trading cities gradually rose along the East African coast. Since ancient times, traders had visited this coast. In the 600s, Arab and Persian merchants set up Muslim communities under the protection of local African rulers. By 1000, port cities were thriving from trade across the Indian Ocean.

Many Peoples, Many Traditions

The ways of life of African societies varied greatly from place to place. Early African peoples hunted, farmed the land, fished along the coasts and rivers, or herded livestock. Generally, farming peoples lived in tight-knit communities. Hunters and herders were often nomadic.

African Kingdoms and Trading States, 1000 B.C. – A.D. 1600

Mercator Projection

0   500   1000 Miles
0   500   1000 Kilometers

Legend:
- Egypt, 712 B.C.–525 B.C.
- Nubia, 1000 B.C.–A.D.150
- Axum, 900 B.C.–A.D. 600
- Ghana, A.D. 800–A.D.1000
- Mali, A.D.1200–A.D.1450
- Ethiopia, A.D.1270–A.D.1550
- Songhai, A.D.1450–A.D.1600
- Major trade routes

Geography and History
Many kingdoms in East Africa and West Africa developed because of profitable trade with other lands.

Across Africa, religious beliefs were varied and complex. Village Africans worshiped many gods and goddesses. Christianity and Islam also influenced peoples in some parts of Africa. Patterns of family life varied, as well. In some African groups, the **nuclear family** was typical, with parents and children living and working together. In other African communities, people lived in a joint family. Several generations shared the same complex of houses.

African societies preserved their histories and values through both oral and written literature. Oral traditions date back many centuries. In West Africa, **griots** (GREE ohs), or professional poets, recited ancient stories. They preserved

both histories and traditional folk tales. Histories praised the heroic deeds of famous ancestors. Folk tales taught important moral lessons.

Review

1. **Identify:** **(a)** Bantu migrations **(b)** Nubia, **(c)** Ghana, **(d)** Mansa Musa, **(e)** Axum.
2. **Define:** **(a)** nuclear family, **(b)** griot.
3. How did Nubian civilization prosper?
4. How did the gold-salt trade develop between West Africa and North Africa?

6 SPREAD OF CIVILIZATIONS IN EAST ASIA (500–1650)

Key Facts

- China expanded and grew rich under the powerful Tang and Song dynasties.
- During the 1200s and 1300s, the Mongols ruled much of Asia. After the fall of the Mongols, the Ming restored Chinese culture and later imposed a policy of isolation.
- During the 1100s, Japan created a feudal society ruled by powerful military lords.

After the Han dynasty collapsed in A.D. 220, China remained a divided land for nearly 400 years. Various Chinese dynasties rose and fell. Then in the 500s, China re-emerged as a united empire. For a short period, the Sui dynasty ruled. Then a Sui general and his son, Tang Taizong, led a successful revolt and established their own dynasty, the Tang.

Two Golden Ages of China

Under the rule of the Tang dynasty (618–907), China was restored to its earlier glory. Tang armies marched deep into Central Asia and surrounding regions. They forced neighboring lands to become tributary states. That is, while these states remained independent, their rulers had to acknowledge Chinese supremacy and send regular tribute to the Tang emperor. Tang emperors restored the bureaucracy. They redistributed land to the peasants. They also completed a system of canals to encourage internal trade and transportation. The Tang dynasty finally collapsed in 907. The Song dynasty soon rose to take its place.

In 960, the Song reunited much of China to rule for 319 years. The Song period was a golden age. Chinese wealth and culture dominated East Asia even when its armies did not.

Farming and foreign trade expanded. Paper money came into use. Several cities had populations over one million.

Government and Society

Under the Tang and Song, China was a well-ordered society. Besides the emperor and the aristocratic families, the two main classes were the gentry and the peasantry. The gentry were wealthy landowners who valued scholarship more than physical labor. Most scholar-officials at court came from this class. The peasants farmed on the land. However, even peasants could move up in society through education and government service.

Cultural Achievements

A rich economy supported the thriving

A Tang woman

culture of Tang and Song China. Prose and poetry flourished. Scholars produced works on philosophy, religion, and history. Painting and calligraphy became essential skills for the scholar-gentry.

The Mongol and Ming Empires

In the early 1200s, the Mongols dominated Asia. They invaded China and finally toppled the Song dynasty in 1279. The Mongols established peace and order within their domains. Political stability set the stage for economic growth. Under the protection of the Mongols, trade flourished along the Silk Road and across Eurasia.

Ming Dynasty In 1368, a rebel Chinese army pushed the Mongols back beyond the Great Wall. A new dynasty, the Ming—meaning brilliant—sought to reassert Chinese greatness after years of foreign rule. The Ming restored the civil service exams. Confucian learning again became the road to success. Chinese cities were home to many industries, and the economy thrived.

Exploration Early Ming rulers proudly sent Chinese fleets into distant waters. The Chinese admiral Zheng He (DZUHNG HEH) commanded hundreds of vessels carrying 25,000 sailors during a series of expeditions. His goal was to promote trade and collect tribute. Zheng He's fleet explored to the coasts of East Africa.

Korea and Its Traditions

As early as Han times, China extended its influence to peoples beyond the Middle Kingdom. To the northeast, the Korean peninsula lay within the Chinese zone of influence. While Korea absorbed many Chinese traditions over the centuries, it also maintained its own identity. Additionally, Koreans improved on a number of Chinese inventions. They advanced Chinese woodblock printing techniques by creating movable metal type to print books. They also created an alphabet for spoken sounds that was easier to use than Chinese characters. Its use led to an extremely high literacy rate in Korea.

The Emergence of Japan

Like Korea, Japan felt the powerful influence of Chinese civilization early in its history. At the same time, the Japanese continued to maintain their own distinct culture. The surrounding seas both protected and isolated Japan. While Japan was close enough to the mainland to learn from Korea and China, it was too far away for China to conquer.

By about A.D. 500, Japan's first and only dynasty—the Yamato—dominated Honshu, the largest Japanese island. In the early 600s, the Yamato dynasty sent young Japanese nobles to study in China. They returned to Japan spreading Chinese thought, technology, and arts. For a time, the Japanese modeled much of their society on Chinese culture and government. Eventually, however, the Japanese chose to adopt some Chinese ways while discarding or changing others.

Japan's Feudal Age

In theory, the emperor headed Japanese society. In fact, he was a powerless, though revered, figurehead. Real power lay in the hands of the shogun, or supreme military commander. He distributed lands to vassal lords who agreed to support him with their armies in time of need. These great warrior lords

FEUDAL SOCIETY IN JAPAN

Emperor
Held highest rank in society but had no political power

Shogun
Actual ruler

Daimyo
Large landowners

Samurai
Warriors loyal to daimyo

Peasants
Three fourths of population

Artisans

Merchants
Low status but gradually gained influence

were called **daimyo** (DĪ myoh). They, in turn, granted land to lesser warriors called **samurai,** meaning "those who serve." Samurai were the fighting aristocracy in the constant struggle for power. Japan had evolved into a feudal society.

In 1603, Tokugawa Ieyasu (toh kuh GAH wah ee YAY yah soo) founded the Tokugawa shogunate, which ruled Japan until 1868. The Tokugawas brought peace and stability to Japan. They imposed central government control on all of Japan and created a unified, orderly society. Trade flourished, merchants prospered, and prosperity contributed to a flowering of culture. Still, the

shoguns were extremely conservative. They tried to preserve samurai virtues and ancient beliefs. This commitment would bring them into sharp conflict with the foreigners who arrived in the 1500s.

Review

1. **Identify:** (a) Tang, (b) Song, (c) Mongols, (d) Ming, (e) Tokugawa.
2. **Define:** (a) tributary state, (b) shogun, (c) daimyo, (d) samurai.
3. How did the Tang and Song dynasties benefit China?
4. Who held the most power in feudal Japan?

UNIT 1

Early Modern Times

1300–1800

OUTLINE

Chapter 1 **The Renaissance and Reformation**
(1300–1650)

Chapter 2 **The First Global Age: Europe and Asia**
(1415–1796)

Chapter 3 **The First Global Age: Europe, the Americas, and Africa** (1492–1750)

Chapter 4 **The Age of Absolutism**
(1550–1800)

Themes

As you read about developments that led to the emergence of modern Europe and the first age of global interaction, you will encounter the following unit themes.

Economics and Technology A scientific revolution enabled explorers to travel the world in search of trade and riches. Dramatic economic developments, such as the rise of capitalism, affected all social classes.

Global Interaction Exploration by powerful nations led to increased competition for trade. The spread of cultural beliefs and the exchange of material goods often were accomplished by conquest and by destruction of native cultures.

Political and Social Systems Absolute monarchs forged modern nation-states with strong central governments. The struggle between monarchs and Parliament in England was an important step in the development of modern democracy.

Religions and Value Systems Classical and Christian humanist ideals shaped the Renaissance. While the Protestant Reformation shattered the religious unity of Europe, Christianity continued to spread to new lands.

Unit Theme Activity

For Your Portfolio The chapters in this unit illustrate changes that led to the first era of global interaction. As you read the chapters, prepare a portfolio project highlighting these developments. Your project might take one of the following forms:
• **Chart or other detailed graphic organizer**
• **Debate**
• **Diary**

The Palace of Versailles was designed to glorify the power of France and its monarch, Louis XIV. It served as the capital of France and as the royal residence from 1682 until the French Revolution.

Prepare to Read

Prepare to read this unit by previewing the
main ideas and main events of each chapter.

Chapter 1

The Renaissance and Reformation
(1300–1650)

Between the 1300s and 1500s, Europe experienced a period of cultural rebirth known as the Renaissance. During the same period, the Protestant Reformation and the Scientific Revolution reshaped European civilization.

- Beginning in Italy and later spreading to northern Europe, the Renaissance reached its most glorious expression in painting, sculpture, and architecture.
- The intellectual movement known as humanism stressed the study of classical Greek and Roman cultures and the development of the individual.
- Reformers like Martin Luther and John Calvin challenged church corruption and eventually broke away from the Roman Catholic Church entirely.
- In response to the Protestant Reformation, the Catholic Church undertook its own vigorous reform movement.
- Religious fervor led to widespread intolerance and persecution by both Protestants and Catholics.
- During the Scientific Revolution, startling discoveries by individuals such as Copernicus, Newton, and Galileo changed the way Europeans viewed the physical world.

Chapter 2

The First Global Age: Europe and Asia
(1415–1796)

Beginning in the 1500s, European powers gradually built trading empires in Asia. Thus began a period of increasing global interdependence that has continued to the present day.

- Improvements in technology helped European explorers navigate the vast oceans of the world.
- In his search for a sea route to Asia, Christopher Columbus came upon the Americas, two continents previously unknown to Europeans.
- Although they were strongly influenced by China and India, the nations of Southeast Asia retained their own unique cultural identities.
- The desire for spices led Europeans to seek control of the Indian Ocean trade network.
- By the late 1500s, the Dutch replaced the Portuguese as the major European power in Asia. In the 1700s, England and France vied for dominance.
- During the 1500s and 1600s, China and Korea restricted contact with the outside world.
- The Japanese initially welcomed western traders, but they later adopted a similar policy of isolation.

	1300	1400	1500
AFRICA	**1300s** Kingdom of Benin flourishes		**1460s** Sonni Ali founds Songhai
THE AMERICAS		**1400s** Aztec and Incan empires expand	**1492** Columbus reaches the Caribbean
ASIA AND OCEANIA		**1405–1433** Voyages of Zheng He	**1510** Portuguese seize Goa
EUROPE	**Mid–1300s** Renaissance begins in Italy	**1456** Gutenberg Bible printed	**1517** 95 Theses

Chapter 3

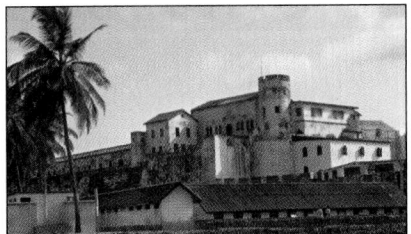

The First Global Age: Europe, the Americas, and Africa (1492–1750)

During the age of exploration, European powers built colonial empires in the Americas. New patterns of conquest and global exchange had an enormous impact on the civilization of Africa as well.

- Spanish conquistadors vanquished the Aztec and Incan civilizations and set up a vast empire in the Americas.
- By the 1600s, Spain, France, England, and the Netherlands were competing for trade and colonies.
- The arrival of European settlers in the Americas brought disaster to Native Americans.
- Beginning in the 1400s, Europeans began establishing trading outposts in Africa.
- Millions of slaves were imported from Africa to meet labor needs in American colonies. The slave trade led to the fall of some African states and the rise of others.
- The Columbian Exchange was a vast global interchange of people, animals, culture, ideas, and technology.
- Beginning in the 1500s, Europe experienced a commercial revolution that brought about dramatic economic changes, including the rise of capitalism.

Chapter 4

The Age of Absolutism (1550–1800)

During the 1500s and 1600s, European monarchs struggled to centralize their power. As they vied for the lead in overseas empires, the center of world civilization shifted to Europe.

- During the 1500s, wealth from the Americas helped make Spain the most powerful nation in Europe.
- Following a period of religious and social turmoil, Louis XIV achieved royal absolutism and helped France become the most powerful nation in Europe during the 1600s.
- Despite efforts at absolutism by several English monarchs, Parliament successfully asserted itself against royal power.
- The Thirty Years' War involved most of Europe. After the Peace of Westphalia, Prussia emerged as a new Protestant power.
- The Hapsburgs expanded Austrian territory but were unable to develop a strong centralized system.
- Peter the Great of Russia centralized royal power, embarked on a program of modernization, and sought to expand Russian territory from Europe to the Pacific.

1600   1700   1800

1500s Zulus migrate into southern Africa

1652 Dutch build Cape Town

1500s Atlantic slave trade grows

Late 1600s Asante kingdom established

1607 British found Jamestown

1608 French build Quebec

1754 French and Indian War begins

1556 Akbar begins reign in India

1600 Tokugawas gain power in Japan

1644 Manchus found Qing dynasty

1736 Qianlong becomes emperor of China

1643 Age of Louis XIV begins

1700s Peter the Great modernizes Russia

1558 Elizabeth begins reign

1687 Newton explains theory of gravity

The Renaissance and Reformation

1300–1650

Chapter Preview

1 The Renaissance in Italy
2 The Renaissance Moves North
3 The Protestant Reformation
4 Reformation Ideas Spread
5 The Scientific Revolution

CHAPTER EVENTS

1300s
The Renaissance begins in Italian city-states. The cathedral in Florence, topped by this magnificent dome, reflects the wealth and artistic brilliance of Renaissance Italy.

1434
The Medici family gains control of the government of Florence.

1456
The first Gutenberg Bible is printed. The introduction of the printing press with movable type ushers in a printing revolution in Europe.

1300 • • 1375 • 1450

GLOBAL EVENTS

1324 Mansa Musa makes hajj.

1368 The Ming dynasty is founded in China.

1453 Constantinople falls to the Ottoman Turks.

Artists of the Renaissance

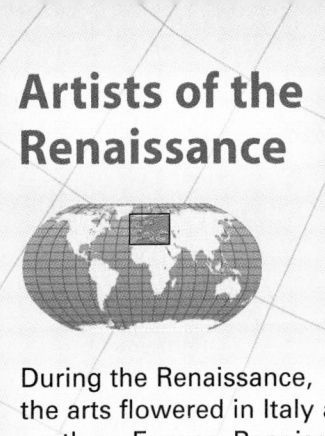

During the Renaissance, the arts flowered in Italy and northern Europe. Renaissance artists built on Greek and Roman traditions and pioneered new techniques.

NORWAY

SCOTLAND

North Sea

SWEDEN

PSKOV

IRELAND

DENMARK

Baltic Sea

TEUTONIC ORDER

ENGLAND

Pieter Bruegel
1525–1569

Peter Paul Rubens
1577–1640

NETHER-LANDS

(SMALL STATES)

POLAND-LITHUANIA

Elbe R.

FLANDERS

Rhine R.

Jan van Eyck
1395–1441

BOHEMIA

Seine R.

Oder R.

Loire R.

Albrecht Dürer
1471–1528

AUSTRIA

MOLDAVIA

50°N

FRANCE

ALPS

HUNGARY

Danube R.

40°N

ATLANTIC OCEAN

PYRENEES MTS.

SAVOY

MILAN

VENICE

Leonardo da Vinci
1452–1519

Rhône R.

NAVARRE

Ebro R.

GENOA

FLORENCE

Michelangelo
1475–1564

PORTUGAL

SPAIN

Tagus R.

Donatello
1386–1466

PAPAL STATES

Adriatic Sea

MONTENEGRO

OTTOMAN EMPIRE

Boundary of Holy Roman Empire

SARDINIA
(Ruled by Spain)

NAPLES
(Ruled by Spain)

Raphael
1483–1520

Mediterranean Sea

SICILY
(Ruled by Spain)

20°E

N
W E
S

Azimuthal Equal Area Projection

0   200   400 Miles

0   200   400 Kilometers

1506
Leonardo da Vinci completes the *Mona Lisa*, one of the greatest paintings of the Italian Renaissance.

1517
Martin Luther posts his 95 Theses in Wittenberg, Germany. This protest against Church policy launches the Protestant Reformation.

1633
Galileo is tried before the Inquisition for claiming that the Earth moves around the sun.

1525   1600   1675

1532 Spanish forces defeat the Incan empire of South America.

1620 Pilgrims found the Plymouth Colony in Massachusetts.

The Renaissance in Italy

Reading Focus

- Why were the Italian city-states a favorable setting for a cultural rebirth?
- What was the Renaissance?
- What themes and techniques did Renaissance artists and writers explore?

Vocabulary

patron
humanism
humanities
perspective

Taking Notes

As you read, prepare an outline of this section. Use Roman numerals to indicate major headings, capital letters for the sub-headings, and numbers for the supporting details. The sample at right will help you get started.

I. The Italian city-states
   A. Why Italy?
      1. Remains of Roman heritage
      2. Prosperous city-states
      3.
   B. Florence and the Medicis
      1.
      2.
II.

Main Idea The Renaissance that began in Italy was characterized by an interest in learning and the arts and a desire to explore the human experience.

Discovery CHANNEL SCHOOL Video
Learn about Machiavelli's *The Prince.*

The Merchants of Venice
The city-state of Venice was built on islands at the northern end of the Adriatic Sea. By Renaissance times, Venetian merchants were bringing back a wealth of trade goods from all over the known world.

Theme: Geography and History How did geography benefit the Venetians?

Setting the Scene The philosopher Marsilio Ficino smiled with pleasure as he watched the sun cast a golden glow over his native city of Florence. To Ficino, this glow symbolized the revival of art and thought taking place in Italy. Dipping his pen in ink, he began to write. "This century," he wrote, "like a golden age has restored to light the liberal arts, which were almost extinct: grammar, poetry, rhetoric, painting, sculpture, architecture, music." What a glorious time to be alive, he thought.

As Ficino recognized, a new age had dawned in Western Europe. Europeans called it the Renaissance, meaning "rebirth." It began in the 1300s and reached its peak around 1500.

The Italian City-States

The Renaissance began in Italy, then spread north to the rest of Europe. Italy was the birthplace of the Renaissance for several reasons.

Why Italy? The Renaissance was marked by a new interest in the culture of ancient Rome. Because Italy had been the center of the Roman empire, it was a logical place for this reawakening to begin. Architectural remains, statues, coins, and inscriptions—all were visible reminders of Roman grandeur.

Italy differed from the rest of Europe in other ways. Its cities survived the Middle Ages. In the north, city-states like Florence, Milan, Venice, and Genoa grew into prosperous centers of trade and manufacturing. Rome, in central Italy, and Naples, in the south, along with a number of smaller city-states, also contributed to the Renaissance cultural revival.

A wealthy and powerful merchant class in these city-states further promoted the cultural rebirth. These merchants exerted both political and economic leadership, and their attitudes and interests helped to shape the Italian Renaissance. They stressed education and individual achievement. They also spent lavishly to support the arts.

Florence and the Medicis Florence, perhaps more than any other city, came to symbolize the energy and brilliance of the Italian Renaissance. Like the ancient city of Athens, it produced a dazzling number of gifted poets, artists, architects, scholars, and scientists in a short span of time.

In the 1400s, the Medici (MEH dee chee) family of Florence organized a successful banking business. Before long, the family expanded into wool manufacturing, mining, and other ventures. The Medicis ranked among the richest merchants and bankers in Europe. Money translated into cultural and political power. Cosimo de' Medici gained control of the Florentine government in 1434, and the family continued as uncrowned rulers of the city for many years.

Cosimo's grandson Lorenzo, known as "the Magnificent," represented the Renaissance ideal. A clever politician, he held Florence together in the late 1400s during difficult times. He was also a generous patron, or financial supporter, of the arts. Under Lorenzo, poets and philosophers frequently visited the Medici palace. Artists learned their craft by sketching ancient Roman statues displayed in the Medici gardens.

What Was the Renaissance?

The Renaissance was a time of creativity and change in many areas—political, social, economic, and cultural. Perhaps most important, however, were the changes that took place in the way people viewed themselves and their world.

A New Worldview Spurred by a reawakened interest in the classical learning of Greece and Rome, creative Renaissance minds set out to transform their own age. Their era, they felt, was a time of rebirth after what they saw as the disorder and disunity of the medieval world.

In reality, Renaissance Europe did not break completely with its medieval past. After all, monks and scholars of the Middle Ages had preserved much of the classical heritage. Latin had survived as the language of the Church and of educated people. And the mathematics of Euclid, the astronomy of Ptolemy, and the works of Aristotle were well known to late medieval scholars.

Yet the Renaissance did produce new attitudes toward culture and learning. Unlike medieval scholars, who were more likely to focus on life after death, Renaissance thinkers explored the richness and variety of human experience in the here and now. At the same time, there was a new emphasis on individual achievement. Indeed, the Renaissance ideal was the person with talent in many fields.

A Spirit of Adventure The Renaissance supported a spirit of adventure and a wide-ranging curiosity that led people to explore new worlds. The Italian navigator Christopher Columbus, who sailed to the Americas in 1492, represented that spirit. So did Nicolaus Copernicus, a Polish scientist who revolutionized the way people viewed the universe. Renaissance writers and artists, eager to experiment with new forms, were also products of that adventurous spirit.

Humanism At the heart of the Italian Renaissance was an intellectual movement known as humanism. Based on the study of classical culture, humanism focused on worldly subjects rather than on the religious issues that had occupied medieval thinkers. Most humanist scholars were pious

Renaissance Italy, 1505

Skills Assessment

Geography At the time of the Renaissance, Italy was made up of numerous republics, kingdoms, and city-states.

1. **Location** On the map, locate (a) Florence, (b) Venice, (c) Rome, (d) Papal States, (e) Duchy of Milan.
2. **Place** (a) In which state was Pisa an important city? (b) Who controlled Corsica and Sicily?
3. **Critical Thinking Making Inferences** Based on this map, why was Venice in a good position to trade with the Muslim world?

Christians who hoped to use the wisdom of the ancients to increase their understanding of their own times.

Humanists believed that education should stimulate the individual's creative powers. They returned to the humanities, the subjects taught in ancient Greek and Roman schools. The main areas of study were grammar, rhetoric, poetry, and history, based on Greek and Roman texts. Humanists did not accept the classical texts without question, however. Rather, they studied the ancient authorities in light of their own experiences.

Francesco Petrarch (PEE trahrk), a Florentine who lived in the 1300s, was an early Renaissance humanist. In monasteries and churches, he found and assembled a library of Greek and Roman manuscripts. Through his efforts and those of others encouraged by his example, the works of Cicero, Homer, and Virgil again became known to Western Europeans. Petrarch also wrote literature of his own. His *Sonnets to Laura*, love poems inspired by a woman he knew only from a distance, greatly influenced later writers.

A Golden Age in the Arts

The Renaissance attained its most glorious expression in its paintings, sculpture, and architecture. Wealthy patrons played a major role in this artistic flowering. Popes and princes supported the work of hundreds of artists. Wealthy and powerful women such as Isabella d'Este of Mantua were important patrons of the arts as well.

Humanist Concerns Renaissance art reflected humanist concerns. Like artists of the Middle Ages, Renaissance artists portrayed religious figures such as Jesus and Mary. However, they often set these figures against Greek or Roman backgrounds. Painters also produced portraits of well-known figures of the day, reflecting the humanist interest in individual achievement.

Perspective
Renaissance artists used perspective to create an illusion of depth. The diagram below shows how the lines in this painting by Antonello da Messina recede from the viewer toward a single vanishing point.

Theme: Arts and Literature
How does the size of objects in this painting add to the sense of depth?

Renaissance artists studied ancient Greek and Roman works and revived many classical forms. The sculptor Donatello, for example, created a life-size statue of a soldier on horseback. It was the first such figure done since ancient times.

New Techniques Roman art had been very realistic, and Renaissance painters developed new techniques for representing both humans and landscapes in a realistic way. Renaissance artists learned the rules of perspective. By making distant objects smaller than those close to the viewer, artists could paint scenes that appeared three-dimensional.

Renaissance painters used shading to make objects look round and real. Painters and sculptors also studied human anatomy and drew from live models. As a result, they were able to portray the human body more accurately than medieval artists had done.

Women Artists Some women overcame the limits on education and training to become professional artists. Sometimes, these women kept their work secret, allowing their husbands to pass it off as their own. Still, a few women artists did gain acceptance. In the 1500s, Sofonisba Anguissola (soh foh NIHZ bah ahn gwee SOH lah), an Italian noblewoman, became court painter to King Philip II of Spain.

Architecture Renaissance architects rejected the Gothic style of the late Middle Ages as cluttered and disorderly. Instead, they adopted the columns, arches, and domes that had been favored by the Greeks and Romans. For the cathedral in Florence, Filippo Brunelleschi (broo nehl LEHS kee) created a majestic dome, which he modeled on the dome of the Pantheon in Rome.

Three Geniuses of Renaissance Art

Renaissance Florence was home to many outstanding painters and sculptors. The three most celebrated Florentine masters were Leonardo da Vinci, Michelangelo, and Raphael.

Leonardo Leonardo da Vinci (dah VIHN chee) was born in 1452. His exploring mind and endless curiosity fed a genius for invention. He made sketches of nature and of models in his studio. He even dissected corpses to learn how bones and muscles work. "Indicate which are the muscles and which the tendons, which become prominent or retreat in the different movements of each limb," he wrote in his notebook.

Today, people admire Leonardo's paintings for their freshness and realism. Most popular is the *Mona Lisa,* a portrait of a woman whose mysterious smile has baffled viewers for centuries. *The Last Supper,* showing Christ and his apostles on the night before the crucifixion, is both a moving religious painting and a masterpiece of perspective. Because Leonardo was experimenting with a new type of paint, much of *The Last Supper* decayed over the years, but it has recently been restored.

Leonardo thought of himself as an artist, but his talents and accomplishments ranged over many areas. His interests extended to botany, anatomy, optics, music, architecture, and engineering. He made sketches for flying machines and undersea boats centuries before the first airplane or submarine was actually built.

Michelangelo Like Leonardo, Michelangelo was a many-sided genius— sculptor, engineer, painter, architect, and poet. As a young man, he shaped marble into masterpieces like the *Pietà,* which captures the sorrow of Mary as she cradles the dead Christ on her knees. Michelangelo's statue of David, the biblical shepherd who killed the giant Goliath, recalls the harmony and grace of ancient Greek tradition.

Primary Source

The Genius of Leonardo
Italian artist and architect Giorgio Vasari is best known for his engaging book of biographies of Italian artists, including Leonardo da Vinci (pictured above):

"Leonardo practiced not one art but all of those that are dependent upon design, and he had great talent for geometry besides being very musical, playing the lute with great ability and being excellent in the art of improvisation. . . . In entertaining, Leonardo was so pleasant that he won everyone's heart. Although he may well be said to have owned nothing and to have worked little, he always kept a servant as well as horses."

—Giorgio Vasari, *Lives of the Most Eminent Italian Painters, Sculptors, and Architects*

Skills Assessment

Primary Source What personal details did Vasari include about Leonardo da Vinci?

A Masterpiece by Michelangelo
Michelangelo spent four years painting biblical scenes on the ceiling of the Sistine Chapel. One of the most dramatic images, the *Creation of Adam*, shows God bringing the first man to life with a touch.

Theme: Religions and Value Systems How does Michelangelo suggest the power of God?

One of Michelangelo's greatest projects was painting a huge mural to decorate the ceiling of the Sistine Chapel in Rome. It was an enormous task, depicting the biblical history of the world, from the Creation to the Flood. For four years, the artist lay on his back on a wooden platform suspended just a few inches below the chapel ceiling. In a poem, Michelangelo later described his ordeal:

"My stomach is thrust toward my chin
 My beard curls up toward the sky
 My head leans right over onto my back . . .
 The brush endlessly dripping onto my face."
—Michelangelo, *Poems*

Michelangelo was also a talented architect. His most famous design was for the dome of St. Peter's Cathedral in Rome. It served as a model for many later structures, including the United States Capitol building in Washington, D.C.

Raphael A few years younger than Leonardo and Michelangelo, Raphael (RAF ee uhl) studied the works of those great masters. His paintings blend Christian and classical styles. He is probably best known for his tender portrayals of the madonna, the mother of Jesus.

In *The School of Athens,* Raphael pictures an imaginary gathering of great thinkers and scientists, such as Plato, Aristotle, Socrates, and the Arab philosopher Averroës. With typical Renaissance self-confidence, Raphael included the faces of Michelangelo, Leonardo—and himself.

Italian Renaissance Writers

Poets, artists, and scholars mingled with politicians at the courts of Renaissance rulers. A literature of "how-to" books sprang up to help ambitious men and women who wanted to rise in the Renaissance world.

Castiglione's Ideal Courtier The most widely read of these handbooks was *The Book of the Courtier.* Its author, Baldassare Castiglione (bahl dahs

SAHR ray kahs steel YOHN ay), describes the manners, skills, learning, and virtues that a member of the court should have. Castiglione's ideal courtier was a well-educated, well-mannered aristocrat who mastered many fields, from poetry to music to sports.

Castiglione's ideal differed for men and women. The ideal man, he wrote, is athletic but not overactive. He is good at games, but not a gambler. He plays a musical instrument and knows literature and history but is not arrogant. The ideal woman offers a balance to men. She is graceful and kind, lively but reserved. She is beautiful, "for outer beauty," wrote Castiglione, "is the true sign of inner goodness."

Machiavelli's Successful Prince Niccolò Machiavelli (mahk ee uh VEHL ee) wrote a different kind of handbook. Machiavelli had served Florence as a diplomat and had observed kings and princes in foreign courts. He also had studied ancient Roman history. In *The Prince,* published in 1513, Machiavelli combined his personal experience of politics with his knowledge of the past to offer a guide to rulers on how to gain and maintain power.

Unlike earlier political writers, such as Plato, Machiavelli did not discuss leadership in terms of high ideals. Instead, *The Prince* looked at real rulers, such as the Medicis, in an age of ruthless power politics. Machiavelli stressed that the end justifies the means. He urged rulers to use whatever methods were necessary to achieve their goals. On the issue of honesty in government, for example, he taught that getting results was more important than keeping promises. He wrote:

"How praiseworthy it is for a prince to keep his word and live with integrity rather than craftiness, everyone understands; yet . . . those princes have accomplished most who paid little heed to keeping their promises, but who knew how craftily to manipulate the minds of men."
—Niccolò Machiavelli, *The Prince*

Machiavelli saw himself as an enemy of oppression and corruption. But critics attacked his cynical advice. Some even claimed that he was inspired by the devil. (In fact, the term "Machiavellian" came to refer to the use of deceit in politics.) Later students of government, however, argued that Machiavelli provided a realistic look at politics. His work continues to spark debate because it raises important ethical questions about the nature of government and the use of power.

Primary Sources and Literature

See "Niccolò Machiavelli: Discourses," in the Reference Section at the back of this book.

SECTION 1 Assessment

Recall

1. **Identify:** **(a)** Lorenzo de' Medici, **(b)** Francesco Petrarch, **(c)** Leonardo da Vinci, **(d)** Michelangelo, **(e)** Raphael, **(f)** Baldassare Castiglione, **(g)** Niccolò Machiavelli.
2. **Define:** **(a)** patron, **(b)** humanism, **(c)** humanities, **(d)** perspective.

Comprehension

3. What conditions in Italy contributed to the emergence of the Renaissance?
4. Identify the concerns and attitudes emphasized during the Renaissance.

5. How did Renaissance art reflect humanist concerns?

Critical Thinking and Writing

6. **Making Inferences** Why might powerful rulers and wealthy business people choose to become patrons of the arts during the Renaissance?
7. **Linking Past and Present** In *The Prince,* Machiavelli advised rulers that it "is much safer to be feared than loved." **(a)** What did he mean by that? **(b)** Do you think a political leader today would be wise to follow that advice? Why or why not?

PHSchool.com

Use the Internet to learn more about a major artist of the Italian Renaissance. You may choose one of the artists mentioned in this section or another artist such as Fra Angelico, Benvenuto Cellini, Sandro Botticelli, or Titian. Prepare a report on one artwork. Include a copy of the work. For help with this activity, use **Web Code mkd-1441.**

Reading Focus

- Which artists brought the Renaissance to northern Europe?
- What themes did humanist thinkers and other writers explore?
- What impact did the printing revolution have on Europe?

Vocabulary

engraving

vernacular

utopian

Taking Notes

On a sheet of paper begin a table like the one shown here. Add information about the Renaissance under each heading as you read the section.

DUTCH	GERMAN	FLEMISH	ENGLISH	FRENCH	SPANISH
Erasmus	Dürer				

Main Idea The Renaissance slowly spread to northern Europe, where artists and writers experimented with new methods and ideas.

Setting the Scene "Had I not torn myself from Rome, I could never have resolved to leave," wrote Dutch priest Desiderius Erasmus. "There one enjoys sweet liberty, rich libraries, the charming friendship of writers and scholars, and the sight of antique monuments." Inspired by his visit to Italy, Erasmus helped spread the Renaissance to northern Europe.

Unlike Italy, northern Europe recovered slowly from the ravages of the Black Death. Only after 1450 did the north enjoy the economic growth that had earlier supported the Renaissance in Italy.

Artists of the Northern Renaissance

The northern Renaissance began in the prosperous cities of Flanders, a region that included parts of present-day northern France, Belgium, and the Netherlands. Spain, France, Germany, and England enjoyed their great cultural rebirth 100 years later, in the 1500s.

A "German Leonardo" Albrecht Dürer traveled to Italy in 1494 to study the techniques of the Italian masters. Returning home, he employed these methods in paintings and, especially, in engravings. In this form of art, an artist etches a design on a metal plate with acid. The artist then uses the plate to make prints. Many of Dürer's engravings portray the religious upheaval of his age.

Through his art as well as through essays, Dürer helped to spread Italian Renaissance ideas in his homeland. Because of his wide-ranging interests, which extended far beyond art, he is sometimes called the "German Leonardo."

Flemish Painters Among the many artists of Flanders in the 1400s, Jan and Hubert van Eyck (van ĪK) stand out. Their portrayals of townspeople as well as religious scenes abound in rich, realistic details. The van Eycks also developed oil paint. Northern artists used this new medium to produce strong colors and a hard surface that could survive the centuries.

In the 1500s, Pieter Bruegel (PEE tuhr BROY guhl) used vibrant colors to portray lively scenes of peasant life. Bruegel's work influenced later Flemish artists, who painted scenes of daily life rather than religious or classical themes.

In the 1600s, Peter Paul Rubens blended the realistic tradition of Flemish painters like Bruegel with the classical themes and artistic freedom of the Italian Renaissance. Many of his enormous paintings portray pagan figures from the classical past.

Northern Humanists

Like Italian humanists, northern European humanist scholars stressed education and classical learning. At the same time, they emphasized religious themes. They believed that the revival of ancient learning should be used to bring about religious and moral reform.

Erasmus The great Dutch priest and humanist Desiderius Erasmus used his knowledge of classical languages to produce a new Greek edition of the New Testament. He also called for a translation of the Bible into the vernacular, or everyday language of ordinary people. He scorned "those who are unwilling that Holy Scripture, translated into the vernacular, be read by the uneducated . . . as if the strength of the Christian religion consisted in the ignorance of it."

To Erasmus, an individual's chief duties were to be open-minded and of good will toward others. As a priest, he was disturbed by corruption in the Church and called for reform. In *The Praise of Folly,* Erasmus uses humor to expose the ignorant and immoral behavior of many people of his day, including the clergy.

More Erasmus's friend, the English humanist Thomas More, also pressed for social reform. In *Utopia,* More describes an ideal society in which men and women live in peace and harmony. No one is idle, all are educated, and justice is used to end crime rather than to eliminate the criminal. Today, the word utopian has come to describe any ideal society.

Writers for a New Audience

Scholars like More and Erasmus wrote mostly in Latin. In northern towns and cities, the growing middle class demanded new works in the vernacular. This audience particularly enjoyed dramatic tales and earthy comedies.

Rabelais The French humanist François Rabelais had a varied career as a monk, physician, Greek scholar, and author. In *Gargantua and Pantagruel,* he chronicles the adventures of two gentle giants. On the surface, the novel is

Dürer, the "German Leonardo"
Albrecht Dürer, shown in a self-portrait (below right), helped bring the genius of the Italian Renaissance to northern Europe. Many of his finest works were engravings, such as the portrait of a peasant couple (below left).
Theme: Arts and Literature How do these works reflect the Renaissance interest in the individual?

Shakespeare's World of Drama

"He was not of an age, but for all time," said one of Shakespeare's contemporaries of him. A later poet said, "He was the man who of all modern, and perhaps ancient poets, had the largest and most comprehensive soul." Today, no plays are performed more frequently around the world than those of William Shakespeare.

In *A Midsummer Night's Dream,* a love potion causes confusion among two young couples and makes Titania, the queen of the fairies, fall in love with a man who has the head of a donkey. One character comments:

"Alas, poor Yorick! I knew him, Horatio, a fellow of infinite jest."

Prince Hamlet mourns his father's deceased court jester.

"What fools these mortals be"

"All the world's a stage, / And all the men and women merely players:/ They have their exits and their entrances;/And one man in his time plays many parts."

—William Shakespeare, *As You Like It*

Portfolio Assessment

Conduct research to find out more about the dramas of William Shakespeare. Form small groups, and have each group choose a different play. Then, pick out a passage from the play, cast and rehearse it, and perform it for the rest of the class.

a comic tale of travel and war. But Rabelais uses his characters to offer opinions on religion, education, and other serious subjects.

Shakespeare The towering figure of Renaissance literature was the English poet and playwright William Shakespeare. Between 1590 and 1613, he wrote 37 plays that are still performed around the world.

Shakespeare's comedies, such as *Twelfth Night,* laugh at the follies of young people in love. His history plays, such as *Richard III,* depict the power struggles of English kings. His tragedies show people crushed by powerful forces or their own weaknesses. In *Romeo and Juliet,* two teenagers fall victim to an old family feud.

Shakespeare's love of words vastly enriched the English language. More than 1,700 words appeared for the first time in his works, including *bedroom, lonely, generous, gloomy, heartsick, hurry,* and *sneak.*

Cervantes The Renaissance in Spain in the early 1600s also led to the production of great works. Best known is *Don Quixote* (DAHN kee HOH tay), by Miguel de Cervantes (suhr VAN teez), an entertaining tale that mocks romantic notions of medieval chivalry. The novel follows the adventures of Don Quixote, a foolish but idealistic knight, and Sancho Panza, his faithful servant. (You will read more about *Don Quixote* in a later chapter.)

The Printing Revolution

In 1456, Johann Gutenberg of Mainz, Germany, printed the first complete edition of the Bible using the first printing press and printing inks in the West. Within twenty years, the development of movable type made book production even easier. A printing revolution had begun that would transform Europe. By 1500, more than 20 million volumes had been printed.

Gutenberg and his successors built on earlier advances. Methods of making paper had reached Europe from China about 1300. The Chinese and Koreans had been using movable metal type for centuries, although Europeans may have developed their technology independently.

The printing revolution brought immense changes. Printed books were cheaper and easier to produce than hand-copied works. With books more readily available, more people learned to read. Readers gained access to a broad range of knowledge, from medicine and law to astrology and mining. Printed books exposed educated Europeans to new ideas, greatly expanding their horizons. As you will read, the new presses would contribute to the religious turmoil that engulfed Europe in the 1500s.

SECTION 2 Assessment

Recall

1. **Identify:** (a) Albrecht Dürer, (b) Jan van Eyck, (c) François Rabelais, (d) William Shakespeare, (e) Miguel de Cervantes, (f) Johann Gutenberg.
2. **Define:** (a) engraving, (b) vernacular, (c) utopian.

Comprehension

3. How did Dürer help bring the Renaissance to northern Europe?
4. What themes did Erasmus and More raise in their writings?

5. What were three effects of the printing revolution?

Critical Thinking and Writing

6. **Recognizing Causes and Effects** Why do you think the cultural flowering of the northern Renaissance did not begin until after economic growth had taken place?
7. **Linking Past and Present** What are some ways in which Shakespeare's plays and sonnets still "live" today?

Activity

Creating Compound Words Shakespeare invented new words by combining two existing words. Examples of these compound words are *eyesore, heartsick, hot-blooded, leapfrog,* and *tongue-tied.* Look up definitions of these words. Then, create five compound words of your own.

The Protestant Reformation

Reading Focus

- How did abuses in the Church spark widespread criticism?
- How did Martin Luther challenge Catholic authority and teachings?
- What role did John Calvin play in the Reformation?

Vocabulary

indulgence

recant

predestination

theocracy

Taking Notes

On a sheet of paper draw a flowchart like the one shown here. As you read this section, add important events and ideas that contributed to the Protestant Reformation.

Church involved in worldly affairs

↓

Tetzel sells indulgences to raise money for new cathedral

↓

↓

Main Idea The ideas of Martin Luther and John Calvin led people to separate from the Roman Catholic Church and form new Protestant churches.

Setting the Scene During the Renaissance, the Church increasingly came under fire. Christians at all levels of society accused the clergy of corruption and worldliness. One peasant even compared the clergy to "wicked wolves." He protested, "Instead of saving the souls of the dead and sending them to Heaven, they gorge themselves at banquets after funerals."

During the Middle Ages, the Church had renewed itself from within. In the 1500s, though, new calls for reform unleashed forces that would shatter Christian unity. This movement is known as the Protestant Reformation.

Abuses in the Church

Beginning in the late Middle Ages, the Church had become increasingly caught up in worldly affairs. Popes competed with Italian princes for political power. They fought long wars to protect the Papal States against invasions by secular rulers. They intrigued against powerful monarchs who tried to seize control of the Church within their lands.

Like other Renaissance rulers, popes maintained a lavish lifestyle. Popes were also patrons of the arts. They hired painters and sculptors to beautify churches.

To finance such projects, the Church increased fees for services such as marriages and baptisms. Some clergy also promoted the sale of indulgences. According to Church teaching, an indulgence was a lessening of the time a soul would have to spend in purgatory, a place where souls too impure to enter heaven atoned for sins committed during their lifetimes. In the Middle Ages, the Church had granted indulgences only for good deeds, such as going on a crusade. By the late 1400s, however, indulgences could also be obtained in exchange for money gifts to the Church.

Many Christians protested such practices, especially in northern Europe. Christian humanists such as Erasmus urged a return to the simple ways of the early Christian Church. They stressed Bible study and rejected what they saw as the worldliness of the Church.

Luther's Protest

In 1517, protests against Church abuses erupted into a full-scale revolt. The man who triggered the revolt was a German monk and professor of theology named Martin Luther.

As a young man, Luther prayed and fasted and tried to lead a holy life. Still, he believed he was doomed to eternal damnation. He also grew disillusioned with what he saw as Church corruption and worldliness. At last, an incident in the town of Wittenberg prompted him to take action.

The 95 Theses In 1517, a priest named Johann Tetzel set up a pulpit on the outskirts of Wittenberg. He offered indulgences to any Christian who contributed money for the rebuilding of the Cathedral of St. Peter in Rome. Tetzel claimed that purchase of these indulgences would assure entry into heaven not only for the purchasers but for their dead relatives as well. "Don't you hear the voices of your dead parents and other relatives crying out?" he demanded.

To Luther, Tetzel's actions were the final outrage. He drew up 95 theses, or arguments, against indulgences. Among other things, he argued that indulgences had no basis in the Bible, that the pope had no authority to release souls from purgatory, and that Christians could be saved only through faith. In accordance with the custom of the time, he posted his list on the door of Wittenberg's All Saints Church.

Luther Versus the Church Almost overnight, copies of Luther's 95 Theses were printed and distributed across Europe, where they stirred furious debate. The Church called on Luther to recant, or give up his views. Luther refused. Instead, he developed even more radical new doctrines. Before long, he was urging Christians to reject the authority of Rome. Because the Church would not reform itself, he wrote, it must be reformed by secular authorities.

In 1521, the pope excommunicated Luther. Later that year, the new Holy Roman emperor, Charles V, summoned Luther to the diet, or assembly of German princes, at Worms. Luther went, expecting to defend his writings. Instead, the emperor simply ordered him to give them up. Luther again refused to recant:

> "Unless I am convicted by Scripture and plain reason—I do not accept the authority of popes and councils, for they have contradicted each other—I am captive to the Word of God. I cannot and will not recant anything, for to go against conscience is neither right nor safe."
> —Martin Luther, Speech Before the Diet of Worms

Charles declared Luther an outlaw, making it a crime for anyone in the empire to give him food or shelter. Still, Luther had many powerful supporters. One prince hid him at a castle in Wartburg. Luther remained in hiding for nearly a year. Throughout Germany, in the meantime, thousands hailed him as a hero. They accepted his teachings and, following his lead, renounced the authority of the pope.

Selling Indulgences
This 1517 cartoon shows Johann Tetzel selling indulgences to the people of Wittenberg. A jingle in the upper left corner said, "As soon as the coin in the coffer rings, a soul from purgatory springs."

Theme: Religions and Value Systems Do you think the artist who drew this picture approved of Tetzel's actions? Why or why not?

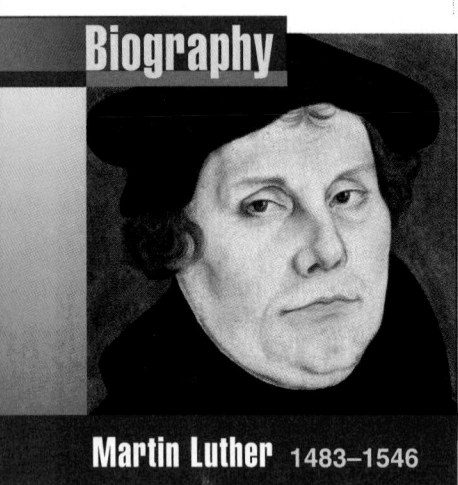
Luther's Teachings At the heart of Luther's teachings were several beliefs. First, he rejected the Church doctrine that good deeds were necessary for salvation. Instead, Luther argued that salvation was achieved through faith alone.

Second, Luther upheld the Bible as the sole source of religious truth. He denied other authorities, such as Church councils or the pope.

Third, Luther rejected the idea that priests and the Church hierarchy had special powers. Instead, he talked of a "priesthood of all believers." All Christians, he said, had equal access to God through faith and the Bible. Luther translated the Bible into the German vernacular so that ordinary people could study it by themselves. Every town, he said, should have a school so that girls and boys could learn to read the Bible.

Luther wanted to change other church practices. He rejected five of the seven sacraments because the Bible did not mention them. He banned indulgences, confession, pilgrimages, and prayers to saints. He simplified the elaborate ritual of the mass and instead emphasized the sermon. And he permitted the clergy to marry. These and other changes were adopted by the Lutheran churches that were set up by Luther's followers.

Spread of Lutheran Ideas

Luther's ideas found a fertile field in northern Germany and Scandinavia. While the new printing presses spread Luther's writings, fiery preachers denounced Church abuses. By 1530, the Lutherans were using a new name, Protestant, for those who "protested" papal authority.

Widespread Support Why did Lutheranism win widespread support? Many clergy saw Luther's reforms as the answer to Church corruption. A number of German princes, however, embraced Lutheran beliefs for more selfish reasons. Some saw Lutheranism as a way to throw off the rule of both the Church and the Holy Roman emperor. Others welcomed a chance to seize Church property in their territory. Still other Germans supported Luther because of feelings of national loyalty. They were tired of German money going to support churches and clergy in Italy.

The Peasants' Revolt Many peasants also took up Luther's banner. They hoped to gain his support for social and economic change.

In 1524, a Peasants' Revolt erupted across Germany. The rebels called for an end to serfdom and demanded other changes in their harsh lives. Luther, however, strongly favored social order and respect for political authority. As the Peasants' Revolt grew more violent, Luther denounced it. With his support, nobles suppressed the rebellion, killing tens of thousands of people and leaving thousands more homeless.

The Peace of Augsburg During the 1530s and 1540s, Holy Roman emperor Charles V tried to force Lutheran princes back into the Catholic Church, but with little success. Finally, after a number of brief wars, Charles and the princes reached a settlement. The Peace of Augsburg, signed in 1555, allowed each prince to decide which religion—Catholic or Lutheran—would be followed in his lands. Most northern German states chose Lutheranism. The south remained largely Catholic.

John Calvin

Two other reformers, Ulrich Zwingli and John Calvin, presented further challenges to the Catholic Church. Zwingli, a priest and an admirer of Erasmus, lived in the Swiss city of Zurich. Like Luther, he rejected elaborate church rituals and stressed the importance of the Bible. John Calvin had a logical, razor-sharp mind. His ideas had a profound effect on the direction of the Reformation.

What Is the Goal of Education?

Both the Renaissance and the Reformation stressed the importance of education. What is your goal in pursuing an education? Think about the goals of modern-day schools as you compare the following viewpoints.

China 500 B.C.

Chinese philosopher Confucius explained how learning was essential for both the individual and the community:

66 Extension of knowledge comes from the investigation of things. When things are investigated, knowledge is extended. When knowledge is extended, the will becomes sincere. When the will is sincere, the heart can be set right. When the heart is right, the personal life can be cultivated. When the personal life is cultivated, the community can be regulated. When the community is regulated, the government can be made orderly. And when the government is orderly, there will be peace in the world. 99

Germany 1524

Protestant reformer Martin Luther called for German communities to set up and pay for Christian schools:

66 The world has need of educated men and women to the end that men may govern the country properly and women may properly bring up their children, care for their domestics, and direct the affairs of the household. . . . The welfare of the state depends on the intelligence and virtue of its citizens. 99

United States 1990s

This poster was designed for school guidance counselors.

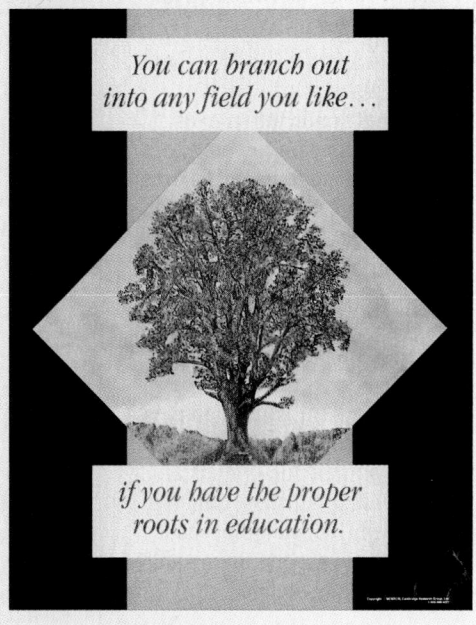

You can branch out into any field you like...

if you have the proper roots in education.

Cuba 1883

José Martí, a poet and political leader, turned away from classical ideas about what should be taught:

66 The schools teach classes in ancient geography, rules of rhetoric, and similar things of long ago, but in their place there should be courses in health; advice on hygiene; practical counseling; clear and simple studies of the human body, its parts, functions, ways of adjusting one to the other, economizing one's strength, and directing it well so that there will be no reason to restore it later. 99

Skills Assessment

1. What goal of education is stressed by both Confucius and Luther?
   - **A** gaining knowledge for its own sake
   - **B** making a good living
   - **C** cultivating the personal life
   - **D** contributing to the community

2. Who would be most likely to favor classes in physical education?
   - **E** Confucius
   - **F** Luther
   - **G** Martí
   - **H** the designer of the poster

3. **Critical Thinking Making Decisions** Identify a future career for yourself. Which educational theory would be most useful in helping you achieve this goal? Why? Explain why more than one type of education would be helpful.

Skills Tip

It is important to recognize that a writer may express his or her point of view as an absolute truth to convince others of its validity.

Teachings Calvin was born in France and trained as a priest and lawyer. In 1536, Calvin published the *Institutes of the Christian Religion.* In this book, which was read by Protestants everywhere, he set forth his religious beliefs. He also provided advice on how to organize and run a Protestant church.

Like Luther, Calvin believed that salvation was gained through faith alone. He, too, regarded the Bible as the only source of religious truth. But Calvin put forth a number of ideas of his own. He preached predestination, the idea that God had long ago determined who would gain salvation. To Calvinists, the world was divided into two kinds of people—saints and sinners. Calvinists tried to live like saints, believing that only those who were saved could live truly Christian lives.

Calvin's Geneva In 1541, Protestants in the city-state of Geneva in Switzerland asked Calvin to lead their community. In keeping with his teachings, Calvin set up a theocracy, or government run by church leaders.

Calvin's followers in Geneva came to see themselves as a new "chosen people" entrusted by God to build a truly Christian society. Calvinists stressed hard work, discipline, thrift, honesty, and morality. Citizens faced fines or other harsher punishments for offenses such as fighting, swearing, laughing in church, or dancing. Calvin closed theaters and frowned on elaborate dress. To many Protestants, this emphasis on strict morality made Calvinist Geneva seem a model community.

Like Luther, Calvin believed in religious education for girls as well as for boys. Women, he felt, should read the Bible—in private. Calvin also allowed women to sing in church, a practice that many church leaders criticized.

Spread of Calvinism Reformers from all over Europe visited Geneva and then returned home to spread Calvin's ideas. By the late 1500s, Calvinism had taken root in Germany, France, the Netherlands, England, and Scotland. This new challenge to the Roman Catholic Church set off bloody wars of religion across Europe.

In Germany, Calvinists faced opposition not only from Catholics, but from Lutherans as well. In France, wars raged between French Calvinists, called Huguenots, and Catholics. Calvinists in the Netherlands organized the Dutch Reformed Church. To avoid persecution, "field preachers" gave sermons in the countryside, away from the eyes of town authorities.

In Scotland, a Calvinist preacher named John Knox led a religious rebellion. Under Knox, Scottish Protestants overthrew their Catholic queen. They then set up the Scottish Presbyterian Church.

Calvin on Greed

John Calvin warns his followers in Geneva and elsewhere against worldly values:

"We have a frenzied desire, an infinite eagerness, to pursue wealth and honor, intrigue for power, accumulate riches, and collect all those frivolities [extras] which seem conducive to luxury and splendor. On the other hand, we have a remarkable dread, a remarkable hatred of poverty, mean birth, and a humble condition, and feel the strongest desire to guard against them. . . . The course which Christian men must follow is this: first, they must not long for, or hope for, or think of any kind of prosperity apart from the blessing of God; on it they must cast themselves, and there safely and confidently recline."

—John Calvin, *On the Christian Life*

Skills Assessment

Primary Source What activities did John Calvin warn against?

SECTION 3 Assessment

Recall

1. **Identify:** (a) Protestant Reformation, (b) Martin Luther, (c) Peace of Augsburg, (d) John Calvin, (e) Huguenot, (f) John Knox.
2. **Define:** (a) indulgence, (b) recant, (c) predestination, (d) theocracy.

Comprehension

3. Why did many Christians call for Church reform?
4. (a) How did Martin Luther's ideas differ from those expressed by the Catholic Church?
   (b) Why did Luther gain wide-spread support?
5. Identify five ideas taught by John Calvin.

Critical Thinking and Writing

6. **Synthesizing Information** How did the Reformation reflect humanist ideas?
7. **Analyzing Information** Why do you think Luther's teachings caused a split in the Catholic Church when earlier reform movements did not?

Activity

Writing an Obituary
Read some obituaries, or death notices, in a current newspaper. Then, using the same style of writing, prepare a brief obituary of Martin Luther. The obituary should list key events in Luther's life and explain why he will be remembered. Try to avoid bias.

Reformation Ideas Spread

Reading Focus

- What ideas did radical reformers support?
- Why did England form a new church?
- How did the Catholic Church reform itself?
- Why did some groups face persecution?

Vocabulary

annul

canonize

compromise

scapegoat

ghetto

Taking Notes

On a sheet of paper draw a Venn diagram like the one shown here. As you read the section, add information from the text.

ENGLISH REFORMATION
- King Henry VIII establishes Church of England

• Widespread persecution

CATHOLIC REFORMATION
- Council of Trent

Main Idea Both the Protestant and Catholic reformations brought sweeping changes to Europe.

Setting the Scene Henry III, the Catholic king of France, was deeply disturbed by Calvinist reformers in Geneva. "It would have been a good thing," he wrote, "if the city of Geneva were long ago reduced to ashes, because of the evil doctrine which has been sown from that city."

Throughout Europe, Catholic monarchs and the Catholic Church fought back against the Protestant challenge. They also took steps to reform the Church and to restore its spiritual leadership of the Christian world. At the same time, Protestant ideas continued to spread.

Radical Reformers

As the Reformation continued, hundreds of new Protestant sects sprang up. These sects often had ideas that were even more radical than those of Luther and Calvin. A number of groups, for example, rejected infant baptism. Infants, they argued, are too young to understand what it means to accept the Christian faith. Only adults, they felt, should receive the sacrament of baptism. They became known as Anabaptists.

A few Anabaptist sects sought radical social change as well. Some wanted to abolish private property. Others sought to speed up the coming of God's day of judgment by violent means. When radical Anabaptists took over the city of Munster in Germany, even Luther advised his supporters to join Catholics in suppressing the threat to the traditional order.

Most Anabaptists were peaceful. They called for religious toleration and separation of church and state. Despite harsh persecution, these groups influenced Protestant thinking in many countries. Today, the Baptists, Quakers, Mennonites, and Amish all trace their ancestry to the Anabaptists.

The English Reformation

In England, religious leaders such as John Wycliffe had called for Church reform as early as the 1300s. By the 1520s, some English clergy were toying with Protestant ideas. The break with the Catholic Church, however, was the work not of religious leaders but of King Henry VIII. For political reasons, Henry wanted to end papal control over the English church.

Seeking an Annulment At first, Henry VIII stood firmly against the Protestant revolt. The pope even awarded him the title "Defender of the Faith" for a pamphlet that he wrote denouncing Luther.

Henry VIII
Henry VIII wrote love songs, played tennis, and married six times. He was also ruthless to his enemies. He had dozens of people beheaded, including his second and fifth wives.

Theme: Impact of the Individual What impression of Henry do you get from this picture?

In 1527, an issue arose that set Henry at odds with the Church. After 18 years of marriage, Henry and his Spanish wife, Catherine of Aragon, had one surviving child, Mary Tudor. Henry felt that England's stability depended on his having a male heir. He wanted to marry Anne Boleyn, hoping that she would bear him a son. Because Catholic law does not permit divorce, he asked the pope to annul, or cancel, his marriage. Popes had annulled royal marriages before. But the current pope refused. He did not want to offend the Holy Roman emperor Charles V, Catherine's nephew.

Break With Rome   Henry was furious. Spurred on by his advisers, many of whom leaned toward Protestant teachings, he decided to take over the English church. Acting through Parliament, he had a series of laws passed. They took the English church from the pope's control and placed it under Henry's rule. In 1534, the Act of Supremacy made Henry "the only supreme head on Earth of the Church of England." Many loyal Catholics refused to accept the Act of Supremacy and were executed for treason. Among them was Sir Thomas More, the great English humanist. More was later canonized, or recognized as a saint, by the Catholic Church.

At the same time, Henry appointed Thomas Cranmer archbishop. Cranmer annulled the king's marriage. Henry then wed Anne Boleyn, who bore him a second daughter, Elizabeth. In the years ahead, Henry married four more times but had only one son, Edward.

The Church of England   Between 1536 and 1540, royal officials investigated English convents and monasteries. Claiming that they were centers of immorality, Henry ordered them closed. He then confiscated, or seized, their lands and wealth. Henry shrewdly granted some of these lands to nobles and other high-ranking citizens. He thus secured their support for the Anglican Church, as the new Church of England was called.

Despite these actions, Henry was not a religious radical. He rejected most Protestant doctrines. Aside from breaking away from Rome and allowing use of the English Bible, he kept most Catholic forms of worship.

Religious Turmoil   When Henry died in 1547, his 10-year-old son, Edward VI, inherited the throne. The young king's advisers were devout Protestants. Under Edward, Parliament passed new laws that brought the Protestant reforms to England. Thomas Cranmer drew up the *Book of Common Prayer.* It imposed a moderate form of Protestant service, while keeping many Catholic doctrines. Even so, the changes sparked uprisings that were harshly suppressed.

When Edward died in his teens, his half-sister, Mary Tudor, became queen. She was determined to return England to the Catholic faith. Under Queen Mary, hundreds of English Protestants were burned at the stake.

The Elizabethan Settlement   On Mary's death in 1558, the throne passed to Elizabeth. For years, Elizabeth had survived court intrigues, including the religious swings under Edward and Mary. As queen, Elizabeth had to determine the future of the Church of England. Moving cautiously at first, she slowly enforced a series of reforms that later were called the Elizabethan settlement.

The queen's policies were a compromise, or acceptable middle ground, between Protestant and Catholic practices. The Church of England preserved much Catholic ceremony and ritual. It kept the hierarchy of bishops and archbishops, but the queen reaffirmed that the monarch was the head of the Anglican Church. At the same time, Elizabeth restored a version of the *Book of Common Prayer,* accepted moderate Protestant doctrine, and allowed English to replace Latin in church services.

During a long reign, Elizabeth used all her skills to restore unity to England. Even while keeping many Catholic traditions, she made England a firmly Protestant nation. After her death, England faced new religious

Biography

Elizabeth I   1533–1603

"She takes great pleasure in dancing and music," noted an English observer of Queen Elizabeth I. "In her youth she danced very well and composed measures and music and had played them herself." The normally thrifty queen employed some 50 singers, 40 musicians, and several songwriters to stage concerts for her.

Elizabeth also loved to see plays. She especially enjoyed the works of William Shakespeare, whom she helped to promote. The queen provided financial support and prestige for major acting groups, which led to a flowering of English theater.

Elizabeth's popular 45-year reign inspired other writers of the day. Poet Edmund Spenser dedicated *The Faerie Queene* to Elizabeth.

Theme: Impact of the Individual How did Queen Elizabeth help promote English arts?

Major European Religions About 1600

Legend:
- Mainly Roman Catholic
- Mainly Anglican
- Mainly Lutheran
- Areas of Calvinist minorities
- Areas of Muslim minorities
- Mainly Orthodox Christian
- Boundary of Holy Roman Empire

Note: Not all minority religious groups are shown. Jews were dispersed throughout Europe.

Azimuthal Equal Area Projection
0   250   500 Miles
0   250   500 Kilometers

storms. But it escaped the endless religious wars that tore apart France and many other European states during the 1500s.

The Catholic Reformation

As the Protestant Reformation swept across northern Europe, a vigorous reform movement took hold within the Catholic Church. The leader of this movement, known as the Catholic Reformation, was Pope Paul III. During the 1530s and 1540s, he set out to revive the moral authority of the Church and roll back the Protestant tide. To end corruption within the papacy itself, he appointed reformers to key posts. They and their successors guided the Catholic Reformation for the rest of the century.

Council of Trent To establish the direction that reform should take, the pope called the Council of Trent in 1545. It met off and on for almost 20 years. The council reaffirmed traditional Catholic views, which Protestants had challenged. Salvation comes through faith and good works, it declared. The Bible, while a major source of religious truth, is not the only source.

The council also took steps to end abuses in the Church. It provided stiff penalties for worldliness and corruption among the clergy. It also established schools to create a better-educated clergy who could challenge Protestant teachings.

The Inquisition To deal with the Protestant threat more directly, Pope Paul strengthened the Inquisition. As you have read, the Inquisition was a Church court set up during the Middle Ages. The Inquisition used secret testimony, torture, and execution to root out heresy. It also prepared the Index of Forbidden Books, a list of works considered too immoral or irreligious for Catholics to read. It included books by Luther and Calvin.

Ignatius of Loyola In 1540, the pope recognized a new religious order, the Society of Jesus, or Jesuits. Founded by Ignatius of Loyola, the Jesuit order was determined to combat heresy and spread the Catholic faith.

Ignatius was a Spanish knight raised in the crusading tradition. After his leg was shattered in battle, he found comfort reading about saints who had overcome mental and physical torture. Vowing to become a "soldier of God," Ignatius drew up a strict program for the Jesuits. It included spiritual and moral discipline, rigorous religious training, and absolute obedience to the Church. Led by Ignatius, the Jesuits embarked on a crusade to defend and spread the Catholic faith throughout the world.

To further the Catholic cause, Jesuits became advisers to Catholic rulers, helping them combat heresy in their lands. They set up schools that taught humanist and Catholic beliefs and enforced discipline and obedience. Daring Jesuits slipped into Protestant lands in disguise to minister to the spiritual needs of Catholics. Jesuit missionaries spread their Catholic faith to distant lands, including Asia, Africa, and the Americas.

Teresa of Avila As the Catholic Reformation spread, many Catholics experienced renewed feelings of intense faith. Teresa of Avila symbolized this renewal. Born into a wealthy Spanish family, Teresa entered a convent in her youth. Finding convent routine not strict enough, she set up her own order of nuns. They lived in isolation, eating and sleeping very little and dedicating themselves to prayer and meditation.

Impressed by her spiritual life, her superiors in the Church asked Teresa to reorganize and reform convents and monasteries throughout Spain. Teresa was widely honored for her work, and after her death the Church canonized her. Her mystical writings rank among the most important Christian texts of her time.

Results Did the Catholic Reformation succeed? By 1600, Rome was a far more devout city than it had been 100 years earlier. Across Catholic Europe, piety and charity flourished. The reforms did slow the Protestant tide and even returned some areas to the Catholic Church. Still, Europe remained divided into a Catholic south and a Protestant north.

Widespread Persecution

During this period of heightened religious passion, persecution was widespread. Both Catholics and Protestants fostered intolerance. Catholic mobs attacked and killed Protestants. Protestants killed Catholic priests and wrecked Catholic churches. Both Catholics and Protestants persecuted radical sects like the Anabaptists.

Witch Hunts Almost certainly, the religious fervor of the times contributed to a wave of witch hunting. Those accused of being witches, or agents of the devil, were usually women, although some men faced similar attacks. Between 1450 and 1750, tens of thousands of women and men died as victims of witch hunts.

Scholars have offered various reasons for this persecution. At the time, most people believed in magic and spirits. They saw a close link between magic and heresy. In addition, during times of trouble, people often look for scapegoats on whom they can blame their problems. People accused of witchcraft were often social outcasts—beggars, poor widows, midwives blamed for infant deaths, or herbalists whose potions were seen as gifts from the devil.

Most victims of the witch hunts died in the German states, Switzerland, and France, all centers of religious conflict. When the wars of religion came to an end, the persecution of witches also declined.

Jews and the Reformation The Reformation brought hard times to Europe's Jews. For many Jews in Italy, the early Renaissance had been a time of relative prosperity. Unlike Spain, which had expelled its Jews in 1492, Italy allowed Jews to remain. Some Jews followed the traditional trades they had

Global Connections

Witch Hunt in Salem

Witch hunts were not just a European phenomenon. They also took place across the Atlantic in the English colonies. In 1692, a witch hunt broke out in the town of Salem Village, Massachusetts. The panic began when two girls suffered strange fits. When coaxed to explain their behavior, the girls accused neighbors of casting spells on them. Soon, accusations spread like wildfire throughout the town. Before the witch hunt ended the following year, at least 200 people had been named, and 20 people had been executed as witches.

Theme: Political and Social Systems How did witch hunts disrupt communities during the Renaissance?

been restricted to in medieval times. They were goldsmiths, artists, traders, and moneylenders. Others expanded into medicine, law, government, and business. Still, pressure remained strong on Jews to convert. By 1516, Venice ordered Jews to live in a separate quarter of the city, which became known as a ghetto. Other Italian cities also forced Jews into walled ghettos.

During the Reformation, restrictions on Jews increased. At first, Luther hoped that Jews would be converted to his teachings. However, when they did not convert, he called for them to be expelled from Christian lands and for their synagogues and books to be burned. In time, some German princes did expel Jews. Others confined Jews to ghettos, requiring them to wear a yellow badge if they traveled outside.

In the 1550s, Pope Paul IV placed added restrictions on Jews. Even Emperor Charles V, who supported toleration of Jews in the Holy Roman Empire, banned them from Spanish colonies in the Americas. After 1550, many Jews migrated to Poland-Lithuania and to parts of the Ottoman empire, where they were permitted to prosper. Dutch Calvinists allowed Jewish families who were driven out of Portugal and Spain to settle in the Netherlands.

Looking Ahead

The upheavals of the Catholic and Protestant reformations sparked wars of religion in Europe until the mid-1600s. At that time, issues of religion began to give way to issues of national power. As you will read, Catholic and Protestant rulers often made decisions based on political interests rather than for purely religious reasons.

Cause and Effect

Long-Term Causes	Immediate Causes
• Roman Catholic Church becomes more worldly • Humanists urge a return to simple religion • Strong national monarchs emerge	• Johann Tetzel sells indulgences in Wittenberg • Martin Luther posts 95 Theses • Luther translates the Bible into German • Printing press allows spread of reform ideas • Calvin and other reformers preach against Roman Catholic traditions

Protestant Reformation

Immediate Effects	Long-Term Effects
• Peasants' Revolt • Founding of Lutheran, Calvinist, Anglican, Presbyterian, and other Protestant churches • Weakening of Holy Roman Empire • Luther calls for Jews to be expelled from Christian lands	• Religious wars in Europe • Catholic Reformation • Strengthening of the Inquisition • Jewish migration to Eastern Europe • Increased antisemitism

Connections to Today

• About one fourth of Christians are Protestant
• Religious conflict in Northern Ireland

Skills Assessment **Chart** The Protestant Reformation brought sweeping changes to Western Europe. **Identify one religious and one political effect of the Reformation.**

SECTION 4 **Assessment**

Recall
1. **Identify:** (a) Henry VIII, (b) Elizabeth I, (c) Council of Trent, (d) Inquisition, (e) Jesuits, (f) Teresa of Avila.
2. **Define:** (a) annul, (b) canonize, (c) compromise, (d) scapegoat, (e) ghetto.

Comprehension
3. Why were the Anabaptists considered radical?
4. Describe the steps by which England became a Protestant country.
5. What were the goals of the Catholic Reformation?

6. Why did persecution increase after the Reformation?

Critical Thinking and Writing
7. **Recognizing Causes and Effects** If the Catholic Church had undertaken reform earlier, do you think that the Protestant Reformation would have occurred? Explain.
8. **Recognizing Point of View** The Protestant term for the Catholic Reformation was the Counter-Reformation. (The prefix *counter* means "against.") How do these two terms reflect different points of view?

Activity
Writing a News Report Prepare a script for a TV news program reporting on King Henry VIII and his break with the Catholic Church. You might wish to include visuals and interviews as well.

The Scientific Revolution

Reading Focus

- How did astronomers change the way people viewed the universe?

- What was the new scientific method?

- What advances did Newton and other scientists make?

Vocabulary

heliocentric
hypothesis
scientific method
gravity

Taking Notes

On a sheet of paper, begin a concept web like this one. As you read this section, fill in the blank circles with information about the Scientific Revolution. Add as many other circles as you need.

Main Idea **A new way of thinking, based on experimentation and observation, changed the way Europeans looked at the world.**

Galileo
In addition to his work in astronomy, Galileo made important discoveries about the motion of pendulums and falling objects. This statue honors Galileo.

Theme: Impact of the Individual In this statue, what might be the meaning of the object Galileo holds in his hand?

Setting the Scene In 1609, Galileo Galilei trained his new telescope on the night sky. Its specially ground lens allowed him to view amazing sights. He saw mountains on the moon, fiery spots on the sun, and four moons circling the planet Jupiter. "I did discover many particulars in Heaven that had been unseen and unheard of until this our age," he later wrote. Galileo's observations supported a new view of the universe.

Leaders of the Renaissance and the Reformation looked to the past for models. Humanists turned to ancient classical ideas. Religious reformers were inspired by the Bible and early Christian times. By contrast, the profound change that took place in science in the mid-1500s pointed ahead, toward a future shaped by a new way of thinking about the physical universe. We call that historical change the Scientific Revolution.

Changing Views of the Universe

Until the mid-1500s, European scholars accepted the theory of the ancient Greek astronomer Ptolemy. Ptolemy taught that the Earth was the center of the universe. Not only did this view seem to agree with common sense, it also matched the teachings of the Church. In the 1500s and 1600s, some startling discoveries radically changed the way Europeans viewed the physical world.

A Revolutionary Theory In 1543, Polish scholar Nicolaus Copernicus (koh PER nuh kuhs) published *On the Revolutions of the Heavenly Spheres.* In it, he proposed a heliocentric, or sun-centered, model of the universe. The sun, he said, stood at the center of the universe. The Earth was just one of several planets that revolved around the sun.

Most experts rejected this revolutionary theory. In Europe at the time, all scientific knowledge and many religious teachings were based on the arguments developed by classical thinkers. If Ptolemy's reasoning about the planets was wrong, they believed, then the whole system of human knowledge might be called into question. But in the late 1500s, the Danish astronomer Tycho Brahe (TEE koh BRAH uh) provided evidence that supported Copernicus's theory. Brahe set up an astronomical observatory. Every night for years, he carefully observed the sky, accumulating data about the movement of the heavenly bodies.

After Brahe's death, his assistant, the brilliant German astronomer and mathematician Johannes Kepler, used Brahe's data to calculate the orbits of the planets revolving around the sun. His calculations supported Copernicus's heliocentric view. At the same time, however, they showed that each planet did not move in a perfect circle, as both Ptolemy and Copernicus believed, but in an oval-shaped orbit called an ellipse.

Galileo Scientists of many lands built on the foundations laid by Copernicus and Kepler. In Italy, Galileo Galilei assembled an astronomical telescope. As you have read, he observed the four moons of Jupiter moving slowly around that planet—exactly, he realized, the way Copernicus said that the Earth moved around the sun.

Galileo's discoveries caused an uproar. Other scholars attacked him because his observations contradicted ancient views about the world. The Church condemned him because his ideas challenged the Christian teaching that the heavens were fixed, unmoving, and perfect.

In 1633, Galileo was tried before the Inquisition. Threatened with death unless he withdrew his "heresies," Galileo agreed to state publicly that the Earth stood motionless at the center of the universe. "Nevertheless," he is said to have muttered as he left the court, "it does move."

A New Scientific Method

Despite the opposition of religious authorities, by the early 1600s a new approach to science had emerged. Unlike most earlier approaches, it did not rely on authorities like Aristotle or Ptolemy or even the Bible. It depended instead upon observation and experimentation.

A Step-by-Step Process The new approach to science required scientists to collect and accurately measure data. To explain the data, scientists used reasoning to propose a logical hypothesis, or possible explanation. They then tested the hypothesis with further observation or experimentation. Complex mathematical calculations were used to convert the observations and experiments into scientific laws. After reaching a conclusion, scientists repeated their work at least once—and usually many times—to confirm their findings. This step-by-step process of discovery became known as the scientific method.

Bacon and Descartes The new scientific method was really a revolution in thought. Two giants of this revolution were the Englishman Francis Bacon and the Frenchman René Descartes (ruh NAY day KAHRT). Each devoted himself to the problem of knowledge.

Skills Assessment

Chart The scientific method, still used today, was based on careful observation and measurement of objective data. **Why do you think step 7 is important?**

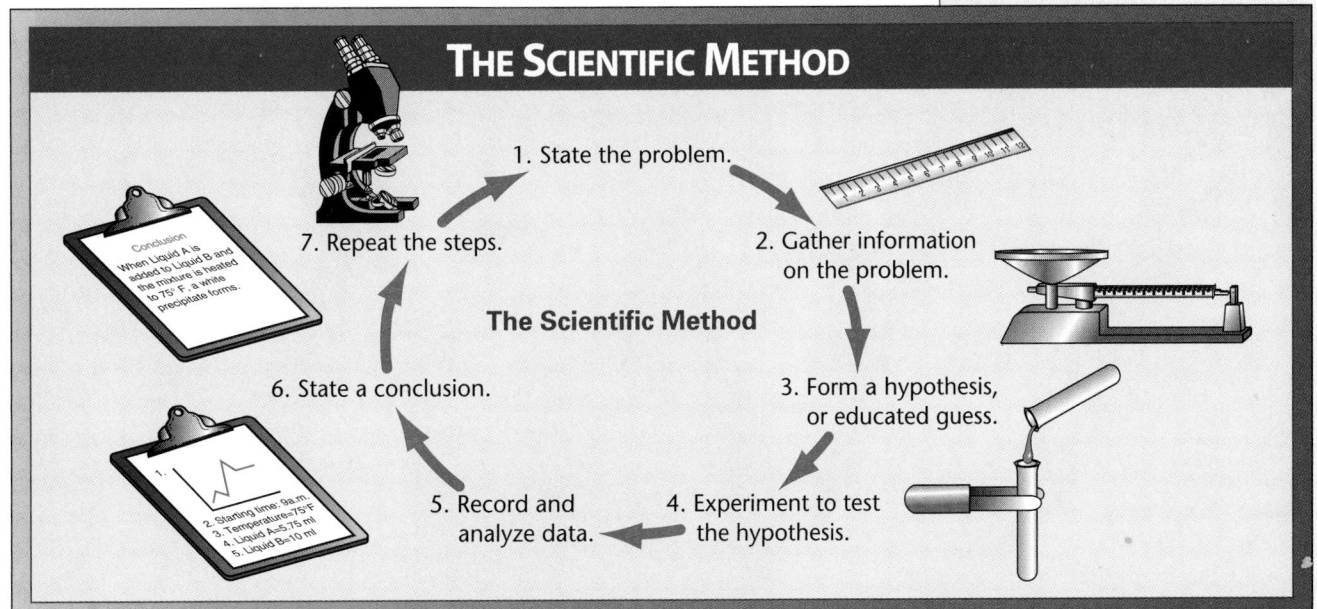

THE SCIENTIFIC METHOD

The Scientific Method

1. State the problem.
2. Gather information on the problem.
3. Form a hypothesis, or educated guess.
4. Experiment to test the hypothesis.
5. Record and analyze data.
6. State a conclusion.
7. Repeat the steps.

Conclusion
When Liquid A is added to Liquid B and the mixture is heated to 75° F, a white precipitate forms.

1.
2. Starting time: 9a.m.
3. Temperature=75°F
4. Liquid A=5.75 ml
5. Liquid B=10 ml

Both Bacon and Descartes rejected Aristotle's scientific assumptions. They also challenged the scholarly traditions of the medieval universities that sought to make the physical world fit in with the teachings of the Church. Both argued that truth is not known at the beginning of inquiry but at the end, after a long process of investigation.

Bacon and Descartes differed in their methods, however. Bacon stressed experimentation and observation. He wanted science to make life better for people by leading to practical technologies. Descartes emphasized human reasoning as the best road to understanding. In his *Discourse on Method,* he explains how he decided to discard all traditional authorities and search for provable knowledge. Left only with doubt, he concluded that the doubter had to exist and made his famous statement, "I think, therefore I am."

Newton Ties It All Together

As a student in England, Isaac Newton devoured the works of the leading scientists of his day. By age 24, he had formed a brilliant theory to explain why the planets moved as they did. According to one story, Newton saw an apple fall from a tree. He wondered whether the force that pulled that apple to the Earth might not also control the movements of the planets.

In the next 20 years, Newton perfected his theory. Using mathematics, he showed that a single force keeps the planets in their orbits around the sun. He called this force gravity.

In 1687, Newton published *Mathematical Principles of Natural Philosophy,* explaining the law of gravity and other workings of the universe. Nature, argued Newton, follows uniform laws. All motion in the universe can be measured and described mathematically.

To many, Newton's work seemed to link physics and astronomy, to bind the new science as gravity itself held the universe together. An English poet caught the spirit of what would later be called the Newtonian revolution:

"Nature and Nature's Laws lay hid in night,
God said, Let Newton be! and all was light."
—Alexander Pope, *Epitaphs*

For over 200 years, Newton's laws held fast. In the early 1900s, startling new theories of the universe called some of Newton's ideas into question.

Exploring Human Anatomy
Leonardo da Vinci dissected more than 30 corpses in order to create precise sketches of the human body (PAST). Today, doctors study anatomy with the aid of advanced computer technology (PRESENT).

Theme: Economics and Technology **How were anatomical drawings useful to Leonardo? How is computer imaging useful to doctors today?**

PAST

PRESENT

Yet Newton's laws of motion and mechanics continue to have many practical uses. Newton also helped develop an important new branch of mathematics—calculus.

Other Scientific Advances

The 1500s and 1600s saw breakthroughs in many branches of science. Some of the most significant advances occurred in chemistry and medicine.

Chemistry   Chemistry slowly freed itself from the magical notions of medieval alchemists, who had believed it was possible to transform ordinary metals into gold. In the 1600s, Robert Boyle distinguished between individual elements and chemical compounds. He also explained the effect of temperature and pressure on gases. Boyle's work opened the way to modern chemical analysis of the composition of matter.

Medicine   Medieval physicians relied on the ancient works of Galen. Galen, however, had made many errors, in part because he had limited knowledge of human anatomy. During the Renaissance, artists and physicians made new efforts to study the human body. In 1543, Andreas Vesalius published *On the Structure of the Human Body*, the first accurate and detailed study of human anatomy. A French physician, Ambroise Paré, developed a new and more effective ointment for preventing infection. He also developed a technique for closing wounds with stitches.

In the early 1600s, William Harvey, an English scholar, described the circulation of the blood for the first time. He showed how the heart serves as a pump to force blood through veins and arteries. Later in the century, the Dutch inventor Anthony van Leeuwenhoek perfected the microscope and became the first human to see cells and microorganisms. These pioneering scientists opened the way for further advances.

Looking Ahead

The rapid advance in science and technology that began in the 1500s has continued to this day. Thinkers like Bacon, Descartes, and Newton applied the scientific method to the pursuit of knowledge. Their work encouraged others to search for scientific laws governing the universe. Such ideas opened the way to the Enlightenment of the 1700s and a growing belief in human progress.

SECTION 5 Assessment

Recall

1. **Identify:** **(a)** Nicolaus Copernicus, **(b)** Johannes Kepler, **(c)** Galileo Galilei, **(d)** Francis Bacon, **(e)** René Descartes, **(f)** Isaac Newton, **(g)** Robert Boyle.
2. **Define:** **(a)** heliocentric, **(b)** hypothesis, **(c)** scientific method, **(d)** gravity.

Comprehension

3. Why did some people oppose the heliocentric theory of the universe?
4. How did the scientific method differ from earlier approaches?

5. How did Newton try to explain the workings of the universe?

Critical Thinking and Writing

6. **Making Inferences**   Newton wrote, "If I have seen further [than others] it is by standing on the shoulders of giants." **(a)** What do you think he meant? **(b)** Who might be some of the "giants" to whom Newton was referring?
7. **Applying Information**   Identify three ways in which your life today might have been different if the Scientific Revolution had never occurred.

Go Online
PHSchool.com

Use the Internet to learn more about the life and work of William Harvey. Then, prepare a brief biographical sketch of Harvey. Include a diagram of the circulatory system that he described. For help with this activity, use **Web Code mkd-1459**.

Creating a Chapter Summary

On a sheet of paper make a table like the one shown here. Use it to summarize major events that you have learned about in this chapter. Some cells have been partly filled in to help you get started.

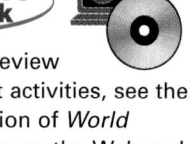

For additional review and enrichment activities, see the interactive version of *World History* available on the Web and on CD-ROM.

	RENAISSANCE	PROTESTANT REFORMATION	CATHOLIC REFORMATION	SCIENTIFIC REVOLUTION
WHAT IT WAS	• Time of creativity and change			
CAUSES				
IMPORTANT EVENTS		• Luther posts 95 Theses •		
KEY PEOPLE			• Ignatius of Loyola •	

Go Online
PHSchool.com
For practice test questions for Chapter 1, use **Web Code mka-1460.**

Building Vocabulary

Write sentences using the chapter vocabulary words listed below, leaving blanks where the vocabulary words would go. Then, exchange your sentences with another student, and fill in the blanks in each other's sentences.

1. patron
2. humanism
3. vernacular
4. utopian
5. indulgence
6. predestination
7. annul
8. ghetto
9. heliocentric
10. hypothesis

Recalling Key Facts

11. (a) What was the Renaissance?
    (b) When and where did it begin?
12. What three different kinds of plays did William Shakespeare write?
13. Why did Martin Luther post his 95 Theses?
14. How did the English Reformation occur?
15. What is the scientific method?
16. What did Descartes mean by the statement "I think, therefore I am"?

Critical Thinking and Writing

17. **Connecting to Geography** How did artists translate new techniques of the Renaissance to their landscape paintings?
18. **Comparing** (a) Compare and contrast the Renaissance in Italy with the Renaissance in northern Europe. (b) How would you account for the differences?
19. **Understanding Sequence** An English author wrote, "The preaching of sermons is speaking to a few of mankind, but printing books is talking to the whole world." How does this statement suggest a relationship between two of the key events discussed in this chapter?
20. **Recognizing Causes and Effects** Why did England escape the kinds of religious wars that tore apart other European nations?
21. **Linking Past and Present** Modern scientists refer to the discoveries of Copernicus as the Copernican Revolution. Why do you think they use that term?

The passage below is from the Council of Trent called by Pope Paul III in 1545 to establish the direction of Catholic reform. Read the passage, then answer the questions that follow.

"This holy Council cautions all bishops so to live . . . that they can bring together truth and behavior as a kind of constant example of thrift, modesty, and decency, and especially of that holy humility that so strongly commends men to God. Therefore, following the example set by our fathers at the Council of Carthage, it is ordered that bishops shall content them-selves not only with modest household furniture and simple food, but with regard to the rest of their manner of living and to their whole house, so that nothing appears that is alien to this holy institution of the Church and that does not show simplicity, zeal for God, and contempt for worldly things."

—Canons and Decrees of the
Holy Council of Trent

22. To what group of people is this passage mainly addressed?
23. **(a)** What orders are given in the passage? **(b)** On what authority are these orders given?
24. What does this document imply about the situation in the Church before the Council?
25. How can you tell that the reformers at the Council of Trent looked to the example of the early Christian Church?
26. **(a)** Do you think the reformers at Trent would agree with Protestant reformers about world-liness in the Church? **(b)** Do you think they would agree about the subject of papal authority?

Go Online
PHSchool.com

Use the Internet to research the invention of the printing press and its effects on Renaissance Europe. Then, write an essay in which you try to persuade the reader that the invention of the Internet either will or will not have a similar effect on world civilization in the future. For help with this activity, use **Web Code mkd-1461.**

Michelangelo sculpted this huge statue of the Israelite prophet Moses for the tomb of Pope Julius II. It stands almost eight feet tall and took years to complete. Study the statue, then answer the following questions:

27. How was this choice of subject typical of the Renaissance?
28. How does the sculpture show Renaissance humanism?
29. How does the sculpture show Michelangelo's attention to anatomical detail?
30. Why would an artist like Michelangelo need the support of a powerful patron like the pope?

Skills Tip

When you study a work of art, use what you know about the period in which it was created. In particular, it is important to understand what themes and topics were of con-cern to artists of that period.

The First Global Age: Europe and Asia

1415–1796

Chapter Preview

1 **The Search for Spices**
2 **Diverse Traditions of Southeast Asia**
3 **European Footholds in Southeast Asia and India**
4 **Encounters in East Asia**

CHAPTER EVENTS

1498
Portuguese explorer Vasco da Gama reaches India after rounding Africa. His voyage sets the stage for the rise of a Portuguese trading empire.

1511
Portugal seizes Malacca.

1522
The *Vittoria* completes the first circumnavigation of the globe. The expedition's original leader, Ferdinand Magellan, and four other ships do not survive the voyage.

1400   1480   1560

GLOBAL EVENTS

1456 The Gutenberg Bible is printed.

1500 The kingdom of Kongo thrives.

1519 Hernan Cortés lands in Mexico.

Trade Between Europe, Africa, and Asia About 1700

Ocean trade routes permitted the development of cultural and economic ties between Europe, Africa, and Asia.

Ports controlled by
- England
- Portugal
- France
- Netherlands
- Spain
- — Trade routes

EUROPE
ENGLAND
NETHERLANDS
FRANCE
PORTUGAL
SPAIN

ASIA

JAPAN
Deshima

CHINA
Macao
East China Sea

PACIFIC OCEAN
From Mexico

Canary Islands

PERSIA

ARABIA

INDIA
Bombay
Goa
Madras
Cochin

Calcutta

Manila
PHILIPPINES

Cape Verde Islands
Bissau

AFRICA

Arabian Sea

Bay of Bengal

South China Sea

Accra
São Tomé

INDIAN OCEAN

Malacca

Batavia
EAST INDIES

ATLANTIC OCEAN

From Europe

Mombasa
Zanzibar

Mozambique
Sofala

MADAGASCAR
Ft. Dauphin

AUSTRALIA

Cape Town

N W E S

Robinson Projection

0   500   1000 Miles
0 500 1000 Kilometers

1641
The Dutch seize Malacca from the Portuguese.

1736
China's Emperor Qianlong, shown here, begins a long reign. Qianlong expands China's territory but rejects western efforts to increase trade with China.

1640

1720

1800

1630s Japan bars western merchants.

1642 The English Civil War begins.

1789 The French Revolution begins.

The Search for Spices

Reading Focus

- Why did Europeans cross the seas?

- How did Portugal's eastward explorations lead to the development of a trading empire?

- How did Columbus's voyages affect the search for a passage to the Indies?

Vocabulary

cartographer

astrolabe

caravel

scurvy

circumnavigate

Taking Notes

Copy the table below. As you read the section, add information about the explorations of Portugal and Spain in the 1400s and 1500s.

PORTUGAL	SPAIN
• Henry the Navigator sponsors voyages •	• Columbus sails for India; reaches Caribbean •

Main Idea A desire to share in the rich spice trade of the East spurred Europeans to explore the oceans.

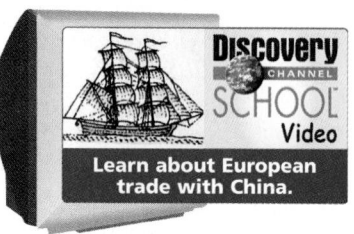

Learn about European trade with China.

The Spice Trade
Voyages of exploration were driven by the desire for cloves, pepper, and other spices.

Theme: Economics and Technology Why were spices so costly?

Setting the Scene Today, we take pepper for granted. To Europeans of past ages, though, this spice was as valuable as gold. Ancient Romans paid as much as $125 for 12 ounces of pepper. During the Middle Ages, the pepper in your local supermarket could have paid a year's rent. By the late 1400s, the desire to share in the rich spice trade of the East spurred Europeans to explore the oceans.

Europeans Explore the Seas

Europeans had traded with Asia long before the Renaissance. The Crusades introduced Europeans to many luxury goods from Asia. Later, when the Mongol empire united much of Asia in the 1200s and 1300s, Asian goods flowed to Europe along complex overland trade routes.

The Black Death and the breakup of the Mongol empire disrupted trade. By the 1400s, though, Europe was recovering from the plague. As its population grew, so did the demand for trade goods. The most valued items were spices, such as cinnamon, cloves, nutmeg, and pepper. People used spices in many ways—to preserve food, add flavor to dried and salted meat, and make medicines and perfumes. The chief source of spices was the Moluccas, an island chain in present-day Indonesia, which Europeans then called the Spice Islands.

Motives In the 1400s, Muslim and Italian merchants controlled most trade between Asia and Europe. Muslim traders brought prized goods to eastern Mediterranean ports. Traders from Venice and other Italian cities then carried the precious cargoes to European markets. Europeans, however, wanted to gain direct access to the riches of Asia. To do so, the Atlantic powers—first Portugal, then Spain—sought a route to Asia that bypassed the Mediterranean.

The desire for wealth was not the only motive that lured people to sea. Some voyagers were still fired by the centuries-old desire to crusade against the Muslims. The Renaissance spirit of inquiry further fired people's desire to learn more about the lands beyond Europe.

Improved Technology Several improvements in technology helped Europeans conquer the vast oceans of the world. Cartographers, or mapmakers, created more accurate maps and sea charts. European sailors also learned to use the astrolabe, an instrument developed by the ancient Greeks and perfected by the Arabs, to determine their latitude at sea.

Along with more reliable navigational tools, Europeans designed larger and better ships. The Portuguese developed the caravel, which combined the square sails of European ships with Arab lateen, or triangular, sails. Caravels also adapted the sternpost rudder and numerous masts of Chinese ships. The new rigging made it easier to sail across or even into the wind. Finally, European ships added more weaponry, including sturdier cannons.

Portugal Sails Eastward

Portugal, a small nation on the western edge of Spain, led the way in exploration. By the 1400s, Portugal was strong enough to expand into Muslim North Africa. In 1415, the Portuguese seized Ceuta (say oo tah) on the North African coast. The victory sparked the imagination of Prince Henry, known to history as Henry the Navigator.

Mapping the African Coast Prince Henry embodied the crusading drive and the new spirit of exploration. He hoped to expand Christianity and find the source of African gold.

At Sagres, in southern Portugal, Henry gathered scientists, cartographers, and other experts. They redesigned ships, prepared maps, and trained captains and crews for long voyages. Henry then sent out ships that slowly worked their way south to explore the western coast of Africa.

Henry died in 1460, but the Portuguese continued their quest. In 1488, Bartholomeu Dias rounded the southern tip of Africa. Despite the turbulent seas, the tip became known as the Cape of Good Hope because it opened the way for a sea route to Asia.

On to India In 1497, Vasco da Gama led four ships around the Cape of Good Hope. After a 10-month voyage, da Gama finally reached the great spice port of Calicut on the west coast of India. The long voyage home took a heavy toll. The Portuguese lost half their ships. Many sailors died of hunger, thirst, and scurvy, a disease caused by a lack of vitamin C in their diets during months at sea. Still, the venture proved highly profitable to the survivors. In India, da Gama had acquired a cargo of spices that he sold at a profit of 3,000 percent.

Da Gama quickly outfitted a new fleet. In 1502, he forced a treaty of friendship on the ruler of Calicut. Da Gama then left Portuguese merchants there to buy spices when prices were low and to store them near the dock until the next fleet could return. Soon, the Portuguese seized key ports around the Indian Ocean to create a vast trading empire.

Columbus Sails to the West

News of Portugal's successes spurred other nations to look for a sea route to Asia. An Italian navigator from the port of Genoa, Christopher Columbus, sought Portuguese backing for his own plan. He wanted to reach the Indies* by sailing west across the Atlantic. Like most educated Europeans, Columbus knew that the Earth was a sphere. A few weeks

---

*The Indies, or East Indies, was the European name for a group of islands in Southeast Asia. Today, they are a part of Indonesia.

Biography

Henry the Navigator
1394–1460

As a younger son of Portugal's King John I and Queen Philippa, Henry was not destined to rule his nation. This did not stop him, however, from carving out a place in history. During the campaign to conquer Ceuta, in northern Africa, he found his true calling. Inspired by stories of gold beyond the Sahara, he recognized Portugal's need for a sea route to distant lands.

Henry's interest in gaining wealth for Portugal was equaled by his desire to spread Christianity. In 1420, he was made a knight in a religious order. Already the governor of a province in southern Portugal, Henry paid for voyages of exploration with funds provided by the order. Each ship that set out from his court in Sagres bore a red cross on its sails, indicating the dual quest to find new lands and new converts to Christianity.

Theme: Impact of the Individual How might Portugal's history have been different if Henry had been the oldest son?

Early Voyages of European Exploration, 1487–1609

Explorers for Portugal

- - → Dias, 1487–1488

——→ Da Gama, 1497–1499

Explorers for Spain

- - → Columbus, 1492–1493

——→ Balboa, 1510–1513

- · - → Magellan and Elcano, 1519–1522

Explorers for England

——→ Cabot, 1497

Explorers for France

——→ Cartier, 1534–1535

Explorers for the Netherlands

——→ Hudson, 1609

Skills Assessment

Geography Beginning in the later 1400s, European nations sent explorers across the oceans in search of riches. New technology, such as the astrolabe and the caravel, made these voyages possible.

1. **Location** On the map, locate **(a)** Ottoman empire, **(b)** West Indies, **(c)** Strait of Magellan.
2. **Movement (a)** What region seems to have been of the most interest to explorers for England and the Netherlands? **(b)** What tool would they have used to determine location during their voyage?
3. **Critical Thinking Making Inferences** Why do you think explorers tended to take similar routes?

sailing west, he reasoned, would bring a ship to eastern Asia. His plan made sense, but Columbus made two errors. First, he greatly underestimated the size of the Earth. Second, he had no idea that two continents lay in his path.

Voyages of Columbus After Portugal refused to help him, Columbus persuaded Ferdinand and Isabella of Spain to finance his "enterprise of the Indies." In 1492, the Catholic rulers had driven the Muslims from their last stronghold in Spain. To strengthen their power, they sought new sources of wealth. Queen Isabella was also anxious to spread Christianity in Asia.

On August 3, 1492, Columbus sailed west with three small ships, the *Pinta*, the *Niña*, and the *Santa María*. Although the expedition encountered good weather and a favorable wind, no land came into sight. Provisions ran low, and the crew became anxious. Finally, on October 12, a lookout yelled, "Land! Land!"

Columbus then spent several months cruising the islands of the Caribbean. Because he thought he had reached the Indies, he called the people of the region Indians. In 1493, he returned to Spain to a hero's welcome. In three later voyages, Columbus remained convinced he had reached the coast of East Asia. Before long, though, other Europeans realized that Columbus had found a route to continents previously unknown to them.

Line of Demarcation Spain and Portugal pressed rival claims to the lands Columbus explored. In 1493, Pope Alexander VI stepped in to keep the peace. He set a Line of Demarcation dividing the non-European world

Tools of Ocean Navigation

Astrolabe This device was used to measure the angles of the sun and stars above the horizon. It was difficult to use accurately in rough seas.

Caravel This ship combined the square sails of European vessels with the lateen (triangular) sails of their Arab counterparts. The new rigging made it easier to sail across and into the wind.

ASIA

KOREA

JAPAN

MING EMPIRE

MUGHAL EMPIRE

PACIFIC OCEAN

Philippine Islands

Malay Pen.

Sumatra

East Indies

INDIAN OCEAN

AUSTRALIA

90°E

Robinson Projection

0   1000   2000 Miles

0   1000   2000 Kilometers

120°E   150°E   180°

into two zones. Spain had trading and exploration rights in any lands west of the line. Portugal had the same rights east of the line.

In 1500, the Portuguese captain Pedro Alvarez Cabral was blown off course as he sailed around Africa. Landing in Brazil, which lay east of the Line of Demarcation, he claimed it for Portugal.

Naming the "New World" In 1507, a German cartographer read reports about the "New World" written by an Italian sailor, Amerigo Vespucci. The mapmaker labeled the region America. The islands Columbus had explored in the Caribbean became known as the West Indies.

The Search Continues

Europeans continued to seek new routes around or through the Americas. In 1513, the Spanish adventurer Vasco Núñez de Balboa, with the help of Native Americans, hacked a passage through the tropical forests of Panama. From a ridge on the west coast, he gazed at a huge body of water that he called the South Sea. On September 20, 1519, a minor Portuguese noble named Ferdinand Magellan set out from Spain with five ships. His crew included men from Europe, Africa, and Southeast Asia.

Perils at Sea As the ships sailed south and west, through storms and calms and tropical heat, Magellan had to put down more than one mutiny. At last, the fleet reached the coast of South America. Carefully, they explored each bay, hoping for one that would lead to the Pacific.

In November 1520, Magellan's ships entered a bay at the southern tip of South America. Amid brutal storms, rushing tides, and unpredictable winds, Magellan charted a passage that became known as the Strait of Magellan. The ships emerged from this lashing into Balboa's South Sea, which Magellan renamed the Pacific—peaceful—Ocean.

Circumnavigating the Globe   Their mission accomplished, most of the crew wanted to return to Spain the way they had come. Magellan, however, insisted they push on across the Pacific to the East Indies. Three more weeks, he thought, would bring them to the Spice Islands.

Magellan soon found that the Pacific was much wider than he imagined. For nearly four months, the ship plowed across the uncharted ocean. Finally in March 1521, the fleet reached the Philippines. There, Magellan was killed when he got involved in a local conflict. In the end, only one ship and 18 sailors completed the voyage. On September 8, 1522, nearly three years after setting out, the survivors reached Seville. The Spanish hailed them as the first people to circumnavigate, or sail around, the world.

Search for a Northwest Passage   "I believe that never more will any man undertake to make such a voyage," predicted Antonio Pigafetta, a survivor of the Magellan voyage. But he was wrong. While Spain and Portugal claimed their zones, English, Dutch, and French explorers searched the coast of North America for a northwest passage to Asia.

In 1497, King Henry VII of England sent a Venetian navigator known as John Cabot to seek a more northerly route than the one Columbus had charted. Cabot found rich fishing grounds off Newfoundland, which he claimed for England. Later the French captain Jacques Cartier explored the St. Lawrence River, while Henry Hudson, sailing for the Dutch, explored the Hudson River. None of them found the hoped-for route to Asia, but the search for a Northwest Passage continued for centuries.

Looking Ahead

The European age of exploration set off a period of growing global interdependence that continues today. Yet the activities of European explorers brought both tragedy and triumph. As trade increased, conflicts between Europe and other civilizations would become more pronounced. These conflicts emerged first in Asia.

SECTION 1 Assessment

Recall
1. **Identify: (a)** Henry the Navigator, **(b)** Vasco da Gama, **(c)** Christopher Columbus, **(d)** Vasco Núñez de Balboa, **(e)** Ferdinand Magellan.
2. **Define: (a)** cartographer, **(b)** astrolabe, **(c)** caravel, **(d)** scurvy, **(e)** circumnavigate.

Comprehension
3. Why did European nations seek a sea route to Asia?
4. **(a)** Describe the routes taken by explorers for Portugal during the 1400s and early 1500s. **(b)** How did this affect Portugal's trade?

5. **(a)** Why did Columbus decide to sail westward? **(b)** What influence did his voyages have on other explorers?

Critical Thinking and Writing
6. **Making Decisions** What pros and cons would you weigh if you were a sailor trying to decide whether to sign on with da Gama, Columbus, or Magellan?
7. **Comparing (a)** In what way were the mistakes that Columbus and Magellan made similar? **(b)** How did their mistakes differ?

Go Online
PHSchool.com

Use the Internet to find out about the coat of arms that Christopher Columbus used after his voyages. How did Columbus modify the original plan for his coat of arms? Present your findings and a drawing of the coat of arms to the class. For help with this activity, use **Web Code mkd-1568.**

Diverse Traditions of Southeast Asia

Reading Focus

■ What are the key geographic features of Southeast Asia?

■ What impact did Indian civilization have on new kingdoms and empires?

■ What factors contributed to the growth of Vietnamese culture?

Vocabulary

matrilineal

stupa

padi

Taking Notes

As you read this section, prepare an outline of the contents. Use Roman numerals to indicate major headings. Use capital letters for the subheadings and numbers for the supporting details. The sample at right will help you get started.

I. Geography of Southeast Asia
  A. Location
    1. Mainland set apart by mountains and plateaus
    2.
  B. Trade routes in the southern seas

Main Idea Because of its location, Southeast Asia was affected by the cultures of both China and India.

Setting the Scene
According to the chronicles of early Burma (modern Myanmar), King Anawrata spoke to a Buddhist monk named Thera Arahanta.

> "'Preach to me somewhat—yea, but a little—of the Law preached by the Lord, the Master.'
> And Arahanta preached the Law, beginning with the things not to be neglected. . . . Then the king's heart was full of faith, steadfast, and immovable. Faith sank into him as oil filtered a hundred times soaks into cotton."
> —*The Glass Palace Chronicle of the Kings of Burma*

Buddhism was one of many exports from India that had a profound effect on the peoples of Southeast Asia. Sandwiched between China and India, the region known today as Southeast Asia was strongly influenced by both of these powerful neighbors. Yet the distinct cultures of Southeast Asia retained their own unique identities.

Geography of Southeast Asia

Southeast Asia is made up of two major regions. The first region, mainland Southeast Asia, includes several peninsulas that jut south between India and China. Today, the mainland is home to Myanmar (MEE uhn mahr), Thailand, Cambodia, Laos, Vietnam, and part of Malaysia. The second region, island Southeast Asia, consists of more than 20,000 islands scattered between the Indian Ocean and the South China Sea. It includes the present-day nations of Indonesia, Singapore, Brunei (bru NĪ), and the Philippines.

Location The mainland is separated from the rest of Asia by mountains and high plateaus. Still, traders and invaders did push overland into the region. Mountains also separate the four main river valleys of Southeast Asia—the Irrawaddy (ihr uh WAHD ee), Chao Phraya, Mekong, and Red. These river valleys were home to early civilizations.

Island Southeast Asia has long been of strategic importance. All seaborne trade between China and India had to pass through either the Malacca or Sunda straits. Whoever commanded the straits controlled rich trade routes.

Trade Routes in the Southern Seas The monsoons, or seasonal winds, shaped trading patterns in the "southern seas." Ships traveled northeast in

Southeast Asia
As the Irrawaddy River reaches the sea, its valley flattens out into a broad delta. The Irrawaddy River valley, like other Southeast Asian river valleys, served as a home to the region's early civilizations.

Theme: Geography and History What are the other major rivers of Southeast Asia?

Go Online
PHSchool.com

For: More on Angkor Wat
Visit: PHSchool.com
Web Code: mkd-1570

Khmer Temple
Although Angkor Wat in Cambodia lies in ruins today, its intricate carvings suggest the magnificence of the original complex. The central towers represent the peaks of mythical Mount Meru, which was believed to be the home of the gods.

Theme: Religions and Value Systems Why might the builders of Angkor Wat have chosen to represent Mount Meru in their design?

summer and southwest in winter. Between seasons, while waiting for the winds to shift, merchants harbored their vessels in Southeast Asian ports, which became important centers of trade and culture. Soon, an international trade network linked India, Southeast Asia, and China to East Africa and the Middle East.

The key products of Southeast Asia were spices. Only a fraction of the spices traded in the region was destined for markets in Europe. Most cargoes went to East Asia, the Middle East, and East Africa.

Early Traditions The peoples of Southeast Asia developed their own cultures before Indian or Chinese influences shaped the region. At Bang Chiang in Thailand, archaeologists have found jars and bronze bracelets at least 5,000 years old. This evidence is challenging old theories about when civilization began in the region.

Over the centuries, diverse ethnic groups speaking many languages settled in Southeast Asia. Living in isolated villages, they followed their own religious and cultural patterns. Many societies were built around the nuclear family rather than the extended families of India and China.

Women had greater equality in Southeast Asia than elsewhere in Asia. Female merchants took part in the spice trade, gaining fame for their skill in bargaining, finance, and languages. In some port cities, they gained enough wealth and influence to become rulers. Matrilineal descent, or inheritance through the mother, was an accepted custom in Southeast Asia. Women also had some freedom in choosing or divorcing marriage partners. Even after Indian and Chinese influences arrived, women retained their traditional rights.

Impact of India

Indian merchants and Hindu priests filtered into Southeast Asia, slowly spreading their culture. Later, Buddhist monks and scholars introduced Theravada beliefs. Following the path of trade and religion came the influence of writing, law, government, art, architecture, and farming.

Increasing Contacts In the early centuries A.D., Indian traders settled in port cities in growing numbers. They gave presents to local rulers and married into influential families. Trade brought prosperity as merchants exchanged products such as cottons, jewels, and perfume for raw materials such as timber, spices, and gold.

In time, local Indian families exercised considerable power. Also, people from Southeast Asia visited India as pilgrims or students. As these contacts increased, Indian beliefs and ideas won widespread acceptance. Indian influence reached its peak between 500 and 1000.

Islam Long after Hinduism and Buddhism took root in Southeast Asia, Indians carried a third religion, Islam, into the region. By the 1200s, Muslims ruled northern India. From there, traders spread Islamic beliefs and Muslim civilization throughout the islands of Indonesia and as far east as the Philippines.* Arab merchants, too, spread the new faith. The prevalence of Islam in lands surrounding the Indian Ocean contributed to the growth of a stable, thriving trade network.

New Kingdoms and Empires

The blend of Indian influences with local cultures produced a series of kingdoms and empires in Southeast Asia. Some of these states rivaled those of India.

Pagan The kingdom of Pagan (pah GAHN) arose in the fertile rice-growing Irrawaddy Valley in present-day Myanmar. In 1044, King Anawrata (ah nuh RAH tuh) united the region. He is credited with bringing Buddhism to the Burman people. Buddhism had reached nearby cultures long before, but Anawrata made Pagan a major Buddhist center. He filled his capital city with magnificent stupas, or dome-shaped shrines, at about the same time that people in medieval Europe were beginning to build Gothic cathedrals.

Pagan flourished for some 200 years after Anawrata's death, but fell in 1287 to conquering Mongols. When the Burmans finally threw off foreign rule, they looked back with pride to the great days of Pagan.

The Khmer Empire Indian influences also helped shape the Khmer (kuh MEHR) empire, which reached its peak between 800 and 1350. Its greatest rulers controlled much of present-day Cambodia, Thailand, and Malaysia. The Khmer people adapted Indian writing, mathematics, architecture, and art. Khmer rulers became pious Hindus. Like the princes and emperors of India, they saw themselves as god-kings. Most ordinary people, however, preferred Buddhism.

In the 1100s, King Suryavarman II built the great temple complex at Angkor Wat. The ruins that survive today, though overgrown with jungle and pocked by the bullets of recent wars, are among the most impressive in the world. Hundreds of carved figures tell Hindu myths and glorify the king. Although the images of Vishnu, Shiva, and the Buddha reflect strong Indian influence, the style is uniquely Khmer.

Srivijaya The trading empire of Srivijaya (shree vah JI yah), in Indonesia, flourished from the 600s to the 1200s. Srivijaya controlled the Strait of

Empires and Kingdoms of Southeast Asia

Pagan kingdom, A.D. 1044–A.D. 1287		Srivijaya empire, A.D. 600s–A.D. 1200s	Mongol invasion, A.D. 1287
Khmer empire, A.D. 800–A.D. 1350		Vietnam kingdom, A.D. 939–A.D. 1883	

Azimuthal Equal Area Projection

0   400   800 Miles

0   400   800 Kilometers

Skills Assessment

Geography The region we call Southeast Asia consists of both a mainland area and thousands of islands. It was home to numerous ancient and diverse cultures.

1. **Location** On the map, locate **(a)** Pagan kingdom, **(b)** Angkor Wat, **(c)** the Moluccas, **(d)** Sunda Strait.
2. **Movement** From which direction did the Mongol invasion take place?
3. **Critical Thinking Understanding Sequence** During which centuries were these empires and kingdoms most likely to have come into contact with one another?

---

*Today, Indonesia has the largest Muslim population of any nation in the world.

Malacca, which, as you have learned, was vital to shipping. Both Hinduism and Buddhism reached this island empire. As elsewhere in Southeast Asia, however, the local people often blended Indian beliefs into their own forms of worship, based on nature spirits.

Later, Islam spread to Sumatra, Java, and other islands. Local rulers adopted the new religion, which cemented commercial links with other Muslim trading centers around the Indian Ocean.

Vietnam Emerges

In most of Southeast Asia, Indian influence outweighed Chinese influence. Indian traditions spread mostly through trade rather than conquest. China, however, sent military forces to conquer the neighboring state of Annam (now northern Vietnam).

The heart of northern Vietnam was the Red River delta, around present-day Hanoi. There, the river irrigated fertile rice padis, or fields, which provided food for a growing population. The Vietnamese had their own distinct culture. As in other parts of Southeast Asia, women often held positions of authority.

Chinese Domination   In 111 B.C., Han armies conquered the region. China remained in control for 1,000 years. During that time, the Vietnamese absorbed Confucian ideas. They adopted the Chinese civil service system and built a government bureaucracy similar to that found in China. Vietnamese nobles learned to speak the Chinese language and read Chinese characters. Unlike the rest of Southeast Asia, where Theravada Buddhism had the strongest impact, Vietnam adopted Mahayana beliefs from China. Daoism also helped shape Vietnamese society.

Resistance   Despite these powerful Chinese influences, the Vietnamese preserved a strong sense of their separate identity. In A.D. 39, two noble sisters, Trung Trac and Trung Nhi, led an uprising that briefly drove the Chinese occupiers from the land. They tried to restore a simpler form of government based on ancient Vietnamese traditions. To this day, the Trung sisters are remembered as great martyrs and heroes. Finally in 939, as the Tang dynasty collapsed in China, Vietnam was able to break free from China. The Vietnamese turned back repeated Chinese efforts to reconquer their land, but did remain a tributary state of China.

Biography

Trung Sisters
d. A.D. 42(?)

Although the Chinese conquest of Annam introduced Confucian values, many local traditions continued for centuries. Women remained involved in politics, law, and trade. Still, officials were surprised when sisters Trung Trac and Trung Nhi forged a legacy for themselves as freedom fighters.

The sisters managed to do what no one else could. They forced the conquering Chinese out and established home rule. They did this by recruiting and training over 80,000 men and women to fight. Thirty-six of their generals were women.

After three years, however, the Chinese emperor sent an army against the sisters. According to legend, after a terrible defeat, the Trung sisters drowned themselves to avoid capture.

Theme: Impact of the Individual Why are the Trung sisters still revered in Vietnam today?

SECTION 2 Assessment

Recall
1. **Identify:** (a) Pagan, (b) Anawrata, (c) Khmer, (d) Suryavarman II, (e) Trung sisters.
2. **Define:** (a) matrilineal, (b) stupa, (c) padi.

Comprehension
3. How did geography make Southeast Asia of strategic importance?
4. How did India influence Pagan, the Khmer empire, and Srivijaya?
5. (a) How did China influence Vietnam? (b) How did Vietnam preserve its identity?

Critical Thinking and Writing
6. **Analyzing Information** Women's social status was limited in both India and China. Why do you think Southeast Asian women were able to retain their equality despite strong Indian and Chinese cultural influence?
7. **Comparing** How did the spread of Indian influence through Southeast Asia differ from the spread of Chinese influence through the same region?

Activity

Making a Map
Create a map showing foreign influences in Southeast Asia. First, draw or trace an outline map of the region. Use arrows to show the origins and directions of influences— for example, blue arrows for trade routes, red arrows for invasion routes. Then, show what products or ideas traveled along these routes.

Reading Focus

■ How did the Portuguese and the Dutch build empires in the East?

■ How did Spain control the Philippines?

■ How did the decline of Mughal India affect European traders?

Vocabulary

outpost

sepoy

Taking Notes

Begin a concept web like this one. As you read this section, fill in the blank circles with information about European influence in Southeast Asia and India. Add more circles as necessary.

Main Idea Europeans used military power to build trading empires in Southeast Asia.

Setting the Scene

In 1511, a Portuguese fleet commanded by Afonso de Albuquerque (ahl boo KEHR keh) dropped anchor off Malacca, a rich Muslim trading port that controlled the sea route linking India, Southeast Asia, and China. "Have you come in peace or in war?" asked the sultan. "Peace," replied Albuquerque. The true goal of the Portuguese, however, was not peace, but conquest.

The fleet remained at anchor for several weeks. Then they opened fire. The Portuguese quickly took the city, killing its inhabitants and seizing its wealth. On the ruins of a mosque, Albuquerque built a fort. The sultan had fled, thinking the invaders would loot and leave. But when he heard about the fort, he realized that the Portuguese had come to stay.

Portugal was the first European power to gain a foothold in Asia. The Portuguese ships were small in size and number, but the firepower of their shipboard cannons was unmatched. In time, this superior firepower helped them win control of the rich Indian Ocean spice trade and build a Portuguese trading empire in Asia. Before long, however, other European nations would challenge Portugal.

Portugal's Empire in the East

After Vasco da Gama's voyage, the Portuguese, under Albuquerque's command, burst into the Indian Ocean. In 1510, they seized the island of Goa off the coast of India, making it their major military and commercial base. Albuquerque then moved to end Muslim power and turn the Indian Ocean into a "Portuguese lake."

Trading Outposts Albuquerque burned coastal towns and crushed Arab fleets at sea. The Portuguese attacked Aden, at the entrance to the Red Sea, and took Ormuz, gateway to the Persian Gulf. In 1511, Albuquerque took Malacca, massacring the city's Muslims and making the Europeans hated and feared.

In less than 50 years, the Portuguese had built a trading empire with military and merchant outposts, or distant areas under their control, rimming the southern seas. They seized cities on the east coast of Africa so they could resupply and repair their ships. For most of the 1500s, Portugal controlled the spice trade between Europe and Asia.

Impact Despite their sea power, the Portuguese remained on the fringe of Asian trade. They had neither the strength nor the resources to conquer

Primary Source

The Portuguese in India

Afonso de Albuquerque explained to his soldiers why the Portuguese wanted to capture Malacca:

"The king of Portugal has often commanded me to go to the Straits, because . . . this was the best place to intercept the trade which the Moslems . . . carry on in these parts. So it was to do Our Lord's service that we were brought here; by taking Malacca, we would close the Straits so that never again would the Moslems be able to bring their spices by this route. . . . I am very sure that, if this Malacca trade is taken out of their hands, Cairo and Mecca will be completely lost."

—*The Commentaries of the Great Afonso de Albuquerque*

Skills Assessment

Primary Source Why did Portugal want to control Malacca?

much territory on land. In India and China, where they faced far stronger empires, they merely sought permission to trade.

The intolerance of Portuguese missionaries caused resentment. In Goa, they attacked Muslims, destroyed Hindu temples, and introduced the Inquisition. Portuguese ships even sank Muslim pilgrim ships on their way to Mecca. Some Asian merchants chose to trade with the Portuguese. Others, however, chose to bypass Portuguese-controlled towns and continue their older trade patterns.

Rise of the Dutch

The Dutch were the first Europeans to challenge Portuguese domination in Asia. The land we know today as the Netherlands included a group of provinces and prosperous cities on the North Sea. The region had long been a center of handicrafts and trade. Through royal marriages, it fell under Spanish rule in the early 1500s. Later, the Protestant northern provinces won independence.

Sea Power In 1599, a Dutch fleet returned to Amsterdam from Asia after more than a year's absence. It carried a cargo of pepper, cloves, and other spices. Church bells rang to celebrate this "Happy Return." Those who had invested in the venture received 100 percent profit. The success of this voyage led to a frenzy of overseas activity.

By the late 1500s, Dutch warships and trading vessels put the Netherlands in the forefront of European commerce. They used their sea power to set up colonies and trading posts around the world. At the southwestern tip of Africa, the Dutch built the Cape Town settlement, where they could repair and resupply their ships.

Dutch Dominance In 1602, a group of wealthy Dutch merchants formed the Dutch East India Company. In the next decades, the Dutch strove to make themselves the major European power in the east. In 1641, they captured Malacca from the Portuguese and opened trade with China. Before long, they were able to enforce a monopoly in the Spice Islands, controlling shipments to Europe as well as much of the trade within Southeast Asia.

Like the Portuguese, the Dutch used military force to further their trading goals. At the same time, they forged closer ties with local rulers than the Portuguese had. Many Dutch merchants married Asian women.

Trade brought the Dutch enormous wealth. At home, Dutch merchants built tall mansions along the canals of Amsterdam and hired artists like Rembrandt to paint their portraits. In the 1700s, however, the growing power of England and France contributed to the decline of the Dutch trading empire in the East.

Spain Seizes the Philippines

While the Portuguese and Dutch set up bases on the fringes of Asia, Spain took over the Philippines. Magellan had claimed the archipelago for Spain in 1521. Within about 50 years, Spain had conquered and colonized the islands, renaming them for the Spanish king Philip II. Unlike most other peoples of Southeast Asia, the Filipinos were not united. As a result, they could be conquered more easily.

In the spirit of the Catholic Reformation, Spanish priests set out to convert the Filipino people to Christianity. Later, missionaries from the Philippines tried to spread Catholic teachings in China and Japan.

The Philippines became a key link in Spain's overseas trading empire. The Spanish shipped silver mined in Mexico and Peru across the Pacific to the Philippines. From there, they used the silver to buy goods in China. In this way, large quantities of American silver flowed into the economies of East Asian nations.

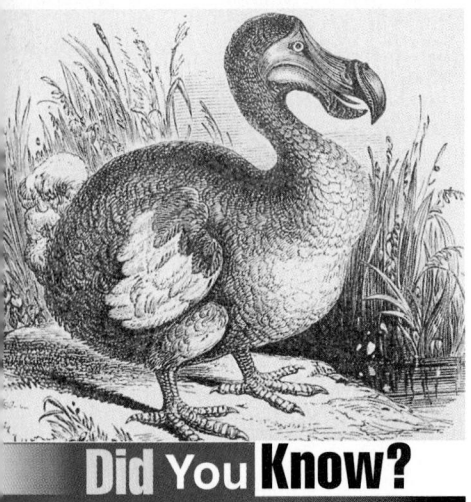

Disaster!

CYCLONE RIPS THROUGH CALCUTTA

When the English East India Company chose the location for the port city of Calcutta (Kolkata) in 1696, they did not realize its danger. Calcutta was built on the Hooghly River, part of the Ganges River delta system that flows into the Bay of Bengal. The bay is hit several times a year with devastating tropical storms. On October 11, 1737, the region was hit by one of the most destructive cyclones in history.

The storm surge—walls of water pushed by powerful winds—is the deadliest part of a cyclone. Waves start small, but as the storm approaches the shore, the surge grows. Finally, huge waves crash onto the shore, flooding the land.

Violent winds and rain struck Calcutta. Breaking waves caused a deafening roar. Then, a monstrous 40-foot wave crashed down on the shore. According to some reports, as many as 300,000 people died and 20,000 boats sank.

Desperate sailors were tossed from their ships and drowned. Of the nine British ships anchored in the Ganges before the storm hit, only one remained afloat. After the storm, bits of the shattered ships were found hanging in trees six miles upriver.

Portfolio Assessment

Conduct research to learn about other tropical storms such as a hurricane in the United States. Make a chart listing precautions that people in coastal areas can take to minimize damage and loss of life.

Mughal India and European Traders

Before the 1700s, European traders made very little impression on India, which was enjoying one of its greatest periods of strength and prosperity. In 1526, Babur had founded the Mughal dynasty. European merchants were dazzled by India's splendid court and its many luxury goods. There seemed little of value that Europeans could offer to the sophisticated civilization of Mughal India.

Industry and Commerce Besides producing spices, India was the world leader in textile manufacturing. It exported large quantities of silk and cotton cloth, from sheer muslins to elaborate chintzes. Handicrafts and shipbuilding added to the country's wealth.

The Mughal empire was larger, richer, and more powerful than any kingdom in Europe. When Europeans sought trading rights, Mughal emperors saw no threat in granting such concessions. The Portuguese and later the Dutch, English, and French thus were permitted to build forts and warehouses in coastal towns.

Turmoil and Decline When Akbar's successors ended his policy of religious toleration, conflicts rekindled between Hindu and Muslim princes. Years of civil war drained Mughal resources. Rulers then increased taxes, sparking peasant rebellions. Several weak rulers held the throne in the early 1700s. Corruption became widespread, and the central government eventually collapsed.

British-French Rivalry As Mughal power faltered, French and English traders played off rival Indian princes against one another. Both the English and French East India companies made alliances with local officials and independent rajahs. Each company organized its own army of sepoys, or Indian troops.

By the mid-1700s, the British and the French had become locked in a bitter struggle for global power. In 1756, war between Britain and France erupted in Europe. The fighting soon spread, involving both nations' lands in Asia and the Americas.

In India, Robert Clive, an agent of the British East India Company, used an army of British troops and sepoys to drive the French from their trading posts. The Company then forced the Mughal emperor to recognize its right to collect taxes in Bengal in the northeast. By the late 1700s, the Company had become the real ruler of Bengal, able to use its great wealth to spread its influence into other parts of India.

Prized Imports
Indian artisans created products like this hand-painted cotton wall hanging for European markets. Indian cottons became so popular in England that, to protect the English textile industry, Parliament tried to ban them.

Theme: Global Interaction
How does this wall hanging reflect both Indian and European culture?

SECTION 3 Assessment

Recall
1. **Identify:** **(a)** Afonso de Albuquerque, **(b)** Robert Clive.
2. **Define:** **(a)** outpost, **(b)** sepoy.

Comprehension
3. **(a)** How did the Portuguese gain control of the spice trade? **(b)** How were they challenged by the Dutch?
4. **(a)** Why was Spain easily able to conquer the Philippines? **(b)** Why did Spain want to control the islands?
5. **(a)** Why did Mughal power decline? **(b)** What effect did the decline have on France and Britain?

Critical Thinking and Writing
6. **Analyzing Information** How did Europeans build on existing trade networks in the Indian Ocean?
7. **Drawing Conclusions** Some people have argued "to the victors belong the spoils [riches] of the enemy." How do events in this section support this statement?

Go Online
PHSchool.com

Use the Internet to learn more about Goa, the Portuguese base in the East. Plan a visit that a modern-day tourist might take to this island. Include historical background that visitors should have, as well as sites that they should see. For help with this activity, use **Web Code mkd-1576.**

Encounters in East Asia

Reading Focus

- How was European trade with China affected by the Manchu conquest?

- What factors led Korea to isolate itself from other nations?

- What attitude did the Tokugawa shoguns have toward foreign traders?

Taking Notes

As you read this section, make a table to show how westerners acted and were received in East Asia. Use this table as a model.

	CHINA	KOREA	JAPAN
WESTERN BEHAVIOR AND ATTITUDES	• Matteo Ricci speaks Chinese • Macartney offends emperor		
RESPONSE TO WESTERNERS	• Restrict trade		

Main Idea China, Korea, and Japan limited contact with western nations.

Setting the Scene The Europeans who reached Asia in the 1500s often made a poor impression on their hosts. The Italian traveler Niccoló Manucci told how Asians thought that Europeans "have no polite manners, that they are ignorant, wanting in ordered life, and very dirty."

Europeans, by contrast, wrote enthusiastically about China. In 1590, a visitor described Chinese artisans "cleverly making devices out of gold, silver and other metals." He was also impressed with their abilities in handicrafts and gunsmithing, and wrote: "They daily publish huge multitudes of books."

Portuguese ships first reached China by way of the South China Sea during the Ming dynasty. To the Chinese, the Portuguese were "southern barbarians." Like other foreigners, they lacked the civilized ways of the Middle Kingdom.

European Trade With China

The Ming dynasty, you will recall, ended its overseas explorations in the mid-1400s. Confucian officials had little use for foreigners. "Since our empire owns the world," said a Ming document, "there is no country on this or other sides of the seas which does not submit to us."

Strict Limits on Trade Portuguese traders reached China by sea in 1514. To the Chinese, the newcomers had little to offer in exchange for silks and porcelains. European textiles and metalwork were inferior to Chinese products. The Chinese therefore demanded payment in gold or silver.

The Ming eventually allowed the Portuguese a trading post at Macao, near Canton, present-day Guangzhou (gwahng JOH). Later, they let Dutch, English, and other Europeans trade with Chinese merchants, but only under strict limits. Foreigners could trade only at Canton under the supervision of imperial officials. When each year's trading season ended, they had to sail away.

Scholars and Missionaries A few European scholars, like the brilliant Jesuit priest Matteo Ricci, did make a positive impression on Ming China.

China and Foreign Trade This fan shows the harbor in Canton, with European flags flying over warehouses in the background. Strict limits on foreign trade kept Europeans from gaining a foothold in China.

Theme: Economics and Technology How does the scene on this fan suggest the limitations placed on European merchants?

In the 1580s, Ricci learned to speak Chinese and adopted Chinese dress. Ricci and other priests had little success spreading their religious beliefs, although Chinese rulers welcomed the chance to learn the arts and sciences of Renaissance Europe.

The Manchu Conquest

By the early 1600s, the aging Ming dynasty was decaying. Revolts erupted, and Manchu invaders from the north pushed through the Great Wall. The Manchus ruled a region in the northeast that had long been influenced by Chinese civilization. In 1644, victorious Manchu armies seized Beijing and made it their capital.

Qing Rule The Manchus set up a new dynasty called the Qing (CHIHNG), meaning "pure." To preserve their distinct identity, the Manchus barred intermarriage between Manchus and Chinese. Manchu women were forbidden to follow the traditional Chinese practice of footbinding. Still, the Manchus won the support of the Chinese scholar-officials because they adopted the Confucian system of government. For each top government position, the Qing chose two people, one Manchu and one Chinese. Local government remained in the hands of the Chinese, but Manchu troops stationed across the empire ensured loyalty.

Two rulers oversaw the most brilliant age of the Qing. Kangxi (kahng SHEE), who ruled from 1661 to 1722, was an able administrator and military leader. He extended Chinese power into Central Asia and promoted Chinese culture. Kangxi's grandson Qianlong (chyehn LOHNG) had an equally successful reign from 1736 to 1796. He expanded China's borders to rule the largest area in the nation's history. Qianlong retired after 60 years because he did not want to rule longer than his grandfather had.

Prosperity The Chinese economy expanded under both emperors. New crops from the Americas, such as potatoes and corn, boosted farm output, which in turn contributed to a population boom. China's population rose from 140 million in 1740 to over 300 million by 1800. Peace and prosperity encouraged further growth in handicraft industries, including silk, cotton, and porcelain. Internal trade grew, as did the demand for Chinese goods from all over the world.

Response to Westerners The Qing maintained the Ming policy of restricting foreign traders. Still, Europeans kept pressing to expand trade to cities other than Guangzhou. In 1793, Lord Macartney arrived in China at the head of a British diplomatic mission. He brought samples of British-made goods to show the Chinese the advantages of trade with westerners. The Chinese thought the goods were gifts offered as tribute to the emperor and looked on them as rather crude products.

Further misunderstandings followed. Macartney insisted on an audience with the emperor. The Chinese told Macartney he would have to perform the traditional kowtow, touching his head to the ground to show respect to the emperor. Macartney refused. He also offended the Chinese by speaking of the natural superiority of the English. The negotiations faltered. In the end, Qianlong did receive Macartney, but the meeting accomplished nothing. Later, in a letter to King George III of Britain, Qianlong rejected the request for trading rights.

At the time, Qianlong's attitude seemed justified by China's successes. After all, he already ruled the world's greatest empire. Why should he negotiate with a nation as distant as Britain? In the long run, however, his policy proved disastrous. Even then, there was much the Chinese could have learned from the West. In the 1800s, China would learn about western advances—especially in military technology—the hard way.

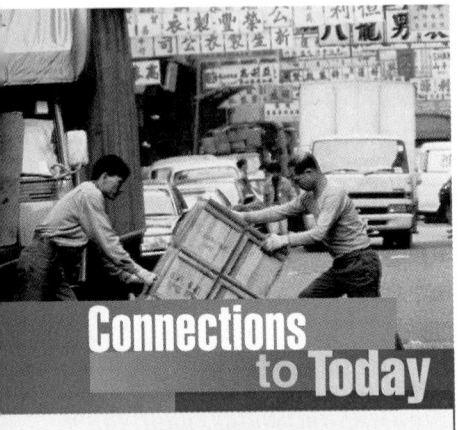

Connections to Today

Guangzhou's International Trade

For centuries, the thriving port of Guangzhou has welcomed merchants from many lands. Today, thousands of business people from all over the world attend the twice-yearly Guangzhou Fair. There they buy Chinese products to sell overseas and market their own goods to sell in China.

Many foreign companies have opened branches in Guangzhou. They have done so because of its status as one of 14 "coastal open cities." This special designation allows Guangzhou to extend privileges, including lower taxes, to foreign companies that want to do business there.

Theme: Economics and Technology How has Guangzhou continued to thrive from international trade?

Letter From the Celestial Emperor to the "Barbarian" King

In the following excerpt, Emperor Qianlong denies the request of King George III for greater trading rights in China.

"We have perused [read] the text of your state message and the wording expresses your earnestness. From it your sincere humility and obedience can clearly be seen. It is admirable and we fully approve. . . .

As to what you have requested in your message, O King, namely to be allowed to send one of your subjects to reside in the Celestial Empire to look after your country's trade, this does not conform to the Celestial Empire's ceremonial system, and definitely cannot be done. . . .

Moreover, the territories ruled by the Celestial Empire are vast, and for all the envoys of vassal [inferior] states coming to the capital there are definite regulations. . . . There has never been any precedent for allowing them to suit their own convenience. . . . Furthermore, there are a great many Western Ocean countries altogether, and not merely your one country. If, like you, O King, they all beg to send someone to reside at the capital, how could we grant their request in every case? It would be absolutely impossible for us to do so. How can we go so far as to change the regulations of the Celestial Empire . . . because of the request of one man—of you, O King? . . .

We have never valued ingenious articles, nor do we have the slightest need of your country's manufacturers. . . . You, O King, should simply act in conformity with our wishes by strengthening your loyalty and swearing perpetual obedience so as to ensure that your country may share the blessings of peace."

—Qianlong, letter to George III

Lord Macartney's Mission Artist William Alexander traveled to China with Lord Macartney. He did not attend the British meeting with the emperor, however, and had to rely on a British officer's firsthand drawings to produce this picture.

Skills Tip

When you analyze a primary source, pay careful attention to the author's point of view. Point of view is the author's beliefs or values that color his or her perceptions.

Skills Assessment

1. Emperor Qianlong seems to treat King George as
   - **A** an equal.
   - **B** an inferior.
   - **C** a superior.
   - **D** a threat.

2. What reason does the emperor not give for denying the king's request?
   - **E** historical precedent
   - **F** current regulations
   - **G** lack of interest in British goods
   - **H** fear of foreign influence

3. **Critical Thinking Recognizing Points of View** **(a)** What words or phrases convey Emperor Qianlong's view of the British king? **(b)** How does the emperor characterize his own nation?

Japanese Screens
Shoguns and daimyo filled their castles with brilliant, multipaneled screen paintings. Many screens depicted the beauties of nature or scenes of everyday life. This screen shows the activities of Japanese and Portuguese sea-farers aboard a large ship.

Theme: Art and Literature
How did the artist create a sense of motion?

Korea and Isolation

Like China, Korea restricted outside contacts in the 1500s and 1600s. Earlier, Korean traders had far-ranging contacts across East Asia. A Korean map from the 1300s accurately outlines lands from Japan to the Mediterranean. Koreans probably acquired this knowledge from Arab traders who had visited Korea.

The Choson dynasty, you will recall, firmly embraced Confucian ideas. Like the Chinese, Koreans felt that Confucian learning was the most advanced in the world. The low status of merchants in Confucianism also led Koreans to look down on foreign traders.

Two other events led the Koreans to turn inward. A Japanese invasion in the 1590s devastated the land of Korea. Then in 1636, the Manchus conquered Korea before overrunning Ming China. When the Manchus set up the Qing dynasty in China, Korea became a tributary state, run by its own government but forced to acknowledge China's supremacy. The two invasions left Korea feeling like "a shrimp among whales."

In response, the Koreans chose isolation, excluding all foreigners except the Chinese and a few Japanese. When European sailors were shipwrecked on Korean shores, they were imprisoned or killed. As a result, Korea became known in the West as the "Hermit Kingdom."

Even though Korea had few contacts with the world for about 250 years, this period was a great age for Korean arts and literature. In one satirical tale, author Pak Chi-won describes a poor scholar who breaks with tradition to become a merchant. Here, Master Ho describes doing business in an isolated country:

> "Our country has no trade with other countries, and . . . everything we use is produced and consumed in the same province. . . . With ten thousand yang, you can buy just about all of one particular item produced in the country. You can buy the whole lot, whether you load it on a cart or on a boat."
>
> —Pak Chi-won, "The Story of Ho"

Japan and Foreign Traders

Unlike the Chinese or Koreans, the Japanese at first welcomed western traders. In 1543, the Portuguese reached Japan. Later came the Spanish, Dutch, and English. They arrived at the turbulent time when strong daimyo were struggling for power. The Japanese quickly acquired western firearms and built castles modeled on European designs. In fact, the new weapons may have helped the Tokugawa shoguns centralize power and impose order.

Japan was much more open to European missionaries than China. Jesuits, like the Spanish priest Francis Xavier, found the Japanese curious and eager to learn about Christianity. A growing number of Japanese adopted the new faith.

The Tokugawa shoguns, however, grew increasingly hostile toward foreigners. After learning how Spain had seized the Philippines, they may have seen the newcomers as agents of an invading force. In addition, Japanese officials disliked the intrigues and competition among Christian missionaries. They also suspected that Japanese Christians—who may have numbered as many as 300,000—owed their allegiance to the pope, rather than to Japanese leaders. In response, the Tokugawas expelled foreign missionaries. They brutally persecuted Japanese Christians, killing many thousands of people.

By 1638, the Tokugawas had barred all western merchants and forbidden Japanese to travel abroad. To further their isolation, they outlawed the building of large ships, thereby ending foreign trade. In order to keep informed about world events, they permitted just one or two Dutch ships each year to trade at a small island in Nagasaki harbor. Through this tiny gateway, a few Japanese did learn about some foreign ideas. They studied Dutch medical texts, for example, which they found to be more accurate than Chinese ones.

Looking Ahead

Japan maintained its policy of strict isolation for more than 200 years. Isolation had a profound effect on Japan. Without outside influence, Japanese culture turned inward. Still, art and literature spread beyond the upper classes. Artists found new ways to interpret traditions.

During this time, internal trade boomed. Cities grew in size and importance, and some merchant families gained wealth and status. By the early 1700s, Edo (present-day Tokyo) had a million inhabitants, more than either London or Paris.

In 1853, Japan was forced to reopen contacts with the western world. Renewed relations unleashed an extraordinary period of change that helped Japan emerge as a major world power.

Global Connections

The Jesuits in Asia

Although Jesuit missionaries in Asia failed to win many converts to Christianity, they succeeded in spreading western ideas and technology. In China, Jesuit priest Matteo Ricci introduced an accurate world map and helped manufacture European-style cannons. Later Jesuits served as heads of the bureau that planned China's official calendar. The Jesuits also translated more than 100 books on science, math, and technology into Chinese. In Japan, Jesuits introduced the printing press.

Cultural influences also flowed in the other direction. The Jesuits introduced Europeans to the works of Confucius.

Theme: Religions and Value Systems What western ideas did the Jesuits introduce in Asia?

SECTION 4 **Assessment**

Recall
1. **Identify:** (a) Matteo Ricci, (b) Manchus, (c) Kangxi, (d) Qianlong, (e) Hermit Kingdom, (f) Francis Xavier.

Comprehension
2. (a) How was economic prosperity reflected in Qing China? (b) How did the Qing restrict trade with other nations?
3. Why did Korea pursue a policy of isolation?
4. Why did the Japanese policy toward trade and foreigners change over time?

Critical Thinking and Writing
5. **Linking Past and Present** Why do some people in the United States today support limited overseas ties?
6. **Making Generalizations** (a) Based on your reading, what generalization might you make about the attitude of European traders to the countries of East Asia? (b) What generalization might you make about how East Asians felt toward Europeans? (c) What evidence might you give to support each generalization?

Activity

Writing a Dialogue Write a dialogue between two officials in China, Korea, or Japan. One official should express a willingness to establish relations with European powers. The other should argue in favor of a policy of isolation.

Creating a Chapter Summary

On a sheet of paper make a cause-and-effect diagram like the one shown here. Fill in the causes and effects of European exploration to help you review this chapter. Add more boxes as needed.

Demand for Asian goods

EUROPEAN EXPLORATION AND FOOTHOLDS IN ASIA

| Portuguese gain Goa, Macao | Dutch East India Company formed | | | |

Interactive Textbook

For additional review and enrichment activities, see the interactive version of *World History* available on the Web and on CD-ROM.

Go Online
PHSchool.com
For practice test questions for Chapter 2, use **Web Code mka-1582.**

Building Vocabulary

Review the meaning of the chapter vocabulary words listed below. Then, write a sentence for each word in which you define the word and describe its relation to the first global age.

1. cartographer
2. astrolabe
3. caravel
4. scurvy
5. circumnavigate
6. matrilineal
7. stupa
8. padi
9. outpost
10. sepoy

Recalling Key Facts

11. What different motives led Europeans to explore the oceans?
12. What was the Line of Demarcation?
13. Why was Magellan's voyage of 1519–1522 important?
14. How did Christianity spread to the Philippines?
15. Which two European nations competed for influence in India?
16. What important policy did Japanese leaders follow between 1638 and 1853?

Critical Thinking and Writing

17. **Linking Past and Present** (a) Why were spices such valued trading goods in the 1400s? (b) What goods and resources play a similar role in the world economy today?
18. **Analyzing Information** How did European encounters with India, China, and Japan link economic, religious, and political activity?
19. **Identifying Alternatives** How might Tokugawa policy have been changed to encourage greater contact with other civilizations?
20. **Recognizing Points of View** Many people admire explorers such as Columbus and da Gama as bold adventurers. Others condemn them as vicious conquerors. (a) Who do you think might hold each of these viewpoints? (b) What evidence can be given to support each opinion?
21. **Connecting to Geography** How did weather conditions in the "southern seas" contribute to travel in the region and cultural exchange in Southeast Asian ports?

The following diary entry is from the log that Christopher Columbus kept on his first voyage. To dispel the crew's fears of how long the voyage was, Columbus always reckoned "fewer leagues than we actually made" and kept confidential records of the actual distance traveled. Martín Alonso Pinzón was the captain of the *Pinta*. Read the entry, then answer the questions that follow.

"Saturday, 6 October 1492
I maintained my course to the west and made 120 miles between day and night, but told the people 99. This evening Martín Alonso Pinzón told me that he thought it would be wise to steer to the SW by west in order to reach the island of Japan, which is marked on the chart that I had shown him. In my opinion it is better to continue directly west until we reach the mainland. Later we can go to the islands on the return voyage to Spain. My decision has not pleased the men, for they continue to murmur and complain. Despite their grumblings I held fast to the west."

—*The Log of Christopher Columbus* (Fuson, tr.)

22. Where did Martín Alonso Pinzón think they were?
23. What mainland did Columbus think they were near?
24. **(a)** What problem did Columbus face with the crew? **(b)** How did Columbus respond?
25. How might a captain like Martín Alonso Pinzón be a problem for Columbus?

Empires and Kingdoms of Southeast Asia

- Pagan kingdom, A.D. 1044–A.D. 1287
- Khmer empire, A.D. 800–A.D. 1350
- Srivijaya empire, A.D. 600s–A.D. 1200s
- Vietnam kingdom, A.D. 939–A.D. 1883
- → Mongol invasion, A.D. 1287

Azimuthal Equal Area Projection

Use the map to answer the following questions:

26. In which empire was Angkor Wat located?
27. What is the location of the Philippine Islands in relation to China?
28. Why did the location of the city of Malacca make the city important to Southeast Asian trade?
29. **(a)** Is China north or south of the Equator? **(b)** Is Java north or south of the Equator? **(c)** Identify the islands through which the Equator runs.
30. Does the region shown in this map lie in the Eastern Hemisphere or the Western Hemisphere?

Go Online
PHSchool.com

Use the Internet to research one of the European voyages that began the first global age. If possible, find a primary source from the voyage, such as the letters of Christopher Columbus. Then, write a series of news reports that the voyager might have written if he had been able to send news flashes about his travels back to his home country. For help with this activity, use **Web Code mkd-1583**.

Skills Tip

Lines of latitude run horizontally and identify whether an area is north or south of the Equator. Lines of longitude show if an area is in the Eastern or Western Hemisphere.

The First Global Age: Europe, the Americas, and Africa 1492–1750

Chapter Preview

1 Conquest in the Americas
2 Spanish and Portuguese Colonies in the Americas
3 Struggle for North America
4 Turbulent Centuries in Africa
5 Changes in Europe

1492

Columbus lands in the Americas. A global exchange of goods and ideas begins.

1521

Cortés completes conquest of the Aztecs, acquiring for Spain vast stores of gold, including ornaments such as this one.

1607

Jamestown is founded by British colonists.

CHAPTER
EVENTS

1500

1550

1600

GLOBAL
EVENTS

1498 Portuguese explorer da Gama rounds Africa and reaches India.

Land Claims in the Americas and Africa, 1675

Legend:
- Dutch territory
- English territory
- French territory
- Portuguese territory
- Spanish territory
- Independent African states

By 1675, Spain, France, Britain, and Portugal possessed sizable overseas empires. Oceangoing trade ships carried tons of goods between Europe and the Americas and Africa.

Map labels: NETHERLANDS, ENGLAND, FRANCE, SPAIN, PORTUGAL, New France, Newfoundland, Nova Scotia, English Colonies, Florida, Mexico, Gulf of Mexico, Caribbean Sea, ATLANTIC OCEAN, Mississippi R., Danube R., Mediterranean Sea, MOROCCO, Nile R., Futa Toro, SENEGAMBIA, ASANTE, Niger R., HAUSA STATES, DAHOMEY, Gold Coast, Congo R., KONGO, Angola, Zambezi R., Amazon R., Brazil, Peru, Paraná R., PACIFIC OCEAN, Chile

Robinson Projection
0 1000 2000 Miles
0 1000 2000 Kilometers

140°W 120°W 100°W 80°W 60°W 40°W 20°W 0° 20°E 40°E
40°N 20°N 0° 20°S 40°S

1600s
Enslaved Africans continue to be shipped to the Americas. Europeans use forts on the west coast of Africa as trading posts. The one shown here, in Ghana, is held at various times by the Portuguese, Dutch, and British.

1700s
Islamic revival spreads across West Africa.

1759
British defeat French at Quebec.

1650   **1700**   **1750**

1630s Japan bars western merchants.

1736 Reign of Emperor Qianlong of China begins.

Conquest in the Americas

Reading Focus

- What were the results of the first encounters between the Spanish and Native Americans?

- How did Spanish conquistadors conquer the Aztec and Incan empires?

- Why were the Spanish victorious?

Main Idea Various factors enabled the Spanish to conquer the Aztec and Incan empires.

Vocabulary

conquistador

immunity

alliance

civil war

Taking Notes

Copy this diagram. As you read, add other factors that help to explain why the Spanish were able to conquer Native American empires. Add as many boxes as you need.

Disease weakens Native Americans

EUROPEANS CONQUER NATIVE AMERICANS

Setting the Scene Spanish soldiers who reached the Aztec capital of Tenochtitlán in 1519 were amazed by its size and splendor. From the emperor's palace, reported one soldier, "We had a clear view of the . . . [majestic temples] of the nearby cities, built in the form of towers and fortresses, . . . and others . . . all whitewashed, and wonderfully brilliant."

Within a few years, the Spanish had captured and destroyed the Aztec capital. In its place, they built a new capital, Mexico City, that became the heart of the Spanish empire in the Americas.

First Encounters

In 1492, Christopher Columbus landed in the islands that are now called the West Indies, in the Caribbean. There, he encountered the Taíno people. The Taínos lived in villages and grew corn, yams, and cotton, which they wove into cloth. They were friendly and generous toward the Spanish.

Friendly relations soon evaporated, however. Spanish conquistadors (kahn KEES tuh dohrz), or conquerors, followed in the wake of Columbus. They settled on the islands of Hispaniola (now the Dominican Republic and Haiti), Cuba, and Puerto Rico. They seized the gold ornaments worn by the Taínos, then made them pan for more gold. At the same time, the newcomers forced the Taínos to convert to Christianity.

Meanwhile, a deadly but invisible invader was at work—disease. Europeans unknowingly carried diseases such as smallpox, measles, and influenza to which Native Americans had no immunity, or resistance. These diseases spread rapidly and wiped out village after village. As a result, the Native American population of the Caribbean islands declined by as much as 90 percent in the 1500s. This cycle of disease and death was repeated in many other places across the Western Hemisphere.

The Conquistadors

From Cuba, Spanish explorers probed the coasts of the Americas. They spread stories of empires rich in gold. Attracted by the promise of riches as well as by religious zeal, a flood of adventurers soon followed.

Cortés in Mexico Among the earliest conquistadors was Hernan Cortés. Cortés landed on the coast of Mexico in 1519 with about 600 men, 16 horses, and a few cannons. As he headed inland toward Tenochtitlán, he was helped

Go Online
PHSchool.com
For: More about the Aztecs and the Spanish conquest
Visit: PHSchool.com
Web Code: mkd-1687

Conquistadors in Mexico
Pedro de Alvarado was one of the Spanish conquistadors who conquered Mexico. This illustration shows Alvarado and his men facing off against a troop of Aztec soldiers.

Theme: Economics and Technology Based on this picture, identify two technological advantages the Spanish had over the Aztecs.

by Malinche (mah LIHN chay), a young Indian woman who served as his translator and adviser. The Spanish called her Doña Marina. Malinche knew both the Mayan and Aztec languages, and she learned Spanish quickly.

From Malinche, Cortés learned that many conquered peoples hated their Aztec overlords. The Aztecs, you will recall, sacrificed thousands of captives to their gods each year. Malinche helped Cortés arrange alliances with these discontented groups. They would help one another fight the Aztecs.

Moctezuma's Dilemma Meanwhile, messengers brought word about the newcomers to the Aztec emperor Moctezuma. He wondered if the leader of the pale-skinned, bearded strangers might be Quetzalcoatl, the god-king who had long ago vowed to return from the east. Moctezuma sent gifts of gold and silver, but urged the strangers not to continue to Tenochtitlán.

Cortés had no intention of turning back. Fighting and negotiating by turns, he led his forces inland toward the capital. At last, they arrived in Tenochtitlán, where they were dazzled by the grandeur of the city.

Fall of Tenochtitlán Moctezuma welcomed Cortés to his capital. However, relations between the Aztecs and Spaniards soon grew strained, and the Aztecs drove the Spanish from the city. Moctezuma was killed in the fighting.

Cortés retreated to plan an assault. In 1521, in a brutal struggle, Cortés and his Indian allies captured and demolished Tenochtitlán. An unknown Aztec lamented, "Broken spears lie in the road; / We have torn our hair with grief. / The houses are roofless now, and their walls are red with blood." On the ruins of Tenochtitlán, the Spanish later built Mexico City.

Pizarro in Peru Cortés's success inspired other adventurers. Among them was Francisco Pizarro. He arrived in Peru in 1532, just after the Incan ruler Atahualpa (ah tah WAHL pah) won the throne from his brother in a bloody civil war. A civil war is fought between groups of people in the same nation.

Helped by Indian allies, Pizarro captured Atahualpa after slaughtering thousands of his followers. The Spanish demanded a huge ransom for the ruler. The Incas paid it, but the Spanish killed Atahualpa anyway.

Despite continuing resistance, the invaders overran the Incan heartland. From Peru, Spanish forces surged across Ecuador and Chile. Before long, Spain added much of South America to its growing empire.

▶ **Primary Sources and Literature**

See "Bernal Díaz: The True History of the Conquest of New Spain" in the Reference Section at the back of this book.

FACT FINDER

Native American Population of Central Mexico

Millions of People (estimated) vs. *Year* (1500–1620)

Source: Nicolás Sánchez-Albornoz, *The Population of Latin America*

Skills Assessment

Graph Disease and conquest combined to reduce drastically the Native American population. This graph shows what happened to central Mexico's Native Americans after the arrival of the Spanish in 1519. **How did the Native American population change during the period shown on the graph?**

Reasons for Victory

How could a few hundred European soldiers conquer huge Native American empires with populations in the millions? Several reasons explain the amazing Spanish success.

1. Superior military technology was a key factor. The Spaniards' horses frightened some Indians, who had never seen such animals. Spanish muskets and cannons killed Indian soldiers, while metal helmets and armor protected the Spanish from the Indians' arrows and spears.
2. Division and discontent among the Indians aided the Spanish. The Spanish won allies by playing on old hatreds among rival Indian groups. In fact, Indians provided Cortés and Pizarro with much of their fighting power.
3. Disease brought by the Europeans weakened the Aztecs and Incas. As tens of thousands of Indians died, some of the bewildered and demoralized survivors felt that their gods were less powerful than the god of their conquerors.
4. Many Indians believed that the disasters they suffered marked the world's end. To Aztecs, the destruction of Tenochtitlán signaled the end of the reign of the sun god.

Ongoing Resistance Native Americans continued to resist the invaders, however. For years, Mayas fought Spanish rule. Long after the death of Atahualpa, revolts erupted among the Incas. Throughout the Americas, Indians resisted Europeans by preserving aspects of their own culture, such as language, religious traditions, and clothing.

Looking Ahead

The Spanish seized gold and silver statues and ornaments from the Aztecs and Incas. After depleting these sources, they forced Native Americans to mine silver in Peru and Mexico. In the 1500s and early 1600s, treasure fleets sailed each year to Spain or the Spanish Philippines loaded with gold and silver. As you will read, this flood of wealth created both benefits and problems for the economy of Europe.

SECTION 1 Assessment

Recall

1. **Identify:** (a) Taínos, (b) Hernan Cortés, (c) Malinche, (d) Moctezuma, (e) Francisco Pizarro, (f) Atahualpa.
2. **Define:** (a) conquistador, (b) immunity, (c) alliance, (d) civil war.

Comprehension

3. How were Native Americans of the Caribbean region affected by their early encounters with Europeans?
4. What methods did Pizarro use to conquer the Incan empire?
5. (a) How did divisions within the Aztec and Incan empires help the Spanish? (b) What other reasons explain the rapid success of the Spanish conquistadors over Native Americans?

Critical Thinking and Writing

6. **Comparing** Compare the Spanish conquest of the Americas with the Reconquista or the Crusades. (a) How were they similar? (b) How were they different?
7. **Identifying Main Ideas** Review the three paragraphs under the heading First Encounters. For each paragraph, write a single sentence identifying the main idea of the paragraph.

Go Online
PHSchool.com

Use the Internet to research the life of Malinche, whose name means "traitor." Then, write a paragraph explaining why you believe she does or does not deserve this name. For help with this activity, use **Web Code mkd-1688.**

Spanish and Portuguese Colonies in the Americas

Reading Focus

- How did Spain rule its empire in the Americas?
- What were the chief features of colonial society and culture?
- How did Portugal and other European nations challenge Spanish power?

Vocabulary

viceroy
plantation
encomienda
peon
peninsular
creole
mestizo
mulatto
privateer

Taking Notes

Copy this partially completed concept web. As you read, write key facts and ideas about the Spanish empire in the Americas in the appropriate circles. Add as many circles as you need.

[Concept web diagram with central circle "SPANISH EMPIRE" connected to: Economy, Government, Society, Culture]

Main Idea Native American, African, and European traditions blended to form new cultures in the Americas.

Setting the Scene

Spain was immensely proud of its rich silver mines in the Potosí region of Peru. By the 1540s, tons of Potosí silver filled Spanish treasure ships. Year after year, thousands of Native Americans were forced to extract the rich ore from dangerous shafts deep inside the Andes Mountains. Many Indians died in the terrible conditions, only to be replaced by thousands more.

Scenes such as this were repeated in Mexico, the Caribbean, and other parts of Spain's empire. A flood of Spanish settlers and missionaries followed the conquistadors. Wherever they went, they claimed the land and its people for their king and Church. When there was resistance, the newcomers imposed their will by force. As devout Christians, they thought it was their duty to bring their religion and civilization to the Indians.

From the first, though, Christian Europeans had much to learn from the peoples that they conquered. In the end, a new culture emerged that reflected European, Native American, and African traditions.

Ruling the Spanish Empire

In the 1500s, Spain claimed a vast empire stretching from California to South America. In time, it divided these lands into five provinces. The most important were New Spain (Mexico) and Peru.

Spain was determined to maintain strict control over its empire. To achieve this goal, the king set up the Council of the Indies to pass laws for the colonies. He also appointed viceroys, or representatives who ruled in his name, in each province. Lesser officials and *audiencias,* or advisory councils of Spanish settlers, helped the viceroy rule. The Council of the Indies in Spain closely monitored these colonial officials to make sure they did not assume too much authority.

The Catholic Church To Spain, winning souls for Christianity was as important as gaining land. The Catholic Church played a key role in the colonies, working with the government to convert Native Americans to Christianity. Church leaders often served as royal officials and helped to regulate the activities of Spanish settlers. As Spain's American empire expanded, Church authority expanded along with it.

Franciscan, Jesuit, and other missionaries baptized thousands of Native Americans. In frontier regions, they built mission churches and worked to turn new converts into loyal subjects of the Catholic king of Spain. They forcibly imposed European culture over Native American culture.

They also introduced European clothing, the Spanish language, and new crafts such as carpentry and locksmithing.

The Economy   To make the empire profitable, Spain closely controlled its economic activities, especially trade. Colonists could export raw materials only to Spain and could buy only Spanish manufactured goods. Laws forbade colonists from trading with other European nations or even with other Spanish colonies. The most valuable resources shipped from Spanish America to Spain were silver and gold.

Sugar cane was introduced into the West Indies and elsewhere and quickly became a profitable resource. The cane was refined into sugar, molasses, and rum. Sugar cane, however, had to be grown on plantations, large estates run by an owner or the owner's overseer. Finding the large numbers of workers needed to make the plantations profitable was a major problem.

At first, Spanish monarchs granted the conquistadors encomiendas, the right to demand labor or tribute from Native Americans in a particular area. The conquistadors used this system to force Native Americans to work under the most brutal conditions. Those who resisted were hunted down and killed. Disease, starvation, and cruel treatment caused catastrophic declines in the population.

Bartolomé de las Casas   A few bold priests, like Bartolomé de las Casas, condemned the evils of the encomienda system. In vivid reports to Spain, Las Casas detailed the horrors that Spanish rule had brought to Native Americans and pleaded with the king to end the abuse.

Prodded by Las Casas, Spain passed the New Laws of the Indies in 1542, forbidding enslavement of Native Americans. The laws were meant to end abuses against Native Americans, but Spain was too far away to enforce them. Many Native Americans were forced to become peons, workers forced to labor for a landlord in order to pay off a debt. Landlords advanced them food, tools, or seeds, creating debts that workers could never pay off in their lifetime.

Bringing Workers From Africa   To fill the labor shortage, Las Casas urged colonists to import workers from Africa. Africans were immune to tropical diseases, he said, and had skills in farming, mining, and metalworking. Las Casas later regretted that advice because it furthered the brutal African slave trade. The Spanish began bringing Africans as slave laborers to the Americas by the 1530s.

As demand for sugar products skyrocketed, the settlers imported millions of Africans as slaves. They were forced to work as field hands, miners, or servants in the houses of wealthy landowners. Others became peddlers, skilled artisans, artists, and mechanics.

In time, Africans and their American-born descendants greatly outnumbered European settlers in the West Indies and parts of South America. Often, they resisted slavery by rebelling or running away. In the cities, some enslaved Africans earned enough money to buy their freedom.

Colonial Society and Culture

In Spanish America, the mix of diverse peoples gave rise to a new social structure. The blending of Native American, African, and European peoples and traditions resulted in a new American culture.

Social Structure   At the top of colonial society were peninsulares, people born in Spain. (The term *peninsular* referred to the Iberian Peninsula, on which Spain is located.) Peninsulares filled the highest positions in both colonial governments and the Catholic Church. Next came creoles,

Primary Source

A Brutal System
Bartolomé de las Casas, a conquistador turned priest, spoke out against the encomienda system and the treatment of Native Americans:

"It is impossible to recount the burdens with which their owners loaded them, more than [75 to 100 pounds], making them walk [hundreds of miles]. . . . They had wounds on their shoulders and backs, like animals. . . . To tell likewise of the whip-lashings, the beatings, the cuffs, the blows, the curses, and a thousand other kinds of torments to which their masters treated them, while in truth they were working hard, would take much time and much paper; and would be something to amaze mankind."

—Bartolomé de las Casas,
Short Description of the Destruction of the Indies

Skills Assessment

Primary Source How were the conditions Las Casas describes linked to the encomienda system?

American-born descendants of Spanish settlers. Creoles owned most of the plantations, ranches, and mines.

Other social groups reflected the mixing of populations. They included mestizos, people of Native American and European descent, and mulattoes, people of African and European descent. Native Americans and people of African descent formed the lowest social classes.

Cities Spanish settlers preferred to live in towns and cities. The population of Mexico City grew so quickly that by 1550 it was the largest Spanish-speaking city in the world.

Colonial cities were centers of government, commerce, and European culture. Around the central plaza, or square, stood government buildings and a Spanish-style church. Broad avenues and public monuments symbolized European power and wealth. Cities were also centers of intellectual and cultural life. Architecture and painting, as well as poetry and the exchange of ideas, flourished.

Education To meet the Church's need for educated priests, the colonies built universities. The University of Mexico was established as early as 1551. A dozen Spanish American universities were busy educating young men long before Harvard, the first university in the 13 English colonies, was founded in 1636.

Women wishing an education might enter a convent. One such woman was Sor Juana Inés de la Cruz. Refused admission to the University of Mexico because she was a girl, Juana entered a convent at the age of 16. There, she devoted herself to study and the writing of poetry. She earned a reputation as one of the greatest poets ever to write in the Spanish language.

Cultural Blending Although Spanish culture was dominant in the cities, the blending of diverse traditions changed people's lives throughout the Americas. Settlers learned Native American styles of building, ate foods native to the Americas, and traveled in Indian-style canoes. Indian artistic styles influenced the newcomers. At the same time, settlers taught their religion to Native Americans. They also introduced animals, especially the horse, that transformed the lives of many Native Americans.

Africans added to this cultural mix with their farming methods, cooking styles, and crops, including okra and palm oil. African drama, dance, and song heightened Christian services. In Cuba, Haiti, and elsewhere, Africans forged new religions that blended African and Christian beliefs.

The Portuguese Colony in Brazil

A large area of South America remained outside the Spanish empire. By the Treaty of Tordesillas in 1494, Portugal claimed Brazil. (See the map in Section 3.) Portugal issued grants of land to Portuguese nobles, who agreed to develop the land and share profits with the crown. Landowners sent settlers to build towns, plantations, and churches.

The Economy Unlike Spain's American lands, Brazil offered no instant wealth from silver or gold. Early settlers clung to the coast, where they cut and exported brazilwood, used to produce a precious dye. Before long,

A New Society and Culture
The social structure and culture of Spain's American empire reflected its unique blend of people. This portrait depicts a Spanish man, his Mexican wife, and their mestizo daughter.

Theme: Diversity What were the social classes in Spain's American empire?

Southwestern Architecture: A Blending of Cultures

When the Spanish explorers entered what is today the American Southwest, they found Native American buildings that had existed for centuries. The Spanish settlers and the Native Americans influenced each other's building styles and created a unique architecture that survives to this day.

The Pueblo Indians used a mixture of mud and sand, called adobe, to construct the Taos Pueblo in New Mexico (below). Built around 1350, this collection of apartment-style houses has flat roofs formed by long poles, closely grouped rooms, and small windows. For protection, the main entrances were in the rooftops. The front doorways are a modern addition.

Known as "The White Dove of the Desert," San Xavier del Bac (right) was completed in the late 1700s. Spanish priests directed the work of Tohono O'odham Indian laborers to create this outpost of Spanish culture in the desert near Tucson, Arizona.

Built in the 1920s in Santa Fe, New Mexico, the Institute of American Indian Arts Museum, (right) blends Native American and Spanish architecture. The twin towers resemble the bell towers of a Spanish church. The main contours of the building follow the shape of an Indian pueblo.

Portfolio Assessment

Conduct research to find out more about the architecture of the American Southwest. Then, prepare a class presentation that identifies Native American and Spanish features of a particular building. If possible, include photographs, drawings, or a model of the building you have selected.

Fast Facts

- Pueblo Indians used "puddled," or poured, adobe before the Spanish arrived. Spanish settlers introduced the use of adobe bricks.

- Both the Pueblos and the Spanish built their communities around a central plaza, or square.

- Taos Pueblo is still inhabited today.

they turned to plantation agriculture and cattle raising. They forced Indians and Africans to clear land for sugar plantations. As many as five million Africans were sent to Brazil.

The thickly forested Amazon basin remained largely unexplored by settlers. However, ruthless adventurers slowly pushed inland. They attacked and enslaved Native American peoples and claimed for themselves land for immense cattle ranches. Some even discovered gold.

A New Culture As in Spanish America, a new culture emerged in Brazil that blended European, Native American, and African patterns. European culture dominated the upper and middle classes, but Native American and African influences left their mark. Portuguese settlers, for example, eagerly adopted Indian hammocks. A settler expressed his enthusiasm:

> "Would you believe that a man could sleep suspended in a net in the air like a bunch of hanging grapes? Here this is the common thing. . . . I tried it, and will never again be able to sleep in a bed, so comfortable is the rest one gets in the net."
>
> —quoted in *Latin America: A Concise Interpretive History* (Burns)

Challenging Spanish Power

In the 1500s, the wealth of the Americas helped make Spain the most powerful country in Europe. Its lofty position fueled envy among its European rivals. Many English and Dutch shared the resentment that French king Francis I felt when he declared, "I should like to see Adam's will, wherein he divided the Earth between Spain and Portugal."

European nations challenged Spain's power in various ways. To get around Spain's strict control over colonial trade, smugglers traded illegally with Spanish colonists. In the Caribbean and elsewhere, Dutch, English, and French pirates preyed on Spanish treasure ships. Some pirates, called privateers, even operated with the approval of European governments. England's Queen Elizabeth, for example, knighted Francis Drake for his daring raids on Spanish ships and towns.

Like the Spanish, the Dutch, English, and French hunted for gold empires and for a northwest passage to Asia. As you will read, these nations explored the coasts and planted settlements in North America.

Geography and History

Piracy on the Seas

Of all the privateers who plundered Spanish colonies, none was bolder than the Englishman whom the Spanish called *El Draque* (the Dragon). But Sir Francis Drake was more than just a pirate. He was also a skilled and daring explorer.

Drake led the second expedition ever to sail around the world. After a violent storm, he rounded the tip of South America in 1578 with only his flagship, the *Golden Hind*. But that one ship was enough. Spain's settlements along the Pacific coast were unguarded. After all, no hostile ship had ever made it into these waters before! Drake plundered one Spanish town and captured two treasure ships before continuing on his mission. Thanks to these raids and others, *El Draque* enriched his queen—and won the lasting hatred of the Spanish.

 Theme: Geography and History Why was Drake able to surprise the Spanish?

SECTION **2** Assessment

Recall

1. **Identify: (a)** Council of the Indies, **(b)** Bartolomé de las Casas, **(c)** New Laws of the Indies, **(d)** Sor Juana Inés de la Cruz.
2. **Define: (a)** viceroy, **(b)** plantation, **(c)** encomienda, **(d)** peon, **(e)** peninsular, **(f)** creole, **(g)** mestizo, **(h)** mulatto, **(i)** privateer.

Comprehension

3. Describe how Spain controlled its American empire.
4. **(a)** How did the mix of peoples in Spanish America result in a new social structure? **(b)** Give three examples of cultural blending in Spain's American empire.
5. How did other European nations challenge Spanish power in the Americas?

Critical Thinking and Writing

6. **Comparing (a)** In what ways were the Spanish and Portuguese empires in the Americas similar? **(b)** In what ways were they different?
7. **Solving Problems** How might the Spanish have solved the problem of finding a dependable labor supply without resorting to the use of slavery?

Activity

Making a Poster
Review what you have read about Spanish treatment of Native Americans. Then, design a poster Bartolomé de las Casas could have used to rouse public opinion in Spain to protect the Indians.

Struggle for North America

Reading Focus

■ What problems did settlers in New France face?

■ What traditions of government evolved in the 13 English colonies?

■ How did competition for power affect Europeans and Native Americans?

Vocabulary

missionary

revenue

compact

Taking Notes

Copy this partially completed table. As you read, fill in key information on the French and English colonies in North America.

	FRENCH COLONIES	ENGLISH COLONIES
LOCATION		East coast of North America
ECONOMY	Based mostly on fishing and fur trading	
GOVERNMENT		
GROWTH		

Main Idea France and England set up colonies and competed for dominance in North America.

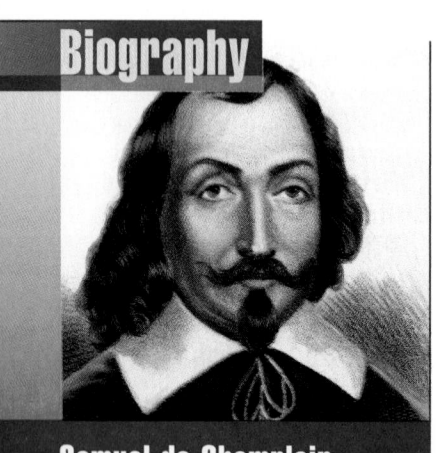

Biography

Samuel de Champlain
1567(?)–1635

Samuel de Champlain was an explorer, geographer, and mapmaker. As founder and first governor of the French colony of Quebec, he is known as the Father of New France, the French colonial empire in North America.

Champlain explored many of the waterways of New France. He especially loved the St. Lawrence River, which he said was "beautiful as the Seine, rapid as the Rhône, and deep as the sea." He helped to make it the main highway for trade through New France and to make himself the force behind the colony's settlement.

Theme: Impact of the Individual Why is Champlain considered the Father of New France?

Setting the Scene

In the 1600s, other European powers moved into the Americas and began building settlements. France, the Netherlands, England, and Sweden joined Spain in claiming parts of North America.

At first, the Europeans were disappointed. North America did not yield vast treasure or offer a water passage to Asia, as they had hoped. Before long, though, the English and French were turning large profits by growing tobacco in Virginia, fishing off the North Atlantic coast, and trading fur from New England to Canada.

By 1700, France and England controlled large parts of North America. As their colonies grew, they developed their own governments, different from each other and from that of Spanish America.

Building New France

By the early 1500s, French fishing ships were crossing the Atlantic each year to harvest rich catches of cod off Newfoundland, Canada. Distracted by wars at home, however, French rulers at first paid little attention to Canada—New France, as they called it. Not until 1608 did Samuel de Champlain build the first permanent French settlement in Quebec. Jesuits and other missionaries, hoping to spread Christianity to Native Americans, soon followed. They advanced into the wilderness, trying to convert Native Americans they met.

Slow Growth Helped by Native American allies, French explorers and fur traders traveled inland, claiming vast territory. Soon, France's American empire reached from Quebec to the Great Lakes and down the Mississippi to Louisiana and the Gulf of Mexico.

The population of New France grew slowly. Wealthy landlords owned huge tracts, or areas of land, along the St. Lawrence River. They sought settlers to farm the land, but the harsh Canadian climate attracted few French peasants.

Many who went to New France soon abandoned farming in favor of fur trapping and trading. They faced a hard life in the wilderness, but the soaring European demand for fur ensured good prices. Fishing, too, supported settlers who lived in coastal villages and exported cod and other fish to Europe.

Government Policy In the late 1600s, the French king Louis XIV set out to strengthen royal power and boost revenues, or income from taxes, from his overseas empire. He appointed officials to oversee justice and economic activities in New France. He also sent more settlers and soldiers to North America. The Catholic Louis, however, prohibited Protestants from settling in New France.

By the early 1700s, French forts, missions, and trading posts stretched from Quebec to Louisiana. Yet the population of New France remained small compared to that of the 13 English colonies expanding along the Atlantic coast.

The 13 English Colonies

The English built their first permanent colony at Jamestown, Virginia, in 1607. Its early years were filled with disaster. Many settlers died of starvation and disease. The rest survived with the help of friendly Native Americans. The colony finally made headway when the settlers started to grow and export tobacco, a crop they learned about from the Indians.

In 1620, other English settlers, the Pilgrims,* landed at Plymouth, Massachusetts. They were seeking religious freedom, rather than commercial profit. Before coming ashore, they signed the Mayflower Compact, in which they set out guidelines for governing their North American colony. A compact is an agreement among people. Today, we see this document as an important early step toward self-government. It read:

> "We, whose names are underwritten . . . having undertaken for the Glory of God, and Advancement of the Christian Faith . . . a voyage to plant [a] colony in the [Americas] . . . do enact, constitute, and frame, such just and equal Laws . . . as shall be thought most [fitting] and convenient for the general Good of the Colony."
> —Mayflower Compact

Many Pilgrims died in the early years of the Plymouth colony. Local Indians, however, taught them to grow corn and helped them survive in the new land. Soon, a new wave of Puritan immigrants arrived to establish the Massachusetts Bay Colony.

Growth In the 1600s and 1700s, the English established 13 colonies. Some, like Virginia and New York, were commercial ventures, organized for profit. Others, like Massachusetts, Pennsylvania, and Maryland, were set up as havens for persecuted religious groups.

Geographic conditions helped shape different ways of life in the New England, middle, and southern colonies. In New England, many settlers were farmers who transferred to North America the village life they had enjoyed in England. In parts of the South, there emerged a plantation economy based on tobacco, rice, and other crops.

Like New Spain, the English colonies needed workers to clear land and raise crops. A growing number of Africans were brought to the colonies and sold as slaves. In several mainland colonies, enslaved Africans and their descendants outnumbered people of European descent.

Government Like the rulers of Spain and France, English monarchs asserted control over their American colonies. They appointed royal governors to oversee colonial affairs and had Parliament pass laws to regulate colonial trade. Yet, compared with settlers in the Spanish and French colonies, English colonists enjoyed a large degree of self-government. Each

Primary Source

Pilgrim Courage
Governor William Bradford of Plymouth Colony wrote a first-hand account of its early days, describing what happened after half the Pilgrims had died:

"[Of the 50 left . . . only six or seven were sound. These six or seven] . . . spared no pains night nor day, but with abundance of toil and hazard of their own health, fetched them wood, made them fires, dressed them meat, made their beds, washed their [filthy] clothes, clothed and unclothed them. . . . All this [was done] willingly and cheerfully, without any grudging in the least, showing herein their true love unto their friends and brethren."
—William Bradford, *Of Plymouth Plantation: 1620–1647*

Skills Assessment

Primary Source Why were the "sound" Pilgrims' actions necessary to the survival of Plymouth Colony?

---

*Pilgrims were a band of English Puritans, a Protestant group, who rejected the practices of the official Church of England.

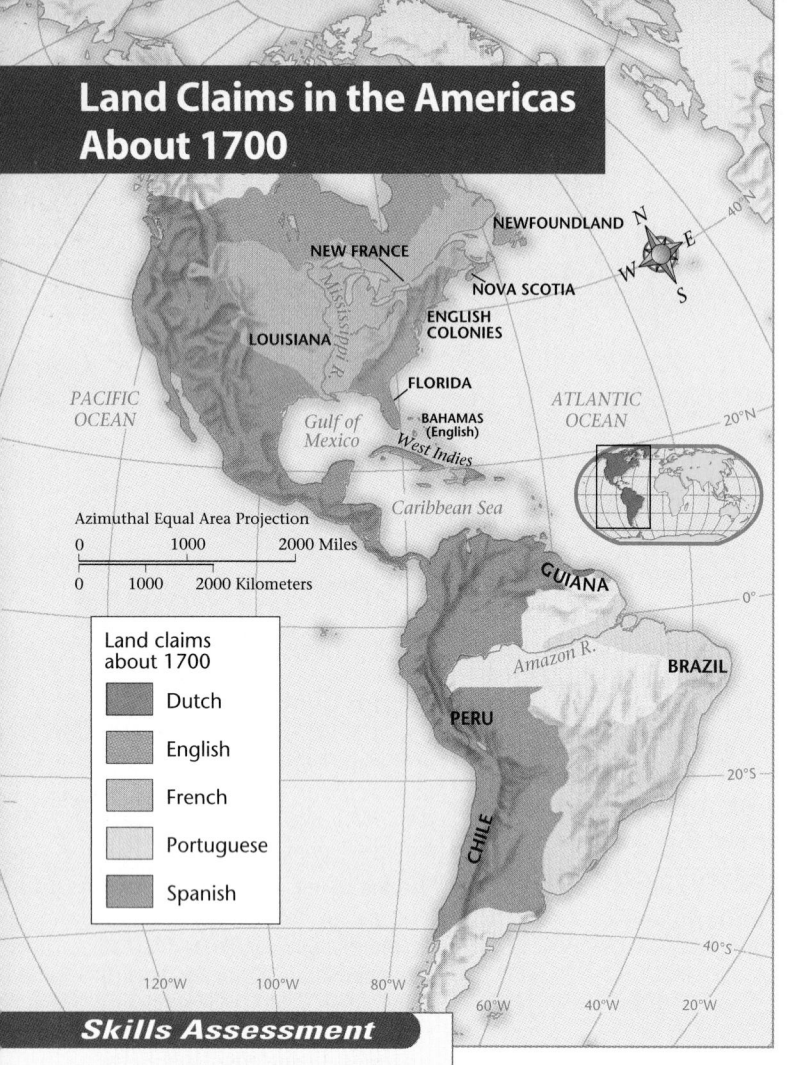

Land Claims in the Americas About 1700

NEWFOUNDLAND

NEW FRANCE

NOVA SCOTIA

ENGLISH COLONIES

LOUISIANA

Mississippi R.

FLORIDA

BAHAMAS (English)

West Indies

PACIFIC OCEAN

Gulf of Mexico

ATLANTIC OCEAN

20°N

Caribbean Sea

Azimuthal Equal Area Projection

0   1000   2000 Miles

0   1000   2000 Kilometers

GUIANA

Amazon R.

BRAZIL

PERU

CHILE

0°

20°S

40°S

120°W   100°W   80°W   60°W   40°W   20°W

N W E S
40°N

Land claims about 1700

- ■ Dutch
- ■ English
- ■ French
- ■ Portuguese
- ■ Spanish

Skills Assessment

Geography In the 1700s, European nations competed for colonies and trade in the Americas.

1. **Location** On the map, locate **(a)** New France, **(b)** Florida, **(c)** West Indies.
2. **Region** In what regions of North America did England have colonies?
3. **Critical Thinking Synthesizing Information** Based on the map and what you have read, why did England and France clash several times during the 1700s?

colony had its own representative assembly elected by propertied men. The assemblies advised the royal governor and made decisions on local issues.

The tradition of consulting representative assemblies grew out of the English experience. Beginning in the 1200s, Parliament had played an increasingly important role in English affairs. Slowly, too, English citizens had gained certain legal and political rights. England's American colonists expected to enjoy the same rights. When colonists later protested British policies in North America, they viewed themselves as "freeborn Englishmen" who were defending their traditional rights.

Competing for Power

By the 1600s, Spain, France, England, and the Netherlands were competing for colonies and trade around the world. All four of these nations had colonies in North America, where they often fought over territory. After several naval wars with the Netherlands, the English seized the Dutch colony of New Netherland in 1664 and renamed it New York. English settlers in Georgia clashed with the Spanish in nearby Florida.

Competition was also fierce in the Caribbean region. Dutch planters developed sugar production in the Caribbean into a big business. The French acquired Haiti, the richest of the sugar colonies, as well as Guadeloupe and Martinique. The English took Barbados and Jamaica. By the 1700s, the French and English Caribbean islands, worked by enslaved Africans, had surpassed the whole of North America in exports to Europe.

British-French Rivalry During the 1700s, Britain and France emerged as bitter rivals for power around the globe. They clashed in Europe, North America, Africa, and Asia. In North America, the French and Indian War raged from 1754 to 1763. A worldwide struggle, known as the Seven Years' War, erupted in Europe in 1756 and spread to India and Africa.

Although France held more territory in North America, the British colonies had more people. Trappers, traders, and farmers from the English colonies were pushing west into the Ohio Valley, a region claimed by France. The French, who had forged alliances with local Indians, fought to oust the intruders.

During the war, British soldiers and colonial troops launched a series of campaigns against the French in Canada and on the Ohio frontier. At first, France won several victories. Then, in 1759, the tide turned in Britain's favor. From ships anchored in the St. Lawrence River, British troops launched an attack on Quebec, the capital of New France. The British scaled steep cliffs along the river and captured the city. Though the war dragged on until 1763, the British had won control of Canada.

The Peace Treaty The 1763 Treaty of Paris officially ended the worldwide war. The treaty ensured British dominance in North America. France ceded Canada and its lands east of the Mississippi River to Britain. As you have read, the British also forced the French out of India. France, however, regained the rich sugar-producing islands in the Caribbean and the slave-trading outposts in Africa that the British had seized during the war.

Impact on Native Americans

As in Spanish America, the arrival of European settlers in North America had a profound impact on Native Americans. Some Native Americans traded or formed alliances with the newcomers. On the Great Plains, as we will see, the arrival of the horse transformed the lifestyle of buffalo-hunting Indians.

War and Disease   Frequently, however, clashes erupted. As settlers claimed more land, Native Americans resisted their advance. Bitter fighting resulted. In the end, superior weapons helped the English to victory. Year by year, the flood of new settlers pushed the frontier—and the Indians—slowly westward.

As elsewhere, the Native American population of North America plummeted. Disease weakened or killed large numbers. For example, in 1608, an estimated 30,000 Algonquins lived in Virginia. By 1670, there were only about 2,000 Algonquins remaining.

Native American Legacy   While encounters with Europeans often brought disaster to Native American societies, the Indian way of life helped shape the emerging new culture of North America. Settlers adopted Native American technologies. From Indians, they learned to grow corn, beans, squash, and tomatoes and to hunt and trap forest animals. Today's Thanksgiving menu of turkey and pumpkin pie reflects Indian foods.

Trails blazed by Indians became highways for settlers moving west. Across the continent, rivers like the Mississippi, lakes like Okeechobee, and mountains like the Appalachians bear Indian names. Some Europeans came to respect Native American medical knowledge. Today, many people are taking a new look at Indian religious traditions that stress respect for the natural environment.

Impact on Native Americans
In their contest for North America, European nations enlisted Indian allies. This leader of the Iroquois sided with the English.

Theme: Global Interaction   How did the flood of European settlers affect the Indians of North America?

SECTION 3 Assessment

Recall
1. **Identify:** (a) Samuel de Champlain, (b) Louis XIV, (c) Jamestown, (d) Pilgrims, (e) Mayflower Compact, (f) French and Indian War, (g) Treaty of Paris.
2. **Define:** (a) missionary, (b) revenue, (c) compact.

Comprehension
3. Why did New France grow slowly?
4. What form of government did the 13 English colonies set up?
5. (a) How did Britain come to dominate North America? (b) What impact did European competition for colonies have on Native Americans?

Critical Thinking and Writing
6. **Connecting to Geography** Study the map in this section and the physical map of North America in the Reference Section of this book. (a) Which waterways were vitally important to French colonies in North America? (b) How might France's rivals take advantage of this geographic dependence?
7. **Comparing** Compare New France and the 13 English colonies in terms of (a) population, (b) government, (c) economy.

Activity

Making a Travel Brochure Suppose you are a minister to Louis XIV of France. To attract people to New France, he has asked you to advertise the benefits of life in the Americas. Make a colorful brochure with maps, illustrations, and persuasive messages.

Turbulent Centuries in Africa

Reading Focus

■ How did the arrival of Europeans in Africa lead to the Atlantic slave trade?

■ How did the slave trade contribute to the rise of new African states?

■ What groups battled for power in southern Africa?

Vocabulary

triangular trade

repeal

monopoly

Taking Notes

Copy this partially completed flowchart. As you read, fill in key events in the development of the Atlantic slave trade. Add as many boxes to the chart as you need.

Enslaved Africans taken to Muslim empires

↓

↓

↓

Millions taken from West Africa to the Americas

Main Idea The Atlantic slave trade, the rise of new states, and power struggles created turbulence in Africa.

Witness the horrors of the Atlantic slave trade.

Setting the Scene "The first object which saluted my eyes when I arrived on the coast was the sea, and a slave ship which was then riding at anchor and waiting for its cargo. These filled me with astonishment, which was soon converted into terror when I was carried on board." So wrote Olaudah Equiano. In the 1750s, when he was 11 years old, Equiano was seized from his Nigerian village by slave traders. He was then transported as human cargo from West Africa to the Americas.

Enslaved Africans like Equiano formed part of an international trade network that arose during the first global age. Encounters between Europeans and Africans had been taking place since the 1400s. By then, as you have read, Africa was home to diverse societies, and Islam had become an important force in some parts of the continent. As Europeans arrived, they would bring their own influences to Africa.

European Outposts in Africa

In the 1400s, Portuguese ships explored the coast of West Africa, looking for a sea route to India. They built small forts along the West African coast to trade for gold, collect food and water, and repair their ships.

The Portuguese lacked the power to push into the African interior. They did, however, attack the coastal cities of East Africa, such as Mombasa and Malindi, which were hubs of international trade. With cannons blazing, they expelled the Arabs who controlled the East African trade network and took over this thriving commerce for themselves.

The Portuguese, however, gained little profit from their victories. Trade between the interior and the coast soon dwindled. By 1600, the once-prosperous East African coastal cities had sunk into poverty.

Other Europeans soon followed the Portuguese into Africa. The Dutch, the English, and the French established forts along the western coast of Africa. Like the Portuguese, they exchanged muskets, tools, and cloth for gold, ivory, hides, and slaves.

The Atlantic Slave Trade

In the 1500s, Europeans began to view slaves as the most important item of African trade. Slavery had existed in Africa, as elsewhere around the world, since ancient times. Egyptians, Greeks, Romans, Persians, Indians, and Aztecs often enslaved defeated foes. Our word *slave* comes from the large number of Slavs taken from southern Russia to work as unpaid laborers in Roman times.

The Arab empire also used slave labor, often captives taken from Africa. In the Middle East, many enslaved Africans worked on farming estates or large-scale irrigation projects. Others became artisans, soldiers, or merchants. Some rose to prominence in the Muslim world even though they were officially slaves.

European and African Slave Traders   The Atlantic slave trade began in the 1500s, to fill the need for labor in Spain's American empire. In the next 300 years, it grew into a huge and profitable business. Each year, traders shipped tens of thousands of enslaved Africans across the Atlantic to work on tobacco and sugar plantations in the Americas.

Europeans seldom went into the interior to take part in slave raids. Instead, they relied on African rulers and traders to seize captives in the interior and bring them to coastal trading posts and fortresses. There, the captives were exchanged for textiles, metalwork, rum, tobacco, weapons, and gunpowder. The slave trade intensified as the demand for slaves increased in the Americas and as the demand for luxury goods increased in Africa.

Triangular Trade   The Atlantic slave trade formed one part of a three-legged trade network known as the triangular trade. On the first leg, merchant ships brought goods to Africa to be traded for slaves. On the second leg, known as the Middle Passage, the slaves were transported to the West Indies. There, the enslaved Africans were exchanged for sugar, molasses, and other products. On the final leg, these products were shipped to Europe or European colonies in the Americas. The prosperity of port cities such as Nantes in France, Bristol in England, and Salem in Massachusetts thus depended in large part on the slave trade.

Horrors of the Middle Passage   For enslaved Africans, the Middle Passage was a horror. Once purchased, Africans were packed below the decks of slave ships. Hundreds of men, women, and children were crammed into a single vessel. Slave ships became "floating coffins" on which up to half the Africans on board died from disease or brutal mistreatment.

The Slave Trade
Merchants from many lands engaged in the slave trade. Arabs, such as those on the ship below, brought human cargoes out of East Africa. Portuguese traders carried slaves to the Americas from West Africa. A Portuguese soldier is depicted in the delicate ivory carving.

Theme: Global Interaction
Why was there a growing demand for slaves in the Americas?

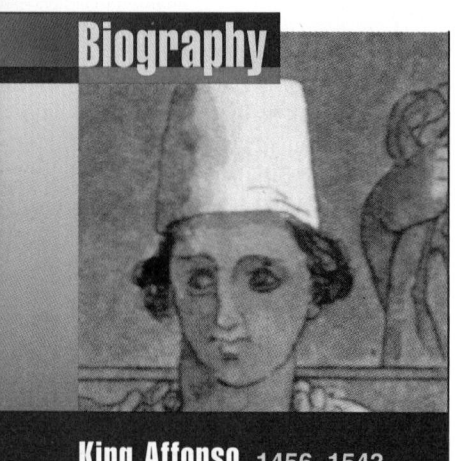

King Affonso 1456–1543

"Most powerful and excellent King of the Kongo, We convey you greetings in that We much love and esteem you." So wrote the king of Portugal to King Affonso in 1512. Affonso (born Nzinga Mbemba) had a long and warm relationship with the Portuguese. However, some years later, in 1526, Affonso wrote in dismay to the king of Portugal: "Merchants are taking every day our natives, sons of the land and sons of our nobles and vassals and our relatives, because the thieves and men of bad conscience . . . grab them and get them to be sold. . . . Our country is being completely depopulated."

In the end, Affonso's ties to Portugal were not strong enough. He sought help to build modern ships, but no Portuguese shipbuilders ever arrived. And his attempts to end the slave trade had no effect.

Theme: Impact of the Individual Why do you think Affonso is admired today, even though his efforts failed?

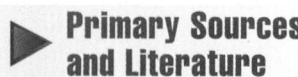

Primary Sources and Literature

See "King Affonso I: Letter to King John of Portugal" in the Reference Section at the back of this book.

Some enslaved Africans resisted. A few tried to seize control of the ship and return to Africa. Others committed suicide by leaping overboard. One African recalled such an incident during the Middle Passage:

> "One day . . . two of my wearied countrymen who were chained together . . . jumped into the sea; immediately another . . . followed their example. . . . two of the wretches were drowned, but [the ship's crew] got the other, and afterwards flogged him unmercifully for thus attempting to prefer death to slavery."
>
> —Olaudah Equiano, *The Life of Gustavus Vassa*

African Leaders Resist Some African leaders tried to slow down the transatlantic slave trade or even to stop it altogether. They used different forms of resistance. But in the end, the system that supported the trade was simply too strong for them.

An early voice raised against the slave trade was that of Affonso I, ruler of Kongo in west-central Africa. As a young man, Affonso was tutored by Portuguese missionaries. After becoming king in 1505, he called on the Portuguese to help him develop Kongo as a modern Christian state.

Before long, however, Affonso grew alarmed. Each year, more and more Portuguese came to Kongo to buy slaves. They offered high prices, and government officials and local chiefs eagerly entered the trade. Even Christian missionaries began to buy and sell Africans.

Affonso insisted that "it is our will that in these Kingdoms there should not be any trade of slaves nor outlet for them." Kongo, he stated, could benefit from contacts with Europe, but the trade in human lives was evil. His appeal failed, and the slave trade continued.

In the late 1700s, another African ruler, the almamy of Futa Toro in northern Senegal, tried to halt the slave trade in his lands. Since the 1500s, French sea captains had bought slaves from African traders in Futa Toro. The almamy decided to put a stop to this practice. In 1788, he forbade anyone to transport slaves through Futa Toro for sale abroad. The sea captains and local chiefs protested, and called on the almamy to repeal, or cancel, the law. The almamy refused. He returned the presents the captains had sent him in hopes of winning him over to their cause. "All the riches in the world would not make me change my mind," he said.

The almamy's victory was short-lived, however. The inland slave traders simply worked out a new route to the coast. Sailing to this new market, the French captains easily purchased the slaves that the almamy had prevented them from buying in Senegal. There was nothing the almamy could do to stop them.

Impact of the Atlantic Slave Trade Historians are still debating the number of Africans who were affected by the Atlantic slave trade. In the 1500s, they estimate, about 2,000 enslaved Africans were sent to the Americas each year. In the 1780s, when the slave trade was at its peak, that number topped 80,000 a year. By the mid-1800s, when the overseas slave trade was finally stopped, an estimated 11 million enslaved Africans had reached the Americas. Another 2 million probably died under the brutal conditions of the voyage between Africa and the Americas.

The slave trade caused the decline of some African states and the rise of others. In West Africa, the loss of countless numbers of young women and men resulted in some small states disappearing forever. At the same time, there arose new African states whose way of life depended on the slave trade. The rulers of these powerful new states waged war against other Africans so they could gain control of the slave trade in their region and reap the profits.

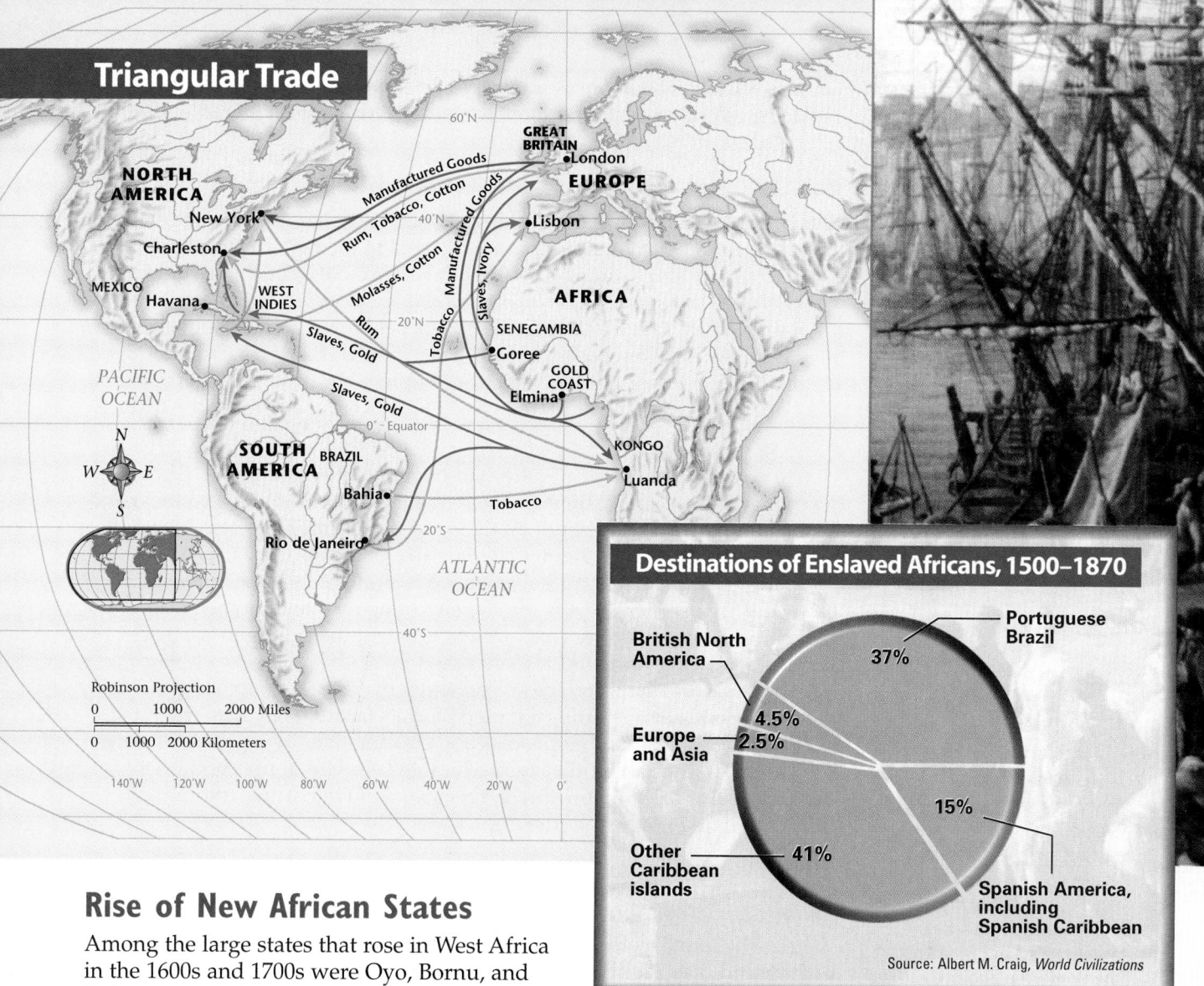

Triangular Trade

Manufactured Goods
Rum, Tobacco, Cotton
Manufactured Goods
Molasses, Cotton
Rum
Slaves, Gold
Tobacco Manufactured Goods
Slaves, Ivory
Slaves, Gold
Tobacco

NORTH AMERICA
New York
Charleston
MEXICO
Havana
WEST INDIES
PACIFIC OCEAN
SOUTH AMERICA
BRAZIL
Bahia
Rio de Janeiro
ATLANTIC OCEAN

GREAT BRITAIN
London
EUROPE
Lisbon
AFRICA
SENEGAMBIA
Goree
GOLD COAST
Elmina
KONGO
Luanda

Robinson Projection
0   1000   2000 Miles
0   1000   2000 Kilometers

Destinations of Enslaved Africans, 1500–1870

Portuguese Brazil 37%
British North America 4.5%
Europe and Asia 2.5%
Spanish America, including Spanish Caribbean 15%
Other Caribbean islands 41%

Source: Albert M. Craig, *World Civilizations*

Rise of New African States

Among the large states that rose in West Africa in the 1600s and 1700s were Oyo, Bornu, and Dahomey. Another state, the Asante kingdom, emerged in the area occupied by modern Ghana.

The Asante Kingdom   In the late 1600s, an able military leader, Osei Tutu, won control of the trading city of Kumasi. From there, he conquered neighboring peoples and organized the Asante kingdom. Osei Tutu claimed that his right to rule came from heaven. Leading chiefs served as a council of advisers but were subject to the royal will.

Officials chosen by merit rather than by birth supervised an efficient bureaucracy. They managed the royal monopolies over gold mining and the slave trade. A monopoly is the exclusive control of a business or industry. The Asante traded with Europeans on the coast, exchanging gold and slaves for firearms. But they shrewdly played off rival Europeans against one another to protect their own interests.

Islamic Crusades   In the 1700s and early 1800s, an Islamic revival spread across West Africa. It began among the Fulani people in northern Nigeria. The scholar and preacher Usman dan Fodio denounced the corruption of the local Hausa rulers. He called for social and religious reforms based on the Sharia, or Islamic law. In the early 1800s, Usman inspired Fulani herders and Hausa townspeople to rise up against their rulers.

Usman and his successors set up a powerful Islamic state. Under their rule, literacy increased, local wars quieted, and trade improved. Their success inspired other Muslim reform movements in West Africa. Between

Skills Assessment

Geography The Atlantic slave trade was part of the triangular trade network that linked merchants in Africa, Europe, and the Americas.

1. **Location** *On the map, locate (a) Africa, (b) West Indies, (c) New York, (d) Charleston.*
2. **Movement** *What goods were sent to Africa?*
3. **Critical Thinking Analyzing Information** *Between 1500 and 1870, most enslaved Africans were taken to what two regions of the Americas?*

about 1780 and 1880, more than a dozen Islamic leaders rose to power, replacing old rulers or founding new states in the western Sudan.

Battles for Power in Southern Africa

Over many centuries, Bantu-speaking peoples had migrated into southern Africa. In 1652, Dutch immigrants also arrived in the region. They built Cape Town to supply ships sailing to or from the East Indies. Dutch farmers, called Boers, settled around Cape Town. Over time, they ousted or enslaved the Khoisan herders who lived there. The Boers held to a Calvinist belief that they were the elect, or chosen, of God. They looked on Africans as inferiors.

In the 1700s, Boer herders and ivory hunters began to push north from the Cape Colony. As they did, they had to battle several powerful African groups.

Shaka and the Zulus   The Zulus had migrated into southern Africa in the 1500s. In the early 1800s, they emerged as a major force under a ruthless and brilliant leader, Shaka. He built on the successes of earlier leaders who had begun to organize young fighters into permanent regiments.

Between 1818 and 1828, Shaka waged relentless war and conquered many nearby peoples. He absorbed their young men and women into Zulu regiments. By encouraging rival groups to forget their differences, he cemented a growing pride in the Zulu kingdom.

Shaka's wars disrupted life across southern Africa. Groups driven from their homelands by the Zulus adopted Shaka's tactics. They then migrated north, conquering still other peoples and creating their own powerful states.

Later Shaka's half brother took over the Zulu kingdom. About this time, the Zulus faced a new threat, the arrival of well-armed, mounted Boers migrating north from the Cape Colony.

Boers Versus Zulus   In 1815, the Cape Colony passed from the Dutch to the British. Many Boers resented British laws that abolished slavery and otherwise interfered in their way of life. To escape British rule, they loaded their goods into covered wagons and started north. In the late 1830s, several thousand Boer families joined this "Great Trek."

As the migrating Boers came into contact with Zulus, fighting quickly broke out. At first, Zulu regiments held their own. But in the end, Zulu spears could not defeat Boer guns. The struggle for control of the land would rage until the end of the century, as you will read later.

Zulu Weapons
The Zulus developed a new type of stabbing spear with a short shaft and a broad blade. For protection, they used ox-hide shields that were four feet high. Zulu armies won battles against the Boers, the English, and neighboring African peoples.

Theme: Economics and Technology Why were Europeans eventually able to defeat the Zulus?

SECTION 4 Assessment

Recall

1. **Identify:** **(a)** Middle Passage, **(b)** Asante, **(c)** Usman dan Fodio, **(d)** Boer, **(e)** Shaka, **(f)** Great Trek.
2. **Define:** **(a)** triangular trade, **(b)** repeal, **(c)** monopoly.

Comprehension

3. **(a)** Describe attempts by Africans to stop the slave trade. **(b)** What was the impact of the slave trade on life in Africa?
4. What steps did the Asante ruler take to ensure his power?
5. How did southern Africa become a battleground for rival groups?

Critical Thinking and Writing

6. **Solving Problems** **(a)** What kinds of information would a modern historian need to determine the number of Africans involved in the slave trade? **(b)** Why might a historian have trouble finding this information?
7. **Analyzing Information** **(a)** Why do you think European traders rarely took part directly in slave raids? **(b)** What effect did participation in the slave trade have on West African states?

Go Online
PHSchool.com

Use the Internet to research the Zulu leader, Shaka. Then, write a newspaper article that describes his life, his character, and his role in the history of southern Africa. For help with this activity, use **Web Code mkd-1602.**

Reading Focus

- How did European explorations lead to a global exchange?

- What impact did the commercial revolution and mercantilism have on European economies?

- How did these changes affect ordinary people?

Vocabulary

inflation

capitalism

entrepreneur

joint stock company

mercantilism

tariff

Taking Notes

Copy this diagram. As you read, fill in ways in which exploration and increased trade affected life in Europe. To help you get started, part of the diagram has been filled in.

EUROPEAN EXPLORATION AND TRADE

New foods from the Americas

Main Idea European exploration and increased trade stimulated a global exchange, a commercial revolution, and other changes in Europe.

Setting the Scene In 1570, Joseph de Acosta visited the Americas. He wrote in amazement about the many strange forms of life that he saw there. "[There are] a thousand different kinds of birds and beasts of the forest, which have never been known, neither in shape nor name. . . ." To Europeans like Acosta, the Americas seemed like a "new world."

As you have read, European explorations between 1500 and 1700 brought major changes to Asia, Africa, and the Americas. Here, we will look at the impact that these explorations had on Europe itself.

A Global Exchange

When Columbus returned to Spain in March 1493, he brought with him "new" plants and animals that he had found in the Americas. Later that year, Columbus returned to the Americas. With him were some 1,200 settlers and a collection of European animals and plants. In this way, Columbus began a vast global exchange that would have a profound effect on the world. In addition to people, plants, and animals, it included technology and even disease. Because this global exchange began with Columbus, we call it the Columbian Exchange.

New Foods From the Americas, Europeans brought home a variety of foods, including tomatoes, pumpkins, and peppers. Perhaps the most important foods from the Americas, however, were corn and the potato. Easy to grow, the potato helped feed Europe's rapidly growing population. Corn spread all across Europe and to Africa and Asia, as well.

At the same time, Europeans carried a wide variety of plants and animals to the Americas. Foods included wheat and grapes from Europe itself, and bananas and sugar cane from Africa and Asia. Cattle, pigs, goats, and chickens, unknown before the European encounter, added protein to the Native American diet. Horses and donkeys also changed the lives of Native Americans. The horse, for example, gave the nomadic peoples of western North America a new, more effective way to hunt buffalo.

Impact on Population The transfer of food crops from continent to continent took time. By the 1700s, however, corn, potatoes, manioc, beans, and tomatoes were contributing to population growth around the world. While other factors help account for the population explosion that began at this time, new food crops from the Americas were probably a key cause.

Global Connections

Europe's Sweet Tooth

Today, we take sugar for granted. But at one time, it was strictly a luxury item that few European households could afford. Then, in 1493, Columbus brought sugar cane plants to the Caribbean. The new crop thrived. As sugar supplies increased, sugar prices fell, and the former luxury item appeared on more and more European tables. It was also used to sweeten a popular new treat from the Americas— chocolate.

Still, Europe's new "sweet tooth" had a tragic side effect. In just 150 years, close to 4 million Africans were shipped as slaves to the Caribbean and Brazil to work the sugar plantations there.

Theme: Global Interaction
Who was originally responsible for bringing sugar cane to the Americas?

The Columbian Exchange sparked the migration of millions of people. Each year, shiploads of European settlers sailed to the Americas. Europeans also settled on the fringes of Africa and Asia. As you have read, the Atlantic slave trade forcibly brought millions of Africans to the Americas. The Native American population declined drastically.

The vast movement of peoples led to the transfer of ideas and technologies. Language also traveled. Words such as *pajama* (from India) or *hammock* and *canoe* (from the Americas) entered European languages.

A Commercial Revolution

The opening of direct links with Asia, Africa, and the Americas had far-reaching economic consequences for Europeans. Among these consequences were an upsurge in prices, known as the price revolution, and the rise of modern capitalism.

The Price Revolution   In the early modern age, prices began to rise in parts of Europe. The economic cycle that involves a rise in prices linked to a sharp increase in the amount of money available is today called inflation.

European inflation had several causes. As the population grew, the demand for goods and services rose. Because goods were scarce, sellers could raise their prices. Inflation was also fueled by an increased flow of silver and gold. By the mid-1500s, tons of these precious metals were flowing into Europe from the Americas. Rulers used much of the silver and gold to make coins. The increased money in circulation, combined with the scarcity of goods, caused prices to rise.

Growth of Capitalism   Expanded trade and the push for overseas empires spurred the growth of European capitalism, the investment of money to make a profit. Entrepreneurs, or enterprising merchants, organized, managed, and assumed the risks of doing business. They hired workers and paid for raw materials, transport, and other costs of production.

As trade increased, entrepreneurs sought to expand into overseas ventures. Such ventures were risky. Capitalist investors were more willing to take the risks when demand and prices were high. Thus, the price revolution of the early modern age gave a boost to capitalism.

Entrepreneurs and capitalists made up a new business class devoted to the goal of making profits. Together, they helped change the local European economy into an international trading system.

New Business Methods   Early capitalists discovered new ways to create wealth. From the Arabs, they adapted methods of bookkeeping to show profits and losses from their ventures. During the late Middle Ages, as you have read, banks sprang up, allowing wealthy merchants to lend money at interest. The joint stock company, also developed in late medieval times, grew in importance. It allowed people to pool large amounts of capital needed for overseas ventures.

Bypassing the Guilds   The growing demand for goods led merchants to find ways to increase production. Traditionally, guilds controlled the manufacture of goods. But guild masters often ran small-scale businesses without the capital to produce for large markets. They also had strict rules regulating quality, prices, and working conditions.

Enterprising capitalists devised a way to bypass the guilds. The "putting-out" system, as it was called, was first used to produce textiles but later spread to other industries. Under the "putting-out" system, a merchant capitalist distributed raw wool to peasant cottages. Cottagers spun the wool into thread and then wove the thread into cloth. Merchants bought the wool cloth from the peasants and sent it to the city for finishing and dyeing. Finally, the merchants sold the finished product for a profit.

Synthesizing Information

The Commercial Revolution

The Commercial Revolution spurred trade, promoted new business methods, and increased competition for profits among European nations. Use the quotation, picture, and graph to learn about this revolution.

The Port of Marseille, France, 1700s

The Clove Market

In his book published in 1998, journalist Charles Corn described one way the Dutch East India Company maintained its profits in cloves:

"The Dutch East India Company by now had gained the power to restrict production to meet Europe's demand for cloves, thereby maintaining high prices and preventing a glutted market. To achieve this end, the company engaged in a ploy . . . : balancing off the island's supply of spices against what it perceived to be the world's demand for them. Such a scheme introduced the practice of [required] cultivation of spice trees in groves officially authorized and the careful [destruction] of those the company did not approve."
—Charles Corn, *The Scents of Eden*

First Five Voyages of the English East India Company

Year	Rate of Profit (percentage)
1609	234%
1608	No profits due to shipwrecks
1607	234%
1604	95%
1601	95%

Source: Sir William Wilson Hunter, *A History of British India*

Skills Assessment

1. The range of profits on the English East India Company's first five voyages was from
   A 95 percent to 234 percent.
   B total loss to 234 percent.
   C 1601 to 1609.
   D $0 to $234.

2. The Dutch East India Company tried to improve its profits on cloves by
   E planting more clove trees.
   F using extra ships to bring cloves to market.
   G keeping production low in relation to demand.
   H increasing the supply of cloves on the market.

3. **Critical Thinking Drawing Conclusions (a)** What evidence here might lead you to conclude that shipping was important to the Commercial Revolution? **(b)** What role did the profit motive play in the Commercial Revolution? Use evidence to support your answer.

Skills Tip

Bar graphs have both a vertical axis and a horizontal axis, with each measuring a different element. Distinguish between the two before turning to the rest of the graph.

"TAKE US TO YOUR LEADER . . .
WE'VE COME TO NEGOTIATE A
FREE TRADE AGREEMENT WITH
EARTH."

Connections to Today

The Banana Wars

Governments have been using tariffs to protect their own industries for years. This practice continues today, as the "Banana Wars" between the United States and Europe demonstrate. American multinational companies produce bananas in countries like Honduras and Ecuador. Former European colonies in the Caribbean also produce bananas. European governments decided to let Caribbean bananas come into their countries more cheaply than the bananas produced by American firms, thus taking market share from the American firms. To retaliate, the United States government placed a 100 percent tariff on certain goods from Europe, making them much more expensive. Some 500 years after they began, tariff wars go on.

Theme: Continuity and Change Why do tariff wars develop?

The "putting-out" system separated capital and labor for the first time. From this system controlled by merchants, the next step would be the capitalist-owned factories of the Industrial Revolution of the 1700s, as you will read.

Mercantilism

European monarchs enjoyed the benefits of the commercial revolution. In the fierce competition for trade and empire, they adopted a new economic policy, known as **mercantilism**, aimed at strengthening their national economies.

Mercantilists supported several basic ideas. They believed that a nation's real wealth was measured in its gold and silver treasure. To build its supply of gold and silver, they said, a nation must export more goods than it imported.

The Role of Colonies Overseas empires were central to the mercantile system. Colonies, said mercantilists, existed for the benefit of the parent country. They provided resources and raw materials not available in Europe. In turn, they enriched a parent country by serving as a market for its manufactured goods.

To achieve these goals, European powers passed strict laws regulating trade with their colonies. Colonists could not set up their own industries to manufacture goods. They were also forbidden to buy goods from a foreign country. In addition, only ships from the parent country or the colonies themselves could be used to send goods in or out of the colonies.

Increasing National Wealth Mercantilists urged rulers to adopt policies to increase national wealth and government revenues. To boost production, governments exploited mineral and timber resources, built roads, and backed new industries. They imposed a single national currency and established standard weights and measures.

Governments also sold monopolies to large producers in certain industries as well as to big overseas trading companies. Finally, governments imposed **tariffs,** or taxes on imported goods. Tariffs were designed to protect local industries from foreign competition by increasing the price of imported goods.

The Lives of Ordinary People

How did these economic changes affect Europeans? In general, their impact depended on a person's social class. Merchants who invested in overseas ventures acquired wealth. But the price revolution hurt nobles. Their wealth was in land, and they had trouble raising money to pay higher costs for stylish clothing and other luxuries. Some sold off land, which in turn reduced their income. In towns and cities, the wages of hired workers did not keep up with inflation, creating poverty and discontent.

Most Europeans were still peasants. Europe's growing involvement in the world had little immediate effect on their lives. Changes took generations, even centuries, to be felt. For example, tradition-bound peasants were often reluctant to grow foods brought from the Americas. Only in the later 1700s did German peasants begin to raise potatoes. Even then, many complained that these strange-looking tubers tasted terrible.

Within Europe's growing cities, there were great differences in wealth and power. Successful merchants dominated city life. Guilds, too, remained powerful. And as trade grew, another group—lawyers—gained importance for their skills in writing contracts. Middle-class families enjoyed a comfortable life. Servants cooked, cleaned, and waited on them. Other city residents, such as journeymen and other laborers, were not so lucky. They often lived in crowded quarters on the edge of poverty.

Regardless of social class, European families were patriarchal. As husband and father, a man was responsible for the behavior of his wife and children. Women had almost no property or legal rights. A woman's chief roles were as wife and mother. Society stressed such womanly virtues as modesty, household economy, obedience, and caring for the family. Middle-class women might help their husbands in a family business. Peasant women worked alongside their husbands in the fields.

Looking Ahead

In the 1500s and 1600s, Europe emerged as a powerful new force on the world scene. The voyages of exploration marked the beginning of what would become European domination of the globe. In the centuries ahead, competition for empire would spark wars in Europe and on other continents.

European expansion would spread goods and other changes throughout the world. It would also revolutionize the European economy and transform its society. The concept of "the West" itself emerged as European settlers transplanted their culture to the Americas and, later, to Australia and New Zealand.

For centuries, most Europeans knew little or nothing about other lands. Exposure to different cultures was both unsettling and stimulating. As their horizons broadened, they had to reexamine old beliefs and customs.

Cause *and* Effect

Long-Term Causes	Immediate Causes
• Scientific Revolution • Europeans search for a sea route to Asia	• Columbus and other Europeans arrive in the Americas • Europeans encounter new plants and animals in the Americas

Columbian Exchange

Immediate Effects	Long-Term Effects
• Millions of Native Americans die from diseases • Enslaved Africans sent to the Americas • American foods introduced into Europe	• Exchange of ideas, foods, art, and language between Europe and the Americas • Population migration from Europe to the Americas • Growth of capitalism

Connections to Today

• Multicultural societies in the Americas
• Worldwide reliance on staples such as corn and potatoes

Skills Assessment **Chart** The arrival of Columbus in the Americas set off a global exchange of people, goods, and ideas. **Based on the chart, name one immediate and one long-term effect of the Columbian Exchange.**

SECTION 5 Assessment

Recall
1. **Identify:** (a) Columbian Exchange, (b) commercial revolution, (c) "putting-out" system.
2. **Define:** (a) inflation, (b) capitalism, (c) entrepreneur, (d) joint stock company, (e) mercantilism, (f) tariff.

Comprehension
3. How did the voyages of Columbus lead to global exchanges of goods and ideas?
4. Explain how each of the following contributed to economic changes in Europe: (a) the price revolution, (b) capitalism, (c) mercantilism.

5. How did the economic changes of the 1500s and 1600s affect the lives of ordinary people?

Critical Thinking and Writing
6. **Linking Past and Present** Global exchanges of goods, ideas, and even diseases continue today. How has modern technology quickened the speed with which global exchanges occur? Provide examples to support your answer.
7. **Inferring** Do you think the European policy of mercantilism was beneficial or harmful for the people of Africa and the Americas? Explain.

Activity
Creating a Map
Create an illustrated map of the world showing the movement of items in the Columbian Exchange. Label Europe, Asia, Africa, and North and South America. Create symbols to stand for products and use arrows to indicate the direction in which they traveled.

Creating a Chapter Summary

Copy this graphic organizer. Complete the organizer by writing in major changes that occurred in Europe, the Americas, and Africa as a result of the first global age from 1492 through the 1700s.

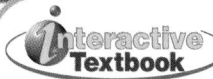

For additional review and enrichment activities, see the interactive version of *World History* available on the Web and on CD-ROM.

For practice test questions for Chapter 3, use **Web Code mka-1608.**

Building Vocabulary

Use the chapter vocabulary words listed to create a crossword puzzle. Exchange your puzzle with a classmate. Complete the puzzle and then check each other's answers.

1. conquistador
2. civil war
3. encomienda
4. creole
5. mestizo
6. missionary
7. compact
8. capitalism
9. mercantilism
10. tariff

Recalling Key Facts

11. How did the Spanish conquistadors treat the Native Americans they encountered?
12. Describe three examples of cultural blending in Spain's empire in the Americas.
13. How did Britain gain control of North America from the French?
14. Why were Africans brought to Spanish colonies in the Americas?
15. Why was there conflict in southern Africa in the 1700s and 1800s?
16. What was the Columbian Exchange?

Critical Thinking and Writing

17. **Connecting to Geography** Look at the map of the world in the Reference Section at the back of the book. How might geography have contributed to Spain and Portugal becoming the first European nations to explore the Americas?

18. **Linking Past and Present** How might your life be different if France had defeated England in the Seven Years' War?

19. **Recognizing Points of View** How might each of the following people have viewed European conquests in the 1500s and 1600s: (a) a Spaniard, (b) a Native American, and (c) an African?

20. **Recognizing Causes and Effects** (a) What were three causes of the growth of the Atlantic slave trade? (b) What were three immediate effects of the slave trade on Africa? (c) What do you think might have been some long-term effects of the slave trade on Africa's later development? Explain.

Read the excerpt below about the Middle Passage. Then, answer the questions that follow.

"I now saw myself deprived of all chances of returning to my native country. . . [and] my present situation. . .was filled with horrors of every kind. . . .The stench of the hold, while we were on the coast was so intolerably loathsome that it was dangerous to remain there for any time. . . .The closeness of the place, and the heat of the climate, added to the number in the ship, which was so crowded that each had scarcely room to turn himself, almost suffocated us. . . .The shrieks of the women, and the groans of the dying, rendered the whole a scene of horror almost inconceivable."

—Olaudah Equiano, *The Life of Gustavus Vassa*

21. **(a)** Who was the author of the excerpt? **(b)** Do you consider him a reliable source of information about the Middle Passage? Why or why not?

22. **(a)** What are some of the descriptive words used by the author about conditions aboard a slave ship? **(b)** What emotions are these words likely to arouse in the reader?

23. How did climate conditions affect the Middle Passage?

24. **(a)** Did the author think that he might one day return to Africa? **(b)** Why do you think he felt this way?

25. Many enslaved Africans died during the Middle Passage. Based on the above account, what were some of the reasons for the high death toll?

Go Online
PHSchool.com

Use the Internet to research the exports of Brazil or another European colony in the Americas during the first global age. Then, write a business report describing how that colony helped increase the wealth of the colonizing nation. If possible, compare the colonial exports with the exports that the area produces as an independent nation today. For help with this activity, use **Web Code mkd-1609.**

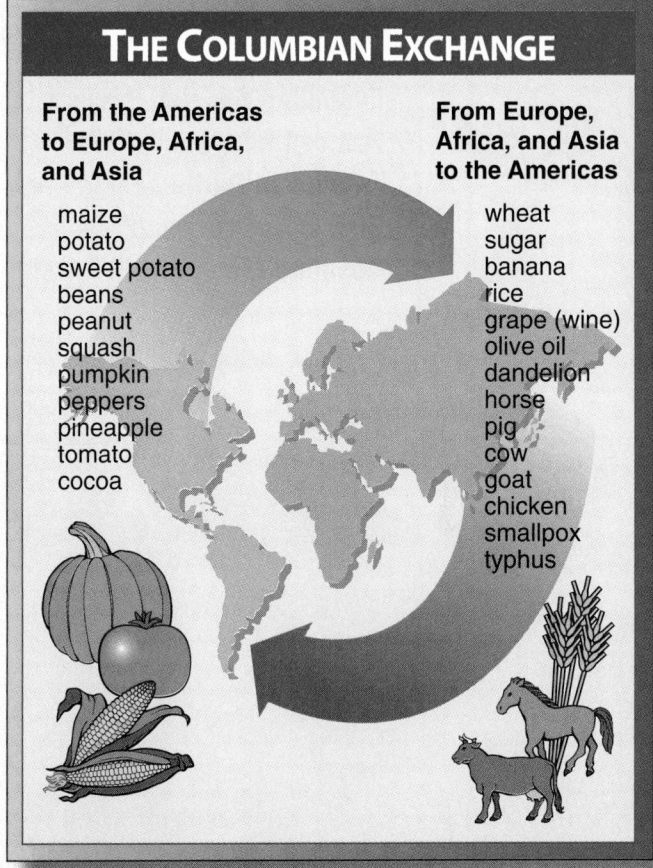

THE COLUMBIAN EXCHANGE

From the Americas to Europe, Africa, and Asia

maize
potato
sweet potato
beans
peanut
squash
pumpkin
peppers
pineapple
tomato
cocoa

From Europe, Africa, and Asia to the Americas

wheat
sugar
banana
rice
grape (wine)
olive oil
dandelion
horse
pig
cow
goat
chicken
smallpox
typhus

Use the chart above and information that you have learned in this chapter to answer the following questions:

26. When and with what event did this global exchange begin?

27. **(a)** Name three food crops that spread from the Americas to Europe, Africa, and Asia. **(b)** Name three domesticated animals that were introduced to the Americas.

28. How did the exchange cause a decline in the Native American population?

29. What effects did the Columbian Exchange have on the European economy?

30. How would life improve for people in both Europe and the Americas as a result of the global exchange?

Skills Tip

A flowchart represents a process in a simplified form. Some show a step-by-step process. Others show a cycle. Look at the arrows to understand the direction of the process.

The Age of Absolutism

1550–1800

Chapter Preview

1 **Extending Spanish Power**
2 **France Under Louis XIV**
3 **Triumph of Parliament in England**
4 **Rise of Austria and Prussia**
5 **Absolute Monarchy in Russia**

THE
Exercife of the English, in the
Militia of the Kingdome of
ENGLAND.

1642

The English Civil War begins, pitting the king's troops (left) against the armies of Parliament (right).

1556

Philip II (second from right) becomes king of Spain. Under Philip, Spain is the wealthiest and most powerful state in Europe.

1618

Religious conflict between German Protestants and Catholics sparks the Thirty Years' War.

CHAPTER EVENTS

1550

1600

1650

GLOBAL EVENTS

1556 Akbar the Great becomes emperor of India.

1607 British colonists found Jamestown.

European Nation-States, 1700

By 1700, powerful European monarchs had set aside the feudal past and built strong, centralized nation-states. Most of these rulers held absolute power.

Major European monarchies

ATLANTIC OCEAN

SWEDEN

North Sea

Baltic Sea

Moscow

RUSSIA

ENGLAND
London

Berlin
PRUSSIA

POLAND

Rhine R.

Vistula R.

Dnieper R.

Paris

Prague

FRANCE

Vienna

AUSTRIA

ALPS

PYRENEES MTS.

Danube R.

Black Sea

Madrid

SPAIN

Rome

O T T O M A N   E M P I R E

50°N

40°N

10°W

0°

Mediterranean Sea

N
W   E
S

Azimuthal Equidistant Projection

0   250   500 Miles
0   250   500 Kilometers

10°E   20°E   30°E   40°E   50°E

1697
Czar Peter the Great of Russia tours Europe to study western technology and ideas.

1715
King Louis XIV of France dies. The palace of Versailles, shown here, is a symbol of his 72-year reign.

1795
Russia, Prussia, and Austria complete the partition of Poland.

1700

1750

1800

1680s Asante kingdom is organized in West Africa.

1754 The French and Indian War erupts in North America.

1793 The emperor of China rejects British trade.

Extending Spanish Power

Reading Focus

- How did Spanish power increase under Charles V and Philip II?
- How did the arts flourish during Spain's golden age?
- Why did the Spanish economy decline in the 1600s?

Vocabulary

absolute monarch

divine right

armada

Taking Notes

As you read this section, prepare an outline of the contents. Use Roman numerals to indicate major headings. Use capital letters for the subheadings and numbers for the supporting details. The example will help you get started.

I. Charles V and the Hapsburg Empire
  A. Wearing two crowns
    1. Spain
    2. Holy Roman Empire and Netherlands
  B. An empire divided
    1.
    2.
II.

Main Idea   Philip II extended Spain's power and helped establish a golden age.

Global Connections

Cartloads of Silver and Gold

Old Spanish shipping records tell a tale about amazing wealth: "On 22 March 1595, ships from the Indies . . . began to discharge and deposit with the Chamber of Commerce 332 cartloads of silver, gold, and pearls of great value." This was the haul for *just one day*—and the flow of riches continued for *years!*

A major part of this wealth enriched the royal family. Most of the rest went into the hands of private traders. For Spain, American silver and gold financed a golden age of art, literature—and power.

Theme: Economics and Technology What impact could wealth from the Americas have on the arts in Renaissance Spain?

Setting the Scene   "It is best to keep an eye on everything," Philip II of Spain often said—and he meant it. As king of the most powerful nation in Europe, he gave little time to pleasure. Instead, he plowed through a mountain of paperwork each day, making notes on even the most trivial matters. Once the Spanish ambassador to England wrote about an unfamiliar kind of insect he had seen in London. "Probably fleas," Philip scribbled on the letter.

Philip's determination to "keep an eye on everything" extended far beyond trivia. It helped him build Spain into a strong centralized state. By the late 1500s, he had concentrated all power into his own hands. Over the next 200 years, other European monarchs would pursue similar goals.

Charles V and the Hapsburg Empire

By the 1500s, Spain had shaken off the feudal past and emerged as the first modern European power. Under Queen Isabella and King Ferdinand, Spain had expelled the last Muslim rulers and enforced religious unity. In 1492, Isabella financed Columbus's voyage across the Atlantic, leading to the Spanish conquest of the Americas.

Wearing Two Crowns   In 1519, Charles V,* grandson of Ferdinand and Isabella, inherited a huge empire. The new king faced a nearly impossible challenge. He not only inherited the crown of Spain but was also the heir of the Austrian Hapsburgs. The sprawling Hapsburg empire included the Holy Roman Empire and the Netherlands.

Ruling two empires involved Charles in constant warfare. As a devout Catholic, he fought to suppress the Protestant movement in the German states. After years of religious warfare, however, Charles was forced to allow the German princes to choose their own religions.

His greatest foe was the Ottoman empire. Under Suleiman, Ottoman forces advanced across central Europe to the walls of Vienna, Austria. Although Austria held firm, the Ottomans occupied much of Hungary. Ottoman naval forces also challenged Spanish power in the Mediterranean.

An Empire Divided   Perhaps the Hapsburg empire was too scattered and diverse for any one person to rule. Exhausted and disillusioned, Charles V gave up his titles and entered a monastery in 1556. He divided his empire,

---

* Within Spain, the king was known as Charles I. However, historians usually refer to him as Charles V, his title as ruler of the Austrian Hapsburg empire.

leaving the Hapsburg lands in central Europe to his brother Ferdinand, who became Holy Roman emperor. He gave Spain, the Netherlands, southern Italy, and Spain's overseas empire to his 29-year-old son Philip.

Philip II and Divine Right

Like his father, King Philip II was hard-working, devout, and ambitious. During his 42-year reign, he sought to expand Spanish influence, strengthen the Catholic Church, and make his own power absolute. Thanks in part to silver from the Americas, he made Spain the foremost power in Europe.

Unlike many other monarchs, Philip devoted much time to government work. He seldom hunted, never jousted, and lived as sparsely as a monk. His isolated, somber palace outside Madrid reflected the King's character. Known as the Escorial (ehs KOHR ee uhl), it served as a church, a residence, and a tomb for members of the royal family.

As did Ferdinand and Isabella, Philip further centralized royal power, making every part of the government responsible to him. He reigned as an **absolute monarch,** a ruler with complete authority over the government and the lives of the people. Like other European rulers, Philip asserted that he ruled by **divine right.** That is, he believed that his authority to rule came directly from God.

Partly as a result of the concept of divine right, Philip saw himself as the guardian of the Roman Catholic Church. The great undertaking of his life was to defend the Catholic Reformation and turn back the rising Protestant tide in Europe. Within his own lands, Philip enforced religious unity. He turned the Inquisition against Protestants and other people thought to be heretics.

The Wars of Philip II

Philip fought many wars as he attempted to advance Spanish Catholic power. At the battle of Lepanto in 1571, Spain and its Italian allies soundly defeated an Ottoman fleet in the Mediterranean. Although Christians hailed this as a great victory, the Ottoman empire remained a major power in the Mediterranean region.

Revolt in the Netherlands During the last half of his reign, Philip battled Protestant rebels in the Netherlands. At the time, the region included 17 provinces that are today Belgium, the Netherlands, and Luxembourg. It was the richest part of Philip's empire. Protestants in the Netherlands resisted Philip's efforts to crush their faith. Protestants and Catholics alike opposed high taxes and autocratic Spanish rule, which threatened local traditions of self-government.

In the 1560s, riots against the Inquisition sparked a general uprising in the Netherlands. Savage fighting raged for decades. In 1581, the northern, largely Protestant provinces declared their independence from Spain and became known as the Dutch Netherlands. They did not gain official recognition, however, until 1648. The southern, mostly Catholic provinces of the Netherlands remained part of the Spanish empire.

Invading England By the 1580s, Philip saw England's Queen Elizabeth I as his chief Protestant enemy. First secretly, then openly, Elizabeth had supported the Dutch against Spain. She even encouraged English captains,

Philip II of Spain
From 1556 to 1598, Philip II ruled the wealthiest, most powerful nation in Europe. Devoted to his family and to the Catholic Church, Philip could also be ruthless toward his enemies.

Theme: Impact of the Individual What impression of Philip II does this painting give you? Explain.

The Wars of Philip II, 1571–1588

SWEDEN

SCOTLAND

North Sea

DENMARK

Baltic Sea

Moscow

RUSSIA

IRELAND

LITHUANIA

ENGLAND

London •

NETHERLANDS

BRANDENBURG
Berlin •

Vistula R.

POLAND

Dnieper R.

Defeat of the
Spanish Armada
(1588)

Netherlands revolts
(1572–1581)

English
Channel

Paris •

Rhine R.

Prague •
BOHEMIA

ATLANTIC
OCEAN

FRANCE

SWITZERLAND

BAVARIA

Vienna •

AUSTRIA

HUNGARY

TRANSYLVANIA

Black Sea

ALPS

Milan •

VENICE

Danube R.

OTTOMAN EMPIRE

PYRENEES MTS.

PAPAL
STATES

Rome •

Constantinople •

PORTUGAL

Madrid •

SPAIN

CORSICA

Naples •
NAPLES

SARDINIA

SICILY

Battle of Lepanto
(1571)

Strait
of Lepanto

Mediterranean Sea

Azimuthal Equal Area Projection

0   250   500 Miles

0   250   500 Kilometers

★ Battle site

▬ Boundary of Holy
Roman Empire

Spanish Hapsburg
possessions

Skills Assessment

Geography To defend
Spanish power and Roman
Catholicism, Philip II sent
Spanish forces across Europe.

1. **Location** On the map,
locate **(a)** Spain,
(b) Madrid, **(c)** Ottoman
empire, **(d)** Strait of
Lepanto, **(e)** Netherlands,
(f) English Channel.
2. **Region** Which battles
shown on the map took
place in a territory ruled
directly by Spain?
3. **Critical Thinking**
Analyzing Information
Why do you think Spain
joined Italy in defending
the Strait of Lepanto?

known as Sea Dogs, to plunder Spanish treasure ships. Francis Drake, the
most daring Sea Dog, looted Spanish cities in the Americas. To Philip's
dismay, instead of punishing the pirate, Elizabeth made him a knight.

To end English attacks and subdue the Dutch, Philip prepared a huge
armada, or fleet, to carry a Spanish invasion force to England. In 1588, the
Armada sailed with more than 130 ships, 20,000 men, and 2,400 pieces of
artillery. The Spanish were confident of victory. "When we meet the English,"
predicted one Spanish commander, "God will surely arrange matters so
that we can grapple and board them, either by sending some strange freak
of weather or, more likely, just by depriving the English of their wits."

The "strange freak of weather," however, favored the other side. In the
English Channel, lumbering Spanish ships took losses from the lighter, faster
English ships. Suddenly, a savage storm blew up, scattering the Armada.
After further disasters at sea, the tattered remnants limped home in defeat.

While the defeat of the Spanish Armada ended Philip's plan to invade
England, it had little short-term effect on his power. In the long term, however, Spain's naval superiority did dwindle. In the 1600s and 1700s, Dutch,
English, and French fleets challenged—and surpassed—Spanish power
both in Europe and around the world.

Spain's Golden Age

The century from 1550 to 1650 is often called Spain's *siglo de oro,* or "golden
century," for the brilliance of its arts and literature. Philip II was a patron of
the arts and also founded academies of science and mathematics.

Painters Among the famous painters of this period was El Greco, meaning "the Greek." Born on the Greek island of Crete, El Greco had studied in

Renaissance Italy before settling in Spain. He produced haunting religious pictures, dramatic views of the city of Toledo, and striking portraits of Spanish nobles, done in a dramatically elongated style.

El Greco's use of vibrant colors influenced the work of Diego Velázquez (vuhl LAHS kehs), court painter to King Philip IV. Velázquez is perhaps best known for his vivid portraits of Spanish royalty.

Writers Spain's golden century produced outstanding writers like Lope de Vega. A peasant by birth, he wrote more than 1,500 plays, including witty comedies and action-packed romances. In *The Sheep Well,* Lope de Vega shows King Ferdinand and Queen Isabella saving a village from the hands of a villainous feudal lord.

Miguel de Cervantes wrote *Don Quixote,* the first modern novel in Europe. It pokes fun at medieval tales of chivalry. Dressed in rusty armor, the madman Don Quixote rides out on his broken-down plowhorse in search of adventure. He battles a windmill, which he thinks is a giant, and mistakes two flocks of sheep for opposing armies. He is accompanied by Sancho Panza, a practical-minded peasant.

Don Quixote mocked the traditions of Spain's feudal past. Yet Cervantes admired both the unromantic, earthy realism of Sancho Panza and the foolish but heroic idealism of Don Quixote.

> ▶ **Primary Sources and Literature**
>
> *See "Miguel de Cervantes: Don Quixote" in the Reference Section at the back of this book.*

Economic Decline

In the 1600s, Spanish power and prosperity slowly declined. Lack of strong leadership was one reason. The successors of Philip II were far less able rulers than he.

Economic problems were also greatly to blame. Costly overseas wars drained wealth out of Spain almost as fast as it came in. Then, too, treasure from the Americas led Spain to neglect farming and commerce. The government heavily taxed the small middle class, weakening a group that in other European nations supported royal power. The expulsion of Muslims and Jews from Spain deprived the economy of many skilled artisans and merchants. Finally, American gold and silver led to soaring inflation, with prices rising much higher in Spain than elsewhere in Europe.

Even though Spain continued to rule a huge colonial empire, its strength slipped away. By the late 1600s, France had replaced Spain as the most powerful European nation.

SECTION 1 Assessment

Recall

1. **Identify: (a)** Hapsburgs, **(b)** *siglo de oro,* **(c)** El Greco, **(d)** Diego Velázquez, **(e)** Miguel de Cervantes.
2. **Define: (a)** absolute monarch, **(b)** divine right, **(c)** armada.

Comprehension

3. **(a)** How did Philip II ensure absolute power? **(b)** How did he try to further Catholicism?
4. Why is the period from 1550 to 1650 considered Spain's golden age?
5. Why did Spanish power and prosperity decline?

Critical Thinking and Writing

6. **Recognizing Points of View** The English referred to the fierce storm that battered the Spanish Armada in 1588 as "the Protestant wind." **(a)** What does this nickname mean? **(b)** What nickname might the Spanish have given to the storm?
7. **Understanding Sequence** Create a time line showing key events in Spain's history between the rise of King Ferdinand and Queen Isabella and the end of its "golden century." Include events from this chapter and earlier chapters.

> **Go Online**
> PHSchool.com
>
> Use the Internet to learn more about the life and times of Miguel de Cervantes and his famous novel *Don Quixote.* Then, prepare a presentation giving examples of how the author used the characters of Don Quixote and Sancho Panza to satirize society. For help with this activity, use **Web Code mkd-1715.**

France Under Louis XIV

Reading Focus

- How did France rebuild after its wars of religion?

- How did Louis XIV strengthen royal power?

- What successes and failures did Louis XIV experience?

Vocabulary

intendant

levée

balance of power

Taking Notes

Begin a concept web like this one. As you read this section, fill in the blank circles with relevant information about Louis XIV. Add as many circles as you need.

Sun as symbol

LOUIS XIV

No meetings of Estates General

Main Idea Under the absolute rule of Louis XIV, France became the leading power of Europe.

Setting the Scene "I have had an idea that will . . . give much pleasure to the people here," wrote Louis XIV, the young king of France. His plan was to throw a grand party. Each guest would receive a lottery ticket for a prize of jewelry—and every ticket would be a winner. At Louis's bidding, some 600 noble guests flocked to the royal palace for a week of sumptuous feasts, pageants, sports, dances, plays, and music. This extravaganza was the first of many spectacles organized by Louis XIV.

By the late 1600s, Louis was absolute monarch of France and the most powerful ruler in Europe. Yet, just 100 years earlier, France had been torn apart by turbulent wars of religion.

Rebuilding France

From the 1560s to the 1590s, religious wars between Huguenots (French Protestants) and the Catholic majority tore France apart. Leaders on both sides used the strife to further their own ambitions.

The worst incident began on St. Bartholomew's Day, August 24, 1572. As Huguenot and Catholic nobles gathered to celebrate a royal wedding, violence erupted that led to the massacre of 3,000 Huguenots. In the next few days, thousands more were slaughtered. For many, the St. Bartholomew's Day Massacre symbolized the complete breakdown of order in France.

Catholics vs. Huguenots In the war between French Catholics and Protestants, both sides committed acts of violence. Here, Huguenot rioters destroy and loot a Catholic church.

Theme: Political and Social Systems Why did some French nobles encourage actions like these?

Henry IV   In 1589, a Huguenot prince inherited the French throne as Henry IV. Knowing that a Protestant would face severe problems ruling a largely Catholic land, he became Catholic. "Paris is well worth a Mass," he is supposed to have said. To protect Protestants, however, he issued the Edict of Nantes in 1598. It granted the Huguenots religious toleration and let them fortify their own towns and cities.

Henry IV then set out to heal his shattered land. His goal, he said, was not the victory of one sect over another, but "a chicken in every pot"—a good Sunday dinner for every peasant. Under Henry, the government reached into every area of French life. Royal officials administered justice, improved roads, built bridges, and revived agriculture. By building the royal bureaucracy and reducing the influence of nobles, Henry IV laid the foundations for royal absolutism.

Richelieu   When Henry IV was killed by an assassin in 1610, his nine-year-old son, Louis XIII, inherited the throne. For a time, nobles reasserted their power. Then, in 1624, Louis appointed Cardinal Armand Richelieu (RIHSH uh loo) as his chief minister. This cunning, capable leader spent the next 18 years strengthening the central government.

Richelieu sought to destroy the power of the Huguenots and nobles, two groups that did not bow to royal authority. He smashed the walled cities of the Huguenots and outlawed their armies, while still allowing them to practice their religion. At the same time, he defeated the private armies of the nobles and destroyed their fortified castles. While reducing their independence, Richelieu tied nobles to the king by giving them high posts at court or in the royal army.

Richelieu handpicked his able successor, Cardinal Jules Mazarin. When five-year-old Louis XIV inherited the throne in 1643, the year after Richelieu's death, Mazarin was in place to serve as chief minister. Like Richelieu, Mazarin worked tirelessly to extend royal power.

Louis XIV, the Sun King

Soon after Louis XIV became king, disorder again swept France. In an uprising called the *Fronde,* nobles, merchants, peasants, and the urban poor rebelled—each group for its own reasons. On one occasion, rioters drove the boy king from his palace. It was an experience Louis would never forget.

When Mazarin died in 1661, Louis resolved to take over the government himself. "I have been pleased to entrust the government of my affairs to the late Cardinal," he declared. "It is now time that I govern them myself."

"I Am the State"   Like his great-grandfather Philip II of Spain, Louis XIV firmly believed in divine right. He wrote:

> "God's power is felt in an instant from one end of the world to the other; royal power takes the same time to act throughout the kingdom. It preserves the order of the whole kingdom, as does God with the whole world."
> —Louis XIV, quoted in *From Absolutism to Revolution* (Rowen)

Louis took the sun as the symbol of his absolute power. Just as the sun stands at the center of the solar system, he argued, so the Sun King stands at the center of the nation. Louis is often quoted as saying, *"L'etat, c'est moi"*—"I am the state."

During his reign, Louis did not once call a meeting of the Estates General, the medieval council made up of representatives of all French social classes. In fact, the Estates General did not meet between 1614 and 1789. Thus, unlike the English Parliament, the Estates General played no role in checking royal power.

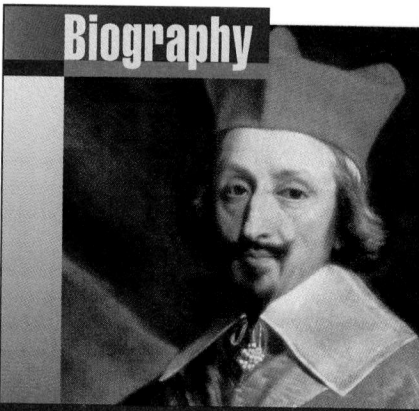

Biography

Cardinal Armand Richelieu
1585–1642

Armand Richelieu's parents expected great things from him. They even invited the king of France to attend Armand's christening, promising that someday he would be a leader of France.

The young boy also aspired to greatness as he was growing up. At first, he received training to become a disciplined and authoritative military officer. Then, at his family's request, he switched directions. At age 17, he began training to become a bishop in the church. The path was different but the purpose was the same: to become a leader and to serve the king.

Over the next 40 years, Armand Richelieu rose to the top of France in both religious and political circles. He became the true power behind the throne of King Louis XIII.

Theme: Impact of the Individual How did Richelieu's training as both a soldier and a bishop prepare him to be a strong political leader?

A High-Maintenance King

"No expense is too great." Applying this rule certainly helped Louis XIV make sure his every wish was fulfilled. For example:

- As much as $1.5 billion may have been taken from France's treasury to build his lavish palace at Versailles. Tens of thousands of workers spent several decades building the palace.

- One minor item for the Versailles palace was his bathtub, which was carved out of a single piece of priceless Languedoc marble.

- Guards were stationed at every fountain in Versailles's gardens. The guards' job was to whistle whenever the king approached so that the water would be turned on fully.

Theme: Impact of the Individual What does the extravagance of Louis XIV say about the power of the French monarch?

Strengthening Royal Power Louis spent many hours each day attending to government affairs. To strengthen the state, he followed the policies of Richelieu. He expanded the bureaucracy and appointed intendants, royal officials who collected taxes, recruited soldiers, and carried out his policies in the provinces. The office of intendant and other government jobs often went to wealthy middle-class men. In this way, Louis cemented ties between the middle class and the monarchy.

Under Louis XIV, the French army became the strongest in Europe. The state paid, fed, trained, and supplied up to 300,000 soldiers. Louis used this highly disciplined army to enforce his policies at home and abroad.

Colbert and the Economy Louis's brilliant finance minister, Jean Baptiste Colbert (kohl BEHR), followed mercantilist policies to bolster the economy. Colbert had new lands cleared for farming, encouraged mining and other basic industries, and built up luxury trades such as lacemaking. To protect French manufacturers, he put high tariffs on imported goods. He also encouraged overseas colonies, such as New France in North America, and regulated trade with the colonies to enrich the royal treasury.

Colbert's policies helped make France the wealthiest state in Europe. Yet Louis XIV was often short of cash. Not even the financial genius of Colbert could produce enough income to support the huge costs of Louis's court or pay for his many foreign wars.

Versailles, Symbol of Royal Power

In the countryside near Paris, Louis XIV turned a royal hunting lodge into the immense palace of Versailles (ver sī). He spared no expense to make it the most magnificent building in Europe. Its halls and salons displayed the finest paintings and statues, and glittering chandeliers and mirrors. In the royal gardens, millions of flowers, trees, and fountains were set out in precise geometric patterns.

Versailles became the perfect symbol of the Sun King's wealth and power. As both the king's home and the seat of government, it housed at least 10,000 people, from nobles and officials to servants.

Court Ceremonies Louis XIV perfected elaborate ceremonies that emphasized his own importance. Each day began in the king's bedroom with a major ritual known as the levée, or rising. High-ranking nobles competed for the honor of holding the royal wash basin or handing the king his diamond-buckled shoes. At night, the ceremony was repeated in reverse. Wives of nobles vied to attend upon women of the royal family.

Rituals such as the levée served a serious purpose. French nobles were descendants of the feudal lords who held power in medieval times. Left at their estates, these nobles were a threat to the power of the monarchy. By luring nobles to Versailles, Louis turned them into courtiers angling for privileges rather than warriors battling for power. Louis carefully protected their prestige and left them free from paying taxes.

Cultural Flowering The king and his court supported a "splendid century" of the arts. Louis sponsored musical entertainments and commissioned plays by the best writers. The age of Louis XIV was the classical age of French drama. Jean Racine (rah SEEN) wrote tragedies based on ancient Greek myths. The actor-playwright Molière (mohl YAIR) turned out comedies, such as *The Miser*, that poked fun at French society.

In painting, music, architecture, and decorative arts, French styles became the model for all Europe. A new form of dance drama, ballet, gained its first great popularity at the French court. As a leading patron of culture, Louis sponsored the French Academies, which set high standards for both the arts and the sciences.

You Are There . . .

Living at Versailles

King Louis XIV has summoned you to live at Versailles. As a French noble, you are both honored and intimidated. After all, life at court can be demanding. Dress, conduct, and events are strictly prescribed. One mistake and you may be ridiculed—or even banished. But the chance is too good to miss!

As you ride through the front gate, under the golden seal, you are stunned by the size of the main palace. It stretches for more than a quarter of a mile and contains 1,300 rooms.

An explosion of color commands your attention as you stroll through the formal gardens of Versailles with other nobles. Flower beds are divided into geometric patterns, and you are amazed at the endless variety of plants, bubbling fountains, and impressive statues.

You find it easy to believe that the king has said, "My dominant passion is certainly love of glory." Everything you have seen at Versailles is extravagant. All this magnificence does not come without a price, however. The kitchen is so far away from your apartments that your food often arrives cold.

Portfolio Assessment

To gain favor with the king, you decide to create a tour brochure of Versailles. You are so taken by the beauty of a particular site within the palace or on the grounds that you focus the guide on that area.

Successes and Failures

Louis XIV ruled France for 72 years, far longer than any other monarch. During his reign, French culture, manners, and customs replaced those of Renaissance Italy as the standard for European taste. In both foreign and domestic affairs, however, many of Louis's policies were costly failures.

Wars of Louis XIV Louis XIV poured vast resources into wars to expand French borders. At first, he did gain some territory. His later wars were disastrous, though, because rival rulers joined forces to check French ambitions. Led by the Dutch or the English, these alliances fought to maintain the balance of power, a distribution of military and economic power that would prevent any one nation from dominating Europe.

In 1700, Louis's grandson Philip V inherited the throne of Spain. Louis declared that France and Spain "must regard themselves as one." But neighboring powers led by England were determined to prevent this union. The War of the Spanish Succession dragged on until 1713, when an exhausted France signed the Treaty of Utrecht. Philip remained on the Spanish throne, but France agreed never to unite the two crowns.

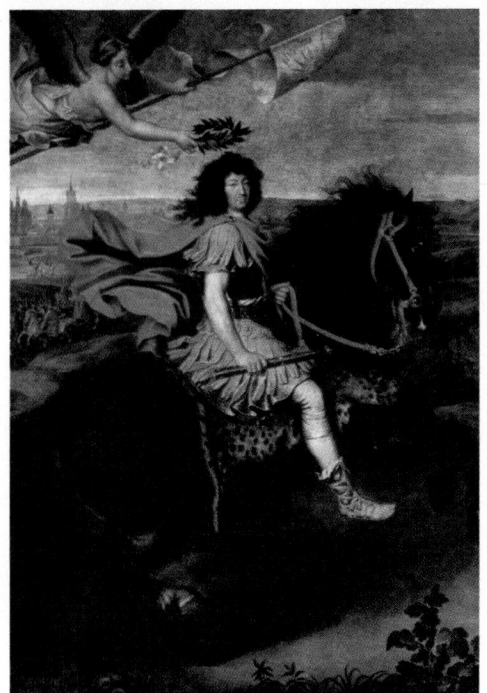

The King as Warrior
Although Louis XIV is best remembered for his extravagant court, he also expanded France's military might. This painting depicts Louis as a gallant warrior.

Theme: Impact of the Individual What symbols does this artist use to glorify Louis XIV?

Persecution of the Huguenots Louis saw France's Protestant minority as a threat to religious and political unity. In 1685, he revoked the Edict of Nantes. More than 100,000 Huguenots fled France.

The persecution of the Huguenots was perhaps the king's most costly blunder. The Huguenots had been among the most hard-working and prosperous of Louis's subjects. Their loss was thus a serious blow to the French economy, just as the expulsion of Muslims and Jews had hurt Spain.

Looking Ahead

Louis XIV outlived his sons and grandsons. When he died in 1715, his five-year-old great-grandson inherited the throne as Louis XV. Although France was then the strongest state in Europe, years of warfare had drained the treasury. The prosperity nurtured by Colbert evaporated under the burden of bad harvests, heavy taxes, and other problems.

Louis XV was too weak a king to deal with such problems. He devoted his days to pleasure, ignoring the growing need for reform. He often quoted an old proverb, "After us, the deluge." As you will read, the deluge came during the reign of the next king.

SECTION **2 Assessment**

Recall
1. **Identify: (a)** St. Bartholomew's Day Massacre, **(b)** Edict of Nantes, **(c)** *Fronde,* **(d)** Versailles, **(e)** War of the Spanish Succession.
2. **Define: (a)** intendant, **(b)** levée, **(c)** balance of power.

Comprehension
3. **(a)** What were the effects of the French wars of religion? **(b)** How did Henry IV rebuild French unity?
4. Describe how Louis XIV strengthened the power of the monarchy.

5. How did Louis's persecution of the Huguenots harm France?

Critical Thinking and Writing
6. **Comparing** How were the ideas of Louis XIV about monarchy similar to those of Philip II of Spain?
7. **Applying Information** On his deathbed, Louis XIV told his heir, "I have loved war too well; do not copy me in this, nor in the lavish expenditures I have made." Why do you think Louis gave this advice?

Activity

Designing a Set
Imagine that your school is putting on a play about Louis XIV at Versailles. You have been asked to design the set. Make a list of furniture, paintings, and other items you would want to include in the set.

Triumph of Parliament in England

Reading Focus

- How did the Tudors and Stuarts differ in their relations with Parliament?
- How did the English Civil War lead to the rise of the Commonwealth?
- What were the causes and results of the Glorious Revolution?

Vocabulary

dissenter

habeas corpus

limited monarchy

Taking Notes

Create a flowchart that shows the events in England that ultimately led to the strengthening of Parliament. Use this chart as a model, and add boxes as needed.

Tudors consult with and control Parliament
↓
James asserts claim to absolute power and clashes with Parliament
↓
↓

Main Idea During the 1600s, the British Parliament asserted its rights against royal claims to absolute power.

Setting the Scene "The most high and absolute power in the realm consists in the Parliament," wrote an English statesman in the 1560s. He was voicing a tradition that had roots in the Middle Ages. But in 1603, a monarch with far different ideas took the throne of England. "Kings are called gods," declared James I, "because they sit upon God's throne on Earth." Before long, James was on a collision course with Parliament.

In the 1600s, while Louis XIV perfected royal absolutism in France, England developed in a different direction. In this section, we will look at why and how Parliament asserted itself against royal power.

The Tudors and Parliament

From 1485 to 1603, England was ruled by the Tudor dynasty. Although the Tudors believed in divine right, they shrewdly recognized the value of good relations with Parliament. As you have read, when Henry VIII broke with the Roman Catholic Church, he turned to Parliament to legalize his actions. Parliament approved the Act of Supremacy, making the monarch head of the Church of England.

A constant need for money also led Henry to consult Parliament frequently. Although he had inherited a bulging treasury, he quickly used up his funds fighting overseas wars. To levy new taxes, the king had to seek the approval of Parliament. Members of Parliament tended to vote as Henry's agents instructed. Still, they became accustomed to being consulted on important matters.

Like her father, Elizabeth I both consulted and controlled Parliament. Her advisers conveyed the queen's wishes to Parliament and forbade discussion of certain subjects, such as foreign policy or the queen's marriage. Her skill in handling Parliament helped make "Good Queen Bess" a popular and successful ruler.

The Early Stuarts

Elizabeth died in 1603 without a direct heir. The throne passed to her relatives the Stuarts, the ruling family of Scotland. The Stuarts were neither as popular as the Tudors nor as skillful in dealing with Parliament. They also inherited problems that Henry and Elizabeth had long suppressed. The result was a "century of revolution" that pitted the Stuart monarchs against Parliament.

The Royal Challenge The first Stuart monarch, James I, had agreed to rule according to English laws and customs. Soon, however, he was lecturing Parliament about divine right. "I will not be content that my power be disputed upon," he declared. Leaders in the House of Commons fiercely resisted the king's claim to absolute power.

James repeatedly clashed with Parliament over money and foreign policy. He needed funds to finance his lavish court and wage wars. When members wanted to discuss foreign policy before voting funds, James dissolved Parliament and collected taxes on his own.

James also found himself embroiled in disputes with dissenters, Protestants who differed with the Church of England. One group, called Puritans, sought to "purify" the church of Catholic practices. Puritans called for simpler services and a more democratic church without bishops. James rejected their demands, vowing to "harry them out of this land or else do worse."

A positive result of the king's dispute with the Puritans was his call for a new translation of the Bible. The King James version that appeared in 1611 has had a lasting influence on English language and literature.

Parliament Responds In 1625, Charles I inherited the throne. Like his father, Charles behaved like an absolute monarch. He imprisoned his foes without trial and squeezed the nation for money. By 1628, though, his need to raise taxes forced Charles to summon Parliament. Before voting any funds, Parliament insisted that Charles sign the Petition of Right. It prohibited the king from raising taxes without the consent of Parliament or from imprisoning anyone without just cause.

Charles did sign the petition, but he then dissolved Parliament in 1629. For 11 years, he ignored the petition and ruled the nation without Parliament. During that time, he created bitter enemies, especially among Puritans. His Archbishop of Canterbury, William Laud, tried to force all clergy to follow strict Anglican rules, dismissing or imprisoning dissenters. Many people felt that the archbishop was trying to revive Catholic practices.

In 1637, Charles and Laud tried to impose the Anglican prayer book on Scotland. The Calvinist Scots revolted. To get funds to suppress the Scottish rebellion, Charles finally had to summon Parliament in 1640. When it met, however, Parliament launched its own revolt.

The Long Parliament The 1640 Parliament became known as the Long Parliament because it lasted on and off until 1653. Its actions triggered the greatest political revolution in English history. In a mounting struggle with the king, Parliament tried and executed his chief ministers, including Archbishop Laud. It further declared that the Parliament could not be dissolved without its own consent and called for the abolition of bishops.

Charles lashed back. In 1642, he led troops into the House of Commons to arrest its most radical leaders. They escaped through a back door and soon raised their own army. The clash now moved to the battlefield.

The English Civil War

The civil war that followed lasted from 1642 to 1649. Like the *Fronde* that occurred about the same time in France, the English Civil War posed a major challenge to absolutism. But while the forces of royal power won in France, in England the forces of revolution triumphed.

Cavaliers and Roundheads At first, the odds seemed to favor the Cavaliers, or supporters of Charles I. Many Cavaliers were wealthy nobles, proud of their plumed hats and fashionably long hair. Well trained in dueling and warfare, the Cavaliers expected a quick victory. But their foes proved to be tough fighters with the courage of their convictions. The

Virtual Field Trip

PHSchool.com

For: More on Oliver Cromwell
Visit: PHSchool.com
Web Code: mkd-1723

A Victory for Parliament
The Battle of Marston Moor was a turning point in the English Civil War. Though wounded in the neck, Oliver Cromwell (center, on horse) rallied his troops to defeat the forces of King Charles I.

Theme: Continuity and Change How would a modern battle scene differ from this one?

forces of Parliament were composed of country gentry, town-dwelling manufacturers, and Puritan clergy. They were called Roundheads because their hair was cut close around their heads.

The Roundheads found a leader of genius in Oliver Cromwell. A Puritan member of the lesser gentry, Cromwell was a skilled general. He organized the "New Model Army" for Parliament into a disciplined fighting force. Inspired by Puritan chaplains, Cromwell's army defeated the Cavaliers in a series of decisive battles. By 1647, the king was in the hands of parliamentary forces.

Execution of a King Eventually, Parliament set up a court to put the king on trial. It condemned him to death as "a tyrant, traitor, murderer, and public enemy." On a cold January day in 1649, Charles I stood on a scaffold surrounded by his foes. "I am a martyr of the people," he declared.

Showing no fear, the king told the executioner that he himself would give the sign for him to strike. After a brief prayer, Charles knelt and placed his neck on the block. On the agreed signal, the executioner severed the king's head with a single stroke.

The execution sent shock waves throughout Europe. In the past, kings had occasionally been assassinated or died in battle. But for the first time, a ruling monarch had been tried and executed by his own people. The parliamentary forces had sent a clear signal that, in England, no ruler could claim absolute power and ignore the rule of law.

The Commonwealth

After the execution of Charles I, the House of Commons abolished the monarchy, the House of Lords, and the official Church of England. It declared England a republic, known as the Commonwealth, under the leadership of Oliver Cromwell.

Challenges to the Commonwealth The new government faced many threats. Supporters of Charles II, the uncrowned heir to the throne, attacked England by way of Ireland and Scotland. Cromwell led forces into Ireland to crush the uprising. He then took harsh measures against the Irish Catholic majority. In 1652, Parliament passed a law exiling most Catholics to barren

Decades before the Puritans gained power in England, a group of settlers tried their hand at building a Puritan society across the Atlantic. Massachusetts Bay was a new colony without any traditions of established churches, strong government, or historic communities. The Puritans knew that to assure survival of their beliefs and culture, they would have to educate their children in their own ways. That was one reason the Puritans built schools, including Harvard College.

Eventually, the colonies became the United States. Over time, the rest of the country adopted the Puritan tradition of establishing public schools to help train children to become good citizens of their community. A literate, well-informed citizenry has continued to be a major aim of American schools to this day.

Theme: Political and Social Systems What other institutions help to train American children to be good citizens?

land in the west of Ireland. Any Catholic found disobeying this order could be killed on sight.

Squabbles also splintered forces within the Commonwealth. One group, called Levellers, thought that poor men should have as much say in government as the gentry, lawyers, and other leading citizens. "The poorest he that is in England hath a life to live as the greatest he," wrote one Leveller. In addition, female Levellers asserted their right to petition Parliament.

These Leveller ideas horrified the gentry who dominated Parliament. Cromwell and his generals suppressed the Levellers, as well as more radical groups who threatened property ownership. As the challenges to order grew, Cromwell took the title Lord Protector in 1653. From then on, he ruled through the army.

Puritan Society Under the Commonwealth, Puritan preachers tried to root out godlessness and impose a "rule of saints." The English Civil War thus ushered in a social revolution as well as a political one.

Parliament enacted a series of laws designed to make sure that Sunday was set aside for religious observance. Anyone over the age of 14 who was caught "profaning the Lord's Day" could be fined. To the Puritans, theaters were "spectacles of pleasure too commonly expressing mirth and levity." So, like John Calvin in Geneva, Cromwell closed all theaters. Puritans also frowned on lewd dancing, taverns, and gambling.

Puritans felt that every Christian, rich and poor, must be able to read the Bible. To spread religious knowledge, they encouraged education for all people. By mid-century, families from all classes were sending their children to school, girls as well as boys.

Puritans pushed for changes in marriage to ensure greater fidelity. In addition to marriages based on business interests, they encouraged marriages based on love. As in the past, women were seen mainly as caretakers of the family, subordinate to men. When some radical Protestant groups allowed women to preach sermons, most Puritans were shocked.

Although Cromwell could not accept open worship by Roman Catholics, he believed in religious freedom for other Protestant groups. He even welcomed Jews back to England, after more than 350 years of exile.

End of the Commonwealth Oliver Cromwell died in 1658. Soon after, the Puritans lost their grip on England. Many people were tired of military rule and strict Puritan ways. In 1660, a newly elected Parliament invited Charles II to return to England from exile.

England's "kingless decade" ended with the restoration of the monarchy. Yet Puritan ideas about morality, equality, government, and education endured. In the following century, these ideas would play an important role in shaping the United States of America.

From Restoration to Glorious Revolution

In late May 1660, cheering crowds welcomed Charles II back to London. One supporter wrote:

> "This day came his Majesty, Charles the Second to London, after a sad and long exile . . . with a triumph of above 20,000 horse and [soldiers], brandishing their swords, and shouting with inexpressible joy; the ways strewd with flowers, the bells ringing, the streets hung with tapestry."
> —John Evelyn, *Diary*

With his charm and flashing wit, young Charles II was a popular ruler. He reopened theaters and taverns and presided over a lively court in the manner of Louis XIV. Charles restored the official Church of England but tolerated other Protestants such as Presbyterians, Quakers, and Baptists.

Synthesizing Information

The Struggle Between King and Parliament

In England, a battle for power raged between king and Parliament during the 1600s. The monarchy was abolished and then restored. The picture, the source, and the time line depict a few highlights of that struggle.

King Versus Parliament

James I and Divine Right (1603)

"Kings are called gods because they sit upon God's throne on earth."

English Bill of Rights (1689)

"1. That . . . suspending of laws . . . by regal authority, without consent of Parliament is illegal.
4. That levying money for or to the use of the crown . . . without grant of Parliament . . . is illegal."

Restoration: Charles II in Triumph

1603 Stuart rule begins	1629 Charles I dissolves Parliament	1649 Parliament orders execution of Charles I; Cromwell rules	1688 Glorious Revolution	1689 Parliament passes Bill of Rights

1600	1620	1640	1660	1680	1700

1640 Long Parliament meets **1642** English Civil War **1660** Parliament restores Stuart rule; Charles II is crowned

Skills Tip

On a time line, equal intervals of time should be represented by an equal amount of space.

Skills Assessment

1. In which of the following years did Parliament seem to have the most power?
   A 1629
   B 1640
   C 1660
   D 1689

2. The person who painted the picture of Charles II probably
   E favored the monarchy.
   F fought for Cromwell.
   G supported Parliament.
   H disliked the new king.

3. **Critical Thinking Applying Information (a)** What advice would you give to an English monarch in the 1600s who wanted to keep his or her throne? **(b)** What advice would you give to a member of Parliament in the 1600s who wanted the monarchy to continue?

Although Charles accepted the Petition of Right, he shared his father's faith in absolute monarchy and secretly had Catholic sympathies. Still, he shrewdly avoided his father's mistakes in dealing with Parliament.

A New Clash With Parliament Charles's brother, James II, inherited the throne in 1685. Unlike Charles, James flaunted his Catholic faith. He further angered his subjects by suspending laws at whim and appointing Catholics to high office. Many English Protestants feared that James would restore the Roman Catholic Church.

In 1688, alarmed parliamentary leaders invited James's Protestant daughter, Mary, and her Dutch Protestant husband, William III of Orange, to become rulers of England. When William and Mary landed with their army late in 1688, James II fled to France. This bloodless overthrow of a king became known as the Glorious Revolution.

English Bill of Rights Before they could be crowned, William and Mary had to accept several acts passed by Parliament in 1689 that became known as the English Bill of Rights. The Bill of Rights ensured the superiority of Parliament over the monarchy. It required the monarch to summon Parliament regularly and gave the House of Commons the "power of the purse." A king or queen could no longer interfere in Parliamentary debates or suspend laws. The Bill of Rights also barred any Roman Catholic from sitting on the throne.

The Bill of Rights also restated the traditional rights of English citizens, such as trial by jury. It abolished excessive fines and cruel or unjust punishment. It affirmed the principle of habeas corpus. That is, no person could be held in prison without first being charged with a specific crime.

Later, the Toleration Act of 1689 granted limited religious freedom to Puritans, Quakers, and other dissenters, though not yet to Catholics. Still, only members of the Church of England could hold public office.

▶ **Primary Sources and Literature**

See "The English Bill of Rights" in the Reference Section at the back of this book.

Looking Ahead

The Glorious Revolution did not create democracy, but a type of government called limited monarchy, in which a constitution or legislative body limits the monarch's powers. English rulers still had much power, but they had to obey the law and govern in partnership with Parliament. In the age of absolute monarchy elsewhere in Europe, the limited monarchy in England was radical enough.

SECTION 3 Assessment

Recall
1. **Identify:** (a) James I, (b) Charles I, (c) Petition of Right, (d) Cavalier, (e) Roundhead, (f) Oliver Cromwell, (g) Leveller, (h) English Bill of Rights.
2. **Define:** (a) dissenter, (b) habeas corpus, (c) limited monarchy.

Comprehension
3. (a) How did Tudor monarchs handle Parliament? (b) Why did the early Stuarts clash with Parliament?
4. (a) Explain two causes of the English Civil War. (b) Why did many people welcome the return of the monarchy?
5. Describe two results of the Glorious Revolution.

Critical Thinking and Writing
6. **Analyzing Information** (a) How might Puritan teachings have led some women to seek greater liberties? (b) Why do you think many men were upset by the idea of women speaking in public?
7. **Linking Past and Present** Which aspects of Commonwealth society are part of American society today? Which are not?

Activity
Drawing a Political Cartoon
Draw a political cartoon that might have appeared in England in 1649 about the execution of Charles I. Take the point of view of either a Roundhead or a Cavalier.

4 Rise of Austria and Prussia

Reading Focus

- What were the causes and results of the Thirty Years' War?

- How did Austria and Prussia emerge as great powers?

- How did European diplomats try to maintain a balance of power?

Vocabulary

elector

mercenary

depopulation

Taking Notes

On a sheet of paper, copy the chart shown at right. As you read this section, add events that occurred before and after the Peace of Westphalia.

PEACE OF WESTPHALIA

Before	After
• Thirty Years' War	• Germany divided into many states
• Frederick becomes Holy Roman emperor	•

Main Idea Two great empires, Austria and Prussia, rose out of the ashes of the Thirty Years' War.

Setting the Scene
Year after year, war ravaged the German states of central Europe. Bodies of victims littered fields and roads. As the Thirty Years' War dragged on, almost every European power was sucked into the conflict. "We have had blue coats and red coats and now come the yellow coats," cried the citizens of one German town. "God have pity on us!"

Finally, two great German-speaking powers, Austria and Prussia, rose out of the ashes. Like Louis XIV in France, their rulers perfected skills as absolute monarchs.

The Thirty Years' War

The French philosopher Voltaire noted that, by early modern times, the Holy Roman Empire was neither holy, nor Roman, nor an empire. Instead, it was a patchwork of several hundred small, separate states. In theory, these states were under the authority of the Holy Roman emperor, who was chosen by seven leading German princes called electors. In practice, the emperor had little power over the many rival princes. Religion further divided the German states. The north was largely Protestant, and the south was Catholic. This power vacuum sparked the Thirty Years' War.

The War Begins The war had both religious and political causes. It began in Bohemia, the present-day Czech Republic. Ferdinand, the Hapsburg king of Bohemia, sought to suppress Protestants and to assert royal power over local nobles. In May 1618, a few rebellious Protestant noblemen tossed two royal officials out of a castle window in Prague. This act sparked a general revolt, which Ferdinand moved to suppress. As both sides sought allies, what began as a local conflict widened into a general European war.

The following year, Ferdinand was elected Holy Roman emperor. With the support of Spain, Poland, and other Catholic states, he tried to roll back the Reformation. In the early stages of the war, he defeated the Bohemians and their Protestant allies. Alarmed, Protestant powers like the Netherlands and Sweden sent troops into Germany.

Before long, political motives outweighed religious issues. Catholic and Protestant rulers shifted alliances to suit their own interests. At one point, Catholic France joined Lutheran Sweden against the Catholic Hapsburgs.

The Thirty Years' War Begins

In an act known as the Defenestration of Prague, rebellious nobles in Bohemia tossed two royal officials out of a castle window. Both men survived, but the defiant act sparked the terrible Thirty Years' War.

Theme: Diversity What opposing groups do the men shown in this picture represent?

Europe After the Thirty Years' War

A Brutal Conflict The fighting took a terrible toll. Roving armies of mercenaries, or soldiers for hire, burned villages, destroyed crops, and killed without mercy. A novel of the time describes episodes of nightmare violence, such as the plundering of a village by marauding soldiers:

> "For one of [the peasants] they had taken they thrust into the baking oven and there lit a fire under him, . . . as for another, they put a cord around his head and twisted it so tight with a piece of wood that the blood gushed from his mouth and nose and ears. In a word each had his own device to torture the peasants."

> —Jacob von Grimmelshausen, *Simplicissimus*

Murder and torture were followed by famine and disease. Wolves, not seen in settled areas since the Middle Ages, stalked the deserted streets of once-bustling villages. The war led to severe depopulation, or reduction in population. Although exact population statistics do not exist, historians estimate that as many as one third of the people in the German states may have died as a result of the war.

Peace at Last Finally, in 1648, the exhausted combatants accepted a series of treaties, known as the Peace of Westphalia. Because so many powers had been involved in the conflict, the war ended with a general European peace and an attempt to settle other international problems as well.

France emerged a clear winner, gaining territory on both its Spanish and German frontiers. The Hapsburgs were big losers because they had to accept the almost total independence of all the princes of the Holy Roman Empire. The Netherlands and the Swiss Federation (present-day Switzerland) won recognition as independent states.

The Thirty Years' War left Germany divided into more than 360 separate states, "one for every day of the year." These states still formally acknowledged the leadership of the Holy Roman emperor. Yet each state had its own government, coinage, state church, armed forces, and foreign policy. Germany, potentially the most powerful nation in Europe, thus remained fragmented for another 200 years.

Hapsburg Austria

Though weakened by war, the Hapsburgs still wanted to create a strong united state. They kept the title of Holy Roman emperors, but focused their attention on expanding their own lands. To Austria, they added Bohemia, Hungary, and, later, parts of Poland and Italy.

Unity and Diversity Uniting these lands proved difficult. Divided by geography, they also included diverse peoples and cultures. By the 1700s, the Hapsburg empire included Germans, Magyars, Slavs, and others. In many parts of the empire, people had their own languages, laws, assemblies, and customs.

The Hapsburgs did exert some control over these diverse peoples. They sent German-speaking officials to Bohemia and Hungary and settled Austrians on confiscated lands in these provinces. The Hapsburgs also put down revolts in Bohemia and Hungary. Still, the Hapsburg empire never developed a centralized system like that of France.

Maria Theresa In the early 1700s, the emperor Charles VI faced a new crisis. He had no son. His daughter, Maria Theresa, was intelligent and capable, but no woman had yet ruled Hapsburg lands in her own name. Charles persuaded other European rulers to recognize his daughter's right to succeed him. When he died, however, many ignored their pledge.

The greatest threat came in 1740, when Frederick II of Prussia seized the rich Hapsburg province of Silesia. Maria Theresa set off for Hungary to appeal for military help from her Hungarian subjects. The Hungarians were ordinarily unfriendly to the Hapsburgs. But she made a dramatic plea before an assembly of Hungarian nobles. According to one account, the nobles rose to their feet and shouted, "Our lives and blood for your Majesty!" She eventually got further help from Britain and Russia.

During the eight-year War of the Austrian Succession, Maria Theresa was not able to force Frederick out of Silesia. Still, she did preserve her empire and win the support of most of her people. Equally important, she strengthened Hapsburg power by reorganizing the bureaucracy and improving tax collection. She even forced nobles and clergy to pay taxes and tried to ease the burden of taxes and labor services on peasants. As you will read, many of her reforms were later extended by her son and successor, Joseph II.

The Rise of Prussia

While Austria was molding a strong Catholic state, Prussia emerged as a new Protestant power. In the 1600s, the Hohenzollern (HOH uhn tsahl ern) family ruled scattered lands across north Germany. After the Peace of Westphalia, ambitious Hohenzollern rulers united their lands by taking over the states between them. Like absolute rulers elsewhere, they set up an efficient central bureaucracy and reduced the independence of their nobles, called Junkers (YOON kerz).

To achieve their goals, Prussian rulers like Frederick William I forged one of the best-trained armies in Europe. Great emphasis was placed on military values. One Prussian military leader boasted, "Prussia is not a state which possesses an army, but an army which possesses a state."

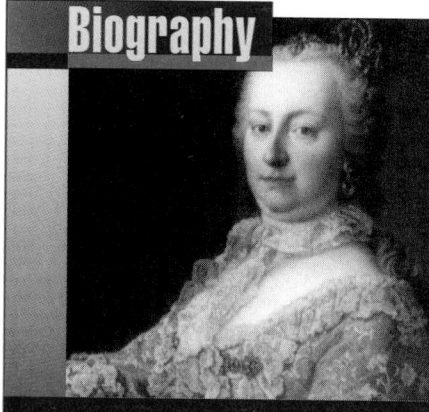

Biography

Maria Theresa 1717–1780

When Maria Theresa became Hapsburg empress at the age of 23, her chances of remaining in power seemed very slim. She later said, "I found myself . . . without money, without credit, without army, without experience and knowledge of my own, and finally without counsel, because each one of them first wanted to wait and see what would happen."

But the determined empress survived. She appointed superb advisers and was able to maintain control of her empire. During her 40-year reign, Vienna became a center for music and the arts.

Maria Theresa had one thing in common with most women of her day—her duties included motherhood. She gave birth to a total of 16 children—11 girls and 5 boys. Among them were future emperors Joseph II and Leopold II and Queen Marie Antoinette of France.

Theme: Impact of the Individual What traits did Maria Theresa need to stay in power?

Frederick William won the loyalty of the Junkers by giving them positions in the army and government. By 1740, Prussia was strong enough to challenge its rival Austria.

Frederick II Frederick William made sure that, from an early age, his son Frederick was trained in the art of war:

> "His tutor must take the greatest pains to imbue my son with a sincere love for the soldier's profession and to impress upon him that nothing else in the world can confer upon a prince such fame and honor as the sword."
> —Frederick William, quoted in *The Heritage of World Civilizations* (Craig)

In fact, young Frederick preferred playing the flute and writing poetry. Frederick William despised these pursuits and treated the young prince so badly that he tried to flee the country. Discovering these plans, Frederick William put his son in solitary confinement. A friend who had helped Frederick was beheaded while the 18-year-old prince was forced to watch.

Military Successes Frederick's harsh military training did have an effect. After becoming king in 1740, Frederick II lost no time in using his army. As you read, he boldly seized Silesia from Austria, sparking the War of the Austrian Succession. In several later wars, Frederick made brilliant use of his disciplined army, forcing all to accept Prussia as a great power. His exploits earned him the name Frederick the Great.

Keeping the Balance of Power

By 1750, the great powers of Europe included Austria, Prussia, France, England, and Russia. They formed various alliances to maintain the balance of power. Though nations sometimes switched partners, two rivalries persisted. Prussia battled Austria for control of the German states, while Britain and France competed for overseas empire.

On occasion, European rivalries ignited a worldwide conflict. The Seven Years' War, which lasted from 1756 until 1763, was fought on four continents. Prussia, Austria, Russia, France, and Britain battled in Europe. Britain and France also fought in India and Africa. In North America, the French and Indian War also involved Native American nations. The Treaty of Paris ending the wars gave Britain a huge empire.

SECTION 4 Assessment

Recall
1. **Identify:** (a) Peace of Westphalia, (b) Maria Theresa, (c) War of the Austrian Succession, (d) Frederick the Great, (e) Seven Years' War.
2. **Define:** (a) elector, (b) mercenary, (c) depopulation.

Comprehension
3. What impact did the Thirty Years' War have on the German states?
4. (a) What two major powers emerged in Europe at the end of the Thirty Years' War? (b) How were the goals of these two nations similar?

5. (a) Why did European nations seek a balance of power? (b) What methods did they use?

Critical Thinking and Writing
6. **Linking Past and Present** Westphalia was the first modern peace conference. (a) Why was such a conference needed? (b) How do nations try to settle disputes today?
7. **Making Inferences** "Prussia is not a state which possesses an army, but an army which possesses a state." What values do you think would be emphasized in such a state?

Activity

Mentoring a Monarch Both Louis XIV and Frederick William wrote instructions for training their sons to rule. With a partner, create a list of eight to ten rules for a successful absolute monarch in the 1600s and 1700s.

Absolute Monarchy in Russia

Reading Focus

- How did Peter the Great try to make Russia into a modern state?
- What steps did Peter take to expand Russia's borders?
- How did Catherine the Great strengthen Russia?

Vocabulary

westernization
boyar
warm-water port
partition

Taking Notes

As you read this section, make a Venn diagram to compare events in the reigns of Peter the Great and Catherine the Great. Use this diagram as a model, and add more information.

PETER
- Visited western countries

- Adopted western ideas

CATHERINE
- Established port on the Black Sea

Main Idea Czar Peter the Great and his successor, Catherine the Great, strengthened Russia and expanded Russian territory.

Setting the Scene

Along the Dutch waterfront, curious observers noticed that Peter Mikhailov was no ordinary man. For one thing, he stood almost seven feet tall. He had a booming laugh but also a furious temper. By day, he dressed in shabby clothes and worked as a shipyard carpenter. At night, he was entertained by royalty. For Peter Mikhailov was none other than Peter the Great, czar of Russia. His mission was to learn all he could about the more advanced nations of Western Europe.

In the early 1600s, Russia was still a medieval state, untouched by the Renaissance and Reformation and largely isolated from Western Europe. As you have read, the "Time of Troubles" had plunged the state into a period of disorder and foreign invasions. The reign of the first Romanov czar in 1613 restored a measure of order. Not until 1682, however, did a czar emerge who was strong enough to regain the absolute power of earlier czars. Peter the Great pushed Russia on the road to becoming a great modern power.

Learn more about the life of Peter the Great.

Peter Westernizes Russia
As part of his program of westernization, Peter the Great ordered nobles to shave their beards or else pay a "beard tax."

Theme: Continuity and Change How is the noble in this cartoon reacting to Peter's beard policy?

Peter the Great

Peter, just 10 years old when he came to the throne, did not take control of the government until 1689. Though he was not well educated, the young czar was immensely curious. He spent hours in the "German quarter," the Moscow suburb where many Dutch, Scottish, English, and other foreign artisans and soldiers lived. There, he heard of the advanced technology that was helping Western European monarchs forge powerful empires.

Journey to the West In 1697, Peter set out to study western technology for himself. He spent hours walking the streets of European cities, noting the manners and homes of the people. He visited factories and art galleries, learned anatomy from a doctor, and even had a dentist teach him how to pull teeth. In England, Peter was impressed by Parliament. "It is good," he said, "to hear subjects speaking truthfully and openly to their king."

Returning to Russia, Peter brought along a group of technical experts, teachers, and soldiers he had recruited in the West. He then embarked on a policy of westernization, that is, the adoption of western ideas, technology, and culture. But persuading fellow Russians to change their way of life proved difficult. To impose his will, Peter became the most autocratic of Europe's absolute monarchs.

Expansion of Russia, 1689–1796

Legend:
- Russia, 1689
- Land added by Peter the Great by 1725
- Land added by Catherine the Great by 1795
- Land added by 1796
- Austria, 1796
- Prussia, 1796
- Trade routes
- Bering's exploration route, 1725–1729

Azimuthal Equal Area Projection
0   500   1000 Miles
0   500   1000 Kilometers

Skills Assessment

Geography During the 1600s and 1700s, Russia expanded both eastward and westward to become the largest nation in the world.

1. **Location** On the map, locate **(a)** Sweden, **(b)** Baltic Sea, **(c)** St. Petersburg, **(d)** Black Sea, **(e)** Siberia, **(f)** Bering Sea.
2. **Place** Why were ports on the Black Sea more appealing to Russia than those on the Baltic?
3. **Critical Thinking Predicting Consequences** How might this map look different if Peter the Great had not modernized Russia?

Autocrat and Reformer At home, Peter pursued several related goals. He wanted to strengthen the military, expand Russian borders, and centralize royal power. To achieve his ends, he brought all Russian institutions under his control, including the Russian Orthodox Church. He forced the haughty boyars, or landowning nobles, to serve the state in civilian or military jobs.

Under Peter, serfdom spread in Russia, long after it had died out in Western Europe. By tying peasants to land given to nobles, he ensured that nobles could serve the state. Further, he forced some serfs to become soldiers or labor on roads, canals, and other government projects.

Using autocratic methods, Peter pushed through social and economic reforms. He imported western technology, improved education, simplified the Russian alphabet, and set up academies for the study of mathematics, science, and engineering. To pay for his sweeping reforms, Peter adopted mercantilist policies, such as encouraging exports. He improved the waterways and canals, developed mining and textile manufacturing, and backed new trading companies.

Some changes had a symbolic meaning. As you read, after returning from the West, Peter insisted that boyars shave their beards. He also forced them to replace their old-fashioned robes with Western European clothes. To end the practice of secluding upper-class women in separate quarters, he held grand parties at which women and men were expected to dance together. Russian nobles resisted this radical mixing of the sexes in public.

Peter had no mercy for any who resisted the new order. When elite palace guards revolted, he had over 1,000 of the rebels tortured and executed. As an example of his power, he left their rotting corpses outside the palace walls for months.

Expansion Under Peter

From his earliest days as czar, Peter worked to build Russian's military power. He created the largest standing army in Europe and set out to extend Russian borders to the west and south.

Search for a Warm-Water Port Russian seaports, located along the Arctic Ocean, were frozen over in the winter. To increase Russia's ability to trade with the West, Peter desperately wanted a warm-water port—one that would be free of ice all year round.

The nearest warm-water coast was located along the Black Sea. To gain control of this territory, Peter had to push through the powerful Ottoman empire. In the end, Peter was unable to defeat the Ottomans and gain his warm-water port. However, the later Russian monarch Catherine the Great would achieve that goal before the century ended.

War With Sweden In 1700, Peter began a long war against the kingdom of Sweden. At the time, Sweden dominated the Baltic region. Early on, Russia suffered humiliating defeats. A Swedish force of only 8,000 men defeated a Russian army five times its size. Undaunted, Peter rebuilt his army along western lines. In 1709, he defeated the Swedes and won land along the Baltic Sea.

Peter's City On land won from Sweden, Peter built a magnificent new capital city, St. Petersburg. Seeking to open a "window on the West," he located the city on the swampy shores of the Neva River near the Baltic coast. He forced tens of thousands of serfs to drain the swamps. Many thousands died, but Peter got his city. He then invited Italian architects and artisans to design great palaces in western style. Peter even planned the city's parks and boulevards himself.

Just as Versailles became a monument to French absolutism, St. Petersburg became the great symbol of Peter's desire to forge a modern Russia. A hundred years later, Russia's best-known poet, Alexander Pushkin, portrayed Peter as a larger-than-life ruler, determined to tame nature no matter what the cost:

> "Here we at Nature's own behest
> Shall break a window to the West,
> Stand planted on the ocean level;
> Here flags of foreign nations all
> By waters new to them will call
> And unencumbered we shall revel."
> —Alexander Pushkin, *The Bronze Horseman*

Toward the Pacific Russian traders and raiders also crossed the plains and rivers of Siberia, blazing trails to the Pacific. Under Peter, Russia signed a treaty with Qing China, defining their common border in the east. The treaty recognized Russia's right to lands north of Manchuria.

In the early 1700s, Peter hired the Danish navigator Vitus Bering to explore what became known as the Bering Strait between Siberia and Alaska. Russian pioneers crossed into Alaska and migrated as far south as California. Few Russians moved east of the Ural Mountains at this time, but on a map, Russia was already the largest country in the world, as it still is today.

Legacy of Peter the Great

When Peter died in 1725, he left behind a mixed legacy. He had expanded Russian territory, gained ports on the Baltic Sea, and created a mighty army. He had also ended Russia's long period of isolation. From the 1700s on, Russia would be increasingly involved in the affairs of Western Europe. Yet

Geography and History

Being "Sent to Siberia"

Russia's absolute monarchs needed a place to exile both criminals and political opponents for long periods of time. What place was better than the arctic region of Siberia to the north? Siberia had an extremely inhospitable climate—temperatures could average –59°F in winter—and it was far away from everything Russian. There was little chance for escape, as it was almost impossible to survive the vast, frozen, sparsely populated region. In fact, approximately 10 to 15 percent of the exiles never made it to Siberia. They died along the way.

Exiles started with a trickle in the early 1600s, but by the early 1800s, the number grew to 2,000 a year. After a revolt in 1825, the czar sent 150,000 people off to their freezing fate. Today, the expression "sent to Siberia" still implies that a person is being punished or has become an outcast.

Theme: Geography and History Why was Siberia chosen as a place for exile?

The Wealth of Catherine the Great

Catherine the Great (pictured above) enjoyed the splendor of being an absolute monarch. The ornate horse-drawn carriage was a gift from one of the Russian nobles who had conspired in the murder of her husband.

Theme: Political and Social Systems Compare this picture to pictures of the French court at Versailles in this chapter. Why do you think great displays of wealth were important to absolute monarchs?

many of Peter's ambitious reforms died with him. Nobles, for example, soon ignored his policy of service to the state.

Like earlier czars, Peter the Great had brandished terror to enforce his absolute power. His policies contributed to the growth of serfdom, which served only to widen the gap between Russia and the West that Peter had sought to narrow.

Catherine the Great

Peter died without naming a successor, setting off power struggles among various Romanovs. Under a series of ineffective rulers, Russian nobles reasserted their independence. Then, a new monarch took the reins of power firmly in hand. She became known to history as Catherine the Great.

A German princess by birth, Catherine had come to Russia at the age of 15 to wed the heir to the Russian throne. She learned Russian, embraced the Russian Orthodox faith, and won the loyalty of the people. In 1762, her mentally unstable husband, Czar Peter III, was murdered by a group of Russian army officers. Whether or not Catherine was involved in the assassination plot, she certainly benefited from it. With the support of the military, she ascended the Russian throne herself.

An Efficient Ruler Catherine proved to be an efficient, energetic empress. She reorganized the provincial government, codified laws, and began state-sponsored education for boys and girls.

Like Peter the Great, she embraced western ideas. At court, she encouraged French language and customs, wrote histories and plays, and organized court performances. As you will read in the next chapter, she was also a serious student of the French thinkers who led the intellectual movement known as the Enlightenment.

A Ruthless Absolute Monarch Like other absolute monarchs, Catherine could be ruthless. She granted a charter to the boyars outlining important rights, such as exemption from taxes. At the same time, she allowed them to increase their stranglehold on the peasants. When peasants rebelled against the harsh burdens of serfdom, Catherine took firm action to repress them. As a result, conditions grew worse for Russian peasants. Under Catherine, even more peasants were forced into serfdom.

Like Peter the Great, Catherine was determined to expand Russia's borders. After a war against the Ottoman empire, she finally achieved Peter's dream of a warm-water port on the Black Sea. She also took steps to seize territory from neighboring Poland.

Partition of Poland As you have read, Poland had once been a great European power. However, Polish rulers were unable to centralize their power or diminish the influence of the Polish nobility. The divided Polish government was ill prepared to stand up to the increasing might of its neighbors Russia, Prussia, and Austria.

In the 1770s, Catherine the Great, Frederick the Great, and Emperor Joseph II of Austria hungrily eyed Poland. To avoid fighting one another, the three monarchs agreed to partition, or divide up, Poland. At the first partition, in 1772, Catherine took part of eastern Poland, where many Russians and Ukrainians lived. Frederick and Joseph nibbled at Polish territory from the west.

Poland was partitioned again in 1793 and a third time in 1795. By the time Austria, Prussia, and Russia had taken their final slices, the independent kingdom of Poland had vanished from the map. Not until 1919 would a free Polish state reappear.

Looking Ahead

By the mid-1700s, absolute monarchs ruled four of the five leading powers in Europe. Britain, with its strong Parliament, was the only exception. As these five nations competed with one another, they often ended up fighting to maintain the balance of power.

At the same time, new ideas were in the air. Radical changes would soon shatter the French monarchy, upset the balance of power, and revolutionize European societies. In the next unit, you will read about how the Enlightenment, the French Revolution, the rise of Napoleon Bonaparte, and the Industrial Revolution would transform Europe.

SECTION 5 Assessment

Recall
1. **Identify:** **(a)** Peter the Great, **(b)** St. Petersburg, **(c)** Vitus Bering, **(d)** Catherine the Great.
2. **Define:** **(a)** westernization, **(b)** boyar, **(c)** warm-water port, **(d)** partition.

Comprehension
3. **(a)** List three goals of Peter the Great. **(b)** Explain one reform that Peter undertook to achieve each goal.
4. Why did Peter seek to expand Russian territory?
5. Describe how two policies of Catherine the Great strengthened Russia.

Critical Thinking and Writing
6. **Comparing** Compare the goals and policies of Peter the Great to those of *one* of the following monarchs: **(a)** Louis XIV of France, **(b)** Frederick II of Prussia, **(c)** Maria Theresa of Austria.
7. **Drawing Conclusions** Peter the Great said of the English Parliament, "It is good to hear subjects speaking truthfully and openly to their king." Based on what you have read, do you think Peter followed this idea in his own kingdom? Give a reason to support your answer.

Use the Internet to learn about the city of St. Petersburg today. Then, write a commentary that Peter the Great might make on the city if he were to see it today. Tell how he would react to a statue such as *The Bronze Horseman* or to the Hermitage Museum. For help with this activity, use **Web Code mkd-1735.**

Creating a Chapter Summary

On a sheet of paper make a table to compare the nations of Europe during the Age of Absolutism. Use the table shown here as a guide to get started.

	SPAIN	FRANCE	ENGLAND	AUSTRIA/ PRUSSIA	RUSSIA
GOVERNMENT	Philip II; absolute ruler				
WARS	Defeats Ottomans in 1571				
RELIGION	Catholic				
ECONOMY					
OTHER					

For additional review and enrichment activities, see the interactive version of *World History* available on the Web and on CD-ROM.

Go Online
PHSchool.com
For practice test questions for Chapter 4, use **Web Code mka-1736.**

Building Vocabulary

Use the chapter vocabulary words listed below to create a crossword puzzle. Exchange puzzles with a classmate. Complete the puzzles and then check each other's answers.

1. **absolute monarch**
2. **divine right**
3. **balance of power**
4. **habeas corpus**
5. **limited monarchy**
6. **mercenary**
7. **depopulation**
8. **westernization**
9. **boyar**
10. **partition**

Recalling Key Facts

11. What was the Spanish Armada?
12. Explain what the statement "I am the state" meant.
13. Describe the results of the English Civil War.
14. How did the Glorious Revolution limit royal power in England?
15. What reforms did Peter the Great carry out?
16. How and when did the kingdom of Poland lose its independence?

Critical Thinking and Writing

17. **Connecting to Geography** **(a)** How did resources of Spanish colonies in the Americas contribute to the decline of Spain? **(b)** How did resources from French colonies enrich France?

18. **Analyzing Primary Sources** Bishop Bossuet, a court preacher under Louis XIV, wrote, "Let God take away his hand and the world will fall back into nothingness; let authority fail in the kingdom, and total confusion will result." **(a)** According to Bossuet, what is the benefit of absolute monarchy? **(b)** What assumption does he make about the source of royal power? **(c)** How might the history of France in the late 1500s have influenced Bossuet's viewpoint?

19. **Recognizing Causes and Effects** **(a)** What were the immediate causes of the English Civil War? **(b)** What were some of the long-term causes?

20. **Recognizing Points of View** How might each of the following have viewed Peter the Great: **(a)** a boyar, **(b)** a serf, **(c)** Catherine the Great?

This passage is from a letter written to Louis XIV by a tutor to the king's children. Read the excerpt, then answer the questions that follow.

> "For nearly thirty years, your principal Ministers have destroyed and reversed all the ancient customs of the state in order to raise your authority to its highest pitch. They no longer speak of the state and its constitution; they only speak of the King and his royal pleasure. They have pushed your revenues and your expenses to unprecedented heights. They have raised you up to the sky in order, they say, to outshine the grandeur of all your predecessors; that is to say, in order to impoverish the whole of France for the introduction of monstrous luxuries of court. . . .
>
> Meanwhile, your people die of hunger. The cultivation of the soil is almost stagnant, and no longer offers employment to working men. All commerce is destroyed."
>
> —Archbishop François de Fénelon, *Letters*

21. **(a)** What did Fénelon criticize about the rule of Louis XIV? **(b)** Whom did he blame besides the king?
22. Fénelon wrote the letter anonymously, that is, unsigned. Why do you think he sent it this way?
23. What reforms do you think Fénelon would have welcomed?
24. Do you think the letter is a reliable source of information about the reign of Louis XIV? Why or why not?
25. How do you think the king might have responded to the charges made in the letter? Explain.

Go Online
PHSchool.com

Use the Internet to research one of the absolute monarchs described in the text. Then, write a brief biography of the monarch. Focus on the characteristics that made this person an example of absolutism, and on how this ruler affected the country he or she ruled. Be sure to list the sources you used in writing your biography. For help with this activity, use **Web Code mkd-1737.**

The maps below, which show Poland in three different years, make it possible to see how the area changed over time. Study the maps, then answer the questions that follow.

Partitions of Poland 1701–1795

26. What country was divided into two separate territories by Poland in 1701?
27. **(a)** How did the size of Poland's territory change from 1701 to 1772? **(b)** What was the status of Warsaw in 1795?
28. **(a)** What had happened to Poland by 1795? **(b)** What three countries divided the Polish territory?
29. In addition to the partition of Poland, what other territorial change can you see on these maps?
30. What do you think happened to the Polish people after the final partition?

Skills Tip

When you compare maps of a place over time, first make sure that you are looking at the same area on each map. Then, note any changes.

TEST PREPARATION

Use the quotation and your knowledge of social studies to answer the following question.

> "Observe how the shoulder changes with all the movements of the arm, moving up and down, inward and outward, backward and forward, and so also with turning movements or any other movements. And do the same with the neck, the hands and feet, and the chest above the hips."
>
> **—Leonardo da Vinci, *Notebooks***

1. This quotation could best be used to support which generalization?

   A   Renaissance artists produced greater paintings than artists of the Middle Ages.

   B   Renaissance artists developed techniques to show perspective.

   C   Renaissance artists were interested in portraying anatomy accurately.

   D   Renaissance artists based their paintings of human figures on Greek and Roman models.

2. One major effect of the European slave trade on Africa was that the slave trade

   A   led to a rapid decrease in tribal warfare.

   B   hastened the decline of older African kingdoms.

   C   strengthened traditional African economies.

   D   caused a severe population shortage in southern Africa.

3. During the Age of Absolutism, European monarchs sought to

   A   increase human rights for their people.

   B   centralize political power in their nations.

   C   seize all lands owned by powerful nobles.

   D   replace mercantilism with capitalism.

4. Which development listed below was an effect of the other three?

   A   Muslim and Italian merchants control overland trade routes to Asia.

   B   Demand for spices increases in Europe.

   C   European sailors learn to use the compass and astrolabe.

   D   European navigators explore the world's oceans.

5. Which statement best summarizes the view of knowledge held by thinkers during the Scientific Revolution?

   A   Scientific knowledge arises out of inquiry and investigation.

   B   Scientific knowledge must fit the teachings of the Church.

   C   Scientific knowledge is based on the learning of the ancient Greeks.

   D   It is impossible to gain scientific knowledge through human reason.

Use the chart and your knowledge of social studies to answer the following question.

Most Power   **Fewest People**

Peninsulares
People born in Spain

Creoles
People of European descent born in the colonies

Mestizos
People of mixed Native American and European descent

Mulattoes
People of mixed African and European descent

Native Americans and People of African descent

Least Power   **Most People**

6. Based on the chart, what conclusion can you draw about the social structure of the Spanish colonies?

   A Power was evenly distributed among many people.

   B Native American populations rapidly decreased.

   C Native Spaniards dominated society.

   D Creoles made up a majority of the population.

7. The Glorious Revolution and the English Bill of Rights are most closely associated with the development of

   A absolutism.

   B Puritanism.

   C divine right.

   D limited monarchy.

8. Which was a major result of the Protestant Reformation?

   A New Christian denominations emerged.

   B Religious warfare decreased in Europe.

   C The power of the pope was strengthened.

   D The Crusades began.

Writing Practice

9. In 1620, Francis Bacon said that the printing press, gunpowder, and the compass "have changed the whole face and state of things throughout the world." Explain why you think Bacon chose those three inventions. State whether you agree or disagree.

10. "In the 1600s, England moved in a different political direction than the other major powers of Europe." Explain the meaning of this statement using specific events and developments you have read about in this unit.

Enlightenment and Revolution

1707–1850

OUTLINE

Chapter 5 **The Enlightenment and the American Revolution** (1707–1800)

Chapter 6 **The French Revolution and Napoleon** (1789–1815)

Chapter 7 **The Industrial Revolution Begins** (1750–1850)

Chapter 8 **Revolutions in Europe and Latin America** (1790–1848)

Themes

As you read about the revolutionary ideas that brought dramatic changes to western society and government, you will encounter the following themes.

Continuity and Change Enlightenment ideas about society and government stood in sharp contrast to the prevailing standards. Since the 1700s, Enlightenment ideas have spread around the world.

Economics and Technology During the 1700s, advances in farming, transportation, and manufacturing contributed to the Industrial Revolution. Production of goods shifted from the home to the factory. Laissez-faire economists, utilitarians, and socialists offered plans to deal with the consequences of this change.

Impact of the Individual Thinkers such as John Locke, Voltaire, and Jean-Jacques Rousseau and political leaders such as Napoleon Bonaparte and Simón Bolívar encouraged national pride and human rights.

Political and Social Systems Revolutionaries, inspired by the Enlightenment, urged radical changes in government. Early industrialization created a new working class, while merchants and skilled artisans formed a growing new middle class.

Unit Theme Activity

For Your Portfolio The chapters in this unit describe the revolutionary changes in governments and economies that occurred in the 1700s. As you read the chapters, prepare a portfolio project showing the impact of development of factories. Your project might take one of the following forms:
• Diary
• Report
• Illustration

These monuments at the Plaza General San Martin in Buenos Aires, Argentina, display pride in national revolutionary heroes. Most nations in Latin America had won their independence by 1825.

Prepare to Read

Prepare to read this unit by previewing the main ideas and main events of each chapter.

Chapter 5

The Enlightenment and the American Revolution (1707–1800)

The Enlightenment was a movement in Western Europe and North America that sought to discover natural laws and apply them to social, political, and economic problems. Since the 1700s, Enlightenment ideas have spread around the world, creating upheaval and change as they have challenged established traditions.

- The ideas of thinkers such as Locke, Montesquieu, and Rousseau would justify revolutions and inspire principles of representative government.
- Enlightenment thinkers called *philosophes* applied the methods of science to their efforts to understand and improve society.
- Physiocrats rejected mercantilism in favor of laissez-faire economics.
- Despite a growing middle class, most Europeans remained peasants who lived in small rural villages, untouched by Enlightenment ideas.
- England established a constitutional monarchy and built the most powerful commercial empire in the world.
- After years of growing dissent, Britain's North American colonies won independence in the American Revolution.
- Inspired by Enlightenment ideas, the United States adopted a constitution that would serve as a model for other democratic nations.

Chapter 6

The French Revolution and Napoleon (1789–1815)

Between 1789 and 1815, the French Revolution destroyed an absolute monarchy and disrupted a social system that had existed for over a thousand years. These events ushered in the modern era in European politics.

- France was burdened by an outdated class system, a severe financial crisis, and a monarchy too indecisive to enact reforms.
- In 1789, dissatisfied members of the middle class called for a constitution and other reforms. Meanwhile, hunger and social resentment sparked rioting among peasants and poor city dwellers.
- In the first phase of the French Revolution, moderates attempted to limit the power of the monarchy and guarantee basic rights of the people.
- In 1793, as enemies outside France denounced the revolution, radicals executed the king and queen and began a Reign of Terror.
- From 1799 to 1815, Napoleon Bonaparte consolidated his power within France and subdued the combined forces of the greatest powers of Europe.
- Under Napoleon, French armies spread the ideas of revolution across Europe.
- In 1815, the Congress of Vienna sought to undo the effects of the French Revolution and the Napoleonic era.

1725 **1750** **1775**

AFRICA

1700s
Islamic revival
in Africa

THE AMERICAS

1763 Britain
wins control
of Canada

1775 American
Revolution
begins

ASIA AND OCEANIA

1756 Seven Years' War affects India

1770 Cook claims
Australia for Britain

EUROPE

1751 Diderot publishes *Encyclopedia*

1764 Spinning
jenny invented

Chapter 7

The Industrial Revolution Begins
(1750–1850)

During the 1700s, production began to shift from simple hand tools to complex machines, and new sources of energy replaced human and animal power. Known as the Industrial Revolution, this transformation marked a crucial turning point in history and changed the lives of people all over the world.

- An agricultural revolution contributed to a population explosion that, in turn, fed the growing industrial labor force.
- Abundant resources and a favorable business climate allowed Britain to take an early lead in industrialization.
- New sources of energy, such as coal and steam, fueled factories and paved the way for faster means of transporting people and goods.
- A series of remarkable inventions revolutionized the British textile industry and led to the creation of the first factories.
- Rapid urbanization and the rise of the factory system at first created dismal living and working conditions.
- Laissez-faire economists, utilitarians, and socialists put forth their own ideas for solving the problems of industrial society.
- Karl Marx promoted communism, a radical form of socialism that would have a worldwide influence.

Chapter 8

Revolutions in Europe and Latin America
(1790–1848)

With the Congress of Vienna, the great powers sought to return to the political and social order that had existed prior to 1789. However, in the early 1800s, a wave of violent uprisings swept across Western Europe and Latin America, fueled by the political ideas of the French Revolution and the economic problems of the Industrial Revolution.

- Two opposing ideologies emerged in Europe. Liberals embraced Enlightenment ideas of democracy and individual rights, while conservatives sought to preserve the old political and social order.
- Nationalism inspired independence movements among peoples with a shared heritage but also bred intolerance and persecution of minorities.
- In 1830 and 1848, ideological tensions and social inequalities sparked uprisings in France and elsewhere in Europe. Although most of these democratic revolutions were suppressed, they served to hasten reform later in the century.
- In Latin America, discontent with foreign domination led to a series of independence movements that freed most of the region from colonial rule by 1825.

1800 **1825** **1850**

1788 Futa Toro outlaws slave trade

1818 Shaka begins
Zulu conquests

1830s Boers begin Great Trek

1847 Liberia becomes independent

1789 United States
Constitution
takes effect

1819 Bolívar captures Bogotá

1810 "El Grito de Dolores" in Mexico

1793 Emperor Qianlong rejects British trade

1839
Opium War
begins in China

1789
French
Revolution
begins

1804
Napoleon
becomes
emperor

1815
Congress
of Vienna

1830
First railway
opens in Britain

1848
Revolutions sweep Europe; *The Communist Manifesto* published

The Enlightenment and the American Revolution

1707–1800

Chapter Preview

1 Philosophy in the Age of Reason
2 Enlightenment Ideas Spread
3 Britain at Mid-Century
4 Birth of the American Republic

1707

The Act of Union unites England and Scotland. This British flag uses symbols from each country's flag to show unity.

1721

Johann Sebastian Bach publishes his Brandenburg Concertos. Bach composes music for the harpsichord, shown here, and for many other instruments.

1740

Frederick II begins his reign in Prussia.

CHAPTER EVENTS

1700   1720   1740

GLOBAL EVENTS

1736 Qianlong begins a 60-year reign as emperor of China.

North America, 1783

The American Revolution transformed maps of North America as the United States became an independent nation.

Legend:
- United States territory
- British territory
- French territory
- Russian territory
- Spanish territory
- Claimed by U.S. and Great Britain
- Claimed by U.S. and Spain
- Claimed by Russia, Spain, and Great Britain

Map labels: ALASKA, Yukon R., Mackenzie R., Arctic Circle, 60°W, Hudson Bay, CANADA, 40°W, Saskatchewan R., St. Lawrence R., Quebec, Halifax, 40°N, Boston, New York, Philadelphia, LOUISIANA, UNITED STATES, ATLANTIC OCEAN, CALIFORNIA, Snake R., Colorado R., Missouri R., Ohio R., Mississippi R., Charleston, New Orleans, NEW SPAIN, FLORIDA, Rio Grande, Gulf of Mexico, BAHAMAS (Br.), HISPANIOLA, PACIFIC OCEAN, Tropic of Cancer, BELIZE, CUBA, PUERTO RICO, MARTINIQUE (Fr.), Mexico City, JAMAICA, GUADELOUPE (Fr.), 20°N, Caribbean Sea, 140°W, 120°W, 100°W, 80°W, 60°W, MOSQUITO COAST, SOUTH AMERICA

Azimuthal Equal Area Projection
0   500   1000 Miles
0   500   1000 Kilometers

N W E S

1759
The *philosophe* Voltaire, shown here, publishes *Candide*. The novel mocks French society.

1762
Jean-Jacques Rousseau publishes *The Social Contract*.

1781
The British army surrenders to the Americans after the Battle of Yorktown. This painting shows American and French officers planning the siege.

1760   **1780**   **1800**

1763 The Treaty of Paris is signed by France and Great Britain.

1789 Parisians storm the Bastille.

Reading Focus

- How did scientific progress promote trust in human reason?
- How did the social contract and separation of powers affect views on government?
- How did new ideas affect society and the economy?

Vocabulary

natural law

social contract

natural right

philosophe

physiocrat

laissez faire

Taking Notes

Make a table like the one here. Add information about each thinker as you read this section.

THINKER	WORKS AND IDEAS
Hobbes	• Wrote *Leviathan* •
Locke	
Montesquieu	
Voltaire	
Diderot	
Rousseau	
Wollstonecraft	
Smith	

Main Idea Enlightenment thinkers tried to apply reason and the laws of nature to human society.

Smallpox Vaccinations
In this painting, Edward Jenner vaccinates a child against smallpox. The smallpox vaccine was one of many scientific developments of the 1700s.

Theme: Art and Literature What elements of the painting suggest that smallpox was a major problem before Jenner developed his vaccine?

Setting the Scene By the early 1700s, European thinkers felt that nothing was beyond the reach of the human mind. The following lines by the English poet Alexander Pope celebrated the successes of humans—the "wondrous creature"—in the Scientific Revolution:

> "Go, wondrous creature! mount where Science guides;
> Go, measure earth, weigh air, and state the tides;
> Instruct the planets in what orbs to run,
> Correct old Time, and regulate the sun."
> —Alexander Pope, *Essay on Man*

Progress and Reason

The Scientific Revolution of the 1500s and 1600s had transformed the way people in Europe looked at the world. In the 1700s, other scientists expanded European knowledge. Joseph Priestley and Antoine Lavoisier (ahn TWAHN lah vwah ZYAY), for example, built the framework for modern chemistry. Edward Jenner developed a vaccine against smallpox, a disease whose path of death spanned the centuries.

Scientific successes convinced educated Europeans of the power of human reason. If people used reason to find laws that governed the physical world, why not use reason to discover natural laws, or laws that govern human nature? Using the methods of the new science, reformers set out to study human behavior and solve the problems of society. Thus, the Scientific Revolution led to another revolution in thinking, known as the Enlightenment. Through the use of reason, insisted Enlightenment thinkers, people and governments could solve every social, political, and economic problem. Heaven could be achieved here on Earth.

Two Views of the Social Contract

In the 1600s, two English thinkers, Thomas Hobbes and John Locke, set forth ideas that were to become key to the Enlightenment. Both men lived through the upheavals of the English Civil War. Yet they came to very different conclusions about human nature and the role of government.

Hobbes Thomas Hobbes set out his ideas in a work titled *Leviathan.* In it, he argued that people were naturally cruel, greedy, and selfish. If not strictly controlled, they would fight, rob, and oppress one another. Life in the "state of nature"—without laws or other control—would be "solitary, poor, nasty, brutish, and short."

To escape that "brutish" life, said Hobbes, people entered into a social contract, an agreement by which they gave up the state of nature for an organized society. Hobbes believed that only a powerful government could ensure an orderly society. For him, such a government was an absolute monarchy, which could impose order and compel obedience.

Locke John Locke had a more optimistic view of human nature. People were basically reasonable and moral, he said. Further, they had certain natural rights, or rights that belonged to all humans from birth. These included the right to life, liberty, and property.

In *Two Treatises of Government*, Locke argued that people formed governments to protect their natural rights. The best kind of government, he said, had limited power and was accepted by all citizens. Thus, unlike Hobbes, Locke rejected absolute monarchy.

Locke then set out a radical idea. A government, he said, has an obligation to the people it governs. If a government fails its obligations or violates people's natural rights, the people have the right to overthrow that government. This right to revolution would echo across Europe and around the world in the centuries that followed.

Separation of Powers

In the 1700s, France saw a flowering of Enlightenment thought. An early and influential thinker was the Baron de Montesquieu (MON tehs kyoo). Montesquieu studied the governments of Europe, from Italy to England. He read all he could about ancient and medieval Europe and learned about Chinese and Native American cultures. His sharp criticism of absolute monarchy opened the doors for later debate.

In 1748, Montesquieu published *The Spirit of the Laws.* In it, he discussed governments throughout history and wrote admiringly about Britain's limited monarchy. Montesquieu felt that the British had protected themselves against tyranny by dividing the various functions and powers of government among three separate branches: the legislative, executive, and judicial. (In fact, he had misunderstood the British system, which did not separate powers in this way.) Still, he felt that the separation of powers was the best way to protect liberty. Montesquieu also felt that each branch of government should be able to serve as a check on the other two, an idea that we call checks and balances.

The *Philosophes* and Society

In France, a group of Enlightenment thinkers applied the methods of science to better understand and improve society. They believed that the use of reason could lead to reforms of government, law, and society. These thinkers were called *philosophes,* which means "lovers of wisdom." Their ideas soon spread beyond France and even beyond Europe.

Voltaire Defends Freedom of Thought Probably the most famous of the *philosophes* was François-Marie Arouet, who took the name Voltaire. "My trade," said Voltaire, "is to say what I think," and he did so throughout his long, controversial life. Voltaire used biting wit as a weapon to expose the abuses of his day. He targeted corrupt officials and idle aristocrats. With his pen, he battled inequality, injustice, and superstition. He detested the slave trade and deplored religious prejudice.

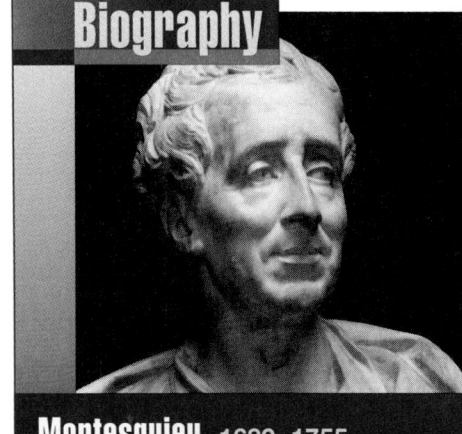

Biography

Montesquieu 1689–1755

Born to wealth, Charles Louis de Secondat inherited the title Baron de Montesquieu. Like many other reformers, his privileged status did not keep him from becoming a voice for democracy. His *Persian Letters* ridiculed the French elite. In *The Spirit of the Laws,* he advanced the idea of separation of powers—a foundation of modern democracy.

Montesquieu's belief in democracy did not mean that he considered all people equal. For example, he held a common view of his time that men were superior to women. However, he thought that women would make good government officials. According to Montesquieu, women's "weakness" would make them "gentle" rulers, thus benefiting the people.

Theme: Impact of the Individual What reforms did Montesquieu promote?

Comparing Viewpoints

What Limits Should There Be on Freedom of Speech?

"I do not agree with a word that you say, but I will defend to the death your right to say it." Whether or not Voltaire said these exact words, he passionately believed in this idea. But his idea has not been universally accepted. To consider whether there should be limits on freedom of speech, examine these viewpoints.

England 1643

John Milton, Puritan writer, expressed views about freedom of expression that later influenced Enlightenment thinkers:

66 Give me liberty to know, to utter, and to argue freely according to conscience, above all liberties. 99

China 1957

Mao Zedong led a government in China based on the ideals of the communist philosopher Karl Marx:

66 What should our policy be toward non-Marxist ideas? As far as unmistakable counterrevolutionaries and saboteurs of the socialist cause are concerned, the matter is easy. We simply deprive them of their freedom of speech. 99

Canada 1985

The criminal code of Canada outlaws public remarks against religious, racial, or ethnic groups:

66 Everyone who, by communicating statements other than in private conversation, willfully promotes hatred against any identifiable group is guilty of . . . an indictable offense and is liable to imprisonment for a term not exceeding two years. 99

United States 1942

Uncle Sam silences an American who is careless in his speech during World War II. "Loose talk" could reveal important secrets to the enemy, costing American lives.

QUIET!

LOOSE TALK CAN COST LIVES

Skills Assessment

1. Who seems to support complete freedom of speech, free from all restrictions?
   - A John Milton
   - B Uncle Sam
   - C Mao Zedong
   - D Karl Marx

2. According to Canadian law, freedom of speech
   - E does not apply to immigrants.
   - F is everyone's right.
   - G should be limited under certain circumstances.
   - H exists only in public situations.

3. **Critical Thinking Analyzing Information (a)** Study the poster. What does it seem to say about freedom of speech? **(b)** Should freedom of speech ever be limited? If so, under what conditions?

Skills Tip

Before comparing points of view, you must identify the main idea of each separate point of view. Then, look for ways in which the views are the same or different.

Voltaire's outspoken attacks offended both the French government and the Catholic Church. He was imprisoned and forced into exile. Even as he saw his books outlawed and even burned, he continued to defend the principle of freedom of speech.

The *Encyclopedia* Another *philosophe*, Denis Diderot (dee DROH), labored for some 25 years to produce a 28-volume *Encyclopedia*. As the editor of this huge work, Diderot did more than just gather articles on human knowledge. His purpose was "to change the general way of thinking" by explaining the new ideas on topics such as government, philosophy, and religion. Diderot's *Encyclopedia* included articles by leading thinkers of the day, including Montesquieu and Voltaire.

In their *Encyclopedia* articles, the *philosophes* denounced slavery, praised freedom of expression, and urged education for all. They attacked divine-right theory and traditional religions. Critics raised an outcry. The French government argued that the *Encyclopedia* was an attack on public morals, and the pope threatened to excommunicate Roman Catholics who bought or read the volumes.

Despite these and other efforts to ban the *Encyclopedia*, as many as 20,000 copies were printed between 1751 and 1789. When translated into other languages, it helped spread Enlightenment ideas throughout Europe and across the Atlantic to the Americas.

Rousseau The most controversial *philosophe*, Jean-Jacques Rousseau (ZHAHN ZHAHK roo SOH), was a strange, difficult man. Coming from a poor family, he never felt comfortable in the glittering social world of Enlightenment thinkers.

Rousseau believed that people in their natural state were basically good. This natural innocence, he felt, was corrupted by the evils of society, especially the unequal distribution of property. This view was later adopted by many reformers and revolutionaries.

In 1762, Rousseau set forth his ideas about government and society in *The Social Contract*. Rousseau felt that society placed too many limitations on people's behavior. He believed that some controls were necessary, but that they should be minimal. Additionally, these controls should be imposed only by governments that had been freely elected.

Rousseau put his faith in the "general will," or the best conscience of the people. The good of the community as a whole, he said, should be placed above individual interests. Thus, unlike many Enlightenment thinkers who put the individual first, Rousseau felt that the individual should be subordinate to the community.

Rousseau has influenced political and social thinkers for more than 200 years. Woven through his work is a profound hatred of all forms of political and economic oppression. His bold ideas would help fan the flames of revolt in years to come.

Women and the Enlightenment The Enlightenment slogan "free and equal" did not apply to women. Women did have "natural rights," said the *philosophes*. But unlike the natural rights of men, these rights were limited to the areas of home and family.

By the mid-1700s, a small but growing number of women protested this view. They questioned the notion that women were by nature inferior to men and that men's domination of women was therefore part of "nature's plan." Germaine de Staël in France and Catharine Macaulay and Mary Wollstonecraft in Britain argued that women were being excluded from the social contract itself. Their arguments, however, were ridiculed and often sharply condemned.

Wollstonecraft was a well-known British social critic. She accepted that a woman's first duty was to be a good mother. At the same time, however,

The *Encyclopedia*
Diderot's *Encyclopedia* contains this passage on the concept of liberty:

"The first state that man acquires by nature and that is esteemed the most precious of all his possible possessions is the state of liberty. He can neither exchange himself for another, nor sell himself, nor be enslaved, for all men are naturally born free. . . .

By virtue of this state, all men hold from nature itself the power to do what seems right to them and to regulate their actions and their property at will, provided they do not act against the laws of the government. . . ."

—Diderot, *Encyclopedia, or Classified Dictionary of the Sciences, Arts, and Occupations*

Skills Assessment

Primary Source What arguments does Diderot offer against slavery?

Germaine de Staël
Madame de Staël argued that women had been excluded from the ideals of the Enlightenment. She wrote a number of books, including an analysis of Rousseau.

Theme: Diversity According to the *philosophes*, how were natural rights different for men and for women?

she felt that a woman should be able to decide what is in her own interest and should not be completely dependent on her husband. In 1792, Wollstonecraft published *A Vindication of the Rights of Woman*. In it, she called for equal education for girls and boys. Only education, she argued, could give women the tools they needed to participate equally with men in public life.

New Economic Thinking

Other thinkers known as physiocrats focused on economic reforms. Like the *philosophes*, physiocrats looked for natural laws to define a rational economic system.

Laissez Faire Physiocrats rejected mercantilism, which required government regulation of the economy to achieve a favorable balance of trade. Instead, they urged a policy of laissez faire (LEHS ay FAIR), allowing business to operate with little or no government interference. Unlike mercantilists, who called for acquiring gold and silver wealth through trade, the physiocrats claimed that real wealth came from making the land more productive. Extractive industries, they said, such as agriculture, mining, and logging, produced new wealth. Physiocrats also supported free trade and opposed tariffs, or taxes on trade.

Adam Smith British economist Adam Smith greatly admired the physiocrats. In his influential work, *The Wealth of Nations*, he argued that the free market should be allowed to regulate business activity. Smith tried to show how manufacturing, trade, wages, profits, and economic growth were all linked to the market forces of supply and demand. Wherever there is a demand for goods or services, he said, suppliers will seek to meet it. They do so because of the profits and other economic rewards they can get from fulfilling the demand.

Smith was a strong supporter of laissez faire. He believed that the marketplace was better off without any government regulation. At the same time, however, he argued that government had a duty to protect society, administer justice, and provide public works.

Adam Smith's ideas would gain increasing influence as the Industrial Revolution spread across Europe and beyond. His emphasis on the free market and the law of supply and demand would help to shape immensely productive economies in the 1800s and 1900s.

SECTION 1 Assessment

Recall
1. **Identify: (a)** Thomas Hobbes, **(b)** John Locke, **(c)** Baron de Montesquieu, **(d)** Voltaire, **(e)** Denis Diderot, **(f)** Jean-Jacques Rousseau, **(g)** Mary Wollstonecraft, **(h)** *The Wealth of Nations*.
2. **Define: (a)** natural law, **(b)** social contract, **(c)** natural right, **(d)** *philosophe*, **(e)** physiocrat, **(f)** laissez faire.

Comprehension
3. How did the achievements of the Scientific Revolution contribute to the Enlightenment?

4. Explain the views of Thomas Hobbes, John Locke, and the Baron de Montesquieu.
5. How did the *philosophes* influence ideas on society and the economy?

Critical Thinking and Writing
6. **Defending a Position** Rousseau put the common good over the interest of the individual. Do you agree with that position? Explain.
7. **Predicting Consequences** Suppose that Mary Wollstonecraft encountered another important *philosophe*. What course might their conversation follow?

Activity

Creating a Cartoon
Draw a cartoon to illustrate the ideas of one or more of the *philosophes* you read about in this section. Write a brief caption to accompany your cartoon.

Enlightenment Ideas Spread

Reading Focus

- What roles did censorship and salons play in the spread of new ideas?
- How did *philosophes* influence enlightened despots?
- How did the Enlightenment affect arts and literature?
- Why were the lives of the majority unaffected?

Vocabulary

censorship
salon
enlightened despot
baroque
rococo

Taking Notes

On a sheet of paper draw a concept web to help you record information from this section. The web at right has been started for you. Add more circles as needed.

SPREAD OF ENLIGHTEN- MENT IDEAS

Salons

Courts of monarchs

Main Idea Enlightenment ideas spread across Europe and prompted some rulers to make reforms.

Setting the Scene

Paris, the heart of the Enlightenment, drew many intellectuals and others eager to debate the new ideas. Reforms proposed one evening became the talk of the town the next day. Even an enemy of the Enlightenment admitted that "an opinion launched in Paris was like a battering ram launched by 30 million men."

From France, Enlightenment ideas flowed across Europe and beyond. Everywhere, thinkers examined traditional beliefs and customs in the light of reason and found them flawed. Even absolute monarchs experimented with Enlightenment ideas, although they drew back when changes threatened the established way of doing things.

The Challenge of New Ideas

The ideas of the Enlightenment spread quickly through many levels of society. Educated people all over Europe eagerly read not only Diderot's *Encyclopedia* but also the small, cheap pamphlets that printers churned out on a broad range of issues. More and more, they saw the need for reform to achieve a just society.

During the Middle Ages, most Europeans had accepted without question a society based on divine-right rule, a strict class system, and a belief in heavenly reward for earthly suffering. In the Age of Reason, such ideas seemed unscientific and irrational. A just society, Enlightenment thinkers taught, should ensure social justice and happiness in this world.

Censorship Government and church authorities felt they had a sacred duty to defend the old order. They believed that the old order had been set up by God. To protect against the attacks of the Enlightenment, they waged a war of censorship, or restricting access to ideas and information. They banned and burned books and imprisoned writers.

Philosophes and writers like Montesquieu and Voltaire sometimes disguised their ideas in works of fiction. In the *Persian Letters*, Montesquieu uses two fictional Persian travelers, named Usbek and Rica, to mock French society. The hero of Voltaire's humorous novel *Candide*, published in 1759, travels across Europe and even to the Americas and the Middle East in search of "the best of all possible worlds." Voltaire slyly uses the tale to expose the corruption and hypocrisy of European society.

Salons The new literature, the arts, science, and philosophy were regular topics of discussion in salons, informal social gatherings at which writers,

Global Connections

An American *Philosophe*

Benjamin Franklin first traveled to Europe when he was just 18. There, he wrote in his *Autobiography*, ". . . I spent little upon myself except . . . in books. I had improved my knowledge, . . . though I had by no means improved my fortune. But I had made some very ingenious acquaintance, whose conversation was of great advantage to me, and I had read considerably."

Franklin's activities in Europe gave him firsthand exposure to Enlightenment ideas. He carried this new knowledge back to the American colonies, where he helped to create a country based on those ideas—the United States.

Theme: Global Interaction
How was the transmission of ideas across the Atlantic different in Franklin's time than it is today?

Salons provided a way for people to gather and share ideas. Today, many people do this without ever meeting—through the Internet.

Every day, millions of people use the Internet to exchange ideas easily. In "chat rooms," people send messages instantly, even if the recipient is on the other side of the world. In "newsgroups," people submit thoughts on a given topic and respond to the comments of others.

Many discussions on the Internet lack the serious-minded tone of a salon conversation. And because participants meet only through computers, there is no way to be sure who is on the other end of the line. But the popularity of the Internet shows that people will find a way to gather and discuss their ideas, even in a "virtual" living room.

Theme: Continuity and Change How does a "virtual" salon compare to the salons of the 1700s?

artists, *philosophes*, and others exchanged ideas. The salon originated in the 1600s, when a group of noblewomen in Paris began inviting a few friends to their homes for poetry readings. By the 1700s, some middle-class women began holding salons. In the drawing rooms of these *salonières* (sah lohn YAIR), middle-class citizens could meet with the nobility on an equal footing to discuss and spread Enlightenment ideas.

One of the most respected salons was run by Madame Geoffrin. In her home on the Rue St. Honoré, she brought together the brightest and most talented people of her day. The young musical genius Wolfgang Amadeus Mozart played for her guests, and Diderot was a regular at her weekly dinners for philosophers and poets.

Enlightened Despots

Discussions of Enlightenment ideas also enlivened the courts of Europe. *Philosophes* tried to persuade European rulers to adopt their ideas. If they could "enlighten" the ruling classes, they thought, they could bring about reform. Some monarchs did accept Enlightenment ideas. They became enlightened despots, or absolute rulers who used their power to bring about political and social change.

Frederick the Great As king of Prussia from 1740 to 1786, Frederick II exerted extremely tight control over his subjects. Still, he saw himself as the "first servant of the state," with a duty to work for the common good.

Frederick admired Voltaire's work and lured the *philosophe* to Berlin to develop a Prussian academy of science. When Frederick was not busy fighting wars, he had swamps drained and forced peasants to grow new crops such as the potato. He had seed and tools distributed to peasants who had suffered in Prussia's wars. Frederick also tolerated religious differences, welcoming victims of religious persecution. "In my kingdom," he said, "everyone can go to heaven in his own fashion."

Frederick's reforms were directed mainly at making the Prussian government more efficient. He reorganized the civil service and simplified laws. But a "rationalized" bureaucracy also meant a stronger monarchy—and more power for Frederick himself.

Catherine the Great Catherine II of Russia read the works of the *philosophes* and exchanged letters with Voltaire and Diderot. She praised Voltaire as someone who had "fought the united enemies of humankind: superstition, fanaticism, ignorance, trickery."

Catherine, who became empress in 1762, toyed with Enlightenment ideas. Early in her reign, she made some limited reforms in law and government. She granted nobles a charter of rights and criticized the institution of serfdom. Still, like Frederick in Prussia, Catherine intended to give up no power. In the end, her political contribution to Russia was not reform but an expanded empire.

Joseph II The most radical of the enlightened despots was the Hapsburg emperor Joseph II, son and successor of Maria Theresa. An eager student of the Enlightenment, Joseph traveled in disguise among his subjects to learn of their problems. His efforts to improve their lives won him the nickname the "peasant emperor."

Maria Theresa had begun to modernize Austria's government. Joseph continued her reforms. Despite opposition, he granted toleration to Protestants and Jews in his Catholic empire. He ended censorship and attempted to bring the Catholic Church under royal control. He sold the property of many monasteries and convents and used the proceeds to build hospitals. Joseph even abolished serfdom. Like many of his other reforms, however, this measure was canceled after his death.

Virtual Field Trip

For: Enlightenment paintings
Visit: PHSchool.com
Web Code: mkd-1853

Enlightenment Painters
During the 1700s, many artists began painting very personal, detailed scenes. In *The Marquise de Peze and the Marquise de Rouget with Her Two Children*, French artist Elisabeth Vigée LeBrun shows the relationships between mothers and young children.

Theme: Art and Literature
What elements of this painting identify its style as rococo rather than baroque?

The Arts and Literature

In the 1600s and 1700s, the arts evolved to meet changing tastes. As in earlier periods, artists and composers had to please their patrons, the men and women who commissioned works from them or gave them jobs.

Courtly Art In the age of Louis XIV, courtly art and architecture were either in the Greek and Roman tradition or in a grand, complex style known as baroque. Baroque paintings were huge, colorful, and full of excitement. They glorified historic battles or the lives of saints. Such works matched the grandeur of European courts.

By the mid-1700s, architects and designers developed the rococo style. Unlike the heavy splendor of the baroque, rococo art was personal, elegant, and charming. Furniture and tapestries featured delicate shells and flowers. Portrait painters showed noble subjects in charming rural settings, surrounded by happy servants and pets.

Middle-Class Audiences A new audience, the growing middle class, emerged with its own requirements. Successful merchants and prosperous town officials wanted their portraits painted, but without frills. They liked pictures of family life or realistic town or country scenes. Dutch painters such as Rembrandt van Rijn (REHM brant van RĪN) conferred great dignity on merchants and other ordinary, middle-class subjects.

Trends in Music New kinds of musical entertainment evolved during this era. Ballets and operas—plays set to music—were performed at royal courts. Before long, opera houses sprang up from Italy to England to amuse the paying public. The music of the period followed ordered, structured forms well suited to the Age of Reason.

Among the towering musical figures of the era was Johann Sebastian Bach. A devout German Lutheran, Bach wrote complex and beautiful religious works for organ and choirs. Another German-born composer, George Frederick Handel, spent much of his life in England. There, he wrote *Water Music* and other pieces for King George I, as well as many operas. His most celebrated work, the *Messiah*, combines instruments and voices. Today, it is a standard at Christmas and Easter concerts.

The Great Mozart

Wolfgang Amadeus Mozart died when he was just 35 years old. His musical genius, however, has lived for centuries. Today, his work is celebrated around the world.

Mozart was a prolific composer. He wrote operas, symphonies, piano concertos, string quartets, and scores of other works, including church music. In all, he composed more than 600 pieces of music.

Mozart wrote the opera *The Magic Flute* during the last year of his life. Here, the high priest is passing judgment on a kidnapper. Mozart's operas are famous for their outstanding arias (solos), recitatives (sung dialogues), and ensembles (group singing).

Mozart's music is admired throughout the world today. It can be playful, serious, uplifting, or somber. Many of his melodies are instantly recognized. People use his music in everything from car commercials to Internet greeting cards.

Portfolio Assessment

Listen to a recording of one of Mozart's compositions. Then, write a journal entry in which you tell how the music affected you. What feelings did it evoke? What images did it bring to mind? Explain why you think Mozart's music is held in such high regard.

Fast Facts

- Mozart was a child prodigy. He played the harpsichord at age 4 and began to compose music at age 5. A year later, he performed for the empress of Austria.
- Mozart's father, Leopold, was an accomplished musician. He took his young son on performing tours throughout Europe. Wolfgang never attended school.

In 1762, a six-year-old prodigy, Wolfgang Amadeus Mozart, burst onto the European scene to gain instant celebrity as a composer and performer. Over the next three decades, his brilliant operas, graceful symphonies, and moving religious music helped define the new style of composition. Although he died in poverty at age 35, his musical legacy thrives today.

The Novel By the 1700s, literature developed new forms and a wide new audience. Middle-class readers, for example, liked stories about their own times told in straightforward prose. One result was an outpouring of novels, or long works of prose fiction. English novelists created many popular works. Daniel Defoe wrote *Robinson Crusoe*, an exciting tale about a sailor shipwrecked on a tropical island. In *Pamela*, Samuel Richardson used a series of letters to tell a story about a servant girl. This technique was adopted by other authors of the period.

Lives of the Majority

Most Europeans were untouched by either courtly or middle-class culture. They remained what they had always been—peasants living in small rural villages. Their culture, based on centuries-old traditions, changed slowly.

Peasant life varied across Europe. Villages in Western Europe were relatively more prosperous than those in Eastern Europe. In the West, serfdom had largely disappeared. Instead, some peasants worked their own patches of land. Others were tenants of large landowners, paying a yearly rent for the land they farmed. Still others were day laborers who hired themselves out to work on other people's farms.

In central and Eastern Europe, however, serfdom was firmly rooted. In Russia, it spread and deepened in the 1700s. Peasants owed labor services to their lords and could be bought and sold with the land.

Despite advances, some echoes of serfdom survived in Western Europe. In France, peasants still had to provide free labor, repairing roads and bridges after the spring floods just as their ancestors had done. In England, country squires had the right to hunt foxes across their tenants' lands, tearing up plowed and planted fields.

By the late 1700s, radical ideas about equality and social justice seeped into peasant villages. While some peasants eagerly sought to topple the old order, others resisted efforts to bring about change. In the 1800s, war and political upheaval, as well as changing economic conditions, would transform peasant life in Europe.

SECTION 2 Assessment

Recall

1. **Identify:** **(a)** *Candide*, **(b)** Joseph II, **(c)** Johann Sebastian Bach, **(d)** George Frederick Handel, **(e)** Wolfgang Amadeus Mozart, **(f)** Daniel Defoe.
2. **Define:** **(a)** censorship, **(b)** salon, **(c)** enlightened despot, **(d)** baroque, **(e)** rococo.

Comprehension

3. Explain how each of the following affected the spread of new ideas: **(a)** censorship, **(b)** salons.
4. What were the goals of enlightened despots?

5. How did the Enlightenment affect **(a)** arts and literature, **(b)** the lives of the majority?

Critical Thinking and Writing

6. **Analyzing Information** **(a)** What did Frederick II mean when he said, "In my kingdom, everyone can go to heaven in his own fashion"? **(b)** How did his actions reflect that idea?
7. **Making Inferences** How did the Enlightenment bring together ideas of both the Renaissance and the Reformation?

Go Online
PHSchool.com

Search the Internet for information about salons in the 1700s. Identify types of people who attended salons in the 1700s, and create a list of people you would invite to a modern salon. Explain your choices. For help with this activity, use **Web Code mkd-1855.**

Reading Focus

- What influences spurred Britain's rise to global power?
- How did the growth of constitutional government reflect conditions in politics and society?
- How did George III reassert royal power?

Vocabulary

constitutional government

cabinet

prime minister

oligarchy

Taking Notes

As you read this section, make an outline of the information. Use Roman numerals for the main headings. Use capital letters for the subheadings, and use numbers for the supporting details. The outline at right has been started for you.

I. Rise to global power
   A. Geography
      1. Location good for trade
      2. From outposts to empire
   B. Success in war
      1. Won Nova Scotia and Newfoundland
      2.

Main Idea Britain's island location, colonial possessions, and powerful navy contributed to its rise to world power.

A Powerful Navy
By the mid-1700s, Britain controlled territories in North America, South America, Asia, and the Pacific. These scattered holdings required a strong navy, including men-of-war like the one shown here.

Theme: Political and Social Systems How might a strong navy benefit trade?

Setting the Scene Supporters of mercantilism found success in England. In the mid-1600s, a mercantilist wrote, "Foreign trade is . . . the honor of the kingdom, the noble profession of the merchant, . . . the means of our treasure, the sinews of our wars, the terror of our enemies."

Over the next century, Britain embraced mercantilism and built a colonial and commercial empire that reached around the world. At the same time, Britain developed a constitutional monarchy, a political system somewhere between the absolute monarchies of Europe and later democracies.

Rise to Global Power

Why did Britain, a small island kingdom on the edge of Europe, rise to global prominence in the 1700s? Here, we can look at a few reasons for the nation's success.

Geography Location placed England in a position to control trade during the Renaissance. In the 1500s and 1600s, English merchants sent ships across the world's oceans and planted outposts in the West Indies, North America, and India. From these tiny settlements, England would build a global empire.

Success in War In the 1700s, Britain was generally on the winning side in European conflicts. Each victory brought valuable rewards. With the Treaty of Utrecht, France gave Britain Nova Scotia and Newfoundland in North America. Britain also monopolized the slave trade in Spanish America. The slave trade brought enormous wealth to British merchants, who invested their profits in other ventures. In 1763, the Treaty of Paris ending the French and Indian War and the Seven Years' War brought Britain all of French Canada. The British East India Company also pushed the French out of India.

Unlike its European rivals, Britain had no large standing army. Instead, it built up its fleet. By 1763, Britain had developed a more powerful navy than its greatest rival, France. With superior naval power, it could protect its growing empire and trade.

A Favorable Business Climate England offered a more favorable climate to business and commerce than did its European rivals. Although England followed mercantilist policies, it put fewer restrictions on trade than France. Also, while British nobles, like most other nobles in Europe, looked down on trade, some did engage in business activities.

Union With Scotland At home, England expanded by merging with its neighbor, Scotland. In 1707, the Act of Union joined the two countries in the United Kingdom of Great Britain. The United Kingdom also included Wales. The union brought economic advantages to both lands. Free trade between the two created a larger market for farmers and manufacturers. Many Scots, however, resented the union. On two occasions, they supported the claims of Stuart princes who sought to regain the British throne. Eventually, though, growing prosperity made the union more acceptable.

Ireland England had controlled Ireland since the 1100s. In the 1600s, English rulers tried to subdue Catholic Ireland by sending Protestants from England and Scotland to settle there. They gave Protestant settlers title to Irish Catholics' lands. The Irish fiercely resisted Protestant rule. Uprisings led to increased repression. Catholics were forbidden to own weapons, marry non-Catholics, or teach.

Growth of Constitutional Government

In the century following the Glorious Revolution, three new political institutions arose in Britain: political parties, the cabinet, and the office of prime minister. The appearance of these institutions was part of the evolution of Britain's constitutional government—that is, a government whose power is defined and limited by law. The British constitution is not a single document. Instead, it consists of all acts of Parliament over the centuries. It also includes documents such as the Magna Carta and Bill of Rights, as well as unwritten traditions that protect citizens' rights.

Political Parties Two political parties emerged in England in the late 1600s—Tories and Whigs. Tories were generally landed aristocrats who

Skills Assessment

Geography During the 1600s in Ireland, England gave Irish lands to English and Scottish settlers. In Scotland, failed rebellions in 1715 and 1745–1746 marked the end of armed resistance to English control.

1. **Location** On the map, locate **(a)** Irish Sea, **(b)** Dublin, **(c)** Edinburgh, **(d)** London.
2. **Region** What percentage of land in Ireland was owned by Catholics in 1603? In 1685?
3. **Critical Thinking** **Drawing Conclusions** How might it benefit England economically to join with its neighbors?

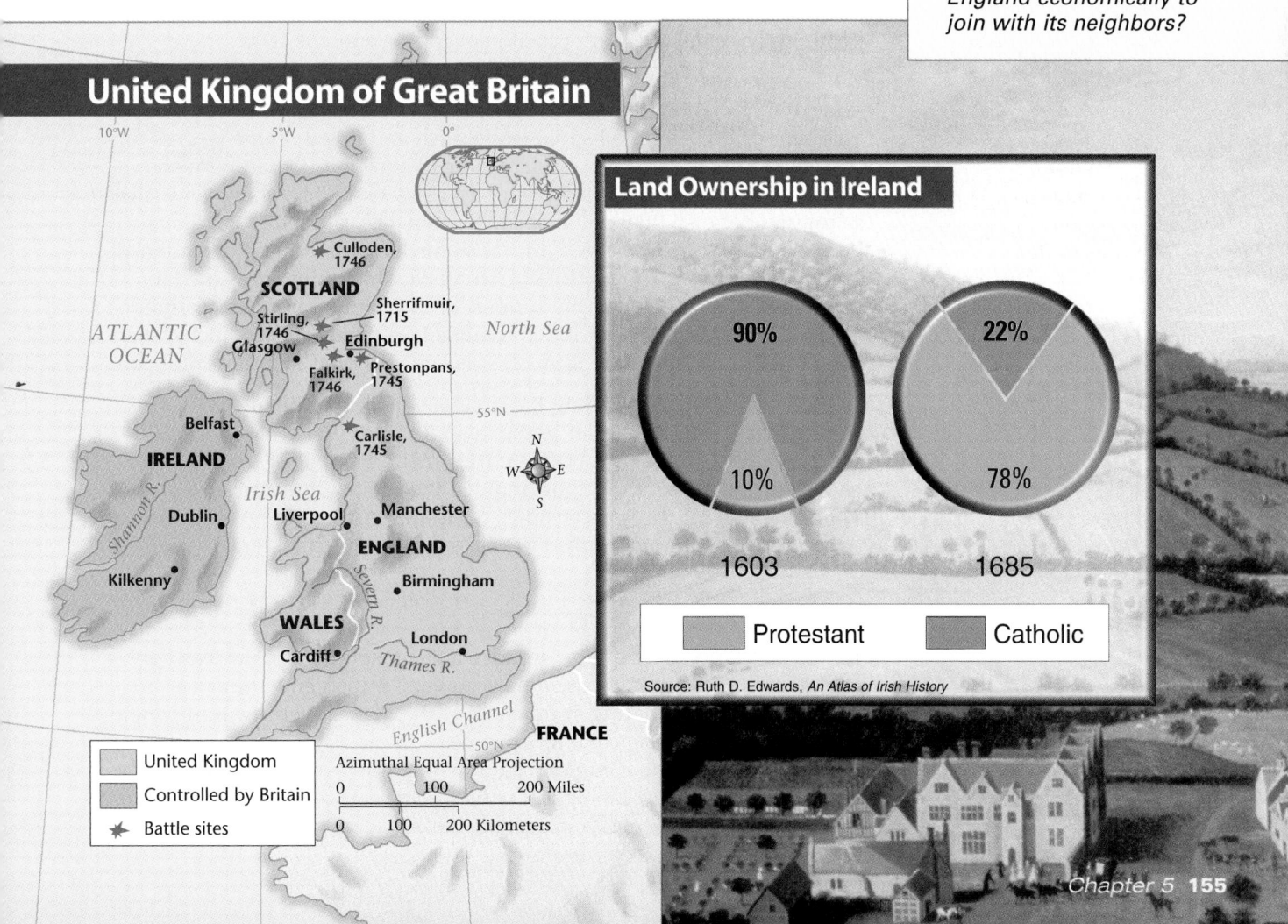

United Kingdom of Great Britain

Culloden, 1746
SCOTLAND
Sherrifmuir, 1715
Stirling, 1746
Edinburgh
Glasgow
Falkirk, 1746
Prestonpans, 1745
ATLANTIC OCEAN
North Sea
Belfast
Carlisle, 1745
IRELAND
Irish Sea
Dublin
Liverpool
Manchester
ENGLAND
Kilkenny
Birmingham
WALES
London
Cardiff
Thames R.
English Channel
FRANCE
Shannon R.
Severn R.

55°N
50°N
10°W 5°W 0°

United Kingdom
Controlled by Britain
Battle sites

Azimuthal Equal Area Projection
0   100   200 Miles
0   100   200 Kilometers

Land Ownership in Ireland

90%   22%
10%   78%
1603   1685

Protestant   Catholic

Source: Ruth D. Edwards, *An Atlas of Irish History*

Political Campaigns
William Hogarth's painting *The Election II—Canvassing for Votes* shows campaigners trying to win votes for their candidates. In England during the 1700s, only men who owned land could vote.

Theme: Political and Social Systems Why might leaders have thought that voting should be limited to landowning men?

sought to preserve older traditions. They supported broad royal powers and a dominant Anglican Church. Whigs backed the policies of the Glorious Revolution. They were more likely to reflect urban business interests, support religious toleration, and favor Parliament over the crown.

These early political parties were unlike the party organizations that we know today. They represented exclusive social circles among rich, powerful men in Parliament. The modern political party, which represents groups of voters and has a distinct platform, did not appear until the 1800s.

The Cabinet System The cabinet, another new feature of government, evolved in the 1700s after the British throne was inherited by a German Protestant prince. George I spoke no English and relied on the leaders in Parliament to help him rule. Under George I and his German-born son George II, a handful of parliamentary advisers set policy. They were called the cabinet because they met in a small room, or "cabinet."

In time, the cabinet gained official status. It was made up of leaders of the majority party in the House of Commons. The cabinet remained in power so long as it enjoyed the support of the Commons. If the Commons voted against a cabinet decision, the cabinet resigned. This cabinet system (also called a parliamentary system) was later adopted by other countries.

The Prime Minister Heading the cabinet was the prime minister. The prime minister was the leader of the majority party in Parliament and in time the chief official of the British government. From 1721 to 1742, the able Whig leader Robert Walpole molded the cabinet into a unified body, requiring all members to agree on major issues. Although the title was not yet used, Walpole is often called Britain's first prime minister.

Politics and Society

The age of Walpole was a time of peace and prosperity. But even as Parliament and the cabinet assumed new powers, British government was far from democratic. Rather, it was an oligarchy—a government in which the ruling power belongs to a few people.

In Britain as on the continent, landowning aristocrats were seen as the "natural" ruling class. The highest nobles held seats in the House of Lords. Other wealthy landowners and rich business leaders in the cities controlled elections to the House of Commons. The right to vote was limited to a relatively few male property owners, and their votes were bought openly.

The lives of most people contrasted sharply with those of the ruling elite. The majority made a meager living from the land. In the 1700s, even that poor existence was threatened. Wealthy landowners bought up farms and took over common lands, evicting tenant farmers and small landowners. Many landless families drifted into towns, where they faced a harsh existence.

A small but growing middle class included successful merchants and manufacturers. They controlled affairs in the towns and cities. Some improved their social standing by marrying into the landed gentry. The middle class also produced talented inventors and entrepreneurs who helped usher in the Industrial Revolution.

George III Reasserts Royal Power

In 1760, George III began a 60-year reign. Unlike his father and grandfather, the new king was born in England. He spoke English and loved Britain. But George was eager to recover the powers the crown had lost. Following his mother's advice, "George, be a king!" he set out to reassert royal power. He wanted to end Whig domination, choose his own ministers, dissolve the cabinet system, and make Parliament follow his will.

Personal Rule Gradually, George found seats in Parliament for "the king's friends." Then, with their help, he began to assert his leadership. Many of his policies, however, would prove disastrous.

After the Seven Years' War, George and his advisers decided that English colonists in North America must pay the costs of their own defense. When colonists protested, Parliament passed harsh measures to force them to obey. In 1775, these and other conflicts triggered the American Revolution, which ended in a loss for Britain.

Cabinet Rule Restored Britain's loss of its American colonies discredited the king. Increasingly, too, he suffered from bouts of mental illness. In the crisis of leadership that followed, cabinet rule was restored in 1788.

In the decades ahead, revolution engulfed France, and Napoleon Bonaparte's armies stormed across Europe, dragging Britain into long wars. During that time, the cabinet controlled the government. The British came to see the prime minister as their real political leader.

George III
This portrait shows the king just a few years after the start of his reign. One of his priorities was to regain power for the throne.

Theme: Art and Literature
What elements of the painting reflect the king's authority?

SECTION 3 Assessment

Recall
1. **Identify:** **(a)** Act of Union, **(b)** Tories, **(c)** Whigs, **(d)** Robert Walpole, **(e)** George III.
2. **Define:** **(a)** constitutional government, **(b)** cabinet, **(c)** prime minister, **(d)** oligarchy.

Comprehension
3. Explain how each of the following contributed to Britain's rise to global power: **(a)** geography, **(b)** success in war, **(c)** attitudes toward business and commerce.

4. How did the British cabinet and office of prime minister develop?
5. What goals did George III have when he became king?

Critical Thinking and Writing
6. **Analyzing Information** How did the British political party system affect most people in Britain?
7. **Predicting Consequences** How might people in Ireland and the American colonies react to British attempts to increase control over those regions?

Activity

Creating a Diagram
Make a diagram showing the relationship among the English crown, prime minister, cabinet, and Parliament during the reigns of George I and George II.

Reading Focus

- What were the chief characteristics of the 13 English colonies?

- How did growing discontent lead to the American Revolution?

- How did the new constitution reflect the ideas of the Enlightenment?

Vocabulary

popular sovereignty

Loyalist

federal republic

Taking Notes

On a sheet of paper draw a time line to show important dates leading up to the emergence of the United States government. Use the time line shown here to help you get started.

French and Indian War ends	Boston Massacre		
1763	**1770**	**1776**	**1789**

Main Idea Colonial opposition to British trade and tax policies led to independence and the founding of the United States of America.

Learn about the American Revolution.

Colonial Unity

Benjamin Franklin created this political cartoon at the beginning of the French and Indian War. The segmented snake represents Britain's colonies in North America.

Theme: Political and Social Systems How does this cartoon suggest Franklin's attitude toward colonial involvement in the war?

JOIN, or DIE.

Setting the Scene

Early in 1776, English colonists in North America eagerly read the newly published *Common Sense*. The pamphlet called on them to declare their independence from Britain. Its author, Thomas Paine, a recent immigrant from England, wrote with passion tempered by reason. "In the following pages," he declared, "I offer nothing more than simple facts, plain arguments, and common sense."

In *Common Sense*, Paine echoed the themes of the Enlightenment. He rejected ancient prejudice and tyranny, while appealing to reason, natural laws, and the promise of freedom. He wrote:

"'Tis repugnant to reason, to the universal order of things, to all examples from former ages, to suppose that this Continent can long remain subject to any external power."

—Thomas Paine, *Common Sense*

Colonists hotly debated Paine's arguments. As resentment of British policies grew, however, many came to agree with his radical ideas.

The 13 English Colonies

By 1750, a string of 13 prosperous colonies stretched along the eastern coast of North America. They were part of Britain's growing empire. Colonial cities such as Boston, New York, and Philadelphia were busy commercial centers that linked North America to the West Indies, Africa, and Europe. Colonial shipyards produced many vessels used in that global trade.

Britain applied mercantilist policies to its colonies. In the 1600s, Parliament had passed the Navigation Acts to regulate colonial trade and manufacturing. For the most part, these acts were not rigorously enforced. Smuggling was common and was not considered a crime by the colonists. Even prominent colonists might gain part of their wealth from smuggled goods.

By the mid-1700s, too, the colonies were home to diverse religious and ethnic groups. Social distinctions were more blurred than in Europe, although government and society were dominated by wealthy landowners and merchants. In politics as in much else, there was a good deal of free discussion. Colonists felt entitled to the rights of English citizens, and their colonial assemblies exercised much control over local affairs.

Although the ways of life between the colonists of New England and those in the south differed, they all shared common values, respect for individual enterprise, and a growing self-confidence. Many also had an increasing sense of their own destiny separate from Britain.

Growing Discontent

After 1763, relations between Britain and the 13 colonies grew strained. The Seven Years' War and the French and Indian War in North America had drained the British treasury. King George III and his advisers thought that the colonists should help pay for the war and for troops still stationed along the frontier. Britain began to enforce the long-neglected laws regulating colonial trade, and Parliament passed new laws to increase the taxes paid by the colonies.

The British measures were not burdensome, but colonists bitterly resented what they saw as an attack on their rights. "No taxation without representation," they protested. Because they had no representatives in Parliament, they believed, Parliament had no right to tax them. Parliament did repeal some of the hated measures, such as a tax on all paper, but in general, it asserted its right to impose taxes on the colonies.

Early Clashes A series of violent clashes intensified the crisis. In March 1770, British soldiers in Boston opened fire on a crowd that was pelting them with stones and snowballs. Colonists called the death of five protesters the "Boston Massacre." In December 1773, a handful of colonists hurled a cargo of recently arrived British tea into the harbor to protest a tax on tea. The incident became known as the Boston Tea Party. When Parliament passed harsh laws to punish Massachusetts for the destruction of the tea, other colonies rallied to oppose the British response.

As tensions increased, fighting spread, representatives from each colony gathered in Philadelphia. There, they met in a Continental Congress to decide what action to take. Members included some extraordinary men. Among the participants were the radical yet fair-minded Massachusetts lawyer John Adams, who had defended at trial the British soldiers involved in the Boston Massacre; Virginia planter and soldier George Washington; and political and social leaders from all 13 colonies.

Declaring Independence The Congress set up a Continental Army, with George Washington in command. In April 1775, the crisis exploded into war. Although many battles ended in British victories, they showed that the Patriots were determined to fight at any cost. In 1776, the Second Continental Congress took a momentous step, voting to declare independence from Britain. Thomas Jefferson of Virginia was the principal author of the Declaration of Independence, a document that clearly reflects the ideas of John Locke.

The Declaration claimed that people had the right "to alter or to abolish" unjust governments—a right to revolt. It also emphasized the principle of popular sovereignty, which states that all government power comes from the people. Jefferson carefully detailed the colonists' grievances against Britain. Because the king had trampled colonists' natural rights, he argued, the colonists had the right to rebel and set up a new government that would protect them. Aware of the risks involved, on July 4, 1776, American leaders adopted the Declaration, pledging "our lives, our fortunes, and our sacred honor" to creating and protecting the new United States of America.

Primary Source

Inspiring Words
The Declaration of Independence stands as one of the most important documents in all of history. It still serves as inspiration for people around the world. Here is one of its most moving passages:

"We hold these truths to be self-evident, that all men are created equal, that they are endowed by their Creator with certain unalienable Rights, that among these are Life, Liberty and the pursuit of Happiness. That to secure these rights, Governments are instituted among Men, deriving their just powers from the consent of the governed; That whenever any Form of Government becomes destructive of these ends it is the Right of the People to alter or to abolish it, and to institute new Government, laying its foundation on such principles and organizing its powers in such form, as to them shall seem most likely to effect their Safety and Happiness."

—Declaration of Independence

Skills Assessment

Primary Source How does this excerpt reflect the ideas of John Locke?

The American Revolution in the East

Map labels:
- Quebec
- Montreal
- St. Lawrence R.
- Fort Ticonderoga, 1775, 1777
- NH
- Saratoga, 1777
- To England, 1776
- Bunker Hill, 1775
- Boston
- MA
- NY
- RI
- CT
- Lexington/Concord, 1775
- Lake Huron
- Lake Ontario
- Lake Erie
- Hudson R.
- Delaware R.
- PA
- NJ
- New York
- Valley Forge, 1777–78
- Trenton, 1776
- From England, 1776
- Brandywine Creek, 1777
- Philadelphia
- MD
- Baltimore
- DE
- Potomac R.
- ATLANTIC OCEAN
- VA
- Yorktown
- Chesapeake Bay
- Yorktown, 1781
- French blockade, 1781
- APPALACHIAN MTS.
- NC
- King's Mountain, 1780
- Moores Creek Bridge, 1776
- Camden, 1780
- SC
- GA
- Charleston
- Savannah

Legend:
- ★ Battle sites
- → Route of American forces
- → Route of British forces

Albers Equal Area Projection
0   250   500 Miles
0   250   500 Kilometers

Skills Assessment

Geography Battles were fought across the colonies, but toward the end of the war, most took place in the southern colonies.

1. **Location** On the map, locate **(a)** Saratoga, **(b)** Valley Forge, **(c)** Yorktown.
2. **Movement** What route did British troops take after landing at Charleston?
3. **Critical Thinking** **Making Inferences** How was the arrival of the French fleet important during the Battle of Yorktown?

The American Revolution

At first, the American cause looked bleak. The British had professional soldiers, a huge fleet, and plentiful money. They occupied most major American cities. Also, about one third of the colonists were Loyalists, who supported Britain. Many others refused to fight for either side.

The Continental Congress had few military resources and little money to pay its soldiers. Still, colonists battling for independence had some advantages. They were fighting on their own soil for their farms and towns. Although the British held New York and Philadelphia, rebels controlled the countryside.

To counteract these advantages, the British worked to create alliances within the colonies. A number of Native American groups sided with the British, while others saw potential advantages in supporting the Patriot cause. Additionally, the British offered freedom to any enslaved people who were willing to fight the colonists.

The French Alliance A turning point in the war came in 1777, when the Americans triumphed over the British at the Battle of Saratoga. This victory persuaded France to join the Americans against its old rival, Britain. The alliance brought the Americans desperately needed supplies, trained soldiers, and French warships. Spurred by the French example, the Netherlands and Spain added their support.

Hard times continued, however. In the brutal winter of 1777–1778, Continental troops at Valley Forge suffered from cold, hunger, and disease. Throughout this crisis and others, Washington proved a patient, courageous, and determined leader able to hold the ragged army together.

Treaty of Paris Finally in 1781, with the help of the French fleet, which blockaded the Chesapeake Bay, Washington forced the surrender of a British army at Yorktown, Virginia. With that defeat, the British war effort crumbled. Two years later, American, British, and French diplomats signed the Treaty of Paris ending the war. In that treaty, Britain recognized the independence of the United States of America. It also accepted the new nation's western frontier as the Mississippi River.

A New Constitution

The national government set up by a document that Americans called the Articles of Confederation was too weak to rule the new United States effectively. To address this problem, the nation's leaders gathered once more in Philadelphia. During the hot summer of 1787, they met in secret to hammer out the Constitution of the United States. This framework for a strong yet flexible government has adapted to changing conditions for more than 200 years.

The Impact of Enlightenment Ideas The framers of the Constitution had absorbed the ideas of Locke, Montesquieu, and Rousseau and had studied history. They saw government in terms of a social contract into which "We the People of the United States" entered. They provided not only for an elective legislature but also for an elected president rather than a hereditary monarch. For the first president, voters would choose George Washington, who had led the army during the war.

The Constitution created a federal republic, with power divided between the federal, or national, government and the states. A central feature of the new federal government was the separation of powers among the legislative, executive, and judicial branches, an idea borrowed directly from Montesquieu. Within that structure, each branch of government was provided with checks and balances on the other branches.

The Bill of Rights, the first 10 amendments to the Constitution, recognized the idea that people had basic rights that the government must protect. These rights included freedom of religion, speech, and the press, as well as the rights to trial by jury and to private property.

Limited Freedom In 1789, the Constitution became the supreme law of the land. It set up a representative government with an elected legislature to reflect the wishes of the governed.

Yet most Americans at the time did not have the right to vote. Only white men who were able to meet certain property requirements could vote. Women could not cast a ballot, nor could African Americans—enslaved *or* free—or Native Americans. It would take more than a century of struggle before the right to vote and equal protection under the law were extended to all adult Americans.

Looking Ahead

Despite these limitations, the Constitution of the United States created the most progressive government of its day. From the start, the new republic shone as a symbol of freedom to European countries and to reformers in Latin America. Its constitution would be copied or adapted by many lands throughout the world.

The Enlightenment ideals that had inspired American colonists brought changes in Europe, too. In 1789, a revolution in France toppled the monarchy in the name of liberty and equality. Before long, other Europeans took up the cry for freedom. By the mid-1800s, most absolute monarchs across Europe would see their powers greatly reduced.

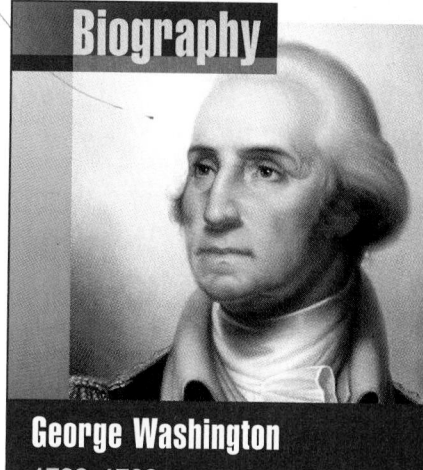

Biography

George Washington
1732–1799

As president, George Washington acted on the Enlightenment ideals given form in the Constitution. Some leaders felt that the president should have a grand title. Instead, Washington chose to be addressed as "Mr. President." He believed that a simple form of address was more appropriate for the leader of a republic.

Toward the end of his second term in office, some hoped that he would run again, becoming a president for life. Again, Washington disagreed. Later presidents followed this example. No president would run for a third term until 1940—nearly 150 years after Washington left office.

Theme: Impact of the Individual How did Washington's presidency reflect the ideas of the Enlightenment?

SECTION 4 Assessment

Recall
1. **Identify:** (a) Navigation Acts, (b) Continental Congress, (c) George Washington, (d) Battle of Saratoga, (e) Treaty of Paris of 1783, (f) Bill of Rights.
2. **Define:** (a) popular sovereignty, (b) Loyalist, (c) federal republic.

Comprehension
3. Describe colonial law, society, and politics in the mid-1700s.
4. Explain why conflict between the colonists and Britain increased after 1763.
5. Give an example of how Enlightenment ideas were reflected in each of the following: (a) the Declaration of Independence, (b) the United States Constitution.

Critical Thinking and Writing
6. **Analyzing Information** Describe the idea of separation of powers. Then, give two examples of how your life would be different if the Constitution did not guarantee separation of powers.
7. **Recognizing Point of View** What reasons might a Loyalist have for opposing the American Revolution?

Go Online
PHSchool.com

Use the Internet to research the Battle of Saratoga during the American Revolution. Then, write a letter that an American officer might have written home describing the battle and its significance. For help with this activity, use **Web Code mkd-1863.**

Creating a Chapter Summary

On a sheet of paper, draw a web like the one shown here. Add information to the empty circles to help you recall important ideas of the Enlightenment and important ideas from the Enlightenment that were used in the American Constitution.

For additional review and enrichment activities, see the interactive version of *World History* available on the Web and on CD-ROM.

For practice test questions for Chapter 5, use **Web Code mka-1864**.

Building Vocabulary

Classify each of the chapter vocabulary words listed below under *one* of the following themes: art and literature; political and social systems; religions and value systems.

1. natural law
2. *philosophe*
3. enlightened despot
4. baroque
5. rococo
6. constitutional government
7. cabinet
8. prime minister
9. Loyalist
10. federal republic

Recalling Key Facts

11. According to John Locke, what should happen if a government violates people's natural rights?
12. According to Adam Smith, how should wages and prices be regulated?
13. How did serfdom differ in Eastern and Western Europe?
14. What areas combined to form the United Kingdom of Great Britain?
15. How did taxation create tensions between the American colonies and the British government?

Critical Thinking and Writing

16. **Linking Past and Present** Today, we talk about human rights rather than natural rights. **(a)** Describe a human rights issue that has been in the news recently. **(b)** Choose one *philosophe* from this chapter and describe how he or she might respond to the issue.
17. **Analyzing Information** **(a)** What ideas about government do you think English settlers brought with them to the Americas? **(b)** How might those ideas have contributed to the outbreak of the American Revolution?
18. **Defending a Position** During the American Revolution, Thomas Paine used the following words to encourage the colonists during a particularly grim time: "What we obtain too cheaply, we esteem too light; it is [costliness] only that gives everything its value." **(a)** What did he mean by this? **(b)** Do you agree or disagree? Give an example to defend your position.
19. **Connecting to Geography** **(a)** During the American Revolution, how did the location of the war help the Americans? **(b)** Why was it a problem for the British?

This passage is from a selection by Voltaire titled "Tolerance." In it, Voltaire describes people who abuse their power. In the first part of the excerpt, he uses the first person, "I," to show how these people think. In the remainder, he uses the third person, "they," to describe the effects of their actions on others. Read the passage, then answer the questions that follow.

"I possess a dignity and power founded on ignorance; I walk on the heads of the men who lie at my feet; if they should rise and look me in the face, I am lost; I must bind them to the ground, therefore, with iron chains. Thus have reasoned the men whom centuries of bigotry have made powerful. They have other powerful men beneath them, and these have still others, who all grow rich with the spoils of the poor, grow fat on their blood, and laugh at their stupidity. They all hate tolerance, as . . . tyrants dread the word liberty."

—Voltaire, *Philosophical Dictionary*

20. Why would people who abuse their power be "lost" if others were to "rise and look me in the face"?
21. What do you think Voltaire meant by the phrase "grow fat on their blood"?
22. What is Voltaire's tone in this passage? How does it suggest Voltaire's own beliefs?
23. Who are some of the intolerant people Voltaire might have had in mind when he wrote this?
24. **(a)** Identify a simile used in this excerpt. **(b)** Identify a metaphor in the excerpt.

Skills Tip

To illustrate a point, authors may use similes and metaphors. A simile is a description that uses "like" or "as" to draw comparisons. A metaphor uses the comparison as the description itself.

Go Online
PHSchool.com

Use the Internet to research one of the political thinkers described in the text. Then, write a letter to that person explaining whether you think his or her ideas continue to be relevant in the present day. For help with this activity, use **Web Code mkd-1865**.

SEPARATION OF POWERS

Executive Branch
(President)
Carries out laws
Proposes laws
Can veto laws
Negotiates foreign treaties
Serves as commander in chief of the armed forces
Appoints federal judges, ambassadors, and other high officials
Can grant pardons to federal offenders

Legislative Branch
(Congress)
Passes laws
Can override President's veto
Approves treaties and presidential appointments
Can impeach and remove President and other high officials
Creates lower federal courts
Appropriates money
Prints and coins money
Raises and supports the armed forces
Can declare war
Regulates foreign and interstate trade

Judicial Branch
(Supreme Court and Other Federal Courts)
Interprets laws
Can declare laws unconstitutional
Can declare executive actions unconstitutional

This table shows the powers held by each branch of the United States government. Study the table and answer the following questions:

25. Who heads the executive branch?
26. What is the main role of the legislative branch?
27. In 1748, Montesquieu wrote, "There is no liberty, if the power of judging is not separated from the legislative and executive powers. Were it joined with the legislative, the life and liberty of the subject would be exposed to arbitrary control, for the judge would then be the legislator. Were it joined to the executive power, the judge might behave with all the violence of an oppressor." How does this table relate to Montesquieu's statement?

The French Revolution and Napoleon
1789–1815

Chapter Preview

1 On the Eve of Revolution
2 Creating a New France
3 Radical Days
4 The Age of Napoleon Begins
5 The End of an Era

1793

During the Reign of Terror, which begins in 1793, the guillotine is used to execute thousands of French citizens.

1789

After a battle with royal troops, Parisians capture the Bastille on July 14, 1789.

1799

Napoleon overthrows the Directory.

CHAPTER EVENTS

1790   1795   1800

GLOBAL EVENTS

1789 The United States Constitution is ratified.

1793 China rejects British trade offer.

Revolutionary France at War, 1793

France, 1793

Allied countries against France

Boundary of Holy Roman Empire

By 1793, the French Revolution had plunged France into a general European war that would last on and off for more than 20 years and transform Europe.

IRELAND

GREAT BRITAIN

North Sea

KINGDOM OF DENMARK AND NORWAY

SWEDEN

PRUSSIA

NETHERLANDS

HANOVER

AUSTRIAN NETHERLANDS

PRUSSIA

PRUSSIA

Vistula R.

POLAND

RUSSIAN EMPIRE

Baltic Sea

SAXONY

Oder R.

Rhine R.

Elbe R.

PRUSSIA

BAVARIA

AUSTRIA

HUNGARY

ATLANTIC OCEAN

50°N

FRANCE

Seine R.

Loire R.

SWISS CONFED.

ALPS

Rhône R.

Po R.

VENETIAN REPUBLIC

Adriatic Sea

PAPAL STATES

Tiber R.

O T T O M A N   E M P I R E

Danube R.

PYRENEES MTS.

PORTUGAL

Tagus R.

SPAIN

Ebro R.

KINGDOM OF SARDINIA

40°N

10°W

0°

Mediterranean Sea

10°E

KINGDOM OF NAPLES

20°E

Azimuthal Equal Area Projection

0   150   300 Miles

0   150   300 Kilometers

N
W   E
S

1804

In a magnificent ceremony, Napoleon crowns himself emperor of the French.

1812

Napoleon invades Russia.

1815

Napoleon abdicates after British and Prussian forces defeat him at Waterloo. The Duke of Wellington is the victorious British general.

1805

1810

1815

1804 Haiti declares independence from France.

1812 The United States declares war on Britain.

On the Eve of Revolution

Reading Focus

- What was the social structure of the old regime?

- Why did France face economic troubles in 1789?

- Why did Louis XVI call the Estates General?

- Why did a Paris crowd storm the Bastille?

Vocabulary

bourgeoisie

deficit spending

Taking Notes

As you read this section, create a chart to identify causes of the French Revolution. Use the incomplete chart below as a model. Add more arrows for causes if you need them.

Burden of debt

THE FRENCH REVOLUTION

Main Idea Social unrest, economic troubles, and the desire for political reforms led to the French Revolution.

Setting the Scene On April 28, 1789, unrest exploded at a Paris wallpaper factory. A rumor had spread that the factory owner was planning to cut wages even though bread prices were soaring. Enraged workers vandalized the owner's home. Later, they stopped some nobles returning from an afternoon at the racetrack. They forced the nobles to shout: "Long live the Third Estate [the common people]!"

Riots like these did not worry most nobles. They knew that France faced a severe economic crisis but thought that financial reforms would ease the problem. Then, rioters would be hanged, as they deserved.

The nobles were wrong. The crisis went deeper than government finances. Reform would not be enough. By July, the hungry, unemployed, and poorly paid people of Paris had taken up arms. Their actions would push events further and faster than anyone could have foreseen.

The Old Regime

In 1789, France, like the rest of Europe, still clung to an outdated social system that had emerged in the Middle Ages. Under this *ancien regime,* or old order, everyone in France belonged to one of three classes: the First Estate, made up of the clergy; the Second Estate, made up of the nobility; or the Third Estate, the vast majority of the population.

The Clergy In the Middle Ages, the Church had exerted great influence throughout Christian Europe. In 1789, the French clergy still enjoyed enormous wealth and privilege. The Church owned about 10 percent of the land, collected tithes, and paid no direct taxes to the state. High Church leaders such as bishops and abbots were usually nobles who lived very well. Parish priests, however, often came from humble origins and might be as poor as their peasant congregations.

The First Estate did provide some social services. Nuns, monks, and priests ran schools, hospitals, and orphanages. But during the Enlightenment, *philosophes* targeted the Church for reform. They criticized the idleness of some clergy, Church interference in politics, and its intolerance of dissent. In response, many clergy condemned the Enlightenment for undermining religion and moral order.

The Nobles The Second Estate was the titled nobility of French society. In the Middle Ages, noble knights had defended the land. In the 1600s, Richelieu and Louis XIV had crushed the nobles' military power but given them other rights—under strict royal control. Those rights included top jobs in government, the army, the courts, and the Church.

At Versailles, ambitious nobles competed for royal appointments while idle courtiers enjoyed endless entertainments. Many nobles, however, lived far from the center of power. Though they owned land, they had little money income. As a result, they felt the pinch of trying to maintain their status in a period of rising prices.

Many nobles hated absolutism and resented the royal bureaucracy that employed middle-class men in positions that once had been reserved for the aristocracy. They feared losing their traditional privileges, especially their freedom from paying taxes.

The Third Estate In 1789, the Third Estate numbered about 27 million people, or 98 percent of the population. It was a diverse group. At the top sat the bourgeoisie (boor zhwah ZEE), or middle class. The bourgeoisie included prosperous bankers, merchants, and manufacturers. It also included the officials who staffed the royal bureaucracy, as well as lawyers, doctors, journalists, professors, and skilled artisans.

The bulk of the Third Estate—9 out of 10 people in France—were rural peasants. Some were prosperous landowners who hired laborers to work for them. Others were tenant farmers or day laborers.

The poorest members of the Third Estate were urban workers. They included apprentices, journeymen, and others who worked in industries such as printing or clothmaking. Many women and men earned a meager living as servants, stable hands, porters, construction workers, or street sellers of everything from food to pots and pans. A large number of the urban poor were unemployed. To survive, some turned to begging or crime.

Discontent From rich to poor, members of the Third Estate resented the privileges enjoyed by their social "betters." Wealthy bourgeois families could buy political office and even titles, but the best jobs were still reserved for nobles. Urban workers earned miserable wages. Even the smallest rise in the price of bread, their main food, brought the threat of greater hunger or even starvation.

The Old Regime
In this cartoon, a priest and a noble stand on a stone crushing a peasant. The stone represents burdensome taxes and feudal dues. Taken together, the pie graphs below show inequalities among France's three estates.

Theme: Political and Social Systems Why did the Third Estate consider the distribution of land unfair?

Population and Land Ownership in France, 1789

Population by Estate

98%
1.5%
0.5%

First Estate
Second Estate
Third Estate

Land Owned by Estate

70%
20%
10%

Bread Riots in France
The British embassy in Paris sent regular reports to London. The excerpts below describe the effects of rising bread prices:

"November 27, 1788
The price of bread has again been raised . . . the consequences of which has already been felt in the instance of more than 40 bakers having been obliged to shut up shop. In the provinces these discontents have still risen higher. . . . The public magazines of wheat have been broken open and pillaged.

December 11, 1788
Bread has again been raised. . . . The distress of the poor is already very great as may be conceived, and the unusual severity of the weather is at this moment pecu-liarly unfortunate for them; nor on this account, is it very surprising that robberies should be frequent, which at present is the case in an alarming degree. It is by no means safe to walk the streets late in the evening."

—O. Browning, *Dispatches from Paris*

Skills Assessment

Primary Source What were the effects of the rising prices?

Peasants were burdened by taxes on everything from land to soap to salt. Though they were technically free, many owed fees and services that dated back to medieval times, such as the corvée (kohr VAY), which was unpaid labor to repair roads and bridges. Peasants were also incensed when nobles, hurt by rising prices, tried to reimpose old manor dues. Also, only nobles had the right to hunt wild game. Peasants were even forbidden to kill rabbits that ate their crops.

In towns and cities, Enlightenment ideas led people to question the inequalities of the old regime. Why, people demanded, should the first two estates have such great privileges at the expense of the majority? It did not meet the test of reason! Throughout France, the Third Estate called for the privileged classes to pay their share.

Economic Troubles

Economic woes added to the social unrest and heightened tensions. One of the causes of the decline was a mushrooming financial crisis that was due in part to years of deficit spending, that is, a government's spending more money than it takes in.

The Burden of Debt Louis XIV had left France deeply in debt. Wars like the Seven Years' War and the American Revolution strained the treasury even further. Costs generally had risen in the 1700s, and the lavish court soaked up millions. To bridge the gap between income and expenses, the government borrowed more and more money. By 1789, half its tax income went just to pay interest on this enormous debt.

To solve the financial crisis, the government would have to increase taxes, reduce expenses, or both. However, the nobles and clergy fiercely resisted any attempt to end their exemption from taxes.

Poor Harvests Other economic troubles added to the financial crisis. A general economic decline had begun in the 1770s. Then, in the late 1780s, bad harvests sent food prices soaring and brought hunger to poorer peasants and city dwellers.

Hard times and lack of food inflamed these people. In towns, people rioted, demanding bread. In the countryside, peasants began to attack the manor houses of the nobles. Arthur Young, an English visitor to France, witnessed the violence:

"Everything conspires to render the present period in France critical: the [lack] of bread is terrible; accounts arrive every moment from the provinces of riots and disturbances, and calling in the military, to preserve the peace of the markets."
—Arthur Young, *Travels in France During the Years 1787–1789*

Failure of Reform The heirs of Louis XIV were not the right men to solve the economic crisis that afflicted France. Louis XV, who ruled from 1715 to 1774, pursued pleasure before serious business and ran up more debts. His grandson, Louis XVI, was well-meaning but weak and indecisive. He wise-ly chose Jacques Necker, a financial wizard, as an adviser. Necker urged the king to reduce extravagant court spending, reform government, and abol-ish burdensome tariffs on internal trade. When Necker proposed taxing the First and Second estates, however, the nobles and high clergy forced the king to dismiss the would-be reformer.

As the crisis deepened, the pressure for reform mounted. Finally, the wealthy and powerful classes demanded that the king summon the Estates General before making any changes. French kings had not called the Estates General for 175 years, fearing that nobles would use it to recover the feudal powers that they had lost under absolute rule. To reform-minded nobles, the Estates General seemed to offer a chance to carry out changes

Virtual Field Trip

Go Online
PHSchool.com

For: Other works by Jacques Louis David
Visit: PHSchool.com
Web Code: mkd-1971

The Tennis Court Oath
In this painting, Jacques Louis David captures the moment when delegates at the National Assembly took the Tennis Court Oath.

Theme: Continuity and Change Why did the Third Estate want to change the voting system used in the Estates General?

like those that had come with the Glorious Revolution in England. They hoped that they could bring the absolute monarch under the control of the nobles and guarantee their own privileges.

Louis XVI Calls the Estates General

As 1788 came to a close, France tottered on the verge of bankruptcy. Bread riots were spreading, and nobles, fearful of taxes, were denouncing royal tyranny. A baffled Louis XVI finally summoned the Estates General to meet at Versailles the following year.

The Cahiers In preparation, Louis had all three estates prepare *cahiers* (kah YAY), or notebooks, listing their grievances. Many cahiers called for reforms such as fairer taxes, freedom of the press, or regular meetings of the Estates General. In one town, shoemakers denounced regulations that made leather so expensive they could not afford to make shoes. Some peasants demanded the right to kill animals that were destroying their crops. Servant girls in the city of Toulouse demanded the right to leave service when they wanted and that "after a girl has served her master for many years, she receive some reward for her service."

The cahiers testified to boiling class resentments. One called tax collectors "bloodsuckers of the nation who drink the tears of the unfortunate from goblets of gold." Another one of the cahiers condemned the courts of nobles as "vampires pumping the last drop of blood" from the people. Another complained that "20 million must live on half the wealth of France while the clergy . . . devour the other half."

The Tennis Court Oath Delegates to the Estates General from the Third Estate were elected, though only propertied men could vote. Thus, they were mostly lawyers, middle-class officials, and writers. They were familiar with the writings of Voltaire, Rousseau, and other *philosophes.* They went to Versailles not only to solve the financial crisis but also to insist on reform.

The Estates General convened in May 1789. From the start, the delegates were deadlocked over the issue of voting. Traditionally, each estate had met and voted separately. Each group had one vote. Under this system, the First and Second estates always outvoted the Third Estate two to one.

This time, the Third Estate wanted all three estates to meet in a single body, with votes counted "by head."

After weeks of stalemate, delegates of the Third Estate took a daring step. Claiming to represent the people of France, they declared themselves to be the National Assembly. They then invited delegates from the other estates to help them write a constitution, a document that describes the basic rules and laws of government.

A few days later, the National Assembly found its meeting hall locked and guarded. Fearing that the king planned to dismiss them, the delegates moved to a nearby indoor tennis court. As curious spectators looked on, the delegates took their famous Tennis Court Oath. They swore "never to separate and to meet wherever the circumstances might require until we have established a sound and just constitution."

When reform-minded clergy and nobles joined the Assembly, Louis XVI grudgingly accepted it. But royal troops gathered around Paris, and rumors spread that the king planned to dissolve the Assembly.

Suspicion and rumor continued to poison the atmosphere as the crisis deepened in early July. The king, who had brought back Necker to deal with the financial crisis, again dismissed the popular minister. Food shortages were also getting worse because of the disastrous harvest of 1788.

Storming the Bastille

On July 14, 1789, Paris seized the spotlight from the National Assembly meeting in Versailles. The streets buzzed with rumors that royal troops were going to occupy the capital. More than 800 Parisians assembled outside the Bastille, a grim medieval fortress used as a prison for political and other prisoners. The crowd was demanding weapons and gunpowder believed to be stored there.

The commander of the Bastille refused to open the gates and opened fire on the crowd. In the battle that followed, many people were killed. Finally, the enraged mob broke through the defenses. They killed the commander and five guards and released a handful of prisoners, but found no weapons.

When told of the attack, Louis XVI asked, "Is it a revolt?" "No, sire," replied a noble. "It is a revolution." The storming of the Bastille quickly became a symbol of the French Revolution. Supporters saw it as a blow to tyranny, a step toward freedom. Today, the French still celebrate July 14 as Bastille Day, the French national holiday.

SECTION 1 Assessment

Recall

1. **Identify:** (a) *ancien regime,* (b) Jacques Necker, (c) cahiers, (d) Tennis Court Oath, (e) National Assembly, (f) Bastille.
2. **Define:** (a) bourgeoisie, (b) deficit spending.

Comprehension

3. Why were members of the Third Estate discontented with conditions under the old regime?
4. What economic troubles did France have in 1789?
5. What issues arose when Louis XVI called the Estates General in 1789?
6. What was the significance of the storming of the Bastille?

Critical Thinking and Writing

7. **Understanding Sequence** List key decisions and events of 1788 and 1789 in the order in which they occurred. Briefly explain the significance or effects of each decision and event in your list.
8. **Defending a Position** Suppose that you are Jacques Necker. Write a paragraph or two explaining how your economic reform program will benefit France.

Activity

Writing a Cahier
Imagine that you belong to one of the following groups in 1789 France: nobles, high clergy, parish priests, bourgeoisie, peasants, urban workers. Write a cahier describing who you are and what you think is the chief problem facing the nation.

Creating a New France

Reading Focus

- How did popular revolts contribute to the French Revolution?

- What moderate reforms did the National Assembly enact?

- How did foreign reaction to the revolution help lead to war?

Vocabulary

faction

émigré

republic

Taking Notes

As you read this section, prepare an outline following this model. Use Roman numerals for major headings, capital letters for subheadings, and numbers for supporting details.

   I. **Revolts in Paris and the provinces**
      A. The Great Fear
         1. Inflamed by famine and rumors
         2.
      B. Paris in arms
   II. **Moderate reforms**

Main Idea The National Assembly instituted political and social reforms in the moderate first stage of the revolution.

Setting the Scene Excitement, wonder, and fear engulfed France as the revolution unfolded at home and spread abroad. Today, historians divide this revolutionary era into four phases. The moderate phase of the National Assembly (1789–1791) turned France into a constitutional monarchy. Then, a phase (1792–1793) of escalating violence led to a Reign of Terror (1793-1794). There followed a period of reaction against extremism, known as the Directory (1795–1799). Finally, the Age of Napoleon (1799–1815) consolidated many revolutionary changes. In this section, you will read about the moderate start of the French Revolution.

Revolts in Paris and the Provinces

The political crisis of 1789 coincided with the worst famine in memory. Starving peasants roamed the countryside or flocked to the towns, where they swelled the ranks of the unemployed. As grain prices soared, even people with jobs had to spend up to 80 percent of their income on bread.

The Great Fear In such desperate times, rumors ran wild and set off what was later called the "Great Fear." Tales of attacks on villages and towns spread panic. Other rumors asserted that government troops were seizing peasant crops.

Inflamed by famine and fear, peasants unleashed their fury on nobles who were trying to reimpose medieval dues. Defiant peasants attacked the homes of nobles, set fire to old manor records, and stole grain from storehouses. The violent attacks died down after a period of time, but they clearly demonstrated peasant anger with an unjust regime.

Paris in Arms Paris, too, was in turmoil. As the capital and chief city of France, it was the revolutionary center. A variety of factions, or small groups, competed to gain power. Moderates looked to the Marquis de Lafayette, the aristocratic "hero of two worlds" who had fought alongside George Washington in the American Revolution. Lafayette headed the National Guard, a largely middle-class militia organized in response to the arrival of royal troops in Paris. The Guard was the first group to don the tricolor—a red, white, and blue badge which was eventually adopted as the national flag of France.

Paris in Arms
In this engraving, an angry mob of men and women march through the streets of Paris.

Theme: Geography and History Why do you think Paris was the center of the French Revolution?

Global Connections

The American Revolution and the French Revolution

The Marquis de Lafayette and Thomas Paine were leading figures in both the American and French revolutions. Lafayette, a French nobleman and military commander, helped the Americans defeat the British at Yorktown. He admired the American Declaration of Independence and American democratic ideals. With these in mind, Lafayette wrote the first draft of the French Declaration of the Rights of Man and the Citizen.

Thomas Paine was a famous American patriot and writer whose ideas in *Common Sense* had a great influence on the American Revolution. During the French Revolution, Paine moved to France. There, he defended the ideals of the revolution and was elected to serve in the revolutionary government.

Theme: Political and Social Systems How did the American Revolution influence the French Revolution?

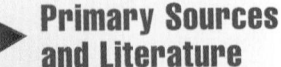

Primary Sources and Literature

See the "Declaration of the Rights of Man and the Citizen" in the Reference Section at the back of this book.

A more radical group, the Paris Commune, replaced the royalist government of the city. It could mobilize whole neighborhoods for protests or violent action to further the revolution. Newspapers and political clubs—many even more radical than the Commune—blossomed everywhere. Some demanded an end to the monarchy and spread scandalous stories about the royal family and members of the court.

Moderate Reforms

Peasant uprisings and the storming of the Bastille stampeded the National Assembly into action. On August 4, in a combative all-night meeting, nobles in the National Assembly voted to end their privileges. They agreed to give up their old manorial dues, exclusive hunting rights, special legal status, and exemption from taxes.

An End to Special Privilege "Feudalism is abolished," announced the proud and weary delegates at 2 A.M. As the president of the Assembly later observed, "We may view this moment as the dawn of a new revolution, when all the burdens weighing on the people were abolished, and France was truly reborn."

Were the votes on the night of August 4 voluntary? Both contemporary observers and modern historians note that the nobles gave up nothing that they had not already lost. In the months ahead, the National Assembly turned the reforms of August 4 into law, meeting a key Enlightenment goal—the equality of all citizens before the law.

Declaration of the Rights of Man In late August, as a first step toward writing a constitution, the Assembly issued the Declaration of the Rights of Man and the Citizen. The document was modeled in part on the American Declaration of Independence, written 13 years earlier. All men, the French declaration announced, were "born and remain free and equal in rights." They enjoyed natural rights to "liberty, property, security, and resistance to oppression." Like the writings of Locke and the *philosophes*, the constitution insisted that governments exist to protect the natural rights of citizens.

The Declaration further proclaimed that all male citizens were equal before the law. Every Frenchman had an equal right to hold public office "with no distinction other than that of their virtues and talents." In addition, the Declaration asserted freedom of religion and called for taxes to be levied according to ability to pay. Its principles were captured in the enduring slogan of the French Revolution, "Liberty, Equality, Fraternity."

Uncertain and hesitant, Louis XVI was slow to accept the reforms of the National Assembly. Parisians grew suspicious as more royal troops arrived. Nobles continued to enjoy gala banquets while people were starving. By autumn, anger again turned to action.

Women March on Versailles On October 5, thousands of women streamed down the road that led from Paris to Versailles. "Bread!" they shouted. They demanded to see the king.

Much of the crowd's anger was directed at the queen, Marie Antoinette. Ever since she had married Louis in 1770, she had come under attack for being frivolous and extravagant. She eventually grew more serious and even advised the king to compromise with moderate reformers. Still, she remained a source of scandal. Early in the revolution, the radical press spread the story that she had answered the cries of hungry people for bread by saying, "Let them eat cake." Though the story was untrue, it helped inflame feelings against the queen.

The women refused to leave Versailles until the king met their most important demand—to return to Paris. Not too happily, the king agreed. The next morning, the crowd, with the king in tow, set out for the city. At the head of the procession rode women perched on the barrels of seized cannons. They told bewildered spectators that they were bringing Louis XVI, Marie Antoinette, and their son back to Paris. "Now we won't have to go so far when we want to see our king," they sang. Crowds along the way cheered the king, who now wore the tricolor.

In Paris, the royal family moved into the Tuileries (TWEE luh reez) palace. For the next three years, Louis was a virtual prisoner.

The National Assembly Presses Onward

The National Assembly soon followed the king to Paris. Its largely bourgeois members worked to draft a constitution and to solve the continuing financial crisis. To pay off the huge government debt—much of it owed to the bourgeoisie—the Assembly voted to take over and sell Church lands.

Reorganizing the Church In an even more radical move, the National Assembly put the French Catholic Church under state control. Under the Civil Constitution of the Clergy, issued in 1790, bishops and priests became elected, salaried officials. The Civil Constitution ended papal authority over the French Church and dissolved convents and monasteries.

Reaction was swift and angry. Many bishops and priests refused to accept the Civil Constitution. The pope condemned it. Large numbers of French peasants, who were conservative concerning religion, also rejected the changes. When the government punished clergy who refused to support the Civil Constitution, a huge gulf opened between revolutionaries in Paris and the peasantry in the provinces.

Constitution of 1791 The National Assembly completed its main task by producing a constitution. The Constitution of 1791 set up a limited monarchy in place of the absolute monarchy that had ruled France for centuries. A new Legislative Assembly had the power to make laws, collect taxes, and decide on issues of war and peace. Lawmakers would be elected by taxpaying male citizens. Still, only about 50,000 men in a population of more than 27 million could qualify as candidates to run for the Assembly.

To make government more efficient, the constitution replaced the old provinces with 83 departments of roughly equal size. It abolished the old provincial courts, and it reformed laws. The middle-class framers of the constitution protected private property and supported free trade. They compensated nobles for land seized by the peasants, abolished guilds, and forbade urban workers to organize labor unions.

Women March on Versailles
As famine gripped Paris, poor mothers did not have enough food for their children. On October 5, 1789, thousands of women decided to bring Louis XVI to Paris, where he could no longer ignore their suffering.

Theme: Continuity and Change Based on this painting, in what ways do you think the march challenged traditional roles of women?

REFORMS OF THE NATIONAL ASSEMBLY

Political

- Proclaimed all male citizens equal before the law
- Limited the power of the monarchy
- Established the Legislative Assembly to make laws
- Granted all tax-paying male citizens the right to elect members of the Legislative Assembly

Social and Economic

- Abolished special privileges of the nobility
- Announced an end to feudalism
- Called for taxes to be levied according to ability to pay
- Abolished guilds and forbade labor unions
- Compensated nobles for lands seized by peasants

Religious

- Declared freedom of religion
- Took over and sold Church lands
- Placed the French Catholic Church under control of the state
- Provided that bishops and priests be elected and receive government salaries

To moderate reformers, the Constitution of 1791 seemed to complete the revolution. Reflecting Enlightenment goals, it ended Church interference in government and ensured equality before the law for all male citizens. At the same time, it put power in the hands of men with the means and leisure to serve in government.

Louis's Failed Flight Meanwhile, Marie Antoinette and others had been urging the king to escape their humiliating situation. Louis finally gave in. One night in June 1791, a coach rolled north from Paris toward the border. Inside sat the king disguised as a servant, the queen dressed as a governess, and the royal children.

The attempted escape failed. In a town along the way, Louis's disguise was uncovered by someone who held up a piece of currency with the king's face on it. A company of soldiers escorted the royal family back to Paris, as onlooking crowds hurled insults at the king. To many, Louis's dash to the border showed that he was a traitor to the revolution.

Reaction Outside France

Events in France stirred debate all over Europe. Supporters of the Enlightenment applauded the reforms of the National Assembly. They saw the French experiment as the dawn of a new age for justice and equality. European rulers and nobles, however, denounced the French Revolution.

Widespread Fears European rulers increased border patrols to stop the spread of the "French plague." Fueling those fears were the horror stories that were told by émigrés (EHM ih grayz)—nobles, clergy, and others who had fled France and its revolutionary forces. Émigrés reported attacks on their privileges, their property, their religion, and even their lives. "Enlightened" rulers turned against French ideas. Catherine the Great of Russia burned Voltaire's letters and locked up her critics.

In Britain, Edmund Burke, who earlier had defended the American Revolution, bitterly condemned revolutionaries in Paris. He predicted all too accurately that the revolution would become more violent. "Plots and assassinations," he wrote, "will be anticipated by preventive murder and preventive confiscation." Burke warned: "When ancient opinions and rules of life are taken away . . . we have no compass to govern us."

Threats From Abroad The failed escape of Louis XVI brought further hostile rumblings from abroad. In August 1791, the king of Prussia and the emperor of Austria—who was Marie Antoinette's brother—issued the Declaration of Pilnitz. In this document, the two monarchs threatened to intervene to protect the French monarchy. The declaration may have been mostly bluff, but revolutionaries in France took the threat seriously and prepared for war. The revolution was about to enter a new, more radical phase of change and conflict.

War at Home and Abroad

In October 1791, the newly elected Legislative Assembly took office. Faced with crises at home and abroad, it would survive for less than a year. Economic problems fed renewed turmoil. Assignats, the revolutionary currency, dropped in value, which caused prices to rise rapidly. Uncertainty about prices led to hoarding and additional food shortages.

Internal Divisions   In Paris and other cities, working-class men and women, called sans-culottes* (sanz kyoo LAHTZ), pushed the revolution into more radical action. By 1791, many sans-culottes demanded a republic, or government ruled not by a monarch, but by elected representatives.

Within the Legislative Assembly, several hostile factions competed for power. The sans-culottes found support among radicals in the Legislative Assembly, especially the Jacobins. A revolutionary political club, the Jacobins were mostly middle-class lawyers or intellectuals. They used pamphleteers and sympathetic newspaper editors to advance the republican cause. Opposing the radicals were moderate reformers and political officials who wanted no more reforms at all.

War on Tyranny   The radicals soon held the upper hand in the Legislative Assembly. In April 1792, the war of words between French revolutionaries and European monarchs moved onto the battlefield. Eager to spread the revolution and destroy tyranny abroad, the Legislative Assembly declared war first on Austria, then on Prussia, Britain, and other states. The great powers expected to win an easy victory against France, a land divided by revolution. In fact, however, the fighting that began in 1792 lasted on and off until 1815.

---

*Sans-culottes means "without culottes," the fancy knee breeches worn by upper-class men. Shopkeepers, artisans, and other working-class men wore trousers, not culottes.

Connections to Today

Knowing Left From Right

Have you ever wondered how political positions came to be described as *right* or *left*?

It began in France's Legislative Assembly in 1791. Members with similar views always sat together in the meeting hall in Paris. On the right sat those who felt that reform had gone far enough; some even wanted to turn the clock back to 1788. In the center of the hall sat supporters of moderate reform. On the left were the Jacobins and other republicans who wanted to abolish the monarchy and promote radical changes.

Today, the terms *right, center,* and *left* continue to reflect those long-ago seating arrangements.

Theme: Political and Social Systems   To what kind of political position might *far right* refer? *Far left?*

SECTION 2 Assessment

Recall

1. **Identify: (a)** Great Fear, **(b)** tricolor, **(c)** Legislative Assembly, **(d)** Declaration of Pilnitz, **(e)** Jacobins.
2. **Define: (a)** faction, **(b)** émigré, **(c)** republic.

Comprehension

3. What role did the people of Paris play in the French Revolution?
4. Describe one reform that the National Assembly enacted through each of the following documents: **(a)** the Declaration of the Rights of Man and the Citizen, **(b)** the Civil Constitution of the Clergy, **(c)** the Constitution of 1791.
5. **(a)** Why did some people outside France react negatively to the French Revolution? **(b)** How did these feelings lead to war?

Critical Thinking and Writing

6. **Comparing** Compare the women's march on Versailles to the storming of the Bastille in terms of goals and results.
7. **Defending a Position** The Declaration of the Rights of Man has been called the "death certificate" of the old regime. Do you agree? Why or why not?

Go Online
PHSchool.com

Use the Internet to research the life of Marie Antoinette. Then, write a feature article about her as it might appear in a popular magazine of today. Include interesting details about her family, friends, and habits that would appeal to your readers. For help with this activity, use **Web Code mkd-1977.**

Radical Days

Reading Focus

- Why did radicals abolish the monarchy?
- How did the excesses of the Convention lead to the Directory?
- What impact did the revolution have on women and daily life?

Vocabulary

suffrage

nationalism

secular

Taking Notes

On a sheet of paper, make a time line like the one begun here. The time line should extend from August 1792 to July 1794. Add dates and important events as you read this section.

August 1792	September 1792	January 1793	July 1794
Mob invades royal palace	September massacres		

Main Idea A radical phase of the revolution led to the monarchy's downfall and a time of violence known as the Reign of Terror.

Did You Know?

The Origin of Madame Tussaud's Wax Museum

In the 1780s, Marie Tussaud ran two wax museums in Paris and was art tutor to the sister of Louis XVI. During the revolution, she was imprisoned as a royalist. Even so, the leaders of the revolution admired her art skills. Tussaud escaped the guillotine by agreeing to make wax models of the revolutionaries and their victims, such as Louis XVI and Marie Antoinette, shown above.

After the revolution, Tussaud took her collection to London. There she established the wax museum that still bears her name. Today, tourists from around the world marvel at the realistic sculptures of the famous and infamous in Madame Tussaud's Wax Museum.

Theme: Art and Literature
How did Tussaud's art skills save her life?

Setting the Scene Someone who had left Paris in 1791 and returned in 1793 could have gotten lost. Almost 4,000 streets had new names. Louis XV Square was renamed the Square of the Revolution. King-of-Sicily Street, named for the brother of Louis XVI, had become the Rights of Man Street.

Renaming streets was one way that Jacobins tried to wipe out all traces of the old order. In 1793, the revolution entered a radical phase. For a year, France experienced one of the bloodiest regimes in its long history as determined leaders sought to extend and preserve the revolution.

The Monarchy Abolished

Dismal news about the war heightened tensions. Well-trained Prussian forces were cutting down raw French recruits. Royalist officers deserted the French army, joining émigrés and others hoping to restore the king's power.

Outbreaks of Violence Battle disasters quickly inflamed revolutionaries who thought the king was in league with the invaders. On August 10, 1792, a crowd of Parisians stormed the Tuileries and slaughtered the king's guards. The royal family fled to the Legislative Assembly.

A month later, citizens attacked prisons that held nobles and priests accused of political offenses. These prisoners were killed, along with many ordinary criminals. Historians disagree about the people who carried out the "September massacres." Some call them bloodthirsty mobs. Others describe them as patriots defending France from its enemies. In fact, most were ordinary citizens fired to fury by real and imagined grievances.

The French Republic Backed by Paris crowds, radicals took control of the Assembly. Radicals called for the election of a new legislative body called the National Convention. Suffrage, the right to vote, was to be extended to all male citizens, not just to property owners.

The Convention that met in September 1792 was a more radical body than earlier assemblies. It voted to abolish the monarchy and declare France a republic. Deputies then drew up a new constitution for France. The Jacobins, who controlled the Convention, set out to erase all traces of the old order. They seized lands of nobles and abolished titles of nobility.

Death of the King and Queen During the early months of the Republic, the Convention also put Louis XVI on trial as a traitor to France. The king was convicted by a single vote and sentenced to death. On a foggy morning

Analyzing Primary Sources

Execution of a King

The following excerpt is from an eyewitness report of the execution of King Louis XVI, January 21, 1793. It was written by Henry Essex Edgeworth de Firmont, a priest who accompanied the king to the scaffold.

"The path leading to the scaffold was extremely rough and difficult to pass; the King was obliged to lean on my arm, and from the slowness with which he proceeded, I feared for a moment that his courage might fail; but what was my astonishment, when arrived at the last step, I felt that he suddenly let go my arm, and I saw him cross with a firm foot the breadth of the whole scaffold; silence, by his look alone, fifteen or twenty drums that were placed opposite to me; and in a voice so loud, that it must have been heard at the Pont Tourant, I heard him pronounce distinctly these memorable words: 'I die innocent of all the crimes laid to my charge; I pardon those who have occasioned my death; and I pray to God that the blood you are going to shed may never be visited on France.'

He was proceeding, when a man on horseback, in the national uniform, and with a ferocious cry, ordered the drums to beat. Many voices were at the same time heard encouraging the executioners. They seemed reanimated themselves, in seizing with violence the most virtuous of Kings, they dragged him under the axe of the guillotine, which with one stroke severed his head from his body. All this passed in a moment. The youngest of the guards, who seemed about eighteen, immediately seized the head, and showed it to the people as he walked around the scaffold; he accompanied this monstrous ceremony with the most atrocious and indecent gestures. At first an awful silence prevailed; at length some cries of 'Vive la République! [Long live the republic!]' were heard. By degrees the voices multiplied, and in less than ten minutes this cry, a thousand times repeated, became the universal shout of the multitude, and every hat was in the air."

—Henry Essex Edgeworth de Firmont, *Report by a Priest of His Majesty's Household*

The Machine of Terror
The guillotine made it easy to behead large numbers of people quickly. It became a symbol of the Reign of Terror.

Skills Tip

Bias is a leaning in favor of or against someone or something. When analyzing an eyewitness account, look for words that indicate the writer's bias.

Skills Assessment

1. Based on this account, how would you describe the king's manner at his execution?
   A frightened and confused
   B cold and unemotional
   C proud and brave
   D angry and violent

2. The man on horseback orders the drums to beat in order to
   E silence the crowd.
   F signal that the execution is about to take place.
   G show respect for the king.
   H announce that the king is dead.

3. **Critical Thinking** **Drawing Conclusions** **(a)** Based on this account, what was Father Firmont's attitude toward the king? Toward the revolutionaries? How can you tell? **(b)** Do you think Firmont's feelings affected his account? Explain.

in January 1793, Louis mounted a scaffold in a public square in Paris. He tried to speak, but his words were drowned out by a roll of drums. Moments later, the king was beheaded.

In October, Marie Antoinette was also executed. The popular press celebrated her death. The queen, however, showed great dignity as she went to her death. Their son, the uncrowned Louis XVII, died of unknown causes in the dungeons of the revolution.

The Convention Defends the Republic

By early 1793, danger threatened France on all sides. The country was at war with much of Europe, including Britain, the Netherlands, Spain, and Prussia. In the Vendée (vahn DAY) region of France, royalists and priests led peasants in rebellion against the government. In Paris, the sans-culottes demanded relief from food shortages and inflation. The Convention itself was bitterly divided between Jacobins and a rival group, the Girondins.

Committee of Public Safety To deal with the threats to France, the Convention created the Committee of Public Safety. The 12-member committee had almost absolute power as it battled to save the revolution. The Committee prepared France for all-out war, issuing a *levée en masse,* or mass levy that required all citizens to contribute to the war effort:

> "All Frenchmen are in permanent requisition for the service of the armies. The young men shall go to battle; the married men shall forge arms and transport provisions; the women shall make tents and clothing and shall serve in the hospitals; the children shall turn old lint into linen; the aged shall take themselves to the public places in order to arouse the courage of the warriors and preach the hatred of kings and the unity of the Republic."
> —*Proclamation of the National Convention,* August 23, 1793

Spurred by revolutionary fervor, French recruits marched off to defend the republic. Young officers developed effective new tactics to win battles with masses of ill-trained but patriotic forces. Soon, French armies overran the Netherlands. They later invaded Italy. At home, they crushed peasant revolts. European monarchs shuddered as the revolutionaries carried "freedom fever" into conquered lands.

Robespierre At home, the government battled counterrevolutionaries under the guiding hand of Maximilien Robespierre (ROHBZ pyair). Robespierre, a shrewd lawyer and politician, quickly rose to the leadership of the Committee of Public Safety. Among Jacobins, his selfless dedication to the revolution earned him the nickname "the incorruptible." The enemies of Robespierre called him a tyrant.

Robespierre had embraced Rousseau's idea of the general will as the source of all legitimate law. He promoted religious toleration and wanted to abolish slavery. Though cold and humorless, he was popular with the sans-culottes, who hated the old regime as much as he did. He believed that France could achieve a "republic of virtue" only through the use of terror, which he coolly defined as nothing more than "prompt, severe, inflexible justice." "Liberty cannot be secured," Robespierre cried, "unless criminals lose their heads."

The Reign of Terror Robespierre was one of the chief architects of the Reign of Terror, which lasted from about July 1793 to July 1794. Revolutionary courts conducted hasty trials. Spectators greeted death sentences with cries of "Hail the Republic!" or "Death to the traitors!"

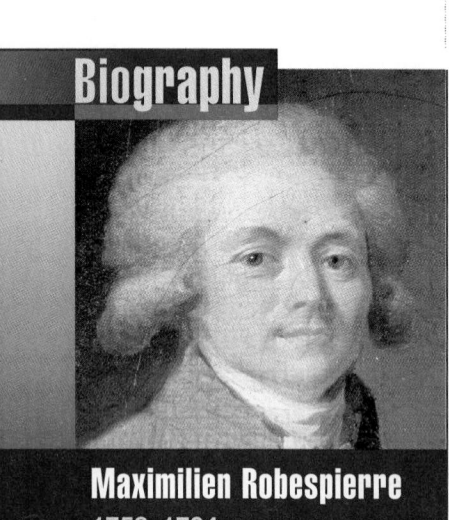

Biography

Maximilien Robespierre
1758–1794

Robespierre was the son and grandson of lawyers, but his early life was difficult. His mother died when he was only 6 years old. Just two years later, his father abandoned him and his three siblings. The children were raised by their grandfather and their aunts.

As a result, Robespierre had to assume responsibilities at an early age. He also experienced poverty. However, with the help of a scholarship, he was able to study law at the University of Paris. His performance was so noteworthy that he was chosen to deliver a speech to Louis XVI on the occasion of the king's coronation. But young Robespierre was snubbed. After listening to the address in a pouring rainstorm, the king and queen quickly left without acknowledging Robespierre in any way. Years later, in 1789, Robespierre was elected to the Estates General where his career as a revolutionary began.

Theme: Impact of the Individual How do you think Robespierre's early life might have influenced his political ideas?

Perhaps 40,000 people died during the Terror. About 15 percent were nobles and clergy. Another 15 percent were middle-class citizens, often moderates who had supported the revolution in 1789. The rest were peasants and sans-culottes involved in riots or revolts against the Republic. Many were executed, including victims of mistaken identity or false accusations by their neighbors. Many more were packed into hideous prisons, where deaths were common.

The engine of the Terror was the guillotine. Its fast-falling blade extinguished life instantly. A member of the legislature, Dr. Joseph Guillotin (GEE oh tan), had introduced it as a more humane method of beheading than the uncertain ax. But the guillotine quickly became a symbol of horror. In a speech given on February 5, 1794, Robespierre explained why the horror was necessary to achieve the goals of the revolution:

> "It is necessary to stifle the domestic and foreign enemies of the Republic or perish with them. . . . The first maxim of our politics ought to be to lead the people by means of reason and the enemies of the people by terror. . . . If the basis of popular government in time of peace is virtue, the basis of popular government in time of revolution is both virtue and terror."
>
> —Maximilien Robespierre, quoted in *Pageant of Europe* (Stearns)

Within a year, however, the Reign of Terror consumed its own. Weary of bloodshed and fearing for their own lives, members of the Convention turned on the Committee of Public Safety. On the night of July 27, 1794, Robespierre was arrested. The next day he was executed. After the heads of Robespierre and other radicals fell, executions slowed down dramatically.

Reaction and the Directory

In reaction to the Terror, the revolution entered a third stage. Moving away from the excesses of the Convention, moderates produced another constitution, the third since 1789. The Constitution of 1795 set up a five-man Directory and a two-house legislature elected by male citizens of property.

The Reign of Terror
During the Reign of Terror, lists of those to be executed, such as the one below, were posted for all to see. In Paris and other cities, cartloads of the condemned rolled to the guillotine.

Theme: Impact of the Individual Why did Robespierre think the Terror was justified?

LISTE
DES
GUILLOTINÉS
Sur la place de la Révolution, et au ci-devant Carouzel

The middle-class and professional people of the bourgeoisie were the dominant force during this stage of the French Revolution. The Directory held power from 1795 to 1799.

Weak but dictatorial, the Directory faced growing discontent. Peace was made with Prussia and Spain, but war with Austria and Great Britain continued. Corrupt leaders lined their own pockets but failed to solve pressing problems. When rising bread prices stirred hungry sans-culottes to riot, the Directory quickly suppressed them. Another threat to the Directory was the revival of royalist feeling. Many émigrés were returning to France, and they were being welcomed by devout Catholics, who resented measures that had been taken against the Church. In the election of 1797, supporters of a constitutional monarchy won the majority of seats in the legislature.

As chaos threatened, politicians turned to Napoleon Bonaparte, a popular military hero who had won a series of brilliant victories against the Austrians in Italy. The politicians planned to use him to advance their own goals—a bad miscalculation! Before long, Napoleon would outwit them all to become ruler of France.

Women in the Revolution

As you have seen, women of all classes participated in the revolution from the very beginning. Working-class women protested and fought in street battles. In Paris and elsewhere, women formed their own political clubs. A few women, like Jeanne Roland, were noted leaders. Roland supported the revolution through her writings, her salon, and her influence on her husband, a government minister.

Rights for Women Many women were very disappointed when the Declaration of the Rights of Man did not grant equal citizenship to women. Olympe de Gouges (oh LAMP duh GOOZH), a journalist, demanded equal rights in her *Declaration of the Rights of Woman.* "Woman is born free," she proclaimed, "and her rights are the same as those of man." Therefore, Gouges reasoned, "all citizens, be they men or women, being equal in the state's eyes, must be equally eligible for all public offices, positions, and jobs." After opposing the Terror and accusing certain Jacobins of corruption, Gouges was sent to the guillotine.

Women did gain some rights for a time. The government made divorce easier, a move that was aimed at weakening Church authority. Government officials also allowed women to inherit property, hoping to undermine the tradition of nobles leaving large estates to their oldest sons. These reforms and others did not last long after Napoleon gained power.

Setbacks As the revolution progressed, women's right to express their views in public came under attack. In 1793, a committee of the National Convention declared that women lacked "the moral and physical strength necessary to practice political rights." Women's revolutionary clubs were banned and violators were arrested.

Women were imprisoned and sent to the guillotine. Among the many women who became victims of the Terror were republicans like Gouges and moderates like Roland. As she mounted the steps to the guillotine, Roland cried, "O liberty, what crimes are committed in your name!"

Changes in Daily Life

By 1799, the 10-year-old French Revolution had dramatically changed France. It had dislodged the old social order, overthrown the monarchy, and brought the Church under state control.

New symbols such as the red "liberty caps" and the tricolor confirmed the liberty and equality of all male citizens. The new title "citizen" applied to people of all social classes. Titles were eliminated. Before he was executed, Louis XVI was called Citizen Capet, from the name of the dynasty that had ruled France in the Middle Ages. Elaborate fashions and powdered wigs gave way to the practical clothes and simple haircuts of the sans-culottes. To show their revolutionary spirit, enthusiastic parents gave their children names like Constitution, Republic, or August Tenth.

Nationalism Revolution and war gave the French people a strong sense of national identity. In earlier times, people had felt loyalty to local authorities. As monarchs centralized power, loyalty shifted to the king or queen. Now, the government rallied sons and daughters of the revolution to defend the nation itself.

Nationalism, a strong feeling of pride in and devotion to one's country, spread throughout France. The French people attended civic festivals that celebrated the nation and the revolution. A variety of dances and songs on themes of the revolution became immensely popular.

By 1793, France was a nation in arms. From the port city of Marseilles (mahr SAY), troops marched to a rousing new song. It urged the "children of the fatherland" to march against the "bloody banner of tyranny." This song, "La Marseillaise" (mahr say EHZ), would later become the French national anthem. The second verse and chorus appear at right.

Social Reform Revolutionaries pushed for social reform and religious toleration. They set up state schools to replace religious ones and organized systems to help the poor, old soldiers, and war widows. With a major slave revolt raging in the colony of St. Domingue (Haiti), the government also abolished slavery in their Caribbean colonies.

The Convention tried to de-Christianize France. It created a secular, or nonreligious, calendar with 1793 as the Year I of the new era of freedom. It banned many religious festivals, replacing them with secular celebrations. Huge public ceremonies boosted support for republican and nationalist ideals.

The Arts In the arts, France adopted a grand classical style that echoed the grandeur of ancient Rome. A leading artist of this period was Jacques Louis David (dah VEED). He immortalized on canvas such stirring events as the Tennis Court Oath and, later, Napoleon's coronation. David helped shape the way future generations pictured the French Revolution.

Primary Source

La Marseillaise
The stirring lyrics of "La Marseillaise" inspired French soldiers to defend their country and the ideals of the revolution:

"Sacred love of the fatherland
  Guide and support our vengeful
    arms.
  Liberty, beloved liberty,
  Fight with your defenders;
  Fight with your defenders.
  Under our flags, so that victory
  Will rush to your manly strains;
  That your dying enemies
  Should see your triumph and glory.

To arms, citizens!
  Form up your battalions.
  Let us march, let us march!
  That their impure blood
  Should water our fields."

—"La Marseillaise"

Skills Assessment

Primary Source Which of the above lines seem most nationalistic? Explain.

SECTION 3 Assessment

Recall

1. **Identify:** (a) Committee of Public Safety, (b) Maximilien Robespierre, (c) Directory, (d) Olympe de Gouges, (e) "La Marseillaise," (f) Jacques Louis David.
2. **Define:** (a) suffrage, (b) nationalism, (c) secular.

Comprehension

3. Why did radical revolutionaries oppose the monarchy?
4. How did the Reign of Terror cause the National Convention to be replaced by the Directory?

5. Describe one effect of the French Revolution on each of the following: (a) women, (b) daily life.

Critical Thinking and Writing

6. **Analyzing Primary Sources** Robespierre wrote, "Terror is nothing but prompt, severe, inflexible justice." Explain why you agree or disagree with Robespierre.
7. **Predicting Consequences** How do you think French nationalism affected the war between France and the powers of Europe?

Activity

Presenting a Poster
Create a poster that might have been used to support or oppose *one* of the following: the goals of the Jacobins; the abolition of the monarchy; the policies of the Committee of Public Safety; French nationalism; equal rights for women.

The Age of Napoleon Begins

Reading Focus

- How did Napoleon rise to power?
- How were revolutionary reforms changed under Napoleon?
- How did Napoleon build an empire in Europe?

Vocabulary

plebiscite
annex
blockade

Taking Notes

Begin a concept web like this one. As you read, fill in the blank circles with relevant information about Napoleon. Add as many circles as you need.

Main Idea Napoleon rose to power in France and built a vast empire that included much of Europe.

Setting the Scene

"He was like an expert chess player, with the human race for an opponent, which he proposed to checkmate." Thus did Madame Germaine de Staël (STAHL), a celebrated writer and intellectual, describe Napoleon Bonaparte. Napoleon himself expressed a more humble view of his rise to power. "Nothing has been simpler than my elevation," he once observed. "It is owing to the peculiarities of the time."

From 1799 to 1815, Napoleon would dominate France and Europe. A hero to some, an evil force to others, he gave his name to the final phase of the revolution—the Age of Napoleon.

FACT FINDER

The Rise of Napoleon

1769	Born on island of Corsica
1785	Becomes officer in French army
1793	Helps capture Toulon from British; promoted to brigadier general
1795	Crushes rebels opposed to the National Convention
1796–1797	Becomes commander in chief of the army of Italy; wins victories against Austria
1798–1799	Loses to the British in Egypt and Syria
1799	Overthrows Directory and becomes First Consul of France
1804	Crowns himself emperor of France

Skills Assessment

Chart Napoleon's successes on the battlefield helped him become emperor. **Where and when did Napoleon experience a military setback? Did that setback affect his rise to power? Explain.**

Napoleon's Rise to Power

Napoleon Bonaparte was born in Corsica, a French-ruled island in the Mediterranean. His family were minor nobles, but had little money. At age nine, he was sent to France to be trained for a military career. When the revolution broke out, he was an ambitious 20-year-old lieutenant, eager to make a name for himself.

Napoleon favored the Jacobins and republican rule. However, he found the conflicting ideas and personalities of the French Revolution confusing. He wrote to his brother in 1793: "Since one must take sides, one might as well choose the side that is victorious, the side which devastates, loots, and burns."

Early Successes During the turmoil of the revolution, Napoleon rose quickly in the army. In December 1793, he drove British forces out of the French port of Toulon (too LOHN). He then went on to win several dazzling victories against the Austrians, capturing most of northern Italy and forcing the Hapsburg emperor to make peace. Hoping to disrupt British trade with India, he led a colorful expedition to Egypt in 1798. The Egyptian campaign proved to be a disaster, but Napoleon managed to hide stories of the worst losses from his admirers in France.

Success fueled his ambition. By 1799, he moved from victorious general to political leader. That year, he helped overthrow the weak Directory and set up a three-man governing board known as the Consulate. Another constitution was drawn up, but Napoleon soon took the title First Consul. In 1802, he had himself named consul for life.

A Self-made Emperor   Two years later, Napoleon had acquired enough power to assume the title Emperor of the French. He invited the pope to preside over his coronation in Paris. During the ceremony, however, Napoleon took the crown from the pope's hands and placed it on his own head. By this action, Napoleon meant to show that he owed his throne to no one but himself.

At each step on his rise to power, Napoleon had held a plebiscite (PLEHB ih sīt), or ballot in which voters say yes or no. Each time, the French strongly supported him. To understand why, we must look at his policies.

France Under Napoleon

During the consulate and empire, Napoleon consolidated his power by strengthening the central government. Order, security, and efficiency replaced liberty, equality, and fraternity as the slogans of the new regime.

Reforms   To restore economic prosperity, Napoleon controlled prices, encouraged new industry, and built roads and canals. To ensure well-trained officials and military officers, he set up a system of public schools under strict government control.

At the same time, Napoleon backed off from some of the revolution's social reforms. He made peace with the Catholic Church in the Concordat of 1801. The Concordat kept the Church under state control but recognized religious freedom for Catholics. Revolutionaries who opposed the Church denounced the agreement, but Catholics welcomed it.

Napoleon won support across class lines. He encouraged émigrés to return, provided that they took an oath of loyalty. Peasants were relieved when he recognized their right to lands they had bought from the Church and nobles during the revolution. The middle class, who had benefited most from the revolution, approved Napoleon's economic reforms and the restoration of order after years of chaos. Napoleon also made jobs "open to

The Coronation
David depicted the splendor and power of the new French emperor in the painting *Napoleon Crowning the Empress Josephine.* Years later, Napoleon would divorce Josephine and marry an Austrian princess.

Theme: Impact of the Individual   How did Napoleon emphasize his personal power at the coronation ceremony?

Napoleon's Power in Europe, 1812

Map Legend:
- French territory
- States ruled by Napoleon's family
- States under French influence
- French allies, 1812
- ★ Battle sites, 1800–1815
- → Route of Napoleon's invasion of Russia

Skills Assessment

Geography Napoleon won a vast empire in Europe. But resistance in Spain and a disastrous invasion of Russia would turn the tide against him.

1. **Location** *On the map, locate (a) Spain, (b) Moscow, (c) Waterloo.*
2. **Place** *What part of the Italian peninsula was French territory?*
3. **Critical Thinking Drawing Conclusions** *Do you think the spread of nationalism would weaken or strengthen Napoleon's power? Explain.*

all talent," a popular policy among those who remembered the old aristocratic monopoly of power.

Napoleonic Code Among Napoleon's most lasting reforms was a new law code, popularly called the Napoleonic Code. It embodied Enlightenment principles such as the equality of all citizens before the law, religious toleration, and advancement based on merit.

But the Napoleonic Code undid some reforms of the French Revolution. Women, for example, lost most of their newly gained rights and could not exercise the rights of citizenship. Male heads of households regained complete authority over their wives and children. Again, Napoleon valued order and authority over individual rights.

Building an Empire

From 1804 to 1814, Napoleon furthered his reputation on the battlefield. He successfully faced down the combined forces of the greatest European powers. He took great risks and even suffered huge losses. "I grew up on the field of battle," he once said, "and a man such as I am cares little for the life of a million men." By 1810, his Grand Empire reached its greatest extent.

As a military leader, Napoleon valued rapid movements and made effective use of his large armies. He developed a new plan for each battle, so opposing generals could never anticipate what he would do next. His enemies paid tribute to his leadership. Napoleon's presence on the battlefield, said one, was "worth 40,000 troops."

The Grand Empire As Napoleon created a vast French empire, he redrew the map of Europe. He annexed, or added outright, some areas to France, including the Netherlands, Belgium, and parts of Italy and Germany. He also abolished the tottering Holy Roman Empire and created a 38-member Confederation of the Rhine under French protection. He cut Prussian territory in half, turning part of old Poland into the Grand Duchy of Warsaw.

Napoleon controlled much of Europe through forceful diplomacy. One tactic was to put friends and relatives on the thrones of Europe. For example, after unseating the king of Spain, he placed his own brother, Joseph

Bonaparte, on the throne. He also forced alliances on European powers from Madrid to Moscow. At various times, the rulers of Austria, Prussia, and Russia reluctantly signed treaties with the "Corsican upstart," as his enemies called him.

In France, Napoleon's successes boosted the spirit of nationalism. Great victory parades filled the streets of Paris with cheering crowds. The people celebrated the glory and grandeur that Napoleon had won for France.

France Versus Britain Britain alone remained outside Napoleon's European empire. With only a small army, Britain relied on its sea power to stop Napoleon's drive to rule the continent. In 1805, Napoleon prepared to invade England. But at the Battle of Trafalgar, fought off the southwest coast of Spain, British admiral Horatio Nelson smashed a French fleet.

With an invasion ruled out, Napoleon struck at Britain's lifeblood, its commerce. He waged economic warfare through the Continental System, which closed European ports to British goods. Britain responded with its own blockade of European ports. A blockade involves shutting off ports to keep people or supplies from moving in or out. During their long struggle, both Britain and France seized neutral ships suspected of trading with the other side. British attacks on American ships sparked anger in the United States and eventually triggered the War of 1812.

In the end, Napoleon's Continental System failed to bring Britain to its knees. Although British exports declined, its powerful navy kept open vital trade routes to the Americas and India. Meanwhile, trade restrictions created a scarcity of goods in Europe, sent prices soaring, and intensified resentment against French power.

Cause *and* Effect

Long-Term Causes	Immediate Causes
• Corrupt, inconsistent, and insensitive leadership • Prosperous members of Third Estate resent privileges of First and Second estates • Spread of Enlightenment ideas	• Huge government debt • Poor harvests and rising price of bread • Failure of Louis XVI to accept financial reforms • Formation of National Assembly • Storming of Bastille

The French Revolution

Immediate Effects	Long-Term Effects
• Declaration of the Rights of Man and the Citizen adopted • France adopts its first written constitution • Monarchy abolished • Revolutionary France fights coalition of European powers • Reign of Terror	• Napoleon gains power • Napoleonic Code established • French public schools set up • French conquests spread nationalism • Revolutions occur in Europe and Latin America

Connections to Today

• French law reflects Napoleonic Code
• France is a democratic republic

Skills Assessment   **Chart** The French Revolution was a major turning point. Its impact spread far beyond France. **How did Napoleon spread the ideas of the French Revolution?**

SECTION 4 Assessment

Recall

1. **Identify:** (a) Consulate, (b) Concordat of 1801, (c) Napoleonic Code, (d) Confederation of the Rhine, (e) Battle of Trafalgar, (f) Continental System.
2. **Define:** (a) plebiscite, (b) annex, (c) blockade.

Comprehension

3. Describe Napoleon Bonaparte's rise to power.
4. (a) What revolutionary reforms were undone by Napoleon? (b) How did Napoleon preserve some of the principles of the Enlightenment?

5. (a) How did Napoleon come to dominate most of Europe? (b) Why did his efforts to subdue Britain fail?

Critical Thinking and Writing

6. **Analyzing Information** What opinions do you think each of the following had of Napoleon? (a) royalists, (b) Catholic priests, (c) soldiers, (d) republicans.
7. **Making Decisions** Suppose you were a French voter in 1803. How would you have voted on the plebiscite to make Napoleon emperor? Explain your reasons.

Go Online
PHSchool.com

Use the Internet to research one of the battles identified on the map in this section. Make a map that shows the terrain of the battle site, and the positions, strengths, and movements of the opposing forces. Write a paragraph or two explaining the outcome. For help with this activity, use **Web Code mkd-1987.**

The End of an Era

Reading Focus

- What challenges threatened Napoleon's empire?
- What events led to Napoleon's downfall?
- What were the goals of the Congress of Vienna?

Vocabulary

guerrilla warfare
abdicate
legitimacy

Taking Notes

On a sheet of paper, make a flowchart like the partially completed one at right. As you read this section, add events that led to the downfall of Napoleon. Add as many boxes as you need.

DOWNFALL OF NAPOLEON

Nationalism spurs opposition to French rule

↓

↓

↓

Waterloo

Main Idea   Napoleon was finally defeated, but revolutionary ideals and the postwar peace settlement affected Europe for many years.

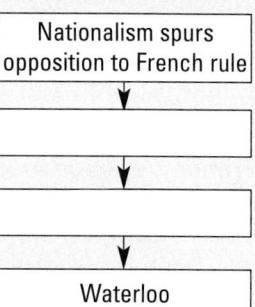

Learn more about Napoleon and his empire.

Biography

Napoleon 1769–1821

Perhaps history has seen no greater believer in nepotism than Napoleon. Nepotism is favoritism shown to relatives by a person in high office.

"I am building a family of kings," Napoleon proudly said. In addition to making his brother Joseph king of Spain, he made Louis king of Holland and Jerome king of Westphalia. His sister Caroline became queen of Naples, and Elisa was named Grand Duchess of Tuscany. Then, his mother wanted a title, too! He named her Imperial Highness, Lady, Mother of the Emperor. His final family appointment went to his son, whom he named king of Rome.

Theme: Impact of the Individual How do you think nepotism benefited Napoleon?

Setting the Scene

Napoleon watched the battle for the Russian city of Smolensk from a chair outside his tent. As fires lit up the walled city, he exclaimed:

"It's like Vesuvius erupting. Don't you think this is a beautiful sight?"

"Horrible, Sire," replied an aide.

"Bah!" snorted Napoleon. "Remember, gentlemen, what a Roman emperor said: 'The corpse of an enemy always smells sweet.'"

In 1812, Napoleon pursued his dream of empire by invading Russia. The campaign began a chain of events that eventually led to his downfall. Napoleon's final defeat brought an end to the era of the French Revolution.

Challenges to Napoleon's Empire

Under Napoleon, French armies spread the ideas of the revolution across Europe. They backed liberal reforms in the lands they conquered. In some places, they helped install revolutionary governments that abolished titles of nobility, ended Church privileges, opened careers to men of talent, and ended serfdom and manorial dues. The Napoleonic Code, too, was carried across Europe. French occupation sometimes brought economic benefits as well, by reducing trade barriers and stimulating industry.

Impact of Nationalism Napoleon's successes, however, contained the seeds of defeat. Although nationalism spurred French armies to success, it worked against them, too. Many Europeans who had welcomed the ideas of the French Revolution nevertheless saw Napoleon and his armies as foreign oppressors. They resented the Continental System and Napoleon's effort to impose French culture.

From Rome to Madrid to the Netherlands, nationalism unleashed revolts against France. In the German states, leaders encouraged national loyalty among German-speaking people to counter French influence.

Resistance in Spain Resistance to foreign rule bled French occupying forces in Spain. In 1808, Napoleon replaced the king of Spain with his own brother, Joseph Bonaparte. He also introduced reforms that sought to undermine the Spanish Catholic Church. But many Spaniards remained loyal to their former king and devoted to the Church. When the Spanish resisted the invaders, well-armed French forces responded with brutal repression. Far from crushing resistance, however, the French reaction further inflamed Spanish nationalism. Efforts to drive out the French intensified.

Spanish patriots conducted a campaign of guerrilla warfare, or hit-and-run raids, against the French. (In Spanish, *guerrilla* means "little war.") Small bands of guerrillas ambushed French supply trains or troops before melting into the countryside. These attacks kept large numbers of French soldiers tied down in Spain, when Napoleon needed them elsewhere. Eventually, the British sent an army under Arthur Wellesley, later the Duke of Wellington, to help the Spanish fight France.

War With Austria Spanish resistance encouraged Austria to resume hostilities against the French. In 1805, at the Battle of Austerlitz, Napoleon had won a crushing victory against an Austro-Russian army of superior numbers. Now, in 1809, the Austrians sought revenge. But once again, Napoleon triumphed—this time at the battle of Wagram. By the peace agreement that followed, Austria surrendered lands populated by more than three million subjects.

The next year, after divorcing his wife Josephine, Napoleon married the Austrian princess Marie Louise. By marrying the daughter of the Hapsburg emperor, he and his heirs could claim kinship with the royalty of Europe.

Defeat in Russia Napoleon's alliance with the Austrian royal family was especially disturbing to Czar Alexander I of Russia. The Russians were also unhappy with the economic effects of Napoleon's Continental System. Yet another cause for concern was that Napoleon had enlarged the Grand Duchy of Warsaw that bordered Russia on the west. These and other issues led the czar to withdraw Russia from the Continental System. Napoleon responded to the czar's action by assembling his Grand Army.

In 1812, more than 400,000 soldiers from France and other countries invaded Russia. To avoid battles with Napoleon, the Russians retreated eastward, burning crops and villages as they went. This "scorched earth" policy left the French hungry and cold as winter came. Napoleon entered Moscow in September. He realized, though, that he

Resistance in Spain
Spanish artist Francisco Goya stressed raw human emotions. Goya's *The Third of May, 1808* shows French soldiers executing Spanish prisoners. His drawing *And They Are Like Wild Beasts* depicts a furious battle between Spanish women and the French.

Theme: Art and Literature How did Goya emphasize nationalism in these artworks?

was not able to feed and supply his army through the long Russian winter. In October, he turned homeward.

The 1,000-mile retreat from Moscow turned into a desperate battle for survival. Russian attacks and the brutal Russian winter took a terrible toll. Philippe Paul de Ségur, an aide to Napoleon, described the grim scene as the remnants of the Grand Army returned:

"In Napoleon's wake [was] a mob of tattered ghosts draped in . . . odd pieces of carpet, or greatcoats burned full of holes, their feet wrapped in all sorts of rags. . . . [We] stared in horror as those skeletons of soldiers went by, their gaunt, gray faces covered with disfiguring beards, without weapons . . . with lowered heads, eyes on the ground, in absolute silence."
—*Memoirs of Philippe Paul de Ségur*

Only about 10,000 soldiers of the once-proud Grand Army survived. Many died. Others deserted. French general Michel Ney sadly concluded: "General Famine and General Winter, rather than Russian bullets, have conquered the Grand Army." Napoleon rushed to Paris to raise a new force to defend France. His reputation for success had been shattered.

Downfall of Napoleon

The disaster in Russia brought a new alliance of Russia, Britain, Austria, and Prussia against a weakened France. In 1813, they defeated Napoleon in the Battle of the Nations at Leipzig.

Exile and Return The next year, Napoleon abdicated, or stepped down from power. The victors exiled him to Elba, an island in the Mediterranean. They then recognized Louis XVIII, brother of Louis XVI, as king of France.

The restoration of Louis XVIII did not go smoothly. The Bourbon king agreed to accept the Napoleonic Code and honor the land settlements made during the revolution. However, many émigrés rushed back to France bent on revenge. An economic depression and the fear of a return to the old regime helped rekindle loyalty to Napoleon.

As the victorious allies gathered in Vienna for a general peace conference, Napoleon escaped his island exile and returned to France. Soldiers flocked to his banner. As citizens cheered Napoleon's advance, Louis XVIII fled. In March 1815, the emperor of the French entered Paris in triumph.

Battle of Waterloo Napoleon's triumph was short-lived. His star soared for only 100 days, while the allies reassembled their forces. On June 18, 1815, the opposing armies met near the town of Waterloo in Belgium. British forces under the Duke of Wellington and a Prussian army commanded by General Blücher crushed the French in an agonizing day-long battle. Once again, Napoleon was forced to abdicate and to go into exile on St. Helena, a lonely island in the South Atlantic. This time, he would not return.

Legacy of Napoleon Napoleon died in 1821, but his legend lived on in France and around the world. His contemporaries as well as historians have long debated his legacy. Was he "the revolution on horseback," as he claimed? Or was he a traitor to the revolution?

No one, however, questions Napoleon's impact on France and on Europe. The Napoleonic Code consolidated many changes of the revolution. The France of Napoleon was a centralized state with a constitution. Elections were held with expanded, though limited, suffrage. Many more citizens had rights to property and access to education than under the old regime. Still, French citizens lost many rights promised so fervently by republicans during the Convention.

On the world stage, Napoleon's conquests spread the ideas of the revolution. He failed to make Europe into a French empire. Instead, he sparked

Geography and History

The Battle of Waterloo

Waterloo—to this day it symbolizes utter defeat. But on the morning of the battle, Napoleon felt certain of victory. "This whole affair will not be more serious than swallowing one's breakfast," he said.

But both weather and terrain conspired against him. First, he held off his attack until the rain-soaked ground could dry. (Cannonballs just stick in mud; they can do more damage bouncing along dry ground.) These lost hours gave the enemy time to move in more troops. Second, Napoleon ordered a frontal attack against an enemy positioned on an upward slope. The crest of its ridge helped shield the opposition from French artillery barrages. At Waterloo, more than 20,000 French soldiers died, and Napoleon suffered his final defeat.

Theme: Geography and History How did geography help defeat Napoleon at Waterloo?

Disaster!

Napoleon's Retreat From Moscow

"My greatest and most difficult enterprise," said Napoleon in June 1812 as he eagerly took on the challenge of conquering Russia. A few months later, he would see things differently, and so would his troops. After a disheartening defeat, Napoleon had to hurry back to Paris to squelch rumors that he had been killed, leaving his shrinking army to face the long, brutal winter in Russia.

Fast Facts

- Russian soldiers set Moscow ablaze to avoid handing it over intact to Napoleon's army.
- When the Grand Army retreated from Moscow in October, the line of French troops stretched for more than 50 miles.
- French troops experienced temperatures as low as −40° F.

As French troops stumbled their way through blinding snow, they grew desperate for shelter. Soldiers resorted to building huts using the frozen corpses of their fallen comrades, stacking them like logs to create walls.

Russian forces harassed the retreating French army throughout November.

The Grand Army of France was forced to follow the same path retreating from Moscow that it used to get there. As the army passed over an old battlefield, one observer commented, "It was covered with the debris of helmets . . . wheels, weapons, rags of uniforms—and 30,000 corpses half-eaten by wolves."

Napoleon's Troops in Russia

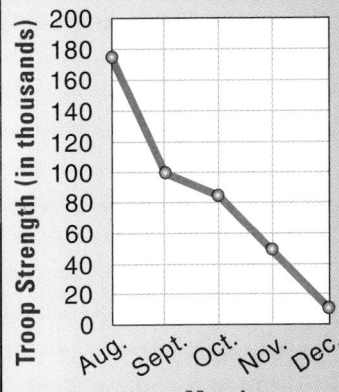

Troop Strength (in thousands): 200, 180, 160, 140, 120, 100, 80, 60, 40, 20, 0

Month: Aug., Sept., Oct., Nov., Dec.

Source: Charles Joseph Minard, 1861

Starting with 422,000 troops in June, Napoleon lost almost half of his forces to fighting, desertion, and famine by August. Grand Army troop strength continued to fall drastically from August through December.

Portfolio Assessment

Conduct research to learn about another disastrous march in history. Some such marches were the Trail of Tears in North America in 1838–1839, the Long March in China in 1934–1935, or the Bataan Death March in the Philippines in 1942. Write a news story in which you include a map of the route and statistics on loss of life.

Boundary of the
German Confederation

Quadruple Alliance, 1815

Great Britain

Prussia

Austrian Empire

Russian Empire

Azimuthal Equal Area Projection

0   250   500 Miles

0   250   500 Kilometers

Geography At the Congress of Vienna, European leaders redrew the map of Europe in order to contain France and keep a balance of power.

1. **Location** On the map, locate (a) German Confederation, (b) Netherlands, (c) Vienna.
2. **Region** Name three states that were in the German Confederation.
3. **Critical Thinking Recognizing Causes and Effects** Why did the Congress enlarge some of the countries around France?

nationalist feeling across Europe. The abolition of the Holy Roman Empire would eventually help in creating a new Germany. Napoleon also had a dramatic impact across the Atlantic. In 1803, his decision to sell France's vast Louisiana Territory to the American government doubled the size of the United States and ushered in an age of American expansion.

The Congress of Vienna

After Waterloo, diplomats and heads of state again sat down at the Congress of Vienna. They faced the monumental task of restoring stability and order in Europe after years of revolution and war.

Gathering of Leaders The Congress met for 10 months, from September 1814 to June 1815. It was a brilliant gathering of European leaders. Diplomats and royalty dined and danced, attended concerts and ballets, and enjoyed parties arranged by their host, Emperor Francis I of Austria.

While the entertainment kept thousands of minor players busy, the real work fell to Prince Clemens von Metternich of Austria, Czar Alexander I of Russia, and Lord Robert Castlereagh (KAS uhl ray) of Britain. Defeated France was represented by Prince Charles Maurice de Talleyrand.

Goals of the Congress The chief goal of the Vienna decision makers was to create a lasting peace by establishing a balance of power and protecting the system of monarchy. Each of the leaders also pursued his own goals. Metternich, the dominant figure at the Congress, wanted to restore the *status quo* (Latin for "the way things are") of 1792. Alexander I urged a "holy alliance" of Christian monarchs to suppress future revolutions. Lord Castlereagh was determined to prevent a revival of French military power.

The aged diplomat Talleyrand shrewdly played the other leaders against one another to get defeated France accepted as an equal partner.

Balance of Power The peacemakers also redrew the map of Europe. To contain French ambitions, they ringed France with strong countries. In the north, they added Belgium and Luxembourg to Holland to create the kingdom of the Netherlands. To prevent French expansion eastward, they gave Prussia lands along the Rhine River. They also allowed Austria to reassert control over northern Italy. This policy of containment proved fairly successful in maintaining the peace.

Restoration of Monarchs To turn back the clock to 1792, the architects of the peace promoted the principle of legitimacy, restoring hereditary monarchies that the French Revolution or Napoleon had unseated. Even before the Congress began, they had put Louis XVIII on the French throne. Later, they restored "legitimate" monarchs in Portugal, Spain, and the Italian states.

Problems of the Peace To protect the new order, Austria, Russia, Prussia, and Great Britain extended their wartime alliance into the postwar era. In the Quadruple Alliance, the four nations pledged to act together to maintain the balance of power and to suppress revolutionary uprisings.

The Vienna statesmen achieved their immediate goals, but they failed to foresee how powerful new forces such as nationalism would shake the foundations of Europe. They redrew national boundaries without any concern for national cultures. In Germany, they created a loosely organized German Confederation with Austria as its official head. But many Germans who had battled Napoleon were already dreaming of a strong, united German nation. Their dream would not come true for more than 50 years, but the story of German unification began in this period.

Looking Ahead

Despite clashes and controversies, the Congress created a framework for peace. Its decisions influenced European politics for the next 100 years. Europe would not see war on a Napoleonic scale until 1914.

The ideals of the French Revolution were not destroyed at Vienna. In the next decades, the French Revolution would inspire people in Europe and Latin America to seek equality and liberty. The spirit of nationalism ignited by Napoleon also remained a powerful force.

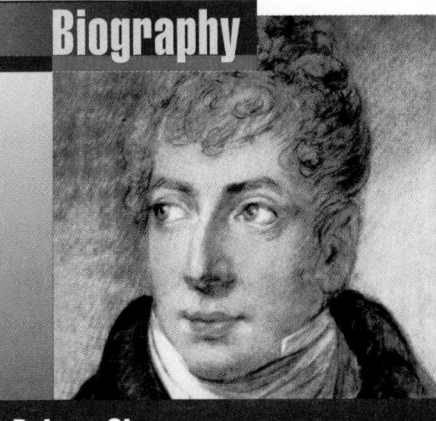

Biography

Prince Clemens von Metternich 1773–1859

As Austria's foreign minister, Metternich used a variety of means to achieve his goals. In 1809, when Napoleon seemed vulnerable, Metternich favored war against France. In 1810, after France had crushed Austria, he supported alliance with France. When the French army was in desperate retreat from Russia, Metternich became the "prime minister of the coalition" that defeated Napoleon. At the Congress of Vienna, Metternich helped create a new European order and made sure that Austria had a key role in it. He would skillfully defend that new order for more than 30 years.

Theme: Impact of the Individual Why did Metternich's policies toward France change?

SECTION 5 Assessment

Recall
1. **Identify:** (a) Joseph Bonaparte, (b) Duke of Wellington, (c) Marie Louise, (d) scorched earth policy, (e) Waterloo, (f) Clemens von Metternich, (g) Quadruple Alliance.
2. **Define:** (a) guerrilla warfare, (b) abdicate, (c) legitimacy.

Comprehension
3. What challenges did Napoleon face in: (a) Spain, (b) Austria?
4. How did the defeat in Russia lead to Napoleon's downfall?
5. What were the chief goals of the Congress of Vienna?

Critical Thinking and Writing
6. **Linking Past and Present** The powers of Europe used the Quadruple Alliance to protect the postwar order. How do international alliances and organizations help provide order in the world today?
7. **Connecting to Geography** Review the map on the preceding page. (a) What two states were the leading powers in the German Confederation? (b) How do you think this affected future attempts to unify Germany?

Go Online
PHSchool.com

Use the Internet to research the Congress of Vienna. Suppose that you have recently returned from attending the Congress and are writing an editorial about its decisions. Explain how the agreements will affect your nation. For help with this activity, use **Web Code mkd-1993.**

Creating a Chapter Summary

On a sheet of paper, make a time line to recall the chief events of the French Revolution and Napoleonic era. Use the model shown here as a guide for getting started.

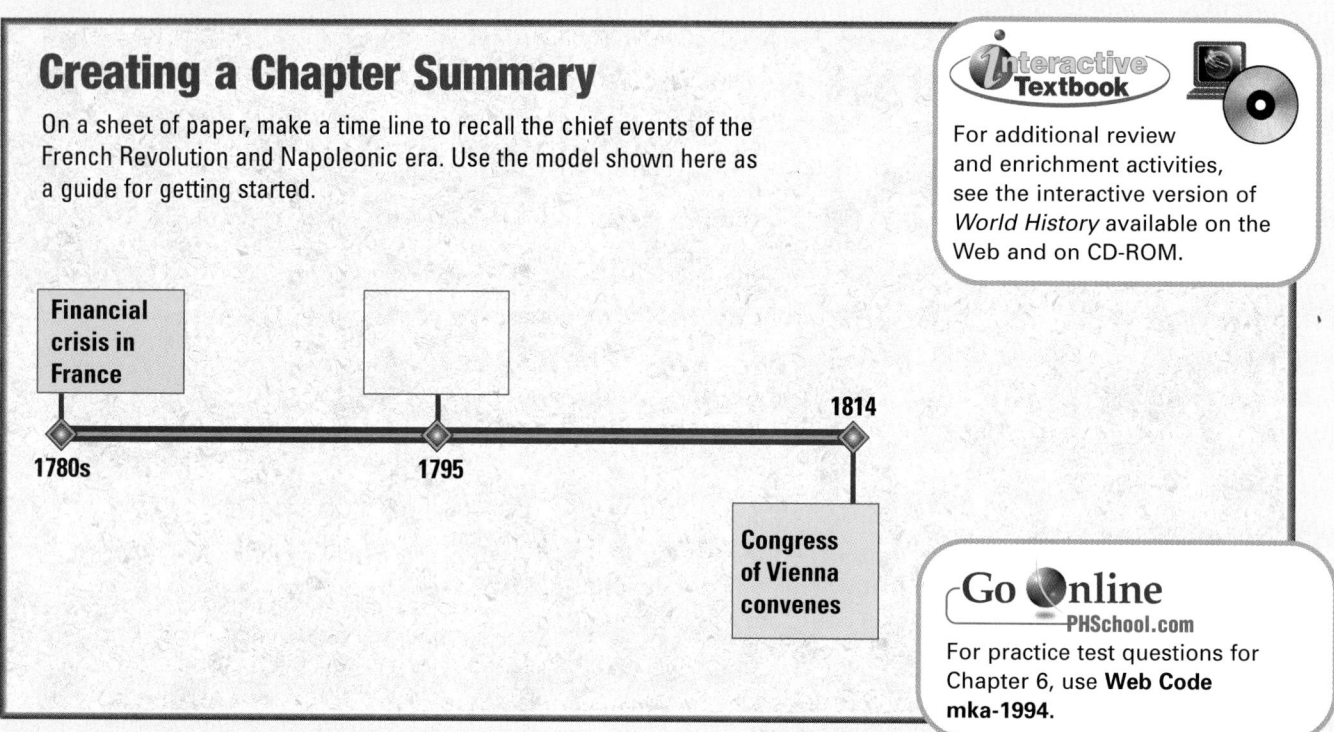

Financial crisis in France

1780s

1795

1814

Congress of Vienna convenes

Interactive Textbook

For additional review and enrichment activities, see the interactive version of *World History* available on the Web and on CD-ROM.

Go Online PHSchool.com

For practice test questions for Chapter 6, use **Web Code mka-1994**.

Building Vocabulary

Use these vocabulary words and their definitions to create a matching quiz. Exchange quizzes with another student. Check each other's answers when you are finished.

1. bourgeoisie
2. deficit spending
3. émigré
4. republic
5. suffrage
6. nationalism
7. plebiscite
8. annex
9. abdicate
10. legitimacy

Recalling Key Facts

11. Why was there discontent with the old regime in France?
12. Why did a crowd storm the Bastille?
13. What was the slogan of the French Revolution?
14. What was the Reign of Terror?
15. List the reforms that Napoleon made as leader of France.
16. (a) How did Napoleon build an empire in Europe? (b) What were two reasons for his downfall?
17. How did the Congress of Vienna try to restore the balance of power in Europe?

Critical Thinking and Writing

18. **Synthesizing Information** A French noble wrote this on the causes of the revolution: "The most striking of the country's troubles was the chaos in its finances, the result of years of extravagance. . . . No one could think of any remedy, except to search for fresh funds." (a) What did the noble mean by "chaos in its finances"? (b) How were fresh funds raised? (c) How did this lead to revolution?

19. **Connecting to Geography** (a) How did the geography of the Russian empire work against Napoleon's Grand Army? (b) Do you think geography can affect the outcome of modern warfare? Explain.

20. **Analyzing Primary Sources** Review the words of "La Marseillaise," which appears in Section 3. How does the song express some of the ideals of the French Revolution?

21. **Comparing** Review the English Civil War. (a) How were the English Civil War and the French Revolution similar? (b) How were they different?

Read the excerpt below from an eyewitness account of the battle at Waterloo. Then answer the questions that follow.

> "Our division, which had stood upwards of 5000 men at the commencement of the battle, had gradually dwindled down into a solitary line of skirmishers. . . . Presently a cheer which we knew to be British commenced far to the right, and made everyone prick up his ears; it was Lord Wellington's long-wished-for orders to advance. . . . [To] people who had been so many hours enveloped in darkness, in the midst of destruction, and naturally anxious about the result of the day, the scene which now met the eye conveyed a feeling of more exquisite gratification than can be conceived. . . . The French were flying in one confused mass. British lines were seen in close pursuit, and in admirable order, as far as the eye could reach to the right, while the plain to the left was filled with Prussians."

—Captain J. Kincaid,
Adventures in the Rifle Brigade

22. What nationality is the writer?
23. What evidence is given that the French fought fiercely?
24. Why do the soldiers cheer?
25. How does the writer feel about victory?
26. How does this battle differ from the guerrilla warfare fought against the French in Spain?

Go Online
PHSchool.com

Use the Internet to research one of the symbols of the French Revolution or the French republic, such as the Bastille, the tricolor, or "La Marseillaise." Then, write a brief historical analysis of the symbol. Explain how it originated, what it represented to French citizens during the revolution, and how it continues to be an important symbol to the French people today. For help with this activity, use **Web Code mkd-1995.**

*The Plumb-pudding in danger,
or State Epicures taking un Petit Soup
the great Globe itself and all which it went is too small to
satisfy such insatiable appetites*

In the political cartoon (above), the figure at left represents the British and the figure at right represents Napoleon. Use the cartoon to answer the following questions:

27. What is represented by the meal on the table?
28. Why are the two figures carving the meal?
29. Does the cartoonist portray Napoleon favorably? Explain.
30. How would people of the time have known which nations were represented by the two men in the cartoon?
31. Which of the two sides, if any, does the cartoon favor? Explain.
32. (a) Compose a title for the cartoon. (b) Explain the meaning of the title you created.

Skills Tip

To understand a political cartoon's point of view, first try to figure out the meaning of the cartoon's various figures and symbols.

The Industrial Revolution Begins

1750–1850

Chapter Preview

1 Dawn of the Industrial Age
2 Britain Leads the Way
3 Hardships of Early Industrial Life
4 New Ways of Thinking

CHAPTER EVENTS

1760s
James Watt improves on the steam engine. Watt's engine, shown here, provides a vital source of power.

1800
Robert Owen begins social reforms at New Lanark.

1807
Robert Fulton develops the first successful steamboat, the *Clermont.* Steam power allows the vessel, shown here, to travel against the current without difficulty.

1750

1775

1800

GLOBAL EVENTS

1762 Catherine the Great comes to power in Russia.

1804 Napoleon becomes emperor of France.

Major Centers of Industry in Great Britain, 1825

The Industrial Revolution first took hold in Britain, encouraging the growth of cities and factory towns.

Population of urban centers
- •   30,000 or more
- •   80,000 or more
- ●   1,000,000 or more

SCOTLAND

ATLANTIC OCEAN

Glasgow   Edinburgh

Newcastle

Tyne R.

North Sea

Belfast

Irish Sea

Mersey R.   *Humber R.*

IRELAND

Liverpool   Manchester

ENGLAND

Severn R.

Birmingham

WALES

Bristol

Thames R.

London

55°N

50°N

15°W   10°W   5°W   0°   5°E

Lambert Azimuthal Equal Area Projection

0   100   200 Miles
0   100   200 Kilometers

N W E S

1830
The Liverpool-Manchester Railroad opens.

1848
Karl Marx and Friedrich Engels publish *The Communist Manifesto.*

1851
The Great Exhibition is held in London. A display of industrial developments, housed in the Crystal Palace, is shown here.

1825   1850   1875

1847 Liberia, settled by freed African Americans, becomes an independent nation.

Dawn of the Industrial Age

Reading Focus

- Why was the Industrial Revolution a turning point in world history?

- How did an agricultural revolution contribute to population growth?

- What new technologies helped trigger the Industrial Revolution?

Vocabulary

anesthetic

enclosure

smelt

Taking Notes

As you read, create a chart of causes of the Industrial Revolution. This sample will help you get started. Add categories as needed.

Agricultural Revolution	Population Explosion	New Technology	
• Dikes • Fertilizer	• Declining death rates •	• •	

INDUSTRIAL REVOLUTION

Main Idea The Industrial Revolution had an impact on every aspect of life in Western Europe and the United States.

Setting the Scene

For thousands of years following the rise of civilization, most people lived and worked in small farming villages. However, a chain of events set in motion in the mid-1700s changed that way of life for all time. Today, we call this period of change the Industrial Revolution.

The Industrial Revolution started in Britain. In contrast with most political revolutions, it was neither sudden nor swift. Instead, it was a long, slow, uneven process in which production shifted from simple hand tools to complex machines. New sources of power replaced human and animal power. In the 250 years since it began, the Industrial Revolution has spread from Britain to the rest of Europe, to North America, and around the globe.

A Turning Point in History

In 1750, most people worked the land, using handmade tools. They lived in simple cottages lit by firelight and candles. They made their own clothes and grew their own food. In nearby towns, they might exchange goods at a weekly outdoor market.

Like their ancestors, these people knew little of the world that existed beyond their village. The few who left home traveled only as far as their feet or a horse-drawn cart could take them. Those bold adventurers who dared to cross the seas were at the mercy of the winds and tides.

With the beginning of the Industrial Revolution, the rural way of life began to disappear. By the 1850s, many country villages had grown into industrial towns and cities. Their inhabitants bought food and clothing in stores that offered a large variety of machine-made goods. Their homes were crowded, multistory apartment buildings.

Industrial-age travelers moved rapidly between countries and continents by train or steamship. Urgent messages flew along telegraph wires. New inventions and scientific "firsts" poured out each year. Between 1830 and 1855, for example, an American dentist first used an anesthetic, or drug that prevents pain during surgery; an American inventor patented the first sewing machine; a French physicist measured the speed of light; and a Hungarian doctor introduced antiseptic methods to reduce the risk of women dying in childbirth.

Still more stunning changes occurred in the next century, creating our familiar world of skyscraper cities and carefully tended suburbs. How and why did these great changes occur? Historians point to a series of interrelated causes that helped trigger the industrialization of the West.

A New Agricultural Revolution

Oddly enough, the Industrial Revolution was made possible in part by a change in the farming fields of Western Europe. The first agricultural revolution took place some 11,000 years ago, when people learned to farm and domesticate animals. About 300 years ago, a second agricultural revolution took place. It greatly improved the quality and quantity of farm products.

Improved Methods of Farming   The Dutch led the way in this new agricultural revolution. They built earthen walls known as dikes to reclaim land from the sea. They combined smaller fields into larger ones to make better use of the land and used fertilizer from livestock to renew the soil.

In the 1700s, British farmers expanded on Dutch experiments. Some farmers mixed different kinds of soils to get higher crop yields. Others tried out new methods of crop rotation. Lord Charles Townshend urged farmers to grow turnips, which restored exhausted soil. Jethro Tull invented a new mechanical device, the seed drill, to aid farmers. It deposited seeds in rows rather than scattering them wastefully over the land.

Educated farmers exchanged news of experiments through farm journals. King George III himself, nicknamed "Farmer George," wrote articles about his model farm near Windsor Castle.

Enclosure Movement   Meanwhile, rich landowners pushed ahead with enclosure, the process of taking over and fencing off land formerly shared by peasant farmers. In the 1500s, they had enclosed land to gain pastures for sheep and increased wool output. By the 1700s, they wanted to create larger fields that could be cultivated more efficiently.

As millions of acres were enclosed, farm output rose. Profits also rose because large fields needed fewer workers. But such progress had a human cost. Many farm laborers were thrown out of work, and small farmers were forced off their land because they could not compete with large landholders. Villages shrank as cottagers left in search of work.

In time, jobless farmworkers migrated to towns and cities. There, they formed a growing labor force that would tend the machines of the Industrial Revolution.

Changes in Agriculture
New inventions contributed to an agricultural revolution during the 1600s and 1700s. Today, the development of new sources of fuel encourages even more use of machine power in farming.

Theme: Economics and Technology How might agricultural developments increase farm productivity and efficiency?

PAST

This four Wheel Drill Plow, with a Seed and a Manure Hopper was first Invented in the Year 1745 and is now in Use with Wm Ellis at Little Gaddesden near Hempstead in Hertfordshire. where any person may View the same. It is so light that a Man may Draw it. but Generally drawn by a pony or little Horse

PRESENT

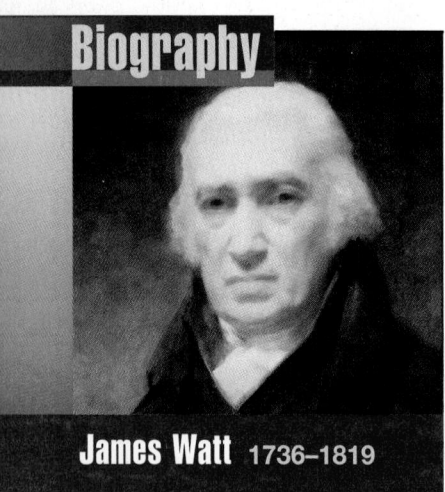

James Watt 1736–1819

How did a clever Scottish engineer become the "Father of the Industrial Revolution"? After repairing a Newcomen steam engine, James Watt had become fascinated with the idea of improving the device. Within a few months, he knew he had a product that would sell.

Still, Watt lacked the money needed to produce and market it. Fortunately, he found a series of partners, including the shrewd Matthew Boulton. Soon, Boulton could boast, "I have at my disposal what the whole world demands, something which will uplift civilization more than ever by relieving man of all undignified drudgery. I have *steam power.*"

Theme: Impact of the Individual How might the Industrial Revolution have been different if Watt had not found a business partner?

The Population Explosion

The agricultural revolution contributed to a rapid growth of population that continues today. Precise population statistics for the 1700s are rare, but those that do exist are striking. Britain's population, for example, soared from about 5 million in 1700 to almost 9 million in 1800. The population of Europe as a whole shot up from roughly 120 million to about 190 million during the same period. Such growth had never before been seen.

The population boom of the 1700s was due more to declining death rates than to rising birthrates. The agricultural revolution reduced the risk of famine. Because they ate better, women were healthier and had stronger babies. In the 1800s, better hygiene and sanitation, along with improved medical care, further slowed deaths from disease.

New Technology

A third factor that helped trigger the Industrial Revolution was the development of new technology. New sources of energy, along with new materials, enabled business owners to change the ways work was done.

An Energy Revolution From the beginning of human history, the energy for work was provided mostly by the muscles of humans and animals. In time, water mills and windmills were added to muscle power.

During the 1700s, people began to harness new sources of energy. One vital power source was coal, used to develop the steam engine. In 1712, inventor Thomas Newcomen had developed a steam engine powered by coal to pump water out of mines. About 1769, Scottish engineer James Watt improved on Newcomen's engine. Watt's engines would become a key power source of the Industrial Revolution.

Improved Iron Coal was also a vital source of fuel in the production of iron, a material needed for construction of machines and steam engines. The Darby family of Coalbrookdale pioneered new methods of producing iron. In 1709, Abraham Darby used coal to smelt iron, or separate iron from its ore. When he discovered that coal gave off impurities that damaged the iron, Darby found a way to remove the impurities from coal.

Darby's experiments led him to produce better-quality and less expensive iron, and his son and grandson continued to improve on his methods. In the decades that followed, high-quality iron was used more and more widely, especially after the world turned to building railroads.

SECTION 1 Assessment

Recall
1. **Identify: (a)** Charles Townshend, **(b)** Jethro Tull, **(c)** Thomas Newcomen, **(d)** James Watt, **(e)** Abraham Darby.
2. **Define: (a)** anesthetic, **(b)** enclosure, **(c)** smelt.

Comprehension
3. Describe how the Industrial Revolution changed daily life, becoming a turning point in history.
4. Identify three causes of the population explosion in Europe.

5. Explain the impact of each of the following technologies: **(a)** steam power, **(b)** improved iron.

Critical Thinking and Writing
6. **Recognizing Causes and Effects** What were the immediate and long-term effects of the agricultural revolution?
7. **Predicting Consequences** How do you think increased population contributed to the Industrial Revolution?

Activity

Creating a Mechanical Drawing
Suppose that you are trying to develop a way to draw water from a well that is faster than pulling up one bucket of water at a time. Draw a sketch of a machine that would speed up the process and require less human labor.

SECTION 2 Britain Leads the Way

Reading Focus

- Why was Britain the starting point for the Industrial Revolution?
- What changes transformed the textile industry?
- What new technologies were part of the revolution in transportation?

Vocabulary

capital
factory
turnpike

Taking Notes

Copy this concept web. As you read, fill in the circles with key factors that helped Britain take an early lead in industry.

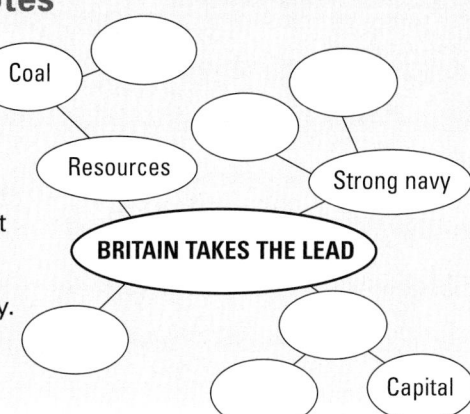

Concept web: Coal, Resources, Strong navy, BRITAIN TAKES THE LEAD, Capital

Main Idea The Industrial Revolution originated in Britain.

Setting the Scene Visitors crowded into London's Crystal Palace in 1851. The immense structure housed the Great Exhibition, a display of the "Works of Industry of all Nations." The palace itself was specially built for the occasion. A vast cavern of glass and iron, it symbolized the triumph of the industrial age.

In the century before the exhibition, Britain had been the first nation to industrialize. Its success became the model for other countries, in Europe and around the world.

Why Britain?

Why did the Industrial Revolution begin in Britain? Historians have identified a number of key factors that helped Britain lead the way.

Resources Britain was a small nation in area. However, it had large supplies of coal to power steam engines. It also had plentiful iron to build the new machines. In addition to natural resources, a labor supply was necessary. Large numbers of workers were needed to mine the coal and iron, build the factories, and run the machines. The agricultural revolution of the 1600s and 1700s freed many people in Britain from farm labor and led to a population boom.

New Technology In the 1700s, Britain had plenty of skilled mechanics who were eager to meet the growing demand for new, practical inventions. Technology was an important part of the Industrial Revolution, but it did not cause it. After all, other societies, such as the ancient Greeks or Chinese, had advanced technology for their time but did not move on to industrialization. Only when other necessary conditions existed, including demand and capital, did technology pave the way for industrialization.

Economic Conditions From the mid-1600s to 1700s, trade from a growing overseas empire helped the British economy prosper. Beginning with the slave trade, the business class accumulated capital, or wealth to invest in enterprises such as shipping, mines, railroads, and factories. Many were ready to risk their capital in new ventures.

At home, the population explosion boosted demand for goods. However, a growing population alone would not have resulted in increased production. General economic prosperity also helped make the new consumer goods affordable to members of every social class.

British Cotton Trade About 1850

Import routes of raw cotton
Export routes of cotton cloth

Robinson Projection

Skills Assessment

Geography As its textile industry grew, Great Britain needed more raw cotton. It also sought out new markets for finished cotton cloth.

1. **Location** On the map, locate **(a)** Great Britain, **(b)** United States, **(c)** British West Indies.
2. **Movement (a)** Name two overseas sources that supplied raw cotton to Britain. **(b)** Name two overseas markets to which Britain exported its cotton cloth.
3. **Critical Thinking Predicting Consequences** What might have happened to the British cotton industry if Britain had lost control of India?

Political and Social Conditions Britain had a stable government that supported economic growth. It built a strong navy to protect its empire and overseas trade. Although the upper class tended to look down on business people, it did not reject the wealth produced by the new entrepreneurs.

Religious attitudes also played a role. Many entrepreneurs came from religious groups that encouraged thrift and hard work. At the same time, many people focused more on worldly concerns than on the afterlife. Thus, risk takers such as inventors and bankers felt free to devote their energies to material achievements.

Changes in the Textile Industry

The Industrial Revolution first took hold in Britain's largest industry, textiles. In the 1600s, cotton cloth imported from India had become popular. British merchants tried to organize a cotton cloth industry at home. They developed the putting out system, in which raw cotton was distributed to peasant families who spun it into thread and then wove the thread into cloth. Skilled artisans in the towns then finished and dyed the cloth.

Major Inventions Under the "putting-out" system, production was slow. As the demand for cloth grew, inventors came up with a string of remarkable devices that revolutionized the British textile industry. For example, using John Kay's flying shuttle, weavers worked so fast that they soon outpaced spinners. James Hargreaves solved that problem by producing the spinning jenny in 1764, which spun many threads at the same time. A few years later, Richard Arkwright invented the waterframe, which used water power to speed up spinning still further.

The First Factories The new machines doomed the "putting-out" system. They were too large and expensive to be operated at home. Instead, manufacturers built long sheds to house the machines. At first, they located the sheds near rapidly moving streams, which provided water power to run the machines. Later, machines were powered by steam engines.

Spinners and weavers came each day to work in these first factories—places that brought together workers and machines to produce large quantities of goods. Early observers were awed at the size and output of these establishments. One onlooker noted: "The same [amount] of labor is now performed in one of these structures which formerly occupied the industry of an entire district."

Synthesizing Information

Impact of the Railroad

The steam locomotive was one of the key inventions of the Industrial Revolution. The maps, the cartoon, and the graph below all relate to the growth of railroads in Great Britain.

English Cartoon, Early 1800s

Railways in Great Britain

1840

1850

—— Railway lines

Travel Times to London

Source: E. J. Hobsbaum, *Industry and Empire*

Skills Assessment

1. Between 1750 and 1830, travel time from Birmingham to London decreased by about

   A 12 hours.

   B 24 hours.

   C 36 hours.

   D 48 hours.

2. Which of the three pieces of evidence above supports the conclusion that railroads reached more places in 1850 than in 1830?

   E the maps only

   F the graph only

   G the maps and the graph

   H the maps and the cartoon

3. **Critical Thinking Drawing Conclusions** **(a)** Based on the evidence provided here, what were some of the benefits and drawbacks of railroads? **(b)** What other positive or negative effects do you think railroads might have had? Give two examples.

Skills Tip

Bar graphs often show change over time. To determine the amount of change, subtract the smaller measure from the larger one.

Revolution in Transportation

As production increased, entrepreneurs needed faster and cheaper methods of moving goods from place to place. Some capitalists invested in turnpikes, which were privately built roads that charged a fee to travelers who used them. Others had canals dug to link rivers or connect inland towns with coastal ports. Engineers also built stronger bridges and upgraded harbors to help the expanding overseas trade.

On Land The great revolution in transportation, however, was the invention of the steam locomotive. It was this invention that made possible the growth of railroads. In the early 1800s, pioneers like George Stephenson developed steam-powered locomotives to pull carriages along iron rails. The railroad did not have to follow the course of a river. This meant that tracks could go places rivers did not, allowing factory owners and merchants to ship goods over land.

The world's first major rail line, from Liverpool to Manchester, opened in England in 1830. In the following decades, railroad travel became faster and railroad building boomed. By 1870, rail lines crisscrossed Britain, Europe, and North America.

On Sea Other inventors applied steam power to improve shipping. In 1807, an American, Robert Fulton, used Watt's steam engine to power the *Clermont* up the Hudson River in New York. Fulton's steamboat traveled at a record-breaking speed of more than five miles an hour!

Designing steamships for ocean voyages was more difficult. The coal needed for the voyage took up much of the cargo space. But by the late 1800s, steam-powered freighters with iron hulls were carrying 10 to 20 times the cargo of older wooden ships.

Looking Ahead

As the Industrial Revolution got under way, it triggered a chain reaction. In response to growing demand, inventors developed machines that could produce large quantities of goods more efficiently. As the supply of goods increased, prices fell. Lower prices made goods more affordable and thus created more consumers who further fed the demand for goods. The Industrial Revolution affected not only how goods were made but also how people lived. It brought a tidal wave of economic and social changes that swept the industrializing nations of the world.

Geography and History

Europe's Canal Boom

People have dug canals since ancient times, but it took the Industrial Revolution to set off a canal-building frenzy in Europe. During the late 1700s and early 1800s, European factories needed an efficient, inexpensive way to receive coal and raw materials and then to ship finished goods to market. The many navigable rivers in Europe did not reach every town and sometimes followed indirect—and lengthy—courses. Canals solved the problem. They connected towns to more distant rivers and provided direct routes from factories to markets.

The canals soon lost some of their importance to railroads, but today Europe is still crisscrossed by a 13,000-mile network of canals and rivers.

Theme: Geography and History How did canals help to advance the Industrial Revolution?

SECTION 2 Assessment

Recall
1. **Identify:** (a) John Kay, (b) James Hargreaves, (c) Richard Arkwright, (d) George Stephenson.
2. **Define:** (a) capital, (b) factory, (c) turnpike.

Comprehension
3. Describe four factors that helped bring about the Industrial Revolution in Britain.
4. How did the Industrial Revolution transform the textile industry?
5. How did transportation improve in the early 1800s? Give three examples.

Critical Thinking and Writing
6. **Analyzing Information** Explain how each of the following helped contribute to demand for consumer goods in Britain: (a) population explosion, (b) general economic prosperity.
7. **Connecting to Geography** Look at the map of the British cotton trade in this section. (a) To what continents did Britain export its cotton cloth? (b) Explain how advances in transportation, such as the steamboat, contributed to Britain's global cotton trade.

Use the Internet to research connections between mining and transportation. Write a brief explanation of how canals affected the coal industry. For help with this activity, use **Web Code mkd-2004.**

Hardships of Early Industrial Life

Reading Focus

- What was life like in the new industrial city?
- How did the factory system change the way people worked?
- What benefits and problems did industrialization bring to the working class and the new middle class?

Vocabulary

urbanization

tenement

labor union

Taking Notes

Copy this table. As you read, list the characteristics of the working class and the middle class. Add more entries as needed.

THE WORKING CLASS	THE MIDDLE CLASS
Factory and mine workers	Merchants, inventors, skilled artisans
Tenement housing	

Main Idea The Industrial Revolution created material benefits as well as social problems.

Setting the Scene The Industrial Revolution brought great riches to most of the entrepreneurs who helped set it in motion. For the millions of workers who crowded into the new factories, however, the industrial age brought poverty and harsh living conditions. One observer commented on the disease-ridden neighborhoods and polluted air:

"The population . . . is crowded into one dense mass of cottages separated by unpaved and almost pestilential streets. This is an atmosphere loaded with the exhalation of a large manufacturing city."
—J. P. Kay, quoted in *Mill Life at Styal*

In time, reforms would curb many of the worst abuses of the early industrial age in Europe and the Americas, and people at all levels of society would benefit from industrialization. Until then, working people could look forward only to lives marked by dangerous working conditions; unsafe, unsanitary, and overcrowded housing; and unrelenting poverty.

The New Industrial City

The Industrial Revolution brought rapid urbanization, or the movement of people to cities. Changes in farming, soaring population growth, and an ever-increasing demand for workers led masses of people to migrate from farms to cities. Almost overnight, small towns around coal or iron mines mushroomed into cities. Other cities grew up around the factories that entrepreneurs built in once-quiet market towns.

The British market town of Manchester numbered 17,000 people in the 1750s. Within a few years, it exploded into a center of the textile industry. Its population soared to 40,000 by 1780 and 70,000 by 1801. Visitors described the "cloud of coal vapor" that polluted the air, the pounding noise of steam engines, and the filthy stench of its river.

In Manchester, as elsewhere, a gulf divided the urban population. The wealthy and the middle class lived in pleasant neighborhoods. Vast numbers of poor, however, struggled to survive in foul-smelling slums. They packed into tiny rooms in tenements, multistory buildings divided into crowded apartments. These buildings had no running water, only community pumps. There was no sewage or sanitation system, and wastes and garbage rotted in the streets. Cholera and other diseases spread rapidly. In time, reformers pushed for laws to improve conditions in city slums.

Find out more about the industrial age.

Primary Sources and Literature

See "Charles Dickens: Hard Times" in the Reference Section at the back of this book.

For: More about iron production during the Industrial Revolution
Visit: PHSchool.com
Web Code: mkd-2006

Forging the Anchor
This painting by William James Muler shows workers laboring to make an anchor of iron. The image provides a glimpse of the factory system.

Theme: Art and Literature
How would you describe the artist's opinion of factories?

The Factory System

The heart of the new industrial city was the factory. There, the technology of the machine age imposed a harsh new way of life on workers.

Rigid Discipline   The factory system differed greatly from farmwork. In rural villages, people worked hard, but their work varied according to the season. In factories, workers faced a rigid schedule set by the factory whistle. "While the engine runs," said an observer, "people must work—men, women, and children are yoked together with iron and steam."

Working hours were long. Shifts lasted from 12 to 16 hours. Exhausted workers suffered accidents from machines that had no safety devices. They might lose a finger, a limb, or even their lives. Workers were exposed to other dangers, as well. Coal dust destroyed the lungs of miners, and textile workers constantly breathed air filled with lint. If workers were sick or injured, they lost their jobs.

Women Workers   Employers often preferred to hire women workers rather than men. They thought women could adapt more easily to machines and were easier to manage than men. More important, they were able to pay women less than men, even for the same work.

Factory work created special problems for women. Their new jobs took them out of their homes for 12 hours or more a day. They then returned to crowded slum tenements to feed and clothe their families, clean, and cope with sickness and other problems. Family life had been hard for poor rural cottagers. In industrial towns, it was even grimmer.

Child Labor   Factories and mines also hired many boys and girls. Often, nimble-fingered and quick-moving children changed spools in textile mills. Others clambered through narrow mine shafts, pushing coal carts. Because children had helped with farmwork, parents accepted the idea of child labor. And the wages the children earned were needed to keep their families from starving.

Employers often hired orphans, making deals with local officials who were glad to have the children taken off their hands. Overseers beat children accused of idling. A few enlightened factory owners did provide basic education and a decent life for child workers. More often, though, children, like their parents, were slaves to the machines.

You Are There . . .

Spinning Thread in a Textile Mill

It is your first day at work and you're already exhausted. You wanted to help your family by earning extra money, so you came to Manchester to work with your uncle in a textile mill. You must work on several machines at once, keeping the thread from tangling and breaking. The factory still seems so strange.

The thunder of the spinning mule vibrates through the floor. This machine allows you to make thread faster by yourself than hundreds of people spinning by hand.

It is hard to breathe. Cotton dust flies out of the machines. You hear other workers coughing, their lungs filled with the thick dust.

Children dart in and out, untying knots in the thread. You wince as you see a little boy almost get his hand caught in a machine. The boss gives you a disapproving look, so you try to focus on your own work.

Portfolio Assessment

After a 12-hour day at the mill, you decide to write a letter to your family. In your letter, describe your new job and say whether you want to keep working here in Manchester or go back home to the farm.

Worker Protests
On a hot August day in 1819, workers gathered in St. Peter's Fields in Manchester to hear reformers speak. Suddenly, soldiers attacked the crowd. The incident became known as the Peterloo Massacre.

Theme: Art and Literature
Did the artist who created this cartoon favor the workers or the soldiers? Explain.

In the 1830s and 1840s, British lawmakers looked into abuses in factories and mines. Government commissions heard about children as young as five years old working in factories. Some died; others were stunted in growth or had twisted limbs. Most were uneducated. Slowly, Parliament passed laws to regulate child labor in mines and factories.

The Working Class

In rural villages, farm families had strong ties to a community in which they had lived for generations. When they moved to the new industrial cities, many felt lost and bewildered. In time, though, factory and mine workers developed their own sense of community.

Protests As the Industrial Revolution began, weavers and other skilled artisans resisted the new "labor-saving" machines that were costing them their jobs. Some smashed machines and burned factories. In England, such rioters were called Luddites after a mythical figure, Ned Ludd, who supposedly destroyed machines in the 1780s.

Protests met harsh repression. When workers held a rally in Manchester in 1819, soldiers charged the crowd, killing a dozen and injuring hundreds more. Workers were forbidden to organize in groups to bargain for better pay and working conditions. Strikes were outlawed.

Spread of Methodism Many working-class people found comfort in a new religious movement. In the mid-1700s, John Wesley had founded the Methodist Church. Wesley stressed the need for a personal sense of faith. He urged Christians to improve their lot by adopting sober, moral ways.

Methodist meetings featured hymns and sermons promising forgiveness of sin and a better life to come. Methodist preachers took this message of salvation into the slums. There, they tried to rekindle hope among the working poor. They set up Sunday schools where followers not only studied the Bible but also learned to read and write. Methodists helped channel workers' anger away from revolution and toward social reform.

The New Middle Class

Those who benefited most from the Industrial Revolution were the entrepreneurs who set it in motion. This new middle class came from several sources. Some members were merchants who invested their growing profits in factories. Others were inventors or skilled artisans who developed new technologies. Some rose from "rags to riches," a pattern that the age greatly admired.

Middle-class families lived in solid, well-furnished homes. They dressed and ate well. Middle-class men gained influence in Parliament, where they opposed any effort to improve conditions for workers.

As a sign of their new standard of living, middle-class women were encouraged to become "ladies." They took up "ladylike" activities, such as drawing, embroidery, or playing the piano. A "lady" did not work outside the home or do housework. Instead, the family hired a maid-servant. The family then set about educating its daughters to provide the same type of happy, well-furnished home for their future husbands. Sons gained an education that allowed them to become businessmen.

The new middle class valued hard work and the determination to "get ahead." They had confidence in themselves and often little sympathy for the poor. If they thought of the faceless millions in the factories and mines, they generally supposed the poor to be responsible for their own misery. Some believed the poor were so lazy or ignorant that they could not "work their way up" out of poverty.

Benefits and Problems

Since the 1800s, people have debated whether the Industrial Revolution was a blessing or a curse. The early industrial age brought terrible hardships. Said English writer Thomas Carlyle, "Something [ought] to be done."

In time, "something" would be done. Reformers pressed for laws to improve working conditions. Workers' organizations called labor unions won the right to bargain with employers for better wages, hours, and working conditions. Eventually, working-class men gained the right to vote, which gave them political power.

Despite the social problems created by the Industrial Revolution—low pay, unemployment, dismal living conditions—the industrial age did bring material benefits. As demand for mass-produced goods grew, new factories opened, creating more jobs. Wages rose so that workers had enough left after paying rent and buying food to buy a newspaper or visit a music hall. As the cost of railroad travel fell, people could visit family in other towns. Horizons widened; opportunities increased.

Industrialization has spread around the world today. Often, it begins with great suffering. In the end, however, it produces more material benefits for more people.

SECTION 3 Assessment

Recall

1. **Identify:** (a) Luddite, (b) John Wesley, (c) Methodism.
2. **Define:** (a) urbanization, (b) tenement, (c) labor union.

Comprehension

3. Describe life in the new industrial city.
4. (a) What were the main characteristics of factory work? (b) What special problems did factory work create for women?

5. How did the conditions of the early industrial age improve?

Critical Thinking and Writing

6. **Comparing** Compare the life of a farmworker with that of an early factory worker.
7. **Connecting to Geography** Look at the chapter opener map. What geographic feature do many of the industrial centers share? Why do you think this is so?

Go Online
PHSchool.com

Search the Internet for information about working conditions during the Industrial Revolution. Draw a political cartoon that illustrates the life of factory workers. Write a caption for your cartoon. For help with this activity, use **Web Code mkd-2009**.

New Ways of Thinking

Reading Focus

- What was laissez-faire economics?

- How did the views of utilitarians differ from those of socialists?

- What were the ideas of "scientific socialism," introduced by Karl Marx?

Vocabulary

utilitarianism

socialism

means of production

communism

proletariat

Taking Notes

As you read this section, prepare an outline of its contents. Use Roman numerals to indicate major headings. Use capital letters for subheadings, and use numbers for the supporting details. The example here will help you get started.

I. Laissez-faire economics
   A. Legacy of Adam Smith
      1. Benefits of free market
      2.
   B. Malthus on population
      1. Population outpaces food supply
      2.

Main Idea The Industrial Revolution fostered new ideas about business and economics.

Biography

Adam Smith 1723–1790

If anyone fit the image of the "absent-minded professor," it was Adam Smith. He forgot things, spoke awkwardly, and rambled as he walked. "I am a beau in nothing but my books," Smith once said. Still, he had one of history's keenest minds.

At the age of 14, Smith was a student at a university in his native Scotland. There, and later in Paris, he met many influential thinkers of the Enlightenment. He also met local merchants, gaining practical knowledge about business.

Smith spent 10 years writing *The Wealth of Nations.* Published in 1776, it became an instant bestseller. Readers embraced Smith's ideas about laissez-faire and the benefits of capitalism.

Theme: Impact of the Individual How did Smith's education shape his work?

Setting the Scene

Everywhere in Britain, Thomas Malthus saw the effects of the population explosion—crowded slums, hungry families, unemployment, and widespread misery. After careful study, in 1798 he published his "Essay on the Principle of Population." Poverty and misery, he concluded, were unavoidable because the population was increasing faster than the food supply. Malthus wrote: "The power of population is [far] greater than the power of the Earth to produce subsistence for man."

Malthus was one of many thinkers who tried to understand the staggering changes taking place in the early industrial age. As heirs to the Enlightenment, these thinkers looked for natural laws that governed the world of business and economics.

Laissez-Faire Economics

During the Enlightenment, physiocrats argued that natural laws should be allowed to operate without interference. As part of this philosophy, they believed that government should not interfere in the free operation of the economy. In the early 1800s, middle-class business leaders embraced this laissez-faire, or "hands-off," approach.

Legacy of Adam Smith The main prophet of laissez-faire economics was Adam Smith, author of *The Wealth of Nations.* Smith asserted that a free market—the unregulated exchange of goods and services—would come to help everyone, not just the rich.

The free market, Smith said, would produce more goods at lower prices, making them affordable by everyone. A growing economy would also encourage capitalists to reinvest profits in new ventures. Supporters of this free-enterprise capitalism pointed to the successes of the industrial age, in which government had played no part.

Malthus on Population Like Smith's book, Thomas Malthus's writings on population shaped economic thinking for generations. Malthus grimly predicted that population would outpace the food supply. The only checks on population growth, he said, were war, disease, and famine. As long as population kept increasing, he went on, the poor would suffer. He thus urged families to have fewer children.

During the early 1800s, many people accepted Malthus's bleak view. It proved to be too pessimistic, however. Although the population boom did continue, the food supply grew even faster. As the century progressed, living conditions for the western world also slowly improved—and then people began having fewer children. By the 1900s, population growth was no longer a problem in the West, but it did continue to afflict many nations elsewhere.

Ricardo on Wages Another influential British economist, David Ricardo, agreed with Malthus that the poor had too many children. In his "iron law of wages," Ricardo pointed out that when wages were high, families had more children. But more children meant a greater supply of labor, which led to lower wages and higher unemployment. Like Malthus, Ricardo did not hold out hope for the working class to escape poverty. Because of such gloomy predictions, economics became known as the "dismal science."

Neither Malthus nor Ricardo was a cruel man. Yet both opposed any government help for the poor. To these supporters of laissez-faire economics, the best cure for poverty was not government relief but the unrestricted "laws of the free market." They felt that individuals should be left to improve their lot through thrift, hard work, and limiting the size of their families.

The Utilitarians

Others adapted laissez-faire doctrines to justify some government intervention. By 1800, Jeremy Bentham was preaching utilitarianism, the idea that the goal of society should be "the greatest happiness for the greatest number" of its citizens. To Bentham, all laws or actions should be judged by their "utility." Did they provide more pleasure (happiness) than pain? He strongly supported individual freedom, which he believed guaranteed happiness. Still, he saw the need for government to become involved under certain circumstances.

Bentham's chief follower, John Stuart Mill, also argued that actions are right if they promote happiness and wrong if they cause pain. He reexamined the idea that unrestricted competition in the free market was always good. Often, he said, it favored the strong over the weak.

Although he believed strongly in individual freedom, Mill wanted the government to step in to improve the hard lives of the working class. "The only purpose for which power can be rightfully exercised over any member of a civilized community, against his will," Mill wrote, "is to prevent harm to others. His own good, either physical or moral, is not a sufficient warrant [cause]." While middle-class business and factory owners were entitled to increase their own happiness, therefore, government should prevent them from doing so in a manner that harmed workers.

Mill further called for giving the vote to workers and women. These groups could then use their political power to win reforms. Utilitarians also worked for reforms in many other areas affecting workers and the poor, from child labor to public health.

Most middle-class people rejected Mill's ideas. Only in the later 1800s were his views slowly accepted. Today's democratic governments, however, have absorbed many ideas from Mill and the other utilitarians.

Emergence of Socialism

While the champions of laissez-faire economics praised individual rights, other thinkers focused on the good of society in general. They condemned the evils of industrial capitalism, which they believed had created a gulf between rich and poor. To end poverty and injustice, they offered a radical solution—socialism. Under socialism, the people as a whole rather than private individuals would own and operate the means of production—the

Overcrowded Conditions
Thomas Malthus warned that population growth could exhaust the food supply, bringing misery to the poor. In *Bishopsgate Street*, artist Gustave Doré captures the squalor and overcrowded conditions of a London slum.
Theme: Political and Social Systems What did Malthus recommend as a solution to the problems of the early industrial age?

farms, factories, railways, and other large businesses that produced and distributed goods.

Socialism grew out of the Enlightenment faith in progress, its belief in the basic goodness of human nature, and its concern for social justice. Socialists wanted to develop a world in which society would operate for the benefit of all members, rather than just for the wealthy. In a socialist society, one reformer predicted:

> "There will be no war, no crime, no administration of justice, as it is called, no government. Besides there will be neither disease, anguish, melancholy, nor resentment. Every man will seek . . . the good of all."
> —William Godwin, "Political Justice"

Connections to Today

Day Care

Robert Owen founded a model village, shown above, for his workers. Owen was not the last employer to provide for the children of his employees. Today, many businesses provide child-care services, either on site or at a separate day care center.

Companies find that child care is an important issue for many people seeking jobs. One center in Denmark has tried to go a step further. Staff at the day care center will also do laundry, shop for groceries, and cook take-out dinners. Additionally, the center has a video camera hooked up to the Internet so parents can log on and see how their child is doing.

Theme: Economics and Technology Why might some companies choose to provide day care for employees' children?

The Utopians Early socialists tried to build self-sufficient communities in which all work was shared and all property was owned in common. When there was no difference between rich and poor, they felt, fighting between people would disappear. These early socialists were called Utopians, after Thomas More's ideal community. The name implied that they were impractical dreamers. However, the Utopian Robert Owen did set up a model community to put his ideas into practice.

Robert Owen A poor Welsh boy, Owen became a successful mill owner. Unlike most industrialists at the time, he refused to use child labor. He campaigned vigorously for laws that limited child labor and encouraged the organization of labor unions.

Owen insisted that the conditions in which people lived shaped their character. To prove his point, he set up his factory in New Lanark, Scotland, as a model village. He built homes for workers, opened a school for children, and generally treated employees well. He showed that an employer could offer decent living and working conditions and still run a profitable business. By the 1820s, many people were visiting New Lanark to study Owen's reforms.

The "Scientific Socialism" of Karl Marx

In the 1840s, Karl Marx, a German philosopher, condemned the ideas of the Utopians as unrealistic idealism. He put forward a new theory, "scientific socialism," which he claimed was based on a scientific study of history.

As a young man in Germany, Marx agitated for reform. Forced to leave his homeland because of his radical ideas, he lived first in Paris and then settled in London. He teamed up with another German socialist, Friedrich Engels, whose father owned a textile factory in England.

Marx and Engels wrote a pamphlet, *The Communist Manifesto*, which they published in 1848. "A spectre is haunting Europe," it began, "the spectre of communism." Communism is a form of socialism that sees class struggle between employers and employees as unavoidable.

Marxism In *The Communist Manifesto*, Marx theorized that economics was the driving force in history. The entire course of history, he argued, was "the history of class struggles" between the "haves" and the "have-nots." The "haves" have always owned the means of production and thus controlled society and all its wealth. In industrialized Europe, Marx said, the "haves" were the bourgeoisie. The "have-nots" were the proletariat, or working class.

According to Marx, the modern class struggle pitted the bourgeoisie against the proletariat. In the end, he predicted, the proletariat would be triumphant. It would then take control of the means of production and set up a classless, communist society. Such a society would mark the end of the struggles people had endured throughout history, because wealth and power would be equally shared.

Marx despised capitalism. He believed it created prosperity for only a few and poverty for many. He called for an international struggle to bring about its downfall. "Working men of all countries," he urged, "unite!"

Looking Ahead

At first, Marxism gained popularity with many people around the world. Leaders of a number of reform movements adopted the idea that power should be held by workers rather than by business owners. Marx's ideas would never be practiced exactly as he imagined them, however.

Failures   As time passed, the failures of Marxist governments would illustrate the flaws in his arguments. Marx claimed that his ideas were based on scientific laws. However, many of the assumptions on which he based his theories were wrong. He predicted that the misery of the proletariat would touch off a world revolution. Instead, by 1900, the efforts of reformers and governments led to improved conditions for the working class. As a result, Marxism lost some of its appeal in the industrially developed countries of Europe and North America.

Marx also predicted that workers would unite across national borders to wage class warfare. Instead, nationalism won out over working-class loyalty. In general, people felt stronger ties to their own countries than to the international communist movement.

Revolutions   These failures did not doom the movement instantly. In the late 1800s, Russian socialists embraced Marxism, and the Russian Revolution of 1917 set up a communist-inspired government. For much of the 1900s, revolutionaries around the world would adapt Marxist ideas to their own needs. Independence leaders in Asia, Latin America, and Africa would turn to Marxism. By the 1990s, however, nearly every nation would incorporate elements of free-market capitalism. To many people, Adam Smith's ideas seemed to be of more lasting value than those of Karl Marx.

SECTION 4 Assessment

Recall
1. **Identify: (a)** Thomas Malthus, **(b)** iron law of wages, **(c)** John Stuart Mill, **(d)** Utopians, **(e)** Karl Marx.
2. **Define: (a)** utilitarianism, **(b)** socialism, **(c)** means of production, **(d)** communism, **(e)** proletariat.

Comprehension
3. Describe the views of laissez-faire economists **(a)** Adam Smith, **(b)** Thomas Malthus, and **(c)** David Ricardo.
4. Contrast the approaches of utilitarians and socialists to solving economic problems.

5. **(a)** Describe Karl Marx's view of history. **(b)** How have events challenged that view?

Critical Thinking and Writing
6. **Linking Past and Present** Choose one economic or political theory discussed in this section. Does that theory seem to apply to the American economy today? Explain.
7. **Applying Information** How might the rise of Methodism and workplace reforms alter Marxist predictions of world revolution?

Activity

Asking Questions
Write five questions you might ask if you were conducting an interview with Robert Owen. Include questions about his goals, how he tried to accomplish them, and whether he succeeded.

Creating a Chapter Summary

Copy this chart on a sheet of paper. Complete the chart by naming the invention or idea developed by each person on the left. One row has been filled in to help you get started.

INVENTORS AND THINKERS	INVENTIONS AND IDEAS
Jethro Tull	
Thomas Newcomen	
Richard Arkwright	
George Stephenson	
John Wesley	Methodism
Adam Smith	
David Ricardo	
Jeremy Bentham	
Robert Owen	
Karl Marx	

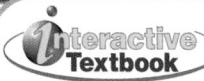

For additional review and enrichment activities, see the interactive version of *World History* available on the Web and on CD-ROM.

For practice test questions for Chapter 7, use **Web Code mka-2014**.

Building Vocabulary

(a) Classify each of the chapter vocabulary words listed below under *one* of the following themes: Continuity and Change; Political and Social Systems; Economics and Technology. **(b)** Choose one word in each category and write a sentence explaining how that word relates to the theme.

1. anesthetic
2. smelt
3. capital
4. factory
5. urbanization
6. labor union
7. utilitarianism
8. means of production
9. proletariat

Recalling Key Facts

10. How did the enclosure movement affect people?
11. What new source of energy helped trigger the Industrial Revolution?
12. List three reasons why the Industrial Revolution began in Britain.
13. Why did large numbers of people migrate to cities?
14. List the government reforms sought by John Stuart Mill.

Critical Thinking and Writing

15. **Connecting to Geography** Explain the link between Britain's natural resources and its rise as an industrial nation.
16. **Analyzing Political Cartoons** Study the political cartoon in Section 3. **(a)** What is the subject of the cartoon? **(b)** Who are the men on horseback? **(c)** Who are the people under attack? **(d)** What do you think was the artist's purpose in creating the cartoon?
17. **Analyzing Information** Describe how the Industrial Revolution affected each of the following: **(a)** size of population, **(b)** cities, **(c)** working and living conditions, **(d)** women and children.
18. **Linking Past and Present** **(a)** How did thinkers in the 1800s disagree about the role of government in helping the poor? **(b)** Give three examples to show that this debate continues today.
19. **Defending a Position** Do you think that the negative social consequences of the Industrial Revolution could have been avoided? Use material from this chapter to defend your position.

In the excerpt below, a British newspaper correspondent details the daily life of cotton-mill workers in the northern industrial town of Manchester. Read the excerpt, then answer the questions that follow.

"The streets in the neighborhood of the mills are thronged with men and women and children flocking to their labour. . . . The factory bell rings from five minutes before six until the hour strikes. Then—to the moment—the engine starts and the day's work begins. Those who are [late], be it but a moment, are fined twopence, and in many mills, after the expiration of a very short time of grace, the doors are locked, and the laggard, besides the fine, loses his morning work.

. . . I fear that I cannot say much for the cleanliness of the workpeople. They have an essentially greasy look, which makes me sometimes think that water would run off their skins, as it does off a duck's back. In this respect the women are just as bad as the men. . . . The spinners and piecers . . . fling shoes and stockings aside, but I fear it is very seldom that their feet see the interior of a tub, with plenty of hot water and soap."

—from "A Working Day" in *Labour and the Poor in England and Wales, 1849–1851*

20. Who made up the work force at the mill?
21. How were workers punished for being late?
22. How did the correspondent view the workers' personal hygiene habits?
23. Why might the spinners and piecers work barefoot?
24. Based on what you have read, would the correspondent view himself as a member of the proletariat? Explain your answer.

Skills Tip

When you read a primary source, try to determine whether the writer identifies with the people or events being described. Is the writer's viewpoint sympathetic or unsympathetic?

BRITISH OUTPUT OF COAL, 1820–1850

Coal Output (in thousands of metric tons)

Year

Source: B. R. Mitchell, *European Historical Statistics 1750–1970*

BRITISH EXPORTS OF COAL, 1820–1850

Coal Export (in thousands of metric tons)

Year

Source: B. R. Mitchell, *European Historical Statistics 1750–1970*

Use the graphs to answer the following questions:

25. By what year had the coal output of 1820 doubled?
26. **(a)** By about how many metric tons did coal output increase between 1820 and 1840? **(b)** Between 1840 and 1850?
27. Write a sentence that summarizes the information about coal output and exports presented in these graphs.

Go Online
PHSchool.com

Use the Internet to research primary or secondary sources on the daily life of factory workers during the Industrial Revolution. Then, write a paper explaining why you do or do not think that the benefits of living in an industrialized nation today outweigh some of the social consequences of the Industrial Revolution. For help with this activity, use **Web Code mkd-2015.**

Revolutions in Europe and Latin America

1790–1848

Chapter Preview

1   An Age of Ideologies
2   Revolutions of 1830 and 1848
3   Latin American Wars of Independence

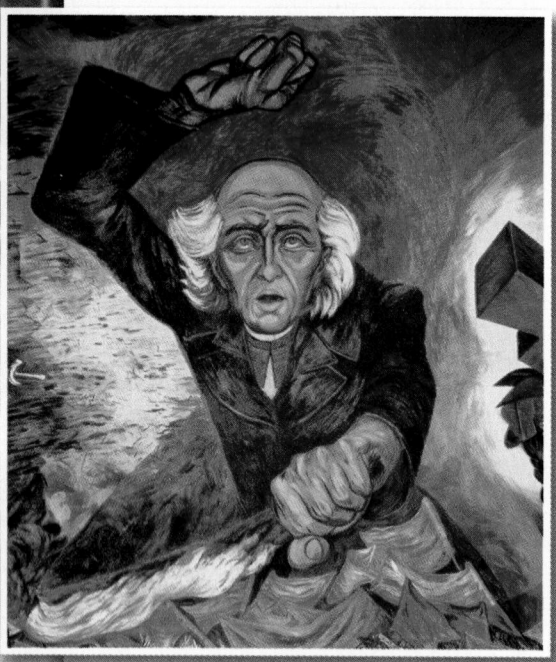

1810

Father Miguel Hidalgo
urges Mexicans to fight for
independence from Spain.

1804

Haiti declares independence
from France.

1819

Simón Bolívar, later known
as "The Liberator," seizes
Bogota from the Spanish.

**CHAPTER
EVENTS**

1800   1810   1820

**GLOBAL
EVENTS**

1803 United States buys
Louisiana from France.

1820 Several thousand British
colonists settle in South Africa.

Revolutions in Europe, 1815–1829

Despite the order imposed by the Congress of Vienna, several revolutions erupted in Europe between 1815 and 1829. The spread of revolutionary ideals would ignite new uprisings in 1830 and 1848.

DENMARK

NETHERLANDS

HANOVER

PRUSSIA

Vistula R.

RUSSIA

Elbe R.

Oder R.

Rhine R.

BAVARIA

SAXONY

Seine R.

Loire R.

AUSTRIAN EMPIRE

Danube R.

FRANCE

SWITZ.

ALPS

LOMBARDY–VENETIA

Po R.

Rhône R.

PAPAL STATES

SERBIA

Black Sea

TUSCANY

PIEDMONT–SARDINIA

Tiber R.

Adriatic Sea

OTTOMAN EMPIRE

PORTUGAL

SPAIN

Ebro R.

PYRENEES MTS.

Tagus R.

ATLANTIC OCEAN

KINGDOM OF THE TWO SICILIES

GREECE

Mediterranean Sea

50°N

40°N

30°E

30°N

20°E

10°E

0°

10°W

Azimuthal Equal Area Projection

0   150   300 Miles

0   150   300 Kilometers

N W E S

Legend:
- Areas where revolutions occurred
- Repression of revolutions
  - → French forces
  - → Austrian forces
  - → Ottoman forces

1830
French revolutionaries battle the king's troops in the streets of Paris.

1848
Revolutions break out across much of Europe.

1830 | **1840** | **1850**

1839 China and Britain clash in the Opium War.

1850 Taiping Rebellion begins in China.

An Age of Ideologies

Reading Focus

- What were the goals of conservatives?
- How did liberalism and nationalism challenge the old order?
- Why was Europe plagued by revolts after 1815?

Vocabulary

ideology

universal manhood suffrage

autonomy

Taking Notes

Copy this chart. As you read this section, list the ideas of conservatism, liberalism, and nationalism.

CONSERVATISM	LIBERALISM	NATIONALISM

Main Idea After 1815, the clash of people with opposing ideologies plunged Europe into an era of turmoil that lasted more than 30 years.

The Conservative Order Conservatives were determined to preserve the old order. At the heart of that order was the monarchy, symbolized in the Austrian empire by the Hapsburg coat of arms shown here.

Theme: Political and Social Systems What other institutions besides the monarchy were part of the old order?

Setting the Scene
A "revolutionary seed" had been planted in Europe, warned Prince Clemens von Metternich. The ideas spread by the French Revolution and Napoleon Bonaparte, he believed, not only threatened Europe's monarchs but also undermined its basic social values:

> "Passions are let loose . . . to overthrow everything that society respects as the basis of its existence: religion, public morality, laws, customs, rights, and duties, all are attacked, confounded, overthrown, or called in question."
> —*Memoirs of Prince Metternich*

At the Congress of Vienna, the powers of Europe tried to uproot that "revolutionary seed." Other voices, however, kept challenging the order imposed in 1815. The clash of people with opposing ideologies, or systems of thought and belief, plunged Europe into more than 30 years of turmoil.

Conservatives and the Old Order

The Congress of Vienna was a victory for the conservative forces, which included monarchs and their officials, noble landowners, and church leaders. Conservatives supported the political and social order that had existed before the French Revolution. Conservative ideas also appealed to peasants, who wanted to preserve traditional ways.

Conservatives of the early 1800s wanted to turn the clock back to the way things had been before 1789. After all, they had benefited under the old order. They wanted to restore royal families to the thrones they had lost when Napoleon swept across Europe. They supported a social hierarchy in which lower classes were expected to respect and obey their social superiors. Conservatives also backed an established church—Catholic in Austria and southern Europe, Protestant in northern Europe, and Orthodox in eastern Europe.

Conservatives believed that talk about natural rights and constitutional government could lead only to chaos, as it had in France in 1789. If change had to come, they argued, it must come slowly. Conservatives felt that they benefited all people by defending peace and stability. Conservative leaders like Metternich sought to suppress revolutionary ideas. Metternich urged monarchs to oppose freedom of the press, crush protests in their own countries, and send troops to douse the flames of rebellion in neighboring lands.

The Liberal and Nationalist Challenge

Challenging the conservatives at every turn were liberals and nationalists who were inspired by the Enlightenment and the French Revolution. Liberalism and nationalism ignited a number of revolts against established rule.

Liberal Goals Because liberals spoke mostly for the bourgeoisie, or middle class, their ideas are sometimes called "bourgeois liberalism." Liberals included business owners, bankers, and lawyers, as well as politicians, newspaper editors, writers, and others who helped to shape public opinion.

Liberals wanted governments to be based on written constitutions and separation of powers. Liberals spoke out against divine-right monarchy, the old aristocracy, and established churches. They defended the natural rights of individuals to liberty, equality, and property. They called for rulers elected by the people and responsible to them. Thus, most liberals favored a republican form of government over a monarchy, or at least wanted the monarch to be limited by a constitution.

The liberals of the early 1800s saw the role of government as limited to protecting basic rights such as freedom of thought, speech, and religion. They believed that only male property owners or others with a financial stake in society should have the right to vote. Only later in the century did liberals support the principle of universal manhood suffrage, giving all adult men the right to vote.

Liberals strongly supported the laissez-faire economics of Adam Smith and David Ricardo. They saw the free market as an opportunity for capitalist entrepreneurs to succeed. As capitalists and often employers, liberals had different goals from those of workers laboring in factories, mines, and other enterprises of the early Industrial Revolution.

Nationalist Goals For centuries, European rulers had gained or lost lands through wars, marriages, and treaties. They exchanged territories and the people in them like pieces in a game. As a result, by 1815 Europe had several empires that included many nationalities. The Austrian, Russian, and Ottoman empires, for example, each included diverse peoples.

In the 1800s, national groups who shared a common heritage set out to win their own states. Within the diverse Austrian empire, for example, various nationalist leaders tried to unite and win independence for each particular group. Nationalism gave people with a common heritage a sense of identity and the goal of creating their own homeland. At the same time, however, nationalism often bred intolerance and led to persecution of other ethnic or national groups.

The Serb Revolt
In 1804, the Serb leader Karageorge, shown below, led a revolt against Ottoman rule. Ottoman troops crushed this rebellion by 1813, but renewed resistance would eventually lead to Serbian independence.

Theme: Political and Social Systems Why did the Ottoman empire face frequent rebellions in the 1800s?

Revolts Against the Old Order

Spurred by the ideas of liberalism and nationalism, revolutionaries fought against the old order. During the early 1800s, rebellions erupted in the Balkan Peninsula and elsewhere along the southern fringe of Europe. The Balkans, in southeastern Europe, were inhabited by people of various religions and ethnic groups. These peoples had lived under Ottoman rule for more than 300 years.

Independence for Serbia

The first Balkan people to revolt were the Serbs. From 1804 to 1813, the Serb leader Karageorge led a guerrilla war against the Ottomans. The bitter struggle was unsuccessful, but it fostered a sense of Serbian identity. A revival of Serbian literature and culture added to the sense of nationhood.

In 1815, Milos Obrenovic led the Serbs in a second, more successful rebellion. One reason for the success was that Obrenovic turned to Russia for assistance. Like the Serbs, the Russian people were Slavic in language and Christian Orthodox in religion. By 1830, Russian support helped the Serbs win **autonomy,** or self-rule, within the Ottoman empire. The Ottoman sultan later agreed to formal independence. In the future, Russia would continue to defend Serbian interests and affect events in the Balkans.

Independence for Greece

In 1821, the Greeks, too, revolted, seeking to end centuries of Ottoman rule. At first, the Greeks were badly divided. But years of suffering in long, bloody wars of independence helped shape a national identity. Leaders of the rebellion justified their struggle as "a national war, a holy war, a war the object of which is to reconquer the rights of individual liberty." They sought help from Western Europeans, who admired ancient Greek civilization.

The Greeks won sympathy in the West. In the late 1820s, Britain, France, and even conservative Russia forced the Ottomans to grant independence to some Greek provinces. By 1830, Greece was independent. The European powers, however, pressured the Greeks to accept a German king, a move meant to show that they did not support revolution. Still, liberals were enthusiastic, and nationalists everywhere saw reasons to hope for a country of their own.

Other Challenges

Several other challenges to the Vienna peace settlement erupted in the 1820s. Revolts occurred along the southern fringe of Europe. In Spain, Portugal, and various states in the Italian peninsula, rebels struggled to gain constitutional governments.

Metternich urged conservative rulers to act decisively and crush the dangerous uprisings. In response, a French army marched over the Pyrenees to suppress a revolt in Spain. Austrian forces crossed the Alps to smash rebellious outbreaks in Italy.

Troops dampened the fires of liberalism and nationalism, but could not smother them. In the next decades, sparks would flare anew. Added to liberal and nationalist demands were the goals of the new industrial working class. By the mid-1800s, social reformers and agitators were urging workers to support socialism or other ways of reorganizing property ownership.

Primary Source

Byron, Glory, and Greece

The English poet Lord Byron went to Greece to aid the fight for independence. He wrote these lines:

"The sword, the banner, and the field,
  Glory and Greece, around me see!
The Spartan, borne upon his shield,
  Was not more free.

Awake! (not Greece—she is awake!)
  Awake, my spirit! Think through whom
Thy lifeblood tracks its parent lake,
  And then strike home! . . ."

—George Gordon, Lord Byron, "On This Day I Complete My Thirty-Sixth Year"

Skills Assessment

Primary Source Why did Lord Byron admire Greece?

SECTION 1 Assessment

Recall

1. **Identify: (a)** conservatives, **(b)** liberals, **(c)** nationalists, **(d)** Karageorge, **(e)** Milos Obrenovic.
2. **Define: (a)** ideology, **(b)** universal manhood suffrage, **(c)** autonomy.

Comprehension

3. What were the goals of conservative leaders?
4. **(a)** How did the political goals of liberals differ from those of conservatives? **(b)** How did nationalists threaten the system set up by Metternich?
5. **(a)** Why did the Serbs and Greeks revolt? **(b)** Why were there uprisings in Spain, Portugal, and the Italian states?

Critical Thinking and Writing

6. **Applying Information** How did ideologies like liberalism and nationalism contribute to unrest?
7. **Analyzing Information** Why do you think liberals of the early 1800s supported limited voting rights?

Go Online
PHSchool.com

On the Internet, find a site that contains some of the writings of Metternich. Print an excerpt that describes one of the key ideas of conservatism. Explain the main idea of the excerpt. For help with this activity, use **Web Code mkd-2120.**

Reading Focus

- Why did revolutions occur in France in 1830 and 1848?
- How did revolution spread in 1830?
- What were the results of the 1848 revolutions?

Vocabulary

ultraroyalist
recession

Taking Notes

Copy this graphic organizer. As you read, fill in information about conditions before and after the revolutions of 1848.

REVOLUTIONS OF 1848	
Before	**After**
• France is a monarchy	• France is a republic
•	•

Main Idea Revolutions broke out across Europe in 1830 and 1848, but most failed to achieve their goals.

Setting the Scene The quick suppression of liberal and nationalist uprisings in the 1820s did not end Europe's age of revolutions. "We are sleeping on a volcano," warned Alexis de Tocqueville, a liberal French leader who saw widespread discontent. "Do you not see that the Earth trembles anew? A wind of revolution blows, the storm is on the horizon."

In 1830 and 1848, Europeans saw street protests explode into full-scale revolts. As in 1789, the upheavals began in Paris and radiated out across the continent.

DISCOVERY CHANNEL SCHOOL Video
Experience the spirit of revolution.

The French Revolution of 1830

When the Congress of Vienna restored Louis XVIII to the French throne, he wisely issued a constitution, the Charter of French Liberties. It created a two-house legislature and allowed limited freedom of the press. Still, although Louis was careful to avoid absolutism, the king retained much power.

Sources of Unrest Louis's efforts at compromise satisfied few people. Ultraroyalists, the king's supporters on the far right, despised constitutional government and wanted to restore the old regime. The "ultras" included many high clergy and émigré nobles who had returned to France in the years after the revolution.

The ultras faced bitter opposition from other factions. Liberals wanted to extend suffrage and win a share of power for middle-class citizens like themselves. On the left, radicals yearned for a republic like that of the 1790s. And in working-class slums, men and women wanted what they had wanted in 1789—a decent day's pay and bread they could afford.

The July Revolution When Louis XVIII died in 1824, his younger brother, Charles X, inherited the throne. Charles, a strong believer in absolutism, rejected the very idea of the charter. In July 1830, he suspended the legislature, limited the right to vote, and restricted the press.

Liberals and radicals responded forcefully to the king's challenge. In Paris, angry citizens threw up barricades across the narrow streets. From behind them, they fired on the soldiers and pelted them with stones and roof tiles. Within days, rebels controlled Paris. The revolutionary tricolor flew from the towers of Notre Dame cathedral. A frightened Charles X abdicated and fled to England.

With the king gone, radicals wanted to set up a republic. Moderate liberals, however, insisted on a constitutional monarchy. The Chamber of

Deputies, the lower house of the French legislature, chose Louis Philippe as king. He was a cousin of Charles X and in his youth had supported the revolution of 1789.

The "Citizen King" The French called Louis Philippe the "citizen king" because he owed his throne to the people. Louis got along well with the liberal bourgeoisie. Like them, he dressed in a frock coat and top hat. Sometimes, he strolled the streets, shaking hands with well-wishers. Liberal politicians and professionals filled his government.

Under Louis Philippe, the upper bourgeoisie prospered. Louis extended suffrage, but only to France's wealthier citizens. The vast majority of the people still could not vote. The king's other policies also favored the middle class at the expense of the workers.

The French Revolution of 1848

In the 1840s, discontent grew. Radicals formed secret societies to work for a French republic. Utopian socialists called for an end to private ownership of property. (See the previous chapter.) Even liberals denounced Louis Philippe's government for corruption and called for expanded suffrage.

Near the end of the decade, discontent was heightened by a recession, or period of reduced economic activity. Factories shut down and people lost their jobs. Poor harvests caused bread prices to rise. Newspapers blamed government officials for some of the problems. As in 1789, Paris was ripe for revolution.

"February Days" In February 1848, when the government took steps to silence critics and prevent public meetings, angry crowds took to the streets. During the "February Days," iron railings, overturned carts, paving stones, and toppled trees again blocked the streets of Paris. Church bells rang alarms, while women and men on the barricades sang the revolutionary "La Marseillaise." A number of demonstrators clashed with royal troops and were killed.

As the turmoil spread, Louis Philippe abdicated. A group of liberal, radical, and socialist leaders proclaimed the Second Republic. (The First Republic had lasted from 1792 until 1804, when Napoleon became emperor.)

From the start, deep differences divided the new government. Middle-class liberals wanted moderate political reforms. Socialists wanted far-reaching social and economic change that would help hungry workers. In the early days of the new republic, the socialists forced the government to set up national workshops to provide jobs for the unemployed.

"June Days" By June, however, upper- and middle-class interests had won control of the government. They saw the national workshops as a waste of money, and they shut them down.

Furious, workers took to the streets of Paris, rallying to the cry "Bread or Lead!" This time, however, bourgeois liberals turned violently against the protesters. Peasants, who feared that socialists might take their land, also attacked the rioting workers. At least 1,500 people were killed before the government crushed the rebellion.

The fighting of the "June Days" left a bitter legacy. The middle class both feared and distrusted the left, while the working class nursed a deep hatred for the bourgeoisie.

Louis Napoleon By the end of 1848, the National Assembly, dominated by members who wanted to restore order, issued a constitution for the Second Republic. It created a strong president and a one-house legislature. But it also gave the vote to all adult men, the widest suffrage in the world at the time. Nine million Frenchmen now could vote, compared with only 200,000 who had that right before.

Art and Revolution

Art became more than an expression of beauty and truth in Europe during the mid-1800s. Many European painters, writers, and composers took an active role in the politics of the time. They used their artistic works to fuel the revolutionary spirit.

This painting (above), called *The Uprising,* captures the passion of the French revolutionaries. The painter Honoré Daumier (1808–1879), who was a revolutionary in his own right, used a paintbrush as others might have used a gun or a sword. As a young man, Daumier was imprisoned for drawing caricatures of Emperor Louis Philippe. Daumier's satirical works helped inspire further protests, and much of his work captured the spirit of the revolution he helped to create.

French writer Victor Hugo is still revered as a champion of French democracy. His novel *Les Misérables* offers a bleak view of French society in the years leading up to the revolution of 1848. The above poster was created to promote the modern theatrical version of *Les Misérables.*

European composers, such as Richard Wagner of Germany (right), also felt the revolutionary spirit and expressed it through their music. The popular music of the day was marked by a new passion and freedom of expression. It seemed to carry the revolutionary and republican spirit through the air.

Portfolio Assessment

INTERNET Using the Internet or library resources, create a display of revolutionary art. You may use works of art, including paintings or drawings. You may choose to illustrate the display with excerpts of revolutionary writings, including poetry, song lyrics, or prose.

Revolutions in Europe, 1830 and 1848

Gained independence, 1830–1831
Revolutions of 1830
Revolutions of 1848
Repression of revolutions in 1830
Repression of revolutions in 1848

Azimuthal Equal Area Projection
0   300   600 Miles
0 300 600 Kilometers

RUSSIA
PRUSSIA
Berlin
Warsaw
BELGIUM
Brussels
Cracow
Paris   Frankfurt   Prague
Vienna
ATLANTIC OCEAN
FRANCE   AUSTRIA   Budapest
Venice
Livorno
Rome
Naples   OTTOMAN EMPIRE
ITALY
GREECE
Mediterranean Sea

Skills Assessment

Geography In 1830 and again in 1848, revolutions in France sparked uprisings throughout Europe. Although most rebellions were quickly crushed, their ideals survived.

1. **Location** On the map, locate **(a)** Paris, **(b)** Warsaw, **(c)** Budapest.
2. **Place** Which countries gained independence in 1830 and 1831?
3. **Critical Thinking Making Inferences** How can you tell from the map that the revolution in Budapest was unsuccessful?

When elections for president were held, the overwhelming winner was Louis Napoleon, nephew of Napoleon Bonaparte. The "new" Napoleon attracted the working classes by presenting himself as a man who cared about social issues such as poverty. At the same time, his famous name, linked with order and past French glory, helped him with conservatives.

Once in office, Louis Napoleon used his position as a steppingstone to greater power. By 1852, he had proclaimed himself emperor, taking the title Napoleon III. (He was the third Napoleon because the son of Napoleon I had died in his youth without ever ruling France.) Thus ended the short-lived Second Republic.

Like his celebrated uncle, Louis Napoleon used a plebiscite to win public approval for his seizure of power. A stunning 90 percent of voters supported his move to set up the Second Empire. Many thought that a monarchy was more stable than a republic. Millions of French hoped that Napoleon III would restore the glory days of Napoleon Bonaparte.

Napoleon III, like Louis Philippe, ruled at a time of rapid economic growth. For the bourgeoisie, the early days of the Second Empire brought prosperity and contentment. In time, however, Napoleon III would embark on foreign adventures that would bring down his empire and end French leadership in Europe.

The Spread of Revolution

In both 1830 and 1848, the revolts in Paris inspired uprisings to break out elsewhere in Europe. As Metternich said, "When France sneezes, Europe catches cold." Most of the uprisings were suppressed by military force. But here and there, rebels did win changes from conservative governments. Even when they failed, revolutions frightened rulers badly enough to encourage reform later in the century.

Belgium The one notable success for Europe's revolutionaries in 1830 took place in Belgium. In 1815, the Congress of Vienna had united the Austrian Netherlands (present-day Belgium) and the Kingdom of Holland under the Dutch king. The Congress had wanted to create a strong barrier to help prevent French expansion in the future.

The Belgians resented the new arrangement. The Belgians and Dutch had different languages, religions, and economic interests. The Belgians were Catholic, while the Dutch were Protestant. The Belgian economy was based on manufacturing; the Dutch, on trade.

In 1830, news of the Paris uprising that toppled Charles X ignited a revolutionary spark in Belgium. Students and workers threw up barricades in Brussels, the capital. The Dutch king turned to the other European powers for help. Britain and France knew that the Belgians were threatening to disrupt the boundaries set up by the Congress of Vienna, but they believed that they would benefit from the separation of Belgium and Holland. They therefore supported Belgian demands for independence. The conservative powers—Austria, Prussia, and Russia—were too busy putting down revolts of their own to help the Dutch king. As a result, in 1831, Belgium became an independent state with a liberal constitution.

Poland Nationalists in Poland also staged an uprising in 1830. But, unlike the Belgians, the Poles failed to win independence for their country.

In the late 1700s, Russia, Austria, and Prussia had divided up Poland. Poles had hoped that the Congress of Vienna would restore their homeland in 1815. Instead, the great powers handed most of Poland to Russia.

In 1830, Polish students, army officers, and landowners rose in revolt. The rebels failed to gain widespread support, however, and were brutally crushed by Russian forces. Some survivors fled to Western Europe and the United States, where they kept alive the dream of freedom.

1848: Another Wave of Rebellion

In 1848, revolts in Paris again unleashed a tidal wave of revolution across Europe. For opponents of the old order, it was a time of such hope that they called it the "springtime of the peoples."

Sources of Discontent Although events in France touched off the revolts, grievances had been piling up for years. Unrest came from many sources. Middle-class liberals wanted a greater share of political power for themselves, as well as protections for the basic rights of all citizens. Workers demanded relief from the miseries of the Industrial Revolution. And nationalists of all classes ached to throw off foreign rule. By 1848, discontent was so widespread that it was only a matter of time before it exploded into full-scale revolution.

Metternich Falls In the Austrian empire, a revolt broke out in Vienna, taking the government by surprise. Metternich, who had dominated Austrian politics for more than 30 years, tried to silence the students who took to the streets. But when workers supported the students, Metternich resigned and fled in disguise. The Austrian emperor then promised reform.

Revolution quickly spread to other parts of the empire. In Budapest, Hungarian nationalists led by Louis Kossuth demanded an independent government. They also called for an end to serfdom and a written constitution to protect basic rights. In Prague, the Czechs made similar demands. Overwhelmed by events, the Austrian government agreed to the reforms.

The gains were temporary. Austrian troops soon regained control of Vienna and Prague. With Russian help, Austrian forces also smashed the rebels in Budapest. Many were imprisoned, executed, or forced into exile.

Revolution in Italy Uprisings also erupted in the Italian states. Nationalists wanted to end domination of Italy by the Austrian Hapsburgs. As elsewhere, nationalist goals were linked to demands for liberal reforms such as constitutional government. Workers suffering economic hardships demanded even more radical changes. From Venice in the north to Naples in the south, Italians set up independent republics. Revolutionaries even expelled the pope from Rome and installed a nationalist government.

Before long, however, the forces of reaction surged back here, too. Austrian troops ousted the new governments in northern Italy. A French army restored the pope to power in Rome. In Naples, local rulers canceled the reforms they had reluctantly accepted.

Turmoil in the German States In the German states, university students passionately demanded national unity and liberal reforms. Economic hard times and a potato famine brought peasants and workers into the struggle. Workers destroyed the machines that threatened their livelihood, while peasants burned the homes of wealthy landowners.

In Prussia, liberals forced King Frederick William IV to agree to a constitution written by an elected assembly. Within a year, though, he dissolved the assembly. Later, he issued his own constitution keeping power in his own hands or those of the upper classes.

Biography

Louis Kossuth 1802–1894

For two decades, Louis Kossuth had been an activist, writing pamphlets designed to inflame patriotic feelings in the Hungarians. As a result, he was imprisoned by Austrian officials for three years. When he was released, he immediately renewed his activities. He became editor of a nationalistic newspaper and was recognized as the leading voice for Hungarian independence.

Kossuth went on to organize Hungarian revolutionary forces and to declare Hungary's independence in 1848. When Russia intervened, however, Kossuth was forced to flee.

He traveled to the United States, where he spoke before both houses of Congress. His subsequent tour of the country was so well received that a county in Iowa and towns in five states were named in his honor. Tragically, Kossuth would never return to his Hungarian homeland.

Theme: Impact of the Individual Why was Kossuth unable to win Hungarian independence?

THE GREAT SEA SERPENT OF 1848

An Eventful Year
This English cartoon comments on the revolutions of 1848 and the reaction of European rulers.

Theme: Political and Social Systems Based on the cartoon, (a) What ideal caused the revolutions of 1848? (b) How did the revolutions affect Europe's monarchs?

Frankfurt Assembly Throughout 1848, delegates from German states met in the Frankfurt Assembly. "We are to create a constitution for Germany, for the whole land," declared one leader with great optimism.

Divisions soon emerged. Delegates debated endlessly on such topics as whether the new Germany should be a republic or a monarchy, and whether or not to include Austria in a united German state. Finally, the assembly offered Prussia's Frederick William IV the crown of a united Germany. To their dismay, the conservative king rejected the offer because it came not from the German princes but from the people—"from the gutter," as he described it. By early 1849, the assembly was dissolved, under threat from the Prussian military. Outside the assembly, middle-class reformers and workers with radical demands clashed. Conservative forces rallied, dousing the last flames of revolt. Hundreds of people were killed. Many more went to prison. Thousands of Germans left their homeland. Most traveled to the United States, attracted by the young nation's promise of democratic government and economic opportunity.

Looking Ahead

By 1850, rebellion faded, ending the age of liberal revolution that had begun in 1789. Why did the uprisings fail? The rulers' use of military force was just one reason. In general, revolutionaries did not have mass support. In Poland in 1830, for example, peasants did not take part in the uprising. In 1848, a growing gulf divided workers seeking radical economic change and liberals pursuing moderate political reform.

By mid-century, Metternich was gone from the European scene. Still, his conservative system remained in force. In the decades ahead, liberalism, nationalism, and socialism would win successes not through revolution but through political activity. Ambitious political leaders would unify Germany and Italy. Workers would campaign for reforms through unions and the ballot box, as they increasingly won the right to vote.

SECTION 2 Assessment

Recall
1. **Identify:** (a) Charter of French Liberties, (b) Charles X, (c) Louis Philippe, (d) Louis Napoleon, (e) Louis Kossuth, (f) Frankfurt Assembly, (g) Frederick William IV.
2. **Define:** (a) ultraroyalist, (b) recession.

Comprehension
3. Describe one cause and one effect of (a) the French revolution of 1830, (b) the French revolution of 1848.
4. (a) To what lands did revolution spread in 1830? (b) Were these revolutions successful? Explain.

5. Why did most of the revolutions of 1848 fail to achieve their goals?

Critical Thinking and Writing
6. **Identifying Alternatives** Do you think that European rulers could have prevented nationalist revolts by granting autonomy to some groups of people? Why or why not?
7. **Making Decisions** Suppose you had been a conservative adviser to King Frederick William IV of Prussia. Would you have advised the king to accept the crown offered by the Frankfurt Assembly? Explain the reasons for your decision.

Go Online
PHSchool.com

In recent years, various ethnic groups have sought independence, just as national groups did in 1830 and 1848. Use the Internet to find news articles about a country where people have recently struggled to win an independent nation. Write a brief essay describing their struggle. For help with this activity, use **Web Code mkd-2126.**

Latin American Wars of Independence

Reading Focus

- What caused discontent in Latin America?
- How did Haitians, Mexicans, and people in Central America win independence?
- How did the nations of South America win independence?

Vocabulary

peninsular
creole
mestizo
mulatto
truce

Taking Notes

Copy the partially completed table below. As you read, fill in the left column with the names of leaders who led independence movements in Latin America. Fill in the right column with the name of the country or countries that each leader helped liberate.

LEADERS	COUNTRIES
Iturbide	Mexico
San Martín	Argentina, Chile, Peru

Main Idea   In the early 1800s, many new nations emerged in Latin America as independence movements freed people from European rule.

Setting the Scene   Like many wealthy Latin Americans,* young Simón Bolívar (boh LEE vahr) was sent to Europe to complete his education. There, he became a strong admirer of the ideals of the Enlightenment and the French Revolution.

One afternoon, Bolívar and his Italian tutor sat talking about freedom and the rights that ordinary people should have. Bolívar's thoughts turned to his homeland, held as a colony by Spain. He fell on his knees and swore a solemn oath: "I swear before God and by my honor never to allow my hands to be idle nor my soul to rest until I have broken the chains that bind us to Spain."

In later years, Bolívar would fulfill his oath, leading the struggle to liberate northern South America from Spain. Elsewhere in Latin America, other leaders organized independence movements. By 1825, most of Latin America had been freed from colonial rule.

Sources of Discontent

By the late 1700s, the revolutionary fever that gripped Western Europe had spread to Latin America. There, discontent was rooted in the social, racial, and political system that had emerged during 300 years of Spanish rule.

Ethnic and Social Hierarchy   Spanish-born peninsulares dominated Latin American political and social life. Only they could hold top jobs in government and the Church. Many creoles—the European-descended Latin Americans who owned the haciendas, ranches, and mines—bitterly resented their second-class status. Merchants fretted under mercantilist policies that tied the colonies to Spain.

Meanwhile, a growing population of mestizos, people of Native American and European descent, and mulattoes, people of African and European descent, were angry at being denied the status, wealth, and power that were available to whites. Native Americans suffered economic misery under the Spanish, who had conquered the lands of their ancestors. In the Caribbean region and parts of South America, masses of enslaved Africans who worked on plantations longed for freedom.

The Ruling Class
This is a portrait of Don Tomas Mateo Cervantes, an aristocrat and government official of Cuba in the late 1700s. The portrait was painted by Vincente Escobar, a Cuban of African descent.

Theme: Political and Social Systems   How was ethnic background linked to class in Latin America?

---

*Latin America refers to the regions in Middle and South America colonized by Europeans, especially the Spanish, French, and Portuguese, whose languages are rooted in Latin. It includes Spanish-speaking countries from Mexico to Argentina, Portuguese-speaking Brazil, and French-speaking Haiti.

Beyond dissatisfaction with Spanish rule, the different classes had little in common. In fact, they distrusted and feared one another. At times, they worked together against the Spanish. But once independence was achieved, the creoles, who had led the revolts, dominated the governments.

Enlightenment Ideas   In the 1700s, educated creoles read the works of Enlightenment thinkers. They watched colonists in North America throw off British rule. Translations of the Declaration of Independence and the Constitution of the United States even circulated among the creole elite.

Women actively participated in the exchange of ideas. In some cities, women hosted and attended salons, called tertulias, where independence and revolution were discussed.

During the French Revolution, young creoles like Simón Bolívar traveled in Europe and were inspired by the ideals of "liberty, equality, and fraternity." Despite their admiration for Enlightenment ideas and revolutions in other lands, most creoles were reluctant to act.

Napoleon Bonaparte   The spark that finally ignited widespread rebellion in Latin America was Napoleon's invasion of Spain in 1808. Napoleon ousted the Spanish king and placed his brother Joseph on the Spanish throne. In Latin America, leaders saw Spain's weakness as an opportunity to reject foreign domination and demand independence from colonial rule.

Haiti's Struggle for Independence

Even before Spanish colonists hoisted the flag of freedom, revolution had erupted elsewhere in Latin America, in a French-ruled colony on the island of Hispaniola. Haiti, as it is now called, was France's most valued possession in the 1700s.

In Haiti, French planters owned very profitable sugar plantations worked by nearly a half million enslaved Africans. Sugar plantations were labor intensive. The slaves were overworked and underfed. Haiti also had about 25,000 free mulattoes. Many were wealthy, and some also owned slaves. However, they did not have full equality with the French creoles.

A Slave Revolt   In the 1790s, revolutionaries in France were debating ways to abolish slavery in the West Indies. However, debating the issue in Paris did not help enslaved Haitians gain their freedom. Embittered by suffering and inspired by the talk of liberty and equality, Haiti's slaves exploded in revolt in 1791.

The rebels were fortunate to find an intelligent and skillful leader in Toussaint L'Ouverture (too SAN loo vuhr TYOOR), a self-educated former slave. Although untrained, Toussaint was a brilliant general. He was also an inspiring commander. On the eve of one crucial battle, he rallied his troops with these stirring words: "We are fighting so that liberty—the most precious of all earthly possessions—may not perish."

The struggle was long and complex. Toussaint's army of former slaves faced many enemies. Some mulattoes joined French planters against the rebels. France, Spain, and Britain each sent armies to Haiti. The fighting took more lives than any other revolution in the Americas.

By 1798, the rebels had achieved their goal; enslaved Haitians had been freed. And even though Haiti was still a French colony, Toussaint's forces controlled most of the island.

Independence   In France, meantime, Napoleon Bonaparte rose to power. In 1802, he sent a large army to reconquer Haiti. Toussaint urged Haitians once again to take up arms, this time to fight for full independence from France. The guerrilla forces were aided by a deadly ally, yellow fever, a disease which took a growing toll on the invaders. In April 1802, the French agreed to a **truce,** or temporary peace.

Geography and History

A Deadly, Microscopic Enemy

French forces in Haiti were up against much more than Toussaint L'Ouverture's brilliant leadership and brave soldiers. They also had to fight an enemy they couldn't see or begin to understand. It was yellow fever.

The source of the disease was the mosquito, so prevalent in tropical Haiti. Mosquitoes can carry the yellow fever virus and transmit it by biting humans.

Soldiers who caught the virus became dizzy and developed high fevers and muscle aches. Their gums would bleed. Many became comatose and eventually died. Historians estimate that of the 33,000 French troops sent to the Caribbean, 29,000 contracted yellow fever within a year.

Theme: Geography and History Why didn't the French take steps to protect themselves from mosquitoes and yellow fever?

Toussaint L'Ouverture on Slavery

In the late 1700s, Toussaint L'Ouverture led a successful revolt in Haiti to eliminate slavery. But Toussaint was haunted by the fear that the French, who still held Haiti as a colony, would try to reestablish slavery. Many French officials, as well as colonists, had already expressed such a desire. Toussaint wrote to the French Directory to oppose any plans to reimpose slavery.

"The attempts on . . . liberty which the colonists propose are all the more to be feared because it is with the veil of patriotism that they cover their detestable plans. We know that they seek to impose some of them on [the French government] by illusory and [deceptive] promises, in order to see renewed in this colony its former scenes of horror. . . . My attachment to France, my knowledge of the blacks, make it my duty not to leave you ignorant either of the crimes which they meditate or the oath that we renew, to bury ourselves under the ruins of a country revived by liberty rather than suffer the return of slavery. . . .

Blind as they are! They cannot see how [their] odious conduct . . . can become the signal of new disasters and irreparable misfortunes, and far from making them regain what in their eyes liberty for all has made them lose, they expose themselves to a total ruin and the colony to its inevitable destruction. Do they think that men who have been unable to enjoy the blessing of liberty will calmly see it snatched away? They supported their chains only so long as they did not know any condition of life more happy than that of slavery. But today when they have left it, if they had a thousand lives they would sacrifice them all rather than be forced into slavery again. . . .

But if, to re-establish slavery in [Haiti], this was to be done, then I declare to you it would be to attempt the impossible: we have known how to face dangers to obtain our liberty, we shall know how to brave death to maintain it."

—Toussaint L'Ouverture, quoted in *The Black Jacobins* (James)

Above, Toussaint L'Ouverture and his army of former slaves battle for independence from France.

Skills Tip

Italics in excerpts from old documents may represent underlining or some other form of emphasis in the original document.

Skills Assessment

1. What is the tone of Toussaint's letter?
   A diplomatic
   B peaceful
   C warning
   D friendly

2. What does Toussaint say will happen if the French try to reestablish slavery?
   E The British will take over.
   F The colony will be ruined by war.
   G The blacks will feel resentful.
   H The French will be condemned.

3. **Critical Thinking Making Inferences (a)** Why do you think Toussaint emphasized that one paragraph in his letter? **(b)** What might you infer about Toussaint himself from this letter?

Independent Nations of Latin America About 1844

Independent nations with date of independence

*United Provinces of Central America had dissolved by 1841

**Gran Colombia had dissolved by 1830

Azimuthal Equal Area Projection

Gulf of Mexico

MEXICO 1821
Mexico City
BELIZE (Br.)
BAHAMAS (Br.)
HAITI 1804
CUBA (Sp.)
DOMINICAN REPUBLIC 1844
JAMAICA (Br.)
PUERTO RICO (Sp.)

UNITED PROVINCES OF CENTRAL AMERICA*
GUATEMALA 1839
EL SALVADOR 1839
HONDURAS 1838
NICARAGUA 1838
COSTA RICA 1838
PANAMA (part of Colombia)

TRINIDAD (Br.)
BRITISH GUIANA
DUTCH GUIANA
FRENCH GUIANA

Caracas
VENEZUELA 1830
Bogotá
COLOMBIA 1819
GRAN COLOMBIA**

PACIFIC OCEAN

Quito
ECUADOR 1822

PERU 1824
Lima

BRAZIL 1822

La Paz
BOLIVIA 1825

PARAGUAY 1811
Rio de Janeiro
Asunción

CHILE 1818
ARGENTINA 1816
URUGUAY 1828

ATLANTIC OCEAN

Santiago
Buenos Aires
Montevideo

PATAGONIA

FALKLAND ISLANDS (Argentine 1820–1833)
Cape Horn

Equator 0°
20°N
20°S
40°S
80°W
60°W
40°W
20°W
0°

Latin America About 1790

NEW SPAIN
UNITED STATES
BAHAMAS (Br.)
Mexico City
CUBA
HISPANIOLA
West Indies
GUIANAS
Bogotá
NEW GRANADA
BRAZIL
Lima
PERU
LA PLATA
Rio de Janeiro
Buenos Aires

British
Dutch
French
Portuguese
Spanish

Skills Assessment

Geography In the early 1800s, many Latin American nations won independence from European rule.

1 **Location** On the main map locate **(a)** Mexico, **(b)** Gran Colombia, **(c)** Haiti.
2. **Place** Which nation of South America was once a Portuguese colony?
3. **Critical Thinking Synthesizing Information** Why did so many nations of Latin America gain independence by 1830?

Shortly after, the French captured Toussaint and carried him in chains to France. Ten months later, he died there in a cold mountain prison. But Haiti's struggle for freedom continued. In 1804, Haitian leaders declared independence. With yellow fever destroying his army, Napoleon abandoned Haiti. In the following years, rival Haitian leaders fought for power. Finally, in 1820, Haiti became a republic.

Independence for Mexico and Central America

The slave revolt in Haiti frightened creoles in Spanish America. Although they wanted power themselves, most had no desire for economic or social changes that might threaten their way of life. In 1810, however, a creole priest in Mexico, Father Miguel Hidalgo (hih DAHL goh), raised a cry for freedom that would echo across the land.

El Grito de Dolores Father Hidalgo presided over the poor rural parish of Dolores. On September 15, 1810, he rang the church bells summoning the people to prayer. When they gathered, he startled them with an urgent appeal. We do not know his exact words, but his message is remembered: "My children, will you be free? Will you make the effort to recover the lands stolen from your forefathers by the hated Spaniards 300 years ago?" Father Hidalgo's speech became known as "el Grito de Dolores"—the cry of Dolores. It called Mexicans to fight for "Independence and Liberty."

A ragged army of poor mestizos and Native Americans rallied to Father Hidalgo and marched to the outskirts of Mexico City. At first, some creoles supported the revolt. However, they soon rejected Hidalgo's call for an end to slavery and his plea for reforms to improve conditions for Native Americans. They felt that these policies would cost them power.

After some early successes, the rebels faced growing opposition. Less than a year after he issued the "Grito," Hidalgo was captured and executed, and his followers scattered.

José Morelos Another priest picked up the banner of revolution. Father José Morelos was a mestizo who called for wide-ranging social and political reform. He wanted to improve conditions for the majority of Mexicans, abolish slavery, and give the vote to all men. For four years, Morelos led rebel forces before he, too, was captured and shot in 1815.

Spanish forces, backed by conservative creoles, hunted down the surviving guerrillas. They had almost succeeded in ending the rebel movement when events in Spain had unexpected effects on Mexico.

Independence Achieved In Spain in 1820, liberals forced the king to issue a constitution. This move alarmed Agustín de Iturbide (ee toor BEE day), a conservative creole in Mexico. He feared that the new Spanish government might impose liberal reforms on the colonies as well.

Iturbide had spent years fighting Mexican revolutionaries. Suddenly in 1821, he reached out to them. Backed by creoles, mestizos, and Native Americans, he overthrew the Spanish viceroy. Mexico was independent at last. Iturbide took the title Emperor Agustín I. Soon, however, liberal Mexicans toppled the would-be monarch and set up the Republic of Mexico.

Although Mexico was free of Spanish rule, the lives of most people changed little. Military leaders dominated the government and ruled by force of arms. The next 100 years would see new struggles to improve conditions for Mexicans.

New Republics in Central America Spanish-ruled lands in Central America declared independence in the early 1820s. Iturbide tried to add these areas to his Mexican empire. After his overthrow, local leaders set up a republic called the United Provinces of Central America. The union was short-lived. It soon fragmented into the separate republics of Guatemala, Nicaragua, Honduras, El Salvador, and Costa Rica. Like Mexico, the new nations faced many social and economic problems.

Independence in South America

In South America, Native Americans had rebelled against Spanish rule as early as the 1700s. These rebellions had limited results, however. It was not until the 1800s that discontent among the creoles sparked a widespread drive for independence.

A Native American Revolt The strongest challenge to Spanish rule by Native Americans was led by Tupac Amaru, who claimed descent from Incan kings. He demanded that the government end the brutal system of forced Indian labor. Spanish officials rejected the demand for reform. In 1780, Tupac Amaru organized a Native American revolt. A large army crushed the rebels and captured and killed their leader. Still, the revolt did have some positive effects. The Spanish king ordered officials to look into the system of forced labor and eventually abolished it.

 Primary Sources and Literature

See "Miguel Hidalgo: Decree of Hidalgo" in the Reference Section at the back of this book.

Connections to Today

Mexican Independence Day
Today, the people of Mexico remember Father Hidalgo's speech as "el Grito de Dolores," which means "the cry of Dolores." Every September 15, the anniversary of the speech, the president of Mexico rings a bell—suggestive of the church bell in Dolores. The president then honors the Grito de Dolores by repeating it.

The next day, September 16, marks the anniversary of the beginning of the fight against the Spanish. It is celebrated as Mexican Independence Day, a national holiday. Schools and businesses shut down, and people throw huge parties. Fireworks light the night sky.

The massive celebration is very different from the event at Dolores that it celebrates, but the spirit of independence is the same.

Theme: Continuity and Change Why is the ringing of bells an important custom of Mexican Independence Day?

Virtual Field Trip

For: More on Latin American independence
Visit: PHSchool.com
Web Code: mkd-2132

San Martín Crossing the Andes

In this painting, José de San Martín and Bernardo O'Higgins lead their army in a dramatic march over the Andes into Chile. San Martín won independence for Chile when he defeated the Spanish at the battle of Maipú in 1818.

Theme: Geography and History How do you think the successful march across the Andes affected San Martín's army?

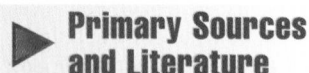

Primary Sources and Literature

See "Simón Bolívar: Address to the Congress of Venezuela" in the Reference Section at the back of this book.

Bolívar In the early 1800s, discontent spread across South America. Educated creoles like Simón Bolívar admired the French and American revolutions. They dreamed of winning their own independence from Spain.

In 1808, when Napoleon Bonaparte occupied Spain, Bolívar and his friends saw it as a signal to act. In 1810, Bolívar led an uprising that established a republic in his native Venezuela. Bolívar's new republic was quickly toppled by conservative forces. For years, civil war raged in Venezuela. The revolutionaries suffered many setbacks. Twice Bolívar was forced into exile on the island of Haiti.

Then, Bolívar conceived a daring plan. He would march his army across the Andes and attack the Spanish at Bogotá, the capital of the viceroyalty of New Granada (present-day Colombia). First, he cemented an alliance with the hard-riding *llañeros*, or Venezuelan cowboys. Then, in a grueling campaign, he led an army through swampy lowlands and over the snowcapped Andes. Finally, in August 1819, he swooped down to take Bogotá from the surprised Spanish.

Other victories followed. By 1821, Bolívar had succeeded in freeing Caracas, Venezuela. "The Liberator," as he was now called, then moved south into Ecuador, Peru, and Bolivia. There, he joined forces with another great South American leader, José de San Martín.

San Martín Like Bolívar, San Martín was a creole. He was born in Argentina but went to Europe for military training. In 1816, this gifted general helped Argentina win freedom from Spain. He then joined the independence struggle in other areas. He, too, led an army across the Andes, from Argentina into Chile. He defeated the Spanish in Chile before moving into Peru to strike further blows against colonial rule.

Bolívar and San Martín tried to work together, but their views were too different. In 1822, San Martín stepped aside, letting Bolívar's forces win the final victories against Spain.

Dreams and Disappointments The wars of independence had ended by 1824. Bolívar now worked tirelessly to unite the lands he had liberated into a single nation, called Gran Colombia. Bitter rivalries, however, made that dream impossible. Before long, Gran Colombia split into three independent countries: Venezuela, Colombia, and Ecuador.

Bolívar faced another disappointment as power struggles among rival leaders triggered destructive civil wars. Spain's former South American colonies faced a long struggle to achieve stable governments—and an even longer one for democracy. Before his death in 1830, a discouraged Bolívar wrote, "We have achieved our independence at the expense of everything else." Contrary to his dreams, no social revolution took place. South America's common people had simply changed one set of masters for another.

Independence for Brazil When Napoleon's armies conquered Portugal, the Portuguese royal family fled to Brazil. During his stay in Brazil, the Portuguese king introduced many reforms, including free trade. He encouraged the development of local industries and allowed Brazilian merchants to trade with nations other than Portugal.

When the king returned to Portugal, he left his son Dom Pedro to rule Brazil. "If Brazil demands independence," the king advised Pedro, "proclaim it yourself and put the crown on your own head."

In 1822, Pedro followed his father's advice. A revolution had brought new leaders to Portugal. They planned to abolish the reforms that had benefited Brazil and they demanded that Dom Pedro return to Portugal. Dom Pedro refused to leave and submit to the Portuguese officials. Instead, he became emperor of an independent Brazil. He accepted a constitution that provided for freedom of the press, freedom of religion, and an elected legislature. Brazil remained a monarchy until 1889, when social and political turmoil led it to become a republic.

Cause *and* Effect

Long-Term Causes	Immediate Causes
• European domination of Latin America • Spread of Enlightenment ideas • American and French revolutions • Growth of nationalism in Latin America	• People of Latin America resent colonial rule and social injustices • Revolutionary leaders emerge • Napoleon invades Spain and ousts Spanish king

Independence Movements in Latin America

Immediate Effects	Long-Term Effects
• Toussaint L'Ouverture leads slave revolt in Haiti • Bolívar, San Martín, and others lead successful revolts in Latin America • Colonial rule ends in much of Latin America • Attempts made to rebuild economies	• 18 separate republics set up • Continuing efforts to achieve stable democratic governments and to gain economic independence

Connections to Today

• Numerous independent nations in Latin America
• Ongoing efforts to expand prosperity and democracy in Latin America

Skills Assessment **Chart** The French Revolution and the Napoleonic wars had a lasting impact on Latin America. **What difficulties did Latin Americans face after independence?**

SECTION 3 Assessment

Recall
1. **Identify: (a)** Toussaint L'Ouverture, **(b)** Miguel Hidalgo, **(c)** el Grito de Dolores, **(d)** José Morelos, **(e)** Tupac Amaru, **(f)** Simón Bolívar, **(g)** Dom Pedro.
2. **Define: (a)** peninsular, **(b)** creole, **(c)** mestizo, **(d)** mulatto, **(e)** truce.

Comprehension
3. How did social structure contribute to discontent in Latin America?
4. **(a)** What was the first step on Haiti's road to independence?
   (b) Why did creoles refuse to support Hidalgo or Morelos?
5. How did successful military campaigns lead to the creation of independent nations in South America?

Critical Thinking and Writing
6. **Comparing** Compare the ways in which Mexico and Brazil achieved independence.
7. **Connecting to Geography** Review the subsection Independence in South America and the map in this section. How does the map show that Bolívar failed to achieve one of his dreams?

Activity

Creating a Poster
Imagine that you are an artist in the service of Bolívar or San Martín. You have been hired to create a poster urging people to join the armies fighting against Spain. Your poster should highlight the goals of the revolutionary armies. It should also be eye-catching and convincing.

Creating a Chapter Summary

Below is a partially completed graphic organizer on the causes of revolution in Europe and Latin America between 1800 and 1848. Copy the organizer and fill in the causes that led to revolutions.

For additional review and enrichment activities, see the interactive version of *World History* available on the Web and on CD-ROM.

Enlightenment ideas spread

REVOLUTIONS IN EUROPE AND LATIN AMERICA

Go Online PHSchool.com

For practice test questions for Chapter 8, use **Web Code mka-2134**.

Building Vocabulary

For each term below, write a sentence in which you show some connection between the term and the revolutions that occurred between 1800 and 1848.

1. ideology
2. autonomy
3. ultraroyalist
4. recession
5. peninsular
6. creole
7. mestizo
8. mulatto

Recalling Key Facts

9. In the early 1800s, what were the main goals of **(a)** conservatives, **(b)** liberals, **(c)** nationalists?
10. What were the causes of the French revolution of 1830?
11. Describe the outcomes of the 1848 rebellions in Europe.
12. How did Napoleon spark the revolutions that erupted in Latin America?
13. **(a)** How did Mexico gain independence from Spain? **(b)** How did Mexico's independence change the lives of its people?
14. Why is Simón Bolívar known as "The Liberator"?

Critical Thinking and Writing

15. **Recognizing Causes and Effects** How did the clash of conservatism, liberalism, and nationalism contribute to unrest in Europe in the 1800s?
16. **Recognizing Points of View** In the 1820s, Britain, France, and Russia supported the Greek struggle for independence. **(a)** Why did these European powers support the Greeks? **(b)** Did the European powers usually respond to revolution in this way? Explain.
17. **Analyzing Information** You have read Metternich's comment: "When France sneezes, Europe catches cold." **(a)** What did he mean by those words? **(b)** Was Metternich correct? Explain.
18. **Predicting Consequences** Do you think that the suppression of nationalist revolutions in the mid-1800s put an end to nationalism? Why or why not?
19. **Connecting to Geography** **(a)** How did climatic conditions help Haitians defeat the French? **(b)** Do you think the distance between Europe and Latin America affected the Latin American wars for independence? Explain.

In 1814, after a defeat in Caracas, Venezuela, Simón Bolívar fled to the British colony of Jamaica. There, he wrote a letter stating his principles. Read the excerpt below and answer the questions that follow.

> "There is nothing we have not suffered at the hands of that unnatural stepmother—Spain. . . . Americans, under the existing Spanish system, occupy a position in society no better than that of serfs suitable for labor. . . . And even this status is surrounded with galling restrictions, such as the prohibition against the cultivation of European crops, the existence of royal monopolies, or the ban on factories. . . . To this add the exclusive trading privileges. . . . In short, do you wish to know what our future was?—simply the cultivation of the fields of indigo, grain, coffee, sugar cane, cacao, and cotton; raising cattle on the empty plains, hunting wild game in the wilderness; digging in the earth to mine gold for the insatiable greed of Spain."

—Simón Bolívar, "Letter From Jamaica"

20. Why do you think Bolívar calls Spain an "unnatural stepmother"?
21. According to Bolívar, what position in society did Latin Americans occupy?
22. What restriction was placed on Latin American farmers?
23. Who had monopolies on some industries?
24. Why do you think there was a ban on factories?
25. What does Bolívar say was the ultimate purpose of all Latin American labor?
26. What do you think were the effects of the publication of this letter?

Go Online
PHSchool.com

Use the Internet to do an in-depth study of one of the revolutions that you have studied in this chapter. Create an outline that identifies the causes, key events, and results of the revolution. Note the Internet sites that you used by listing their titles, authors, and addresses. For help with this activity, use **Web Code mkd-2135.**

"You have the floor; explain yourself!"

In his satirical cartoons, French artist Honoré Daumier (1808–1879) protested unfair social conditions, legal injustices, and middle-class corruption. He was once imprisoned for drawing an unflattering caricature of the king. Study his cartoon titled "You have the floor; explain yourself!" Then, answer the following questions:

27. In this court scene, **(a)** who is the speaker? **(b)** What do his words mean?
28. How well do you think the accused will be able to defend himself?
29. In this cartoon, what do the unbalanced scales of justice symbolize?
30. Based on the cartoon, what was Daumier's view of the French justice system?
31. Do you think Daumier's cartoons helped bring about change? Explain.

Skills Tip

A political cartoon expresses one person's point of view. The cartoon may be fac tually accurate or inaccurate. To amuse the reader, a cartoon's message is often exaggerated.

TEST PREPARATION

1. In England, the rise of political parties and the growing power of the prime minister were steps in the development of

   A laissez-faire.

   B enlightened despotism.

   C socialism.

   D constitutional government.

2. An important result of the Industrial Revolution was the

   A concentration of workers in urban areas.

   B formation of powerful craft guilds.

   C reduction of wages for all workers.

   D decline of the middle class.

3. As a result of Napoleon's conquests in Europe,

   A the Congress of Vienna collapsed.

   B nationalist feelings grew across Europe.

   C the Reign of Terror spread to other countries.

   D France issued the Declaration of the Rights of Man and the Citizen.

Use the quotation and your knowledge of social studies to answer the following question.

> "Each of us puts his person and all his power in common under the supreme direction of the general will; and in a body we receive each member as . . . part of the whole."

4. This statement reflects

   A Locke's ideas on natural rights.

   B Montesquieu's ideas on separation of powers.

   C Voltaire's ideas on freedom of speech.

   D Rousseau's ideas on the social contract.

5. One of the chief goals of middle-class European liberals in the early 1800s was

   A suppression of revolutionary ideas.

   B restoration of legitimate monarchs.

   C adoption of written constitutions.

   D creation of strong labor unions.

6. Marxism was based on the idea of constant struggle between

   A different social classes.

   B different nations.

   C liberals and conservatives.

   D democracy and monarchy.

South America, 1790

South America, 1828

Use the maps above and your knowledge of social studies to answer the following question.

7. How many of the independent nations shown on the map of 1828 were once colonies of Spain?

   A 1

   B 5

   C 9

   D 10

8. Which leader of the Industrial Revolution is correctly matched with his major contribution?

   A James Hargreaves: new means of transportation

   B James Watt: new sources of power

   C Robert Fulton: new methods of farming

   D Thomas Newcomen: new technology in the textile industry

Writing Practice

9. Compare and contrast the American Revolution and the French Revolution in terms of: (a) causes; (b) immediate effects; (c) long-term effects.

10. The word *revolution* is used to describe both political events, such as the French Revolution and the American revolution, and technological developments, such as the Agricultural Revolution and the Industrial Revolution. Write a definition of the word *revolution*. Explain how your definition fits the different kinds of revolutions you learned about in this unit.

UNIT 3

Industrialism and a New Global Age

1800–1914

OUTLINE

Chapter 9 **Life in the Industrial Age** (1800–1914)

Chapter 10 **Nationalism Triumphs in Europe** (1800–1914)

Chapter 11 **Growth of Western Democracies** (1815–1914)

Chapter 12 **The New Imperialism** (1800–1914)

Chapter 13 **New Global Patterns** (1800–1914)

Themes

As you read about imperialism and the new global age, you will encounter the following themes.

Diversity Rulers strengthened their nations by incorporating surrounding states and colonies. Conflicts arose as new subjects, often of different ethnic backgrounds, demanded independence. Women struggled to end restrictions on their lives and gain recognition of their rights.

Economics and Technology Developing factory systems, improved transportation and communication, and scientific advances contributed to overseas expansion by European powers. Industrialized nations grew wealthy, often at the expense of colonies.

Impact of the Individual Nationalist leaders in Italy and Germany used warfare and political alliances to forge new nations out of fragmented provinces.

Political and Social Systems In the 1800s, as the middle class grew, democratic rights were extended in Britain, France, and the United States. Urbanization and the impact of industrialization led to major changes in social values.

Unit Theme Activity

For Your Portfolio The chapters in this unit describe the effects of developing technology on national growth. As you read the chapters, prepare a portfolio project showing the significance of industrialization to imperialism. Your project might take one of the following forms:
• Editorial
• Debate
• Time line

The Gateway of India was built in 1911 to honor the visit of King George V and Queen Mary to India. Located on the harbor of Mumbai (Bombay), it combines Indian, Islamic, and Persian styles of art and architecture.

Prepare to Read

Prepare to read this unit by previewing the main ideas and main events of each chapter.

Chapter 9

Life in the Industrial Age (1800–1914)

From the mid-1800s, industrialism spread rapidly across Europe to North America and beyond. This second Industrial Revolution transformed the economies of the world and solidified patterns of life familiar to us today.

- By the mid-1800s, other western nations—particularly Germany and the United States—were challenging Britain's position as the world's industrial giant.
- Steel, electricity, and advances in communications and transportation marked the second Industrial Revolution.
- By the late 1800s, "big business" came increasingly to dominate industry.
- With the spread of industry, a more complex social structure, dominated by middle-class values, evolved. Although the poor endured harsh conditions, the overall standard of living for workers improved.
- Artistic movements such as romanticism, realism, and expressionism reflected various responses to social and technological changes.

Chapter 10

Nationalism Triumphs in Europe (1800–1914)

The 1800s saw an upsurge of nationalism in Europe. Nationalism unified some countries and sparked divisiveness and conflict in others.

- Between 1862 and 1890, Otto von Bismarck molded the German states into a powerful empire. To strengthen the German state, Bismarck promoted economic development, aggressive foreign policy goals, and domestic reforms.
- Although nationalist forces unified Italy in 1870, a long history of fragmentation created a host of problems for the new state.
- Nationalist feelings among diverse ethnic groups in Eastern Europe created widespread unrest and helped hasten the decline of the Ottoman and Hapsburg empires.
- Reluctant to surrender absolute power, Russian czars of the 1800s swung between reform and repression.

Chapter 11

Growth of Western Democracies (1815–1914)

In Britain, France, and the United States, reformers struggled for an extension of democratic rights and social change. Although many inequalities persisted, these efforts paved the way for great improvements in the quality of life.

- The British Parliament passed a series of reforms designed to help those whose labor supported the new industrial society. Suffrage was extended to all male citizens, prompting women to seek the vote as well.
- Following its defeat in the Franco-Prussian War and a fierce internal revolt, France established the Third Republic, which instituted a series of important reforms.
- By 1900, the United States had become the world's leading industrial giant, a global power, and a magnet for immigrants seeking freedom and opportunity.

	1800	1825	1850
AFRICA		**1805** Muhammad Ali becomes governor of Egypt	**1830** France conquers Algeria	
THE AMERICAS	**1803** Louisiana Purchase	**1823** Monroe Doctrine issued	**1840** Act of Union unites Canada
ASIA AND OCEANIA		**1814** Missionaries arrive in New Zealand	**1842** Treaty of Nanjing	**1857** Sepoy Rebellion
EUROPE	**1807** Industrial Revolution spreads to Belgium	**1832** Reform Bill in Britain	**1845** Great Hunger in Ireland

Chapter 12

The New Imperialism
(1800–1914)

During the 1800s, European powers embarked on a period of aggressive expansion known as the Age of Imperialism. Despite fierce resistance, these powers brought much of the world under their control between 1870 and 1914.

- The Industrial Revolution gave western powers both the means and the motives to seek global domination.
- With little regard for traditional patterns of settlement, European powers partitioned almost the entire African continent.
- Taking advantage of the slowly crumbling Ottoman empire, Britain, France, and Russia competed to extend their influence over Algeria, Egypt, and other Ottoman lands.
- Britain set up a profitable system of colonial rule, controlling over 60 percent of India.
- Western powers carved out spheres of influence along the Chinese coast. China tried unsuccessfully to resist foreign influence with belated efforts at modernization and reform.
- By the early 1900s, leaders in many colonized regions were forging their own nationalist movements.

Chapter 13

New Global Patterns
(1800–1914)

Imperialism resulted in a global exchange that profited industrial nations but disrupted local economies in Africa, Asia, and Latin America. Radical changes reshaped the lives of both subject peoples and westerners.

- As a defense against western imperialism, Japan transformed itself into a modern industrial power and set out on its own imperialist path.
- By 1900, western powers had claimed most islands in the Pacific and divided up most of Southeast Asia.
- The British colonies of Canada, Australia, and New Zealand won independence relatively quickly.
- Although Latin American nations struggled to set up stable governments and economies, a pattern of military rule and economic dependency emerged.
- The United States created its own sphere of influence in the Western Hemisphere.
- Europeans forced subject peoples to accept western ideas about government, technology, and culture.

1875   **1900**   **1925**

1869 Suez Canal opens
1884 Berlin Conference carves up Africa
1896 Ethiopia defeats Italy at Battle of Adowa

1876
Diaz gains
power in Mexico

1898 Spanish-
American War

1914
Panama Canal
opens

1868
Meiji restoration
begins

1885
Indian National
Congress formed

1900 Boxer Uprising in China

1908 Young Turks overthrow sultan

1870 Italy unified
1871 Germany unified

1894
Dreyfus
affair begins

1905
Bloody Sunday
in Russia

1918
Women win suffrage
in Britain

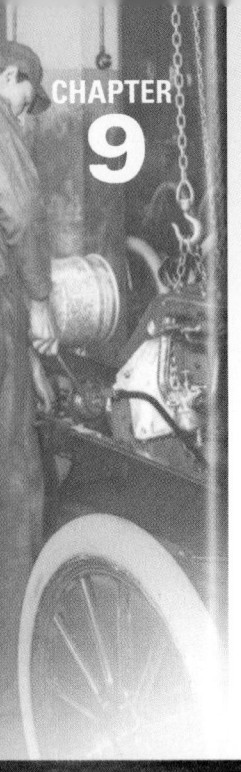

CHAPTER 9

Life in the Industrial Age 1800–1914

Chapter Preview

1 The Industrial Revolution Spreads
2 The World of Cities
3 Changing Attitudes and Values
4 A New Culture

Early 1800s
Romanticism shapes western art and literature. Painters such as J.M.W. Turner seek to glorify nature and stir powerful emotions.

1807
First factories open in Belgium, setting off the Industrial Revolution on the European continent.

1839
French inventor Louis Daguerre perfects an effective method of photography.

CHAPTER EVENTS

1790 — 1815 — 1840

GLOBAL EVENTS

1819 Simón Bolívar establishes Gran Colombia.

1842 The Treaty of Nanjing gives Britain trading rights in China.

Industrial Growth, 1800–1900

From its beginnings in eighteenth-century Britain, the Industrial Revolution spread through Europe and beyond.

Industrializing by 1800
Industrializing by 1850
Industrializing by 1900

Robinson Projection

0   1500   3000 Miles
0   1500   3000 Kilometers

1859
Charles Darwin publishes *On the Origin of Species*. His theory of evolution is denounced by many religious leaders.

1869
Germany legalizes labor unions.

1903
Wilbur and Orville Wright demonstrate the first airplane at Kitty Hawk, North Carolina.

1861 Czar Alexander II emancipates Russian serfs.

1884 European nations carve up Africa at the Berlin Conference.

1914 The Panama Canal opens.

1865   1890   1915

The Industrial Revolution Spreads

Reading Focus

- What industrial powers emerged in the 1800s?
- What impact did new technology have on industry, transportation, and communication?
- How did big business emerge in the late 1800s?

Vocabulary

dynamo
interchangeable parts
assembly line
stock
corporation
cartel

Taking Notes

Copy the diagram below. As you read, fill in the major developments of the Industrial Revolution.

THE SECOND INDUSTRIAL REVOLUTION			
Countries • Belgium • Germany •	**Methods of production**		

Main Idea The second Industrial Revolution was marked by the spread of industry, the development of new technologies, and the rise of big business.

Setting the Scene By the 1880s, steel had replaced steam as the great symbol of the Industrial Revolution. Steel girders could support stronger bridges and taller buildings. Steel rails could carry faster steel railway cars. In huge steel mills, visitors watched with awe as tons of molten metal were poured into giant mixers:

> "At night the scene is indescribably wild and beautiful. The flashing fireworks, the terrific gusts of heat, the gaping, glowing mouth of the giant chest, the quivering light from the liquid iron, the roar of a near-by converter . . . combine to produce an effect on the mind that no words can translate."
> —J. H. Bridge, *History of the Carnegie Steel Company*

The first phase of industrialization had largely been forged from iron, powered by steam engines, and driven by the British textile industry. By the mid-1800s, the Industrial Revolution entered a new phase. New industrial powers emerged. New factories powered by new sources of energy used new processes to turn out new products. And new forms of business organization contributed to the rise of giant new companies. As the twentieth century dawned, this second Industrial Revolution transformed the economies of the western world.

New Industrial Powers

During the early Industrial Revolution, Britain stood alone as the world's industrial giant. To protect its head start, Britain tried to enforce strict rules against exporting inventions.

For a while, the rules worked. Then, in 1807, British mechanic William Cockerill opened factories in Belgium to manufacture spinning and weaving machines. Belgium became the first European nation outside Britain to industrialize. By the mid-1800s, other nations had joined the race, and several newcomers were challenging Britain's industrial supremacy.

The New Pacesetters How were other nations able to catch up to Britain so quickly? First, nations such as Germany, France, and the United States had more abundant supplies of coal, iron, and other resources than did Britain. Also, they had the advantage of being able to follow Britain's lead. Like Belgium, latecomers often borrowed British experts or technology. The first American textile factory was built in Pawtucket, Rhode Island, with plans smuggled out of Britain. American inventor Robert Fulton powered his steamboat with one of James Watt's steam engines.

Two countries in particular thrust their way to industrial leadership. Germany united into a powerful nation in 1871. (See the next chapter.) Within a few decades, it became Europe's leading industrial power. Across the Atlantic, the United States advanced even more rapidly, especially after the Civil War. By 1900, American industry led the world in production.

Uneven Development Other nations industrialized more slowly, particularly those in eastern and southern Europe. These nations often lacked natural resources or the capital to invest in industry. Although Russia did have resources, social and political conditions slowed its economic development. Only in the late 1800s, more than 100 years after Britain, did Russia lumber toward industrialization.

In East Asia, however, Japan offered a remarkable success story. Although it lacked many basic resources, it industrialized rapidly after 1868. Canada, Australia, and New Zealand also built thriving industries.

Impact Like Britain, the new industrial nations underwent social changes, such as rapid urbanization. Men, women, and children worked long hours in difficult and dangerous conditions. As you will read, by 1900, these conditions had begun to improve in many industrialized nations.

The factory system produced huge quantities of new goods at lower prices than ever before. In time, workers were buying goods that in earlier times only the wealthy could afford. The demand for goods created jobs, as did the building of cities, railroads, and factories. Politics changed, too, as leaders had to meet the demands of an industrial society.

Globally, industrial nations competed fiercely, altering patterns of world trade. Thanks to their technological and economic advantage, western powers came to dominate the world more than ever before, as you will read.

Centers of Industry, 1871

Technology and Industry

During the early Industrial Revolution, inventions such as the steam engine were generally the work of gifted tinkerers. They experimented with simple machines to make them better. By the 1880s, the pace of change quickened as companies hired professional chemists and engineers to create new products and machinery. The marriage of science, technology, and industry spurred economic growth.

Steel In 1856, British engineer Henry Bessemer developed a process to purify iron ore and produce a new substance, steel. Steel was lighter, harder, and more durable than iron. Others improved on the Bessemer process, so steel could be produced very cheaply. It rapidly became the major material used in tools, bridges, and railroads.

As steel production soared, industrialized countries measured their success in steel output. In 1880, for example, the average German steel mill produced less than five million metric tons of steel a year. By 1910, that figure had reached nearly fifteen million metric tons.

Chemicals Chemists created hundreds of new products, from medicines such as aspirin to perfumes and soaps. Newly developed chemical fertilizers played a key role in increasing food production.

In 1866, the Swedish chemist Alfred Nobel invented dynamite, an explosive much safer than others used at the time. It was widely used in construction and, to Nobel's dismay, in warfare. Dynamite earned Nobel a huge fortune, which he willed to fund the famous Nobel prizes that are still awarded today.

Electricity In the late 1800s, a new power source—electricity—replaced steam as the dominant source of industrial power. Scientists like Benjamin Franklin had tinkered with electricity a century earlier. The Italian scientist Alessandro Volta developed the first battery about 1800. Later, the English chemist Michael Faraday created the first simple electric motor and the first dynamo, a machine that generates electricity. Today, all electrical generators and transformers work on the principle of Faraday's dynamo.

In the 1870s, the American inventor Thomas Edison made the first electric light bulb. Soon, Edison's "incandescent lamps" illuminated whole cities. The pace of city life quickened, and factories could continue to operate after dark. By the 1890s, cables carried electrical power from dynamos to factories.

New Methods of Production The basic features of the factory system remained the same during the 1800s. Factories still used large numbers of workers and power-driven machines to mass-produce goods. To improve efficiency, however, manufacturers designed products with interchangeable parts, identical components that could be used in place of one another. Interchangeable parts simplified both assembly and repair.

By the early 1900s, manufacturers introduced another new method of production, the assembly line. Workers on an assembly line add parts to a product that moves along a belt from one work station to the next. Like interchangeable parts, the assembly line made production faster and cheaper, lowering the price of goods.

Technology Speeds Transportation and Communication

During the second Industrial Revolution, transportation and communications were transformed by technology. Steamships replaced sailing ships, and railroad building took off. In Europe and North America, rail lines connected inland cities and seaports, mining regions and industrial centers. In

Connections to Today

When the Lights Go Out

The role of electric power in our lives has come a long way since the days of Thomas Edison. In December 1998, residents of San Francisco found out just how much their lives depend on electricity. When mistakes during a routine repair led to a widespread power outage, more than one million people were affected for seven hours. Lights and elevators stopped working in skyscrapers, and workers had to carefully make their way down darkened stairways. Others were trapped on trains or stuck in traffic jams caused by nonfunctioning traffic lights. Business slowed when phone systems crashed, computerized cash registers could not ring up sales, and ATM machines went down. With today's linked power grids, such blackouts have the potential to disrupt the lives of millions of people across county and state lines.

Theme: Economics and Technology What economic effects might a power outage have?

Comparing Viewpoints

Is Technology a Blessing or a Curse?

After the second Industrial Revolution, technology began to have an increasing influence on people's lives. Does technology always benefit us, or can it have some harmful effects? Think about the influence of technology as you compare the following viewpoints.

United States 1876

Writer William Dean Howells attended the Centennial Exposition in Philadelphia. He marveled at Machinery Hall, filled with examples of recent American technology:

66 The superior elegance, aptness, and ingenuity of our machinery is observable at a glance. Yes, it is still in these things of iron and steel that the national genius speaks most freely; by and by the inspired marbles, the breathing canvases, the great literature [will be recognized]; for the present America is [expressed] in the strong metals and their infinite uses. 99

South Africa 1986

This cartoon uses imagery borrowed from the pyramid builders of ancient Egypt to comment on modern technology.

BERRY
THE STAR
Johannesburg
SOUTH AFRICA

CARTOONISTS & WRITERS SYNDICATE: http://CartoonWeb.com

India 1955

After India's independence, Prime Minister Jawaharlal Nehru commented on its need for industrial development:

66 There can be no real well-being or advance in material standards in India without the big factory. I shall venture to say that we cannot even maintain our freedom and independence as a nation without the big factory and all it represents. 99

Japan 1984

Ikeda Daisaku spoke of the effects of technology from the viewpoint of a Buddhist philosopher:

66 The man who rides in a car all of the time loses the ability to walk long distances vigorously. Even when we employ mechanical devices, we must realize that it is we humans who are at the controls and that whether the machine is a blessing or a curse depends on what is inside us. 99

Skills Assessment

1. The viewpoints most favorable toward technology are expressed by
   A Howells and Daisaku.
   B Nehru and Daisaku.
   C Howells and Nehru.
   D Nehru and the cartoon.

2. Ikeda Daisaku would probably agree with the cartoonist that technology
   E can rule people.
   F expresses the ideals of a nation.
   G is key to economic development.
   H is always destructive.

3. **Critical Thinking Making Decisions** Decide whether you think technology is a blessing or a curse in today's society. Write a short essay explaining your point of view. Be sure to provide several clear examples to support your decision.

Skills Tip

A person's point of view may be influenced by such factors as time and place of birth, historical period, occupation, economic status, religious values, and political opinions.

the United States, a transcontinental railroad provided rail service from the Atlantic to the Pacific. In the same way, Russians built the Trans-Siberian Railroad, linking Moscow in European Russia to Vladivostok on the Pacific. Railroad tunnels and bridges crossed the Alps in Europe and the Andes in South America. Passengers and goods rode on rails in India, China, Egypt, and South Africa.

The Automobile Age Begins The transportation revolution took a new turn when a German engineer, Nikolaus Otto, invented a gasoline-powered internal combustion engine. In 1886, Karl Benz received a patent for the first automobile, which had three wheels. A year later, Gottlieb Daimler (DĪM luhr) introduced the first four-wheeled automobile. People laughed at the "horseless carriages," which quickly transformed transportation.

The French nosed out the Germans as early automakers. Then the American Henry Ford started making models that reached the breathtaking speed of 25 miles an hour. In the early 1900s, Ford began using the assembly line to mass-produce cars, making the United States a leader in the automobile industry.

Conquest of the Air The internal combustion engine powered more than cars. Motorized threshers and reapers boosted farm production. Even more dramatically, the internal combustion engine made possible the dream of human flight. In 1903, two American bicycle makers, Orville and Wilbur Wright, designed and flew a flimsy airplane at Kitty Hawk, North Carolina. Although their flying machine stayed aloft for only a few seconds, it ushered in the air age.

Soon, daredevil pilots were flying airplanes across the English Channel and over the Alps. Commercial passenger travel, however, would not begin until the 1920s.

Rapid Communication A revolution in communications also made the world smaller. An American inventor, Samuel F. B. Morse, developed the telegraph, which could send coded messages over wires by means of electricity. His first telegraph line went into service between Baltimore and Washington, D.C., in 1844. By the 1860s, an undersea cable was relaying messages between Europe and North America.

Communication soon became even faster. In 1876, the Scottish-born American inventor Alexander Graham Bell patented the telephone. By the

Ford's Automobile Assembly Line
The use of the assembly line allowed cars to be produced more quickly and cheaply. These pictures show three stages in the creation of the Ford Model T.

Theme: Economics and Technology Based on these pictures, what words would you use to describe working on an assembly line?

Unfinished car frames move along a belt.

At this station, workers attach the engine.

1890s, the Italian pioneer Guglielmo Marconi had invented the radio. In 1901, Marconi transmitted a radio message from Britain to Canada, using Morse's dot-and-dash code. Radio would become a cornerstone of today's global communications network that links every corner of the world.

New Directions for Business

New technologies required the investment of large amounts of money. To get the needed capital, entrepreneurs developed new ways of organizing businesses. Owners sold stock, or shares in their companies, to investors. Each stockholder thus became owner of a tiny part of a company.

Rise of Big Business   By the late 1800s, what we call "big business" came to dominate industry. Large-scale companies such as steel foundries needed so much capital that they sold hundreds of thousands of shares. These businesses formed giant corporations, businesses that are owned by many investors who buy shares of stock. Stockholders risk only the amount they invest in the company and cannot be held personally responsible for any debts of the corporation.

With large amounts of capital, corporations could expand into many areas. In the novel *Germinal* by the French writer Émile Zola, two investors discuss the growth of a large coal mining company. "And is your company rich?" one asks. "Ah! yes. Ah! yes," the other replies:

> "Ten thousand workers, concessions reaching over sixty-seven towns, an output of five thousand tons a day, a railway joining all the pits, and workshops, and factories! Ah! yes! Ah, yes! There's money there!"
>
> —Émile Zola, *Germinal*

Move Toward Monopolies   Powerful business leaders created monopolies and trusts, huge corporate structures that controlled entire industries or areas of the economy. In Germany, Alfred Krupp inherited a steelmaking business from his father. He bought up coal and iron mines as well as ore-shipping lines that fed the steel business. Later, he and his son acquired plants that made tools, railroad cars, and weapons. In the United States, John D. Rockefeller built Standard Oil Company of Ohio into an empire. By

Primary Source

The Radio Age Begins
Guglielmo Marconi describes receiving the first overseas radio transmission in 1901:

"Shortly before mid-day I placed the single earphone to my ear and started listening. . . . The answer came at 12:30 when I heard, faintly but distinctly, *pip-pip-pip*. I handed the phone to Kemp: 'Can you hear anything?' I asked. 'Yes,' he said, 'the letter S'—he could hear it. I knew then that all my anticipations had been justified. The electric waves sent out into space from Poldhu had traversed the Atlantic—the distance, enormous as it seemed then, of 1,700 miles. . . . I now felt for the first time absolutely certain that the day would come when mankind would be able to send messages without wires not only across the Atlantic, but between the farthermost ends of the earth."

—Guglielmo Marconi, quoted in *Scrapbook, 1900–1914* (Bailey)

Skills Assessment

Primary Source Did Marconi's prediction come true? Explain.

Car bodies slide down a wooden ramp and are attached to the frame.

A family enjoys a ride in its new Model T.

gaining control of oil wells, oil refineries, and oil pipelines, he dominated the American petroleum industry.

In their pursuit of profit, ruthless business leaders destroyed competing companies. Then, with the competition gone, they were free to raise prices to any level. Sometimes, a group of large corporations would join forces and form a cartel, an association to fix prices, set production quotas, or control markets. In Germany, a single cartel fixed prices for 170 coal mines. An international shipping cartel of British, German, French, Dutch, and Japanese shippers came close to setting freight rates on the sea lines of the world.

Move Toward Regulation The rise of big business and the creation of such great wealth sparked a stormy debate. Some people saw the Krupps and Rockefellers as "captains of industry" and praised their vision and skills. They pointed out that capitalists invested their wealth in worldwide ventures, such as railroad building, that employed thousands of workers and added to the general prosperity.

To others, the aggressive magnates were "robber barons." Any effort to destroy competition, critics argued, damaged the free-enterprise system. Reformers called for laws to prevent monopolies and regulate large corporations. By the early 1900s, some governments did move against monopolies. However, the political and economic power of business leaders often hindered efforts at regulation.

One View of Big Business
To some critics, the growth of monopolies had a dangerous effect on society. This American cartoon of 1899 shows a monopoly as an octopus-like monster.

Theme: Economics and Technology Do you think this cartoonist favored or opposed government regulation of business? Explain.

Looking Ahead

By the late 1800s, European and American corporations were setting up factories, refineries, and other production facilities around the world. Banks, too, were involved in this global economy. They invested vast sums—the money coming from rich and small depositors—in undertakings such as building ports, railroads, and canals. As western capital flowed into Africa, Asia, and Latin America, western governments became increasingly involved in these areas.

SECTION 1 Assessment

Recall
1. **Identify:** **(a)** Bessemer process, **(b)** Alfred Nobel, **(c)** Michael Faraday, **(d)** Thomas Edison, **(e)** Henry Ford, **(f)** Orville and Wilbur Wright, **(g)** Guglielmo Marconi, **(h)** Alfred Krupp.
2. **Define:** **(a)** dynamo, **(b)** interchangeable parts, **(c)** assembly line, **(d)** stock, **(e)** corporation, **(f)** cartel.

Comprehension
3. How did the Industrial Revolution spread in the 1800s?

4. How did technology help industry expand?
5. How did the need for capital lead to new business methods?

Critical Thinking and Writing
6. **Connecting to Geography** "The availability of natural resources is the most important condition for industrialization." Do you agree or disagree? Explain.
7. **Ranking** Which three technological advances in this section do you think were the most important? Explain.

Activity

Drawing a Political Cartoon
Draw a political cartoon that might have appeared in a newspaper in the late 1800s. In your cartoon, take a stand for or against the passage of laws to prevent monopolies or regulate big business.

Reading Focus

- What was the impact of medical advances in the late 1800s?
- How had cities changed by 1900?
- How did working-class struggles lead to improved conditions for workers?

Vocabulary

germ theory

urban renewal

mutual-aid society

standard of living

Taking Notes

As you read, prepare an outline of this section. Use Roman numerals to indicate the major headings, capital letters for the subheadings, and numbers for the supporting details. The sample at right will help you get started.

I. Medicine and population
  A. The fight against disease
    1.
    2.
  B. In the hospital
    1.
    2.
II. The life of the cities

Main Idea The population of cities grew as people moved to urban centers for jobs.

Setting the Scene

In the 1870s, a citizen of Berlin, Germany, boasted of his city's rapid growth. "We have already 800,000 inhabitants, next year we shall have 900,000, and the year after that a million." He predicted that Berlin's population would soon rival those of Paris and even London.

The population explosion that had begun during the 1700s continued through the 1800s. Cities grew as rural people streamed into urban areas. By the end of the century, European and American cities had begun to take on many of the features of cities today.

Discovery CHANNEL **SCHOOL** Video
Explore city life during the industrial age.

Medicine and Population

Between 1800 and 1900, the population of Europe more than doubled. This rapid growth was not due to larger families. In fact, families in most industrializing countries had fewer children. Instead, populations soared because the death rate fell. People ate better, thanks in part to improved methods of farming, food storage, and distribution. Medical advances and improvements in public sanitation also slowed death rates.

The Fight Against Disease Since the 1600s, scientists had known of microscopic organisms, or microbes. Some scientists speculated that certain microbes might cause specific infectious diseases. Yet most doctors scoffed at this germ theory. Not until 1870 did French chemist Louis Pasteur clearly show the link between microbes and disease. Pasteur went on to make other major contributions, including the development of vaccines against rabies and anthrax and the discovery of a process called pasteurization, named after him, for killing disease-carrying microbes in milk.

In the 1880s, the German doctor Robert Koch identified the bacteria that caused tuberculosis, a respiratory disease that claimed about 30 million human lives in the 1800s. The search for a tuberculosis cure, however, took half a century. By 1914, yellow fever and malaria had been traced to microbes carried by mosquitoes.

As people understood how germs caused disease, they bathed and changed their clothes more often. In western cities, better hygiene caused a marked drop in the rate of disease and death.

FACT FINDER

Average Life Expectancy in Selected Industrial Areas, 1850–1910

Year	Male	Female
1850	40.3 years	42.8 years
1870	42.3 years	44.7 years
1890	45.8 years	48.5 years
1910	52.7 years	56.0 years

Source: E. A. Wrigley, *Population and History* (based on data for parts of Western Europe and the United States)

Skills Assessment

Chart Improved medicine and sanitation played a major role in increasing life expectancy in the industrialized world. **Between 1850 and 1910, how much did life expectancy increase for men? For women?**

In the Hospital In the early 1840s, anesthesia was first used to relieve pain during surgery. The use of anesthetics allowed doctors to experiment with operations that had never before been possible.

Yet, throughout the century, hospitals could be dangerous places. Surgery was performed with dirty instruments in dank operating rooms. Often, a patient would survive an operation, only to die days later of infection. For the poor, being admitted to a hospital was often a death sentence. Wealthy or middle-class patients insisted on treatment in their own homes.

"The very first requirement in a hospital," said British nurse Florence Nightingale, "is that it should do the sick no harm." As an army nurse during the Crimean War, Nightingale insisted on better hygiene in field hospitals. After the war, she worked to introduce sanitary measures in British hospitals. She also founded the world's first school of nursing.

The English surgeon Joseph Lister discovered how antiseptics prevented infection. He insisted that surgeons wash their hands before operating and sterilize their instruments. Eventually, the use of antiseptics drastically reduced deaths from infection.

The Life of the Cities

As industrialization progressed, cities came to dominate the West. City life, as old as civilization itself, underwent dramatic changes.

The Changing City Landscape Growing wealth and industrialization altered the basic layout of western cities. City planners gouged out spacious new squares and boulevards. They lined these avenues with government buildings, offices, department stores, and theaters.

The most extensive urban renewal, or rebuilding of the poor areas of a city, took place in Paris in the 1850s. Georges Haussmann, chief planner for Napoleon III, destroyed many tangled medieval streets full of tenement housing. In their place, he built wide boulevards and splendid public buildings. The project put many people to work, decreasing the threat of social unrest. The wide boulevards also made it harder for rebels to put up barricades and easier for troops to reach any part of the city.

Gradually, settlement patterns shifted. In most American cities, the rich lived in pleasant neighborhoods on the outskirts of the city. The poor crowded into slums near the city center, within reach of factories. Trolley lines made it possible to live in one part of the city and work in another.

Sidewalks, Sewers, and Skyscrapers Paved streets made urban areas much more livable. First gas lamps, then electric street lights, increased safety at night. Cities organized police forces and expanded fire protection.

Beneath the streets, sewage systems made cities healthier places to live. City planners knew that clean water supplies were needed to combat epidemics of cholera and tuberculosis. The massive new sewer systems of London and Paris were costly, but they cut death rates dramatically.

By 1900, architects were using steel to construct soaring buildings. The steel Eiffel Tower became a symbol of Paris. American architects like Louis Sullivan pioneered a new structure, the skyscraper. In large cities, single-family middle-class homes gave way to multistory apartment buildings.

Slums Despite efforts to improve cities, urban life remained harsh for the poor. Some working-class families could afford better clothing, newspapers, or tickets to a music hall. But they went home to small, cramped row houses or tenements in overcrowded neighborhoods.

In the worst tenements, whole families were often crammed into a single room. Unemployment or illness meant lost wages that could ruin a family. High rates of crime and alcoholism were a constant curse. Conditions had improved somewhat from the early Industrial Revolution, but slums remained a fact of city life.

Biography

Florence Nightingale
1820–1910

When Florence Nightingale arrived at a British military hospital in the Crimea in 1854, she was horrified by what she saw. The sick and wounded lay on bare ground. With no sanitation and a shortage of food, some 60 percent of all patients died. But Nightingale was a fighter. Bullying the military and medical staff, she soon had every available person cleaning barracks, digging latrines, doing laundry, and caring for the wounded. Six months later, the death rate had dropped to 2 percent.

Back in England, Nightingale was hailed as a saint. Ballads were even written about her. She took advantage of her popularity and connections to pressure the government for reforms.

Nightingale lived most of the last 50 years of her life as an invalid. Yet from her couch, she continued to write letters and reports and to command her vast network of supporters.

Theme: Impact of the Individual How did Nightingale achieve reforms in British army hospitals?

The Lure of the City   Despite their drawbacks, cities attracted millions. New residents were drawn as much by the excitement as by the promise of work. For tourists, too, cities were magnetic centers of action. One reporter described the hustle and bustle of holiday crowds in London:

> "Cyclists of both sexes covered the roads. River steamers and pleasure boats carried their thousands to Kew and the upper reaches of the Thames. The London parks were crowded. The Botanic Gardens and Zoological Gardens formed great attractions, and the flowers of Battersea Park drew large crowds all day."
>
> —*Times* (London), quoted in *Crises in English History, 1066–1945* (Henning)

Music halls, opera houses, and theaters provided entertainment for every taste. Museums and libraries offered educational opportunities. Sports, from tennis to bare-knuckle boxing, drew citizens of all classes. Few of these enjoyments were available in country villages.

Working-Class Struggles

Workers tried to improve the harsh conditions of industrial life. They protested low wages, long hours, unsafe conditions, and the constant threat of unemployment. At first, business owners and governments tried to silence protesters. Strikes and unions were illegal. Demonstrations were crushed.

By mid-century, workers slowly began to make progress. They formed mutual-aid societies, self-help groups to aid sick or injured workers. Men and women joined socialist parties or organized unions. The revolutions of 1830 and 1848 left vivid images of worker discontent.

By the late 1800s, most western countries had granted all men the vote. Workers also won the right to organize unions to bargain on their behalf.

The Lure of a City
The photograph of Paris in 1900 (bottom) shows two of its most famous attractions—the Eiffel Tower and a giant Ferris wheel. The city also won worldwide fame for its theaters, music halls, museums, and circuses.

Theme: Continuity and Change   How might this photograph of Paris look different if it were taken today?

Cause and Effect

Causes

- Increased agricultural productivity
- Growing population
- New sources of energy, such as steam and coal
- Growing demand for textiles and other mass-produced goods
- Improved technology
- Available natural resources, labor, and money
- Strong, stable governments that promoted economic growth

Industrial Revolution

Immediate Effects	Long-Term Effects
• Rise of factories • Changes in transportation and communication • Urbanization • New methods of production • Rise of urban working class • Growth of reform movements	• Growth of labor unions • Inexpensive new products • Spread of industrialization • Rise of big business • Expansion of public education • Expansion of middle class • Competition for world trade among industrialized nations • Progress in medical care

Connections to Today

- Improvements in world health
- Growth in population
- Industrialization in developing nations
- New energy sources, such as oil and nuclear power
- Mass media and mass entertainment
- Efforts to regulate world trade

Skills Assessment **Chart** The long-term effects of the Industrial Revolution touched nearly every aspect of life. **Identify two social and two economic effects of the Industrial Revolution.**

Germany legalized labor unions in 1869. Britain, Austria, and France followed. Unions grew rapidly. In France, membership grew from 140,000 in 1890 to over a million in 1912.

Pressured by unions, reformers, and working-class voters, governments passed laws to regulate working conditions. Over time, laws were passed outlawing child labor and banning the employment of women in mines. Other laws limited work hours and improved safety. By 1909, British coal miners had won an eight-hour day, setting a standard for workers in other countries.

First in Germany, and then elsewhere, western governments established old-age pensions, as well as disability insurance for workers who were hurt or became ill. These programs protected workers from poverty once they were no longer able to work.

Rising Standards of Living Wages varied throughout the industrialized world, with unskilled laborers earning much less than skilled workers. Women received less than half the pay of men doing the same work. Farm laborers barely scraped by during the economic slump of the late 1800s. Periods of unemployment brought desperate hardships to industrial workers and helped boost union membership.

Overall, though, standards of living for workers did rise. The standard of living measures the quality and availability of necessities and comforts in a society. Families ate more varied diets, lived in better homes, and dressed in inexpensive, mass-produced clothing. Advances in medicine improved health. Some workers moved to suburbs, traveling to work on subways and trams. Still, the gap between workers and the middle class widened.

SECTION 2 Assessment

Recall

1. **Identify: (a)** Louis Pasteur, **(b)** Robert Koch, **(c)** Florence Nightingale, **(d)** Joseph Lister.
2. **Define: (a)** germ theory, **(b)** urban renewal, **(c)** mutual-aid society, **(d)** standard of living.

Comprehension

3. Why did the rate of population growth increase in the late 1800s?
4. Describe three ways that city life changed in the 1800s.

5. What laws helped workers in the late 1800s?

Critical Thinking and Writing

6. **Analyzing Information** What were the advantages and disadvantages of city life in the late 1800s?
7. **Linking Past and Present** By the early 1900s, governments had passed many laws that improved conditions for the working class. What are some laws that regulate working conditions today?

Activity

Writing a Letter
You have moved from a rural village to London or Paris in the late 1800s. Write a letter home describing your feelings about city life. Suggest both positive and negative aspects.

Changing Attitudes and Values

Reading Focus

- What values shaped the new social order?
- How did women and educators seek change?
- How did science challenge existing beliefs?
- What role did religion play in urban society?

Vocabulary

cult of domesticity

temperance movement

women's suffrage

racism

social gospel

Taking Notes

Copy this chart. As you read, list new attitudes and values in the left-hand column. List supporting details in the right-hand column.

CHANGES IN ATTITUDES AND VALUES

1. A new social order	• Upper class—old nobility, new industrialists, and business families •
2. Middle-class values	•
3.	•

Main Idea The Industrial Revolution changed the social order in the western world, and new ideas challenged long-held traditions.

Setting the Scene "Once a woman has accepted an offer of marriage, all she has . . . becomes virtually the property of the man she has accepted as husband." This advice appeared in an 1859 British publication called *The What-Not or Ladies' Handbook.* But not all women accepted such restrictions. One Italian crusader for women's rights denounced the inferior legal status of women:

> "For her, taxes but not an education; for her, sacrifices but not employment; . . . strong enough to be laden with an array of painful duties, but sufficiently weak not to be allowed to govern herself."
>
> —Anna Mazzoni, *La Liberazione della Donna*

Demand for women's rights was one of many issues that challenged the traditional social order in the late 1800s. By then, the social order itself was changing. In many countries, the middle class increasingly came to dominate society.

A New Social Order

The Industrial Revolution slowly changed the old social order in the western world. For centuries, the two main classes were nobles and peasants. Their roles were defined by their relationship to the land. While middle-class merchants, artisans, lawyers, and officials played important roles, they still occupied a secondary position in society. With the spread of industry, a more complex social structure emerged.

By the late 1800s, Western Europe's new upper class included superrich industrial and business families as well as the old nobility. Wealthy entrepreneurs married into aristocratic families, gaining the status of noble titles. Nobles needed the money brought by the industrial rich to support their lands and lifestyle. By tradition, the upper class held the top jobs in government and the military.

Below this tiny elite, a growing middle class was pushing its way up the social ladder. Its highest rungs were filled with midlevel business people and professionals such as doctors, scientists, and lawyers. With comfortable incomes, they enjoyed a wide range of material goods. Next came the lower middle class, which included teachers, office workers, shopkeepers, and clerks. Even though they earned much smaller incomes, they struggled to keep up with their "betters."

At the base of the social ladder were workers and peasants. In highly industrialized Britain, workers made up more than 30 percent of the population in 1900. In Western Europe and the United States, the number of farmworkers dropped, but many families still worked the land. The rural population was even higher in eastern and southern Europe, where industrialization was limited.

Middle-Class Values

By mid-century, the modern middle class had developed its own way of life. The nuclear family lived in a large house, or perhaps in one of the new apartment houses. Rooms were crammed with large overstuffed furniture, and paintings and photographs lined the walls. Clothing reflected middle-class tastes for luxury and respectability. A strict code of etiquette governed social behavior. Rules dictated how to dress for every occasion, how to give a dinner party, how to pay a social call, when to write letters, and how long to mourn for relatives who died.

Parents strictly supervised their children, who were expected to be "seen but not heard." A child who misbehaved was considered to reflect badly on the entire family. Servants, too, were seen as a reflection of their employers. Even a small middle-class household was expected to have at least a cook and a housemaid.

Courtship and Marriage   As in the past, middle-class families had a large say in choosing whom their children married. At the same time, young people had more freedom to choose a marriage partner. The notion of "falling in love" was more accepted than ever before.

Yet most women and men carefully considered the practical side of marriage. Mothers and daughters discussed the "likely prospects" of a possible husband. A young man was expected to court his bride-to-be with tender sentiments, but he also had to convince her father that he could support her in style. Until the late 1800s in most western countries, a husband controlled his wife's property, so marriage contracts were drawn up to protect a daughter's property rights.

The Ideal Home   Within the family circle, the division of labor between wife and husband changed. In earlier times, middle-class women had often helped run family businesses out of the home. By the later 1800s, most middle-class husbands went to work in an office or shop. A successful husband was one whose income was enough to keep his wife at home. Women spent their working hours raising children, directing the servants, and perhaps doing religious or charitable service.

Books, magazines, and popular songs supported a cult of domesticity that idealized women and the home. Sayings like "home, sweet home" were stitched into needlework and hung on parlor walls. The ideal woman was seen as a tender, self-sacrificing caregiver who provided a nest for her children and a peaceful refuge for her husband.

This ideal rarely applied to the lower classes. Working-class women labored for low pay in garment factories or worked as domestic servants. Young women might leave domestic service after they married but often had to seek other employment. Despite long days working for wages, they were still expected to take full responsibility for child care and homemaking.

Rights for Women

Some individual women and women's groups protested restrictions on women. Like earlier pioneers Olympe de Gouges and Mary Wollstonecraft, they sought a broad range of rights. Across Europe and the United States, politically active women campaigned for fairness in marriage, divorce, and

Sipping Tea in a Victorian Parlor

You are visiting friends in London. As part of Victorian England's middle class, they think of their home as an island of peace away from the hustle and bustle of the new factories. As you gaze at their lavishly decorated parlor, you are impressed with their good taste.

Heavy velvet drapes and leaded-glass windows make the room quite dark. Pictures, mirrors, and richly colored wallpaper decorate the walls. Almost every surface is covered with knickknacks and flower arrangements. The rest of the house is considered very private, so the parlor is the only room you will see.

You notice that the parlor is crowded with fancy, overstuffed chairs. That is only proper, because everyone should have a fresh seat. It is considered extremely rude for someone to be offered a seat that is still warm.

The butler has just come in to announce another caller. He presents your friend with the visitor's calling card—a small, decorative card that contains the visitor's name. Good manners demand that the lady of the house return the visit, or at least a card, to every caller within three days.

Portfolio Assessment

When you get home from your visit, you decide to redecorate your parlor in the Victorian style. Draw up a floor plan with doorways, windows, and furniture. Write an explanation of how the room will impress your visitors.

property laws. Women's groups also supported the temperance movement, a campaign to limit or ban the use of alcoholic beverages. Temperance leaders argued that drinking threatened family life.

These reformers faced many obstacles. In Europe and the United States, women could not vote. They were barred from most schools and had little, if any, protection under the law. A woman's husband or father controlled her property.

Early Voices Before 1850, some women had become leaders in the union movement. Others, mostly from the middle class, had campaigned for the abolition of slavery. In the process, they realized the severe restrictions on their own lives. In the United States, Elizabeth Cady Stanton and Susan B. Anthony crusaded against slavery before organizing a movement for women's rights.

Many women broke the barriers that kept them out of universities and professions. By the late 1800s, a few brave women overcame opposition to train as doctors or lawyers. Others became explorers, researchers, or inventors, often without recognition. For example, Julia Brainerd Hall worked with her brother to develop an aluminum-producing process. Their company became hugely successful, but Charles Hall received almost all of the credit.

The Suffrage Struggle By the late 1800s, married women in some countries had won the right to control their own property. The struggle for political rights proved far more difficult. In the United States, the Seneca Falls Convention of 1848 demanded that women be granted the right to vote. In Europe, groups dedicated to women's suffrage, or women's right to vote, emerged in the later 1800s.

Among men, some liberals and socialists supported women's suffrage. In general, though, suffragists faced intense opposition. Some critics claimed that women were too emotional to be allowed to vote. Others argued that women needed to be "protected" from grubby politics or that a woman's place was in the home, not in government. To such claims, Sojourner Truth, an African American suffragist, is believed to have replied, "Nobody ever helps me into carriages, or over mudpuddles, or gives me any best place! And ain't I a woman?"

On the edges of the western world, women made faster strides. In New Zealand, Australia, and some western territories of the United States, women won the vote before 1900. There, women who had "tamed the frontier" alongside men were not dismissed as weak and helpless. In Europe and most of the United States, however, the suffrage struggle succeeded only after World War I. (You will read more about the suffrage movement in later chapters.)

Growth of Public Education

By the late 1800s, reformers persuaded many governments to set up public schools and require basic education for all children. Teaching "the three Rs"—reading, writing, and 'rithmetic—was thought to produce better citizens. In addition, industrialized societies recognized the need for a literate work force. Schools taught punctuality, obedience to authority, disciplined work habits, and patriotism. In European schools, children also received basic religious education.

Public Education At first, elementary schools were primitive. Many teachers had little schooling themselves. In rural areas, students attended class only during the times when they were not needed on the farm or in their parents' shops.

By the late 1800s, more and more children were in school, and the quality of elementary education improved. Also, governments began to expand secondary schools, known as high schools in the United States.

In secondary schools, students learned the "classical languages," Latin and Greek, along with history and mathematics.

In general, only middle-class families could afford to have their sons attend these schools, which trained students for more serious study or for government jobs. Middle-class girls were sent to school primarily in the hope that they might marry well and become better wives and mothers.

Higher Education Colleges and universities expanded in this period, too. Most university students were the sons of middle- or upper-class families. The university curriculum emphasized ancient history and languages, philosophy, religion, and law. By the late 1800s, universities added courses in the sciences, especially in chemistry and physics. At the same time, engineering schools trained students who would have the knowledge and skills to build the new industrial society.

Some women sought greater educational opportunities. By the 1840s, a few small colleges for women opened, including Bedford College in England and Mount Holyoke in the United States. In 1863, the British reformer Emily Davies campaigned for female students to be allowed to take the entrance examinations for Cambridge University. She succeeded, but as late as 1897, male Cambridge students rioted against granting degrees to women.

New Directions in Science

As you have seen, science in the service of industry brought great changes in the later 1800s. At the same time, researchers advanced startling theories about the natural world. Their new ideas challenged long-held beliefs.

Atomic Theory A crucial breakthrough in chemistry came in the early 1800s when the English Quaker schoolteacher John Dalton developed modern atomic theory. The ancient Greeks had speculated that all matter was made of tiny particles called atoms. Dalton showed how different kinds of atoms combine to make all chemical substances. In 1869, the Russian chemist Dmitri Mendeleyev (mehn duh LAY ehv) drew up a table that grouped

Public Education
By the late 1800s, poor children often attended elementary school, although many would drop out before high school. Above left, students in a cramped New York City classroom copy their lessons.

Theme: Continuity and Change Why are poor children today more likely to attend high school than the children shown here?

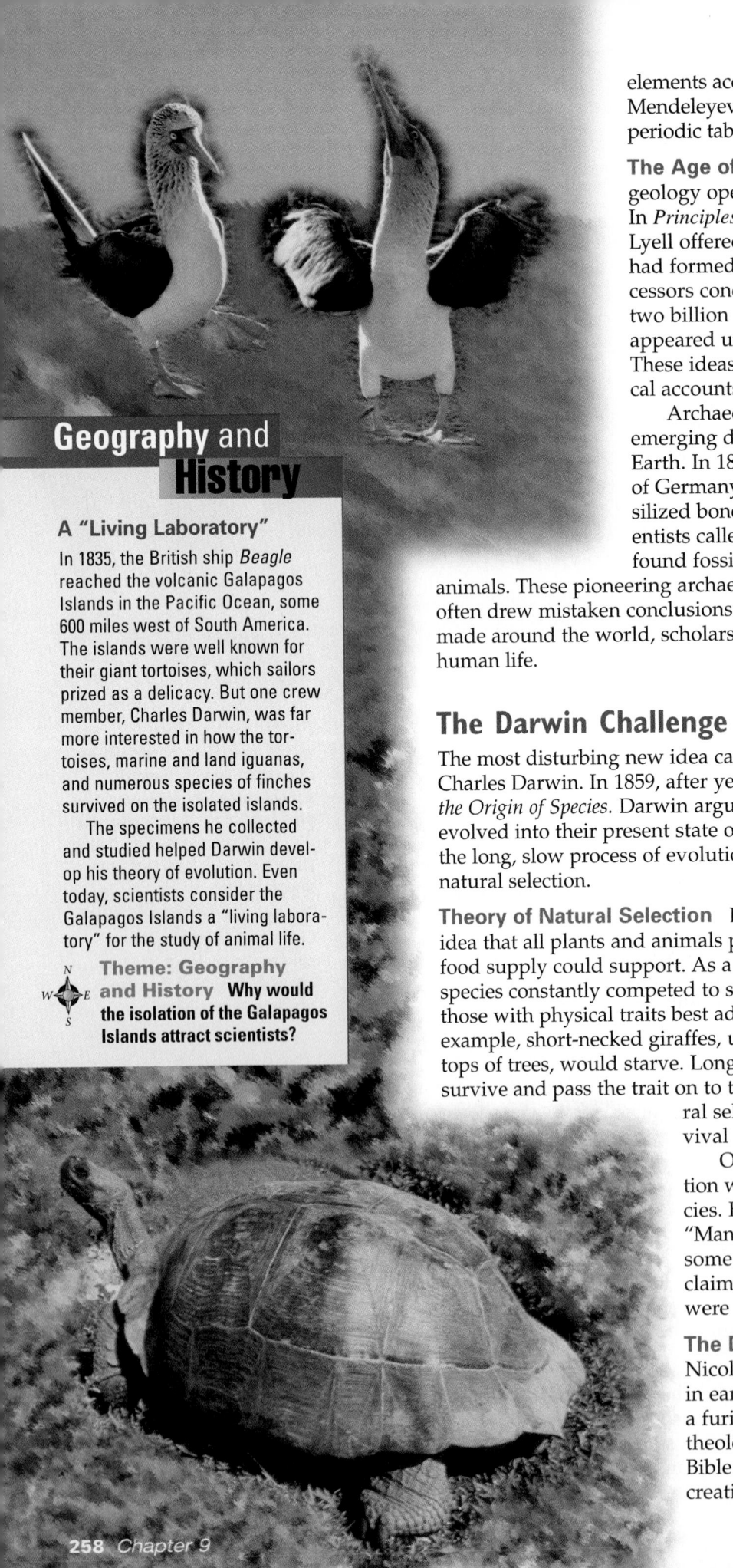

elements according to their atomic weights. Mendeleyev's table became the basis for the periodic table of elements used today.

The Age of the Earth The new science of geology opened disturbing avenues of debate. In *Principles of Geology* (1830–1833), Charles Lyell offered evidence to show that the Earth had formed over millions of years. His successors concluded that the Earth was at least two billion years old and that life had not appeared until long after Earth was formed. These ideas did not seem to agree with biblical accounts of creation.

Archaeology added other pieces to an emerging debate about the origins of life on Earth. In 1856, workers in the Neander valley of Germany accidentally uncovered the fossilized bones of prehistoric people, whom scientists called Neanderthal. Later scholars found fossils of other prehistoric humans and animals. These pioneering archaeologists had limited evidence and often drew mistaken conclusions. But as more discoveries were made around the world, scholars developed new ideas about early human life.

The Darwin Challenge

The most disturbing new idea came from the British naturalist Charles Darwin. In 1859, after years of research, he published *On the Origin of Species*. Darwin argued that all forms of life had evolved into their present state over millions of years. To explain the long, slow process of evolution, he put forward his theory of natural selection.

Theory of Natural Selection Darwin adopted Thomas Malthus's idea that all plants and animals produced more offspring than the food supply could support. As a result, he said, members of each species constantly competed to survive. Natural forces "selected" those with physical traits best adapted to their environment. For example, short-necked giraffes, unable to reach the leaves at the tops of trees, would starve. Longer-necked giraffes, however, would survive and pass the trait on to their offspring. This process of natural selection came to be known as "survival of the fittest."

Over time, said Darwin, natural selection would give rise to entirely new species. He applied this theory to humans. "Man," he declared, "is descended from some less highly organized form." He claimed that humans, like all life forms, were still evolving.

The Darwin Furor Like the ideas of Nicolaus Copernicus and Galileo Galilei in earlier times, Darwin's theory ignited a furious debate between scientists and theologians. To many Christians, the Bible contained the only true account of creation. It told how God created the

Geography and History

A "Living Laboratory"

In 1835, the British ship *Beagle* reached the volcanic Galapagos Islands in the Pacific Ocean, some 600 miles west of South America. The islands were well known for their giant tortoises, which sailors prized as a delicacy. But one crew member, Charles Darwin, was far more interested in how the tortoises, marine and land iguanas, and numerous species of finches survived on the isolated islands.

The specimens he collected and studied helped Darwin develop his theory of evolution. Even today, scientists consider the Galapagos Islands a "living laboratory" for the study of animal life.

Theme: Geography and History Why would the isolation of the Galapagos Islands attract scientists?

world and all forms of life in six days. Darwin's theory, they argued, reduced people to the level of animals and undermined belief in God and the soul.

While some Christians eventually came to accept the idea of evolution, others did not. Controversy over Darwin's theory has continued to the present day, especially in the United States.

Social Darwinism   Darwin himself never promoted any social ideas. However, some thinkers used Darwin's theories to support their own beliefs about society. Their ideas became known as Social Darwinism, applying the idea of survival of the fittest to war and economic competition. Industrial tycoons, argued Social Darwinists, were more "fit" than those they put out of business. War brought progress by weeding out weak nations. Victory was seen as proof of superiority.

Social Darwinism encouraged racism, the belief that one racial group is superior to another. By the late 1800s, many Europeans and Americans claimed that the success of western civilization was due to the supremacy of the white race. Karl Pearson, a British mathematician, wrote, "History shows me one way, and one way only, in which a high state of civilization has been produced, namely the struggle of race with race, and the survival of the physically and mentally fitter race." By the end of the century, as you will read, such ideas would be used to justify the global expansion of imperialism, as well as racial discrimination and segregation.

Religion in an Urban Age

Despite the challenge of new ideas, religion continued to be a major force in western society. Christian churches and Jewish synagogues remained at the center of communities. Religious leaders influenced political, social, and educational developments.

The grim realities of industrial life stimulated feelings of compassion and charity. In Europe, Christian labor unions and political parties pushed for reforms. Individuals and church groups tried to help the working poor. Catholic priests and nuns set up schools and hospitals in urban slums. In the United States, Jewish organizations such as B'nai B'rith provided similar social services.

In Europe and the United States, many Protestant churches backed the social gospel, a movement that urged Christians to social service. They campaigned for reforms in housing, health care, and education. By 1878, William and Catherine Booth had set up the Salvation Army in London. It both spread Christian teachings and provided social services.

Comfort for the Poor
Evangeline Booth, daughter of William and Catherine, helped bring the Salvation Army from Britain to the United States and Canada. This picture shows Booth with two slum children.

Theme: Religions and Value Systems How does this picture express the values of groups like the Salvation Army?

SECTION 3 Assessment

Recall
1. **Identify:** (a) atomic theory, (b) Charles Lyell, (c) natural selection, (d) Social Darwinism, (e) Salvation Army.
2. **Define:** (a) cult of domesticity, (b) temperance movement, (c) women's suffrage, (d) racism, (e) social gospel.

Comprehension
3. (a) How did the social order change in industrial nations? (b) Describe three values associated with the middle class.

4. (a) What were the main goals of the women's movement? (b) Why did it face strong opposition?
5. Why did the ideas of Charles Darwin cause controversy?
6. What services did religious organizations provide?

Critical Thinking and Writing
7. **Defending a Position** Why do you think reformers pushed for free public education?
8. **Linking Past and Present** What charitable services do religious organizations perform today?

Go Online
PHSchool.com
Use Internet resources to find out about entertaining in a middle-class English home in the 1800s. Then, with two other students, plan a party. Write an invitation, plan a menu, and demonstrate a game that you might play. For help with this activity, use **Web Code mkd-2261.**

Reading Focus

- What themes shaped romantic art, literature, and music?

- How did realists respond to the industrialized, urban world?

- How did the visual arts change?

Vocabulary

romanticism

realism

impressionism

Taking Notes

Copy the diagram below. As you read, fill in the major features of the artistic movements in the 1800s. To help you get started, some answers have been provided.

	GOALS	CHARACTERISTICS	MAJOR FIGURES
ROMANTICISM	• Rebellion against the Enlightenment emphasis on reason •	• Romantic hero in literature •	• Lord Byron • Wordsworth •
REALISM			
IMPRESSIONISM			

Main Idea New artistic styles emerged as a reaction to the Industrial Revolution.

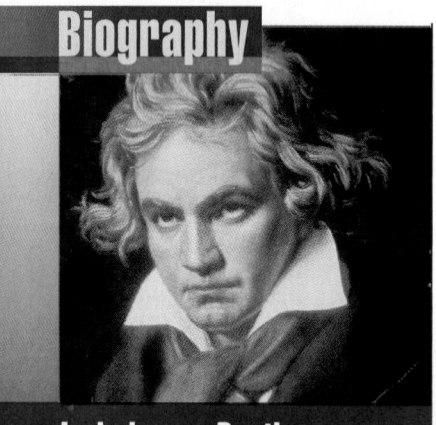

Biography

Ludwig van Beethoven
1770–1827

Composer Ludwig van Beethoven wrote from the heart. An accomplished musician by age 12, he agonized over every note of every composition. The result was stunning music that expresses intense emotion. The famous opening of his Fifth Symphony conveys the sense of fate knocking at the door. His Sixth Symphony captures a joyful day in the countryside, interrupted by a violent thunderstorm.

Beethoven's career was haunted by perhaps the greatest tragedy a musician can face. In 1798, he began to lose his hearing. Still, he continued to compose music he could hear only in his mind.

Theme: Impact of the Individual How did Beethoven's music reflect romanticism?

Setting the Scene In the 1800s, many writers turned away from the harsh realities of industrial life to celebrate the natural world. The English poet William Wordsworth described the peace and beauty of sunset:

> "It is a beauteous evening, calm and free,
> The holy time is quiet as a Nun
> Breathless with adoration; the broad sun
> Is sinking down in its tranquillity."
> —William Wordsworth,
> *Complete Poetical Works*

Other writers, however, made the new industrialized, urban society the subject of their work.

The Romantic Revolt Against Reason

Wordsworth was part of a cultural movement called romanticism. From about 1750 to 1850, romanticism shaped western literature and arts. Romantic writers, artists, and composers rebelled against the Enlightenment emphasis on reason and progress. They glorified nature and sought to excite strong emotions in their audiences.

The Romantic Hero Romantic writers created a new kind of hero—a mysterious, melancholy figure who felt out of step with society. "My joys, my grief, my passions, and my powers, / Made me a stranger," wrote Britain's Lord Byron. He himself was a larger-than-life figure equal to those he created. Public interest in his poetry and adventures was so great that moody, isolated romantic heroes came to be described as "Byronic."

The romantic hero often hid a guilty secret and faced a grim destiny. Germany's greatest writer, Johann Wolfgang von Goethe (GEH tuh), wrote the dramatic poem *Faust*. The aging scholar Faust makes a pact with the devil, exchanging his soul for youth. After much agony, Faust wins salvation by accepting his duty to help others. In *Jane Eyre*, British novelist Charlotte Brontë weaves a tale about a quiet governess and her brooding, Byronic employer, whose large mansion conceals a terrifying secret.

Romance of the Past Romantic writers combed history, legend, and folklore. Sir Walter Scott's novels and ballads evoked the turbulent history of Scottish clans or medieval knights. Alexandre Dumas (doo MAH) re-created France's past in novels like *The Three Musketeers*.

Music Romantic composers also tried to stir deep emotions. The passionate music of German composer Ludwig van Beethoven combined classical forms with a stirring range of sound. He was the first composer to take full advantage of the broad range of instruments in the modern orchestra. In all, Beethoven produced nine symphonies, five piano concertos, a violin concerto, an opera, two masses, and dozens of shorter pieces. To many, he is considered the greatest composer of his day.

Other romantic composers wove traditional folk melodies into their works to glorify their nations' pasts. In his piano works, Frederic Chopin (shoh PAN) used Polish peasant dances to convey the sorrows and joys of people living under foreign occupation.

Romanticism in Art Painters, too, broke free from the discipline and strict rules of the Enlightenment. Landscape painters like J.M.W. Turner sought to capture the beauty and power of nature. Using bold brush strokes and colors, Turner showed tiny human figures struggling against sea and storm.

Romantics painted many subjects, from simple peasant life to medieval knights to current events. Bright colors conveyed violent energy and emotion. The French painter Eugène Delacroix (deh luh KRWAH) filled his canvases with dramatic action. In *Liberty Leading the People*, the Goddess of Liberty carries the revolutionary tricolor as French citizens rally to the cause.

The Call to Realism

By the mid-1800s, a new artistic movement, realism, took hold in the West. Realism was an attempt to represent the world as it was. Realists often focused their work on the harsh side of life in cities or villages. Many writers and artists were committed to improving the lot of the unfortunates whose lives they depicted.

Realism in Art
After seeing two men working on a road, Gustave Courbet invited them to pose for him in his studio. In 1849, *The Stone Breakers* became his first important work of realist art.

Theme: Arts and Literature Many critics denounced Courbet's work for being vulgar and unspiritual. Why do you think his work caused such a reaction?

Virtual Field Trip

Go Online
PHSchool.com

For: More works by Claude Monet and other impressionists
Visit: PHSchool.com
Web Code: mkd-2264

Impressionism
In his many paintings of Rouen Cathedral, Claude Monet showed how light and atmosphere can affect perception. These three paintings show the cathedral at different times of day and in different weather conditions.

Theme: Arts and Literature Why do you think Monet always painted the cathedral from a similar angle?

The Novel The English novelist Charles Dickens vividly portrayed the lives of slum dwellers and factory workers, including children. In *Oliver Twist*, he tells the story of a nine-year-old orphan raised in a grim poorhouse. One day, young Oliver gets up the nerve to ask for extra food:

> "Child as he was, he was desperate with hunger, and reckless with misery. He rose from the table, and advancing on the master, basin and spoon in hand, said somewhat alarmed at his own [boldness]:
> 'Please, sir, I want some more.'"
> —Charles Dickens, *Oliver Twist*

In response to that simple request, Oliver is smacked on the head and sent away to work. Later, he runs away to London. There he is taken in by Fagin, a villain who trains homeless children to become pickpockets. *Oliver Twist* shocked many middle-class readers with its picture of poverty, mistreatment of children, and urban crime. Yet, Dickens's humor and colorful characters made him one of the most popular novelists in the world.

French novelists also portrayed the ills of their time. In *Les Misérables* (LAY mih zehr AHB bluh), Victor Hugo revealed how hunger drove a good man to crime and how the law hounded him ever after. The novels of Émile Zola painted an even grimmer picture. In *Germinal*, Zola exposed class warfare in the French mining industry. To Zola's characters, neither the Enlightenment's faith in reason nor romantic feelings mattered at all.

Drama Norwegian dramatist Henrik Ibsen brought realism to the stage. His plays attacked the hypocrisy he observed around him. *A Doll's House* showed a woman caught in a straitjacket of social rules. In *An Enemy of the People*, a doctor discovers that the water in a local spa is polluted. Because the town's economy depends on its spa, the citizens denounce the doctor and suppress the truth. Ibsen's realistic dramas had a wide influence in Europe and the United States.

Realism in Art Painters also represented the realities of their time. Rejecting the romantic emphasis on imagination, they focused on ordinary subjects, especially working-class men and women. "I cannot paint an angel," said the French realist Gustave Courbet (koor BAY), "because I have never seen one." Instead, he painted works such as *The Stone Breakers*, which shows two rough laborers on a country road. Later in the century, *The Gross Clinic,* by American painter Thomas Eakins, shocked viewers with its realistic depiction of a medical class conducting a dissection.

New Directions in the Visual Arts

By the 1840s, a new art form, photography, was emerging. Louis Daguerre (dah GAYR) in France and William Fox Talbot in England had improved on earlier technologies to produce successful photographs. At first, many photos were stiff, posed portraits of middle-class families or prominent people. Other photographs reflected the romantics' fascination with faraway places.

In time, photographers used the camera to present the grim realities of life. During the American Civil War, Mathew B. Brady preserved a vivid, realistic record of the corpse-strewn battlefields. Other photographers provided vivid evidence of harsh conditions in industrial factories or slums.

The Impressionists Photography posed a challenge to painters. Why try for realism, some artists asked, when a camera could do the same thing better? By the 1870s, a group of painters took art in a new direction, seeking to capture the first fleeting impression made by a scene or object on the viewer's eye. The new movement, known as impressionism, took root in Paris, capital of the western art world.

Since the Renaissance, painters had carefully finished their paintings so that not a brush stroke showed. But impressionists like Claude Monet (moh NAY) and Edgar Degas (day GAH) brushed strokes of color side by side without any blending. According to new scientific studies of optics, the human eye would mix these patches of color.

By concentrating on visual impressions rather than realism, artists achieved a fresh view of familiar subjects. Monet, for example, painted the cathedral at Rouen (roo AHN), France, dozens of times from the same angle, capturing how it looked in different lights at different times of day.

The Postimpressionists Later painters, called postimpressionists, developed a variety of styles. Georges Seurat (suh RAH) arranged small dots of color to define the shapes of objects. The Dutch painter Vincent van Gogh experimented with sharp brush lines and bright colors.

Paul Gauguin (goh GAN) developed a bold, personal style. He rejected the materialism of western life and went to live on the island of Tahiti. In his paintings, people look flat, as in "primitive" folk art. But his brooding colors and black outlining of shapes convey intense feelings and images.

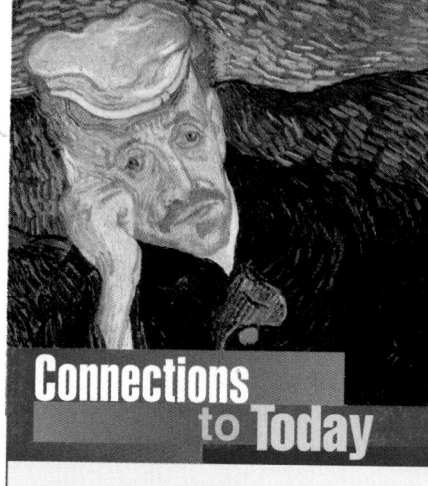

Connections to Today

A Van Gogh at Auction

Vincent van Gogh sold few paintings during his short, unhappy life. In 1890, after several attacks of epilepsy and depression, he began to see the noted doctor Paul-Ferdinand Gachet. Soon after, his doctor became his model. Van Gogh wrote that he had painted Gachet "with the heart-broken expression of our time."

Van Gogh died nearly penniless a year later, but his *Portrait of Dr. Gachet* became one of the most valuable paintings of all time. In 1990, exactly 100 years after it was painted, the portrait sold at an auction in New York for more than $82 million—then an all-time record for any work of art sold at auction.

Theme: Art and Literature
How has the value of Van Gogh's paintings changed?

SECTION 4 Assessment

Recall

1. **Identify:** **(a)** Lord Byron, **(b)** Johann Wolfgang von Goethe, **(c)** Ludwig van Beethoven, **(d)** Charlotte Brontë, **(e)** Charles Dickens, **(f)** Gustave Courbet, **(g)** Claude Monet, **(h)** postimpressionists.
2. **Define:** **(a)** romanticism, **(b)** realism, **(c)** impressionism.

Comprehension

3. **(a)** How did romantics respond to the Enlightenment? **(b)** Describe three subjects romantics favored.

4. How did Dickens and Ibsen explore realistic themes?
5. How did photography influence the development of painting?

Critical Thinking and Writing

6. **Recognizing Causes and Effects** In what ways were the new artistic styles of the 1800s a reaction to changes in society?
7. **Defending a Position** **(a)** What did Courbet mean when he said, "I cannot paint an angel because I have never seen one"? **(b)** Do you agree with his attitude? Explain.

Go Online PHSchool.com

Use the Internet to research one of the artists mentioned in this section. Then, write a review of one of his paintings. Consider such questions as the following: What style is used? What is the artist trying to do? What is your opinion of the work? For help with this activity, use **Web Code mkd-2265.**

Creating a Chapter Summary

Copy this graphic organizer on a piece of paper. Include information about the developments that occurred in each category during the 1800s. Add more circles as needed.

For additional review and enrichment activities, see the interactive version of *World History* available on the Web and on CD-ROM.

For practice test questions for Chapter 9, use **Web Code mka-2266.**

Building Vocabulary

Review the meaning of the chapter vocabulary words listed below. Then, write a sentence for each word in which you define the word and describe its relationship to life in the Industrial Revolution.

1. **assembly line**
2. **corporation**
3. **cartel**
4. **urban renewal**
5. **standard of living**
6. **cult of domesticity**
7. **temperance movement**
8. **social gospel**
9. **romanticism**
10. **realism**

Recalling Key Facts

11. Which two nations became industrial leaders in the late 1800s?
12. What arguments were made for and against the rise of big business?
13. What kinds of attractions did cities offer their residents?
14. What improvements in working conditions occurred in the late 1800s?
15. Name three characteristics or concerns of romanticism.
16. How did the visual arts change in response to new technology?

Critical Thinking and Writing

17. **Connecting to Geography** How did technology affect the movement of people and goods in the 1800s and early 1900s?
18. **Linking Past and Present** **(a)** How did the second Industrial Revolution differ from the first? **(b)** Some historians believe that we are now in the midst of a "third" Industrial Revolution. Do you agree or disagree? Explain.
19. **Recognizing Points of View** How might each of the following have viewed the Industrial Revolution: **(a)** an inventor, **(b)** an entrepreneur, **(c)** a worker?
20. **Applying Information** Did the lives of women improve as a result of the Industrial Revolution? Why or why not?
21. **Making Inferences** Referring to *Oliver Twist,* Dickens wrote that "to show [criminals] as they really are, for ever skulking uneasily through the dirtiest paths of life . . . would be a service to society." **(a)** What do you think he meant? **(b)** How does his claim reflect the goals of realism?

John Hollingshead was an English journalist who had himself been raised in poverty in London. He wrote this description of city life in 1862. Read the passage and answer the questions that follow.

"We are a little too apt to pride ourselves on our national growth and to overlook the quality in the quantity of our population. Thirty millions of people in the United Kingdom, one-tenth of whom belong to London proper . . . show an undoubted advance in capital and prosperity. Taken in detail [however] they show that the spreading limbs of a great city may be healthy and vigorous, while its heart may gradually become more choked and decayed. A vast deal of life that skulks or struggles in London is only familiar to the hard-working clergy, certain medical practitioners, and a few [parish] officers. It burrows in holes and corners at the back of busy thoroughfares. . . . Its records, if truthfully given, have little romance, little beauty, and less variety. Poverty, ignorance, dirt, immorality, and crime are the five great divisions of its history."

—John Hollingshead, "London Poor"

22. According to the author, what percentage of people in London had experienced an improvement in their standard of living as a result of the Industrial Revolution?
23. What does Hollingshead say are the main problems facing the poor?
24. What does the author mean when he says that "the spreading limbs of a great city may be healthy and vigorous, while its heart may gradually become more choked and decayed"?
25. How does this passage reflect what you have learned about the role of religion in urban society?
26. **(a)** Who do you think was the intended audience for this article? **(b)** Why does Hollingshead say, "We are a little too apt to pride ourselves on our national growth"? **(c)** What effect do you think the author hoped to have on his audience?
27. Do you think Hollingshead's description of London in the 1860s could also apply to cities today? Explain.

STEEL PRODUCTION, 1880–1910

Sources: *European Historical Statistics, 1750–1970,* and *Historical Statistics of the United States*

The graph above shows the amount of steel produced by three major industrialized nations. Look at the graph and answer the following questions:

28. About how much steel did Britain produce in 1880? In 1910?
29. List the three countries shown in the graph in order from highest to lowest steel production in **(a)** 1890, **(b)** 1900.
30. Between 1890 and 1910, which nation had the greatest increase in steel production? The smallest?
31. Based on what you have read, how can you explain Germany's rise in steel production?

Skills Tip

When you analyze a graph, look for increases and decreases, as well as similarities and differences over time.

Go Online
PHSchool.com

Use the Internet to research an invention or breakthrough from the second Industrial Revolution. Then, create and deliver a presentation about it. Include when and how it was discovered or created, its importance at the time it was discovered or created, and whether it is still in use today. For help with this activity, use **Web Code mkd-2267**.

CHAPTER 10

Nationalism Triumphs in Europe

1800–1914

Chapter Preview

1 Building a German Nation
2 Strengthening Germany
3 Unifying Italy
4 Nationalism Threatens Old Empires
5 Russia: Reform and Reaction

Early 1800s

Nationalism rises in Germany. The folk tales collected by Jacob and William Grimm, such as "Hansel and Gretel" (above), were one attempt to foster a common German heritage.

1814

The Congress of Vienna begins.

1831

Giuseppe Mazzini, shown here, founds a secret society called Young Italy. The society encourages Italian unification.

CHAPTER EVENTS

1800   1825   1850

GLOBAL EVENTS

1804 Haiti declares independence from France.

1848 Revolutions take place throughout Europe.

Unification in Europe, 1873

Nationalist movements led to the creation of several new nations across Europe.

ATLANTIC OCEAN

UNITED KINGDOM

NETHERLANDS

KINGDOM OF SWEDEN AND NORWAY

DENMARK

St. Petersburg

RUSSIA

Don R.

Elbe R.

Berlin

GERMANY

Oder R.

Vistula R.

Dnieper R.

BELGIUM

Rhine R.

LUXEMBOURG

SWITZERLAND

Seine R.

Loire R.

FRANCE

50°N

Dniester R.

AUSTRIA–HUNGARY

Vienna

Budapest

Danube R.

Black Sea

ALPS

Rhône R.

Po R.

PORTUGAL

SPAIN

PYRENEES MTS.

Ebro R.

Tagus R.

10°W

40°N

Tiber R.

Adriatic Sea

Rome

ITALY

OTTOMAN EMPIRE

10°E

20°E

30°E

40°E

Mediterranean Sea

N W E S

Azimuthal Equal Area Projection

0   200   400 Miles
0   200   400 Kilometers

1885
Construction begins on the parliament building in Budapest. Although Austria and Hungary have been united under the Dual Monarchy since 1867, each state has its own parliament.

1905
In Russia, the czar's troops, standing in front of the arch, fire on peaceful protesters. The massacre becomes known as Bloody Sunday.

1914
World War I begins.

1875

1900

1925

1898 The Philippines declares independence from Spain.

1903 In North Carolina, the Wright brothers complete the first flight in an airplane.

Building a German Nation

Reading Focus

- What early changes promoted German unity?
- How did Bismarck unify Germany?
- What was the basic political organization of the new German empire?

Vocabulary

chancellor
Realpolitik
annex
kaiser
Reich

Taking Notes

On a sheet of paper, make a flowchart showing the key events that led to a united Germany. Use this flowchart to help you get started. Add more boxes as needed

```
┌─────────────────────────────────────┐
│ Bismarck becomes chancellor          │
└─────────────────────────────────────┘
                  │
                  ▼
┌─────────────────────────────────────┐
│ Bismarck enters alliance with        │
│ Austria to "liberate" Holstein       │
│ and Schleswig                        │
└─────────────────────────────────────┘
                  │
                  ▼
┌─────────────────────────────────────┐
│                                      │
└─────────────────────────────────────┘
```

Main Idea Otto von Bismarck, the chancellor of Prussia, led the drive for German unity.

Setting the Scene The Prussian legislators waited restlessly for Otto von Bismarck to speak. They knew he wanted them to vote more money to build up the Prussian army. Liberal members of the parliament, however, opposed the move. At last, Bismarck rose and dismissed their concerns:

> "Germany does not look to Prussia's liberalism, but to her power. . . . The great questions of the day are not to be decided by speeches and majority resolutions—that was the mistake of 1848 and 1849—but by blood and iron!"
> —Otto von Bismarck, quoted in *Modern and Contemporary European History, 1815–1940* (Schapiro)

Bismarck delivered his "blood and iron" speech in 1862. It set the tone for his policies in the years ahead. Bismarck was determined to build a strong, unified German state, with Prussia at its head.

Steps Toward Unity

In the early 1800s, German-speaking people lived in a number of small and medium-sized states as well as in Prussia and the Austrian Hapsburg empire. Napoleon's invasions unleashed new forces in these territories.

Impact of Napoleon Between 1807 and 1812, Napoleon made important territorial changes in German-speaking lands. He annexed lands along the Rhine River for France. He dissolved the Holy Roman Empire and organized a number of German states into the Rhine Confederation.

At first, some Germans welcomed the French emperor as a hero with enlightened, modern policies. He encouraged freeing the serfs, made trade easier, and abolished laws against Jews. However, not all Germans appreciated Napoleon and his changes. As people fought to free their lands from French rule, they began to demand a unified German state.

Napoleon's defeat did not resolve the issue. At the Congress of Vienna, Metternich pointed out that a united Germany would require dismantling the government of each German state. Instead, the peacemakers created the German Confederation, a weak alliance headed by Austria.

Prussian Leadership In the 1830s, Prussia created an economic union called the *Zollverein* (TSAWL fuh rīn). It dismantled tariff barriers between many German states. Still, Germany remained politically fragmented.

In 1848, liberals meeting in the Frankfurt Assembly again demanded German political unity. They offered the throne of a united German state to Frederick William IV of Prussia. The Prussian ruler, however, rejected the notion of a throne offered by "the people."

Bismarck and German Unity

Otto von Bismarck succeeded where others had failed. Bismarck came from Prussia's Junker (YUNG ker) class, made up of conservative landowning nobles. Bismarck first served Prussia as a diplomat. In 1862, King William I made him chancellor, or prime minister. Within a decade, the new chancellor had united the German states under Prussian rule.

Master of *Realpolitik* Bismarck's success was due in part to his strong will. He was a master of *Realpolitik,* or realistic politics based on the needs of the state. Power was more important than principles.

Although Bismarck was the architect of German unity, he was not really a German nationalist. His primary loyalty was to the Hohenzollerns, the ruling dynasty of Prussia. Through unification, he hoped to bring more power to the Hohenzollerns.

Strengthening the Army As chancellor, Bismarck moved first to build up the Prussian army. Despite his "blood and iron" speech, the liberal legislature refused to vote funds for the military. In response, Bismarck strengthened the army with money that had been collected for other purposes. He then was ready to pursue an aggressive foreign policy.

In the next decade, Bismarck led Prussia into three wars. Each war increased Prussian power and paved the way for German unity.

Skills Assessment

Geography In the early 1800s, people living in German-speaking states had local loyalties. By the mid-1800s, however, they were developing a national identity.

1. **Location** On the map, locate **(a)** Prussia, **(b)** Silesia, **(c)** Bavaria, **(d)** Schleswig.
2. **Region** What area did Prussia add to its territory in 1866?
3. **Critical Thinking Analyzing Information** Why do you think Austrian influence was greater among the southern German states than among the northern ones?

Unification of Germany, 1865–1871

Legend:
- Prussia, 1865
- Added to Prussia, 1866
- Added to form North German Confederation, 1867
- Added to form German empire, 1871
- Boundary of German empire, 1871
- ★ Battle sites
- → Route of Prussian armies in Austro-Prussian War
- → Route of German armies in Franco-Prussian War

Azimuthal Equal Area Projection

Analyzing Primary Sources

Crowning the German Emperor

This painting by Anton von Werner shows the coronation of William I (center on the steps) as emperor of the united Germany. The ceremony took place at Versailles in 1871.

Skills Tip

Keep in mind that a painting is an artist's vision of an event. Unlike a photograph of an actual scene, a painting may embellish or exaggerate certain aspects of an event.

Skills Assessment

1. In the painting, William I is saluted by
   A common citizens.
   B the royal court.
   C uniformed men.
   D foreign dignitaries.

2. How is Otto von Bismarck (at center, in white jacket) portrayed?
   E as equal to the emperor
   F as superior to the emperor
   G as unimportant to the coronation
   H as a central part of the coronation

3. **Critical Thinking Analyzing Primary Sources (a)** What feelings does the painting evoke about the coronation and the union of Germany? Which details support your view? **(b)** Write three questions that the painting raises about the event, then find the answers through further research.

Wars With Denmark and Austria   Bismarck's first maneuver was to form an alliance in 1864 with Austria. They seized the provinces of Schleswig and Holstein from Denmark. Prussia and Austria "liberated" the two provinces, which were largely inhabited by Germans, and divided up the spoils.

In 1866, Bismarck invented an excuse to attack Austria. The Austro-Prussian War lasted just seven weeks and ended in a decisive Prussian victory. Prussia then annexed, or took control of, several other north German states.

Bismarck dissolved the Austrian-led German Confederation and created a new confederation dominated by Prussia. He allowed Austria and four other southern German states to remain independent. Bismarck's motives, as always, were strictly practical. "We had to avoid leaving behind any desire for revenge," he later wrote.

The Franco-Prussian War   In France, the Prussian victory over Austria worried Napoleon III. A growing rivalry between the two nations led to the Franco-Prussian War of 1870.

Germans recalled only too well the invasions of Napoleon I some 60 years earlier. Bismarck played up the image of the French menace to spur German nationalism. For his part, Napoleon III did little to avoid war, hoping to mask problems at home with military glory.

Bismarck furthered the crisis by rewriting and then releasing to the press a telegram that reported on a meeting between King William I and the French ambassador. Bismarck's editing of the "Ems dispatch" made it seem that William I had insulted the Frenchman. Furious, Napoleon III declared war on Prussia, as Bismarck had hoped.

A superior Prussian force, supported by troops from other German states, smashed the badly organized and poorly supplied French soldiers. Napoleon III, old and ill, surrendered within a few weeks. France had to accept a humiliating peace.

The German Empire

Delighted by the victory over France, princes from the southern German states and the North German Confederation persuaded William I of Prussia to take the title kaiser (KĪ zer), or emperor. In January 1871, German nationalists celebrated the birth of the Second Reich, or empire. They called it that because they considered it heir to the Holy Roman Empire.

A constitution drafted by Bismarck set up a two-house legislature. The Bundesrat, or upper house, was appointed by the rulers of the German states. The Reichstag, or lower house, was elected by universal male suffrage. Because the Bundesrat could veto any decisions of the Reichstag, real power remained in the hands of the emperor and his chancellor.

Primary Source

War and Power
In 1866, Field Marshal Helmuth von Moltke analyzed the importance of Prussia's war against Austria:

"The war of 1866 was entered on not because the existence of Prussia was threatened, nor was it caused by public opinion and the voice of the people; it was a struggle, long foreseen and calmly prepared for, recognized as a necessity by the Cabinet, not for territorial expansion, for an extension of our domain, or for material advantage, but for an ideal end—the establishment of power. Not a foot of land was exacted from Austria. . . . Its center of gravity lay out of Germany; Prussia's lay within it. Prussia felt itself called upon and strong enough to assume the leadership of the German races."

—Helmuth von Moltke, quoted in *Readings in European History* (Robinson)

Skills Assessment

Primary Source Why, according to von Moltke, did Prussia go to war against Austria?

SECTION 1 Assessment

Recall

1. **Identify:** (a) *Zollverein*, (b) Otto von Bismarck, (c) William I.
2. **Define:** (a) chancellor, (b) *Realpolitik*, (c) annex, (d) kaiser, (e) Reich.

Comprehension

3. What territorial and economic changes promoted German unity?
4. Describe the techniques Bismarck used to unify the German states.
5. How did the emperor and his chancellor retain power in the new German government?

Critical Thinking and Writing

6. **Applying Information** Identify three examples of Bismarck's use of *Realpolitik*.
7. **Comparing** How did the nationalism represented by Bismarck differ from that embraced by liberals in the early 1800s?

Activity

Making a Map
Create an illustrated map and time line showing the unification of Germany. Include a legend that explains symbols on your map, such as those used for battle sites.

Strengthening Germany

Reading Focus

- What marked Germany as an industrial giant?
- Why was Bismarck called the Iron Chancellor?
- What policies did Kaiser William II follow?

Vocabulary

Kulturkampf
social welfare

Taking Notes

On a sheet of paper, make a diagram like the one started here. As you read the section, add other causes that led to a strong German nation.

- Plentiful resources for industry
- Educated work force
-
-

STRONG GERMAN NATION

Main Idea Germany increased its power by building up its industry and armed forces.

Setting the Scene

In January 1871, German princes gathered in the glittering Hall of Mirrors at the French palace of Versailles. They had just defeated Napoleon III in the Franco-Prussian War. The palace of Louis XIV seemed the perfect place to proclaim the new German empire. To the winners as well as to the losers, the symbolism was clear. French domination of Europe, dating from the age of Louis XIV, had ended. Germany, headed by William I and his chancellor, Otto von Bismarck, was now the dominant power in Europe.

The German Industrial Giant

In the aftermath of unification, the German empire emerged as the industrial giant of the European continent. By the late 1800s, German chemical and electrical industries were setting the standard worldwide. German shipping was second only to Britain's among the European powers.

Economic Progress Germany, like Great Britain, possessed several of the factors that made industrialization possible. Germany's spectacular growth was due in part to ample iron and coal resources, the basic ingredients for industrial development. A disciplined and educated work force also helped the economy, and a rapidly growing population—from 41 million in 1871 to 67 million by 1914—provided a huge home market along with a larger supply of industrial workers.

The new nation also benefited from earlier progress. During the 1850s and 1860s, Germans had founded large companies and built many railroads. The house of Krupp boomed after 1871. It became an enormous industrial complex that produced steel and weapons for a world market. Between 1871 and 1914, the business tycoon August Thyssen built a small steel factory of 70 workers into a giant empire with 50,000 employees.

Science, Government, and Industry German industrialists were the first to see the value of applied science in developing new products such as synthetic chemicals and dyes. They supported research and development in the universities and hired trained scientists to solve technological problems in their factories.

German Industry
The Krupp works was a major German industrial company. This huge cannon was displayed at an international industrial exhibition to demonstrate the might of the house of Krupp and of Germany.

Theme: Economics and Technology What advantages would a cannon like this one offer to an army?

The German government promoted economic development. After 1871, it issued a single currency for Germany, reorganized the banking system, and coordinated railroads built by the various German states. When a worldwide depression hit in the late 1800s, Germany raised tariffs to protect home industries from foreign competition. The leaders of the new German empire were determined to maintain economic strength as well as military power.

The Iron Chancellor

As chancellor of the new German empire, Bismarck pursued several foreign-policy goals. He wanted to keep France weak and isolated while building strong links with Austria and Russia. He respected British naval power but did not seek to compete in that arena. "Water rats," he said, "do not fight with land rats." Later, however, he would take a more aggressive stand against Britain as the two nations competed for colonies to expand their overseas empires.

On the domestic front, Bismarck applied the same ruthless methods he had used to achieve unification. The Iron Chancellor, as he was called, sought to erase local loyalties and crush all opposition to the imperial state. He targeted two groups—the Catholic Church and the socialists. In his view, both posed a threat to the new German state.

Campaign Against the Church After unification, Catholics made up about a third of the German population. The Lutheran Bismarck distrusted Catholics—especially the clergy—whose first loyalty, he believed, was to the pope instead of to Germany.

In response to what he saw as the Catholic threat, Bismarck launched the *Kulturkampf*, or "battle for civilization." His goal was to make Catholics put loyalty to the state above allegiance to the Church. The chancellor had laws passed that gave the state the right to supervise Catholic education and approve the appointment of priests. Other laws closed some religious orders, expelled the Jesuits from Prussia, and made it compulsory for couples to be married by civil authority.

Bismarck's moves against the Catholic Church backfired. The faithful rallied behind the Church, and the Catholic Center party gained strength in the Reichstag. A realist, Bismarck saw his mistake and worked to make peace with the Church.

Campaign Against the Socialists Bismarck also saw a threat to the new German empire in the growing power of socialism. By the late 1870s, German Marxists had organized the Social Democratic party, which called for parliamentary democracy and laws to improve conditions for the working class. Bismarck feared that socialists would undermine the loyalty of German workers and turn them toward revolution. He had laws passed that dissolved socialist groups, shut down their newspapers, and banned their meetings. Once again, repression backfired. Workers were unified in support of the socialist cause.

Bismarck then changed course. He set out to woo workers away from socialism by sponsoring laws to protect them. Bismarck made it clear that *Realpolitik* influenced social reform as well as foreign policy:

"Give the workingman the right to work as long as he is healthy, assure him care when he is sick, and maintenance when he is old . . . then the socialists will sing their siren songs in vain, and the workingmen will cease to throng to their banner."

—Otto von Bismarck, quoted in *Economic Development of Europe* (Ogg and Sharp)

Biography

Otto von Bismarck
1815–1898

Bismarck spent his early years on his father's country estate. He worked briefly as a civil servant, but found the work boring. At 24, Bismarck resigned his post as a bureaucrat. "My ambition strives more to command than to obey," the independent-minded young man explained.

The resignation did not end his career in government. While he was a delegate to the Prussian assembly in 1847, his conservative views and passionate speeches in defense of government policies won him the support of the Prussian king. He was rewarded with appointment to the post of prime minister, a position he held for 28 years.

Theme: Impact of the Individual What path did Bismarck take to win political power?

Photography and Daily Life
The invention of photography in the mid-1800s provided artists with a new way to reflect and comment on real life. This photograph is from a series depicting workers at the beginning of the 1900s.

Theme: Art and Literature
What do you think the photographer is trying to say about German workers?

By the 1890s, Germans had health and accident insurance as well as old-age insurance to provide retirement benefits. Thus, under Bismarck, Germany was a pioneer in social reform. Its system of economic safeguards became the model for other European nations.

Bismarck's plan was only partly successful. Although workers benefited from his measures, they did not abandon socialism. In fact, the Social Democratic party continued to grow in strength. By 1912, it had more seats in the Reichstag than were held by any other party. Yet Bismarck's program showed that conditions for workers could be improved without the upheaval of a revolution. Later, Germany and other European nations would build on Bismarck's social policies, greatly increasing government's role in providing for the needs of its citizens.

Kaiser William II

In 1888, William II succeeded his grandfather as kaiser. The new emperor was supremely confident of his abilities and wished to put his own stamp on Germany. In 1890, he shocked Europe by asking the dominating Bismarck to resign. "There is only one master in the Reich," he said, "and that is I."

William II seriously believed that his right to rule came from God. He expressed this view when he said:

> "My grandfather considered that the office of king was a task that God had assigned to him. . . . That which he thought I also think. . . . Those who wish to aid me in that task . . . I welcome with all my heart; those who oppose me in this work I shall crush."
> —William II, quoted in *Europe Since 1815* (Hazen)

Not surprisingly, William resisted efforts to introduce democratic reforms. At the same time, his government provided services, from programs for social welfare, or programs to help certain groups of people, to cheap transportation and electricity. An excellent system of public schools, begun under Bismarck, taught students obedience to the emperor along with reading, writing, and mathematics.

Like his grandfather, William II lavished funds on the German military machine, already the most powerful in Europe. He also launched an ambitious campaign to expand the German navy and win an overseas empire to rival those of Britain and France. You will read in later chapters how William's nationalism and aggressive militarism helped increase tensions on the eve of World War I.

SECTION 2 Assessment

Recall
1. **Identify:** **(a)** house of Krupp, **(b)** August Thyssen, **(c)** Iron Chancellor.
2. **Define:** **(a)** *Kulturkampf,* **(b)** social welfare.

Comprehension
3. How did Germany become an industrial giant in the late 1800s?
4. Why did Bismarck try to crush the Catholic Church and socialists?
5. What policies did William II introduce?

Critical Thinking and Writing
6. **Recognizing Causes and Effects** Why do you think supporters of democratic government had little hope of success in Germany in the late 1800s?
7. **Defending a Position** Were Bismarck's methods justified by his social reforms? Explain.

Go Online
PHSchool.com

Use the Internet to research the Krupp family of Germany. Then, write a report explaining their role in the military and industrial history of Germany. For help with this activity, use **Web Code mkd-2376.**

3 Unifying Italy

Reading Focus

- What were the key obstacles to Italian unity?
- What roles did Count Camillo Cavour and Giuseppe Garibaldi play in the struggle for Italy?
- What challenges faced the new nation of Italy?

Vocabulary

anarchist
emigration

Taking Notes

As you read, make a time line to show events from 1831 to 1871 in Italy. Use the time line shown here to help you get started.

1831	1849	1852	1871
Mazzini founds Young Italy	Mazzini's revolutionary republic in Rome toppled	Cavour becomes prime minister in Sardinia	

Main Idea — During the 1800s, influential leaders helped to create a unified Italy.

Setting the Scene

At the Congress of Vienna, Italian nationalists hoped to end centuries of foreign rule and achieve unity. To Metternich, the idea of a unified Italy was laughable. Italy, he was convinced, was a mere "geographic expression."

Although the people of the Italian peninsula spoke the same language, they had not experienced political unity since Roman times. By the early 1800s, though, Italian patriots were determined to build a new, united Italy. As in Germany, unification was brought about by the efforts of a strong state and a shrewd, ruthless politician—Count Camillo Cavour.

Obstacles to Italian Unity

For centuries, Italy had been a battleground for ambitious foreign and local princes. Frequent warfare and foreign rule had led people to identify with local regions. The people of Florence considered themselves Tuscans, those of Venice Venetians, the people of Naples Neapolitans, and so on. But as in Germany, the invasions of Napoleon had sparked dreams of national unity.

The Congress of Vienna, however, ignored the nationalists. At Vienna, Austria took control of much of northern Italy, while Hapsburg monarchs ruled various other Italian states. In the south, a French Bourbon ruler was put in charge of Naples and Sicily.

In response, nationalists organized secret patriotic societies and focused their efforts on expelling Austrian forces from northern Italy. Between 1820 and 1848, nationalist revolts exploded across the region. Each time, Austria sent in troops to crush the rebels.

Mazzini's Young Italy In the 1830s, the nationalist leader Giuseppe Mazzini founded Young Italy. The goal of this secret society was "to constitute Italy, one, free, independent, republican nation." In 1849, Mazzini helped set up a revolutionary republic in Rome, but French forces soon toppled it. Like many other nationalists, Mazzini spent much of his life in exile, plotting and dreaming of a united Italy.

The Tide of Nationalism "Ideas grow quickly," Mazzini once said, "when watered by the blood of martyrs." Although revolution had failed, nationalist agitation had planted seeds for future harvests.

To nationalists like Mazzini, a united Italy made sense not only because of geography, but also because of a common language and history. Nationalists reminded Italians of the glories of ancient Rome and the medieval

Primary Source

First Stirrings of Nationalism

After the failed revolution in northern Italy, many rebels came through Genoa, begging for funds to pay for safe passage to Spain. An impressionable Giuseppe Mazzini described his reaction to the situation:

"He held out a white handkerchief, merely saying, 'For the refugees of Italy.' My mother . . . dropped some money into the handkerchief. . . . That day was the first in which a confused idea presented itself to my mind—I will not say of country or of liberty—but an idea that we Italians could and ought to struggle for the liberty of our country. . . . The idea of an existing wrong on my own country, against which it was a duty to struggle, flashed before my mind on that day for the first time, never again to leave me."

—Giuseppe Mazzini,
Life and Writings

Skills Assessment

Primary Source How did the man's request influence Mazzini's thinking?

papacy. To others, unity made practical economic sense. It would end trade barriers among the Italian states and stimulate industry.

The Struggle for Italy

After 1848, leadership of the Risorgimento (ree sor jee MEHN toh), or Italian nationalist movement, passed to the kingdom of Sardinia. Its constitutional monarch, Victor Emmanuel II, hoped to join other states to his own, thereby increasing his power.*

Cavour In 1852, Victor Emmanuel made Count Camillo Cavour his prime minister. Cavour came from a noble family but favored liberal goals. He was a flexible, practical, crafty politician, willing to use almost any means to achieve his goals. Like Bismarck in Prussia, Cavour was a monarchist who believed in *Realpolitik*.

Once in office, Cavour moved first to reform Sardinia's economy. He improved agriculture, had railroads built, and encouraged commerce by supporting free trade. Cavour's long-term goal, however, was to end Austrian power in Italy and annex its provinces of Lombardy and Venetia.

Intrigue With France In 1855, led by Cavour, Sardinia joined Britain and France in the Crimean War against Russia. Sardinia did not win territory, but it did have a voice at the peace conference. Sardinia also gained the attention of Napoleon III.

In 1858, Cavour negotiated a secret deal with Napoleon, who promised to aid Sardinia in case it faced a war with Austria. A year later, the shrewd

*The kingdom of Sardinia included Piedmont, Nice, and Savoy, as well as the island of Sardinia.

Giuseppe Garibaldi
As leader of a volunteer army (below, right) that fought to unify Italy, Garibaldi told his troops, "I offer hunger, thirst, . . . battles, and death. Let him who loves his country in his heart, and not with his lips only, follow me."

Theme: Impact of the Individual What leadership qualities might someone like Garibaldi have?

Cavour provoked that war. With help from France, Sardinia defeated Austria and annexed Lombardy. Meanwhile, nationalist groups overthrew Austrian-backed rulers in several other northern Italian states. These states then joined with Sardinia.

Garibaldi's Red Shirts Next, attention shifted to the kingdom of the Two Sicilies in southern Italy. There, Giuseppe Garibaldi, a long-time nationalist and an ally of Mazzini, was ready for action. Like Mazzini, Garibaldi wanted to create an Italian republic. He did not, however, hesitate to accept aid from the monarchist Cavour. By 1860, Garibaldi had recruited a force of 1,000 red-shirted volunteers. Cavour provided weapons and allowed two ships to take Garibaldi and his "Red Shirts" south to Sicily.

With surprising speed, Garibaldi's forces won control of Sicily, crossed to the mainland, and marched triumphantly north to Naples. An English volunteer recalled his impression of Garibaldi during one battle:

"I saw Garibaldi, with his red shirt wringing wet with perspiration, his eye sternly gleaming, his face flushed with the heat of conflict. . . . I heard his voice commanding—but it was no longer now the calm, clear voice of quieter times. It was hoarse and guttural, and choked with emotion. For the good general saw his gallant band unfalteringly pouring out their life-blood."
—W. B. Brooke, quoted in *Garibaldi: Great Lives Observed* (Smith)

Unity at Last Garibaldi's success alarmed Cavour, who feared that the nationalist hero would set up his own republic in the south. To prevent this, Cavour urged Victor Emmanuel to send Sardinian troops to deal with Garibaldi. Instead, the Sardinians overran the Papal States and linked up with Garibaldi and his forces in Naples.

In a patriotic move, Garibaldi turned over Naples and Sicily to Victor Emmanuel. Shortly afterward, southern Italy voted to approve the move, and in 1861, Victor Emmanuel II was crowned king of Italy.

Two areas remained outside the new Italian nation: Rome and Venetia. Cavour died in 1861, but his successors completed his dream. In a deal negotiated with Bismarck, Italy acquired Venetia after the Austro-Prussian War. Then, during the Franco-Prussian War in 1870, France was forced to withdraw its troops from Rome. For the first time since the fall of the Roman empire, Italy was a united land.

Challenges Facing the New Nation

Italy faced a host of problems. Like the many states Bismarck cemented into the German empire, Italy had no tradition of unity. Few Italians felt ties to the new nation. Strong regional rivalries left Italy unable to solve critical national issues.

Unification of Italy, 1858–1870

Mercator Projection

Kingdom of Sardinia, 1858

Added to Sardinia, 1859 and 1860

→ Route of Garibaldi's expedition, 1860

Added to Italy, 1866

Added to Italy, 1870

Skills Assessment

Geography By 1871, Italy was a united nation with its capital in Rome. Giuseppe Garibaldi and his Red Shirts played a vital role in achieving unification.

1. **Location** On the map, locate **(a)** Sicily, **(b)** Naples, **(c)** Rome, **(d)** Venetia.
2. **Movement** Describe the route of Garibaldi's expedition in 1860.
3. **Critical Thinking Identifying Main Ideas** What is the main idea of this map? Explain.

Divisions The greatest regional differences were between the north and the south. The north was richer and had more cities than the south. For centuries, northern Italian cities had flourished as centers of business and culture. The south, on the other hand, was rural and poor. Its population was booming, but illiterate peasants could wring only a meager existence from the exhausted farmland.

Hostility between Italy and the Roman Catholic Church further divided the nation. Popes bitterly resented the seizure of the Papal States and of Rome. The government granted the papacy the small territory of the Vatican. Popes, however, saw themselves as "prisoners" and urged Italian Catholics—almost all Italians—not to cooperate with their new government.

Turmoil Under Victor Emmanuel, Italy was a constitutional monarchy with a two-house legislature. The king appointed members to the upper house, which could veto bills passed by the lower house. Although the lower house consisted of elected representatives, only a small number of men had the right to vote.

In the late 1800s, unrest increased as radicals on the left struggled against a conservative government. Socialists organized strikes while anarchists, people who want to abolish all government, turned to sabotage and violence. Slowly, the government extended suffrage to more men and passed laws to improve social conditions. Still, the turmoil continued. To distract attention from troubles at home, the government set out to win an overseas empire.

Progress Despite its problems, Italy did develop economically, especially after 1900. Although the nation lacked important natural resources such as coal, industries did sprout up in northern regions. Industrialization, of course, brought urbanization as peasants flocked to the cities to find jobs in factories. As in other countries, reformers campaigned to improve education and working conditions.

The population explosion of this period created tensions. One important safety valve for many people was emigration, or movement away from their homeland. Many Italians left for the United States, Canada, and Latin American nations.

Looking Ahead

Although unification brought great challenges, it also brought increased strength. By 1914, Italy was significantly better off than it had been in 1861. But it was hardly prepared for the great war that broke out in that year and into which it was soon drawn.

Connections to Today

Vatican City

As Italian nationalists unified Italy, the Papal States lost their independence. Today, only one Papal State exists: Vatican City. Located in Rome, Vatican City is the world's smallest and least populated nation. At just over 108 acres, it is "just big enough to keep body and soul together," noted Pope Pius XI. In 1929, the Italian government granted the pope control of Vatican City. This gave him political independence as head of the Catholic Church. Named a United Nations world heritage site, Vatican City houses St. Peter's Basilica, the Sistine Chapel, and other churches and museums.

Theme: Political and Social Systems Why do you think the government granted the pope control of Vatican City?

SECTION 3 Assessment

Recall

1. **Identify:** (a) Giuseppe Mazzini, (b) Risorgimento, (c) Victor Emmanuel II, (d) Camillo Cavour, (e) Giuseppe Garibaldi.
2. **Define:** (a) anarchist, (b) emigration.

Comprehension

3. (a) What obstacles to unity did Italian nationalists face? (b) What conditions favored unity?
4. How did Cavour and Garibaldi work for Italian unity?

5. Describe the problems Italians faced after unification.

Critical Thinking and Writing

6. **Comparing** Compare the goals and methods of Cavour in Italy and Bismarck in Germany. (a) How were they similar? (b) How were they different?
7. **Analyzing Information** (a) What was the source of conflict between Garibaldi and Cavour? (b) How was the conflict resolved?

Activity

Creating a Comic Strip Create a historical comic strip that illustrates the events leading to Italian unification. Include important historical figures and locations.

Nationalism Threatens Old Empires

Reading Focus

- How did nationalism contribute to the decline of the Austrian empire?
- What were the main characteristics of the Dual Monarchy?
- How did the growth of nationalism affect the Balkans?

Taking Notes

Start a table like the one shown here. As you read this section, add information about the threats and changes that led to the decline of the Hapsburg and Ottoman empires.

HAPSBURGS	OTTOMAN TURKS
• Oldest ruling house in Europe	•
•	•

Main Idea Desires for national independence threatened to break up the Austrian and Ottoman empires.

Setting the Scene

The Hapsburgs had controlled the Holy Roman Empire for nearly 400 years when Napoleon invaded the German-speaking states. Austria's center of power now lay in Eastern Europe. Further wars resulted in continued loss of territory to Germany and Italy. Why did nationalism bring new strength to some countries and weaken others?

In Eastern Europe, the Austrian Hapsburgs and the Ottoman Turks ruled lands that included diverse ethnic groups. Nationalist feelings among these subject people contributed to tensions building across Europe.

A Declining Empire

In 1800, the Hapsburgs were the oldest ruling house in Europe. In addition to their homeland of Austria, over the centuries they had acquired the territories of Bohemia and Hungary, as well as parts of Romania, Poland, Ukraine, and northern Italy.

Challenge of Change Since the Congress of Vienna, the Austrian emperor Francis I and Metternich, his foreign minister, had upheld conservative goals against liberal forces. "Rule and change nothing," the emperor told his son. Under Francis and Metternich, newspapers could not even use the word *constitution*, much less discuss this key demand of liberals. The government also tried to limit industrial development, which would threaten traditional ways of life.

Austria, however, could not hold back the changes that were engulfing the rest of Europe. By the 1840s, factories were springing up. Soon, the Hapsburgs found themselves facing the problems of industrial life that had long been familiar in Britain—the growth of cities, worker discontent, and the stirrings of socialism.

A Patchwork of People Equally disturbing to the old order were the urgent demands of nationalists. The Hapsburgs presided over a multinational empire. Of its 50 million people at mid-century, fewer than a quarter were German-speaking Austrians. Almost half belonged to different

The Imperial Hub
Vienna was a glittering, glamorous city that attracted many of the best minds and talents of Europe. Here, Vienna's leading citizens enjoy an evening of gaiety at an imperial ball.

Theme: Political and Social Systems Based on this painting, what generalization might you make about the Hapsburg ruling class?

Virtual Field Trip

Go Online
PHSchool.com

For: More information about the Austrian empire
Visit: PHSchool.com
Web Code: mkd-2382

The Hapsburg Empire
Schönbrunn Palace in Vienna was the summer home of Hapsburg rulers. The imposing structure and extensive gardens were designed during the 1700s and 1800s to show the power of the Hapsburgs.

Theme: Political and Social Systems Why might the Hapsburgs have wanted a showplace palace?

Slavic groups, including Czechs, Slovaks, Poles, Ukrainians, Romanians, Serbs, Croats, and Slovenes. Often, rival groups shared the same region. The empire also included large numbers of Hungarians and Italians.

The Hapsburgs ignored nationalist demands as long as they could. "Peoples?" Francis I once exclaimed. "What does that mean? I know only subjects." As you have read, when nationalist revolts broke out across the Hapsburg empire in 1848, the government crushed them.

Early Reforms Amid the turmoil, 18-year-old Francis Joseph inherited the Hapsburg throne. He would rule until 1916, presiding over the empire during its fading days into World War I.

An early challenge came when Austria suffered its humiliating defeat at the hands of France and Sardinia in 1859. Francis Joseph realized he needed to strengthen the empire at home. Accordingly, he made some limited reforms. He granted a new constitution that set up a legislature. This body, however, was dominated by German-speaking Austrians. The reforms thus satisfied none of the other national groups that populated the empire. The Hungarians, especially, were determined to settle for nothing less than total self-government.

The Dual Monarchy

Austria's disastrous defeat in the 1866 war with Prussia brought renewed pressure for change from Hungarians within the empire. One year later, Francis Deák (deh AHK), a moderate Hungarian leader, helped work out a compromise that created a new political power known as the Dual Monarchy of Austria-Hungary.

Under the agreement, Austria and Hungary were separate states. Each had its own constitution and parliament. Francis Joseph ruled both, as emperor of Austria and king of Hungary. The two states also shared ministries of finance, defense, and foreign affairs, but were independent of each other in all other areas.

Although Hungarians welcomed the compromise, other subject peoples resented it. Restlessness increased among various Slavic groups, especially the Czechs in Bohemia. Some nationalist leaders called on Slavs to unite, insisting that "only through liberty, equality, and fraternal solidarity" could Slavic peoples fulfill their "great mission in the history of mankind." By the early 1900s, nationalist unrest often left the government paralyzed in the face of pressing political and social problems.

Balkan Nationalism

Like the Hapsburgs, the Ottomans ruled a multinational empire. It stretched from Eastern Europe and the Balkans to North Africa and the Middle East. There, as in Austria, nationalist demands tore at the fabric of the empire.

In the Balkans, Serbia had won autonomy in 1817, and southern Greece won independence in the 1830s. But many Serbs and Greeks still lived in the Balkans under Ottoman rule. The Ottoman empire was home to other national groups, such as Bulgarians and Romanians. During the 1800s, various subject peoples staged revolts against the Ottomans, hoping to set up their own independent states.

Such nationalist stirrings became mixed up with the ambitions of the great European powers. In the mid-1800s, Europeans came to see the Ottoman empire as "the sick man of Europe." Eagerly, they scrambled to divide up Ottoman lands. Russia pushed south toward the Black Sea and Istanbul, which Russians still called Constantinople. Austria-Hungary took control of the provinces of Bosnia and Herzegovina. This action angered the Serbs, who also had hoped to expand into that area. Meanwhile, Britain and France set their sights on other Ottoman lands in the Middle East and North Africa.

In the end, a complex web of competing interests contributed to a series of crises and wars in the Balkans. Russia fought several wars against the Ottomans. France and Britain sometimes joined the Russians and sometimes the Ottomans. Germany supported Austrian authority over the discontented national groups. But Germany also encouraged the Ottomans because of their strategic location in the eastern Mediterranean. In between, the subject peoples revolted and then fought among themselves. By the early 1900s, observers were referring to the region as the "Balkan powder keg." The explosion that came in 1914 helped set off World War I.

The Balkans, 1878

Independent Balkan states

Ottoman empire

RUSSIA

AUSTRIA-HUNGARY

Danube R.

BOSNIA–HERZEGOVINA (occupied by Austria)

ROMANIA

SERBIA

MONTENEGRO

BULGARIA (autonomous)

EASTERN RUMELIA (administered by Turkey)

Constantinople

Black Sea

Adriatic Sea

ITALY

40°N

Azimuthal Equal Area Projection

0   200   400 Miles

0   200   400 Kilometers

GREECE

Aegean Sea

Mediterranean Sea

20°E

Crete

30°E

Skills Assessment

Geography In the late 1800s, the Balkans had become a center of conflict, as various peoples and empires competed for power.

1. **Location** On the map, locate (a) Black Sea, (b) Ottoman empire, (c) Serbia, (d) Greece, (e) Austria-Hungary.
2. **Place** Which four large seas border the Balkan Peninsula?
3. **Critical Thinking Predicting Consequences** Why do you think competing interests in the Balkans led the region to be called a powder keg?

SECTION 4 Assessment

Recall
1. **Identify:** (a) Francis Joseph, (b) Dual Monarchy.

Comprehension
2. Explain how nationalism affected the Austrian empire.
3. (a) How was the Dual Monarchy organized? (b) Why did it fail to end nationalist demands?
4. How did Balkan nationalism contribute to the decline of the Ottoman empire?

Critical Thinking and Writing
5. **Solving Problems** Do you think that either the Hapsburgs or the Ottoman Turks could have built a modern, unified nation from their multinational empires? Explain.
6. **Identifying Alternatives** (a) What actions did Francis Joseph take to maintain power in Austria-Hungary? (b) How else might he have responded to nationalist demands?

Activity

Studying Current Events Research recent developments in the Balkans. Organize your findings into a report that can be presented orally or in writing.

Reading Focus

- How did conditions in Russia affect progress?
- Why did czars follow a cycle of absolutism, reform, and reaction?
- How did the problems of industrialization contribute to the growing crisis and outbreak of revolution?

Vocabulary

colossus
emancipation
zemstvo
pogrom
Duma

Taking Notes

As you read this section, make an outline of the information. Use Roman numerals for the main headings. Use capital letters for the subheadings, and use numbers for the supporting details. The outline has been started for you.

I. Conditions in Russia
  A. Obstacles to progress
    1. Economically undeveloped
    2. Rigid social structure
  B. Serfdom
II. Russian absolutism
  A. Alexander I
    1. Initially open to liberal ideas
    2.

Main Idea Industrialization and reform came more slowly to Russia than to Western Europe.

See the struggle for reform in Russia.

Setting the Scene Although serfdom had almost disappeared in Western Europe by the 1700s, it survived and spread in Russia. Masters exercised almost total power over their serfs. In the 1800s, a noble who became a revolutionary described the brutal treatment of serfs:

> "I heard . . . stories of men and women torn from their families and their villages, and sold, or lost in gambling, or exchanged for a couple of hunting dogs, and then transported to some remote part of Russia to create a [master's] new estate; . . . of children taken from their parents and sold to cruel masters."
> —Peter Kropotkin, *Memoirs of a Revolutionist*

Reformers hoped to free Russia from autocratic rule, economic backwardness, and social injustice. But efforts to modernize Russia had little success, as czars imprisoned critics or sent them into icy exile in Siberia.

Conditions in Russia

By 1815, Russia was not only the largest, most populous nation in Europe but also a great world power. Since the 1600s, explorers had pushed the Russian frontier eastward across Siberia to the Pacific. Peter the Great and Catherine the Great had added lands on the Baltic and Black seas, and czars in the 1800s had expanded into Central Asia. Russia had thus acquired a huge multinational empire, part European and part Asian.

Other European nations looked on the Russian colossus, or giant, with a mixture of wonder and misgiving. It had immense natural resources. Russia's vast size gave it global interests and influence. But Western Europeans disliked its autocratic government and feared its expansionist aims.

Obstacles to Progress Despite efforts by Peter and Catherine to westernize Russia, it remained economically undeveloped. By the 1800s, czars saw the need to modernize but resisted reforms that would undermine their absolute rule. While the czars wavered, Russia fell further behind Western Europe in economic and social developments.

A great obstacle to progress was the rigid social structure. Landowning nobles dominated society and rejected any change that would threaten their privileges. The middle class was too small to have much influence. The majority of Russians were serfs, laborers bound to the land and to masters who controlled their fates.

Serfdom Most serfs were peasants. Others might be servants, artisans, or soldiers forced into the czar's army. As industry expanded, some masters sent serfs to work in factories but took much of their pay.

Many enlightened Russians knew that serfdom was inefficient. As long as most people had to serve the whim of their masters, Russia's economy would remain backward. Landowning nobles had no reason to improve agriculture and took little interest in industry.

Russian Absolutism

For centuries, czars had ruled with absolute power, imposing their will on their subjects. The changes brought about by the Enlightenment and the French Revolution had almost no effect on Russian autocracy.

Alexander I When Alexander I inherited the throne in 1801, however, he seemed open to liberal ideas. The new czar eased censorship and promoted education. He even talked about freeing the serfs.

By the time Napoleon invaded Russia in 1812, Alexander had drawn back from reform. Like earlier czars, he feared losing the support of nobles. At the Congress of Vienna, he joined the conservative powers in opposing liberal and nationalist impulses in Europe.

Revolt and Repression When Alexander I died in 1825, a group of army officers led an uprising known as the Decembrist Revolt. They had picked up liberal ideas while fighting Napoleon in Western Europe and now demanded a constitution and other reforms. The new czar, Nicholas I, suppressed the Decembrists and cracked down on all dissent.

Nicholas used police spies to hunt out critics. He banned books from Western Europe that might spread liberal ideas. Only approved textbooks were allowed in schools and universities. Many Russians with liberal or revolutionary ideas were judged to be insane and shut up in mental hospitals. Up to 150,000 others were exiled to Siberia.

Nicholas I and Absolutism To bolster his regime, Nicholas I embraced the three pillars of Russian absolutism symbolized in the motto "Orthodoxy, Autocracy, and Nationalism." *Orthodoxy* referred to the strong ties between the Russian Orthodox Church and the government. *Autocracy* was the absolute power of the state. *Nationalism* involved respect for Russian traditions and suppression of non-Russian groups within the empire.

Still, Nicholas realized that Russia needed to modernize. He issued a new law code and made some economic reforms. He even tried to limit the power of landowners over serfs. But he could see no way to change the system completely without angering Russian nobles and weakening the power of the czar. Before he died, he told his son, "I am handing you command of the country in a poor state."

Reforms of Alexander II

Alexander II came to the throne in 1855 during the Crimean War. The war had broken out after Russia tried to seize Ottoman lands along the Danube. Britain and France stepped in to help the Turks, invading the Crimean peninsula that juts into the Black Sea. The war, which ended in a Russian defeat, revealed the country's backwardness. It had only a few miles of

Russian Serfs
Masters held great power over serfs in Russia, and a large labor supply meant that few landowners invested in machines that could speed up agricultural labor. Here, women clear large stones from a field.

Theme: Economics and Technology How did the continuation of serfdom keep the Russian economy from advancing as quickly as that of Western Europe?

railroads, and the military bureaucracy was hopelessly inefficient. Many felt that dramatic changes were needed.

Emancipation   A widespread popular reaction followed. Liberals demanded changes, and students demonstrated for reform. Pressed from all sides, Alexander II finally agreed to reforms. In 1861, he issued a royal decree that required emancipation, or freeing the serfs.

Freedom brought problems. Former serfs had to buy the land they had worked for so long. Many were too poor to do so. Also, the lands allotted to peasants were often too small to farm efficiently or to support a family. As a result, peasants remained poor, and discontent festered.

Still, emancipation was a turning point. Many peasants moved to the cities, taking jobs in factories and building Russian industries. Equally important, freeing the serfs boosted the drive for further reform.

Other Reforms   Along with emancipation, Alexander set up a system of local government. Elected assemblies, called zemstvos, were made responsible for matters such as road repair, schools, and agriculture. At the local level, at least, Russians gained some experience of self-government.

The czar also introduced legal reforms based on ideas such as trial by jury. He eased censorship and tried to reform the military. A soldier's term of service was reduced from 25 years to 15, and brutal discipline was limited. Alexander also encouraged the growth of industry in Russia, which still relied almost entirely on agriculture.

A movement to liberate women also swept the urban centers of Russia. Since they were denied education in Russia, hundreds of privileged young women left their homes and families to study abroad in the few universities that would accept them. Many came to support revolutionary goals.

Reaction to Change

Alexander's reforms failed to satisfy many Russians. Peasants had freedom but not land. Liberals wanted a constitution and an elected legislature. Radicals, who had adopted socialist ideas from the West, demanded even more revolutionary changes. The czar, meantime, moved away from reform and toward repression.

Revolutionary Currents   In the 1870s, some socialists carried the message of reform to the peasants. They went to live and work among the peasants, sometimes preaching rebellion. These educated young men and women had little success. The peasants scarcely understood them and sometimes turned them over to the police.

The failure of this "Go to the People" movement, combined with renewed government repression, sparked anger among radicals. Some turned to terrorism. A revolutionary group calling itself the People's Will assassinated officials and plotted to kill the czar. Their first attempts failed. Then, on a cold March day in 1881, terrorists hurled two bombs at Alexander's carriage. One struck down several guards. The second killed the leader known to some as the "czar emancipator."

Crackdown   Alexander III responded to his father's assassination by reviving the harsh methods of Nicholas I. To wipe out liberals and revolutionaries, he increased the power of the secret police, restored strict censorship, and exiled critics to Siberia. He relied on his adviser and former tutor, Constantine Pobedonostsev (puh beh duh NAWS tsehv), who rejected all talk of democracy and constitutional government as "the lies of hollow and flabby people."

The czar also launched a program of Russification aimed at suppressing the cultures of non-Russian peoples within the empire. Alexander insisted on one language, Russian, and one church, the Russian Orthodox Church.

Global Connections

Freedom for Enslaved Americans

Emancipation was a troublesome issue around the world. For many years, the United States had been divided over slavery. In 1861, civil war erupted, in part over slavery. President Abraham Lincoln issued the Emancipation Proclamation in 1863, declaring the slaves in rebel areas to be free.

Neither Lincoln's action nor four years of bloody fighting settled the question. Finally, in 1865, the Thirteenth Amendment to the United States Constitution abolished slavery throughout the United States.

Even after emancipation, African Americans continued to face great challenges. Former slaves, like former serfs in Russia, had trouble acquiring farm land. Many worked for wages on the farms of former slaveholders, and others left to work in factories.

Theme: Political and Social Systems What settled the issue of slavery in the United States?

Humanities Link

Russian Ballet

Although French and Italian in origin, ballet took on a bold, unique form in Russia. Beginning in the eighteenth century, European ballet teachers introduced the classical style to Russia. By the late 1800s, Russian choreographers and dancers had developed an expressive, muscular style that was to rejuvenate and dominate ballet in the twentieth century.

Russian dancer and choreographer Vaslav Nijinsky won worldwide fame while touring with the Ballet Russe in the early 1900s. Many consider him the greatest male ballet dancer of the twentieth century.

The ballet *Firebird*, shown here in a modern production, debuted in Paris in 1910. It was one of the first ballets to be created by a Russian choreographer and inspired by a Russian folk tale.

Twice destroyed by fires, Moscow's ornate Bolshoi ("Big") Theater took on its present form in 1856. Tiers of seats line the opulent interior of the theater, which can seat more than 2,000. Today, the grand theater is considered "the main theater of the country."

Fast Facts

- Until the early 1900s, common people in Russia were thought to be too ignorant to understand and appreciate ballet. Only nobles and people from the wealthy classes attended performances.

- In 1911, Sergey Diaghilev's Ballet Russe began to spread the influence of Russian dance worldwide.

- During World War II, dancers from the Bolshoi traveled from place to place, entertaining Russian troops in the field.

Portfolio Assessment

Conduct research to find out more about Russian ballet. Then, prepare a presentation on the significance of a particular Russian choreographer or dancer. If possible, include photographs or drawings of the individual you have selected.

Poles, Ukrainians, Finns, Armenians, and many others suffered persecution. The Russification campaign also targeted Jews and Muslims in the empire.

Persecution and Pogroms Russia had acquired a large Jewish population when it carved up Poland and expanded into Ukraine. Under Alexander III, persecution of Russian Jews increased. The czar limited the number of Jews who were allowed to study in universities and practice professions such as law and medicine. He revived old laws that forced Jews to live in certain restricted areas.

Official persecution encouraged pogroms, or violent mob attacks on Jews. Gangs beat and killed Jews and looted and burned their homes and stores. The police did nothing to stop the violence. Faced with savage persecution, many Jews escaped from Russia. They became refugees, or people who flee their homeland to seek safety elsewhere. Large numbers of Russian Jews went to the United States. Though they often faced prejudice and great hardship there, they were safe from pogroms and official persecution. Jewish immigrants sent joyful news back to Russia: "There is no czar in America!"

Building Russian Industry

Under Alexander III and his son, Nicholas II, Russia finally entered the industrial age. In the 1890s, Count Serge Witte, finance minister to Nicholas, focused on economic development. Witte encouraged railroad building to connect iron and coal mines with factories and to transport goods across Russia. He secured foreign capital to invest in transportation systems and industry. Loans from France helped build the Trans-Siberian Railroad. Begun in the 1890s, it linked European Russia to the Pacific Ocean.

The drive to industrialize increased political and social problems. Government officials and business leaders applauded and encouraged economic growth. Nobles and peasants opposed it, fearing the changes brought by the new ways.

Industrialization also created new social ills as peasants flocked to cities to work in factories. Instead of a better life, they found long hours and low pay in dangerous conditions. In the slums around the factories, poverty, disease, and discontent multiplied.

Radicals sought supporters among the new industrial workers. At factory gates, socialists handed out pamphlets that preached the revolutionary ideas of Karl Marx. Among the revolutionaries of the 1890s was young Vladimir Ulyanov, whose older brother had been executed for plotting to kill Alexander III. Like many revolutionaries, Ulyanov used an alias, or false name—Lenin. In 1917, Lenin would take power in a revolution that transformed Russia.

Turning Point: Crisis and Revolution

War broke out between Russia and Japan in 1904. Nicholas II called on his people to fight for "the Faith, the Czar, and the Fatherland." But despite their efforts, the Russians suffered one humiliating defeat after another.

A Peaceful March News of the military disasters unleashed pent-up discontent created by years of oppression. Protesters poured into the streets. Workers went on strike with demands for shorter hours and better wages. Liberals called for a constitution and reforms to overhaul the inefficient, corrupt government.

As the crisis deepened, a young Orthodox priest, Father George Gapon, organized a march for Sunday, January 22, 1905. Father Gapon felt certain that the "Little Father," as many Russians called the czar, would help his people if only he understood their sufferings. The parade flowed through

Geography and History

Russia's Long Iron Road

Beginning in the 1890s, Russian workers laid more than 5,000 miles of track to build the Trans-Siberian Railroad, the longest railroad in the world at that time. Siberia's harsh landscape and climate challenged workers. Iron, stone, hardwoods, and food had to be shipped thousands of miles to the crews.

In the chilling winters, many workers died from hypothermia. With no safety devices, some fell to their deaths onto frozen rivers. To lay tracks in some areas, workers had to dynamite permanently frozen soil. These explosions often proved fatal, as did epidemics of bubonic plague, anthrax, and cholera.

Theme: Geography and History What geographic and climatic challenges did the railroad builders face in Siberia?

the icy streets of St. Petersburg toward the czar's lavish Winter Palace. Chanting prayers and singing hymns, workers carried holy icons and pictures of the czar. They also brought a petition for justice and freedom, which was addressed to Nicholas.

Bloody Sunday Fearing the marchers, the czar had fled the palace and called in soldiers. As the people approached, they saw troops lined up across the square. Suddenly, gunfire rang out. Men and women ran and fell. More shots left hundreds dead or wounded in the snow.

A woman stumbling away from the scene of the massacre moaned: "The czar has deserted us! They shot away the orthodox faith." Indeed, the slaughter marked a turning point for Russians. "Bloody Sunday" killed the people's faith and trust in the czar.

The Revolution of 1905 In the months that followed Bloody Sunday, discontent exploded across Russia. Strikes multiplied. In some cities, workers took over local government. In the countryside, peasants revolted and demanded land. Minority nationalities called for autonomy from Russia. Terrorists targeted officials, and some assassins were cheered as heroes by discontented Russians.

At last, the clamor grew so great that Nicholas was forced to announce sweeping reforms. In the October Manifesto, he promised "freedom of person, conscience, speech, assembly, and union." He agreed to summon a Duma, or elected national legislature. No law, he declared, would go into effect without approval by the Duma.

Results of the Revolution The manifesto won over moderates, leaving socialists isolated. These divisions helped the czar, who had no intention of letting strikers, revolutionaries, and rebellious peasants challenge him.

In 1906, the first Duma met, but the czar quickly dissolved it when leaders criticized the government. Nicholas then appointed a new prime minister, Peter Stolypin (stuh LEE pihn). Arrests, pogroms, and executions followed as the conservative Stolypin sought to restore order.

Stolypin soon realized that Russia needed reform, not just repression. To regain peasant support, he introduced moderate land reforms. He strengthened the zemstvos and improved education. These reforms were too limited to meet the broad needs of most Russians, and dissatisfaction still simmered. Stolypin was assassinated in 1911. Several more Dumas met during this period, but new voting laws made sure they were conservative. By 1914, Russia was still an autocracy, simmering with unrest.

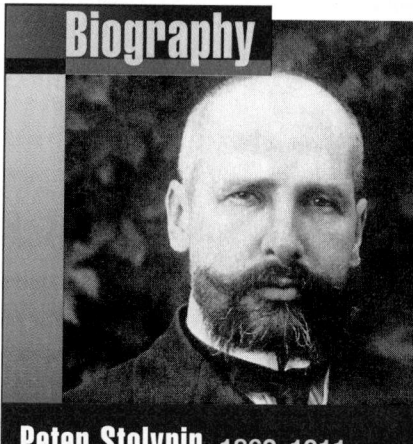

Biography

Peter Stolypin 1862–1911

Violence surrounded Peter Stolypin, who was once described as "a tall stiff man with a dead white face and a dead white beard." As governor and later prime minister, he used harsh measures to silence opposition. On his orders, trials of terrorists were held within 24 hours of arrest; executions were held immediately upon conviction. More than 1,000 suspected terrorists were executed in less than a year. The noose used to hang them came to be known as "Stolypin's necktie."

Stolypin and his family were also the targets of violence. In 1907, his opponents bombed his house, killing many servants and severely injuring his children. Four years later, Stolypin himself was assassinated while attending the theater.

Theme: Impact of the Individual How did Stolypin deal with terrorism?

SECTION 5 Assessment

Recall
1. **Identify:** (a) Decembrist Revolt, (b) Alexander II, (c) Russification, (d) Bloody Sunday, (e) October Manifesto, (f) Peter Stolypin.
2. **Define:** (a) colossus, (b) emancipation, (c) zemstvo, (d) pogrom, (e) Duma.

Comprehension
3. What conditions in Russia posed challenges during the early 1800s?
4. How did Russian czars often react to change?

5. (a) What were the causes of the revolution of 1905? (b) How did Nicholas II respond?

Critical Thinking and Writing
6. **Analyzing Information** Alexander II declared that it is "better to abolish serfdom from above than to wait until it will be abolished by a movement from below." Explain his statement.
7. **Making Inferences** What does Bloody Sunday suggest about the relationship between the czar and the Russian people?

Go Online
PHSchool.com

Use the Internet to find the decree of Alexander II to free the serfs. Write a paragraph that summarizes Alexander's reasons for emancipation. For help with this activity, use **Web Code mkd-2389.**

Creating a Chapter Summary

On a sheet of paper, make a table like the one shown here to list events that led to nationalism in Germany, Italy, Austria, the Balkans, and Russia in the 1800s.

GERMANY	ITALY	AUSTRIA	BALKANS	RUSSIA
• German states unite under William I • Empire takes leading role in Europe • Bismarck/Iron Chancellor		• Francis I and Metternich uphold conservative goals •		

For additional review and enrichment activities, see the interactive version of *World History* available on the Web and on CD-ROM.

For practice test questions for Chapter 10, use **Web Code mka-2390**.

Reviewing Vocabulary

Review the meaning of the chapter vocabulary words listed below. Then, write a sentence for each word in which you define the word and describe its relation to nationalism in Europe.

1. *Realpolitik*
2. annex
3. Reich
4. *Kulturkampf*
5. anarchist
6. colossus
7. emancipation
8. zemstvo
9. pogrom
10. Duma

Recalling Key Facts

11. What factors aided German economic growth in the late 1800s?
12. How did Bismarck try to persuade workers not to support the socialists?
13. What was the goal of Mazzini's Young Italy society?
14. How did the Hapsburg leaders deal with the ethnic diversity of their empire?
15. How did European powers react to Ottoman weakness?
16. How did war with Japan contribute to the Revolution of 1905 in Russia?

Critical Thinking and Writing

17. **Analyzing Information** Study the painting that appears in the feature in Section 1. **(a)** What is the subject of the painting? **(b)** Where does the scene take place? **(c)** Who seems to be the central figure of the painting? **(d)** What conclusions can you draw from this about the power structure in Germany at the time?
18. **Predicting Consequences** Based on your reading of the chapter, predict the consequences of the following: **(a)** defeat of France in the Franco-Prussian War, **(b)** growth of German nationalism and militarism in the late 1800s, **(c)** failure to satisfy nationalist ambitions in Austria-Hungary, **(d)** weakening of the Ottoman empire.
19. **Connecting to Geography** How did regional differences contribute to continued divisions in Italy after unification?
20. **Linking Past and Present** Is nationalism a force in the world today? Give examples from current events to support your answer.

On January 22, 1905, Father George Gapon led Russian workers to the Winter Palace to deliver a petition to the czar. Unfortunately, Nicholas II had called in soldiers and fled. The result was the massacre known as Bloody Sunday. Read the workers' petition, then answer the questions that follow.

"We, the workers of the town of St. Petersburg, with our wives, our children and our aged and feeble parents, have come to you, Sire, in search of justice and protection. We have fallen into poverty, we are oppressed, we are loaded with a crushing burden of toil, we are insulted, we are not recognized as men, we are treated as slaves who should bear their sad and bitter lot in patience and silence. . . . Do not refuse to protect your people; raise [Russia] from the grave of arbitrary power, poverty and ignorance; permit it to dispose of its own fate; free it from the intolerable oppression of officials; destroy the wall between yourself and your people—and let it govern the country with you."

—quoted in *Revolution From 1789 to 1906* (Postgate)

21. **(a)** On whose behalf is the petition presented? **(b)** Whom does the petition blame?
22. What hardships does the petition describe?
23. What are the demonstrators' goals?
24. What is the tone of this petition?
25. If Nicholas had stayed to receive this petition, do you think he would have acted differently? Why or why not?

Go Online
PHSchool.com

Use the Internet to research the history of the Hapsburgs and their roles in European history. Create a time line that shows major political events relating to the Hapsburgs. Illustrate your time line with copies of photographs or paintings of significant locations, battles, and rulers. For help with this activity, use **Web Code mkd-2391.**

Unification of Italy, 1858–1870

Use the map to answer the following questions:

26. **(a)** When was the largest part of Italy added to the Kingdom of Sardinia? **(b)** When was the last part added?
27. To what country did Corsica belong?
28. In degrees of longitude, approximately how much farther east is Naples than Rome?
29. What body of water lies between Italy and the Ottoman empire?
30. **(a)** Describe the route of Garibaldi's expedition in 1860. **(b)** About how many miles did the expedition travel?
31. Why, in your opinion, was Rome the last area to become part of unified Italy?

Skills Tip

Degrees of longitude tell you how far east or west a point lies from the Prime Meridian.

Growth of Western Democracies 1815–1914

Chapter Preview

1 Britain Becomes More Democratic
2 A Century of Reform
3 Division and Democracy in France
4 Expansion of the United States

CHAPTER EVENTS

1832
The Great Reform Act gives more British men the right to vote. The houses of Parliament, shown here, will be the center of a century of political reform.

1845
Ireland's Great Hunger begins, leading to widespread death and disease and mass emigration.

1861
The American Civil War begins. The four-year battle between North and South will lead to the end of slavery in the United States.

1815

1835

1855

GLOBAL EVENTS

1821 Mexico wins independence from Spain.

1858 Britain begins direct rule of India.

Western Democracies, 1900

PACIFIC OCEAN

UNITED STATES

Washington, D.C.

ATLANTIC OCEAN

Gulf of Mexico

GREAT BRITAIN   St. Petersburg
GERMANY   RUSSIA
London   Paris   Berlin
FRANCE   Vienna   Budapest
Black Sea
Mediterranean Sea

40°N
20°N
0°

| | Democratic governments |
| | Autocratic governments |

The Industrial Revolution uprooted old ways of life. While Germany and Russia tried to stem the tide of change, Britain, France, and the United States slowly extended democratic rights.

N
W   E
S

Robinson Projection

0   1000   2000 Miles
0   1000   2000 Kilometers

120°W   100°W   80°W   60°W   40°W   20°W   0°   20°E   40°E

1897
Theodor Herzl organizes the First Zionist Congress for the purpose of founding a Jewish state.

1870
The Franco-Prussian War leads to the fall of Napoleon III and the founding of a new French republic.

1900s
The women's suffrage movement grows in Britain. This 1911 cartoon expresses the determination of British women to win the vote.

Mr. John Bull - No it does not. John I must have one OF MY own

THE VOTE

John Bull My umbrella protects us all!

1875   1895   1915

1869 The French-built Suez Canal opens in Eygpt.

1889 Brazil becomes a republic.

1893 New Zealand is the first nation to give women the vote.

1910 The Union of South Africa is formed.

Britain Becomes More Democratic

Reading Focus

- Why did reformers seek to change Parliament in the 1800s?
- What values did Queen Victoria represent?
- How did the Liberal and Conservative parties help bring a new era to British politics?

Vocabulary

rotten borough
electorate
secret ballot

Taking Notes

As you read this section, prepare an outline of the contents. Use Roman numerals to indicate major headings. Use capital letters for subheadings, and use numbers for the supporting details. The example at right will help you get started.

I. Reforming Parliament
   A. Pressure for change
      1. Religious restrictions on voting
      2.
      3.
   B. Reform Act of 1832
      1.
      2.

Main Idea Throughout the 1800s, political reform gradually expanded suffrage and made Parliament more democratic.

Setting the Scene Charles Egremont, a wealthy young man, is proud to be British. One day, he boasts to strangers that Victoria, the queen of England, "reigns over the greatest nation that ever existed." "Which nation?" asks one of the strangers, "for she reigns over two":

> "Two nations: between whom there is no [communication] and no sympathy; who are as ignorant of each other's habits, thoughts, and feelings, as if they were . . . inhabitants of different planets; who are formed by a different breeding, are fed by a different food, are ordered by different manners, and are not governed by the same laws."
>
> —Benjamin Disraeli, *Sybil*

What are these "two nations," Egremont wonders. "THE RICH AND THE POOR," the stranger replies.

Egremont is the hero of Benjamin Disraeli's novel *Sybil*. Disraeli, a leading political figure at the time of the Industrial Revolution, had seen both the world of aristocratic luxury and the appalling poverty of factory towns and rural villages. In the 1800s, Disraeli and other political leaders slowly worked to bridge Britain's "two nations" and extend democratic rights. Unlike some of its neighbors in Europe, Britain generally achieved change through reform rather than revolution.

Reforming Parliament

In 1815, Britain was a constitutional monarchy with a parliament and two political parties. Still, it was far from democratic. Although members of the House of Commons were elected, less than five percent of the people had the right to vote. Wealthy nobles and squires, or country landowners, dominated politics and heavily influenced voters. In addition, the House of Lords—made up of hereditary nobles and high-ranking clergy—could veto any bill passed by the House of Commons.

Pressure for Change Long-standing laws kept many people from voting. Catholics and non-Anglican Protestants, for example, could not vote or serve in Parliament. In the 1820s, reformers pushed to end religious restrictions. After fierce debate, Parliament finally granted Catholics and non-Anglican Protestants equal political rights.

An even greater battle soon erupted over making Parliament more representative. During the Industrial Revolution, centers of population shifted.

Some rural towns lost so many people that they had few or no voters. Yet local landowners in these rotten boroughs still sent members to Parliament. At the same time, populous new industrial cities like Manchester and Birmingham had no seats in Parliament at all because they had not existed as important population centers in earlier times.

Reform Act of 1832 By 1830, Whigs and Tories* were battling over a bill to reform Parliament. In the streets, supporters of reform chanted, "The Bill, the whole Bill, and nothing but the Bill!" Their shouts seemed to echo the cries of revolutionaries on the continent.

Parliament finally passed the Great Reform Act in 1832. It redistributed seats in the House of Commons, giving representation to large towns and cities and eliminating rotten boroughs. It also enlarged the electorate, the body of people allowed to vote, by granting suffrage to more men. The Act did, however, keep a property requirement for voting.

The Reform Act of 1832 did not bring full democracy, but it did give a greater political voice to middle-class men. Landowning nobles, however, remained a powerful force in the government and in the economy.

The Chartist Movement The reform bill did not help rural or urban workers. Some of them demanded more radical change. In the 1830s, protesters known as Chartists drew up the People's Charter. This petition demanded universal male suffrage, annual parliamentary elections, and salaries for members of Parliament. Another key demand was for a secret ballot, which would allow people to cast their votes without announcing them publicly.

Twice the Chartists presented petitions with over a million signatures to Parliament. Both petitions were ignored. In 1848, as revolutions swept Europe, the Chartists prepared a third petition and organized a march on Parliament. Fearing violence, the government moved to suppress the march. Soon after, the unsuccessful Chartist movement declined. In time, however, Parliament would pass most of the major reforms proposed by the Chartists.

The Victorian Age

From 1837 to 1901, the great symbol in British life was Queen Victoria. Her reign was the longest in British history. Although she exercised little real political power, she set the tone for what is now called the Victorian age.

Symbol of a Nation's Values As queen, Victoria came to embody the values of her age. These Victorian ideals included duty, thrift, honesty, hard work, and—above all—respectability. Today, we associate most of these qualities with the Victorian middle class. However, people at all levels of society shared these ideals, even if they could not always live up to them.

Victoria herself embraced a strict code of morals and manners. As a young woman, she married a German prince, Albert, and they raised a large family. Albert held a lower rank than Victoria. Still, she treated him with the devotion a dutiful wife was expected to have for her husband. When he died in 1861, Victoria went into deep mourning and dressed in black for the rest of her reign.

Victoria, Queen of England
Although she held little political power, Queen Victoria came to stand for the values of her age. This plate was presented to Victoria on the occasion of her fiftieth year on the throne.

Theme: Political and Social Systems How do the words and images on this plate reflect Britain's sense of optimism and self-confidence?

---

*The Whig party largely represented middle-class and business interests. The Tory party spoke for nobles, landowners, and others whose interests and income were rooted in agriculture.

Two Political Giants
As the leading political figures of Victorian England, Benjamin Disraeli (left) and William Gladstone (right) were often the subjects of caricatures.

Theme: Political and Social Systems Why are political caricatures like these often seen as a sign of a healthy democracy?

A Confident Age Under Victoria, the British middle class—and growing numbers of the working class—felt great confidence in the future. That confidence grew as Britain expanded its already huge empire. Victoria, the empress of India and ruler of some 300 million subjects around the world, became a revered symbol of British might.

As she aged from teenaged monarch to grieving widow to revered national symbol, Victoria witnessed growing agitation for social reform. The queen herself commented that the lower classes "earn their bread and riches so deservedly that they cannot and ought not to be kept back." As the Victorian era went on, reformers continued the push toward greater social and economic justice.

A New Era in British Politics

In the 1860s, a new era dawned in British politics. The old political parties regrouped under new leadership. Benjamin Disraeli forged the Tories into the modern Conservative party. The Whigs, led by William Gladstone, evolved into the Liberal party. Between 1868 and 1880, as the majority in Parliament swung between the two parties, Gladstone and Disraeli alternated as prime minister. Both fought for important reforms.

Expanding Suffrage Disraeli and the Conservative party pushed through the Reform Bill of 1867. By giving the vote to many working-class men, the new law almost doubled the size of the electorate.

In the 1880s, it was the turn of Gladstone and the Liberal party to extend suffrage. Their reforms gave the vote to farmworkers and most other men. By century's end, almost-universal male suffrage, the secret ballot, and other Chartist ambitions had been achieved.

Limiting the Lords In the early 1900s, Liberals in the House of Commons pressed ahead with social reforms. But many bills passed by the Commons met defeat in the House of Lords. In particular, the Lords used their veto power to block any attempt to increase taxes on the wealthy.

In 1911, a Liberal government passed measures to restrict the power of the Lords, including their power to veto tax bills. The Lords resisted. Finally, the government threatened to create enough new lords to approve the law, and the Lords backed down. People hailed the change as a victory for democracy. In time, the House of Lords would become largely a ceremonial body with little power. The elected House of Commons would reign supreme.

SECTION 1 Assessment

Recall
1. **Identify:** (a) Benjamin Disraeli, (b) Chartism, (c) Victoria, (d) William Gladstone.
2. **Define:** (a) rotten borough, (b) electorate, (c) secret ballot.

Comprehension
3. How did the Reform Act of 1832 change Parliament?
4. What middle-class values are associated with the Victorian age?
5. What reforms did the Liberal and Conservative parties achieve?

Critical Thinking and Writing
6. **Drawing Conclusions** Why do you think the Chartists demanded (a) a secret ballot, (b) salaries for members of Parliament?
7. **Analyzing Literature** Reread the excerpt from *Sybil* at the beginning of this section. (a) Restate the stranger's main idea in your own words. (b) Why is Egremont surprised by this view of Britain? (c) Would you consider this novel a reliable source of information about Britain in the early 1800s? Why or why not?

PHSchool.com

Use the Internet to research the life of Queen Victoria. Then, present your findings in a "This Is Your Life" format. Have one student play Victoria and another the host. Other students will play surprise guests who can discuss Victoria's life. For help with this activity, use **Web Code mkd-2496.**

A Century of Reform

Reading Focus

- What social and economic reforms benefited British workers and others?
- How did British women work to win the vote?
- What were the goals of Irish nationalists?

Vocabulary

free trade
repeal
capital offense
penal colony
absentee landlord
home rule

Taking Notes

On a sheet of paper, create a concept web like this one. As you read the section, add information to the web. Add as many circles as you need.

REFORMS IN BRITAIN
Free trade established
Slavery banned in colonies

Main Idea Parliament passed a wide variety of reform measures, but women's suffrage and the status of Ireland remained difficult issues.

Setting the Scene Her aristocratic family would have been shocked. Here was Lady Constance Lytton, disguised as a seamstress—and lying in a prison hospital! Lytton had been arrested for taking part in a women's suffrage protest. Now, she refused to eat. Her hunger strike, she vowed, would go on until the British government granted the vote to women. Lytton later recalled:

> "I was visited again by the Senior Medical Officer, who asked me how long I had been without food. I said I had eaten a buttered scone and a banana sent in by friends to the police station on Friday at about midnight. He said, 'Oh, then, this is the fourth day; that is too long, I shall feed you, I must feed you at once.'"
> —Constance Lytton, *Prisons and Prisoners*

In the end, the doctor—with the help of five prison matrons—force-fed Lytton through a tube. Yet the painful ordeal failed to weaken her resolve. "No surrender," she whispered. "No surrender."

Lytton's 1910 hunger strike was part of the long struggle for women's suffrage in Britain. Suffragists were not the only people to fight for change. Between 1815 and 1914, Parliament responded to widespread discontent with a series of social and economic reforms. At the same time, the question of British control over Ireland was becoming a dominant and divisive political issue.

Social and Economic Reforms

During the early and mid-1800s, Parliament passed a wide variety of important new laws. One of the most controversial measures involved the issue of free trade, or trade between countries without quotas, tariffs, or other restrictions.

Free Trade and the Corn Laws In the early 1800s, Britain, like other European nations, taxed foreign imports in order to protect local economies. But supporters of free trade demanded an end to such protective tariffs. Free traders, usually middle-class business leaders, agreed with Adam Smith that a policy of laissez faire would increase prosperity for all. If tariffs were abolished, merchants everywhere would have larger markets in which to sell their goods, and consumers would benefit from open competition.

DISCOVERY CHANNEL SCHOOL Video
Witness the Great Hunger in Ireland.

Punishing Crime
These pictures are from an 1862 study of Britain's new system of reformed prisons. The cell at left reflects the new idea that prisoners should be confined to individual cells instead of milling around a common prison yard. At right, female convicts take care of their children in a prison nursery.

Theme: Political and Social Systems What does the picture on the left show you about how many prisoners spent their day?

Some British tariffs were repealed in the 1820s. However, fierce debate erupted over the Corn Laws, which imposed high tariffs on imported grain. (In Britain, "corn" refers to all cereal grains, such as wheat, barley, and oats.) Farmers and wealthy landowners supported the Corn Laws because they kept the price of British grain high. Free traders, however, wanted Parliament to repeal, or cancel, the Corn Laws. They argued that repeal of these laws would lower the price of grain, make bread cheaper for city workers, and open up trade in general.

Parliament finally repealed the Corn Laws in 1846, after widespread crop failures swept many parts of Europe. Liberals hailed the repeal as a victory for free trade and laissez-faire capitalism. However, in the late 1800s, economic hard times led Britain and other European countries to impose protective tariffs on many goods again.

Campaign Against Slavery During the 1700s, Enlightenment thinkers had turned the spotlight on the evils of the slave trade. At the time, British ships were carrying more Africans to the Americas than was any other European country. Under pressure from middle-class reformers, the campaign against the slave trade and slavery slowly took off. In 1807, Britain became the first leading European power to abolish the slave trade.

Banning the slave trade did not end slavery. Although the Congress of Vienna had condemned slavery, it had taken no action. In Britain, liberals preached the immorality of slavery. Finally, in 1833, Parliament passed a law banning slavery in all British colonies. Yet British textile manufacturers still imported cheap cotton produced by enslaved African Americans in the United States.

Crime and Punishment Other reforms were aimed at the criminal justice system. In the early 1800s, more than 200 crimes were punishable by death. Such capital offenses included not only murder but also shoplifting, sheep stealing, and impersonating an army veteran. In practice, some juries refused to convict criminals, because the punishments were so harsh. Executions were public occasions, and the hanging of a well-known murderer might attract thousands of curious spectators. Afterward, instead of receiving a proper burial, the criminal's body might be given to a medical college for dissection.

Victorian reformers began to reduce the number of capital offenses. By 1850, the death penalty was reserved for murder, piracy, treason, and arson. Many petty criminals were instead transported to penal colonies, or special settlements for convicts, in the new British territories of Australia and New

Zealand. In 1868, Parliament ended public hangings. Additional reforms improved prison conditions and outlawed imprisonment for debt.

Victories for the Working Class

"Four [ghosts] haunt the Poor: Old Age, Accident, Sickness and Unemployment," declared Liberal politician David Lloyd George in 1905. "We are going to [expel] them." By the early 1900s, Parliament gradually passed a series of reforms designed to help the men, women, and children whose labor supported the new industrial society.

Working Conditions As you have read, working conditions in the early industrial age were grim and often dangerous. Gradually, Parliament passed laws to regulate conditions in factories and mines. In 1842, for example, mineowners were forbidden to employ women or children under age 10. An 1847 law limited women and children to a 10-hour day. Later in the 1800s, the government regulated many safety conditions in factories and mines—and sent inspectors to see that the laws were enforced. Other laws set minimum wages and maximum hours of work.

Labor Unions Early in the Industrial Revolution, labor unions were outlawed. Under pressure, government and business leaders slowly accepted worker organizations. Trade unions were made legal in 1825. At the same time, though, strikes remained illegal.

Despite restrictions, unions spread, and gradually they won additional rights. Between 1890 and 1914, union membership soared. Besides winning higher wages and shorter hours for workers, unions pressed for other laws to improve the lives of the working class.

Later Reforms During the late 1800s and early 1900s, both political parties enacted social reforms to benefit the working class. Disraeli sponsored laws to improve public health and housing for workers in cities. Under Gladstone, an Education Act called for free elementary education for all children. Gladstone also pushed to open up government jobs based on merit rather than on birth or wealth.

Another force for reform was the Fabian Society, a socialist organization founded in 1883. The Fabians promoted gradual change through legal means rather than by violence. Though small in number, the Fabians had a strong influence on British politics.

In 1900, socialists and union members backed the formation of a new political party, which became the Labour party. ("Labour" is the British spelling of "labor.") The Labour party would grow in power and membership until, by the 1920s, it surpassed the Liberal party as one of Britain's two major parties.

In the early 1900s, Britain began to pass social welfare laws to protect the well-being of the poor and disadvantaged. These laws were modeled on those Bismarck had introduced in Germany. They protected workers with accident, health, and unemployment insurance as well as old-age pensions. One result of such reforms was that Marxism gained only limited support among the British working classes. The middle class hailed reforms as proof that democracy was working.

Votes for Women

In Britain, as elsewhere, women struggled for the right to vote against strong opposition. Just as Parliament had rejected the Chartist demand for universal male suffrage in 1848, so it resisted the demands of the women's suffrage movement 50 years later.

Women themselves were divided on the issue. Some women opposed suffrage altogether. Queen Victoria, for example, called the suffrage struggle

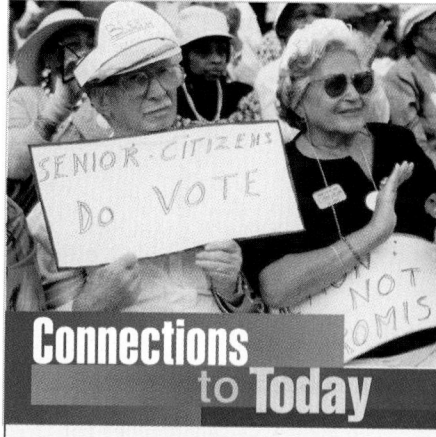

Connections to Today

Your Senior Years: Is Your Future Secure?

The United States created its Social Security system in 1935. It is similar to some of the social reforms Britain introduced years earlier. But Social Security was designed to supplement other pension plans and personal savings. Today, it has become a primary source of retirement income for many older Americans.

Social Security is now facing increasing challenges. The rising cost of living forces retirees to stretch their Social Security benefits more than ever. Also, life expectancies have increased dramatically. In 1900, only 4 percent of the American population was age 65 or over. By the year 2000, that figure was almost 13 percent—and growing. In the future, there will be many more retirees who live longer and healthier lives. These changes will put strains on the Social Security system, and some experts predict that funds will be exhausted by 2032.

Theme: Continuity and Change What might happen if the Social Security system were to run completely out of funding?

Emmeline Pankhurst
1858–1928

From the time she attended her first women's suffrage meeting at the age of 14, Emmeline Pankhurst was a "conscious and confirmed suffragist." Years of peaceful protest and demonstrations did little to win women the vote, however. After newspapers stopped reporting on suffrage rallies, Pankhurst turned to more aggressive tactics.

Tireless and fiercely determined, Pankhurst fought for her cause on many fronts—on the streets, from a prison cell, and in the courtroom. She even went on 10 hunger strikes within 18 months. With England's entrance into World War I in 1914, Pankhurst suspended her militant activities to support the war effort. Continuing to fight from the podium, however, Pankhurst spoke at home and abroad, refusing to let women's suffrage be forgotten.

Theme: Impact of the Individual Why did Emmeline Pankhurst believe that strong measures were necessary?

"mad, wicked folly." Even women in favor of suffrage disagreed about how best to achieve it.

Suffragists Revolt By the early 1900s, Emmeline Pankhurst, a leading suffragist, had become convinced that only aggressive tactics would bring victory. Pankhurst and other radical suffragists interrupted speakers in Parliament, shouting, "Votes for women!" until they were carried away. They collected petitions and organized huge public demonstrations. During one suffragist rally in London's Hyde Park, organizers brought demonstrators from all over Britain. An astonished newspaper reporter wrote, "It is probable that so many people have never before stood in one square mass anywhere in England."

When mass meetings and other peaceful efforts brought no results, some women turned to violent protest. They smashed windows or even burned buildings. Pankhurst justified such tactics as necessary to achieve victory. "There is something that governments care far more for than human life," she declared, "and that is the security of property, so it is through property that we shall strike the enemy."

Pankhurst and other women, including her daughters Christabel and Sylvia, were arrested and jailed. As you have read, some went on hunger strikes, risking their lives to achieve their goals. One radical suffragist died when she threw herself in front of the king's horse.

A Belated Victory Many middle-class women disapproved of such radical and violent actions. Yet they, too, spoke up in increasing numbers, demanding votes for women and equality under the law. Still, Parliament refused to grant women's suffrage. Not until 1918 did Parliament finally grant suffrage to women over age 30. Younger women did not win the right to vote for another decade.

The Irish Question

Throughout the 1800s, Britain faced the ever-present "Irish question." The English had begun conquering Ireland in the 1100s. In the 1600s, English and Scottish settlers colonized Ireland, taking possession of much of the best farmland.

The Irish never accepted English rule. They bitterly resented settlers, especially absentee landlords who owned large estates but did not live on them. Many Irish peasants lived in desperate poverty, while paying high rents to landlords living in England. In addition, the Irish, most of whom were Catholic, had to pay tithes to support the Church of England. Under these conditions, resistance and rebellion were common.

Irish Nationalism Like the national minorities in the Austrian empire, Irish nationalists campaigned vigorously for freedom and justice in the 1800s. Nationalist leader Daniel O'Connell, nicknamed "the Liberator," organized an Irish Catholic League and held mass meetings to demand repeal of unfair laws. "My first object," declared O'Connell, "is to get Ireland for the Irish."

Under pressure from O'Connell and other Irish nationalists, Britain slowly moved to improve conditions in Ireland. In 1829, Parliament passed the Catholic Emancipation Act, which allowed Irish Catholics to vote and hold political office. Yet many injustices remained. Absentee landlords could evict tenants almost at will. Other British laws forbade the teaching and speaking of the Irish language.

The Great Hunger Under British rule, three quarters of Irish farmland was used to grow crops that were imported to England. The potato, introduced from the Americas, became the main source of food for most of the Irish people themselves. Still, potatoes were abundant and nutritious enough to support a growing population.

Famine Devastates Ireland

The first potatoes harvested in the Irish countryside in October 1845 looked fine. But within days the potatoes had turned black and rotten. Soon, half the potato crop was ruined, the result of a deadly plant disease. For seven years the potato blight lingered, leading to a disastrous famine.

Like this family bound for Detroit, many Irish during the famine chose to emigrate rather than face certain starvation. The number of Irish who left between 1845 and 1851 totaled more than one million—greater than the number who had emigrated in the previous 30 years. The majority went to the United States.

During the "Great Hunger," many Irish homes such as this one were stripped of food and belongings. Many farmers sold furniture and clothing to buy food. Few families could even afford to buy fuel for heat.

In 1846, Mary Rush of Ardnaglass, Ireland, wrote to her parents in Quebec, Canada:
"Pen cannot dictate the poverty of this country at present. . . . For God's sake take us out of the poverty, and don't let us die with the hunger."
— Mary Rush, letter to her parents

Portfolio Assessment

Conduct research to find out more about a recent famine. Then, prepare a class presentation on the causes and results of the famine. If possible, include first-person accounts or photographs of the topic you have selected.

Fast Facts

- Irish peasants could not afford to buy the wheat, meat, and dairy products that continued to be shipped from Ireland to England.

- When the Irish protested against taxes, rents, and evictions, thousands of British troops arrived in Ireland to restore order.

- Due to rampant malnutrition, more people died from diseases such as typhus and cholera than from starvation during the famine.

Americans from all walks of life rushed to the aid of the starving Irish. Quakers were the first to organize relief efforts. Catholic churches, Jewish synagogues, and women's groups worked to raise funds. The American government encouraged food shipments by announcing that no road or canal tolls would be charged on any supplies headed for Ireland.

The Choctaw people, whose own forced relocation in the 1830s resulted in great hardship and many deaths, identified with the plight of the Irish people. Still recovering from food shortages of their own, the Choctaws contributed over $700—a large sum in the 1840s.

Theme: Global Interaction
How do groups and individuals today respond to disasters around the world?

Then, in 1845, disaster struck. A blight, or disease, destroyed the potato crop. Other crops, such as wheat and oats, were not affected. Yet British landowners continued to ship these crops outside Ireland, leaving little for the Irish except the blighted potatoes. The result was a terrible famine that the Irish called the "Great Hunger."

Witnesses described many "scenes of frightful hunger." One official told of entering what he thought was a deserted village. In one home, he saw "six famished and ghastly skeletons, to all appearances dead . . . huddled in a corner on some filthy straw."

"I approached with horror, and found by a low moaning they were alive—they were in a fever, four children, a woman and what had once been a man. . . . In a few minutes I was surrounded by at least 200 such phantoms, such frightful spectres as no words can describe, either from famine or from fever."
—letter to the *Times* (London), December 24, 1846

In four years, at least one million Irish men, women, and children died of starvation or disease. More than one million emigrated to the United States and Canada. The Great Hunger left a legacy of Irish bitterness toward the English that still exists today.

Struggle for Home Rule Throughout the century, Irish demands for self-rule intensified. In the 1850s, some Irish militants organized the Fenian Brotherhood. Its goal was to liberate Ireland from British rule by force. In the 1870s, moderate Irish nationalists found a rousing leader in Charles Stewart Parnell. He rallied Irish members of Parliament to press for home rule, or local self-government. The debate dragged on for decades.

The "Irish question" disrupted English politics. At times, political parties were so deeply split over the Irish question that they could not take care of other business. As prime minister, Gladstone pushed for reforms in Ireland. He ended the use of Irish tithe money to support the Anglican church and tried to ease the hardships of Irish tenant farmers. New laws prevented landlords from charging unfair rents and protected the rights of tenants to the land they worked.

Finally, in 1914, Parliament passed a home rule bill. But it delayed putting the new law into effect when World War I broke out that year. As you will read, the southern counties of Ireland finally became independent in 1921.

SECTION 2 Assessment

Recall
1. **Identify:** (a) Corn Laws, (b) Fabian Society, (c) Emmeline Pankhurst, (d) Catholic Emancipation Act, (e) Great Hunger, (f) Charles Stewart Parnell.
2. **Define:** (a) free trade, (b) repeal, (c) capital offense, (d) penal colony, (e) absentee landlord, (f) home rule.

Comprehension
3. Describe three social reforms that helped the British working class.
4. What actions did women suffragists take to achieve their goals?

5. (a) Why did Irish nationalists oppose British rule? (b) Describe two reforms that improved conditions in Ireland.

Critical Thinking and Writing
6. **Analyzing Ideas** How is the idea of free trade linked to the principles of laissez faire and competition?
7. **Defending a Position** Do you agree that the tactics used by suffragists like Emmeline Pankhurst were necessary at the time? Why or why not?

Activity
Designing a Poster
Design a poster that an Irish nationalist of the late 1800s or early 1900s might have used in the struggle for home rule. First, decide whether your main goal is to win support from the Irish or to persuade members of the British Parliament.

Reading Focus

- What domestic and foreign policies did Napoleon III pursue?

- What impact did the Dreyfus affair and other challenges have on the Third Republic?

- How did the French government take steps toward reform in the early 1900s?

Vocabulary

provisional
premier
coalition
libel

Taking Notes

On a sheet of paper, draw a time line to show the main events of this section. Use the time line shown here to help you get started.

1848	1860s	1863	1914
Second Empire	Napoleon III eases controls	Napoleon III tries to put Maximilian on throne of Mexico	

Main Idea Democratic reforms in France took place under the Second Empire of Napoleon III and its successor, the Third Republic.

Setting the Scene

The news sent shock waves throughout Paris. An entire French army under the emperor Napoleon III had surrendered to the Prussians at the city of Sedan. Still worse, Prussian forces were now about to advance on Paris. Could the city survive?

Georges Clemenceau (KLEHM uhn soh), a young French doctor who had entered politics, rallied the people of Paris to defend their city and their homeland. "Citizens," he cried, "must France destroy herself and disappear, or shall she resume her old place in the vanguard of nations?" Clemenceau concluded:

> "Each of us knows his duty. We are children of the Revolution. Let us seek inspiration in the example of our forefathers in 1792, and like them we shall conquer. *Vive la France!* [Long Live France!]"
> —Georges Clemenceau, quoted in *Clemenceau and the Third Republic* (Jackson)

For four months, Paris did resist the German onslaught. But finally, in January 1871, the French government at Versailles was forced to accept Prussian surrender terms.

The Franco-Prussian War ended a long period of French domination of Europe that had begun under Louis XIV. Yet the Third Republic rose from the ashes of the Second Empire of Napoleon III. Economic growth, democratic reforms, and the fierce nationalism expressed by Clemenceau all played a part in shaping modern France.

France Under Napoleon III

After the revolution of 1848, Napoleon III set up the Second Empire. His appeal cut across lines of class and ideology. The bourgeoisie saw him as a strong leader who would restore order. His promise to end poverty gave hope to the lower classes. People of all classes were attracted by his name, a reminder of the days when France had towered over Europe. Unlike his famous uncle, however, Napoleon III would bring France neither glory nor an empire.

Limits on Liberty On the surface, the Second Empire looked like a constitutional monarchy. In fact, Napoleon III ruled almost as a dictator, with the power to appoint his cabinet, the upper house of the legislature, and

Napoleon III
This portrait of Emperor Napoleon III suggests his pride and love of pomp. Like many monarchs of his day, Napoleon often had himself painted or photographed in military garb.

Theme: Political and Social Systems Why do you think many monarchs favored military dress?

The Siege of Paris, 1870

Paris

Versailles

Seine R.

Marne R.

Seine R.

N
W E
S

| 0 | 2 | 4 Miles |
| 0 | 2 | 4 Kilometers |

—— Prussian siege line
🔫 Prussian batteries
→ Prussian attacks
—— French defensive line
🏰 French forts
→ French attacks
▭ City walls

Skills Assessment

Geography For four months, Prussian troops surrounded Paris. In the painting at right, a hot air balloon leaves the city.

1. **Location** On the map, locate **(a)** Paris, **(b)** Seine River, **(c)** Marne River, **(d)** Versailles.
2. **Movement** In what area did the Prussians launch attacks?
3. **Critical Thinking Synthesizing Information** Based on the map, why do you think Parisians made use of hot air balloons during the Prussian siege?

many officials. Although the assembly was elected by universal male suffrage, appointed officials "managed" elections so that supporters of the emperor would win. Debate was limited, and newspapers faced strict censorship.

In the 1860s, the emperor began to ease controls. He lifted some censorship and gave the legislature more power. On the eve of his disastrous war with Prussia, Napoleon III even issued a new constitution that extended democratic rights.

Economic Growth Like much of Europe, France prospered at mid-century. Napoleon III promoted investment in industry and large-scale ventures such as railroad building and the urban renewal of Paris. During this period, a French entrepreneur, Ferdinand de Lesseps (duh LEHS uhps), organized the building of the Suez Canal to link the Mediterranean with the Red Sea and thus the Indian Ocean.

Workers enjoyed some benefits from economic growth. Napoleon legalized labor unions, extended public education to girls, and created a small public health program. Still, in France, as in other industrial nations, many people lived in great poverty.

Foreign Adventures Napoleon's worst failures were in foreign affairs. In the 1860s, he tried to place Maximilian, an Austrian Hapsburg prince, on the throne of Mexico. Through Maximilian, Napoleon hoped to turn Mexico into a French satellite. But after a large commitment of troops and money, the adventure failed. Mexican patriots resisted fiercely, and the United States protested. After four years, France withdrew its troops. Maximilian was overthrown and shot by Mexican patriots.

Napoleon's successes were almost as costly as his failures. He helped Italian nationalists defeat Austria, gaining Nice (NEES) and Savoy. But this victory backfired when a united Italy emerged as a rival on France's border. And, though France and Britain won the Crimean War, France had little to show for its terrible losses except a small foothold in the Middle East.

War With Prussia At this time, France grew increasingly concerned about the rise of a great rival, Prussia. The Prussian leader Otto von Bismarck shrewdly manipulated French worries to lure Napoleon into war in 1870.

As you have read, the Franco-Prussian War was a disaster for France. After Napoleon III was captured at Sedan, German forces began the four-month siege of Paris. Encircled by Prussian troops, starving Parisians were reduced to catching rats and killing circus animals for food.

Challenges of the Third Republic

After Napoleon's capture, republicans in Paris had declared an end to the Second Empire. They set up a provisional, or temporary, government that evolved into France's Third Republic.

In 1871, the newly elected National Assembly accepted a harsh peace with Germany. France had to surrender the provinces of Alsace and Lorraine and pay a huge sum to Germany. The French burned to avenge their loss.

The Paris Commune In 1871, an uprising broke out in Paris. Rebels set up the Paris Commune. Like the radical government during the French Revolution, its goal was to save the Republic from royalists. Communards, as the rebels were called, included workers and socialists as well as bourgeois republicans. As patriots, they rejected the harsh peace that the National Assembly had signed with Germany. Radicals dreamed of creating a new socialist order.

The National Assembly ordered the Commune to disband. When the Communards refused, the government sent troops to besiege Paris. For weeks, civil war raged. As government troops advanced, the rebels toppled great Paris monuments and slaughtered hostages. Finally, government forces butchered some 20,000 Communards. The suppression of the Paris Commune left bitter memories that deepened social divisions within France.

Government Structure Despite its shaky beginnings, the Third Republic remained in place for 70 years. The new republic had a two-house legislature. The powerful lower house, or Chamber of Deputies, was elected by universal male suffrage. Together with the Senate, it elected the president of the republic. However, he had little power and served mostly as a figurehead. Real power was in the hands of the premier (prih MIR), or prime minister.

Unlike Britain, with its two-party system, France had many parties, reflecting the wide splits within the country. Among them were divine-right royalists, constitutional monarchists, moderate republicans, and radicals. With so many parties, no single party could win a majority in the legislature. In order to govern, politicians had to form coalitions, or alliances of various parties. Once a coalition controlled enough votes, it could then name a premier and form a cabinet.

Multiparty systems and coalition governments are common in Europe. Such alliances allow citizens to vote for a party that most nearly matches their own beliefs. Coalition governments, however, are often unstable. If one party deserts a coalition, the government might lose its majority in the legislature. The government then falls, and new elections must be held. In the first 10 years of the Third Republic, 50 different coalition governments were formed and fell.

Scandals Despite frequent changes of governments, France made economic progress. It paid Germany the huge sum required by the peace treaty and expanded its overseas empire. But in the 1880s and 1890s, a series of political scandals shook public trust in the government.

Le Petit Journal

Le Petit Journal
Le Supplement illustré

SUPPLÉMENT ILLUSTRÉ
Huit pages : CINQ centimes

ABONNEMENTS

Sixième année

DIMANCHE 13 JANVIER 1895

Numero 217

Dreyfus in Disgrace
The cover of this 1895 French magazine shows Alfred Dreyfus being drummed out of the army. By tradition, a disgraced officer stood at attention while his shoulder pads were ripped off and his sword was broken.

Theme: Diversity **How do you think people in France reacted to this magazine cover?**

One crisis erupted when a popular minister of war, General Georges Boulanger (boo lahn ZHAY), rallied royalists and ultranationalists eager for revenge on Germany. Accused of plotting to overthrow the republic, Boulanger fled to Belgium and later committed suicide. In another scandal, a nephew of the president was caught selling nominations for the Legion of Honor, France's highest award. The president was forced to resign.

The Dreyfus Affair

The most divisive scandal began in 1894, when a high-ranking army officer, Alfred Dreyfus, was accused of spying for Germany. At his military trial, neither Dreyfus nor his lawyer was allowed to see the evidence against him. The injustice was rooted in antisemitism. The military elite detested Dreyfus, the first Jew to reach such a high position in the army. Although Dreyfus proclaimed his innocence, he was convicted and condemned to life imprisonment on Devil's Island, a desolate penal colony off the coast of South America.

By 1896, new evidence pointed to another officer, Ferdinand Esterhazy, as the spy. Still, the army refused to grant Dreyfus a new trial.

Deep Divisions The Dreyfus affair, as it was called, scarred French politics and society for decades. Royalists, ultranationalists, and Church officials charged Dreyfus supporters, or "Dreyfusards," with undermining France. Paris echoed with cries of "Long live the army!" and "Death to traitors!" Dreyfusards, mostly liberals and republicans, upheld ideals of justice and equality in the face of massive public anger. In 1898, French novelist Émile Zola joined the battle. In an article headlined *J'Accuse!* (I Accuse!), he charged the army and government with suppressing the truth. As a result, Zola was convicted of libel, or the knowing publication of false and damaging statements. He fled into exile.

Slowly, though, the Dreyfusards made progress. They revealed that the evidence against Dreyfus was forged. In 1906, a French court finally cleared Dreyfus of all charges and restored his honors. That move was a victory for justice, but the political scars of the Dreyfus affair took longer to heal.

Calls for a Jewish State The Dreyfus case reflected the rise of antisemitism in Europe. The Enlightenment and the French Revolution had spread ideas about religious toleration. In Western Europe, some Jews had gained jobs in government, universities, and other areas of life. A few were successful in banking and business, though most struggled to survive in the ghettos of Eastern Europe or slums of Western Europe.

By the late 1800s, however, antisemitism was again on the rise. Antisemites were often members of the lower middle class who felt insecure in their social and economic position. Steeped in the new nationalist fervor, they adopted an aggressive intolerance for outsiders and a violent hatred of Jews.

The Dreyfus case and the pogroms in Russia stirred Theodor Herzl (HEHRT suhl), a Hungarian Jewish journalist living in France. He called for Jews to form their own separate state, where they would have the rights denied to them in European countries. Herzl helped launch modern Zionism, a movement devoted to rebuilding a Jewish state in Palestine. Many Jews had kept alive this dream since the Roman destruction of Jerusalem. In 1897, Herzl organized the First Zionist Congress in Basel, Switzerland.

Reforms in France

Though shaken by the Dreyfus affair, France achieved serious reforms in the early 1900s. Like Britain, France passed laws regulating wages, hours, and safety conditions for workers. It set up a system of free public elementary schools. Creating public schools was also part of a campaign to reduce the power of the Roman Catholic Church, which controlled education.

Separating Church and State Like Germany, France tried to end Church involvement in government. Republicans viewed the Church as a conservative force that opposed progressive policies. In the Dreyfus affair, it had backed the army and ultranationalists.

The government closed Church schools, along with many convents and monasteries. In 1905, it passed a law to separate church and state and stopped paying the salaries of the clergy. Catholics, Protestants, and Jews enjoyed freedom of worship, but none had any special treatment from the government.

Women's Rights Under the Napoleonic Code, French women had few rights. Women could not even control their own property. By the 1890s, a growing women's rights movement sought legal reforms. It made some gains, such as an 1896 law giving married women the right to their own earnings.

In 1909, Jeanne-Elizabeth Schmahl founded the French Union for Women's Suffrage. Rejecting the radical tactics used in Britain, Schmahl favored legal protests. Yet even liberal men were reluctant to grant women suffrage. They feared that women would vote for Church and conservative causes. In the end, French women did not win the vote until after World War II.

Looking Ahead

By 1914, France was the largest democratic country in Europe, with a constitution that protected basic rights. France's economy was generally prosperous, and its overseas empire was second only to that of Britain.

Yet the outlook was not all smooth. Coalition governments rose and fell at the slightest pressure. To the east loomed the industrial might of Germany. Many French citizens were itching for a chance to avenge the defeat in the Franco-Prussian War and liberate the "lost provinces" of Alsace and Lorraine. That chance came in 1914, when all of Europe exploded into World War I.

SECTION 3 Assessment

Recall
1. **Identify:** (a) Paris Commune, (b) Georges Boulanger, (c) Alfred Dreyfus, (d) Theodor Herzl, (e) Jeanne-Elizabeth Schmahl.
2. **Define:** (a) provisional, (b) premier, (c) coalition, (d) libel.

Comprehension
3. Describe the government of France during the Second Empire.
4. Explain how each of the following heightened divisions in France: (a) the Paris Commune, (b) the Dreyfus affair.

5. Describe two reforms enacted in France in the early 1900s.

Critical Thinking and Writing
6. **Comparing** (a) How does the French system of political parties differ from the American system? (b) How do these differences affect the stability of governments under each system?
7. **Solving Problems** (a) What solution did Zionists propose for the problem of widespread anti-semitism? (b) Why do you think they felt it was the best solution?

Activity

Drawing a Political Cartoon Draw a political cartoon about one event or development during the reign of Napoleon III. You may focus either on domestic affairs, such as limitations on liberty, or on foreign affairs, such as the Franco-Prussian War.

Expansion of the United States

Reading Focus

- How did the United States extend its territory?
- How did American democracy grow before and after the Civil War?
- What impact did economic growth and social reform have on the United States?

Vocabulary

expansionism
abolitionist
secede
segregation
isolationism

Taking Notes

On a sheet of paper, start a before-and-after chart like the one shown here. As you read this section, list events under the appropriate columns.

CIVIL WAR	
Before	After
• Expansion and western settlement • Manifest Destiny • Calls for abolition of slavery	

Main Idea In the United States, the 1800s were a time of changing borders, growing industry, and expanding democracy.

Setting the Scene

For many Irish families fleeing hunger, Russian Jews escaping pogroms, or poor Italian farmers seeking economic opportunity, the answer was the same—America! A poem inscribed on the base of the Statue of Liberty expressed the hopes of millions of immigrants:

"Give me your tired, your poor,
Your huddled masses yearning to breathe free,
The wretched refuse of your teeming shore.
Send these, the homeless, tempest-tossed to me.
I lift my lamp beside the golden door."
—Emma Lazarus, "The New Colossus"

In the 1800s, the United States was a beacon of hope for many people. The American economy was growing rapidly, offering jobs to newcomers. The Constitution and Bill of Rights held out the hope of political and religious freedom. Not everyone shared in the prosperity or the ideals of democracy. Still, by the turn of the century, Americans were increasingly proud of their status as an emerging world power.

Territorial Expansion

From the earliest years of its history, the United States followed a policy of expansionism, or extending a nation's boundaries. At first, the United States stretched only from the Atlantic coast to the Mississippi River. In 1803, President Thomas Jefferson bought the Louisiana territory from France. In one stroke, the Louisiana Purchase virtually doubled the size of the nation.

Manifest Destiny By 1846, the United States had expanded to include Florida, Oregon, and the Republic of Texas. The Mexican War (1846–1848) added California and the Southwest. With growing pride and confidence, Americans claimed that their nation was destined to spread across the entire continent, from sea to sea. This idea became known as Manifest Destiny. Some expansionists even hoped to absorb Canada and Mexico. In fact, the United States did go far afield. In 1867, it bought Alaska from Russia and in 1898 annexed the Hawaiian Islands.

Settling the West During the 1800s, settlers flocked to newly acquired western lands. The discovery of gold in California drew floods of easterners.

Other people, like the Mormons, sought a place to practice their religion freely. Still others headed west in the spirit of adventure.

The waves of settlers brought tragedy to Native Americans. Following a pattern that began in colonial days, newcomers pushed the Indians off their lands, sometimes by treaty, but more often by force. Some Native American nations resisted the invaders, but they were outgunned and outnumbered. As settlers moved westward, they destroyed the buffalo herds on which the Plains Indians depended. By the 1890s, most surviving Native Americans had been driven onto reservations, usually the least desirable parts of a territory.

Expanding Democracy

In 1800, the United States had the most liberal suffrage in the world, but still only white men who owned property could vote. States slowly chipped away at requirements. By the 1830s, most white men had the right to vote. Democracy was far from complete, however. Women, Native Americans, and free blacks had no vote. Enslaved African Americans had no rights at all.

By mid-century, reformers were campaigning for many changes. Some demanded a ban on the sale of alcoholic beverages. Others called for better treatment of the mentally ill or pushed for free elementary schools. Two crusades, especially, highlighted the limits of American democracy—the abolition movement and the women's rights movement.

Calls for Abolition In the early 1800s, a few Americans demanded an immediate and complete end to slavery. These abolitionists included William Lloyd Garrison, who pressed the antislavery cause through his newspaper, the *Liberator.* Frederick Douglass, who had himself escaped slavery, spoke eloquently in the North about the evils of slavery.

Expansion of the United States, 1783–1898

Chapter 11 **307**

Synthesizing Information

The Growth of American Suffrage

The right to vote in the United States has gradually expanded over time. When the Constitution was approved, only white men over age 21 who owned property could vote. The chart, cartoon, and primary source below all relate to the growth of American suffrage.

Expansion of Suffrage in the United States

Year	People Granted the Vote
Late 1700s	Most white men aged 21 or older who meet property requirements (state laws)
Early 1800s–1850s	Most white men aged 21 or older (state laws)
1870	Black men (Amendment 15)
1920	Women (Amendment 19)
1961	People in the District of Columbia in presidential elections (Amendment 23)
1971	People aged 18 or older (Amendment 26)

"The Latest Suffrage Recruit"

Secretary of State William Jennings Bryan unfurls the suffragist flag in 1915.

Fifteenth Amendment

"Section 1. The right of citizens of the United States to vote shall not be denied or abridged by the United States or by any state on account of race, color, or previous condition of servitude.
Section 2. The Congress shall have power to enforce this article by appropriate legislation."
　　　—Fifteenth Amendment to the United States Constitution, adopted 1870

Skills Tip

Be careful not to draw conclusions from political cartoons when you do not have enough information. Political cartoons can be misleading, particularly when they depict events that happened a long time ago.

Skills Assessment

1. According to the chart, which amendment to the Constitution gave all citizens aged 18 or older the right to vote in the United States?
   A Fifteenth
   B Nineteenth
   C Twenty-third
   D Twenty-sixth

2. What can you conclude about William Jennings Bryan from this cartoon?
   E He supported votes for women.
   F Defending women's suffrage helped his political career.
   G His endorsement alone earned women the right to vote.
   H He sponsored the Fifteenth Amendment.

3. **Critical Thinking Making Inferences (a)** By what means was suffrage extended to an increasingly broader group of people? **(b)** Based on these sources, how would you describe the expansion of suffrage in the United States?

By the 1850s, the battle over slavery intensified. As new states entered the union, proslavery and antislavery forces met in violent confrontations to decide whether slavery would be legal in the new state. Harriet Beecher Stowe's novel *Uncle Tom's Cabin* helped convince many northerners that slavery was a great social evil.

Women's Rights Movement   Women worked hard in the antislavery movement. Lucretia Mott and Elizabeth Cady Stanton traveled to London for the World Antislavery Convention—only to find they were forbidden to speak because they were women. Gradually, American women began to protest the laws and customs that limited their lives.

In 1848, in Seneca Falls, New York, Mott and Stanton organized the first women's rights convention. The convention passed a resolution, based on the Declaration of Independence. It began, "We hold these truths to be self evident: that all men and women are created equal." The women's rights movement set as its goal equality before the law, in the workplace, and in education. Some women also demanded the vote.

The Civil War and Its Aftermath

Economic differences, as well as the slavery issue, drove the North and South apart. The division reached a crisis in 1860 when Abraham Lincoln was elected president. Lincoln opposed extending slavery into new territories. Southerners feared that he would eventually abolish slavery altogether and that the federal government would infringe on their states' rights.

North Versus South   Soon after Lincoln's election, most southern states seceded, or withdrew, from the Union and formed the Confederate States of America. This action sparked the Civil War. From 1861 to 1865, the agonizing ordeal divided families as well as a nation.

The South had fewer resources, people, and industry than the North. Still, southerners fought fiercely to defend their cause. They won many early victories. At one point, Confederate armies under General Robert E. Lee drove northward as far as Gettysburg, Pennsylvania. In a bloody three-day battle, the Union army turned back the southern advance for good.

In the last years of the war, General Ulysses S. Grant used the massive resources of the North to launch a full-scale offensive against the South. The Confederacy finally surrendered in 1865. The struggle cost more than 600,000 lives—the largest casualty figures of any American war. Although the war left a bitter legacy, it did guarantee that the nation would remain united.

Challenges for African Americans   During the war, Lincoln declared that enslaved African Americans in the South were free. After the war, three amendments to the Constitution banned slavery throughout the country and granted political rights to African Americans. Under the Fifteenth Amendment, African American men won the right to vote.

Still, African Americans faced many restrictions. In the South, laws imposed segregation, or legal separation of the races, in hospitals, schools, and other public places. Other laws bypassed the Fifteenth Amendment to prevent African Americans from voting. Thus, in the United States, as in Europe, democracy remained a goal rather than a reality for many citizens.

African Americans also faced economic hardships. Freed from slavery but without land, many ended up working as tenant farmers. To escape the bleak poverty of the postwar South, some headed west. Others migrated to the northern cities, seeking jobs in the factories that were springing to life.

Economic Growth and Social Reform

After the Civil War, the United States grew to lead the world in industrial and agricultural production. With seemingly unlimited natural resources

Biography

Abraham Lincoln 1809–1865

When he arrived in Washington in 1861, Abraham Lincoln was an unpolished Illinois lawyer with little political experience and no formal education. Yet for four years, he skillfully led the Union through the Civil War, the bloodiest conflict in American history. Throughout the long ordeal, Lincoln's dedication to preserving the Union never faltered.

He has been called "the Grand Harmonizer of the North" for his ability to solidify public opinion behind him as the war raged on. Yet Lincoln looked beyond the war to the future of the whole nation. In his second inaugural address, he expressed his dream for a reunited country: "With malice toward none; with charity for all; let us strive . . . to bind up the nation's wounds . . . to do all which may achieve and cherish a just, and a lasting peace, among ourselves, and with all nations."

Theme: Impact of the Individual How would you describe the popular image of Abraham Lincoln today?

Virtual Field Trip

Go Online
PHSchool.com

For: More photographs of immigrants in the late 1800s and early 1900s
Visit: PHSchool.com
Web Code: mkd-2412

New Immigrants to the United States
In this 1902 photograph, European immigrants crowd onto the deck of a ship as they sail into New York Harbor. For many, their first stop in the United States was the immigration center at Ellis Island.

Theme: Global Interaction
Why do you think these immigrants might have decided to come to the United States?

and the help of European capital, the economy boomed. Farm output soared as settlers flooded into the fertile farmlands of the Midwest. Mechanical reapers, plows, and threshers led to huge increases in farm production.

Industry and Transportation Industry grew even more rapidly. As in Europe, early progress came in the textile industry. Cotton mills used machines and cheap labor to turn out great quantities of mass-produced goods. Rich coal and iron resources fed other industries. A huge work force, swelled by waves of immigrants, labored in mines and factories.

A growing network of transportation and communication aided economic growth. The first transcontinental railroad was completed in 1869, opening up new opportunities for settlement and growth. In the early 1900s, Americans took to the automobile faster than Europeans. Henry Ford's "Model T" became the symbol of a new automobile era.

Immigration and the Growth of Cities The Industrial Revolution brought rapid urbanization. Millions of Americans left farms for jobs in the growing industrial cities. The nation's population soared as millions of immigrants arrived in the 1800s and early 1900s. They represented nearly every nationality and ethnic group, including Irish, German, Chinese, Italian, Scandinavian, Japanese, Eastern European Jews, and many others.

Most European immigrants settled first in cities on the Atlantic coast, while Asian immigrants filled cities on the Pacific coast. In time, newcomers spread out across the country. They worked in mines and factories, built railroads, and opened up farmlands in the West. Immigration made the United States "a nation of nations," with roots around the world.

Immigrants faced harsh conditions in crowded slum tenements. Often, newcomers suffered from prejudice and even violence from native-born Americans. In the West, whites hostile to Chinese workers pushed for laws to end immigration from China. For the first time, the United States began to close its "golden door."

Business and Labor By 1900, giant monopolies controlled whole industries. Scottish-born Andrew Carnegie built the nation's largest steel company, while John D. Rockefeller's Standard Oil Company dominated the world's petroleum industry. Big business enjoyed tremendous profits.

But the growing prosperity was not shared by all. In factories, wages were low and conditions were often brutal. To defend their interests, American workers organized labor unions such as the American Federation of Labor. Unions sought better wages, hours, and working conditions. Struggles with management sometimes erupted into violent confrontations. Slowly, however, workers made gains.

Populists and Progressives In the economic hard times of the late 1800s, farmers, too, organized to defend their interests. In the 1890s, they joined city workers to support the new Populist party. The Populists never became a major party, but their platform of reforms, such as an eight-hour workday, eventually became law.

By 1900, reformers known as Progressives again pressed for change. They sought laws to ban child labor, limit working hours, regulate monopolies, and give voters more power. Another major goal of the Progressives was votes for women. After a long struggle, American suffragists finally won the vote in 1920, when the Nineteenth Amendment went into effect.

Looking Ahead

By 1900, the United States was the world's largest democracy and its leading industrial giant. It was also acquiring a new role—that of a global power. In the Spanish American War of 1898, the United States acquired overseas territories, including the Philippines, Guam, and Puerto Rico.

Many Americans wanted to maintain their tradition of isolationism, or limited involvement in world affairs. This tradition dated back to George Washington, who had advised Americans to "steer clear of permanent alliances" with other nations. Expansionists, however, urged the nation to pursue global economic and military interests. "Whether they will or no, Americans must now begin to look outward," wrote influential expansionist Alfred T. Mahan. "The growing production of the country demands it."

In 1914, rivalries among European nations exploded into war. Although Americans sought to stay out of the conflict, World War I would eventually force the United States to take an even greater role on the world stage.

SECTION 4 Assessment

Recall

1. **Identify:** (a) Louisiana Purchase, (b) Manifest Destiny, (c) Frederick Douglass, (d) Abraham Lincoln, (e) Fifteenth Amendment, (f) Progressives.
2. **Define:** (a) expansionism, (b) abolitionist, (c) secede, (d) segregation, (e) isolationism.

Comprehension

3. Describe how the United States grew in each of these areas in the 1800s: (a) territory, (b) population, (c) economy.
4. Describe two ways that democracy expanded.

5. (a) How did immigrants benefit from economic growth in the United States after the Civil War? (b) What problems did workers face?

Critical Thinking and Writing

6. **Recognizing Causes and Effects** How do you think economic growth helped make the United States a world power?
7. **Linking Past and Present** Reread the poem by Emma Lazarus at the beginning of this section. How do these words still apply to the United States today?

Use the Internet to research the legacy of Andrew Carnegie's philanthropic efforts. Then, prepare a map of the United States showing places that benefited from his libraries and other gifts. For help with this activity, use **Web Code mkd-2413.**

Creating a Chapter Summary

On a sheet of paper, create a concept web to identify the main democratic reforms in Britain, France, and the United States during the 1800s. Use the web shown here to help you get started. Add as many circles as you need.

interactive Textbook

For additional review and enrichment activities, see the interactive version of *World History* available on the Web and on CD-ROM.

Go Online
PHSchool.com

For practice test questions for Chapter 11, use **Web Code mka-2414.**

Building Vocabulary

Use the chapter vocabulary words listed below to create a crossword puzzle. Exchange puzzles with a classmate. Complete the puzzles, and then check each other's answers.

1. **rotten borough**
2. **secret ballot**
3. **free trade**
4. **penal colony**
5. **home rule**
6. **provisional**
7. **coalition**
8. **abolitionist**
9. **segregation**
10. **isolationism**

Recalling Key Facts

11. What were the effects of the Reform Bill of 1832?

12. How did British policy toward slavery change in 1833?

13. How did British women's suffragists try to win the vote?

14. How did the party system in France's Third Republic differ from the British party system?

15. What was the main goal of the Zionist movement?

16. List two goals of progressive reformers in the United States.

Critical Thinking and Writing

17. **Identifying Main Ideas** Reread the subsection "A New Era in British Politics" in Section 1. Then, write a sentence summarizing the main idea of this subsection.

18. **Drawing Conclusions** Britain and France faced many similar political and social problems in the 1800s. Why do you think Britain was able to avoid the upheavals that plagued France?

19. **Recognizing Causes and Effects** **(a)** List two long-term and two immediate causes of the Great Hunger. **(b)** List two immediate effects. **(c)** Why do you think the famine sparked lasting feelings of bitterness against Britain?

20. **Applying Information** Describe how each of the following was related to nationalism: **(a)** the prestige of Queen Victoria, **(b)** the revolt of the Paris Commune, **(c)** the rise of Zionism.

21. **Connecting to Geography** How did the location of the United States encourage the American government to achieve its goal of Manifest Destiny?

The passage below is from *"J'Accuse!"* the letter that Émile Zola published in 1898. Read the passage, then answer the questions that follow.

> *"It is a crime to misdirect public opinion and to pervert it until it becomes delirious. It is a crime to poison small and simple minds, to rouse the passions of intolerance and reaction through the medium of that miserable antisemitism of which great and liberal France, with her Rights of Man, will expire if she is not soon cured. It is a crime to exploit patriotism for motives of hatred and it is a crime, finally, to make of the sword the modern god when all human science is at work to bring about a future of truth and justice. . . .*
>
> *I have but one passion—that of light. . . . Let them dare to bring me before the court of appeals and let an inquiry be made in broad daylight. I wait."*
>
> —Émile Zola, *Aurore,* January 13, 1898

22. What historical event is Zola describing?
23. **(a)** Whom is Zola accusing of crimes? **(b)** What are the crimes that Zola lists?
24. What does Zola say will happen to France if intolerance and antisemitism continue?
25. How does Zola appeal to the French people's pride in their history?
26. What does Zola mean when he says, "I have but one passion—that of light"?
27. What is the tone of this passage?
28. **(a)** What does Zola dare his opponents to do? **(b)** Why does he want them to do this? **(c)** Based on what you have read, did Zola succeed in his aim?

Go Online
PHSchool.com

Use the Internet to research leading figures in the women's suffrage movement in Britain, such as Emily Davidson, Constance Lytton, Christabel Pankhurst, or Annie Kenney. Then, with a partner, conduct a mock interview with one of these women. Include questions about her goals and what actions she took to achieve them. If possible, include actual quotations. For help with this activity, use **Web Code mkd-2415.**

This cartoon appeared in Britain in 1831. The man on the stilts is saying, "REFORM is become absolutely necessary—the Representation is corrupt—we have now representatives of Green Mounds, of Stone Walls, even of a Pig-sty, while many of our most populous manufacturing towns remain unrepresented." Study the cartoon, then answer the following questions:

29. What are "Green Mounds," "Stone Walls," and "Pig-sty"?
30. Why does the man on stilts say reform is necessary?
31. **(a)** What political position do the people on the ground represent? **(b)** Why are they in danger?
32. **(a)** Why would a British newspaper publish a cartoon about this issue in 1831? **(b)** How do you think the cartoonist felt about the issue? **(c)** Could the same cartoon have appeared in 1833? Why or why not?

Skills Tip

A political cartoon comments on events of its time. Knowing the date of a cartoon and the issues that were important at that time can help you understand the meaning of the cartoon.

The New Imperialism
1800–1914

Chapter Preview

1 **A Western-Dominated World**
2 **The Partition of Africa**
3 **European Challenges to the Muslim World**
4 **The British Take Over India**
5 **China and the New Imperialism**

1857

The Sepoy Rebellion breaks out in India. At the battle of Cawnpore, shown here, Indian cavalry charges a British line.

1805

Muhammad Ali is named governor of Egypt. This mosque in Cairo is named in his honor.

1830

France begins efforts to conquer Algeria in North Africa.

CHAPTER EVENTS

1800   1825   1850

GLOBAL EVENTS

1807 In the United States, Robert Fulton uses a steam engine to power a ship.

1848 Revolutions break out through much of Europe.

Imports From Africa and Asia About 1870

Legend:
- Industrialized nations
- Coal
- Coffee
- Copper
- Cotton
- Jute
- Silk
- Sugar
- Timber
- Wheat
- → Trade routes

EUROPE

ASIA

AFRICA

ATLANTIC OCEAN

INDIAN OCEAN

PACIFIC OCEAN

AUSTRALIA

N W E S

Robinson Projection

0 — 1000 — 2000 Miles
0 — 1000 — 2000 Kilometers

In the late 1800s, during the Age of Imperialism, the industrial powers of Europe sought raw materials from Africa and Asia.

1884
European officials meet at the Berlin Conference to settle rival land claims in Africa. No Africans are invited.

1899
Boer War erupts in South Africa.

1911
Sun Yixian becomes president of Chinese republic.

1875

1900

1925

Mid 1880s German engineers develop the first automobile.

1914 World War I begins in Europe.

A Western-Dominated World

Reading Focus

- What were the causes of the "new imperialism"?
- Why was western imperialism so successful?
- How did governments rule their empires?

Vocabulary

imperialism
protectorate
sphere of influence

Taking Notes

As you read, make an organizer like the model below showing the causes of imperialism in the 1800s. Add as many boxes as you need.

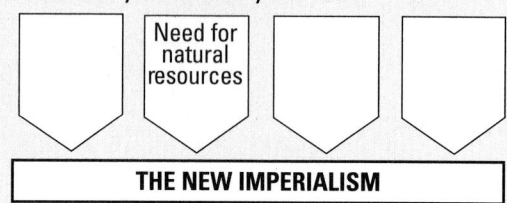

Need for natural resources

THE NEW IMPERIALISM

Main Idea In the late 1800s, industrial nations of the West engaged in imperialism and dominated much of the world.

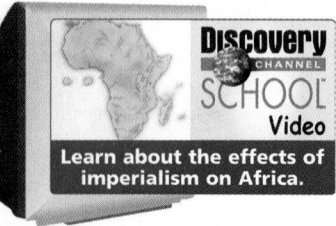

Learn about the effects of imperialism on Africa.

Setting the Scene When Edward VII inherited the British throne in 1901, his empire extended far beyond Britain. One writer boasted, "The sun never sets" on the British empire. In other words, because the empire circled the globe, the sun always shone on some part of it.

Like Britain, other western powers built overseas empires in the late 1800s. The Industrial Revolution and the growth of science and technology had transformed the West. Armed with new economic and political power, western nations set out to dominate the world.

The New Imperialism and Its Causes

European imperialism did not begin in the 1800s. Imperialism is the domination by one country of the political, economic, or cultural life of another country or region. As you have learned, European states won empires in the Americas after 1492, established colonies in South Asia, and gained toeholds on the coasts of Africa and China. Despite these gains, between 1500 and 1800, Europe had little influence on the lives of the peoples of China, India, or Africa.

By the 1800s, however, Europe had gained considerable power. Strong, centrally governed nation-states had emerged, and the Industrial Revolution had greatly enriched European economies. Encouraged by their new economic and military strength, Europeans embarked on a path of aggressive expansion that today's historians call the "new imperialism." Like other key developments in world history, the new imperialism exploded out of a combination of causes.

Economic Interests The Industrial Revolution created needs and desires that spurred overseas expansion. Manufacturers wanted access to natural resources such as rubber, petroleum, manganese for steel, and palm oil for machinery. They also hoped for new markets where they could sell their factory goods. In addition, colonies offered a valuable outlet for Europe's growing population. Lord Frederick Lugard, a British empire builder, tried to justify imperialism in Africa with these words:

> "The necessity that is upon us [is] to provide for our ever-growing population—either by opening new fields for emigration, or by providing work and employment . . . and to stimulate trade by finding new markets."
> —Lord Lugard, *The Rise of Our East African Empire*

Political and Military Interests Closely linked to economic motives were political and military issues. Steam-powered merchant ships and naval vessels needed bases around the world to take on coal and supplies. Industrial powers seized islands or harbors to satisfy these needs.

Nationalism played an important role, too. When France, for example, moved into West Africa, rival nations like Britain and Germany seized lands nearby to halt further French expansion. Western leaders claimed that colonies were needed for national security. They also felt that ruling a global empire increased a nation's prestige around the world.

Humanitarian Goals Many westerners felt a genuine concern for their "little brothers" beyond the seas. Missionaries, doctors, and colonial officials believed they had a duty to spread what they saw as the blessings of western civilization, including its medicine, law, and Christian religion.

Social Darwinism Behind the idea of a civilizing mission was a growing sense in the West of racial superiority. Many westerners had embraced the ideas of Social Darwinism. They applied Darwin's ideas about natural selection and survival of the fittest to human societies. European races, they argued, were superior to all others, and imperial conquest and destruction of weaker races were simply nature's way of improving the human species!

The Success of Western Imperialism

In just a few decades, from about 1870 to 1914, imperialist nations gained control over much of the world. Leading the way were soldiers, merchants, settlers, missionaries, and explorers. In Europe, imperial expansion found favor with all classes, from bankers and manufacturers to workers. Western imperialism succeeded for a number of reasons.

Weakness of Nonwestern States While European nations had grown stronger in the 1800s, several older civilizations were in decline, especially the Ottoman Middle East, Mughal India, and Qing China. In West Africa, wars among African peoples and the draining effect of the slave trade had undermined established empires, kingdoms, and city-states. Newer African states were not strong enough to resist the western onslaught.

Western Advantages Europeans had the advantages of strong economies, well-organized governments, and powerful armies and navies. Superior technology and improved medical knowledge also played a role. Quinine and other new medicines helped Europeans survive deadly tropical diseases. And, of course, advances such as Maxim machine guns, repeating rifles, and steam-driven warships were very strong arguments in persuading Africans and Asians to accept western control. As an English writer sarcastically noted: "Whatever happens, we have got the Maxim gun, and they have not."

Resistance Africans and Asians strongly resisted western expansion into their lands. Some people fought the invaders, even though they had no weapons to equal the Maxim gun. As you will read, ruling groups in certain areas tried to strengthen their societies against outsiders by reforming their own Muslim, Hindu, or Confucian traditions. Finally, many western-educated Africans and Asians organized nationalist movements to expel the imperialists from their lands.

Primary Source

"The White Man's Burden"
In the photo above, British writer Rudyard Kipling (front right) is one of several journalists in South Africa. Kipling promoted imperialism in his controversial poem, "The White Man's Burden":

"Take up the White Man's burden—
    Send forth the best ye breed—
Go bind your sons to exile
    To serve your captives' need. . . .
Take up the White Man's burden—
    The savage wars of peace—
Fill full the mouth of Famine,
    And bid the sickness cease;
And when your goal is nearest
    (The end for others sought)
Watch sloth and heathen folly
    Bring all your hope to nought.
                    —Rudyard Kipling,
            "The White Man's Burden"

Skills Assessment

Primary Source Why did Kipling consider imperialism to be beneficial?

The Maxim Gun
Britain's future King Edward VII tries his hand at the Maxim machine gun. Standing next to him is Sir Hiram Maxim, the gun's inventor.

Theme: Economics and Technology Why were European armies often able to defeat African or Asian forces?

Criticism at Home In the West itself, a small group of anti-imperialists emerged. Some argued that colonialism was a tool of the rich. Others said it was immoral. Westerners, they pointed out, were moving toward greater democracy at home but were imposing undemocratic rule on other people. "The new imperialism stood," one English critic protested, "not for a widened and ennobled sense of national responsibility, but for a hard assertion of racial supremacy and material force."

Forms of Imperial Rule

The new imperialism took several forms. In some areas, imperial powers established colonies. Elsewhere, they set up protectorates and spheres of influence.

Colonies France and Britain, the leading imperial powers, developed different kinds of colonial rule. The French practiced direct rule, sending officials and soldiers from France to administer their colonies. Their goal was to impose French culture on their colonies and turn them into French provinces.

The British, by contrast, relied on a system of indirect rule. To govern their colonies, they used sultans, chiefs, or other local rulers. They then encouraged the children of the local ruling class to get an education in Britain. In that way, they groomed a new "westernized" generation of leaders to continue indirect imperial rule and to spread British civilization. Like France and other imperialist nations, however, Britain could still resort to military force if its control over a colony was threatened in any way.

Protectorates In a protectorate, local rulers were left in place but were expected to follow the advice of European advisers on issues such as trade or missionary activity. A protectorate cost less to run than a colony did, and usually did not require a large commitment of military forces.

Spheres of Influence A third form of western control was the sphere of influence, an area in which an outside power claimed exclusive investment or trading privileges. Europeans carved out these spheres in China and elsewhere to prevent conflicts among themselves. The United States claimed Latin America as its sphere of influence.

SECTION 1 Assessment

Recall
1. **Identify:** (a) new imperialism, (b) direct rule, (c) indirect rule.
2. **Define:** (a) imperialism, (b) protectorate, (c) sphere of influence.

Comprehension
3. Describe three causes of the new imperialism.
4. (a) What were three reasons for the success of western imperialism? (b) How did people oppose western imperialism?
5. Describe three different forms of imperial rule.

Critical Thinking and Writing
6. **Analyzing Primary Sources** Review the words of Lord Lugard quoted at the start of this section. Explain why Lugard thought that it was necessary for Britain to pursue a policy of imperialism in Africa.
7. **Recognizing Bias** Western colonial officials and missionaries thought that they had a duty to spread the "blessings of western civilization" to their "little brothers" in Africa and Asia. How was this a biased viewpoint?

Activity

Making a Graphic Organizer
Make a graphic organizer that shows the various reasons for the success of western imperialism. Use the graphic organizers at the start of each section and at the end of each chapter for ideas on how to design your chart.

Reading Focus

- What forces were shaping Africa in the early 1800s?
- How did European contact with Africa increase?
- How did Leopold II start a scramble for colonies?
- How did Africans resist imperialism?

Vocabulary

missionary

elite

Taking Notes

As you read, create a concept web like the model below that lists examples of African resistance against imperialism. Add as many circles as needed to complete the web.

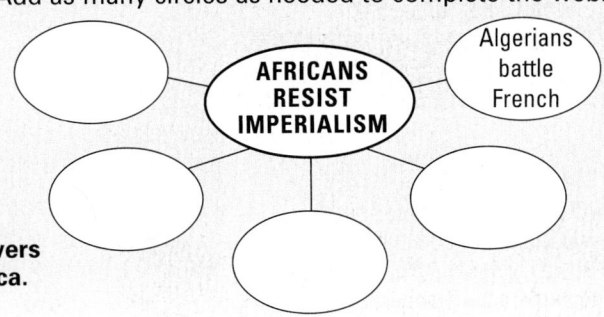

AFRICANS RESIST IMPERIALISM

Algerians battle French

Main Idea By the end of the 1800s, the imperialist powers of Europe claimed control over most of Africa.

Setting the Scene

In the late 1800s, Britain, France, Germany, and other European powers swept into Africa. Chief Machemba of the Yao people in East Africa wrote in Swahili to a German officer:

> "If it be friendship that you desire, then I am ready for it . . . but to be your subject, that I cannot be. . . . I do not fall at your feet, for you are God's creature just as I am."
>   —Chief Machemba, Letter to Herman von Wissman

Though the Yao and others resisted, they could not prevent European conquest. Within about 20 years, the Europeans had carved up the continent and dominated millions of Africans.

Chicago 4 lyfe

Africa in the Early 1800s

To understand the impact of European domination, we must look at Africa in the early 1800s, before the scramble for colonies began. Africa is a huge continent, four times the size of Europe. Across its many regions, people spoke hundreds of languages and had developed varied governments. Some people lived in large centralized states, others in village communities.

North Africa North Africa includes the enormous Sahara and the fertile land along the Mediterranean. Since long before 1800, the region had close ties to the Muslim world. In the early 1800s, much of North Africa remained under the rule of the declining Ottoman empire.

West Africa In West Africa, a reform movement stimulated the growth of Islam throughout the region and led to the creation of a new Muslim empire. Leaders like Usman dan Fodio urged followers to revive and purify Islam. Under these leaders, Muslim revolutionaries overthrew their rulers and established the Sokoto caliphate.

In the forest regions, strong states like the Asante kingdom had arisen. The Asante traded with Europeans and Muslims and controlled several smaller states. However, these tributary states were ready to turn to Europeans or others who might help them defeat their Asante rulers.

East Africa Islam had long influenced the east coast of Africa, where port cities like Mombasa and Kilwa carried on profitable trade. The cargoes were often slaves. Captives were marched from the interior to the coast to be shipped as slaves to the Middle East. Ivory and copper from Central Africa were also exchanged for goods such as cloth and firearms from India.

The Ivory Trade
East African merchants profited from the ivory trade. For centuries, artists around the world made beautiful ivory carvings. Today, international law severely limits the trade in order to protect declining elephant populations.

Theme: Economics and Technology Besides ivory, what was another source of profits for merchants in East Africa?

Go Online
PHSchool.com

For: Further information on the life and work of Dr. David Livingstone
Visit: PHSchool.com
Web Code: mkd-2522

Livingstone and Victoria Falls

After recovering from bouts of malaria and rheumatic fever, Dr. David Livingstone set out in 1853 to explore the Zambesi River valley. On November 17, 1855, he viewed the magnificent site that we know today as Victoria Falls.

Theme: Geography and History Why was exploration of Africa difficult?

Southern Africa In the early 1800s, southern Africa was in turmoil. Shaka, you will recall, united the Zulu nation. His conquests, however, set off mass migrations and wars, creating chaos across much of the region. By the 1830s, the Zulus were also battling the Boers, who were migrating north from the Cape Colony.

The Slave Trade In the early 1800s, European nations began to outlaw the transatlantic slave trade, though it took years to end it. Meanwhile, the East African slave trade, continued to the Middle East and Asia.

Some people in Britain and the United States helped freed slaves resettle in Africa. In 1787, the British organized Sierra Leone in West Africa as a colony for former slaves. Later, some free blacks from the United States settled in nearby Liberia. By 1847, Liberia became an independent republic.

European Contacts Increase

From the 1500s through the 1700s, Europeans traded along the African coast. Difficult geography and diseases kept them from reaching the interior. Medical advances and river steamships changed all that in the 1800s.

Explorers In the early 1800s, European explorers began pushing into the interior of Africa. Daring adventurers like Mungo Park and Richard Burton set out to map the course and sources of the great African rivers such as the Niger, the Nile, and the Congo. These explorers were fascinated by African geography, but they had little understanding of the peoples they met. All, however, endured great hardships in pursuit of their dreams.

Missionaries Catholic and Protestant missionaries followed the explorers. All across Africa, they sought to win people to Christianity. The missionaries were sincere in their desire to help Africans. They built schools and medical clinics alongside churches. They also focused attention on the evils of the slave trade.

Still, missionaries, like most westerners, took a paternalistic view of Africans. They saw them as children in need of guidance. To them, African cultures and religions were "degraded." They urged Africans to reject their own traditions in favor of western civilization.

Livingstone The best known explorer-missionary was Dr. David Livingstone. For 30 years, he crisscrossed Africa. He wrote about the many peoples he met with more sympathy and less bias than did most Europeans. He relentlessly opposed the slave trade, which remained a profitable business for some African rulers and foreign traders. The only way to end this cruel traffic, he believed, was to open up the interior of Africa to Christianity and trade.

Livingstone blazed a trail that others soon followed. In 1869, the journalist Henry Stanley trekked into Central Africa to find Livingstone, who had not been heard from for years. He finally tracked him down in 1871 in what is today Tanzania, greeting him with the now-legendary phrase "Dr. Livingstone, I presume?"

A Scramble for Colonies

Shortly afterward, King Leopold II of Belgium hired Stanley to explore the Congo River basin and arrange trade treaties with African leaders. Publicly, Leopold spoke of a civilizing mission to carry the light "that for millions of men still plunged in barbarism will be the dawn of a better era." Privately, he dreamed of conquest and profit.

Skills Assessment

Geography During the late 1800s, European countries took part in a scramble for Africa. They claimed control of nearly the whole continent by 1914.

1. **Location** On the map, locate (a) Algeria, (b) Belgian Congo, (c) Ethiopia.
2. **Region** In which part of Africa were most of France's colonies located?
3. **Critical Thinking** **Making Inferences** How can you tell from the map that Africans did not willingly accept European domination?

Imperialism in Africa to 1914

SPANISH MOROCCO 1912
Tangier
Algiers • Tunis
Mediterranean Sea
FRENCH MOROCCO 1912
TUNISIA 1881
• Tripoli
IFNI 1860
Alexandria
Suez Canal
Cairo
ATLANTIC OCEAN
RIO DE ORO 1885
ALGERIA 1830
LIBYA 1912
EGYPT 1882
Red Sea
30°N

FR. SOMALILAND 1884
ERITREA 1890
• Adowa
BR. SOMALILAND 1889
15°N

FRENCH WEST AFRICA 1874
GAMBIA 1888
PORTUGUESE GUINEA 1901
SIERRA LEONE 1808
GOLD COAST 1874
NIGERIA 1884
ANGLO-EGYPTIAN SUDAN 1889
• Fashoda
• Addis Ababa
ETHIOPIA (Independent)
ITALIAN SOMALILAND 1884
INDIAN OCEAN

LIBERIA (Independent)
TOGO 1884
CAMEROONS 1884
UGANDA 1895
BRITISH EAST AFRICA (KENYA) 1886

FRENCH EQUATORIAL AFRICA 1910
RÍO MUNI 1900
BELGIAN CONGO 1908
GERMAN EAST AFRICA (TANGANYIKA) 1885
ZANZIBAR (British Protectorate) 1890
Equator 0°

CABINDA 1886
ANGOLA 1891
NORTHERN RHODESIA 1891
NYASALAND 1891
MOZAMBIQUE 1500
MADAGASCAR 1895
15°S

GERMAN SOUTHWEST AFRICA 1884
SOUTHERN RHODESIA 1890
BECHUANALAND 1885
Johannesburg
SWAZILAND 1907
UNION OF SOUTH AFRICA 1910
BASUTOLAND 1871
• Cape Town
30°S

Mercator Projection
0   500   1000 Miles
0   500   1000 Kilometers

N W E S

Legend:
- Belgian
- British
- French
- German
- Italian
- Portuguese
- Spanish
- ★ Outbreaks of anticolonial resistance
- Dates on map indicate year of official colonization

European Colonies in Africa About 1850

0   1000   2000 Miles
0   1000   2000 Kilometers

Niger R.
Nile R.
Congo R.
Zambezi
Orange R.

15°E   30°E   45°E

King Leopold's activities in the Congo set off a scramble by other European nations. Before long, Britain, France, and Germany were pressing rival claims to the region.

Berlin Conference To avoid bloodshed, European powers met at an international conference in 1884. It took place not in Africa but in Berlin, Germany. No Africans were invited to the conference.

At the Berlin Conference, European powers recognized Leopold's private claims to the Congo Free State but called for free trade on the Congo and Niger rivers. They further agreed that a European power could not claim any part of Africa unless it had set up a government office there. This principle led Europeans to send officials who would exert their power over local rulers and peoples.

The rush to colonize Africa was on. In the 20 years after the Berlin Conference, the European powers partitioned almost the entire continent. As Europeans carved out their claims, they established new borders and frontiers. They redrew the map of Africa with little regard for traditional patterns of settlement or ethnic boundaries.

Horrors in the Congo Leopold and other wealthy Belgians, meantime, exploited the riches of the Congo, including its copper, rubber, and ivory. Soon, there were horrifying reports of Belgian overseers brutalizing villagers. Forced to work for almost nothing, laborers were savagely beaten or mutilated. The population of some areas declined drastically.

Eventually, international outrage forced Leopold to turn over his colony to the Belgian government. It became the Belgian Congo in 1908. Under Belgian rule, the worst abuses were ended. Still, the Belgians regarded the Congo as a possession to be exploited. Africans were given little or no role in either the government or the economy of the colony.

French Expansion France took a giant share of Africa. In the 1830s, it had invaded and conquered Algeria in North Africa. The victory cost tens of thousands of French lives and killed many times more Algerians. In the late 1800s, France extended its influence along the Mediterranean into Tunisia. It also won colonies in West and Central Africa. At its height, the French empire in Africa was as large as the continental United States.

Britain Takes Its Share Britain's share of Africa was smaller and more scattered than that of France. However, it included more heavily populated regions with many rich resources. Britain took chunks of West and East Africa. It gained control of Egypt, and pushed south into the Sudan.

In southern Africa, Britain clashed with the Boers, who were descendants of Dutch settlers. Britain had acquired the Cape Colony from the Dutch in 1815. At that time, many Boers fled British rule. They migrated north and set up their own republics. In the late 1800s, however, the discovery of gold and diamonds in the Boer lands led to conflict with Britain. The Boer War, which lasted from 1899 to 1902, involved bitter guerrilla fighting. The British won, but at great cost.

In 1910, the British united the Cape Colony and the former Boer republics into the Union of South Africa. The new constitution set up a government run by whites and laid the foundation for a system of complete racial segregation that would remain in force until 1993.

Others Join the Scramble Other European powers joined the scramble for colonies, in part to bolster their national image, in part to further their economic growth and influence. The Portuguese carved out large colonies in Angola and Mozambique. Italy reached across the Mediterranean to occupy Libya and then pushed into the "horn" of Africa, at the southern end of the Red Sea. The newly united German empire took lands in eastern and southwestern Africa. A German politician, trying to ease the worries of

A Royal Gift
In 1908, German colonizers met with Njoya, ruler of the West African kingdom of Bamum. King Njoya presented this ornate throne as a gift for Kaiser William II.

Theme: Global Interaction
Why do you think Njoya wanted to give a gift to the German ruler?

A Schoolroom in East Africa

This photograph, dated 1903, was taken in a German missionary school in East Africa. The pictures on the wall are of Kaiser William II and his wife, Augusta.

Skills Tip

Although photographs show real scenes, be careful not to draw conclusions that are too broad. A single photograph may not show important details. A different picture might suggest a different story.

Skills Assessment

1. When this picture was taken, the students were taking a lesson in
   A arithmetic.
   B reading.
   C art.
   D music.

2. Which is the most valid conclusion that you can draw from this photograph?
   E Africans resented German colonial rule.
   F Germany educated young Africans to help rule their colonies.
   G Colonial classrooms did not allow girls.
   H In some lands, colonial powers provided basic education.

3. **Critical Thinking** **Drawing Conclusions** Select three details that you see in this photograph. **(a)** What does each detail suggest about this classroom and the people in it? **(b)** What additional information might help you check if your conclusions are valid?

Biography

Menelik II 1844–1913

Before becoming emperor of Ethiopia, Menelik II ruled the Shoa region in central Ethiopia. He ensured that he would succeed John IV as emperor by marrying John's daughter. After John died in 1889, Menelik took the throne.

Menelik used profits from ivory sales to buy modern weapons. He then hired European advisers to teach his soldiers how to use the new guns. Menelik's army conquered neighboring lands and won a stunning victory over the Italians at Adowa. European nations rushed to establish diplomatic ties with Ethiopia. Around the world, people of African descent hailed Menelik's victory over European imperialism.

Theme: Impact of the Individual How did Menelik preserve Ethiopian independence?

European rivals, explained, "We do not want to put anyone in the shade, but we also demand our place in the sun."

Africans Resist Imperialism

Europeans met armed resistance across the continent. The Algerians battled the French for years. Samori Touré fought French forces in West Africa, where he was building his own empire. The British battled the Zulus in southern Africa and the Asante in West Africa. When their king was exiled, the Asante put themselves under the command of their queen, Yaa Asantewaa. She led the fight against the British in the last Asante war. Another woman who became a military leader was Nehanda, of the Shona in Zimbabwe. Although a clever tactician, Nehanda was captured and executed. However, the memory of her achievements inspired later generations to fight for freedom.

In East Africa, the Germans fought wars against people like the Yao and Herero. Fighting was especially fierce in the Maji-Maji Rebellion of 1905. The Germans triumphed only after using a scorched-earth policy. To crush resistance, they burned acres and acres of farmland, leaving thousands of local people to die of starvation.

Ethiopia Survives Successful resistance was mounted by Ethiopia. This ancient Christian kingdom had survived in the highlands of East Africa. But, like feudal Europe, it had been divided up among a number of rival princes who ruled their own domains.

In the late 1800s, a reforming ruler, Menelik II, began to modernize his country. He hired European experts to plan modern roads and bridges and set up a western school system. He imported the latest weapons and European officers to help train his army. Thus, when Italy invaded Ethiopia in 1896, Menelik was prepared. At the battle of Adowa (ah DUH wah), the Ethiopians smashed the Italian invaders. Ethiopia was the only African nation, aside from Liberia, to preserve its independence.

New African Elite During the Age of Imperialism, a western-educated African elite, or upper class, emerged. Some middle-class Africans admired western ways and rejected their own culture. Others valued their African traditions and condemned western societies that upheld liberty and equality for whites only. By the early 1900s, African leaders were forging nationalist movements to pursue self-determination and independence.

SECTION 2 Assessment

Recall

1. **Identify:** (a) Asante, (b) Liberia, (c) David Livingstone, (d) Berlin Conference, (e) Boer War, (f) Nehanda, (g) Menelik II.
2. **Define:** (a) missionary, (b) elite.

Comprehension

3. Describe one development in each region of Africa in the early 1800s.
4. How did European contact with Africa increase?
5. Which European nations were most successful in the scramble for African colonies?

6. Describe two examples of African resistance to European imperialism.

Critical Thinking and Writing

7. **Making Inferences** (a) Why do you think the Europeans did not invite Africans to the Berlin Conference? (b) What might be the effect of this exclusion upon later African leaders?
8. **Connecting to Geography** Review the maps of Africa in this section. Why do you think Britain, France, and Italy were all interested in controlling part of Somaliland?

PHSchool.com

Use the Internet to find out more about David Livingstone. Then, prepare a brief biography of him. You may wish to illustrate the biography with a map showing Livingstone's explorations and a chart describing his missionary activities. For help with this activity, use **Web Code mkd-2526.**

European Challenges to the Muslim World

Reading Focus

- What were sources of stress in the Muslim world?
- What problems did the Ottoman empire face?
- How did Egypt seek to modernize?
- Why were European powers interested in Iran?

Vocabulary

pasha
genocide
concession

Taking Notes

As you read, prepare an outline. Use Roman numerals for major headings, capital letters for subheadings, and numbers for supporting details. The incomplete model below will help you get started.

> I. Stresses in the Muslim world
>   A. Empires in decline
>   1.
>   2.
>   B.
>   C.
> II. Problems for the Ottoman empire
>   A.

Main Idea During the 1800s, European nations extended their power into parts of the Muslim world.

Setting the Scene "Europe is a molehill," said Napoleon Bonaparte in 1797. He felt it offered too few chances for glory. "We must go to the East," he declared. "All great glory has been acquired there." In 1798, he put his thoughts into action by invading Egypt, a province of the Ottoman empire.

Napoleon's Egyptian campaign highlighted Ottoman decline and opened a new era of European contact with the Muslim world. In the early 1800s, European countries were just nibbling at the edges of the Muslim world. Before long, they would strike at its heartlands.

Stresses in the Muslim World

The Muslim world extended from western Africa to Southeast Asia. In the 1500s, three giant Muslim empires ruled much of this world—the Mughals in India, the Ottomans in the Middle East, and the Safavids in Iran.

Empires in Decline By the 1700s, all three Muslim empires were in decline. The decay had many causes. Central governments had lost control over powerful groups such as landowning nobles, military elites, and urban craft guilds. Corruption was widespread. In some places, Muslim scholars and religious leaders were allied with the state. In other areas, they helped to stir discontent against the government.

Islamic Reform Movement In the 1700s and early 1800s, reform movements sprang up across the Muslim world. Most stressed religious piety and strict rules of behavior. The Wahhabi movement in Arabia, for example, rejected the schools of theology and law that had emerged in the Ottoman empire. In their place, they wanted to recapture the purity and simplicity of Muhammad's original teachings. An Arab prince led the Wahhabis against Ottoman rule. Although the revolt was crushed, the Wahhabi movement survived. Its teachings are influential in the kingdom of Saudi Arabia today.

Islamic revivals rose in Africa, too. As you have read, Usman dan Fodio led the struggle to reform Muslim practices. In the Sudan, south of Egypt, Muhammad Ahmad announced that he was the Mahdi, the long-awaited savior of the faith. In the 1880s, the Mahdi and his followers fiercely resisted British expansion into the region.

European Imperialism In addition to internal decay and stress, the old Muslim empires faced western imperialism. Through diplomacy and military threats, European powers won treaties giving them favorable

Constantinople
People from all over the world met and traded at Constantinople. The capital of the Ottoman empire was located on the Bosporus.
Theme: Geography and History Why did Russia hope to gain control of the Bosporus?

trading terms. They then demanded special rights for Europeans residing in Muslim lands. At times, European powers protected those rights by intervening in local affairs. Sometimes, they took over an entire region.

Problems for the Ottoman Empire

At its height, the Ottoman empire had extended across the Middle East, North Africa, and Southeastern Europe. By the early 1800s, however, it faced serious challenges. Ambitious pashas, or provincial rulers, had increased their power. Economic problems and corruption added to Ottoman decay.

Nationalist Revolts As ideas of nationalism spread from Western Europe, internal revolts weakened the multiethnic Ottoman empire. Subject peoples in Eastern Europe, the Middle East, and North Africa threatened to break away. In the Balkans, Greeks, Serbs, Bulgarians, and Romanians gained their independence. Revolts against Ottoman rule also erupted in Arabia, Lebanon, and Armenia. The Ottomans suppressed these uprisings, but another valuable territory, Egypt, slipped out of their control.

European Pressure European states sought to benefit from the slow crumbling of the Ottoman empire. After seizing Algeria in the 1830s, France hoped to gain more Ottoman territory. Russia schemed to gain control of the Bosporus and the Dardanelles. Control of these straits would give the Russians access to the Mediterranean Sea. Britain tried to thwart Russia's ambitions, which it saw as a threat to its own power in the Mediterranean and beyond it to India. And in 1898, the new German empire jumped onto the bandwagon, hoping to increase its influence in the region by building a Berlin-to-Baghdad railway.

Efforts to Westernize Since the late 1700s, several Ottoman rulers had seen the need for reform and looked to the West for ideas. They reorganized the bureaucracy and system of tax collection. They built railroads, improved education, and hired European officers to train a modern military. Young men were sent to the West to study the new sciences and technology. Many returned home with western ideas about democracy and equality.

The reforms also brought better medical care and revitalized farming. These improvements, however, were a mixed blessing. Better living conditions resulted in a population explosion. The growing population increased competition for the best land, which led to unrest.

The adoption of western ideas about government also increased tension. Many officials objected to changes that were inspired by a foreign culture. For their part, repressive sultans rejected reform and tried to rebuild the autocratic power enjoyed by earlier rulers.

Young Turks In the 1890s, a group of liberals formed a movement called the Young Turks. They insisted that reform was the only way to save the empire. In 1908, the Young Turks overthrew the sultan. Before they could achieve their planned reforms, however, the Ottoman empire was plunged into the world war that erupted in 1914.

Massacre of Armenians Traditionally, the Ottomans had let minority nationalities live in their own communities and practice their own religions. By the 1890s, however, nationalism was igniting new tensions, especially between

Turkish nationalists and minority peoples who sought their own states. These tensions triggered a brutal genocide of the Armenians, a Christian people concentrated in the eastern mountains of the empire. **Genocide** is a deliberate attempt to destroy an entire religious or ethnic group.

The Muslim Turks distrusted the Christian Armenians and accused them of supporting Russian plans against the Ottoman empire. When Armenians protested repressive Ottoman policies, the sultan had tens of thousands of them slaughtered. Over the next 25 years, a million or more Armenians in the Ottoman empire were killed.

Egypt Seeks to Modernize

Egypt in 1800 was a semi-independent province of the Ottoman empire. In the early 1800s, it made great strides toward reform. Its success was due to Muhammad Ali, who was appointed governor of Egypt in 1805.

Muhammad Ali Muhammad Ali is sometimes called the "father of modern Egypt." To strengthen Egypt, he introduced a number of political and economic reforms. He improved tax collection, reorganized the landholding system, and backed large irrigation projects to increase farm output. By expanding cotton production and encouraging the development of local industry, he increased Egyptian participation in world trade.

Muhammad Ali also brought western military experts to Egypt to help him build a well-trained, modern army. He conquered the neighboring lands of Arabia, Syria, and Sudan. Before he died in 1849, he had set Egypt on the road to becoming a major Middle Eastern power.

The Suez Canal Muhammad Ali's successors lacked his skills, and Egypt came increasingly under foreign control. In 1859, a French entrepreneur, Ferdinand de Lesseps, organized a company to build the Suez Canal. This

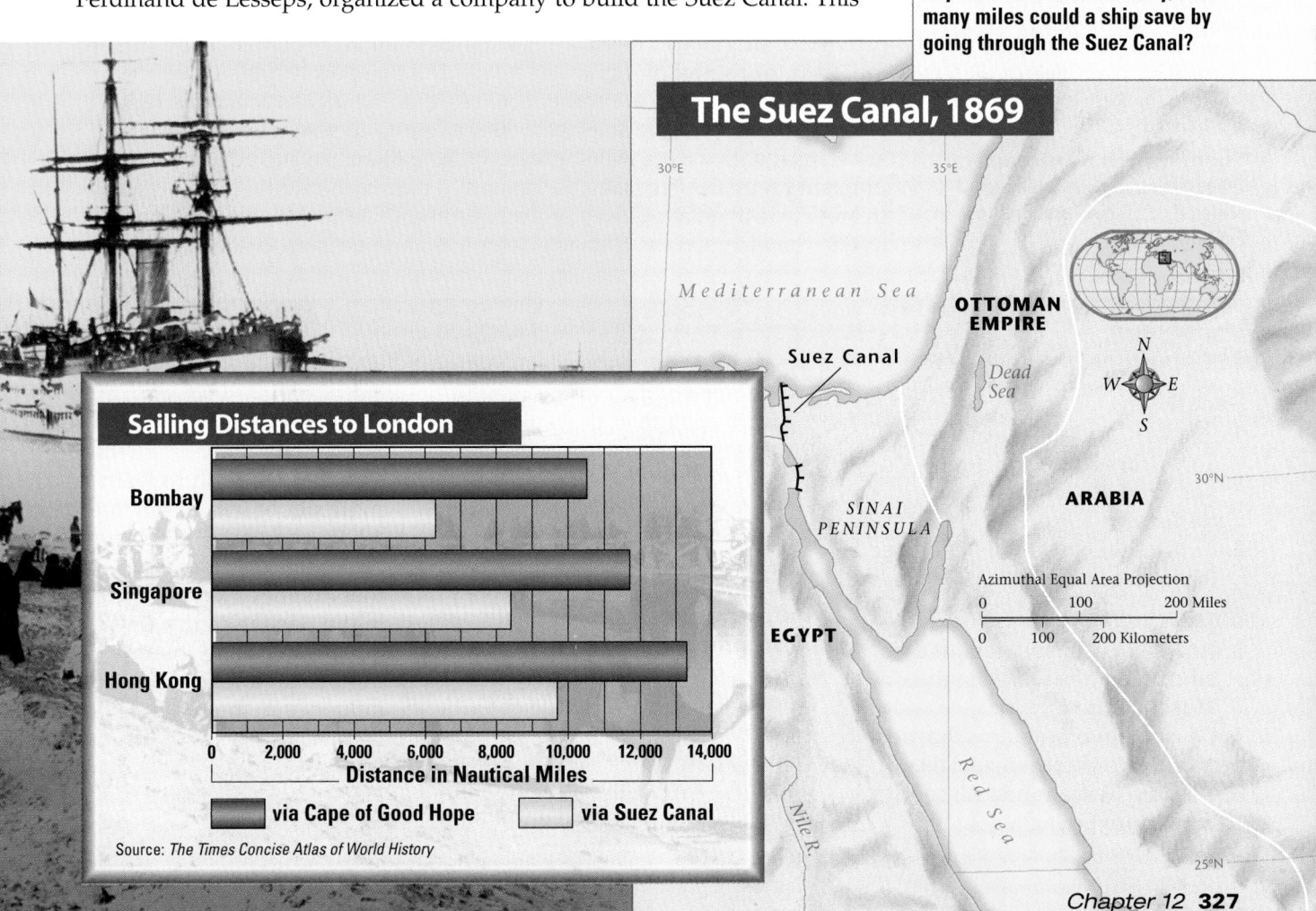

The Suez Canal, 1869

Mediterranean Sea

OTTOMAN EMPIRE

Suez Canal

Dead Sea

ARABIA

SINAI PENINSULA

30°N

EGYPT

Azimuthal Equal Area Projection

0   100   200 Miles

0   100   200 Kilometers

Red Sea

Nile R.

25°N

Sailing Distances to London

Bombay

Singapore

Hong Kong

0   2,000   4,000   6,000   8,000   10,000   12,000   14,000
Distance in Nautical Miles

■ via Cape of Good Hope   □ via Suez Canal

Source: *The Times Concise Atlas of World History*

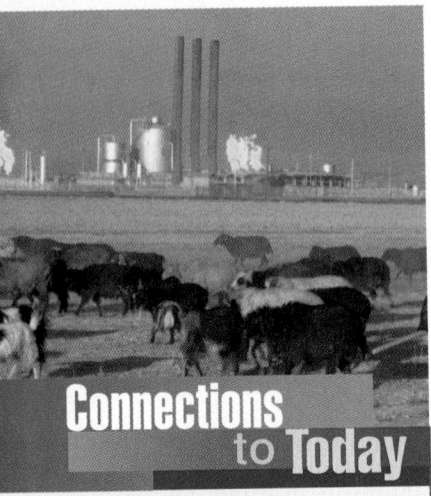

Connections to Today

The Power of Oil
In the early 1900s, Russia and Britain competed for oil in the Middle East. Today, the vast petroleum deposits in the region are controlled by Middle Eastern countries themselves.

Oil produces enormous wealth for countries in the Middle East. Industrialized nations rely on imported oil to produce electricity, run factories, and fuel vehicles. In the Organization of Petroleum Exporting Countries (OPEC), oil-producing countries of the Middle East and other world regions try to maximize their profits through cooperation. They influence oil prices by controlling how much oil is produced.

Theme: Global Interaction
What do you think happens to oil prices if OPEC cuts production? Explain.

100-mile waterway links the Mediterranean and Red seas. (See the map on the previous page.) Europeans hailed its opening in 1869 because it greatly shortened the sea route from Europe to South and East Asia. To Britain, especially, the canal was a "lifeline" to India.

In 1875, the ruler of Egypt was unable to repay loans he had contracted for the canal and other modernization projects. To pay his debts, he was forced to sell his shares in the canal. British prime minister Disraeli quickly bought the shares, giving Britain a controlling interest in the canal.

A British Protectorate When Egyptian nationalists revolted against foreign influence in 1882, Britain made Egypt a protectorate. In theory, the governor of Egypt was still an official of the Ottoman government. In fact, he followed policies dictated by Britain. Under British influence, Egypt continued to modernize. At the same time, however, nationalist discontent simmered and flared into protests and riots well into the next century.

Iran and the European Powers

Like the Ottoman empire, Iran faced major challenges in the 1800s. The Qajar (kah JAHR) shahs, who ruled Iran from 1794 to 1925, exercised absolute power like the Safavids before them. Still, they did take steps to introduce reforms. The government improved finances, sponsored the building of telegraph lines and railroads, and even experimented with a liberal constitution.

Reform, however, did not save Iran from western imperialism. Both Russia and Britain battled for influence in the area. Russia wanted to protect its southern frontier and expand into Central Asia. Britain was concerned about protecting its interests in India.

For a time, each nation set up its own sphere of influence in Iran. Russia operated in the north and Britain in the south. The discovery of oil in the early 1900s heightened foreign interest in the region. Both Russia and Britain intrigued for control of Iranian oil fields. The two powers persuaded the Iranian government to grant them concessions, or special economic rights given to foreign powers. To protect their interests, they sent troops into Iran.

Iranian nationalists were outraged. The nationalists included two very different groups. Some Iranians, especially the urban middle class, wanted to move swiftly to adopt western ways. Others, led by Muslim religious leaders, condemned the Iranian government and western influences.

SECTION 3 Assessment

Recall
1. **Identify:** (a) Mahdi, (b) Young Turks, (c) Armenians, (d) Muhammad Ali, (e) Suez Canal, (f) Qajars.
2. **Define:** (a) pasha, (b) genocide, (c) concession.

Comprehension
3. How did European nations take advantage of stresses in the Muslim world?
4. Describe two problems that contributed to Ottoman decline.
5. How did Muhammad Ali seek to modernize Egypt?

6. Why did Russia and Britain compete for power in Iran?

Critical Thinking and Writing
7. **Linking Past and Present** (a) How did Turkish nationalism lead to intolerance of minorities in the Ottoman empire? (b) Describe a present-day example of nationalism's causing intolerance of others.
8. **Solving Problems** Suppose you are an Ottoman government official in the 1800s. Recommend and explain a series of actions that you think will solve the problems afflicting the Ottoman empire.

Activity

Making a Time Line
Conduct research to learn more about Iran in the late 1800s and early 1900s. Then, make a time line that identifies key events in the decline of the Qajar government and the rise of Russian and British influence in the region.

The British Take Over India

Reading Focus

- What were the causes and effects of the Sepoy Rebellion?
- How did British rule affect India?
- How did Indians view western culture?
- What were the origins of Indian nationalism?

Vocabulary

sati
sepoy
viceroy
deforestation
purdah

Taking Notes

As you read this section, make a flowchart to show the events that led to increased British control of India. Use the incomplete chart below as a model.

```
┌─────────────────────────────────┐
│   British East India Company     │
│        gets trading rights       │
└─────────────────────────────────┘
                 ↓
┌─────────────────────────────────┐
│      British officials introduce │
│     western education and law    │
└─────────────────────────────────┘
                 ↓
┌─────────────────────────────────┐
│                                  │
└─────────────────────────────────┘
                 ↓
┌─────────────────────────────────┐
│                                  │
└─────────────────────────────────┘
```

Main Idea Despite Indian opposition, Britain gradually extended its control over most of India.

Setting the Scene Ranjit Singh ruled the large Sikh empire in northwestern India during the early 1800s. He had cordial dealings with the British but saw only too well where their ambitions were headed. One day, he was looking at a map of India on which British-held lands were shaded red. "All will one day become red!" he predicted.

Not long after Ranjit Singh's death in 1839, the British conquered the Sikh empire. They added its 100,000 square miles to their steadily growing lands. As Singh had forecast, India was falling under British control.

East India Company and Sepoy Rebellion

In the early 1600s, the British East India Company won trading rights on the fringe of the Mughal empire. As Mughal power declined, the company's influence grew. By the mid-1800s, it controlled three fifths of India.

Exploiting Indian Diversity The British were able to conquer such a vast territory by exploiting the diversity of India. Even when Mughal power was at its height, India was home to many people and cultures. As Mughal power crumbled, India fragmented. Indians with different traditions and dozens of different languages were not able to unite against the newcomers. The British took advantage of Indian divisions by encouraging competition and disunity among rival princes. Where British diplomacy or intrigue did not work, their superior weapons overpowered local rulers.

British Policies The East India Company's main goal in India was to make money, and leading officials often got very rich. At the same time, the company did work to improve roads, preserve peace, and reduce banditry.

By the early 1800s, British officials introduced western education and legal procedures. Missionaries tried to convert Indians to Christianity, which they felt was far superior to Indian religions. The British also pressed for social change. They worked to end slavery and the caste system and to improve the position of women within the family. One law outlawed sati, a Hindu custom practiced mainly by the upper classes. It called for a widow to join her husband in death by throwing herself on his funeral fire.

Causes of Discontent In the 1850s, the East India Company made several unpopular moves. First, it required sepoys, or Indian soldiers in its service, to serve anywhere, either in India or overseas. For high-caste Hindus, however, overseas travel was an offense against their religion. Second, it

Global Connections

"Thank God for Tea!"

The British East India Company made a fortune by importing tea—a drink with a long history. According to legend, a Chinese emperor discovered tea thousands of years ago when windblown leaves fell into a pot of boiling water. Buddhist monks brought the drink to Japan and made it part of their meditation rites. Europeans did not become acquainted with the pleasure of tea until the 1600s—but they caught on quickly.

In England, tea was first used as a medicinal drink only. However, it soon became common to have tea every afternoon. The custom became a regular social event. People invited friends for afternoon tea served with cake, bread, and butter. By the 1800s, tea was considered an essential part of English culture, moving one writer to offer special thanks: "Thank God for tea! What would the world do without tea?—how did it exist? I am glad I was not born before tea."

Theme: Global Interaction
Why did the British East India Company earn huge profits?

Imperialism in India to 1858

British colonies in 1765

Territory under British rule in 1805

Territory under British rule in 1858

Main area affected by Sepoy Rebellion

KASHMIR

PUNJAB

Indus R.

Brahmaputra R.

30°N

Delhi

NORTHWEST PROVINCES

RAJPUTANA

SIND

BIHAR

Ganges R.

ASSAM

BENGAL

Calcutta

ARAKAN

Narmada R.

BERAR

Bombay

HYDERABAD

Arabian Sea

Bay of Bengal

15°N

Goa (Portuguese)

MYSORE

Madras

Andaman Islands

Pondicherry (French)

N W E S

CEYLON

Mercator Projection

0   300   600 Miles

0   300   600 Kilometers

INDIAN OCEAN

75°E

90°E

Skills Assessment

Geography Britain controlled all of India by 1858. British officials ruled some areas directly and other areas through local Indian rulers.

1. **Location** On the map, locate **(a)** Punjab, **(b)** Delhi, **(c)** Hyderabad, **(d)** Madras.
2. **Region** Which regions were most greatly affected by the Sepoy Rebellion?
3. **Critical Thinking**
   Asking Questions Write three questions based on information on the map.

passed a law that allowed Hindu widows to remarry. Hindus viewed both moves as a Christian conspiracy to undermine their beliefs.

Then, in 1857, the British issued new rifles to the sepoys. Troops were told to bite off the tips of cartridges before loading them into the rifles. The cartridges, however, were greased with animal fat—either from cows, which Hindus considered sacred, or from pigs, which were forbidden to Muslims. When the troops refused the order to "load rifles," they were sent home without pay.

Rebellion and Aftermath Angry sepoys rose up against their British officers. The Sepoy Rebellion swept across northern and central India. Several sepoy regiments marched off to Delhi, the old Mughal capital. There, they hailed the last Mughal ruler as their leader.

The sepoys brutally massacred British men, women, and children in some places. But the British soon rallied and crushed the revolt. They then took terrible revenge for their earlier losses, torching villages and slaughtering thousands of unarmed Indians.

The Sepoy Rebellion left a bitter legacy of fear, hatred, and mistrust on both sides. It also brought major changes in British policy. In 1858, Parliament ended the rule of the East India Company and put India directly under the British crown. It sent more troops to India, taxing Indians to pay the cost of these occupying forces. While it slowed the "reforms" that had angered Hindus and Muslims, it continued to develop India for Britain's own economic benefit.

British Colonial Rule

After 1858, Parliament set up a system of colonial rule in India. A British viceroy in India governed in the name of the queen, and British officials held the top positions in the civil service and army. Indians filled most other jobs. With their cooperation, the British made India the "brightest jewel" in the crown of their empire.

British policies were designed to fit India into the overall British economy. At the same time, British officials felt they were helping India to modernize. In their terms, modernizing meant adopting not only western technology but also western culture.

An Unequal Partnership Britain saw India as a market and as a source of raw materials. To this end, the British built roads and an impressive railroad network. Improved transportation let the British sell their factory-made goods across the subcontinent and carry Indian cotton, jute, and coal to coastal ports for transport to factories in England. New methods of communication, such as the telegraph, also gave Britain better control of India.

After the Suez Canal opened in 1869, British trade with India soared. But it remained an unequal partnership, favoring the British. The British flooded India with inexpensive, machine-made textiles, ruining India's once-prosperous hand-weaving industry.

Britain also transformed Indian agriculture. It encouraged nomadic herders to settle into farming and pushed farmers to grow cash crops, such as cotton and jute, that could be sold on the world market. Clearing new farmlands led to massive **deforestation,** or cutting of trees.

Population Growth and Famine The British introduced medical improvements and new farming methods. Better health care and increased food production led to rapid population growth. The rising numbers, however, put a strain on the food supply, especially as farmland was turned over to growing cash crops instead of food. In the late 1800s, terrible famines swept India.

Benefits of British Rule On the positive side, British rule brought peace and order to the countryside. The British revised the legal system to promote justice for Indians regardless of class or caste. Railroads helped Indians move around the country, while the telegraph and postal system improved communication. Greater contact helped bridge regional differences and opened the way for Indians to develop a sense of national unity.

The upper classes, especially, benefited from some British policies. They sent their sons to British schools, where they were trained for posts in the civil service and military. Indian landowners and princes, who still ruled their own territories, grew rich from exporting cash crops.

Different Views on Culture

During the Age of Imperialism, Indians and British developed different views of each other's culture. Both the British and the Indians were divided in their opinions.

Indian Attitudes Some educated Indians were impressed by British power and technology and urged India to follow a western model of progress. These mostly upper-class Indians learned English and adopted western ways. Other Indians felt that the answer to change lay with their own Hindu or Muslim cultures.

In the early 1800s, Ram Mohun Roy combined both views. A great scholar, he knew Sanskrit, Persian, and Arabic classics, as well as English, Greek, and Latin works. Roy felt that India could learn from the West. At the same time, he wanted to revitalize and reform traditional Indian culture.

Roy condemned some traditions, such as rigid caste distinctions, child marriage, sati, and **purdah,** the isolation of women in separate quarters. But he also set up educational societies that helped revive pride in Indian culture. Because of his influence on later leaders, he is often hailed today as the founder of Indian nationalism.

Western Attitudes The British disagreed among themselves about India. A few admired Indian theology and philosophy. As western scholars translated Indian classics, they acquired respect for India's ancient heritage. Western writers and philosophers borrowed ideas from Hinduism and Buddhism.

However, most British people knew little about Indian achievements and dismissed Indian culture with contempt. In an essay on whether Indians should be taught in English or their own languages, the English historian Thomas Macaulay wrote that "a single shelf of a good European library is worth the whole native literature of India and Arabia."

Cotton: A Valuable Cash Crop
In the 1800s, British officials encouraged Indian farmers to grow cash crops rather than food crops. Today, India is one of the world's largest producers of cotton.

Theme: Global Interaction
How did British policy contribute to famine in India?

The British railway system in India was massive in size and importance. By 1900, 25,000 miles of track crisscrossed the Asian subcontinent, providing easy transportation for tea, cotton, jute, and other goods destined to enrich the British economy.

The vast rail network aided India as well. India had long been divided by geography, cultural differences, and rival rulers. British railroads helped to bridge some of these divisions and promote a sense of nationalism. They enabled Indians to travel across the country. The trains also helped ideas spread by transporting books, newspapers, and letters.

One British official compared the railroad system in India to "the aqueducts of Rome, the pyramids of Egypt, the great wall of China . . . monuments not merely of intelligence and power, but of utility and beneficence."

Theme: Geography and History How did railroads encourage Indian nationalism?

Indian Nationalism

During the years of British rule, a class of western-educated Indians emerged. In the view of Macaulay and others, this elite class would bolster British power:

> "We must at present do our best to form a class who may be interpreters between us and the millions whom we govern; a class of persons, Indian in blood and color, but English in taste, in opinions, in morals, and in intellect."
>
> —Thomas Macaulay, quoted in
> *Sources of Indian Tradition* (deBary)

As it turned out, exposure to European ideas had the opposite effect. By the late 1800s, western-educated Indians were spearheading a nationalist movement. Schooled in western ideals such as democracy and equality, they dreamed of ending imperial rule.

Indian National Congress In 1885, nationalist leaders organized the Indian National Congress, which became known as the Congress party. Its members were mostly professionals and business leaders who believed in peaceful protest to gain their ends. They called for greater democracy, which they felt would bring more power to Indians like themselves. The Indian National Congress looked forward to eventual self-rule but supported western-style modernization.

Muslim League At first, Muslims and Hindus worked together for self-rule. In time, however, Muslims grew to resent Hindu domination of the Congress party. They also worried that a Hindu-run government would oppress Muslims. In 1906, Muslims formed the Muslim League to pursue their own goals. Soon, they were talking of a separate Muslim state.

Looking Ahead

By the early 1900s, protests and resistance to British rule increased. Some Indian nationalists urged that Indian languages and cultures be restored. More and more Indians demanded not simply self-rule but complete independence. Their goal finally would be achieved in 1947, but only after a long struggle against the British and a nightmare of bloody conflict between Hindus and Muslims.

SECTION 4 Assessment

Recall
1. **Identify:** (a) East India Company, (b) Sepoy Rebellion, (c) Ram Mohun Roy, (d) Indian National Congress, (e) Muslim League.
2. **Define:** (a) sati, (b) sepoy, (c) viceroy, (d) deforestation, (e) purdah.

Comprehension
3. What were the causes and effects of the Sepoy Rebellion?
4. Describe three effects of British colonial rule on India.
5. How did Indians differ in their views on Indian and British culture?

6. How did British rule lead to growing Indian nationalism?

Critical Thinking and Writing
7. **Analyzing Primary Sources** Review the words of Thomas Macaulay, quoted above. What kind of education did Macaulay favor for Indians? Why?
8. **Defending a Position** Do you think that the British were right to pass laws that tried to reform the caste system and end sati? Explain and defend your position.

Activity
Drawing a Political Cartoon
Draw a cartoon that either praises or criticizes a British colonial policy in India. Give your cartoon a title and a caption. Consider using symbolism such as a lion, which is a traditional symbol of Britain.

SECTION 5 China and the New Imperialism

Reading Focus

- What trade rights did westerners seek in China?
- What internal problems did Chinese reformers try to solve?
- How did the Qing dynasty come to an end?

Vocabulary

trade surplus
trade deficit
indemnity
extraterritoriality

Taking Notes

As you read, create a concept web, like this partially completed model, to show key events and developments in the decline of Qing China. Add as many circles as you need to finish the web.

- Opium War
- Boxer Uprising
- DECLINE OF QING CHINA

Main Idea During the 1800s, Qing China declined as western powers used diplomacy and war to gain power in East Asia.

Setting the Scene By the 1830s, British merchant ships were arriving in China loaded with opium to sell to the Chinese. One Chinese official complained bitterly to Britain's Queen Victoria. "I have heard that smoking opium is strictly forbidden in your country," he wrote. "Why do you let this evil drug be sent to harm people in other countries?"

For centuries, Chinese regulations had ensured that China had a favorable balance of trade with other nations. The phrase *balance of trade* refers to the difference between how much a country imports and how much it exports. By the 1800s, however, western nations were using their growing power to gain more influence over East Asia.

The Trade Issue

Prior to the 1800s, Chinese rulers placed strict limits on foreign traders. European merchants were restricted to a small area in southern China. China sold them silk, porcelain, and tea in exchange for gold and silver. Under this arrangement, China enjoyed a trade surplus, exporting more than it imported. Westerners, on the other hand, had a trade deficit with China, buying more from the Chinese than they sold to them.

By the late 1700s, two developments were underway that would transform China's relations with the western world. First, China entered a period of decline. Second, the Industrial Revolution created a need for expanded markets for European goods. At the same time, it gave the West superior military power.

The Opium War During the late 1700s, British merchants began making huge profits by trading opium grown in India for Chinese tea, which was popular in Britain. Soon, many Chinese had become addicted to the drug. Silver flowed out of China in payment for the drug, disrupting the economy.

The Chinese government outlawed opium and executed Chinese drug dealers. They called on Britain to stop the trade. The British refused, insisting on the right of free trade.

The Opium War
The Opium War began when Chinese officials tried to keep British ships from bringing the addictive drug into China. Here, a British warship sinks Chinese junks during the war.

Theme: Economics and Technology How does the picture suggest Britain's superior military technology?

Chapter 12 **333**

In 1839, Chinese warships clashed with British merchants, triggering the Opium War. British gunboats, equipped with the latest in firepower, bombarded Chinese coastal and river ports. With outdated weapons and fighting methods, the Chinese were easily defeated.

Unequal Treaties In 1842, Britain made China accept the Treaty of Nanjing. Britain received a huge indemnity, or payment for losses in the war. The British also gained the island of Hong Kong. (See the map later in this section.) China had to open five ports to foreign trade and grant British citizens in China extraterritoriality, the right to live under their own laws and be tried in their own courts.

The treaty was the first of a series of "unequal treaties" that forced China to make concessions to western powers. During the mid-1800s, under pressure from the West, China agreed to open more ports to foreign trade and to let Christian missionaries preach in China.

Internal Problems

By the 1800s, the Qing dynasty was in decline. Irrigation systems and canals were poorly maintained, leading to massive flooding of the Huang He valley. The population explosion that had begun a century earlier created a terrible hardship for China's peasants. An extravagant court, tax evasion by the rich, and widespread official corruption added to the peasants' burden. Even the honored civil service system was rocked by bribery scandals.

The Taiping Rebellion As poverty and misery increased, peasants rebelled. The Taiping Rebellion, which lasted from 1850 to 1864, was probably the most devastating peasant revolt in history. The leader, Hong Xiuquan (howng shyoo CHWAHN), was a village schoolteacher. Inspired by religious visions, he set himself up as a revolutionary prophet. He wanted to establish a "Heavenly Kingdom of Great Peace"—the Taiping (tī PIHNG).

Influenced by the teachings of Christian missionaries, Hong endorsed social ideas that Chinese leaders considered radical. These included land reform, community ownership of property, and equality of women and men. Above all, he called for an end to the hated Qing dynasty.

The Taiping rebels won control of large parts of China. They held out for 14 years. However, with the help of loyal regional governors and generals, the government crushed the rebellion in the end.

Effects The Taiping Rebellion almost toppled the Qing dynasty. It is estimated to have caused the deaths of between 20 million and 30 million Chinese. The Qing government survived, but it had to share power with regional commanders. During the rebellion, Europeans kept up pressure on China. Russia seized lands in northern China.

Reform Efforts

By the mid-1800s, educated Chinese were divided over the need to adopt western ways. Most scholar-officials saw no reason for new industries because China's wealth and taxes came from land. Although Chinese merchants were allowed to do business, they were not seen as a source of prosperity.

Scholar-officials also disapproved of the ideas of western missionaries, whose emphasis on individual choice challenged the Confucian order. They saw western technology as dangerous, too, because it threatened Confucian ways that had served China successfully for so long.

The imperial court was a center of conservative opposition. By the late 1800s, the empress Ci Xi (tsee SHYEE) had gained power. A strong-willed ruler, she surrounded herself with advisers who were deeply committed to Confucian traditions.

Primary Source

The Taiping Rebellion
The rebels of the Taiping Rebellion were peasants. Here, some of the captured rebels explain why they joined the rebellion:

"We men from Kwangtung . . . were born in a time of prosperity and were good people. We lived in towns and were taught to distinguish right from wrong. But because of continuous flooding in our area, we could not get a grain of rice to eat even if we worked hard in the fields, and we could not engage in business because we lacked the funds. As a result we all joined the bandits.

Not long ago we came to Kwangsi to try to make a living. We met others who had come from our hometowns. We pitied each other because of our sad situation, and together we began to imitate outlaws in order to relieve our hungry stomachs . . . no one forced us to join the outlaws. We were driven to join them because we were desperate. Given the chance, we would have returned gladly to our normal way of life."

—Kwangsi Bandit Group,
quoted in *Chinese Civilization and Society* (Ebrey)

Skills Assessment

Primary Source Why did these men join the rebellion?

Meeting the Emperor

After years of education, you have finally made it. You are about to be installed as a government official in the service of the emperor. You stand in the throne room known as the Hall of Supreme Harmony. Yet today, there is little harmony. Wars and rebellion have weakened China, and the foreigners are gaining power. Here in Beijing, meanwhile, leaders quarrel over what to do.

The room fell silent when Emperor Guang Xu entered. Now, as he begins the ceremony, you reflect on his recent actions as emperor. You know that he is trying to modernize China. However, conservatives in the government are fighting his reforms.

The Dowager Empress Ci Xi is not present. You have heard that she does not approve of the emperor's reforms. When the ceremony ends, you feel confused. You want to be loyal to your emperor, but you have spent years studying traditional Confucian ways of governing. Should you support reform?

Portfolio Assessment

In your new government post, you can either support or oppose the emperor's reforms. Write a poem explaining your decision. Be sure to include both reasons for and possible consequences of your decision.

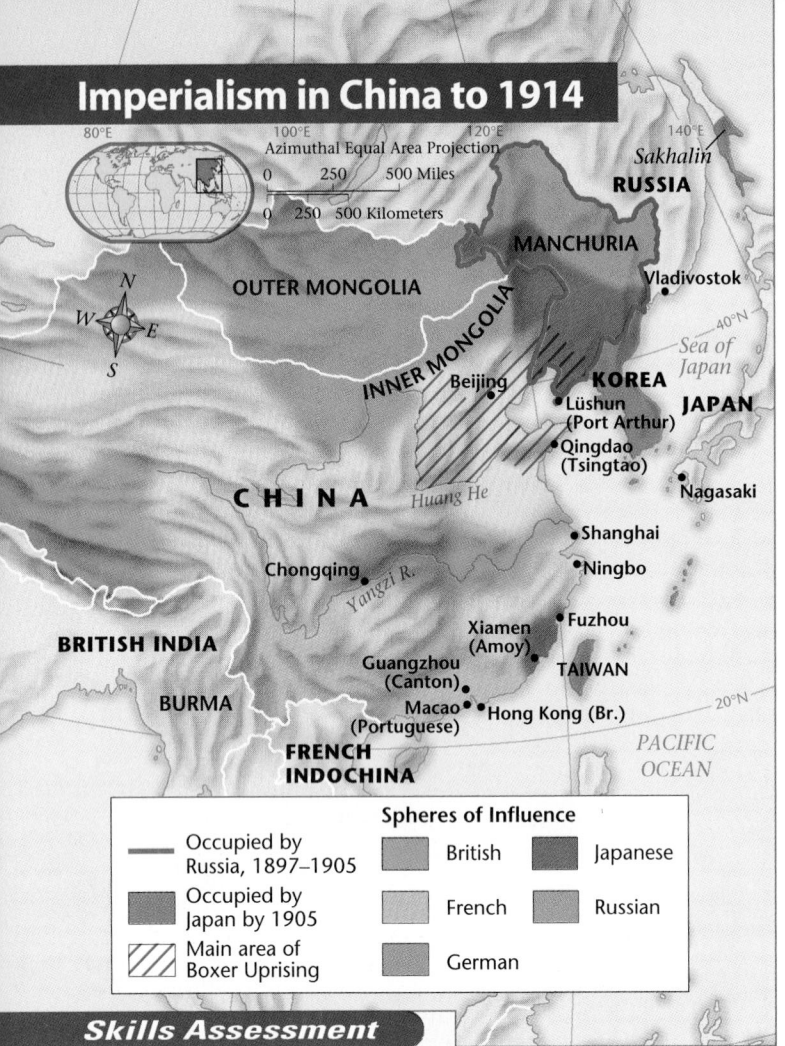

Imperialism in China to 1914

Azimuthal Equal Area Projection

0   250   500 Miles

0   250   500 Kilometers

RUSSIA

Sakhalin

MANCHURIA

OUTER MONGOLIA

Vladivostok

Sea of Japan

INNER MONGOLIA

Beijing

KOREA

Lüshun (Port Arthur)

Qingdao (Tsingtao)

JAPAN

Nagasaki

CHINA

Huang He

Shanghai

Chongqing

Ningbo

Yangzi R.

Fuzhou

Xiamen (Amoy)

TAIWAN

BRITISH INDIA

Guangzhou (Canton)

BURMA

Macao (Portuguese)

Hong Kong (Br.)

PACIFIC OCEAN

FRENCH INDOCHINA

Spheres of Influence

— Occupied by Russia, 1897–1905

■ Occupied by Japan by 1905

▨ Main area of Boxer Uprising

■ British   ■ Japanese

■ French   ■ Russian

■ German

Skills Assessment

Geography The European powers and Japan carved China into spheres of influence.

1. **Location** On the map, locate **(a)** Vladivostok, **(b)** Korea, **(c)** Hong Kong, **(d)** Taiwan.

2. **Place** What river was the center of Britain's sphere of influence?

3. **Critical Thinking Recognizing Causes and Effects** Use information on the map to identify causes of the growth of Chinese nationalism.

Self-Strengthening Movement In the 1860s, reformers launched what became known as the "self-strengthening movement." They imported western technology, setting up factories to make modern weapons. They developed shipyards, railroads, mining, and light industry. The Chinese translated western works on science, government, and the economy. However, the movement made limited progress because the government did not rally behind it.

War With Japan Meanwhile, the western powers and nearby Japan moved rapidly ahead. Japan began to modernize after 1868. It then joined the western imperialists in the competition for a global empire.

In 1894, Japanese pressure on China led to the Sino-Japanese War. It ended in disaster for China, with Japan gaining the island of Taiwan off the coast of China. When the two powers met at the peace table, there was a telling difference. Japanese officials were dressed in western clothes, the Chinese in traditional robes.

Spheres of Influence The crushing defeat revealed China's weakness. Western powers moved swiftly to carve out spheres of influence along the Chinese coast. The British took the Yangzi River valley. The French acquired the territory near their colony of Indochina. Germany and Russia gained territory in northern China.

The United States, a longtime trader with the Chinese, did not take part in the carving up of China. It feared that European powers might shut out American merchants. A few years later, in 1899, it called for a policy to keep Chinese trade open to everyone on an equal basis. The imperial powers more or less accepted the idea of an Open Door Policy, as it came to be called. No one, however, consulted the Chinese about the policy.

Hundred Days of Reform Defeated by Japan and humiliated by westerners, the Chinese looked for a scapegoat. Reformers blamed conservative officials for not modernizing China. They urged conservative leaders to stop looking back at China's past golden ages and instead to modernize as Japan had.

In 1898, a young emperor, Guang Xu (gwawng SHYOO), launched the Hundred Days of Reform. New laws set out to modernize the civil service exams, streamline government, and encourage new industries. Reforms affected schools, the military, and the bureaucracy. Conservatives soon rallied against the reform effort. The emperor was imprisoned, and the aging empress Ci Xi reasserted control. Reformers fled for their lives.

The Qing Dynasty Falls

As the century ended, China was in turmoil. Anger grew against Christian missionaries who belittled Chinese thinkers like Confucius. The presence of foreign troops was another source of discontent. Protected by extraterritoriality, foreigners ignored Chinese laws and lived in their own communities.

Boxer Uprising Antiforeign feeling finally exploded in the Boxer Uprising. In 1899, a group of Chinese had formed a secret society, the Righteous

Harmonious Fists. Westerners watching them train in the martial arts dubbed them Boxers. Their goal was to drive out the "foreign devils" who were polluting the land with their un-Chinese ways, strange buildings, machines, and telegraph lines.

In 1900, the Boxers attacked foreigners across China. In response, the western powers and Japan organized a multinational force. It crushed the Boxers and rescued foreigners besieged in Beijing. The empress Ci Xi had at first supported the Boxers but reversed her policy as they retreated.

Aftermath of the Uprising China once again had to make concessions to foreigners. The defeat, however, forced even Chinese conservatives to support westernization. In a rush of reforms, China admitted women to schools and stressed science and mathematics in place of Confucian thought. More students were sent abroad to study.

China expanded economically, as well. Mining, shipping, railroads, banking, and exports of cash crops grew. With foreign capital, small-scale Chinese industry developed. A Chinese business class emerged, and a new urban working class began to press for rights as western workers had done.

Three Principles of the People Although the Boxer Uprising failed, the flames of Chinese nationalism spread. Reformers wanted to strengthen China's government. By the early 1900s, they had introduced a constitutional monarchy. Some reformers called for a republic.

A passionate spokesman for a Chinese republic was Sun Yixian* (soon yee SHYAHN). Sun had studied in the West. In the early 1900s, he organized the Revolutionary Alliance. His goal was to rebuild China on "Three Principles of the People." The first principle was nationalism, freeing China from foreign domination. The second was democracy, or representative government. The third was "livelihood," or economic security for all Chinese.

Birth of a Republic When Ci Xi died in 1908 and a two-year-old boy inherited the throne, China slipped into chaos. In 1911, uprisings in the provinces swiftly spread. Peasants, students, local warlords, and even court politicians helped topple the Qing dynasty.

Sun Yixian hurried home from a trip to the United States. In December 1911, he was named president of the new Chinese republic. From the outset, the republic faced overwhelming problems. For the next 37 years, China was almost constantly at war with itself or fighting off foreign invasion.

*In earlier history books, this name appears as Sun Yat-sen.

Biography

Sun Yixian 1866–1925

Sun Yixian was not born to power. His parents were poor farmers. Sun's preparation for leadership came from his travels, education, and personal ambitions. In his teen years, he lived with his brother in Hawaii and attended British and American schools. Later on, he earned a medical degree.

Sun left his career in medicine to struggle against the Qing government. After a failed uprising in 1895, he went into exile. Sun visited many nations, seeking support against the Qing dynasty. When revolution erupted in China, Sun was in Denver, Colorado. He returned to China to begin his leading role in the new republic.

Theme: Impact of the Individual How did Sun's background prepare him to lead?

SECTION 5 **Assessment**

Recall
1. **Identify: (a)** Opium War, **(b)** Treaty of Nanjing, **(c)** Taiping Rebellion, **(d)** Ci Xi, **(e)** Open Door Policy, **(f)** Boxer Uprising, **(g)** Sun Yixian.
2. **Define: (a)** trade surplus, **(b)** trade deficit, **(c)** indemnity, **(d)** extraterritoriality.

Comprehension
3. How did western powers gain greater trading rights in China?
4. **(a)** What internal problems threatened the Qing dynasty? **(b)** What were the goals of Chinese reformers?

5. How was the Qing dynasty replaced by a republic?

Critical Thinking and Writing
6. **Making Generalizations** Based on what you have learned about western imperialism in Africa and Asia, what methods did European states use to gain power around the world?
7. **Making Decisions** If you had been a Chinese government official in the 1800s, would you have decided to support or oppose reform efforts designed to westernize China? Explain the reasons for your decision.

Activity

Planning a Debate
Work with a partner to plan a debate between a British merchant and a Chinese government official. The topic is extraterritoriality in China. Each of you should be prepared to present and defend your own position and to criticize the opposing position. Conduct your debate before the class.

Creating a Chapter Summary

On a sheet of paper, create a chart showing the effects of imperialism in the late 1800s and early 1900s. Use the partially completed model below to help you get started. Add as many boxes as you need.

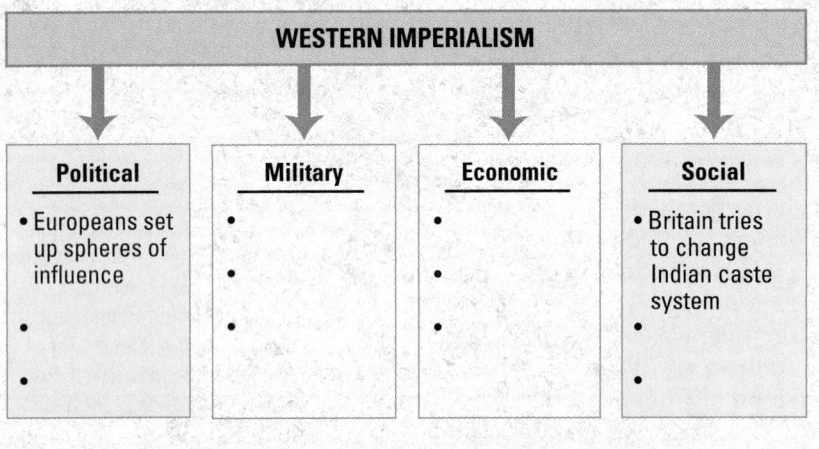

WESTERN IMPERIALISM

Political
- Europeans set up spheres of influence
-
-

Military
-
-
-

Economic
-
-
-

Social
- Britain tries to change Indian caste system
-
-

For additional review and enrichment activities, see the interactive version of *World History* available on the Web and on CD-ROM.

For practice test questions for Chapter 12, use **Web Code mka-2540.**

Building Vocabulary

Use these words and their definitions to create a matching quiz. When you are finished, exchange quizzes with another student and check each other's answers.

1. imperialism
2. protectorate
3. sphere of influence
4. missionary
5. pasha
6. genocide
7. sepoy
8. viceroy
9. indemnity
10. extraterritoriality

Recalling Key Facts

11. List the four main motives of the new imperialists.
12. How did Ethiopia successfully resist European imperialism?
13. How did the Ottoman empire try to westernize?
14. (a) What were the causes of the Sepoy Rebellion? (b) What were its effects?
15. Give two main reasons that China's policy of limiting trade with foreigners ended after the 1700s.
16. (a) What was the goal of the Boxer Uprising? (b) Describe the three principles that guided Sun Yixian.

Critical Thinking and Writing

17. **Linking Past and Present** (a) How did the opening of the Suez Canal in 1869 transform world trade? (b) Do you think the canal might be less important today? Why or why not?
18. **Analyzing Information** Western industrial nations set up colonies in Africa and India. In China, however, they established spheres of influence rather than colonies. Why do you think they did not colonize China?
19. **Comparing** In the late 1800s, several nonwestern nations instituted programs of western reforms and modernization. (a) Describe the reform efforts of two of the following: Egypt, the Ottoman empire, China. (b) Compare the results of these efforts.
20. **Connecting to Geography** Why were the natural resources of African and Asian lands so important to Europeans in the 1800s?
21. **Predicting Consequences** How do you think rivalries between religious groups affected anti-imperialism efforts in India? Explain your answer.

In 1896, Liang Ch'i-ch'ao, an influential Chinese thinker, was unhappy with conditions in China. Read the excerpt below and answer the questions that follow.

"The age of China as a country is equal to that of India and the fertility of her land is superior to that of Turkey, but her conformity to the defective ways which have accumulated and her incapacity to stand up and reform make her also like a brother of these two countries. . . . Whenever there is a flood or drought, communications are severed, there is no way to transport famine relief, the dead are abandoned to fill the ditches or are disregarded, and nine out of ten houses are emptied. . . . The members of secret societies are scattered over the whole country, waiting for the chance to move. Industry is not developed, commerce is not discussed, the native goods daily become less salable. . . ."

—Liang Ch'i-ch'ao,
On the Harm of Not Reforming

22. According to Liang Ch'i-ch'ao, how is China similar to India and Turkey?
23. What does he say are some of China's most serious problems?
24. What kind of "move" do you think "secret societies" were waiting to make? Explain.
25. What do you think Liang Ch'i-ch'ao wanted Chinese leaders to do?
26. **(a)** What important event occurred in China four years after this was written? **(b)** Based on what you have read, how do you think Liang Ch'i-ch'ao may have felt about this event?

Go Online
PHSchool.com

Use the Internet to find primary sources having to do with imperialism in the late 1800s and early 1900s. Select two documents or excerpts of documents and print them out. Explain the meaning of each primary source in your own words. For help with this activity, use **Web Code mkd-2541.**

The cartoon above was published in France in 1904, at the height of the Age of Imperialism. The figure at left is a French soldier. The figure at right is a British soldier. Study the cartoon and answer the following questions:

27. What continent appears on the map?
28. Why are the soldiers in the cartoon ripping the map apart?
29. **(a)** Which part of the continent are the British getting? **(b)** Which part of the continent are the French getting?
30. Why do you think part of the continent was not colored red?
31. How do you think the situation depicted in the cartoon affected relations between Britain and France?
32. How do you think people of the time knew which nations the two figures represented?
33. What prediction about future international relations can you make based on information in the cartoon? Explain.
34. Create an interesting title for the political cartoon. Explain the reason for your choice of title.

Skills Tip

Use information that you already have about a historical topic to help you understand a political cartoon.

New Global Patterns
1800–1914

Chapter Preview

1 **Japan Modernizes**
2 **Southeast Asia and the Pacific**
3 **Self-Rule for Canada, Australia, and New Zealand**
4 **Economic Imperialism in Latin America**
5 **Impact of Imperialism**

1840
Britain annexes New Zealand, leading to devastation for the Maori population. This carved figure is an example of Maori art.

1853
American ships commanded by Commodore Matthew Perry arrive in Japan. This woodblock print shows the American "black ships" and Japanese onlookers.

1823
The United States issues the Monroe Doctrine.

CHAPTER EVENTS

1800 • 1825 • 1850

GLOBAL EVENTS

1804 Haiti declares independence from France.

1818 Shaka begins Zulu conquests.

1845 Potato blight leads to the Great Hunger in Ireland.

Imperialism in Asia, the Pacific, and the Americas, 1900

Industrialized nations competed for control of territories around the world.

PACIFIC OCEAN

Caribbean Sea

INDIAN OCEAN

Arctic Circle

Tropic of Cancer 20°N

Equator 0°

Tropic of Capricorn 20°S

40°N

40°S

60°E 80°E 100°E 120°E 140°E 160°E 180° 160°W 140°W 120°W

N
W — E
S

Robinson Projection

0   1500   3000 Miles
0   1500   3000 Kilometers

Colonial possessions:
- British
- Dutch
- French
- German
- Japanese
- United States
- Russian
- Portuguese

Spheres of influence:
- British
- French
- German
- Japanese
- Russian
- United States
- British and French

1885
The Canadian Pacific Railway opens, linking eastern and western Canada.

1898
The Philippines declares independence from Spain.

1914
The Panama Canal opens, linking the Pacific Ocean and the Caribbean Sea. Construction of the canal, shown here, will lead to greater United States involvement in Latin America.

1875 1900 1925

1871 Germany is unified under Prussian leadership in the Second Reich.

1914 World War I begins.

Japan Modernizes

Reading Focus

- How did discontent in Japanese society and the opening of Japan lead to the Meiji restoration?

- What were the main reforms under the Meiji?

- How did Japanese military strength promote imperialism?

Vocabulary

Diet

zaibatsu

homogeneous society

Taking Notes

Copy this chart. As you read, fill in the major reforms of the Meiji restoration. The sample has been started for you.

REFORMS DURING MEIJI RESTORATION		
Political	**Economic**	**Social**
• Adopted German model of government	•	•
•		

Main Idea During the late 1800s, Japan opened its doors to foreign influence and became a modern industrial power.

Setting the Scene In 1853, the United States displayed its new military might, sending a naval force to make Japan open its ports to trade. Japanese leaders debated how to respond. While some resisted giving up their 215-year-old policy of seclusion, others felt that it would be wiser to learn from the foreigners. One Japanese lord pointed out:

> "There is a saying that when one is besieged in a castle, to raise the drawbridge is to imprison oneself. . . . Even though the Shogun's ancestors set up seclusion laws, they left the Dutch and Chinese to act as a bridge. . . . Might this bridge not now be of advantage to us, . . . providing us with the means whereby we may for a time avert the outbreak of hostilities and then, after some time has elapsed, gain a complete victory?"
> —Ii Naosuke, quoted in *Selected Documents on Japanese Foreign Policy* (Beasley)

In the end, Japan chose to abandon its centuries of isolation and to learn from the West. The country swiftly transformed itself into a modern industrial power and then set out on its own imperialist path.

Discontent in Tokugawa Japan

After the Tokugawa shoguns gained power in 1600, they reimposed centralized feudalism, closed Japan to foreigners, and forbade Japanese to travel overseas. The nation's only window on the world was through Nagasaki, where the Dutch were allowed very limited trade.

For more than 200 years, Japan developed in isolation. Although internal commerce expanded, economic changes introduced severe strains in Japanese society. By the 1800s, shoguns were no longer strong leaders, and corruption was common. Discontent simmered throughout Japan.

Many daimyo suffered financial hardship. Money was needed in a commercial economy, but a daimyo's wealth was in land rather than cash. Daimyo also had the heavy expense of maintaining households in both Edo and their own domains. Lesser samurai were unhappy, too, because they were no longer fighters. Many were bureaucrats. Even though they were noble, they lacked the money to live as well as urban merchants.

Merchants in turn resented their place at the bottom of the social ladder. No matter how rich they were, they had no political power. Peasants, meanwhile, suffered under heavy taxes.

The government responded by trying to revive old ways, emphasizing farming over commerce and praising traditional values. These efforts at reform, however, had scant success. Many groups felt little loyalty to the old system.

Opening Up Japan

While the shogun faced troubles at home, disturbing news reached him from abroad during the 1830s and 1840s. He was alarmed by news of the British victory over China in the Opium War. Even more disturbing was the way in which imperialists had forced China to sign the unequal treaties. Surely, the shogun reasoned, it would not be long before western powers began seeking trading rights in Japan.

External Pressure and Internal Revolt Then, in July 1853, a fleet of well-armed American ships commanded by Commodore Matthew Perry sailed into Tokyo Bay. Perry had a letter from the President of the United States. The letter demanded that Japan open its ports to diplomatic and commercial exchange.

The shogun's advisers debated what to do. As Lord Ii noted, Japan did not have the ability to defend itself against the powerful United States Navy. In the Treaty of Kanagawa in 1854, the shogun agreed to open two Japanese ports to American ships, though not for trade.

The United States soon won trading and other rights, including the right of extraterritoriality and a "most favored nation" clause. European nations demanded and won similar rights. Like the Chinese, the Japanese deeply resented the terms of these unequal treaties, which they found humiliating. Some bitterly criticized the shogun for not taking a strong stand against the foreigners.

Foreign pressure deepened the social and economic unrest. In 1867, discontented daimyo and samurai led a revolt that unseated the shogun and "restored" the 15-year-old emperor to power. He moved from the old imperial capital in Kyoto to the shogun's palace in Edo, which was renamed Tokyo, or "eastern capital."

Tea Ceremony
In Japan, the tea ceremony was developed to provide a peaceful setting for social activity (PAST). Today, the rituals provide a reminder of the nation's cultural heritage, as well as an oasis of calm in an otherwise busy world (PRESENT).

Theme: Continuity and Change Why might people choose to maintain traditions along with modernization?

Industrialization in Japan

The emperor Meiji wrote a poem to provide inspiration for Japan's efforts to become a modern country: "May our country, / Taking what is good, / and rejecting what is bad, / Be not inferior / To any other." The picture, the song, and the chart on this page relate to Japan's efforts to modernize in the late 1800s.

Children's Game

In 1878, a song composed for Japanese children impressed on them the 10 objects that their country should adopt from the West to be truly modern. As they named each object, the children bounced a ball:

"Gas Lamps
Steam Engines
Horse Carriages
Cameras
Telegrams
Lightning Conductors
Newspapers
Schools
[Postal System]
Steamboats"

Clothing Manufacturing in Japan

Japanese manufacturing grew rapidly in the late 1800s. As in Europe and the United States, women played a key role in Japan's industrial revolution. In this 1897 print, women make clothing in a Japanese workshop.

Investments by Industry in Meiji Japan

Activity	1877	1883	1893
Agriculture	–	1,053,000	2,542,000
Trading	454,000	35,904,000	57,616,000
Manufacturing	–	14,725,000	68,259,000
Railways	–	12,080,000	57,945,000
Banking	24,981,000	75,375,000	111,635,000

All figures are in yen.
Source: S. Uyehara, *The Industry and Trade of Japan*

Skills Tip

In tables containing numbers, a dash is often used to indicate a value of zero or to indicate that no value is given.

Skills Assessment

1. According to the picture, Japanese women
   A adopted western ways.
   B worked long hours.
   C opposed organized labor unions.
   D earned less than men.

2. In which economic activity did the investments increase by about 46 million yen between 1883 and 1893?
   E agriculture
   F trading
   G manufacturing
   H railways

3. **Critical Thinking Evaluating Information** Name two things about modernization in Japan that you cannot learn from the sources on this page. Explain why it would be useful to have that information.

Meiji Restoration The young emperor began a long reign known as the Meiji (MAY jee) restoration. This period, which lasted from 1868 to 1912, was a major turning point in Japanese history. *Meiji* means "enlightened rule." The Meiji reformers, who ruled in the emperor's name, were determined to strengthen Japan. Their goal was summarized in their motto, "A rich country, a strong military."

The new leaders set out to study western ways, adapt them to Japanese needs, and eventually beat westerners at their own game. In 1871, members of the government traveled overseas to learn about western governments, economies, technology, and customs. The government brought experts from western countries to Japan and sent young samurai to study abroad.

Reforms Under the Meiji

The Meiji reformers faced an enormous task. They were committed to replacing the rigid feudal order with a completely new political and social system and to building a modern industrial economy. Change did not come easily. In the end, however, Japan adapted foreign ideas with amazing speed and success.

Government The reformers wanted to create a strong central government, equal to those of western powers. After studying various European governments, they adapted the German model. In 1889, the emperor issued the Meiji constitution. It set forth the principle that all citizens were equal before the law. Like the German system, however, it gave the emperor autocratic power. A legislature, or Diet, was formed, made up of one elected house and one house appointed by the emperor. Additionally, voting rights were sharply limited.

Japan then established a western-style bureaucracy with separate departments to supervise finance, the army, the navy, and education. To strengthen the military, it turned to western technology and ended the special privilege of samurai. In the past, samurai alone were warriors. In modern Japan, as in the West, all men were subject to military service.

Economic Reforms Meiji leaders made the economy a major priority. They encouraged Japan's business class to adopt western methods. The government set up a banking system, built railroads, improved ports, and organized a telegraph and postal system.

To get industries started, the government typically built factories and then sold them to wealthy business families who developed them further. With such support, business dynasties like the Kawasaki family soon ruled over industrial empires that rivaled those of the Rockefellers in the United States or the Krupps in Germany. These powerful banking and industrial families were known as zaibatsu (zī baht soo).

By the 1890s, industry was booming. With modern machines, silk manufacturing soared. Shipyards, copper and coal mining, and steel making also helped make Japan an industrial powerhouse. As in other industrial countries, the population grew rapidly, and many peasants flocked to the growing cities for work.

Social Change The constitution ended legal distinctions between classes, thus providing the opportunity for more people to become involved in nation-building. The government set up schools and a university. It hired westerners to teach the new generation modern technology.

Despite the reforms, class distinctions survived in Japan as they did in the West. Also, although literacy increased and some women gained an education, women in general were still assigned a secondary role in society.

The reform of the Japanese family system, and women's position in it, became the topic of major debates in the 1870s. Reformers wanted women to become full partners in the process of nation-building and to learn skills

Primary Sources and Literature

See "Fukuzawa Yukichi: Autobiography" in the Reference Section at the back of this book.

Go Online
PHSchool.com

For: More about transportation in Japan after the Meiji restoration
Visit: PHSchool.com
Web Code: mkd-2648

A Railway in Japan
One of the most important techno-logical advances that the Meiji bor-rowed from the West was the steam locomotive. This woodblock print shows a celebration to mark the opening of a Tokyo rail line.

Theme: Continuity and Change How does this picture show the continuity of some Japanese cultural traditions?

that would allow them to live on their own. Although the government agreed to some increases in education for women, it dealt harshly with other attempts at change. After 1898, Japanese women were forbidden any political participation and legally were lumped together with minors.

Amazing Success During the Meiji period, Japan modernized with amazing speed. Its success was due to a number of causes. It was a homogeneous society—that is, it had a common culture and language that gave it a strong sense of identity. Economic growth during Tokugawa times had set Japan on the road to development. Also, the Japanese had experience in learning from foreign nations, such as China.

Like other people faced with western imperialism, the Japanese were determined to resist foreign rule. In fact, in the 1890s, Japan was strong enough to force western powers to revise the unequal treaties. By then, it was already acquiring its own overseas empire.

Growing Military Strength

As with western industrial powers, Japan's economic needs fed its imperi-alist desires. A small island nation, Japan lacked many basic resources that were essential for industrial growth. Yet, spurred by nationalism and a strong ambition to equal the West, Japan built an empire. With its modern army and navy, it maneuvered for power in East Asia.

Japan Gains Power In 1894, competition between Japan and China led to the Sino-Japanese War. Although China had greater resources, Japan had benefited from modernization. To the surprise of China and the West, Japan won easily. It used its victory to gain treaty ports in China and control over the island of Taiwan, thus joining the West in the race for empire.

Ten years later, Japan successfully challenged Russia, its rival for power in Korea and Manchuria. During the Russo-Japanese War, Japan's armies defeated Russian troops in Manchuria, and its navy destroyed almost an entire Russian fleet. For the first time in modern history, an Asian power humbled a European nation. In the 1905 Treaty of Portsmouth, Japan gained control of Korea as well as rights in parts of Manchuria. This foothold on the East Asian mainland would fuel its ambitions.

Competition for Korea Imperialist rivalries put the spotlight on Korea. Located at a crossroads of East Asia, the Korean peninsula was a focus of competition among Russia, China, and Japan.

Although Korea had long been influenced by its powerful neighbor, it had its own traditions and government. Like China and Japan, Korea had shut its doors to foreigners. It did, however, maintain relations with China and sometimes with Japan.

By the 1800s, Korea faced pressure from outsiders. As Chinese power declined, Russia expanded into East Asia. Then, as Japan industrialized, it too eyed Korea. In 1876, Japan used its superior power to force Korea to open its ports to Japanese trade. Faced with similar demands from western powers, the "Hermit Kingdom" had to accept unequal treaties.

As Japan extended its influence in Korea, it came into conflict with China, which still saw Korea as a tributary state. After defeating China and then Russia, Japan made Korea a protectorate. In 1910, it annexed Korea outright, absorbing the kingdom into the Japanese empire.

Japan Rules Korea Japan ruled Korea for 35 years. Like western imperialists, the Japanese set out to modernize their newly acquired territory. They built factories, railroads, and communications systems. Development, however, generally benefited Japan. Under Japanese rule, Koreans produced more rice than ever before, but most of it went to Japan.

The Japanese were as unpopular in Korea as western imperialists were elsewhere. They imposed harsh rule on their colony and deliberately set out to erase the Korean language and identity. Repression bred resentment. And resentment, in turn, nourished a Korean nationalist movement.

Nine years after annexation, a nonviolent protest against the Japanese began on March 1, 1919, and soon spread throughout Korea. The Japanese crushed the uprising and massacred many Koreans. The violence did not discourage people who worked to end Japanese rule. Instead, the March First Movement became a rallying symbol for Korean nationalists.

Looking Ahead

The Koreans would have to wait many years for freedom. By the early 1900s, Japan was the strongest power in Asia. It continued to expand in East Asia during the years that followed, seeking natural resources and territory. In time, Japanese ambitions to control a sphere of influence in the Pacific would put it on a collision course with several western powers, especially Britain and the United States.

Global Connections

The Russo-Japanese War

The Russo-Japanese War began and ended on the sea. On February 19, 1904, Japanese torpedo boats made a surprise attack on part of the Russian fleet, near Manchuria. Most of those ships were wiped out.

The rest of the Russian navy was based in the Baltic Sea, more than 10,000 miles away. The Russian ships began a slow 15-month journey around Africa. When they chugged into the waters of East Asia on May 27, 1905, the Japanese navy attacked again. Japan's faster ships and more accurate gunnery forced the Russians to surrender within a single day.

Theme: Economics and Technology Why were the Japanese forces able to defeat their opponents so easily?

SECTION 1 Assessment

Recall

1. **Identify:** **(a)** Matthew Perry, **(b)** Treaty of Kanagawa, **(c)** Meiji restoration, **(d)** Russo-Japanese War, **(e)** Treaty of Portsmouth.
2. **Define:** **(a)** Diet, **(b)** zaibatsu, **(c)** homogeneous society.

Comprehension

3. **(a)** What problems did Tokugawa Japan face in the early 1800s? **(b)** Why did Japan end 200 years of seclusion?
4. **(a)** List three ways in which Japan modernized. **(b)** Explain how each of these actions helped strengthen Japan so it could resist western pressure.
5. How did Japan demonstrate its growing military strength?

Critical Thinking and Writing

6. **Connecting to Geography** How did the geographic location of Korea make it desirable to both China and Japan?
7. **Predicting Consequences** What might have happened to Japan if the Meiji reformers had not decided to modernize in the late 1800s? Explain.

Go Online
PHSchool.com

Use the Internet to research the opening of Japan by Matthew Perry. Then, write a news article for either an American or a Japanese newspaper describing the event. For help with this activity, use **Web Code mkd-2649.**

Southeast Asia and the Pacific

Reading Focus

- What impact did European colonization have on Southeast Asia?

- How did Siam maintain its independence?

- How did imperialism spread to the Philippines and other Pacific islands?

Taking Notes

Copy this table. As you read, fill in information on imperialism in Asia and the Pacific. To help you get started, portions of the table have been completed.

REGION	IMPERIALIST POWER	REASONS FOR COLONIZATION
INDONESIA	The Netherlands	
MALAYA		Rubber and tin
INDOCHINA		
SIAM		
HAWAII		
PHILIPPINES		

Main Idea   Western industrialized powers divided up Southeast Asia in pursuit of raw materials, new markets, and converts to Christianity.

Setting the Scene   A Vietnamese official, Phan Thanh Gian, faced a dilemma in 1867. The French were threatening to invade. As a patriot, Phan Thanh Gian wanted to resist. But as a devoted follower of Confucius, he was obliged "to live in obedience to reason." And based on the power of the French military, he concluded that the only reasonable course was to surrender. Phan Thanh Gian made his choice with a heavy heart. By avoiding a useless war that would hurt his people, he became a traitor to his king. For that decision, he wrote, "I deserve death."

Leaders throughout Southeast Asia faced the same dilemma during the Age of Imperialism. As they had in Africa, western industrial powers gobbled up the region in their relentless race for raw materials, new markets, and Christian converts.

Europeans Colonize Southeast Asia

Southeast Asia commanded the sea lanes between India and China and had been influenced by both civilizations. From the 1500s through the 1700s, European merchants gained footholds in the region, but most of the area remained independent. This changed in the 1800s. Westerners— notably the Dutch, British, and French—played off local rivalries and used modern armies and technology to colonize much of Southeast Asia.

During the 1600s, the Dutch East India Company gained control of the fabled riches of the Moluccas, or Spice Islands. They then reached out to dominate the rest of Indonesia. The Dutch expected their Southeast Asian colonies to produce profitable crops of coffee and indigo as well as spices.

In the early 1800s, rulers of Burma (present-day Myanmar) clashed with the British, who were expanding eastward from India. In several wars, the Burmese suffered disastrous defeats. They continued to resist British rule, however, even after Britain annexed Burma in 1886.

The British also pushed south through Malaya. The bustling port of Singapore, on the sea route between the Indian Ocean and the China Sea, grew up at the southern tip of the peninsula. Soon, natural resources and profits from Asian trade flowed through Singapore to enrich Britain.

The French, meanwhile, were building an empire on the Southeast Asian mainland. In the early 1800s, French missionaries began winning converts in what is today Vietnam. The region had long been influenced by Confucian traditions. Vietnamese officials tried to suppress Christianity by killing converts and missionary priests.

As with Burma and the British, the Vietnamese misjudged European power. In the 1860s, the French invaded and seized a chunk of Vietnam. Over the next decades, they added more lands, eventually seizing all of Vietnam, Laos, and Cambodia. The French and other westerners referred to these holdings as French Indochina.

By the 1890s, Europeans controlled most of Southeast Asia. They introduced modern technology and expanded commerce and industry. They set up new enterprises to mine tin and harvest rubber, brought in new crops of corn and cassava, and built harbors and railroads. But these changes benefited Europeans far more than the people of Southeast Asia.

Many Chinese migrated to Southeast Asia to escape hardship and turmoil at home and to benefit from growing economic opportunities. Despite persistent local resentment, these communities of "overseas" Chinese formed vital networks in trade, banking, and other economic activities.

Siam Survives

Sandwiched between British-ruled Burma and French Indochina lay the kingdom of Siam—present-day Thailand. King Mongkut, who ruled from 1851 to 1868, did not underestimate western power. Before inheriting the throne, he had studied foreign languages and read widely on modern science and mathematics. He thus had a greater understanding of the West than many other Asian rulers.

Although Mongkut had to accept some unequal treaties, Siam escaped becoming a European colony. He and his son, Chulalongkorn, set Siam on the road to modernization. They reformed government, modernized the army, and hired western experts to train Thais in the new technology. They abolished slavery and gave women some choice in marriage. As Siam modernized, Chulalongkorn bargained to remove the unequal treaties.

In the end, both Britain and France saw the advantage of making Siam a buffer, or neutral zone, between them. In the early 1900s, they guaranteed its independence.

Imperial Powers in the Pacific

In the 1800s, the industrial powers began to take an interest in the islands of the Pacific.* At first, American, French, and British whaling and sealing ships looked for bases to take on supplies. Missionaries, too, moved into the Pacific region and opened the way for political involvement.

In 1878, the United States secured an unequal treaty from Samoa, gaining rights such as extraterritoriality and a naval station. Other nations gained similar agreements. As their rivalry increased, the United States, Germany, and Britain agreed to a triple protectorate over Samoa.

From the mid-1800s, American sugar growers pressed for power in Hawaii. When the Hawaiian queen Liliuokalani (lee lee oo oh kah LAH nee)

---

*The thousands of islands splashed across the Pacific are known as Oceania. Besides Australia and New Zealand, Oceania includes three regions: Melanesia, Micronesia, and Polynesia. (See the map in the Reference Section at the back of this book.)

Skills Assessment

Geography Spices first attracted Europeans to Southeast Asia. Later, the Industrial Revolution encouraged the search for raw materials and new markets.

1. **Location** On the map, locate **(a)** New Guinea, **(b)** Siam, **(c)** Singapore, **(d)** Philippines, **(e)** Indochina.
2. **Region** Which European countries claimed territory on the mainland?
3. **Critical Thinking Making Inferences** According to the map, which countries had the widest variety of resources?

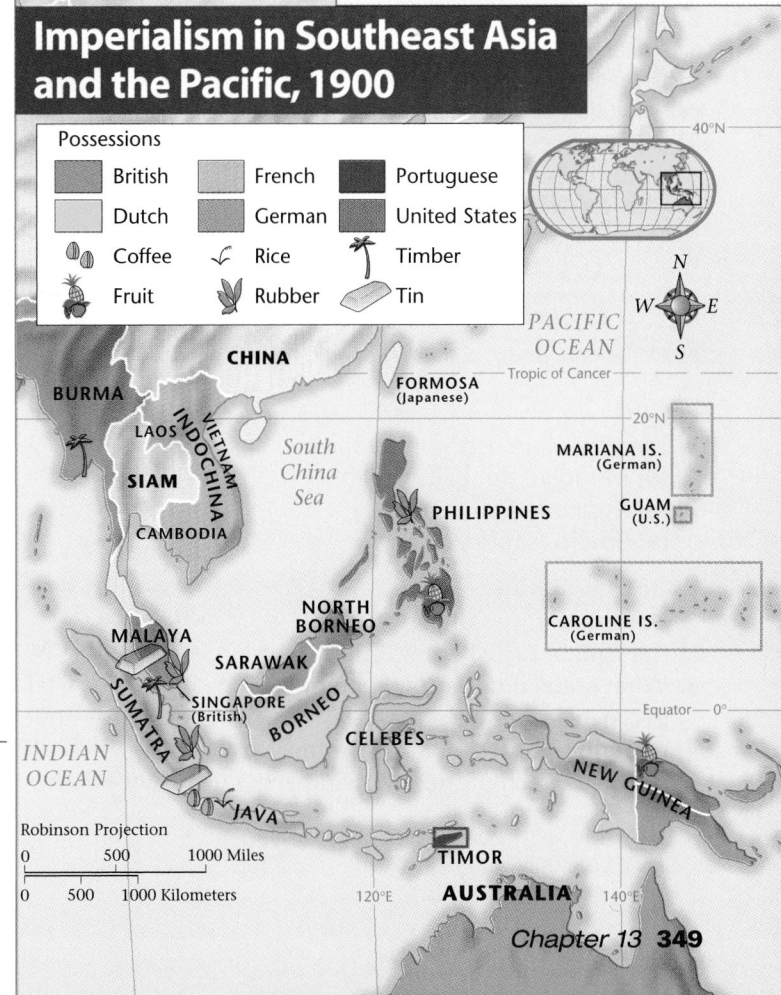

Imperialism in Southeast Asia and the Pacific, 1900

Possessions

British	French	Portuguese
Dutch	German	United States
Coffee	Rice	Timber
Fruit	Rubber	Tin

CHINA
BURMA
LAOS
VIETNAM
INDOCHINA
SIAM
CAMBODIA
South China Sea
FORMOSA (Japanese)
PHILIPPINES
MARIANA IS. (German)
GUAM (U.S.)
CAROLINE IS. (German)
MALAYA
SARAWAK
NORTH BORNEO
SINGAPORE (British)
SUMATRA
BORNEO
CELEBES
INDIAN OCEAN
JAVA
TIMOR
NEW GUINEA
AUSTRALIA
PACIFIC OCEAN
Tropic of Cancer
40°N
20°N
Equator — 0°
120°E
140°E

Robinson Projection

0   500   1000 Miles
0   500   1000 Kilometers

tried to reduce foreign influence, American planters overthrew her in 1893. They then asked the United States to annex Hawaii, which it did in 1898. Supporters of annexation argued that if the United States did not take Hawaii, Britain or Japan might do so.

The United States and the Philippines

In the 1500s, Spain had seized the Philippines. Catholic missionaries spread Christianity among the Filipinos, and the Catholic Church gained enormous power and wealth. Many Filipinos accused the Church of abusing its position. By the late 1800s, their anger had fueled strong resistance to Spanish rule. Inspired by leaders such as José Rizal, many Filipinos worked to end Spanish control of the islands.

The United States became involved in the fate of the Philippines almost by accident. In 1898, war broke out between Spain and the United States over Cuba's independence from Spain. During the Spanish-American War, American battleships destroyed the Spanish fleet, which was stationed in the Philippines. Seizing the moment, Filipino leaders declared their independence from Spain. Rebel soldiers threw their support into the fight against Spanish troops.

In return for their help, the Filipino rebels had expected the Americans to recognize their independence. The peace settlement with Spain, however, placed the Philippines under American control.

Bitterly disappointed, Filipino nationalists renewed their struggle. From 1899 to 1901, Filipinos led by Emilio Aguinaldo (ah gee NAHL doh) battled American forces. Thousands of Americans and hundreds of thousands of Filipinos died. In the end, the Americans crushed the rebellion. The United States set out to modernize the Philippines through education, improved health care, economic reform, and construction of dams, roads, railways, and ports. Additionally, the United States promised Filipinos self-rule some time in the future.

Looking Ahead

By 1900, the United States, Britain, France, and Germany had claimed nearly every island in the Pacific. Japan, too, wanted a share of the region. Eventually, it would gain control of German possessions in the Pacific. Japanese territorial expansion would set the stage for a growing rivalry with the United States.

Biography

José Rizal 1861–1896

José Rizal was a pacifist and never fought in any battle himself. Still, he inspired other Filipinos to fight for independence from Spain.

Rizal was a talented man. He was a doctor, sculptor, novelist, and philosopher who spoke many languages fluently. He also wrote two novels that criticized Spanish leaders in the Philippines. The books were banned and even burned. The rulers later arrested Rizal as a revolutionary and had him executed by a firing squad. He is still recognized as a martyr of the cause for independence and a national hero.

Theme: Impact of the Individual Why does Rizal's life make him a national hero?

SECTION 2 Assessment

Recall
1. **Identify: (a)** French Indochina, **(b)** Mongkut, **(c)** Liliuokalani, **(d)** Spanish-American War, **(e)** Emilio Aguinaldo.

Comprehension
2. Compare imperialist policies of the Dutch, British, and French.
3. What steps did Siam take to preserve its independence?
4. Describe how the United States acquired each of the following territories in the Pacific: **(a)** Samoa, **(b)** Hawaii, **(c)** Philippines.

Critical Thinking and Writing
5. **Comparing** Compare the partition of Southeast Asia to the partition of Africa during the Age of Imperialism. **(a)** How was it similar? **(b)** How was it different?
6. **Connecting to Geography** Why were the Philippines, Singapore, and Indonesia of strategic value?

Activity

Creating a Time Line Create a time line showing the colonialization of Southeast Asia and the Pacific during the Age of Imperialism.

Self-Rule for Canada, Australia, and New Zealand

Reading Focus

- How did Canada achieve self-rule?
- How did European settlement change the course of Australian history?
- How did New Zealand emerge as an independent nation?

Vocabulary

indigenous
confederation
dominion

Taking Notes

Copy this Venn diagram. As you read, fill in the information on the similarities and differences between the colonial experiences of Canada and those of Australia. To help you get started, some entries have been made.

CANADA
- Two distinct populations, British and French
•

- Set up government based on British model

AUSTRALIA
- Established as penal colony for Britain
•

Main Idea The British colonies of Canada, Australia, and New Zealand won independence faster and with greater ease than territories in other regions.

Setting the Scene

The pattern of imperialism in the British colonies of Australia and New Zealand differed from that in other parts of the world. The indigenous (ihn DIHJ uh nuhs), or original, inhabitants of these regions were relatively few in number, and white settlers quickly subdued and replaced them. Still, the process of "replacement" was as deadly as it had been in the Americas some 200 years earlier.

These two English-speaking colonies, as well as Canada, won independence faster and with greater ease than England's territories in Africa or Asia. One reason was that they, unlike nonwestern peoples, had cultural roots in western-style government. However, western racial attitudes also played a part. Imperialist nations like Britain felt that whites could govern themselves. Nonwhites in places like India were thought to be incapable of shouldering such responsibility.

DISCOVERY CHANNEL SCHOOL Video
Learn about Europeans in Australia.

Canada Achieves Self-Rule

Canada's first European rulers were the French. When France lost Canada to Britain in 1763, thousands of French-speaking settlers remained. After the American Revolution, an estimated 30,000 or more colonists who had remained loyal to Britain fled to Canada. Unlike the French-speaking Catholics, the newcomers were English-speaking and Protestant.

Native Americans formed another strand of the Canadian heritage. In the 1790s, various Native American people still lived in eastern Canada. Others, in the west and the north, remained largely undisturbed by the movement of white settlers.

The Two Canadas To ease ethnic tensions, Britain passed the Canada Act in 1791. It created two provinces: English-speaking Upper Canada (now Ontario) and French-speaking Lower Canada (now Quebec). Each had its own laws, legislature, and royal governor. French traditions and the Catholic Church were protected in Lower Canada, while English traditions and laws guided Upper Canada.

During the early 1800s, unrest grew in both colonies. The people of Upper Canada resented the power held by a small British elite. In Lower Canada, too, people felt that British officials ignored their needs. In 1837, discontent flared into rebellion in both Upper and Lower Canada. "Put down the villains who oppress and enslave our country," cried William Lyon Mackenzie, a leader of the Upper Canada revolt.

Connections to Today

A Quandary for Quebec

Many Quebecers want Quebec to become independent. They believe that the cultural differences between French and English speakers are too deep for them to share the same country. They feel allegiance to Quebec rather than to Canada as a whole.

In 1995, a referendum on secession was held in Quebec. The final vote was almost a tie, with 50.5 percent voting against separation and 49.5 percent supporting the idea. Thus, the stage is set for continuing tension.

Theme: Diversity In what ways are Quebecers different from citizens of other Canadian provinces?

Canada, 1867–1914

Westward expansion
(Color value indicates the passing of time)

1891 ————————————————→ 1914

Natural resources

Gold   Coal

Silver   Timber

Copper   Fish

Iron Ore   Lobster

ARCTIC OCEAN

Azimuthal Equal Area Projection

0   250   500 Miles

0   250   500 Kilometers

YUKON TERRITORY 1898

NORTHWEST TERRITORIES 1870

CANADA

BRITISH COLUMBIA 1871

ALBERTA 1905

SASKATCHEWAN 1905

MANITOBA 1870

Hudson Bay

QUEBEC 1867

ATLANTIC OCEAN

ONTARIO 1867

PACIFIC OCEAN

ROCKY MTS.

Peace R.

Mackenzie R.

Fraser R.

Saskatchewan R.

PRINCE EDWARD I. 1873

NEW BRUNSWICK 1867

NOVA SCOTIA 1867

UNITED STATES

L. Superior   L. Huron   L. Michigan   L. Erie   L. Ontario

St. Lawrence R.

Skills Assessment

Geography By the end of the 1800s, railroads were moving people from one coast of Canada to the other.

1. **Location** *On the map, locate (a) Quebec, (b) Ontario, (c) Alberta, (d) British Columbia.*
2. **Region** *Which of the provinces on this map was organized last?*
3. **Critical Thinking Drawing Conclusions** *What major geographic feature might have provided an obstacle to large-scale migration before the construction of railroads?*

The Durham Report The British had learned a lesson from the American Revolution. While they hurried to put down the disorder, they sent an able politician, Lord Durham, to study the causes of the unrest. In 1839, the Durham Report called for the two Canadas to be reunited and given control over their own affairs.

In 1840, Parliament passed the Act of Union, a major step toward self-government. It gave Canada an elected legislature to determine domestic policies. Britain kept control of foreign policy and trade.

Dominion of Canada Like the United States, Canada expanded westward in the 1800s. As the country grew, two Canadians, John Macdonald and George Étienne Cartier, urged confederation, or unification, of all Canada's provinces. Like many Canadians, Macdonald and Cartier feared that the United States might try to dominate Canada. A strong union, they felt, would strengthen the nation against United States ambitions and help Canada develop economically.

Britain finally agreed. In 1867, it passed the British North America Act of 1867, creating the Dominion of Canada. It united four provinces into a dominion, or self-governing nation. Six additional provinces later joined the union.

As a dominion, Canada had its own parliament, modeled on that of Britain. By 1900, Canada had also been granted some control over its own foreign policy. Still, although self-governing, Canada maintained close ties with the British monarchy.

Expansion John Macdonald, Canada's first prime minister, encouraged expansion across the continent. To unite the far-flung regions of Canada, he called for a transcontinental railroad. In 1885, the Canadian Pacific Railway opened, linking eastern and western Canada. Wherever the railroad went, settlers followed. It moved people and products, such as timber and manufactured goods, across the country.

As in the United States, westward expansion destroyed the way of life of Native Americans in Canada. Most were forced to sign treaties giving up their lands. Some resisted. Louis Riel led a revolt of the métis, people of mixed Native American and European descent. Many were French-speaking Catholics who accused the government of stealing their land and trying to destroy their language and religion. Government troops put down the uprising and executed Riel.

Immigration In the late 1800s and early 1900s, immigration increased as people flooded into Canada from across Europe and Asia. Newcomers from Germany, Italy, Poland, Russia, Ukraine, China, and Japan enriched Canada economically and culturally.

By 1914, Canada was a flourishing nation. Two issues continued to plague it, however. First, French-speaking Canadians were determined to preserve their separate heritage, making it hard for Canadians to create a single national identity. Second, the United States exerted a powerful economic and cultural influence that threatened to dominate its neighbor to the north. Both issues have continued to affect Canada to the present day.

Europeans in Australia

The Dutch in the 1600s were the first Europeans to reach Australia—the world's smallest continent. In 1770, Captain James Cook claimed Australia for Britain. For a time, however, it remained too distant to attract European settlers.

The First Settlers Like most regions claimed by imperialist powers, Australia had long been inhabited by other people. The first settlers had reached Australia perhaps 50,000 years earlier, probably from Southeast Asia, and spread across the continent. Cut off from the larger world, the Aborigines, as Europeans later called them,* lived in small hunting and food-gathering bands, much as their Stone Age ancestors had. Aborigine groups spoke as many as 250 distinct languages. When white settlers arrived in Australia, the indigenous population suffered disastrously.

A Penal Colony Events halfway around the world in North America and Britain ended Australia's isolation and brought Europeans to the island continent. During the 1700s, Britain had sent convicts to its North American colonies, especially to Georgia. The American Revolution closed that outlet just when the Industrial Revolution was disrupting British society. Prisons in London and other cities were jammed with poor people arrested for crimes such as stealing food or goods to pawn, agitating against the government, or murder.

To fulfill the need for prisons, Britain made Australia into a penal colony. The first ships, carrying about 700 convicts, arrived in Botany Bay, Australia, in 1788. The men, women, and children who survived the grueling eight-month voyage faced more hardships on shore. Many were city dwellers with no farming skills. Under the brutal discipline of soldiers, work gangs cleared land for the settlement.

Among these first arrivals was Matthew Everingham, who at the age of 14 had been sentenced to seven years in Australia for stealing two books.

---

*Aborigine was a word used by Europeans to denote the earliest people to live in a place. Today, many Australian Aborigines call themselves Kooris.

Primary Source

A Convict's Life
Convicts in the Australian penal colonies found that the attitudes of their masters determined the quality of their lives. Here, a son describes his father's life as a shepherd:

"He became a dreadful spectacle ... weak and helpless as a child. . . . After my father had been out in the bush from sunrise to sunset, he had then to retire for repose to the watchbox, 6 feet by 18 inches, with a small bed and one blanket, where he could lie and gaze upon the starry heavens, and where the wind blew in at one end and out of the other, with nothing to ward off the pitiless storm. . . . Besides this he had to walk four miles [at night] for his rations."

—John Standfield, quoted in *The Fatal Shore* (Hughes)

Skills Assessment

Primary Source Why did a convict-shepherd have such a terrible life in Australia?

Geography of Australia and New Zealand

Legend:
- Penal settlements
- Coal
- Copper
- Gas
- Gold
- Iron
- Oil
- Other metals
- Sheep
- Silver
- Timber

Map labels: Timor Sea, Darwin, Arafura Sea, CAPE YORK PEN., INDIAN OCEAN, GREAT SANDY DESERT, AUSTRALIA, WESTERN PLATEAU, SIMPSON DESERT, Great Barrier Reef, GREAT DIVIDING RANGE, Coral Sea, Tropic of Capricorn, PACIFIC OCEAN, CENTRAL LOWLANDS, Moreton Bay, Brisbane, GREAT VICTORIA DESERT, NULLARBOR PLAIN, Port Macquarie, DARLING RANGE, Perth, Great Australian Bight, GREAT DIVIDING RANGE, Newcastle, Sydney, Adelaide, Canberra, Melbourne, Mercator Projection, 0 300 600 Miles, 0 300 600 Kilometers, Bass Strait, Tasman Sea, NEW ZEALAND, Auckland, NORTH ISLAND, Wellington, Christchurch, SOUTH ISLAND, TASMANIA

Skills Assessment

Geography Australia is both a continent and a country. Australia and its neighbor New Zealand feature a great variety of landforms.

1. **Location** On the map, locate **(a)** Great Barrier Reef, **(b)** Great Victoria Desert, **(c)** Central Lowlands, **(d)** Tasmania.
2. **Region (a)** In which region was gold found? **(b)** What geographic features did people encounter during the 1851 gold rush?
3. **Critical Thinking Drawing Conclusions** How does the map help you conclude that the population of Australia is not evenly distributed?

Despite illness and beatings during the course of his sentence, Everingham continued to have hope for the future:

> "I have now two years and seven months to remain a convict and then I am at liberty to act as a free-born Englishman ought to. . . . I am yet but young, only 19. If my health is spared I shall not be one jot the worse for being transported."
> —Matthew Everingham, quoted in "Children of the First Fleet," *National Geographic*

Everingham later married another convict, Elizabeth Rimes, and stayed in Australia. Their descendants, like those of other convicts and early settlers, carved out farms. Some prospered in their new homeland.

Into the Outback In the early 1800s, Britain encouraged free citizens to emigrate to Australia by offering them land and tools. As the newcomers occupied coastal lands, they thrust aside or killed the Aborigines. After settlers found that sheepherding was suited to the land and climate, a prosperous wool industry grew up in Australia.

In 1851, a gold rush in eastern Australia brought a population boom. Many gold hunters stayed on to become ranchers and farmers. They pushed into the rugged interior known as the Outback, displacing the Aborigines and carving out huge sheep ranches and wheat farms. By the late 1800s, Australia had won a place in a growing world economy.

Achieving Self-Government Like Canada, Australia was made up of separate colonies scattered around the continent. During the Age of Imperialism, Britain worried about interference from other powers. To counter this threat and to boost development, it responded to Australian demands for self-rule. In 1901, Britain helped the colonies unite into the independent Commonwealth of Australia. The new country kept its ties to Britain by recognizing the British monarch as its head of state.

The Australian constitution drew on both British and American models. Like the United States Constitution, it set up a federal system that limited the power of the central government. As in Britain, Australia's executive is a prime minister chosen by the majority party in Parliament. Unlike Britain and the United States, Australia quickly granted women the right to vote. It also was the first nation to introduce the secret ballot.

New Zealand

Far to the southeast of Australia lies New Zealand. In 1769, Captain Cook claimed its islands for Britain. Missionaries landed there in 1814 to convert the local people, the Maoris, to Christianity.

Maori Struggles Unlike Australia, where the Aborigines were spread thinly across a large continent, the Maoris were concentrated in a smaller area. They were descended from seafaring people who had reached New Zealand from Polynesia in the 1200s. The Maoris were settled farmers. They were also determined to defend their land.

Missionaries were followed by white settlers, who were attracted by the mild climate and good soil. These settlers introduced sheep and cattle and were soon exporting wool, mutton, and beef. In 1840, Britain annexed New Zealand.

As colonists poured in, they took over more and more of the land, leading to fierce wars with the Maoris. Many Maoris died in the struggle. Still more perished from disease, alcoholism, and other misfortunes that followed European colonization.

By the 1870s, resistance crumbled. The Maori population had fallen drastically, from 250,000 to less than 50,000. Only in recent years has the Maori population started to grow once more.

Self-Government Like settlers in Australia and Canada, white New Zealanders sought self-rule. In 1907, they won independence, with their own parliament, prime minister, and elected legislature. They, too, preserved close ties to the British empire.

New Zealand pioneered in several areas of democratic government. In 1893, it became the first nation to give suffrage to women. Later, it was in the forefront of other social reforms, passing laws to guarantee old-age pensions and a minimum wage for all workers.

SECTION 3 Assessment

Recall
1. **Identify:** (a) Upper Canada, (b) Lower Canada, (c) British North America Act, (d) Aborigines, (e) Maoris.
2. **Define:** (a) indigenous, (b) confederation, (c) dominion.

Comprehension
3. What steps led to Canadian self-rule?
4. How did the British settle Australia?

5. Why did Maoris fight colonists in New Zealand?

Critical Thinking and Writing
6. **Analyzing Information** Why might young nations like Australia and New Zealand have been willing to grant women the right to vote before European nations did so?
7. **Synthesizing Information** What ethnic tensions did Australia, Canada, and New Zealand face?

Go Online
PHSchool.com

Use the Internet to research the British Commonwealth. Then, write a report identifying the member countries and the purpose of the organization. For help with this activity, use **Web Code mkd-2657.**

SECTION 4

Economic Imperialism in Latin America

Reading Focus

- What political and economic problems faced new Latin American nations?
- How did Mexico struggle for stability?
- How did the United States influence Latin America?

Vocabulary

regionalism

caudillo

economic dependence

peonage

Taking Notes

Copy this concept web. As you read, fill in the major problems facing Latin American countries during the 1800s. To help you get started, parts of the diagram have been completed.

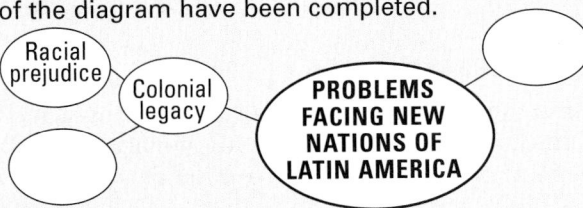

Main Idea The economy of Latin America became dependent on industrialized nations for investment, technology, and manufactured goods.

Setting the Scene The new technology of the Industrial Revolution allowed European nations to import goods from around the world. Meat, which spoiled easily and traditionally required drying before being transported, could now be shipped across the globe in refrigerated vessels. One observer noted: "Great Britain supplies Brazil with its steam and sailing ships, and paves and repairs its streets, lights its cities with gas, . . . carries its mail." These and other developments contributed to the intertwining of nations that might be thousands of miles apart.

During the Age of Imperialism, Latin American nations found their economies increasingly dependent on those of more developed countries. Britain, and later the United States, invested heavily in Latin America.

Lingering Political Problems

Simón Bolívar had hoped to create strong ties among the nations of Latin America. After all, most people shared a common language, religion, and cultural heritage. But feuds among leaders, geographic barriers, and local nationalism shattered that dream of unity. In the end, 20 separate nations emerged.

These new nations wrote constitutions modeled on that of the United States. They set up republics with elected legislatures. During the 1800s, however, most Latin American nations were plagued by revolts, civil war, and dictatorships.

Colonial Legacy Many problems had their origins in colonial rule, as independence barely changed the existing social and political hierarchy. Creoles simply replaced peninsulares as the ruling class. The Roman Catholic Church kept its privileged position and still controlled huge amounts of land.

For most people—mestizos, mulattoes, blacks, and Indians—life did not improve after independence. The new constitutions guaranteed equality before the law, but deep-rooted inequalities remained. Voting rights were limited. Racial prejudice was widespread, and land remained in the hands of a few. Owners of haciendas ruled their great estates, and the peasants who worked them, like medieval European lords.

A City in Brazil
By 1900, the city of Rio de Janeiro, Brazil (below), was a bustling modern seaport. Yet much of the nation's wealth flowed out of the harbor and across the ocean to Europe.

Theme: Global Interaction Why might industrialized nations be eager to invest in Latin American countries?

Instability With few roads and no tradition of unity, the new nations were weakened by regionalism, loyalty to a local area. Local strongmen, called *caudillos,* assembled private armies to resist the central government. At times, popular *caudillos* gained national power. They looted the treasury, ignored the constitution, and ruled as dictators. Power struggles led to frequent revolts that changed little except the name of the leader. In the long run, power remained in the hands of a privileged few who had no desire to share it.

As in Europe, the ruling elite in Latin America were divided between conservatives and liberals. Conservatives defended the old social order, favored press censorship, and strongly supported the Catholic Church. Liberals backed laissez-faire economics, religious toleration, greater access to education, and freedom of the press. Liberals saw themselves as enlightened supporters of progress but often showed little concern for the needs of the majority of the people.

The Economics of Dependence

Under colonial rule, mercantilist policies made Latin America economically dependent on Spain and Portugal. Colonies sent raw materials such as sugar, cotton, or precious metals to the parent country and had to buy manufactured goods from them. Strict laws kept colonists from trading with other countries or building local industries that might compete with the parent country.

After independence, this pattern changed very little. The new republics did adopt free trade, welcoming all comers. Britain and the United States rushed into the new markets, replacing Spain as the chief trading partners with Latin American nations. But the region remained as economically dependent as before.

Economic dependence occurs when less-developed nations export raw materials and commodities to industrial nations and import manufactured goods, capital, and technological know-how. The relationship is unequal because the more developed—and wealthier—nation can control prices and the terms of trade.

Foreign Influence In the 1800s, foreign goods flooded Latin America, creating large profits for foreigners and for a handful of local business people. Foreign investment, which could yield enormous profits, was often accompanied by interference. Investors from Britain, the United States, and other nations might pressure their own governments to take action if political events or reform movements in a Latin American country seemed to threaten their interests.

Economic Growth After 1850, some Latin American economies did grow. With foreign capital, they were able to develop mining and agriculture. Chile exported copper and nitrates, and Argentina expanded livestock and wheat production. Brazil exported coffee and rubber as well as sugar. By the early 1900s, both Venezuela and Mexico were developing important oil industries.

Throughout the region, foreigners invested in modern ports and railroads to carry goods from the interior to coastal cities. As in the United States, European immigrants poured into Latin America. The newcomers helped to promote economic activity, and a small middle class emerged.

Thanks to trade, investment, technology, and migration, Latin American nations moved into the world economy. Yet development was limited. The tiny elite at the top benefited from the economic upturn, but very little trickled down to the masses of people at the bottom. The poor earned too little to buy consumer goods. Without a strong demand, many industries failed to develop.

Primary Source

Imitating European Fashions
The wealthy in Brazil in the late 1800s regarded European goods and culture as superior to their own. Here, a Brazilian writer describes how the elite of his country copied British ways:

"At that time . . . Brazil did not manufacture a yard of silk, a shoe, a spool of thread; everything was imported. . . . Men's clothing for a tropical climate was made of English wool suitable for life in the unheated homes of an English winter. I asked myself: how did they stand the heat? The ladies when they took off their shoes at home used slippers of heavy wool, as if they were in Siberia. . . . Except for the poor, I never saw in the Pernambuco [his hometown] of my time anyone dressed in light clothing."

—Gilbert Amado,
História da Minha Infância

Skills Assessment

Primary Source Why did the elite in Pernambuco dress so impractically?

Imperialism in the Caribbean and South America, 1898–1917

United States possessions
Under United States influence
British possessions
Dutch possessions
French possessions

Fishing
Timber
Bananas
Coffee
Sugar
Cacao
Tobacco

UNITED STATES

Gulf of Mexico

ATLANTIC OCEAN

MEXICO

Tropic of Cancer

30°N
20°N

BAHAMA ISLANDS (Br.)

Grand Cayman
Little Cayman
CAYMAN IS. (Br.)

CUBA

DOMINICAN REPUBLIC

PUERTO RICO

U.S. VIRGIN ISLANDS

ANTIGUA (Br.)

HAITI

JAMAICA

GUADELOUPE (Fr.)

DOMINICA

MARTINIQUE (Fr.)

ST. LUCIA

ST. VINCENT

BARBADOS

GRENADA

TOBAGO

TRINIDAD

BRITISH HONDURAS

Caribbean Sea

GUATEMALA
HONDURAS
EL SALVADOR
NICARAGUA

DUTCH ANTILLES
Aruba Curaçao
Bonaire

PACIFIC OCEAN

COSTA RICA

CANAL ZONE

PANAMA

VENEZUELA

COLOMBIA

BRITISH GUIANA
DUTCH GUIANA
FRENCH GUIANA

N W E S

100°W   90°W   80°W   70°W   60°W

0° Equator

10°N

Azimuthal Equal Area Projection
0   200   400 Miles
0   200   400 Kilometers

Geography In the early 1900s, foreign governments often intervened in the Caribbean to protect business interests there.

1. **Location** On the map, locate (a) Caribbean Sea, (b) Cuba, (c) Canal Zone, (d) Honduras.
2. **Place** (a) Which country controlled Martinique? (b) Name two United States possessions. (c) Which islands were controlled by the Dutch?
3. **Critical Thinking Applying Information** Why did the United States have a particularly strong interest in Caribbean affairs?

Mexico's Struggle for Stability

During the 1800s, each Latin American country followed its own course. In this section, we will explore the experiences of Mexico as an example of the challenges facing Latin American nations.

Large landowners, army leaders, and the Catholic Church dominated Mexican politics. However, bitter battles between conservatives and liberals led to revolts and the rise of dictators. Deep social divisions separated wealthy creoles from mestizos and Indians who lived in desperate poverty.

Santa Anna and War Between 1833 and 1855, an ambitious and cunning *caudillo*, Antonio López de Santa Anna, gained and lost power many times. At first, he posed as a liberal reformer. Soon, however, he reversed his stand and crushed efforts at reform.

In Mexico's northern territory of Texas, discontent grew. Settlers from the United States and other countries began an independence movement. In 1835, American settlers and some Mexicans in Texas revolted. The next year they set up an independent republic. In 1845, the United States annexed Texas. Mexicans saw this act as a declaration of war. In the fighting that followed, the United States invaded and defeated Mexico. In the treaty ending the war, Mexico lost almost half its territory. This defeat shook the creole ruling class and triggered new violence between conservatives and liberals.

La Reforma In 1855, Benito Juárez (WAHR ehz) and other liberals seized power and opened an era of reform known as La Reforma. Juárez, a Zapotec Indian, offered hope to the oppressed people of Mexico. He and his fellow reformers revised the Mexican constitution to strip the military of power and end the special privileges of the Church. They ordered the Church to sell unused lands to peasants.

Although conservatives resisted La Reforma and unleashed a civil war, Juárez was elected president in 1861. He used his new office to expand reforms. His opponents turned to Europe for help. In 1863, Napoleon III sent troops to Mexico and set up Austrian archduke Maximilian as emperor.

For four years, Juárez led Mexicans in battle against conservative and French forces. When France withdrew its troops, Maximilian was captured and shot. In 1867, Juárez was returned to power. Although he tried to renew reform, opponents resisted. Juárez, who died in office in 1872, never achieved all the reforms he envisioned. He did, however, help unite Mexico, bring mestizos into political life, and separate church and state.

Growth and Oppression   After Juárez died, General Porfirio Díaz, a hero of the war against the French, gained power. From 1876 to 1880 and 1884 to 1911, he ruled as a dictator. In the name of "Order and Progress," he strengthened the army, local police, and central government. Any opposition was brutally crushed.

Under his harsh rule, Mexico made impressive economic advances. It built railroads, increased foreign trade, developed some industry, and expanded mining. Growth, however, had a high cost. Capital for development came from foreign investors, to whom Díaz granted special rights. He also let wealthy landowners buy up Indian lands.

The rich prospered, but most Mexicans remained poor. Many Indians and mestizos fell into peonage to their employers. In the peonage system, hacienda owners would give workers advances on their wages and require them to stay on the hacienda until they had paid back what they owed. Wages remained low, and workers were rarely able to repay the hacienda owner. Many children died in infancy. Others worked 12-hour days and never learned to read or write.

In the early 1900s, pressure mounted for real change. Middle-class Mexicans demanded democracy. Urban and rural workers joined protests and strikes. In 1910, Mexico plunged into revolution. It was the first true social revolution in Latin America.

The Influence of the United States

As nations like Mexico tried to build stable governments, a neighboring republic, the United States, was expanding across North America. At first, the young republics in the Western Hemisphere looked favorably on each other. Bolívar praised the United States as a "model of political virtues and moral enlightenment." In time, however, Latin American nations felt threatened by the "Colossus of the North," the giant power that cast its shadow over the entire hemisphere.

The Monroe Doctrine   In the 1820s, Spain plotted to recover its American colonies. Britain opposed any move that might close the door to trade with Latin America. It asked the United States to join it in a statement opposing any new colonization of the Americas.

President James Monroe, however, wanted to avoid any "entangling alliance" with Britain. Acting alone, in 1823 he issued the Monroe Doctrine. "The American continents," it declared, "are henceforth not to be considered as subjects for future colonization by any European powers." The United States lacked the military power to enforce the doctrine. But knowledge that Britain was willing to use its strong navy to support the doctrine discouraged European interference. For more than a century, the Monroe Doctrine would be the key to United States policy in the Americas.

Expansion   As a result of the war with Mexico, in 1848 the United States acquired the thinly populated regions of northern Mexico, including the Colorado River valley and California. The victory fed dreams of future

Global Connections

The Monroe Doctrine in Action

The statement of President Monroe has been interpreted many different ways since 1823. In 1845, President Polk used the doctrine to lay claim to all of the disputed Oregon territory and also to warn European powers not to interfere in the Mexican War of 1846–1848. In the early 1900s, President Theodore Roosevelt claimed that the Monroe Doctrine gave the United States the right to exercise an "international police power."

In 1939, the interpretation of the doctrine was narrowed. President Franklin Roosevelt declared that the doctrine only warranted opposition to European interference in the Western Hemisphere, not to United States interference in the affairs of other countries.

Theme: Global Interaction
Why would presidents interpret the Monroe Doctrine differently at different times?

expansion. Before the century had ended, the United States controlled much of North America and was becoming involved in overseas conflicts.

For decades, Cuban patriots had battled to free their island from Spanish rule. As they began to make headway, the United States joined their cause, declaring war on Spain in 1898. The brief Spanish-American War ended in a crushing defeat for Spain.

In the peace treaty ending the war, the United States acquired Puerto Rico in the Caribbean and the Philippines and Guam in the Pacific. Cuba was granted independence, but in 1901 the United States forced Cubans to add the Platt Amendment to their constitution. It gave the United States naval bases in Cuba and the right to intervene in Cuban affairs.

Intervention American investments in Latin America soared in the early 1900s. Citing the need to protect those investments, in 1904 the United States issued the Roosevelt Corollary to the Monroe Doctrine. Under this policy, the United States claimed "international police power" in the Western Hemisphere. When the Dominican Republic failed to pay its foreign debts, the United States sent in troops. It collected customs duties, paid off the debts, and remained there for years.

In the next decades, the United States sent troops to Cuba, Haiti, Mexico, Honduras, Nicaragua, and other countries in Central America and the Caribbean. Like European powers in Africa and Asia, the United States intervened in the Caribbean to protect American lives and investments.

Panama Canal From the late 1800s, the United States had wanted to build a canal across Central America. A canal would let the American fleet move swiftly between the Atlantic and Pacific oceans and protect its coastlines on either side of the continent. It would also greatly reduce the cost of trade between the two oceans.

Panama, however, belonged to Colombia, which refused to sell the United States land for the canal. In 1903, the United States backed a revolt by Panamanians against Colombia. The Panamanians quickly won independence and gave the United States land to build the canal.

The Panama Canal opened in 1914. It was an engineering marvel that boosted trade and shipping worldwide. To people in Latin America, however, the canal was another example of "Yankee imperialism." In those years, nationalist feeling in the hemisphere was often expressed as anti-Americanism. (In 1978, the United States agreed to a series of treaties that would grant Panama control over the Canal Zone by the year 2000.)

Geography and History

French Failure in Panama

In 1879, even before the United States envisioned a canal in Panama, Frenchman Ferdinand de Lesseps dreamed of completing the engineering achievement for the honor of his country. He had built the Suez Canal in Egypt, but disease and disaster plagued him in Panama. As fast as De Lesseps could send engineers and construction workers to Panama, they died of malaria, yellow fever, and snakebite. Asked one magazine, "Is De Lesseps a canal digger or a grave digger?"

High costs drove his company into bankruptcy within 10 years. It would take another 25 years before American engineers successfully completed the canal.

 Theme: Geography and History What problems did De Lesseps face in Panama that he had not confronted in Egypt?

SECTION 4 Assessment

Recall

1. **Identify:** (a) Antonio López de Santa Anna, (b) Benito Juárez, (c) Porfirio Díaz, (d) Monroe Doctrine, (e) Roosevelt Corollary.
2. **Define:** (a) regionalism, (b) *caudillo,* (c) economic dependence, (d) peonage.

Comprehension

3. What problems faced new nations in Latin America?
4. How did imperialism encourage economic dependence?
5. Describe two ways the United States influenced Latin America.

Critical Thinking and Writing

6. **Identifying Main Ideas** Reformers introduced many changes to Latin America during the late 1800s and early 1900s. Describe the reforms and identify those that seem to have been most successful. Explain.
7. **Defending a Position** (a) Why might developing nations encourage foreign investment? (b) Do you think foreign investors should have the right to intervene in another nation's affairs to protect their investments? Explain.

Use the Internet to research the building of the Panama Canal. Write a diary describing a week in the life of a worker on the canal. For help with this activity, use **Web Code mkd-2662.**

Impact of Imperialism

Reading Focus

- How did imperialism lead to new economic patterns?
- What was the cultural impact of imperialism?
- How did new political tensions develop as the result of imperialism?

Taking Notes

Copy this concept web. As you read, fill in the information on the impact of imperialism on the different cultures. To help you get started, parts of the diagram have been completed.

Western culture — IMPACT OF IMPERIALISM — Traditional cultures — Technology — Money for investment

Main Idea Imperialism brought both benefits and challenges to every region of the world.

Setting the Scene

In 1900, Rudyard Kipling was among the most popular writers in the English-speaking world. Kipling was born in British-ruled India and, after being educated in England, returned to India as a journalist for a number of years. His stories and poems often glorified imperialism or presented it as a romantic adventure.

Like most British imperialists, Kipling emphasized the differences between what he saw as "exotic" India and his own English culture. In one famous poem, however, he recounted a dramatic clash between equals: a gallant Afghan chief and a heroic British officer. Though enemies, the two men respect each other and act with great nobility and courage. The poem begins and ends with these lines:

"Oh, East is East, and West is West; and never the
    twain shall meet,
Till Earth and Sky stand presently at God's great
    Judgment Seat;
But there is neither East nor West, Border, nor Breed,
    nor Birth,
When two strong men stand face to face, though
    they come from the ends of the Earth!"
—Rudyard Kipling, "The Ballad of East and West"

The Age of Imperialism brought confrontations between differing cultures "from the ends of the Earth." By 1900, western nations had unfurled their flags over much of the globe. That expansion set off radical changes that reshaped the lives of subject people from Africa to Southeast Asia and the Pacific. For their western rulers, too, imperialism would bring about dramatic economic, political, and cultural changes.

New Economic Patterns

During the Age of Imperialism, a truly global economy emerged. It was dominated by the industrialized nations of the West, especially the United States, Britain, France, and Germany. From these nations, machine-made goods, investment capital, and technology flowed to the rest of the world. In return, the people of Africa, Asia, and Latin

One Link in a Global Economy

By the early 1900s, imperialism had created a global economy. The coffee grown at this plantation on the island of Java might have ended up in an American or Dutch dining room.

Theme: Economics and Technology Who might profit from this growing global economy?

America provided agricultural goods, natural resources, and cheap labor. Most profits from this global exchange went to the industrialized nations.

The demands of the new world economy disrupted traditional local economies in Africa and Asia. As in Europe before the Industrial Revolution, most people on these continents grew and produced goods by hand for local use. Under colonial rule, they were forced to supply products such as rubber, copper, and coffee needed by the industrial world.

Money Economy   Western capitalists developed plantations and mines but relied on a steady supply of local labor to work them. At the same time, colonial rulers introduced a money economy that replaced the old barter system that existed in some countries. To cover the expense of governing their colonies, colonial authorities imposed heavy taxes on their subjects. The only way that people could earn money to pay the taxes was by working on plantations, in mines, or on projects such as railroad building.

Families were disrupted as men left their homes and villages to work in distant mines or cities. In southern and eastern Africa, especially, many men became migrant workers. Their departure shattered families and undermined village life as women were left alone to grow food and support their children. In other parts of the world, such as Japan and Latin America, sons were kept at home to farm while daughters were sent to cities to find work as domestics or in the growing textile industry.

Economic Dependency   Mass-produced goods from the industrialized world further disrupted traditional economies. India, for example, was seen by Britain as a great market for its goods. It flooded the subcontinent with cheap, factory-made cloth. The British textile industry flourished. Indian weavers who produced cloth by hand, however, could not compete and were ruined. Elsewhere, too, artisan-run businesses and handicraft industries were destroyed.

Local economies that had once been self-sufficient became dependent on the industrial powers, which bought their raw materials and supplied them with manufactured goods. When the demand and prices for crops or minerals were high, colonies prospered. When demand and prices fell, people suffered. In addition, because many workers were producing export crops rather than food for local consumption, famines occurred in lands that had once fed themselves.

Modernization   Colonial rule did bring some economic benefits. Westerners laid the groundwork for modern banking systems. They introduced new technology and built modern communication and transportation networks. Capitalists invested huge sums in railroad building to boost the export economy. Railroads linked plantations and mines to ports, which developers also modernized.

From China to Chile, some local leaders and business people benefited from the new economic system. Countries like Argentina, Brazil, and Chile, for example, used export profits to develop industry, buy modern farm equipment, and promote growth.

Cultural Impact

Like many other peoples in history, Europeans were convinced of their own superiority. During the Age of Imperialism, they also believed that they had a mission to "civilize" the world. Cecil Rhodes, a leading promoter of British imperialism, declared: "The more of the world we inhabit the better it is for the human race. . . . If there be a God, I think what he would like me to do is to paint as much of the map of Africa British red as possible."

Westernization   As westerners conquered other lands, they pressed subject people to accept "modern" ways. By this, they meant western ideas,

Biography

Cecil Rhodes 1853–1902

Cecil Rhodes arrived in South Africa at age 17, determined to make his fortune. He got off to a slow start. His first venture, a cotton-farming project, failed. Then Rhodes turned to diamond and gold mining. By the age of 40, he had become one of the richest men in the world.

However, money was not his real interest. "For its own sake I do not care for money," he once wrote. "I want the power." Rhodes strongly supported British imperialism in Africa. He helped Britain extend its African empire by 1,000,000 square miles and had an entire British colony named after himself—Rhodesia (now Zimbabwe). Rhodes also helped promote the policy of the separation of races in southern Africa.

Theme: Impact of the Individual   How was Cecil Rhodes's desire for power illustrated by his actions?

government, technology, and culture. Thus, during the Age of Imperialism, modernization and westernization came to be seen as one and the same.*

Many nonwesterners, especially in conquered lands, came to accept a belief in western superiority. The overwhelming successes of the western imperialist nations sapped people's confidence in their own leaders and cultures. To share in the material advantages offered by western society, business and professional people and others who had contact with westerners learned western languages, wore western clothing, adopted western manners, and embraced many western ways.

Other nonwesterners, however, had great misgivings about abandoning their own age-old traditions. They greatly resented—and often strongly resisted—western efforts to force new ways on them.

The new imperialism spread western culture around the world. Still, many regions were able to escape much of its influence. In remote areas of Africa, the Middle East, and Asia, many farming villagers and nomadic herders had virtually no contact with westerners. As a result, their lives continued with relatively few changes.

Schools and Hospitals Western culture was often spread by missionaries who built schools and hospitals. They taught children basic literacy and trained young men for jobs in colonial governments.

Western medicine brought many benefits. Missionaries introduced medical breakthroughs such as vaccines and modern methods of hygiene that saved lives. At the same time, however, modern medicine undermined traditional herbalists and local healers, who sometimes possessed useful knowledge of the medicinal value of plants.

Religion Imperialism enabled missionaries to spread their Christian faith across the globe. They had great success in some areas. In southern Africa, for example, Christianity became widespread, although Africans generally adapted its teachings and beliefs to their own traditions. In regions where other world religions or belief systems such as Islam, Hinduism, Buddhism, and Confucianism were deeply rooted, Christian missionaries won fewer converts.

Old and New Ways The pressure to westernize forced colonized people to reevaluate their traditions. In Asia, for example, people were proud of their ancient civilizations. On the other hand, they did work to discourage some customs, such as sati in India or footbinding in China, which they now saw as harmful. In the end, many nonwestern cultures created a complex blend of old and new ways.

As people moved into cities that had become westernized, many still felt the pull of the past. "People come to the city because they want to live

Westernization and Tradition
In French colonies, local rulers kept their titles while real power was held by colonial officials. In this photo, a French colonial governor (left) meets with the king of Laos (right).

Theme: Continuity and Change What element of the king's clothing shows European influence?

---

*The process of modernization along western lines has continued to the present. In today's world, however, modernization and westernization are often seen as separate and different courses.

The Influence of African Art on Picasso

In 1907, Pablo Picasso was inspired while viewing an exhibition of African masks and sculpture in the Trocadéro museum in Paris. He rushed to his studio and repainted the heads of several figures in his painting *Les Demoiselles d' Avignon*. From then on, many of his portraits showed the influence of African art.

The distinctive abstract patterns of stripes and hatchmarks on this mother and child from 1907 show the influence of African art on Picasso's portraits.

Mother and child constituted a frequent theme in Picasso's work. He did this painting in 1903, before his introduction to African art.

Masks like this one inspired Picasso to move in a new direction. He wrote of his visit to the Trocadéro, "If you give spirits a shape, you break free from them. . . . I grasped why I was a painter. All alone in that museum, surrounded by masks. . . ."

Fast Facts

- Picasso's first word was "lápiz," the Spanish word for pencil, and he began drawing almost as soon as he began walking.

- Though many of his works are abstract, Picasso maintained a huge photography collection in his studio and often painted from photographs.

- Picasso lived to age 91 and continued to experiment with new styles until his death.

Portfolio Assessment

Conduct research to find examples of cubist paintings by Picasso and his contemporaries, Juan Gris and Georges Braque. Assemble your examples into a class display. Then, use the display to identify similarities among the three artists' work.

like Europeans," admitted one Nigerian, "but we still feel close to our village and always go back to visit it."

Impact on Western Culture Western cultures changed, too, during the Age of Imperialism. The Columbian Exchange that had begun in 1492 picked up speed in the 1800s. Westerners drank coffee from Brazil and tea from Sri Lanka. They ate bananas from Honduras and pineapples from Hawaii. Their factories turned out products made from rubber harvested on plantations in Southeast Asia or South America.

Archaeologists and historians slowly unearthed evidence about ancient civilizations previously unknown to the West. Westerners who studied Hindu and Buddhist texts, Chinese histories, or Japanese poetry realized that they had much to learn from other civilizations. The arts of Japan, Persia, Africa, and Southeast Asia influenced western sculptors and painters. Western manufacturers also copied designs from other lands, launching fashions for Egyptian furniture, Japanese kimonos, and Chinese embroidery screens.

New Political Tensions

Imperialism had global political consequences, as you have seen. Europeans claimed and conquered large empires in Africa and Asia. They disrupted traditional political units such as tribes and small kingdoms. Often, they united rival peoples under a single government, imposing stability and order where local conflicts had raged for centuries.

By the early 1900s, however, resistance to imperialism was taking a new course. In Africa and Asia, western-educated elites were organizing nationalist movements to end colonial rule.

At the same time, the competition for imperial power was fueling tensions among western nations. In the Sudan in 1898, British forces expanding south from Egypt and French forces pushing east from West Africa met at Fashoda. An armed clash was barely avoided.

Elsewhere, the British and Russians played a cat-and-mouse game in Central Asia. The Great Powers—Germany, Britain, France, and Russia—tried to thwart one another's ambitions in Ottoman lands. More than once, Germany and France teetered on the brink of war over Morocco in North Africa. In 1914 and again in 1939, imperialist ambitions would contribute to the outbreak of two shattering world wars.

SECTION 5 Assessment

Recall
1. **Identify: (a)** Rudyard Kipling, **(b)** Cecil Rhodes.

Comprehension
2. Describe how each of the following affected industrialized nations and traditional cultures: **(a)** money economy, **(b)** dependency, **(c)** modernization.
3. How did imperialism affect cultures around the world?
4. Why did imperialism lead to increased tensions among the industrialized powers of Europe?

Critical Thinking and Writing
5. **Drawing Conclusions** List the benefits and disadvantages brought by colonial rule. Do you think subject people were better or worse off as a result of the Age of Imperialism? Explain.
6. **Recognizing Points of View** How might a subject person respond to the quotation by Cecil Rhodes in this section?

Activity

Creating a Chart
Create a chart showing the movement of goods and money in the global economy that emerged in the late 1800s. Be sure to include effects on traditional economies. Illustrate your chart with original drawings or pictures from magazines.

Creating a Chapter Summary

Copy this graphic organizer on a piece of paper. Include facts that describe the impact of the Age of Imperialism on different areas of the world.

REGION	IMPACT OF IMPERIALISM
JAPAN	• Meiji restoration and westernization • Becomes imperialist power
SOUTHEAST ASIA	• •
CANADA	
AUSTRALIA	
LATIN AMERICA	
WESTERN EUROPE	

Interactive Textbook

For additional review and enrichment activities, see the interactive version of *World History* available on the Web and on CD-ROM.

Go Online
PHSchool.com

For practice test questions for Chapter 13, use **Web Code mka-2668**.

Building Vocabulary

Review the meaning of the chapter vocabulary words listed below. Then, write a sentence for each word in which you define the word.

1. zaibatsu
2. homogeneous society
3. indigenous
4. confederation
5. regionalism
6. *caudillo*
7. economic dependence
8. peonage

Recalling Key Facts

9. How did modernization encourage Japan to seek its own colonies?
10. How did Siam avoid colonization by a European nation?
11. How did the creation of the Dominion of Canada encourage expansion?
12. What role did the United States play in the construction of the Panama Canal?
13. Which nations dominated the global economy that emerged in the late 1800s?
14. How did imperialism encourage economic dependence?

Critical Thinking and Writing

15. **Synthesizing Information** How did the Industrial Revolution contribute to imperialism?
16. **Comparing** Compare Japan's response to western imperialism with that of China. **(a)** How were the two responses similar? **(b)** How were they different?
17. **Connecting to Geography** Would you expect westernization to have a stronger impact in coastal cities or in rural areas? Explain.
18. **Applying Information (a)** What principle did the United States express in the Monroe Doctrine? **(b)** How did the Roosevelt Corollary alter the Monroe Doctrine?
19. **Defending a Position** Mexican President Porfirio Díaz defended his regime: "We were harsh. Sometimes we were harsh to the point of cruelty. But it was necessary then to the life and progress of the nation." Do you agree or disagree with Díaz's view that the end justifies the means? Explain.

In the excerpt below, future Mexican president Benito Juárez describes growing up as a poor Zapotec Indian. Read the excerpt, then answer the questions that follow.

> "As soon as I could think at all, I dedicated myself, insofar as my young age permitted, to work in the fields. In the few intervals in which we were not working, my uncle taught me to read; he showed me how useful and advantageous it would be for me to know the Spanish language, and since at that time it was extremely difficult for poor people, and especially for Indians, to follow any learned career except holy orders, he revealed that he wanted me to study for [the priesthood]. His desire, and the examples that I had before me of fellow countrymen who knew how to read, write, and speak the Spanish language, and of others in the priesthood, awakened in me a vehement desire to learn. . . . However, my uncle's work, and my own, in the fields, frustrated my ambition, and I advanced very little in my lessons. Furthermore, in a village as small as mine, which had hardly 20 families, at a time when hardly anyone was concerned with the education of youth, there was no school."

> —Benito Juárez, *Notes for My Children*

20. What did Juárez's uncle encourage him to learn?
21. Why did his uncle want him to study for the priesthood?
22. What challenges did Juárez encounter?
23. Based on this excerpt, what reforms do you think Juárez might have introduced as president?

Go Online
PHSchool.com

Use the Internet to research the history of one of the colonies in this chapter. Write a report summarizing its history since colonization. Include information on how it gained independence and major events that have occurred since independence. For help with this activity, use **Web Code mkd-2669.**

Cause *and* Effect

Causes

- Industrial Revolution strengthens the West
- Newly industrialized nations seek new markets
- Western nations compete for power
- Westerners feel duty to spread their culture

New Imperialism

Effects

- Europeans claim and conquer large empires in Africa and Asia
- Europeans gain control of global trading empires
- Western powers spread their ideas and adopt elements of nonwestern cultures
- Local people resist western domination
- Some nonwestern leaders attempt reforms in an effort to modernize

Connections to Today

- Nations in Africa, Asia, and Latin America struggle to build stable governments

Use the cause-and-effect chart to answer the following questions:

24. What did newly industrialized nations seek?
25. How did nonwestern peoples respond to colonization?
26. What is the central idea of this chart?
27. How do the events and developments identified in this chart continue to affect the world today?

Skills Tip

When reading a cause-and-effect chart, pay careful attention to the outcomes of events and developments.

TEST PREPARATION

1. The need for natural resources, the desire to spread Christianity, and the ideas of Social Darwinism were all causes of

   A isolationism.

   B imperialism.

   C Zionism.

   D regionalism.

Use the quotation and your knowledge of social studies to answer the following question.

> "Hosts of families who have been evicted from their small holdings in the surrounding country . . . have taken refuge in ditches and other places in the vicinity . . . . Their mode of living levels them almost with brutes."
>
> **—the *Cork Examiner*, September 1847**

2. The scene described in this newspaper report most likely took place in a

   A slum in London.

   B penal colony in Australia.

   C rural village in Ireland.

   D Jewish village in Russia.

3. Nationalism is most likely to develop in an area that has

   A land suited to agriculture.

   B adequate industry to support consumer demands.

   C large numbers of immigrants.

   D common customs, language, and history.

4. During the Age of Imperialism, the relationship between France and Indochina was most similar to the relationship between

   A the United States and Japan.

   B Italy and Ethiopia.

   C Great Britain and Canada.

   D Belgium and the Congo.

Use the graphs and your knowledge of social studies to answer the following question.

Population of the United States

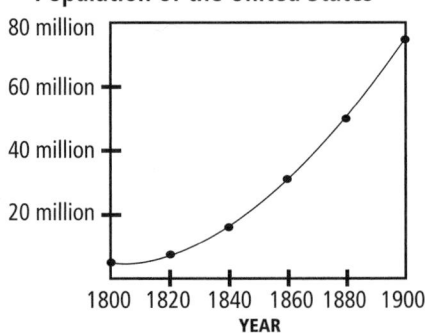

Population of Great Britain

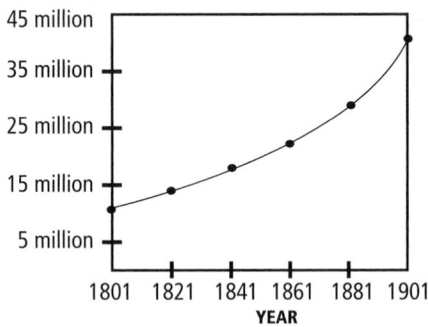

Sources: *The World Almanac and Book of Facts*, 1996
Chronology of the Modern World, 1763–1992

5. Which of the following was a cause of the trend shown on BOTH graphs?

   A improved medical care

   B increased immigration

   C westward expansion

   D decline in rural populations

6. In Britain, the Reform Act of 1832 and the Reform Bill of 1867

   A extended suffrage to women.

   B ended child labor.

   C increased the number of voters.

   D outlawed slavery.

Use the map and your knowledge of social studies to answer the following question.

Spheres of Influence in China to 1914

7. From this map, you can conclude that, by 1914,

   A China was completely under the control of European powers.

   B Shanghai was an important port for British traders.

   C Russia's sphere of influence included the city of Peking.

   D the United States did not participate in trade with China.

8. Otto von Bismarck and Giuseppe Garibaldi were similar in that each

   A worked to unify his nation.

   B became the leader of a powerful new empire.

   C believed strongly in democracy.

   D led a war against France.

9. Interchangeable parts, the assembly line, and other means of mass production led to

   A a decline in the standard of living.

   B lower prices for consumer goods.

   C the rise of labor unions.

   D the invention of the electric light.

Writing Practice

10. Rank what you consider the three most important technological developments you read about in this unit. Then, discuss the development you ranked as first. Explain both the impact of that development at the time and its continuing impact today.

11. Discuss the benefits and drawbacks of imperialism, using India as an example. Then, explain whether you think the effects of British rule in India were mostly positive or mostly negative.

UNIT 4

World Wars and Revolutions

1910–1955

OUTLINE

Chapter 14 **World War I and Its Aftermath** (1914–1919)

Chapter 15 **Revolution in Russia** (1917–1939)

Chapter 16 **Nationalism and Revolution Around the World** (1910–1939)

Chapter 17 **Crisis of Democracy in the West** (1919–1939)

Chapter 18 **World War II and Its Aftermath** (1931–1955)

Themes

As you read about global wars and revolutions, you will encounter the following themes.

Continuity and Change Nationalists in Asia, Latin America, and Africa challenged foreign domination and encouraged a revival of traditional culture. Tools of change ranged from civil disobedience in India to armed rebellion in Mexico.

Economics and Technology The Great Depression caused major economic problems around the world. Fascists and communists offered their own extreme solutions to the crisis.

Global Interaction Two world wars were fought in the first half of the twentieth century. Developed nations in the global North and developing countries in the global South became increasingly interdependent. Common concerns encouraged nations to support international organizations and agreements.

Political and Social Systems Democracy, communism, and fascism competed for influence and political power. Totalitarian dictatorships attempted to regulate all aspects of life and to place the needs of the state above individual rights.

Unit Theme Activity

For Your Portfolio The chapters in this unit examine economic challenges around the world. As you read the chapters, prepare a portfolio project comparing various solutions to the issues. Your project might take one of the following forms:
• **PowerPoint presentation**
• **Interview**
• **Photo essay**

The official Japanese surrender was signed on September 2, 1945, on board the USS *Missouri* in Tokyo Bay. General Douglas MacArthur, commander in the Southwest Pacific and supreme commander for the Allied Powers, accepted the formal document, ending World War II.

Prepare to Read

Prepare to read this unit by previewing the main ideas and main events of each chapter.

Chapter 14

World War I and Its Aftermath (1914–1919)

Many forces—including nationalism, militarism, and imperialist rivalries—propelled Europe into World War I. This massive conflict engulfed much of the world for four years and ushered in a new age of modern warfare.

- Two huge alliances emerged in Europe: the Central Powers, dominated by Germany and Austria-Hungary, and the Allies, led by France, Britain, and Russia.
- Although the assassination of Archduke Francis Ferdinand in 1914 ignited World War I, historians agree that all the major powers share blame for the conflict.
- Trench warfare and new weapons contributed to a stalemate on the Western Front.
- In 1917, the United States entered the war, allowing the Allies to achieve victory.
- The Paris Peace Conference imposed heavy penalties on Germany and redrew the map of Eastern Europe.

Chapter 15

Revolution in Russia (1917–1939)

Lenin and his successors transformed czarist Russia into the communist Soviet Union. This experiment in single-party politics and a state-run economy would exert a powerful influence over the modern world for almost 75 years.

- In March 1917, political, social, and economic conditions in Russia sparked a revolution that overthrew the czar and paved the way for more radical changes.
- After leading the Bolsheviks to power in November 1917, Lenin hoped to build a communist state based on the ideas of Marx.
- Lenin's successor, Stalin, imposed "five-year plans" to build industry and increase farm output.
- Stalin created a totalitarian state, employing censorship, propaganda, and terror to ensure personal power and push the Soviet Union toward modernization.

Chapter 16

Nationalism and Revolution Around the World (1910–1939)

Between 1919 and 1939, the desire for democracy and self-determination contributed to explosive struggles in many regions. New leaders in Africa, Latin America, and Asia built liberation movements that would change the world.

- The Mexican revolution opened the door to social and economic reforms.
- African leaders opposed imperialism and reaffirmed traditional cultures.
- Arab Nationalism led to Pan-Arabism, uniting Arabs against foreign domination.
- In India, Gandhi led a campaign of nonviolent resistance to British rule.
- In China, foreigners extended their spheres of influence. Later, communists and nationalists engaged in civil war.
- In the 1920s and 1930s, extreme nationalism and economic upheaval set Japan on a militaristic and expansionist path.

1910 **1920** **1930**

 AFRICA

1912 African National Congress formed in South Africa   **1919** First Pan-African Congress held in Paris

 THE AMERICAS

1910 Mexican Revolution begins   **1919** Red Scare in United States   **1929** Stock market crash

 ASIA AND OCEANIA

1911 Civil War in China   **1923** Atatürk begins modernization of Turkey

 EUROPE

1914 World War I begins   **1917** Russian Revolution   **1922** Mussolini rules Italy   **1933** Hitler rules Germany

Chapter 17

Crisis of Democracy in the West
(1919–1939)

After World War I, western nations worked to restore prosperity and ensure peace. At the same time, political and economic turmoil in the 1920s and 1930s challenged democratic traditions and led to the rise of dictators.

- The Great Depression of the 1930s created financial turmoil and widespread suffering throughout the industrialized world.
- Scientific discoveries, new trends in literature and the arts, and social changes all contributed to a sense of uncertainty.
- Unrest in Italy helped Mussolini lead his Fascist party to power in the 1920s.
- In Germany, Hitler rose to power by appealing to extreme nationalism, antisemitism, anti-communism, and resentment of the Treaty of Versailles. In the 1930s, he turned the German state into a totalitarian Nazi dictatorship.
- Three systems of government—democracy, communism, and fascism—competed for influence in postwar Europe.

Chapter 18

World War II and Its Aftermath
(1931–1955)

Between 1939 and 1945, nations all over the globe fought World War II, the largest and most costly conflict in history. The war shifted the balance of world power from Western Europe to the United States and the Soviet Union.

- The Axis powers—Germany, Italy, and Japan—embarked on a course of aggression in the late 1930s. France and Britain first adopted a policy of appeasement but declared war when Hitler invaded Poland.
- During the Holocaust, the Nazis systematically killed more than six million Jews, as well as millions of other people the Nazis considered undesirable.
- The United States, the Soviet Union, and the Allied Powers joined to defeat Germany.
- To force a Japanese surrender, the United States dropped two atomic bombs.
- The Cold War followed World War II, pitting the western democracies, led by the United States, against the communist bloc, dominated by the Soviet Union.

1940   **1950**   **1960**

1935
Italy invades
Ethiopia

1948 South Africa makes
apartheid the law of the land

1941
Bombing of
Pearl Harbor

1947
United States announces
Marshall Plan

1930s
Gandhi leads anti-British
protests in India

1945
Japan
surrenders and World War II ends

1949 People's Republic of China established

1939 World War II begins   **1949** NATO formed
1941 Holocaust begins   **1955** Warsaw Pact formed

World War I and Its Aftermath

1914–1919

Chapter Preview

1 **The Stage Is Set**
2 **The Guns of August**
3 **A New Kind of Conflict**
4 **Winning the War**
5 **Making the Peace**

1914

Archduke Francis Ferdinand of Austria-Hungary and his wife are killed in Sarajevo. The assassination sparks World War I.

1915

German submarines sink the ocean liner *Lusitania*.

1916

More than one million soldiers are killed in the battle of the Somme, shown above, but the war in Europe remains deadlocked.

CHAPTER EVENTS

1914   1915   1916

GLOBAL EVENTS

1914 The Panama Canal opens.

1916 Japan tries to establish a protectorate over China.

The World at War, 1914–1918

World War I began in Europe. However, other world powers, as well as European colonies around the world, were drawn into the conflict.

**Map labels:**
NORTH AMERICA
SOUTH AMERICA
EUROPE
ASIA
AFRICA
AUSTRALIA
ATLANTIC OCEAN
PACIFIC OCEAN
INDIAN OCEAN
PACIFIC OCEAN

Robinson Projection
0   1500   3000 Miles
0   1500   3000 Kilometers

Legend:
- Allies
- Central Powers
- Colonial possessions of Allies
- Colonial possessions of Central Powers

I WANT YOU FOR U.S. ARMY
NEAREST RECRUITING STATION

1917
The United States ends its policy of neutrality and enters the war. This famous poster is used to recruit American soldiers for the war effort.

1918
An armistice ends the war on November 11. This painting by George Luks shows an armistice celebration in New York.

1919
Delegates to the Paris Peace Conference draft the Treaty of Versailles, which blames Germany for the war.

1917   **1918**   **1919**

1917 The czar is overthrown in the Russian Revolution.

1919 The first Pan-African Congress meets in Paris.

The Stage Is Set

Reading Focus

- What efforts in the early 1900s were made toward peace?
- How did nationalism and international rivalries push Europe toward war?
- What were the causes and effects of the European alliance system?

Vocabulary

pacifism

militarism

entente

Taking Notes

Copy this table. As you read, fill in the left-hand column with developments that promoted peace. In the right-hand column, list forces that were pushing Europe toward war.

EFFORTS AT PEACE	FORCES FOR WAR
• Modern Olympic games	• Aggressive nationalism
•	•
•	•

Main Idea In the late 1800s and early 1900s, a number of forces were pushing Europe to the brink of war.

Setting the Scene By 1914, Europe had enjoyed a century of relative peace. Many idealists hoped for a permanent end to the scourge of war. "The future belongs to peace," said French economist Frédéric Passy.

Others were less hopeful. "I shall not live to see the Great War," warned German chancellor Otto von Bismarck, "but you will see it, and it will start in the east." It was Bismarck's prediction, rather than Passy's, that came true.

The Pursuit of Peace

By the early 1900s, many efforts were underway to end war and foster understanding between nations. In 1896, the first modern Olympic games were held in Athens. Its founder hoped the games would promote "love of peace and respect for life." Alfred Nobel, the Swedish inventor of dynamite, regretted the military uses of his invention. In his will, he set up the annual Nobel Peace Prize to reward people who worked for peace.

The struggle for women's suffrage supported the peace movement. Dutch doctor Aletta Jacobs argued that if women won the vote, they could prevent war. "They don't feel as men do about war," Jacobs said. "They are the mothers of the race." Organizations such as the Women's International League for Peace and Freedom promoted pacifism, or opposition to all war.

Governments, too, backed peace efforts. In 1899, many world leaders attended the First Universal Peace Conference in the Netherlands. They set up the Hague Tribunal, a world court to settle disputes between nations. The Hague Tribunal could not force nations to submit their disputes, nor could it enforce its rulings. Still, it was a step toward keeping the peace.

Aggressive Nationalism

At the same time, other powerful forces were pushing Europe to the brink of war. Aggressive nationalism was one leading cause of international tension.

France and Germany Nationalist feelings were strong in both Germany and France. Germans were proud of their new empire's military power and industrial leadership. France longed to regain its position as Europe's leading power. The French were especially bitter about their 1871 defeat in the Franco-Prussian War and the German occupation of the border provinces of Alsace and Lorraine. Patriotic French citizens yearned for revenge against Germany and recovery of the "lost provinces."

Comparing Viewpoints

Is War Ever Justified?

In the years leading up to World War I, militarists glorified warfare, and pacifists strongly denounced war. Is war ever justified? Think about this enduring issue as you look at the following viewpoints.

China 300s B.C.

The warrior-philosopher Sun Tzu wrote *The Art of War,* an influential handbook of military strategy:

❝ A government should not mobilize an army out of anger, military leaders should not provoke a war out of wrath. Act when it is beneficial, desist when it is not. Anger can revert to joy, wrath can revert to delight, but a nation destroyed cannot be restored to existence, and the dead cannot be restored to life. ❞

Germany 1913

Helmuth von Moltke, chief of the German General Staff, directed Germany's strategy at the beginning of World War I:

❝ The German people must be made to see that we have to attack because of our enemies' provocation. Things must be so built up that war will seem as a deliverance from the great armaments, the financial burdens, the political tensions. . . . Germany must regain what formerly she lost. ❞

United States 1970s

The group Another Mother Against War created this poster.

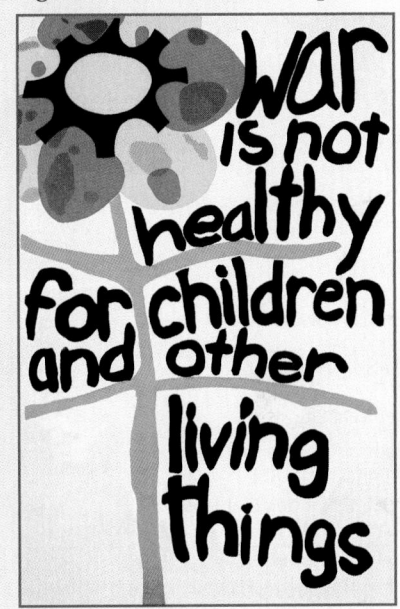

Zimbabwe 1978

Bishop Abel Muzorewa joined the struggle for majority rule in his nation and later served as prime minister:

❝ I question whether God himself would wish me to hide behind the principles of nonviolence while innocent persons were being slaughtered. ❞

Skills Assessment

1. Which of the following would agree with the position that war should be avoided at all costs?
   A Sun Tzu
   B Helmuth von Moltke
   C Another Mother Against War
   D Abel Muzorewa

2. Sun Tzu and Bishop Muzorewa would probably agree that war
   E is justified in certain situations.
   F should be used by governments to gain revenge.
   G is a glorious and noble activity.
   H should be fought only to save innocent lives.

3. **Critical Thinking** **Making Decisions** You are running for the office of president of the United States. Write a brief position statement in which you explain under what circumstances you might send United States troops into action.

Skills Tip

Do not make hasty judgments about people's viewpoints. For example, you cannot automatically assume that every monarch will be against democracy or that every general will be in favor of war.

European Alliances, 1914

NORWAY

SWEDEN

DENMARK

GREAT BRITAIN

London

NETH.

BELGIUM

Berlin

GERMANY

RUSSIA

ATLANTIC OCEAN

Paris

LUX.

ALSACE-LORRAINE

FRANCE

SWITZ.

Vienna

Budapest

AUSTRIA-HUNGARY

North Sea

PORTUGAL

SPAIN

ITALY

Rome

Sarajevo

SERBIA

MONTENEGRO

ALBANIA

ROMANIA

BULGARIA

Black Sea

Constantinople

OTTOMAN EMPIRE

GREECE

Mediterranean Sea

Legend:
- Central Powers
- Allies
- Neutral Nations
- Neutral Nations that later joined the Central Powers
- Neutral Nations that later joined the Allies

Azimuthal Equal Area Projection

0   250   500 Miles

0   250   500 Kilometers

Standing Armies in Europe, 1914

Number of Soldiers (in millions)

ALLIES: Great Britain, France, Russia

CENTRAL POWERS: Austria-Hungary, Germany

Source: *The International Internet Encyclopedia*

Skills Assessment

Geography By 1914, most of Europe was divided into two armed camps. Millions of troops stood ready for war.

1. **Location** On the map, locate (a) Germany, (b) Austria-Hungary, (c) Serbia, (d) Russia, (e) France, (f) Great Britain.
2. **Region** Why would Germany worry about the alliance between France and Russia?
3. **Critical Thinking** **Synthesizing Information** Based on the map and the graph, which alliance do you think had the greater advantage in 1914?

Eastern Europe In Eastern Europe, Russia sponsored a powerful form of nationalism called Pan-Slavism. It held that all Slavic peoples shared a common nationality. As the largest Slavic country, Russia felt that it had a duty to lead and defend all Slavs. By 1914, it stood ready to support Serbia, a proud young nation that dreamed of creating a South Slav state.

Two old multinational empires particularly feared rising nationalism. Austria-Hungary worried that nationalism might foster rebellion among the many minority populations within its empire. Ottoman Turkey felt threatened by new nations on its borders, such as Serbia and Greece.

In 1912, several Balkan states attacked Turkey. The next year, the new Balkan states fought among themselves over the spoils of war. These brief but bloody Balkan wars raised tensions to a fever pitch. By 1914, the Balkans were the "powder keg of Europe"—a tiny spark might lead to an explosion.

Rivalries Among European Powers

Economic rivalries further poisoned the international atmosphere. Britain felt threatened by Germany's rapid economic growth. By 1900, Germany's new factories were outproducing Britain's older ones. Britain, therefore, had strong economic reasons to oppose Germany in any conflict. The Germans, in turn, thought the other great powers did not give them enough respect.

Imperialism Imperial rivalries also divided European nations. In 1905 and again in 1911, competition for colonies brought France and Germany to the brink of war. Germany wanted to prevent France from imposing a protectorate on Morocco. Although diplomats kept the peace, Germany did gain some territory in central Africa. As a result of the two Moroccan crises, Britain and France began to form closer ties against Germany.

Militarism and the Arms Race The 1800s saw a rise in militarism, the glorification of the military. It grew partly out of Social Darwinism. Echoing the idea of "survival of the fittest," one German militarist called war "a biological necessity of the first importance." Militarists painted war in romantic colors. Young men dreamed of blaring trumpets and dashing cavalry charges—not at all the sort of conflict they would soon face.

With international tensions on the rise, the great powers expanded their armies and navies. The result was an arms race that further increased suspicions and made war more likely. The fiercest competition was the naval rivalry between Britain and Germany. To protect its vast overseas empire, Britain had built the world's most respected navy. As Germany began acquiring overseas colonies, it began to build up its own navy. Suspicious of Germany's motives, Britain in turn increased naval spending.

As readiness for war came to dominate national policy, military leaders came to gain wider influence. On matters of peace and war, governments turned to military leaders for advice. German generals and British admirals enjoyed great respect and got more funds to build up their forces.

A Tangle of Alliances

Distrust led the great powers to sign treaties pledging to defend one another. These alliances were intended to create powerful combinations that no one would dare attack. Gradually, two huge alliances emerged.

The first of these alliances had its origins in Bismarck's day. He knew that France longed to avenge its defeat in the Franco-Prussian War. Sure that France would not attack Germany without help, Bismarck signed treaties with other powers. In 1882, he formed the Triple Alliance with Italy and Austria-Hungary. In 1914, when war did erupt, Germany and Austria-Hungary fought on the same side. They became known as the Central Powers.

A rival bloc took shape in 1894, when France and Russia formed an alliance. In 1904, France and Britain signed an entente (ahn TAHNT), a nonbinding agreement to follow common policies. Though not as formal as a treaty, the entente led to close military and diplomatic ties. Britain later signed a similar agreement with Russia. When war began, these powers became known as the Allies.

Other alliances also formed. Germany signed a treaty with the Ottoman empire, while Britain drew close to Japan. The growth of rival alliance systems increased international tensions. A local conflict could easily mushroom into a general war.

Biography

Kaiser William II
1859–1941

"All the long years of my reign," William II complained, "my colleagues, the monarchs of Europe, have paid no attention to what I have to say." As kaiser, he fought to win respect for himself and his empire.

William's rivalry with other rulers was in many ways a family feud. He and George V of Britain were cousins, grandchildren of Queen Victoria. Czar Nicholas II was another cousin. When war broke out in 1914, the kaiser blamed "George and Nicky. . . . If my grandmother had been alive, she would never have allowed it!"

Theme: Impact of the Individual How did the kaiser's desire for respect influence his policies?

SECTION 1 Assessment

Recall
1. **Identify: (a)** Hague Tribunal, **(b)** Pan-Slavism, **(c)** Central Powers, **(d)** Allies.
2. **Define: (a)** pacifism, **(b)** militarism, **(c)** entente.

Comprehension
3. Identify three peace efforts of the late 1800s and early 1900s.
4. Describe how each of the following served to inflame tensions in Europe: **(a)** nationalism, **(b)** imperial rivalries, **(c)** militarism.

5. **(a)** Why did European nations form alliances? **(b)** How did alliances increase fears of war?

Critical Thinking and Writing
6. **Applying Information** Reread Bismarck's statement at the start of this section. Why do you think he made this prediction?
7. **Linking Past and Present** Do you think the idea of going to war excites young people today in the same way that it did 100 years ago? Why or why not?

Go Online
PHSchool.com

Use Internet sources to find out about peace efforts today. Then, choose someone whom you would nominate for the Nobel Peace Prize. Write a brief paragraph explaining why you think he or she deserves the honor. For help with this activity, use **Web Code mkd-2781.**

The Guns of August

Reading Focus

- How did ethnic tensions in the Balkans spark a political assassination?
- How did conflict between Austria-Hungary and Serbia widen?
- How do historians view the outbreak of World War I?

Vocabulary

ultimatum
mobilize
neutrality

Taking Notes

Copy this flowchart. Include at least five empty boxes. As you read, fill in the chain of events in the summer of 1914 that led to an all-out war.

Francis Ferdinand is assassinated
↓
[ ]
↓
[ ]
↓
[ ]
↓
Britain declares war on Germany

Main Idea The assassination of Archduke Francis Ferdinand ignited the Balkan "powder keg" and sparked World War I.

Connections to Today

A New Balkan Powder Keg?

"Crisis in the Balkans! Threat of War!" Some 80 years after the assassination of Francis Ferdinand, headlines like these flared in the world's newspapers. In 1991, rivalries among Eastern Orthodox Serbs, Muslim Bosnians, and Catholic Croats led to civil war in Bosnia. More than 250,000 people died, and millions fled their homes. In 1995, American and European troops helped restore peace.

Tensions flared again when Serbia moved to suppress an independence movement by Muslim Albanians in the province of Kosovo. In 1999, the United States and its allies took military action against the Serbian government.

Theme: Geography and History Identify two other places where religious or ethnic differences have led to conflict.

Setting the Scene

Bertha von Suttner devoted her life to peace. Though the daughter of a noble Austrian military family, she wrote a best-selling antiwar novel and organized a peace society. Her tireless work won her the nickname "Peace Bertha." Yet, in April 1913, Suttner wrote in her diary that "the great European disaster is well on its way. If so many seeds have been sown, surely the weeds will sprout up soon and surely so much stockpiled gunpowder will explode."

"Peace Bertha" died on June 20, 1914. Eight days later, an assassin's bullet set off the "gunpowder" and ignited a war that engulfed much of the world for four bloody years.

Assassination in Sarajevo

The crisis began when Archduke Francis Ferdinand of Austria-Hungary announced that he would visit Sarajevo (sar uh YAY voh), the capital of Bosnia. At the time, Bosnia was under the rule of Austria-Hungary. But it was also the home of many Serbs and other Slavs.

Serbian Outrage News of the royal visit angered many Serbian nationalists. They viewed the Austrians as foreign oppressors. Even worse, the date chosen for the archduke's visit, June 28, was a special date in Serbian history. It was on that date in 1389, Serbia had been conquered by the Ottoman empire. On the very same date in 1912, Serbia had at last freed itself from Turkish rule.

Some members of Unity or Death, a Serbian terrorist group commonly known as the Black Hand, vowed to take action. As one conspirator later recalled, "Our decision was taken almost immediately. Death to the tyrant!"

The Fatal Shots The archduke ignored warnings of anti-Austrian unrest in Sarajevo. On June 28, 1914, he and his wife, Sophie, rode through Sarajevo in an open car. Stationed along the route were several Black Hand conspirators. As the cars passed, one of the conspirators hurled a bomb. It missed the archduke but injured an officer in another car.

Later that day, the archduke asked to visit the wounded officer in the hospital. He did not know that one of the conspirators, Gavrilo Princip (GAHV ree loh PREEN tseep), was still waiting. As the car set out, Princip sprang forward and fired twice into the back seat. Moments later, the archduke and his wife were dead.

The Conflict Widens

The news of his nephew's death shocked the aging Austrian emperor, Francis Joseph. Still, he was reluctant to go to war. His government in Vienna, however, saw the incident as an excuse to crush Serbia for good.

A Harsh Ultimatum Austria sent Serbia a sweeping ultimatum, or final set of demands. To avoid war, said the ultimatum, Serbia must end all anti-Austrian agitation and punish any Serbian official involved in the murder plot. It must even let Austria join in the investigation.

Serbia agreed to most, but not all, of the terms of Austria's ultimatum. This partial refusal gave Austria the opportunity it was seeking. On July 28, 1914, Austria declared war on Serbia.

From Capital to Capital A war between a major power and a small Balkan state might have been another "summer war," like most European wars of the past century. But as diplomats sent notes from capital to capital, larger forces drew the great powers deeper into conflict.

Austria-Hungary might not have pushed Serbia into war at all without the backing of its longtime ally, Germany. In Berlin, Kaiser William II was horrified at the assassination of a royal heir. He wrote to Francis Joseph, advising him to take a firm stand toward Serbia. The kaiser assured the emperor of Germany's full support. Thus, instead of urging restraint, William II gave Austria a "blank check."

Serbia meanwhile sought help from Russia, the champion of Slavic nations. From St. Petersburg, Nicholas II telegraphed William II. The czar asked the kaiser to urge Austria to soften its demands. When this plea failed, Russia began to mobilize, or prepare its military forces for war. Germany responded by declaring war on Russia.

Russia, in turn, appealed to its ally France. In Paris, nationalists saw a chance to avenge France's defeat in the Franco-Prussian War. Though French leaders had some doubts, they gave Russia the same kind of backing Germany offered Austria. When Germany demanded that France keep out of the conflict, France refused. Germany then declared war on France. By early August, the battle lines were hardening.

The Schlieffen Plan Italy and Britain remained uncommitted. Italy chose to remain neutral for the time being. Neutrality is a policy of supporting neither side in a war. Britain had to decide quickly whether or not to support its ally France. Then, Germany's war plans suddenly made the decision for Britain.

Years earlier, General Alfred von Schlieffen (SHLEE fuhn) had developed a plan of attack against France. The Schlieffen Plan was designed to avoid a two-front war—against France in the west and Russia to the east. Schlieffen reasoned that Russia's lumbering military would be slow to mobilize. Under the Schlieffen Plan, Germany first had to defeat France quickly. Then, it would fight Russia.

To ensure a swift victory in the west, the Schlieffen Plan required German armies to march through Belgium, then swing south behind French lines. On August 3, Germany invaded Belgium. However, Britain and other European powers had signed a treaty guaranteeing Belgian neutrality. Outraged by the invasion of Belgium, Britain declared war on Germany.

"Who Killed the Peace of Europe?"
One by one, the major powers of Europe were drawn into war. This cartoon appeared in an American newspaper in the summer of 1914.

Theme: Global Interaction What point is this cartoon making about the events leading up to the war?

Off to War
Like most European soldiers in 1914, these young Germans optimistically believed that they would be "home by Christmas." They had no idea of the horrors that lay ahead.

Theme: Geography and History Why did these soldiers write the word "Paris" on their troop train?

The Historians' View

How could an assassination lead to all-out war in just a few weeks? During the war, each side blamed the other. Afterward, the victorious Allies placed all blame on Germany, because it was the first country to invade another. Today, most historians agree that all parties must share blame for a catastrophe nobody wanted.

Each of the great powers believed that its cause was just. Austria-Hungary wanted to punish Serbia for encouraging terrorism. Germany felt that it must stand by its one dependable ally, Austria-Hungary. Russia saw the Austrian ultimatum to Serbia as an effort to oppress Slavic peoples. France feared that if it did not support Russia, it would have to face Germany alone later. Britain felt committed to protect Belgium but also feared the powerful German force on the other side of the English Channel.

Once the machinery of war was set in motion, it seemed impossible to stop. In *The Guns of August,* a widely read study of the outbreak of the war, historian Barbara Tuchman wrote:

> "[Military] staffs, goaded by their relentless timetables, were pounding the table for the signal to move lest their opponents gain an hour's head start. Appalled upon the brink, the chiefs of state who would be ultimately responsible for their country's fate attempted to back away but the pull of military schedules dragged them forward."
> —Barbara Tuchman, *The Guns of August*

Although leaders made the decisions, most people on both sides were equally committed to military action. Young men rushed to enlist, cheered on by women and their elders. Now that war had come at last, it seemed an exciting adventure.

British diplomat Edward Grey was less optimistic. As armies began to move, he predicted, "The lamps are going out all over Europe. We shall not see them lit again in our lifetime."

SECTION 2 Assessment

Recall
1. **Identify: (a)** Francis Ferdinand, **(b)** Gavrilo Princip, **(c)** Schlieffen Plan.
2. **Define: (a)** ultimatum, **(b)** mobilize, **(c)** neutrality.

Comprehension
3. **(a)** Why was Archduke Francis Ferdinand assassinated? **(b)** How did Austria-Hungary react?
4. Describe how each of the following nations was drawn into the conflict: **(a)** Germany, **(b)** Russia, **(c)** France, **(d)** Britain.
5. Who do most modern historians think was responsible for the war?

Critical Thinking and Writing
6. **Drawing Conclusions** Do you think war could have been avoided in 1914? Why or why not?
7. **Connecting to Geography** What role did geography play in the outbreak of World War I?

Activity
Drawing a Political Cartoon
Choose one of the European powers involved in the outbreak of World War I. Then, from that nation's point of view, draw a cartoon assigning blame for the war.

SECTION 3 A New Kind of Conflict

Reading Focus

- Why did a stalemate develop on the Western Front?
- How did technology make World War I different from earlier wars?
- How did the war become a global conflict?

Vocabulary

stalemate
no man's land
zeppelin
U-boat
convoy

Taking Notes

Copy this concept web. As you read, fill in important facts about the various battle fronts of World War I. Add as many circles as you need.

Main Idea Modern weapons resulted in huge numbers of casualties and helped prevent either side from gaining an advantage.

Setting the Scene The "Great War," as newspapers soon called it, was the largest conflict in history up to that time. The French mobilized almost 8.5 million men, the British 9 million, the Russians 12 million, and the Germans 11 million. But for those who fought, the statistics were more personal. "One out of every four men who went out to the World War did not come back again," recalled a survivor, "and of those who came back, many are maimed and blind and some are mad."

The early enthusiasm for the war soon faded. There were no stirring cavalry charges, no quick and glorious victories. This was a new kind of war, far deadlier than any ever fought before.

The Western Front

As the war began, German forces swept through Belgium toward Paris. German generals, however, soon violated the Schlieffen Plan. Russia mobilized more quickly than expected. After Russian forces won a few small victories in eastern Prussia, Germany hastily shifted some troops to the east. That move weakened German forces in the west. In September 1914, when British troops reached France, they joined the French along the Marne River. The battle of the Marne pushed back the German offensive and destroyed Germany's hopes for a quick victory on the Western Front.

Both sides then dug in for the winter. They did not know that the conflict would turn into a long, deadly stalemate, a deadlock in which neither side is able to defeat the other. Battle lines in France would remain almost unchanged for four years.

Trench Warfare On the Western Front, the warring armies burrowed into a vast system of trenches, stretching from the Swiss frontier to the English Channel. An American war correspondent described the scene:

"There were vast stretches of mud, of fields once cultivated, but now scarred with pits, trenches, rusty barbed wires. The roads were rivers of clay. They were lined with dugouts, cellars, and caves. These burrows in the earth were supported by beams, and suggested a shaft in a disused mine."
—Richard H. Davis, *With the French in France and Salonika*

An underground network linked bunkers, communications trenches, and gun emplacements. There, millions of soldiers roasted under the broiling

Learn about the front during World War I.

Did You Know?

The Christmas Truce

On December 24, 1914, British troops reported an amazing sight: Christmas trees and Chinese lanterns along the German front line. They were even more amazed to see some Germans walking toward the British trenches shouting, "Hello! I want to talk to you!" So began the unofficial Christmas Truce. Ignoring orders from headquarters, small groups of enemy soldiers drank a toast and exchanged gifts such as chocolate or jam. One German also recalled playing soccer against a Scottish regiment wearing kilts.

Theme: Global Interaction
Why do you think commanders opposed the Christmas Truce?

You Are There . . .

CARING FOR THE WOUNDED

The echoes of the last exploding shells have died away. The stench of poison gas still lingers, and cries of the wounded fill the air. You and the other medics pick your way through mud and corpses to retrieve the wounded, trying hard to ignore the horror of the scene. . . .

You find a soldier groaning in pain from a head wound. You and three other medics carry him on a stretcher through a long tunnel to a first-aid station in a dugout shelter. A doctor and a nurse evaluate his condition and treat him with the primitive supplies on hand. You hope this soldier survives until he is taken by ambulance or train for further treatment.

You have seen too many men felled by poison gas, which can cause blindness, skin rashes, and even death. To protect themselves, soldiers must wear masks that also allow them to talk and hear.

You pass by these French troops proudly displaying their catch of trench rats. The rats carry disease and feed on corpses.

Portfolio Assessment

After an exhausting day of caring for the wounded, you decide to write a letter to your family back home. In the letter, you describe your feelings of frustration at the hazards faced by soldiers and the limited supplies that you have to treat them.

Europe at War, 1914–1918

Allies, 1918

Central Powers, 1918

Neutral Nations

Farthest advance by Central Powers

★ Battle sites

Azimuthal Equal Area Projection

0   250   500 Miles

0   250   500 Kilometers

Skills Assessment

Geography World War I was fought on many fronts, with massive losses of life and property.

1. **Location** On the map, locate **(a)** Tannenberg, **(b)** Verdun, **(c)** Paris, **(d)** Caporetto, **(e)** the Dardanelles.

2. **Movement** How far into France did the Central Powers advance?

3. **Critical Thinking Making Inferences** Based on this map, why were many Russians demoralized by the progress of the war?

summer sun or froze through the long winters. They shared their food with rats and their beds with lice.

Between the opposing trench lines lay "no man's land." In this empty tract, pocked with shell holes, every house and tree had long since been destroyed. Through coils of barbed wire, soldiers peered over the edges of their trenches, watching for the next attack. They themselves would have to charge into this man-made desert when officers gave the order.

Sooner or later, soldiers would obey the order to go "over the top." With no protection but their rifles and helmets, they charged across no man's land toward the enemy lines. With luck, they might overrun a few trenches. In time, the enemy would launch a counterattack, with similar results. Each side then rushed in reinforcements to replace the dead and wounded. The struggle continued, back and forth, over a few hundred yards of territory.

Costly Battles In 1916, both the Allies and Central Powers launched massive offensives to break the stalemate. German forces tried to overwhelm the French at Verdun (vuhr DUHN). The French sent up the battle cry "They shall not pass." The French defenders held firm, but the 11-month struggle cost more than a half-million casualties on both sides.

An Allied offensive at the Somme (SAHM) River was even more costly. In a single grisly day, 60,000 British soldiers were killed or wounded. In the five-month battle, over one million soldiers were killed, without either side winning an advantage.

Technology of Modern Warfare

Modern weapons added greatly to the destructiveness of the war. Rapid-fire machine guns mowed down waves of soldiers, making it nearly impossible to advance across no man's land. Artillery allowed troops to shell enemy lines and cities from more than 10 miles away.

In 1915, Germany began using poison gas that blinded or choked its victims or caused agonizing burns and blisters. Later that year, the Allies also began to use gas. Though soldiers were eventually given gas masks, poison

World War I Technology

Airplane

A one- or two-seat propeller plane was equipped with a machine gun. At first the planes were used mainly for observation. Later, "flying aces" engaged in individual combat, though such "dogfights" had little effect on the war.

Automatic machine gun

A mounted gun that fired a rapid, continuous stream of bullets made it possible for a few gunners to mow down waves of soldiers. This helped create a stalemate by making it difficult to advance across no man's land.

Submarine

These underwater ships, or U-boats, could launch torpedoes, or guided underwater bombs. Used by Germany to destroy Allied shipping, U-boat attacks helped bring the United States into the war.

Connections to Today

World War I was the first modern, fully industrialized war. Some weapons, such as submarines and machine guns, altered the nature of the fighting. Other new technology, such as airplanes, did not have its greatest impact until years later.

Skills Assessment   **Chart Which invention on this chart do you think has done the most to change how wars are fought? Explain.**

gas remained one of the most dreaded hazards of the war. One British soldier recalled the effects of being gassed:

> "I suppose I resembled a kind of fish with my mouth open gasping for air. It seemed as if my lungs were gradually shutting up and my heart pounded away in my ears like the beat of a drum. . . . To get air into my lungs was real agony."
> —William Pressey, quoted in
> *People at War 1914–1918* (Moynihan)

Although poison gas could be fatal, it was an uncertain weapon. Shifting winds might blow the gas back on the side that launched it.

In 1916, Britain introduced a new weapon, the armored tank. Mounted with machine guns, the tanks were designed to move across broken ground and through barbed wire. Still, the first tanks moved slowly and broke down often. They did little to break the stalemate.

Both sides also used aircraft. At first, planes simply observed enemy troop movements. In 1915, Germany used **zeppelins,** large gas-filled balloons, to bomb the English coast. Later, both sides equipped airplanes with machine guns. Pilots known as "flying aces" battled in the skies. These "dogfights" were spectacular, but had little effect on the course of the war.

Submarines proved much more important. German submarines roamed the Atlantic. These **U-boats** did tremendous damage to the Allied side, sinking merchant ships that carried vital supplies to Britain. To counteract submarine warfare, the Allies organized **convoys,** or groups of merchant ships protected by warships. As you will read, Germany's policy of unrestricted submarine warfare would eventually help bring the United States into the war.

A Global Conflict

On Europe's Eastern Front, battle lines swayed back and forth, sometimes over large areas. Casualties rose even higher than on the Western Front, but the results were just as indecisive.

Eastern Europe   In August 1914, Russian armies pushed into eastern Germany. Then, at the battle of Tannenberg, the Russians suffered one of the worst defeats of the war, causing them to retreat. After Tannenberg, armies in the east fought on Russian soil. As the least industrialized of the great powers, Russia was poorly equipped to fight a modern war. Troops sometimes lacked even rifles. Still, Russian commanders continued to throw masses of peasant soldiers into combat.

Southern Europe   Southeastern Europe was another battleground. In 1915, Bulgaria joined the Central Powers and helped crush its old Balkan rival Serbia. That same year, Italy declared war on Austria-Hungary and, later, on Germany. Italy had signed a secret treaty with the Allies to gain Austrian-ruled lands inhabited by Italians.

In October 1917, the Austrians and Germans launched a major offensive against the Italian position at Caporetto.

The Italians retreated in disarray. British and French forces later helped stop the Central Powers' advance into Italy. Still, Caporetto proved as disastrous for Italy as Tannenberg had been for Russia.

The War Outside Europe Though most of the fighting took place in Europe, World War I was a global conflict. Japan, allied with Britain, used the war as an excuse to seize German outposts in China and islands in the Pacific. It also tried to impose a protectorate on China.

The Ottoman empire joined the Central Powers in 1914. The Turks then closed off Allied ships from the Dardanelles, a vital strait connecting the Black Sea and the Mediterranean. In 1915, the Allies sent a massive force of British, Indian, Australian, and New Zealander troops to open up the strait. At the battle of Gallipoli (guh LIHP uh lee), Turkish troops tied down the trapped Allies on the beaches. In January 1916, after 10 months and more than 200,000 casualties, the Allies finally withdrew from the Dardanelles.

In turn, the Turks were hard hit in the Middle East. The Ottoman empire included vast areas of Arab land. In 1916, Arab nationalists led by Husayn ibn Ali declared a revolt against Ottoman rule. The British sent Colonel T. E. Lawrence—later known as Lawrence of Arabia—to support the Arab revolt. Lawrence led guerrilla raids against the Turks, dynamiting bridges and supply trains. Eventually, the Ottoman empire lost a great deal of territory to the Arabs, including the key city of Baghdad.

War and the Colonies European colonies were drawn into the struggle. The Allies overran scattered German colonies in Africa and Asia. They also turned to their own colonies and dominions for troops, laborers, and supplies. Canada, Australia, and New Zealand sent troops to Britain's aid. Colonial recruits from British India and French West Africa fought on European battlefields.

People in the colonies had mixed feelings about serving. Some were reluctant to serve the imperial powers. "When we speak of joining," remarked a South African man, "our women curse and spit at us, asking us whether the Government, for whom we propose to risk our lives, is not the one which sends the police to our houses at night . . . to trample upon us."

Other colonial troops volunteered eagerly. They expected that their service would be a step toward citizenship or independence. As you will read, such hopes would be dashed after the war.

Primary Source

The Battle of Gallipoli
A British soldier describes the fighting at Gallipoli:

"On June 4th we went over the top. We took the Turks' trench and held it. It was called Hill 13. The next day we were relieved and told to rest for three hours, but it wasn't more than half an hour before the relieving regiment came running back. The Turks had returned and recaptured their trench. On June 6th my favorite officer was killed and no end of us butchered, but we managed to get hold of Hill 13 again. We found a great muddle, carnage, and men without rifles shouting, 'Allah! Allah!' . . . Of the 60 men I had started out to war from Harwich with, there were only three left."

Skills Assessment

Primary Source How many times did Hill 13 change hands in three days?

SECTION 3 Assessment

Recall
1. **Identify: (a)** Western Front, **(b)** Verdun, **(c)** Somme, **(d)** Tannenberg, **(e)** Caporetto, **(f)** Gallipoli, **(g)** T. E. Lawrence.
2. **Define: (a)** stalemate, **(b)** no man's land, **(c)** zeppelin, **(d)** U-boat, **(e)** convoy.

Comprehension
3. Why did the war on the Western Front turn into a stalemate?
4. Describe three ways new technology affected the war.
5. What role did Europe's overseas colonies and dominions play in World War I?

Critical Thinking and Writing
6. **Linking Past and Present** Why do you think most nations today have agreed to ban the use of poison gas and other chemical and biological weapons?
7. **Predicting Consequences** Governments on both sides of World War I tried to keep full casualty figures and other bad news from reaching the public. What effect do you think news about disastrous defeats such as Tannenberg, Caporetto, or Gallipoli would have had on the attitude of people back home?

Activity

Conducting an Interview With a partner, conduct an interview between a war correspondent and a soldier fighting on the Western Front during World War I. Include at least ten questions and answers. You may wish to tape your interview.

Reading Focus

- How did World War I become a total war?
- What effect did the continuing war have on morale?
- What were the causes and results of American entry into the war?

Vocabulary

total war
conscription
propaganda
atrocity
self-determination
armistice

Taking Notes

As you read, prepare an outline of this section. Use Roman numerals for major headings, capital letters for subheadings, and numbers for supporting details. The sample here will help you get started.

I. Total war
  A. Economic impact
    1.
    2.
  B. Propaganda war
    1.
    2.

Main Idea In their efforts to achieve victory, governments committed all their nations' resources to the war effort.

Setting the Scene By 1917, European societies were cracking under the strain of war. Instead of praising the glorious deeds of heroes, war poets began denouncing the leaders whose errors wasted so many lives. British poet and soldier Siegfried Sassoon captured the bitter mood:

> "You smug-faced crowds with kindling eye
> Who cheer when soldier lads march by,
> Sneak home and pray you'll never know
> The hell where youth and laughter go."
> —Siegfried Sassoon, "Suicide in the Trenches"

Three years into the war, a revolution in Russia and the entry of the United States into the war would upset the balance of forces and finally end the long stalemate.

Total War

As the struggle wore on, nations realized that a modern, mechanized war required the total commitment of their whole society. The result was what we today call total war, the channeling of a nation's entire resources into a war effort.

Economic Impact Early on, both sides set up systems to recruit, arm, transport, and supply armies that numbered in the millions. All of the warring nations except Britain imposed universal military conscription, or "the draft," which required all young men to be ready for military or other service. Germany set up a system of forced civilian labor as well.

Governments raised taxes and borrowed huge amounts of money to pay the costs of war. They rationed food and other products, from boots to gasoline. In addition, they introduced other economic controls, such as setting prices and forbidding strikes.

Propaganda War Total war meant controlling public opinion. Even in democratic countries, special boards censored the press. Their aim was to keep complete casualty figures and other discouraging news from reaching the people. Government censors also restricted popular literature, historical writings, motion pictures, and the arts.

Both sides waged a propaganda war. Propaganda is the spreading of ideas to promote a cause or to damage an opposing cause. Allied

Propaganda War
Name-calling is one of the most common techniques of propaganda. Allied propaganda often referred to Germans as Huns, the barbarian tribe who helped destroy Roman civilization.

Theme: Art and Literature How does the picture add to the emotional impact of this propaganda poster?

propaganda often played up Germany's invasion of Belgium as a barbarous act. The British and French press circulated tales of atrocities, horrible acts against innocent people. Often, these stories were greatly exaggerated or completely made up. In Germany, propagandists encouraged people to sing a "Hymn of Hate" against the British:

> "Hate by water and hate by land;
> Hate of the head and hate of the hand;
> We love as one, we hate as one;
> We have one foe and one alone—
> ENGLAND!"
> —Ernst Lissauer, "Hymn of Hate"

Impact on Women Women played a critical role in total war. As millions of men left to fight, women took over their jobs and kept national economies going. Many women worked in war industries, manufacturing weapons and supplies. Others joined women's branches of the armed forces. When food shortages threatened Britain, volunteers in the Women's Land Army went to the fields to grow their nation's food.

Nurses shared the dangers of the men whose wounds they tended. At aid stations close to the front lines, nurses often worked around the clock, especially after a big "push" brought a flood of casualties. In her diary, English nurse Vera Brittain describes sweating through 90-degree days in France, "stopping hemorrhages, replacing intestines, and draining and reinserting innumerable rubber tubes" with "gruesome human remains heaped on the floor."

War work gave women a new sense of pride and confidence. After the war, most women had to give up their jobs to men returning home. Still, they had challenged the idea that women were too "delicate" for demanding and dangerous jobs. In many countries, including Britain and the United States, women's support for the war effort helped them finally win the right to vote, after decades of struggle.

Collapsing Morale

By 1917, the morale of both troops and civilians had plunged. Germany was sending 15-year-old recruits to the front. Britain was on the brink of bankruptcy. Long casualty lists, food shortages, and the failure of generals to win promised victories led to calls for peace.

As morale collapsed, troops mutinied in some French units. In Italy, many soldiers deserted during the retreat at Caporetto. In Russia, soldiers left the front to join in a full-scale revolution back home.

Revolution in Russia Three years of war had hit Russia especially hard. Stories of incompetent generals and corruption destroyed public confidence. In March 1917, bread riots in St. Petersburg mushroomed into a revolution that brought down the Russian monarchy. (You will read more about the causes and effects of the Russian Revolution in the next chapter.)

At first, the Allies welcomed the overthrow of the czar. They hoped Russia would institute a democratic government and become a stronger ally. But later that year, when V. I. Lenin came to power, he promised to pull Russian troops out of the war. Early in 1918, Lenin signed the Treaty of Brest-Litovsk (brehst lih TAWFSK) with Germany. The treaty ended Russian participation in World War I.

Impact on the War Russia's withdrawal had an immediate impact on the war. With Russia out of the struggle, Germany could concentrate its forces on the Western Front. In the spring of 1918, the Central Powers stood ready to achieve the great breakthrough they had sought so long.

Biography

Edith Cavell 1865–1915

Like most ordinary people caught up in war, Edith Cavell did not plan on becoming a hero. An English nurse, she was in charge of a hospital in Belgium. After the German invasion, Cavell cared for wounded soldiers on both sides. She also helped Allied soldiers escape to the Netherlands.

In 1915, the Germans arrested Cavell for spying. As she faced a firing squad, her last reported words were, "Standing as I do in view of God and Eternity, I realize that patriotism is not enough. I must have no hatred or bitterness toward anyone."

Theme: Impact of the Individual Why do you think the British government spread the story of Edith Cavell?

 Primary Sources and Literature

See "Erich Maria Remarque: All Quiet on the Western Front," in the Reference Section at the back of this book.

Go Online
PHSchool.com

For: Other artworks, artifacts, and documents relating to World War I
Visit: PHSchool.com
Web Code: mkd-2792

Allied Push Toward Victory
In September 1918, American troops pushed German forces back through the Argonne Forest of France. This battle was the last Allied offensive of the war.

Theme: Geography and History What does this picture suggest about the environmental impact of the war?

The United States Declares War

Soon after the Russian Revolution began, however, another event altered the balance of forces. The United States declared war on Germany. Why did the United States exchange neutrality for war in 1917?

Unrestricted Submarine Warfare One major reason involved German submarine attacks on merchant and passenger ships carrying American citizens. Many of these ships were transporting supplies to the Allies. But President Woodrow Wilson insisted that Americans, as citizens of a neutral country, had a right to safe travel on the seas.

In May 1915, a German submarine torpedoed the British liner *Lusitania*. Almost 1,200 passengers were killed, including 128 Americans. Germany justified the attack, arguing that the *Lusitania* was carrying weapons. When Wilson threatened to cut off relations with Germany, though, Germany agreed to restrict its submarine campaign. Before attacking any ship, U-boats would surface and give warning, allowing neutral passengers to escape to the lifeboats. In December 1916, however, Germany announced that it would resume unrestricted submarine warfare. Wilson angrily denounced Germany.

Cultural Ties Many Americans supported the Allies. They felt ties of culture and language to Britain and sympathized with France as another democracy. Still, some German Americans favored the Central Powers. So did many Irish Americans, who resented British rule of Ireland, and Russian Jewish immigrants, who did not want to be allied with the czar.

Zimmermann Note In early 1917, the British intercepted a message from the German foreign minister, Arthur Zimmermann, to his ambassador in Mexico. Zimmermann promised that, in return for Mexican support, Germany would help Mexico "to reconquer the lost territory in New Mexico, Texas, and Arizona." Britain revealed the Zimmermann note to the American government. When the note became public, anti-German feeling intensified in the United States.

Declaring War In April 1917, Wilson asked Congress to declare war on Germany. "We have no selfish ends to serve," he stated. Instead, he painted the conflict idealistically as a war "to make the world safe for democracy" and as a "war to end war."

First, the United States needed months to recruit, train, supply, and transport a modern army across the Atlantic. By 1918, about two million fresh, confident American soldiers had joined the war-weary Allied troops fighting on the Western Front. Although relatively few American troops got into combat, they proved to be good fighters. Their arrival gave Allied troops a much-needed morale boost. Just as important to the debt-ridden Allies was the financial aid provided by the United States.

The Fourteen Points Though he had failed to maintain American neutrality, Wilson still hoped to be a peacemaker. In January 1918, he issued the Fourteen Points, a list of his terms for resolving this and future wars. He called for freedom of the seas, free trade, large-scale reductions of arms, and an end to secret treaties. For Eastern Europe, Wilson favored self-determination, the right of people to choose their own form of government. All those issues, he felt, had helped cause the war. Finally, he urged the creation of a "general association of nations" to keep the peace in the future.

Campaign to Victory

A final showdown got underway in early 1918. In March, the Germans launched a huge offensive that pushed the Allies back 40 miles by July. But the effort exhausted the Germans. The Allies then launched a counter-attack, slowly driving German forces back across France and Belgium. In September, German generals told the kaiser that the war could not be won.

The German people showed their monarch their frustration as uprisings exploded among hungry city dwellers. German commanders advised the kaiser to step down, as the czar had done. William II did so in early November, fleeing into exile in the Netherlands.

By autumn, Austria-Hungary was also reeling toward collapse. As the government in Vienna tottered, the subject nationalities revolted, splintering the empire of the Hapsburgs.

The new German government sought an armistice, or agreement to end fighting, with the Allies. At 11 A.M. on November 11, 1918, the Great War at last came to an end.

Geography and History

Getting "Over There"

By July 1918, the United States was sending some 10,000 troops every day to France. But transporting so many soldiers and supplies across the Atlantic Ocean was no easy task. Violent storms plagued the cold waters of the North Atlantic. Even more threatening were the German U-boats that patrolled Atlantic shipping lanes.

To protect the transport of men and supplies, naval destroyers escorted the convoys. Faster and more agile than the submarines, they outmaneuvered the enemy. The United States Navy was so effective that in just two years, 2.5 million American soldiers and 7.5 million tons of supplies reached France with few losses.

Theme: Geography and History What geographic obstacle did the United States face when it entered World War I?

SECTION 4 Assessment

Recall

1. **Identify: (a)** Treaty of Brest-Litovsk, **(b)** Woodrow Wilson, **(c)** *Lusitania,* **(d)** Fourteen Points.
2. **Define: (a)** total war, **(b)** conscription, **(c)** propaganda, **(d)** atrocity, **(e)** self-determination, **(f)** armistice.

Comprehension

3. What measures did wartime governments take to control **(a)** national economies, **(b)** public opinion?
4. What impact did wartime failures have on Russia?

5. **(a)** Why did the United States declare war on Germany? **(b)** What impact did American entry have on the war?

Critical Thinking and Writing

6. **Analyzing Literature** Reread the poem at the beginning of this section. **(a)** To whom is the poem addressed? **(b)** What does it suggest about the effects of trench warfare?
7. **Defending a Position** If you had been a women's suffragist, would you have supported the war effort? Why or why not?

Go Online
PHSchool.com

Create a bibliography of five Web sites dealing with World War I. Rank the sites in order from 1 to 5, with 1 being the best. Consider content, images, and interactivity. For help with this activity, use **Web Code mkd-2793.**

Making the Peace

Reading Focus

- What were the costs of the war?
- What issues faced the delegates to the Paris Peace Conference?
- Why were many people dissatisfied with the Treaty of Versailles and other peace settlements?

Vocabulary

pandemic

reparations

collective security

mandate

Taking Notes

Copy this chart. As you read, fill in the left-hand column with issues that faced the world after World War I. In the right-hand column, write how the Paris Peace Conference dealt with each of these issues.

ISSUE	SETTLEMENT
1. Debt	1. German reparations
2.	2. Reduced size of Germany
3. Nationalism	3.
4.	4. League of Nations
5.	5.

Main Idea As Europe struggled to recover from the devastation of war, world leaders met in Paris to craft a peace treaty.

Setting the Scene Just weeks after the war ended, President Wilson boarded a steamship bound for France. He had decided to go in person to Paris, where Allied leaders would make the peace. Wilson was certain that he could solve the problems of old Europe. "Tell me what is right," Wilson urged his advisers, "and I'll fight for it."

Sadly, it would not be that easy. Europe was a shattered continent. Its problems, and those of the world, would not be solved at the Paris Peace Conference, or for many years afterward.

FACT FINDER

Casualties of World War I

	Deaths in Battle	Wounded in Battle
Allies		
France	1,357,800	4,266,000
British empire	908,371	2,090,212
Russia	1,700,000	4,950,000
Italy	462,391	953,886
United States	50,585	205,690
Others	502,421	342,585
Central Powers		
Germany	1,808,546	4,247,143
Austria-Hungary	922,500	3,620,000
Ottoman empire	325,000	400,000

Source: R. E. Dupuy and T. N. Dupuy, *The Encyclopedia of Military History*

Skills Assessment

Chart World War I resulted in more casualties than any previous war. **Which two nations suffered the most deaths? Why were American casualties relatively low?**

The Costs of War

The human and material costs of the war were staggering. More than 8.5 million people were dead. Double that number had been wounded, many of them handicapped for life. Famine threatened many regions.

The devastation was made even worse in 1918 by a deadly pandemic of influenza. A pandemic is the spread of a disease across an entire country, continent, or—in this case—the whole world. In just a few months, the flu swept around the world, killing more than 20 million people—twice as many as the war itself.

Financial Burdens In battle zones from France to Russia, homes, farms, factories, roads, and churches had been shelled into rubble. The costs of rebuilding and paying off huge national war debts would burden an already battered world.

Shaken and disillusioned, people everywhere felt bitter about the war. The Allies blamed the conflict on their defeated foes and insisted that the losers make reparations, or payments for war damage. The stunned Central Powers, who had viewed the armistice as a cease-fire rather than a surrender, looked for scapegoats on whom they could blame their defeat.

Political Turmoil Under the stress of war, governments had collapsed in Russia, Germany, Austria-Hungary, and the Ottoman empire. Political radicals dreamed of building a new social order from the chaos, as revolutionaries in Russia seemed to be doing. Conservatives warned against the spread of bolshevism, or communism, as it soon came to be called.

Unrest also swept through Europe's colonial empires. African and Asian soldiers had discovered that the imperial powers were not as invincible as they seemed. Colonial troops returned home with a more cynical view of Europeans and renewed hopes for independence.

The Paris Peace Conference

To a weary world, Woodrow Wilson seemed a symbol of hope. His talk of self-determination and democracy raised expectations for a just and lasting peace, even in defeated Germany. Crowds cheered wildly as he rode along the Paris boulevards.

The Big Three Wilson was one of three strong personalities who dominated the Paris Peace Conference. A dedicated reformer, Wilson was so sure of his rightness that he could be hard to work with. Urging "peace without victory," he wanted the Fourteen Points to be the basis of the peace.

The other Allied leaders at the peace conference had different aims. The British prime minister, David Lloyd George, knew that his people demanded harsh treatment for Germany. He promised to build a postwar Britain "fit for heroes"—a goal that would cost money. The French leader, Georges Clemenceau (KLEHM uhn soh), bore the nickname "the Tiger" for his fierce anti-German war policy. His chief goal was to weaken Germany so that it could never again threaten France. "Mr. Wilson bores me with his Fourteen Points," complained Clemenceau. "Why, God Almighty has only ten!"

Difficult Issues Crowds of other representatives circled around the "Big Three" with their own demands and interests. The Italian prime minister, Vittorio Orlando, insisted that the Allies honor their secret agreement to give to Italy lands that were once ruled by Austria-Hungary. Such secret agreements violated Wilson's principle of self-determination.

Self-determination posed other problems. Many people who had been ruled by Russia, Austria-Hungary, or the Ottoman empire now demanded national states of their own. The territories claimed by these peoples often overlapped, so it was impossible to satisfy them all.

Faced with conflicting demands, Wilson had to compromise on his Fourteen Points. On one point, though, he stood firm. His dream was to create an international League of Nations. The League would be based on the idea of collective security, a system in which a group of nations acts as one to preserve the peace of all. With the League in place, Wilson felt sure that any mistakes made in Paris could be corrected in time.

The Treaty of Versailles

In June 1919, the peacemakers summoned representatives of the new German Republic to the palace of Versailles outside Paris. The Germans were ordered to sign the treaty drawn up by the Allies.

The German delegates read the document with growing horror. It forced Germany to assume full blame for causing the war. It also imposed huge reparations that would put an already damaged German economy under a staggering burden. The reparations covered not only the destruction caused by the war, but also pensions for millions of Allied soldiers or their widows and families. The total cost of German reparations would come to over $30 billion.

Other clauses were aimed at weakening Germany. The treaty severely limited the size of the once-feared German military. It returned Alsace and Lorraine to France, removed hundreds of square miles of territory from western and eastern Germany, and stripped Germany of its overseas colonies.

Primary Source

Signing the Peace Treaty
A British delegate describes how the German delegates were brought in to sign the Treaty of Versailles:

"Isolated and pitiable, come the two German delegates. Dr. Müller, Dr. Bell. The silence is terrifying. . . . They keep their eyes fixed away from those two thousand staring eyes, fixed up on the ceiling. They are deathly pale. . . . They are conducted to their chairs. Clemenceau at once breaks the silence. 'Messieurs,' he rasps, '[the meeting is open.]' He adds a few ill-chosen words. 'We are here to sign a Treaty of Peace.' The Germans leap up anxiously when he has finished, since they know that they are the first to sign. William Martin, as if a theater manager, motions them [crossly] to sit down again."
—Harold Nicolson,
Peacemaking, 1919

Skills Assessment

Primary Source Do you think Nicolson approved of the way the German delegates were treated? Explain.

Europe, 1914

NORWAY
SWEDEN
GREAT BRITAIN
DENMARK
North Sea
Baltic Sea
RUSSIA
GERMANY
ATLANTIC OCEAN
FRANCE
AUSTRIA-HUNGARY
ROMANIA
PORTUGAL
SPAIN
ITALY
Black Sea
BULGARIA
GREECE
OTTOMAN EMPIRE
Mediterranean Sea

Azimuthal Equal Area Projection
0   250   500 Miles
0   250   500 Kilometers

Europe, 1920

FINLAND
NORWAY
SWEDEN
ESTONIA Moscow
LATVIA
LITHUANIA
GREAT BRITAIN
DENMARK
North Sea
Baltic Sea
GER.
DANZIG
London •
NETH.
• Berlin
• Warsaw
BELG.
GERMANY
POLAND
RHINELAND
Paris • LUX.
SAAR BASIN
CZECHOSLOVAKIA
ALSACE LORRAINE
• Vienna
RUSSIA
ATLANTIC OCEAN
FRANCE
SWITZ.
AUSTRIA HUNGARY
YUGOSLAVIA
ROMANIA
PORTUGAL
SPAIN
• Madrid
ITALY
• Rome
BULGARIA
Constantinople •
ALBANIA
GREECE
TURK
Mediterranean Sea
DODECANESE (Italy)

Azimuthal Equal Area Projection
0   250   500 Miles
0   250   500 Kilometers

Skills Assessment

Geography The peace treaties that ended World War I redrew the map of Europe.

1. **Location** On the map, locate **(a)** Lithuania, **(b)** Latvia, **(c)** Estonia, **(d)** Poland, **(e)** Yugoslavia.
2. **Region** Which countries lost territory in Eastern Europe?
3. **Critical Thinking**
   Making Inferences Why do you think the war had no effect on national boundaries in southwestern Europe?

The Germans signed because they had no choice. But German resentment of the Treaty of Versailles would poison the international climate for 20 years—and help spark an even deadlier world war.

Widespread Dissatisfaction

The Allies drew up separate treaties with the other Central Powers. Like the Treaty of Versailles, these treaties left widespread dissatisfaction.

Self-Determination in Eastern Europe Where the German, Austrian, and Russian empires had once ruled, a band of new nations emerged. They included the Baltic states of Latvia, Lithuania, and Estonia. Poland regained independence after more than 100 years of foreign rule.

Three new republics—Czechoslovakia, Austria, and Hungary—rose in the old Hapsburg heartland. In the Balkans, the peacemakers created a new South Slav state, Yugoslavia, dominated by Serbia. Eastern Europe, however, remained a center of conflict, as you will read.

Mandate System European colonies in Africa, Asia, and the Pacific had looked to the Paris Peace Conference with high hopes. Many people from these lands had fought alongside Europeans. Colonial leaders expected that the peace would bring new respect and an end to imperial rule. They took up Wilson's call for self-determination.

However, the leaders at Paris applied self-determination only to parts of Europe. Outside Europe, the victorious Allies added to their overseas empires. The treaties created a system of mandates, territories administered by western powers. Britain and France gained mandates over German colonies in Africa and Ottoman lands in the Middle East. In theory, mandates were to be held and modernized until they were able to "stand alone." In practice, they became European colonies. From Africa to the Middle East and across Asia, colonized peoples felt betrayed by the peacemakers.

Unfulfilled Goals Germany was not the only power dissatisfied by the peace. Italy was angry because it did not get all the lands promised in its secret treaty with the Allies. Japan protested the refusal of western nations to recognize its claims in China. At the same time, China was forced to accept former German holdings. Russia, excluded from the peace talks, resented the reestablishment of a Polish nation and three independent Baltic states on lands that had been part of the Russian empire. All of these discontented nations bided their time. They waited for a chance to revise the peace settlements in their favor.

Hopes for Global Peace The Paris Peace Conference did offer one beacon of hope in the League of Nations. In the aftermath of the war, millions of people looked to the League to ensure the peace. More than 40 nations joined the League. They agreed to negotiate disputes rather than resort to war. Members of the League promised to take common action—economic or even military—against any aggressor state.

Wilson's dream had become a reality. Yet his own Senate refused to ratify the treaty, and the United States never joined the League. Disillusioned with war, the United States chose to play a lone hand in world affairs. As time soon revealed, the League was powerless to prevent war. Still, it was a first step toward something genuinely new—an international organization dedicated to maintaining peace and advancing the interests of all peoples.

Cause *and* Effect

Long-Term Causes	Immediate Causes
• Imperialist and economic rivalries among European powers • European alliance system • Militarism and arms race • Nationalist tensions in Balkans	• Austria-Hungary's annexation of Bosnia and Herzegovina • Fighting in the Balkans • Assassination of Archduke Francis Ferdinand • German invasion of Belgium

World War I

Immediate Effects	Long-Term Effects
• Enormous cost in lives and money • Russian Revolution • Creation of new nations in Eastern Europe • Requirement that Germany pay reparations • German loss of its overseas colonies • Balfour Declaration • League of Nations	• Economic impact of war debts on Europe • Emergence of United States and Japan as important powers • Growth of nationalism in colonies • Rise of fascism • World War II

Connections to Today

• Ethnic tensions in Balkans
• International agreement banning poison gas
• Use of airplanes and submarines for military purposes
• Arab-Israeli conflict

Skills Assessment **Chart** Sparked by old rivalries in Europe, World War I helped shape our world today. **Which effect of the war do you think is most important today? Why?**

SECTION 5 Assessment

Recall
1. **Identify:** **(a)** David Lloyd George, **(b)** Georges Clemenceau, **(c)** League of Nations, **(d)** Treaty of Versailles.
2. **Define:** **(a)** pandemic, **(b)** reparations, **(c)** collective security, **(d)** mandate.

Comprehension
3. Describe conditions in Europe after World War I.
4. **(a)** Identify three issues to be settled at the Paris Peace Conference. **(b)** How did Woodrow Wilson's goals at the peace talks differ from those of other Allied leaders?

5. How did the peace treaties both follow and violate Wilson's principle of self-determination?

Critical Thinking and Writing
6. **Connecting to Geography** How might the creation of the mandate system affect the map of Africa after World War I?
7. **Making Inferences** Wilson's closest adviser wrote, "Looking at the conference in retrospect, there is much to approve and much to regret." What do you think he might have approved? What might he have regretted?

Activity

Writing an Editorial Choose *one* of the countries mentioned in this section. Write an editorial about the Paris Peace Conference that might have appeared in a newspaper in that country during or after the peace talks.

Creating a Chapter Summary

Copy this concept web on a sheet of paper. For each statement in the light purple ovals, include two or more facts to support that statement, adding as many ovals as you need. Two examples have been filled in to help you get started.

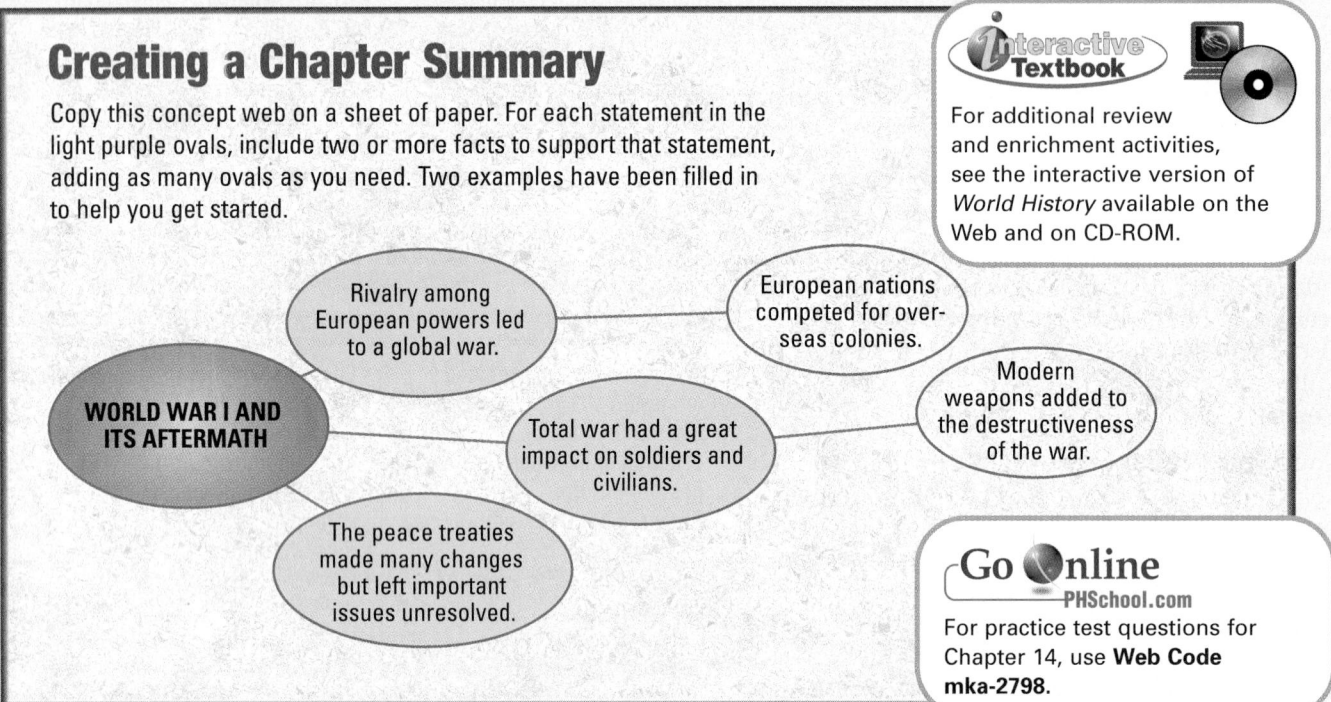

interactive Textbook

For additional review and enrichment activities, see the interactive version of *World History* available on the Web and on CD-ROM.

Rivalry among European powers led to a global war.

European nations competed for over-seas colonies.

WORLD WAR I AND ITS AFTERMATH

Total war had a great impact on soldiers and civilians.

Modern weapons added to the destructiveness of the war.

The peace treaties made many changes but left important issues unresolved.

Go Online
PHSchool.com

For practice test questions for Chapter 14, use **Web Code mka-2798.**

Building Vocabulary

Use the chapter vocabulary words listed below to create a crossword puzzle. Exchange puzzles with a classmate. Complete the puzzles and then check each other's answers.

1. **militarism**
2. **entente**
3. **ultimatum**
4. **mobilize**
5. **neutrality**
6. **propaganda**
7. **atrocity**
8. **armistice**
9. **reparations**
10. **mandate**

Recalling Key Facts

11. **(a)** What event sparked the outbreak of World War I? **(b)** Which nation was the first to declare war?
12. At the start of the war, which nations made up the Central Powers? Which nations made up the Allies?
13. Describe trench warfare.
14. How did troops from Europe's overseas colonies become involved in the war?
15. **(a)** What nation joined the war on the Allied side in 1917? **(b)** What Allied nation dropped out of the war in 1918?
16. How did the Treaty of Versailles punish Germany?

Critical Thinking and Writing

17. **Linking Past and Present (a)** What efforts were made to promote world peace before and after World War I? **(b)** How do individuals and govern-ments work for peace today?

18. **Recognizing Points of View (a)** What arguments could Russia have used to blame Austria-Hungary for the start of World War I? **(b)** What argu-ments could Austria-Hungary have used to blame Russia?

19. **Recognizing Causes and Effects** How did the Industrial Revolution affect the course of World War I?

20. **Connecting to Geography** Review the map of the war in Europe in Section 3. **(a)** Locate the Dardanelles. How would control of the strait have been important to the Allies? **(b)** Why did submarine war-fare play an important role in the war?

21. **Analyzing Ideas (a)** What do you think Woodrow Wilson meant by "peace without victory"? **(b)** Why do you think the European Allies were unwilling to accept this idea?

Read this description of how the declaration of war was greeted in St. Petersburg, the capital of Russia. Then, answer the questions that follow.

> *"There was a crowd in front of a newspaper office. Every few minutes a momentous phrase scribbled in charcoal appeared in the window: 'ENGLAND GIVES UP PEACE NEGOTIATIONS. Germany invades Belgium. Mobilization progressing with Great Enthusiasm.' And at 7:50 p.m.:*
>
> *'GERMANY DECLARES WAR ON RUSSIA.' Spontaneously the crowd started singing the national anthem. . . . The people were staring at the sprawling words, as if trying to understand what they actually meant as far as each personal little life was concerned.*
>
> *Then the edges of the crowd started breaking off and drifting in one direction, up the Nevsky Prospect. I heard the phrase 'German Embassy' repeated several times."*

—Sergyei N. Kurnakov, *Savage Squadrons*

22. Based on what you have read, during what month and year did this scene take place?

23. What is the first reaction of the crowd to news of the declaration of war?

24. "The people were staring at the sprawling words, as if trying to understand what they actually meant as far as each personal little life was concerned." Is this statement a fact, an opinion, or a mixture of both? Explain.

25. What do you think will happen when the crowd moves on up the Nevsky Prospect?

26. Based on what you have read, do you think similar scenes may have been taking place in France or Germany at this time? Explain.

27. How might the mood in St. Petersburg have been different three years later?

Go Online
PHSchool.com

Use the Internet to research important battles, turning points, and changes in methods of warfare that took place during World War I. Then, create an illustrated map of Europe during World War I that highlights some of these events and explains their significance. For help with this activity, use **Web Code mkd-2799.**

The poster above was created in 1916 by Louis Raemaekers, a Dutch artist who was then living in England. Study the poster and then answer the following questions:

28. Whom do the two figures on the poster represent?

29. **(a)** What organization distributed this poster? **(b)** Where was this organization located?

30. **(a)** Who was the intended audience for this poster? **(b)** What did the artist want the people who saw this poster to do?

31. Based on what you have read, why would people in England in 1916 have been sympathetic toward Belgium?

32. Describe how the poster appeals to the following emotions: **(a)** pity; **(b)** anger.

33. Would you consider this poster an effective piece of propaganda? Explain.

Skills Tip

As you analyze a work of propaganda, look for ways in which it tries to stir people to action by appealing to their emotions.

Revolution in Russia

1917–1939

Chapter Preview

1 Two Revolutions in Russia
2 From Lenin to Stalin
3 Life in a Totalitarian State

1917

Two revolutions lead to the creation of a communist government in Russia. In this painting, Bolsheviks storm the Winter Palace.

1921

Lenin, shown in the monument above, adopts the New Economic Policy.

**CHAPTER
EVENTS**

 1915

1920

1925

**GLOBAL
EVENTS**

1919 After World War I, the Paris Peace Conference convenes.

1920s Mexico recovers from revolution and civil war.

Russian Revolution and Civil War, 1917–1922

Between 1917 and 1922, revolution and civil war transformed Russia into the communist Soviet Union.

Murmansk
Barents Sea
Archangel
ESTONIA FINLAND
LATVIA Petrograd
Moscow
LITHUANIA
Brest-Litovsk
Kiev
POLAND
ROMANIA
Black Sea
TURKEY
Mediterranean Sea

R U S S I A
(Union of Soviet Socialist Republics, 1922)

L. Baikal
Sea of Okhotsk
L. Balkhash
Aral Sea
Caspian Sea
MONGOLIA
Vladivostok
JAPAN

IRAN
AFGHANISTAN
CHINA
PACIFIC OCEAN
INDIA

N W E S

Robinson Projection

0   500   1000 Miles
0   500   1000 Kilometers

Lands lost by Russia

★ Revolutionary outbreaks, 1917

✳ Major battle sites, 1918–1920

→ Foreign interventions

КОМСОМОЛ-УДАРНАЯ БРИГАДА ПЯТИЛЕТКИ.

1928
Stalin proposes a five-year plan for Soviet economic growth. This poster urges industrial workers to participate.

1934
Stalin launches the Great Purge. Millions will be executed or sent to forced-labor camps like the one shown here.

1930

1929 Stock market crash in New York triggers global depression of the 1930s.

1935

1934 Chinese Communists make epic retreat known as the Long March.

1940

1939 German forces invade Poland. World War II begins.

Reading Focus

■ Why did revolution occur in Russia in March 1917?

■ Why did Lenin and the Bolsheviks launch the November revolution?

■ How did the Communists defeat their opponents in Russia's civil war?

Vocabulary

proletariat

soviet

commissar

Taking Notes

Copy this partially completed chart on the causes of revolution in Russia. As you read, finish the chart by writing in other causes.

REVOLUTION IN RUSSIA

Main Idea After two revolutions and a civil war, Lenin and the Communist party were the new rulers of Russia.

Geography and History

A Land of Many Nations

Geography had long favored the growth of the Russian empire. The vast plain stretching from Moscow had few natural obstacles to halt the advance of Russian armies. For nearly four centuries, the empire grew steadily. This growth was a mixed blessing, however. In 1897, a census revealed that the Russians were a minority in their own empire. More than half the people under czarist rule were not Russians. The population included Poles, Finns, Ukrainians, Lithuanians, Latvians, Turkic peoples, and other groups.

Nationalism led to the rise of new political parties among these peoples. In addition to social and economic reform, the parties' leaders hoped for some degree of self-rule. Radicals even dreamed of independent nations—a revolutionary idea that contributed to unrest in the Russian empire.

Theme: Geography and History Refer to a modern map of Europe. Name two independent nations of today that were once part of the Russian empire.

Setting the Scene On Easter 1913, Czar Nicholas II gave his wife, Alexandra, a fabulous jeweled egg, made by the famous jewelry firm of Fabergé. The egg's enamel shell held tiny portraits of all the Romanovs who had reigned since Michael Romanov was elected to rule Russia in 1613. Balls, parades, and other festive events celebrated the 300th anniversary of the Romanov dynasty. Everywhere, Russians cheered wildly for the czar and his family.

Czarina Alexandra felt confident that the people loved Nicholas too much to ever threaten him. "They are constantly frightening the emperor with threats of revolution," she told a friend, "and here,—you see it yourself—we need merely to show ourselves and at once their hearts are ours."

Appearances were deceiving. After the Revolution of 1905, Nicholas had failed to solve Russia's basic political, economic, and social problems. Discontent sparked new eruptions. In March 1917, the first of two revolutions would topple the Romanov dynasty and pave the way for even more radical changes.

The March Revolution

In 1914, the huge Russian empire stretched from Eastern Europe to the Pacific Ocean. Unlike industrialized Western Europe, Russia was a backward land dominated by landowning nobles, priests, and an autocratic czar. Much of its majority peasant population endured stark poverty. A small middle class and an urban working class were emerging as Russia began to industrialize.

Long-Term Unrest Under pressure, czars had made some reforms, but too few to ease the nation's crisis. The elected Duma set up after the Revolution of 1905 had no real power. Moderates pressed for a constitution and social change. But Nicholas II, a weak and ineffectual man, blocked attempts to limit his authority. Like past czars, he relied on his secret police and other enforcers to impose his will. Adding to the problems of the government were a corrupt bureaucracy and an overburdened court system.

Revolutionaries hatched radical plots. Some hoped to lead discontented peasants to overthrow the czarist regime. Marxists tried to ignite revolution among the proletariat—the growing class of factory and railroad workers, miners, and urban wage earners. To outwit government spies and informers, revolutionaries worked in secrecy under rigid discipline. A revolution, they believed, would occur, when the time was ripe.

Impact of World War I The outbreak of war in 1914 fired national pride and united Russians. Armies dashed to battle with enthusiasm. But like the Crimean and Russo-Japanese wars, World War I quickly strained Russian resources. Factories could not turn out enough supplies. The transportation system broke down, delivering only a trickle of needed materials to the front. By 1915, many soldiers had no rifles and no ammunition. Badly equipped and poorly led, they died in staggering numbers. In 1915 alone, Russian casualties reached two million.

In a patriotic gesture, Nicholas II went to the front to take personal charge. The decision proved a disastrous blunder. The czar was no more competent than many of his generals. Worse, he left domestic affairs to the czarina, Alexandra. Many Russians already distrusted Alexandra because she was German born. She also knew little about government.

Rasputin Alexandra came to rely on the advice of Gregory Rasputin, an illiterate peasant and self-proclaimed "holy man." Rasputin's powerful personality had helped him gain a wide-spread reputation as a healer. The czarina, especially, came to believe in his "miraculous" powers after he helped ease the suffering of her son, who suffered from hemophilia, a disorder in which even the smallest injury can result in uncontrollable bleeding.

By 1916, Rasputin's influence over Alexandra had reached new heights and weakened confidence in the government. Officials were appointed or dismissed at his say-so. Those who flattered him won top jobs. Yet Alexandra ignored all warnings about Rasputin. Fearing for the monarchy, a group of Russian nobles killed Rasputin on December 29, 1916.

Collapse of the Monarchy By March 1917,* disasters on the battlefield, combined with food and fuel shortages on the home front, brought the monarchy to collapse. In St. Petersburg (renamed Petrograd during the war), workers were going on strike. Marchers, mostly women, surged through the streets, shouting, "Bread! Bread!" Troops refused to fire on the demonstrators, leaving the government helpless. Finally, on the advice of military and political leaders, the czar abdicated.

Duma politicians then set up a provisional, or temporary, government. Middle-class liberals in the government began preparing a constitution for a new Russian republic. At the same time, they continued the war against Germany. That decision proved fatal. Most Russians were fed up with the war. Troops at the front were deserting in droves. Peasants wanted land. City workers demanded food and an end to the desperate shortages.

Outside the provisional government, revolutionary socialists plotted their own course. In Petrograd and other cities, they set up soviets, or councils of workers and soldiers. At first, the soviets worked democratically within the government. Before long, though, the Bolsheviks, a radical socialist group, took charge. The leader of the Bolsheviks was a determined revolutionary, V. I. Lenin.

Lenin and the Bolsheviks

Vladimir Ilyich Ulyanov (ool YAHN awf) was born in 1870 to a middle-class family. Lenin was the name he adopted when he became a revolutionary. When he was 17, his older brother was arrested and hanged for plotting to kill the czar. The execution branded his family as a threat to the state and instilled in young Vladimir a hatred for the czarist government.

A Hard Man to Kill

The death of Gregory Rasputin was perhaps even more bizarre than his strange life.

To get rid of him, a group of nobles lured Rasputin to the palace of Prince Felix Yussoupov, where they served him cakes and wine laced with enough cyanide to kill several men. Incredibly, Rasputin was not affected. Next, Yussoupov shot him through the chest with a revolver. Rasputin fell. As the conspirators examined the body, Rasputin sprang to his feet and began to attack Yussoupov! The prince fled.

Then Rasputin attempted his own escape. He bolted outside and ran across the courtyard toward the gate. Another shot hit him, and he fell into the snow. The conspirators then clubbed him unconscious. Flinging Rasputin into the icy Neva River, they watched him sink.

Later, the body of Rasputin—poisoned, shot twice, and badly beaten—was recovered from the river and autopsied. The cause of death? Drowning.

Theme: Impact of the Individual Why did Yussoupov and others go to so much trouble to murder Rasputin?

---

* The revolutions of March and November 1917 are known to Russians as the February and October revolutions. In 1917, Russia still used an old calendar, which was 13 days behind the one used in Western Europe. Not until 1918 did Russia adopt the western calendar.

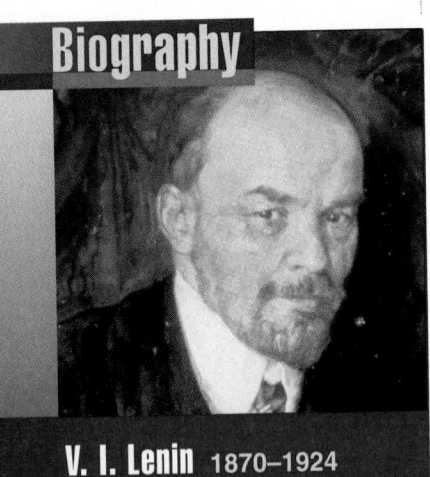

V. I. Lenin 1870–1924

Lenin was the son of a teacher and his wife who lived in a little town on the Volga River. Vladimir lived with his parents and five siblings in a rented wing of a large house. By all accounts it was a happy home. Vladimir excelled at school and looked up to his older brother Alexander. But, when Vladimir was 16, his father died. When he was 17, his beloved brother Alexander was hanged for plotting to kill the czar.

Still reeling from the death of his brother, Vladimir enrolled at Kazan University. There he met other discontented young people. They united to protest the lack of student freedom in the university. Vladimir was expelled within three months for his part in the demonstrations.

Theme: Impact of the Individual How do you think Lenin's early life affected his later political ideas?

Early Career As a young man, Lenin read the works of Karl Marx and participated in student demonstrations. He spread Marxist ideas among factory workers along with other socialists, including Nadezhda Krupskaya (nah DYEZH duh kroop SKĪ uh), the daughter of a poor noble family.

In 1895, Lenin and Krupskaya were arrested and sent to Siberia. During their imprisonment, they were married. After their release, they went into exile in Switzerland. There, they worked tirelessly to spread revolutionary ideas. A rival once described Lenin's total commitment to the cause: "There is no other man who is absorbed by the revolution 24 hours a day, who has no other thoughts but the thought of revolution, and who, even when he sleeps, dreams of nothing but the revolution."

A New View of Marx Lenin adapted Marxist ideas to fit Russian conditions. Marx had predicted that the industrial working class would rise spontaneously to overthrow capitalism. But Russia did not have a large urban proletariat. Instead, Lenin called for an elite group to lead the revolution and set up a "dictatorship of the proletariat." Though this elite revolutionary party represented a small percentage of socialists, Lenin gave them the name Bolsheviks, meaning "majority."

In Western Europe, many leading socialists had come to think that socialism could be achieved through gradual and moderate reforms such as higher wages, increased suffrage, and social welfare programs. The Bolsheviks rejected this approach. To Lenin, reforms of this nature were merely capitalist tricks to repress the masses. Only revolution, he said, could bring about needed changes.

Lenin Returns From Exile In March 1917, Lenin was still in exile. As Russia stumbled into revolution, Germany saw a chance to weaken its enemy by helping Lenin return home. In a special train, it rushed the Bolshevik leader across Germany to the Russian frontier.

On April 16, 1917, Lenin stepped off the train in Petrograd. A crowd of fellow exiles and activists recently released from the czar's prisons met him at the station. Lenin triumphantly addressed the crowd:

> "Dear Comrades, soldiers, sailors and workers! I am happy to greet in your persons the victorious Russian revolution, to greet you as the vanguard of the worldwide proletarian army. . . . Any day now the whole of European capitalism may crash. The Russian revolution accomplished by you has prepared the way and opened a new epoch. Long live the worldwide Socialist revolution!"
> —V. I. Lenin, quoted in *The Russian Revolution, 1917* (Sukhanov)

The November Revolution

Lenin threw himself into the work of furthering the revolution. He was assisted by another committed Marxist revolutionary, Leon Trotsky. To the hungry, war-weary Russian people, Lenin and the Bolsheviks promised "Peace, Land, and Bread."

The provisional government, meanwhile, continued the war effort and failed to deal with land reform. In the summer of 1917, the government launched a disastrous offensive against Germany. By November, according to one official report, the army was "a huge crowd of tired, poorly clad, poorly fed, embittered men." Growing numbers of troops mutinied. At the same time, peasants seized land and drove off fearful landlords.

The Bolshevik Takeover Conditions were ripe for the Bolsheviks to make their move. In November 1917, squads of Red Guards—armed factory workers—joined mutinous sailors from the Russian fleet in attacking the provisional government. In just a matter of days, Lenin's forces overthrew a government that no longer had any support.

In Petrograd, members of the government were meeting in a room at the Winter Palace. Suddenly, a young cadet entered the chamber to announce that Bolsheviks were storming the palace. "What are the provisional government's orders?" he asked.

"It's no use," one politician announced. "We give up. No bloodshed!" A moment later, armed rebels flooded into the room. The provisional government had fallen without a struggle.

The Bolsheviks in Charge   The Bolsheviks quickly seized power in other cities. In Moscow, it took a week of fighting to blast the local government out of the walled Kremlin, the former czarist center of government. Moscow became the Bolsheviks' capital, and the Kremlin their headquarters.

"We shall now occupy ourselves in Russia in building up a proletarian socialist state," declared Lenin. The Bolsheviks ended private ownership of land and distributed land to peasants. Workers were given control of the factories and mines. A new red flag with an entwined hammer and sickle symbolized union between peasants and workers.

Throughout the land, millions thought they had at last gained control over their own lives. In fact, the Bolsheviks—renamed Communists—would soon become their new masters.

Russian Civil War

After the Bolshevik Revolution, Lenin quickly sought peace with Germany. Russia signed the Treaty of Brest-Litovsk in March 1918, giving up a huge chunk of its territory and its population. The cost for peace was extremely high, but the Communist leaders knew that they needed all their energy to defeat a battery of enemies at home.

Opposing Forces   For three years, civil war raged between the "Reds," as the Communists were known, and the "Whites," counterrevolutionaries who remained loyal to the czar. National groups that the czars had conquered also took up arms against the Red Army. Poland, Estonia, Latvia, and Lithuania broke free, but nationalists in Ukraine, the Caucasus, and Central Asia were eventually subdued.

The Allied powers of World War I intervened in the civil war. They hoped that the Whites might overthrow the Communists and support the fight against Germany. Britain, France, and the United States sent forces to help the Whites. Japan seized land in East Asia that czarist Russia had once claimed. The Allied presence, however, did little to help the Whites. The Reds appealed to nationalism and urged Russians to drive out the foreigners. In the long run, the Allied invasion fed Communist distrust of the West.

Turning Points in Russia, 1914–1921

1914

August
World War I begins.

1917

March
Revolution forces the czar to abdicate. A provisional government is formed.

April
Lenin returns to Russia.

July
Russians suffer more than 50,000 casualties in battle against German and Austro-Hungarian forces.

November
A second revolution results in Bolshevik takeover of government.

December
Bolshevik government seeks peace with Germany.

1918

March
Russia signs treaty of Brest-Litovsk, losing a large amount of territory.

July
Civil war between the Reds and Whites begins. The czar and his family are executed.

August
British, American, Japanese, and other foreign forces intervene in Russia.

1921

March
Communist government is victorious. Only sporadic fighting continues.

Skills Assessment   **Chart** Between 1914 and 1921, the Russian people struggled through World War I, two revolutions, and civil war. **How did the events of April and July 1917 contribute to revolution later that year?**

The Whites and the Reds
Like all modern wars, the Russian civil war involved civilians as well as soldiers. Here, an English eyewitness describes people fleeing from the advancing Red Army:

"Tens of thousands of peaceful people had fled . . . during that space of time, rushing away from the Red Terror with nothing but the clothes they stood in, as people rush in their nightdresses out of a house on fire. . . . Peasants had deserted their fields, students their books, doctors their hospitals, scientists their laboratories, workmen their workshops, authors their completed manuscripts. . . . We were being swept away in the wreckage of a demoralized army."

—quoted in *Russia Under the Bolshevik Regime* (Pipes)

Skills Assessment

Primary Source Why do you think people feared the Red Army?

Brutality was common in the civil war. Counterrevolutionary forces slaughtered captured Communists and tried to assassinate Lenin. The Communists, meanwhile, launched their own reign of terror. They organized the Cheka, a secret police force. They executed ordinary citizens, even if they were only suspected of taking action against the revolution. The former czar and czarina and their five children were shot to keep them from becoming a rallying symbol for counterrevolutionary forces.

War Communism The Communists adopted a policy known as "war communism." They took over banks, mines, factories, and railroads. Peasants were forced to deliver "surplus" food to hungry people in the cities. Peasant laborers were drafted into the military or into factory work.

Meanwhile, Trotsky turned the Red Army into an effective fighting force. He used former czarist officers under the close watch of **commissars,** Communist party officials assigned to the army to teach party principles and ensure party loyalty. Trotsky's passionate speeches roused soldiers to fight. So did the order to shoot every tenth man if a unit performed poorly—a tactic borrowed from the armies of ancient Rome.

The great Russian writer Maxim Gorky had supported revolution and was a friend of Lenin, but he opposed the severities of war communism. Gorky later recalled Lenin's response to his complaints:

"'Is it possible to act humanely in a struggle of such unprecedented ferocity? Where is there any place for softheartedness or generosity? We are being blockaded by Europe, we are deprived of the help of the European proletariat, counter-revolution is creeping like a bear on us from every side. What do you want? Are we not right?'"

—Maxim Gorky, "Days With Lenin"

A Costly Triumph By 1921, the Communists had defeated their scattered foes, but Russia was in chaos. Millions had died since the beginning of World War I. Millions more perished from the famine and disease that stalked the land. An American journalist, accompanying an international relief team in Russia, described the horrible desolation. In village after village, he noted, "no one stirred from the little wooden houses . . . where Russian families were hibernating and waiting for death." Although Lenin had triumphed, he faced an immense job of rebuilding a nation and an economy in ruins.

SECTION 1 Assessment

Recall
1. **Identify:** **(a)** Nicholas and Alexandra, **(b)** Gregory Rasputin, **(c)** Bolsheviks, **(d)** Leon Trotsky, **(e)** Red Army, **(f)** Whites, **(g)** Cheka.
2. **Define:** **(a)** proletariat, **(b)** soviet, **(c)** commissar.

Comprehension
3. What were the causes of the March Revolution?
4. **(a)** How did Lenin adapt Marxism to conditions in Russia? **(b)** Why were the Bolsheviks able to seize power in November 1917?

5. Describe the opposing forces in the Russian civil war.

Critical Thinking and Writing
6. **Analyzing Primary Sources** Review the excerpt from "Days With Lenin" by Maxim Gorky, quoted above. **(a)** Did Lenin favor or oppose war communism? **(b)** How did Lenin defend his position? **(c)** Do you agree or disagree with Lenin? Explain.
7. **Recognizing Causes and Effects** What were the causes and effects of the civil war in Russia?

Go Online
PHSchool.com

Use the Internet to find three primary sources on the revolutions or civil war in Russia. Find one source for the Red point of view, one for the White point of view, and a third for the viewpoint of the foreign powers that intervened. Print the documents and summarize the main ideas of each. For help with this activity, use **Web Code mkd-2806.**

From Lenin to Stalin

Reading Focus

- How did the Communist state develop under Lenin?
- What were the effects of Stalin's five-year plans?
- Why did Stalin launch the Great Purge?
- How did Soviet foreign policy affect relations with the western powers?

Vocabulary

command economy
collective
kulak

Taking Notes

Create a table like this one. As you read, list the policies and effects of Lenin's NEP and Stalin's five-year plans. Be sure to make your table large enough to allow a list of facts in each box.

	POLICIES	EFFECTS
THE NEP		Food production rose
THE FIVE-YEAR PLANS	Government made all economic decisions	

Main Idea | **After Lenin helped the country recover from civil war, Stalin established a brutal Communist dictatorship in the Soviet Union.**

Setting the Scene

In January 1924, tens of thousands of people lined up in Moscow's Red Square. They had come to view the body of Lenin, who had died a few days earlier.

Meanwhile, Lenin's party colleagues debated what to do with his corpse. His widow, Krupskaya, wanted him buried simply, next to his mother's grave in Petrograd. Communist party officials—including Joseph Stalin—had other ideas. They wanted Lenin preserved and put on permanent display. In the end, the party had its way. Lenin's body would remain on display in Red Square for more than 65 years.

By having Lenin preserved, Stalin wanted to show that he would carry on the goals of the revolution. In the years that followed, he used ruthless measures to win dictatorial power and impose a new order on Russia.

Building the Communist Soviet Union

Lenin's first years as leader of Russia had been occupied in putting down civil war. Once the Communist victory and his personal power were secure, he turned to the enormous problem of rebuilding a state and an economy that had been shattered by World War I, two revolutions, and years of civil war.

Government   In 1922, the Communists produced a constitution that seemed both democratic and socialist. It set up an elected legislature, later called the Supreme Soviet, and gave all citizens over 18 the right to vote. All political power, resources, and means of production would belong to workers and peasants. The new government united much of the old Russian empire in the Union of Soviet Socialist Republics (USSR), or Soviet Union. (See the map later in this section.) The Soviet Union was a multinational state made up of European and Asian peoples. In theory, all the member republics shared certain equal rights.

Reality, however, differed greatly from theory in the Soviet Union. The Communist party, not the people, reigned supreme. Like the Russian czars, the party used the army and secret police to enforce its will. Russia, which was the largest republic, dominated the other republics.

Lenin's NEP   On the economic front, Lenin retreated from his policy of "war communism," which had brought the economy to near collapse. Under party control, factory and mine output had fallen. Peasants stopped producing grain, knowing it would only be seized by the government.

DISCOVERY CHANNEL SCHOOL Video
Learn about communism in the Soviet Union.

Symbols of the Soviet Union
The hammer and sickle were prominent symbols of the Soviet Union. The hammer represented industrial workers, and the sickle represented agricultural workers.

Theme: Political and Social Systems   Why do you think Communist leaders placed the hammer and sickle over the world in the symbol below?

In 1921, Lenin adopted the New Economic Policy, or NEP. It allowed some capitalist ventures. Although the state kept control of banks, foreign trade, and large industries, small businesses were allowed to reopen for private profit. The government also stopped squeezing peasants for grain. Under the NEP, peasants held on to small plots of land and freely sold their surplus crops.

Lenin's compromise with capitalism helped the Soviet economy recover and ended armed resistance to the new government. By 1928, food and industrial production climbed back to prewar levels. The standard of living improved, too. But Lenin always saw the NEP as just a temporary retreat from communism. His successor would soon put the Soviet Union back on the road to "pure" communism.

Stalin Gains Power   Lenin's sudden death in 1924 set off a power struggle among Communist leaders. The chief contenders were Trotsky and Joseph Stalin. Trotsky was a brilliant Marxist thinker, a skillful speaker, and an architect of the Bolshevik Revolution. Stalin, by contrast, was neither a scholar nor an orator. He was, however, a shrewd political operator and behind-the-scenes organizer.

Stalin was born Joseph Djugashvili (joo guhsh VEE lee) to a poor family in Georgia, a region in the Caucasus Mountains. As a boy, he studied for the priesthood. But his growing interest in revolution brought him under the seminary's harsh discipline. Once, he was confined to a punishment cell for reading a novel about the French Revolution.

By 1900, Djugashvili had joined the Bolshevik underground and had taken the name Stalin, meaning "man of steel." He organized robberies to get money for the party and spent time in prison and in Siberian exile. He played a far less important role in the revolution and the civil war than did Trotsky. But in the 1920s, he became general secretary of the party. He used that position to build a loyal group of Communist officials who owed their jobs to him.

As early as 1922, Lenin had expressed grave doubts about Stalin's ambitious nature: "Comrade Stalin . . . has concentrated an enormous power in his hands; and I am not sure that he always knows how to use that power with sufficient caution." To Lenin, Stalin was "too rude." Lenin urged the party to choose a successor "more tolerant, more loyal, more polite, and more considerate to comrades."

At Lenin's death, Trotsky and Stalin jockeyed for position. They differed on most issues, including the future of communism. Trotsky, a firm Marxist, urged support for a worldwide revolution against capitalism. Stalin took a more cautious view. Efforts to foster Marxist revolutions in Europe after World War I had failed. Instead, he wanted to concentrate on building socialism at home first.

With political cunning, Stalin put his own supporters into top jobs and isolated Trotsky within the party. Stripped of party membership, Trotsky fled the country in 1929. Still, he continued to criticize Stalin. In 1940, Trotsky was murdered in Mexico by a Stalinist agent.

Stalin's Five-Year Plans

Once in power, Stalin set out to make the Soviet Union into a modern industrial power. In the past, said Stalin, Russia had suffered defeats because of its economic backwardness. In 1928, therefore, he proposed the first of several "five-year plans" aimed at building heavy industry, improving transportation, and increasing farm output.

To achieve this growth, he brought all economic activity under government control. The Soviet Union developed a command economy, in which government officials made all basic economic decisions. Under Stalin, the government owned all businesses and allocated financial and other

Biography

Joseph Stalin 1879–1953

"The outstanding characteristic of Stalin's personality," one historian wrote, "was his total ruthlessness. No consideration of sentiment or pity seems to have influenced him in the slightest."

It is hard to disagree. Stalin left a wake of suffering and death that boggles the mind.

Stalin instituted "purges," sending millions of people to lives of misery in forced-labor camps. He sent millions more to their deaths. Many historians think that this one man was responsible for the deaths of some 20 million people. The only thing that stopped his killing was his own death. Just before he died, he was planning yet another wave of mass arrests and executions. Stalin is quoted as saying, "A single death is a tragedy, a million deaths is a statistic."

Theme: Impact of the Individual   Why did Stalin's purges consolidate his power?

Soviet Union, 1917–1938

EUROPE
LITHUANIA
LATVIA
ESTONIA
POLAND
FINLAND
BELORUSSIAN S.S.R.
UKRAINIAN S.S.R.
•Leningrad
•Archangel
•Moscow
Stalingrad•
TURKEY
GEORGIAN S.S.R.
ARMENIAN S.S.R.
AZERBAIJAN S.S.R.
Volga R.
Black Sea
Caspian Sea
Aral Sea
IRAN
AFGHANISTAN
TURKMEN S.S.R.
UZBEK S.S.R.
KAZAKH S.S.R.
L. Balkhash
KIRGHIZ S.S.R.
TADZHIK S.S.R.
INDIA
CHINA
ARCTIC OCEAN
RUSSIAN SOVIET FEDERATED SOCIALIST REPUBLIC
Ob R.
Yenisei R.
Lena R.
L. Baikal
Sea of Okhotsk
Sakhalin
Amur R.
MANCHURIA
MONGOLIA
Vladivostok•
KOREA
JAPAN
PACIFIC OCEAN

Azimuthal Equal Area Projection
0   500   1000 Miles
0   500   1000 Kilometers

	Russian empire, 1914
	Area controlled by Bolsheviks, 1919
	Union of Soviet Socialist Republics, 1938

resources. By contrast, in a capitalist economy, the free market controls most economic decisions. Businesses are privately owned and operated by individuals for profit.

Mixed Industrial Results Stalin's five-year plans set high production goals, especially for heavy industry and transportation. The government pushed workers and managers to meet these goals by giving bonuses to those who succeeded—and by punishing those who did not. Between 1928 and 1939, large factories, hydroelectric power stations, and huge industrial complexes rose across the Soviet Union. Oil, coal, and steel production grew. Mining expanded, and new railroads were built.

Despite the impressive progress in some areas, Soviet workers had little to show for their sacrifices. Some former peasants did improve their lives, becoming skilled factory workers or managers. Overall, though, standards of living remained poor. Wages were low, and consumer goods were scarce. Also, central planning was often inefficient, causing shortages in several areas and surpluses in others. Many managers, concerned only with meeting production quotas, turned out large quantities of low-quality goods.

During and after the Stalin era, the Soviet Union continued to do well in heavy industry, such as the production of farm machinery. However, its planned economy failed to match that of the capitalist world in making consumer goods such as clothing, cars, and refrigerators.

Revolution in Agriculture Stalin also brought agriculture under government control. Under the NEP, peasants had held on to small plots of land. But Stalin saw that system as being inefficient and a threat to state power. He forced peasants to give up their private plots and live on either state-owned farms or collectives, large farms owned and operated by peasants as a group. Peasants were permitted to keep their houses and personal

Skills Assessment

Geography After the Bolshevik Revolution, the Soviet Union extended control over many areas of the former Russian empire.

1. **Location** On the map, locate **(a)** Turkmen S.S.R., **(b)** Poland, **(c)** China.
2. **Region** Name three countries that had been part of the Russian empire but were not part of the Soviet Union in 1938.
3. **Critical Thinking Applying Information** How does the map help explain why Russia was the most influential republic in the Soviet Union?

belongings, but all farm animals and implements were to be turned over to the collective. The state set all prices and controlled access to farm supplies.

On collectives, the government planned to provide tractors, fertilizers, and better seed, and to teach peasants modern farm methods. The government needed increased grain output to feed workers in the cities. Surplus grain would also be sold abroad to earn money to invest in industry.

A Ruthless Policy Peasants resisted collectivization by killing farm animals, destroying tools, and burning crops. The government responded with brutal force. An army officer described his horror at the orders he received:

> "I am an Old Bolshevik. . . . I worked in the underground against the czar and I fought in the civil war. Did I do all that in order that I should now surround villages with machine guns and order my men to fire indiscriminately into crowds of peasants? Oh, no, no!"
> —quoted in *Stalin: A Political Biography* (Deutscher)

Stalin sought to destroy the kulaks, or wealthy peasants. The government confiscated kulaks' land and sent them to labor camps. Thousands were killed or died from overwork.

Collectivization took a horrendous toll. Angry peasants often grew just enough to feed themselves. In response, the government seized all the grain, leaving the peasants to starve. This ruthless policy, combined with poor harvests, led to a terrible famine. Between five and eight million people died in Ukraine alone.

Although collectivization increased Stalin's control, it did not improve farm output. During the 1930s, grain production inched upward, but meat, vegetables, and fruits remained in short supply. Feeding the population would remain a major problem in the Soviet Union.

FACT FINDER

Effects of the Five-Year Plans

Output (in thousands of metric tons)

20,000 — 15,000 — 10,000 — 5,000

1928   1933   1938

Year

— Steel — Brown coal

Source: B. R. Mitchell, *European Historical Statistics, 1750–1970*

Skills Assessment

Chart The five-year plans increased Soviet industrial output. **How much more steel was produced in 1938 than in 1928?**

The Great Purge

Even though Stalin's power was absolute, he harbored obsessive fears that rival party leaders were plotting against him. In 1934, he launched the Great Purge. In this reign of terror, Stalin and his secret police cracked down especially on Old Bolsheviks, or party activists from the early days. His net soon widened to target army heroes, industrial managers, writers, and ordinary citizens. They were charged with a wide range of crimes, from counterrevolutionary plots to failure to meet production quotas.

Between 1936 and 1938, Stalin staged a series of spectacular public "show trials" in Moscow. Former Communist leaders confessed to all kinds of crimes after officials tortured them or threatened their families or friends. Many purged party members were never tried but were sent to forced-labor camps in Siberia and elsewhere. Others were executed. Secret police files reveal that at least four million people were purged during the Stalin years. Some historians estimate the toll to be much greater.

The purges increased Stalin's power. Old revolutionaries were replaced by young party members who owed absolute loyalty to him. All Soviet citizens were now well aware of the consequences of disloyalty.

However, Stalin also paid a price. The victims of the purges included most of the nation's military officers. This loss of military leadership would weigh heavily on Stalin in 1941, when Germany invaded the Soviet Union.

Synthesizing Information

Collectivization

Following their successful revolution, the Communists gave land to peasants. But after 1928, the five-year plans required peasants to give up their land and work on large, state-run farms called collectives. Collectivization was a disaster for farmers, leading to widespread famine and millions of deaths.

Stalin's Propaganda

This propaganda photograph shows farmers at the "Lenin's Way" collective in Vilshanka, Ukraine, as they remain in the field for a communal meal during harvest season.

Soviet Agricultural Output, 1928 and 1932

(Bar graph showing Output (in millions of metric tons) on the y-axis ranging from 0 to 50, and Oats, Wheat, Potatoes on the x-axis. Legend: 1928, 1932.)

Oats: 1928 ≈ 16, 1932 ≈ 11
Wheat: 1928 ≈ 22, 1932 ≈ 20
Potatoes: 1928 ≈ 46, 1932 ≈ 43

Source: B. R. Mitchell, *European Historical Statistics, 1750–1970*

Stalin hoped that collectivization would increase crop yields. Instead, collectivization contributed to a drop in output that continued until the 1950s.

Resistance to Collectivization

Many peasants resisted collectivization. In addition to slaughtering livestock and burning crops, they sold farm animals to keep them out of the hands of the government. The newspaper *Pravda* explained this practice:

"A mass sale of livestock is carried on by the middle and poor farmers before their entrance to the collective farms. . . . Buyers travel to different stations buying livestock at high prices, snatching them away from government markets, which are now at a standstill. . . . This practice is most evident in regions where there is all-out collectivization.

   Before entering collective farming the middle, and even the poor farmers, try to get rid of their livestock, hoarding the money from the sale."

—*Pravda*, January 1930

Skills Assessment

1. What changes occurred in oat production between 1928 and 1932?
   A Production dropped by approximately five million metric tons.
   B Production increased by approximately five million metric tons.
   C It stayed the same.
   D Farmers were not producing oats at this time.

2. Which of the three pieces of evidence above suggests that peasants opposed collectivization?
   E the picture only
   F the primary source only
   G the graph and the picture
   H the picture and the primary source

3. **Critical Thinking** **Drawing Conclusions** (a) For each piece of evidence write a generalization about collective farming. (b) Use these generalizations to reach an overall conclusion about the social and economic impact of collectivization.

Skills Tip

Bar graphs show numerical information in graphic form for ease of comparison. Pay close attention to the labels that identify the quantities being compared.

Soviet Foreign Policy

Between 1917 and 1939, the Soviet Union pursued two very different goals in foreign policy. As Communists, both Lenin and Stalin wanted to bring about the worldwide revolution that Marx had predicted. But as Russians, they wanted to guarantee their nation's security by winning the support of other countries. The result of pursuing these two different goals was a contradictory and generally unsuccessful foreign policy.

Lenin formed the Communist International, or Comintern. It aided revolutionary groups around the world and urged colonial peoples to rise up against imperialist powers. Yet the Soviet Union also sought to join the League of Nations and to improve relations with western governments.

The Comintern's propaganda against capitalism made western powers highly suspicious of the Soviet Union. In the United States, fear of Bolshevik plots led to the "Red Scare" in the early 1920s. Britain broke off relations with the Soviet Union when evidence revealed Soviet schemes to turn a 1926 strike into a revolution. Even so, the Soviet Union slowly won recognition from western powers and increased trade with capitalist countries. It also joined the League of Nations. However, mistrust still poisoned relations, especially after the Great Purge.

Three Revolutions Compared

Historians often compare the Russian, French, and American revolutions. The American Revolution was in many ways the least radical of the three. American leaders did not order mass executions or seize property. French revolutionaries executed thousands and nationalized the lands of the Church and the aristocracy. In Russia, Stalin seized even the lands of the peasant masses. His policies caused millions of deaths.

All three revolutions had a worldwide impact. The Declaration of Independence and the United States Constitution served as models of democratic government. The French Revolution inspired revolts across Europe. As you will see, the Soviet Union supported revolts in many lands and became a model for other communist governments. Yet today, Russia and most of its allies have abandoned the goals of Lenin and Stalin. Democratic nations, meanwhile, continue to build on the principles preached during the American and French revolutions.

SECTION 2 Assessment

Recall

1. Identify: (a) USSR, (b) NEP, (c) Great Purge, (d) Comintern.
2. Define: (a) command economy, (b) collective, (c) kulak.

Comprehension

3. (a) How did Lenin make a compromise between the ideas of capitalism and communism? (b) Why did he think that the compromise was necessary?
4. What were the goals and results of Stalin's five-year plans?
5. What were the causes and effects of the Great Purge?

6. How did Soviet foreign policy lead to difficult relations with the West?

Critical Thinking and Writing

7. Analyzing Information Review the two charts in this section that show the effects of the five-year plans on industry and agriculture. (a) Were the effects on industry and agriculture similar or different? (b) Explain the reasons for the similar or different results.
8. Comparing How did the Soviet command economy under Stalin differ from a capitalist economy?

Activity

Drawing a Political Cartoon
Draw a political cartoon that comments on one of Lenin's or Stalin's policies. Give your cartoon a title and a caption. Try to use symbolism, such as the hammer and sickle.

Life in a Totalitarian State

Reading Focus

■ How did Stalin create a totalitarian state?

■ How did communism change Soviet society?

■ How did state control affect the arts in the Soviet Union?

Vocabulary

totalitarian state

atheism

socialist realism

Taking Notes

Create a chart like this one. Fill in the chart as you read. In the left column, list ways in which people benefited from communist rule. In the right column, list ways in which people suffered.

COMMUNIST RULE	
Benefits	Drawbacks

Main Idea ▸ Stalin turned the Soviet Union into a totalitarian state that regulated every aspect of the lives of its citizens.

Setting the Scene From the 1930s until his death in 1953, Stalin tried to boost morale and faith in the communist system by making himself a godlike figure. His propaganda mills described him as a devoted father of the Soviet people. Poets wrote hymns of praise to "Stalin the Wise" and the "Son of Lenin" who was "the unsinking sun of our times." This "cult of personality" was one more pillar to support Stalin's absolute power.

An Age of Totalitarian Control

Marx had predicted that under communism the state would wither away. The opposite occurred under Stalin. He turned the Soviet Union into a totalitarian state. In this form of government, a one-party dictatorship attempts to regulate every aspect of the lives of its citizens. You have already seen, for example, how Stalin imposed central government control over industry and agriculture.

Terror To ensure obedience, Stalin's Communist party used secret police, censorship, violent purges, and terror. Police spies did not hesitate to open private letters or plant listening devices. Nothing appeared in print without official approval. Grumblers or critics were rounded up and sent to brutal labor camps, where many died.

Propaganda Using modern technology, the party bombarded the public with relentless propaganda. Radios and loudspeakers blared into factories and villages. In movies, theaters, and schools, citizens heard about communist successes and the evils of capitalism. Newsreels and newspapers showed bumper harvests and new hydroelectric dams opening up, or proclaimed the misery of workers in the capitalist West. Billboards and posters urged workers to meet or exceed production quotas.

Stalinist propaganda also revived extreme nationalism. Headlines in the Communist party newspaper, *Pravda*, or "Truth," linked enemies at home to foreign agents seeking to restore power to the landowners and capitalists. Supporters of Stalin's aims were often glorified as national heroes. For example, the government put up statues honoring a 14-year-old boy who turned his own father over to the secret police for associating with kulaks.

Forced-Labor Camp
Accused of drawing an anti-Stalin caricature, Russian artist Nikolai Getman was convicted in a seven-minute trial. He spent the next seven years in forced-labor camps, where he painted haunting scenes such as this.

Theme: Art and Literature How does Getman convey the despair of camp life?

Connections to Today

The Russian Orthodox Church

The Russian Orthodox Church survived more than half a century of Communist persecution. Millions of Russians continued to worship, in private and sometimes in public, in defiance of the government's prohibitions.

Today, the Communist government has fallen, and the Church is enjoying a revival. Its membership has swelled to perhaps as many as 50 million people.

Polls of the Russian people indicate that the Orthodox Church surpasses the government and the military as the most respected institution in the country. One Muscovite put it this way: "The Orthodox Church is perhaps the last, lone symbol of Russian national identity to have survived communism more or less intact. People . . . want and need such a symbol."

Theme: Religions and Value Systems Why is the Russian Orthodox Church experiencing a revival today?

War on Religion In accordance with the ideas of Marx, atheism, or the belief that there is no god, became an official state policy. Early on, the Communists targeted the Russian Orthodox Church, which had strongly supported the czars. The party seized religious property and converted churches into offices and museums. Many priests and other religious leaders were killed or died in prison camps.

Other religions were persecuted as well. At one show trial, 15 Roman Catholic priests were charged with "counterrevolutionary activities," such as teaching religion to the young. The state seized Jewish synagogues and banned the use of Hebrew. Islam was also officially discouraged. However, Muslims living in the Soviet Union generally faced fewer restrictions, partly because the Communists hoped to win support among colonized peoples in the Middle East.

The Communists replaced religion with their own ideology. Like a religion, communist ideology had its own "sacred" texts—the writings of Marx and Lenin—and its own shrines, such as the tomb of Lenin. Portraits of Stalin replaced religious icons in Russian homes.

Changes in Soviet Society

The Communists transformed Russian life. They destroyed the old social order of landowning nobles at the top and serfs at the bottom. But instead of creating a society of equals, as they promised, they created a society where a few elite groups emerged as a new ruling class.

The New Elite At the head of society were members of the Communist party. Only a small fraction of Soviet citizens were allowed to join the party. Many who did so were motivated by a desire to get ahead, rather than a belief in communist ideology.

The Soviet elite also included industrial managers, military leaders, scientists, and some artists and writers. The elite enjoyed benefits denied to most people. They had the best apartments in the cities and vacation homes in the country. They could shop at special stores for scarce consumer goods. Good shoes, noted one western visitor, distinguished the elite from the common citizen.

Social Benefits and Drawbacks Although excluded from party membership, most people did enjoy benefits unknown before the revolution. Free education was offered to all. The state also provided free medical care, day care for children, inexpensive housing, and public recreation.

While these benefits were real, the standard of living remained low. As elsewhere, industrial growth led millions of people to migrate to cities. Although the state built massive apartment complexes, housing was scarce. Entire families might be packed into a single room. Bread was plentiful, but meat, fresh fruit, and other foods were in short supply.

Education After the Russian Revolution, the Communists built schools everywhere and required all children to attend. The state supported technical schools and universities as well. Schools served many important goals. Educated workers were needed to build a modern industrial state. In addition to basic skills, schools taught communist values, such as atheism, the glory of collective farming, and love of Stalin.

The Communist party also set up programs for students outside school. These programs included sports, cultural activities, and political classes to train teenagers for party membership. Sometimes, young Communists would be sent to help harvest crops or to participate in huge parades.

Women Long before 1917, women such as Lenin's wife, Krupskaya, worked for the revolution, spreading radical ideas among peasants and workers. Some urged fellow Socialists to pay attention to women's needs.

Virtual Field Trip

Go Online
PHSchool.com
For: Other examples of socialist realism
Visit: PHSchool.com
Web Code: mkd-2815

Socialist Realism
Bold, heroic images were the trademark of socialist realism. Here, workers and farmers hold aloft the Soviet hammer and sickle. Bright sunbeams suggest a glorious future just ahead.

Theme: Art and Literature
What values did socialist realism try to communicate?

In 1905, Alexandra Kollontai noted "how little our party concerned itself with the fate of women . . . [and] women's liberation." After the revolution, Kollontai became the only high-ranking woman to serve in Lenin's government. She vigorously campaigned for women's rights.

Under the Communists, women won equality under the law. They gained access to education and a wide range of jobs. By the 1930s, many Soviet women were working in medicine, engineering, or the sciences.

By their labor, women contributed to Soviet economic growth. They worked in factories, in construction, and on collectives. Within the family, their wages were needed because men earned low salaries. The government provided day nurseries for children.

The Arts and the State

The Bolshevik Revolution at first meant greater freedom for Russian artists and writers. "Art must serve politics," Lenin had insisted, but he generally did not interfere with artistic freedom. Artists welcomed the chance to experiment with ideas and forms.

Socialist Realism Under Stalin, however, the heavy hand of state control gripped the arts. Stalin forced artists and writers to conform to a style called socialist realism. Its goal was to boost socialism by showing Soviet life in a positive light. Artists and writers could criticize the bourgeois past or even, to a limited degree, point out mistakes under communism. Their overall message, though, had to promote hope in the communist future. Popular themes for socialist-realist artists were peasants, workers, heroes of the revolution, and—of course—Stalin.

Censorship Government controlled what books were published, what music was heard, and which works of art were displayed. Artists who ignored Communist guidelines could not get materials, work space, or jobs.

Under Stalin's totalitarian policies, writers, artists, and composers faced government persecution. The Jewish poet Osip Mandelstam, for example,

Humanities Link

A Revolution in Filmmaking

In the Soviet Union, filmmakers used motion pictures to express revolutionary ideals. "Of all the arts, for us the cinema is the most important," said Lenin, who valued film as a propaganda tool. In 1925, director Sergei Eisenstein's *Battleship Potemkin* went far beyond propaganda. His techniques continue to influence filmmakers around the world.

In the film, sailors on the imperial ship *Potemkin* stage a successful mutiny. In the port city of Odessa, a crowd gathers in support of the mutineers and is fired upon by the czar's soldiers. Eisenstein fictitiously places this dramatic scene on a long flight of steps, where a woman stands among the shadows of the czar's soldiers who have killed her child.

In this dynamic sequence, a baby carriage bounces past murdered and wounded civilians. It evokes the helplessness of the unarmed civilians against armed soldiers. Many later directors from all over the world have copied this image.

Portfolio Assessment

Conduct research to find out more about the "golden era of Soviet film," which took place between 1925 and 1930. Then, prepare a class presentation on an important Soviet director or film from this era. Include photographs, drawings, diagrams, or videos that illustrate important aspects of the chosen director or film.

Eisenstein (right) won acclaim for his use of montage, a technique of cutting back and forth between clashing images. *Battleship Potemkin* was the last film over which Eisenstein had full control. After Stalin came to power, censorship was the rule. Eisenstein's last film was banned for criticizing the new leader. It was not shown in the Soviet Union until after Stalin's death.

was imprisoned, tortured, and exiled for composing a satirical verse that was critical of Stalin. Out of fear for his wife's safety, Mandelstam finally submitted to threats and wrote an "Ode to Stalin." Boris Pasternak, who would later win fame for his novel *Doctor Zhivago*, was afraid to publish anything at all during the Stalin years. Rather than write in the favored style of socialist realism, he became a translator of literary works.

Anna Akhmatova (ahk MAH taw vuh), one of Russia's greatest poets, could not publish her works because she had violated state guidelines. Still, she wrote secretly. In "Requiem," she described the ordeal of trying to visit her 20-year-old son, imprisoned during the Stalinist terrors:

"For seventeen long months my pleas,
My cries have called you home.
I've begged the hangman on my knees,
My son, my dread, my own.
My mind's mixed up for good,
And I'm no longer even clear
Who's man, who's beast, nor how much time
Before the end draws near."
—Anna Akhmatova, "Requiem"

Despite restrictions, some Soviet writers produced magnificent works. *And Quiet Flows the Don,* by Mikhail Sholokhov, passed the censor. The novel tells the story of a man who spends years fighting in World War I, the Russian Revolution, and the civil war. Sholokhov later became one of the few Soviet writers to win the Nobel Prize for literature.

Looking Ahead

By the time Stalin died in 1953, the Soviet Union had become a military superpower and a world leader in heavy industry. Yet Stalin's efforts exacted a brutal toll. The Soviet people were dominated by a totalitarian system based on terror. Most people in the Soviet Union lived meager lives compared with people in the West.

The Soviet Union was not the only totalitarian state to emerge in the decades after World War I. As you will read, in the 1920s and 1930s, dictators arose in Italy and Germany. They, too, created one-party states and cults of personality to impose dictatorial rule on their people.

SECTION 3 Assessment

Recall
1. **Identify:** **(a)** *Pravda,* **(b)** Alexandra Kollontai, **(c)** Osip Mandelstam, **(d)** Anna Akhmatova, **(e)** Mikhail Sholokhov.
2. **Define:** **(a)** totalitarian state, **(b)** atheism, **(c)** socialist realism.

Comprehension
3. What methods did Stalin use to create a totalitarian state?
4. **(a)** Who made up the new elite in Soviet society? **(b)** What special privileges did they enjoy?
5. How did the Soviet government make sure that most writers and artists conformed to the style of socialist realism?

Critical Thinking and Writing
6. **Comparing** Compare life under Stalin's rule with life under the Russian czars. **(a)** Describe two similarities. **(b)** Describe two differences.
7. **Analyzing Information** One historian has said that socialist realism was "communism with a smiling face." What do you think he meant? (See the Virtual Field Trip in this section.)

Activity

Writing Propaganda
Write two propaganda newspaper articles about Stalin or his policies. One article should be similar to what *Pravda* might have printed. The other article should be similar to what an illegal anti-Stalinist newspaper might have printed.

Creating a Chapter Summary

Copy the chart below on a sheet of paper. Review what you have learned about communist dictatorship in the Soviet Union by completing the chart. A few entries have been made to help you get started.

COMMUNIST DICTATORSHIP IN THE SOVIET UNION

POLITICAL	ECONOMIC	SOCIAL	CULTURAL	MILITARY
• One party only	• Government makes all decisions			

Interactive Textbook

For additional review and enrichment activities, see the interactive version of *World History* available on the Web and on CD-ROM.

Go Online
PHSchool.com

For practice test questions for Chapter 15, use **Web Code mka-2818**.

Building Vocabulary

Use the chapter vocabulary words below to create a crossword puzzle. Exchange puzzles with a classmate. Complete the puzzles and then check each other's answers.

1. **proletariat**
2. **soviet**
3. **commissar**
4. **collective**
5. **kulak**
6. **totalitarian state**
7. **atheism**
8. **socialist realism**

Recalling Key Facts

9. How did World War I contribute to the collapse of the Russian monarchy?
10. How and when did the Bolsheviks take power in Russia?
11. What was the final outcome of the Russian civil war?
12. How was the NEP different from "pure communism"?
13. Describe Stalin's policies on agriculture and industry.
14. What was the Great Purge?
15. How did Stalin make use of propaganda?
16. What was the Soviet government's policy toward religion?
17. According to Stalin, what purpose should art serve?

Critical Thinking and Writing

18. **Identifying Alternatives** After the March Revolution, the provisional government of Russia chose a course that led to another revolution. What policies could the provisional government have followed that might have avoided a second revolution?
19. **Comparing** How were the Russian and French revolutions similar or different in terms of **(a)** long-term causes, **(b)** immediate causes, **(c)** effects, **(d)** world reaction?
20. **Synthesizing Information** **(a)** In what ways did Soviet communism conform to the teachings of Marx? **(b)** In what ways did Soviet communism differ from Marxist philosophy?
21. **Linking Past and Present** In the 1990s, the breakup of the Soviet Union led to a revival of religion. Why do you think the Soviets were unsuccessful in their attempt to destroy religion?
22. **Connecting to Geography** Review the map in Section 2. **(a)** How did the Soviet constitution try to satisfy the nationalist aspirations of non-Russians? **(b)** Do you think nationalist leaders in the Soviet Union were satisfied? Explain.

The exerpt below, written by an American news reporter in Russia, is a dramatic eyewitness account of Stalin's brutal campaign against the kulaks. Read the excerpt and then answer the questions that follow.

> "Obliteration of the . . . kulak elements was not only an end in itself, but a means for stampeding the rest of the population into submission to collectivization. . . . A population as large as all of Switzerland's or Denmark's was stripped clean of all their belongings—not alone their land and homes and cattle and tools, but often their last clothes and food and household utensils—and driven out of their villages. They were herded with bayonets at railroad stations, packed indiscriminately into cattle cars and freight cars, and dumped weeks later in the lumber regions of the frozen North, the deserts of Central Asia, wherever labor was needed, there to live or die. Some of this human wreckage was merely flung beyond the limits of their former villages, without shelter or food in those winter months, to start life anew if they could, on land too barren to have been cultivated in the past."

—Eugene Lyons, *Assignment in Utopia*

23. Who were the kulaks?
24. According to the reporter, what were the reasons for the policy toward the kulaks?
25. What do you think the government did with the confiscated property?
26. Do you think the kulaks prospered in the lands to which they were brought? Explain.
27. **(a)** What part of this account is most probably opinion? Explain. **(b)** What part is most probably fact? Explain.

Go Online
PHSchool.com

Use the Internet to find examples of propaganda such as the Soviet poster on this page. You can look for posters, speeches, film clips, or other types. Print out two examples. For each example, identify the author and the intended audience, and explain the message that is being communicated. For help with this activity, use **Web Code mkd-2819.**

Under the czars, few Russian peasants could read. The Soviet government launched a campaign to increase adult literacy. This Soviet propaganda poster proclaims, "Knowledge Will Break the Chains of Serfdom." Study the poster and answer the following questions:

28. **(a)** What symbol in the poster represents serfdom? **(b)** What symbols represent education?
29. Why do you think the Soviet government wanted people to learn to read?
30. Based on what you have read in this chapter, do you agree or disagree that education broke the "chains of serfdom" for the Russian people? Explain.

Skills Tip

To understand propaganda, try to recognize who the author is and who the intended audience is. Remember that propaganda uses lies, truths, or half-truths to sway opinion.

Nationalism and Revolution Around the World

1910–1939

Chapter Preview

1 **Struggle for Change in Latin America**
2 **Nationalist Movements in Africa and the Middle East**
3 **India Seeks Self-Rule**
4 **Upheavals in China**
5 **Empire of the Rising Sun**

CHAPTER EVENTS

1914
New settlement increases the Jewish population of Palestine to 90,000. Leaders promote long-term development of the region's agriculture, as shown in this 1925 poster.

1916
Pancho Villa, shown here, invades the United States during the Mexican Revolution. He kills more than a dozen Americans in New Mexico.

1923
Atatürk begins modernizing Turkey.

1910

1916

1922

GLOBAL EVENTS

1914 World War I begins.

1917 Two revolutions lead to Bolshevik control of Russia.

Major Nationalist Movements, 1910–1939

The end of World War I motivated many people around the world to seek self-government.

ATLANTIC OCEAN

PACIFIC OCEAN

PACIFIC OCEAN

INDIAN OCEAN

MEXICO

TURKEY

IRAN

EGYPT

CHINA

JAPAN

INDIA

NIGERIA

KENYA

SOUTH AFRICA

Robinson Projection

0   1500   3000 Miles

0   1500   3000 Kilometers

N W E S

1930
Thousands of Indians join Mohandas Gandhi in the Salt March to protest British rule.

1934
Mao Zedong leads the Long March.

1937
The Japanese army captures Nanjing. Here, Japanese soldiers enter the Chinese city, which has been under siege for weeks.

1928

1934

1940

1929 The New York Stock Exchange crashes.

1935 Italy invades Ethiopia.

1939 Germany invades Poland.

Struggle for Change in Latin America

Reading Focus

- What were the causes of the Mexican Revolution?
- What reforms were introduced in Mexico?
- How did nationalism affect Mexico?
- What was the Good Neighbor Policy?

Vocabulary

nationalization

economic nationalism

cultural nationalism

Taking Notes

Copy this diagram. As you read, fill in the major events in Mexican history. To help you get started, one part of the diagram has been completed.

STRUGGLE FOR CHANGE IN MEXICO			
1910s	**1920s**	**1930s**	**1940s**
• Dictator Porfirio Díaz rules • Prosperity for wealthy landowners	•	•	•

Main Idea The desire for lands, better wages, and democratic reforms led to the Mexican Revolution.

Setting the Scene The winds of revolution swept through Mexico between 1910 and 1920. "It is like a hurricane," says a peasant fighter in Mariano Azuela's novel *The Underdogs*. "If you're in it, . . . you're a leaf . . . blown by the wind."

The Mexican Revolution unleashed radical forces. As the revolution spread, Indian peasants battled to end centuries of oppression and to win land. A century after Miguel Hidalgo raised the "cry of Dolores," the Mexican Revolution finally opened the door to social and economic reform.

The Mexican Revolution

By 1910, the dictator Porfirio Díaz had ruled Mexico for almost 35 years, winning reelection as president again and again. On the surface, Mexico enjoyed peace and economic growth. Díaz welcomed foreign investors who developed mines, built railroads, and drilled for oil.

Sources of Discontent Prosperity benefited wealthy landowners, business people, and foreign investors. But most Mexicans were peasants who lived in desperate poverty. Without land or education, they had no hope of improving their situation.

Discontent rippled through Mexico in the early 1900s. Factory workers and miners earning meager wages were restless and angry. And middle-class liberals, who embraced democracy, opposed the Díaz dictatorship.

The Battle Begins The unrest boiled over when Francisco Madero, a liberal reformer, demanded free elections in 1910. After being imprisoned by Díaz, he began to encourage revolt. Faced with rebellion in several parts of the country, Díaz resigned in 1911. "Madero has unleashed a tiger, now let us see if he can control it," declared the dictator as he left Mexico. Díaz's taunt proved well founded. Madero became president of Mexico, but within two years he was murdered.

A Complex Upheaval During the power struggle that followed, several leaders emerged. Among them was Francisco "Pancho" Villa, a hard-riding rebel from the north. He fought mostly for personal power but won the loyalty of his followers. In southern Mexico, Emiliano Zapata led a peasant revolt. Zapata, himself an Indian tenant farmer, understood the misery of peasant villagers. His followers were called Zapatistas.

Fighting flared across Mexico for a decade, killing as many as a million people. Peasants, small farmers, ranchers, and urban workers were drawn

Remembering the Revolution

Zeferino Diego Ferreira was a peasant soldier in Pancho Villa's army. His experiences represent those of the Mexican masses who rallied to the revolutionary cause. Decades later, he shared his memories with an interviewer, who recorded the old man's tales of life as a revolutionary.

Poster of Emiliano Zapata
Zeferino Ferreira displayed a poster like this one on his living room wall. Asked years later what Zapata looked like, he snapped: "It's not important what he looked like. What is important was his politics."

"I was born in 1892. . . . We lived in a little room with no furniture . . . nothing. We slept on the floor. The only thing we had was a box with my mother's clothes in it. . . .

When I was about fourteen years old I got a job in some mines owned by an American company near Tlalpujahua. . . . At that time here in Mexico they didn't pay more than eighteen to twenty-five centavos. . . .

It was there in Tlalpujahua where I first saw firearms. . . . [A] friend of mine talked to me a lot about Villa and finally convinced me to go and join up. . . . My friend and I went north looking for Villa. And, yes, Villa was firing a shot here and there! . . .

In those days at the beginning of the revolution we didn't have many people and we weren't very well armed. You could say we were almost fighting without rifles. . . .

During the revolution I slept for only two hours at night, between two and four o'clock in the morning, and was always leaning against a wall or a rock or on my rifle. Sometimes we didn't have any hope of getting food, so we'd eat a mule, a skunk.

Yes! That was how we went through the revolution. . . .

[Villa] used to tell us: 'We are fighting for the people and we have to respect them.' . . . Villa wasn't like some people say. He was a well-liked person. Yes, he had people shot, but he'd also get his fill and stop the shootings. He was always in the battles. Sometimes he disguised himself but we would recognize him by his horse. Black. Villa never hid away all cozy and warm while his troops fought. He was right there in the middle. He said: 'Where my troops die, I'll die there, too.'

I am glad to have fought in the same cause with Zapata . . . and so many of my dear revolutionary friends who were left behind in the hills, their bones eaten by animals. I wasn't afraid. Just the opposite, I was glad. It's a beautiful thing to fight to realize an ideal."

—Zeferino Diego Ferreira, "The Life Story of a Villista"

Skills Assessment

1. Which term best describes Villa's peasant army?
   A well equipped
   B professional
   C poor
   D unmotivated

2. According to Ferreira, Villa was
   E a traitor to the peasant cause.
   F brave and decent.
   G seeking money and fame.
   H selfish and cruel.

3. **Critical Thinking Evaluating Information (a)** Ferreira spoke of events that had taken place more than 50 years earlier. How reliable do you think he is as a source of information about the Mexican Revolution? **(b)** How might a historian determine the truth of Ferreira's words?

into the violent struggle. Women soldiers called *soldaderas* cooked, tended the wounded, and even fought alongside the men.

Reforms in Mexico

In 1917, voters elected Venustiano Carranza, a conservative, president of Mexico. That year, Carranza reluctantly approved a new constitution. With amendments, it is still in force today.

The Constitution of 1917 addressed three major issues: land, religion, and labor. It permitted the breakup of large estates, placed restrictions on foreigners owning land, and allowed nationalization, or government takeover, of natural resources. Church land was made "the property of the nation." The constitution set a minimum wage and protected workers' right to strike.

Although the constitution gave suffrage only to men, it did give women some protection. Women doing the same job as men were entitled to the same pay. In response to women activists, Carranza also passed laws allowing married women to draw up contracts, take part in legal suits, and have equal authority with men in spending family funds.

Social Change At first, the constitution was just a set of goals to be achieved sometime in the future. But in the 1920s, as the government finally restored order after years of civil war, it began to carry out reforms.

The government helped some Indian communities regain lands that had been taken from them. It supported labor unions and launched a massive effort to combat illiteracy. Schools and libraries were set up.

Dedicated teachers, often young women, worked for low pay. While they taught basic skills, they spread ideas of nationalism that began to bridge the gulf between the regions and the central government. As the revolutionary era ended, Mexico became the first Latin American nation to pursue real social and economic reforms for the majority of its people.

The PRI In 1929, government leaders organized what later became the Institutional Revolutionary Party (PRI). It has dominated Mexican politics ever since. The PRI managed to accommodate all groups in Mexican society, including business and military leaders, peasants, and workers. It backed reform but suppressed opposition. In 1938, the government nationalized foreign oil holdings, part of a program to reduce foreign influence.

Rising Tide of Nationalism

Mexico's move to reclaim its oil fields from foreign investors reflected a growing spirit of nationalism in Latin America. This spirit focused in part on ending economic dependence on the industrial powers, especially the United States.

Economic Nationalism During the 1920s and 1930s, world events affected Latin American economies. After World War I, trade fell off with Europe. The Great Depression that struck the United States in 1929 spread around the world in the 1930s. Prices for Latin American exports plunged as demand dried up. At the same time, the cost of imported consumer goods rose.

Murals
Diego Rivera painted murals with scenes of Mexico's history. The top portion of this mural section depicts people in the Mexican Revolution.

Theme: Art and Literature
How does Rivera show that people from all levels of society were involved in the revolution?

A tide of economic nationalism, or emphasis on domestic control of the economy, swept Latin American countries. They were determined to develop their own economies and end foreign economic control. Local entrepreneurs set up factories to produce goods. They urged their governments to raise tariffs to protect the new industries. Following Mexico's lead, some nations also nationalized resources or took over foreign-owned industries. The drive to create domestic industries had limited success. As in the past, the unequal distribution of wealth hampered economic development.

Cultural Nationalism   By the 1920s, Latin American writers, artists, and thinkers began to reject European influences. Instead, they took pride in their own culture, with its blend of western and Indian traditions.

In Mexico, cultural nationalism, or pride in one's own culture, was reflected in the revival of mural painting, a major art form of the Aztecs. In the 1920s and 1930s, Diego Rivera, José Clemente Orozco (oh RAHS koh), David Alfaro Siqueiros (sih KAY rohs), and other muralists created magnificent works. On the walls of public buildings, they portrayed the struggles of the Mexican people for liberty, first from the Spanish and later during the Díaz era. The murals have been a great source of national pride ever since.

The "Good Neighbor" Policy

During and after World War I, investments by the United States in the nations of Latin America soared, especially as British influence declined. The United States continued to play the role of "international policeman," intervening to restore order when it felt its interests were threatened.

During the Mexican Revolution, the United States supported leaders who it thought would protect American interests. In 1914, it attacked the port of Vera Cruz to punish Mexico for imprisoning several American sailors. In 1916, it invaded Mexico after Pancho Villa killed more than a dozen Americans in New Mexico.

These actions stirred up anti-American feelings, which increased during the 1920s. In Nicaragua, Augusto César Sandino led a guerrilla movement against United States forces occupying his country. Many people in Latin America saw Sandino as a hero.

In the 1930s, President Franklin Roosevelt took a new approach to Latin America and pledged to follow "the policy of the good neighbor." Under the Good Neighbor Policy, the United States withdrew troops stationed in Haiti and Nicaragua. It also lifted the Platt Amendment, which had limited Cuban independence.

SECTION 1 Assessment

Recall
1. **Identify:** **(a)** Porfirio Díaz, **(b)** Francisco Madero, **(c)** Zapatistas, **(d)** Venustiano Carranza, **(e)** Diego Rivera, **(f)** Good Neighbor Policy.
2. **Define:** **(a)** nationalization, **(b)** economic nationalism, **(c)** cultural nationalism.

Comprehension
3. Describe three causes of the Mexican Revolution.
4. Explain how the Constitution of 1917 addressed each of these issues: **(a)** land, **(b)** religion, **(c)** labor.

5. Describe how nationalism affected Mexico.
6. How did Franklin Roosevelt change United States policy toward Latin America?

Critical Thinking and Writing
7. **Analyzing Information** How did world events affect the economies of Latin American nations during the 1920s and 1930s?
8. **Synthesizing Information** **(a)** How did opportunities for women change under the 1917 constitution? **(b)** How did women's lives stay the same?

Go Online
PHSchool.com

Use the Internet to research Emiliano Zapata and the Zapatista movement. Then, create a poster publicizing Zapatista goals. For help with this activity, use **Web Code mkd-2925.**

Nationalist Movements in Africa and the Middle East

Reading Focus

- How did Africans resist colonial rule?

- What signs of nationalism developed in Africa?

- How did Turkey and Iran modernize?

- How did European mandates contribute to the growth of Arab nationalism?

Main Idea Following World War I, nationalist sentiment contributed to many changes in Africa and the Middle East.

Vocabulary

apartheid
polygamy

Taking Notes

Copy this table. As you read, fill in the major nationalist developments in Africa and the Middle East. To help you get started, one row of the table has been completed.

NATION	LEADER	PROTESTS AGAINST	RESULTS
KENYA	Jomo Kenyatta	• Loss of land •	• Jailing of nationalist leaders •
SOUTH AFRICA			
EGYPT			
TURKEY			
IRAN			

Discovery CHANNEL

SCHOOL Video

Learn about life under apartheid.

An African Speaks Out Against Colonialism

Jomo Kenyatta was a leader in Kenya's struggle for independence from British rule. In the following quotation, he dramatizes his view of European colonialism:

"If you woke up one morning and found that somebody had come to your house, and had declared that house belonged to him, you would naturally be surprised, and you would like to know by what arrangement. Many Africans found that, on land that had been in the possession of their ancestors from time immemorial, they were now working as squatters or as laborers."

—Jomo Kenyatta, quoted in *A History of the African People* (July)

Skills Assessment

Primary Source Why was Kenyatta's house comparison an effective device for dramatizing the injustices of colonialism?

Setting the Scene

The Kikuyu people of Kenya were outraged. Not only had the British taken their land, but they also treated the Kikuyu like second-class citizens.

The Kikuyu were among many African people who resented colonial rule. During the 1920s and 1930s, a new generation of leaders, proud of their unique heritage, struggled to stem the tide of imperialism and restore Africa for Africans.

Resistance to Colonial Rule

During the early 1900s, Africans felt the impact of colonial rule. In Kenya and Rhodesia, for example, white settlers forced Africans off the best land. The few who kept their land were forbidden to grow the most profitable crops, such as coffee and sisal—only Europeans could grow these. In Kenya, too, the British made all Africans carry identification cards, imposed a tax, and restricted where they could live or travel.

Everywhere, Africans were forced to work on European-run plantations or in mines. The money they earned was needed to pay taxes to the colonial government. Farmers who had kept their land had to grow cash crops, such as cotton, instead of food. This led to famines in some regions. Increasingly, they lost their self-sufficiency and became dependent on European-made goods.

Resistance Opposition to imperialism grew among Africans. Resistance took many forms. Those who had lost their lands to Europeans sometimes squatted, or settled illegally, on European-owned plantations. In cities, workers began to form labor unions, even though such activity was illegal under the law codes imposed by imperialist nations.

Many western-educated Africans criticized the injustice of imperial rule. Although they had trained for professional careers, the best jobs went to Europeans. Inspired by President Woodrow Wilson's call for self-determination, they condemned the system that excluded Africans from political control of their own lands. Some eagerly read Lenin's writings that claimed imperialism was the final stage of a corrupt and dying capitalist society. In Africa, as in other regions around the world, socialism found a growing audience.

Protests Although large-scale revolts were rare, protests were common. In Kenya, the Kikuyu protested the loss of their land, forced labor, heavy taxes, and the hated identification cards. The British jailed the Kikuyu leaders, but protests continued.

In West Africa, women traditionally had controlled the marketplaces and the farmland. In the 1920s, Ibo women in Nigeria denounced British policies that threatened their rights and their economic role. They demanded a voice in decisions that affected them and their business activities. The "Women's War," as it was called, soon became a full-fledged revolt. Women armed with machetes and sticks mocked British troops and shouted down officials who ordered them to disperse.

Racial Segregation and Nationalism in South Africa Between 1910 and 1940, whites strengthened their grip on South Africa. They imposed a system of racial segregation. Their goal was to ensure white economic and political power and social supremacy. New laws, for example, restricted better-paying jobs in mines to whites only. Blacks were pushed into low-paid, less-skilled work. As in Kenya, South African blacks had to carry passes at all times. They were evicted from the best land, which was set aside for whites, and forced to live on crowded "reserves," which were located in dry, infertile areas.

Other laws chipped away at the rights of blacks. In one South African province, educated blacks who owned property had been allowed to vote in local elections. In 1936, the government abolished that right. The system of segregation set up at this time would become even more restrictive after 1948, when apartheid (uh PAHRT tīd) became law.

Yet South Africa was also home to a vital nationalist movement. African Christian churches and African-run newspapers demanded rights for black South Africans. In 1912, educated Africans organized a political party, later known as the African National Congress (ANC). Its members worked through legal means, protesting laws that restricted the freedom of black Africans. Their efforts, however, had no effect on South Africa's white government. Still, the ANC did build a framework for political action in later years.

Rise of Nationalism

During the 1920s, a movement known as Pan-Africanism began to nourish the nationalist spirit. Pan-Africanism emphasized the unity of Africans and people of African descent around the world. Among its most inspiring leaders was Jamaican-born Marcus Garvey. He preached a forceful and appealing message of "Africa for Africans" and demanded an end to colonial rule. Although Garvey never visited Africa, his ideas influenced a new generation of African leaders.

Pan-African Congress Led by African American scholar and activist W.E.B. DuBois (doo BOYS), Pan-Africanists tried to forge a united front. DuBois organized the first Pan-African Congress in 1919. It met in Paris, where the victorious Allies were holding their peace conference. Delegates from African colonies, the West Indies, and the United States called on the Paris peacemakers to approve a charter of rights for Africans. Although the western powers ignored their demands, the Pan-African Congress established cooperation among African and African American leaders.

Négritude French-speaking writers in West Africa and the Caribbean further awakened self-confidence among Africans. They expressed pride in their African roots through the *négritude* movement. Best known among them was the Senegalese poet Léopold Senghor, who celebrated Africa's rich cultural heritage. He fostered African pride by rejecting the negative views of Africa spread by colonial rulers. In his poem "Black Woman," he uses the image of an African woman to reflect on the beauty of Africa. Later, Senghor would take an active role in Senegal's drive to independence, and he would serve as its first president.

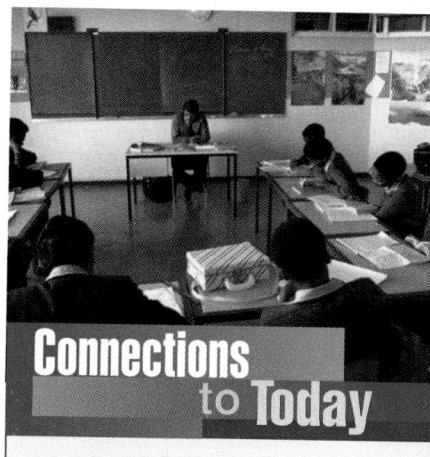

Connections to Today

Rekindling Hope in South Africa

Soweto, a poor suburb of Johannesburg, was a harsh symbol of apartheid. Created in the 1930s to house South Africa's black gold miners, it became a center of violent protest against apartheid in the 1970s. Forced into tiny hovels, Soweto's blacks lived lives marked by gunfire and tear gas and midnight visits from the police.

Today, Soweto has changed. In 1989, South Africa held its first all-race elections and began to dismantle apartheid. The new government brought electricity to most residents, built roads, and set up schools and libraries.

Life in post-apartheid Soweto is not perfect. Poverty is still widespread, and crime is a serious problem. Still, Soweto's residents have begun to feel hope for the future.

Theme: Continuity and Change How did the end of apartheid make it possible for Soweto to make social and economic gains?

Egyptian Independence African nationalism brought little political change, except to Egypt. During World War I, Egyptians had been forced to provide food and workers to help Britain. Simmering resistance to British rule flared as the war ended. Western-educated officials, peasants, landowners, Christians, and Muslims united behind the Wafd (WAHFT) party, which launched strikes and riots.

In 1922, the British finally agreed to declare Egypt independent. In fact, however, British troops stayed in Egypt to guard the Suez Canal, and Britain remained the real power behind Egypt's King Faud.

In the 1930s, many young Egyptians were attracted to an organization called the Muslim Brotherhood. This group fostered a broad Islamic nationalism that rejected western culture and denounced widespread corruption in the Egyptian government.

Modernization in Turkey and Iran

Nationalist movements brought immense changes to the Middle East in the aftermath of World War I. The defeated Ottoman empire collapsed in 1918. Its Arab lands, as you have read, were divided up between Britain and France. In Asia Minor, however, Turks resisted western control and fought to build a modern nation.

Atatürk Led by the determined and energetic Mustafa Kemal, Turkish nationalists overthrew the sultan, defeated western occupation forces, and declared Turkey a republic. Kemal later took the name Atatürk, meaning "father of the Turks." Between 1923 and his death in 1938, Atatürk forced through an ambitious program of radical reforms. His goals were to modernize Turkey along western lines and to separate religion from government.

Modernizing Turkey
Atatürk pushed radical reforms to make Turkey a modern nation. One of his changes was the replacement of Arabic with western script. Here, Atatürk reveals the new Turkish alphabet to a crowd in an Istanbul park.

Theme: Impact of the Individual Why do you think Atatürk introduced the new alphabet himself in a public ceremony?

Westernization Atatürk swept away centuries-old traditions when he replaced Islamic law with a new law code based on European models. He discarded the Muslim calendar in favor of the calendar based on western (Christian) traditions and moved the day of rest from Friday, traditional with Muslims, to Sunday, in line with Christian practice.

Like Peter the Great in Russia, Atatürk forced his people to wear western dress. He replaced Arabic script with the western (Latin) alphabet, stating it was easier to learn. He closed religious schools but opened thousands of state schools to prepare young Turks for the challenges of modern society.

Other reforms transformed the lives of women. They no longer had to veil their faces and were allowed to vote. Polygamy—the custom allowing men to have more than one wife—was banned. Given freedom to work outside the home, women became teachers, doctors, lawyers, and even politicians.

Under Atatürk, the government encouraged industrial expansion. The government built roads and railroads, set up factories, and hired westerners to advise on how to make Turkey economically independent.

To achieve his reforms, Atatürk ruled with an iron hand. To many Turks, he was a hero who was transforming Turkey into a strong,

modern power. Some Turkish Muslims, however, rejected his secular government. To them,
the Quran and Islamic customs provided all
needed guidance, from personal concerns such
as prayer and behavior to national matters such
as government, commerce, and education.

Nationalism and Reform in Iran The success
of Atatürk's reforms inspired nationalists in
neighboring Iran. They greatly resented the
British and Russians, who had won spheres of
influence in their land. In 1925, an ambitious
army officer, Reza Khan, overthrew the shah.
He set up his own Pahlavi dynasty, with himself
as shah.

Like Atatürk, Reza Khan rushed to modernize Iran and make it fully independent. He built
factories, roads, and railroads and strengthened
the army. He, too, adopted the western alphabet,
forced Iranians to wear western clothing, and set
up modern, secular schools. In addition, he
moved to replace Islamic law with secular law
and encouraged women to take part in public
life. Although many wealthy Iranians in cities
supported Reza Khan, Muslim religious leaders
fiercely condemned his efforts to introduce western ways to the nation.

As Iran modernized, it won better terms
from the British company that controlled its oil
industry. It persuaded the British to give it a
larger share of the profits and insisted that
Iranian workers be hired at all levels of the company. In the decades ahead,
oil would become a major factor in Iranian economic and foreign affairs.

European Mandates and Arab Nationalism

Arab nationalism blossomed after World War I and gave rise to Pan-
Arabism. This nationalist movement built on the shared heritage of Arabs
who lived in lands from the Arabian Peninsula through North Africa.* It
emphasized their common history and language and recalled the golden
age of Arab civilization. Pan-Arabism sought to free Arabs from foreign
domination and unite them in their own state. The national pact written
at the First Arab Students' Conference spoke of this mission:

> "I am an Arab, and I believe that the Arabs constitute one
> nation. The sacred right of this nation is to be sovereign in
> her own affairs . . . to liberate the Arab homeland, to unite
> all its parts and to found [distinctively Arab] political,
> economic, and social institutions."
> —Arab pledge, quoted in *Arab Nationalism:*
> *An Anthology* (Haim)

Betrayal at the Peace Conference The mandates—territories administered by European nations—set up by the Paris Peace Conference outraged
Arabs. During World War I, they had helped the Allies against the Central
Powers, especially the Ottomans. In return, they had been promised independence. Instead, the Allies carved up the Ottoman lands, giving France

---

* The Arab lands included areas from the Arabian Peninsula through North Africa. Today,
this area includes nations such as Syria, Jordan, Iraq, Egypt, Algeria, and Morocco.

Building New Settlements

During the early 1900s, many Jewish settlers in Palestine wanted to develop a new way of life. They organized collective farms, called *kibbutzim*. Members shared belongings, labor, and proceeds. The settlements were communal, with cooking done in a central dining hall. Children were raised in a home, separate from their parents, so that women could join the kibbutz work force.

Together, the settlers, called *kibbutzniks*, introduced new techniques of drainage and irrigation. Their efforts helped Israel become a world leader in agricultural production. The kibbutzniks grew grain, fruit trees, and vegetables. For meat, they raised chickens and cows. Cypress and palm trees were planted to provide shade from the desert sun.

Theme: Geography and History What were the main characteristics of the kibbutzim?

mandates in Syria and Lebanon and Britain mandates in Palestine and Iraq. Later, Trans-Jordan was added to the British mandate.

Arabs felt betrayed by the West—a feeling that has endured to this day. During the 1920s and 1930s, their anger erupted in frequent protests and revolts against western imperialism. A major center of turmoil was the British mandate of Palestine. There, Arab nationalists faced European Zionists, or Jewish nationalists, with dreams of a homeland of their own.

Promises in Palestine Since Roman times, Jews had dreamed of returning to Palestine. In 1897, Theodor Herzl (HER tsuhl) responded to growing antisemitism in Europe by founding the modern Zionist movement. His goal was to rebuild a Jewish state in Palestine, "our ever-memorable historical home." Soon, some Jews, mostly from Eastern Europe, migrated to Palestine. There they joined the small Jewish community that had survived since biblical times.

During World War I, the Allies made two vague sets of promises. First, they promised Arabs their own kingdoms in former Ottoman lands, including Palestine. Then, in 1917, the British issued the Balfour Declaration to win support of European Jews. In it, Britain supported the idea of setting up "a national home for the Jewish people" in Palestine. The declaration noted, however, that "nothing shall be done which may prejudice the civil and religious rights of existing non-Jewish communities in Palestine." Those communities were Arab. The stage was thus set for conflict between Arab and Jewish nationalists.

A Bitter Struggle In the 1930s, antisemitism, primarily in Germany and Eastern Europe, forced many Jews to seek safety in Palestine. Despite great hardships, they set up factories, built new towns, and turned arid desert into irrigated farmland.

At first, some Arabs welcomed the money and modern technical skills that the newcomers brought with them. But as Jews poured into the land of Palestine, tensions between the two groups developed. Sometimes, Jewish settlers bought land from absentee Arab landowners. In the cities, some Jewish factory owners refused to hire Arabs. These tensions were heightened by religious differences between Jews and Arabs. Although most Arabs were Muslim, some were Christian. Angry Arabs staged attacks on Jewish settlements, hoping to oust the Jews. For the rest of the century, Arab nationalists battled Zionists over the land that Arabs called Palestine and Jews called Israel.

SECTION 2 Assessment

Recall
1. **Identify:** **(a)** "Women's War," **(b)** African National Congress, **(c)** Pan-Africanism, **(d)** négritude, **(e)** Pan-Arabism, **(f)** Zionist.
2. **Define:** **(a)** apartheid, **(b)** polygamy.

Comprehension
3. How did Africans resist the impact of colonialism?
4. Describe three examples of the rise of nationalism in Africa.
5. What reforms were introduced in **(a)** Turkey, **(b)** Iran?

6. **(a)** Why were many Arabs angered by decisions made at the Paris Peace Conference after World War I? **(b)** Why did Palestine become a center of conflict?

Critical Thinking and Writing
7. **Synthesizing Information** **(a)** How did nationalist leaders in Africa oppose colonial rule? **(b)** How did colonial powers control African countries?
8. **Drawing Conclusions** How did the Balfour Declaration affect the Middle East?

Activity
Writing a Speech
Imagine that you are a member of the Pan-African movement in the 1920s. Use what you have learned about African culture in this and earlier chapters to write a speech extolling your unique heritage.

India Seeks Self-Rule

Reading Focus

- What sparked the Indian independence movement after World War I?

- How did Mohandas Gandhi influence the independence movement?

- What did the Salt March symbolize?

Vocabulary

ahimsa

civil disobedience

Taking Notes

Copy this time line. As you read, fill in the key events in India's move to independence. To help you get started, one part of the time line has been completed.

1900	1910	1920	1930	1940

1858
Britain takes control of India

1914

Main Idea Mohandas Gandhi and the Congress party led the drive for independence in India.

Setting the Scene Tensions were running high in Amritsar, a city in northern India. Protests against British rule had sparked riots and attacks on British residents. On April 13, 1919, a large but peaceful crowd jammed into a walled field in the heart of the city. The British commander, General Reginald Dyer, had banned public meetings, but Indians either ignored or had not heard the order. As Indian leaders addressed the crowd, Dyer arrived with 50 soldiers. To clear the field, they opened fire on the unarmed men, women, and children. Within 10 minutes, they had killed 379 people and wounded more than 1,100. The Amritsar massacre was a turning point for many Indians. It convinced them of the evils of British rule.

Moves Toward Independence

The tragedy at Amritsar was linked to broader Indian frustrations after World War I. During the war, more than a million Indians had served overseas, suffering heavy casualties. As thousands died on distant battlefields, Indian nationalists grew angry that they had no freedom at home.

To quiet nationalist demands, the British promised India greater self-government after the war. But when the fighting ended, Britain proposed only a few minor reforms.

Since 1885, the Congress party had pressed for self-rule within the British empire. After Amritsar, it began to call for full independence. But party members were mostly a middle-class, western-educated elite who had little in common with the masses of Indian peasants. In the 1920s, a new leader emerged and united all Indians. Adoring Indians dubbed him Mahatma, or "Great Soul."

Mohandas Gandhi

The new leader was Mohandas Gandhi. Gandhi came from a middle-class Hindu family. At age 19, he went to England to study law. Like thousands of Indians before him, Gandhi went to South Africa. There he joined an Indian law firm. Although Gandhi was more successful financially than many Indians in South Africa, he too faced racial prejudice. For 20 years, Gandhi fought laws that discriminated against Indians in South Africa. In his struggle against injustice, he

Serving the Empire
Large numbers of Indians served in World War I. Here, Indian troops repel an air attack in Mesopotamia.

Theme: Political and Social Systems How did Indian nationalists respond to World War I?

Primary Source and Literature

See "Mohandas Gandhi:
Hind Swaraj" in the
Reference Section at the
back of this book.

adopted the weapon of nonviolent (passive) resistance. He called it *satya-graha*, or "soul-force." In 1914, Gandhi returned to India, where his ideas inspired Indians of all religions and ethnic backgrounds.

Nonviolence   While leaders like Atatürk adopted western solutions to national problems, Gandhi embraced Hindu traditions. Above all, he preached the ancient doctrine of ahimsa (uh HIM sah), or nonviolence and reverence for all life. By using the power of love, he believed, people could convert even the worst wrongdoer to the right course of action.

Gandhi's philosophy reflected western as well as Indian influences. He admired Christian teachings about love and had read the works of Henry David Thoreau, an American philosopher of the 1800s who believed in civil disobedience, the refusal to obey unjust laws. Gandhi also embraced western ideas of democracy and nationalism. He rejected the inequalities of the caste system and fought hard to end the harsh treatment of untouchables. He urged equal rights for all Indians, women as well as men.

Gandhi Sets an Example   Abandoning western-style clothing, Gandhi dressed in the *dhoti*, the simple white garment traditionally worn by village Indians. During the 1920s and 1930s, he launched a series of nonviolent actions against British rule. He called for boycotts of British goods, especially textiles, and urged Indians to wear only cotton grown and woven in India. He worked to restore pride in India's traditional industries, making the spinning wheel a symbol of the nationalist movement. Many women joined the self-sufficiency movement, producing as much as they could in their homes.

Through his own example, Gandhi inspired Indians to "get rid of our helplessness." His campaigns of civil disobedience attracted wide support. But when protests led to violent riots, Gandhi was deeply upset. He would fast, pray, and call on patriots to practice self-control.

The Salt March

To mobilize mass support, Gandhi set out to end the British salt monopoly. Everyone needs salt to survive. But while natural salt was available in the sea, Indians were forbidden to touch it. They could buy only salt sold by the British government. To Gandhi, the government salt monopoly was a symbol of British oppression. Early in 1930, he wrote to the British viceroy in India, stating his intention to break the law.

Breaking the Law   On March 12, Gandhi set out with 78 followers on a 240-mile march to the sea. As the tiny band passed through villages, crowds responded to Gandhi's message. By the time they reached the sea, the marchers numbered in the thousands. On April 6, Gandhi waded into the surf and picked up a lump of sea salt. Raising it over his head, he declared, "With this, I am shaking the foundations of the British empire."

Gandhi was arrested and jailed. Still, Indians followed his lead. Coastal villages started collecting salt. Congress party leaders sold salt on city streets, displayed it to enormous rallies—and were arrested. As Gandhi's campaign gained force, tens of thousands of Indians were imprisoned.

Toward Freedom   All around the world, newspapers thundered against Britain. Stories revealed how police brutally clubbed peaceful marchers who tried to occupy a government saltworks. "Not one of the marchers even raised an arm to fend off the blows," wrote an outraged American reporter.

Gandhi's campaign of nonviolence and the self-sacrifice of his followers slowly forced Britain to agree to hand over some power to Indians. Britain also agreed to meet other demands of the Congress party. Complete independence, however, would not be achieved until 1947.

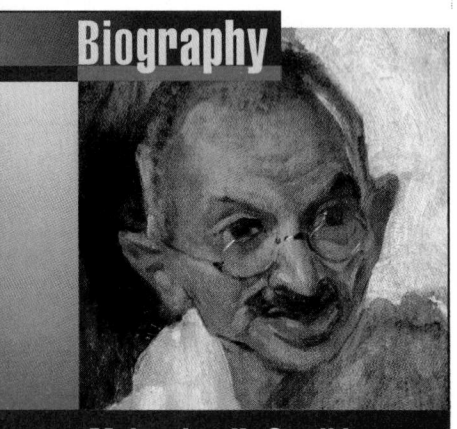

Biography

Mohandas K. Gandhi
1869–1948

A train trip in South Africa changed Gandhi's life. One day, the neatly dressed young lawyer bought a first-class ticket for a train. As he seated himself, a train official ordered him to move to a rear compartment.

At that time, South Africa had laws that required "coloured" travelers to sit separately from "whites." When Gandhi protested, the official forced him off the train.

This event inspired Gandhi to oppose injustice. Gradually, he developed his belief in nonviolent resistance. He pursued this battle—first in South Africa and later in India—for the rest of his life.

Theme: Impact of the Individual   How did Gandhi's personal experience influence India's struggle for independence?

Virtual Field Trip

Go Online
PHSchool.com

For: More information about Gandhi and the Salt March
Visit: PHSchool.com
Web Code: mkd-9230

Defying British Law
The Salt March focused the attention of all India on Gandhi's challenge to the British. Supporters followed him from village to village until they reached the sea. Here, women boil ocean water to collect salt.

Theme: Global Interaction How did other countries react to the Salt March?

Looking Ahead

As India came closer to independence, Muslim fears of the Hindu majority increased. While millions of Muslims responded to Gandhi's campaigns, tensions between Hindus and Muslims often erupted into violence.

A Separate Muslim State During the 1930s, the Muslim League gained an able leader in Muhammad Ali Jinnah. Like Gandhi, Jinnah came from a middle-class background and had studied law in England. At first, he represented Muslim interests within the Congress party. Later, he threw his support behind the idea of a separate state for Muslims. It would be called Pakistan, meaning "land of the [ritually] pure."

World War II India was moving toward independence when a new world war exploded in 1939. Britain outraged Indian leaders by postponing further action on independence and then bringing India into the war without consulting them. Angry nationalists launched a campaign of noncooperation and were jailed by the British. Millions of Indians, however, did help Britain during the war. When the war ended in 1945, independence could no longer be delayed.

SECTION 3 Assessment

Recall
1. **Identify: (a)** Amritsar massacre, **(b)** Mohandas Gandhi, **(c)** Muhammad Ali Jinnah.
2. **Define: (a)** ahimsa, **(b)** civil disobedience.

Comprehension
3. How did the Amritsar massacre affect the movement for Indian independence?
4. How did Gandhi revive Indian pride?

5. Why did Gandhi organize the Salt March?

Critical Thinking and Writing
6. **Recognizing Causes and Effects** Why do you think Gandhi was able to unite Indians when earlier attempts had failed?
7. **Predicting Consequences** What conflicts would you expect to emerge in India after World War II?

Go Online
PHSchool.com

Use the Internet to research the Amritsar massacre. Then, write two headlines about the event—one for an Indian newspaper and one for a British newspaper. For help with this activity, use **Web Code mkd-2933.**

Upheavals in China

Reading Focus

- What were the key challenges to the Chinese republic?

- What leaders emerged in the "new" China?

- How did invasion by Japan affect China?

Taking Notes

As you read this section, prepare an outline of its contents. Use Roman numerals to indicate major headings. Use capital letters for subheadings, and use numbers for the supporting details. The example here will help you get started.

I. **The Chinese republic**
  A. **Internal problems**
    1. **Yuan Shikai sets up dynasty with himself as emperor**
    2.
  B. **Foreign imperialism**
    1.
    2.

Main Idea   Civil war and foreign invasions plagued the new Chinese republic.

Setting the Scene Sun Yixian, "father" of the Chinese revolution, painted a grim picture of China after the overthrow of the Qing dynasty. "In comparison with other nations," he wrote, "we have the greatest population and the oldest culture, of 4,000 years' duration." In spite of this, he noted, China was "the poorest and weakest state in the world." Other countries were "the carving knife and the serving dish," and China was "the fish and the meat."

As the new Chinese republic took shape, nationalists like Sun Yixian set the goal of "catching up and surpassing the powers, east and west." But that goal would remain a distant dream as China suffered the turmoil of civil war and foreign invasion.

The Chinese Republic

In China, as you recall, the Qing dynasty collapsed in 1911. Sun Yixian hoped to rebuild China on the Three Principles of the People. But he made little progress. China quickly fell into chaos.

Internal Problems In 1912, Sun Yixian stepped down as president in favor of a powerful general, Yuan Shikai. Sun hoped that Yuan would restore order and create a strong central government. Instead, the ambitious general tried to set up a new dynasty, with himself as emperor. The military, however, did not support him, and opposition divided the nation. When Yuan died in 1916, China plunged into still greater disorder.

In the provinces, local warlords seized power. As rival armies battled for control, the economy collapsed and millions of peasants suffered terrible hardships. Warlords forced them to pay taxes to support their armies. The constant fighting ravaged the land. Famine and attacks by bandits added to their misery.

Foreign Imperialism During this period of upheaval, foreign powers increased their influence over Chinese affairs. Foreign merchants, missionaries, and soldiers dominated the ports China had opened to trade. They also exerted influence inland.

In 1915, Japan had begun to put new pressure on its once-powerful neighbor. While the attentions of the western powers were focused on World War I, Japan presented Yuan Shikai with the Twenty-One Demands, which sought to make China a Japanese protectorate. Too weak to resist, Yuan gave in to some of the demands.

Then, in 1919, at the Paris Peace Conference, the victorious Allies gave Japan control over former German possessions in China. That news infuriated Chinese nationalists, who blamed their leaders for "selling out" China in the Treaty of Versailles.

May Fourth Movement On May 4, 1919, student protests erupted in Beijing and later spread to cities across China—a startling event in those days. "China's territory may be conquered," they declared, "but it cannot be given away! The Chinese people may be massacred, but they will not surrender." Students organized boycotts of Japanese goods.

Student protests set off a cultural and intellectual ferment known as the May Fourth Movement. As with earlier reform movements, its goal was to strengthen China. Western-educated leaders blamed the imperialists' successes on China's own weakness. As in Meiji Japan, Chinese reformers wanted to learn from the West and use that knowledge to end foreign domination. Most reformers rejected Confucian traditions, and many turned to western science and ideas such as democracy and nationalism to solve China's problems.

Women played a key role in the May Fourth Movement, just as they had in earlier uprisings. They joined marches and campaigned to end a number of traditional practices, such as arranged marriages, footbinding, and the seclusion of women within the home. Their work helped open doors for women in education and the economy.

The Appeal of Marxism Some Chinese turned to the revolutionary ideas of Marx and Lenin. The Russian Revolution seemed to offer a model of how a strong, well-organized party could transform a nation. And Soviet Russia was more than willing to train Chinese students and military officers to become the vanguard, or elite leaders, of a communist revolution. By the 1920s, a small group of Chinese communists had formed their own political party.

Leaders for a New China

In 1921, Sun Yixian and his Guomindang (gwoh meen DAWNG), or Nationalist, party established a government in south China. Sun planned to raise an army, defeat the warlords, and spread his government's rule over all of China. When western powers ignored pleas for help in building a democratic China, Sun decided "that the one real and genuine friend of the

May Fourth Movement
In 1919, student protests spread across China. Reformers wanted to modernize the nation so that China would be able to expel foreign powers.

Theme: Political and Social Systems Why did some Chinese reformers adopt the ideas of Marx and Lenin?

Civil War in China, 1925–1935

Legend:
→ Route of Jiang Jieshi, 1926–1928
→ Route of Long March, 1934–1935
▨ Controlled by Guomindang, 1927
▢ Communist bases

Skills Assessment

Geography Beginning in 1925, the Guomindang and the Communists waged a long and bitter war for control of China.

1. **Location** On the map, locate **(a)** Beijing, **(b)** Nanjing, **(c)** Yenan, **(d)** Chongqing.
2. **Movement** Describe the route of the Long March.
3. **Critical Thinking Synthesizing Information** What types of natural features made the Long March difficult?

Chinese Revolution is Soviet Russia." Russian experts helped the Nationalists plan and carry out their campaign against the warlords.

Jiang Jieshi After Sun's death in 1925, an energetic young army officer, Jiang Jieshi* (jyawng jeh SHEE), took over the Guomindang. He had received military training in Japan. While he was determined to smash the power of the warlords and reunite China, Jiang had little interest in either democracy or communism.

In 1926, Jiang Jieshi began a march into northern China, crushing local warlords as he advanced and capturing Beijing. In midcampaign, he stopped to strike at the Chinese Communist party, which he saw as a threat to his power. While Jiang had the support of landlords and business leaders, the Communists were winning converts among the small proletariat in cities like Shanghai.

Early in 1927, on orders from Jiang, Guomindang troops slaughtered Communist party members and the workers who supported them. In Shanghai and elsewhere, thousands of people were killed. Anger over the massacre would fuel a bitter civil war that lasted for 22 years.

Mao Zedong Among the Communists who escaped Jiang's attack was a young revolutionary of peasant origins, Mao Zedong. Unlike earlier Chinese Communists, Mao believed that the Communists should seek support not among the small urban working class but among the large peasant masses.

Although the Communists were pursued at every turn by Guomindang forces, Mao was optimistic about eventual success. "A single spark can start a prairie fire," he once observed. For a time, Mao and the Communists organized the peasants in southeastern China. They redistributed land to peasants and offered them schooling and health care.

The Long March Jiang Jieshi, however, was determined to destroy the "Red bandits," as he called the Communists. He led the Guomindang in a series of "extermination campaigns" against them.

In 1934, in an epic retreat known as the Long March, Mao and about 100,000 of his followers fled the Guomindang. During the next year, they trekked more than 6,000 miles, facing daily attacks as they crossed rugged mountains, deep gorges, and mighty rivers. Only about 20,000 people survived the ordeal. For decades, the Long March stood as a symbol of Communist heroism to Chinese who opposed the Guomindang. The march also inspired new recruits to follow Mao.

During the Long March, the Communists enforced strict discipline. Soldiers had to follow three main rules: Obey orders, "do not take a single needle or a piece of thread from the people," and turn in everything you capture. Further, they were to treat peasants politely, pay for goods they wanted, and avoid damaging crops. Such behavior made Mao's forces welcome among peasants, many of whom had suffered greatly at the hands of the Guomindang.

At the end of the Long March, the Communists set up a new base in a remote region of northern China. There, Mao rebuilt his forces and plotted

---

* In earlier textbooks, this name is spelled Chiang Kai-shek.

new strategies for fighting the Guomindang. He claimed the great retreat as a victory. As he observed:

> "The Long March is also a seeding-machine. It has sown many seeds in eleven provinces, which will sprout, grow leaves, blossom into flowers, bear fruit, and yield a crop."
> —Mao Zedong, "On the Tactics of Fighting Japanese Imperialism"

Japanese Invasion

While Jiang was pursuing the Communists across China, the country faced another danger. In 1931, Japan invaded Manchuria in northeastern China, adding it to the growing Japanese empire. As Japanese aggression increased, some of Jiang's own generals began to doubt him. Why, they demanded, did he waste valuable resources fighting other Chinese instead of mobilizing against the foreign invaders? In the end, Jiang was forced to form a united front with the Communists against Japan.

In 1937, the Japanese struck again. As airplanes bombed Chinese cities, highly disciplined and well-equipped Japanese troops overran eastern China, including Beijing and Guangzhou. Jiang Jieshi retreated to the interior and set up his capital at Chongqing (chawng CHIHNG).

After a lengthy siege, Japanese troops marched into the city of Nanjing on December 13. Nanjing was an important cultural center, and had been the Nationalist capital before Chongqing. After the city's surrender, the Japanese killed hundreds of thousands of soldiers and civilians and brutalized still more. The cruelty and destruction became known around the world as the "rape of Nanjing."

Looking Ahead

From 1937 to 1945, the Guomindang, the Communists, and the Japanese were locked in a three-sided struggle. The bombing of Pearl Harbor in 1941 brought the United States not only into the war against Japan but into an alliance with the Chinese, as well. After Japan's defeat, the United States, which supported Jiang, tried to prevent renewed civil war in China, but with no success. Within a few years, the Communists would triumph, and Mao would move to impose revolutionary change on China.

Primary Source

Massacre in Nanjing
From December 1937 to March 1938, the Japanese army terrorized the people of Nanjing. This account is from a classified Chinese document on the incident:

"In the last ten days of December, the campaign to clear the streets began.... Japanese soldiers, in groups of three to five, went from door to door wielding long swords, loudly screaming out orders, and insisting the doors be opened.... those who had been hiding inside ... could not help but poke their heads out their doors to look around and see what had happened outside. Then catastrophe befell them. The moment they opened their doors ... the Japanese opened fire. On this one day alone, the dead and wounded numbered in the thousands...."

> —Gao Xingzu, Wu Shimin, Hu Yungong, and Cha Ruizhen, *Japanese Imperialism and the Massacre in Nanjing*

Skills Assessment

Primary Source How might people in Nanjing respond to this type of violence?

SECTION 4 Assessment

Recall
1. **Identify:** (a) Sun Yixian, (b) May Fourth Movement, (c) Guomindang, (d) Jiang Jieshi, (e) Mao Zedong, (f) Long March.

Comprehension
2. Why did the new republic of China fall into chaos after 1912?
3. Describe the goals of each of the following: (a) Sun Yixian, (b) Jiang Jieshi, (c) Mao Zedong.
4. Why did Jiang side with the Communists after 1931?

Critical Thinking and Writing
5. **Recognizing Causes and Effects** (a) How did the actions of foreign imperialist powers help to strengthen nationalism in China? (b) How do you think the "rape of Nanjing" affected Japan's reputation around the world?
6. **Defending a Position** Do you think that Mao's order not to take a single needle or piece of thread from the people was a wise decision? Why or why not?

Activity

Drawing a Political Cartoon Review Mao's statement about the Long March as a "seeding-machine." Draw a political cartoon illustrating this statement. Include a title and a caption for your political cartoon.

Empire of the Rising Sun

Reading Focus

■ How did liberal changes affect Japan during the 1920s?

■ How did nationalists react to Japan's problems during the Great Depression?

■ How did the militarists use their power?

Vocabulary

Diet
ultranationalist

Taking Notes

Copy this graphic organizer on a piece of paper. Include facts that describe the causes and effects of the rise of militarism in Japan. To help you get started, part of the graphic organizer has been completed.

Causes
• Unhappiness over loss of tradition
•

↓

RISE OF MILITARISM IN JAPAN

↓

Effects
• Withdrawal from League of Nations
•

Main Idea By the 1930s, the Japanese military dominated a government that emphasized service to the nation and a policy of imperialistic expansion.

Biography

Hirohito 1901–1989

Hirohito became emperor of Japan in 1926. As emperor, according to Japanese tradition, he was a living god and the nation's supreme authority—no one could look at his face or even mention his name. In practice, however, he merely approved the policies that his ministers formulated.

Hirohito was a private man who preferred marine biology to power politics. As a result, his role in Japan's move toward aggression is unclear. Some historians believe that Hirohito did not encourage Japanese military leaders. Others assert that he was actively involved in expansionist policies.

Theme: Impact of the Individual Why was Hirohito given great respect?

Setting the Scene Solemn ceremonies marked the start of Emperor Hirohito's reign. A few honored participants gathered in the Secret Purple Hall. Other high-ranking guests sat in an outer chamber, able to hear but not to see the emperor.

In the hall, the new emperor sat on the ancient throne of Japan. Beside him was his wife, the empress Nagako. With great care, he performed purification rituals that were sacred going back thousands of years. Calling on the spirits of his ancestors, he pledged "to preserve world peace and benefit the welfare of the human race."

The prime minister then made his own brief speech, ending with a ringing cry: "May the Lord Emperor live 10,000 years!" This traditional wish for a long and successful reign echoed across Japan.

In fact, Hirohito reigned from 1926 to 1989—an astonishing 63 years. During those decades, Japan experienced remarkable successes and appalling tragedies. In this section, we will focus on the 1920s and 1930s, when the pressures of extreme nationalism and economic upheaval set Japan on a militaristic and expansionist path that would engulf all of Asia.

Liberal Changes of the 1920s

During the 1920s, Japan moved toward greater democracy. Political parties grew stronger, and elected members of the Diet—the Japanese parliament—exerted their power. By 1925, all adult men had won the right to vote. Western ideas about women's rights had brought a few changes. Overall, however, Japanese women remained subordinate to men, and they would not win suffrage until 1947.

Economic Growth During World War I, the Japanese economy enjoyed phenomenal growth. Its exports to Allied nations soared. Also, while western powers battled in Europe, Japan expanded its influence throughout East Asia. Additionally, it sought further rights in China with the Twenty-One Demands.

By the 1920s, the powerful business leaders known as the zaibatsu strongly influenced politics through donations to political parties. They pushed for policies to favor international trade and their own interests. At the same time, in the spirit of world peace, Japan signed an agreement with the United States and Britain to limit the size of its navy. The government also reduced military spending.

Serious Problems Behind this seeming well-being, Japan faced some grave problems. The economy grew more slowly in the 1920s than at any time since Japan had modernized. Rural peasants enjoyed none of the prosperity of city dwellers. In the cities, factory workers earning low wages were attracted to the socialist ideas of Marx and Lenin. As these workers won the right to vote, many of them elected socialists to the Diet.

In the cities, members of the younger generation were also in revolt against tradition. They adopted western fads and fashions and rejected family authority for the western notion of individual freedom.

During the 1920s, tensions between the government and the military simmered not far below the surface. Conservatives, especially military officers, blasted government corruption, including payoffs by powerful zaibatsu. They also condemned western influences for undermining basic Japanese values of obedience and respect for authority.

The Nationalist Reaction

In 1929, the Great Depression rippled across the Pacific, striking Japan with devastating force. Trade suffered as foreign buyers could no longer afford to purchase Japanese silks and other exports. Unemployment in the cities soared, while in the countryside peasants were only a mouthful from starvation.

A Worsening Crisis Economic disaster fed the discontent of the leading military officials and extreme nationalists, or **ultranationalists.** They condemned politicians for agreeing to western demands to stop overseas expansion. Western industrial powers, they pointed out, had long ago grabbed huge empires. By comparison, Japan's empire was tiny.

Japanese nationalists were further outraged by racial policies in the United States, Canada, and Australia that shut out Japanese immigrants. The Japanese took great pride in their industrial achievements and bitterly resented being treated as second-class citizens in other parts of the world.

As the crisis worsened, nationalists demanded renewed expansion. An empire in Asia, they argued, would provide much-needed raw materials as well as an outlet for Japan's rapidly growing population. They set their sights on the Chinese province of Manchuria. This region was rich in natural resources, and Japanese businesses had already invested heavily there.

The Manchurian Incident In 1931, a group of Japanese army officers provoked an incident that would provide an excuse to seize Manchuria. They set explosives and blew up tracks on a Japanese-owned railroad line. Then, they claimed that the Chinese had committed the act. In "self-defense," the army attacked Chinese forces. Without consulting their own government, the Japanese military forces conquered all of Manchuria and set up a puppet state there that they called Manzhouguo (mahn joh GWOH).

When the League of Nations condemned Japanese aggression against China, Japan simply

Geography Between 1918 and 1934, Japan expanded its territory in Asia. From their conquered lands, the Japanese acquired natural resources to fuel their industries.

1. **Location** On the map, locate **(a)** Japan, **(b)** Sakhalin, **(c)** Manchuria, **(d)** Korea, **(e)** Taiwan.
2. **Region** In what regions were Japan's main manufacturing areas located?
3. **Critical Thinking Identifying Main Ideas** Based on this map, which area was the most likely source of raw materials for Japanese industry? Explain.

Japan's Expanding Empire to 1934

▢ Japan, 1890		📦 Bauxite	
▢ Territory added by 1918		⛏ Coal	
▢ Territory added by 1934		✳ Copper	
▢ Main manufacturing areas		◇ Gold	
		🔨 Iron ore	
		⛏ Petroleum	

Azimuthal Equal Area Projection

Disaster!

The Tokyo Earthquake of 1923

Fleeing the flames and destruction, people poured into the streets. They used bicycles and wagons to salvage whatever belongings they could carry.

On September 1, 1923, an earthquake of historic proportions struck the Tokyo-Yokohama area. One of the most destructive quakes in history, it was followed by widespread fires. The main quake, which lasted only four minutes, measured 8.3 on the Richter scale. It was followed by about 300 aftershocks.

An office worker in Yokohama reported, "Without warning, came the first rumbling jar of an earthquake, a sickening sway, the vicious grinding of timbers and, in a few seconds, a crescendo of turmoil as the floor began to heave and the building to lurch drunkenly. . . . Walls bulged, spread and sagged, pictures danced on their wires, flew out and crashed to splinters."

—Otis Manchester Poole, *The Death of Old Yokohama*

Most buildings were constructed in the traditional style with wood and paper, making them very vulnerable to fire.

Fast Facts

- An average of 1,500 earthquakes strike Japan each year.

- The 1923 earthquake caused the deaths of about 140,000 people and damaged as many as 700,000 buildings.

- Possibly 45 percent of surviving workers lost their jobs because so many businesses were destroyed.

Portfolio Assessment

Conduct research to learn more about world earthquakes. List three of the most destructive earthquakes in modern history and pinpoint them on a map. Why are some regions of the world more vulnerable to earthquakes than others? How can buildings be designed to combat the effects of earthquakes?

withdrew itself from the League. When politicians in Tokyo objected to the army's highhanded actions, public opinion sided with the military.

Militarists in Power

By the early 1930s, ultranationalists were winning popular support for foreign conquests and a tough stand against the western powers. Members of "patriotic" societies assassinated a number of politicians and business leaders who opposed expansion. Military leaders plotted to overthrow the government and, in 1936, briefly occupied the center of Tokyo.

Traditional Values Revived Civilian government survived, but by 1937 it had been forced to accept military domination. To please the ultranationalists, it cracked down on socialists and ended most democratic freedoms. It revived ancient warrior values and built a cult around the emperor, who was believed to be descended from the sun goddess.

To spread its nationalist message, the government focused on the schools. A government pamphlet, which became required reading in schools, criticized the Japanese adoption of western ideas:

> "With the influx of European and American culture into this country, . . . individualism, liberalism, utilitarianism, and materialism began to assert themselves, with the result that the traditional character of the country was much impaired and the virtuous habits and customs bequeathed by our ancestors were affected unfavorably."
> —from *The Way of Subjects,* quoted in *Human Record: Sources of Global History* (Andrea)

To practice "the way of subjects," students were taught absolute obedience to the emperor and service to the state.

Renewed Expansion During the 1930s, Japan took advantage of China's civil war to increase its influence there. Japan expected to complete its conquest of China within a few years. But in 1939, while the two nations were locked in deadly combat, World War II broke out in Europe. That conflict swiftly spread to Asia.

By 1939, Japan had joined with two aggressive European powers, Germany and Italy, in the alliance known as the Axis Powers. That alliance, combined with renewed Japanese conquests, would turn World War II into a brutal, wide-ranging conflict waged not only across the continent of Europe but across Asia and the islands of the Pacific as well.

SECTION 5 Assessment

Recall
1. **Identify:** **(a)** Hirohito, **(b)** Manzhouguo.
2. **Define:** **(a)** Diet, **(b)** ultranationalist.

Comprehension
3. What liberal changes occurred in Japan in the 1920s?
4. How did nationalists deal with the Great Depression?
5. **(a)** What goals did Japanese militarists pursue at home? **(b)** What goals did they pursue overseas?

Critical Thinking and Writing
6. **Comparing** Compare the policies pursued by Japanese liberals to those followed by Japanese conservatives during the 1920s and 1930s.
7. **Recognizing Cause and Effect** Why might a nation turn to military leaders and extreme nationalists during a time of crisis?

Activity

Creating a Time Line
Create a time line of the major events in Japan's shift from liberalism to militarism during the 1920s and 1930s. Briefly describe each event on the time line.

Creating a Chapter Summary

Copy this chart on a piece of paper. Then, fill in the chart with facts about revolutions and national movements around the world. Some entries have been completed to serve as a sample.

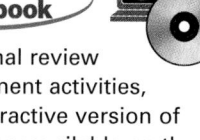

For additional review and enrichment activities, see the interactive version of *World History* available on the Web and on CD-ROM.

NATIONALISM AND REVOLUTION AROUND THE WORLD (1910–1939)

SOURCES OF DISCONTENT		RESULTS
• Lack of land and education for peasants •	MEXICO	• Civil war •
•	AFRICA	•
•	MIDDLE EAST	•
•	INDIA	•
•	CHINA	•
•	JAPAN	•

Go Online
PHSchool.com

For practice test questions for Chapter 16, use **Web Code mka-2942.**

Building Vocabulary

Review the chapter vocabulary words listed below. Then, use the words and their definitions to create a matching quiz. Exchange quizzes with another student. Check each other's answers when you are finished.

1. nationalization
2. apartheid
3. polygamy
4. ahimsa
5. civil disobedience
6. ultranationalist

Recalling Key Facts

7. How did the Good Neighbor Policy change United States relations with Latin America?
8. How did Pan-Africanism affect people around the world?
9. How did Atatürk try to transform Turkey into a modern, secular state?
10. How did World War I affect relations between India and Britain?
11. What three-sided struggle took place in China from 1937 to 1945?
12. How did the Great Depression affect political activity in Japan?

Critical Thinking and Writing

13. **Making Inferences** **(a)** What were the three main issues addressed by the Mexican Constitution of 1917? **(b)** What groups do you think welcomed the constitution? **(c)** What groups might have opposed the constitution? Explain.
14. **Connecting to Geography** Why did some European Jews choose to move to Palestine in the early 1900s?
15. **Linking Past and Present** **(a)** Describe Gandhi's methods of nonviolence and civil disobedience. **(b)** How are methods used by other groups seeking social or political change similar to those used by Gandhi?
16. **Drawing Conclusions** Do you think the rise of militarism in Japan could have been avoided? Explain.
17. **Synthesizing Information** How is political independence related to economic independence? Explain your answer using examples from the nations in this chapter.

Delegates to the Second Pan-African Congress wrote a manifesto to state their beliefs and goals. Use this excerpt from the *Manifesto* to answer the questions that follow.

> *"The absolute equality of races—physical, political and social—is the founding stone of world peace and human advancement. . . .*
>
> *That in the vast range of time, one group should in its industrial technique, or social organization, or spiritual vision, lag a few hundred years behind another, or forge fitfully ahead, . . . is proof of the essential richness and variety of human nature. . . . The doctrine of racial equality does not interfere with individual liberty, rather, it fulfills it. . . .*
>
> *It is the duty of the world to assist in every way the advance of the backward and suppressed groups of mankind. . . .*
>
> *The habit of democracy must be made to encircle the earth. Despite the attempt to prove that its practice is the secret and divine gift of the few, no habit is more natural or more widely spread, . . . or more easily capable of development among masses. . . . "*
>
> —Manifesto of the Second Pan-African Congress

18. What, according to the *Manifesto*, is proved by different levels of accomplishment among groups of people?
19. Why should wealthier nations aid poorer nations?
20. What does the *Manifesto* say about the spread of democracy?
21. How might the *Manifesto* encourage African pride and nationalism?

Go Online
PHSchool.com

Use the Internet to research nationalist movements in Mexico, China, or an African nation during the early 1900s. Then, create a piece of artwork that reflects the ideals of the movement. You may want to create a sculpture or painting, or design a small mural. For help with this activity, use **Web Code mkd-2943**.

Civil War in China, 1925–1935

- Route of Jiang Jieshi, 1926–1928
- Route of Long March, 1934–1935
- Controlled by Guomindang, 1927
- Communist bases

MANCHURIA (MANZHOUGUO)
Beijing
CHINA
Yenan
SHAANXI   *Huang He*
KOREA (controlled by Japan)
Yellow Sea
JAPAN
Han R.
Yangzi R.
Nanjing
Shanghai
Chongqing
East China Sea
HUNAN
JIANGXI
Guangzhou
FORMOSA (controlled by Japan)
PACIFIC OCEAN
South China Sea
HAINAN
Azimuthal Equal Area Projection
0   200   400 Miles
0   200   400 Kilometers

Use this map, as well as information from the chapter, to answer the following questions:

22. What areas were controlled by Japan?
23. When did Jiang Jieshi's march take place?
24. When did the Long March take place?
25. **(a)** In what region did the Long March begin? **(b)** In what city did it end?
26. Based on the map, which group would seem more likely to come into conflict with Japanese armies? Explain your answer.

Skills Tip

Many maps present information within a certain time period. Read the title, legend, and caption carefully to identify the time period shown in the map.

Crisis of Democracy in the West 1919–1939

Chapter Preview

1 The Western Democracies

2 A Culture in Conflict

3 Fascism in Italy

4 Hitler and the Rise of Nazi Germany

CHAPTER EVENTS

1920s

Modern art flourishes in Europe. Paintings like *Composition No. 4* by Fernand Leger challenge realistic traditions and disturb many viewers.

1922

Benito Mussolini comes to power in Italy. Mussolini will create Europe's first fascist dictatorship.

1925

Seven European nations sign the Locarno treaties, raising hopes for world peace.

| 1915 | 1920 | 1925 |

GLOBAL EVENTS

1919 Amritsar massacre takes place in India.

1922 Britain declares Egypt independent.

Rise of Dictatorships in Europe, 1917–1939

Legend:
- State controlled by communist regime
- Areas controlled by fascist or right-wing regimes
- Dates on map indicate year of rise of communist or fascist regime

After World War I, political and economic turmoil challenged democratic traditions. Dictatorships arose in many European countries.

**Map labels:**

FINLAND

NORWAY

SWEDEN

DENMARK

ESTONIA 1933

LATVIA 1934

LITHUANIA 1926

IRELAND

UNITED KINGDOM

NETH.

BELGIUM

LUX.

GERMANY 1933

EAST PRUSSIA (Germany)

POLAND 1926

UNION OF SOVIET SOCIALIST REPUBLICS 1917

FRANCE

SWITZ.

To Germany 1938–1939

CZECHOSLOVAKIA

To Hungary 1938–1939

AUSTRIA To Germany 1938

HUNGARY 1932

ROMANIA 1938

PORTUGAL 1926

SPAIN 1939

ITALY 1922

YUGOSLAVIA 1929

BULGARIA 1935

ALBANIA To Italy 1939

GREECE 1936

ATLANTIC OCEAN

Mediterranean Sea

Adriatic Sea

Baltic Sea

Black Sea

Lambert Azimuthal Equal Area Projection

0   250   500 Miles
0   250   500 Kilometers

N W E S

"Mates! help me get a job."

1929
The Great Depression begins in the United States. Economic collapse also causes hardship for people in other countries, as this British poster shows.

1933
Nazi leader Adolf Hitler comes to power in Germany and begins building a totalitarian state.

1938
During *Kristallnacht,* or the "Night of Broken Glass," Nazi mobs attack Jewish communities in Germany.

Timeline:

1930

1931 Japan conquers Manchuria.

1935

1934 Stalin launches Great Purge in the Soviet Union.

1938 Mexico nationalizes foreign oil holdings.

1940

The Western Democracies

Reading Focus

- What issues faced Europe after World War I?
- How did the Great Depression begin and spread?
- How did Britain, France, and the United States try to meet the challenges of the 1920s and 1930s?

Vocabulary

disarmament
overproduction
margin buying
general strike

Taking Notes

On a sheet of paper, make a table like this one. As you read this section, add information about the three democracies in the years after World War I.

BRITAIN	FRANCE	UNITED STATES
Economic problems		
Political drift to right		

Main Idea Following World War I, the leading democratic powers moved to ensure peace but faced difficult political and economic challenges.

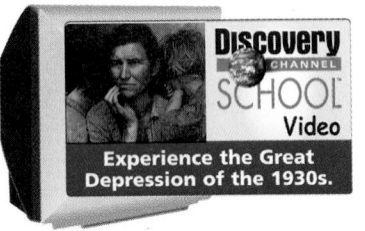
Experience the Great Depression of the 1930s.

Disillusion in Postwar Europe
German artist Käthe Kollwitz lost a son in World War I. In her 1923 woodcut *The Parents* (below), Kollwitz mirrors the sense of despair that gripped postwar Europe.

Theme: Art and Literature How does this picture make a universal statement about war?

Setting the Scene In his 1929 novel, *All Quiet on the Western Front*, German writer Erich Maria Remarque captured the disillusionment of the World War I generation. The novel's hero, a young German soldier, endures three years of grueling trench warfare. His friends are dead—butchered by bullets, shrapnel, artillery, or poison gas. In the last chapter, he wonders how he can return to civilian life feeling dead inside:

> "Had we returned home in 1916, out of the suffering and the strength of our experience we might have unleashed a storm. Now if we go back we will be weary, broken, burnt out, rootless, and without hope. We will not be able to find our way any more."
> —Erich Maria Remarque, *All Quiet on the Western Front*

The catastrophe of World War I shattered the sense of optimism that had grown in the West since the Enlightenment. Despair gripped survivors on both sides as they added up the staggering costs of the war. Especially among the democracies, economic and political crises only added to the growing pessimism of the 1920s and 1930s.

Postwar Issues

In 1919, three western democracies—Great Britain, France, and the United States—appeared powerful. They had ruled the Paris Peace Conference and boosted hopes for democracy among the new nations of Eastern Europe.

Underlying Problems Beneath the surface, however, postwar Europe faced grave problems. At first, the most pressing issues were finding jobs for returning veterans and rebuilding war-ravaged lands. Many nations also owed huge debts because they had borrowed heavily to pay for the war. In the early postwar years, economic problems fed social unrest and made radical ideas more popular. The Russian Revolution unleashed fears of the spread of communism. Some people saw socialism as the answer to hardships. Others embraced nationalistic political movements.

Other troubles clouded the international scene. As you have read, the peace settlements dissatisfied many Europeans, especially in Germany and among various ethnic groups in Eastern Europe. Finally, Europe lacked strong leaders just when they were most needed. The war had killed many of those who might have helped solve critical problems.

The Pursuit of Peace   During the 1920s, diplomats worked hard for peace. Hopes soared in 1925 when representatives from seven European nations signed a series of treaties at Locarno, Switzerland. These treaties settled Germany's disputed borders with France, Belgium, Czechoslovakia, and Poland. The Locarno treaties became the symbol of a new era. "France and Germany Ban War Forever," trumpeted a *New York Times* headline.

The hopeful "spirit of Locarno" was echoed in the Kellogg-Briand Pact of 1928. Almost every independent nation signed this agreement, promising to "renounce war as an instrument of national policy." In this optimistic spirit, the great powers pursued disarmament, the reduction of armed forces and weapons. The United States, Britain, France, Japan, and other nations signed treaties to reduce the size of their navies. However, they failed to agree on limiting the size of their armies.

Despite grumblings about the Versailles treaty, people around the world put great hopes in the League of Nations. From its headquarters in Geneva, Switzerland, the League encouraged cooperation and tried to get members to make a commitment to stop aggression. In 1926, after signing the Locarno agreements, Germany joined the League. Later, the Soviet Union was also admitted.

Obstacles to Peace   Although the Kellogg-Briand Pact outlawed war, there was no way of enforcing the ban. The League of Nations, too, was powerless to stop aggressors. It had also been damaged by the American refusal to join. In 1931, the League vigorously condemned Japan's invasion of Manchuria, but to no effect. Noting the League's weakness, ambitious dictators rearmed their military forces and pursued aggressive foreign policies, as you will read.

HAVING AN INSURANCE POLICY DOESN'T MEAN YOU CAN DO WITHOUT FIRE PREVENTION

An End to War?
The Kellogg-Briand Pact raised hopes for an end to war. But not everyone was so optimistic, as this 1929 American cartoon shows.

Theme: Global Interaction Summarize the main idea of this cartoon in your own words.

Recovery and Depression

During the 1920s, Europe made a shaky recovery. Economies returned to peacetime manufacturing and trade. Veterans gradually found jobs. Middle-class families generally enjoyed a rising standard of living, with money to buy new products such as cars, refrigerators, and radios.

The United States emerged from the war as the world's leading economic power. American banks and businesses controlled a global network of trade and finance. American loans and investments backed the recovery in Europe. As long as the American economy was healthy, the global economy remained relatively prosperous.

A Dangerous Imbalance   Both the American and the world economy had weak spots, however. One major problem was overproduction, a condition in which production of goods exceeds the demand for them. The war had increased demand for raw materials from Latin America, Africa, and Asia. Improved technology and farming methods also contributed to higher output. After the war, the demand for raw materials dwindled and prices fell. Consumers benefited from the lower prices. But farmers, miners, and other suppliers of raw materials suffered severe hardships.

At the same time, industrial workers won higher wages, which raised the price of manufactured goods. An imbalance emerged. Because farmers' earnings had fallen, they could afford fewer manufactured goods. Despite the slowing demand, factories kept pouring out goods. This imbalance, combined with other problems, undermined industrial economies. By the late 1920s, conditions were ripe for disaster.

The Great Depression in Europe
British author George Orwell describes the desperation of the unemployed poor:

"In the 'dirt' that is sent up from the [coal] pits there is a certain amount of broken coal. . . . In Wigan the competition among unemployed people for [this] waste coal has become so fierce that it has led to an extraordinary custom called 'scrambling for the coal.' . . . [The process] consists in getting on to the train while it is moving.

No one was hurt the afternoon I was there, but a man had had both his legs cut off a few weeks earlier, and another man lost several fingers a week later. Technically it is stealing but, as everybody knows, if the coal were not stolen, it would simply be wasted."

—George Orwell,
The Road to Wigan Pier

Skills Assessment

Primary Source What dangers were involved in "scrambling for the coal"?

Crash and Collapse Few people saw the danger. In the United States, prices on the New York Stock Exchange soared. Eager investors acquired stocks through **margin buying**, paying part of the cost and borrowing the rest from brokers. In the autumn of 1929, jitters about the economy caused brokers to call in these loans. Investors who were unable to repay were forced to sell their stocks. Financial panic set in. Stock prices crashed, wiping out the fortunes of many investors.

The stock market crash triggered the Great Depression of the 1930s, a painful time of global economic collapse. The crash created financial turmoil in the industrial world as American banks stopped making loans abroad and demanded repayment of foreign loans.

In the United States and elsewhere, banks failed and businesses closed, throwing millions out of work. The cycle spiraled steadily downward. The jobless could not afford to buy goods, so more factories had to close, which in turn increased the numbers of unemployed. In once-prosperous western cities, people slept on park benches and lined up to eat in charity soup kitchens. Former business leaders sold apples in the street.

Global Impact Desperate governments tried to protect their economies from foreign competition. The United States imposed the highest tariffs in its history. The policy backfired because other nations retaliated by raising their tariffs. In the end, all countries lost access to the larger global market. As you have read, the Great Depression spread misery from the industrial world to the suppliers of agricultural goods and raw materials.

As the depression dragged on, many people lost faith in the ability of democratic governments to solve the problems. Misery and hopelessness created fertile ground for extremists who promised radical solutions. Communists gloated that capitalism had collapsed. Right-wing extremists played on themes of intense nationalism, the failure of democracy, the virtues of authoritarian rule, and the need to rearm.

Britain in the Postwar Era

Even before the depression, Britain faced economic problems. Although it emerged victorious from the war, much of its overseas trade was lost. German U-boats had wreaked havoc on British shipping. The nation was deeply in debt, and its factories were out of date.

During the 1920s, unemployment was severe. Wages remained low, leading to worker unrest and frequent strikes. In 1926, a **general strike**, or strike by workers in many different industries at the same time, lasted nine days and involved some three million workers.

Economics and Politics During the 1920s, the Labour party surpassed the Liberal party in strength. Labour leaders gained support among workers by promoting a gradual move toward socialism. The middle class, however, firmly backed the Conservative party, which held power during much of this period. Widespread fear of communism contributed to a drift toward the right. After the general strike, Conservatives passed legislation limiting the power of workers to strike.

The Great Depression intensified the nation's economic woes. As the crisis worsened, Britain set up a coalition government made up of leaders from all three major political parties. The coalition government provided some unemployment benefits to ease the worst problems. Despite such efforts, millions of people suffered great hardships.

Irish Independence At the war's end, Britain still faced the "Irish question." In 1914, you will recall, Parliament passed a home-rule bill that was shelved when the war began. Militant Irish nationalists, however, were unwilling to wait. On Easter 1916, a small group launched a revolt against British rule. Although the Easter Rising was quickly suppressed, the execution of 15 rebel leaders stirred wider support for their cause.

When Parliament again failed to grant home rule in 1919, revolution erupted in Ireland. Members of the Irish Republican Army (IRA) carried on a guerrilla war against British forces and their supporters. Civilians were often caught in the middle of the violence.

In 1922, moderates in Ireland and England reached an agreement. Most of Ireland became the self-governing Irish Free State.* The largely Protestant northern counties (Ulster) remained under British rule. However, the IRA and other opponents of the treaty never accepted the division. Civil war broke out. Although peace was restored in 1923, the status of Northern Ireland would remain a thorny issue through the end of the century.

Commonwealth and Empire In 1931, four former colonies—Canada, Australia, New Zealand, and South Africa—became fully self-governing dominions within the newly formed British Commonwealth of Nations. Although linked by economic and cultural ties, each member of the Commonwealth pursued its own course.

Despite challenges from nationalists, Britain retained its colonies. To the British, their vast empire remained a source of wealth and pride. At the same time, Britain worked to improve agriculture and education in its colonies while planning for gradual independence at some uncertain date.

Foreign Policy Britain's postwar foreign policy created tensions with its ally France. Almost from the signing of the Treaty of Versailles, British leaders wanted to relax the treaty's harsh treatment of Germany. They feared that if Germany became too weak, the Soviet Union would be able to expand and France might gain too much control on the continent. Britain's leniency toward Germany helped push France in the opposite direction.

---

*Ireland later became a fully independent republic known as Eire.

Ireland's Easter Rising
Although the Easter Rising of 1916 failed, it was a turning point in the struggle for Irish independence. This photograph shows the ruins of a nationalist base of operations in Dublin.

Theme: Political and Social Systems How was the Easter Rising both a success and a failure?

France Pursues Security

Like Britain, France emerged from World War I both a victor and a loser. Fighting on the Western Front had devastated northern France. The French had suffered enormous casualties. Survivors felt battered and insecure.

The French economy recovered fairly rapidly, thanks in part to German reparations and to territories gained from Germany, including Alsace and Lorraine. Later, the Great Depression did not hurt France as much as it did some countries. French industry was not as centralized in the hands of big business. Small workshops served local regions and were less affected by global trends.

Coalition Governments Economic swings did occur, adding to an unstable political scene. Political divisions and financial scandals continued to plague the Third Republic. Many parties—from conservatives to communists—competed for power. During the postwar years, France was again ruled by a series of coalition governments.

In 1936, several leftist parties united behind the socialist leader Leon Blum. His Popular Front government tried to solve labor problems and passed some social legislation. But it could not satisfy more radical leftists. Strikes soon brought down Blum's government. Thus, France, like Britain, muddled through a series of crises. Democracy survived, but the country lacked strong leadership that could respond to the clamor for change.

The Maginot Line France's chief concern after the war was securing its borders against Germany. The French remembered with distrust the German invasions of 1870 and 1914. To prevent a third invasion, France built massive fortifications along the border. The Maginot (MA zhee noh) Line, as this defensive "wall" was called, offered a sense of security—a false one. The line would be of little use when Germany again invaded in 1940.

In its quest for security, France strengthened its military and sought alliances with other countries, including the Soviet Union. It insisted on strict enforcement of the Versailles treaty and complete payment of reparations, hoping to keep the German economy weak.

Prosperity and Depression in the United States

The United States emerged from World War I in excellent shape. A late entrant into the war, it had suffered relatively few casualties and little loss of property. It led the world in industrial and agricultural output. American money helped finance the European recovery.

Postwar Issues As you have read, the United States stayed out of the League of Nations. Arguing that membership might lead to involvement in future foreign wars, many Americans insisted that the nation maintain its free hand in foreign affairs. Still, during the 1920s, the United States took a leading role in international diplomacy. It sponsored the Kellogg-Briand Pact, pressed for disarmament, and worked to reduce German reparations.

Fear of bomb-throwing radicals and the Bolshevik Revolution in Russia set off a "Red Scare" in 1919 and 1920. Police rounded up suspected foreign-born radicals, and a number were expelled from the United States.

The "Red Scare" fed growing demands to limit immigration. Millions of immigrants from southern and eastern Europe had poured into the United States between 1890 and 1914. Some native-born Americans sought to exclude these newcomers, whose cultures differed from those of earlier settlers from northern Europe. In response, Congress passed laws limiting immigration from Europe. Earlier laws had already excluded or limited Chinese and Japanese immigration.

Boom and Bust In the boom years of the 1920s, middle-class Americans were enjoying the benefits of capitalism. They stocked their homes with

---

Geography and History

The Maginot Line

The Maginot Line was a masterpiece of engineering. Most of the line was built underground, with interconnecting tunnels that stretched for miles. Main forts, placed strategically to protect river crossings and crossroads, were located about every three to five miles. These were self-contained underground structures over 20 feet beneath the surface. Large enough to accommodate about 1,200 men, the forts contained barracks, kitchens, infirmaries, storage depots, telephone systems, electrical generating systems, and railways to move supplies. All that could be seen above ground were the barrels of the huge guns and gun placements.

In the end, the line failed to prevent a German invasion. In 1940, German troops simply bypassed the Maginot Line and marched into France.

Theme: Geography and History Look at a map of Europe. What routes could a German army take to bypass the German–French border and invade France?

radios, refrigerators, and automobiles. Most Americans agreed with President Calvin Coolidge that "the business of America is business."

The 1929 stock market crash shattered this mood of prosperity. President Herbert Hoover firmly believed that the government should not intervene in private business matters. However, as hard times got worse, he did try a variety of limited measures to solve the crisis. Nothing seemed to work.

The New Deal In 1932, Americans elected a new President, Franklin D. Roosevelt. "FDR" projected a sense of energy and optimism. Arguing that the government had to take an active role in combating the Great Depression, he introduced the New Deal, a massive package of economic and social programs.

Under the New Deal, the federal government became more directly involved in people's everyday lives than ever before. New laws regulated the stock market and protected bank depositors' savings. Government programs created jobs for the unemployed and gave aid to farmers. A new Social Security system provided old-age pensions and other benefits that major European countries had introduced years earlier.

The New Deal failed to end the Great Depression, but it did ease the suffering for many. Still, some critics fiercely condemned FDR's expansion of the role of government. As a result of the New Deal, many Americans came to expect the government to intervene directly to promote their economic well-being. The debate about the size and role of the federal government continues to this day.

Cause *and* Effect

Long-Term Causes	Immediate Causes
• Worldwide interrelationship of governments and economies • Huge war debts • American loans to Europe • Widespread use of credit • Overproduction of goods • Industrial wages rise as farm earnings fall	• New York stock market crash • Farmers unable to repay loans • Banks demand repayment of loans • American loans to other countries dry up • Without capital, businesses and factories fail

Worldwide Economic Depression

Immediate Effects	Long-Term Effects
• Vast unemployment and misery • Protective tariffs imposed • Loss of faith in capitalism and democracy • Authoritarian leaders emerge	• Rise of fascism and Nazism • Governments experiment with social programs • People blame scapegoats • World War II begins

Connections to Today

• Government monitoring of or control of national economies, banks, credit, and stock markets
• Continuation of social programs
• Monitoring of worldwide economic developments by international agencies

Skills Assessment **Chart** Economists still debate the causes and effects of the Great Depression. **How do governments today deal with the kinds of conditions that caused the depression?**

SECTION 1 Assessment

Recall
1. **Identify:** (a) Locarno treaties, (b) Kellogg-Briand Pact, (c) IRA, (d) Commonwealth of Nations, (e) Leon Blum, (f) Maginot Line, (g) New Deal.
2. **Define:** (a) disarmament, (b) overproduction, (c) margin buying, (d) general strike.

Comprehension
3. (a) What steps did the major powers take to protect the peace? (b) Why did these moves have limited effects?
4. Explain how each of the following contributed to the outbreak or spread of the Great Depression: (a) overproduction, (b) margin buying, (c) high tariffs.
5. How did the Great Depression affect political developments in the United States?

Critical Thinking and Writing
6. **Understanding Causes and Effects** Why do you think the 1926 general strike in Britain strengthened the Conservative party?
7. **Applying Information** How did Britain and France emerge from World War I as both victors and losers?

Activity

Creating a Political Cartoon Draw a political cartoon that might have appeared in an American or British newspaper in 1932. The cartoon should show how the effects of the Great Depression often undermined confidence in democracy.

SECTION 2 A Culture in Conflict

Reading Focus

- How did new views revolutionize modern science and thought?
- What artistic and literary trends emerged in the 1920s?
- How did western society change after World War I?

Vocabulary

psychoanalysis
abstract
surrealism
stream of consciousness
flapper

Taking Notes

On a sheet of paper, draw a concept web like the one shown here. As you read this section, fill in important information about cultural changes. Add as many circles as you need.

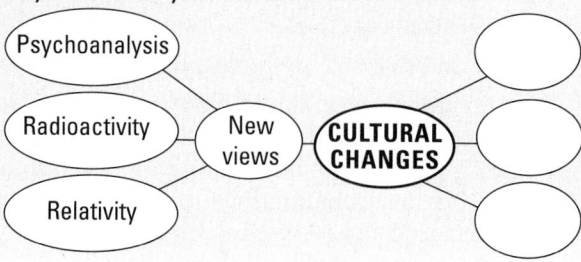

Main Idea Western culture experienced great changes in the years following World War I.

Setting the Scene

In 1921, the Irish poet William Butler Yeats summed up the mood of many postwar writers and artists:

> "Things fall apart; the centre cannot hold;
> Mere anarchy is loosed upon the world,
> The blood-dimmed tide is loosed, and everywhere
> The ceremony of innocence is drowned."
> —William Butler Yeats, "The Second Coming"

It was not only the war that fostered this sense of uncertainty, of civilization falling apart. New ideas and scientific discoveries were challenging long-held ideas about the nature of the world.

New Views of the Universe

The ancient Greeks were the first to propose that all matter is composed of tiny, indivisible atoms. Over the centuries, most scientists came to accept this idea. But discoveries made in the late 1800s and early 1900s showed that the atom was more complex than anyone suspected.

Radioactivity By the early 1900s, the Polish-born French scientist Marie Curie and others were experimenting with radioactivity. They found that the atoms of certain elements, such as radium and uranium, spontaneously release charged particles. As scientists studied radioactivity further, they discovered that it could change atoms of one element into atoms of another. Such findings proved that atoms were not solid and indivisible.

Relativity By 1905, the German-born physicist Albert Einstein advanced his theories of relativity. Einstein argued that measurements of space and time are not absolute but are determined by many factors, some of them unknown. This idea raised questions about Newtonian science, which compared the universe to a machine operating according to absolute laws.

In the postwar years, many scientists came to accept the theories of relativity. To much of the general public, however, Einstein's ideas seemed to reinforce the unsettling sense of old certainties crumbling and a universe whirling beyond the understanding of human reason.

Probing the Mind The Austrian physician Sigmund Freud (FROID) also challenged faith in reason. He suggested that the subconscious mind drives much human behavior. Freud said that, in civilized society, learned values such as morality and reason help people repress, or check, powerful urges.

Biography

Marie Curie 1867–1934

Marie Curie won two Nobel prizes, one in physics and one in chemistry. Still, like many other women, she had to balance her work with home duties. "I have a great deal of work," she said, "what with the housekeeping, the children, the teaching, and the laboratory, and I don't know how I shall manage it all."

Curie won worldwide fame for her groundbreaking research on radioactivity. But she paid a high price for knowledge. Her fingertips were often burned from handling radioactive material. Although she shrugged off the health dangers, she died from radiation poisoning.

Theme: Impact of the Individual Why do you think Marie Curie's achievements were unique for her time?

---

450 *Chapter 17*

Virtual Field Trip

PHSchool.com

For: Other works by the artist
Salvador Dali
Visit: PHSchool.com
Web Code: mkd-3053

**A Masterpiece
of Modern Art**
The Persistence of Memory, by the
Spanish artist Salvador Dali, is one
of the most famous works of modern art. This 1931 painting seems to
suggest a dream world where
nothing is certain, not even time.

Theme: Art and Literature
**How do you think people who
admired traditional painting would
have reacted to Dali's work?**

But an individual feels constant tension between repressed drives and
social training. This tension, argued Freud, may cause psychological illness
or physical symptoms, such as paralysis or blindness.

Freud pioneered psychoanalysis, a method of studying how the mind
works and treating mental disorders. He analyzed dreams for clues to subconscious desires and developed ways to treat mental illnesses. His ideas
had an impact far beyond medicine. Freud's work led artists and writers to
explore the subconscious mind.

Modern Art and Architecture

In the early 1900s, many western artists rejected traditional styles. Instead
of trying to reproduce the real world, they explored other dimensions of
color, line, and shape. Painters, like Henri Matisse (mah TEES), outraged the
public with their bold use of color and odd distortions. He and fellow
artists were dubbed fauves (FOHVZ), or Wild Beasts.

New Directions in Painting   Before the war, the Spanish artist Pablo
Picasso and his friend Georges Braque (BRAHK) had created a revolutionary
new style, called cubism. They broke three-dimensional objects into fragments and composed them into complex patterns of angles and planes. By
redefining objects into separate shapes, they offered a new view of reality.

Later, the Russian Vasily Kandinsky and the German Paul Klee (KLAY)
moved even further away from representing reality. Their artwork was
abstract, composed of lines, colors, and shapes with no recognizable subject
matter at all.

During and after the war, dada burst onto the Paris art world. Dada
was a revolt against civilization. One dadaist proclaimed, "Dada is life
without discipline or morality and we spit on humanity." Paintings by
artists like Hans Arp and Max Ernst were intended to shock and disturb
middle-class viewers.

Cubism and dada helped inspire surrealism, a movement that attempted to portray the workings of the unconscious mind. The Spanish surrealist
Salvador Dali used images of melting clocks or burning giraffes to suggest
the chaotic dream state described by Freud.

Architecture Architects, too, rejected classical traditions and developed new styles to match an industrial, urbanized world. The famous Bauhaus school in Germany influenced architecture by blending science and technology with design. Bauhaus designers used glass, steel, and concrete but little ornamentation.

The American architect Frank Lloyd Wright reflected the Bauhaus belief that the function of a building should determine its form. When designing a house, he used materials and forms that fit its environment.

The New Literature

In the 1920s, war novels, poetry, plays, and memoirs flowed off the presses. Works like Remarque's *All Quiet on the Western Front* exposed the grim horrors of modern warfare. Other writers heaped scorn on blundering military and political leaders. Their works reflected a powerful disgust with war that would color the European scene for decades.

A Loss of Faith To many postwar writers, the war symbolized the moral breakdown of western civilization. In 1922, the American-born English poet T. S. Eliot published *The Waste Land.* This long poem portrays the modern world as spiritually empty and barren. In *The Sun Also Rises,* the American novelist Ernest Hemingway shows the rootless wanderings of young people who lack deep convictions. "I did not care what it was all about," says the narrator. "All I wanted to know was how to live in it."

Literature of the Inner Mind As Freud's ideas became popular, some writers experimented with stream of consciousness. In this technique, a writer appears to probe a character's random thoughts and feelings without imposing any logic or order. In novels like *Mrs. Dalloway,* British novelist Virginia Woolf used stream of consciousness to explore the hidden thoughts of people as they go through the ordinary actions of their everyday lives.

The Irish novelist James Joyce went even further. In *Finnegans Wake,* he explores the inner mind of a hero who remains sound asleep throughout the novel. To convey the freedom and playfulness of the unconscious mind, Joyce invented many words—including some, like bababadalgharagtakamminarronnkonnbronntonnerronntuonnthunntrovarrhounawnskawntoohoohoordenenthurnuk, 100 letters long!

A Changing Society

In the aftermath of World War I, many people yearned to return to "normalcy"—to life as it had been before 1914. But rapid social changes would make it hard to turn back the clock.

A New Popular Culture New technologies helped create a mass culture shared by millions in the world's developed countries. Affordable cars gave middle-class people greater mobility. Movie stars such as Charlie Chaplin had fans on every continent. Radios brought news, music, and sports into homes throughout the western world.

Many radios were tuned to the new sounds of jazz. Jazz was pioneered by African American musicians who combined western harmonies with African rhythms. Jazz musicians, like trumpeter Louis Armstrong, took simple melodies and improvised endless subtle variations in rhythm and beat. They produced music that was both original and popular.

Europeans embraced American popular culture, with its greater freedom and willingness to experiment. The nightclub and the sound of jazz were symbols of that freedom. In fact, the 1920s are often called the Jazz Age.

The Younger Generation After the war, rebellious young people rejected the moral values and rules of the Victorian Age and chased after excitement.

Humanities Link

JAZZ!

Jazz is a lively improvisational musical style that first appeared in the bustling port of New Orleans in the early 1900s. It is actually a blend of many different musical traditions, including African rhythms and spirituals. Jazz caught on quickly, and by the 1920s there were jazz clubs in many cities across North America and Europe. Much of today's music, including rock and rap, has been influenced by jazz.

Louis Armstrong was one of the early jazz musicians from New Orleans. In 1922, he left New Orleans to play in Chicago. His improvised trumpeting and "scat" singing set a standard for later musicians.

Duke Ellington was a gifted piano player and composer. Born in Washington, D.C., he went to New York to pursue his career. His popular tunes include "Take the A Train."

Portfolio Assessment

Conduct research to find out more about jazz and listen to some recordings of jazz music. Then, write a song or a poem, either in the style of jazz lyrics or describing the sound of the music.

In the 1920s, record companies began to record jazz music. The music was pressed onto vinyl discs, which were often marked with colorful labels.

The Flapper
The flapper became a symbol of the rebellious "new woman" of the 1920s. Still, relatively few young women were flappers. Most continued to follow traditional lifestyles.

Theme: Continuity and Change What was new and shocking about this flapper's "look"? How are women's fashions today different from those of the 1920's?

Gertrude Stein, an American writer living in Paris, called them the "lost generation." Others saw them as immoral pleasure seekers.

The symbol of rebellious Jazz Age youth was the liberated young woman called the flapper. The first flappers were American, but their European sisters soon adopted the fashion. Flappers rejected old ways. Shocking their elders, they bobbed their hair and wore skirts far shorter than those of prewar fashions. They went out on dates unchaperoned, enjoyed wild new dance fads such as the Charleston, smoked cigarettes, and drank in nightclubs.

Women's Lives For most women, the postwar period brought limited progress. During the war, women had held a wide range of jobs. Although most women returned to the home when the war ended, their war work helped them win the vote in many western countries. A few women were elected to public office, such as Texas governor Miriam Ferguson or Lady Nancy Astor, the first woman to serve in the British Parliament.

By the 1920s, labor-saving devices had become common in middle-class homes. Washing machines, vacuum cleaners, and canned foods freed women from many time-consuming household chores. Some women found paid work outside the home. Others took volunteer jobs, providing social services or raising funds for charities.

In the new atmosphere of emancipation, women pursued careers in many arenas—from sports to the arts. Women golfers, tennis players, swimmers, and pilots set new records. Women worked as newspaper reporters, published bestselling novels, and won recognition for their artwork. Most professions, though, were still dominated by men. Women doing the same work as men earned much less.

Social Classes The war had changed social values and the class system itself. In Europe, noble families had lost sons in the fighting, while Russia's noble class was destroyed by the revolution. Peasants had suffered heavy losses. After the war, many filtered into the cities, adding their voices to protests against economic conditions. For many factory workers, wages improved in the postwar decades. Wealthy capitalists prospered in the boom times of the 1920s.

The lower middle class, however, often felt pinched. It resented the successes of big business and the rising wages of workers. As the Great Depression struck, many people from this class were attracted to radical right-wing groups.

SECTION 2 Assessment

Recall
1. **Identify:** (a) Marie Curie, (b) cubism, (c) Bauhaus, (d) T. S. Eliot, (e) Virginia Woolf, (f) James Joyce, (g) Jazz Age.
2. **Define:** (a) psychoanalysis, (b) abstract, (c) surrealism, (d) stream of consciousness, (e) flapper.

Comprehension
3. How did the ideas of Einstein and Freud contribute to a sense of uncertainty?
4. (a) How did postwar artists challenge older western traditions?
(b) What themes did postwar writers stress?
5. How did flappers symbolize changes in western society?

Critical Thinking and Writing
6. **Linking Past and Present** (a) How did technology shape popular culture in the 1920s? (b) What technologies are shaping popular culture today?
7. **Synthesizing Information** Choose one postwar writer and one postwar artist. Explain how the work of each reflected a new view of the world.

Go Online
PHSchool.com

Use the Internet to find out more about Paul Klee and the ideas that affected his paintings. Choose one painting and prepare a description and explanation based on Klee's ideas, the period in which he worked, and your own reaction to the work. For help with this activity, use **Web Code mkd-3056.**

Fascism in Italy

Reading Focus

- How did conditions in Italy favor the rise of Mussolini?
- How did Mussolini reshape Italy?
- What were the values and goals of fascist ideology?

Taking Notes

As you read this section, prepare an outline of its contents. Use Roman numerals to indicate major headings. Use capital letters for subheadings, and use numbers for the supporting details. The example here will help you get started.

I. Rise of Mussolini
  A. A leader emerges
    1.
    2.
  B. Seizing power
    1. Combat squads
    2.
    3.
  C.

Main Idea | **Angered by political and economic problems, many Italians turned to fascism for solutions.**

Setting the Scene "I hated politics and politicians," said Italo Balbo. Like many Italian veterans of World War I, he had come home to a land of economic chaos and political corruption. Italy's constitutional government, he felt, "had betrayed the hopes of soldiers, reducing Italy to a shameful peace." Disgusted and angry, Balbo rallied behind a fierce nationalist, Benito Mussolini. Mussolini's rise to power in the 1920s served as a model for ambitious strongmen elsewhere in Europe.

Rise of Mussolini

In 1919, Italian nationalists were outraged by the Paris peace treaties. As one of the victorious Allies, Italy had expected to gain territory on the Adriatic. Instead, these lands became part of the new Yugoslavia.

At home, disorders multiplied. Inspired in part by the revolution in Russia, peasants seized land, and workers went on strike or seized factories. Amid the chaos, returning veterans faced unemployment. Trade declined and taxes rose. The government, split into feuding factions, seemed powerless to end the crisis.

A Leader Emerges Into this turmoil stepped Benito Mussolini. The son of a socialist blacksmith and a teacher, Mussolini had been a socialist in his youth. During the war, however, he rejected socialism for intense nationalism. In 1919, he organized veterans and other discontented Italians into the Fascist party. They took the name from the Latin *fasces*, a bundle of sticks wrapped around an ax—a symbol of authority in ancient Rome.

With his jutting jaw and slashing phrases, Mussolini was a fiery speaker. He promised to end corruption and replace turmoil with order. He also spoke of reviving Roman greatness, pledging to turn the Mediterranean into a "Roman lake" once again.

Seizing Power Mussolini organized his supporters into black-shirted "combat squads." Rejecting the democratic process in favor of violent action, "Black Shirts" broke up socialist rallies, smashed leftist presses, and attacked farmers' cooperatives. Through intimidation and terror, Fascist gangs ousted elected officials in northern Italy. Many Italians accepted these moves because they, too, had lost faith in constitutional government.

In 1922, the Fascists made a bid for power. At a rally in Naples, they announced a "march on Rome" to demand that the government make changes. Tens of thousands of Fascists swarmed into the capital. Fearing civil war, King Victor Emmanuel III asked Mussolini to form a government as prime minister. Without firing a shot, Mussolini thus obtained a "legal" appointment from the king, undermining constitutional democracy.

Mussolini's Italy

At first, Fascists held only a few cabinet posts. By 1925, though, Mussolini had assumed more power and taken the title Il Duce (eel DOO chay), "The Leader." He suppressed rival parties, muzzled the press, rigged elections, and replaced elected officials with Fascist supporters.

In theory, Italy remained a parliamentary monarchy. In fact, it was a dictatorship upheld by terror. Critics were thrown into prison, forced into exile, or murdered. Secret police and propaganda bolstered the regime.

Economic Policy To encourage economic growth and end conflicts between owners and workers, Mussolini brought the economy under state control. Unlike socialists, though, he preserved capitalism. Under Mussolini's "corporate state," representatives of business, labor, government, and the Fascist party controlled industry, agriculture, and trade. Although production increased, this success came at the expense of workers. They were forbidden to strike, and their wages lagged.

Social Policies To Fascists, the individual was unimportant except as a member of the state. Men, women, and children were bombarded with slogans glorifying the state and Mussolini. "Believe! Obey! Fight!" loudspeakers blared and posters proclaimed. Men were urged to be ruthless, selfless warriors for the glory of Italy. Women were pushed out of paying jobs. Instead, Mussolini called on women to "win the battle of motherhood." Those who bore more than 14 children were given a medal by Il Duce himself.

Shaping the young was a major Fascist goal. Fascist youth groups toughened children and taught them to obey strict military discipline. Boys and girls learned about the glories of ancient Rome. Young Fascists marched in torchlight parades, singing patriotic hymns and chanting, "Mussolini is always right." By the 1930s, a generation of young soldiers stood ready to back Il Duce's drive to expand Italian power.

What Is Fascism?

Historians still debate the real nature of fascist ideology. Mussolini coined the term, but fascists had no single unifying set of beliefs, as Marxists did. Today, we generally use the term to describe any authoritarian government that is not communist. In the 1920s and 1930s, though, fascism meant different things in different countries.

All forms of fascism, however, shared some basic features. It was rooted in extreme nationalism. Fascists glorified action, violence, discipline, and, above all, blind loyalty to the state. "Fascism conceives of the State as an absolute," declared Mussolini, "in comparison with which all individuals or groups are relative, only to be conceived of in their relation to the State."

Fascists were antidemocratic. They rejected the Enlightenment faith in reason and the concepts of equality and liberty spread by the French Revolution. To them, democracy led to corruption and weakness and put individual or class interests above national goals. Instead, fascists emphasized emotion and the need for the citizen to serve the state.

Fascists also pursued aggressive foreign expansion. Echoing the Social Darwinist idea of "survival of the fittest," Fascist leaders glorified warfare as a necessary and noble struggle for survival.

Compared to Communism Fascists were the sworn enemies of socialists and communists. While communists had hopes for international change, fascists pursued nationalist goals. Fascists found allies among business

Mussolini's Plaster Rome

"The nation is in our hands now," declared Mussolini, "and we swear to lead her back to her ways of ancient greatness." In 1937, he inaugurated a celebration known as "The Augustan Exhibit of Roman Spirit" to commemorate the two-thousandth anniversary of the birth of Augustus Caesar. Many of the exhibits are still on display, including a scale plaster model of the city of Rome as it appeared in the 300s. Today the model, known as "Plastico," can be seen in the Museum of Roman Civilization, located in the heart of Rome. The Plastico is about 860 square feet, taking up an entire room in the museum.

Theme: Political and Social Systems Why do you think Mussolini wanted to glorify ancient Rome?

Synthesizing Information

Totalitarianism

In 1922, Benito Mussolini set up a fascist government, making Italy the first totalitarian state in Europe. Shortly afterward, Germany and the Soviet Union also came under totalitarian rule. Use the quotation, the poster, and the photograph to learn about the nature of totalitarianism.

Admiring the Leader

"[Only joy at finding such a leader] can explain the enthusiasm [Mussolini] evoked at gathering after gathering, where his mere presence drew the people from all sides to greet him with frenzied acclamations. Even the men who at first came out of mere curiosity and with indifferent or even hostile feelings gradually felt themselves fired by his personal magnetic influence. . . .

The women of the Abruzzi . . . strove to touch his hand as they would to touch a shrine or a relic. . . . The mayor of a little Sicilian village stopped his motor-car and said to him, 'I have nothing to ask of you, but this only. Perhaps you will never again pass over this ground of ours. Dismount that you may touch it with your feet!' "
—Margherita G. Sarfatti, *The Life of Benito Mussolini*
(tr. Frederic Whyte)

Fascist Propaganda

FERROVIE DELLO STATO

LE PIU' RECENTI CARROZZE DI 3ª CLASSE

This propaganda poster celebrates the introduction of new passenger cars for the Italian state railroad. The words say, "State Railroad. The Newest Third-Class Carriages."

Fascist Youth

A company of uniformed Italian boys, shouldering packs and rifles, proudly parades during a military drill.

Skills Tip

When you analyze a work of propaganda, notice how images can convey an emotional impact, even when the words do not.

Skills Assessment

1. What value is reflected in both the photograph and the poster?
   A personal freedom
   B national pride
   C prosperity
   D individuality

2. According to Sarfatti, many Italians greeted Mussolini with
   E petitions for jobs.
   F complaints about his fascist government.
   G calls for him to resign.
   H deep respect.

3. Critical Thinking **Synthesizing Information** (a) How do the quotation, the poster, and the photograph illustrate some of the features of totalitarian states? (b) Based on your reading in the chapter and using the list (from the next page) of six basic features of a totalitarian state, name three additional traits of fascist Italy.

leaders, wealthy landowners, and the lower middle class. Communists won support among urban and agricultural workers.

Despite such differences, these two ideologies had much in common. Both flourished during economic hard times by promoting extreme programs of social change. In Communist Russia as well as Fascist Italy, dictators imposed totalitarian governments in order to bring about social revolutions. In both, a party elite claimed to rule in the name of the national interest.

Totalitarian Rule Mussolini built the first totalitarian state, which became a model for others. Fascist rule in Italy was not as absolute as those of Stalin in the Soviet Union or Adolf Hitler in Germany. Still, all three governments shared these basic features: (1) a single-party dictatorship, (2) state control of the economy, (3) use of police spies and terror to enforce the will of the state, (4) strict censorship and government monopoly of the media, (5) use of schools and the media to indoctrinate and mobilize citizens, and (6) unquestioning obedience to a single leader.

Appeal Given its restrictions of individual freedom, why did fascism appeal to many Italians? First, it promised a strong, stable government and an end to the political feuding that had paralyzed democracy. Mussolini's intense nationalism also struck a chord among most ordinary Italians. He revived national pride, pledging to make the Mediterranean Sea a "Roman lake" once more. Finally, Mussolini projected a sense of power and confidence at a time of disorder and despair.

At first, Il Duce received good press outside Italy, too. Newspapers in Britain, France, and North America applauded the discipline and order of his government. "He got the trains running on time," admirers said. Only later, when Mussolini embarked on a course of foreign conquest, did western democracies protest his actions.

Looking Ahead

Three systems of government competed for influence in postwar Europe. Democracy endured in Britain and France but faced an uphill struggle in hard times. Communism emerged in Russia and won support elsewhere, but many people saw it as a dangerous threat.

In Italy, fascism offered a different formula. Its chest-thumping calls for action, national unity, and dedication to the state ignited patriotic feeling. As the Great Depression spread, other nations—most notably Germany—looked to leaders who preached fascist ideology.

Global Connections

Authoritarian Rule in Eastern Europe

Italy was not the only European nation to embrace authoritarian rule. The newly formed countries of Eastern Europe were in turmoil after World War I. They embraced democracy, but struggled with nationalist sentiments, ethnic tensions, wars, and economic problems. In 1926, General Joseph Pilsudski, a military hero who had helped liberate Poland, used the army to seize control of the country. Eventually every country in Eastern Europe, except Czechoslovakia, turned to some form of authoritarian government.

In the 1930s, President Franklin Roosevelt tried to explain why many nations had rejected democracy. "People . . . have grown tired of unemployment and insecurity," he said. "Finally, in desperation, they chose to sacrifice liberty in the hope of getting something to eat."

Theme: Political and Social Systems What methods might dictators use to reduce ethnic tensions?

SECTION 3 Assessment

Recall
1. **Identify: (a)** Black Shirts, **(b)** Il Duce.

Comprehension
2. **(a)** What problems did Italy face after World War I? **(b)** How did these problems help Mussolini win power?
3. Describe two economic or social goals of Mussolini, and explain the actions he took to achieve each goal.
4. **(a)** What values did fascism promote? **(b)** List two similarities and two differences between fascism and communism.

Critical Thinking and Writing
5. **Analyzing Information** Why do you think the Fascists blamed democracy for problems in Italy?
6. **Analyzing Primary Sources** Mussolini said, "Machines and women are the two main causes of unemployment." **(a)** What do you think he meant? **(b)** How did Mussolini's policies reflect his attitude toward women?

Reading Focus

- What problems did the Weimar Republic face?
- How did Hitler come to power?
- What political, social, economic, and cultural policies did Hitler pursue?
- How did Hitler take action against German Jews?

Vocabulary

chancellor

repudiate

concentration camp

Taking Notes

Make a cause-and-effect diagram about the rise of Hitler. This sample will help you get started.

Versailles Treaty	Inflation		

RISE OF HITLER

Main Idea Under Adolf Hitler, the Nazi government used terror, repression, and one-party rule to establish a totalitarian state.

Setting the Scene In November 1923, a German army veteran and leader of an extremist party, Adolf Hitler, tried to follow Mussolini's example. His brown-shirted thugs burst into a beer hall in Munich, where a political meeting was set to start. Hitler climbed onto a table and fired his pistol. "The National Socialist revolution has begun!" he shouted.

The coup failed, and Hitler was soon behind bars. But Hitler was a force that could not be ignored forever. Within a decade, he made a new bid for power. This time, he succeeded by legal means.

Hitler's rise to power raises disturbing questions that we still debate today. Why did Germany, which had a democratic government in the 1920s, become a totalitarian state in the 1930s? How could a ruthless, hate-filled dictator gain the enthusiastic support of many Germans?

The Weimar Republic

As World War I drew to a close, Germany tottered on the brink of chaos. Under the threat of a socialist revolution, the kaiser abdicated. Moderate leaders signed the armistice and later, under protest, the Versailles treaty.

In 1919, German leaders drafted a constitution in the city of Weimar (vī mahr). It created a democratic government known as the Weimar Republic. The constitution set up a parliamentary system led by a chancellor, or prime minister. It gave women the vote and included a bill of rights.

Struggles of the Republic The republic faced severe problems from the start. Politically, it was weak because Germany, like France, had many small parties. The chancellor had to form coalitions that easily fell apart.

The government, led by moderate democratic socialists, came under constant fire from both the left and right. Communists demanded radical changes like those Lenin had brought to Russia. Conservatives—including the old Junker nobility, military officers, and wealthy bourgeoisie—attacked the government as too liberal and weak. They longed for another strong leader like Bismarck or the kaiser. Germans of all classes blamed the Weimar Republic for the hated Versailles treaty, with its war-guilt clause and heavy reparations. In their bitterness, they looked for scapegoats. Many blamed German Jews for economic and political problems.

Inflation Economic disaster fed unrest. In 1923, when Germany fell behind in reparations payments, France occupied the coal-rich Ruhr Valley. Ruhr Germans turned to passive resistance, refusing to work. To support them,

German Inflation

In 1923, runaway inflation caused prices in Germany to soar. Here, a housewife prepares to light her stove with several million marks.

Theme: Economics and Technology What does this picture suggest about the price of fuel at the time?

the government printed huge quantities of paper money. This move set off inflation that spiraled out of control. The German mark became almost worthless. An item that cost 100 marks in July 1922 cost 944,000 marks by August 1923. A loaf of bread cost tens of thousands of marks.

Runaway inflation spread misery and despair. Salaries rose by billions of marks, but they still could not keep up with skyrocketing prices. Many middle-class families saw their savings wiped out.

Recovery and Collapse With help from the western powers, the government did bring inflation under control. In 1924, the United States gained British and French approval for a plan to reduce German reparations payments. Under the Dawes Plan, France withdrew its forces from the Ruhr, and American loans helped the German economy recover.

Germany began to prosper. Then, the Great Depression hit, reviving memories of the miseries of 1923. Germans turned to an energetic leader, Adolf Hitler, who promised to solve the economic crisis and restore Germany's former greatness.

Adolf Hitler

Hitler was born in Austria in 1889. When he was 18, he went to Vienna, hoping to enter art school, but he was turned down. Vienna was then the capital of the multinational Hapsburg empire. Austrian Germans made up just one of many ethnic groups. Yet they felt superior to Jews, Serbs, Poles, and other groups. While living in Vienna, Hitler developed the fanatical antisemitism that would later play a major role in his rise to power.

Hitler later moved to Germany and fought in the German army during World War I. Like many ex-soldiers, he despised the Weimar government which he perceived as weak and ineffectual. In 1919, he joined a small group of right-wing extremists. Within a year, he was the unquestioned leader of the National Socialist German Workers, or Nazi, party. Like Mussolini, Hitler organized his supporters into fighting squads. Nazi "Storm Troopers" battled in the streets against their political enemies.

Mein Kampf In 1923, as you have read, Hitler made a failed attempt to seize power in Munich. He was arrested, tried, and found guilty of treason. While in prison, Hitler wrote *Mein Kampf* ("My Struggle"). It would later become the basic book of Nazi goals and ideology.

Mein Kampf reflected Hitler's obsessions—extreme nationalism, racism, and antisemitism. Germans, he said, belonged to a superior "master race" of Aryans, or light-skinned Europeans, whose greatest enemies were the Jews. Hitler viewed Jews not as members of a religion but as a separate race. (He defined a Jew as anyone with one Jewish grandparent.) Echoing a familiar right-wing theme, he claimed that Germany had not lost the war but had been betrayed by a conspiracy of Marxists, Jews, corrupt politicians, and business leaders.

In his recipe for revival, Hitler urged Germans everywhere to unite into one great nation. Germany must expand, he said, to gain *Lebensraum,* or living space, for its people. Slavs and other inferior races must bow to Aryan needs. To achieve its greatness, Germany needed a strong leader, or *Führer* (FYOO ruhr). Hitler was determined to become that leader.

The Road to Power After serving less than a year, Hitler left prison. He soon renewed his table-thumping speeches. He found enthusiastic followers among veterans and lower-middle-class Germans who felt frustrated about their future. The Great Depression played into Hitler's hands. As unemployment rose, Nazi membership grew to almost a million. Hitler's program appealed to workers, the lower middle classes, small-town Germans, and business people alike. He promised to end reparations, create jobs, and defy the Versailles treaty by rearming Germany.

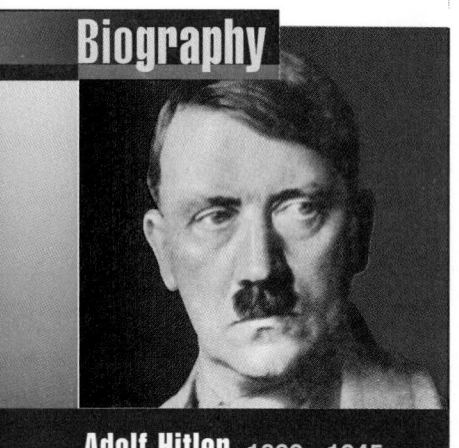

With the government paralyzed by divisions, both Nazis and Communists won more seats in the Reichstag, or lower house of the legislature. Fearing the growth of communist political power, conservative politicians turned to Hitler. Although they despised him, they believed they could control him. Thus, with conservative support, Hitler was elected chancellor in 1933 through legal, democratic means under the Weimar constitution.

Within a year, Hitler was master of Germany. He suspended civil rights, destroyed the socialists and Communists, and disbanded other political parties. Germany became a one-party state. Nazi flags, with their black swastikas, waved across the country. Like Stalin in Russia, Hitler purged his own party, brutally executing Nazis he felt were disloyal. Nazis learned that Hitler, the Führer, demanded unquestioning obedience.

Hitler's Third Reich

Once in power, Hitler moved to build a new Germany. Like Mussolini, Hitler appealed to nationalism by recalling past glories. Germany's First Reich, or empire, was the medieval Holy Roman Empire. The Second Reich was the empire forged by Bismarck in 1871. Under Hitler's new Third Reich, he boasted, the German master race would dominate Europe for 1,000 years.

Hitler soon **repudiated,** or rejected, the hated Treaty of Versailles. He began scheming to unite Germany and Austria. "Today Germany belongs to us," sang young Nazis. "Tomorrow, the world."

A Totalitarian State To achieve his goals, Hitler organized an efficient but brutal system of terror, repression, and totalitarian rule. Nazis controlled all areas of German life—from government to religion to education. Elite, black-uniformed SS troops enforced the Führer's will. His secret police, the Gestapo, rooted out opposition.

Few Germans saw or worried about this terror apparatus taking shape. Instead, they cheered Hitler's accomplishments in ending unemployment and reviving German power.

Economic Policy To combat the Great Depression, Hitler launched large public works programs (as did Britain and the United States). Tens of thousands of people were put to work building highways and housing or replanting forests. Hitler also began a crash program to rearm Germany, in violation of the Versailles treaty. Demand for military hardware stimulated business and helped eliminate unemployment.

Nazis March
Militarism was a key element of Nazi ideology. Here, German soldiers march at a Nazi party rally in Nuremberg. The swastika, which the Nazis adopted as a party symbol, actually dates back to ancient times.

Theme: Political and Social Systems **Why would mass meetings and marches be important in a totalitarian state?**

Purging German Culture
The Nazis tried to "purify" German culture by destroying ideas they felt were dangerous. Here, enthusiastic youngsters participate in book burning.

Theme: Political and Social Systems What impression does this photograph give you of youth in Nazi Germany?

Like Mussolini, Hitler preserved capitalism but brought big business and labor under government control. Few objected to this loss of freedom because their standard of living rose. Propaganda highlighted the improvements. "Strength Through Joy" programs offered workers vigorous outdoor vacations that also made them physically fit for military service.

Social Policy Like the Fascists in Italy and the Communists in the Soviet Union, the Nazis indoctrinated young people with their ideology. In passionate speeches, the Führer spewed his message of racism. He urged young Germans to destroy their so-called enemies without mercy:

"Extremes must be fought by extremes. Against the infection of [Marxism], against the Jewish pestilence, we must hold aloft a flaming ideal. And if others speak of the World and Humanity, we must say the Fatherland—and only the Fatherland!"
—Adolf Hitler, *My New Order*

On hikes and in camps, the "Hitler Youth" pledged absolute loyalty to Germany and undertook physical fitness programs to prepare for war.

Like Fascists in Italy, Nazis sought to limit women's roles. Women were dismissed from upper-level jobs and turned away from universities. To raise the birthrate, Nazis offered "pure-blooded Aryan" women rewards for having more children. Still, Hitler's goal to keep women in the home and out of the work force applied mainly to the privileged. As German industry expanded, women factory workers were needed.

Purging German Culture

Nazis used education as a propaganda tool. School courses and textbooks were rewritten to reflect Nazi racial views. "We teach and learn history," said one Nazi educator, "not to say how things actually happened but to instruct the German people from the past."

The Arts The Nazis sought to purge, or purify, German culture. They denounced modern art, saying that it was corrupted by Jewish influences. They condemned jazz because of its African roots. Instead, the Nazis glorified old German myths such as those re-created in the operas of Richard Wagner.

At huge public bonfires, Nazis burned books of which they disapproved. *All Quiet on the Western Front* was one of many works that went up in flames. The Nazis viewed Remarque's novel as an insult to the German military.

Nazism and the Churches Hitler despised Christianity as "weak" and "flabby." He sought to replace religion with his racial creed. In an attempt to control the churches, the Nazis combined all Protestant sects into a single state church. They closed Catholic schools and muzzled the Catholic clergy.

Although some clergy supported the new regime or remained silent, others courageously denounced Hitler. Martin Niemoller, a Lutheran minister, preached against Nazi policies and was later jailed. He later commented:

"The Nazis came first for the Communists. But I wasn't a Communist, so I didn't speak up. Then they came for the Jews, but I wasn't a Jew so I didn't speak up. . . . Then they came for the Catholics, but I was a Protestant so I didn't speak up.

Then they came for me. By that time, there was no one left to speak up."
—Martin Niemoller, quoted in *Time* magazine

The Campaign Against the Jews Begins

In his fanatical antisemitism, Hitler set out to drive Jews from Germany. In 1935, the Nuremberg Laws placed severe restrictions on Jews. They were prohibited from marrying non-Jews, attending or teaching at German schools or universities, holding government jobs, practicing law or medicine, or publishing books. Nazis beat and robbed Jews and roused mobs to do the same. Many German Jews, including the brilliant scientist, Albert Einstein, fled the growing menace and sought refuge in other countries.

Night of Broken Glass On November 7, 1938, a young Jew, whose parents had been mistreated in Germany, shot and wounded a German diplomat in Paris. Hitler used the incident as an excuse to stage an attack on all Jews.

Kristallnacht (krihs TAHL nahkt), or the "Night of Broken Glass," took place on November 9 and 10. Nazi-led mobs attacked Jewish communities all over Germany, shouting "Revenge for Paris! Down with the Jews!" They smashed windows, looted shops, and burned synagogues. Many Jews were dragged from their homes and beaten in the streets.

Aftermath World reaction to *Kristallnacht* was swift and negative. Still, Hitler was unmoved. He even made the Jewish victims pay for the damage.

In the years that followed, Hitler's campaign against the Jews intensified. Tens of thousands of Jews were sent to concentration camps, detention centers for civilians considered enemies of the state. Before long, Hitler and his henchmen were making even more sinister plans for what they called the "final solution"—the extermination of all Jews.

Looking Ahead

In the 1930s, Germany became Europe's second fascist state. Germans of all classes responded to Hitler's hypnotic speeches and programs, which restored their national pride. Despite the warnings of some courageous Germans, most individuals ignored the ugly side of Nazi rule. Those who opposed Nazism were not united and were soon silenced.

While Hitler won absolute power at home, he moved boldly to expand Germany's power in Europe. In the next chapter, you will see how Nazi aggression set the stage for the largest war the world has yet seen.

SECTION 4 Assessment

Recall

1. **Identify:** (a) Ruhr Valley, (b) Dawes Plan, (c) *Mein Kampf,* (d) Third Reich, (e) Gestapo, (f) Nuremberg Laws, (g) *Kristallnacht.*
2. **Define:** (a) chancellor, (b) repudiate, (c) concentration camp.

Comprehension

3. List three problems faced by the Weimar Republic.
4. How did the depression pave the way for the rise of Hitler?
5. (a) How did Hitler create a one-party dictatorship? (b) What racial and nationalistic ideas did Nazis promote?
6. What were some of the restrictions that Hitler placed on German Jews?

Critical Thinking and Writing

7. **Defending a Position** Do you think that there are any circumstances under which a government would be justified in banning books or censoring ideas? Explain.
8. **Drawing Conclusions** Both Stalin in the Soviet Union and Hitler in Germany instituted ruthless campaigns against supposed enemies of the state. Why do you think dictators need to find scapegoats for their nation's ills?

Go Online
PHSchool.com

Use the Internet to learn more about the rise of Hitler. Then, write a newspaper editorial for a western paper describing the day when Hitler became chancellor of Germany. For help with this activity, use **Web Code mkd-3055.**

Creating a Chapter Summary

On a sheet of paper, draw a Venn diagram to compare Italy and Germany in the postwar years. Place information relating to Italy in the circle marked Italy and information relating to Germany in the circle marked Germany. Place information that relates to both countries in the part of the circles that overlaps.

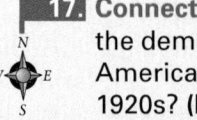

Italy
- Mussolini becomes *Il Duce*
- Black Shirts use intimidation and violence
-

Single-party dictatorship
-

Germany
- Hitler becomes *Führer*
-

For additional review and enrichment activities, see the interactive version of *World History* available on the Web and on CD-ROM.

Go Online
PHSchool.com
For practice test questions for Chapter 17, use **Web Code mka-3066.**

Building Vocabulary

Write sentences, using the chapter vocabulary words listed below, leaving blanks where the vocabulary words would go. Exchange your sentences with another student and fill in the blanks in each other's sentences.

1. disarmament
2. overproduction
3. margin buying
4. psychoanalysis
5. surrealism
6. stream of consciousness
7. flapper
8. chancellor
9. repudiate
10. concentration camp

Recalling Key Facts

11. What imbalances helped cause the Great Depression of the 1930s?
12. What was the Maginot Line?
13. How did the literature of the 1920s reflect the influence of World War I?
14. Why did the ideology of fascism appeal to many Italians?
15. Describe the economic policies that Hitler pursued as German leader.
16. How did racist theories shape Hitler's social policies?

Critical Thinking and Writing

17. **Connecting to Geography (a)** Why did the demand for raw materials from Latin America, Africa, and Asia fall in the 1920s? **(b)** How did this change in demand affect the world economy?
18. **Linking Past and Present** The manners and culture of the 1920s created a "generation gap" between young people and their elders. Do present-day manners and culture create a similar "generation gap"? Explain.
19. **Recognizing Propaganda (a)** Give three examples of Hitler's use of propaganda. **(b)** Why was propaganda an important Nazi tool?
20. **Identifying Main Ideas** Reread Martin Niemoller's words about Nazism. Then, restate Niemoller's main point in your own words.
21. **Recognizing Points of View** "England can only be saved by direct action. When it's saved, we can begin to think about Parliament again." Based on what you have read, which of the three competing postwar ideologies does this statement express—democracy, fascism, or communism? Explain.

Gaetano Salvemini was an Italian college professor. In the 1920s, he was forced to resign his position and go into exile. Here, Salvemini describes events after an attempt was made on Mussolini's life in 1926. Read the passage, then answer the questions that follow.

"At Como, the Fascists got hold of many of the Opposition and painted their faces in three colors. Amongst the persons who suffered this vile treatment were the proprietor of a clock factory at Monte Olimpino, the proprietor of a cement factory at Pontchiano, and Commendatore Rosasco, one of the most important silk weavers of the district. The houses of Signor Noseda, a Member of Parliament, of the lawyer Beltramini-Frontini, and of the priest Primo Noiana, were sacked. . . .

At Brescia, the printing establishment of the paper Il Cittadino di Brescia, *and the headquarters of the Christian-Democrat organizations were smashed and burnt."*

—Gaetano Salvemini, *The Fascist Dictatorship in Italy*

22. How did the Fascists respond to the assassination attempt on Mussolini?

23. (a) Why do you think the Fascists painted the faces of some people? (b) Do you think this was an effective tactic?

24. (a) How would you describe the people persecuted by the Fascists? (b) Why do you think these people were chosen?

25. What message do you think the Fascists were trying to send?

26. Reread the description of *Kristallnacht* at the end of Section 4. (a) How were the tactics used by Italian Fascists and German Nazis similar? (b) Why do you think fascist dictatorships often used such tactics?

Go Online
PHSchool.com

Use the Internet to research the economic systems of capitalism, socialism, and communism *or* the political systems of democracy and totalitarianism. Then, make a graphic organizer that compares and contrasts the systems you chose. For help with this activity, use **Web Code mkd-3067.**

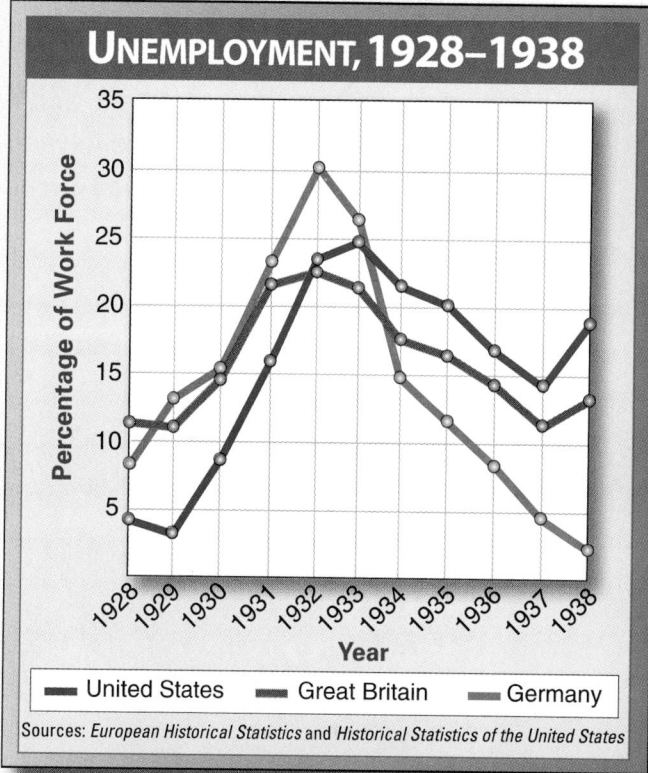

UNEMPLOYMENT, 1928–1938

Percentage of Work Force vs *Year*

— United States   — Great Britain   — Germany

Sources: *European Historical Statistics* and *Historical Statistics of the United States*

Among the nations hardest hit by the Great Depression were the three titans of the Industrial Revolution—Britain, Germany, and the United States. Study the graph, then answer the following questions:

27. What was Britain's unemployment rate in 1928? In 1931?

28. Which nation shown here had the lowest unemployment rate in 1928? In 1933?

29. (a) During what year did unemployment in Germany reach its highest point? (b) In what year did Hitler become chancellor? (c) How are these events related?

30. (a) What trend do you see in the unemployment rate in the United States from 1933 to 1937? (b) Based on what you have read, how might you explain this trend?

31. (a) What trend do you see in Germany's unemployment rate from 1932 to 1938? (b) Based on what you have read, how might you explain this trend?

Skills Tip

When you look at a graph, be aware of what was going on during that time period. Knowing key events may indicate the causes of certain trends.

CHAPTER 18

World War II and Its Aftermath 1931–1955

Chapter Preview

1 Aggression, Appeasement, and War
2 The Global Conflict: Axis Advances
3 The Global Conflict: Allied Successes
4 Toward Victory
5 From World War to Cold War

¡a las armas!

EL DEBER NO ADMITE DISCULPAS

1936
Spanish Civil War begins. This anti-fascist poster reads, "To Arms! No one is excused from duty."

1939
Germany invades Poland, sparking World War II. Here, a German tank and motorcycle corps speeds through the Polish countryside.

1935
Italy invades Ethiopia.

CHAPTER EVENTS

1930   1935   1940

GLOBAL EVENTS

1930 Mohandas K. Gandhi leads the Salt March in India.

1934 Chinese Communists flee the Guomindang in the Long March.

Major Battles of World War II, 1939–1945

World War II was fought on land and sea. Battles took place on several continents.

Legend:
- Allied powers and areas under Allied control, 1939
- Axis powers and areas under Axis control, 1939
- ★ Battle sites

1939: German invasion of Poland

1942: Battle of Midway

1945: Fall of Berlin

1944: Allied invasion of France (D-Day)

1941: Japanese attack on Pearl Harbor

1942–1943: Battle of Stalingrad

1945: Atomic bombing of Hiroshima and Nagasaki

Robinson Projection
0   1500   3000 Miles
0   1500   3000 Kilometers

PACIFIC OCEAN

ATLANTIC OCEAN

INDIAN OCEAN

PACIFIC OCEAN

Honolulu Star-Bulletin 1st EXTRA

(Associated Press by Transpacific Telephone)

SAN FRANCISCO, Dec. 7.—President Roosevelt announced this morning that Japanese planes had attacked Manila and Pearl Harbor.

WAR!
OAHU BOMBED BY JAPANESE PLANES

1941
Japan bombs Pearl Harbor, on the the Hawaiian island of Oahu, and the United States enters the war.

1945
World War II ends. To honor the occasion, Allied troops in Paris march through the Arc de Triomphe.

1955
Postwar conflict between the Soviets and their former allies leads to the creation of the Warsaw Pact.

1945   1950   1955

1947 Britain grants independence to India, and the separate nation of Pakistan is created.

1949 Mao Zedong founds the People's Republic of China.

Aggression, Appeasement, and War

Reading Focus

- How did dictators and the Spanish Civil War challenge world peace?
- How did continuing German aggression lead Europe toward war?
- What factors encouraged the coming of war?

Vocabulary

sanction
appeasement
pacifism
Anschluss

Taking Notes

On a sheet of paper, make a table like the one shown here. As you read this section, complete the table by adding information about how dictators challenged world peace.

JAPAN	ITALY	GERMANY	SPAIN
• 1931 Manchuria seized	•	•	•
•			

Main Idea During the 1930s, dictators undermined world peace.

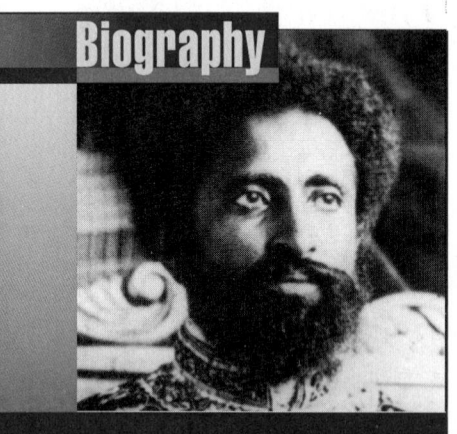

Biography

Haile Selassie 1892–1975

When Tafari Makonnen became emperor of Ethiopia in 1930, he took the name Haile Selassie, which means "Might of the Trinity," to show that his power was conferred by God. The Ethiopian people believed that their leader was descended from King Solomon.

Selassie was exiled during the Italian occupation, but returned after four years. He wanted to modernize his country. Selassie oversaw the writing of a constitution, established a parliament and cabinet, initiated land reforms, and encouraged all adults to vote. He remained in office until 1974, when a military group seized power.

Theme: Impact of the Individual How did Selassie share his power?

Setting the Scene During the 1920s, the western democracies tried to strengthen the framework for peace. In the 1930s, that structure crumbled. Dictators in Spain, Germany, and Italy, along with militarists in Japan, pursued ambitious goals for empire. They scorned peace and glorified war.

Unlike these dictators, leaders of the western democracies were haunted by memories of the Great War. Spurred by voters who demanded "no more war," the leaders of Britain, France, and the United States tried to avoid conflict through diplomacy. During the 1930s, the two sides tested each other's commitment and will.

Dictators Challenge World Peace

Challenges to peace followed a pattern throughout the 1930s. Dictators took aggressive action but met only verbal protests and pleas for peace from the democracies. Mussolini and Hitler viewed that desire for peace as weakness and responded with new acts of aggression. With hindsight, we can see the shortcomings of the democracies' policies. We must remember, however, that these policies were the product of long and careful deliberation. At the time, people strongly believed they would work.

Japan on the Move One of the earliest tests had been posed by Japan. Japanese military leaders and ultranationalists thought that Japan should have an empire equal to those of the western powers. In pursuit of this goal, Japan seized Manchuria in 1931. When the League of Nations condemned the aggression, Japan withdrew from the organization.

Japan's easy success strengthened the militarists. In 1937, Japanese armies overran much of eastern China. Once again, western protests had no effect on the conqueror.

Italy Invades Ethiopia In Italy, Mussolini used his new, modern military to pursue his own imperialist ambitions. He looked first to Ethiopia, in northeastern Africa. Italy's defeat by the Ethiopians at the battle of Adowa in 1896 still rankled.

In 1935, Italy invaded Ethiopia. Although the Ethiopians resisted bravely, their outdated weapons were no match for Mussolini's tanks, machine guns, poison gas, and airplanes. The Ethiopian king Haile Selassie (HĪ lee suh LAS ee) appealed to the League of Nations for help. The League voted sanctions, or penalties, against Italy for having violated international law. But the League had no power to enforce the sanctions, and by early 1936, Italy had conquered Ethiopia.

Hitler's Challenge By then, Hitler, too, had tested the will of the western democracies and found it weak. First, he built up the German military in defiance of the Versailles treaty. Then, in 1936, he sent troops into the "demilitarized" Rhineland bordering France—another treaty violation.

Germans hated the Versailles treaty, and Hitler's successful challenge won him greater popularity at home. Western democracies denounced his moves but took no real action. Instead, they adopted a policy of appeasement, giving in to the demands of an aggressor to keep the peace.

Appeasement and Neutrality The western policy of appeasement developed for a number of reasons. France was demoralized, suffering from political divisions at home. It could not move against Hitler without British support.

The British, however, had no desire to confront the German dictator. Some even thought that Hitler's actions constituted a justifiable response to the terms of the Versailles treaty, which they believed had been too harsh against Germany.

In both Britain and France, many saw Hitler and fascism as a defense against a worse evil—the spread of Soviet communism. Additionally, the Great Depression sapped the energies of the western democracies. Finally, widespread pacifism, or opposition to all war, and disgust with the destruction during the previous war pushed many governments to seek peace at any price.

As war clouds gathered in Europe in the mid-1930s, the United States Congress passed a series of Neutrality Acts. One law forbade the sale of arms to any nation at war. Others outlawed loans to warring nations and prohibited Americans from traveling on ships of warring powers. The fundamental goal of American policy, however, was to avoid involvement in a European war, not to prevent such a conflict.

Rome-Berlin-Tokyo Axis In the face of the democracies' apparent weakness, Germany, Italy, and Japan formed what became known as the Rome-Berlin-Tokyo Axis. The Axis powers agreed to fight Soviet communism. They also agreed not to interfere with one another's plans for expansion. The agreement cleared the way for these anti-democratic, aggressor powers to take even bolder steps.

Axis Leaders
Benito Mussolini (left) and Adolf Hitler (right) were two of the leaders in the Rome-Berlin-Tokyo Axis. Here, they view a parade staged in Mussolini's honor during his 1937 visit to Germany.

Theme: Political and Social Systems What did the Axis powers agree to do?

The Spanish Civil War

In 1936, Spain plunged into civil war. Although the Spanish Civil War was a local struggle, it soon drew other European powers into the fighting.

From Monarchy to Republic In the 1920s, Spain was a monarchy dominated by a landowning upper class, the Catholic Church, and the military. Most Spaniards were poor peasants or urban workers. In 1931, popular unrest against the old order forced the king to leave Spain. A republic was set up with a new, more liberal constitution.

The republican government passed a series of controversial reforms. It took over some Church lands and ended Church control of education. It redistributed some land to peasants, gave women the vote, and ended some privileges of the old ruling class. Spanish public opinion was divided. Leftists demanded more radical reforms. Conservatives, who were backed by the military, rejected change. Although most Spaniards wanted a peaceful democracy, clashes between leftists and rightists created chaos.

Global Connections

Fighting and Writing in Spain

Although the United States government remained neutral in the Spanish Civil War, nearly 3,000 American citizens, as members of the Abraham Lincoln Brigade, joined the Loyalists.

Some American journalists in Spain covered the war for newspapers or magazines. One was Ernest Hemingway, who described Madrid following a German air raid: ". . . with the air still full of heavy granite dust and high explosive smoke, the sidewalks scattered by new round jagged holes with blood trails leading into half the doorways you passed." Hemingway later turned his articles into a novel, *For Whom the Bell Tolls*.

Theme: Art and Literature
How might Hemingway's war experiences have contributed to the success of his novel?

Nationalists Versus Loyalists   In 1936, a conservative general named Francisco Franco led a revolt that touched off a bloody civil war. Fascists and supporters of right-wing policies rallied to the banner of Franco's forces, called Nationalists. Supporters of the republic, known as Loyalists, included communists, socialists, and supporters of democracy.

Hitler and Mussolini sent arms and forces to help Franco. Close to 37,000 volunteers from Germany, Italy, the Soviet Union, and the western democracies joined the International Brigades and fought alongside the Loyalists against fascism. The governments of Britain, France, and the United States, however, remained neutral.

A Dress Rehearsal   Both sides committed horrible atrocities. The ruinous struggle took almost one million lives. One of the worst horrors was a German air raid on Guernica, a small Spanish market town that lacked any military value. One April morning in 1937, German bombers streaked over the market square. They dropped their load of bombs and then swooped low to machine-gun anyone in the streets who had survived the first attack. An estimated 1,600 innocent people were killed.

To Nazi leaders, the attack on Guernica was an "experiment" to identify what their new planes could do. To the world, it was a grim warning of the destructive power of modern warfare.

By 1939, Franco had triumphed. Once in power, he created a fascist dictatorship like those of Hitler and Mussolini. He rolled back earlier reforms, killed or jailed enemies, and used terror to promote order.

German Aggression Continues

In the meantime, Hitler pursued his goal of bringing all German-speaking people into the Third Reich. He also took steps to gain "living space" for Germans in Eastern Europe. Hitler, who believed in the superiority of the German, or "Aryan race," thought that Germany had a right to conquer the inferior Slavs to the east. "Nature is cruel," he claimed, "so we may be cruel, too. . . . I have a right to remove millions of an inferior race that breeds like vermin."

Austria Annexed   From the beginning, Nazi propaganda had found fertile ground in Austria. By 1938, Hitler was ready to engineer the Anschluss, or union of Austria and Germany. Early that year, he forced the Austrian chancellor to appoint Nazis to key cabinet posts. When the Austrian leader balked at other demands, Hitler sent in the German army "to preserve order." To indicate his new role as ruler of Austria, Hitler made a speech from the Hofburg Palace, the former residence of the Hapsburg emperors.

The Anschluss violated the Versailles treaty and created a brief war scare. But Hitler quickly silenced any Austrians who opposed him. And since the western democracies took no action, Hitler easily had his way.

The Czech Crisis   Germany's next victim was Czechoslovakia. At first, Hitler insisted that the three million Germans in the Sudetenland—a region of western Czechoslovakia—be given autonomy. The demand set off new alarms among the democracies.

Czechoslovakia was one of only two remaining democracies in Eastern Europe. (Finland was the other.) Still, Britain and France were not willing to go to war to save it. As British and French leaders searched for a peaceful solution, Hitler increased his demands. The Sudetenland, he said, must be annexed to Germany.

At the Munich Conference in September 1938, British and French leaders again chose appeasement. They caved in to Hitler's demands and then persuaded the Czechs to surrender the Sudetenland without a fight. In exchange, Hitler assured Britain and France that he had no further plans to expand his territory.

Aggression in Europe to 1939

Legend:
- Under German control September 1, 1939
- Under Italian control September 1, 1939
- Maginot Line
- German concentration camps, 1939

Azimuthal Equal Area Projection

0 — 250 — 500 Miles
0 — 250 — 500 Kilometers

Map labels: NORWAY, SWEDEN, ESTONIA, LATVIA, LITHUANIA, IRELAND, GREAT BRITAIN, North Sea, DENMARK, Baltic Sea, Danzig, POLISH CORRIDOR, USSR, NETH., Sachsenhausen, GERMANY, Buchenwald, POLAND, BELG., LUX., RHINELAND March 1936, CZECHOSLOVAKIA March 1939, SUDETENLAND September 1938, Mauthausen, Dachau, ATLANTIC OCEAN, FRANCE, SWITZ., AUSTRIA March 1938, HUNGARY, ROMANIA, PORTUGAL, SPAIN, CORSICA, ITALY, YUGOSLAVIA, Black Sea, BULGARIA, SARDINIA, ALBANIA April 1939, GREECE, TURKEY, Mediterranean Sea, SICILY

"Peace for Our Time" Returning from Munich, British prime minister Neville Chamberlain told cheering crowds that he had achieved "peace for our time." To Parliament, he declared that the Munich Pact had "saved Czechoslovakia from destruction and Europe from Armageddon." French leader Edouard Daladier had a different reaction to the joyous crowds that greeted him in Paris. "The fools, why are they cheering?" he asked.

The Czech crisis revealed the Nazi menace. British politician Winston Churchill, who had long warned of the Nazi threat, judged the diplomats harshly: "They had to choose between war and dishonor. They chose dishonor; they will have war."

Europe Plunges Toward War

Just as Churchill predicted, Munich did not bring peace. Instead, Europe plunged rapidly toward war. In March 1939, Hitler gobbled up the rest of Czechoslovakia. The democracies finally accepted the fact that appeasement had failed. At last thoroughly alarmed, they promised to protect Poland, most likely the next target of Hitler's expansion.

Nazi-Soviet Pact In August 1939, Hitler stunned the world by announcing a nonaggression pact with his great enemy—Joseph Stalin, the Soviet dictator. Publicly, the Nazi-Soviet Pact bound Hitler and Stalin to peaceful relations. Secretly, the two agreed (1) not to fight if the other went to war and (2) to divide up Poland and other parts of Eastern Europe.

The pact was based not on friendship or respect but on mutual need. Hitler feared communism as Stalin feared fascism. But Hitler wanted a free hand in Poland. Also, he did not want to fight a war with the western democracies and the Soviet Union at the same time.

Skills Assessment

Geography Between 1936 and 1939, Germany and Italy repeatedly threatened the peace in Europe.

1. **Location** On the map, locate **(a)** Germany, **(b)** Italy, **(c)** Sudetenland, **(d)** Rhineland, **(e)** Albania, **(f)** Dachau.
2. **Region** Locate the region called the Polish Corridor. Why is that an appropriate name for the region?
3. **Critical Thinking Applying Information (a)** What example of Italian aggression is not on the map? **(b)** How could the map be changed to show that aggression?

For his part, Stalin had sought allies among the western democracies against the Nazi menace. Mutual suspicions, however, kept them apart. By joining with Hitler, Stalin bought time to build up Soviet defenses. He also saw a chance for important territorial gains.

Invasion of Poland On September 1, 1939, a week after the Nazi-Soviet Pact, German forces invaded Poland. Two days later, Britain and France honored their commitment to Poland and declared war on Germany. World War II had begun. One British poet caught the overwhelming mood of gloom in these lines:

"In the nightmare of the dark
All the dogs of Europe bark,
And the living nations wait,
Each sequestered in its hate."
—W. H. Auden, "In Memory of W. B. Yeats"

Why War Came

Many factors contributed to the outbreak of World War II. You have learned some of the reasons behind Axis aggression. You have also seen why western democracies adopted a policy of appeasement. Today, historians often see the war as an effort to revise the 1919 peace settlement. The Versailles treaty had divided much of the world into two camps—those who were satisfied with its terms and those who were not. Germany, Italy, Japan, and the Soviet Union all felt betrayed or excluded by the settlement.

Since 1939, people have debated issues such as why the western democracies failed to respond forcefully to the Nazi threat, and whether they could have stopped Hitler if they had responded. Dreading war, the democracies hoped that diplomacy and compromise would right old wrongs and prevent further aggression. They were distracted by their own political and economic problems and misread Hitler's intentions. Most disregarded even Hitler's declared goals in *Mein Kampf*.

Some historians assert that Britain and France could have stopped Hitler in 1936 by aiding Loyalist Spain before Germany was fully rearmed. But neither country was willing to risk war. The devastation of World War I, combined with awareness of the destructive power of modern technology, made the idea of more fighting unbearable. Unfortunately, when war came, it proved to be even more horrendous than anyone had imagined.

SECTION 1 Assessment

Recall

1. **Identify:** (a) Haile Selassie, (b) Rome-Berlin-Tokyo Axis, (c) Guernica, (d) Munich Conference, (e) Neville Chamberlain, (f) Nazi-Soviet Pact.
2. **Define:** (a) sanction, (b) appeasement, (c) pacifism, (d) Anschluss.

Comprehension

3. (a) How did Japan, Italy, and Germany test the resolve of western democracies before 1937? (b) Explain how other countries participated in the Spanish Civil War.

4. Identify major acts of German aggression in 1938 and 1939.
5. How did appeasement lead to the outbreak of war?

Critical Thinking and Writing

6. **Recognizing Causes and Effects** How was the Munich Conference a turning point in the road toward world war?
7. **Analyzing Information** Why do you think some historians call the period between 1919 and 1939 the 20-year armistice?

Go Online
PHSchool.com

Use the Internet to find out more about the Munich Conference of 1938. Write a letter to the editor describing your opinion of Prime Minister Chamberlain's actions at the conference. For help with this activity, use **Web Code mkd-3174.**

The Global Conflict: Axis Advances

Reading Focus

- What early gains allowed the Axis powers to control much of Europe?

- What were the Battle of Britain and Operation Barbarossa?

- How did Japan respond to growing American involvement?

Vocabulary

blitzkrieg

radar

sonar

Taking Notes

As you read this section, make a time line on a separate sheet of paper. Record key events in the global conflict from 1939 to 1942. The sample on this page will help you get started.

1939	1940	1941	1942
Germany invades Poland			

Main Idea The early years of World War II were marked by Axis victories.

Setting the Scene

"Hitler will collapse the day we declare war on Germany," predicted a confident French general on the eve of World War II. He could not have been more wrong. World War II, the costliest war in history, lasted six years—from 1939 to 1945. It pitted the Axis powers, chiefly Germany, Italy, and Japan, against the Allied powers, which eventually included Britain, France, the Soviet Union, China, the United States, and 45 other nations.

Early Axis Gains

On September 1, 1939, Nazi forces stormed into Poland, revealing the enormous power of Hitler's blitzkrieg, or "lightning war." First, German planes bombed airfields, factories, towns, and cities, and screaming dive bombers fired on troops and civilians. Then, fast-moving tanks and troop transports roared into the country. The Polish army fought back unsuccessfully.

While Germany attacked from the west, Stalin's forces invaded from the east, grabbing lands promised to them under the Nazi-Soviet Pact. Within a month, Poland ceased to exist.

Hitler passed the winter without much further action. Stalin's armies, however, pushed on into the Baltic states of Estonia, Latvia, and Lithuania. Soviet forces also seized part of Finland, which put up stiff but unsuccessful resistance.

The "Phony War" During that first winter, the French hunkered down behind the Maginot Line. Britain sent troops to wait with them. Some reporters referred to this quiet time as the "phony war."

Then, in April 1940, the war exploded into action. Hitler launched a blitzkrieg against Norway and Denmark, both of which soon fell. Next, his forces slammed into the Netherlands and Belgium.

Miracle of Dunkirk By May, German forces were pouring into France. Retreating British forces were soon trapped between the advancing Nazis and the waters of the

Invasion of Poland
World War II was the first war to use airplanes in large-scale attacks. Here, German Stuka dive bombers fly over Poland.

Theme: Economics and Technology How would airplanes be used in wartime?

English Channel. In a desperate gamble, the British sent all available naval vessels, merchant ships, and even fishing and pleasure boats across the channel to pluck stranded troops off the beaches of Dunkirk and Ostend.

Despite German air attacks, the improvised armada ferried more than 300,000 troops to safety in Britain. This heroic rescue, dubbed the "miracle of Dunkirk," greatly raised British morale.

France Falls   Meanwhile, German forces headed south toward Paris. Italy declared war on France and attacked from the south. Overrun and demoralized, France surrendered. On June 22, 1940, in a forest clearing in northeastern France, Hitler avenged the German defeat of 1918. He forced the French to sign the surrender documents in the same railroad car in which Germany had signed the armistice ending World War I. Following the surrender, Germany occupied northern France. In the south, the Germans set up a "puppet state," with its capital at Vichy (VIHSH ee).

Some French officers escaped to England and set up a government-in-exile. Led by Charles de Gaulle, these "free French" worked to liberate their homeland. Within France, resistance fighters used guerrilla tactics against German forces.

Africa and the Balkans   Axis armies also pushed into North Africa and the Balkans. In September 1940, Mussolini ordered forces from Italy's North African colony of Libya into Egypt. When the British army repulsed these invaders, Hitler sent a brilliant commander, General Erwin Rommel, to North Africa. The "Desert Fox," as he was called, chalked up a string of successes in 1941 and 1942. He pushed the British back across the desert toward Cairo, in Egypt.

In October 1940, Italian forces invaded Greece. They encountered stiff resistance, and in 1941 German troops once again provided reinforcements. Both Greece and Yugoslavia were added to the growing Axis empire. Even after the Axis triumph, however, Greek and Yugoslav guerrillas plagued the occupying forces.

Meanwhile, both Bulgaria and Hungary had joined the Axis alliance. By 1941, the Axis powers or their allies controlled most of Western Europe.

The Technology of Modern Warfare   The whirlwind Nazi advance revealed the awesome power of modern warfare. Air power took a prominent role. After its tryout in Spain, the Luftwaffe, or German air force, perfected methods of bombing civilian as well as military targets. Hitler also used fast-moving armored tanks and troop carriers along with parachute troops to storm through Europe.

Technology created a war machine with even greater destructive power. Scientists and engineers improved the design and effectiveness of airplanes and submarines. They produced ever more deadly bombs and invented hundreds of new devices, such as radar to detect airplanes and sonar to detect submarines. At the same time, research also led to medical advances to treat the wounded and new synthetic products to replace scarce strategic goods.

The Battle of Britain and the Blitz

With the fall of France in June 1940, Britain stood alone in Western Europe. Hitler was sure that the British would sue for peace. But Winston Churchill, who had replaced Neville Chamberlain as prime minister, had other plans. For many years, Churchill had been a lone voice against the Nazi threat. In 1940, he rallied the British to fight on:

> "We shall defend our island, whatever the cost may be.
> We shall fight on the beaches, we shall fight on the landing
> grounds, we shall fight in the fields and in the streets, we
> shall fight in the hills; we shall never surrender."
> —Winston Churchill, radio address, June 4, 1940

Rationing and New Products

What do nylon, margarine, and synthetic rubber have in common? All three were used during World War II to replace consumer goods needed for the war effort.

Before the war, women often wore silk stockings. The supply of silk dried up, however, as the army used it to make parachutes. In response, stocking manufacturers switched to nylon, a synthetic fabric developed just before the war.

During World War II, butterfat was needed to make cheese for soldiers. Stores replaced butter with margarine, a little-used vegetable oil substance that had been developed in the 1860s.

When the Japanese invaded Southeast Asia, they cut off the supply of rubber. The United States responded by developing synthetic rubber, modeled on a German invention from World War I.

Theme: Economics and Technology How did technology reduce the impact of shortages during World War II?

Surviving the Blitz

You are glad you heeded Churchill's warnings and prepared for a German assault on London. For the forty-fifth night in a row, the air-raid sirens wail. Soon, the unmistakable drone of German bomber engines will fill the air. This will be followed by the high-pitched shriek of falling bombs and the booming of antiaircraft guns.

You race with members of your family to the nearest shelter—an underground (subway) station. No trains run through it now. Instead, you and hundreds of others can sleep here for the night—safely, you hope. Someone begins an upbeat song. . . .

Bombs pound the city, turning buildings to rubble. At dawn, hours after the "all-clear" sirens sound, you climb up to the street and head home. Miraculously, the high dome of St. Paul's Cathedral stands proud above the damage. It is a symbol that "London can take it."

Portfolio Assessment

As a Londoner living through the wartime blitz, you are keeping a journal of your experiences. Write a journal entry describing your night in the underground during the raid and what you saw on your walk home in the morning.

Faced with this defiance, Hitler ordered his generals to make plans for Operation Sea Lion—the invasion of Britain. In preparation for the invasion, he launched massive air strikes against the island nation.

The London Blitz Beginning on August 12, 1940, German bombers began a daily bombardment of England's southern coast. For a month, the British Royal Air Force valiantly battled the German Luftwaffe. Then, the Germans changed their tactics, turning their attention from military targets in the south to the blitz, or bombing, of London and other cities.

German bombers first appeared over London late on September 7. All through the night, relays of aircraft showered high explosives and fire-bombs on the sprawling capital. The bombing continued for 57 nights. Much of the city was destroyed, and some 15,000 people lost their lives.

London did not break under the blitz. Defiantly, Parliament continued to meet. Citizens carried on their daily lives, seeking protection in shelters and then emerging when the all-clear sounded to resume their routines. Even the British king and queen chose to support Londoners by joining them in bomb shelters rather than fleeing to the countryside.

Failure of the Blitz German planes continued to bomb London and other cities off and on until June 1941. But contrary to Hitler's hopes, British morale was not destroyed. In fact, the bombing only made the British more determined to turn back the enemy.

Operation Sea Lion was a failure. Hitler turned to a new target—the Soviet Union. The decision to invade Russia helped save Britain. It also proved to be one of Hitler's costliest mistakes.

Operation Barbarossa

In June 1941, Hitler embarked on Operation Barbarossa—the conquest of the Soviet Union.* Hitler made his motives clear. "If I had the Ural Mountains with their incalculable store of treasures in raw materials," he declared, "Siberia with its vast forests, and the Ukraine with its tremendous wheat fields, Germany under National Socialist leadership would swim in plenty." He also wanted to crush communism in Europe and defeat his powerful rival Joseph Stalin.

The German Advance In Operation Barbarossa, Hitler unleashed a new blitzkrieg. About three million Germans poured into the Soviet Union. They caught Stalin unprepared, his army still suffering from the purges that had wiped out many of its top officers.

The Russians lost two and a half million soldiers trying to fend off the invaders. As they were forced back, Russian troops destroyed factories and farm equipment and burned crops to keep them out of enemy hands. But they could not stop the German war machine. By autumn, the Nazis had smashed deep into Russia and were poised to take Moscow and Leningrad.

There, however, the German advance stalled. Like Napoleon's Grand Army in 1812, Hitler's forces were not prepared for the fury of Russia's "General Winter." By early December, temperatures plunged to –4 degrees. Thousands of German soldiers froze to death.

Siege of Leningrad The Russians, meanwhile, suffered appalling hardships. In September 1941, the two-and-a-half-year siege of Leningrad began. Food was soon rationed to two pieces of bread a day. Desperate Leningraders ate almost anything. They boiled wallpaper scraped off walls because its paste was said to contain potato flour. Owners of leather briefcases boiled and ate them—"jellied meat," they called it.

---

*The plan took its name from the Holy Roman emperor Frederick Barbarossa, a medieval Germanic leader who had won great victories in the East.

Although more than a million Leningraders died during the German siege, the survivors struggled to defend their city. Hoping to gain some relief for the exhausted Russians, Stalin urged Britain to open a second front in Western Europe. Although Churchill could not offer much real help, the two powers did agree to work together.

American Involvement Grows

When the war began in 1939, the United States declared its neutrality. Although isolationist feeling remained strong, many Americans sympathized with those who battled the Axis powers. Later, President Roosevelt found ways around the Neutrality Acts to provide aid, including warships, to Britain as it stood alone against Hitler.

The Arsenal of Democracy In early 1941, FDR persuaded Congress to pass the Lend-Lease Act. It allowed him to sell or lend war materials to "any country whose defense the President deems vital to the defense of the United States." The United States, said Roosevelt, would not be drawn into the war, but it would become "the arsenal of democracy," supplying arms to those who were fighting for freedom.

Atlantic Charter In August 1941, Roosevelt and Churchill met secretly on a warship in the Atlantic. The two leaders issued the Atlantic Charter, which set goals for the war—"the final destruction of the Nazi tyranny"—and for the postwar world. They pledged to support "the right of all peoples to choose the form of government under which they will live" and called for a "permanent system of general security."

Japan Attacks

In December 1941, the Allies gained a vital boost when a surprise action by Japan suddenly pitched the United States into the war. From the late 1930s, Japan had been trying to conquer China. Although Japan occupied much of eastern China, the Chinese would not surrender. When war broke out in Europe in 1939, the Japanese saw a chance to grab European possessions in Southeast Asia. The rich resources of the region, including oil, rubber, and tin, would be of immense value in fighting the Chinese war.

Growing Tensions In 1940, Japan advanced into French Indochina and the Dutch East Indies (present-day Indonesia). To stop Japanese aggression, the United States banned the sale to Japan of war materials, such as iron, steel, and oil for airplanes. This move angered the Japanese.

Japan and the United States held talks to ease the growing tension. But extreme militarists such as General Tojo Hideki were gaining power in Japan. They hoped to seize lands in Asia and the Pacific, and the United States was interfering with their plans.

Attack on Pearl Harbor With talks at a standstill, General Tojo ordered a surprise attack on the American fleet at Pearl Harbor, Hawaii. Early on December 7, 1941, Japanese airplanes damaged or destroyed 19 ships, smashed American planes on the ground, and killed more than 2,400 people.

The Eastern Front
In 1941, the German army attacked the Soviet Union. Here, Soviet soldiers crawl through the snow as they try to halt the German advance.

Theme: Geography and History Why was Russia's winter so devastating to the German army?

 Primary Sources and Literature

See "Franklin D. Roosevelt: The Four Freedoms" in the Reference Section at the back of this book.

Go Online
PHSchool.com

For: More about the attack on Pearl Harbor
Visit: PHSchool.com
Web Code: mkd-8031

Pearl Harbor
On December 7, 1941, Japan attacked the United States naval base at Pearl Harbor, Hawaii. Here, the *Arizona* sinks after being destroyed by Japanese planes.

Theme: Global Interaction
Why did the Japanese attack Pearl Harbor, and how did the United States respond?

The next day, a grim-faced President Roosevelt told the nation that December 7 was "a date which will live in infamy." He asked Congress to declare war on Japan. On December 11, Germany and Italy, as Japan's allies, declared war on the United States.

Japanese Victories In the long run, the Japanese attack on Pearl Harbor would be as serious a mistake as Hitler's invasion of Russia. But the months after Pearl Harbor gave no such hint. Instead, European and American possessions in the Pacific fell one by one to the Japanese. They captured the Philippines and seized other American islands across the Pacific. They overran the British colonies of Hong Kong, Burma, and Malaya, pushed deeper into the Dutch East Indies, and completed the takeover of French Indochina.

By the beginning of 1942, the Japanese empire stretched from Southeast Asia to the western Pacific Ocean. The Axis powers had reached the high point of their successes.

SECTION 2 Assessment

Recall
1. **Identify:** **(a)** "phony war," **(b)** Dunkirk, **(c)** Winston Churchill, **(d)** Battle of Britain, **(e)** Operation Barbarossa, **(f)** Lend-Lease Act, **(g)** Pearl Harbor.
2. **Define:** **(a)** blitzkrieg, **(b)** radar, **(c)** sonar.

Comprehension
3. How did the Axis powers achieve victories in 1939 and 1940?
4. How did Operation Barbarossa affect the Battle of Britain?

5. **(a)** What goals did Japan pursue in Asia? **(b)** Why did General Tojo order a surprise attack on the United States?

Critical Thinking and Writing
6. **Identifying Alternatives** Could the United States have stayed out of the war?
7. **Recognizing Causes and Effects** **(a)** Describe three technological advances during World War II. **(b)** How did this technology make war more destructive?

Go Online
PHSchool.com

Use the Internet to learn more about the attack on Pearl Harbor in 1941. Prepare a radio broadcast giving a firsthand account of the attack and its toll on American ships. For help with this activity, use **Web Code mkd-3180.**

Reading Focus

- How did Germany and Japan treat people in occupied lands?
- How did the Allies turn the tide of war?
- How did the Red Army and the Allied invasion of France undo German plans?

Vocabulary

genocide

collaborator

reparations

Taking Notes

As you read this section, make an outline of its contents. Use Roman numerals for major headings. Use capital letters for subheadings, and use numbers for supporting details. The example at right will help you get started.

I. Occupied lands
  A. Nazi Europe
    1. Slavs considered inferior
    2. Plundered occupied lands
  B. Nazi genocide
  C.

Main Idea   In 1942 and 1943, the tide of the war began to turn as Allied forces won key victories.

Setting the Scene   World War II was fought on a larger scale and in more places than any other conflict in history. It was also more costly in terms of human life than any previous war. Civilians, as well as soldiers, were targets. In 1941, a reporter visited a Russian town that had been home to 10,000 people before the German invasion. The reporter found a lone survivor: "[She was] a blind old woman who had gone insane. I saw her wandering barefooted around the village, carrying a few dirty rags, a rusty pail, and a tattered sheepskin."

From 1939 until mid-1942, the Axis ran up a string of successes. The conquerors blasted villages and towns and divided up the spoils. Then the Allies won some key victories. Slowly, the tide began to turn.

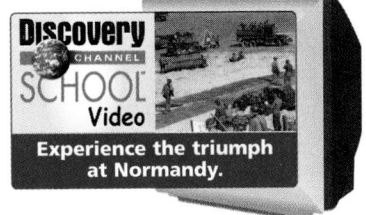

Experience the triumph at Normandy.

Occupied Lands

While the Germans rampaged across Europe, the Japanese conquered an empire in Asia and the Pacific. Each set out to build a "new order" in the occupied lands.

Nazi Europe   Hitler's new order grew out of his racial obsessions. He set up puppet governments in Western European countries that were peopled by "Aryans" or related "races." The Slavs of Eastern Europe were considered to be an inferior "race." They were shoved aside to provide more "living space" for Germans, whom Hitler considered the ideal "race."

To the Nazis, occupied lands were an economic resource to be plundered and looted. The Nazis systematically stripped conquered nations of their works of art, factories, and other resources. They sent thousands of Slavs and others to work as slave laborers in German war industries. As resistance movements emerged to fight German tyranny, the Nazis took savage revenge, shooting hostages and torturing prisoners.

Nazi Genocide   The most savage of Hitler's policies was his program to kill all people he judged "racially inferior," particularly Jews. Other targets included Slavs, Gypsies, and the mentally ill. At first, the Nazis forced Jews in Poland and other countries to live in ghettos and concentration camps. By 1941, however, German leaders had devised plans for the "final solution of the Jewish problem"—the genocide, or deliberate murder, of all European Jews.

To accomplish this goal, Hitler had special "death camps" built in Poland, at places like Auschwitz, Sobibor, and Treblinka. The Nazis

In Southeast Asia, the Japanese captured tens of thousands of Allied prisoners of war (POWs) and turned them into a slave labor force. Nearly half of the POWs were forced to build a 250-mile rail line linking Siam (Thailand) and Burma (Myanmar). Engineers said the line would take from 2 to 5 years to build. Japanese generals ordered it completed in 18 months.

Geography made the task seem impossible. Not only were there mountains and ravines to cross but also winding rivers to be bridged again and again and a tropical jungle to be braved. Wild animals, deadly snakes, and tropical diseases threatened survival everywhere. Equipped only with pickaxes and shovels, the POWs completed the railway at the cost of thousands of lives.

Theme: Geography and History How did geography contribute to the high death toll in building the Burma-Siam Railway?

shipped Jews from all over occupied Europe to the camps. There, Nazi engineers designed the most efficient means of killing millions of men, women, and children.

As Jews reached the camps, they were stripped of their clothes and valuables. Their heads were shaved. Guards separated men from women and children from their parents. The young, old, and sick were targeted for immediate killing. Within a few days, they were herded into "shower rooms" and gassed. The Nazis worked others to death or used them for perverse "medical" experiments. By 1945, the Nazis had massacred some six million Jews in what became known as the Holocaust. Almost as many other "undesirable" people were killed as well.

Jews resisted the Nazis even though they knew their efforts could not succeed. In October 1944, for example, a group of Jews in the Auschwitz death camp destroyed one of the gas chambers. The rebels were all killed. One woman, Rosa Robota, was tortured for days before she was hanged. "Be strong and have courage," she called out to the camp inmates who were forced by the Nazis to watch her execution.

In some cases, friends, neighbors, or strangers protected Jews. Sugihara Chiune, a Japanese diplomat in Lithuania, saved some 6,000 Jews by writing exit visas until he was ordered home by the Japanese government. Italian peasants hid Jews in their villages, and the nations of Denmark and Bulgaria saved almost all their Jewish populations. Most often, however, people pretended not to notice what was happening. Some were collaborators, helping the Nazis hunt down the Jews or, like the Vichy government in France, shipping tens of thousands of Jews to their death.

The scale and savagery of the Holocaust are unequaled in history. The Nazis deliberately set out to destroy the Jews for no reason other than their religious and ethnic heritage. Today, the record of that slaughter is a vivid reminder of the monstrous results of racism and intolerance.

The Co-Prosperity Sphere   As Japan expanded across Asia and the Pacific, it donned the mantle of anti-imperialism. Under the slogan "Asia for Asians," it created the Greater East Asia Co-Prosperity Sphere. Japan's self-proclaimed mission was to help Asians escape western colonial rule. In fact, its real goal was a Japanese empire in Asia.

The Japanese treated the Chinese, Filipinos, Malaysians, and other conquered people with great brutality, killing and torturing civilians throughout East and Southeast Asia. People were shot simply for listening to Allied radio broadcasts. The Japanese seized food crops, destroyed cities and towns, and made local people into slave laborers. Whatever welcome the Japanese had at first met as "liberators" was soon turned to hatred. In the Philippines, Indochina, and elsewhere, nationalist groups waged guerrilla warfare against the Japanese invaders.

The Allied War Effort

After the United States entered the war, the Allied leaders met periodically to hammer out their strategy. In 1942, the Big Three—Roosevelt, Churchill, and Stalin—agreed to finish the war in Europe before turning their attention to Asia.

From the outset, the Allies distrusted one another. Churchill thought Stalin wanted to dominate Europe. Roosevelt felt that Churchill had ambitions to expand British imperial power. Stalin believed that the western powers wanted to destroy communism. At meetings and in writing, Stalin urged Roosevelt and Churchill to relieve the pressure on Russia by opening a second front in Western Europe. Not until 1944, however, did Britain and the United States make such a move. The British and Americans argued that they did not have the resources before then. Stalin saw the delay as a deliberate policy to weaken the Soviet Union.

Analyzing Primary Sources

The Holocaust

As the Allied armies entered territories occupied by Germany, they came upon the concentration camps. The soldiers were horrified by what they saw. General Dwight Eisenhower of the United States insisted on having the camps photographed so others could see the conditions.

After camp inmates were killed, huge ovens like this one were used to cremate their bodies. Between 9 and 12 million people–including about 6 million Jews–died in concentration camps from 1939 to 1945.

These skeletal men were prisoners at Buchenwald camp in Germany. Inmates who escaped execution were used for forced labor. They suffered torture, starvation, and disease.

Children were among the millions of people shipped to the concentration camps. Most suffered the same ghastly fate as their parents.

Skills Tip

Remember that photographs depict real scenes and were also taken for a particular purpose. Knowing this purpose can help you make sense of the photographs.

Skills Assessment

1. Based on the photographs, it can be assumed that
   A families were kept together.
   B conditions were the same in every camp.
   C conditions improved as the war continued.
   D the Nazis cared little about the well-being of their prisoners.

2. The photographs help historians to
   E explain Hitler's motives.
   F document conditions in concentration camps.
   G understand why the Nazis hated Jews.
   H identify the causes of World War II.

3. **Critical Thinking Making Inferences** (a) Based on the photographs, what do you think the Nazis thought about the camp inmates? (b) What does the ultimate purpose of the camps seem to have been?

Women in Wartime
Women's military roles have changed dramatically. Although the British and American armies did not allow women to serve in combat positions during World War II, women did serve in auxiliaries such as the Women's Auxiliary Air Force, or WAAF (PAST). Today, women's roles are more active. During Operation Desert Storm in 1991 (PRESENT), women served as soldiers.

Theme: Continuity and Change What reasons might the military have for allowing women to serve as soldiers?

Total War Like the Axis powers, the Allies were committed to total war. Democratic governments in the United States and Britain increased their political power. They directed economic resources into the war effort, ordering factories to stop making cars or refrigerators and to turn out airplanes or tanks instead. Governments rationed consumer goods, from shoes to sugar, and regulated prices and wages. On the positive side, while the war brought shortages and hardships, it ended the unemployment of the depression era.

Under pressure of war, even democratic governments limited the rights of citizens, censored the press, and used propaganda to win public support for the war. In the United States and Canada, many citizens of Japanese descent lost their jobs, property, and civil rights. Japanese Americans and Japanese Canadians even lost their freedom and were forced into internment camps after governments decided that they were a security risk. The British took similar action against German refugees. Some 40 years later, both the United States and Canada apologized for the wartime policy and provided former internees with **reparations,** or payment for damages caused by the imprisonment.

Women Help Win the War As men joined the military and war industries expanded, millions of women around the world replaced them in essential jobs. Women built ships and planes, produced munitions, and staffed offices. A popular British song recognized women's contributions:

"She's the girl that makes the thing that drills the hole
  that holds the spring
That drives the rod that turns the knob that works the
  thingumebob. . . .
And it's the girl that makes the thing that holds the
  oil that oils the ring
That works the thingumebob
  THAT'S GOING TO WIN THE WAR!"
—from *The People's War: Britain, 1939–1945* (Calder)

British and American women served in the armed forces in many auxiliary roles—driving trucks and ambulances, delivering airplanes, decoding messages, and assisting at antiaircraft sites. In occupied Europe, women fought in the resistance. Marie Fourcade, a French woman, directed 3,000 people in the underground and helped downed Allied pilots escape to safety. Many Soviet women played combat roles. Soviet pilot Lily Litvak, for example, shot down 12 German planes before she herself was killed.

Turning Points

During 1942 and 1943, the Allies won several victories that would turn the tide of battle and push back the Axis powers. The first of these turning points came in North Africa and Italy.

El Alamein In Egypt, the British under General Bernard Montgomery finally stopped Rommel's advance during the long, fierce Battle of El Alamein. They then turned the tables on the Desert Fox, driving the Axis forces back across Libya into Tunisia.

Later in 1942, American general Dwight Eisenhower took command of a joint Anglo-American force in Morocco and Algeria. Advancing on Tunisia from the west, he combined with the British forces to trap Rommel's army, which surrendered in May 1943.

World War II in Europe and North Africa

FINLAND

NORWAY SWEDEN

Leningrad

Moscow

SOVIET UNION

IRELAND

GREAT BRITAIN

DENMARK

Baltic Sea

REICHSKOMMISSARIAT OSTLAND

1943

North Sea

Danzig 1945 1944

1944

ATLANTIC OCEAN

London NETH.

Berlin

Stalingrad

1943

NORMANDY 1944 Dunkirk BELG.

1945

1945 Warsaw

1945

REICHSKOMMISSARIAT UKRAINE

1943

Paris LUX.

1945

GERMANY

Elbe R.

FRANCE

1945

SWITZ.

SLOVAKIA

1945

1944

Vichy

ITALY

HUNGARY

1944

VICHY FRANCE

1944

CROATIA

ROMANIA

Yalta

PORTUGAL

SPAIN

Rome

MONTENEGRO SERBIA

Black Sea

Anzio

Yugoslavian territory under Italian administration

BULGARIA

TURKEY

Salerno

ALBANIA

1944

1944

Palermo 1943

GREECE

Sicily

1943

SYRIA

1942

Algiers Tunis

1943

1942

SP. MOROCCO Oran

Casablanca

1942

LEBANON

IRAQ

Mediterranean Sea

MOROCCO ALGERIA

TUNISIA

PALESTINE

TRANS-JORDAN

Tripoli

El Alamein Cairo

1943

1942

LIBYA

Azimuthal Equal Area Projection

EGYPT

SAUDI ARABIA

0   300   600 Miles

0   300   600 Kilometers

	European Axis Powers, 1942		Allied territory, 1942
	Maximum extent of Axis control, 1942	→	Allied advances
	Neutral nations, 1942	▪	Concentration camps, 1939–1945

Invasion of Italy

Victory in North Africa let the Allies leap across the Mediterranean into Italy. In July 1943, a combined British and American army landed first in Sicily and then in southern Italy. They defeated the Italian forces there in about a month.

Italians, fed up with Mussolini, overthrew Il Duce. The new Italian government signed an armistice, but the fighting did not end. Hitler sent German troops to rescue Mussolini and stiffen the will of Italians fighting in the north. For the next 18 months, the Allies pushed slowly up the Italian peninsula, suffering heavy losses against stiff German resistance. Still, the Italian invasion was a decisive event for the Allies because it weakened Hitler by forcing him to fight on another front.

The Red Army Resists

Another major turning point in the war occurred in the Soviet Union. After their triumphant advance in 1941, the Germans were stalled outside Moscow and Leningrad. In 1942, Hitler launched a new offensive. This

Skills Assessment

Geography Axis power reached its height in Europe in 1942. Then, the tide began to turn.

1. **Location** On the map, locate **(a)** Vichy France, **(b)** Soviet Union, **(c)** El Alamein, **(d)** Berlin, **(e)** Normandy, **(f)** Anzio.
2. **Movement** Describe the extent of the Axis advance to the east by 1942.
3. **Critical Thinking Analyzing Information** How did geography help or hinder Allied advances?

time, he aimed for the rich oil fields of the south. His troops, however, got only as far as the city of Stalingrad.

Stalingrad The Battle of Stalingrad was one of the costliest of the war. Hitler was determined to capture Stalin's namesake city. Stalin was equally determined to defend it. The battle began when the Germans surrounded the city. The Russians then encircled their attackers. As winter closed in, a bitter street-by-street, house-by-house struggle raged. Soldiers fought for two weeks for a single building, wrote a German officer. Corpses "are strewn in the cellars, on the landings and the staircases," he said. Trapped, without food or ammunition and with no hope of rescue, the German commander finally surrendered in early 1943. The battle cost the Germans approximately 300,000 killed, wounded, or captured soldiers.

Counterattack After the Battle of Stalingrad, the Red Army took the offensive and drove the invaders out of the Soviet Union entirely. Hitler's forces suffered irreplaceable losses of both troops and equipment. By early 1944, Soviet troops were advancing into Eastern Europe.

Invasion of France

By 1944, the Allies were at last ready to open a second front in Europe— with the invasion of France. Eisenhower was made the supreme Allied commander. He and other Allied leaders faced the enormous task of planning the operation and assembling troops and supplies. To prepare the way for the invasion, Allied bombers flew constant missions over Germany. They targeted factories and destroyed aircraft that might be used against the invasion force. They also bombed a number of German cities.

The Allies chose June 6, 1944—D-Day, they called it—for the invasion of France. After midnight, Allied planes dropped paratroopers behind enemy lines. Then, at dawn, thousands of ships ferried 176,000 Allied troops across the English Channel. From landing craft, the troops fought their way to shore amid underwater mines and raking machine-gun fire. They clawed their way inland through the tangled hedges of Normandy. Finally, they broke through German defenses and advanced toward Paris. Meanwhile, other Allied forces sailed from Italy to land in southern France.

In Paris, French resistance forces rose up against the occupying Germans. Under pressure from all sides, the Germans retreated. On August 25, the Allies entered Paris. Within a month, all of France was free. Attention focused on conquering Germany itself—and defeating Japan.

SECTION 3 Assessment

Recall
1. **Identify: (a)** Holocaust, **(b)** Greater East Asia Co-Prosperity Sphere, **(c)** Battle of El Alamein, **(d)** Battle of Stalingrad, **(e)** D-Day.
2. **Define: (a)** genocide, **(b)** collaborator, **(c)** reparations.

Comprehension
3. **(a)** How did Hitler try to achieve a "new order" in Europe? **(b)** How did the Japanese treat conquered people?
4. How did democratic governments mobilize their economies for war?

5. Explain how each of the following battles was a turning point in the war: **(a)** El Alamein, **(b)** Stalingrad.

Critical Thinking and Writing
6. **Defending a Position** Do you think that democratic governments should be allowed to limit their citizens' freedoms during wartime? Defend your position.
7. **Applying Information** Hitler translated his hatred of Jews and others into a program of genocide. How do ethnic, racial, and religious hatreds weaken society?

Activity

Creating a Memorial Design a memorial commemorating the millions who died in the Holocaust. Include a brief description of any symbols you will use in your memorial.

Toward Victory

Reading Focus

- How was the Pacific war fought?
- How did the Allies defeat Nazi Germany?
- What debates surrounded the defeat of Japan?

Vocabulary

island-hopping

kamikaze

Taking Notes

On a separate sheet of paper, copy the cause-and-effect chart shown here. As you read the section, complete the chart with information about how the Allies won in the Pacific and in Europe.

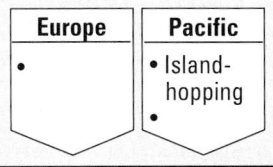

Europe	Pacific
•	• Island-hopping
	•

ALLIES WIN WORLD WAR II

Main Idea — Continued Allied successes led to victory over Germany and Japan in 1945.

Setting the Scene General Douglas MacArthur stood at the dock on Corregidor in March 1942. A boat waited to evacuate him from the fortified island in the Philippines. Although the United States Army and Filipino defense forces had battled to keep the Japanese out of the island chain, they had not been successful. Thousands of Allied civilians—men, women, and children—were being held in prison camps throughout the islands, and American and Filipino soldiers were under attack on the Bataan peninsula. After reaching Australia, MacArthur pledged his determination to free the Philippines with the words "I shall return."

Allied troops found that the war in Southeast Asia and the Pacific was very different from that in Europe. Most battles were fought at sea, on tiny islands, or in deep jungles.

War in the Pacific

At first, the Japanese won an uninterrupted series of victories. They controlled much of Southeast Asia and many Pacific islands. By May 1942, the Japanese had gained control of the Philippines, killing several hundred American soldiers and some 10,000 Filipino soldiers during the 68-mile Bataan Death March. One survivor described the ordeal as "a macabre litany of heat, dust, starvation, thirst, flies, filth, stench, murder, torture, corpses, and wholesale brutality that numbs the memory." Many Filipino

Storming the Beach
The Pacific war relied on the capture of individual islands. Here, United States Marines land on the island of Iwo Jima.

Theme: Geography and History How was the war in the Pacific different from the fighting in Europe?

civilians risked—and sometimes lost—their lives to give food and water to captives on the march.

Soon, however, the tide of the Pacific war began to turn. In May and June 1942, United States warships and airplanes severely damaged two Japanese fleets during the battles of the Coral Sea and Midway Island. These victories greatly weakened Japanese naval power and stopped the Japanese advance.

After the Battle of Midway, the United States took the offensive. That summer, under MacArthur's command, United States Marines landed at Guadalcanal in the Solomon Islands. Victory on Guadalcanal marked the beginning of an "island-hopping" campaign. The goal of the campaign was to recapture some Japanese-held islands while bypassing others. The captured islands served as steppingstones to the next objective. In this way, American forces gradually moved north toward Japan itself. By 1944, the United States Navy, commanded by Admiral Chester Nimitz, was blockading Japan, and American bombers pounded Japanese cities and industries.

In October 1944, MacArthur began the fight to retake the Philippines. The British, meanwhile, were pushing Japanese forces back in the jungles of Burma and Malaya. Despite such setbacks, the Japanese government rejected any suggestions of surrender.

The Nazis Defeated

Hitler, too, scorned talk of surrender. "If the war is to be lost," he declared, "the nation also will perish." To win the assault on "Fortress Europe," the Allies had to use devastating force.

The Allies Advance After freeing France, Allied forces battled toward Germany. As their armies advanced into Belgium in December 1944, Germany launched a massive counterattack. At the bloody Battle of the Bulge, which lasted more than a month, both sides took terrible losses. The Germans were unable to break through. The battle delayed the Allied advance, but it was Hitler's last success. His support within Germany was declining, and he had already survived one assassination attempt by senior officers in the German military.

By this time, Germany was reeling under round-the-clock bombing. For two years, Allied bombers had hammered military bases, factories, railroads, oil depots, and cities. In one 10-day period, bombing almost erased the huge industrial city of Hamburg. Allied raids on Dresden in February 1945 killed as many as 135,000 people.

By March, the Allies had crossed the Rhine into western Germany. From the east, Soviet troops closed in on Berlin. In late April, American and Russian soldiers met and shook hands at the Elbe River. Everywhere, Axis armies began to surrender.

The End in Europe In Italy, guerrillas captured and executed Mussolini. In Berlin, Hitler knew that the end was near. As Soviet troops fought their way into the city, Hitler committed suicide in his underground bunker. After just 12 years, Hitler's "thousand-year Reich" was bomb-ravaged. On May 7, Germany surrendered. Officially, the war in Europe ended the next day, May 8, 1945, which was proclaimed V-E Day (Victory in Europe).

Defeat of Japan

With war won in Europe, the Allies poured their resources into defeating Japan. By mid-1945, most of the Japanese navy and air force had been destroyed. Yet the Japanese still had an army of two million men. The road to victory, it appeared, would be long and costly.

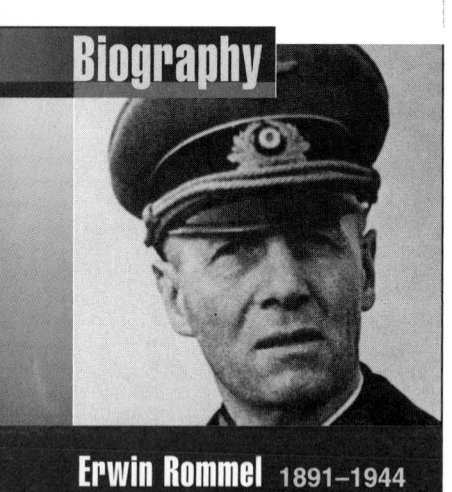

Biography

Erwin Rommel 1891–1944

When the war began, Erwin Rommel was personally responsible for guaranteeing Hitler's safety. Impressed with Rommel, in 1942, Hitler promoted him to field marshal. Rommel was the youngest person to hold that rank in the German army. The two men soon became disillusioned with each other. When Rommel tried to explain setbacks for his command in North Africa, Hitler branded him a defeatist. When Hitler refused to listen to military experts, Rommel came to believe that the Nazi leader was trying to destroy Germany. In 1944, Rommel was connected to a plot to assassinate Hitler, which led to his own destruction.

Theme: Impact of the Individual How did Rommel's attitude toward Hitler change?

World War II in the Pacific

Invasion Versus the Bomb Some American officials estimated that an invasion of Japan would cost a million or more casualties. In bloody battles on the islands of Iwo Jima and Okinawa, the Japanese had shown that they would fight to the death rather than surrender. Beginning in 1944, some young Japanese chose to become kamikaze (kah mih KAH zee) pilots who undertook suicide missions, crashing their explosive-laden airplanes into American warships. They hoped these efforts would stop the Allies and save their nation from defeat.

While Allied military leaders planned for invasion, scientists offered another way to end the war. Since the early 1900s, scientists had understood that matter, made up of atoms, could be converted into pure energy. In military terms, this meant that, by splitting the atom, scientists could create an explosion far more powerful than any yet known. During the war, Allied scientists, some of them German and Italian refugees, raced to harness the atom. In July 1945, they successfully tested the first atomic bomb at Alamogordo, New Mexico.

News of this test was brought to the new American president, Harry Truman. Truman had taken office after Franklin Roosevelt died unexpectedly on April 12. He realized that the atomic bomb was a terrible new force for destruction. Still, after consulting with his advisers, he decided to use the new weapon against Japan.

At the time, Truman was meeting with other Allied leaders in the city of Potsdam, Germany. They issued a warning to Japan to surrender or face "utter and complete destruction." When the Japanese ignored the deadline, the United States took action.

Hiroshima On August 6, 1945, an American plane dropped an atomic bomb on the mid-sized city of Hiroshima. The bomb flattened four square

Skills Assessment

Geography For six months, the Japanese won a series of uninterrupted victories. After the Battle of Midway, however, the Allies took the offensive in the Pacific.

1. **Location** On the map, locate (a) Japan, (b) Midway Island, (c) Pearl Harbor, (d) Iwo Jima, (e) Hiroshima, (f) Manila.
2. **Movement** (a) Did Japan ever gain control of New Guinea? Explain. (b) Which of the Allies advanced into Manchuria?
3. **Critical Thinking Making Inferences** How did geography make it difficult for Japan to maintain control of its empire?

miles and instantly killed more than 70,000 people. In the months that followed, many more would die from radiation sickness, a deadly aftereffect from exposure to radioactive materials.

On August 8, the Soviet Union declared war on Japan and invaded Manchuria. Again, Japanese leaders did not respond. The next day, the United States dropped a second atomic bomb, this time on the city of Nagasaki. More than 40,000 people were killed in this second explosion.

Still, the Japanese cabinet argued. Should they surrender or continue to fight? Finally, on August 10, Emperor Hirohito intervened—an action unheard of for a Japanese emperor—and forced the government to surrender. On September 2, 1945, the formal peace treaty was signed on board the American battleship *Missouri,* which was anchored in Tokyo Bay.

The Atomic Bomb
President Harry Truman warned the Japanese that if they did not surrender, they would face "a rain of ruin from the air the like of which has never been seen on this Earth." This photo shows the destructive effects of the bomb on Hiroshima. The inset shows a watch stopped by the blast.

Theme: Religions and Value Systems What were some of the arguments for and against dropping the atomic bomb on Japan?

An Ongoing Controversy Dropping the atomic bomb brought a quick end to the war. It also unleashed terrifying destruction. Ever since, people have debated whether the United States should have used the bomb.

Why did Truman use the bomb? First, he was convinced that Japan would not surrender without an invasion that would result in an enormous loss of both American and Japanese lives. Truman also may have hoped that the bomb would impress the Soviet Union with American power. At any rate, the Japanese surrendered shortly after the bombs were dropped, and World War II was ended.

Looking Ahead

After the surrender, American forces occupied the smoldering ruins of Japan. In Germany, meanwhile, the Allies had divided Hitler's fallen empire into four zones of occupation. In both countries, the Allies faced difficult decisions about the future. How could they avoid the mistakes of 1919 and build the foundations for a stable world peace?

SECTION **4 Assessment**

Recall

1. **Identify: (a)** Battle of the Coral Sea, **(b)** Battle of the Bulge, **(c)** V-E Day, **(d)** Harry Truman.
2. **Define: (a)** island-hopping, **(b)** kamikaze.

Comprehension

3. How did the United States fight the war in the Pacific?
4. How did the Allies weaken Germany?
5. How was Japan defeated?

Critical Thinking and Writing

6. **Making Decisions** Suppose that you are President Truman. What information would you want before deciding whether to drop an atomic bomb on Japan?
7. **Making Generalizations** How would you describe the attitudes of the Japanese government and of Hitler toward surrendering to the Allies?

Activity

Writing Headlines
Write a series of newspaper headlines reporting the final months of the war in Europe. Suggest photos or other visuals that might accompany a story for one of the headlines.

Reading Focus

■ What issues arose in the aftermath of war?

■ Why did the Allies organize the United Nations?

■ How did the breakup of the wartime alliance lead to new conflicts?

Vocabulary

containment

satellite

Taking Notes

On a sheet of paper, make a concept web like the one shown here. As you read this section, add information about events that occurred after World War II. Add as many circles as you need.

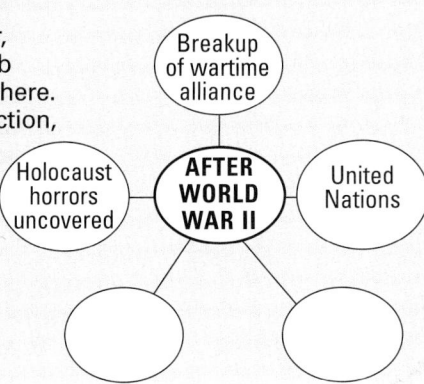

Main Idea As the war ended, new tensions developed between the United States and the Soviet Union.

Setting the Scene "Give me ten years and you will not be able to recognize Germany," said Hitler in 1933. His prophecy proved correct—although not in the way he had intended. In 1945, Germany was an unrecognizable ruin. Poland, Russia, Japan, and many other countries also lay in ruins. Total war had gutted cities, factories, harbors, bridges, railroads, farms, homes—and lives. Millions of refugees, displaced by the fighting or liberated from prison camps, wandered the land. Amid the devastation, hunger and disease took large tolls for years after the fighting ended.

Aftermath of War

Even as the Allies celebrated victory, the appalling costs of the war began to emerge. It had killed as many as 75 million people around the world. In Europe, about 38 million people lost their lives, many of them civilians. The Soviet Union suffered the worst casualties, with more than 22 million dead.

Numbers alone did not tell the story of the Nazi nightmare in Europe or the Japanese brutality in Asia. In the aftermath of war, investigation brought new atrocities to light.

Horrors of the Holocaust During the war, the Allies were aware of the existence of Nazi concentration camps and death camps. But only at war's end did they learn the full extent of the inhumanity and misery of the Holocaust. United States general Dwight Eisenhower, who visited the camps, was stunned to come "face to face with indisputable evidence of Nazi brutality and ruthless disregard of every sense of decency."

Walking skeletons stumbled out of the death camps with tales of mass murder. Rudolf Hoess, Nazi commander at Auschwitz, would later admit that he had supervised the killing of some two and a half million people, not counting those who died of disease or starvation.

War Crimes Trials At wartime meetings, the Allies had agreed that Axis leaders should be tried for "crimes against humanity." In Germany, the Allies held war crimes trials in Nuremberg, where Hitler had staged mass rallies in the 1930s. A total of 177 Germans and Austrians were tried, and 142 were found guilty. A handful of top Nazis received death sentences. Others were imprisoned. Similar war crimes trials were held in Japan and Italy. The trials showed that political and military leaders could be held accountable for actions in wartime.

Allied Occupation The war crimes trials served an additional purpose. By exposing the savagery of the Axis regimes, they further discredited the Nazi, fascist, and militarist ideologies that had led to the war.

Yet disturbing questions haunted people then, as now. What made the Nazi horrors possible? Why had ordinary people in Germany, Poland, France, and elsewhere accepted—and even collaborated in—Hitler's "final solution"? How could the world prevent the rise of future dictators?

The Allies tried to address those issues as their troops occupied Germany and Japan. The United States felt that strengthening democracy would ensure tolerance and peace. The western Allies built new governments with democratic constitutions to protect the rights of all citizens. In German schools, for example, Nazi textbooks and courses were replaced with a new curriculum that taught democratic principles.

The United Nations

As in 1919, the World War II Allies set up an international organization to ensure peace. In April 1945, delegates from 50 nations met in San Francisco to draft a charter for the United Nations. The UN would play a greater role in world affairs than did its predecessor, the League of Nations.

Under the UN Charter, each of the member nations had one vote in the General Assembly. A much smaller body called the Security Council was given greater power. Each of its five permanent members—the United States, the Soviet Union (today Russia), Britain, France, and China—had the right to veto any council decision. The goal was to give these great powers the authority to ensure the peace. Often, however, differences among these nations have kept the UN from taking action.

The UN's work would go far beyond peacekeeping. The organization would take on many world problems—from preventing the outbreak of disease and improving education to protecting refugees and aiding nations to develop economically. UN agencies like the World Health Organization and the Food and Agricultural Organization have provided help for millions of people around the world.

The Alliance Breaks Apart

Amid the rubble of war, a new power structure emerged. In Europe, Germany was defeated. France and Britain were drained and exhausted. Two other powers, the United States and the Soviet Union, had brought about the final victory. Before long, these two nations would become superpowers with the economic resources and military might to dominate the globe. They would also become tense rivals in an increasingly divided world.

Growing Differences During the war, the Soviet Union and the nations of the West had cooperated to defeat Nazi Germany. By 1945, however, the wartime alliance was crumbling. Conflicting ideologies and mutual distrust soon led to the conflict known as the Cold War. The Cold War was a state of tension and hostility among nations, without armed conflict between the major rivals. At first, the focus of the Cold War was Eastern Europe, where Stalin and the western powers had very different goals.*

---

*Stalin was deeply suspicious of other powers. Russia had been invaded by Napoleon's armies and by Germans in World Wars I and II. Also, the United States and Britain had both sent troops into Russia during World War I.

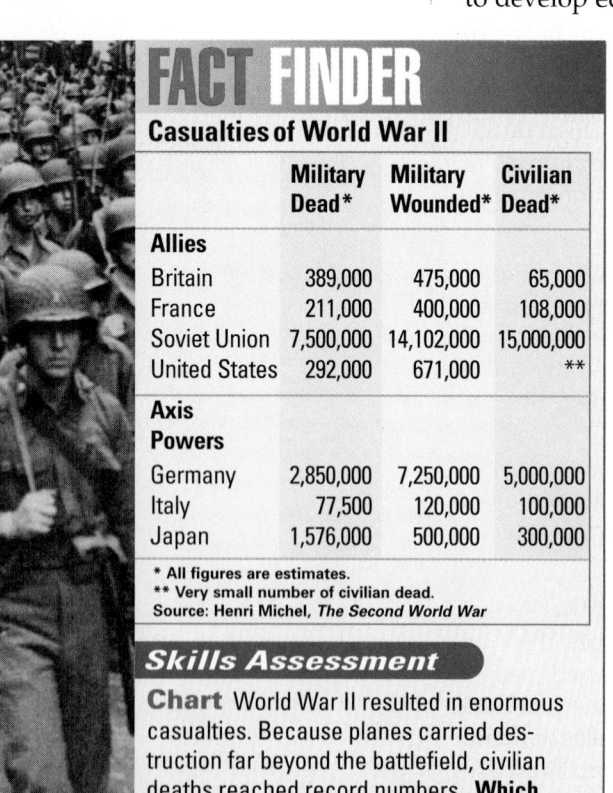

FACT FINDER

Casualties of World War II

	Military Dead*	Military Wounded*	Civilian Dead*
Allies			
Britain	389,000	475,000	65,000
France	211,000	400,000	108,000
Soviet Union	7,500,000	14,102,000	15,000,000
United States	292,000	671,000	**
Axis Powers			
Germany	2,850,000	7,250,000	5,000,000
Italy	77,500	120,000	100,000
Japan	1,576,000	500,000	300,000

* All figures are estimates.
** Very small number of civilian dead.
Source: Henri Michel, *The Second World War*

Skills Assessment

Chart World War II resulted in enormous casualties. Because planes carried destruction far beyond the battlefield, civilian deaths reached record numbers. **Which nation suffered the greatest number of both civilian and military casualties?**

Origins of the Cold War   Stalin had two goals in Eastern Europe. First, he wanted to spread communism into the area. Second, he wanted to create a buffer zone of friendly governments as a defense against Germany, which had invaded Russia during World War I and again in 1941.

As the Red Army had pushed German forces out of Eastern Europe, it had left behind occupying forces. At wartime conferences, Stalin tried to persuade the West to accept Soviet influence in Eastern Europe. He bluntly stated, "Whoever occupies a territory also imposes his own social system. Everyone imposes his own system as far as his armies can reach. It cannot be otherwise."

The Soviet dictator pointed out that the United States was not consulting the Soviet Union about peace terms for Italy or Japan, defeated and occupied by American and British troops. In the same way, Russia would determine the fate of the Eastern European lands overrun by the Red Army on its way to Berlin.

Roosevelt and Churchill rejected Stalin's view, making him promise "free elections" in Eastern Europe. Stalin ignored that pledge. Backed by the Red Army, local communists in Poland, Czechoslovakia, and elsewhere destroyed rival political parties and even assassinated democratic leaders. By 1948, Stalin had installed pro-Soviet communist governments throughout Eastern Europe.

A Divided Europe   Churchill had long distrusted Stalin. As early as 1946, during a visit to the United States, he described Soviet control of Eastern Europe as an "iron curtain" dividing the continent.

In the West, the "iron curtain" became a symbol of the Cold War. It expressed the growing fear of communism. More important, it described the division of Europe into "eastern" and "western" blocs. In the East were the Soviet-dominated, communist countries of Eastern Europe. In the West were the western democracies, led by the United States.

New Conflicts Develop

Like Churchill, President Truman saw communism as an evil force creeping across Europe and threatening countries around the world, including China. To deal with that threat, the United States abandoned its traditional isolationism. After World War I, it had withdrawn from global affairs, but after World War II, the nation took a leading role on the world stage.

Stalin soon showed his aggressive intentions. In Greece, Stalin backed communist rebels who were fighting to overturn a right-wing monarchy supported by Britain. By 1947, however, Britain could no longer afford to defend Greece. Stalin was also menacing Turkey in the Dardanelles, the strait linking the Russian Black Sea coasts and the Mediterranean.

Truman Doctrine   Truman took action. On March 12, 1947, Truman outlined a new policy to Congress: "I believe that it must be the policy of the United States to support free people who are resisting attempted subjugation by armed minorities or by outside pressures."

This policy, known as the Truman Doctrine, would guide the United States for decades. It made clear that Americans would resist Soviet expansion in Europe or elsewhere in the world. Truman soon sent military and economic aid and advisers to Greece and Turkey so that they could withstand the communist threat.

The Truman Doctrine was rooted in the idea of containment, limiting communism to the areas already under Soviet control. George Kennan, the American statesman who first proposed this approach, believed that communism would eventually destroy itself. Stalin, however, saw containment as "encirclement" by the capitalist world that wanted to isolate the Soviet Union.

Primary Source

Curtaining Off Eastern Europe

In 1946, Winston Churchill traveled to Westminster College in Fulton, Missouri, and delivered an address analyzing the Soviet threat in Eastern Europe:

"A shadow has fallen upon the scenes so lately lighted by Allied victory. . . . From Stettin in the Baltic to Trieste in the Adriatic, an iron curtain has descended across the Continent. . . . Warsaw, Berlin, Prague, Vienna, Budapest, Bucharest, and Sofia, all these famous cities and the populations around them lie in what I must call the Soviet sphere, and all are subject . . . not only to Soviet influence but to a very high and, in many cases, increasing measure of control from Moscow. . . . I do not believe that Soviet Russia desires war. What they desire is the fruits of war and the indefinite expansion of their power and doctrines."

—Winston Churchill, speech delivered March 5, 1946

Skills Assessment

Primary Source   What does Churchill believe are Soviet motives for isolating its territories?

Cold War in Europe

Divided Germany, 1945

NATO nations, 1955 · Warsaw Pact nations, 1955 · Other communist countries · Territory added to Soviet Union

The Marshall Plan Postwar hunger and poverty made Western European lands fertile ground for communist ideas. To strengthen democratic governments, the United States offered a massive aid package, called the Marshall Plan. Under it, the United States funneled food and economic assistance to Europe to help countries rebuild. Billions in American aid helped war-shattered Europe recover rapidly.

President Truman also offered aid to the Soviet Union and its satellites, or dependent states, in Eastern Europe. Stalin, however, saw the plan as a trick to win Eastern Europe over to capitalism and democracy. He forbade Eastern European countries to accept American aid, promising help from the Soviet Union in its place.

Divisions in Germany Defeated Germany became another focus of the Cold War. Fearing the danger of a restored Germany, the Soviet Union dismantled factories and other resources in its occupation zone and used them to help rebuild Russia. France, Britain, and the United States, however, decided to unite their zones of occupation, encouraging Germans to rebuild businesses and industries.

Germany thus became a divided nation. In West Germany, the democratic nations allowed the people to write their own constitution and regain self-government. In East Germany, the Soviet Union installed a communist government tied to Moscow.

Berlin Airlift Stalin's resentment at western moves to rebuild Germany as a democracy triggered a crisis over Berlin. The former German capital was occupied by all four victorious Allies, even though it lay deep within the Soviet zone.

In 1948, Stalin tried to force the western Allies out of Berlin by sealing off every railroad and highway into the western sectors of the city. The western powers responded to the blockade by mounting a round-the-clock airlift. For more than a year, cargo planes supplied West Berliners with food and fuel. Their success forced the Soviets to end the blockade. Although the West had won a victory, the crisis deepened hostilities.

Military Alliances Tensions continued to grow. In 1949, the United States, Canada, and nine Western European countries formed a new military alliance called the North Atlantic Treaty Organization (NATO). Members pledged to help one another if any one of them was attacked.

In 1955, the Soviet Union responded by forming its own military alliance, the Warsaw Pact. It included the USSR and seven satellites in Eastern Europe. Unlike NATO, however, the Warsaw Pact was a weapon used by the Soviets to keep its satellites in order.

The Arms Race Each side in the Cold War armed itself to withstand an attack by the other. At first, the United States held an advantage in its control of nuclear power. But Stalin's top scientists were under orders to develop an atomic bomb of their own. They succeeded in 1949, and the arms race was on. For four decades, the superpowers spent fantastic sums to develop new, more deadly nuclear and conventional weapons. They invested still more to improve "delivery systems"—bombers, missiles, and submarines to launch these weapons of mass destruction. Soon, the global balance of power became, in Churchill's phrase, a "balance of terror."

The Propaganda War Both sides participated in a propaganda war. The United States spoke of defending capitalism and democracy against communism and totalitarianism. The Soviet Union claimed the moral high ground in the struggle against western imperialism. Yet linked to those stands, both sides sought world power.

Looking Ahead

In 1945, the world hoped for an end to decades of economic crisis, bloody dictators, and savage war. Instead, it faced new tensions.

The Cold War would last for more than 40 years. Rivalry between the hostile camps would not only divide Europe but also fuel crises around the world. It would strain the resources of the United States and exhaust those of the Soviet Union. Though it would not erupt into large-scale fighting between the two superpowers, many small wars would break out, with the superpowers championing opposite sides. Meanwhile, the spread of ominous new weapons would raise the specter of global destruction.

SECTION 5 Assessment

Recall
1. **Identify:** **(a)** UN, **(b)** "iron curtain," **(c)** Truman Doctrine, **(d)** Berlin airlift, **(e)** NATO, **(f)** Warsaw Pact.
2. **Define: (a)** containment, **(b)** satellite.

Comprehension
3. How did the Allies try to hold the Axis leaders responsible for the suffering they caused during the war?
4. What was the main purpose of the UN?

5. List two causes of the Cold War.

Critical Thinking and Writing
6. **Recognizing Causes and Effects** Some historians argue that the Cold War began in 1918 when the World War I Allies, including the United States, sent forces to Russia to topple the Bolsheviks. How might they support this position?
7. **Linking Past and Present** Why do people feel it is so important to remember the inhumanity of the Holocaust?

Activity

Creating a Political Cartoon Use Churchill's "iron curtain" image to create a political cartoon about the Cold War. Write a caption for your cartoon.

Creating a Chapter Summary

Make a flowchart on a separate sheet of paper to show the main events of World War II and its aftermath, as well as related details. Use the chart below to help you get started.

Dictators challenge world peace/Japan, Italy, Germany

Spanish Civil War/Dress rehearsal

Appeasement fails/Britain, France

Interactive Textbook

For additional review and enrichment activities, see the interactive version of *World History* available on the Web and on CD-ROM.

Go Online
PHSchool.com

For practice test questions for Chapter 18, use **Web Code mka-3196.**

Building Vocabulary

(a) Classify each of the chapter vocabulary words listed below under one of the following themes: economics and technology, global interaction, religions and value systems, geography and history. (b) Choose one word in each category and write a sentence explaining how that word relates to the theme.

1. **sanction**
2. **appeasement**
3. **pacifism**
4. **blitzkrieg**
5. **radar**
6. **sonar**
7. **genocide**
8. **collaborator**
9. **island-hopping**
10. **containment**

Recalling Key Facts

11. What happened at the Munich Conference of 1938?
12. What event started World War II? When did it occur?
13. Why was the Battle of Stalingrad important?
14. When and why was the United Nations established?
15. What was the Truman Doctrine?

Critical Thinking and Writing

16. **Linking Past and Present** What lessons does the Holocaust have for us today?
17. **Analyzing Information** Explain the following statement: World War II brought down several dictatorships but increased the power of the world's largest totalitarian state.
18. **Defending a Position** Agree or disagree with the following statement: The western democracies could have prevented World War II. Explain.
19. **Synthesizing Information** (a) How did the United States help the Allies before entering World War II? (b) Was participation by the United States crucial to winning the war? Explain.
20. **Connecting to Geography** How were Hitler's plans to conquer Europe affected by the geography of (a) Britain, (b) Russia?
21. **Drawing Conclusions** (a) Which battle was most important in the war in Europe? (b) Which battle was most important in the war in the Pacific? Explain your answers.

The passage below is from a dispatch filed by Douglas Williams, a reporter for the London *Daily Telegraph*. The report describes Williams's first-hand observation of the evacuation of Dunkirk in May and June of 1940. Read the passage, then answer the questions that follow.

> "All day long and during the night evacuation continued. Rescue vessels raced across the Channel loaded with men to the fullest capacity as fast as conditions would permit, steamed back at full speed across the narrow strip of water to return again with undiminished enthusiasm for fresh batches. . . .
>
> Their position at Dunkirk becomes hourly more dangerous as German batteries begin to receive a full [supply] of ammunition from their supply columns. . . .
>
> Parts of the town are in flames, and entire quarters in ruins. Outside, the main roads present scenes of confusion and destruction. Innumerable abandoned motorcars and [trucks] lie ditched in every field, while others set alight blaze fiercely.
>
> Bodies of refugees killed by German machinegun bullets are seen at frequent intervals, and everywhere long lines of soldiers hurry down to the sea and safety.
>
> Yet the work of evacuation continues uninterruptedly with calm efficiency, while a powerful rear-guard fights magnificently to delay the constantly increasing masses of German troops. . . ."
>
> —Douglas Williams,
> Dunkirk: May 28–June 4, 1940

22. **(a)** Describe the actions of people involved in the rescue operation. **(b)** According to Williams, what was the attitude of the rescuers?
23. **(a)** Why was the position of the Allied troops at Dunkirk becoming more dangerous? **(b)** How does Williams describe conditions at Dunkirk?
24. How would you describe Williams's point of view?
25. **(a)** How do you think the success of this operation affected British morale? **(b)** An American reporter wrote: "So long as the English tongue survives, the word Dunkirk will be spoken with reverence." What do you think the reporter meant by this?

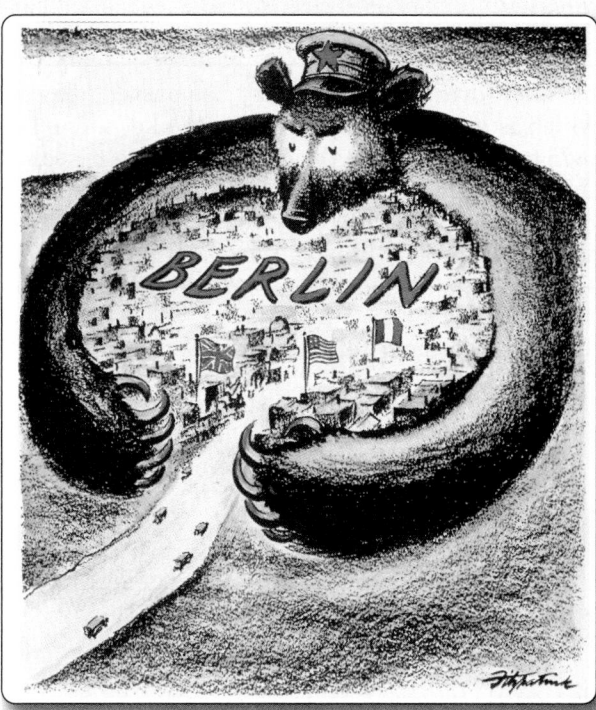

After World War II, relations between Russia and the western nations deteriorated. The cartoon is a comment on developments in Berlin. Study the cartoon, then answer the following questions:

26. What do the flags stand for?
27. **(a)** What does the bear represent? **(b)** What is the bear doing? Why?
28. Based on what you have learned, why did Russia want to close off Berlin?

Skills Tip

Pay careful attention to symbols in political cartoons. Determine how the cartoonist combines symbols to present a point of view.

Go Online
PHSchool.com

Use the Internet to research important events of World War II. Then, create a time line that shows the progression of the war. Use a special color or other design to indicate important dates, such as major turning points. For help with this activity, use **Web Code mkd-3197.**

TEST PREPARATION

Use the quotation and your knowledge of social studies to answer the following question.

> "The Government of the day has passed a law which is applicable to me. I do not like it. If by using violence I force the Government to repeal the law, I am employing what may be termed body-force. If I do not obey the law and accept the penalty for its breach, I use soul-force."

1. This statement reflects one of the major ideas of

   A   Mao Zedong.

   B   Winston Churchill.

   C   Mohandas Gandhi.

   D   Emiliano Zapata.

2. One similarity between the czars of Russia and Joseph Stalin is that both

   A   tried to reduce their nation's involvement in world affairs.

   B   pursued economic policies that limited industrial growth.

   C   worked to suppress the Russian Orthodox Church.

   D   established an authoritarian form of government.

3. A major cause of World War I was

   A   independence movements in Europe's overseas colonies.

   B   the creation of a complex system of alliances.

   C   German U-boat attacks on ships carrying American citizens.

   D   the decline of nationalism in Eastern Europe.

Use the table and your knowledge of social studies to answer the following question.

Industrial Unemployment Rates		
Country	1921–1929	1930–1938
United States	7.9	26.1
United Kingdom	12.0	15.4
France	3.8	10.2
Germany	9.2	21.8

Source (of statistics): Peter Temin, *Lessons from the Great Depression* (Massachusetts Institute of Technology, 1989), page 3.

4. What conclusion about the Great Depression can you draw from this table?

   A   More people were unemployed in the United Kingdom than in France.

   B   Italy did not suffer unemployment during the Great Depression.

   C   Unemployment grew at a greater rate in the United States than in the United Kingdom.

   D   In 1932, the unemployment rate in Germany was 21.8 percent.

5. Which situation contributed to Adolf Hitler's rise to power in Germany?

   A   Economic crises led to increased feelings of resentment and nationalism.

   B   Social Democrats in the Reichstag supported Hitler's radical policies.

   C   In the 1930s, France and Britain demanded that Germany increase its reparations.

   D   The League of Nations refused to admit Germany as a member.

The World at War: World War II

Use the map and your knowledge of social studies to answer the following question.

6. On this map, the areas in gray represent

    A the Allied powers.

    B areas under Axis control.

    C neutral nations.

    D communist countries.

7. Russian peasants supported the Bolsheviks in the 1917 revolution mainly because the Bolsheviks promised to

    A end collective agriculture.

    B bring modern technology to Russian farms.

    C execute the czar and his family.

    D redistribute land owned by the nobility.

8. The Holocaust and the treatment of Armenians in the Ottoman empire are both examples of

    A antisemitism.

    B containment.

    C genocide.

    D appeasement.

Writing Practice

9. Compare Soviet communism to Italian or German fascism. Consider both the goals of each form of government and the methods that both used to maintain power.

10. "The solution of one conflict often contains the seeds of another." Describe EITHER how the ending of World War I led to the start of World War II OR how the ending of World War II led to the start of the Cold War.

UNIT 5

The World Today

1945–Present

This satellite image of Earth shows the Arctic, Europe, Middle East, India, and Africa with a bit of South America. Nations around the world have become increasingly interdependent.

OUTLINE

Chapter 19 **The World Since 1945: An Overview**
(1945–Present)

Chapter 20 **Europe and North America**
(1945–Present)

Chapter 21 **East Asia and Southeast Asia**
(1945–Present)

Chapter 22 **South Asia and the Middle East**
(1945–Present)

Chapter 23 **Africa** (1945–Present)

Chapter 24 **Latin America** (1945–Present)

Themes

As you read about the developments and challenges over the last half of the twentieth century, you will encounter the following themes.

Diversity Conflicts flared between ethnic groups and between old and new ways of life. Urbanization, westernization, and the women's movement challenged the traditional culture.

Economics and Technology After a long struggle for control, communist state-run economies disappeared from Europe. Advances in science and technology dramatically changed human life and thought.

Global Interaction The Cold War between the United States and the Soviet Union dominated international relations in the second half of the century. Colonial empires collapsed as emerging nations in Africa, Asia, and elsewhere won their independence.

Geography and History Economic development often caused serious damage to the natural environment. Global warming, pollution, and diminishing resources were concerns of both rich and poor nations.

Unit Theme Activity

For Your Portfolio The chapters in this unit explore the challenge of ethnic groups to put aside differences and work together for a common good. As you read the chapters, prepare a portfolio project examining how diversity poses concern for a nation's development. Your project might take one of the following forms:
• Poster
• Editorial
• Time line

Chapter 19

The World Since 1945: An Overview (1945–Present)

Since the end of World War II, the world has changed rapidly. Although we cannot yet determine the long-term impact of events of the recent past, we can identify political, social, and economic trends that have shaped the postwar years.

- The collapse of western colonial empires led to the emergence of nearly 100 new countries, mostly in Africa and Asia.
- Nuclear weapons, terrorism, and human rights are enduring issues in an increasingly interdependent world.
- Complex economic ties link the rich nations of the global North and the poor nations of the global South.
- Urbanization, modernization, women's movements, and technology have brought dramatic social changes.
- Technology has revolutionized medicine and agriculture and helped create a global, westernized popular culture.

Chapter 20

Europe and North America (1945–Present)

Western Europe enjoyed tremendous economic growth after World War II. The Cold War pitted the West, led by the United States, against the Soviet Union and its allies. After the Cold War, Eastern and Western Europe moved closer together in regional cooperation.

- In the postwar era, Western European nations expanded social programs and introduced the welfare state. By the 1980s, an economic slowdown forced cuts in social programs.
- The United States led world opposition to communism, pursued economic prosperity, and extended civil rights.
- Efforts to reform inefficiencies in government and the economy led to the collapse of the Soviet Union.
- After shaking off Soviet domination, nations of Eastern Europe faced economic challenges and ethnic conflicts.

Chapter 21

East Asia and Southeast Asia (1945–Present)

China, Japan, and other Asian nations have achieved varying degrees of success in their efforts to modernize. Several of these nations enjoy growing trade and other ties, linking the nations of the Pacific Rim from Asia to the Americas.

- After World War II, Japan introduced democratic reforms and by the 1960s had emerged as an economic superpower.
- Under communist rule, the People's Republic of China achieved modest economic gains while sacrificing individual political freedoms.
- The "Asian tigers"—Taiwan, Hong Kong, Singapore, and South Korea—vaulted into the class of newly industrialized nations.
- Cold War tensions sparked long, devastating conflicts in Korea, Vietnam, and Cambodia.

	1940	1955	1970
AFRICA		**1948** Apartheid is law in South Africa	**1957** Ghana gains independence	**1966** Civil war begins in Nigeria
THE AMERICAS		**1946** Perón becomes president of Argentina	**1962** Cuban missile crisis	
			1954 *Brown* v. *Board of Education of Topeka*	
ASIA AND OCEANIA		**1947** India wins independence		**1966** Cultural Revolution in China
			1954 French leave Vietnam	
EUROPE		**1945** Labour party gains power in Britain	**1956** Hungarian uprising	
			1957 European Community formed	

Chapter 22

South Asia and the Middle East (1945–Present)

In South Asia and the Middle East, nations cast off western rule and set out to modernize. They have often confronted similar challenges—from religious strife and border conflicts to urbanization and population growth.

- Upon achieving independence, India built on the legacy of British rule to create the world's largest democracy.
- Ethnic and religious rivalries have fueled ongoing conflict among people of South Asia.
- Faced with failed development, repressive regimes, and growing Western influence, many Muslim leaders and writers called for a return to traditional Islamic values.
- The long Arab-Israeli struggle, war in Iraq, the war on terrorism, and other conflicts have focused world attention on the Middle East and South Asia.

Chapter 23

Africa (1945–Present)

Leaders of new African nations set out to build strong central governments, achieve economic growth, and raise standards of living. They have faced a variety of obstacles, including economic dependency and political instability.

- After independence, a number of new nations experienced military or one-party rule. Many have since introduced multi-party democracy.
- African nations experimented with different economic systems, including socialism and mixed economies.
- In several regions of Africa, warfare, disease, and drought have resulted in tremendous losses of human lives and property.
- After decades of conflict, South Africa abandoned its system of apartheid in the 1990s and made a transition to democratic rule.

Chapter 24

Latin America (1945–Present)

Despite setbacks, Latin American nations have tried to sustain economic growth and overcome a legacy of poverty and social inequality. Marxism, military rule, and the Roman Catholic Church have been continuing influences in the region.

- In the postwar period, poverty and uneven distribution of wealth fed social unrest in many nations.
- Latin America was a focus of Cold War politics, especially after a communist revolution in Cuba in 1959.
- Through trade, investment, and military intervention, the United States was a dominant force in Latin America.
- Although Mexico enjoyed economic gains in agriculture and manufacturing, most people remained in poverty.
- Argentina and Brazil experienced economic growth and long periods of military rule.

1985　　　　**2000**　　　　**2015**

1980s Drought causes famine in parts of Africa

1994 Mandela wins first multiracial election in South Africa

2003 Death toll from war in central Africa surpasses 3 million

1993 Canada, United States, and Mexico sign NAFTA

2001 U.S. launches war on terrorism after 9/11 attacks

1989 Tiananmen Square massacre in China

1998 India and Pakistan test nuclear weapons

2001 New violence stalls Israeli-Palestinian peace talks

2003 War in Iraq

1979 Revolution in Iran

1970s Greece restores civilian rule

1989 Berlin Wall falls

1991 Breakup of Soviet Union

2000s More nations join NATO and European Union

CHAPTER 19

The World Since 1945: An Overview 1945–Present

Chapter Preview

1 **The Changing Political Climate**
2 **Global Economic Trends**
3 **Changing Patterns of Life**

1969
On July 20, American astronauts become the first people to walk on the moon.

1945
The United Nations is formed. Today, the UN meets in this building in New York City.

1960s
The Green Revolution begins, increasing food production in many developing nations.

CHAPTER EVENTS

1940   1955   1970

The World Economy

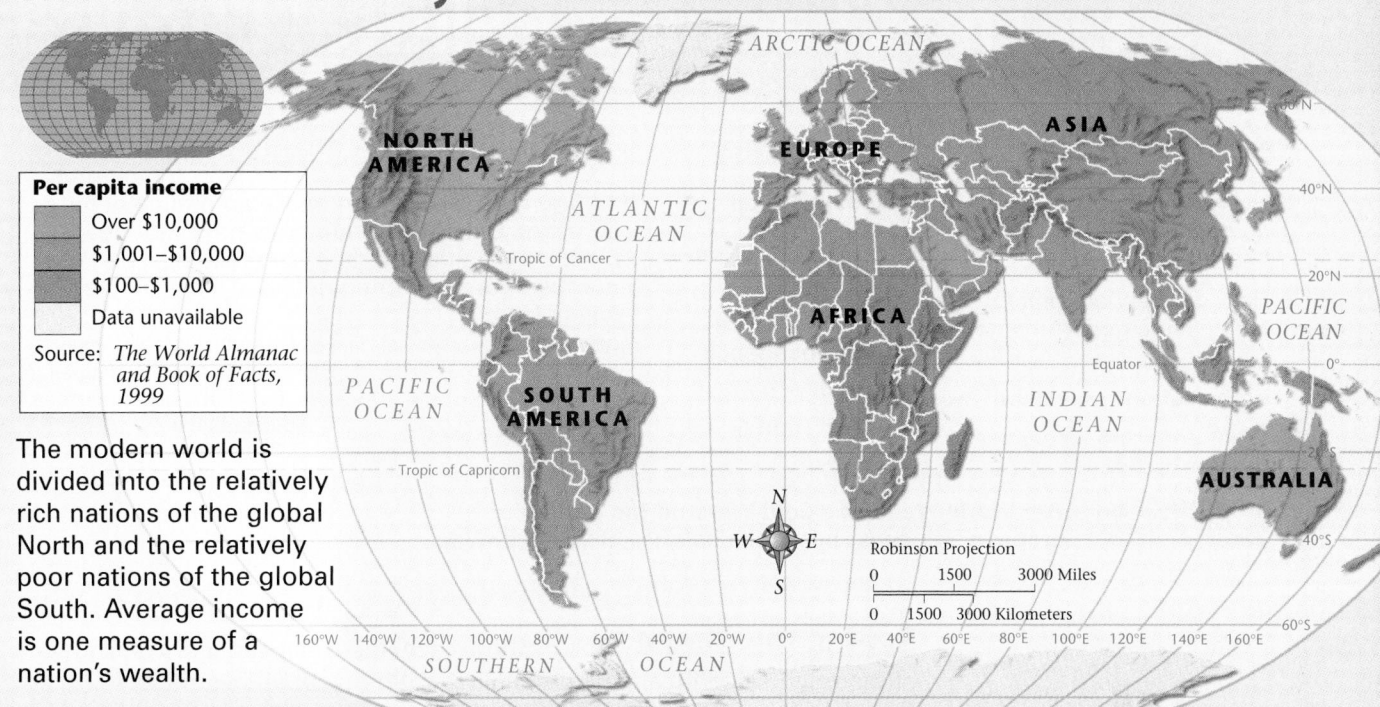

Per capita income

- Over $10,000
- $1,001–$10,000
- $100–$1,000
- Data unavailable

Source: *The World Almanac and Book of Facts, 1999*

The modern world is divided into the relatively rich nations of the global North and the relatively poor nations of the global South. Average income is one measure of a nation's wealth.

1980s

The computer becomes an essential tool in homes and offices. Here, a technician processes data in Senegal.

1991

The global Cold War ends.

2000s

Increased terrorist attacks lead to an international war on terrorism. Here, police guard the site of a 2002 bomb blast in Bali, Indonesia, that killed more than 180 people.

1985   2000   2015

The Changing Political Climate

Reading Focus

- How did the end of colonialism and the Cold War shape the world?
- How did new nations try to form stable governments?
- What role have world organizations played?
- What enduring issues face the world today?

Vocabulary

modernization
superpower
ideology
nonaligned
interdependence
summit
human rights
terrorism

Taking Notes

As you read this section, make an outline of its contents. Use Roman numerals for major headings. Use capital letters for subheadings, and use numbers for supporting details. This example will help you get started.

I. End to European colonial empires
  A. Nationalism and independence
    1. Nationalist leaders insist on independence
    2.
  B. Different roads to freedom
    1.
  C.

Main Idea   After World War II, the Cold War and the decline of European influence shifted the balance of world power.

Setting the Scene   Two centuries ago, the American and French revolutions launched ideals such as the natural rights of all people. In 1972, President Julius Nyerere of Tanzania in East Africa put those ideas in modern terms when he spoke of the goals of new nations that had freed themselves from colonial rule:

> "There is a world-wide movement now—even within the imperialist countries it exists—to put an end to the exploitation [taking advantage] of man by man. This movement will succeed. Eventually, imperialism and racialism will become merely a chapter in the history of man—we shall hear about it in museums."
>
> —Julius K. Nyerere, *Freedom and Development*

The balance of world power changed dramatically after 1945. European influence declined while the United States and the Soviet Union emerged as the world's dominant powers, locked in a tense Cold War. Perhaps the greatest change, however, was the collapse of western overseas empires and the emergence of dozens of new countries.

An End to European Colonial Empires

The postwar decades brought a major turning point in world history. The colonial empires built by western powers during the Age of Imperialism crumbled. In Asia and Africa, people demanded and won freedom. Between 1950 and 1980, more than 50 new nations emerged in Africa alone.

Nationalism and Independence   Resistance to colonial rule had begun long before. By the 1930s, nationalist movements had taken root in Africa, Asia, and the Middle East. After World War II, nationalist leaders such as Gandhi in India insisted on independence.

At first, Britain, France, and other powers tried to hold on to their empires. But the war had exhausted their military and financial resources. With subject peoples ready to fight for freedom, many war-weary Europeans had no desire for further conflict.

The Cold War, too, undermined imperialism. The United States backed the right of colonized people to self-determination. Its rival, the Soviet Union, also had long condemned western imperialism. Soon, both sides were seeking allies among emerging nations.

Connections to Today

The Last Shreds of an Empire

In the great tide of national liberation, Bermuda has gone its own way. It is one of a handful of remaining British colonies, all of them small island remnants of the once-mighty British empire.

A small group of islands that lures half a million visitors per year with soft ocean breezes, Bermuda did experience some political problems. The assassination of the British governor in 1973 and outbreaks of rioting in 1977 delayed independence negotiations. A vote for independence was finally held in August 1995. Prosperous and cautious, the Bermudans voted overwhelmingly to retain their ties to Great Britain.

Theme: Political and Social Systems   Why might a colony choose to vote against independence?

Different Roads to Freedom In most areas, people achieved freedom largely through peaceful means. In a few regions, especially where many whites had settled, colonial rulers were reluctant to leave. Desperate wars of liberation often resulted. France, for example, fought to hold on to Algeria in North Africa and to French Indochina in Southeast Asia. By contrast, it gave up its vast colonial holdings in West Africa without a struggle.

Global Impact Altogether, around 90 new countries emerged during this "great liberation." Some, such as India and Nigeria, were large in area or population. Many others, such as Nepal, Kuwait, and Lesotho, were small.

The new nations of Africa and Asia, as well as the countries of Latin America, became known as the developing world.* Although these nations differed greatly from one another, they shared common goals. All were determined to pursue modernization, which meant building stable governments and developing their countries economically. They followed different paths toward modernization, but many experienced similar challenges.

The needs and goals of developing nations transformed the postwar world. Most joined the United Nations, where they have become an important voice by uniting their interests and often voting as a bloc. Individually and in regional groups, a number of them have played significant roles in global political and economic affairs.

The Cold War Goes Global

The new nations emerged into a world dominated and divided by the Cold War. The United States and Soviet Union emerged as superpowers, nations strong enough to influence the acts and policies of other nations. They competed for influence by offering economic and military aid to developing nations. Each superpower wanted new countries to adopt its ideology, or system of thought or belief—either capitalism or socialism. Many new nations favored socialism, in part because their old colonial rulers had been capitalist. Other nations were attracted by the greater prosperity of the capitalist West.

Nonaligned Nations To avoid superpower rivalry, many new nations chose to remain nonaligned, that is, not allied to either side in the Cold War. The goal of the nonaligned movement was to reduce world tensions and promote economic policies that would benefit developing nations. Giant India, which blended a democratic government with a socialist economy, was a leader in the nonaligned movement.

Hot Spots In Africa, Latin America, and Asia, local conflicts took on a Cold War dimension. Often, the West, led by the United States, supported one side, and the Soviet bloc supported the other. Through such struggles, the superpowers confronted each other indirectly rather than head to head.

Contributing to this tension was the Chinese Communist victory in 1949. When Mao Zedong's forces won control of mainland China, the United States feared that the "red tide" would sweep around the world. American policies, therefore, were designed to stop the communist threat.

On occasion, the Cold War did erupt into "shooting wars," especially in Asia. Both Korea and Vietnam were torn by brutal conflicts in which the United States and the Soviet Union played crucial roles, as you will read.

---

*During the Cold War, the term *Third World* was used to refer to these nations with less-advanced technology than that of the First World (the western industrial powers and Japan) or the Second World (the communist bloc nations).

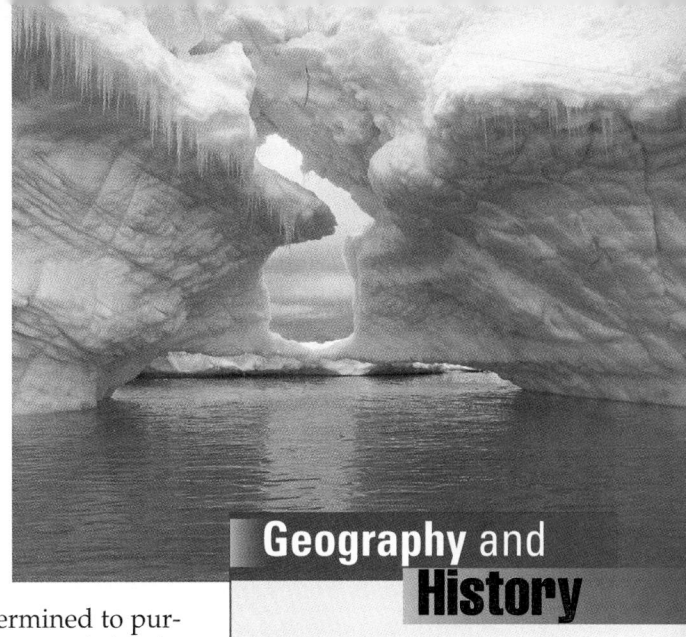

Geography and History

The Coldest Place on Earth

Oddly enough, the coldest place on Earth remained untouched by the Cold War. In 1959, twelve of the world's leading powers—including the United States and the Soviet Union—signed a treaty that made Antarctica a neutral zone of scientific research and cooperation. The continent was now off-limits to military bases, nuclear weapons testing, and radioactive-waste disposal. This treaty was followed in 1991 by a 50-year ban on oil and mineral exploration.

Antarctica is home to as many as 4,000 scientists who may stay for up to a year. Heavily wrapped in special cold-weather gear, they brave temperatures ranging from 32 degrees Fahrenheit to −100 degrees Fahrenheit. These men and women study topics such as global climate changes, ocean life, and geology.

Theme: Geography and History Why is Antarctica a symbol of international cooperation?

The Great Liberation and the Cold War, 1945–1990

Former European colonies that gained independence, 1945–1990   ★ **Cold War hot spots**

Robinson Projection

0   1000   2000 Miles

0   1000 2000 Kilometers

Skills Assessment

Geography As former European colonies won independence, they often became centers of Cold War rivalry.

1. **Location** *On the map, locate (a) United States, (b) Soviet Union, (c) Cuba, (d) Congo, (e) Afghanistan, (f) Vietnam.*
2. **Region** *On which continent did the greatest number of nations win independence?*
3. **Critical Thinking**
   Predicting Consequences *What effect do you think the Cold War might have on new nations seeking to build stable governments?*

The Cold War Ends The Cold War ended suddenly in 1991 when the Soviet Union collapsed. With the western victory in the Cold War, tensions eased and some long-standing conflicts were resolved. But troubling local, regional, and global problems remained.

Ethnic and Religious Conflict Within many nations, ethnic and religious groups have demanded greater independence to protect their cultural and political identity. For example, ethnic Kurds have sought autonomy within Turkey and Iraq, while in Kashmir, Muslims have struggled for independence from predominantly Hindu India. In 2002, after a violent struggle, the Christian people of East Timor won independence from predominantly Muslim Indonesia. In some countries, such as Nigeria, both ethnic and religious differences contribute to violent conflicts.

New Nations Seek Stability

After winning independence, new nations had high hopes for the future. Still, they faced immense problems. Especially in Africa, nations were created out of European colonies that had been carved up during the age of imperialism. People in new nations like Nigeria came from different cultural traditions and had few ties to unite them.

The new nations wrote constitutions modeled on those of western democracies. Only a few, however, like India, were able to sustain democratic rule. In general, colonial rulers had done little to prepare the people for self-government. Many new nations were shaken by revolution or civil war. Often, a wealthy, western-educated elite controlled the government and the economy. The great majority of people remained poor and cut off from advancement.

As problems multiplied, the military or authoritarian leaders often took control. Many times, these were the same people who had led the fight for liberation. They imposed order by building one-party dictatorships. They banned other political parties, claiming that a multiparty system threatened stability. Leaders waved the banner of nationalism, in hope of overcoming ethnic, religious, or regional divisions.

Despite setbacks, democracy did make some progress in the late 1980s and 1990s. In Africa, Asia, and Latin America, nations that had been ruled by dictators or by a single party held multiparty elections. Some of these new democracies have lasted. Others have not. Internal conflicts and lack of experience in representative government upset these fragile experiments in democracy.

Regional and Global Organizations

Since 1945, transportation and communications systems have made the world increasingly interdependent. Interdependence is the dependence of countries on goods, resources, and knowledge from other parts of the world. Political, economic, cultural, and other links have created both problems and opportunities. A number of international organizations deal with issues of global concern.

The United Nations The United Nations was set up at the end of World War II as a forum for settling disputes. Its responsibilities, along with its membership, have expanded greatly since 1945. The UN played a vital role in decolonization. Since then, it has tried to act as peacekeeper from Cambodia to the Middle East and from Africa to the Balkans. Some UN interventions have been successful. Others have failed, often because member nations could not agree on goals and methods.

UN agencies provide services for millions of people worldwide. The World Health Organization (WHO), for example, helped wipe out smallpox through its program of vaccinations. Today, WHO works with other groups to seek a solution to the AIDS crisis. Other UN programs aim to reduce malnutrition or ensure access to safe drinking water. The UN has also sponsored global summits, conferences of leaders and experts from around the world, to discuss issues such as the environment, women, and population.

Other Organizations Many nations formed regional groups to promote trade or meet other common needs. Powerful regional trading blocs have emerged. In later chapters, you will see how such groups as the European Union, the North American Free Trade Association, and the Association of Southeast Asian Nations have worked to lower trade barriers and promote the free exchange of goods and services.

The importance of global trade has been recognized by a series of international treaties. The General Agreement on Tariffs and Trade (GATT), signed in 1947, tried to establish fair trade policies for all nations. In 1995, more than 100 nations joined to form the World Trade Organization (WTO). Its goal was to establish global rules of trade "to ensure that trade flows as smoothly, predictably and freely as possible." Some people have opposed it.

The Group of Eight, or G-8, is another international organization that promotes economic cooperation. The G-8 consists of the world's major industrial democracies: Britain, Canada, France, Germany, Italy, Japan, Russia, and the United States. Representatives of the European Union also attend G-8 summit meetings. Leaders of the G-8 countries meet every year to discuss a wide range of international economic, political, and security issues.

The World Bank and the International Monetary Fund (IMF) play a large role in the world economy, as you will read, by making loans to developing nations. Many other types of nongovernmental organizations

Terrorist Attacks of 9/11
On September 11, 2001, terrorists opposed to American policies in the Middle East crashed several hijacked airplanes into the World Trade Center in New York City (above) and the Pentagon in Washington, D.C. The attacks killed thousands and led to an international war on terrorism.

Theme: Political and Social Systems How can countries cooperate in the fight against terrorism?

▶ **Primary Sources and Literature**

See "The Universal Declaration of Human Rights" in the Reference Section at the back of this book.

(NGOs) have forged valuable global networks, including the International Olympic Committee and the International Red Cross.

Global Issues

Many issues pose a challenge to world peace. Since the United States first exploded two atomic bombs in 1945, many nations have worked to build nuclear weapons. Today, nuclear, biological, and chemical weapons that cause huge casualties are called weapons of mass destruction, or WMD. The spread of such weapons has raised global concerns.

Deadly Weapons During the Cold War, efforts to curb the arms race had only limited success. In 1968, many nations signed the Nuclear Non-Proliferation Treaty (NPT), agreeing to stop the spread of nuclear weapons. In 1995, the treaty was renewed although some nations refused to sign. Why, they asked, could nations like the United States and Russia have nuclear weapons if they could not?

Even after the Cold War ended, many nations kept spending huge sums on the military. By the late 1990s, both India and Pakistan had developed nuclear weapons. In 2003, a crisis erupted when North Korea announced that it had nuclear weapons. In response, countries stepped up their efforts to limit the spread of weapons of mass destruction.

Human Rights In 1948, UN members approved the Universal Declaration of Human Rights. According to the document, all people are entitled to basic rights and freedoms "without distinction of any kind, such as race, color, sex, language, property, birth, or other status." Human rights include "the right to life, liberty, and security of person." In 1975, nations signing the Helsinki Accords guaranteed such basic rights as freedom of speech, religion, and the press as well as the rights to a fair trial, to earn a living, and to live in safety.

Despite these documents, human rights abuses, including torture and arbitrary arrest, occur around the world. At times, the world community has pressed countries to stop abuses. Economic pressure, for example, was used to push South Africa to end its system of apartheid.

In some countries, leaders have accused western nations of trying to impose their own ideas about individual freedom. They claim that their cultures value the community over the individual. Chinese leaders, for example, have argued that economic goals, such as improving the standard of living for their people, are more important than individual political freedom.

Terrorism Since the 1960s, terrorism has increased around the world. Terrorism is the willful use of violence, especially against civilians, to achieve political goals. Terrorists use bombings, kidnappings, airplane hijackings, and shootings to get attention for their causes and to force governments to meet their demands. In Northern Ireland, extremists on both sides murdered civilians. Other terrorists killed Israeli athletes at the 1972 Olympics to push their demands for a Palestinian state.

On September 11, 2001, terrorists opposed to American policies in the Middle East crashed several hijacked airplanes into the World Trade Center in New York and the Pentagon in Washington, D.C. Thousands were killed on this day, which is now commonly called 9/11. The terrorists were members of al-Qaida, an organization led by a Saudi named Osama bin Laden. Al-Qaida had bases in Afghanistan and other countries around the world.

To combat terrorism, governments passed tough laws and increased watchfulness. The United States declared a global war on terrorism and enlisted countries around the world to join the fight.

Intervention Terrorism and human rights violations have raised tough questions. Does the world community have a duty to step in to end abuses? As you will read, the United States and its allies recently took military action against brutal governments in Afghanistan and Iraq. Afghanistan was harboring Osama bin Laden and other terrorists of al-Qaida. The United States believed that Iraq was developing weapons of mass destruction that threatened world peace.

Ethnic conflicts, especially, have led to fierce debates over intervention to protect human rights. The UN has a mixed record on intervention. In the 1990s, UN peacekeepers were sent to northern Iraq to protect the Kurds, an ethnic group suffering brutal government persecution. For complex reasons, though, the UN was slow to move when Serbs persecuted Muslims in Bosnia. Later, the UN did not step in when Hutus massacred an estimated one million Tutsis in Rwanda.

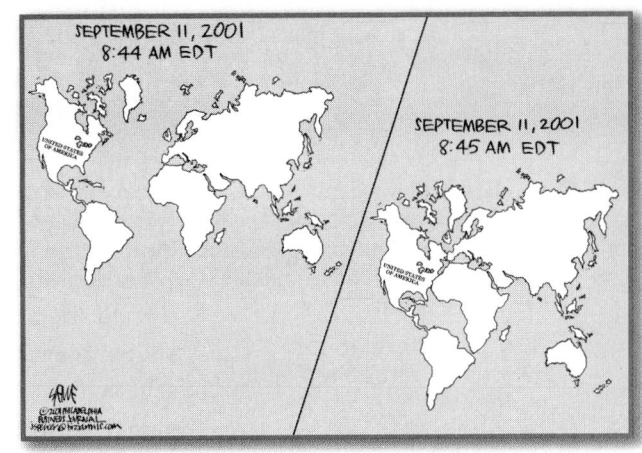

A Smaller World
This American cartoon appeared after the terrorist attack on the World Trade Center in New York.

Theme: Global Interaction According to the cartoon, how did the 9/11 attacks change international relations? Explain.

SECTION 1 Assessment

Recall
1. **Identify:** (a) GATT, (b) International Monetary Fund, (c) NPT, (d) Universal Declaration of Human Rights.
2. **Define:** (a) modernization, (b) superpower, (c) ideology, (d) nonaligned, (e) interdependence, (f) human rights (g) summit, (h) terrorism.

Comprehension
3. (a) Why did European nations lose their colonial empires after World War II? (b) What was one effect of this "great liberation"?
4. Why did political instability plague many developing nations?

5. What two main roles has the UN played in world affairs?
6. Describe one effort nations have made to deal with each of the following issues: (a) the spread of nuclear arms, (b) human rights abuses, (c) terrorism.

Critical Thinking and Writing
7. **Predicting Consequences** Is interdependence likely to make the world more peaceful? Why or why not?
8. **Analyzing Information** (a) Why might lack of experience with representative government be a problem for developing nations? (b) Do you think democracy will help them solve their problems?

Activity

Designing an Invitation
Design an invitation to an international conference on nuclear arms, terrorism, or human rights. Your invitation should clearly state the goals of the meeting and who will participate. You may also design a logo relating to the theme of the meeting.

Global Economic Trends

Reading Focus

- In what ways are the global North and South economically interdependent?
- Why have developing nations had trouble reaching their goals?
- How is economic development linked to the environment?

Vocabulary

multinational corporation
privatization
environmentalist
acid rain
global warming

Taking Notes

On a sheet of paper, draw a Venn diagram like the one shown here. As you read this section, add more information, including the area where the ovals overlap.

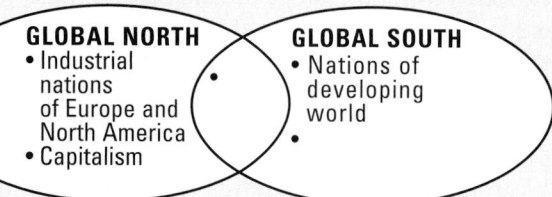

GLOBAL NORTH
- Industrial nations of Europe and North America
- Capitalism

GLOBAL SOUTH
- Nations of developing world

Main Idea The industrial nations of the global North and the developing nations of the global South have become increasingly interdependent.

Setting the Scene "Ours is a time of problems, of gigantic problems," noted Pope Paul VI in 1969. "And every day, if we want to live with open eyes, we have a problem to study, to resolve." Among these difficulties is the growing gulf between rich and poor nations. Yet in today's interdependent world, rich and poor nations are closely linked.

The Global North and South

The Cold War created an ideological split between the communist East and the capitalist West. Today, an economic gulf divides the world into two spheres—the relatively rich nations of the global North and the relatively poor nations of the global South.

Rich Nations The global North includes the industrial nations of Europe and North America, as well as Japan and Australia. Most are located in the temperate zone north of the Equator. They control most of the world's wealth. Although pockets of poverty exist, the standard of living in the North is generally high. Most people are literate, earn adequate wages, and have basic health services.

These rich nations have basically capitalist economies. Decisions about what to produce and for whom are generally regulated by the free market, not by the government. The governments of these nations do support economic growth through transportation and communication systems, public education, and social services. They also regulate their economies in various ways, from requiring pure food and drugs to preventing stock market fraud. Still, in the global North, economic success is driven by the free market.

Poor Nations The global South refers to the developing world. Most of these nations lie in Asia, Africa, and Latin America in the zone between the Tropics of Cancer and Capricorn. The South has 75 percent of the world's population and much of its natural resources. Some nations have enjoyed strong growth, especially the Asian "tigers," the oil-exporting nations of the Middle East, and several Latin American nations. Overall, though, the global South remains generally underdeveloped and poor. Unlike the nations that industrialized before 1900, newer nations have not had enough time to build up their capital, resources, or industries.

For most people in the developing world, life is a daily struggle for survival. About one billion people worldwide live in extreme poverty—many of them children.

Migration Despite some advances in the developing world, the gap between rich and poor nations is widening. The imbalance has sparked migration of people from poor regions to wealthier ones. Every year, refugees flee poverty or war to seek a better life in Western Europe, North America, and Australia. Millions of others, however, remain close to their homes.

Economic Interdependence

Rich and poor nations are linked by many economic ties. The nations of the global North control much of the world's capital, trade, and technology. But they depend increasingly on low-paid workers in developing states to produce manufactured goods as inexpensively as possible. This shift in labor has led to a loss of manufacturing jobs in many western nations.

Huge multinational corporations, with branches in many countries, have invested in the developing world. They bring new technology to mining, agriculture, transportation, and other industries. Rich nations also provide aid, technical advisers, and loans. At the same time, interdependence has often led to resentment. With its great buying power, the North controls the prices of goods and commodities produced by the South. In addition, multinational corporations remove many profits from developing countries and often limit workers' attempts to seek higher wages.

The Oil Crisis In an interdependent world, events in one country or region can affect people everywhere. A drastic example of this was the oil crisis of the 1970s. All nations use oil for transportation and for products ranging from plastics to fertilizers. This demand has allowed nations with oil resources to seek favorable prices on the world market.

Much of the world's oil comes from the Middle East. In 1973, a political crisis in the region led the Organization of Petroleum Exporting Countries (OPEC) to halt its oil exports and raise oil prices. Shortages and soaring fuel prices set off economic shock waves. Suddenly, industrialized nations realized how much they depended on imported oil. While some efforts were made to find other fuels or to conserve energy use, the energy crisis showed what impact a single vital product could have on the world economy.

The Debt Crisis Another complex economic problem involved the growing debt owed by poor nations to rich ones. Developing nations, needing capital to modernize,

The World of Refugees
By 2000, nearly 20 million refugees around the world had fled poverty and turmoil. Many, like these children from Bosnia (top) and Rwanda (bottom), crowded into refugee camps near their home countries.

Theme: Global Interaction
Based on these pictures, how might you react to living in a refugee camp?

took loans offered by western banks. In the 1980s, however, bank interest rates rose, while the world economy slowed down. As demand for many of their goods fell, poor nations were unable to repay their debts or even the interest on their loans. Their economies stalled as they spent their income from exports on payments to their foreign creditors.

The debt crisis hurt rich nations, too, as banks were stuck with billions of dollars of bad debts. To ease the crisis, the International Monetary Fund, the World Bank, and private banks worked out agreements with debtor nations. Lenders lowered interest rates or gave some nations more time to repay the loans. In some cases, debts were even canceled altogether.

In return, debtor nations had to agree to adopt free-market policies. Many ended governmental supports for industry. They turned instead to privatization, selling off state-owned industries to private investors. Nations hoped that more efficient private enterprises would bring prosperity in the long run. Still, the immediate effects of privatization often hurt the poor.

Economic Trouble Spots Other economic crises have shown the interdependence of the world's financial markets. In 1997, Japan, the world's second richest economy, fell into recession. The downturn affected other Asian economies from Singapore to South Korea. The Asian financial crisis, as it was called, also affected Russia as it struggled to replace its old communist system with capitalism.

More recently, Argentina was plunged into crisis after it was unable to pay its debts. Argentina's neighbors, Brazil and Uruguay, also faced economic worries. In many African nations, the AIDS crisis is expected to take a huge economic—and human—toll.

Economic Organizations Various international economic organizations deal with global economic issues. The World Bank, for example, offers loans and advice to developing countries. The International Monetary Fund (IMF) has become a lender of last resort to countries in crisis. It monitors economic developments and provides expert advice to help countries solve economic problems.

Although these organizations seek to ease economic problems, their policies have stirred controversy. Before making loans, they often require governments to make economic reforms and cut costly social programs. The poor in these countries have at times rioted or even overthrown their governments. Recently, a worldwide protest movement has emerged. Its supporters loudly attack the policies of the World Bank and the IMF.

Obstacles to Development

Why have many developing nations been unable to make progress toward modernization? The answers vary from country to country, but many shared problems in five general areas: (1) geography, (2) population and poverty, (3) economic dependence, (4) economic policies, and (5) political instability.

Geography In parts of Africa, Asia, and Latin America, geography has posed an obstacle to development. For example, some of the African countries created since the 1950s are tiny and have few natural resources. Difficult climates, uncertain rainfall, lack of good farmland, and disease have added to the problems of some nations.

Population and Poverty The worldwide population boom that began in the 1700s has continued. Better medical care and increased food supplies have reduced death rates and led to explosive population growth. In the developing world, though, rapid growth is linked to poverty. Each year, the populations of countries like Nigeria and India increase by millions. All those people need food, housing, education, jobs, and medical care. Meeting these needs puts a staggering burden on developing nations.

Health Statistics of Selected Countries

Country	Population (thousands)	Life Expectancy at Birth (male/female)	Physicians (per 1,000 people)	Infant Mortality (deaths per 1,000)
Angola	10,366	37/40	0.05	194
Argentina	37,385	72/79	2.7	18
Guatemala	12,974	64/69	0.9	46
Japan	126,772	78/84	1.9	4
Jordan	5,153	75/80	1.7	20
Myanmar	41,735	54/57	0.3	74
Netherlands	15,981	76/81	2.6	4
Nigeria	126,636	51/51	0.2	73
Poland	38,634	69/78	2.3	9
United States	278,059	74/80	2.7	7

Sources: *World Almanac and Book of Facts* (2002) and *Financial Times World Desk Reference* (2002)

Skills Assessment

Chart Population and poverty can have a critical impact upon a nation's state of health. At right, a doctor in Guatemala treats a poor Indian child. **In which country shown here is life expectancy highest? Which has the fewest physicians per 1,000 people?**

Across the developing world, people are caught in a cycle of poverty. Millions of people die each year from hunger-related illnesses. Children are the most vulnerable. The UN estimates that 35,000 children die each day from malnutrition, disease, and other effects of poverty.

Many developing nations have tried to slow population growth. Few countries, except China, want to force people to limit family size. In farming societies, children are a source of labor. They are seen as an insurance policy to support their parents in old age. Religious traditions often encourage large families. Also, despite education efforts, many people still lack information about or access to family planning.

Economic Dependence Often, economic patterns formed during the Age of Imperialism have survived. Most new nations remained dependent on their former colonial rulers. They sold agricultural products and raw materials to the industrial world. In turn, they relied on the West for manufactured goods, technology, and investment. Also, many new nations had only a single export crop or commodity, such as sugar, cocoa, or copper. Their economies depended on world demand for the product.

As you have read, developing nations borrowed heavily from foreign banks. These funds were intended for development. Once in debt, though, nations had to spend much of their resources to pay interest.

Economic Policies Many newly independent nations saw socialism, rather than capitalism, as a way to modernize quickly. They modeled their economies on those of China or the Soviet Union, rather than on those of their former colonial rulers. Under socialism, the government controls the economy. These nations had little private capital, so only the government could raise the money to finance large-scale development projects.

At first, emerging nations made some gains. But in the long run, socialism often blocked economic growth. Later, like their models China and Russia, many developing nations introduced free-market policies.

Political Instability Political unrest often hindered economic development. El Salvador, Lebanon, Cambodia, and Angola are among the many nations devastated by civil wars. Military dictators or other authoritarian leaders spent huge sums on weapons and warfare instead of on education, housing, or health care. In addition, war created millions of refugees. The loss of their labor further hurt war-torn countries.

Comparing Viewpoints

What Is the Relationship Between People and the Environment?

Today, environmental issues are getting worldwide attention. Is it more important for a poor nation to protect its environment or to develop its resources? How much right do people have to alter the environment in the first place? To begin your investigation, examine the following viewpoints.

Greece 300s B.C.

The scientist and philosopher Aristotle used logic to explain relationships in the natural world:

❝ Plants exist for the sake of animals, and animals exist for the sake of man—the tame for use and food, and the wild, if not all, at least the greater part of them, for food and for the provision of clothing and various instruments. Now, if nature makes nothing in vain, [it follows] that she has made all animals for the sake of man. ❞

Russia 1890s

Concern that humankind is exploiting its environment drove famous Russian author Anton Chekhov to write:

❝ Man has been endowed with reason, with the power to create, so that he can add to what he's been given. But up to now he hasn't been a creator, only a destroyer. Forests keep disappearing, rivers dry up, wildlife's become extinct, the climate's ruined and the land grows poorer and uglier every day. ❞

Indonesia 1980s

Dr. Sumitro Djojohadikusumo, the former minister of trade and industry, gave his views on managing and protecting the environment:

❝ If we are to make further progress, we need the natural resources, we need the timber, we need the water, we need the fish. We can apply science to manage nature so that everyone benefits, even the animals. ❞

United States 1990s

American cartoonist Tom Toles commented on protecting biodiversity, the wide variety of plant and animal species on the planet.

Skills Assessment

1. Whose viewpoint emphasizes the complete dominance of people over nature?
   A Chekhov
   B Toles
   C Djojohadikusumo
   D Aristotle

2. Chekhov and Toles would agree that
   E the environment will continue to improve on its own.
   F humans have done much to alter the environment.
   G there are no environmental problems.
   H Aristotle was right.

3. **Critical Thinking** **Defending a Position** You are going to write a letter to Congress about an environmental issue. Include specific examples that support your point of view.

Skills Tip

When you express a point of view, you should cite specific examples to support your position.

Development and the Environment

For both rich and poor nations, economic development has taken a heavy toll on the environment. Modern industry and agriculture have gobbled up natural resources and polluted much of the world's water, air, and soil.

Growing Threats Since earliest times, people everywhere have taken what they wanted from their environment. In the past, damage was limited because the world's population was relatively small and technology was simple. With the Industrial Revolution and the population explosion, the potential for widespread environmental damage grew.

By the 1970s, environmentalists raised the alarm about threats to the planet's fragile environment. Strip mining provided ores for industry but destroyed much land. Chemical pesticides and fertilizers produced more food crops but harmed the soil and water. Oil spills polluted vital waterways and killed marine life. Gases from power plants and factories produced acid rain, a form of pollution in which toxic chemicals in the air fall back to the Earth as rain, snow, or hail. Acid rain damaged forests, lakes, and farmland, especially in industrial Europe and North America.

Over the last century, world temperatures have increased. Scientists blame this global warming on the emission of gases into the upper atmosphere. Many warn that global warming will continue in the future.

Industrial accidents focused attention on threats to the environment. In Bhopal, India, a leak from a pesticide plant in 1984 killed 3,600 people. In 1986, an accident at the Chernobyl nuclear power plant in the Soviet Union exposed people, crops, and animals to deadly radiation over a wide area. Although industries and governments have developed safety measures, such measures are often expensive and not always successful.

Protecting the Environment Rich nations consume most of the world's resources and produce much of its pollution. At the same time, they have led the campaign to protect the environment. Most have laws to control pollution and ensure conservation.

At environmental summits, world leaders hotly debated how to preserve the planet. Should economic development take priority over protecting the environment? Are people, especially in rich nations, willing to do with less in order to conserve resources? Many agreed that permanent damage to the planet was too high a price for economic progress. Agreeing on solutions, however, is a challenge for the future.

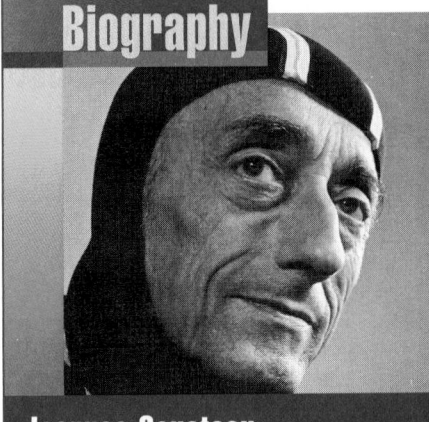

Biography

Jacques Cousteau
1910–1997

Jacques Cousteau introduced millions of people around the world to a wondrous and previously unexplored world within our world—the vast depths of the oceans.

Cousteau helped develop the aqualung, making it possible for divers to remain submerged for hours at a time. Aboard his research ship, the *Calypso*, he documented oceans, rivers, and the marine life they contained. His popular films, books, and television series educated the world about the beauty and fragility of the sea. Today, the Cousteau Society continues its founder's goal of preserving the undersea environment.

Theme: Impact of the Individual How did Cousteau help protect the world's oceans?

SECTION 2 Assessment

Recall
1. **Identify:** **(a)** OPEC, **(b)** Chernobyl.
2. **Define:** **(a)** multinational corporation, **(b)** privatization, **(c)** environmentalist, **(d)** acid rain, **(e)** global warming.

Comprehension
3. How do the nations of the global North and global South depend on one another?
4. What obstacles do developing nations face?
5. How has economic development increased the potential for widespread damage to the environment? Give two examples.

Critical Thinking and Writing
6. **Applying Information** Describe how each of the following showed interdependence: **(a)** the oil crisis, **(b)** the Asian financial crisis.
7. **Making Decisions** Would you be willing to pay much higher prices for manufactured goods such as clothing or your first car if it would help conserve the world's resources? Why or why not?

Go Online
PHSchool.com

Use the Internet to do research on a current environmental issue such as acid rain, desertification, deforestation, waste disposal, or threats to endangered species. Then, write an editorial explaining the issue and taking a stand on it. For help with this activity, use **Web Code mkd-3217.**

Reading Focus

- How are new ways of life replacing old ways?
- How has modernization affected the lives of women?
- What are the benefits and limits of modern science and technology?
- What forces have shaped a new global culture?

Main Idea Forces such as urbanization, religion, and changing roles for women have shaped world societies.

Vocabulary

shantytown
fundamentalist
liberation theology
feminist movement
e-commerce
genetic engineering

Taking Notes

On a sheet of paper, draw a concept web to show the changing patterns of life in the past 50 years. Use this web to help you get started. As you read, add as many circles as you need.

CHANGING PATTERNS OF LIFE · Urbanization · New roles for women · Science and technology

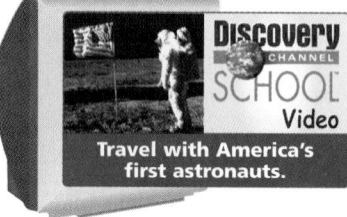

Travel with America's first astronauts.

Endangered Languages

Of the 6,700 different languages spoken in the world today, many are spoken only in isolated rural areas or on remote islands among a handful of elderly residents. As families migrate to cities or other countries, their children often grow up speaking a dominant language, such as English, Hindi, or Spanish. In the next century, some linguists predict that 90 to 95 percent of all current languages will disappear. That is an average of more than one language every two weeks. Scholars are now working to preserve oral and written records of many of these disappearing languages.

Theme: Diversity How has migration affected the diversity of languages spoken?

Setting the Scene

"My village is changing," observed Indian writer Prafulla Mohanti. A road was built there in the 1960s to carry iron ore from a nearby mine to a port city some 40 miles away. Since then, Mohanti said, "Nylon, stainless steel, plastic, [and] fizzy drinks have reached the village."

New products and technology are changing villages around the world. At the same time, millions of villagers have migrated to cities, and that has further transformed the lives of people in the developing world.

Old Ways and New

In the western world, industrialization and urbanization began more than 200 years ago during the Industrial Revolution. In the past 50 years, the rest of the world has experienced similar upheavals.

Urbanization Since 1945, people in the developing world have flocked to cities to find jobs and escape rural poverty. Cities offer economic opportunities and attractions such as stores, concerts, and sports. Today, more than half of the world's population lives in urban areas.

With no money and few jobs, some newcomers settled in shantytowns. These slums on the outskirts of cities are as crowded and dangerous as European cities were in the 1800s. They lack basic services such as running water or sewers. Drugs and crime are constant threats.

In the cities, the extended family of rural villages is giving way to the nuclear family. As urban children go to school and learn how to read, they often reject their parents' ways. Without the support of the village and the extended family, older beliefs and values are undermined by such urban values as material wealth, education, and job status. Many villagers who move to cities suffer a sense of stress and isolation.

Westernization In cities, people frequently adopt western fashions and ideas. During the Age of Imperialism, westerners taught that their civilization was superior. Even after independence, many people in emerging nations felt that the way to modernize was to follow western models.

Some early nationalists, such as Mohandas Gandhi, rejected the rush to abandon traditional ways. Today, leaders in some Muslim lands have called for "modernization without westernization." Although they welcome modern technology, they want to preserve older traditions and religious beliefs. They reject western emphasis on material success and the individual, which they think undermines the community and family.

Village Life Despite urbanization, villages are still home to billions of people, mostly in the global South. Their lives vary widely, depending on climate, geographic isolation, and other factors. Still, village life follows similar patterns in much of the world. Many villagers are farmers. Their workday begins at sunrise. Women wash clothes in local streams. Young and old labor in fields or in workshops. Villagers exchange news at tiny shops in the village center and celebrate centuries-old religious festivals.

Westernization and technology are transforming villages. Changes such as roads, clinics, and television can enrich life. But they also weaken traditional cultures and lure young people to abandon villages for cities.

Religious Influences The major world religions and their offshoots still shape modern societies. In recent times, religious revivals have swept many regions. Christian, Muslim, Jewish, Buddhist, and Hindu reformers offer their own solutions to modern problems. Some of these reformers have been called fundamentalists because they stress what they see as the fundamental, or basic, values of their faiths. Many have sought political power in order to resist changes which they think undermine their beliefs.

In the West, evangelical Protestant groups emphasize salvation through faith and preaching, offering spiritual guidelines in a rapidly changing world. In the 1960s, the Second Vatican Council gave Roman Catholics more freedom to discuss issues and promoted cooperation with other Christian denominations. In Latin America, some Roman Catholic clergy backed a movement called liberation theology. They urged the Church to take a more active role in opposing the social conditions that contributed to poverty. Conservative Catholic forces often oppose such political activities.

In the Muslim world, too, religious reformers have called for change. They rejected what they saw as the West's emphasis on secular goals and the impact of western culture. Instead, they wanted to return to a strict version of Sharia, or Islamic law, to guide governments and people.

New Rights and Roles for Women

After 1945, women's movements brought changes to both the western and the developing nations. The UN Charter supported "equal rights for men and women." By 1950, women had won the right to vote in most European nations, as well as in Japan, China, Brazil, and other countries. In most African nations, both women and men won the vote at independence.

A small but growing number of women won elected office. Women headed democratic governments in Britain, Israel, India, Pakistan, the Philippines, and other countries. Still, a report to the UN noted that while women represent half of the world's people, "they perform nearly two thirds of all working hours, receive only one tenth of the world's income, and own less than one percent of world property."

The West In the industrialized world, more and more women worked outside the home. By the 1970s, the feminist movement sought greater access for women to jobs and promotions, equal pay for equal work, and an end to sexual harassment on the job. Women advanced into high-profile jobs as business owners and executives, astronauts, scientists, and technicians.

Religious Influences
Despite revolutionary changes, religious traditions remain a powerful force throughout the modern world. At top, a Christian woman prays in Kenya. At bottom, Buddhists gather at a temple in Vietnam.

Theme: Religions and Value Systems Besides those represented below, what other religions have millions of followers today?

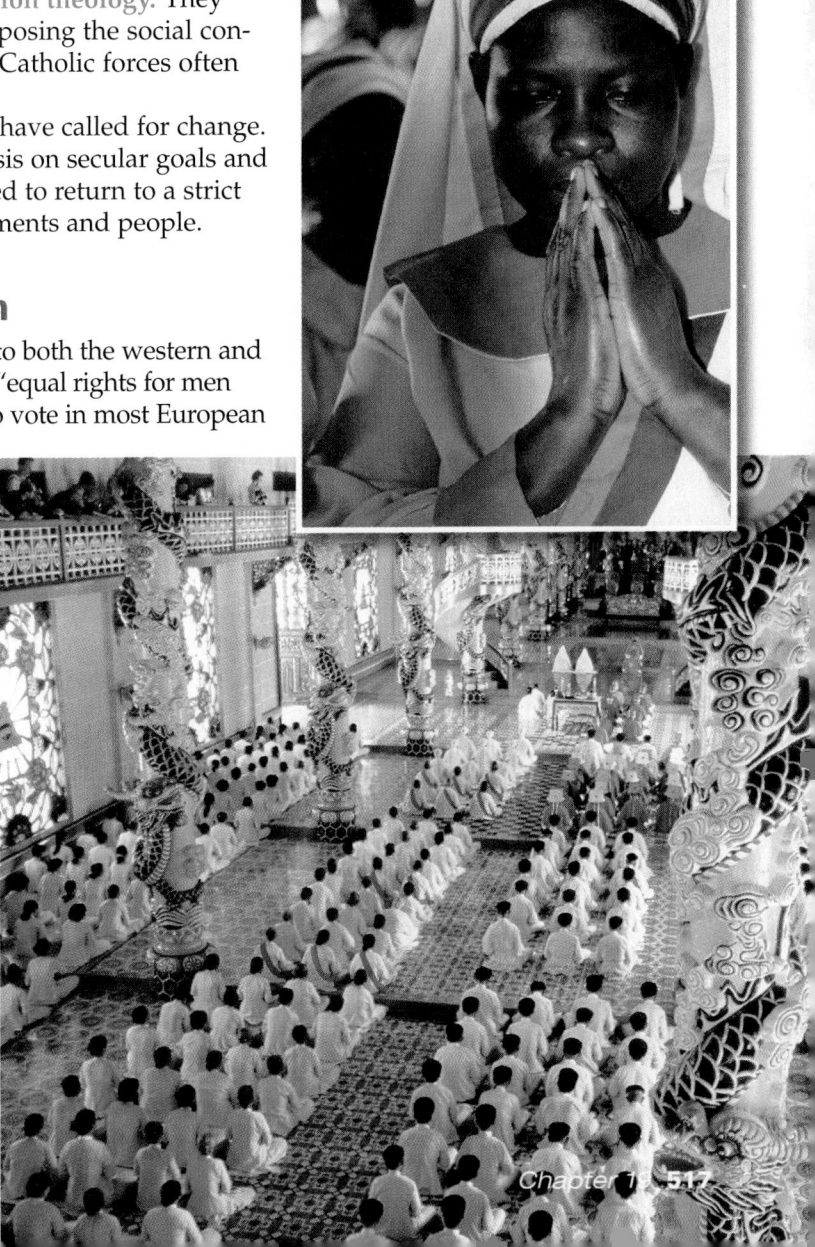

Women's Work
The following is an account of women's lives in the Kenyan countryside:

"One third of all rural households are headed by women, largely because men have migrated to the cities and towns in the hope of finding salaried work. Their wives continue to work the family plots of land and are always busy with some scheme to earn a bit of cash. Everywhere, one sees women walking to market with basketloads of vegetables on their heads, infants strapped to their backs, and older children following behind. Even while they are walking to the market, these women often are weaving baskets or fashioning other handiwork that they hope to exchange for cash needed for the family's support and for the children's education."

—P. Houston, *Third World Women Speak Out*

Skills Assessment

Primary Source According to the passage, why are so many Kenyan women the heads of their households?

New roles for women raised difficult social issues. Working women had to balance jobs with child rearing and household work. Some critics claimed that the growing number of women in the work force was partly responsible for rising divorce rates and a decline in family life. Others responded that many families required two incomes.

The Developing World In emerging nations, women worked actively in nationalist struggles. New constitutions spelled out equality for women, at least on paper. Although women still had less education than men, the gap narrowed. Women from the middle and elite classes entered the work force in growing numbers. Their skills contributed to their nations' wealth.

Still, women often shoulder a heavy burden of work in and out of the home. In rural areas, especially in Africa, women traditionally do much of the farmwork along with household tasks. In recent times, men have gone to cities to find work, leaving women with added responsibilities. In other regions, such as Southeast Asia, it is often young women who leave home to work, helping to support the family or pay for the education of their brothers. In many places, religious and cultural traditions confine women to the home or segregate men and women in the workplace.

Science and Technology

Since 1945, technology has transformed human life and thought. Instant communication via satellites has shrunk the globe. New forms of energy, especially nuclear power, have been added to the steam power, electricity, and gasoline energy of the first industrial age.

The Computer Revolution The computer has brought an information revolution. The first electronic computers, built in the 1940s, were huge, slow machines. Later, the computer was miniaturized, thanks to inventions like the silicon chip. By 2000, a huge computer network linked individuals, governments, and businesses around the world. Computerized robots operated in factories, and computers appeared in more and more homes and schools. E-commerce, or buying and selling on the Internet, contributed to economic growth and vitality. At the same time, however, access to computers widened the gap between the global North and South.

Medical and Biological Breakthroughs In the postwar era, the field of medicine achieved amazing successes. Vaccines helped prevent the spread of smallpox and other diseases. Toward the end of the century, however, the spread of deadly diseases such as AIDS created new challenges for researchers and public health officials.

In the 1970s, surgeons learned to transplant organs to save lives. Lasers made surgery safer. Scientists also had success in treating some cancers. Yet advances in medicine were costly and usually limited to people and nations that could afford them.

A controversial area of medical research is genetic engineering, which alters the chemical code carried by living things. Genetic research has produced new drug therapies. It has also created new strains of fruits and vegetables, which some see as unnatural and dangerous "Frankenfood." The possibility of cloning genetically identical mammals has also raised ethical questions about how far science should go to create and change life.

The Space Age In 1957, the space age started when the Soviet Union launched *Sputnik*, the first artificial satellite, into orbit. *Sputnik* set off a frantic "space race" between the superpowers. In 1969, the United States landed the first man on the moon. Both superpowers explored the military uses of space and sent spy satellites to orbit the Earth. Since the Cold War, the United States and Russia have cooperated in joint space ventures.

COMPUTERS and the Arts

Rapid advances in computer technology have revolutionized the arts. Computers have given artists, writers, musicians, photographers, and filmmakers new tools with which to release their imaginations. From computer-generated graphics to film animation to electronically synthesized music, digital technologies are transforming the practice and content of art.

Using a computer, a graphic artist manipulated reality to create this image of marbles in a maze.

Toy Story (1995) was the first full-length feature film in which all the images were computer-generated.

A composer uses a keyboard hooked up to a computer to create music.

Fast Facts

- It took animators 800,000 hours to generate the images for the movie *Toy Story.*

- The first electronic musical instrument, invented in 1919, was called the theremin. The performer waved his or her hands around two antennas to control the pitch and volume. No physical contact with the instrument was needed.

Portfolio Assessment

Conduct research to find samples of computer-generated graphics. Then, prepare a class presentation on the material you have found. Alternatively, you might research one of the instruments or techniques used to create electronic music, such as synthesizers, drum machines, sequencers, MIDI, or notation-based software. Download one or two selections to share with the class.

Virtual Field Trip

For: More photographs of missions to outer space
Visit: PHSchool.com
Web Code: mkd-3222

The Space Age
The International Space Station was built and is operated by the United States, Canada, Japan, Russia, Brazil, and 11 nations in Europe. An astronaut works on a robotic arm of the station in space.

Theme: Global Interaction
How does the International Space Station reflect changes in the world's political climate?

European nations, as well as Japan and China, launched their own satellites, mostly for peaceful purposes. Satellites mapped weather and tracked droughts, livestock diseases, and plagues. In the weightlessness of space, scientists experimented with promising new drugs and vaccines.

The Green Revolution Scientists applied new technology to increasing food production for the world's growing population. During the 1960s, they touched off the Green Revolution, developing new kinds of rice and other grains that yielded more food per acre than older strains. In India, Indonesia, and elsewhere, the Green Revolution doubled food output.

The Green Revolution had limits, however. It succeeded only in areas with regular moisture. Also, it required chemical fertilizers and pesticides as well as irrigation systems, which only wealthy farmers could afford. Unable to compete with larger, more efficient agricultural enterprises, many poor peasants were forced off their small farms.

Ongoing Issues Technology has improved life for people everywhere. Many people, especially in the industrial world, pin their hopes on technology to solve a variety of economic, medical, and environmental problems. Yet it has not solved such basic problems as hunger or poverty. Also, while technology has created many new kinds of jobs, it has threatened others. For example, a single computer can process thousands of telephone calls that were once handled by human operators.

A New Global Culture

"Radio has changed everything," noted Egyptian leader Gamal Abdel Nasser in the 1950s. "Today, people in the most remote villages hear of what is happening and form their opinions." Modern communications technology has indeed created a "new world." Radio, television, fax machines, satellites, and computer networks have put people everywhere in touch and helped create a new global culture.

Westernized Popular Culture The driving force behind this global culture has been the United States. American fashions, products, and entertainment have captured the world's imagination. American movies and television programs play in Beijing, Buenos Aires, and Cairo. English has become the leading language of international business.

Some critics have compared this westernization of culture to a foreign invasion. Yet the new global culture has sometimes balanced western and nonwestern traditions. From Latin America, popular music such as calypso and reggae gained international popularity. Movie makers like Japan's Akira Kurosawa and India's Satyajit Ray adapted western techniques to express their own distinct traditions.

The Arts Global exchanges have influenced literature and the visual arts for hundreds of years. By the 1700s, Europeans were copying Turkish carpets and Chinese pottery. A century later, European painters adapted the printmaking traditions of Japan. At the same time, Japanese artists were studying the styles of European painters. More recently, writers from Africa to India have adapted literary forms, such as the novel, from the West.

In the last 100 years, the western world has gained a new appreciation for the arts of other civilizations. Western artists studied Southeast Asian and African sculptures, dances, and music.

Global interest in the arts has led nations to value and protect ancient cultural treasures. The UN and other groups are helping countries preserve and restore temples, palaces, manuscripts, and other artifacts. Museums, too, preserve the heritage of the past. Traveling exhibits of Egyptian jewelry, Russian icons, Indian sculpture, or West African masks help modern audiences understand cultures from other times and places.

Looking Ahead

The recent past presents special problems for students of history. We can see the immediate results of recent events, but cannot know their long-term impact. Many recent trends and issues emerged long before 1945 and will continue for decades. At the same time, new issues and new conflicts will almost certainly take shape.

In the next five chapters, we will see how many of the trends and issues discussed in this chapter have affected different regions of the world. As you read, notice the impact of two contradictory trends. Nationalism, along with ethnic politics, is on the rise. Yet global interdependence has become an inescapable fact of life. Across the world, people must reconcile local and global interests.

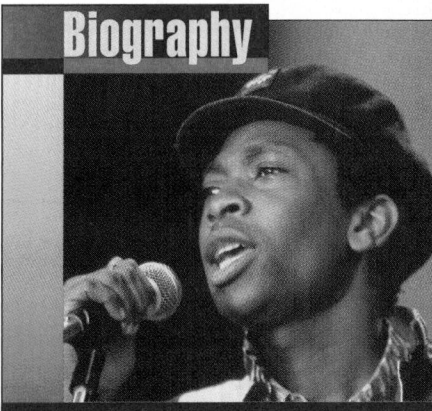

Biography

Youssou N'Dour 1959—

In the 1980s, singer and musician Youssou N'Dour helped popularize "world beat" music. This new global rhythm mixes African, Latin, and western styles.

As a child, N'Dour absorbed the sounds of traditional Senegalese drum music. He was also inspired by reggae, funk, soul, jazz, and Cuban music. These influences created *mbalax*, music in which the "talking drum" is the main instrument.

Today, N'Dour considers himself "a modern griot." His music, he says, is "a representation of not only African music but of African life and the whole image of Africa."

Theme: Impact of the Individual How is N'Dour's music an example of international culture?

SECTION 3 Assessment

Recall

1. **Identify:** **(a)** *Sputnik,* **(b)** Green Revolution.
2. **Define:** **(a)** shantytown, **(b)** fundamentalist, **(c)** liberation theology, **(d)** feminist movement, **(e)** e-commerce, **(f)** genetic engineering.

Comprehension

3. How has urbanization affected people in developing nations?
4. Describe two changes in the roles and rights of women.
5. How have three developments in science or technology affected the modern world?

6. How did American influences shape a new global culture?

Critical Thinking and Writing

7. **Predicting Consequences** What do you think might be some major global issues of the next century?
8. **Applying Information** "Educate a boy," says an African proverb, "and you educate a person. Educate a girl, and you educate a nation." **(a)** What does the proverb assume about the role of women in society? **(b)** What goal could this proverb be used to support?

Go Online
PHSchool.com

Use the Internet to learn about the history of computers and how they have affected contemporary society. Then, make a time line showing key events in the story of computers up to the present. You may illustrate your time line if you choose. For help with this activity, use **Web Code mkd-3223.**

Creating a Chapter Summary

On a sheet of paper, make a concept web like the one shown here.
Add as many circles as you need to show the key ideas of this chapter.

For additional review and enrichment activities, see the interactive version of *World History* available on the Web and on CD-ROM.

For practice test questions for Chapter 19, use **Web Code mka-3224.**

Building Vocabulary

Review the meaning of the chapter vocabulary words listed below. Then, write a sentence for each word in which you define the word and describe its relation to the world in the second half of the twentieth century.

1. **modernization**
2. **superpower**
3. **interdependence**
4. **multinational corporation**
5. **privatization**
6. **acid rain**
7. **global warming**
8. **fundamentalist**
9. **liberation theology**
10. **genetic engineering**

Recalling Key Facts

11. Why did many new nations emerge in the years after World War II?
12. Explain what is meant by the terms "global North" and "global South."
13. What were the causes of the debt crisis of the 1980s?
14. How has urbanization affected life in the developing world?
15. List three medical breakthroughs in the postwar era.

Critical Thinking and Writing

16. **Linking Past and Present** How does the Universal Declaration of Human Rights echo the ideas of the American Bill of Rights and the French Declaration of the Rights of Man and the Citizen?

17. **Understanding Points of View** Why do some people resent the World Bank and IMF?

18. **Connecting to Geography** **(a)** Why has the environment become an area of growing concern in recent years? **(b)** Describe the causes and effects of one global environmental problem.

19. **Distinguishing Facts From Opinions** Harry Truman wrote, "The scientific and industrial revolution which began two centuries ago . . . caught up the peoples of the globe in a common destiny. Two world-shattering wars have proved that no corner of the Earth can be isolated from the affairs of mankind." **(a)** Which parts of Truman's statement are facts? **(b)** Which parts are opinions? **(c)** Do you think Truman's facts support his opinions? Explain.

Nguyen Sa is one of the leading poets of modern Vietnam. Read these excerpts from Sa's poem "No Time," then answer the questions that follow.

> *"I must get far away from this city*
> *with its soot-streaked curbs*
> *and people who pass each other*
> *without a smile or a word.*
> *'No time! I have no time!' she answered me,*
> *the girl dressed all in lavender.*
>
> *Still, she did answer me, and yet*
> *I didn't dare ask her,*
> *'What important things have you time for?'*
> *but whispered to myself instead*
> *—the homeless whispering to the home-*
> *less—*
> *there are those who love but have no time*
> *for loving.*
> *If this is true, how can birds fly back to*
> *their nests?*
> *How can poetry be written?*
> *If this is true, birds and poems will die.*
>
> *Yes, I must get away from the city*
> *if there is no time, no time here*
> *to speak one word,*
> *to share one moment's laughter. . . ."*
>
> —Nguyen Sa, "No Time"

20. According to the first lines of the poem, what two qualities of cities does the speaker dislike?

21. How does the "girl dressed all in lavender" respond to the speaker?

22. Why does the speaker of the poem refer to himself as "homeless"?

23. Write a sentence summarizing the main point of this poem.

24. **(a)** How would you describe the mood of this poem? **(b)** How does it reflect what you have read about the psychological effects of urbanization?

Skills Tip

Modern poems often deal with the impact of modern life on the poet. When analyzing a poem, look for words that reveal the speaker's emotional or psychological state.

This political cartoon appeared in a Bombay newspaper in 1983. The woman in the cartoon is Indira Gandhi, India's prime minister at that time. Study the cartoon, then answer the following questions:

25. What familiar story does this cartoon recall?

26. **(a)** What does the boat represent? **(b)** What do the animals represent?

27. Cartoons often use familiar symbols for certain ideas. What idea does a dove symbolize?

28. **(a)** What dangers do the passengers on the boat face? **(b)** What is their goal?

29. **(a)** How does this cartoon reflect the position of India and many other developing nations during the Cold War? **(b)** Do you think the cartoonist supported or opposed this position? Explain.

Go Online
PHSchool.com

Use the Internet to research one of the present-day issues mentioned in this chapter. You might choose a political issue such as human rights, an economic issue such as debt, an environmental issue such as global warming, or a social issue such as urbanization. Then, write a report on the status of that issue today. You may want to illustrate your report with photographs, diagrams, graphs, or charts. For help with this activity, use **Web Code mkd-3225.**

Europe and North America 1945–Present

Chapter Preview

1 The Western World: An Overview
2 The Western European Democracies
3 North American Prosperity
4 The Soviet Union: Rise and Fall of a Superpower
5 A New Era in Eastern Europe

1957

The Soviet Union launches *Sputnik,* the first artificial satellite, into orbit around the Earth.

1960s

United States begins sending troops to battle communist forces in the Vietnam War. Here, American helicopters patrol a road in Vietnam.

CHAPTER EVENTS

1940

1955

1970

GLOBAL EVENTS

1950 The Korean War begins.

1959 Fidel Castro comes to power in Cuba.

1973 An oil crisis affects nations around the world.

Political Map of Europe

Europe has undergone significant change since World War II. In the 1990s, many nations became independent.

ICELAND

Faroe Islands (Den.)

Norwegian Sea

Shetland Islands (Br.)

NORWAY

FINLAND

SWEDEN

SCOTLAND

North Sea

N. IRELAND

UNITED KINGDOM

IRELAND

WALES

ENGLAND

NETHERLANDS

English Channel

BELGIUM

GERMANY

LUXEMBOURG

CZECH REPUBLIC

LIECHTENSTEIN

FRANCE

SWITZERLAND

AUSTRIA

HUNGARY

SLOVENIA

CROATIA

ANDORRA

SAN MARINO

MONACO

Corsica (Fr.)

ITALY

SLOVAKIA

ROMANIA

BULGARIA

MACEDONIA

ALBANIA

GREECE

Aegean Sea

TURKEY

VATICAN CITY

Sardinia (It.)

Sicily

Mediterranean Sea

MALTA

Crete

PORTUGAL

SPAIN

Balearic Islands (Sp.)

Strait of Gibraltar

Gibraltar (Br.)

ATLANTIC OCEAN

Bay of Biscay

DENMARK

Baltic Sea

ESTONIA

LATVIA

LITHUANIA

RUSSIA

BELARUS

POLAND

UKRAINE

MOLDOVA

RUSSIA

BOSNIA & HERZ.

SERBIA & MONT.

Black Sea

Bosporus

Caspian Sea

60°N

50°N

40°N

10°W

0°

10°E

20°E

40°E

Azimuthal Equal Area Projection

0 — 300 — 600 Miles

0 — 300 — 600 Kilometers

1991

The Soviet Union collapses. In this scene, a man waves a Russian flag as others look upon a fallen statue of Lenin.

2000s

The European Union grows, and more countries change their currency to the euro.

1985

2000

2015

1980s A global economic slowdown causes many governments to reduce spending.

To learn about recent developments in the world, use **Web Code mkc-3327**.

The Western World: An Overview

Reading Focus

- What issues troubled Europe after the Cold War?
- How have recent economic and political trends affected the West?
- How has Europe moved toward greater unity?
- How have social trends changed the West?

Vocabulary

détente
welfare state
recession
service industry
euro

Taking Notes

As you read this section, make an outline of its contents. Use Roman numerals for major headings, capital letters for subheadings, and numbers for supporting details. The model at right will help you get started.

I. Europe: The Cold War and after
  A. The Berlin Wall
    1. Berlin divided into two zones
  B.
II. Economic and political trends
  A.
    1.
    2.
  B. The oil shock

Main Idea In the years since World War II, various economic, political, and social trends have shaped the western world.

Setting the Scene Western Europe rebounded out of the rubble of World War II. During the postwar years, standards of living rose dramatically. People earned higher wages, bought homes with central heating and running water, and enjoyed luxuries unheard of in earlier times. Amid these comforts, many other changes were shaping the western world.

Europe: The Cold War and After

For more than 40 years, the Cold War divided Europe into two hostile military alliances. The communist nations of Eastern Europe, dominated by the Soviet Union, formed the Warsaw Pact. The western democracies, led by the United States, formed NATO. The superpowers avoided direct confrontation in Europe, but some issues brought the continent to the brink of war.

The Berlin Wall Berlin was a focus of Cold War tensions. The city was split into democratic West Berlin and communist East Berlin. In the 1950s, West Berlin became a showcase for West German prosperity. Thousands of low-paid East Germans, discontented with communism, slipped into West Berlin. To stop the exodus, East Germany built a wall in 1961 that separated the two sectors of the city. When completed, the wall was a massive concrete barrier, topped with barbed wire and patrolled by guards.

The Berlin Wall was an ugly symbol of the Cold War and an embarrassment for the Soviets. It showed that workers, far from enjoying a communist paradise, had to be forcibly restrained from fleeing.

The Nuclear Threat The Cold War triggered an arms race, with both sides producing huge arsenals of nuclear weapons. Critics argued that a nuclear war would destroy both sides. Yet the superpowers claimed that they dared not stop. Each side wanted to have the power to deter the other from launching its nuclear weapons. The result was a "balance of terror."

During the arms race, both superpowers spent huge sums of money on weapons. Such spending meant cutbacks in other areas. In 1953, President Dwight Eisenhower warned Americans about the impact: "Every gun that is made, every warship launched . . . signifies . . . a theft from those who hunger and are not fed, those who are cold and are not clothed."

Disarmament and Détente To reduce the threat of nuclear destruction, both sides met at disarmament talks. Although mutual distrust often blocked progress, they did sign some agreements, such as the 1963 Nuclear

The Nuclear Threat
In Europe and other parts of the world, children were taught they could survive a nuclear attack. In 1954, the image above was used to advertise a bogus "radiation-resistant" blanket.

Theme: Economics and Technology How did nuclear weapons change the nature of war?

Test Ban Treaty. It banned the testing of nuclear weapons in the atmosphere. Underground testing was still permitted, however.

By the 1970s, American and Soviet leaders promoted an era of détente (day TAHNT), or relaxation of tensions. The two superpowers made new agreements to reduce nuclear stockpiles. Détente ended, however, after the Soviet Union invaded Afghanistan in 1979.

End of the Cold War By the 1990s, as you will read, economic and foreign policy troubles threatened the Soviet Union. A new Soviet leader, Mikhail Gorbachev (mee kah EEL GOR bah chawf), eased the Soviet grip on Eastern Europe. One by one, communist governments collapsed. Communism even fell from power in the Soviet Union, which broke up into separate independent republics.

When the Cold War ended, nations in Western and Eastern Europe sought normal relations. Germany was reunited. The Warsaw Pact dissolved. NATO, originally formed to defend the West against communism, had to redefine its role in a post–Cold War world.

Troublesome Issues As the century neared its end, Europeans faced troublesome issues, new and old. Russia and the nations of Eastern Europe turned to the West for loans and investments to build capitalist economies. Ethnic clashes, especially in the Balkans, created conflicts that threatened the peace of Europe.

The nuclear peril was reduced, but it still remained. The United States, Russia, and other nations still had nuclear weapons. As disarmament talks continued, there were fears that some Russian nuclear materials might end up in the hands of other nations and groups.

NATO's New Role After the Cold War, Eastern Europe's former communist nations joined NATO despite Russian protests. In 1999, Hungary, Poland, and the Czech Republic joined the alliance. In the early 2000s, several more former communist states were slated for membership.

In the 1990s, conflict in the Balkans posed new challenges to NATO. When ethnic groups in Bosnia and Kosovo tried to break away from Yugoslavia, war erupted. Europeans witnessed the worst fighting since World War II and were shocked by horrible abuses of human rights. As you will read, NATO members finally sent military forces into both Bosnia and Kosovo. Those moves sparked debate over whether NATO should become Europe's peacekeeper and protector of human rights.

Economic and Political Trends

In the 1950s, Western Europeans recovered quickly from World War II. With Marshall Plan aid, their economies boomed. They rebuilt industries, farms, and transportation networks destroyed by the war.

Meanwhile, right-wing parties were discredited because they had supported fascism. Communists and socialists, who had resisted the Nazis during the war, enjoyed growing support. As a result, postwar governments in France, Italy, and Germany adopted many policies favored by the left.

The Welfare State A major goal of leftist parties was to extend the welfare state. Under this system, a government keeps most features of a capitalist economy but takes greater responsibility for the social and economic needs of its people. The welfare state had its roots in

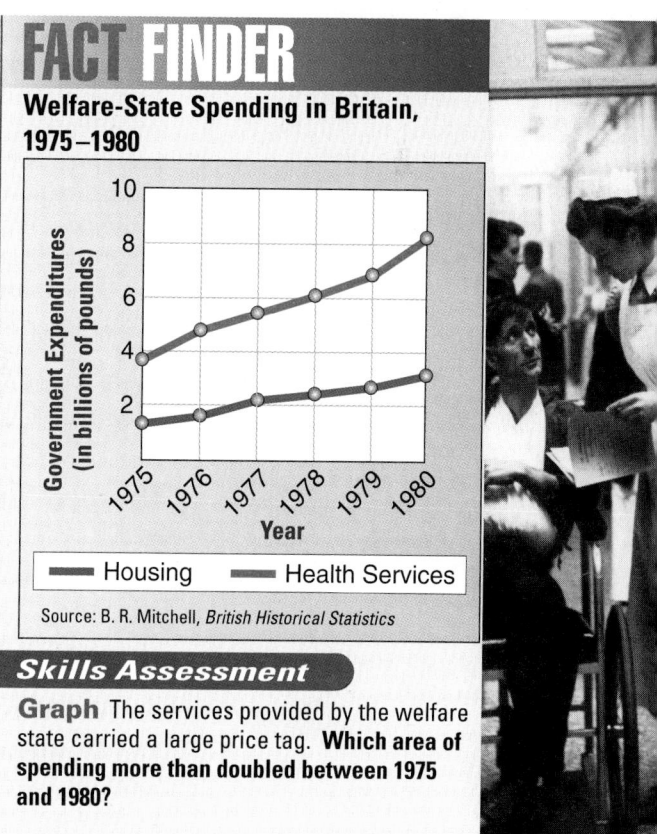

FACT FINDER

Welfare-State Spending in Britain, 1975–1980

Government Expenditures (in billions of pounds)

Housing
Health Services

Source: B. R. Mitchell, *British Historical Statistics*

Skills Assessment

Graph The services provided by the welfare state carried a large price tag. **Which area of spending more than doubled between 1975 and 1980?**

the late 1800s, when governments passed reforms to ease the hardships of the industrial age. During that period, Germany, Britain, and other nations had set up unemployment insurance and old-age pensions.

After 1945, governments expanded these social programs. Both the middle class and the poor enjoyed increasing benefits from national health care, unemployment insurance, and old-age pensions. Other programs gave aid to the poor and created an economic cushion to help people get through difficult times. Still, the welfare state was costly, involving many burdensome taxes and greater government regulation of private enterprise.

Socialists supported the welfare state and a larger role for government in the economy. In Britain, France, and elsewhere, governments nationalized basic industries such as railroads, airlines, banks, steel, and energy. Conservatives condemned the drift from the free enterprise system toward socialism.

The Oil Shock In 1973, the West suffered an economic shock when OPEC cut oil production and raised prices. (See the previous chapter.) Because most Western European countries used imported oil to fuel industries, the higher oil prices caused inflation and slowed economic growth. In 1979, OPEC again raised prices, triggering a severe recession, in which business slowed and unemployment rates rose.

Economic Shifts At the same time, the West faced growing competition from other parts of the world. For 200 years, most manufactured goods came from factories in the West. By the 1980s, that pattern had changed. Japan's industrial economy boomed after World War II. Other countries, such as China and India, also expanded their industries. Western-based multinational corporations set up factories in the developing world, where labor was cheap. From there, they exported goods to the West.

In the West, economies changed. Many factories closed because they could not make goods as cheaply as competing industries did elsewhere. As manufacturing declined in the West, most new jobs were created in service industries. A service industry is one that provides a service rather than a product. Service industries include health care, finance, sales, education, and recreation. The shift from producing goods to services is a key feature of the post-industrial society that emerged in the West after World War II. In a post-industrial society, scientific and technical information dominate.

As economies slowed during the 1970s and 1980s, governments had to cut costs. Some moved away from the welfare state, reducing benefits. Conservative governments privatized state-owned industries. In the new political and economic climate, the gap between rich and poor grew, but most people still enjoyed a relatively high standard of living.

Toward European Unity

Economic cooperation helped Western Europe to recover from World War II. In 1952, six nations—France, West Germany, Belgium, Italy, the Netherlands, and Luxembourg—set up the European Coal and Steel Community. This independent agency set prices and regulated the coal and steel industries of member states. This small start spurred economic growth across Western Europe and led to further regional cooperation.

The Common Market In 1957, the same six nations signed a treaty to form the European Community (EC), or Common Market. Its goal was to expand free trade. The Common Market gradually ended tariffs on goods and allowed workers and capital to move freely across national borders. It

Geography and History

Offshore Oil Rigs

The oil crisis of 1973 spurred the West to search for new sources of oil. Exploration companies discovered rich deposits of petroleum and natural gas beneath the ocean floor. Today's offshore rigs are colossal steel structures that rise to heights taller than most skyscrapers. They are built to withstand 100-foot waves and 160-mph winds. The picture above shows a giant oil rig rising out of the North Sea, off the coast of Western Europe.

Living and working in this harsh environment is hard. Roughnecks, as the rig workers are called, must wrestle with heavy equipment, often in bitter winds or rain. Lodged in cramped quarters, the workers are subject to punishing conditions and long hours. They usually stay on the rigs for just a few weeks at a time. On a regular basis, helicopters or ships bring in a new crew and ferry exhausted workers ashore for rest.

Theme: Geography and History Why did exploration for oil increase after 1973?

The European Union

In ancient times, the Roman empire united much of Europe politically. During the Middle Ages, many Europeans were joined by a common faith in Christianity. Today, some European nations are looking for a common economic bond through the European Union (EU).

A Closely Tied Union—For and Against

For

"[The European Union means that a] great power is being born, one at least as strong commercially, industrially and financially as the United States and Japan."

—French President François Mitterrand, 1991

Against

"We [do not want] a European super-state exercising a new dominance. . . . Europe will be stronger precisely because it has France as France, Spain as Spain, Britain as Britain, each with its own customs, traditions and identity."

—British Prime Minister Margaret Thatcher, 1988

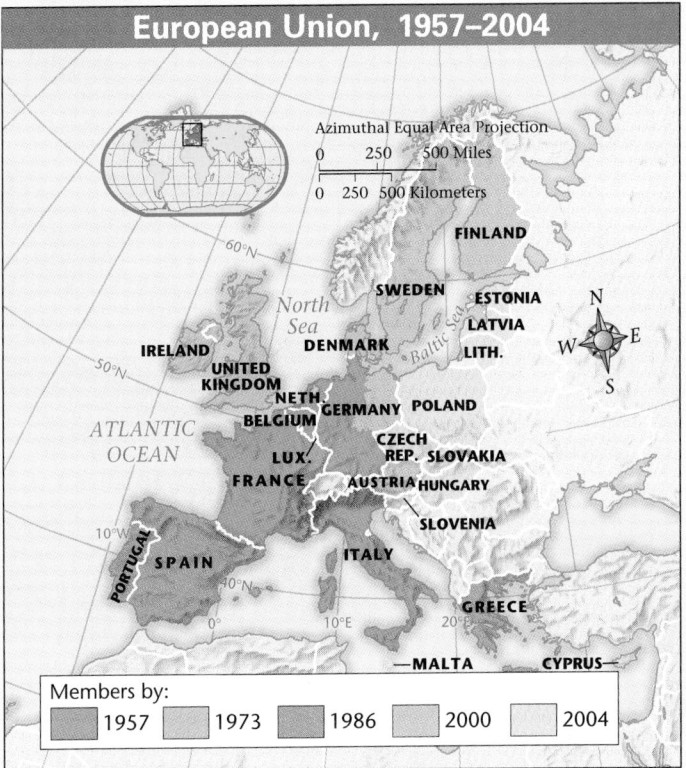

European Union, 1957–2004

Azimuthal Equal Area Projection

Members by:
1957 | 1973 | 1986 | 2000 | 2004

Votes in the European Union Council

State	Votes	State	Votes	State	Votes	State	Votes	State	Votes
France	10	Poland	8	Hungary	5	Denmark	3	Slovenia	3
Germany	10	Netherlands	5	Portugal	5	Finland	3	Estonia	3
Italy	10	Greece	5	Sweden	4	Ireland	3	Cyprus	2
U.K.	10	Czech Rep.	5	Austria	4	Lithuania	3	Lux.	2
Spain	8	Belgium	5	Slovakia	3	Latvia	3	Malta	2

Source: European Union   Note: Member states and vote totals reflect admission of 10 new EU countries in 2004.

The Council of the European Union enacts European Union laws. This chart shows how many votes each member nation can cast in that Council.

Skills Assessment

1. Which of the following items pairs an oldest member with a youngest member of the European Union? (oldest/youngest)
   - **A** Portugal/Italy
   - **B** Germany/Latvia
   - **C** France/Luxembourg
   - **D** Greece/Ireland

2. Who are the most powerful members in the Council of the European Union?
   - **E** France, Netherlands, Sweden, Denmark
   - **F** United Kingdom, Belgium, Austria, Ireland
   - **G** Germany, Spain, Portugal, Finland
   - **H** France, Germany, Italy, United Kingdom

3. **Critical Thinking Making Inferences (a)** What do you think led Mitterrand to favor a united Europe? **(b)** What do you think led Thatcher to oppose the European Union?

Migration to Western Europe

Legend:
→ Major population movements

▨ Countries attractive to immigrants, with foreign population

NORWAY 150,000
SWEDEN 490,000
UNITED KINGDOM 1.9 million
DENMARK 160,000
NETH. 760,000
GERMANY 6.7 million
BELG. 920,000
FRANCE 3.6 million
SWITZ. 1.4 million
AUSTRIA 550,000
SPAIN 480,000
ITALY 1 million

North Sea
Baltic Sea
ATLANTIC OCEAN
Black Sea
Mediterranean Sea

Azimuthal Equal Area Projection
0   250   500 Miles
0   250   500 Kilometers

Skills Assessment

Geography In the 1990s, more than two million immigrants a year arrived in Western Europe.

1. **Location** *On the map, locate (a) France, (b) Spain, (c) Germany, (d) United Kingdom.*
2. **Place** *Which three countries had the largest foreign populations?*
3. **Critical Thinking Drawing Conclusions** *Why did so many people move to Western Europe?*

set up the European Parliament, a multinational body elected by citizens of the Common Market countries. Its powers were limited, however, as member states remained independent. Despite disputes between members, the Common Market prospered. In 1973, after much debate, Britain was admitted, along with Denmark and Ireland.

European Union In the 1980s and 1990s, the Common Market expanded further and took the name European Union (EU). By replacing destructive competition with greater cooperation, the EU promoted regional prosperity, peace, and security.

The EU pushed for greater economic and political unity. It replaced national passports with EU passports and ended most tariffs. In 2002, many Europeans turned in their different national currencies for euros, a single currency for member nations. Despite the benefits of cooperation, nationalist feelings remained strong in some nations. Thus, a United States of Europe seemed unlikely to emerge any time soon.

Still, the EU was a growing force. In the early 2000s, more than a dozen countries joined the Union. Most of the new members were former communist states of Eastern Europe. With the EU controlling about 20 percent of world trade, Europe was able to compete with economic superpowers like the United States and Japan.

Social Trends

Social change speeded up after 1945 and class lines blurred as prosperity spread. For most of western history, a tiny wealthy class had dominated society. By the 1950s, though, more and more people belonged to the middle class. As wages rose, working-class people bought homes and cars, and their children attended universities. Although pockets of poverty remained, most people had opportunities unknown in earlier times.

Ethnic Diversity   Since the 1950s, many immigrants from former colonies in Asia, Africa, and the Caribbean had settled in Europe. In Germany and other European countries, "guest workers" from Turkey and the Middle East provided low-wage labor for booming economies. Many Eastern Europeans fled economic hardships to find work in the West.

Some Europeans resented newcomers who competed with them for scarce jobs and brought new cultural influences. As a result, many newcomers faced discrimination and segregation. In a few countries, ultranationalists and racist thugs attacked and even killed foreign workers and immigrants. In 2000, in Austria, members of an anti-immigrant party assumed a leading role in a new coalition government.

Women   In 1949, French writer Simone de Beauvoir (boh vwAHR) analyzed the status of women in western society:

> "The two sexes have never shared the world in equality. And even today woman is heavily handicapped, though her situation is beginning to change. Almost nowhere is her legal status the same as man's."
> —Simone de Beauvoir, *The Second Sex*

Since then, women in the West have made progress toward legal and economic equality. A growing number of women worked outside the home. Despite efforts to ensure equality, however, women's pay lagged behind that of men. Women often ran into a "glass ceiling," an invisible barrier that kept them from top jobs. However, women gradually chipped away at old attitudes and narrowed the gender gap in hiring, promotion, and pay. As a woman's income increased, so did her family's standard of living.

Family Life   Devotion to family ideals remained strong in the West, but family life changed. Western families had fewer children than in the past. Children stayed in school longer to get needed skills. Family life seemed less stable as the divorce rate climbed. In cases in which a divorced parent failed to fulfill financial responsibilities, children suffered. At the same time, increasing numbers of children were being born to unwed mothers. Often dependent on one income, a growing number of single-parent families found themselves living in poverty.

SECTION 1 Assessment

Recall
1. **Identify:** (a) Berlin Wall, (b) Nuclear Test Ban Treaty, (c) NATO, (d) Common Market, (e) European Union.
2. **Define:** (a) détente, (b) welfare state, (c) recession, (d) service industry, (e) euro.

Comprehension
3. What were two effects of the end of the Cold War?
4. (a) How were western economies affected by growing international competition? (b) How did some governments respond?

5. How did the European Union benefit the economies of its member nations?
6. What social trends affected family life in the West?

Critical Thinking and Writing
7. **Predicting Consequences** Review the Fact Finder chart in this section. Based on the chart statistics, would you expect popular support for the welfare state to increase or decline? Explain.
8. **Connecting to Geography** How did the end of the Cold War change the map of Europe?

Reading Focus

- How did Britain's policies change after World War II?
- How did French power and prosperity revive?
- How did Germany reunify?
- What problems have other democratic nations faced?

Vocabulary

chancellor
coalition

Taking Notes

Make a table like this partially completed model. As you read, identify main ideas about the Western European democracies and list them in the appropriate boxes.

COUNTRY	GOVERNMENT	ECONOMY
BRITAIN		• Industries nationalized •
FRANCE		
GERMANY		
ITALY		

Main Idea As a result of government policies and international cooperation, the people of Western European democracies have enjoyed freedom and prosperity.

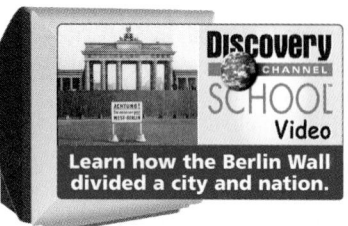

Learn how the Berlin Wall divided a city and nation.

Biography

Tony Blair 1953—

In 2003, British Prime Minister Tony Blair was a strong supporter of President Bush's policy to disarm Iraq "by all means necessary." Blair faced strong opposition from British public opinion, even from within his own party. Risking both his party's popularity and his own personal career, he persevered, convincing the country to send troops to fight in Iraq. "I've learned in this job you should always try to do the right thing, not the easy thing," he said.

Theme: Impact of the Individual Do you think an elected leader should base decisions on his conscience or on public opinion? Explain.

Setting the Scene In 1994, an army of bicycles sped through the English countryside, cheered by countless spectators. The event was the famous Tour de France race. The cyclists had crossed from France to England through the new English Channel tunnel, nicknamed Chunnel. For the first time since the ice age, a land route linked Britain and continental Europe.

The Chunnel reflected closer ties among Britain, France, and other European nations. After World War II, the Western European democracies worked within a framework of international cooperation, including NATO, the EU, and the UN. Each nation, however, faced its own problems and made its own contributions to freedom and prosperity.

Britain: Changing Policies

In 1945, British voters put the Labour party in power, hoping that it could help the nation recover from World War II. The war had helped change old attitudes toward the working class. A Labour official noted that if a working-class boy could save England in a fighter plane, "the same brain can be turned to produce a new world."

Labour and Conservative Governments That "new world" gave rise to the welfare state, in which government expanded benefits such as unemployment insurance and old-age pensions. The British government nationalized major industries, built housing for the poor, and provided free or low-cost medical care. To pay for all this, taxes rose tremendously. By the late 1970s, Britain, like the rest of Europe, was reeling under economic hard times.

In 1979, British voters turned to the Conservative party, which denounced the welfare state as costly and inefficient. The Conservatives were led by Margaret Thatcher, who served 11 years as Britain's prime minister. Stressing individual responsibility, Thatcher's government reduced social welfare programs and returned government-run industries to private control. The changes slowed government spending but did not revive the British economy as much as the Conservatives had hoped. Thatcher retired in 1990, but the Conservatives remained in power.

In 1997, the Labour Party won a majority in Parliament, and Tony Blair became prime minister. Blair tried to follow a "third way" between the traditional left and right. However, in the early 2000s, his failure to solve problems in health care, education, and transportation, along with his unswerving support of U.S. foreign policy, undercut his popularity.

A New World Role After World War II, Britain's role in the world changed. Its empire shrank as colonies won independence. Still, some former colonies kept ties to Britain by joining the Commonwealth of Nations. Weakened by war and the loss of empire, Britain gave up global leadership to its ally, the United States. Even so, Britain remained a leader in the UN and NATO. In recent years, Britain and the United States have worked together in the war against Iraq and the war against terrorism.

Meanwhile, Britain has grown closer to its European neighbors. It joined the Common Market in 1973 and is part of the European Union today. But nationalism has led some Britons to be wary. The British rejected the euro, and many oppose greater European unity.

Northern Ireland When Ireland won independence in 1922, Britain retained control of six northern counties where there was a Protestant majority. Faced with widespread discrimination, Catholics demanded civil rights and the reunification of Ireland. Protestants wanted to remain part of Britain.

Violence escalated in the 1960s and 1970s as extremists on both sides turned to terrorism. The Irish Republican Army (IRA) attacked Protestants, and Protestant militias targeted Catholics. Britain sent soldiers to keep order in Northern Ireland. But their presence inflamed tensions, especially as they jailed IRA members and violated their civil rights.

Peace talks were held on and off for years. Finally, in 1998, the main political parties signed a peace accord. Enacting the agreement proved difficult. Elections were held for a new government that would bring self-rule to Northern Ireland. But lasting peace and political stability were threatened by sporadic acts of violence and by the IRA's slowness to disarm.

France: Revival and Prosperity

Like Britain, France emerged from World War II greatly weakened. The Fourth Republic, set up in 1946, was ineffective and drew criticism from both communists and conservatives. Bloody colonial wars in Vietnam and Algeria further drained and demoralized France. In Algeria, longtime French settlers and the French military opposed Algerian nationalists who wanted independence for the North African country. France itself was so divided over the issue that civil war threatened.

Economic Prosperity in France
In 1981, President François Mitterrand met with industrial workers in the Lorraine region of France. Like British leaders of the time, Mitterrand encouraged the growth of private industry.

Theme: Economics and Technology What is the difference between a nationalized industry and a privatized industry?

De Gaulle As the crisis worsened, French voters turned to General Charles de Gaulle, a hero of World War II. In 1958, de Gaulle set up the Fifth Republic. Its constitution gave him, as president, great power. Although a staunch nationalist, de Gaulle realized that France must give up Algeria. In 1962, he made peace with the Algerians. Other French colonies in Africa soon won freedom without bloodshed.

De Gaulle worked hard to restore French prestige and power. He forged new ties with West Germany, ending the long hostility between the two nations. He developed a French nuclear force and challenged American dominance in Europe. He opposed the Cold War stance of the United States by opening talks with communist China and Cuba.

In 1968, youth revolts shook France. The next year, de Gaulle resigned. Although he was widely disliked by the left, he had successfully reasserted French leadership in Europe.

Economic Revival Like Britain, France nationalized some industries and expanded social welfare benefits after World War II. With government help, industry and business modernized, leading to new prosperity by the 1970s.

In the 1980s, French Socialists, led by François Mitterrand, won power just as a global recession hit. At first, Mitterrand tried to nationalize more industries and expand welfare benefits. But when those policies deepened the crisis, he encouraged the growth of private business.

In 1995, his successor, Jacques Chirac, took an even more conservative approach. Chirac cut government spending, despite protests by farmers, students, and others. Over the years, France overcame internal stresses and global economic swings to build the fourth largest economy in the world.

Germany: Division and Reunification

The early years after World War II were a desperate time for Germany. People were starving amid a landscape of destruction. German cities lay in ruins. "Nothing is left in Berlin," wrote an American reporter:

> "There are no homes, no shops, no transportation, no government buildings. Only a few walls. . . . Berlin can now be regarded only as a geographical location heaped with mountainous mounds of debris."
>
> —*New York Herald Tribune,* May 3, 1945

Germany Divided By 1949, the emerging Cold War had divided Germany. West Germany was a member of the western alliance, and East Germany lay in the Soviet orbit. For 40 years, differences between the two Germanys widened. The Soviet Union opposed a unified Germany that might threaten Soviet security.

West Germany's "Economic Miracle" Early in the Cold War, the United States rushed aid to its former enemy. It wanted to strengthen West Germany against communist Eastern Europe. From 1949 to 1963, Konrad Adenauer (AD ehn ow er) was West Germany's chancellor, or chief minister. He guided the rebuilding of cities, factories, and trade. Despite high taxes to pay for the recovery, West Germans created a booming industrial economy. This "economic miracle" raised European fears of a German revival. But West Germany worked closely with France and the United States, and played a key role in NATO and the European Community. This cooperation helped to reduce fear of German strength.

Later West German chancellors came from the Socialist party. West Germany remained a capitalist country, but the government expanded the social welfare benefits.

Did You Know?

The People's Car

The German Volkswagen Beetle is a popular car with a dark past. Those small, sturdy automobiles were a common sight from the 1950s to the early 1970s. The Beetle furnished cheap, fuel-efficient transportation to more than 20 million people around the world.

But the tiny car was originally a pet project of Adolph Hitler, who, in 1934, began promoting the idea of an inexpensive "people's car." In 1938, he laid the foundation stone of the original Volkswagen plant, which used Russian and Jewish slave labor to turn out military vehicles during World War II.

The Volkswagen company began exporting the Beetle in the 1950s. Its popularity faded in the early 1970s, but the Beetle staged a comeback in 1998.

Theme: Continuity and Change Why was the Volkswagen Beetle so successful?

Virtual Field Trip

Go Online
PHSchool.com

For: More on the fall of the Berlin Wall and Germany today
Visit: PHSchool.com
Web Code: mkd-3337

East Germany Under Communism Under communist rule, East Germany's economy stagnated. The Soviet Union exploited East German workers and industry for its own benefit. Still, unemployment was low, and workers had some basic benefits, such as health care, housing, and free education.

Lured by glittering views of life in the West, however, many East Germans fled. As you have read, this mass exodus led to the building of the Berlin Wall in 1961. Overnight, the migration ended. Occasionally, an East German made a dramatic escape. Many died in the attempt.

Reunification In 1969, West German chancellor Willy Brandt tried to ease tensions with communist neighbors to the east. He called his policy Ostpolitik, or "eastern policy." Brandt kept close ties to the West, but signed treaties with the Soviet Union and Poland. He established economic ties to Eastern Europe and signed a treaty of mutual recognition with East Germany. In the midst of the Cold War, however, Brandt's long-term goal of reunifying Germany seemed impossible.

In 1989, as Soviet communism declined, Germany was able to move toward reunification. Without Soviet backing, East German communist leaders were ousted. In Berlin, people from both Germanys clambered up the hated wall and began to tear it down. West German chancellor Helmut Kohl assured both the Soviet Union and the West that a united Germany would pose no threat to peace. In 1990, German voters approved reunification, and Kohl became chancellor of a united Germany.

Economic Problems German unification brought some economic and social problems. Prosperous West Germans had to pay higher taxes to finance the rebuilding of the east. As old government-run factories closed in the east, unemployment rose. Driven by racism, some neo-Nazis blamed immigrants for the hard times and viciously attacked foreign workers. The vast majority of Germans condemned such actions.

Germans sought solutions to their economic problems. The government tried to control the costs of welfare programs and to balance the budget through tax reform. But a global economic slowdown led to high unemployment rates and many German companies moved to other countries

Fall of the Berlin Wall
In 1989, Germans celebrated as they tore down the wall that had divided communist East Berlin from democratic West Berlin. The entire nation was reunited soon after the collapse of communism in East Germany.

Theme: Political and Social Systems Who built the Berlin Wall? Why was it built?

where labor and tax costs were lower. In the early 2000s, Germany's economy—Europe's most powerful—seemed almost as fragile as Japan's.

Other Democratic Nations

Other parts of Western Europe slowly recovered from the war. The Scandinavian countries of Norway, Sweden, and Denmark created extensive socialist welfare programs. By the 1990s, rising costs revived debate about how much people were willing to pay for the welfare state. Yet many people saw these social programs as essential to a democratic society.

Italy   In Italy, long-term regional differences continued to divide the country. In the urban north, industries rebuilt and prospered after World War II. In the rural south, the largely peasant population remained much poorer.

Political divisions also led to instability. Since no one political party could win a lasting majority, Italy experienced one coalition government after another. A coalition is a temporary alliance of political parties. Corruption and financial scandals added to the instability. Meanwhile, the Mafia, a violent criminal syndicate, defied government efforts to end its power, especially in the south. Despite these problems, Italy made impressive economic gains and ranked as a leading industrial nation.

Spain, Portugal, and Greece   Change came slowly to other countries of southern Europe. In 1945, Spain, Portugal, and Greece were economically undeveloped with large peasant populations. In Spain and Portugal, dictators clung to power for decades.

Finally, in the 1970s, both Spain's Francisco Franco and Portugal's Antonio de Oliveira Salazar died. Their authoritarian governments soon collapsed. Both countries adopted democratic governments and eventually joined NATO and the EU. Their economies have grown rapidly.

Greece faced difficult obstacles on its path to democratic rule. After World War II, the Greek government needed American aid to defeat communist rebels. Then, in 1967, military rulers came to power. A crisis emerged in 1974, when the government supported an attempt to bring Cyprus under Greek rule. Cyprus is a Mediterranean island inhabited by Greeks and Turks. The incident brought Greece and Turkey to the brink of war and led to the downfall of the military regime. Cyprus was divided into two zones, one ruled by Greeks and the other ruled by Turks. In 1975, Greece returned to democratic rule.

SECTION 2 Assessment

Recall

1. **Identify:** **(a)** Margaret Thatcher, **(b)** Tony Blair, **(c)** IRA, **(d)** Charles de Gaulle, **(e)** François Mitterrand, **(f)** Konrad Adenauer, **(g)** Helmut Kohl, **(h)** neo-Nazis.
2. **Define:** **(a)** chancellor, **(b)** coalition.

Comprehension

3. What changes were introduced in Britain by Thatcher and the Conservative party?
4. **(a)** How did de Gaulle revive French power? **(b)** How did Chirac affect the French economy?

5. Why was Germany finally able to reunify?
6. Describe one problem that has troubled Italy in recent years.

Critical Thinking and Writing

7. **Defending a Position**   Some people, especially in France, worried that a reunited Germany would pose a danger to Europe. Using historical evidence, explain why you agree or disagree.
8. **Making Inferences**   Why did President de Gaulle decide that France had to give up Algeria?

Go Online
PHSchool.com

Search online sources for recent articles on peace efforts in Northern Ireland. Print three articles—one from the United States, one from Ireland, and one from Britain. Write a summary in which you point out how the three sources agree and disagree. For help with this activity, use **Web Code mkd-3338.**

North American Prosperity

Reading Focus

- What actions has the United States taken as a global superpower?
- What developments have shaped the economy, government, and society of the United States?
- What issues has Canada faced in recent years?

Vocabulary

deficit

surplus

civil rights movement

segregation

separatism

Taking Notes

Copy this partially completed chart. As you read, list major ideas concerning the foreign policy, economy, and society of the United States since World War II.

UNITED STATES SINCE 1945		
Foreign Policy	**Economy**	**Society**
• Cold War with Soviet Union	•	• Minorities faced segregation
•	•	•

Main Idea — Since the 1940s, the United States has asserted its role as a global superpower, promoted economic prosperity, and extended civil rights.

Setting the Scene In 1961, John F. Kennedy was sworn in as president of the United States. He proclaimed to the world:

> "Let every nation know that we shall pay any price, bear any burden, meet any hardship, support any friend, oppose any foe to assure the survival and the success of liberty."
> —John F. Kennedy, Inaugural Address

Kennedy's vow reflected a commitment to contain communism and promote democracy. During the postwar era, the United States also moved to extend civil rights and boost economic prosperity at home. To the north, meanwhile, Canada carved out its own world role.

The United States: A Global Superpower

During the Cold War, the United States used its vast economic and military resources to protect its interests and the security of the free, or noncommunist, world. In 1945, the United States was the world's greatest military power and the only country that possessed the atomic bomb. Yet it felt threatened by communist expansion, especially after the Soviet Union developed its own atomic bomb.

Global Commitments The United States built bases overseas and organized military alliances from Europe to Southeast Asia. Its fleets patrolled the world's oceans, and its air power provided protection for its allies.

As another way to contain communism, the United States provided economic aid to help Europe rebuild and to assist emerging nations. At times, American aid went to nations that were ruled by anti-communist dictators. Yet presidents such as Jimmy Carter pressed these countries to end human rights abuses.

Korea and Vietnam In 1950, the Korean War began in East Asia when communist North Korean forces invaded noncommunist South Korea. American troops made up the majority of a UN force sent to protect South Korea. During that war, anti-communist fears rose in the United States. Extremists such as Senator Joseph McCarthy charged that many Americans harbored communist sympathies.

By the early 1960s, the United States had become involved in Vietnam. Like Korea, this Southeast Asian nation was divided into a communist northern state and a noncommunist southern state. To prevent communist

Air and Sea Power
United States air and sea power has played a significant role in conflicts and peacekeeping missions around the world. The aircraft carrier *Philippine Sea*, shown above, saw action in the Korean War.

Theme: Global Interaction
Why did the United States become involved in the Korean War?

rebels from winning power in South Vietnam, Presidents Kennedy and Johnson sent economic and military aid plus a growing number of American troops. Soon, American forces there numbered half a million.

The Vietnam War led to bitter divisions among Americans. Many opposed supporting an unpopular government in South Vietnam. Antiwar protests spread from college campuses to city streets. In 1968, Richard Nixon was elected president with a promise to end American involvement in Vietnam. By 1974, Nixon finally negotiated an American withdrawal. Still, the divisions that had built up during the war took years to heal.

The Only Superpower With the collapse of the Soviet Union in the early 1990s, the United States was the world's only superpower. It worked within the UN to resolve conflicts in Southeastern Europe, Africa, and other world regions. The United States and its NATO allies sent peacekeeping forces to end bloody civil wars in Bosnia and Kosovo. In 1991 and 2003, American forces battled Iraq's army, as you will read in Chapter 35. In 2001, the nation faced a deadly new challenge after terrorists used hijacked airplanes to attack New York and Washington, D.C. In response, the United States began an international war on terrorism.

Economy and Government

By the early 1950s, the American economy was booming. Unlike Europe, the United States emerged from World War II with its cities and industries undamaged. American factories quickly shifted from producing tanks and bombers to meeting the peacetime demand for cars and refrigerators.

The United States and the Global Economy In the postwar decades, American businesses expanded into markets around the globe. The United States profited greatly from the growing global economy. But interdependence also brought problems. In the 1970s, OPEC price hikes fed inflation and showed how much Americans relied on imported oil. Inflation also contributed to the Third World debt crisis, which involved American banks.

American industries faced stiff competition from Asian and other nations. Like Western Europe, the United States lost manufacturing jobs to the developing world. Some American corporations even moved operations to Mexico or Asia to take advantage of lower wages.

Wider Role for Government In the United States, as in Western Europe, the government's role in the economy grew. Under President Harry Truman, Congress created generous benefits that helped veterans attend college or buy homes. Other Truman programs expanded FDR's New Deal, providing greater Social Security benefits for the elderly and poor.

Truman's successor, Dwight Eisenhower, tried to reduce the government's role in the economy. At the same time, he approved government funding to build a vast interstate highway system. This program spurred the growth of auto, trucking, and related industries. Highways and home construction changed the face of the nation. As middle-class Americans moved out of cities to booming suburbs, urban neighborhoods declined.

During the 1960s, the government expanded social programs to help the poor and disadvantaged. Urged on by Presidents Kennedy and Johnson and other leaders of the Democratic party, Congress funded Medicare, providing health care for the elderly. Other programs offered job training and housing for the poor. Many Americans came to rely on these programs.

The Conservative Response In the 1980s, conservatives challenged costly social programs and the growth of government. Like Margaret Thatcher in Britain, President Ronald Reagan and the Republican party called for cutbacks in government spending on social programs. Congress ended some welfare programs, reduced government regulation of the economy, and cut taxes. At the same time, however, military spending increased.

Connections to Today

Social Security

The Social Security system of the United States began in the midst of the Great Depression during the presidency of Franklin D. Roosevelt. It provided for old-age assistance, unemployment insurance, and aid for dependent children.

Today, the Social Security system faces an uncertain future. Its funding is strained by the rising costs of benefits. One reason for increasing expenditures is that the population of older Americans who receive Social Security benefits is becoming a larger and larger percentage of the United States population.

Government leaders disagree on what to do. Some think that benefits need to be cut and taxes increased. Another idea is increasing the retirement age. Some recommend that, instead of paying Social Security taxes, people be allowed to save for retirement themselves by investing in stocks and bonds.

Theme: Continuity and Change Why are government leaders thinking about changing the Social Security system?

The combination of government spending and tax cuts greatly increased the national budget deficit, the gap between what a government spends and what it takes in through taxes and other resources. To deal with the deficit, conservatives pushed for deeper cuts in social and economic programs, including education, welfare, and environmental protection.

The New Century During the late 1990s, the American economy boasted record growth, full employment, a booming stock market, and even budget surpluses in Washington. A budget surplus is the amount of money left over after expenditures.

Although Americans entered the new century enjoying peace and prosperity, problems remained. The costs of medical care and social security were growing, as was the gap between rich and poor. To many, moral standards seemed to be declining, a problem illustrated by President Bill Clinton's impeachment for personal misconduct while in office.

By the early 2000s, the economy slowed as the boom in technology industries faded. The jobless rate rose, and budget surpluses were replaced by deficits. Terrorist attacks fed recession worries. But most Americans supported President George Bush's decision to invade Iraq in 2003. As the President waged war on terrorism, he also sought economic growth.

Civil Rights and Society

During the 1950s and 1960s, many social changes took place. Some were linked to the civil rights movement that set out to end discrimination and ensure equal rights for all Americans.

Segregation and Discrimination Although slavery was abolished a century before, many states denied equality to various minority groups. They faced legal segregation, or separation, in education and housing. Minorities also suffered discrimination in jobs and voting. After World War II, President Truman desegregated the armed forces. Then, in 1954, the Supreme Court made a landmark ruling in *Brown* v. *Board of Education of Topeka,* declaring that segregated schools were unconstitutional.

Progress and Problems By 1956, a gifted preacher, Dr. Martin Luther King, Jr., emerged as a leader of the civil rights movement. Inspired by Gandhi's civil disobedience in India, King organized boycotts and led peaceful marches throughout the 1960s to end segregation in the United States. In 1963, at a huge civil rights rally in the nation's capital, King made a stirring speech. "I have a dream," he proclaimed, "that one day this nation will rise up and live out the true meaning of its creed: 'We hold these truths to be self-evident, that all men are created equal.'"

Americans of all races joined the civil rights movement, and their courage in the face of sometimes brutal attacks stirred the nation's conscience. Congress outlawed segregation in public accommodations, protected the rights of black voters, and required equal access to housing and jobs. Despite this, racial prejudice survived and poverty and unemployment still plagued many urban African Americans. Yet others were elected to political office or gained top jobs in business and the military.

Other groups—Asians, Latinos, Native Americans, and women—also campaigned for equality. Civil rights laws banned discrimination based on gender and on race in hiring and promotion. More women won elected offices, and many made progress toward higher salaries and positions in business.

Immigration The United States remained a magnet for immigrants, many of them from Latin America and Asia. New laws sought to end illegal immigration and restrict benefits to legal immigrants. Even tougher laws were issued after the 2001 terrorist attacks. Many new Americans, however, brought labor power and valuable skills to their new homeland.

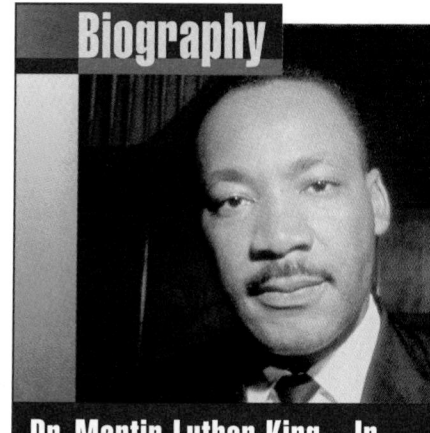

Biography

Dr. Martin Luther King, Jr.
1929–1968

In 1964, the year after his "I have a dream" speech, Martin Luther King, Jr., was awarded the Nobel Peace Prize for his civil rights work. He accepted the prize on behalf of the entire movement. After winning the prize, King continued his struggle to make his "dream" come true.

King led a massive drive to register African American voters in the South in 1965 and was thrown into a Selma, Alabama, jail for his efforts. He began a "Poor People's Campaign" to get help for the poor of all races—and received threats on his life. Even so, on the night of April 3, 1968, he could still say, "I'm not worried about anything. I'm not fearing any man." But he did have cause for fear. On the next day, in Memphis, Tennessee, Dr. King was killed by an assassin's bullet.

Theme: Impact of the Individual Why do you think King was such an effective leader in the civil rights movement?

Canada

After gaining independence, Canada charted its own course but still maintained links with Britain through the Commonwealth of Nations. Canada sided with the Allies in both world wars and became a member of NATO. Through diplomacy, Canada often worked to ease Cold War tensions. Its troops served in UN peacekeeping missions around the world.

Economic Growth Canada is a leading democratic and industrial power. It had a postwar economic boom, due in part to oil and gas deposits found in the western provinces. In 1959, Canada and the United States completed the St. Lawrence Seaway. It opened the Great Lakes to oceangoing ships and linked the interiors of both countries to the Atlantic Ocean.

With a population only a tenth that of the United States, Canada has encouraged immigration. Since the 1950s, Canada's population has grown increasingly diverse, with newcomers from Europe, Asia, Africa, Latin America, and the Caribbean.

Quebec Separatism Defining a national identity has remained a challenge for Canada. Quebec's French-speaking people saw themselves as a "distinct society." To protect their culture, Quebec demanded more autonomy within Canada.

Government leaders tried to meet those demands. But other provinces resisted any solution that gave Quebec special treatment. Some Quebec residents supported separatism, calling for Quebec to separate from Canada and become an independent nation. Today, Quebec separatism remains an explosive issue for Canadians.

United States Influence Another challenge for Canada has been the immense impact of the United States. Although the two nations enjoyed close ties, many Canadians resented their neighbor's cultural domination. Economic competition led to disputes over trade and tariffs. To resolve issues of economic competition, the countries set up the North American Free Trade Association (NAFTA). It created a free trade zone between Canada, the United States, and Mexico.

Other issues between Canada and the United States concerned the environment. Chemical pollution from American smokestacks, for example, contributed to acid rain that fell on northeastern Canada. The two nations agreed to work together for a common solution.

Quebec Separatism
Some French Canadians have urged that Quebec separate from the rest of Canada. Several times, they have come close to succeeding. Shown here are separatist buttons and French Canadians waving the blue-and-white flag of Quebec.

Theme: Diversity Why have some Quebeckers favored separatism?

SECTION 3 Assessment

Recall

1. **Identify:** (a) John F. Kennedy, (b) Richard Nixon, (c) social security, (d) Medicare, (e) Ronald Reagan, (f) *Brown* v. *Board of Education of Topeka,* (g) Martin Luther King, Jr., (h) Quebec.
2. **Define:** (a) deficit, (b) surplus, (c) civil rights movement, (d) segregation, (e) separatism.

Comprehension

3. What goals has the United States tried to achieve as a global superpower?
4. (a) How did government policies affect the American economy in the 1980s and 1990s? (b) How did the civil rights movement affect the economy?
5. What challenges have Canadians faced?

Critical Thinking and Writing

6. **Comparing** How is the situation of French-speaking Canadians similar to or different from that of minority groups within the United States?
7. **Linking Past and Present** Describe three ways the civil rights movement helped shape American life today.

Go Online
PHSchool.com

On the Internet, find sites that specialize in biographies. From these and other sites, gather information and photographs about the life of Martin Luther King, Jr. Use the information and images to create a brief illustrated biography of King. For help with this activity, use **Web Code mkd-3342.**

The Soviet Union: Rise and Fall of a Superpower

Reading Focus

- What ideas guided Soviet political, economic, and foreign policy?
- Why did the Soviet Union collapse?
- What problems have Russia and the other republics faced since the fall of the Soviet Union?

Vocabulary

dissident
glasnost
perestroika
default

Taking Notes

Copy the before-and-after chart at right. As you read, write key facts about conditions before and after the collapse of the Soviet Union in the appropriate columns.

COLLAPSE OF THE SOVIET UNION	
Before	After
• Cold War with the United States	• Attempts to cooperate with the United States
•	•
•	•

Main Idea After years of Communist rule, the Soviet Union collapsed and was replaced by Russia and other independent republics.

Setting the Scene "We shall bury you," Soviet leader Nikita Khrushchev (KROOSH chawf) told the West during the Cold War. He later explained that his statement was not a military threat, as many westerners believed. Instead, he said, it was a reference to his belief that capitalism was doomed and that Soviet communism was the wave of the future.

Khrushchev's prediction did not come true. In fact, it was Soviet communism that was doomed. In the 1980s, the Soviet economy began to crumble. Efforts at reform led the Soviet empire to disintegration.

Soviet Government and Economy

After World War II, the Soviet Union emerged as a superpower. Under Stalin, it established a sphere of influence from the Baltic to the Balkans.

Victory, however, brought few rewards to the Soviet people. Stalin continued his ruthless policies. He filled slave labor camps with "enemies of the state" and seemed ready to launch new purges when he died in 1953.

Stalin's Successors Nikita Khrushchev emerged as the new Soviet leader. In 1956, he shocked top Communist party members when he publicly denounced Stalin's abuse of power. Khrushchev then pursued a policy of de-Stalinization. He did not change Soviet goals but did free many political prisoners and eased censorship. He sought a thaw in the Cold War, calling for a "peaceful coexistence" with the West.

The thaw had limits, though. When discontented Hungarians revolted against communist rule in 1956, Khrushchev sent tanks in to smash them. When critics at home grew too bold, he clamped down. It appeared that a return to Stalinism could happen at any time.

Khrushchev's successor, Leonid Brezhnev (BREHSH nehf) held power from the mid-1960s until he died in

Khrushchev at the UN
Soviet leader Khrushchev was known for strong responses to the West. In 1960 at the UN, he emphasized a point by shaking his fist. *Life* magazine captured the moment and the feeling.

Theme: Global Interaction
How did events in Europe cause the Cold War to heat up?

1982. Brezhnev rigorously suppressed **dissidents,** people who spoke out against the government. Critics faced arrest and imprisonment. Some were locked away in insane asylums, a policy once used by czarist Russia.

Some Successes After World War II, the Soviet Union had rebuilt its shattered industries, using factories and equipment stripped from Germany. As in the 1930s, priority was given to industries such as steel, coal, and heavy machinery. The government also poured resources into weapons, science, and technology. In 1957, the Soviets launched *Sputnik I,* the first artificial satellite to orbit the Earth. *Sputnik* was a propaganda victory for the Soviet Union because it suggested technological superiority over the United States.

The Soviets also claimed other successes. Citizens enjoyed benefits such as low rents, cheap bread, free health care, and day care for children. Although wages were low, unemployment was almost nonexistent.

Failure of the Command Economy In general, however, the Soviet economy was plagued by severe problems. Collectivized agriculture remained so unproductive that the Soviet Union frequently had to import grain to feed its people. Nor could the Soviet command economy match the free-market economies of the West in producing consumer goods. Soviet shoes, suits, and television sets were far inferior to those made in the West, and luxuries like clothes washers or automobiles remained rare. People spent many hours of their lives waiting in line to buy food and other goods.

Low output was the result of inefficiencies in central economic planning. A huge bureaucracy, rather than supply and demand, decided what to produce, how much, and for whom. Government planners in Moscow often had little knowledge of the local conditions. Sometimes, factories were forced to shut down because needed supplies never arrived. At the local level, workers set out to meet production quotas, regardless of quality. Because workers had lifetime job security, they had little incentive to produce better-quality goods.

Foreign Policy Issues

Stalin and his successors forcefully asserted Soviet control over Eastern Europe. In 1955, Khrushchev set up the Warsaw Pact, in theory to defend the communist bloc against NATO. In practice, it was used to suppress dissent within Eastern Europe.

The Developing World Both the Soviet Union and the United States sought allies among the developing nations. One way to win and keep allies was to offer military and economic aid. At times, this policy turned local conflicts into Cold War confrontations. In two bitter wars, Soviet-backed governments in North Korea and North Vietnam battled against American-backed governments in South Korea and South Vietnam.

Rivalry With the United States Soviet-American relations swung back and forth between confrontation and détente. In 1961, the building of the Berlin Wall increased Cold War tensions. A year later, Khrushchev tried to build nuclear missile bases in Cuba. That move triggered the dangerous Cuban missile crisis, which you will read about in a later chapter. The crisis brought the two superpowers to the brink of war.

Brezhnev invested in a huge military buildup. In the Brezhnev Doctrine, he asserted that the Soviet Union had a right to intervene militarily in any Warsaw Pact nation. At the same time, however, he also pursued détente and disarmament with the United States.

Détente came to an abrupt end in 1979, after the Soviets invaded Afghanistan to ensure Soviet influence in that neighboring nation. Like the Vietnam War for the United States, the Afghan War drained the Soviet economy and provoked a crisis in morale at home.

Disaster!

MELTDOWN AT CHERNOBYL

In the early morning hours of April 26, 1986, disaster struck near the Ukrainian city of Prypyat. A full-scale nuclear meltdown had taken place in Reactor No. 4 of the Chernobyl nuclear power plant. The meltdown triggered a fire that released radiation-laden gas and dust particles. Countless civilians were contaminated by the radiation.

Radiation Warning Sign

These two children from Kiev, 65 miles southeast of Chernobyl, are being tested for radiation levels. Right now in the Ukraine, Belarus, and Russia, unusually high numbers of children suffer from thyroid cancer. Even children born after the accident are at risk.

The once thriving city of Prypyat is now a ghost town. People living within a 20-mile radius of the plant were evacuated immediately after the accident. The plant and surrounding area are now fenced, and it is still unsafe for humans to live there. Still, with nowhere else to go, hundreds of people have returned to their homes in Prypyat, despite the danger of contamination.

The area surrounding the Chernobyl nuclear power plant was the worst hit by radiation, but much of the Northern Hemisphere was affected, as well.

Radiation Levels

BELORUSSIAN S.S.R.

Dnieper R.

Savichi

Chernobyl Nuclear Power Plant — **Prypyat**

Prypyat R.

Cooling Pond — **Chernobyl**

Teterev R.

N
W   E
S

Ivankov

0   10 Miles
0   10 Kilometers   **UKRAINIAN S.S.R.**

Dymer

Kiev Reservoir
Desna R.

Kiev

Initial evacuation zone

Severe radiation area

Most severe radiation area

Portfolio Assessment

Nuclear power is only one alternative form of energy. Conduct research to learn more about other energy sources. Create a diagram or model that describes and illustrates how one new alternative energy source works.

Primary Sources and Literature

See "Mikhail Gorbachev: Perestroika" in the Reference Section at the back of this book.

Biography

Mikhail Gorbachev 1931—

Before he led the Soviet Union, Mikhail Gorbachev knew hard times. He was born to a Russian family of peasant farmers. For a time, his mother kept him home from school because he had no shoes.

After falling from leadership, Gorbachev met hard times again. He lost some $80,000 in a Russian bank crisis. To earn money, he made a television commercial for a chain of pizza restaurants. In 1998, few Russians came to a press conference announcing his new book.

Many Russians blamed Gorbachev for their nation's troubles, charging that he had changed the Soviet Union without a plan or goal. In a 1999 interview, Gorbachev rejected the charge. "We had a concept," he said. "Give up the totalitarianism. Lead society to freedom: political, ideological, and religious pluralism. Economic freedom, too. . . . But when such developments get under way, no one can predict specifically what it will lead to."

Theme: Impact of the Individual Did Gorbachev achieve his goals? Explain.

Collapse of the Soviet Empire

In 1985, an energetic new leader, Mikhail Gorbachev, came to power in the Soviet Union. As the war in Afghanistan dragged on, Gorbachev was eager to bring about reforms. The changes he unloosed, however, soon spiraled out of control.

The Gorbachev Revolution In foreign policy, Gorbachev sought an end to costly Cold War tensions. He renounced the Brezhnev Doctrine, signed arms control treaties with the United States, and eventually pulled Soviet troops out of Afghanistan.

At home, Gorbachev launched a two-pronged effort at reform. First, he called for glasnost, or openness. He ended censorship and encouraged people to openly discuss the country's problems. Second, he urged perestroika (pehr uh STROI kuh), which meant the restructuring of the government and economy. He hoped that he could boost efficiency by reducing the size and complexity of the government bureaucracy. He backed some free-market ideas, including limited private enterprise, but he still wanted to keep the essence of communism.

Gorbachev wanted the Soviet economy to produce more and higher-quality consumer goods. To achieve this goal, factory managers, instead of central planners, were made responsible for decisions. To increase food supplies, farmers were allowed more land on which to grow food that they could sell on the free market.

Unexpected Results Gorbachev's reforms brought economic turmoil. Shortages grew worse and prices soared. Factories that could not survive without government help closed, leading to high unemployment. The reforms were denounced by old-line Communists and bureaucrats whose jobs were threatened. At the same time, other critics, like the popular Russian leader Boris Yeltsin, demanded even more radical changes.

Problems increased as glasnost fed unrest in the multinational Soviet empire. The Baltic republics of Estonia, Latvia, and Lithuania, which had been seized in 1940, regained full independence in 1991. In Eastern Europe, countries from Poland and East Germany to Romania and Bulgaria broke out of the Soviet orbit.

In response, hard-liners tried to overthrow Gorbachev and restore the old order. Their attempted coup failed, but it further weakened Gorbachev. In 1991, as more Soviet republics declared independence, Gorbachev resigned as president. After 74 years the Soviet Union ceased to exist.

The Russian Republic

Russia, the largest Soviet republic in size and population, had dominated the Soviet Union since its creation. After the breakup of the Soviet Union, Russia and its president, Boris Yeltsin, faced a difficult future.

Economic Problems To solve Russia's economic problems and gain western aid, Yeltsin privatized more state-run industries and collective farms. The changeover to a market economy was painful. Unemployment soared. Without government controls, prices skyrocketed. Older people on pensions were especially hard hit. Unlike East Germany, which got massive aid from West Germany, Russia got relatively little aid from the West.

Despite these difficulties, some Russians prospered in the new economy. Their success, however, fanned resentment among poorer Russians. Meanwhile, criminals flourished, and ruthless gangs preyed on the new business class.

In 1998, Russia barely avoided financial collapse when it defaulted, or failed to make payments, on much of its foreign debt. The value of Russia's currency, the ruble, collapsed. The economy survived, but many banks and businesses closed. People lost their savings and jobs. In time, a few industries began to recover, but experts predicted further problems. Yeltsin's failure to solve the crisis and frequent change of top officials fed uncertainty and unrest.

Further troubles arose when minorities within Russia sought greater autonomy or independence. In 1994, Yeltsin failed in his brutal attempt to crush a revolt in Chechnya, a region in the Caucasus Mountains. That region was home to a variety of ethnic and religious groups, including Muslims. In 1999, fighting between Russian troops and rebel forces again raged in Chechnya. At the same time, a wave of terrorist violence broke out in Moscow. By early 2000, Russian troops had gained the upper hand and the Muslim rebels were in retreat.

The future of democracy in Russia remained uncertain as politicians—from former communists to ultranationalists—jockeyed for position. In 1999, moderates made a strong showing in parliamentary elections. That same year, Boris Yeltsin resigned and Vladimir Putin, a veteran of the Soviet secret police, became acting president. In the presidential election of 2000, Putin was elected president through the first free elections in Russia's history.

Putin in Charge Putin projected a toughness and strength that many Russians have traditionally admired in their leaders. He brought Russia success in the war with the secessionist province of Chechnya. He also brought more orderly and less corrupt government and some degree of economic improvement.

However, Putin faced some opposition. Some remembered his former ties to the secret police and feared that he was not strongly committed to democracy. Critics worried about the muffling of critical journalists and his treatment of minorities. Others were disturbed by his failure to prevent a new wave of Chechnyan terrorist attacks in the early 2000s.

A World Power On the international scene, the one-time superpower had suffered grievous setbacks in the years since the end of the Cold War. The breakup of the USSR, the absorption of former Warsaw Pact allies into such Western organizations as NATO and the European Union, and the establishment of American military bases on former Soviet territory, as in Central Asia, were major international setbacks.

Even though Russia was no longer a superpower, it retained a large military force and a nuclear arsenal. It still exercised influence around the

Russia's Free-Market Economy
Russia's transition from a command economy to a free-market economy has not brought prosperity to all. While affluent shoppers browse in a new Moscow department store, women in the province of Chechnya receive food handouts from government officials.

Theme: Economics and Technology How is a free-market economy different from a command economy?

Cause *and* Effect

Long-Term Causes	Immediate Causes
• Low output of crops and consumer goods • Cold War led to high military spending • Ethnic and nationalist movements • Denial of rights and freedoms	• War with Afghanistan • Food and fuel shortages • Demonstrations in the Baltic states • Gorbachev's rise to power

Collapse of the Soviet Union

Effects

• Soviet Union breaks up into 15 republics
• Russian republic approves a new constitution
• Changeover to market economy in Russia
• Cold War ends
• War in Chechnya

Connections to Today

• New republics struggle to achieve democratic reforms
• Difficulties adjusting to a free-market economy
• Increased danger of ethnic and religious conflict

Skills Assessment **Chart** It will be many years before the long-term effects of the fall of the Soviet Union are fully understood. **What was one economic cause of the fall of the Soviet Union?**

world. Western nations hoped that Russia might work to resolve global problems. After September 11, 2001, Russia pledged support to the U.S.-led war on terrorism. In return, many world leaders saw Russia's conflict with Chechnyans as a legitimate battle against terrorism. In 2002, a new NATO-Russia Council was established, effectively making Russia a junior partner in NATO. Russia also took a seat at the G-8 meetings of the world's major industrial democracies.

The Other Republics

Like Russia, the other former Soviet republics wanted to build stable governments and improve their economies. They, too, faced unrest, corruption, and political divisions. In some countries, authoritarian rulers gained power. Ethnic conflict erupted in republics with a mix of national groups. Other conflicts arose over border disputes. Armenia, for example, seized a piece of neighboring Azerbaijan, where many Armenians lived. The republic of Georgia survived a bloody civil war.

These new nations endured hard times as they switched to market economies. With help from the UN, the World Bank, and the International Monetary Fund (IMF), the new nations worked to increase trade with the rest of the world. The republics of Ukraine, Kazakhstan, and Belarus gave up the nuclear weapons on their soil in return for trading privileges or investments from the West.

SECTION 4 Assessment

Recall
1. **Identify:** **(a)** Nikita Khrushchev, **(b)** Afghan War, **(c)** Mikhail Gorbachev, **(d)** Boris Yeltsin, **(e)** Chechnya, **(f)** Vladimir Putin.
2. **Define:** **(a)** dissident, **(b)** glasnost, **(c)** perestroika, **(d)** default.

Comprehension
3. What were the effects of each of the following Soviet policies: **(a)** command economy, **(b)** rivalry with the United States?
4. How did Gorbachev's reforms contribute to the collapse of the Soviet Union?

5. Describe two problems that have afflicted Russia and the other new republics since the breakup of the Soviet Union.

Critical Thinking and Writing
6. **Predicting Consequences** What do you think might happen in Russia if the Communist party won control of the government again?
7. **Making Decisions** Do you think the western democracies should invest large sums of money in Russia and other former Soviet republics? Why or why not?

Activity

Writing a Protest Letter
Write a letter to the leaders of the Russian republic in which you protest Russia's policy toward Chechnya. In your letter, demonstrate that you understand the issues involved, make your position clear, and offer reasons as to why Russian officials should change their policy.

Reading Focus

- How did Eastern European nations oppose Soviet domination and strive for democracy?
- What were the effects of the fall of communism?
- What were the causes and effects of civil war in Yugoslavia?

Vocabulary

ethnic cleansing

war crime

Taking Notes

As you read, make a chart showing how the end of Soviet domination affected the countries of Eastern Europe. Use this partially completed chart as a model. Add as many countries as possible to the chart.

END OF SOVIET DOMINATION			
Poland	**East Germany**	**Romania**	
• Solidarity legalized	• Berlin Wall toppled	•	•
		•	•

Main Idea After years of Soviet domination, the countries of Eastern Europe were free of Russian control, facing new and sometimes difficult challenges.

Setting the Scene

For centuries, Eastern Europe lived in the shadow of larger powers. Before World War I, much of the region was divided among the German, Russian, Austrian, and Ottoman empires. Many small nations gained independence in 1919, only to be overrun by Germany in World War II. After the war, the region fell under Soviet domination.

Finally, in 1989, Eastern European nations again won their freedom. Vaclav Havel, a playwright and president of the Czech Republic, saw independence as a challenge. To him, it was not "just a state of being" but a "complex task." Independence, he noted, should benefit all citizens and be something worth fighting for and defending.

> ▶ **Primary Sources and Literature**
>
> See "Vaclav Havel: New Year's Address" in the Reference Section at the back of this book.

Under Soviet Domination

In 1945, as World War II ended, Soviet armies occupied much of Eastern Europe. By the end of the 1940s, most countries in the region were ruled by local Communist parties. Backed by Soviet power, they destroyed rival parties, silenced critics, and campaigned against religion. As in the Soviet Union, Communist leaders in Eastern Europe ended private ownership of businesses and turned to central economic planning. Because the countries of Eastern Europe were held in the orbit of the more powerful Soviet Union, they became known as satellites, or client states.

Unrest In the 1950s, the Soviet Union tightened its grip on its satellites. Stalin forced them to sell natural resources on terms favorable to the Soviet Union and to provide troops and money to support the Warsaw Pact. Soviet troops were stationed throughout Eastern Europe.

Yet in East Germany, Poland, Hungary, and elsewhere, unrest simmered. Despite some economic progress, many people despised the communist monopoly on power. Nationalists resented Russian domination.

Resistance and Repression In 1956, Imre Nagy (NOJ), a communist reformer and strong nationalist, gained power in Hungary. He ended one-party rule and withdrew Hungary from the Warsaw Pact. Khrushchev responded with force. Hungarian "freedom fighters" resisted Soviet

FACT FINDER

Soviet Domination of Eastern Europe

1945	After World War II, Soviet armies occupy much of Eastern Europe.
1949	Most Eastern European countries are under communist rule.
1956	Hungary withdraws from Warsaw Pact and ends one-party rule; Soviet troops crush Hungarian uprising.
1968	Czechoslovakia introduces reforms; Soviets use force to restore communist dictatorship.
1980	Polish government, under Soviet pressure, cracks down on trade union movement and arrests its leaders.

Skills Assessment

Graph The Soviet Union dominated Eastern Europe from 1945 through the 1980s. **How did World War II lead to the establishment of communism in most of Eastern Europe?**

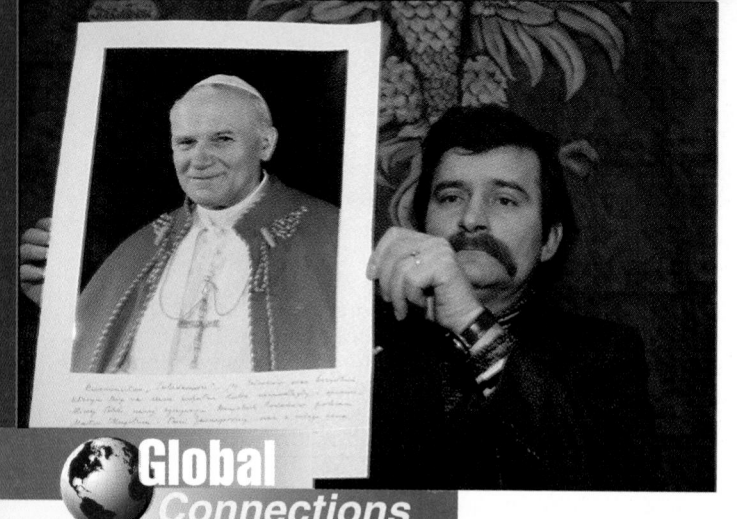

Global Connections

The Enduring Impact of Pope John Paul II

This picture shows Lech Walesa holding a portrait of Pope John Paul II. Walesa knew how important the pope had been in helping to end communism in Poland. So did Soviet leader Mikhail Gorbachev, who said "Everything that happened in Eastern Europe in these last few years would have been impossible without the presence of this pope."

John Paul II was well known for his political activism. During World War II, before becoming a Catholic priest, Karol Wojtyla helped Polish Jews escape the Nazis. After he was elected pope in 1978, he visited well over 100 nations around the world. Wherever he went, he was outspoken. He was a vocal critic of communist dictatorship and other abuses of human rights. In a 1995 address to the UN, Pope John Paul II made a plea to leaders around the world. "The human person," he said, "must be the true focus of all social, political, and economic activity."

Theme: Global Interaction
What do you think was the meaning of the pope's speech at the UN?

► **Primary Sources and Literature**

See "Lech Walesa: Nobel Peace Prize Lecture" in the Reference Section at the back of this book.

tanks and troops, and called on the West for help. None came. Thousands died in the fighting, and Nagy was executed.

A dozen years later, Alexander Dubček introduced liberal reforms in Czechoslovakia. He called for "socialism with a human face." Once again, the Soviets responded with force. Warsaw Pact troops ousted Dubček and restored a communist dictatorship. As you have read, under the Brezhnev Doctrine, the Soviet Union claimed the right to intervene in the affairs of any Eastern European nation.

Yugoslavia's Independent Path Soviet power did not extend to Yugoslavia. During World War II, a fierce guerrilla leader, Josip Tito, had battled German occupying forces. Later, Tito set up a communist government in Yugoslavia, but he pursued a path independent of Moscow. He refused to join the Warsaw Pact and claimed to be neutral in the Cold War.

Poland's Road to Democracy

Poland was the Soviet Union's most troublesome satellite. Like Hungarians and Czechs, Poles wanted greater freedom within the Soviet bloc. Stalin had clamped down hard on Poland, but communist persecution of the Roman Catholic Church backfired. The Church became a rallying point for Poles opposed to the regime. In 1956, economic woes touched off riots and strikes. To end the turmoil, the Polish government made some reforms. Dissatisfaction with communism, however, would continue to surface.

Solidarity In 1980, economic hardships ignited strikes by shipyard workers. Led by Lech Walesa (vah LEHN sah), they organized Solidarity, an independent trade union. It won millions of members and demanded political change. Under pressure from the Soviet Union, the Polish government outlawed the union and arrested its leaders, including Walesa.

Still, unrest simmered. Walesa became a national hero. Pressure from the world community further strained the communist government. Pope John Paul II visited Poland in 1979, met with Solidarity leaders, and criticized communist policies. The pope was the former Karol Wojtyla, archbishop of the Polish city of Cracow.

Peaceful Transition In the late 1980s, Gorbachev declared he would not interfere in Eastern Europe. By then, Poland was introducing radical economic reforms similar to Gorbachev's changes in the Soviet Union. It also legalized Solidarity and, in 1989, held the first free elections in 50 years. Solidarity candidates triumphed. A year later, Lech Walesa was elected president of Poland. The new government began a difficult, but peaceful, transition from a planned to a market economy.

Fall of Communist Governments

By late 1989, a "democracy movement" was sweeping through Eastern Europe. Everywhere, people took to the streets, demanding reform. One by one, communist governments fell. A dissident writer and human rights activist, Vaclav Havel, was elected president of Czechoslovakia. The Berlin Wall was toppled and Germany was reunited. Most changes came peacefully. Only Romania's brutal longtime dictator, Nicolae Ceausescu (chah SHEHS koo), refused to step down. He was overthrown and executed.

For the first time since 1945, Eastern European countries were free to settle their own affairs. They withdrew from the Warsaw Pact and requested that Soviet troops leave. By then, Soviet power itself was crumbling.

New Challenges Like Russia and the former Soviet republics, Eastern European nations set out to build stable governments and free-market economies. Although the experiences of each nation differed, all faced similar challenges. Governments privatized industries and stopped keeping prices for basic goods and services artificially low. As in Russia, the many changes contributed to rising inflation, high unemployment, and crime waves. Consumer goods were certainly more plentiful, but many people could not afford to pay the high prices for them.

By the mid-1990s, some people were disillusioned with reform. As a result, former communists gained seats in some national parliaments. However, after initial hardships, the outlook began to brighten in Hungary, Poland, the Czech Republic, and other Eastern European countries.

With the Cold War over, Eastern European countries assumed a greater role in international affairs. In 1999, Poland, Hungary, and the Czech Republic became members of the NATO military alliance. Other Eastern European states were slated for membership in the early 2000s. The European Union also opened its doors to the east. In 2003, Poland and other European countries sent soldiers to help rebuild war-torn Iraq.

Ethnic Tensions Centuries of migration and conquest left most Eastern European countries with ethnically diverse populations. Most countries had a majority population, along with one or more ethnic minorities. Nationalism helped unite countries like Poland and Hungary, but it worked as a divisive force elsewhere. Hungarians in Romania demanded autonomy. Faced with ethnic tensions, Czechoslovakia peacefully split into two countries, the Czech Republic and Slovakia. In the 1990s, ethnic conflict tore Yugoslavia apart in a long civil war.

Civil War in Yugoslavia

Yugoslavia was created after World War I as a homeland for the South Slavs. It consisted of various republics—Serbia, Croatia, Bosnia and Herzegovina, Macedonia, Slovenia, and Montenegro. Yugoslavia's ethnic and religious groups included Serbs, who were Orthodox Christians; Croats, who were Roman Catholics; and Bosnians, who were Muslims. The groups had distinct customs and religions, but all spoke the same language, Serbo-Croatian. The Serbs dominated the multinational state.

Budapest, Hungary
In 1956, Soviet troops and tanks rolled through the streets of Budapest, crushing the freedom fighters of the Hungarian uprising (PAST). Today, the people of Budapest live in a nation with a democratic government and a free-market economy (PRESENT).

Theme: Continuity and Change Why was Hungary finally able to free itself from Soviet domination?

PAST

PRESENT

New Nations in Eastern Europe

Former territory of

Czechoslovakia	Soviet Union
East Germany	Yugoslavia

SWEDEN

DENMARK

Baltic Sea

ESTONIA

LATVIA

LITHUANIA

RUSSIA

GERMANY

POLAND

BELARUS

RUSSIA

KAZAKHSTAN

50°N

CZECH REP.

SLOVAKIA

UKRAINE

AUSTRIA

HUNGARY

MOLDOVA

SLOVENIA

CROATIA

ROMANIA

Caspian Sea

BOSNIA & HERZEGOVINA

ITALY

SERBIA & MONTENEGRO

Black Sea

GEORGIA

BULGARIA

ARMENIA

40°N

MACEDONIA

ALBANIA

GREECE

TURKEY

AZERBAIJAN

Azimuthal Equal Area Projection

0   150   300 Miles

0   150   300 Kilometers

Skills Assessment

Geography By the end of the 1990s, many nations in Eastern Europe had become newly independent.

1. **Location** On the map, locate (a) Latvia, (b) Ukraine, (c) Georgia, (d) Czech Republic, (e) Slovenia.
2. **Region** What three Baltic nations won independence from the Soviet Union?
3. **Critical Thinking Comparing** Yugoslavia and the Soviet Union were multinational states. How does that help to explain what happened to both nations in the 1990s?

Breakup For decades following World War II, Tito ruled Yugoslavia with an iron hand. He jailed critics and silenced nationalist and religious unrest. However, soon after his death and the fall of communism, nationalism tore Yugoslavia apart. The ruling Serbs tried in vain to keep the multinational state together and to hold onto power. In 1991, Slovenia declared independence. Croatia, Macedonia, and Bosnia and Herzegovina soon followed. Yugoslavia was left with only Serbia and Montenegro.

Fighting in Bosnia In Bosnia, civil war erupted among Muslims, Serbs, and Croats. Bosnian Serbs fought to set up their own autonomous regions. They received money and arms from Yugoslav president Slobodan Milosevic, an extreme Serb nationalist. The Muslims, who were the majority group in Bosnia, did not want the country divided into ethnic regions.

During the war, all sides committed atrocities. In a vicious campaign of ethnic cleansing, Serbs killed people of other ethnic groups or forcibly removed them from the areas they held. Tens of thousands of Bosnian Muslims were brutalized or killed, sometimes in mass executions. Muslim fighters committed acts of revenge. Innocent people were caught in the crossfire, and streams of refugees fled the war zones. To many, Serb efforts at ethnic cleansing recalled the horrors of Nazi Germany and the Holocaust.

The UN, NATO powers, and Russia all tried to bring about peace. Finally, in 1995, NATO launched air strikes against the Bosnian Serb military. Under that pressure, the warring parties began peace talks. Guided by the United States, Bosnia, Croatia, and Serbia signed the Dayton Accords, a series of peace agreements. International forces monitored the peace, but implementing the agreements was often difficult in the face of bitter feelings among the hostile groups.

Fighting in Kosovo As Bosnia reached a tense peace, a new crisis rose in the Yugoslav province of Kosovo, a historic part of Serbia. Over the centuries, many ethnic Albanians, mostly Muslim, had settled in Kosovo. By the 1990s, they made up about 90 percent of the population. The rest of the population were mostly Serbs.

In 1989, President Milosevic ended the limited self-rule that Muslims in Kosovo had long enjoyed in Yugoslavia. Protests by Muslim Kosovars led to repression, and a small Kosovo Liberation Army waged guerrilla war against the Serbs.

Milosevic began ethnic cleansing in Kosovo as he had in Bosnia. When UN and NATO demands for a negotiated settlement failed, NATO launched air strikes against Serbia. As reports of Serbian massacres of Albanian Kosovars spread, hundreds of thousands fled.

Yugoslavia finally withdrew its forces from Kosovo, and NATO peacekeepers moved in, along with returning refugees. The international force had to help Kosovars organize a government and rebuild homes and factories while preventing ethnic Albanians from taking revenge on Serbs.

The tightening of UN sanctions then incited unrest and led to the overthrow of Miloseviç in 2000. In 2003, Yugoslavia became Serbia and Montenegro under a new federal constitution. But government leaders were still plagued by internal disputes. And both republics were guaranteed the option to secede from the country in 2006.

Although peace was restored, the Balkan region remained unstable. New nations needed massive aid to rebuild, and large numbers of refugees remained in temporary shelters. Ethnic feuds continued to simmer.

Looking Ahead

Bosnia and Kosovo were test cases for NATO in the post–Cold War world. In Bosnia, the United States and its European allies were hesitant to intervene militarily. In Kosovo, they took action more quickly.

During the Balkan conflicts, an international court charged Milosevic and others with war crimes for violating rules of war that forbid atrocities such as the mass killings of prisoners or civilians. When captured, they faced trial and possible punishment. To some, the interventions, the punishment of war crimes, and the widespread condemnation of human rights abuses suggested that a new era of international cooperation was emerging.

SECTION 5 Assessment

Recall
1. **Identify:** (a) satellites, (b) Imre Nagy, (c) Alexander Dubçek, (d) Josip Tito, (e) Lech Walesa, (f) Pope John Paul II, (g) Vaclav Havel, (h) Slobodan Milosevic.
2. **Define:** (a) ethnic cleansing, (b) war crime.

Comprehension
3. (a) How did Hungarians resist Soviet domination? (b) How did democracy emerge in Poland?
4. Why were some Eastern Europeans unhappy with the changes that came after the fall of communism?

5. Why did civil war break out in Yugoslavia?

Critical Thinking and Writing
6. **Analyzing Primary Sources** Mikhail Gorbachev said, "Everything that happened in Eastern Europe in these last few years would have been impossible without the presence of this pope." Explain the meaning of Gorbachev's words.
7. **Asking Questions** Suppose you are a journalist interviewing a Serb official. Make a list of questions about recent events in Yugoslavia.

Activity

Preparing a Dialogue With a classmate, prepare a dialogue between two people in an Eastern European nation. Discuss the changes that have occurred in the country and the outlook for the future. Present your dialogue before the class.

Creating a Chapter Summary

To help you review the chapter, prepare a time line like the one below. Above the time line, list key events concerning Western Europe and North America. Below the time line, list key events concerning Eastern Europe and the Soviet Union.

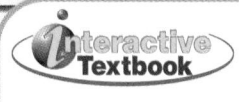

For additional review and enrichment activities, see the interactive version of *World History* available on the Web and on CD-ROM.

| 1945 | 1956 | Youth riots in France | | United States has budget surpluses |

Soviets occupy Eastern Europe

Soviets crush Hungarian revolt

1968

1990s

Go Online
PHSchool.com
For practice test questions for Chapter 20, use **Web Code mka-3354**.

Building Vocabulary

Use the terms below to create a fill-in quiz. Write a sentence for each word, but leave a blank space where the word would appear.

1. recession
2. euro
3. coalition
4. surplus
5. separatism
6. dissident
7. glasnost
8. ethnic cleansing

Recalling Key Facts

9. What were the effects of the Cold War arms race?
10. Describe two steps Western European nations took toward unity.
11. What events led to German reunification?
12. How did NAFTA affect Canada and the United States?
13. Why was the Soviet command economy less successful than western capitalist economies?
14. How did the Soviet Union dominate Eastern Europe?
15. Describe three problems faced by former Soviet republics.

Critical Thinking and Writing

16. **Defending a Position** If you lived in a European country today, would you support a "United States of Europe"? Why or why not?
17. **Comparing** Compare the impact of Labour party leadership and Conservative party leadership on the citizens of Britain.
18. **Understanding Causes and Effects** What were the causes of the collapse of the Soviet Union?
19. **Drawing Conclusions** (a) Why do you think that many Russians considered Putin to be an improvement over Yeltsin? (b) Do you think Putin will benefit Russia in the long run? Explain.
20. **Connecting to Geography** What role might geography have played in Yeltsin's failure to crush revolts in Chechnya?
21. **Solving Problems** List possible solutions to the troubles in Yugoslavia. Describe the strengths and weaknesses of each possible solution.

Read the excerpt below from a news article titled "Liberal Leaders Warn Yeltsin to Protect His People." Then, answer the questions that follow.

"MOSCOW, Oct 6, 1999—Liberal leaders urged Russian President Boris Yeltsin on Wednesday to defend his people by exercising caution in the advance of troops into the breakaway region of Chechnya. Liberal economist Grigory Yavlinsky said the troop movements and a two-week-old campaign of air raids ignored the 'tragic experience' of the 1994-96 Chechen war in which tens of thousands died on Russia's southern rim. . . .

[Yavlinsky] backed punitive measures against Chechen 'terrorists,' accused by Moscow of incursions in a neighboring region and of masterminding bomb blasts in Russian cities. But he urged the Kremlin to start talks with Chechen leaders. 'Russian forces should cooperate with those organizations which exist there . . . only contact with the people and with leaders can change the situation for the better,' he said. 'We insist on finding a balance between our security and your [Chechen] independence.'

. . . 'The development of events in Chechnya along the lines of 1994-96 will lead to Russia's colossal defeat,' Yavlinsky said. 'Russia will not be able to survive it.' "

—Reuters Information Service

22. Why were Russian troops advancing into Chechnya in 1999?
23. What policy does Yavlinsky recommend in Chechnya?
24. Why does Grigory Yavlinsky urge Yeltsin to exercise caution in Chechnya?

Go Online
PHSchool.com

Do Internet research on a major current event or trend in Europe, the United States, or Canada. Use the information to produce a television news report on the topic. Remember to include maps, video, charts, or other visuals to go with the report. For help with this activity, use **Web Code mkd-3355.**

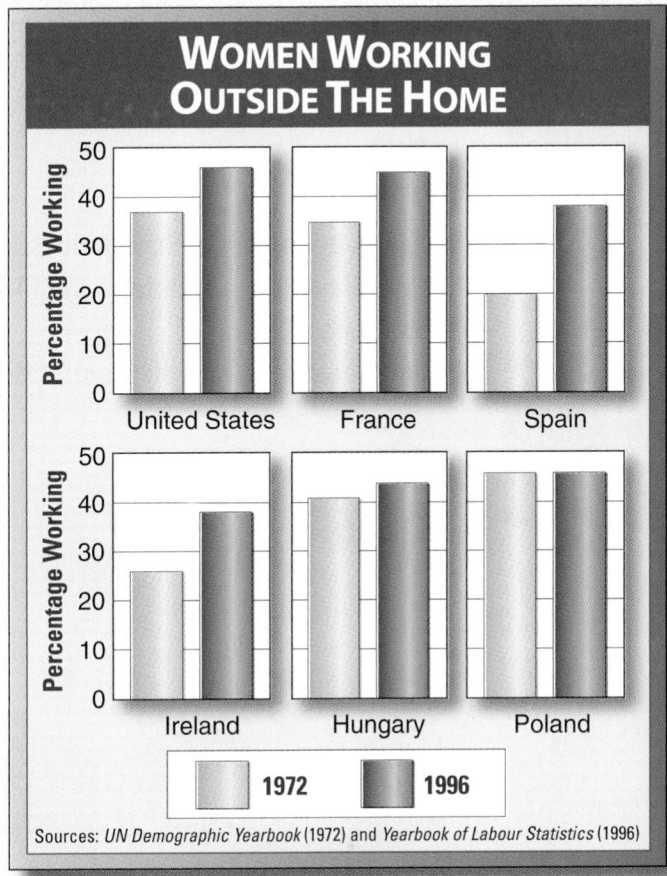

WOMEN WORKING OUTSIDE THE HOME

Sources: *UN Demographic Yearbook* (1972) and *Yearbook of Labour Statistics* (1996)

Study the series of bar graphs and answer the following questions:

25. What percentage of Spanish women worked outside the home in 1972? In 1996?
26. In 1996, which four countries had about the same percentage of women working outside the home?
27. In 1972, which country had the smallest percentage of women working outside the home?
28. **(a)** Which two countries experienced the smallest increase in women working outside the home between 1972 and 1996? **(b)** Based on what you have learned in this chapter, offer a possible explanation for the lack of change in these two countries.

Skills Tip

To understand a bar graph, use the title and key to identify what each bar represents. Read the numbers and labels on the vertical or horizontal axis to determine the measurements being compared.

East Asia and Southeast Asia

1945–Present

Chapter Preview

1 Japan Becomes an Economic Superpower
2 From Revolution to Reform in China
3 The Asian Tigers
4 Southeast Asia and the Pacific Rim

CHAPTER EVENTS

1949

Mao Zedong announces the formation of the People's Republic of China. This idealized portrait of Mao was painted after he had ruled China for 20 years.

1950s

Japan's recovery from World War II begins, sparking an "economic miracle."

1968

During the Vietnam War, the Tet Offensive shows that guerrilla forces are determined to fight, no matter the cost. Here, American medical troops race to rescue a wounded Marine.

1940

1955

1970

GLOBAL EVENTS

1957 In Africa, the nation of Ghana gains independence from Britain.

1962 The Cuban missile crisis heightens Cold War tensions.

Nations of the Pacific Rim

40°E 60°E 80°E 100°E 120°E 140°E 160°E 180° 160°W 140°W 120°W 100°W 80°W 60°W 40°W

Arctic Circle

60°N

CANADA

UNITED STATES

40°N

CHINA **SOUTH KOREA** **JAPAN**

Tropic of Cancer

MEXICO

20°N

TAIWAN
Hong Kong

THAILAND **PHILIPPINES**

PACIFIC OCEAN

BRUNEI
MALAYSIA

N
W—E
S

Equator 0°

INDIAN OCEAN

I N D O N E S I A **PAPUA NEW GUINEA**

SINGAPORE

EAST TIMOR

20°S

Tropic of Capricorn

CHILE

Resources and population enable nations of the Asia-Pacific Economic Cooperation group (APEC) to play a vital role in the global economy.

AUSTRALIA

Robinson Projection

0   1000   2000 Miles

0   1000   2000 Kilometers

40°S

NEW ZEALAND

60°S

1986

In the Philippines, newly elected President Corazon Aquino promotes democracy after long-time dictator Ferdinand Marcos is ousted from power.

1987

South Korea holds direct elections, moving toward democracy.

2003

SARS—severe acute respiratory syndrome—is the first serious new disease of the twenty-first century. It begins in China but infects thousands around the world.

1985   2000   2015

1989 The Berlin Wall falls.

Go Online
PHSchool.com

To learn about recent developments in East and Southeast Asia, use **Web Code mkc-3457.**

Japan Becomes an Economic Superpower

Reading Focus

■ What factors made Japan's recovery an economic miracle?

■ How did Japan interact economically and politically with other nations?

■ How are patterns of life changing in Japan?

Vocabulary

zaibatsu

gross domestic product

trade deficit

Taking Notes

Copy this concept web. Fill in each blank circle with key factors in Japan's emergence as an economic superpower. Add as many circles as you need.

Protectionist policies

JAPAN: ECONOMIC SUPERPOWER

Educated, skilled work force

Main Idea After World War II, Japan rapidly rebuilt and became an economic superpower.

Political and Economic Recovery
United States general Douglas MacArthur (left) led the occupation of Japan after World War II. This picture, showing him with Emperor Hirohito (right), was a great surprise to the Japanese people. MacArthur's casual appearance contrasted sharply with the emperor's formality.

Theme: Political and Social Systems How did political and social changes in Japan affect the nation's economic recovery?

Setting the Scene Wartime destruction left cities crumbling throughout Japan. More than half of the homes in Tokyo had been destroyed. Agricultural production also suffered, as bad weather left rice harvests at only two thirds the prewar level.

With the end of the war came the need to rebuild. As in the past, the Japanese learned from outsiders. They selectively borrowed western ideas and technology and put them to their own use. In time, Japan emerged as an economic superpower.

Recovery and Economic Miracle

In 1945, Japan lay in ruins. It had suffered perhaps the most devastating property damage of any nation involved in World War II. Tens of thousands of Japanese were homeless and hungry.

The Occupation Under General Douglas MacArthur, the American military government set two main objectives for the occupation of Japan—to destroy militarism and to ensure democratic government. To achieve the first, Japan's armed forces were disbanded. As in Germany, trials were held to punish those responsible for wartime atrocities. Along with Japan's defeat, the trials further discredited the military. In 1946, a new constitution provided that "the Japanese people forever renounce war as a sovereign right of the nation." Japan, it said, would never maintain military forces except for its own defense.

The emperor lost all political power, and Japan became a constitutional monarchy. Power was held by the people, who elected representatives to the Diet, or parliament. The constitution also protected basic rights such as freedom of thought, press, and assembly. Occupation forces also brought social reforms. They opened the education system to all people and emphasized legal equality for women.

The Americans introduced economic reforms designed to promote democracy. The constitution protected the right of workers to organize unions.

A sweeping land-reform program divided up large estates among tenant farmers. The former owners received payment, and peasants owned land for the first time. This change erased lingering traces of feudalism in Japan. Although the Americans tried to disband the zaibatsu, or giant business organizations, the Japanese resisted. They felt that large firms were needed to compete internationally.

As Cold War tensions heightened, the United States grew eager to end the occupation. In 1952, it signed a peace treaty with Japan. Still, the two nations kept close ties. American military forces operated out of bases in Japan, which in turn was protected by the American "nuclear umbrella." They also were trading partners, eventually competing with each other in the global economy.

Economic Success Between 1950 and 1970, Japan produced an economic miracle. Its gross domestic product (GDP) soared. GDP refers to the total value of all goods and services produced by a nation within a particular year.

Japan's success was built on producing goods for export. At first, Japan made textiles. Later, it shifted to making steel for shipbuilding and machinery. By the 1970s, Japanese cars, cameras, and televisions found eager buyers on the world market. Its companies also moved into high technology. Soon, Japanese electronic goods were competing with western, and especially American, products.

How did Japan enjoy such success? After World War II, Japan, like Germany, had to rebuild from scratch. Also like Germany, it had successfully industrialized in the past, so it quickly built efficient, modern factories that outproduced older industries in the West.

In addition, Japan benefited from an educated and skilled work force. Until recently, some Japanese companies provided lifetime employment for their workers. In return, workers gave the company total loyalty.

Also, Japanese workers saved much of their pay. Their savings gave banks the capital to invest in industry. Other investment came from the government, which did not have to spend money on a large military force.

Trade and Investment As a small island nation with few natural resources, Japan depended on trade. It imported oil and other raw materials, like iron ore, but it exported the more profitable finished goods, such as steel. It marketed its products so successfully that it built a favorable balance of trade, exporting more than it imported.

As Japan's economy grew, it invested in ventures around the world. The Japanese bought real estate. They financed mines and plantations and built airports and chemical plants. Japanese engineers and managers worked everywhere, meeting and outpacing the West.

Japan's protectionist policies angered its trading partners. The government protected home industries by imposing tariffs and regulations that limited imports. This policy along with the high quality of Japanese exports caused other nations to run a trade deficit with Japan. That is, they bought more goods from Japan than Japan bought from them. Americans, for example, bought so many Japanese-made cars that United States automakers felt threatened.

The United States claimed that unfair trade barriers kept American companies from selling their goods in Japan. To force Japan to ease its restrictions, the United States threatened to raise tariffs on Japanese imports, making them more expensive for American buyers. Frequent trade talks between the two nations had only limited success.

Slowdown After decades of stunning economic growth, the bubble burst in the 1990s. Japan faced its worst economic depression since the 1930s. Unemployment rose. Many workers no longer enjoyed the guarantee of lifetime employment. The government tried to spur growth by easing

Japanese Entrepreneurs Break With Tradition
Executives at the Toyota Corporation in Japan developed a new production system. The following excerpt describes the main features of this revolutionary new technique:

"The two executives [created] an entirely new system of production —dubbed . . . 'lean production.'. . . Its genius was to shift the focus of manufacturing . . . to 'economies of time.'

It did this in [several] ways. The first was by making every employee a quality checker. . . . Toyota gave workers the right to stop the production line as soon as they saw errors.

The second improvement came from introducing 'just-in-time' production. In the rest of the world, manufacturers made their components 'just in case' they were needed. They filled . . . warehouses with . . . costly parts, which gathered dust until they were finally needed. The Japanese started making components 'just in time,' with parts arriving just as they were needed on the production line."

—"The Art and Practice of Japanese Management" (Mickelthwaite)

Skills Assessment

Primary Source How would these techniques save time for Japanese companies?

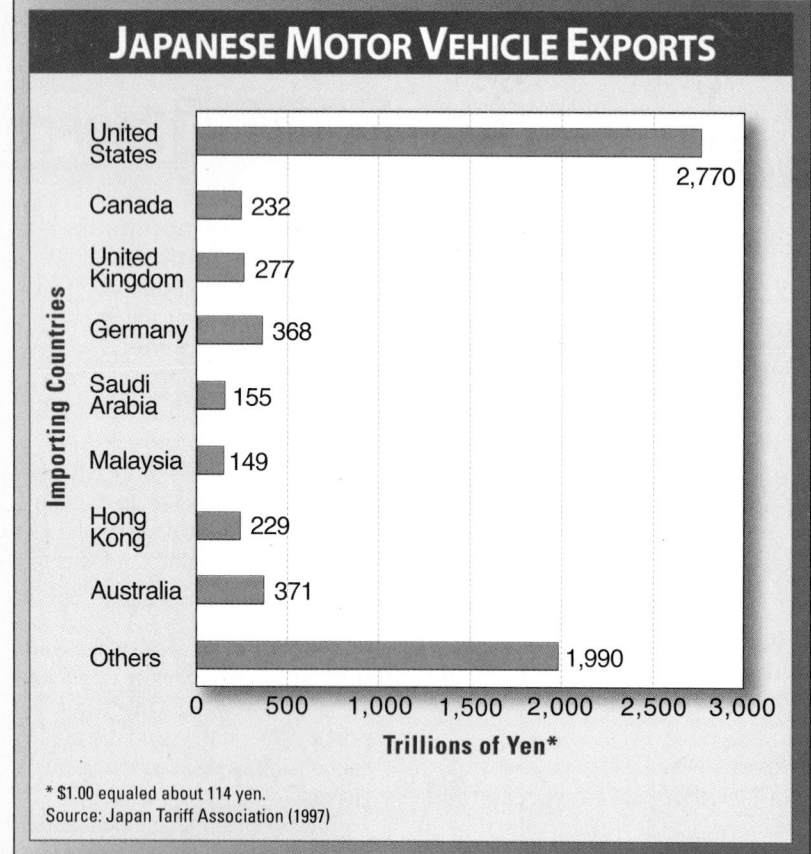

JAPANESE MOTOR VEHICLE EXPORTS

Importing Countries	Trillions of Yen*
United States	2,770
Canada	232
United Kingdom	277
Germany	368
Saudi Arabia	155
Malaysia	149
Hong Kong	229
Australia	371
Others	1,990

* $1.00 equaled about 114 yen.
Source: Japan Tariff Association (1997)

Skills Assessment

Graph International sales of Japanese motor vehicles soared during the 1970s, and remained high through the 1980s and 1990s. The nation that imported the largest number of these vehicles was the United States. **Which individual nation was the second-largest importer of Japanese motor vehicles?**

regulations and reforming the banking system, but with little success. A global economic slowdown in the early 2000s further hindered growth. Despite a slow recovery, Japan remained an economic superpower.

Economic and Political Interaction

Economic success allowed Japan to benefit from the modern global economy. Yet Japan felt the negative effects of interdependence as well, especially because of its need for imported raw materials.

Dependence on Oil Nothing brought home Japan's dependence on world markets more than OPEC's price hikes in the 1970s. Japan's booming industries had fed on cheap imported oil. Higher energy costs sent shock waves through its economy.

In response to this economic challenge, Japan sought better relations with oil-producing nations of the Middle East. It also tried to reduce energy use by building more efficient power plants and expanding and improving public transportation. Still, Japan's modern economy required oil.

Japan and Its Neighbors As Japan sought economic openings in Asia, it had to deal with nations that still held bitter memories of World War II. China, Korea, and parts of Southeast Asia had suffered terribly under Japanese occupation. Japan was slow to apologize for its wartime actions, but it did work hard to regain the trust of neighboring peoples. By the 1980s, Japan was a major investor in China and the emerging nations of Southeast Asia. In the 1990s, Japanese leaders offered some public regrets for the death and destruction of the war years.

International Politics Although Japan was an economic superpower, it took a back seat in international politics for many years. During the Cold War, Japan supported the western alliance. More recently, it has edged toward a larger world role. For decades, Japan has given foreign aid to emerging nations. Today, it ranks as the world's largest donor nation.

In recent years, the United States has urged Japan to rearm and assume more of the costs for its own defense. Asian neighbors oppose Japan's rearmament, and the Japanese themselves are divided on the issue. Some think Japan's status as a world power requires rearmament. Most prefer to avoid the hazards and expense of becoming a military power.

Changing Patterns of Life

After decades of economic growth, the Japanese have struggled to deal with the social challenges presented by the economic downturn of the 1990s and early 2000s. With company cutbacks, many workers lost job security. Confidence diminished. For the future, Japan faced two long-term problems: a lack of usable land and an aging population.

Political Stresses Japan's democracy has survived many crises. The Liberal Democratic Party (LDP) dominated the government from the 1950s to the 1990s. But Japanese political parties, however, differ from those in the United States. The LDP is a coalition, or temporary alliance, of factions that compete behind the scenes for top government positions. In recent years, Japan has been led by a series of prime ministers leading different coalitions. Voters have expressed their desire for economic and political reform.

Crowded Cities Today, most Japanese live in cities, which are hugely overcrowded. Housing is expensive, and space is scarce. Most people live in tiny, cramped apartments. Despite the crowded conditions, however, urban crime and violence are relatively rare. Many space-hungry Japanese move to the suburbs but then face long commutes between home and work.

Because Japan lies in a region often rocked by earthquakes, it built modern structures using "quake-proof" technology. Japanese highways and other structures were supposed to be designed to withstand strong quakes. In 1995, however, a severe earthquake badly damaged the city of Kobe (KOH BEE). The disaster raised questions about just how completely technology can protect against natural forces.

Women Japanese women have legal equality and often control the family finances. But traditional attitudes toward women continue to keep them in subordinate, or lower, positions in the workplace. About half the nation's adult women work outside the home, but most are in low-paying jobs or in family-run businesses. Fewer women than men get a university education, and only a handful have moved into higher-level jobs in business or government.

Work Ethic For decades, the Japanese sacrificed family life to work long hours. They also saved large portions of their earnings. Many younger Japanese, however, want more time to enjoy the benefits of economic success. Some older Japanese worry that the old work ethic is weakening. Also, as the tradition of lifetime employment fades, workers feel less loyalty to individual companies.

Crowded Cities
Japanese cities are so crowded that people must adapt their needs for parking and recreation. Here, people play tennis on a rooftop court.

Theme: Geography and History How have crowded Japanese cities adapted to limited space?

SECTION 1 Assessment

Recall
1. **Identify: (a)** Douglas MacArthur, **(b)** Diet, **(c)** Liberal Democratic Party.
2. **Define: (a)** zaibatsu, **(b)** gross domestic product, **(c)** trade deficit.

Comprehension
3. **(a)** How did Japan achieve political recovery? **(b)** What were three reasons for Japan's economic recovery?
4. What role has Japan played in world affairs in recent years?
5. What challenges face Japanese society today?

Critical Thinking and Writing
6. **Recognizing Points of View** Some nations complained that Japanese policies made it difficult for trading partners to sell goods to Japan, resulting in trade deficits. To the Japanese, however, these policies led to Japan's trade *surplus.* How might these differing perspectives affect trade talks?
7. **Synthesizing Information** How do you think occupation policies regarding Japan's armed forces and the zaibatsu affected the nation's economic success?

Activity

Writing a Letter
Suppose that you are a Japanese teenager. Write a letter to the prime minister supporting or opposing the rearming of Japan. Prepare a bibliography of the sources you used to gather your information about this issue.

From Revolution to Reform in China

Reading Focus

- What were the effects of communist policies in China?
- What challenges did China face during the Cold War?
- How did calls for political reform lead to repression?
- What challenges face China today?

Vocabulary

collectivization

commune

joint venture

special enterprise zone

Taking Notes

Copy this table. As you read, list developments in the People's Republic of China under Mao Zedong and Deng Xiaoping.

MAO ZEDONG	DENG XIAOPING
• Great Leap Forward	• Joint ventures
•	•

Main Idea ▶ **After a series of failed reforms in China, communist leaders introduced elements of capitalism.**

Setting the Scene On October 1, 1999, China celebrated an important anniversary. Exactly 50 years earlier, in 1949, communist leader Mao Zedong had announced the birth of the People's Republic of China. He pledged "to build a new China, independent, . . . prosperous and strong." Under Mao, China experienced a revolution that ranks with Russia's as one of the major social transformations of the 1900s.

Communist Control of China

After World War II, civil war resumed between Mao Zedong's communist forces and Jiang Jieshi's nationalists. Battles raged until Mao's forces swept to victory and set up the People's Republic of China (PRC). Jiang Jieshi and his supporters fled to the island of Taiwan. After decades of struggle, China was finally united—with the communists in control.

Reasons for Victory The communists triumphed for a number of reasons. Mao won the support of China's huge peasant population. Peasants had long suffered from brutal landlords and crushing taxes. The communists pledged to redistribute land to poor peasants and end oppression by landlords.

Additionally, many women backed Mao's forces. The nationalists had made little effort to improve their harsh lives. Women were still seen as inferior to men and often were cruelly mistreated. The communists rejected the inequalities of the old Confucian order. To point out this break with tradition, Mao said: "Women hold up half the sky."

Mao's armies outfought Jiang's, and while support for the communists grew, the nationalists lost popularity. Many educated Chinese saw Jiang's government as morally and politically bankrupt. They hoped that the communists would build a new China and end foreign domination.

Reorganizing the Economy Once in power, the communists set out to turn China from a backward peasant society into a modern industrial nation. To build socialism and repair the economy, China nationalized all businesses. The government also drew up five-year plans to develop agriculture and heavy industry. With Soviet help, the Chinese built hydroelectric plants, railroads, and canals.

To boost agriculture, Mao distributed land to peasants. Then he called for collectivization, the pooling of peasant land and labor in an attempt to increase efficiency.

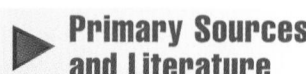

Primary Sources and Literature

See "Mao Zedong: The People's Democratic Dictatorship" in the Reference Section at the back of this book.

Remolding Society Like Lenin in the Soviet Union, Mao Zedong built a one-party totalitarian state, with the Communist party supreme. Communist ideology replaced Confucian beliefs and traditional religions. The government attacked crime and corruption. It did away with the old landlord and business classes. In their place, peasants and workers were honored as the builders of the new China. Many thousands of landlords and middle-class people were beaten and killed. One official justified the attacks, saying:

> "The freedom we uphold is not the same as that based on the type of democracy advocated by the bourgeoisie. . . . We, on the contrary, hold that there must be democratic liberties among the people, but that no freedom should be extended to counterrevolutionaries: for them we have only dictatorship."
> —Lu Ting-yi, speech delivered May 26, 1956

To increase literacy, the government simplified Chinese characters, making it easier to learn to read and write. Schools were opened for young and old. Reading and writing were mixed with political education. Students learned to praise the "Great Helmsman," Mao Zedong, who could do no wrong.

The Communists also sent health-care workers to remote rural areas. Although many of these "barefoot doctors" had limited training, they did help to reduce disease and teach better hygiene.

Changes for Women Under China's new constitution, women won equality under the law. They were expected to work alongside men in fields and factories. State-run nurseries were set up to care for the children. These changes weakened the old ideal of the extended family dominated by the oldest male. In China's cities, as elsewhere in the developing world, the nuclear family became increasingly common.

Although Chinese women made real progress, they did not enjoy full equality. Only a few won promotion to top jobs in government and industry. Women were often paid less than men for the same work. Also, after working at paid jobs, they still were responsible for cleaning, cooking, and child care.

Economic Disasters

Although some reforms did result in more access to education and greater equality, people in China paid a heavy cost for Mao's programs. During the 1950s and 1960s, two efforts in particular led to economic disaster and tremendous loss of life.

The Great Leap Forward In 1958, Mao launched a program known as the "Great Leap Forward." He urged people to make a superhuman effort to increase farm and industrial output. In an attempt to make agriculture more efficient, he created communes. A typical commune included several villages, thousands of acres of land, and up to 25,000 people. It had its own schools, factories, housing, and dining halls. Each commune had production quotas. Communes also mobilized labor brigades to build dams and irrigation systems. Rural communes set up "backyard" industries to produce steel and other products.

The Great Leap Forward was a dismal failure. Backyard industries turned out low-quality, useless goods. The commune system slowed food output. Bad weather and declining food production added to the problems and led to a terrible famine. Between 1959 and 1961, up to 30 million Chinese are thought to have starved to death. In response, China turned to more moderate policies.

The Cultural Revolution China slowly recovered from the Great Leap Forward. Then, in 1966, Mao launched the Great Proletarian Cultural Revolution. Its goal was to purge China of "bourgeois," or nonrevolutionary, tendencies. He urged young Chinese to experience revolution firsthand, as his generation had.

Biography

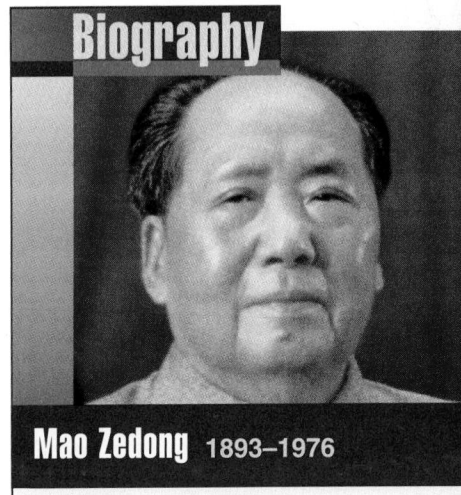

Mao Zedong 1893–1976

During the mid-1950s, divisions arose within the Communist party in China. In response, Mao launched a campaign under the slogan "Let a hundred flowers bloom, let a hundred thoughts contend." Mao hoped that by offering people the opportunity to openly express their views he would gain more support. When people began to criticize the Communist party, however, Mao ended the campaign. Of the nearly 550,000 Chinese who had spoken out, thousands were executed and hundreds of thousands were exiled to the countryside to "rectify their thinking through labor."

Theme: Impact of the Individual What methods did Mao use to keep power for himself?

In response, teenagers formed bands of Red Guards. Waving copies of the "Little Red Book" of Mao's sayings, Red Guards attacked those they claimed were counterrevolutionaries. They targeted people in authority, from party leaders and factory managers to teachers, writers, and artists. The accused were publicly humiliated or beaten, and sometimes even killed.

The Cultural Revolution convulsed China. Schools and factories closed. The economy slowed, and civil war threatened. Finally, Mao had the army restore order. Many Red Guards were sent to work on communes. They became a lost generation, undereducated and cut off from normal family life and careers. In the end, many became disillusioned with communism.

Red Guards
During the Cultural Revolution, groups of teenagers known as Red Guards responded to Mao's call for renewed revolution. Here, young Red Guards read from Mao's "Little Red Book."

Theme: Impact of the Individual How does this photograph show Mao's importance in communist China?

China and the Cold War

The Communist victory over the Nationalists dominated the Cold War in 1949. After Jiang Jieshi fled to Taiwan, the United States continued to support the Nationalist government. The United States refused to recognize the People's Republic of China, which it saw as an aggressive communist power and a threat to all of Asia.

Relations With the United States For years, the United States tried to isolate China. In 1971, however, China won admission to the United Nations. A year later, United States President Richard Nixon visited Mao in Beijing. Slowly, relations improved. Finally, in 1979, the United States set up formal diplomatic relations with China.

Split With the Soviet Union China and the Soviet Union were uneasy allies in the 1950s. Stalin sent economic aid and technical experts to help China modernize, but he and Mao disagreed on many issues.

Mao had adapted Marxism to Chinese conditions. Marx had predicted that the industrial working class—the proletariat—would lead the revolution. Because China had little industry, however, Mao's revolution relied on peasants rather than factory workers. Stalin rejected Mao's views. Mao, in turn, thought that the Soviets were too conservative and accused them of being too willing to "coexist" with the capitalist powers.

China and the Soviet Union also competed for influence in developing nations. In addition, border disputes triggered tensions between the two. By 1960, border clashes and disputes over ideology led the Soviets to withdraw all aid and advisers from China.

Reform and Repression

Mao Zedong died in 1976. Despite disastrous mistakes, many still saw him as the revolutionary hero who had restored order, ended foreign domination, and made China a world power once again.

After Mao, more moderate leaders controlled China. By 1981, Deng Xiaoping (duhng show PIHNG) had set China on a new path. Deng was a practical reformer, more interested in raising output than in political purity. "I don't care if a cat is black or white," he declared, "as long as it catches mice."

Economic Reforms Deng backed a program called the Four Modernizations, which emphasized agriculture, industry, science, and defense. As part of this plan, Deng introduced economic reforms, including some private ownership of property and free-market policies. In agriculture, the responsibility system replaced the communes. Peasant families were allotted plots of farmland. The government took a share of their crops, but the family could sell the rest on the free market.

Entrepreneurs were allowed to set up their own businesses. Managers of state-run factories were given more freedom but were expected to make their plants more efficient. Deng welcomed foreign capital and technology. Investors from Japan, Hong Kong, Taiwan, and the West organized joint ventures with China, in which foreign companies would organize a business with Chinese firms, with profits shared by both participants. The government also set up special enterprise zones, where foreigners could own and operate industries.

Deng's reforms brought a surge of growth and a better standard of living for some Chinese. They were soon buying motor scooters, televisions, and refrigerators. On the downside, crime and corruption grew. Inequalities increased as a new wealthy class emerged. An economic gap also grew between poor rural farmers in the interior and city dwellers on the coast who were exposed to western influences.

Tiananmen Square Massacre By the late 1980s, some Chinese were demanding greater political freedom as well as economic reform. In Beijing and other cities, students, workers, and others supported a democracy movement like those sweeping Eastern Europe. Deng, however, would not talk about political reform.

In May 1989, tens of thousands of demonstrators occupied Tiananmen Square. They raised banners calling for democracy and brought in a huge plaster statue called the Goddess of Democracy and Freedom. When the demonstrators refused to disperse, the government sent in troops and tanks. Thousands of demonstrators were killed or wounded. Many others were arrested and tortured. Some were put to death.

The crackdown showed that China's communist leaders were determined to maintain control. To them, order was more important than political freedom. During the 1990s, efforts to persuade China to end human rights violations had limited effects.

Challenges Today

By the mid-1990s, China had become a major industrial power. Its economy ranked among the fastest growing in the world, and it was building major trade ties with countries worldwide. Yet even as economic gains continued, the nation faced many unresolved issues.

Population Population growth posed a challenge for the future. Since 1949, China's population has more than doubled, to more than 1.2 billion. Such rapid growth strained the economy. In the 1980s, the government instituted

► **Primary Sources and Literature**

See "Harry Wu: The Outlook for China, Human Rights" in the Reference Section at the back of this book.

Population Density
Bicycles, trucks, and buses compete for space at a dangerous Beijing intersection.

Theme: Economics and Technology Why would the bicycle be a common form of transportation in Chinese cities?

You Are There . . .

Helping Protesters in Tiananmen Square

You are bringing food and supplies to the students in Tiananmen Square. They are protesting government corruption and the lack of democratic reform. As each day passes, the crowd of protesters grows—and tensions mount.

The government has declared military rule, and soldiers are moving into Beijing. In response, crowds of protesters build barricades. A wave of excitement ripples through the square as art students from Beijing University arrive. They have brought a statue that they call the "Goddess of Democracy and Freedom."

Finally, soldiers break through the barricades and march into the city. For 20 minutes, a lone man blocks a column of tanks. Eventually, however, the soldiers occupy Tiananmen Square and force the students out.

Portfolio Assessment

After you return home, you record all you have seen in your diary. In your entry, describe what you saw and how you felt about the demonstration.

a one-child-per-family policy. Parents who had only one child were given rewards, such as better housing or improved medical benefits. Those who had more children faced fines and other penalties.

The campaign to slow the birthrate worked better in cities than in rural areas. Farm families, who wanted children to work the land, often paid fines rather than obey the policy. The one-child policy had a tragic effect in a country that still valued boys over girls. Female infanticide, or the killing of girl babies, increased despite efforts to prevent it.

Economic and Political Issues Deng Xiaoping died in 1997. Jiang Zemin and later Hu Jintao continued Deng's economic reforms. Between 1978 and 2000, China's GDP quadrupled. Before long, it had the world's second largest economy after the United States.

Despite a booming economy, China faced problems. Many state-run industries were inefficient, but they could not be closed without risking high unemployment. Cities overflowed with millions of peasants eager to find new opportunities. Inequalities between rich and poor and between urban and rural Chinese grew. In addition, communist ideology weakened. From party officials on down, people were more interested in profit than in socialism. Corruption spread. The government tried to crack down on corruption and other criminal activity but had limited success.

Human Rights Issues The Communist party kept tight political control even as it eased economic controls. The government continued to jail critics. Human rights activists pointed to many abuses such as the lack of free speech and China's use of prison labor to produce cheap goods for export. They charged China with deliberately suppressing Tibetan Buddhist culture. China also cracked down on a religious sect called Falun Gong. The government saw Falun Gong, which claimed millions of members, as a political threat.

Chinese dissidents, human rights activists, and spokespeople for Tibet's exiled religious leader the Dalai Lama, found strong support in the West. China's trading partners, including the United States, also pressured it to end abuses.

Chinese leaders answered critics by declaring that outsiders had no right to interfere with China's internal affairs. Further, communist officials claimed that the West had no right to impose what they deemed "western-style" human rights on other cultures.

Geography and History

The Threat of Disease
SARS—severe acute respiratory syndrome—was the first serious new disease of the twenty-first century. Highly contagious, it is caused by a virus. SARS was first identified in March 2003 by Dr. Carlo Urbani of Italy, an infectious-disease specialist with the World Health Organization (WHO). He was called in after hospital staff in Vietnam became sick after treating a Chinese American businessman who died. The disease was traced back to a case that occurred in southern China in November 2002. Dr. Urbani, who was 46 years old, contracted the disease himself and died. SARS spread around the world in less than a year, sickening thousands and killing hundreds. The epidemic alerted countries to the need to work together to control the spread of new infectious diseases.

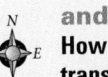

Theme: Economics and Technology
How do modern means of transportation affect the spread of disease?

SECTION 2 Assessment

Recall
1. **Identify:** (a) People's Republic of China, (b) five-year plan, (c) Great Leap Forward, (d) Cultural Revolution, (e) "Little Red Book," (f) Four Modernizations, (g) Tiananmen Square.
2. **Define:** (a) collectivization, (b) commune, (c) joint venture, (d) special enterprise zone.

Comprehension
3. How did Mao's economic policies harm China?
4. What major issues did China face during the Cold War?

5. (a) What economic reforms did Deng Xiaoping introduce? (b) What challenges does China face today?

Critical Thinking and Writing
6. **Predicting Consequences** Do you think economic reforms can be successful without political reforms? Explain.
7. **Comparing** Compare Deng's reforms in China to those of Gorbachev in the Soviet Union. (a) How were the reforms similar? (b) How were they different?

Go Online
PHSchool.com

Use the Internet to research the Tiananmen Square massacre. Create a database of the student protesters' criticisms of the government and the major actions the students took. Then, write a paragraph explaining the role of students in the 1989 demonstrations in Beijing. For help with this activity, use **Web Code mkd-3467.**

Reading Focus

- How has China influenced Taiwan and Hong Kong?

- How did Singapore modernize?

- Why has Korea remained divided for more than 50 years?

Taking Notes

Create an outline of this section. Use Roman numerals for major headings, capital letters for subheadings, and numbers for the supporting details. Use this sample as a starting point.

I. **Taiwan and Hong Kong**
  A. **Taiwan**
    1. Ruled by China until 1895
    2.
  B. **Hong Kong**
    1.

Main Idea   Aggressive economic growth led to world prominence for several nations in East and Southeast Asia.

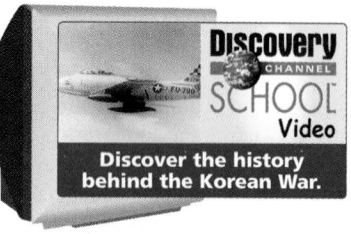

DISCOVERY SCHOOL Video

Discover the history behind the Korean War.

Connections to Today

Taiwan: Rebel Province or Independent State?

Since 1949, the People's Republic of China has considered Taiwan a "rebel province" that must be reunited with the parent country. In 1995, the Chinese drove home that point by conducting missile tests and live-fire exercises in the island's waters.

In 1999, Taiwanese President Lee Teng-hui insisted that China deal with Taiwan as a separate state. The Chinese responded angrily, renewing their threats of force against Taiwan. In Beijing, the *People's Daily* compared Taiwan's efforts to influence China to "an ant trying to topple a tree."

Theme: Political and Social Systems How do you think reunion with mainland China would affect the lives of the Taiwanese?

Setting the Scene   At a university in Taiwan, Professor Xu Wenxing proudly unveiled an invention he had worked on for 10 years. His invention was a computerized fingerprint-recognition device, which was soon put to use. To Xu, however, the most satisfying aspect of his success was that "the technology involved was developed in Taiwan."

Taiwan was one of four small Asian lands that vaulted into the class of "newly industrialized countries" by the 1980s. Besides Taiwan, Hong Kong, Singapore, and South Korea are also known for their aggressive economic growth. The four are often called the "Asian tigers." Although they differ in important ways, all followed similar roads to modernization after 1945. Additionally, all four nations were influenced to some degree by China and by Confucian traditions.

Taiwan and Hong Kong

Both Taiwan and Hong Kong have deep cultural and historical links to China. Both were once part of China. Neither, however, experienced Mao's communist revolution. The island of Taiwan was once ruled by the mainland. Today, the People's Republic still considers it part of China. Hong Kong was returned to China in 1997 after more than a century under British colonial rule.

Taiwan   The island of Taiwan was ruled by China until 1895, when it fell to Japan. The Japanese built some industry, providing a foundation for later growth. In 1945, with Japan defeated, Taiwan reverted to China. But when Jiang Jieshi fled the mainland in 1949, he set up his Nationalist government on Taiwan. Despite Jiang's autocratic rule, Taiwan experienced rapid economic growth and enjoyed United States's support.

First, Taiwan set up light industries such as textiles. Later, it developed heavy industry. The Green Revolution of the 1960s, with its new seeds and fertilizers, helped Taiwan's agriculture become more productive. Trade boomed, industrial cities grew, and in time Taiwan's standard of living rose to one of the highest in Asia.

With economic success, the government slowly allowed people more political freedom. Hostility between Taiwan and the mainland eased somewhat after the Cold War ended. China still saw Taiwan as a breakaway province. In the long term, it insisted that Taiwan must be rejoined with China. Taiwan's government firmly resisted such pressure.

Despite sometimes bitter political disputes, economic ties between Taiwan and China grew. Taiwanese businesses invested in joint ventures on the mainland. Trade also increased. Recently, China pushed to expand trade with Taiwan. It hoped that strong economic links would help resolve their political differences. Even so, occasional Chinese military exercises in the area were a stark reminder of the enduring threat to Taiwan.

Hong Kong Britain gained the tiny island of Hong Kong after the Opium War. Under British rule, Hong Kong and nearby territories grew into a center of trade. In 1949, millions of refugees from the Chinese Revolution flooded into Hong Kong, providing labor and capital to help the area.

Hong Kong's new prosperity was based largely on trade and light industry, such as textiles and electronics. It also became a world financial center with many foreign banks and a busy stock market. Wealth from these profitable industries helped Hong Kong modernize.

Hong Kong's amazing growth was also due in part to its location on China's doorstep. Hong Kong Chinese built commercial ties to the mainland at a time when the People's Republic was largely isolated from the world community. This gave Hong Kong the chance to buy and sell goods with a market that was unavailable to many other countries.

In 1997, Britain returned Hong Kong to China. Beijing agreed not to change Hong Kong's social or economic system for 50 years and to allow its people self-government. Still, many residents remained nervous about China's power and use of repressive measures against protests.

Singapore

The smallest Asian tiger is the city-state of Singapore. It sits on a tiny island at the tip of the Malay Peninsula in Southeast Asia. Its 200 square miles have a population of about two million.

In 1819, British empire builder Sir Stamford Raffles leased the island from a local ruler. Raffles recognized its ideal location on the Strait of Malacca, halfway between China and India. He and his successors turned the island's fishing villages into a seaport.

Under British rule, Singapore grew rapidly. The population came to include Malayans, British merchants and sailors, and Chinese and Indian immigrants. All hoped to prosper in the booming city. The British brought in Chinese workers to work in factories that processed tin and rubber from Malaya. In time, the Chinese, with their Confucian tradition, became the dominant ethnic group.

Order and Prosperity Singapore won independence first from Britain in 1959 and then from nearby Malaya in 1963. For 30 years, Lee Kwan Yew was Singapore's autocratic prime minister. Lee supported a free-market economy. By keeping labor costs low, Lee attracted foreign capital that helped the economy boom. He expanded Singapore's seaport into one of the world's busiest harbors.

The government welcomed skilled immigrants and insisted on education for all its people—in both English and Chinese. It encouraged high-tech industries, manufacturing, finance, and tourism. As Singapore's economy grew, its standard of living rose. The government set up a successful public housing program. Most married couples became homeowners with the help of government loans.

Ongoing Issues Lee's successors continued his strict policies, allowing little opposition. Critics condemned limits on freedom. In response, the government claimed that order was more important than individual freedoms. Still, it faced demands for more rights from many of its young, well-educated citizens.

Did You Know?

Life in Singapore
Unlike most large Asian cities, Singapore is clean, quiet, and orderly. With low pollution, lush tropical greenery, no traffic jams, and low crime, the city is often described by its citizens as "paradise."

But Singaporeans pay a price for stability. To achieve public order, the government levies—and vigorously enforces—hefty penalties on all sorts of behavior. For example, littering brings a $625 fine, eating on the subway merits a $312 penalty, and failing to flush a public toilet costs the offender $94. The sale of chewing gum is outlawed, as is smoking in public.

Many Singaporeans feel that their nation's prosperity and stability justify these limits on personal freedom. They probably would agree with former Prime Minister Lee Kwan Yew when he said: "When you are hungry, when you lack basic services, freedom, human rights and democracy do not add up to much."

Theme: Political and Social Systems How does Singapore emphasize public order?

Korean War, 1950–1953

CHINA

Chongjin

USSR

Conic Projection

0   50   100 Miles

0   50   100 Kilometers

Chosan

40°N

Pyongyang

NORTH
KOREA

Kosong

38th Parallel

Panmunjom

Yangyang

Seoul

Inchon

Samchok

Yellow
Sea

Pyongtaek

SOUTH
KOREA

Sea of
Japan
(East Sea)

N
W   E
S

Taegu
Masan

35°N

Pusan

JAPAN

125°E

130°E

Yalu R.

	Line of farthest North Korean advance, September 1950		Line of farthest Chinese and North Korean advance, January 1951
	UN invasion, September 1950		Armistice line, 1953
	Line of farthest UN advance, November 1950		

Skills Assessment

Geography After North Korean troops stormed across the 38th parallel, the UN sent an army to aid South Korea. Fighting continued for three years, until a cease-fire was signed in 1953.

1. **Location** On the map, locate *(a)* North Korea, *(b)* South Korea, *(c)* 38th parallel, *(d)* Yalu River, *(e)* Inchon.
2. **Movement** How far did UN forces advance into North Korea?
3. **Critical Thinking Making Inferences** Based on the map, why do you think the UN advance beyond the 38th parallel worried the Chinese?

Because Singapore depended heavily on trade, its economy was influenced by events elsewhere. Yet it weathered the Asian financial crisis. Over the years, it also faced ethnic tensions between the Chinese majority and Malay and Indian minorities.

Despite such issues, Singapore was often seen as a model of successful development. With few natural resources, it built a booming economy. How did it succeed? Lee Kwan Yew preached "Confucian values," such as hard work, loyalty toward family, and respectful obedience to authority. Lee and others also spoke of a "Confucian model of development." Singapore and the other Asian tigers, they noted, all had stable governments that invested in education. In each, the Confucian ethic shaped attitudes about work. People worked long hours for low wages. They also saved these wages, which enabled banks to invest in further development.

The Two Koreas

The fourth Asian tiger, South Korea, emerged during the Cold War. It occupies the southern half of the Korean peninsula. In 1910, Japan annexed the Korean peninsula, imposing harsh rule on it. After World War II, the Soviet Union and the United States agreed to a temporary division of Korea along the 38th parallel of latitude. Before long, North Korea, ruled by Kim Il Sung, became a communist ally of the Soviet Union. In South Korea, the United States backed the authoritarian—but noncommunist—leader, Syngman Rhee.

The Korean War Both leaders wanted to end the division. In early 1950, Kim Il Sung called for a "heroic struggle" to reunite Korea. North Korean troops attacked and soon overran most of the south. The United States then organized a UN force to help South Korea.

UN forces were made up mostly of Americans and South Koreans. They were led by United States general Douglas MacArthur, who had commanded troops in World War I and World War II and headed the occupation of Japan. He landed troops behind enemy lines, drove the invaders back across the 38th parallel, and then pushed northward to the Yalu River, along the border of China. MacArthur's success alarmed China. Mao Zedong sent Chinese troops to help the North Koreans, who again advanced southward.

The Korean War turned into a stalemate. Finally, in 1953, both sides signed an armistice, or end to fighting. The armistice has held for nearly 50 years, but no peace treaty has ever been negotiated. More than a million North Korean and South Korean troops dug in on either side of the demilitarized zone (DMZ), an area with no military forces, near the 38th parallel. At the end of the 1990s, American forces were still in South Korea to help guarantee the peace.

After the war, the two Koreas slowly rebuilt economies destroyed by the fighting and by years of Japanese occupation. Both remained centers of Cold War tensions. The United States funneled aid to South Korea, while the Soviets helped the north.

Analyzing Primary Sources

War Refugees in Korea

The power struggle over North and South Korea played a large part in the Cold War tensions of the late 1940s and 1950s. Those not involved in the politics were drawn in when the Cold War escalated into a hot war between Communist and UN-backed forces in 1950. Civilians, such as K. Connie Kang and her mother, were caught up in the fighting.

"On a cold January night in 1951, when North Korean troops were about to invade Seoul, I rode on the rooftop of the last train bound for Pusan with my mother to escape the oncoming Communists. Bone-chilling wind from Siberia whipped across the 'freedom train,' which was jam-packed with soldiers, the sick, and the injured. There was no room for able-bodied civilians—not even children.

'I don't want to go up there, Mommy,' I protested. 'It's too scary.'

'We will be all right,' Mother assured me, even though I could tell she was scared herself. 'See those fellows on the train? They will secure us.' she said, pointing to the men on top of the train with . . . straw rope in their hands. 'If we don't take this train, we will surely die in the hands of Communists. This is the last train to Pusan.'

Mother climbed very slowly up a small staircase at the back of the coach. When I got up on the top of the train, I was surprised to see how roomy it was. . . . My mother sat beside me and held me by the cord tied around my middle with one hand to make sure I didn't fall off the train. The 'freedom train' traveled all through the night. Not everyone was as fortunate as I on that fateful night. That night several youngsters fell accidentally to their death. Life was cheap. I could have been one of them, had my mother not secured me and grasped the rope tied to my waist through the long trip, her hand nearly frozen under her mittens from the exposure to the biting wind. Whenever my mother caught me dozing off, she pinched me. 'Don't fall asleep. . . . You'll fall off the train if you do,' she said, all the while not once letting go of the rope around my waist."

—K. Connie Kang, *Home Was the Land of Morning Calm*

Fleeing South
Thousands of Korean refugees struggle to board a train heading south out of Seoul to escape the advancing North Korean army.

Skills Tip

When you analyze primary source material, be sure to think about the person or persons being quoted, how knowledgeable they might be about the subject, and what their biases might be.

Skills Assessment

1. Why was Kang forced to ride on top of the train with her mother?
   A They had no money.
   B Only soldiers, the sick, and the injured could ride inside.
   C Passengers heading for Pusan had to ride on top.
   D They had lost their tickets.

2. According to this excerpt, many South Koreans risked the train ride from Seoul because
   E it would soon be winter in Seoul.
   F their homes had been destroyed by bombs.
   G they feared that invading Communists would kill them.
   H there was no food left in Seoul.

3. **Critical Thinking** **Drawing Conclusions** List two conclusions you can draw from the information in the passage.

South Korea By the mid-1960s, South Korea's economy had leaped ahead. At first, it exported inexpensive textiles and manufactured goods. Later, it shifted to higher-priced exports such as automobiles and electronics. As in the other Asian tigers, its growth was partly due to low wages, long hours, and other worker sacrifices.

By the 1990s, South Korea was an economic powerhouse. With prosperity, workers won better pay, and the country's standard of living rose greatly. The 1997 Asian financial crisis brought hardships such as business failure and high unemployment. The government undertook difficult economic reforms, and by 2000, the nation's economy was recovering.

For decades after the Korean War, dictators backed by the military ruled in South Korea. By 1987, however, growing prosperity and fierce student protests pushed the government to hold direct elections. Since then, the nation has moved successfully toward democracy.

North Korea Under Kim Il Sung, state-owned industries and collective farms increased output in North Korea. That growth slowed, however, in the late 1960s. Kim's emphasis on self-reliance kept North Korea isolated. Even when its Soviet and Chinese allies undertook economic reforms, North Korea clung to hardline communism.

Propaganda constantly glorified Kim as the "Great Leader." After he died, his son Kim Jong Il, the "Dear Leader," took over. He faced huge problems. Failed government policies and terrible floods destroyed harvests, bringing widespread hunger. During the late 1990s, North Korea had to accept food aid from the United States, South Korea, and other nations to prevent mass starvation. Kim held onto power despite the misery and famine.

Demilitarized Zone
The border between South and North Korea lies in the demilitarized zone, an area in which military forces are prohibited. Here, South Korean soldiers patrol the border along the zone.

Theme: Political and Social Systems Why have tensions remained high between the two nations?

The Nuclear Issue Like several emerging nations, North Korea tried to develop nuclear power for electricity and for nuclear weapons. Under intense pressure from the United States, it agreed to end its nuclear weapons program in exchange for oil and other aid. But North Korea later resumed its nuclear weapons programs, triggering new tensions.

Outlook for Unity Despite differences between the two Koreas, most Koreans want to see their country reunited. After all, they share the same history, language, and culture. Restoring unity is of global interest because of Korea's strategic location in Asia.

SECTION 3 Assessment

Recall
1. **Identify:** **(a)** Asian tigers, **(b)** Lee Kwan Yew, **(c)** Syngman Rhee, **(d)** Kim Jong Il.

Comprehension
2. Describe how China's strength has affected the development of Taiwan and Hong Kong.
3. How did Singapore's leaders encourage economic growth?
4. **(a)** How do the economies of South Korea and North Korea differ? **(b)** How has the North Korean government's policy on isolation affected the nation?

Critical Thinking and Writing
5. **Drawing Conclusions** What characteristic seems to have been most important to the economic success of the "Asian tigers"? Explain.
6. **Linking Past and Present** What conditions existing today in Taiwan, Hong Kong, Singapore, and Korea reflect lingering Cold War tensions?

Activity

Writing a Position Paper In 1950, Kim Il Sung described North Korea's advances on the 38th parallel as the means to "achieve glorious, complete independence." Imagine that you are an official in the South Korean government. Write a position paper reacting to Kim's statement and identifying possible responses.

Southeast Asia and the Pacific Rim

Reading Focus

- How did war affect Vietnam and Cambodia?
- What challenges faced the Philippines and the developing nations of Southeast Asia?
- Why is the Pacific Rim a vital region?

Vocabulary

domino theory
cease-fire
embargo

Taking Notes

Create a time line that includes major events discussed in this section. The sample below will help you get started.

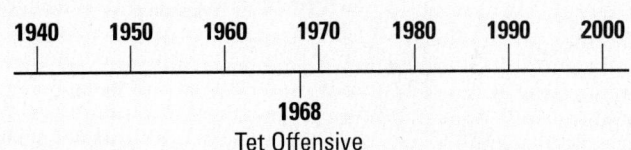

| 1940 | 1950 | 1960 | 1970 | 1980 | 1990 | 2000 |

1968
Tet Offensive

Main Idea Southeast Asian nations sought independence but also fell into divisive conflicts in the decades after World War II.

Setting the Scene Today, Southeast Asia is a key player in the global economy. For decades after the end of World War II, though, the region was shaped by the nationalist drive for independence. Some nations won freedom with little violence. Others faced long wars of liberation against European nations that wanted to reclaim their colonial empires after the war.

War in Vietnam and Cambodia

In mainland Southeast Asia, an agonizing liberation struggle tore apart the region once known as French Indochina. It affected the emerging nations of Vietnam, Cambodia, and Laos. The nearly 30-year conflict had two major phases. First was the battle against the French, dating from 1946 to 1954. Second were the civil war and Cold War conflicts that raged from 1959 to 1975.

In 1946, the French set out to regain Indochina, which Japan had seized during World War II. They faced fierce resistance from guerrilla forces led by Ho Chi Minh. Ho was a nationalist and communist who had fought the Japanese. He and his forces wore down the French and eventually forced them to leave Vietnam.

Vietnam Divided The struggle for Vietnam became part of the Cold War. At an international conference in 1954, western and communist powers agreed to a temporary division of Vietnam. Ho's communists ruled North Vietnam. Ngo Dinh Diem's noncommunist government, supported by the United States, ruled South Vietnam. Cambodia and Laos gained independence.

The agreement called for elections to reunite Vietnam. The elections were never held, however, largely because the Americans and Diem feared that the communists might win. American officials believed in the domino theory. It held that a communist victory in South Vietnam would cause noncommunist governments across Southeast Asia to fall to communism, like a row of dominoes.

American Involvement As the war continued, the United States became increasingly involved. Ho Chi Minh wanted to unite Vietnam under northern rule. He aided the National Liberation Front, communist rebels trying to overthrow Diem in South Vietnam. At first, the United States sent only military advisers and supplies to Diem. Later, it sent troops, turning a local struggle into a major Cold War conflict.

In 1964, the United States began bombing targets in North Vietnam. Eventually, more than 500,000 American troops were committed. At the

Primary Source

Vietnamese Declaration of Independence

Vietnamese nationalists led by Ho Chi Minh proclaimed the Democratic Republic of Vietnam on September 2, 1945. Following is an excerpt from their Declaration of Independence:

"The Declaration of the French Revolution . . . states: 'All men are born free with equal rights, and must always remain free and have equal rights.' . . .

Nevertheless, for more than eighty years, the French imperialists . . . have violated our Fatherland and oppressed our fellow-citizens. They have acted contrary to the ideals of humanity and justice. . . .

For these reasons, we . . . solemnly declare to the world that Vietnam has the right to be a free and independent country. . . . The entire Vietnamese people are determined to . . . sacrifice their lives and property in order to safeguard their independence and liberty."

—Vietnamese Declaration of Independence

Skills Assessment

Primary Source What document does this declaration cite? Why do you think the Vietnamese chose that document?

Vietnam War, 1968–1975

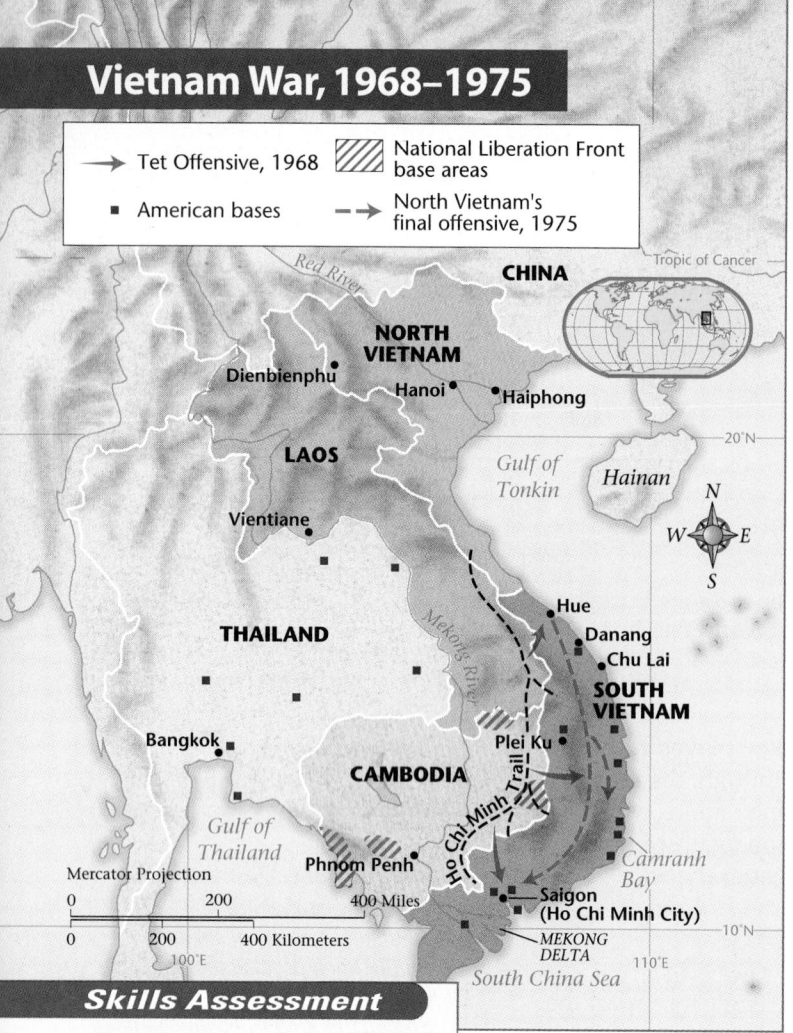

Legend:
- → Tet Offensive, 1968
- ▨ National Liberation Front base areas
- ■ American bases
- ⇢ North Vietnam's final offensive, 1975

(Map showing China, North Vietnam, Laos, Thailand, Cambodia, South Vietnam with cities including Dienbienphu, Hanoi, Haiphong, Vientiane, Hue, Danang, Chu Lai, Plei Ku, Bangkok, Phnom Penh, Saigon (Ho Chi Minh City); features: Red River, Gulf of Tonkin, Hainan, Mekong River, Ho Chi Minh Trail, Gulf of Thailand, Câmranh Bay, Mekong Delta, South China Sea; Mercator Projection; Tropic of Cancer; 20°N, 10°N, 100°E, 110°E; scale 0–400 Miles / 0–400 Kilometers)

Skills Assessment

Geography In the Vietnam War, the United States supported South Vietnam in its struggle against communist North Vietnam. Despite this help, the war ended with a North Vietnamese victory.

1. **Location** On the map, locate **(a)** North Vietnam, **(b)** South Vietnam, **(c)** Cambodia, **(d)** Laos, **(e)** Saigon, **(f)** Ho Chi Minh Trail.
2. **Movement** How did North Vietnam's use of the Ho Chi Minh Trail as a supply route help to spread the war beyond Vietnam?
3. **Critical Thinking** **Applying Information** Use the map to describe the "domino theory."

same time, both the Soviet Union and China sent aid—but no troops—to help North Vietnam.

Despite massive American aid, South Vietnam could not defeat the communist guerrillas and their North Vietnamese allies. In 1968, guerrilla forces launched a massive attack on American and South Vietnamese forces. The assault was unexpected because it took place at Tet, the Vietnamese New Year. Although the communists did not capture any cities, the Tet Offensive marked a turning point in public opinion in the United States. It also showed that the North Vietnamese would fight at any cost.

As the fighting continued, the bombing of North Vietnam and growing American casualties on the ground inflamed antiwar opinion in the United States. Under increasing pressure, President Nixon finally arranged a cease-fire, or halt in the fighting. He began withdrawing American forces in 1973. Two years later, the North Vietnamese captured Saigon, capital of the south, and reunited the country.

The Communist Victory Why did the communists win? In some ways, the Vietnam War mirrored the civil war in China that brought Mao to power in 1949. Diem and his successors in South Vietnam were unpopular leaders of a corrupt government. Ho Chi Minh was admired as a hero who had fought the Japanese and the French. Many Vietnamese saw the United States as another foreign power seeking to dominate their land. Also, despite American air power and advanced technology, guerrillas fought well in the jungle terrain.

Vietnam Today The communist victors imposed harsh rule on the south. Tens of thousands of Vietnamese fled in small boats. Many of these "boat people" drowned. Survivors landed in refugee camps. Eventually, some were accepted into the United States or other countries.

Vietnam had to rebuild a land destroyed by war. Recovery was slow due to government inefficiency and an American-led embargo, or blockage of trade. For years, the country remained mired in poverty and was unable to attract foreign capital.

In the early 1990s, Vietnam introduced some free-market reforms, opening the door to investors. The economy received a further boost after the United States lifted its embargo and restored diplomatic relations. Although Vietnam made some progress, it remained one of the poorest countries in Southeast Asia. The government's monopoly on political power and its complex laws made foreign investment difficult. Vietnam's best hope was the entrepreneurial spirit of its people.

Tragedy in Cambodia During the Vietnam War, fighting spilled over into neighboring Cambodia. North Vietnam sent supplies along the Ho Chi Minh Trail through Cambodia to guerrilla forces in South Vietnam. In 1970, the United States bombed that route and then invaded Cambodia. After the Americans left, Cambodian communist guerrillas called the Khmer Rouge overthrew the government.

Led by Pol Pot, the Khmer Rouge unleashed a reign of terror. To destroy all western influences, they drove people from the cities and forced them to work in the fields. They slaughtered or caused the death of more than a million Cambodians, perhaps a third of the population:

> "There were no more cities. No more markets, stores, restaurants, or cafes. . . . No schools. No books or magazines. No money. No clocks. No holidays and religious festivals. Just the sun that rose and set, the stars at night and the rain that fell from the sky. And work. Everything was work."
> —Haing Ngor, *A Cambodian Odyssey*

In 1979, Vietnam invaded and occupied Cambodia. Pol Pot and his forces retreated to remote areas. In the 1990s, the UN helped Cambodia hold elections. The new government, however, soon grew authoritarian. After Pol Pot died in 1998, a number of Khmer Rouge leaders gave up their guerrilla struggle. Cambodia debated whether to put Khmer Rouge leaders on trial.

Challenges for the Philippines

In 1946, the Philippines gained freedom peacefully after almost 50 years of American rule. The United States, however, continued to influence the country through military and economic aid. Although the Filipino constitution set up a democratic government, a wealthy elite controlled politics and the economy. The peasant majority was desperately poor. For a time, the government battled Huks, local communists with strong peasant support.

Ferdinand Marcos, elected president in 1965, became a dictator. He cracked down on basic freedoms. He even had Benigno Aquino (beh NEE nyoh ah KEE noh), a popular rival, murdered. Under heavy pressure, Marcos finally held elections. Voters elected Corazon Aquino, widow of the slain Benigno. Marcos tried to overturn the results, but the people of Manila forced him to leave in what was called the "people power" revolution.

Under Aquino and her successors, the fragile democracy struggled to survive. The economy grew during the 1990s but then slowed. Most people remained poor. Government corruption continued unchecked. As urbanization increased, unrest grew in crowded slum neighborhoods. Natural disasters added to the problems. Enterprising Filipinos left home to build new lives in the United States and other parts of Asia.

For decades, the government has battled rebels who wage guerrilla warfare. The fighting has taken many lives. Some rebels were communists. Others belonged to Muslim separatist groups. Some Islamic militants supported international terrorism. As part of its war on terrorism, the United States aided the Filipino government.

Conflict in the Philippines
Democracy in the Philippines is threatened by government corruption and social divisions. In the photo above, the guerrilla fighter behind the boy is a member of a Muslim separatist group.

Theme: Political and Social Systems In countries around the world, what do separatist groups want?

Developing Nations of Southeast Asia

Southeast Asian nations faced many problems after independence. They lacked experience in self-government and were often hampered by complex ethnic and religious conflicts. Demands for political freedom and social justice were frequent. Some government leaders, however, claimed that order and economic development must take priority. All pursued the same goal, modernization, but their paths differed. Here, we will look at the experiences of two developing nations: Indonesia and Myanmar (formerly Burma).

Indonesia Geography posed an obstacle to unity in Indonesia, as in many developing nations. Indonesia includes more than 13,000 islands splashed across 3,200 miles of ocean—a distance equal to the width of the United States. Its large population is ethnically diverse. The Javanese dominate,

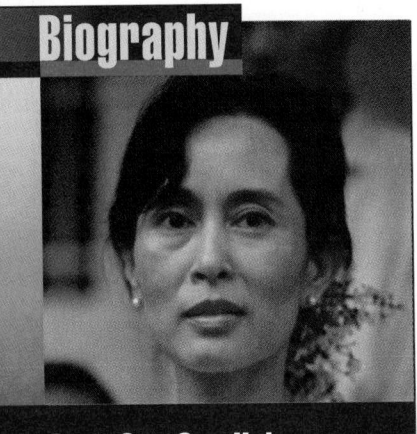

Aung San Suu Kyi 1945—

Aung San Suu Kyi was living in Britain with her husband and their sons when she decided to go home to Myanmar and oppose the military government. For safety, her family remained in Britain. After the 1990 election, the Myanmar government placed her under house arrest.

In 1991, the government announced that if Suu Kyi traveled to Norway to receive her Nobel Peace Prize, she would not be permitted to return to Myanmar. Her 18-year-old son Alexander accepted the award in her place.

Even after releasing Suu Kyi from house arrest in 1995, the government closely monitored her actions. In the years that followed, she continued to protest against injustice and was repeatedly placed under house arrest.

Theme: Impact of the Individual Why do many people in Myanmar consider Aung San Suu Kyi a hero?

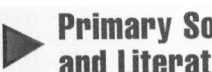

Primary Sources and Literature

See "Aung San Suu Kyi: Freedom From Fear" in the Reference Section at the back of this book.

---

but about 300 other groups, many with their own languages or dialects, also live in Indonesia. Despite this diversity, about 90 percent of Indonesians are Muslims.

For years after independence, Indonesia had an authoritarian, military government. In 1965, the government crushed what looked like a communist uprising and massacred many of the rebels. Mobs also killed hundreds of thousands of Chinese whose ancestors had moved to Indonesia.

But under authoritarian rule, Indonesia made great economic progress. It benefited from exporting oil, tin, rubber, spices, and coffee. The government increased literacy and, in the 1990s, introduced economic reforms that attracted more foreign capital.

Then, the 1997 Asian financial crisis shook Indonesia to its roots. Rioters protested massive government corruption. President Suharto was forced to resign after 32 years in power. An elected government faced grave problems, such as reforming and reviving the economy, restoring confidence in government, and dealing with separatist demands.

A struggle erupted in East Timor, which Indonesia had seized from Portugal in 1975. For years, the government battled the mostly Catholic people of East Timor, who finally won independence in 2002.

Religious and ethnic conflicts fueled violence and separatist movements elsewhere. In the Moluccan Islands, fighting between Muslims and Christians claimed thousands of lives. Discrimination against Chinese led to vicious attacks on their businesses. Separatist groups in various provinces demanded independence. Some Muslim extremists had links to international terrorism. In response to the violence and separatism, the government gave police and military additional powers.

Myanmar Ethnic tensions have also plagued Burma. The majority, Burmans, long dominated the country. For years, repressive military rulers battled rebel ethnic minorities who wanted autonomy. In 1962, the military government isolated the country, thus limiting trade and foreign investment. It imposed state socialism modeled on Mao's system in China. These policies brought little improvement in the standard of living. In 1989, they renamed the country Myanmar, meaning "the People's Country," which recognized that other groups besides Burmans lived there.

Under mounting pressure, the government held elections in 1990. The opposition party won. It was led by Aung San Suu Kyi (AWNG SAHN SOO SHEE), whose father had helped Burma win independence. The military rejected the election results and jailed, killed, or exiled many opponents. Suu Kyi was held under house arrest. While still a prisoner, she won the Nobel Peace Prize for her "nonviolent struggle for democracy and human rights." Suu Kyi was released in 1995. But in 2003, a new crackdown by the military government placed Suu Kyi under house arrest again.

Regional Cooperation Demands for political freedom and social justice remained an issue in Southeast Asia. Some government leaders, however, argued that order and economic development must take priority over democracy. To achieve prosperity and improve regional self-reliance, six Southeast Asian countries formed the Association of Southeast Asian Nations (ASEAN) in 1967. Since then, ASEAN has expanded to include most Southeast Asian nations. They have worked to promote economic and cultural cooperation.

The Pacific Rim

In the modern global economy, Southeast Asia and East Asia are part of a vast region known as the Pacific Rim. It includes countries in Asia and the Americas that border the Pacific Ocean.

The Pacific first became an artery for world trade in the 1500s. By the mid-1900s, links across the Pacific had grown dramatically. By the 1990s,

Virtual Field Trip

Go Online
PHSchool.com

For: More about batik in Indonesia
Visit: PHSchool.com
Web Code: mkd-3477

Indonesian Textiles
Batik is made by applying wax and then dye to fabric. The waxed portions of the fabric do not absorb the dye, creating intricate patterns and shapes.

Theme: Art and Literature
What kinds of skills would a batik artist need?

the volume of trade across the Pacific was greater than that across the Atlantic. Some analysts have predicted that the 2000s will be the "Pacific century" because of this region's potential for further growth.

Countries on the Asian Pacific Rim formed a huge market that lured investors, especially multinational corporations. American companies, too, sought a place on the Asian Pacific Rim. With almost 1.3 billion people, China has a fifth of the world's population. Indonesia, with 235 million people, and Japan, with 127 million, are also among the world's most populous nations. Since the 1960s, Japan has dominated the Asian Pacific Rim economically. By the 1990s, however, China was challenging Japan's economic empire.

Pacific Rim countries are enormously diverse. Indian, Hindu, Buddhist, and Confucian traditions, you will recall, helped shape Southeast Asian cultures. Later, Islam took root in some areas, while the Age of Imperialism brought western and Christian influences.

Today, cultural exchanges occur rapidly as radio and television programs are beamed by satellite across Asia. Businesses and tourists aid the exchange of technology and ideas. The development of the Pacific Rim promises to bring the Americas and Asia into closer contact.

SECTION 4 Assessment

Recall
1. **Identify:** (a) Ho Chi Minh, (b) Khmer Rouge, (c) Corazon Aquino, (d) Aung San Suu Kyi, (e) ASEAN.
2. **Define:** (a) domino theory, (b) cease-fire, (c) embargo.

Comprehension
3. Describe the effects of war on (a) Vietnam, (b) Cambodia.
4. What economic and ethnic issues have faced governments in the Philippines and Indonesia?

5. Why is the Pacific Rim seen as an important link in the global economy?

Critical Thinking and Writing
6. **Linking Past and Present** What effects of the Vietnam War can still be seen in the United States today?
7. **Connecting to Geography** How might Indonesia's geographic features affect its ability to create a national identity?

Go Online
PHSchool.com

Research the ASEAN Promotion Centre on Trade, Investment, and Tourism. Write a paragraph explaining Japan's economic relations with another member country. For help with this activity, use **Web Code mkd-7734.**

CHAPTER 21 **Review and Assessment**

Creating a Chapter Summary

Copy this diagram on a sheet of paper. In the blank circles, write the names of nations that have communist governments and those that have independent or democratic governments. Add more circles as needed.

For additional review and enrichment activities, see the interactive version of *World History* available on the Web and on CD-ROM.

For practice test questions for Chapter 21, use **Web Code mka-3478.**

Building Vocabulary

Write a sentence for each of the following terms.

1. zaibatsu
2. gross domestic product
3. trade deficit
4. five-year plan
5. collectivization
6. commune
7. joint venture
8. special enterprise zone
9. domino theory
10. cease-fire

Recalling Key Facts

11. How did the Great Leap Forward affect China?
12. Why did Taiwan create a separate government from that of mainland China?
13. What was the outcome of the war in Vietnam?
14. How did supporters of democracy in the Philippines overturn Ferdinand Marcos's government?
15. How have Southeast Asian nations increased regional cooperation?
16. What is the Pacific Rim? What has happened to trade in this region?

Critical Thinking and Writing

17. **Recognizing Causes and Effects** How might Japan's emergence as an economic superpower threaten some of the values that contributed to that success?
18. **Comparing** How did Deng Xiaoping's reforms in China compare with Mikhail Gorbachev's reforms in the Soviet Union?
19. **Linking Past and Present** How are the effects of the Cold War still felt in Korea today?
20. **Predicting Consequences** What long-term effects might the takeover of Hong Kong by China have on **(a)** Hong Kong, **(b)** China? Explain your answers.
21. **Connecting to Geography** "Five hundred years ago," notes a modern economist, "the world's economic center moved from the Mediterranean to the Atlantic. Today, it has shifted again to the Pacific." Support this statement using details about Asia from this chapter.

576 *Chapter 21*

China's Cultural Revolution became an assault on intellectuals throughout Chinese society. In the excerpt below, a student describes some of the hardships he endured. Read the excerpt, then answer the questions that follow.

"When the Cultural Revolution began . . . my family was one of the first in the city to be ransacked. . . . At that time all the funds capitalists had in the banks were frozen. You couldn't withdraw anything. . . . My mother didn't know about that. She went to get some money out. The bank clerks immediately called the Red Guards. They showed up in no time at my home and started to search and ransack our apartment. . . .

The next day, I went to see the Red Guards responsible for ransacking my family. I figured I'd take anything from them: insults, criticism, and everything else. I was going to beg them to allow me to go home to have a look. . . .

I glanced over the rooms. . . . Lots of things were in shreds, smashed and torn. . . . The only thing left to me was the desire to survive. I forgot everything else, even hunger."

—quoted in *Voices From the Whirlwind* (Jicai)

22. Why was the student's home ransacked?
23. What type of damage did the student see?
24. What feelings did the student have after seeing his family's home?

Skills Tip

A critical reader of Internet resources must be able to detect bias. Identify the source of information you are using, such as a university, news organization, or individual.

Go Online
PHSchool.com

Use the Internet to research diverse opinions about the possibility of reunifying Taiwan and China. Then, write a paragraph explaining whether or not you support reunification. For help with this activity, use **Web Code mkd-3479.**

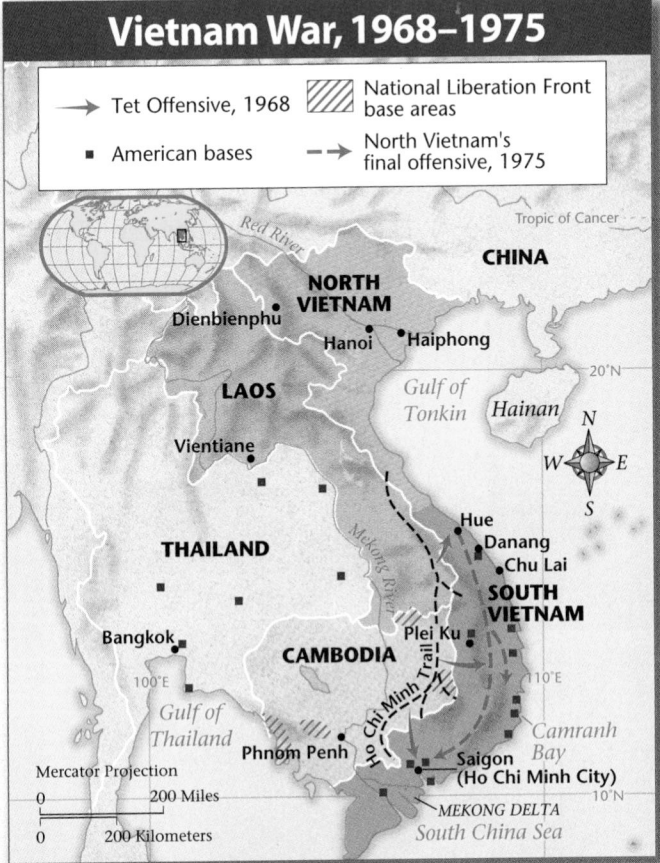

Vietnam War, 1968–1975

→ Tet Offensive, 1968
■ American bases
▨ National Liberation Front base areas
⇢ North Vietnam's final offensive, 1975

Study this map of the Vietnam War. Then, answer the following questions:

25. In what nation did the National Liberation Front have its base areas?
26. What was the starting point for the Tet Offensive?
27. Describe the route of the Ho Chi Minh Trail.
28. What countries provided sites for American bases?
29. Examine the course of the Mekong River. How might different nations have been able to use the river to their advantage during the war?
30. Why do you think the name of the city of Saigon was changed?

South Asia and the Middle East 1945–Present

Chapter Preview

1 **Nations of South Asia**
2 **Forces Shaping the Modern Middle East**
3 **Nation Building in the Middle East: Three Case Studies**
4 **The Middle East and the World**

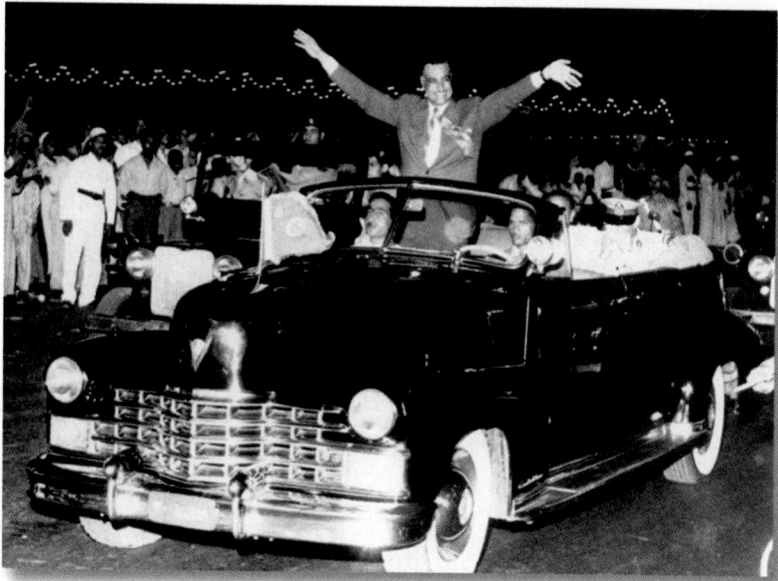

1947

India wins independence from Britain. The subcontinent is divided into Hindu India (top) and Muslim Pakistan (bottom).

1956

Egyptian president Gamal Abdel Nasser (above) nationalizes the Suez Canal, ending British and French control of the vital waterway.

1979

Revolutionaries in Iran oust the shah and declare an Islamic republic.

CHAPTER EVENTS

1940

1955

1970

GLOBAL EVENTS

1941 Nazis begin to implement "Final Solution."

1957 Ghana wins independence.

1966 Cultural Revolution begins in China.

Independence in South Asia and the Middle East

In South Asia and the Middle East, large nations like India and tiny ones like Jordan won independence. Since then, each has charted its own path toward modernization.

Black Sea

Ankara
TURKEY
1923

Caspian Sea

ASIA

Mediterranean Sea

LEBANON
1941
SYRIA
1946
Beirut • Damascus • Baghdad
ISRAEL
1948
Amman
Jerusalem
JORDAN
1946
Cairo •

IRAQ
1932

IRAN

AFGHANISTAN

Islamabad

PAKISTAN
1947

New
Delhi •

NEPAL

KUWAIT
1961 • Kuwait

Persian Gulf

BHUTAN

Ganges R.

BANGLADESH
1971
Dhaka •

BAHRAIN
1971
Manama •
QATAR 1971
Riyadh •
Doha •

Abu
Dhabi •
UNITED
ARAB
EMIRATES
1971

OMAN
1951
• Muscat

Tropic of Cancer

INDIA
1947

EGYPT
1922

Red Sea

SAUDI ARABIA
1932

*Arabian
Sea*

*Bay of
Bengal*

AFRICA

Nile R.

YEMEN
1990

Sanaa •

Mercator Projection

0   400   800 Miles

0   400   800 Kilometers

INDIAN OCEAN

Gulf of Aden

SRI LANKA
1948
• Colombo

Dates on map indicate date
of creation or independence

1984
Sikh separatists clash
with Indian troops at the
Golden Temple in Amritsar.

1991
The Persian Gulf War ends
an Iraqi invasion of Kuwait.
Retreating Iraqi troops set fire
to hundreds of Kuwaiti oil wells.

2003
American and British troops
invade Iraq and topple the
regime of Saddam Hussein.

1985   2000   2015

1991 The Soviet
Union collapses.

To learn about recent developments
in South Asia and the Middle East,
use **Web Code mkc-3581.**

Chapter 22 **579**

Nations of South Asia

Reading Focus

- Why was India partitioned?
- How has India dealt with political, economic, and social change?
- What problems did Pakistan and Bangladesh face?
- How is South Asia linked to world affairs?

Vocabulary

partition
federal system
harijan
deforestation
debt service
cyclone

Taking Notes

On a sheet of paper, make a Venn diagram like this one. As you read, add information about developments in India and Pakistan after winning independence.

INDIA
- World's largest democracy

- Ethnic rivalries

PAKISTAN
- Military leaders seize power

| *Main Idea* | After winning independence, Hindu India and Muslim Pakistan pursued separate roads to modernization. |

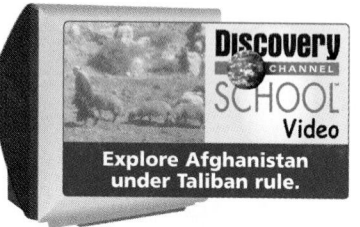

Discovery CHANNEL SCHOOL Video
Explore Afghanistan under Taliban rule.

Primary Source

Nehru's Vision of Independence

As the Indian Assembly met to celebrate independence, Prime Minister Jawaharlal Nehru spoke:

"At the stroke of the midnight hour, when the world sleeps, India will awake to life and freedom. A moment comes, which comes but rarely in history, when we step out from the old to the new, when an age ends and when the soul of a nation long suppressed finds utterance."

—Jawaharlal Nehru, "Tryst With Destiny" speech

Skills Assessment

Primary Source What words or phrases did Nehru use to express his optimism about India's future?

Setting the Scene August 15, 1947, was a joyful day in India. Everywhere, crowds gathered to watch parades and fireworks. At the stroke of midnight, power had passed from British colonial rulers into the hands of Indians themselves. This was India's Independence Day.

Three years later, India adopted a new democratic constitution. It set lofty goals for the nation:

"... to secure to all its citizens: JUSTICE, social, economic, and political; LIBERTY of thought, expression, belief, faith and worship; EQUALITY of status and opportunity; and to promote among them all FRATERNITY assuring the dignity of the individual and the unity of the Nation."
—Indian National Constitution

Achieving those goals would be difficult. Most Indians were poor, uneducated, and divided by caste, region, language, and religious and ethnic background. Other nations on the subcontinent faced similar challenges.

Independence and Partition

As you have read, Indian nationalists had demanded independence since the late 1800s. After World War II, Britain finally agreed to these demands. As independence neared, a long-simmering issue surfaced. What would happen to the Muslim minority in a Hindu-dominated India?

Two Nations Muhammad Ali Jinnah, leader of the Muslim League, insisted that Muslims have their own state, Pakistan. Riots between Hindus and Muslims helped persuade Britain to partition, or divide, the subcontinent. Drawing fair borders was impossible because Hindus and Muslims lived side by side. Still, in 1947, British officials hastily created Hindu India and Muslim Pakistan. Pakistan was made up of two widely separated areas in the northern part of the subcontinent that had large Muslim populations.

Tragedy Unfolds In 1947, millions of Hindus and Muslims crossed the borders of India and Pakistan in both directions. During the mass migration, centuries of mistrust—which the British had exploited to keep the population divided—plunged northern India into savage violence. Sikh and Hindu mobs slaughtered Muslims fleeing into Pakistan. Muslims massacred Hindu and Sikh neighbors. An estimated 10 million refugees fled their homes. One million or more, mostly Muslims, may have died.

Horrified at the partition and the violence, Mohandas Gandhi, the "father of the nation," turned once more to satyagraha to restore peace. But on January 30, 1948, he was shot and killed by a Hindu extremist. Jawaharlal Nehru, India's first prime minister, told a stricken nation, "The light has gone out of our lives and there is darkness everywhere." Gandhi's death discredited the extremists and helped to end the worst violence. Still, Hindu-Muslim tensions persisted.

India: World's Largest Democracy

India built on the legacy of British government, including its system of law and government. Today, with a population of about one billion, it is the world's largest democratic nation.

Unity and Diversity To achieve independence, Indians had united behind the Congress party. Still, the new nation was deeply divided. It included hundreds of princely states that had survived British rule. Indians spoke a wide variety of languages and dialects. The majority of Indians were Hindu, but millions of others were Muslim, Sikh, Christian, or Buddhist.

India's constitution set up a federal system, like that of the United States. Under this system, powers are divided between a strong central government and smaller local governments. In time, the government reorganized the princely states into a smaller number of states. It recognized 15 official languages and 35 major regional languages.

The "Nehru Dynasty" For 40 years after independence, members of the Nehru family led India. From 1947 to 1964, Jawaharlal Nehru worked to build a modern, secular state dedicated to promoting social justice. After he died, his daughter Indira Gandhi and, later, his grandson Rajiv Gandhi, served as prime minister. Both were popular, energetic leaders, but at times their highhanded policies eroded goodwill. In the end, both fell victim to violence, as you will read. Sonia Gandhi, the Italian-born widow of Rajiv, entered politics and became leader of the Congress party in 1998.

Ongoing Divisions In the early 1990s, support deepened for the Hindu fundamentalist Bharatiya Janata party (BJP). For them, India was a Hindu nation. Unlike the Congress party, which wanted to separate religion and government, the BJP called for a government built on Hindu principals. Beginning in the late 1990s, the BJP often won the most seats in India's parliament.

As the BJP rose to power, conflict between Hindus and Muslims increased. In 1992, the BJP backed calls for the destruction of a mosque in Ayodhya (uh YOHD yuh). Hindu fundamentalists claimed that it stood on a sacred Hindu site seized by Muslim invaders centuries earlier. The BJP wanted a Hindu temple there. The conflict ignited rioting at Ayodhya and the mosque was destroyed. In 2002, the BJP state government in Gujarat was accused of backing mob attacks against the Muslim minority there.

Other divisions affected the prosperous Punjab region of northwestern India. There, some Sikhs wanted an independent state. In 1984, these Sikh separatists occupied the Golden Temple in Amritsar. When talks failed to

Partition of India, 1947

India, 1947
Pakistan, 1947
Disputed areas

Skills Assessment

Geography The partition of India created two populous new nations but also led to widespread violence.

1. **Location** On the map, locate **(a)** India, **(b)** East Pakistan, **(c)** West Pakistan, **(d)** Kashmir, **(e)** Afghanistan.
2. **Movement** Based on this map, describe the migration of Hindus and Muslims across the India–West Pakistan border in 1947.
3. **Critical Thinking Linking Past and Present** Compare this map with the map of Asia in the Reference Section. Identify two changes that have taken place since 1947.

Protest at the Golden Temple
Although the Sikh religion has roots in Hinduism, conflict has often erupted between India's Sikh minority and Hindu majority. Here, Sikh separatists occupy the Golden Temple in Amritsar in 1984.

Theme: Diversity What were these protesters demanding?

oust them, Indira Gandhi sent troops. Thousands of Sikhs died in the fighting. A few months later, Gandhi was killed by two of her Sikh bodyguards. The assassination ignited battles between Hindus and Sikhs.

A third center of conflict lay to the south, on the island nation of Sri Lanka. Most Sri Lankans are Buddhists who speak Singhalese. The Tamil-speaking Hindu minority faced discrimination. For years, Tamil rebels have fought to set up a separate nation. In the 1980s, India's Rajiv Gandhi sent troops to smash the rebels. The attempt failed, and outraged Tamil extremists assassinated Gandhi in 1991. The violence has continued despite peace efforts.

Economic Growth and Challenges

Like other developing nations, India wanted to apply modern technology to expand agriculture and industry. The government adopted a largely socialist model, drawing up five-year plans to set economic goals and manage resources.

Industry and Agriculture British-built railroads gave India its basic transportation network. Under Nehru, India built dams to produce hydroelectric power and poured resources into heavy industries such as steel. By the 1960s, India was on its way to becoming an industrial power. Development, however, remained uneven. India lacked oil and natural gas—two resources essential to economic growth. It had to rely on costly imported oil.

To turn out the educated work force essential to a developing industrial economy, the Indian government built schools and universities. The nation's literacy rate climbed, but unevenly. Boys were more likely to attend school than were girls. Also, children from poor families often received little schooling because they were needed to work.

Seeking to make India self-sufficient in food production, Nehru took advantage of the Green Revolution. New seeds, chemical fertilizers, and irrigation methods boosted crop output. Still, only farmers with enough land and money could afford to grow the new crops. Most farmers continued to use the same methods as in the past. They depended on the monsoons and produced enough to survive but had little surplus.

The Population Issue Rapid population growth hurt efforts to improve living conditions. India's population has tripled since independence to more than one billion people. While food output rose, so did demand. More than a third of Indians live below the poverty level, eating only one meal a day.

As the population boomed and the Green Revolution eliminated many agricultural jobs, millions of people streamed into cities like Calcutta and Bombay to find work. But these overcrowded cities did not have enough jobs. Often, they could not provide basic services such as water or sewage. To help the urban poor, Mother Teresa, a Roman Catholic nun, founded an order in Calcutta called the Missionaries of Charity. Its branches in India and elsewhere have provided food and medical care to thousands.

The government encouraged family planning but did not impose harsh population control measures, as China did. Efforts to slow down population growth met with limited success. Many Indians, especially in rural areas, saw children as an economic resource. Children were expected to work the land and to care for parents in old age.

Economic Reform An economic slowdown and pressure from international lenders forced India to make reforms. Turning from the socialist model, it looked to the successes of the Asian tigers. It privatized some industries and made foreign investment easier. By the 1990s, India had a significant role in textiles, technology, and other industries. Computer experts at India's software center at Madras gained a worldwide reputation.

Social Change

In India, as elsewhere, urbanization undermined some traditions. Yet most Indians continued to live in villages, where centuries-old attitudes and values remained strong.

Reforming the Caste System Discrimination based on caste continued. In the 1930s, Gandhi had campaigned to end the inhumane treatment of untouchables, whom he called harijans—children of God. India's 1950 constitution banned discrimination against untouchables. The government set aside jobs and places in universities for these long-mistreated groups.

Despite such programs, deep prejudice persisted. Higher-caste Hindus still received better schooling and jobs. In the 1990s, the government tried to open more jobs to untouchables. Violent protests by higher-caste Hindus who feared losing their jobs forced the government to back off from its plan.

Women At independence, women gained the vote along with other legal rights. A few educated women, like Indira Gandhi, won elected office or entered professions. In the cities, upper- and middle-class families sought to educate their daughters as a sign of modernization and accomplishment.

Yet, because of class and caste differences, many girls from poor families receive little or no education. Women on the lower rungs of society cluster in menial, low-paying jobs. In rural areas, women make up a majority of the work force, but few receive wages for their labor.

Indian women have formed organizations and movements to meet their needs. The Self-Employed Women's Association (SEWA) formed production and marketing cooperatives, opened banks, and provided classes and legal advice for poor women. Women's groups have also fought violence against women, protested dowry laws, and called for environmental protection.

Pakistan and Bangladesh

At independence, Pakistan faced severe problems. Early on, military leaders seized power and ruled as dictators. The country lacked many essential natural resources for industry. Ethnic rivalries also fueled conflicts.

A Divided Nation West Pakistan and East Pakistan were separated by a wide swath of Indian territory. The people of both regions were Muslim, but their languages and cultures differed. Bengalis in the east outnumbered Punjabis in the west, yet Punjabis dominated the government and economy.

As tensions mounted, Bengalis broke away. In 1971, they declared independence for Bangladesh, or "Bengal Nation." The Pakistani military ruler ordered the army to crush the rebels. To escape the bloodbath, millions of Bengalis fled west into India. India responded by attacking and defeating the Pakistani army in Bangladesh.

Government For years, Pakistan alternated between civilian and military governments. After the loss of Bangladesh, Pakistan's ruling general fell from power. A new civilian president, Zulfikar Ali Bhutto, promised progress and prosperity. When it didn't come fast enough, Bhutto was overthrown, tried, and executed by the military. Later, civilian government was restored. Twice between 1988 and 1996, Bhutto's daughter Benazir served as prime minister, but she was ousted from power both times. By 1999, Pakistan's elected government faced economic woes, widespread corruption,

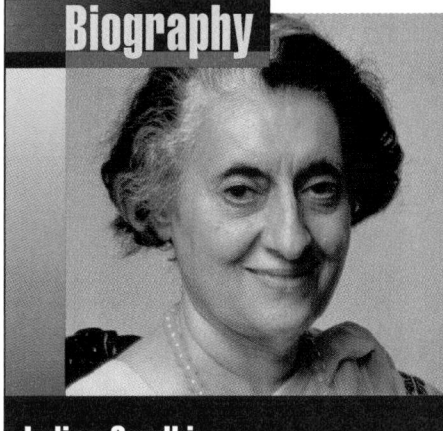

Biography

Indira Gandhi 1917–1984

"On her fragile shoulders rests the huge destiny of India—and they don't shrink from the burden," noted French leader Charles de Gaulle of Prime Minister Indira Gandhi. Early in life, Gandhi's strength was forged by her family's participation in the independence struggle. "I was part of the processions and meetings and everything that took place," she said. As a young woman, she was imprisoned by British authorities for her part in the independence campaign.

Gandhi continued her central role in Indian politics after her father, Jawaharlal Nehru, became prime minister. With him she traveled throughout India and went on official trips abroad. Her experience and connections to Nehru helped her become prime minister after his death.

Theme: Impact of the Individual How did Gandhi's experiences as Nehru's daughter influence her political career?

Geography and History

Afghan Refugees

In 2002, more than 2 million refugees returned to Afghanistan. They hoped that the fall of the Taliban had opened the way to stable peace and protection of human rights. The refugees returned to a country ravaged by decades of civil war, destruction from U.S. bombing, and devastating drought. Basic infrastructure and services were basically non-existent outside cities. The homes of many refugees had been destroyed, and many returnees had no resources with which to resume life. Upon arrival, the UN Refugee Agency provided returnees with an aid package containing plastic tarpaulins, soap, and wheat flour. Countries around the world donated money to help rebuild the country. Even so, in 2003, more than 3.5 million Afghans still lived as refugees in other countries, mainly Iran and Pakistan.

Theme: Geography and History Why did so many Afghans migrate away from their country?

and other severe challenges. Once again, the military stepped in. Led by General Pervez Musharraf, the military dismissed the elected government and suspended the constitution.

However, in 2001, after the 9/11 terrorist attacks on the United States, General Musharraf began to change his ways. He won American support by contributing significantly to President Bush's "war on terrorism." He cooperated with American officials in rounding up a number of key al-Qaida operatives in Pakistan. Musharraf's government also announced that it was committed to the restoration of democracy.

However, foreign critics remained concerned about Muslim militancy in the country. Militants repeatedly slipped across the border to aid Muslim separatist fighters in India. Religious schools were criticized for encouraging anti-western sentiment. And it was believed that Osama bin Laden and other al-Qaida fighters had found refuge in the borderlands of Pakistan.

Economy After independence, Pakistan moved to improve agriculture. It distributed unused lands to landless farmers, experimented with new high-yield crops, and financed irrigation projects. Building dams and clearing land helped boost food production, but at a high cost to the environment. Deforestation, or destruction of forest land, caused terrible floods when monsoon rains were heavy.

To modernize, Pakistan nationalized major industries. More recently, the government has encouraged private or mixed government and private ownership of businesses. Like other developing nations, Pakistan faces an ongoing financial crisis. It has borrowed heavily from lenders such as the World Bank and IMF. Yet debt service, paying interest on loans, takes 40 percent of the nation's budget, leaving little for development.

Trials of Bangladesh Since 1971, Bangladesh has struggled to rise out of poverty, but geography often stands in the way. Its large population is crowded on a low-lying coastal plain. The region is subject to devastating floods when monsoon rains are too heavy or to droughts if the rains are too light. Cyclones, fierce circular windstorms, are another frequent threat.

Explosive population growth has strained resources still further. More than 50 million people, many of them women and children, live below the poverty level. Large amounts of foreign aid have brought little relief, in part because various military governments have misused the assistance.

South Asia and the World

India and Pakistan were affected by the Cold War and its aftermath. India welcomed economic aid from both the United States and Soviet Union but embraced the nonaligned movement. Pakistan, feeling threatened by India and the Soviet Union, accepted military aid from the United States. After the Cold War ended in the early 1990s, both India and Pakistan sought aid from the United States and other western powers.

Conflict Between India and Pakistan Fear and mistrust have marred relations between India, with its Hindu majority, and Pakistan, with its Muslim majority. At independence, border conflicts ignited a war over Kashmir, a princely state in the Himalayas. Its Hindu monarch decided to join India even though the state's Muslim majority wanted to be part of Pakistan. Since then, Pakistan and India have fought several wars over Kashmir. In 2002, war almost erupted again. Over the years, Muslim Kashmiri separatists, supported by activists from neighboring Pakistan, have repeatedly attacked Hindus, seeking to drive them out of Kashmir. Indian military units, in turn, have repeatedly savaged Kashmiri Muslims.

The Nuclear Issue After India tested a nuclear bomb in 1974, Pakistan felt threatened and began to develop its own nuclear capability. In 1998, both India and Pakistan tested nuclear weapons. As fear grew, the two nations agreed to ease tensions and improve relations. Still, both countries faced strong nationalist and religious pressure to use at least the threat of nuclear conflict in future confrontations.

Afghanistan This Central Asian country has suffered years of civil war. From 1979 to 1989, Soviet troops supported a harsh communist government. With American aid, Afghan guerrillas forced the Soviets to withdraw.

The Soviet exit did not end the fighting. Civil war between rival factions went on for years. In the late 1990s, the Taliban, a fundamentalist Muslim group, gained power. They restored order but imposed an extreme form of Islam on Afghanistan. The Taliban government was condemned by the international community for human rights violations and for the destruction of ancient Buddhist statues.

The Taliban was also condemned for supporting al-Qaida, the international terrorist group led by Osama bin Laden. This support persisted even after al-Qaida's attacks on New York City and Washington, D.C., on September 11, 2001. The Taliban defied international opinion and UN sanctions by continuing to shelter bin Laden and his followers.

In response, an international coalition led by the United States invaded Afghanistan. Al-Qaida forces were defeated or forced into hiding and the Taliban government fell from power. Bin Laden seemed to be among the terrorists who escaped. After the war, American troops remained in Afghanistan to continue the hunt for terrorists and to help the new Afghan government rebuild the country.

Cause *and* Effect

Long-Term Causes	Short-Term Causes
• Muslim conquest of northern India in 1100s • British imperialism in India • Nationalists organize the Indian National Congress in 1885 • Muslim nationalists form separate Muslim League in 1906	• World War II weakens European colonial empires • Pressure from Indian nationalists increases • Insistence by Muhammad Ali Jinnah and the Muslim League that Muslims have their own state • Rioting between Hindus and Muslims throughout northern India

Partition of India

Effects

- Violence erupts as millions of Hindus and Muslims cross the border between India and Pakistan
- Gandhi is assassinated by Hindu extremists
- India and Pakistan become centers of Cold War rivalry
- Establishment of the state of Bangladesh

Connections to Today

- Continuing clash between India and Pakistan over Kashmir
- Nuclear arms race as both India and Pakistan refuse to sign Non-Proliferation Treaty

Skills Assessment **Chart** The conflicts that led to the partition of India continue to affect the subcontinent. **How have the long-term effects of the partition spread beyond India and Pakistan?**

SECTION 1 Assessment

Recall

1. Identify: (a) Jawaharlal Nehru, **(b)** Indira Gandhi, **(c)** Rajiv Gandhi, **(d)** BJP, **(e)** Mother Teresa, **(f)** Zulfikar Ali Bhutto, **(g)** Osama bin Laden.

2. Define: (a) partition, **(b)** federal system, **(c)** harijan, **(d)** deforestation, **(e)** debt service, **(f)** cyclone.

Comprehension

3. Why was the Indian subcontinent divided into two nations?

4. (a) What economic goals did India pursue? **(b)** Why has progress been limited?

5. Describe one problem facing **(a)** Pakistan, **(b)** Bangladesh.

6. How has conflict in Afghanistan affected the world? Give two examples.

Critical Thinking and Writing

7. Applying Information "The past still clings to us," said Jawaharlal Nehru. Give two examples that support his statement.

8. Defending a Position (a) Why would nationalists in India and Pakistan favor development of nuclear weapons? **(b)** Why did world leaders worry about the arms race in South Asia?

Go Online
PHSchool.com

Use the Internet to find out more about a recent flood in Bangladesh. Then, with a partner, prepare an action report outlining local and international efforts to relieve flood victims. You may wish to include an illustrated map of the flood plain. For help with this activity, use **Web Code mkd-3587.**

Forces Shaping the Modern Middle East

Reading Focus

- How have diversity and nationalism shaped the Middle East?

- What political and economic patterns have emerged?

- Why has an Islamic revival spread across the region?

- How do women's lives vary in the Middle East?

Vocabulary

recognize

kibbutz

desalinization

hejab

Taking Notes

As you read this section, prepare an outline of its contents. Use Roman numerals to indicate major headings. Use capital letters for subheadings, and use numbers for the supporting details. The example here will help you get started.

I. Diversity and nationalism
   A. Religious and cultural diversity
      1. Judaism, Christianity, Islam
      2. Different languages
      3.
   B. Winning independence

Main Idea Three forces shaping the modern Middle East are nationalism, religious and cultural diversity, and access to resources such as oil and water.

Connections to Today

A People Without a Nation

Numbering some 25 million, the Kurds today are the world's largest ethnic group without a homeland. After World War I, world leaders had promised the Kurds a nation. But these promises were broken. Since then, the Kurds have fought for autonomy and independence.

However, politics has often driven a wedge among Kurds and weakened these efforts. In 1994, a civil war divided the two main Kurdish political parties in northeastern Iraq. In 1994, radical Kurds in Turkey led by rebel leader Abdullah Ocalan began a guerrilla war for independence. In 2000, rebel leaders called a halt to the fighting. They pledged to work for Kurdish rights "within a framework of peace and democratization."

Theme: Geography and History Why might Kurd rebels in Turkey have decided to halt the guerrilla war?

Setting the Scene In the Arab world, as in South Asia, nationalists sought to free themselves from the legacy of imperialism. "We are [erasing] the traces of the past," declared Egyptian president Gamal Abdel Nasser in the 1950s. "We are building our country on strong and sound bases."

Leaders of Nasser's generation embarked on ambitious reforms. Their policies, however, often failed to bring promised improvements. By the 1970s, Islamic reformers began to offer another route to modernization.

Diversity and Nationalism

What does the term *Middle East* mean? Western powers first used the term to refer to the region between Europe and what they called the "Far East"— China, Japan, and Southeast Asia. To avoid this western bias, some people now call the region Southwest Asia. Yet the UN and many scholars and journalists continue to use the term *Middle East*.

Experts differ on what areas lie in the Middle East. In this chapter, we use the term to refer to the region from Egypt in the west to Iran in the east and from Turkey in the north to the Arabian Peninsula in the south.

Religious and Cultural Diversity Judaism, Christianity, and Islam all emerged in the Middle East. Today, most people in the region are Muslims, but many Jews and Christians also live there. Different sects within these religions add to the diversity.

Middle Eastern peoples speak more than 30 different languages, including Arabic, Turkish, Persian, Hebrew, Kurdish, and Armenian. Every country is home to minority groups—some, as many as a dozen. The Kurds, for example, are an ethnic group divided by modern borders among Turkey, Iraq, and Iran. Their efforts to win autonomy have led to repression.

Like Christians in Europe, Muslims in the Middle East share the same basic faith but belong to different national groups. Arabs, Iranians, and Turks have their own cultures, languages, and histories. Often, such differences have created divisions.

Winning Independence In the Middle East, as elsewhere, imperialism and nationalism were powerful forces. In the decades after World War I, Arab nationalists opposed the mandate system that placed Arab territories under European rule. Iraq won freedom from Britain in 1932. After World War II, British and French mandates won complete independence as the nations of Lebanon, Syria, and Jordan.

A Diverse City
The streets of Jerusalem are filled with a wide mix of people, including Jews and Palestinian Arabs. The street sign—written in Hebrew, Arabic, and English—reflects the city's diversity.

Theme: Diversity   Why might Jerusalem become a center of conflict?

The Pan-Arab dream of a united Arab state foundered as nations pursued individual goals. Still, their common heritage linked Arabs across borders. Pan-Arabism survived in the Arab League, which promoted Arab solidarity in times of crisis and worked for common economic goals.

Colonial Legacy   Despite winning independence, Arab nations remained economically dependent on the West. Westerners owned industries and banks. They provided the capital and technology needed for development, as well as the principal market for exports. Ending western economic domination became a key goal of many governments.

Imperialism left another legacy. Britain and France had drawn borders to serve their own interests. At independence, Arab nations inherited these borders, which often led to disputes. For example, Iraq included diverse and sometimes hostile groups. Colonial borders also limited Iraq's access to the Persian Gulf. Religious and ethnic tensions, plus a desire for outlets on the gulf, continue to fuel conflicts in Iraq.

Conflict Over Palestine   As you read, in 1917, Britain issued the Balfour Declaration, which pledged support for a Jewish national home in Palestine. The declaration deepened tensions in that region. Both Jews and Palestinian Arabs claimed a historical right to the land. Jewish migration to Palestine, which began in the late 1800s, increased after World War II. In the United States, especially, the horrors of the Holocaust created strong support for a Jewish homeland. But growing migration and conflicting British policies led to violent clashes.

As turmoil increased, Britain turned over its mandate to the United Nations. In 1947, the UN drew up a plan to partition Palestine into an Arab and a Jewish state. Jews accepted the plan, but Arabs rejected it. They saw it as a plan to relocate European Jews on Arab territory.

The Birth of Israel   After Britain withdrew in 1948, Jews proclaimed the independent state of Israel. The United States and Soviet Union both recognized Israel, that is, they formally agreed to treat it as a legitimate government. Arab states, however, launched a military attack on the new nation. Israeli forces fought well against the poorly equipped and badly led Arab forces. In the end, Israel increased its territory. Other Arab-Israeli wars would follow, as you will read.

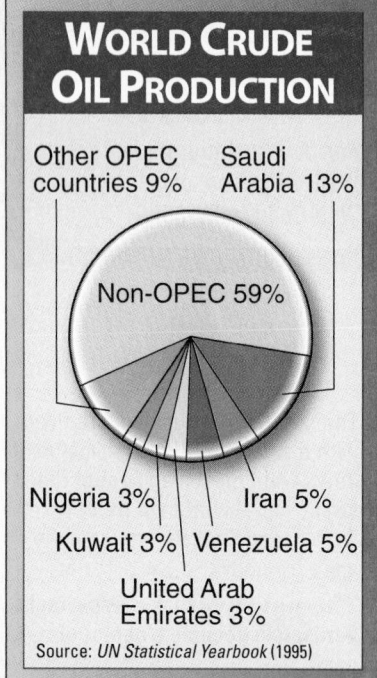

WORLD CRUDE OIL PRODUCTION

Other OPEC countries 9%

Saudi Arabia 13%

Non-OPEC 59%

Nigeria 3%

Iran 5%

Kuwait 3%

Venezuela 5%

United Arab Emirates 3%

Source: *UN Statistical Yearbook* (1995)

Israel developed rapidly after 1948. The government built towns for settlers and provided many services. American aid and high taxes gave Israel the capital to invest in industry and agriculture. In spite of scarce natural resources, a skilled and educated work force made rapid progress. Israelis built factories and developed methods to farm their arid land. Kibbutzim, or collective farms, produced crops for export.

The Refugee Issue The Arab-Israeli War of 1948 uprooted 700,000 Arabs from Palestine. The UN set up temporary shelters for Palestinian refugees. These poverty-stricken camps have since become permanent homes. Recent generations of Palestinian refugees have grown up bitterly determined to win a homeland of their own. Resolving the refugee issue would remain a thorny problem in the peace process for decades.

Political and Economic Patterns

After winning independence, Middle Eastern nations worked to modernize their governments and economies. Parts of the region sit atop the world's largest oil reserves, which brought regional and global consequences.

Governments Most Middle Eastern nations developed authoritarian governments. In Egypt and Iraq, revolutionary military leaders toppled monarchs who were closely tied to western powers. In other countries, such as Jordan and Saudi Arabia, hereditary monarchs remained in power but took steps to adapt to the modern world. In Iraq and Syria, a single party won power. Dictators like Iraq's Saddam Hussein brutally suppressed opponents but enjoyed some popular backing because their social and economic policies improved life for many.

Only Israel and Turkey formed multiparty democratic systems. In both of these countries, however, minority groups—Kurds in Turkey and Arabs in Israel—faced restrictions or serious discrimination.

Impact of Oil Because the Middle East commanded vital oil resources, the United States and other powers increased their political and military presence in the region. At the same time, the 1973 OPEC oil embargo showed that oil could be a powerful diplomatic and economic weapon.

Oil is unevenly distributed. Only a few countries, mostly on the Persian Gulf, have large oil reserves. Oil-rich Saudi Arabia and Kuwait have small populations. Turkey and Egypt, with much larger populations, have little oil. As a result, differences between "haves" and "have-nots" fueled resentments within the region. Oil-rich nations built roads, hospitals, and schools. Poorer countries lacked the capital needed for development.

Water Resources Many experts have predicted that water, not oil, may soon become the most valuable resource in the Middle East. Most of the region has limited rainfall. Growing populations and rising standards of living have increased demands for water. Farmers can produce good crops—if they can get water. Farming accounts for 80 percent of water use in the Middle East. To meet this urgent demand, oil-rich countries have built desalinization plants that convert salty sea water into fresh water.

Individual nations have built dams to supply water both for crops and for hydroelectric power. Turkey, for example, erected 22 dams in the late 1980s, including the giant Atatürk Dam. Its goal was to irrigate southeastern Turkey with water from the Tigris and Euphrates rivers, turning the region into a breadbasket.

Yet dam building has sparked explosive debates over water resources. Many rivers run through several countries. The Euphrates rises in Turkey but flows through Syria and Iraq. Israel, Jordan, and Syria all have claims on the waters of the Jordan River. As water needs grow, nations that share river systems must seek ways to use that scarce resource cooperatively.

Synthesizing Information

Water Scarcity in the Middle East

Arid lands stretch across vast areas of the Middle East, where fresh water and rainfall are scarce. With new technology and massive investment, however, the nations in this dry region are trying to meet the water needs of growing populations.

The Most Important Resource

Water conservation is critical in the Middle East. In many cases, peace hangs in the balance where water is concerned. Anis Muasher, founder of Jordan's Royal Society for the Protection of Nature, had this to say about water rights along the Jordan River:

"It becomes of no use to anybody if we continue behaving with nature the way we are behaving. . . . The whole world knows that water in the Middle East could be the cause of future wars, and we are fed up with wars. So the reasonable thing to do is to sit together, look at what we have, try to analyze it scientifically, take the consequences bravely, and do our job. Anything short of that will get nobody anywhere."

—Anis Muasher, *Audubon* magazine,
September–October 1994

Piping Water In

Once connected, this long line of pipes will snake across the desert in Saudi Arabia. Rather than carrying oil, these pipes will transport water. Pipelines bring treated water from desalinization plants on the coast to Riyadh and other inland cities.

Expensive projects such as dams and desalinization plants help Middle Eastern nations harness rivers and seas to make the desert bloom.

Water Resources in the Middle East

Albers Equal Area Projection

0   300   600 Miles

0   300   600 Kilometers

─ Major dams   • Desalinization plants

Skills Assessment

1. Which Middle Eastern nation has the most desalinization plants?
   A Turkey
   B Syria
   C Saudi Arabia
   D Kuwait

2. Based on the picture, what can you conclude about Saudi Arabia?
   E It lacks natural resources.
   F Its terrain is flat.
   G It has a tropical climate.
   H It has an arid climate.

3. **Critical Thinking Connecting to Geography** Analyze each of the pieces of evidence above to describe how nations have used technology to change their environment. How might these changes affect international relations?

Skills Tip

Map symbols convey important geographic information while summarizing the main idea of the map.

Economic Policies In the 1950s, some Arab nations turned to socialism as a way to end foreign economic control and modernize rapidly. They nationalized banks, oil companies, and factories. Despite such moves, they still depended on the industrial world for much of their technology.

To get capital, governments took foreign loans. They then built large projects in industry and agriculture, especially dams and other irrigation systems. In some countries, they redistributed land to peasants. But small farmers did not produce efficiently, and food output did not keep pace with rapid population growth. By the 1990s, under pressure from the IMF and other international lenders, many governments eased restrictions on foreign ownership. They privatized some state-run enterprises.

The Middle East, like other developing regions, faced grave economic challenges. Heavy borrowing left them deeply in debt and owing massive sums just in debt service. Also, while nations had built some industry and cities had boomed, large segments of the people still lived in poverty.

Islamic Revival

Islam has been a shaping force in the Middle East for more than 1,300 years. As in the past, the Quran and Sharia provide guidance on all aspects of life—from religious faith, law, and government to family and business relationships.

Western Influences During the Age of Imperialism, westerners urged Muslim nations to modernize. To the West, modernization meant adopting western forms of secular government and law. It also meant keeping religion and government separate.

After nearly a century of western influence, some Middle Eastern leaders adopted western models of development, promising economic progress and social justice. In the 1950s and 1960s, western cultural influences increased. In the growing cities, people wore western-style clothing, watched American television programs, and bought foreign products. Yet despite government promises, life improved very little for many people. When their leaders were unable to solve mounting problems, many people became disillusioned.

Call for Reform By the 1970s, in the face of failed development, repressive regimes, and growing western influence, many Muslim leaders and writers called for a return to the Sharia. Islamic reformers, often called fundamentalists by westerners, blamed social and economic ills on blind imitation of western models. They did not reject modernization, but they did reject westernization. They argued that a renewed commitment to Islamic principals was the only way to solve their current problems. The movement appealed to poor and educated Muslims alike.

Impact Across the Muslim world, from Morocco to Indonesia, the Islamic revival sparked heated debates between reformers and secularists and between moderates and extremists. Like Christian fundamentalists, many devout Muslims opposed any scientific view of the world that excluded belief in God as creator and ruler of the universe. Muslim reformers called for political power to be put in the hands of religious leaders. Some reformers supported peaceful methods. Others backed violence. Extremists were willing to wage terrorism to achieve their goals.

By the 1990s, the Islamic revival had spread across the Muslim world. Its impact varied from country to country. In Iran, as you will read, revolutionaries overthrew an unpopular shah. In Algeria, voters supported a political party that pledged to restore the Sharia. In Egypt and elsewhere, some extremists justified terrorist acts as a weapon against authoritarian, secular governments. Al-Qaida and other terrorist groups directed their violence against foreign influences in Muslim lands.

A Profession of Islamic Faith
The Arabic lettering on this ceramic by Iraqi artist Wasma'a K. Chorbachi proclaims, "There is no God but God and Muhammad is his prophet." Chorbachi said that she turned away from western artistic styles to express her "inner identity" as an Arab and Muslim.

Theme: Religions and Value Systems Why do you think Chorbachi chose to inscribe this phrase on a work of art?

Women in the Muslim World

Conditions for women vary greatly from country to country in the modern Middle East. Since the 1950s, women in most countries have won voting rights and equality before the law. They attend schools and universities in growing numbers. Middle- and upper-class women have entered professions such as law, engineering, and medicine.

The changes have taken place at different rates in different places. In Turkey, Syria, and Egypt, many urban women gave up long-held practices such as wearing hejab, or cover.* On the other hand, conservative countries like Saudi Arabia and Iran have opposed the spread of many western secular influences among women.

Return to Hejab   In recent decades, many educated Muslim women have returned to wearing hejab. For some women, the movement symbolized resistance to unpopular governments or a refusal to imitate western culture. "I think of Muslim dress as a kind of uniform," one Egyptian student said. "I can sit in class with men and there is no question of attraction and so on—we are all involved in the same business of learning." Most important, women who elected to return to hejab saw it as an expression of sincere loyalty to Muslim values and practices.

Continuing Issues   Still, some women in Muslim countries were dismayed. They argued against social and political forces that put severe limits on their lives.

Under Sharia, women traditionally held powerful positions in the family and played important economic roles. In some countries, though, laws and traditions emerged that limited women's right to vote, work, or even drive cars. Many Muslim and non-Muslim women spoke out on the need for women to realize their full potential and contribute to national life.

Return to Hejab
Today, many Muslim women have adopted the traditional form of dress known as hejab. Here, these Iranian women shop in a local market.

Theme: Continuity and Change How does the return to hejab reflect continuity in the Muslim world?

---

*The Arabic word *hejab* means "following Islamic guidelines for women's dress in public." The practice includes a variety of head coverings as well as a long, loose-fitting garment. In English, the word is often translated as "veiling," though only a small fraction of Muslim women cover their faces.

SECTION 2 Assessment

Recall
1. **Identify:** **(a)** Kurds, **(b)** Arab League.
2. **Define:** **(a)** recognize, **(b)** kibbutz, **(c)** desalinization, **(d)** hejab.

Comprehension
3. **(a)** What forces have linked Arab nations? **(b)** Give one example of how diversity has caused tension in a Middle Eastern nation.
4. How has oil shaped Middle Eastern economies?
5. How was the Islamic revival linked to social and political development?
6. **(a)** What rights have women gained in the Middle East? **(b)** Why did some Muslim women favor a return to hejab?

Critical Thinking and Writing
7. **Understanding Causes and Effects** **(a)** How did events of the early 1940s increase European and American support for the creation of Israel? **(b)** Why was such support needed?
8. **Defending a Position** Would you agree that water is a more valuable resource than oil? Why or why not?

Activity

Holding a Debate
With a group of classmates, stage a debate about paths to development in the Middle East. Have one team present arguments in favor of modernization and westernization. Have the other team present the opposing viewpoint. Have one student act as moderator.

Nation Building in the Middle East: Three Case Studies

Reading Focus

■ What issues has Turkey faced?

■ Why was Egypt a leader in the Arab world?

■ What were the causes and results of the revolution in Iran?

Vocabulary

delta

ayatollah

theocracy

Taking Notes

Prepare a table comparing the three nations discussed in this section. The table here has been partly filled in to help you get started.

	TURKEY	EGYPT	IRAN
GOVERNMENT	• Multiparty democracy		
ECONOMY	• Expanding agriculture		
CONFLICTS	• Kurds		
OTHER ISSUES			

Main Idea Since World War II, Turkey, Egypt, and Iran have followed different routes to modernization.

Setting the Scene An Iranian religious leader, Ruhollah Khomeini (roo HOH luh koh MAY nee), angrily denounced the government. While the shah lived off the riches of the land, claimed Khomeini, most people lived in misery, especially in the capital city of Tehran:

> "Look at those pits, those holes in the ground where people live, dwellings you reach by going down a hundred steps into the ground, homes people have built out of rush matting or clay so their poor children can have somewhere to live."
> —*Declarations of the Ayatollah Khomeini*

Khomeini's fiery speeches helped spur an Iranian revolution in 1979.

In this section, we will see how three nations pursued modernization. Turkey, Egypt, and Iran are the three most populous nations in the Middle East. While they have faced similar issues, each followed its own course.

Turkey Moves Toward Democracy

In the 1920s, Kemal Atatürk began his campaign to transform Turkey into a modern secular state. At the beginning of the Cold War, the Soviets tried to expand southward into Turkey to gain control of the Bosporus. With American aid, Turkey held off the Soviet threat. Later, Turkey joined NATO and remained an important western ally in the Mediterranean.

Government and Economy Turkey struggled to build a stable government. At first, the military seized power in times of unrest. In time, a multiparty democracy emerged. In recent decades, however, Muslim reformers won support and played a larger role in Turkish politics.

Turkey transformed its economy by expanding agriculture through increased irrigation and by promoting industry. It exported crops and manufactured goods to Europe and hoped to join the European Union. While the EU agreed to build closer ties, it denied Turkey full membership.

As elsewhere, modernization and urbanization brought social turmoil. Istanbul could not provide jobs for millions of newcomers. The jobless and the poor lived in shantytowns, where desperate conditions fed unrest.

Tragic Earthquakes Turkey lies in a region of frequent earthquakes. The nation has the technology to erect buildings that can withstand most tremors. Yet, because of rapid urbanization and poorly enforced building codes, many structures were hastily put up without adequate safeguards.

Poorly built schools, homes, and factories have often collapsed, killing or injuring thousands.

Conflicts For decades, Turkey tried to stamp out the culture of its Kurdish minority. Kurds were forbidden to speak, publish, or broadcast in their own language. Kurdish revolts were fiercely crushed. Although the government finally agreed to abolish laws aimed at erasing Kurdish culture, discrimination against Kurds continued. At the same time, Kurdish separatists kept up their struggle for autonomy.

Turkey also waged a long struggle over Cyprus, an island in the eastern Mediterranean. The roots of the conflict dated back to Ottoman times. In the 1970s, clashes between the Greek majority and Turkish minority led to a Turkish invasion and a partitioning of the island. Today, UN peacekeepers monitor the tense dividing line between Turkish and Greek communities.

Turkey itself was divided politically. On one side stood secular politicians. Along with the military, they were intent on preserving Ataturk's legacy of keeping religion out of government. On the other side stood Islamic-based parties, some of which wanted to revive Sharia. In the early 2000s, voters put an Islamist-based party in power. Its leaders, however, agreed to abide by Turkey's secular constitution. In 2002, Turkey supported the U.S.-led war on terrorism by sending peacekeeping troops to Afghanistan. But in 2003, it denied a U.S. request to base American soldiers in Turkey so they could participate in the war against Iraq.

Earthquake in Turkey
Residents of Istanbul survey the ruins of their apartment building after an earthquake. The disaster sparked a massive international relief and rescue effort.

Theme: Geography and History Why might an earthquake be especially harmful for a developing nation?

Egypt, A Leader in the Arab World

Egypt has roots both in Africa, where it is located, and in the Arab world. Geography has always played a key role in Egypt's destiny. Its location between the Mediterranean and Red seas is strategically important. It shares a long border with Israel and controls the Suez Canal. It is a rich agricultural region. But, since most of Egypt is desert, 99 percent of its people live on four percent of the land, in the fertile Nile Valley.

Nasser In the 1950s, Gamal Abdel Nasser emerged as a towering Arab leader. Like Atatürk, Nasser was a military officer who rose to power after the overthrow of a weak ruler who had allowed foreigners to dominate his country. Nasser set out to modernize Egypt and end western domination. In 1956, he nationalized the Suez Canal, ending British and French control. "The Canal is the property of Egypt," he declared. It "was dug by Egypt's sons and 120,000 of them died while working" on it. Nasser's defiance of the West boosted his prestige in the Arab world.

An outspoken enemy of Israel, Nasser led two wars against the Zionist state. Although defeated each time, he nevertheless remained a symbol of Arab independence and pride.

Economic Development Like leaders of other developing nations, Nasser turned to socialism. He nationalized banks and businesses. He launched land reforms that broke up large estates and distributed the land to peasant farmers. Nasser's economic policies had only limited success.

In the 1960s, with Soviet help, Nasser built the giant Aswan High Dam on the upper Nile. The dam created a huge reservoir, Lake Nasser, as well

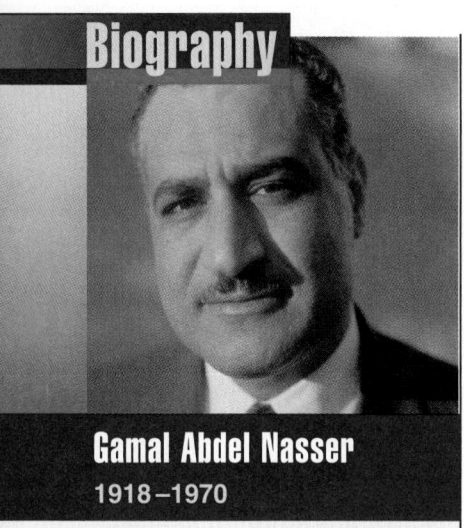

Gamal Abdel Nasser
1918–1970

The military—both as enemy and as ally—played a key role in Gamal Abdel Nasser's life. As a child, the fiery Nasser was beaten and then arrested by British soldiers as he took part in a protest against foreign rule. Later, in high school, he led student demonstrations. During one protest, a British bullet wounded him.

Nasser entered the national military academy in 1937. He felt that the military was the only institution strong enough to free Egypt from British domination and bring social change to Egypt. While in the army, he developed close ties to Anwar Sadat and others who became part of the Free Officers Society. This group staged the coup that later brought Nasser to power.

Theme: Impact of the Individual What role did the military play in Nasser's rise to political power?

as more than two million acres of new farmland. It controlled Nile floodwaters and made year-round irrigation possible. But such benefits had a price. The dam increased the salt content of the Nile, destroyed fish hatcheries in the eastern Mediterranean, and caused erosion of the delta, the triangular area of marshland at the mouth of the river. As Lake Nasser rose, many ancient temples had to be relocated to higher ground.

Sadat After Nasser's death in 1970, the new president, Anwar Sadat, took steps to open Egypt to foreign investment and private business. In foreign affairs, Sadat moved away from the Soviet camp and closer to the United States. In 1979, he became the first Arab leader to make peace with Israel. Although that move angered other Arab states, Sadat promised Egyptians that peace would have economic benefits. It did bring American aid but did not improve life for most Egyptians.

Continuing Issues In 1981, Sadat was assassinated by Muslim extremists. His successor, Hosni Mubarak, reaffirmed the peace with Israel. At the same time, he mended fences with his Arab neighbors. Under Mubarak, Egypt continued to push for peace in the region.

At home, Mubarak faced serious problems. Although industry and farm output expanded, the economy could not keep pace with population growth. Most rural families who streamed into cities like Cairo barely managed to survive in teeming slums. The thousands of families living in the City of the Dead, a Cairo cemetery, symbolized the miseries of urbanization.

Islamic reformers denounced the government's failure to solve economic and social ills. Their model for change, based on Islamic solutions, seemed to offer a vision for a better future. Muslim groups set up schools and offered the poor many other social services, which tight government budgets did not provide. Extremists turned to terrorist attacks, and harsh government crackdowns tended to increase support for the dissenters.

Iran's Ongoing Revolution

Iran is the most ethnically diverse country in the Middle East. About half the people are Persian-speaking Iranians. The rest come from many groups. Unlike their neighbors, most Iranians are Shiite, not Sunni, Muslims.

Nationalism and Oil Because of its vast oil fields, Iran became a focus of British, Soviet, and American interests. In 1945, Shah Muhammad Reza Pahlavi had western backing but faced many opponents at home. Iranian nationalists wanted to end British control of Iran's oil wealth and limit the shah's dictatorial powers.

Led by Muhammad Mosaddiq (MOH sah dehk), nationalists in Iran's parliament voted to nationalize the oil industry. That action set off a long, complex crisis involving the shah, Mosaddiq, Britain, and the United States. In 1953, the United States helped the shah oust Mosaddiq, a move that outraged many Iranians. The United States wanted the anti-communist shah as an ally against the Soviets. For the next 25 years, American weapons and experts helped the shah stay in power.

Reform From Above To strengthen Iran and to quiet unrest, the shah pushed for modernization. He used oil wealth to build roads and industries, redistributed some land to peasants, and extended new rights to women. To separate religion and government, he reduced the power of Islamic scholars, teachers, and legal experts.

The shah's "reform from above" was supported by the army, the westernized elite, and others who prospered under the shah. Opposition came from landowners, merchants, students, and religious leaders. As protests grew, the shah became more repressive. His secret police arrested critics. Some were tortured, executed, or forced into exile.

EXPLORING the HUMAN DRAMA

Naguib Mahfouz: Views of Egypt

Since the 1930s, writer Naguib Mahfouz has woven stories that capture the rich tapestry of twentieth-century Egyptian life. He has long been considered one of the greatest Arabic writers and in 1988 won the Nobel Prize for literature. The following excerpts evoke the sights and sounds of Mahfouz's Egypt.

Naguib Mahfouz

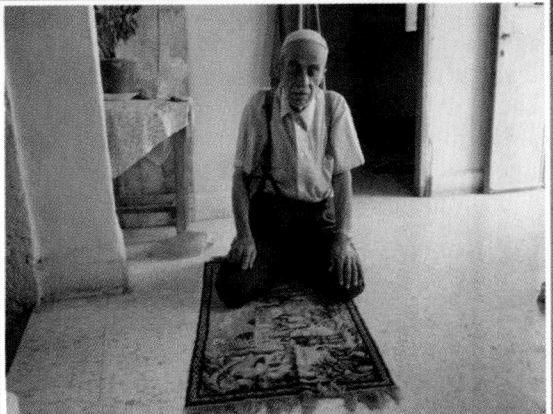

In his 1957 novel *Palace of Desire,* Mahfouz shows how ancient and modern exist side by side:
"The automobile stopped near the foot of the great pyramid. . . . The expanse of land seemed vast and limitless, but the pyramid shot up in the center like a legendary giant. On the far side, beyond the downward-sloping plateau, the city of Cairo was visible with the tops of its trees, a thread of water, and the roofs of its large buildings."

The 1961 novel *The Thief and the Dogs* reflects the continuing traditions of the Egyptian people:
"[He] . . . saw the Sheikh sitting cross-legged on the prayer carpet, absorbed in quiet recitation. The old room had hardly changed. The rush mats had been replaced by new ones, thanks to his disciples, but the Sheikh's sleeping mattress still lay close to the western wall. . . . The other walls of the room were half-covered with rows of books on shelves. The odor of incense lingered."

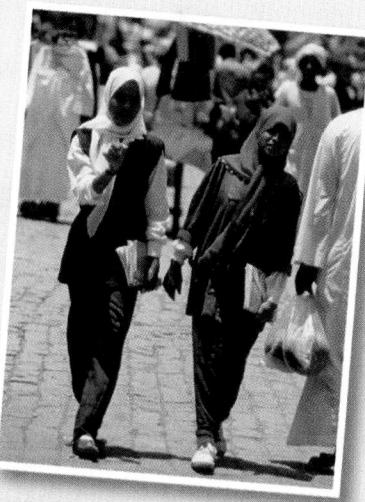

In *Miramar,* written in 1967, two characters discuss the changing lives of Egyptian women:
"'What about this decision to study? What made you think of it?'
  'All girls go to school now. The streets are full of them.'
  'But you never thought of it before.'
  'It's your fault,' she smiled. 'You said . . . there was no reason why they should read and write while I stayed illiterate.' . . .
  'When I learn to read and write,' she said thoughtfully, 'I'll try and learn some profession. Like dressmaking, perhaps.'"

Portfolio Assessment

Conduct research to find out more about twentieth-century Arabic literature. Then, prepare a class presentation on the significance of an important Arabic writer. Summarize a book or story that illustrates the writer's style and themes.

Leader of the Iranian Revolution
In 1979, the Ayatollah Khomeini returned to Iran after a 15-year exile to direct an Islamic revolution. He was almost 80 years old at the time.

Theme: Impact of the Individual Why was Khomeini exiled from Iran?

Islamic Revolution In the 1970s, the shah's foes rallied behind the exiled Ayatollah Ruhollah Khomeini. Ayatollah is a title given to learned Shiite legal experts. He condemned western influences and accused the shah of violating Islamic law. In 1979, massive unrest forced the shah to flee. As Khomeini returned to Iran, his supporters proclaimed an Islamic republic based on the Quran and Sharia. They set up a theocracy, or government ruled by religious leaders.

Revolutionaries attacked corruption. They replaced secular courts with religious ones, abolished the shah's laws favoring women's rights, and banned western books, music, and movies. At first, the new government allowed some open discussion. Before long, though, the revolutionaries suppressed opponents, just as the shah had.

Foreign Policy The new leaders bitterly denounced the West. When the shah was allowed into the United States for medical treatment, angry revolutionaries seized the American embassy in Tehran and held 52 hostages for over a year. Iran also tried to export its revolution. It urged Muslims in countries like Egypt and Turkey to overthrow secular governments. Although the revolution seemed to strengthen the Islamic revival, it was not reproduced in other Muslim lands.

In 1980, as you will read, Iraq took advantage of the turmoil to invade Iran. In Iran, the war helped rally support for the new government, but the eight-year ordeal took a huge economic and human toll.

Moderate Voices The end of the Iran-Iraq War and Khomeini's death in 1989 helped moderate voices resurface. Iran rebuilt its economy. Industries returned to producing consumer goods, but low oil prices in the 1990s slowed economic growth. As moderates gained positions in government, they restored some political and social freedoms. Conservative clerics, however, rejected most changes. In the early 2000s, student protests in favor of reform revealed growing opposition to the hardliners.

Relations with the West gradually improved but suffered a setback in 2002 after U.S. President George Bush grouped Iran with Iraq and North Korea as part of an "axis of evil." Also, there was growing international concern that Iran might try to develop nuclear weapons.

Impact The revolution changed Iran's foreign policy and some forms of public behavior. Although some reforms helped rural people, the revolution did not improve life greatly for most Iranians. Corruption resurfaced. Poverty, unemployment, and other problems remained. More than two decades after Iran's revolution, Iranians still debated how to achieve the goal of modernization within an Islamic republic.

SECTION 3 Assessment

Recall

1. **Identify: (a)** Gamal Abdel Nasser, **(b)** Aswan High Dam, **(c)** Anwar Sadat, **(d)** Muhammad Mosaddiq, **(e)** Ruhollah Khomeini.
2. **Define: (a)** delta, **(b)** ayatollah, **(c)** theocracy.

Comprehension

3. **(a)** What kind of government did Turkey build? **(b)** Describe one challenge Turkey faced.
4. What steps did Egypt take toward modernization?

5. **(a)** Why did discontent spread in Iran under the shah? **(b)** Describe two effects of the Iranian revolution.

Critical Thinking and Writing

6. **Making Inferences** Why do you think Turkey would want to force its Kurdish citizens to abandon their language and culture?
7. **Recognizing Points of View (a)** Who might consider the Iranian revolution a success? Why? **(b)** Who might criticize the revolution? Why?

Use the Internet to find more information about Turkey, Egypt, or Iran. Then, create a statistical profile of that nation. Include information about population, ethnic and religious groups, literacy rate, or the economy. For help with this activity, use **Web Code mkd-3598.**

The Middle East and the World

Reading Focus

- How did the Cold War increase tensions in the Middle East?

- Why has the Arab-Israeli conflict been difficult to resolve?

- Why did conflicts arise in Lebanon and the Persian Gulf?

Vocabulary

client state

intifada

militia

no-fly zone

Taking Notes

Copy this time line. As you read, fill in the time line with important events from the section. Some entries have been included to help you get started.

1960	1967	1980	2000
	Third Arab-Israeli war	Iraq invades Iran	

Main Idea — The Middle East has been the focus of conflicts that have had an impact far beyond the region.

Setting the Scene

To David Ben-Gurion, Israel's first prime minister, the birth of modern Israel in 1948 was the fulfillment of God's promise to the ancient Israelites. He quoted Scripture:

> "The land whereto we have returned to inherit it, it is the inheritance of our fathers and within it no stranger has part or parcel. . . . We have taken unto us our fathers' inheritance."
> —First Book of Maccabees

But to the Arabs then living on the land called Palestine, the creation of Israel was an illegal "invasion." The land, they felt, was rightfully theirs:

> "Palestine is the homeland of the Arab Palestinian people. It is an indivisible part of the Arab homeland, and the Palestinian people are an integral part of the Arab nation."
> —The Palestinian National Charter, Article 1

These conflicting claims to the same land touched off repeated violence. The Arab-Israeli struggle was one of many issues that focused worldwide attention on the Middle East.

The Cold War and After

Today, as in the past, the Middle East is a strategic region. It commands vital oil resources as well as key waterways such as the Bosporus, the Suez Canal, and the Persian Gulf. During the Cold War, both the United States and the Soviet Union were anxious to have access to the oil and the waterways. Superpower rivalries had a far-reaching impact on the region.

Superpower Rivalries In their global rivalry, each of the superpowers tried to line up allies in the Middle East. The United States sent aid to stop a communist threat to Turkey in 1947. For years, it supported the strongly anti-communist shah of Iran despite his repressive actions.

In Egypt, Nasser saw himself as a leader of the nonaligned movement. Still, the Soviets showered aid on Egypt during the Nasser years. Iraq, Syria, and Libya also became Soviet client states, dependent on the support of a stronger power. All of these Arab nations mistrusted their former colonial rulers in the West and condemned western support for Israel.

Weapons Pile Up Each superpower sold arms to its allies in the region. In the Arab-Israeli conflict, the United States helped Israel, while the Soviet

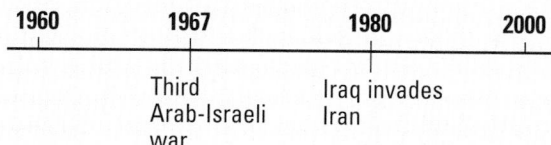

Israel's Citizen Army

At the age of 18, most young men and women in Israel are drafted for military service. The men spend three grueling years training as infantry soldiers, elite paratroopers, or tank soldiers. They must then serve one month a year in the reserves for some 30 years.

After independence, women did not serve in combat. Now, they serve in both support and combat support roles. Since 1995, women can also serve as paramilitary border police in combat positions, and a few have become pilots.

Theme: Political and Social Systems Why do you think Israel introduced such an extensive military draft?

A Palestinian Refugee Camp

A few months before the intifada began, a young Israeli writer visited a refugee camp on the West Bank:

"Twelve thousand Palestinians live here in one of the highest population densities in the world; the houses are piled together, and the house of every extended family branches out in ugly cement growths, rooms and niches, rusty iron beams spread throughout as sinews, jutting like disconnected fingers.

   In Deheisha, drinking water comes from wells. The only running water is the rainwater and the sewage flowing down the paths between the houses. . . .

   Beside each house—a yard. They are small, fenced in with corrugated aluminum, and very clean. A large [jar] filled with springwater and covered with cloth stands in each yard. But every person here will tell you without hesitation that the water from the spring of his home village was sweeter."

—David Grossman,
The Yellow Wind

Skills Assessment

Primary Source Do you think the author feels sympathetic toward the Palestinian refugees? Explain.

Union gave aid to the Arabs. After each Arab-Israeli war, the superpowers rearmed their allies with expensive new weapons. Other nations also benefited from lavish arms sales, including such valued American allies as oil-rich Saudi Arabia.

During and after the Cold War, the development of weapons of mass destruction in the Middle East became a global concern. International military experts believed that Israel was developing nuclear weapons to defend itself against hostile Arab neighbors. Iraq under Saddam Hussein was also thought to be building a nuclear capability, as well as stockpiling chemical and biological weapons. Iraq used some of its poison gas supplies to suppress a Kurdish liberation movement within its own borders.

The Arab-Israeli Conflict

After the 1948 war, Israel and its Arab neighbors fought again in 1956, 1967, and 1973. In these conflicts, Israel defeated Arab attacks and gained territory. In between the wars, Israel faced guerrilla warfare and terrorist activity. Despite the long conflict, the UN, the United States, and others kept pushing for peace negotiations.

The Occupied Territories   In the 1967 war, Israeli forces won the Golan Heights from Syria, East Jerusalem and the West Bank from Jordan, and the Gaza Strip and Sinai Peninsula from Egypt. In 1973, Arabs attacked Israel but failed to regain these occupied territories.

Israel refused to give up the territories until Arab nations recognized Israel's right to exist. Later, Israel annexed East Jerusalem and the Golan Heights. The government helped Jewish settlers build homes in the occupied territories, displacing more Palestinian Arabs.

Palestinian Resistance The number of Palestinians in refugee camps had grown since 1948. Many supported the Palestine Liberation Organization (PLO), headed by Yasir Arafat. Its stated goal was the destruction of Israel, which the PLO claimed had no right to exist on the land they called Palestine.

For years, the PLO waged guerrilla warfare against Israelis at home and abroad. Bombings, airplane hijackings, and the massacre of Israeli athletes at the 1972 Olympic games brought PLO demands to the attention of the world. At the same time, though, such attacks stiffened Israel's resolve not to negotiate with the PLO.

In the late 1980s and again in the early 2000s, many young Palestinians mounted intifadas, or uprisings, against Israeli occupation. Demanding a Palestinian homeland, they broke curfew laws and stoned Israeli troops. Gunmen fired on Israeli soldiers and civilians. Meanwhile, Palestinian suicide bombers blew up buses, stores, and clubs inside Israel, killing hundreds of civilians.

Israel responded to the attacks with force. Thousands of Palestinians were injured or killed in bloody street fights. Israeli troops sealed off Palestinian towns and villages, crippling the fragile Palestinian economy and increasing Palestinian bitterness.

Peace Efforts Despite the fighting, some steps toward peace were taken. As you have read, Israel returned the Sinai Peninsula to Egypt. In the early 1990s, Jordan and Israel reached a peace agreement. However, talks between Israel and Syria stalled over the issue of the Golan Heights.

A further breakthrough occurred in 1993 after Israel and the PLO held direct talks for the first time. Arafat and Israeli Prime Minister Yitzhak Rabin signed the Oslo Accord. It gave Palestinians in Gaza and the West Bank limited self-rule under an independent Palestinian Authority headed by Arafat. Urged by the United States, the two sides made more agreements. While Israel extended Palestinian self-rule, the Palestinian Authority recognized Israel's right to exist and promised to end terrorism against Israel.

Discontent ran high on both sides. Many Palestinians rejected the accords because they did not create an independent Palestinian state. Some Israelis were willing to return occupied territory, but others wanted to keep and settle on the lands that Israel had won.

Violence continued. Radical groups like Hamas and Hizbullah kept up their terrorist attacks, vowing to continue until Israel was destroyed. Israel condemned the new Palestinian Authority for failing to prevent the attacks. A Jewish student who opposed the peace policy assassinated Prime Minister Rabin. As suicide bombings and other attacks increased, more Israelis came to distrust and fear their Arab neighbors.

Peace efforts stalled. After Prime Minister Ariel Sharon took office in Israel, the violence escalated. Under intense pressure to reform the Palestinian Authority, Yasir Arafat agreed to the election of Mahmoud Abbas as prime minister in 2003. The United States pushed to restart peace talks. Still, the level of distrust on both sides remained high. Israelis were still reeling from recent suicide bombings, while Palestinians were bitter about the deaths and destruction caused by Israeli tanks and troops.

Divisive Issues Several issues blocked a peace settlement. Many Palestinians whose families had fled their homes during the Arab-Israeli wars wanted the right to return to the land where their families had lived. But Israelis opposed the return of large numbers of Palestinians.

Many Israelis wanted any peace settlement to guarantee the right of Israeli settlers to remain in the occupied territories. But Palestinians rejected the idea of Israeli settlements scattered across a future Palestinian state.

Jerusalem, sacred to Muslims, Jews, and Christians, was another source of disagreement. Palestinians called for Muslims to control Islamic holy places in the city and for East Jerusalem to become the capital of a future Palestinian nation. Many Israelis insisted that the city remain undivided as the capital of Israel. As long as both sides held such different views, peace remained hard to achieve.

Civil War in Lebanon

After winning independence, Lebanon became a thriving center of international commerce. People of diverse ethnic and religious groups lived mostly in harmony. But the surface prosperity masked deep problems.

Growing Tensions The government depended on a delicate balance among Maronites (a Christian sect), Sunni and Shiite Muslims, Druze (a sect derived from Islam), and others. Maronites held the most power, but local bosses controlled their own districts backed by private armies.

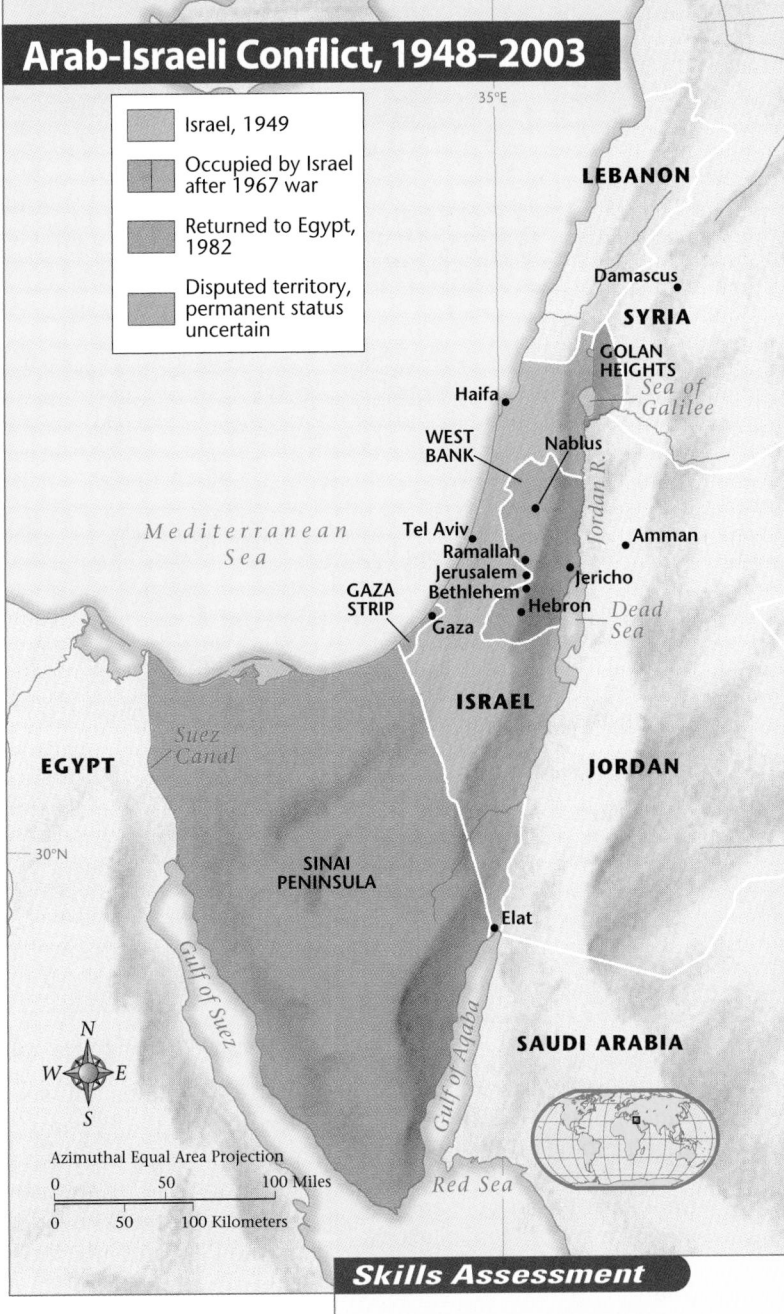

Arab-Israeli Conflict, 1948–2003

Israel, 1949

Occupied by Israel after 1967 war

Returned to Egypt, 1982

Disputed territory, permanent status uncertain

35°E

LEBANON

Damascus

SYRIA

GOLAN HEIGHTS

Haifa

Sea of Galilee

WEST BANK

Nablus

Mediterranean Sea

Tel Aviv

Ramallah

Jerusalem

Bethlehem

GAZA STRIP

Hebron

Dead Sea

Gaza

Amman

Jericho

ISRAEL

JORDAN

EGYPT

Suez Canal

30°N

SINAI PENINSULA

Elat

Gulf of Suez

Gulf of Aqaba

SAUDI ARABIA

N
W   E
S

Azimuthal Equal Area Projection

0   50   100 Miles

0   50   100 Kilometers

Red Sea

Skills Assessment

Geography Israel and its Arab neighbors have fought four wars since 1948.

1. **Location** On the map, locate (a) Israel, (b) Egypt, (c) West Bank, (d) Gaza Strip, (e) Sinai Peninsula, (f) Jerusalem.
2. **Region** What areas did Israel gain as a result of the 1967 war?
3. **Critical Thinking Making Inferences** Why would cities like Hebron and Jericho be likely points of conflict?

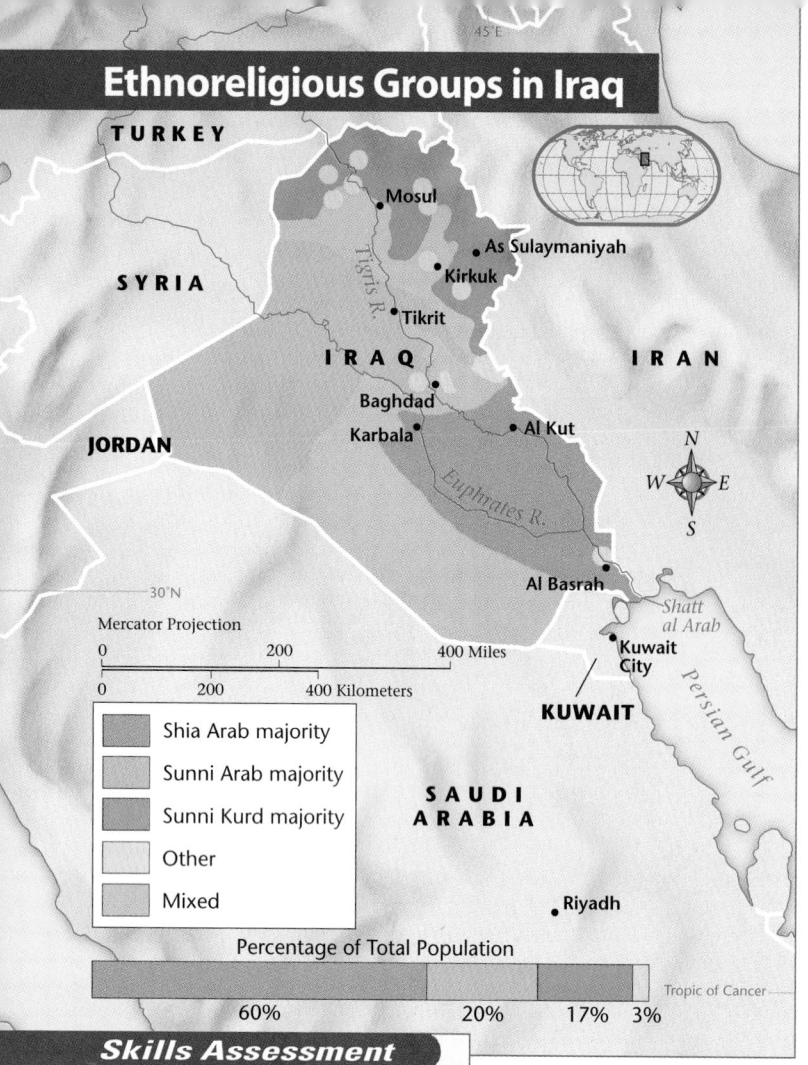

Ethnoreligious Groups in Iraq

TURKEY

Mosul

As Sulaymaniyah

Kirkuk

Tikrit

SYRIA

Tigris R.

I R A Q

I R A N

Baghdad

Karbala

Al Kut

JORDAN

Euphrates R.

30°N

Al Basrah

Shatt al Arab

Mercator Projection

0   200   400 Miles

0   200   400 Kilometers

Kuwait City

KUWAIT

Persian Gulf

- Shia Arab majority
- Sunni Arab majority
- Sunni Kurd majority
- Other
- Mixed

SAUDI ARABIA

Riyadh

Percentage of Total Population

60%   20%   17% 3%

Tropic of Cancer

Skills Assessment

Geography Sunni Arabs are only about 20 percent of the Iraqi population, but they have dominated the country for decades. The Kurds and Shi'ites suffered political injustice and violence atrocities under Saddam Hussein's rule.

1. **Location** On the map, locate the so-called "Sunni Triangle" where Sunnis are a majority of the population.
2. **Place** Which ethnoreligious group is the majority group in Iraq?
3. **Critical Thinking Drawing Conclusions** Do you think there will be continuing violence in Iraq? Explain.

Many Palestinian refugees entered Lebanon from Israeli-occupied lands, straining resources. In time, the Muslim population came to outnumber Christians and stirred unrest. Tensions rose further as PLO guerrillas among the refugees crossed the border to attack Israelis.

Civil War By 1975, Lebanon plunged into a civil war. Christian and Muslim militias, or bands of citizen soldiers, battled across the land. Israel invaded southern Lebanon to destroy PLO bases. Syria occupied eastern Lebanon.

Massacres were committed by all sides. A UN peacekeeping force tried to restore order, but it withdrew after hundreds of French and American peacekeepers were killed by suicide bombers.

Rebuilding By 1990, Lebanese leaders finally restored order and the PLO was forced out of southern Lebanon. Beirut, the ruined capital, was slowly rebuilt. By the early 2000s, Beirut was becoming, as it had once been, a leading economic center of the Middle East.

Despite economic growth, cultural and religious divisions remained. Both Syria and Israel each continued to take an active role in its own interests. The future of Lebanon seemed to depend on the prospects for peace among its more powerful neighbors.

Three Wars in the Persian Gulf

Border disputes, oil wealth, foreign intervention, and ambitious rulers fed tensions in the Persian Gulf region. In 1980, Iraq's dictator, Saddam Hussein, sent his forces into Iran to seize a disputed border region.

Iraq used its superior weapons and poison gas to stop waves of Iranian soldiers. After both sides attacked foreign oil tankers and offshore oil fields in the Persian Gulf, the United States sent naval forces to protect shipping lanes in the region. The war dragged on for eight years, ending in a stalemate. For both Iran and Iraq, the human and economic toll was enormous.

The 1991 Gulf War In 1990, Iraqi troops invaded the oil-rich nation of Kuwait. Saddam Hussein argued that historically the region was part of Iraq. Control of Kuwait would give Iraq one of the world's largest oil-producing areas. Iraq would also gain increased access to the Persian Gulf.

The United States saw the invasion as a threat to its ally, Saudi Arabia, as well as to oil flow from the Persian Gulf. President George H. Bush therefore put together a coalition of American, European, and Arab powers to drive Iraqi forces out of Kuwait. In the 1991 Gulf War, American missiles and bombers destroyed targets in Iraq. Then, under the UN banner, coalition forces liberated Kuwait.

Saddam Remains Defiant Despite defeat, Saddam Hussein remained in power in Iraq. He brutally crushed revolts by Shiite Muslims in the south. He also attacked Kurdish rebels in the north, at times with chemical weapons. Individuals who opposed him were often jailed, tortured, or executed.

The UN took action. To protect the Shiites and Kurds, the UN set up no-fly zones, areas over which Iraqi aircraft were not allowed to fly. The UN also banned Iraq from building weapons of mass destruction. To stop Saddam from using oil profits to build weapons, the UN imposed economic sanctions.

During the 1990s, Iraq frequently violated the no-fly zones and refused to comply with UN weapons inspectors in their search for weapons of mass destruction. In response, the U.S. and Britain launched occasional air strikes against Iraqi military targets. Finally, under intense UN pressure, Saddam allowed weapons inspectors to return in 2002.

The Third Gulf War But by 2003, the United States and Britain were convinced that Saddam Hussein had weapons of mass destruction which he might use. American President George W. Bush also accused Saddam of supporting terrorists. Without UN backing, President Bush and British Prime Minister Tony Blair decided to invade Iraq. The U.S.-led coalition quickly toppled Saddam Hussein and occupied Iraq. In December 2003, American troops captured Saddam.

After large-scale fighting ended, American and British soldiers continued to face guerrilla resistance and terrorism. Many Iraqis welcomed the end of Saddam's vicious regime but resented foreign occupation. Countries from around the world donated money and small peacekeeping forces to help restore peace and order. The peacekeeping forces planned to use revenues from Iraq's rich oil resources to rebuild the country.

Rebuilding Iraq The peacekeeping forces and Iraqi people faced great difficulties as they tried to build a new Iraqi government. Most Iraqis had known only dictatorship. Another problem was ethnic and religious divisions. Central Iraq, home to Arab Sunni Muslims, had been Saddam Hussein's power base. Kurds in the north and Arab Shiite Muslims in the south had suffered under Saddam Hussein. The challenge was to develop a system in which these groups could share power and work together.

Uncertainties Continue

The Middle East remained a focus of many conflicting forces. Nationalist conflicts, clashes between religious and secular goals, and competition for limited water resources were among the issues that might spark future violence. The region's vast oil resources meant that outside powers would continue to intervene.

Terrorism, too, posed challenges for the region, especially after the 2001 al-Qaida attacks on the United States. The United States pressed nations in the Middle East to move more strongly against terrorist groups.

Go Online PHSchool.com

Go to **United We Stand** for updated articles and lessons to guide your classroom discussion of September 11 and beyond. For help with this activity, use **Web Code mkd-4444.**

SECTION 4 Assessment

Recall

1. **Identify: (a)** PLO, **(b)** Yasir Arafat, **(c)** Yitzhak Rabin, **(d)** Palestinian Authority, **(e)** Ariel Sharon, **(f)** Saddam Hussein.
2. **Define: (a)** client state, **(b)** intifada, **(c)** militia, **(d)** no-fly zone.

Comprehension

3. How did the Cold War affect the Middle East?
4. **(a)** Why were the occupied territories a source of conflict? **(b)** What steps were taken toward peace?

5. Describe one cause of each of the following: **(a)** the civil war in Lebanon, **(b)** the Iran-Iraq war, **(c)** the 2003 war in Iraq.

Critical Thinking and Writing

6. **Making Decisions** If you had been an Israeli leader in the late 1980s, what response to the intifada would you have favored? Explain your reasons.
7. **Solving Problems** If you were organizing a Middle East peace conference, whom would you invite and what issues would you put on the table?

Activity

Drawing a Political Cartoon Draw a cartoon about the role of oil in fueling tensions in the Persian Gulf. Take the viewpoint of an Iraqi, a Kuwaiti, a Saudi, or an outside observer. Identify the time period of your cartoon.

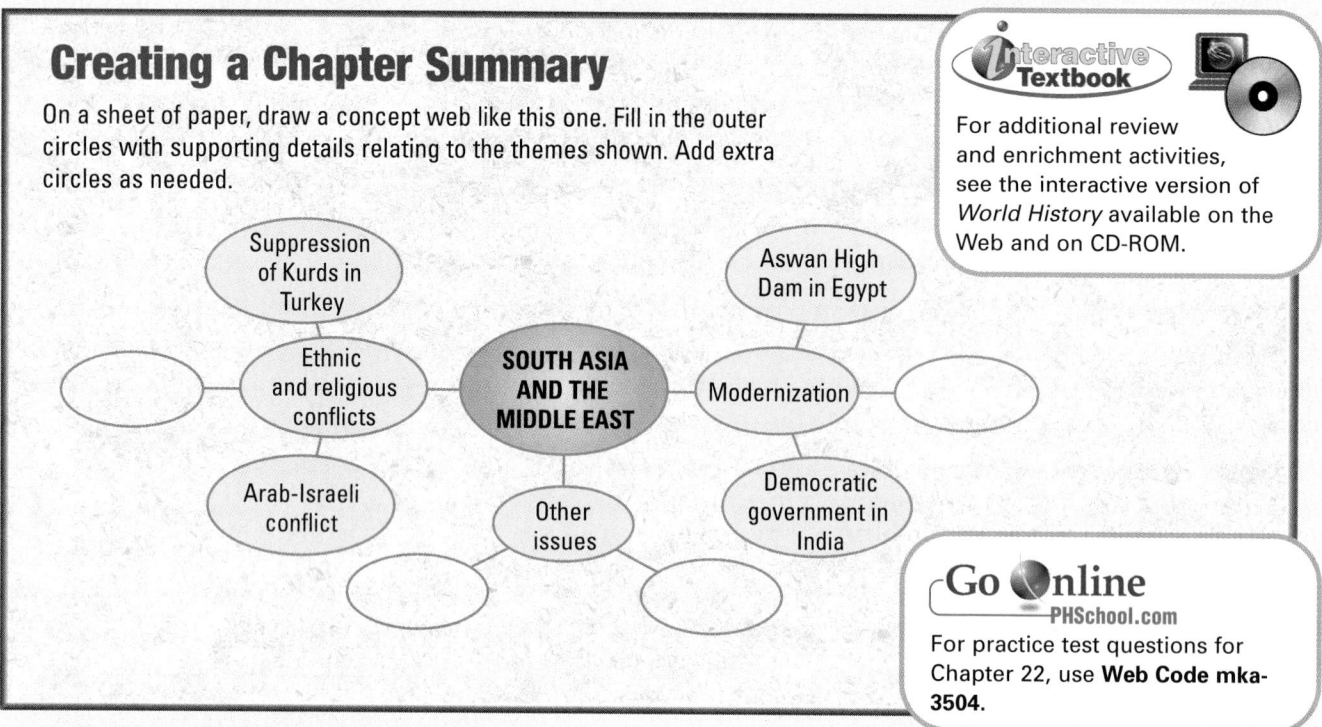

Creating a Chapter Summary

On a sheet of paper, draw a concept web like this one. Fill in the outer circles with supporting details relating to the themes shown. Add extra circles as needed.

Interactive Textbook

For additional review and enrichment activities, see the interactive version of *World History* available on the Web and on CD-ROM.

Go Online
PHSchool.com
For practice test questions for Chapter 22, use **Web Code mka-3504**.

Building Vocabulary

(a) Classify each of the chapter vocabulary words listed below under *one* of the following themes: Political and Social Systems; Economics and Technology; Religions and Value Systems. (b) Choose *one* word in each category and write a sentence explaining how that word relates to the theme.

1. **federal system**
2. **harijan**
3. **deforestation**
4. **debt service**
5. **kibbutz**
6. **desalinization**
7. **hejab**
8. **ayatollah**
9. **theocracy**
10. **intifada**

Recalling Key Facts

11. What economic policies did Nehru pursue in India?
12. How was Bangladesh created?
13. Why did Arab nations oppose the creation of Israel?
14. Why did Islamic reformers oppose westernization?
15. Why did Nasser nationalize the Suez Canal?
16. What were the results of the three wars in the Persian Gulf?

Critical Thinking and Writing

17. **Linking Past and Present** Give three examples of how the legacy of imperialism has influenced recent developments in South Asia and the Middle East.

18. **Comparing** (a) How is India's attempt to reform the caste system similar to the civil rights movement in the United States? (b) How is it different?

19. **Connecting to Geography** (a) What region do historians mean when they refer to the Middle East? (b) Why do some people prefer to use the term *Southwest Asia*? (c) Describe three ways that geographic features have influenced recent events in the region.

20. **Identifying Alternatives** Developing nations have often alternated between periods of military and civilian rule. (a) Identify two nations of South Asia or the Middle East that have followed this pattern. (b) What are the benefits and dangers of each alternative?

21. **Asking Questions** Suppose that you are going to interview the current leaders of Israel and the Palestinian Authority. Write a list of five questions to ask them about their plans for achieving lasting peace.

Zade Teherani was a Shiite preacher and scholar in Iran. In 1986, he was interviewed by a British journalist. Here, Teherani describes how he and other Muslim clergy were arrested by the shah's secret police. Read the passage, then answer the questions that follow.

> "I was arrested in August 1978 with several other members of the clergy. We were told to take off our clerical robes, but we refused. We said to them that only those who had given us our clothes, at the theological [religious] school, could take them away from us. They tried to make us sign a paper saying that we would never preach again. And they asked us questions continually, just as you are doing. But they let us go in the end. It was nothing more than intimidation. They wouldn't have dared to do anything serious to us. Things were so tense in Iran then that it would have caused a real upheaval."
>
> —Zade Teherani, quoted in *Inside Iran* (Simpson)

22. **(a)** Who ruled Iran at the time that Teherani was arrested? **(b)** Who ruled Iran at the time that he gave this interview? **(c)** What significant event occurred between these two dates?

23. **(a)** What did the secret police order Teherani and the other clergy to do? **(b)** How did the clergy respond?

24. How would you describe the attitude shown by the clergy toward the secret police?

25. According to Teherani, why were the prisoners released?

26. Based on what you have read, why would the shah's secret police want to arrest these prisoners?

27. Do you think Teherani was probably a supporter of the Ayatollah Khomeini? Explain.

28. **(a)** What seems to be Teherani's mood as he looks back at past events? **(b)** How might his mood be different if this interview had taken place in 1978?

Skills Tip

Interviews are part of oral history, or a spoken record of events. When you read an interview, make sure that you understand the relationship of the speaker to the events he or she is describing.

This photograph shows a young worker in an Indian textile factory. Look at the photograph and answer the following questions:

29. How would you describe **(a)** the child, **(b)** his surroundings? Identify at least two specific details relating to each.

30. **(a)** How could a human rights activist make use of this photograph? **(b)** How might the factory owner respond?

31. Compare this picture with what you have seen and read about the early Industrial Revolution in Britain. What similarities can you recognize?

Go Online
PHSchool.com

Use the Internet to research modern-day life in one of the countries of South Asia or the Middle East. Then, choose one country as the site of a "virtual vacation." Write a brochure describing sites to visit, as well as the climate and natural features. For help with this activity, use **Web Code mkd-3505.**

Africa
1945–Present

Chapter Preview

1 Achieving Independence
2 Programs for Development
3 Three Nations: A Closer Look
4 Struggles in Southern Africa

1956

The Sudan gains independence from Britain. Here, the changing of the flags symbolizes the transfer of power.

1957

Ghana becomes the first African nation south of the Sahara to free itself from colonial rule. This arch commemorates Ghanaian independence.

1961

Tanzania gains independence.

CHAPTER EVENTS

1940   1955   1970

GLOBAL EVENTS

1947 India wins independence.

1957 The European Community is formed.

1966 Mao Zedong announces the Cultural Revolution in China.

African Independence

In the decades after World War II, African nationalist movements gained strength. More than 50 new nations emerged.

**Map labels:**

TUNISIA 1956
MOROCCO 1956
Mediterranean Sea
ALGERIA 1962
LIBYA 1951
EGYPT 1922
WESTERN SAHARA
Tropic of Cancer
Red Sea
MAURITANIA 1960
MALI 1960
NIGER 1960
CHAD 1960
SUDAN 1956
ERITREA 1993
SENEGAL 1960
DJIBOUTI 1977
THE GAMBIA 1965
BURKINA FASO 1960
ETHIOPIA ~1000
GUINEA 1958
GUINEA-BISSAU 1974
GHANA 1957
BENIN 1960
NIGERIA 1960
CENTRAL AFRICAN REPUBLIC 1960
CÔTE D'IVOIRE 1960
SIERRA LEONE 1961
LIBERIA 1847
TOGO 1960
CAMEROON 1960
SOMALIA 1960
ATLANTIC OCEAN
15°W
0°
EQUATORIAL GUINEA 1968
DEMOCRATIC REPUBLIC OF CONGO 1960
UGANDA 1962
KENYA 1963
0° Equator
SÃO TOMÉ AND PRÍNCIPE 1975
GABON 1960
CONGO 1960
RWANDA 1962
CABINDA (TO ANGOLA)
BURUNDI 1962
TANZANIA 1961
INDIAN OCEAN
ANGOLA 1975
MALAWI 1964
ZAMBIA 1964
MOZAMBIQUE 1975
15°S
NAMIBIA 1990
ZIMBABWE 1980
MADAGASCAR 1960
Tropic of Capricorn
BOTSWANA 1966
SWAZILAND 1968
30°S
SOUTH AFRICA 1910
LESOTHO 1966
15°E
30°E
45°E
30°N

N W E S

Legend:
- Independent nations by 1945
- Gained independence, 1945–1959
- Gained independence since 1959
- Status in dispute
- ✦ Sites of civil wars and ethnic clashes, 1990s and 2000s

Mercator Projection

0   400   800 Miles

0   400   800 Kilometers

1980s
Zimbabwe begins land and economic reforms.

1985

1989 The Berlin Wall falls.

1994
South Africa holds its first all-race elections and elects Nelson Mandela (right) as president. With Mandela is F. W. de Klerk, the previous president of South Africa.

2000

2003
After more than 10 years of fighting, with 3 million dead, UN peacekeepers try to restore peace in central Africa.

2015

Go Online PHSchool.com

To learn about recent developments in Africa, use **Web Code** mkc-3607.

Achieving Independence

Reading Focus

- How did colonialism contribute to a growing spirit of nationalism?

- What routes to freedom did Ghana, Kenya, and Algeria follow?

- How have international organizations affected Africa?

Taking Notes

On a sheet of paper, create a time line to show important events in the struggle for African independence. Use the time line shown here to help you get started.

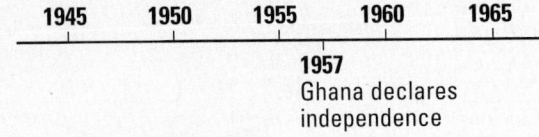

1945   1950   1955   1960   1965

1957
Ghana declares
independence

Main Idea As many African nations won independence in the 1950s and 1960s, they held great hopes and faced great challenges.

Setting the Scene
"Kenya regained her *Uhuru* [freedom] from the British on 12 December 1963," writes Ngugi wa Thiong'o in a novel about Kenya's struggle for independence. One scene describes the moment of independence in Nairobi, Kenya's capital:

"A minute before midnight, lights were put out at the Nairobi stadium. . . . In the dark, the Union Jack [British flag] was quickly lowered. When next the lights came on the new Kenya flag was flying and fluttering, and waving in the air."
—Ngugi wa Thiong'o, *A Grain of Wheat*

In Nairobi and in villages throughout Kenya, bands played the new national anthem and crowds cheered the good news. During the 1950s and 1960s, dozens of new nations emerged in Africa. As people across the continent celebrated their newfound freedom, they also faced many challenges.

The Colonial Legacy

Scholars trace many of Africa's recent problems to the colonial experience. Western imperialism had a complex and contradictory impact on Africa. Some changes brought real gains. Others had a destructive effect on African life that is felt down to the present.

Economics In their colonies, Europeans introduced new crops, technologies, and cash economies. They built roads, railroads, harbors, and cities. The new forms of transportation were meant to make the colonies profitable by linking plantations and mines to ports. Exporting raw materials and cash crops helped pay for European rule. Most Africans, who were subsistence farmers, gained little or nothing from these facilities.

After liberation, the pattern of economic dependence continued. To pay for expensive development projects, African nations exported minerals and agricultural goods to the industrial world. But most profits flowed out of Africa because the new nations had to buy expensive manufactured goods and technology from the West. Also, many large farms and mines were still owned by westerners.

Politics During the colonial period, Europeans undermined Africa's traditional political systems. Even when they left African rulers in place, they told Africans how to govern. In other cases, Europeans denied educated Africans top jobs in colonial governments.

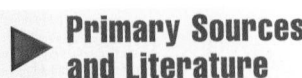

Primary Sources and Literature

See "Chinua Achebe: Things Fall Apart" in the Reference Section at the back of this book.

At independence, colonial powers expected that African leaders would almost immediately transform authoritarian colonies into democratic nations. These powers seemed to forget that many western nations themselves had achieved democracy only after centuries of turmoil—and with the help of strong industrial economies.

Health Care and Education Colonial governments had an impact on health care and education in Africa. Western doctors developed vaccines for yellow fever and smallpox, and helped reduce deaths from malaria. These governments usually did not emphasize general health care, however. Medical attention was more likely to be provided by missionary groups.

By the 1950s, in response to nationalist demands, colonial rulers built more hospitals and schools. They emphasized elementary education, but established relatively few secondary schools and only a handful of universities. With limited access to education, people in liberated colonies faced additional challenges in the modern world.

National Borders At independence, African nations inherited borders drawn by colonial powers. These borders often caused immense problems. Europeans had staked out colonies according to their own political and economic interests, regardless of who lived in a particular region. Colonies therefore included people from diverse ethnic groups and with different—even conflicting—interests. As a result, many new nations were made up of hostile groups forced to live together in the same country. Some borders also split people of the same ethnic group into two separate nations. Rather than draw new borders, leaders of the new nations worked to build a sense of unity where none existed.

A Growing Spirit of Nationalism

In 1945, four European powers—Britain, France, Belgium, and Portugal—controlled almost all of the African continent. Only Egypt, Ethiopia, Liberia, and white-ruled South Africa were independent nations. The rising tide of nationalism, however, was sweeping over European colonial empires. Around the world, liberation would follow this tide.

Impact of World War II World War II sharpened the edges of nationalist movements in Africa. Early Japanese victories in Asia shattered the West's reputation as an unbeatable force. Also, African troops provided support for Allied armies in Africa, the Middle East, and other parts of the world. When they returned to find discrimination and second-class citizenship at home, these ex-soldiers became easy recruits for growing nationalist movements. Nationalists also found support among workers in wartime defense industries. Often, strikes by workers over issues such as pay escalated into demands for freedom.

The Global Setting After the war, most people in Europe had had their fill of fighting. Many were reluctant to return to combat over their overseas colonies. Britain and France, the largest imperialist powers, were faced with growing nationalist demands. In response, they adopted new policies toward their African colonies. Both countries introduced political reforms that would lead to gradual independence. Colonial powers soon learned, however, that they could dictate neither the terms nor the pace of change.

African Soldiers
During World War II, African troops helped Allied armies around the world. Here, members of the Nyasaland Battalion of the King's African Rifles prepare for action.

Theme: Political and Social Systems How did wartime experiences contribute to the growth of nationalist movements?

Ghana Wins Independence

On March 6, 1957, Ghana became the first African nation south of the Sahara to win independence. The following is an eyewitness account of the events celebrating the birth of the new nation.

Kwame Nkrumah (center), prime minister and later president of Ghana, addresses the public during Ghana's independence celebration.

"Nation of Ghana Is Born In Africa
Accra, Ghana, Wednesday, March 6, 1957—A new . . . nation was born at midnight.

As the British flag was lowered from the staff of the Legislative Assembly here and the new red, green and gold flag bearing a star rose in its place, the British colony known as the Gold Coast ceased to exist and the sovereign state of Ghana became the ninth member of the Commonwealth [of Nations].

Prime Minister Kwame Nkrumah had told the final session of the colony's Legislative Assembly a few minutes earlier that the 'chains of imperialism and colonialism which have hitherto bound us to Britain' were left behind as Ghana redeemed 'her lost freedom.'

Ghana is the name of the ancient West African empire that flourished about a thousand years ago. After it disintegrated, it remained a legend of . . . power and magnificence.

Attending the celebration of the rebirth of Ghana are representatives of more than fifty nations, including the Soviet Union and Communist China. Vice President Richard M. Nixon heads the United States delegation. . . .

Thousands of Ghanaians marched in the streets of Accra this morning singing, thumping drums and shooting firecrackers. At least 30,000 of them came from the polo grounds where the Prime Minister had told them in English and in the Fanti language that they were free people—no longer 'slaves'—and that they must throw out their chests when they walk.

Mr. Nkrumah addressed them after his long and serious speech in Parliament House. He was still inside when the flag of Ghana rose on the mast and the crowd in the streets began to cheer and yell. . . .

Mr. Nkrumah told the final session of the Assembly that the Government would seek to help 'all African peoples in their pursuit of freedom and social progress.' He also emphasized that foreign investment would be encouraged."
—Thomas F. Brady, special to *The New York Times*

Skills Tip

Keep in mind that a newspaper article reports only on facts that are available at the moment. Often, additional information emerges through the years that helps historians gain a deeper understanding of events.

Skills Assessment

1. According to this report, the name *Ghana* calls up images of
   A colonial oppression.
   B bloody civil war.
   C past greatness.
   D successful diplomacy.

2. The article conveys the international importance of Ghana's independence mainly in its description of
   E Ghana's new flag.
   F the foreign officials in attendance.
   G the cheering crowds in Accra.
   H Nkrumah's speech.

3. Critical Thinking Making Inferences (a) Based on this account, how did the people of Ghana react to their independence? (b) What issues faced the new nation?

Pressures for independence built up both within and outside Africa. After India won independence from Britain in 1947, African leaders grew impatient. Furthermore, both the United States and the Soviet Union rejected colonialism. Everywhere, the cry rose: "Freedom Now."

Nationalist Leaders Most nationalist leaders were western educated. Many were powerful speakers whose words inspired their supporters. Kwame Nkrumah in Gold Coast (later Ghana), Jomo Kenyatta in Kenya, and Léopold Senghor in Senegal, to name just a few, also were skilled political organizers.

In colonies throughout Africa, leaders organized political parties. In the cities, these political parties published newspapers, held mass rallies, and mobilized support for independence. Demonstrations, strikes, and boycotts were designed to pressure European governments into negotiating timetables for freedom.

Routes to Freedom

During the great liberation, each African nation had its own leaders and its own story. Here, we will look at three examples: Ghana in West Africa, Kenya in East Africa, and Algeria in North Africa.

Ghana The first African nation south of the Sahara to win freedom was the British colony of Gold Coast. During the late 1940s, Kwame Nkrumah (kwah MEE ehn KROO muh) was impatient with Britain's policy of gradual movement toward independence. Nkrumah had spent time in the United States, where he was inspired by the Pan-Africanist Marcus Garvey and other civil rights leaders. He also studied the nonviolent methods of India's Mohandas Gandhi.

Back in Gold Coast, Nkrumah organized a radical political party. Through strikes and boycotts, he tried to win concessions from Britain. When mass actions led to riots, Nkrumah was imprisoned. His supporters continued the struggle.

In 1957, Gold Coast finally won independence. Nkrumah, who had emerged from prison to become prime minister of the new nation, named it Ghana, after the ancient West African empire.* The symbolism was clear. *Gold Coast* reflected European interests in Africa. *Ghana* linked the new nation with the region's African past. "Before the arrival of the Europeans," Nkrumah said, "our ancestors had attained a great empire. . . . Thus we may take pride in the name of Ghana, not out of romanticism, but as an inspiration for the future."

Kenya In Kenya, freedom came only with armed struggle. White settlers had carved out farms in the fertile highlands, where they displaced African farmers, mostly Kikuyu (kih KOO yoo). Settlers saw Kenya as their homeland and had passed laws to ensure their domination.

Even before World War II, Jomo Kenyatta had been a leading spokesman for the Kikuyu. "The land is ours," he said. "When Europeans came, they kept us back and took our land." Kenyatta supported nonviolent methods to end oppressive laws.

More radical leaders turned to guerrilla warfare. They burned farms and destroyed livestock, hoping to scare whites into leaving. In 1952, they began to attack settlers and Africans who worked with the colonial rulers. The British called the guerrillas Mau Mau and pictured them as savages. To stop the violence, the British arrested Kenyatta and forced thousands of Kikuyu into concentration camps. Kikuyu casualties rose when British bombers pounded Mau Mau armed mostly with swords. All told, casualties totaled about 75 dead among the whites, and about 13,000 Kenyans.

*Ancient Ghana was located to the north and west of modern Ghana.

Primary Sources and Literature

See "Kwame Nkrumah: Autobiography" in the Reference Section at the back of this book.

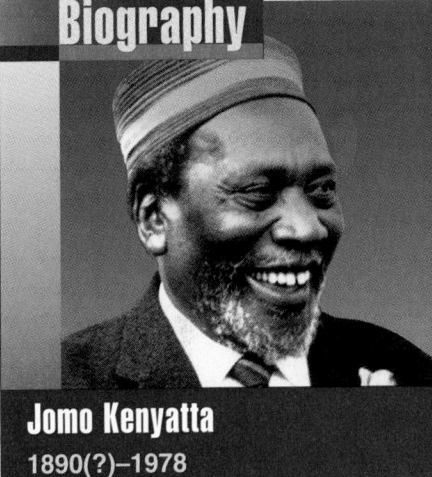
Biography

Jomo Kenyatta
1890(?)–1978

Jomo Kenyatta was born in a small Kikuyu village and educated at a Christian mission. Moving to Nairobi, he was quickly drawn to the first stirrings of the nationalist cause. He became a prominent anticolonial organizer and was eventually elected president of the Kenya Africa Union.

Kenyatta was arrested in 1952 and convicted in 1953 on charges of inciting the Mau Mau uprising against the British. Released in 1961, he resumed leadership of the movement for independence, which was finally granted in December 1963. When Kenya became a republic in 1964, Kenyatta was elected its first president. Under his 15-year rule, Kenya enjoyed political stability and economic advances. Each year, October 20, the date of his arrest, is celebrated as Kenyatta Day.

Theme: Impact of the Individual What role do you think national heroes play in helping to form a nation's identity?

The rebels were crushed, but the movement lived on. Eventually, the British released Kenyatta, whose imprisonment had made him a national hero. In 1963, he became the first prime minister of an independent Kenya. The next year, Kenya became a republic, with Kenyatta as president.

Algeria   From 1954 to 1962, a longer and even costlier war of liberation raged in Algeria. In the 1800s, France had conquered Algeria after a brutal struggle. Over the years, the French had come to see Algeria, located across the Mediterranean from France, as part of their country. Along with the million Europeans who had settled there, they were determined to keep the Arab-Berber people of Algeria from winning independence.

Muslim Algerian nationalists set up the National Liberation Front (FLN). In 1954, the group turned to guerrilla warfare to win freedom. France, which had just lost its Asian colony of Vietnam, was unwilling to retreat from Algeria. As the fighting escalated, a half-million French troops went to Algeria. Thousands of these troops were killed. Additionally, hundreds of thousands of Algerians died during the long war.

Eventually, public opinion in France turned against the war. After Charles de Gaulle, a World War II hero, became president of France in 1958, he began talks to end the war. In 1962, Algeria celebrated its freedom.

The New Nations of Africa

More than 50 new nations were born in Africa during the great liberation. Throughout the continent, Africans had great hopes for the future. People looked forward to rapid political and economic development. African leaders knew they had much to do to build modern nations, but they welcomed the chance to deal on an equal footing with the other nations of the world. After 70 years of colonial rule, Africans were again in control of their destinies.

During the early decades after independence, the new nations took different paths to modernization. Some made progress despite huge obstacles. Others were plunged into crisis by civil war, natural disasters, military rule, or corrupt dictators. In some parts of Africa, standards of living actually fell after liberation. In many countries, a small elite enjoyed wealth and privileges, while the majority lived in poverty.

Africa and the Cold War   African nations emerged during the Cold War between the United States and the Soviet Union. The struggle between the two superpowers and their allies affected many African nations. Each superpower supplied arms to African governments it favored. That policy boosted the power of the military in many countries, contributing to instability.

Cold War rivalries affected local conflicts within Africa. For example, the Soviet Union and the United States supported rival groups in Angola's civil war. The two superpowers also became involved in a long, bloody war between the nations of Ethiopia and Somalia.

The Cold War left a painful legacy. After it ended, weapons supplied by the superpowers remained in the hands of rival African tribes, governments, or guerrilla forces. Armed with modern weapons, these groups spread violence across many lands.

African Regional Organizations   The new nations of Africa were determined to carve out their own position in the world. To do so, they joined regional and global organizations.

The Cold War
Cold War rivalries had devastating effects in Africa. One of the bloodiest struggles took place in Somalia and Ethiopia. In this cartoon, American and Soviet advisers rush to help their allies, but head for their own collision.

Theme: Global Interaction   Why did the two superpowers care about which political system African nations adopted?

In 1963, they set up the Organization of African Unity (OAU). It promoted cooperation among members and sought peaceful settlements of disputes. This organization, however, failed to prevent conflicts between African states and even defended the right of dictators such as Idi Amin of Uganda to rule their peoples as they pleased.

In 2001, African leaders gathered in Zambia to launch a new African Union. Modeled on the successful European Union, the new organization focused on building democratic institutions, coordinating economic development, and seeking increased foreign investment and aid. "Africa must reject the ways of the past," declared UN Secretary General Kofi Annan, "and commit itself to a future of democratic governance."

The UN After independence, African nations joined the United Nations. They contributed to and benefited from the UN and its many agencies. Africans served in UN peacekeeping missions around the world.

African countries and other developing nations focused world attention on issues including health care, literacy, and economic development. They called for an end to racism and imperialism. They also pressed nations of the global North to deal with the unequal distribution of wealth.

Disaster Relief and Military Intervention The UN—along with individual nations and private agencies like the International Red Cross, Oxfam, and Doctors Without Borders—responded to famine and other crises that struck African nations. In the early 1960s, UN peacekeepers helped stop the fighting in Zaire. Later, UN efforts helped save millions from starvation in Biafra during Nigeria's civil war.

Military intervention has been another method of dealing with crises in Africa. These efforts have generally had limited success. In the early 1990s, UN forces, with massive U.S. support, brought food to Somalians caught up in a civil war. But military efforts to end the civil strife failed, and the UN and U.S. forces withdrew. In 2003, French troops entered the Democratic Republic of Congo to protect civilians from rival militia forces. That same year, American troops aided a large West African multinational force as it tried to end a civil war in Liberia.

Turmoil and Survival
Although civil wars caused great hardship, people throughout Africa were determined to create better lives. Here, women build new homes after war in Rwanda forced them to abandon their villages.

Theme: Economics and Technology What economic and political changes did reformers support during the 1980s?

SECTION 1 Assessment

Recall
1. **Identify:** **(a)** Kwame Nkrumah, **(b)** Jomo Kenyatta, **(c)** National Liberation Front, **(d)** Charles de Gaulle, **(e)** Organization of African Unity.

Comprehension
2. **(a)** What challenges faced African nations as a result of colonialism? **(b)** How did nationalist leaders respond to these challenges?
3. Describe the conflicts that arose during independence in the following countries: **(a)** Ghana, **(b)** Kenya, **(c)** Algeria.

4. How have international organizations affected the new nations of Africa?

Critical Thinking and Writing
5. **Connecting to Geography** How might Africa's size and diversity have affected early reform efforts?
6. **Making Inferences** Review the subsection A Growing Spirit of Nationalism. Why might European enthusiasm for colonization have declined after World War II? Provide details from the text to support your answer.

Activity

Creating a Poster
Create a poster that illustrates the goals of one of the independence movements discussed in this section. Be sure to include images that show the legacy of colonialism.

SECTION 2 Programs for Development

Reading Focus

- What were barriers to unity and stability in Africa?
- What economic choices did African nations make?
- What critical issues affect African nations today?
- How has modernization affected patterns of life?

Vocabulary

one-party system
mixed economy
desertification

Taking Notes

As you read this section, prepare an outline of its contents. Use Roman numerals to indicate major headings. Use capital letters for sub-headings, and use numbers for the supporting details. The example here will help you get started.

I. Seeking unity and stability
  A. Divisions
    1. Diversity
    2.
  B. Civil war
  C.
II. Economic choices
  A. Socialism or capitalism
  B.

Main Idea New African nations faced many choices and challenges as they established new governments.

Setting the Scene "Independence is the beginning of a real struggle," declared one liberation leader in Africa. The new nations faced two critical issues. First, they needed to create unified states with stable governments. Second, they had to achieve economic growth that would improve the standard of living of their people. Meeting those challenges would be a long, complex process—one that is still incomplete.

After independence, African governments experimented with various programs. They made some progress but also took some wrong turns. In this section, we will look at the political and economic challenges faced by nations across Africa.

Seeking Unity and Stability

At independence, African nations set up governments modeled on those of departing colonial rulers. But parliamentary systems did not work in the new African countries as they did in European nations, where they had evolved over centuries.

Struggle for Stability
More than half of all African nations have suffered through military coups and civil wars. These heavily armed soldiers are patrolling a town in the Democratic Republic of the Congo, where decades of dictatorship and civil war have resulted in millions of deaths.

Theme: Political and Social Systems Why might new African governments face civil war?

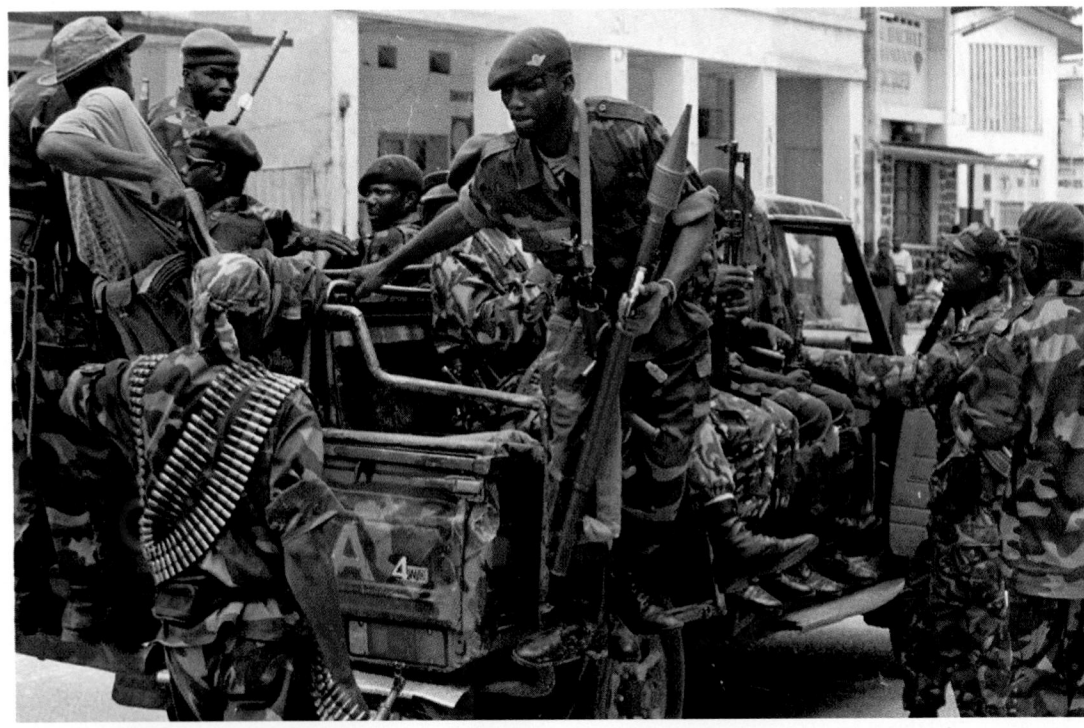

Divisions Colonial borders had left most African nations a patchwork of people with diverse cultures, languages, and histories. Nationalism had helped unify Africans within each colony to end foreign rule. But once freedom was won, many Africans felt their first loyalty was to their own ethnic group, not to a faceless national government.

Like Eastern European nations, African nations were plagued by ethnic and regional conflict. In Sudan, for example, the Arabic-speaking Muslim majority in the north dominated and persecuted the minority, mostly African Christian groups, in the south. These southerners tried to break away, resulting in a civil war that has continued to the present.

Civil War Westerners often blamed African civil wars on old "tribal" rivalries.* But most conflicts were more complex. Some were rooted in colonial history. Britain, for example, often chose to rule a colony through what it called "tribal" leaders. It assigned Africans within a colony to tribes, and then chose one tribe to rule the others. This system fostered ill will that continued long after independence.

Civil wars also erupted when liberation leaders monopolized political and economic power for their own group. In Nigeria and Zaire, civil war erupted when economically successful groups tried to set up their own nations. In Africa, as elsewhere, civil wars unleashed terrible violence.

One-Party Rule Faced with divisions that threatened national unity, many early leaders turned to a one-party system. Under this political structure, a country has a single political party, or only one party that has any real likelihood of winning elections. Multiparty systems, these leaders declared, encouraged disunity. In Tanzania, Julius Nyerere (nyuh RAIR ay) claimed that a one-party system could be democratic and offered voters a choice of candidates within the party.

In fact, most one-party nations became authoritarian states. After the struggle for independence, some nationalist leaders became dictators. Some used their position to enrich themselves and a privileged elite. Others used force to hold onto power.

Military Rule When bad government led to unrest, the military often seized power. More than half of all African nations suffered military coups. Military leaders claimed that they—unlike politicians, who they said sought power and wealth—were motivated by a sense of duty to their country. Some military rulers, like Idi Amin, who murdered thousands of citizens in Uganda, were brutal tyrants. Others sought to end abuses and improve conditions.

Military leaders usually promised to restore civilian rule once they had cleaned up the government. In many cases, however, they gave up power only when they were toppled by other military coups.

Reforms By the mid-1980s, political and economic woes brought Africa to the brink of crisis. Demands for change came from inside and outside the continent. African thinkers looked for African solutions to their problems. They studied precolonial African societies that had limited a ruler's power and allowed people a share in decision making. They did not propose returning to the past, but hoped instead to build on traditions that had worked before.

While some Africans demanded this sort of "people participation," external sources called for democratic reforms. Western governments and the World Bank, for example, required such reforms before making more loans. Under that pressure, some governments eased autocratic policies.

---

*The word *tribe* was used by westerners to describe people living in small-scale societies and implied backwardness. The term is misleading, however. Like societies elsewhere, Africans in precolonial times belonged to ethnic or social groups that shared a common culture or loyalty. But these groups changed over time and continue to change today.

Primary Source

Building New Nations
Kenneth Kaunda delivered this speech in 1966, when he was president of Zambia. In this excerpt, Kaunda emphasizes the need for elected leaders to serve their nation:

"We must think and think and think again about how best we shall serve and not how important we are as leaders of our people or how we can safeguard our own positions as leaders. . . . We must remember we are *not* elected kings. . . .

Selfishness in leaders and followers inevitably leads to corruption. I cannot see, however, that uniformed men replacing elected leaders, by either killing them, imprisoning them, or, indeed, sending them into exile is the answer to this problem. . . .

To my fellow leaders on the continent of Africa I would . . . send this message—that our task and challenge is to try and help establish governments of the people, by the people, and for the people."

—Kenneth Kaunda, speech delivered March 18, 1966

Skills Assessment

Primary Source What is Kaunda's opinion of military rule?

They legalized opposition parties and lifted censorship. In some places, multiparty elections were held, removing long-ruling leaders from office.

Economic Choices

A key to modernization was building productive economies and raising standards of living. Developing modern economies meant improving agriculture and developing industry. To achieve those goals, African nations had to build transportation systems, develop resources, increase literacy, and solve problems of rural poverty. Many had little capital to invest in such projects. As a result, they had to make difficult choices.

Socialism or Capitalism Many newly independent nations chose socialism, which meant that the government made economic decisions about using resources and producing goods. Socialist governments wanted to control scarce resources, using them where government planners thought they were most needed. They hoped to end foreign economic influence and prevent inequalities between rich and poor. But to regulate the economy, socialism created large bureaucracies, which generally were inefficient. Often, policies imposed by the national government were ill suited to local farming communities.

Some African nations set up mixed economies, with both private and state-run enterprises. These, too, had problems. These nations relied heavily on foreign aid from the UN, the World Bank, and industrial nations. Foreign capital was used to build airports, hydroelectric plants, and factories, and to improve farming. Some programs succeeded. Others were costly failures, due partly to mistakes by government planners or foreign advisers.

Although African nations did build some industries, they remained heavily dependent on imports. Most people were subsistence farmers. As a result, there was too little demand for manufactured goods to make local industries prosper.

Cash Crops or Food In the early years, governments pushed programs to increase earnings by growing more cash crops for export. But land used for crops such as cotton, tea, coffee, or sisal could not also be used to produce food. As a result, African countries that once had fed their people from their own land had to import food.

Urban or Rural Needs The food dilemma had another aspect. Many city dwellers earned low wages and needed cheap food to survive. Farmers, however, would grow food crops only if they received good prices for them. Many governments kept food prices artificially low to satisfy poor city people. As a result, farmers either used their land for export crops or produced only for themselves.

Many early government programs neglected rural development in favor of industrial projects. By the 1980s, though, governments realized they must pay more attention to farmers' needs. In Zimbabwe, the government helped small farmers buy tools, fertilizer, and seed. Additionally, it made sure farmers received higher prices for their crops. The policy paid off in higher food output.

The Debt Crisis Soaring oil prices in the 1970s also hurt developing economies. Most African nations were oil importers and had to pay out large amounts of currency for much-needed fuel. Prices for African exports fell, plunging the young nations deep into debt. Governments had to pay so much interest on loans that they had little money for development.

The debt crisis led the World Bank and other lenders to require developing nations to make tough economic reforms before extending new loans. African governments had to privatize businesses, cut spending on

Geography and History

Preserving Africa's Wildlife

Logging, farming, and urban development have devoured nearly 70 percent of Africa's animal habitats. The black rhinoceros, wildebeest, and hartebeest have been pushed to the edge of extinction. Populations of elephant, zebra, and antelope are in decline.

Some governments have responded with strong conservation measures. In fact, national parks and game reserves encompass 185,000 square miles of Africa, a higher proportion than on any other continent. Still, Africa's wildlife faces threats from many sources, among them real estate developers, farmers who view wild beasts as a threat to their crops and livestock, and poachers who traffic in ivory elephant tusks and black rhino horns. Wildlife officials face an uphill battle in persuading Africans that the benefits they will gain from protecting their natural heritage will outweigh the costs.

Theme: Political and Social Systems Why are some African governments having a hard time protecting endangered wildlife?

development projects, and stop subsidizing prices of basic foods for the urban poor. In the long term, the reforms were designed to help economies grow. In the short term, however, they increased unemployment and led to higher prices that the poor could not pay.

Critical Issues

The population explosion put a staggering burden on Africa's developing economies. In 1965, Africa's population was about 280 million. By 1990, that figure had increased to over 650 million. The continent's population was expected to double before 2020. As in other developing nations around the world, rising population meant that the least-developed countries had to find ways to feed, educate, and generate jobs for the fastest-growing number of people.

Drought and Famine In the early 1970s and again in the 1980s, prolonged drought contributed to famine in parts of Africa. Livestock died. As farmland turned to dust and blew away, millions of people became refugees. The Sahel was especially hard hit. This semidesert region stretches across Africa just south of the Sahara. There, overgrazing and farming removed topsoil and speeded up desertification, or the spread of desert areas.

In countries like Ethiopia and Sudan, civil war intensified the effects of drought and famine. Each side in the conflict tried to keep relief supplies from reaching the other. On several occasions, huge international efforts helped save millions of people facing starvation.

Deforestation Rain forests, too, came under attack. To boost badly needed export earnings, African governments allowed hardwood trees to be cut and shipped to the global North. Once forests were cleared, heavy tropical rains washed nutrients from the soil and destroyed its fertility. In Kenya, an environmental activist named Wangari Maathi challenged government policy by starting the Greenbelt movement. She hoped to restore the environment and create job opportunities for women in areas such as planting trees, marketing, and forestry.

AIDS The AIDS epidemic spread rapidly across Africa. Nations such as South Africa, Ethiopia, Nigeria, Kenya, and Botswana were particularly hard hit. In the early 2000s, the UN estimated that almost 30 million people in Africa south of the Sahara were infected with the HIV virus that causes AIDS, and that more than two million died of the disease each year.

Some African nations, however, launched successful programs to drastically lower rates of infection. Government and medical officials focused on educating people about how the HIV virus is transmitted and how people can take precautions to reduce its transmission. Uganda was especially successful, reducing infection rates from 14 percent to 5 percent in a single decade.

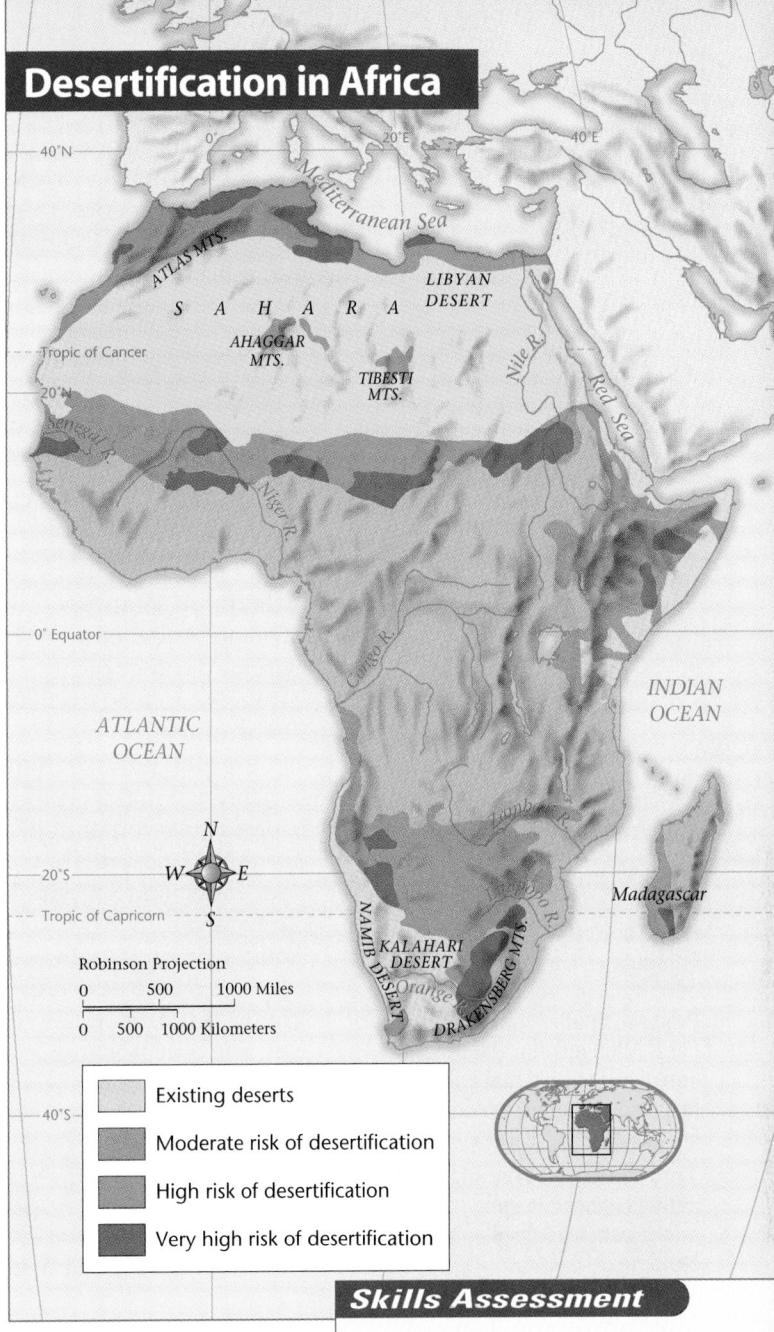

Desertification in Africa

Existing deserts

Moderate risk of desertification

High risk of desertification

Very high risk of desertification

Skills Assessment

Geography The spread of deserts in Africa results in the loss of farmlands and grazing lands.

1. **Location** On the map, locate **(a)** Sahara, **(b)** Kalahari Desert, **(c)** Namib Desert, **(d)** Libyan Desert.
2. **Region** Which regions of Africa are least likely to experience desertification?
3. **Critical Thinking Drawing Conclusions** **(a)** Based on this map, in which direction would you expect the Sahara to expand? **(b)** the Kalahari Desert?

Old and New Patterns

In Africa, as elsewhere, modernization disrupted old ways. Colonial rule also undermined African traditions by promoting western cultural influences. Today, people across Africa face a similar dilemma. On the one hand, they want the high standard of living, advanced technology, and other benefits associated with modern societies. On the other, they value and want to preserve their own culture and traditions.

Impact of Urbanization By 2000, almost half of all Africans lived in towns and cities, and rural people were still migrating to cities at a rapid rate. Although urbanization contributed to the development of a larger national identity, it weakened traditional cultures and undermined ethnic and kinship ties that unified rural communities. Young urban dwellers who returned to their villages often scorned traditional ways. Yet many educated Africans took pride in those traditions.

Effects on Women The great migration to the cities had some effect on women. A few educated women joined the urban elite, working in civil service or other professional positions. Most urban women, however, struggled to feed and keep their families together in poverty-stricken urban slums.

Despite urbanization, most African women still live in rural areas, where they make up the bulk of the population. As men moved to the cities, rural women took on the sole responsibility of caring and providing for their children. They planted and harvested food crops, collected wood and water, and prepared food. In some areas, they found paid work on large farms. In West Africa, their historical role as market traders allowed some women to gain considerable economic power.

The constitutions of most African nations promised women generous rights. But often those rights were not enforced, and women's lives were still ruled by traditional laws. A small but powerful group of well-educated African women has worked to make national governments more responsive to women's issues.

Christianity in Africa Today, as in the past, Africa is home to many religious traditions. Colonialism and modernization disrupted traditional practices, but in rural areas, people remained faithful to their own beliefs. Both Christianity and Islam spread to Africa centuries ago, and both have grown

Urban Growth
Throughout Africa, people continue to seek jobs in cities such as Pretoria, South Africa, shown here. Although such migration can disrupt traditional cultures, it has also promoted national unity.

Theme: Economics and Technology Why might new nations choose to spend money on the construction of modern buildings?

since their introduction. Almost three fourths of African Christians are Roman Catholic. Others belong to Orthodox Christian or Protestant sects. These churches sometimes combine Christian and traditional African beliefs.

At times, African clergy risked their lives to stand up to dictators in Zaire, Uganda, and elsewhere. Sometimes, though, they were unable to stop violence. In Rwanda, for example, most people are Christian. But ethnic conflict in that nation led to mass killings, even in churches where people had taken refuge.

Islamic Revival Islam has long influenced the northern half of Africa and linked it to the Middle East. Islam, you will recall, spread along trade routes into both East and West Africa. Today, Nigeria has the largest Muslim population south of the Sahara.

Muslim African nations felt the effects of the Islamic revival that began in the Middle East. Its message of reform based on Islamic traditions and its call for social justice were welcomed by people in Africa and around the world. So, too, was its rejection of western influences. In the early 1990s, Algeria's Islamic party did so well in elections that the government feared an Islamic revolution like Iran's. The military canceled further elections. That action outraged Islamic extremists, who attacked politicians, scholars, and others, sometimes massacring whole villages. The government responded with force. More than 70,000 people were killed in the fighting.

In other African lands, as in parts of Asia, the Islamic revival stimulated deeper religious commitment. Many Muslims, like some Christians in the West, believed that the world had become too secularized and returned to the faith of their ancestors.

Improving Health Care
Providing medical care has been a goal of many African nations. Because there are few hospitals in many areas, health projects often focus on prevention. Here, doctors at a rural Nigerian clinic teach women about the importance of good nutrition in raising healthy children.

Theme: Political and Social Systems Why is preventive medicine especially important in areas with few doctors or hospitals?

SECTION 2 Assessment

Recall
1. **Identify:** **(a)** Julius Nyerere, **(b)** Wangari Maathi, **(c)** AIDS epidemic.
2. **Define:** **(a)** one-party system, **(b)** mixed economy, **(c)** desertification.

Comprehension
3. Why were unity and stability difficult to achieve?
4. Describe the choices faced by African nations after independence.
5. What environmental challenges does Africa face?

6. How did modernization and the growth of cities change daily life for many Africans?

Critical Thinking and Writing
7. **Analyzing Information** How did governments of new African nations respond to political and economic challenges?
8. **Identifying Alternatives** How might development in Africa have been different if nationalist leaders had chosen to draw new national boundaries based on ethnicity?

Activity

Creating a Development Program
Suppose that you have been elected president of a newly independent nation. Outline a development program that identifies the nation's needs and suggests ways to address them.

Three Nations: A Closer Look

Reading Focus

- What were some pressures for change in Nigeria?

- What effects did dictatorship have on the Congo?

- What was the outcome of Tanzania's experiment in socialism?

Taking Notes

Create a concept web that shows key issues discussed in this section. Use this sample as a starting point, and add more circles as needed.

Wealth from oil — Nigeria — MODERNIZATION — Congo — Tanzania

Main Idea Nigeria, the Congo, and Tanzania provide examples of paths followed by African nations.

Setting the Scene Nigerian poet John Pepper Clark saw his nation torn by civil war. In one poem, he chronicled both the obvious effects and the unseen costs of the war:

> "The casualties are not only those who are dead;
> They are well out of it.
> The casualties are not only those who are wounded,
> Though they await burial by installment. . . .
> The casualties are not only those led away by night;
> The cell is a cruel place. . . .
> The casualties are many, and a good number well
> Outside the scenes of ravage and wreck; . . .
>
> We fall,
> All casualties of the war,
> Because we cannot hear each other speak
> Because eyes have ceased to see the face from the crowd."
> —John Pepper Clark, "The Casualties"

Nigeria was only one of many African nations that suffered a disastrous civil war after independence. In this section, we will take a closer look at Nigeria, the Democratic Republic of Congo (formerly called Zaire), and Tanzania. Their experiences, resources, populations, and leaders differed.

Oil Drilling

Oil produced from wells such as the one shown here provides income for a number of West African countries. Several nations have used their oil wealth to industrialize their economies.

Theme: Economics and Technology In what ways might the people and the government disagree about how income from oil should be spent?

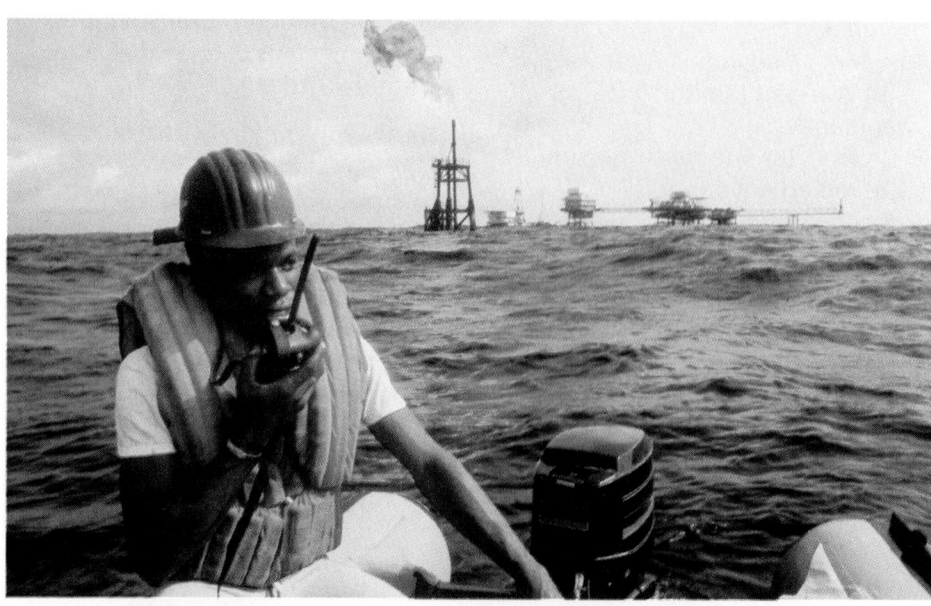

But through their efforts to modernize, they illustrate the patterns that were common during the post-independence years.

Pressures for Change in Nigeria

When Nigeria won independence in 1960, it hoped to develop rapidly. This large West African nation had rich resources, especially oil. Its population was the largest in Africa south of the Sahara, giving it a potentially strong internal market. Its fertile farming areas produced exports of cocoa and palm oil as well as food crops. The Niger and Benue rivers provided a good transportation network.

Diversity and Civil Strife Nigeria's borders, drawn in colonial times, lumped together 250 ethnic groups. Several regional groups competed for power. In the north were the Muslim Hausa and Fulani, heirs to a strong empire since the early 1800s. Christian Ibo dominated the oil-rich south. Some of the Yoruba of the southwest were Christian and others were Muslim. Many others still practiced traditional religions.

At independence, Nigeria drew up a federal constitution to protect various national interests. The system did not work well, however. At first, the Hausa dominated the government, and ethnic rivalries increased. In the 1960s, massacres of tens of thousands of Ibo triggered a bloody civil war. Ibo leaders in the southeast declared their region the independent state of Biafra. The two-and-a-half-year struggle that followed cost hundreds of thousands of lives, including vast numbers who starved to death in the long blockade of Biafra.

Economic Recovery The 1970s oil boom helped Nigeria recover from the war. With its massive oil wealth, the government spent lavishly on development projects. It set up industries, including a steel mill, auto assembly plant, and petrochemical works. To pay for prestige projects like a new capital, it also borrowed heavily from the West.

Rural people flooded into the cities, hoping to share in the economic boom. But while cities grew, the government paid little heed to farmers. Nigeria, once a food exporter, bought expensive imported grain. Local food production fell, and rural poverty increased.

Later, when oil prices fell, the economy almost collapsed. A huge debt burden combined with waste, mismanagement, and corruption strangled the young nation. Though a small elite continued to profit enormously, the majority of the people suffered.

Military and Civilian Rule Since independence, Nigeria has often lived under military rule. The military usually took over in the name of reform, arguing that something needed to be done to end the lavish lifestyle and corrupt practices of civilian politicians. Though many citizens welcomed the military as a force for order and honest government, military dictators imposed rigid political controls, often without providing either greater efficiency or economic progress.

During Nigeria's debt crisis in the 1980s, General Ibrahim Babangida imposed harsh economic reforms to restore economic stability. He attacked corruption, prohibited imports, and raised the prices paid farmers for agricultural produce. But he also cracked down on his critics, outraging the international community by executing Ken Saro-Wiwa, a renowned writer and critic of the regime.

The people democratically elected Babangida's successor, Olusegun Obasanjo, a former dictator. Accepting tight IMF reform requirements, he moved to privatize state industries. Supported by a big rise in world oil prices, he promised more roads, schools, and clinics for Nigeria's people. But sporadic violence between Muslims and Christians continued to plague the country.

Primary Source

A Nigerian Speaks Out
Convicted by a military tribunal in 1995 of inciting violence, Nigerian author Ken Saro-Wiwa tried in vain to read a statement to the court:

"I am a man of peace, of ideas.
Appalled by the deplorable poverty of my people . . . angered by the devastation of their land, anxious to preserve their right to life and to a decent living, and determined to usher to this country as a whole a fair and just democratic system, I have devoted all my intellectual and material resources—my very life—to a cause in which I have total belief and from which I cannot be blackmailed or intimidated. . . .
In my innocence of the false charges I face here, in my utter conviction, I call upon the Ogoni people, the peoples of the Niger delta, and the oppressed ethnic minorities of Nigeria to stand up and fight fearlessly and peacefully for their rights. History is on their side, God is on their side. . . ."

—Ken Saro-Wiwa,
unpublished remarks

Skills Assessment

Primary Source What grievances against the government does Ken Saro-Wiwa cite in his speech?

Dictatorship and War in Congo

After World War II, Belgium, determined to keep the Congo, did nothing to prepare the huge central African colony for freedom. Then, in 1960, fearing a struggle like the French war in Algeria, Belgium suddenly rushed the Congo to independence. Unprepared for self-government and with few trained leaders, the new nation was soon plunged into civil war.

Physically, the new country had many advantages. It had many rich resources, including vast tropical forests, plantations, and great mineral wealth. In addition, the immense Congo River and its tributaries flowed from the interior to the coast, providing water resources as well as an extensive transportation network.

Yet the new nation included some 200 ethnic groups and had no sense of unity. At independence, more than 100 political parties sprang up. They represented diverse regional and ethnic groups. Within months after independence, the nation split apart.

Mobutu in Power Civil war raged for almost three years before the UN peace-keeping troops ended the worst fighting. Two years later, in 1965, an army general, Mobutu Sese Seko, seized power and imposed some kind of order. He renamed the nation Zaire, meaning "big river."

For the next 34 years, Mobutu built an increasingly brutal dictatorship. He slaughtered rivals and ran the economy into the ground. He also bilked the treasury of millions stolen from the nation and stored in foreign bank accounts. Mobutu survived for more than three decades because he represented order in a land formerly torn by civil war and because his strong anti-communist stance won favor with the West during the Cold War.

Conflicts Continue In the late 1990s, ethnic violence spilled across several countries of central Africa, including Zaire. Rebels overthrew Mobutu. They renamed the country Democratic Republic of Congo and promised reforms. But struggles for political power, territory, and control of valuable natural resources continued. Rival armies from nine neighboring countries joined the fighting. The UN began to deploy troops in Congo in 1999 to protect civilians and to monitor shaky cease-fire agreements. By the early 2000s, warfare had led to the deaths of an estimated three million people in central Africa, mainly through hunger and disease.

Tanzania's Experiment in Socialism

In sharp contrast to Zaire's greedy and corrupt dictator, Tanzania's first president, Julius Nyerere, set out on a high-minded crusade. Tanganyika had been a German colony until World War I, when it was transferred to British control. After independence in 1961, nationalist leaders hoped for great changes for their country, which became known as Tanzania. Nyerere's goals included improving rural life, building a classless society, and creating a self-reliant economy.

To carry out his program, Nyerere embraced what he called "African socialism." This system was not a western import, he declared, but was based on African village traditions of cooperation and shared responsibility. Nyerere was a strong supporter of women's rights, claiming that their subservient position was "inconsistent with our socialist conception of the equality of all human beings."

In the 1960s, Nyerere introduced a command economy, nationalizing all banks and foreign-owned businesses. Drawing on traditional images of community, he emphasized the idea that Tanzania was "a rural society where improvement will depend largely upon the efforts of the people in agriculture and village development." Nyerere also tried to prevent the rise of a wealthy elite.

One-Party Rule At independence, Tanzania was a large country with plenty of land and labor but very little capital or technology. Its main exports were coffee, cotton, tea, and tobacco. Most people worked as farmers or herders.

Tanzania included about 120 ethnic groups. Most groups were small, however, and the country escaped the type of conflicts that ravaged Nigeria and Zaire. To promote unity, Nyerere set up a one-party system. Under this system, several candidates could run for each office. They were permitted to debate any topic except those related to ethnic or regional issues.

Mutual Cooperation Nyerere promoted the idea of *ujamaa*, a Swahili word that means "familyhood" or "mutual cooperation." Rural farmers were encouraged to live in large villages and to farm the land collectively. The government pledged to build roads and provide tools, clean water, health care, and schools. Under this arrangement, Nyerere believed, output would increase. The government would then sell the surplus crops to towns or export them for sale in other nations.

Nyerere's bold experiment did not work as planned. Many families refused to leave land they had farmed for generations, so the government forced them to move to *ujamaa* villages. Those farmers who did relocate resented experts who tried to teach them to farm. In the end, farm output did not rise.

Reforms High oil prices, inflation, and a bloated bureaucracy plunged Tanzania into debt. In 1985, Nyerere resigned. His successors introduced new reforms, ending one-party rule, reducing government bureaucracy, and moving the nation toward a free-market economy.

The people of Tanzania had some reason to believe in a brighter future. In the early 2000s, the opening of a huge new gold mine made Tanzania the third largest gold producer in Africa. The government hoped to use the gold profits along with foreign aid to improve basic services such as clean water, schools, and health care.

Farming in Tanzania
New farming methods and seeds are helping some Tanzanian farmers to grow more than they could in the past. Changes like these are designed to improve Tanzania's economy.

Theme: Economics and Technology Under Tanzania's socialist government, who was likely to make decisions about the use of new agricultural techniques?

SECTION 3 Assessment

Recall

1. **Identify:** **(a)** Biafra, **(b)** General Ibrahim Babangida, **(c)** Ken Saro-Wiwa, **(d)** Olusegun Obasanjo, **(e)** Mobutu Sese Seko.

Comprehension

2. How has Nigeria responded to economic pressures?
3. **(a)** What challenges faced the Congo at independence? **(b)** How did Mobutu Sese Seko's policies affect the nation?

4. What programs did Julius Nyerere introduce in Tanzania after independence?

Critical Thinking and Writing

5. **Analyzing Information** What effects did the rise of military dictatorships have on Nigeria and the Congo?
6. **Drawing Conclusions** Why did socialist policies fail in Tanzania?

Research current events in one of the nations discussed in this chapter. Write a paragraph summarizing an important issue or event in that nation. For help with this activity, use **Web Code mkd-3623**.

Struggles in Southern Africa

Reading Focus

■ What challenges faced Zimbabwe?

■ How did the long struggle to end apartheid lead to a new South Africa?

■ How did the Cold War affect nations of southern Africa?

Taking Notes

Create a table that shows important information about southern Africa. Use this sample as a starting point.

	ZIMBABWE	SOUTH AFRICA	NAMIBIA	ANGOLA	MOZAMBIQUE
NATIONAL LEADERS	Robert Mugabe, Joshua Nkomo				
SOCIAL AND POLITICAL CONFLICTS					
REFORMS					

Main Idea Nations in southern Africa experienced turmoil as people sought majority rule and equal rights.

Meet Nelson Mandela.

▶ Primary Sources and Literature

See "Nelson Mandela: Glory and Hope" in the Reference Section at the back of this book.

Setting the Scene On May 10, 1994, Nelson Mandela stood before a wildly cheering crowd. He had just been inaugurated as South Africa's first president elected by voters of all races. "The time for the healing of wounds has come," he told black and white South Africans.

For almost 350 years, whites had dominated South Africa and had denied blacks the most basic civil rights. Mandela's election marked a new beginning for South Africa. In his inauguration speech, he spoke of the need for a new unity, not of revenge for the losses suffered by black South Africans. The crowd sang "Nkosi Sikelel' iAfrika" (God Bless Africa)—the anthem that had come to symbolize South Africa's struggle for freedom.

Zimbabwe's Road to Majority Rule

During the Age of Imperialism, European nations had carved up southern Africa. In the 1890s, British businessman Cecil Rhodes took control of the region known as Southern Rhodesia. Later, white settlers turned the region into a self-governing British colony. Whites made up only five percent of the population but owned half the land and controlled the government. As the tide of nationalism swept through Africa in the 1960s, white Southern Rhodesians flatly rejected any move to give up power to the black majority. When Britain supported demands for majority rule, conservative whites led by Ian Smith declared independence in 1965.

Armed Struggle In response, nationalist groups waged guerrilla war to achieve majority rule. Among their leaders were Robert Mugabe (moo GAH beh) and Joshua Nkomo (uhn KOH moh). The long struggle caused much suffering. As guerrilla forces won more successes, many whites fled. UN sanctions hurt the economy. Smith finally had to accept a negotiated settlement. In 1980, Southern Rhodesia became the nation of Zimbabwe.

Rebuilding The new nation faced severe challenges. International sanctions had damaged the economy, and droughts caused additional problems. Recovery was also slowed by a power struggle between Mugabe and Nkomo. Mugabe won and became the elected president of Zimbabwe.

Mugabe called for a one-party system to promote national unity and tolerated little opposition. In the early 2000s, he encouraged the violent seizure of white-owned farmlands. This policy, combined with severe drought, led to massive food shortages and growing international pressure against the increasingly autocratic leader.

South Africa's Long Struggle

In 1910, South Africa won self-rule from Britain. Freedom, however, was limited to white settlers. Whites, who made up less than 20 percent of the population, controlled vast mineral resources and the most fertile land. Over the next decades, the white-minority government passed racial laws to keep the black majority in a subordinate position.

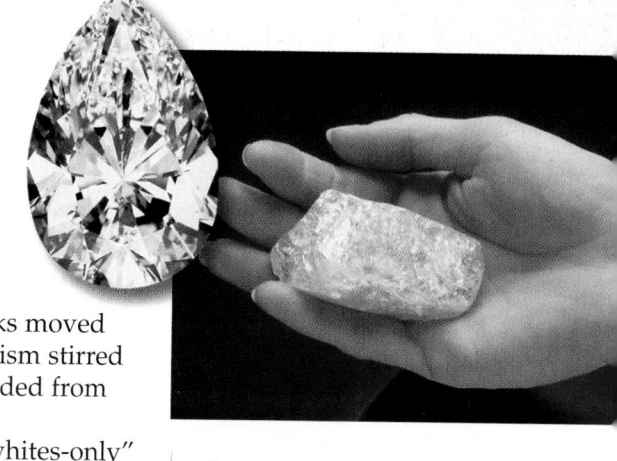

Afrikaner Nationalism After World War II, thousands of blacks moved to towns and cities. There, as elsewhere in Africa, black nationalism stirred demands for equality. In response, Afrikaners, who were descended from Dutch settlers, demanded severe new limits on blacks.

In 1948, the Afrikaner National party won a majority in a "whites-only" parliament. They then extended the existing system of racial segregation, creating what was known as apartheid, or the separation of the races. Under apartheid, all South Africans were registered by race: Black, White, Colored (people of mixed descent), and Asian. Afrikaners claimed that apartheid would allow each race to develop its own culture. In fact, it was designed to give whites control over South Africa.

Apartheid in Action For nonwhites, apartheid meant a life of restrictions. Blacks were treated like foreigners in their own land. They had to get permission to travel and had to carry passbooks or face arrest. The pass laws were an especially heavy burden for women, who had to get permission from their parents, guardian, or husband, as well as from the authorities, in order to move from one district to another.

Blacks were assigned to "homelands" based on their ethnic group. Homelands were located in arid, unproductive parts of the country. More than 80 percent of South Africa, including cities, mines, and the richest farmland, was reserved for whites. Apartheid laws banned marriages between the races and set up segregated restaurants, beaches, schools, and other facilities. Blacks who worked in factories, mines, and other jobs were paid less than whites for the same work. Low wages and inferior schooling condemned blacks to poverty.

Black Resistance From the beginning, black South Africans protested apartheid. In 1912, an organization, later called the African National Congress (ANC), was set up to oppose white domination. In the 1950s, as Afrikaner nationalists imposed harsh new laws, the ANC organized marches, boycotts, and strikes. As protests continued, government violence increased. In 1960, police gunned down 69 men, women, and children taking part in a peaceful demonstration in Sharpeville, a black township outside Johannesburg. In the wake of the incident, the government outlawed the ANC and cracked down on groups that opposed apartheid.

The massacre at Sharpeville stunned the world. At home, it pushed some ANC activists to shift from nonviolent protest to armed struggle. Some leaders left South Africa to wage the battle for freedom from abroad. Others went underground, including Nelson Mandela.

Mandela's Struggle As a young lawyer, Mandela had helped organize the ANC Youth League. With other league leaders, he mobilized young South Africans to take part in acts of civil disobedience against apartheid laws. As government suppression grew, Mandela joined ANC militants who called for armed struggle against the white-minority government.

In the early 1960s, Mandela was arrested, tried, and condemned to life in prison for conspiracy. "I have cherished the ideal of a democratic and free society," he declared at his trial. It was an ideal Mandela hoped "to live for and to achieve." It was also "an ideal for which I am prepared to die." Mandela spent 27 years in prison, often in isolation. Yet he remained a popular leader and powerful symbol of the struggle against apartheid.

Apartheid and Business
The diamond industry provides great wealth for South Africa. Mined in a rough state (right), diamonds later are cut and polished (left). For decades, white-run companies in South Africa have controlled the world's diamond market.

Theme: Economics and Technology How did white-controlled companies benefit from apartheid?

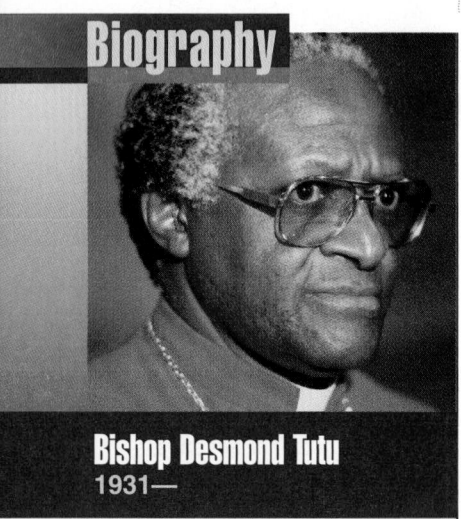
Desmond Tutu grew up in the Transvaal region of South Africa, where he attended mission schools as a child. Lacking the money to pursue his dream of attending medical school, he first became a schoolteacher. Later, he took up the study of theology. He was ordained as an Anglican priest in 1961 and was made bishop in 1976.

Tutu used his growing influence to crusade against the brutal laws of apartheid. Although there was the constant threat of violent rebellion, he never wavered from his message of peace and reconciliation. In 1980, Tutu said, "I will never tell anyone to pick up a gun. But I will pray for the man who picks up a gun, pray that he will be less cruel than he might otherwise have been. . . ."

Theme: Impact of the Individual How did people like Desmond Tutu influence South Africa's battle against apartheid?

By the 1980s, demands for an end to apartheid and for Mandela's release intensified. Many countries, including the United States, imposed strict economic sanctions on South Africa. South African athletes were banned from world sports events such as the Olympic games. In 1984, the black Anglican bishop Desmond Tutu won the Nobel Peace Prize for his nonviolent opposition to apartheid.

Toward Reform Foreign boycotts hurt South Africa's economy. Even worse, in 1985, protests and growing violence at home forced the government to impose a state of emergency. Many South African whites questioned the oppressive measures used by the government.

By 1989, a new South African president, F. W. de Klerk, boldly accepted the need for reform. He abandoned apartheid, repealed the hated pass laws, and lifted the ban on the ANC. A year later, he freed Mandela. Over the next four years, Mandela and de Klerk negotiated the terms by which South Africa would move to majority rule. White voters overwhelmingly approved the reforms that would allow "one person, one vote."

Majority Rule In 1994, South Africa held its first multiracial elections. Black, mixed race, and Asian South Africans, young and old, lined up with white voters to cast their ballots. They elected Nelson Mandela as the first president of a new, democratic South Africa. In a speech to supporters, Mandela echoed the African American civil rights leader Martin Luther King, Jr.: "We can loudly proclaim from the rooftops: Free at last!"

The New South Africa

As president, Mandela offered a striking example to other African nations when he welcomed longtime political foes into his government. If he could work with Afrikaners who had once tyrannized the black majority, perhaps other leaders could learn to accept democratic, multiparty systems. "Let us build together," *masakhane,* was Mandela's slogan and guiding policy.

Mandela's government faced the huge challenge of meeting people's high expectations for change. Mandela had promised a better life to the black majority. Delivering on those promises would be difficult. South Africa was a rich country with a strong industrial base. But it could afford only a limited amount of spending for housing, education, and other programs. The gap between blacks and whites remained large.

Even in Mandela's South Africa, whites owned three fourths of the land, black unemployment remained high, and the crime rate made both cities and the shantytowns around them unsafe. But South Africa's first black president did bring both a peaceful transition to democratic rule and international prestige to his country. He also set up programs to broaden the availability of public housing, education, clean water, and electricity.

In 1999, a second all-race election brought Thabo Mbeki to the presidency. Mbeki also faced many challenges. Crime and poverty remained major problems. And AIDS had emerged as a major health crisis, infecting millions of South Africans. But the democratic process seemed to be successful, and people were hopeful for the future.

Other Nations of Southern Africa

The colonies of southern Africa were among the last to win independence. From the 1960s to the 1980s, South Africa's white-minority government intervened to prevent neighboring peoples from achieving freedom.

Namibia In 1920, South Africa received German Southwest Africa as a mandate from the League of Nations. After World War II, the UN asked South Africa to prepare the territory for independence. Instead, South Africa backed the oppressive regime run by the white minority.

You Are There . . .

Reporting on the Election in South Africa

As an American journalist covering South Africa's second all-race elections, you are excited to find that people here feel strongly about exercising their right to vote. Nelson Mandela, the national hero who became president in 1994, has turned down a second term. Which party's candidate will succeed him? All of South Africa holds its breath to see what happens. . . .

When you arrive at the polling station at 8 A.M., you find a line of voters stretching for more than two miles. Because of the enormous turnout, some people will have to wait more than four hours to vote.

Inside the polling station, voters show signs of weariness. The elderly and sick are ushered to the front of the line. Despite the long wait, most people remain patient, knowing their turn will come.

After the station closes, you learn that someone may have tampered with three of the ballot boxes. If this proves to be true, election officials will have to discard hundreds of votes. Despite the problems, you reflect that South Africans have once again demonstrated their commitment to democracy.

Portfolio Assessment

After you return to the United States, your editor asks you to write an article comparing the attitudes toward democracy and elections in South Africa and in the United States.

Go Online
PHSchool.com

For: More information about Namibia
Visit: PHSchool.com
Web Code: mkd-3628

Freedom for Namibia
Like many African peoples, Namibians waged a long, armed struggle to win independence. Here, a group of Namibian women celebrate the birth of their nation in 1990.

Theme: Global Interaction
How did the Cold War affect Namibia's struggle for independence?

By the 1960s, the Southwest African People's Organization (SWAPO) had turned to armed struggle to win independence. For years, SWAPO guerrillas battled South African troops. The struggle became part of the Cold War, with the Soviet Union and Cuba lending their support to SWAPO. As the Cold War ground to a halt, an agreement was finally reached to hold free elections. In 1990, Namibia—as the new country was called—celebrated independence.

Portuguese Colonies As Britain and France took steps to meet nationalist demands in their African possessions, Portugal clung fiercely to its colonies in Angola and Mozambique. During the 1960s, the Portuguese dictator António Salazar rejected African demands for freedom. In response, nationalists turned to guerrilla warfare. Portugal responded by sending almost its entire army to defend its last outposts of empire.

After 15 years of fighting, many Portuguese army officers realized that they could not succeed in the struggle. In 1974, an army coup in Portugal toppled the dictatorship of Salazar's successor. The new Portuguese government quickly agreed to withdraw from southern Africa. In 1975, Angola and Mozambique celebrated independence.

Wars Continue Independence did not end the fighting in Angola and Mozambique. Bitter civil wars, fueled by Cold War rivalries, raged for years in both countries. Both South Africa and the United States had seen the struggles for freedom in southern Africa as a threat because some liberation leaders were socialists. To undermine the new governments, South Africa aided rebel groups in both countries that wanted power for themselves.

Between 1975 and 1992, nearly a million people died in Mozambique as a result of civil wars, famines, and economic collapse. The end of the Cold War and South Africa's move to majority rule helped stop the civil war. Democracy seemed to be taking root. The economy improved, even though periods of drought and flooding continued to ravage the land.

In Angola, a civil war dragged on for years. The Soviet Union helped one side in the struggle by financing more than 50,000 Cuban troops that went to fight in Angola. The United States and South Africa backed a rival group. Even after the Cold War ended, the civil war continued. After the death of one of the rival leaders in 2002, hope increased that a new peace initiative would finally end the long and bloody struggle.

Outlook and Gains

Making accurate generalizations about Africa is difficult. Every nation is different. Some nations have rich resources to help finance progress. Others lack resources. Each country has its own set of circumstances and its own history. Despite many setbacks, African nations have made progress. As independent nations, they carved out a place on the world scene and won the power to shape their own future. Within each nation, the process of building a national identity went slowly. But education and urbanization did begin to break the localism of the past.

Education and Health Care As governments set up more schools, literacy rates rose. Every year, more students entered high school. Universities trained a new generation of leaders.

A few countries promoted higher education for women, and great strides were made in providing girls with elementary school education. Relatively few girls, however, went on to high school because they were needed to help their mothers with farm work and household chores. As a result, illiteracy among African women remained high, especially in rural areas.

Most African nations sought to improve health care and created family planning programs. Governments saw that population growth had profound effects on the standards of living.

Economic Opportunity Despite often-depressing economic news, Africa has enormous potential for growth. By the 1990s, many nations had learned from failed policies of the past. With free-market reforms, countries such as Ghana enjoyed economic growth. Other nations expanded mining and manufacturing. Some built factories and expanded communication and transportation networks.

Cultural Influence In literature, film, and the arts, Africans made major contributions to global culture. Writing in African languages produced many writers with large local audiences. Other African writers used western languages to reach a world audience. In music and dance, Africans and members of the "African diaspora"—African-descended citizens of other lands—helped shape the culture of the century. Influential diaspora musical forms included jazz, blues, reggae, and samba.

Global Connections

The Scars of War

After Angola gained independence in 1975, a bitter civil war broke out. Angolans found themselves in the middle of a Cold War battlefield. The Soviet Union offered the Popular Liberation Movement of Angola (MPLA), millions of dollars in arms. It also arranged for thousands of Cuban soldiers to travel to Angola to bolster support. The United States, on the other hand, provided aid to the National Union for the Total Independence of Angola (UNITA), which opposed the MPLA's Marxist policies.

Fighting finally ended in 1991, but the unrest continues. Today, UNITA controls about 70 percent of Angola, including most of the diamond trade, while the MPLA retains the oil-rich regions. Caught between the two are thousands of refugees who still wait for life to return to normal.

Theme: Political and Social Systems How did Angola become a victim of the Cold War?

SECTION 4 Assessment

Recall

1. **Identify: (a)** Robert Mugabe, **(b)** Joshua Nkomo, **(c)** African National Congress, **(d)** Nelson Mandela, **(e)** F. W. de Klerk, **(f)** Southwest African People's Organization.

Comprehension

2. How did Zimbabwe achieve independence?
3. **(a)** Identify major events leading to the elimination of apartheid. **(b)** Describe how South Africa has changed since 1989.

4. How did the Cold War affect independence movements in southern Africa?
5. How have African nations worked to improve conditions?

Critical Thinking and Writing

6. **Drawing Conclusions** Would a country be likely to face greater challenges after independence if it won freedom through fighting or through negotiation? Explain.
7. **Identifying Main Ideas** Why was the idea of majority rule so important to people in African nations?

Go Online
PHSchool.com

Research the history of one of the nations discussed in this section. Create an illustrated time line that shows important dates and events in that nation's history. For help with this activity, use **Web Code mkd-3629.**

Creating a Chapter Summary

Complete the concept web by filling in circles with appropriate information from the chapter. Add more circles as needed.

For additional review and enrichment activities, see the interactive version of *World History* available on the Web and on CD-ROM.

Go Online
PHSchool.com
For practice test questions for Chapter 23, use **Web Code mka-3630**.

Building Vocabulary

For each of the terms below, write a sentence using the term.
1. **one-party system**
2. **mixed economy**
3. **desertification**

Recalling Key Facts

4. How did the colonial legacy affect independence movements in Africa?
5. Compare independence movements in Ghana, Kenya, and Algeria.
6. What role did international organizations play in Africa during the Cold War?
7. What choices did new nations face as they tried to build productive economies?
8. Describe the effects of the population explosion on the African environment.
9. Explain how modernization affected (a) cities, (b) women, (c) religious groups.
10. How has oil affected Nigeria's development?

11. What were Julius Nyerere's goals for Tanzania?
12. How did South Africa overcome apartheid?
13. How did the Cold War affect southern Africa?
14. Describe how education and urbanization have encouraged development in Africa.

Critical Thinking and Writing

15. **Synthesizing Information** How were African nations affected by military dictatorships? Support your answer with examples.
16. **Connecting to Geography** How have subsistence farming and population growth affected desertification in Africa?
17. **Making Inferences** Based on information in this chapter, what types of economic development seem to have been most successful? Explain.
18. **Drawing Conclusions** How has majority rule affected political stability in southern African nations?

In 1998, Catherine Bertini, executive director of the World Food Programme, gave a speech about hunger issues in Africa. Read this excerpt and answer the questions that follow.

"In Africa, women provide roughly 80 percent of the labor to grow, process, and store food. They account for 60 percent of the labor needed to harvest and market food. They must be involved and benefit from agricultural innovations and reforms, and from food aid and other forms of assistance. . . .

Emphasizing women is done because it is the most efficient way to improve the nutrition of families. . . . Robert Fogel, a Nobel laureate in economics, . . . estimates . . . that almost a third of the growth in per capita income in Britain in the last two centuries can actually be attributed to better nutrition in the workforce. Study after study . . . has shown a clear connection between nutritional status and the productivity and wage earnings of workers. . . ."

—Catherine Bertini, speech delivered February 19, 1998

19. What role do women play in African agriculture?

20. What assistance does Bertini recommend?

21. Why, according to Bertini, must women be at the center of efforts to improve nutrition?

22. **(a)** What economic information does she use to support her point? **(b)** Does this theory seem reasonable? Explain your answer.

Skills Tip

When you read a primary source, pay careful attention to the information used to support the writer's or speaker's opinion.

Go Online
PHSchool.com

Use the Internet to research current development projects in one African nation. Create a poster that shows how these projects are supposed to affect your chosen nation. For help with this activity, use **Web Code mkd-3631.**

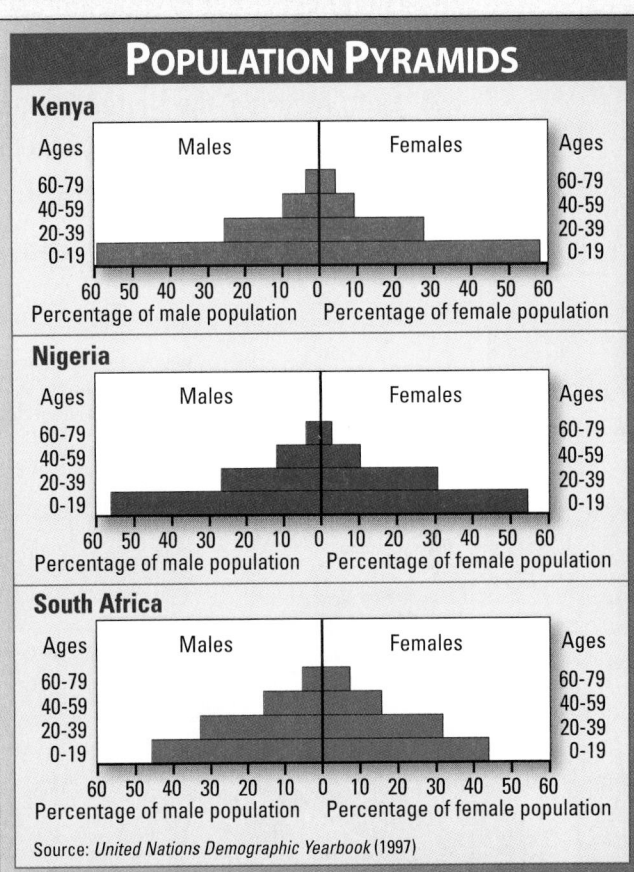

POPULATION PYRAMIDS

Source: *United Nations Demographic Yearbook* (1997)

A population pyramid is a bar graph that shows the percentages of males and females by age group in a particular country. The shape can also tell you whether a population is growing or declining. A wide base indicates growth, and a narrow base indicates decline. Study the graphs and answer the following questions:

23. Which country has the highest percentage of females ages 60–79?

24. Which country has the lowest percentage of males ages 0–19?

25. Which is the largest age group in each of the three countries?

26. How would you explain the great difference in size between age ranges 0–19 and 20–39?

27. According to the population pyramids, which nation seems to be experiencing the fastest rate of growth?

Latin America
1945–Present

Chapter Preview

1 Forces Shaping Modern Latin America
2 Latin America, the United States, and the World
3 Mexico, Central America, and the Caribbean
4 Focus on Argentina and Brazil

1948

The Organization of American States is formed. Its colorful symbol, above, consists of the furled flags of its member nations.

1959

In Cuba, Fidel Castro and his guerrilla army overthrow a corrupt dictator. Later, Castro establishes a communist dictatorship.

CHAPTER EVENTS

1940   1955   1970

GLOBAL EVENTS

1949 The People's Republic of China is founded.

1960s Many African nations gain independence from European rule.

Population Density of Latin America

Latin America is a diverse region that stretches across Mexico, Central America, the Caribbean, and South America. The region's population is very unevenly distributed.
.

Robinson Projection

0 — 1000 Miles
0 — 1000 Kilometers

MEXICO
Gulf of Mexico
BAHAMAS
CUBA
DOMINICAN REPUBLIC
PUERTO RICO (U.S.)
JAMAICA **HAITI**
BELIZE
HONDURAS *Caribbean Sea*
GUATEMALA
EL SALVADOR **NICARAGUA**
COSTA RICA
PANAMA
VENEZUELA **GUYANA**
SURINAME
FRENCH GUIANA (Fr.)
COLOMBIA
Equator
ECUADOR
PACIFIC OCEAN
PERU
BRAZIL
BOLIVIA
PARAGUAY
CHILE
URUGUAY
ARGENTINA
ATLANTIC OCEAN
Tropic of Cancer
120°W
100°W
80°W
60°W
20°N
0°
20°S
Tropic of Capricorn
N W E S

Persons per sq. mi.		Persons per sq. km.
250 +		100 +
100–249		40–99
25–99		10–39
5–24		3–9
0–4		0–2
Data unavailable		Data unavailable

1983
In Argentina, people celebrate the end of military rule and the restoration of democracy.

2000
After more than 70 years of rule by the Institutional Revolutionary Party (PRI), Mexico elects the opposition candidate Vicente Fox as president (above, at left).

1985   2000   2015

1980s A global economic slowdown causes many governments to reduce spending.

Go Online
PHSchool.com

To learn about recent developments in Latin America, use **Web Code mkc-3733.**

Forces Shaping Modern Latin America

Reading Focus

- Why is Latin America a culturally diverse region?
- What conditions contributed to unrest in Latin American countries?
- What forces shaped political, economic, and social patterns in Latin America?

Vocabulary

import substitution
agribusiness
liberation theology

Taking Notes

As you read this section, make an outline of its contents. Use Roman numerals for major headings, capital letters for subheadings, and numbers for supporting details. The model at right will help you get started.

I. A diverse region
  A. Geographic diversity
    1.
    2.
  B. Cultural diversity
II. Sources of unrest
  A. Social structure
    1.
    2.
  B. Population and poverty

Main Idea   **Latin America's development is influenced by geography, culture, social patterns, and political and economic conditions.**

Setting the Scene

For Carolina Maria de Jesus, life in the slums of São Paulo, Brazil, was filled with hardship. Like millions of other poor people, she had moved from the country to the city. To earn money to feed her family, she combed garbage for paper, cans, and other scraps to sell. In her diary, De Jesus described her daily struggle against poverty:

> "July 16. I went to Senhor Manuel, carrying some cans to sell. . . . He gave me 13 [coins]. I kept thinking that I had to buy bread, soap, and milk. . . . The 13 [coins] wouldn't make it. I returned . . . to my shack, nervous and exhausted. I thought of the worrisome life that I led, carrying paper, washing clothes for the children, staying in the street all day long."
> —Carolina Maria de Jesus, *Child of the Dark*

After 1945, Latin American nations faced problems similar to those of other emerging nations—rapid population growth, poverty, illiteracy, political instability, and authoritarian governments. In Latin America, as elsewhere, each country pursued its own course toward modernization.

A Diverse Region

Latin America stretches across an immense region from Mexico, Central America, and the Caribbean through South America. It includes 33 independent countries that range from tiny island nations like Grenada and Haiti to giant Brazil, which is almost as large as the United States.

Skills Assessment

Graph Latin America is a region of ethnic and cultural diversity. **What ethnic group is the largest in each of the following countries? (a) Haiti, (b) Argentina, (c) Peru.**

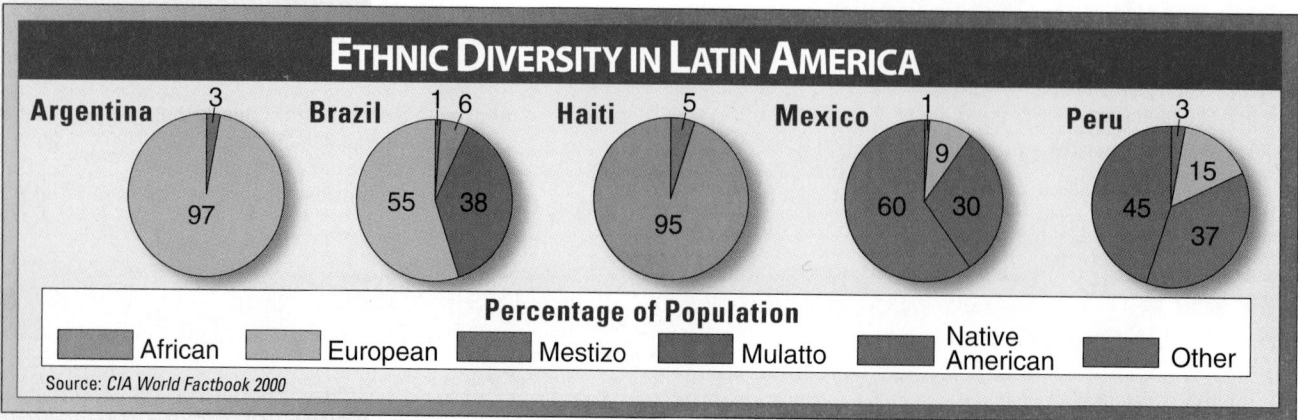

ETHNIC DIVERSITY IN LATIN AMERICA

Argentina	Brazil	Haiti	Mexico	Peru
97, 3	55, 38, 1, 6	95, 5	60, 30, 9, 1	45, 37, 15, 3

Percentage of Population

African   European   Mestizo   Mulatto   Native American   Other

Source: *CIA World Factbook 2000*

Conquest, immigration, and intermarriage made Latin America culturally diverse. After 1492, Europeans imposed their civilization on Native Americans. They later brought millions of Africans to the region. As these populations mingled, they created vital new cultures. Since the late 1800s, immigrants from Europe and Asia have further contributed to the diversity. Today, people of Indian descent are still the majority population in Mexico, Guatemala, Peru, and Bolivia. Brazil has more people of African descent than any other Latin American nation. Although Spanish is the chief language of the region, Portuguese, French, English, Creole, and hundreds of Native American languages and African dialects are also spoken.

Sources of Unrest

For decades after World War II, uprisings and revolutions shook much of Latin America. Although they grew in part out of changes brought by modernization, they also reflected the failure to reform deep-rooted inequalities.

Social Structure Since colonial days, a key feature of Latin America has been the uneven distribution of wealth. In most countries, a tiny elite controlled the land, mines, businesses, and factories. The wealthy few opposed reforms that threatened their economic power. A growing gulf between rich and poor fueled discontent in the postwar era.

Poverty was linked to the social structure that had survived since colonial times. The upper classes were mostly descended from Europeans. The great majority of the population—the urban and rural poor—were mestizos, Native Americans, or people of African descent.

By the mid-1900s, two social classes were emerging as important forces. As cities grew, the middle class and urban working class expanded. They were less tied to particular ethnic groups than the old aristocracy and peasantry. Both had their own hopes for progress and prosperity.

Population and Poverty In Latin America, as elsewhere, the population explosion contributed to poverty. Between 1930 and 1985, for example, the populations of both Brazil and Mexico increased by more than four times. Growth rates in some countries slowed during the 1990s, but economies were still hard pressed to keep pace with population. Overall populations kept rising because a large proportion of the people were young and just starting their own families. Latin America's population reached 400 million in 1990 and exceeded 600 million in 2000.

In rural areas, where most of the people were peasant farmers, population growth put stress on the land. A family might own a small plot for growing food. But most farmers worked for low wages on the estates of wealthy landlords who held the best land. Many had to borrow money from their landlords just to get by from harvest to harvest. Burdened by this so-called debt slavery, they were tied to the land unless they ran away to the cities.

Urbanization Pressure on the land contributed to the great migration that sent millions of peasants to the cities. Today, about 70 percent of all Latin Americans live in cities. Some newcomers found jobs in factories,

Source of Unrest
The gulf between rich and poor contributes to unrest in Latin America. This family lives in a shack near Lima, Peru.

Theme: Political and Social Systems Why do you think poor health is often a problem for people who live in communities such as this?

Military Regimes

Military officers ruled many Latin American countries in the 1960s and 1970s. In other nations, elected officials stayed in power only with the army's support. In this painting, *The Parrots,* Colombian artist Beatriz González uses the repeating image of a civilian president flanked by generals.

Theme: Art and Literature Why do you think the artist did not stress the leaders' facial features?

offices, or stores. Many more survived by working odd jobs such as doing laundry or mending shoes. Others scavenged at the city garbage dump.

In the shantytowns that ringed Latin American cities, people lived in shacks without electricity, sewage, or other services. Yet because they were near urban centers, they were more likely to attend school or have access to health care than were the rural poor. As a result, poor city children were sometimes in a better position to move ahead than rural children.

Politics: Reform, Repression, or Revolution

Most Latin American states had constitutions modeled on those of France or the United States. On paper, they protected the rights of individuals. Yet real democracy seemed difficult to achieve in nations plagued by poverty and inequality.

Competing Ideologies After World War II, various groups pressed for reforms. They included liberals, socialists, students, labor leaders, peasant organizers, and Catholic priests and nuns. Although they differed over how to achieve their goals, all wanted to improve conditions for the poor. Most called for schools, housing, health care, and land reform.

Conservative forces, however, resisted reforms that might undermine their power. These elite groups included the military, the traditional landed aristocracy, and the growing business middle class. They often had strong ties to foreign investors and corporations. Conflict between conservatives and reformers contributed to political instability in many nations.

Military Regimes Military leaders, like *caudillos* of the 1800s, held power in many Latin American nations. They often served conservative interests. However, some supported modest social and economic reforms, in part because a growing number of officers came from the working classes.

In the 1960s and 1970s, as social unrest increased, military governments seized power in Argentina, Brazil, Chile, and elsewhere. Claiming the need to restore order, they imposed harsh regimes. They outlawed political parties, censored the press, and closed universities. In Argentina and Chile, the military imprisoned and executed thousands of dissidents. Others were murdered by illegal "death squads" allied to the government.

Some military rulers tried to solve economic problems by sponsoring capitalism. In Chile, General Augusto Pinochet (pee noh SHAY), who ruled from 1973 to 1990, promoted foreign investment and privatized industry. The Chilean economy did expand. In general, however, most military regimes were unable to solve basic problems.

The Threat of Revolution During the 1960s and 1970s, guerrillas and urban terrorists battled repressive governments in many Latin American countries. Rebel groups used bombings, kidnappings, and assassinations. The leaders of many of these groups supported Marxist goals. Only a socialist revolution, they said, could end inequalities. Marxism won support among peasants, urban workers, and some intellectuals. Other revolutionaries were motivated by nationalism. They condemned economic and cultural domination by the United States.

During the Cold War, the spread of Marxism complicated moderate reform efforts. Conservatives tended to view any effort at reform as a communist threat and often won support from the United States.

Revival of Democracy By the mid-1980s, inflation, debt, and growing protests led repressive leaders to step aside. Argentina, Brazil, Chile, and other countries held multiparty elections to replace military governments with civilian governments. As the twenty-first century began, the only major nonelected ruler in Latin America was Cuba's Fidel Castro.

Still, elections alone could not ensure a truly democratic government. In Peru, for example, President Alberto Fujimori suspended the nation's constitution to crush antigovernment guerrillas and engineered his own reelection before fleeing the country. President Hugo Chavez of Venezuela centralized power in his own hands to advance his populist and nationalist "Bolivarian revolution." Heavy debt burdens and economic slowdowns have threatened the success of Latin America's elected rulers, putting the stability of democratic governments in the region in doubt.

 Primary Sources and Literature

See "Mario Vargas Llosa: Latin America, the Democratic Option" in the Reference Section at the back of this book.

Economic Development

Except during the Great Depression of the 1930s, most Latin American nations experienced economic growth between 1900 and the 1960s. Their economies, though, were influenced by global economic trends and dependence on industrial nations. Many relied on the export of a single crop or commodity, so they were hard hit if harvests failed or demand declined. By the 1960s, Latin America faced growing competition from African and Asian nations seeking to export their crops and commodities.

Industry To reduce dependence on imported goods, many Latin American governments encouraged the development of local industries. This policy, called import substitution, had mixed success. The middle class prospered, but life did not improve for most people. Many of the new industries were inefficient and needed government help or foreign capital

Women in Government

Today, a growing number of women are becoming leaders in government. Mireya Moscoso was elected the first woman president of Panama. She follows in the footsteps of her husband, Arnulfo Arias, a former president.

Theme: Continuity and Change How does Mireya Moscoso represent both continuity and change?

to survive. Also, industry did not expand rapidly enough to produce new jobs for a rapidly growing population. Eventually, governments returned to promoting agricultural exports.

Expanding Agriculture Over the past 60 years, large areas of land were opened up for farming through irrigation and the clearing of forests. Much of the best farmland belonged to agribusinesses, or giant commercial farms owned by multinational corporations. They used modern technology to develop the land and operate processing plants. In Central America and Brazil, developers cleared tropical forests to provide new farmlands.

Commercial agriculture increased the need to import food. Production of some food crops declined as land was turned over to growing crops for export. As a result, more food had to be imported, at a high cost.

Economic Challenges In the 1980s, Latin American nations were shaken by economic storms, including high oil costs, rising interest rates, and a global recession. High interest rates meant nations that had borrowed money to develop industry were crushed by debt.

To ease the debt crisis, nations like Mexico and Brazil took strong steps. They cut spending on social programs, raised prices, and opened their markets to foreign companies. Most governments brought their debt payments under control. Still, most nations continued to be affected by global economic swings, and some suffered severe economic crises.

Since the 1990s, Latin American governments have strengthened regional free trade blocs. Two trade blocs, the Andean Community and the Southern Common Market (Mercosur), have talked about merging. Said one supporter, "Together we are stronger than apart." In addition, the North American Free Trade Association (NAFTA) linked Mexico to markets in the United States and Canada. By expanding markets, free trade organizations opened the way to economic growth.

Changing Social Patterns

In Latin America, as elsewhere, urbanization brought social upheaval. City life weakened the extended family of rural villages and often replaced it with the smaller nuclear family. Instead of raising food, family members had to earn cash. The struggle to make a living caused some families to fall apart. In large cities, thousands of abandoned or runaway children roamed the streets. Many were caught up in crime and violence. To support their families, many women took jobs outside the home.

Women Throughout the 1900s, Latin American women worked hard to increase their role in public life and to win equality, including the right to vote. By 1961, women had won the vote throughout the Americas. By the

1990s, women moved into the political arena in small but growing numbers. Argentina, Nicaragua, and Panama had women presidents, and Benedita da Silva became the first black woman elected to the Brazilian congress.

Women's status varied according to class and race. Generally, women were responsible for the home and for child care. Upper-class women had access to education and professional careers and could hire servants to care for their homes and children. Rural women of Indian or African descent faced prejudice and poverty. They lacked schooling and basic health care, and they often labored for low pay.

A peasant woman from El Salvador, who began harvesting coffee and cotton at age 16, described the injustices she endured. One problem was the quota system: "They'd give you two and a half sacks as a quota for every day and if you didn't manage it, they didn't pay you anything." Another complaint was unequal treatment: "Men have always been paid 5 colones more than women or children and we all do exactly the same work."

Women struggled to win change. To help their families and communities, some peasant women pushed for schools and health care. In Argentina and elsewhere, women protested human rights abuses by brutal military governments. During the harsh Pinochet years in Chile, women in Santiago organized food kitchens to serve meals to the poor. Others protested violence against women or challenged the subordinate position of women within the family.

Religion   The Catholic Church has remained a powerful force throughout Latin America. Traditionally, it was often tied to the conservative ruling class. However, some Church leaders had always spoken up for the poor. During the 1960s and 1970s, many priests, nuns, and church workers crusaded for social justice and an end to poverty. Their movement became known as liberation theology. These activists saw Jesus as a "liberator of the poor." They urged the Church to become a force for reform. Many joined the struggle against oppressive governments. Some became objects of violence themselves. In El Salvador, for example, Archbishop Oscar Romero was assassinated by a right-wing death squad.

Some evangelical Protestant groups won a growing following among the poor. Their message, which emphasized the power of faith, had an especially strong appeal among women, who then brought other family members into the faith.

Primary Source

Catholics Take Action
Dom Hélder Câmara, a Catholic bishop, outlined his vision for the Catholic Church in Brazil:

"We will [help] to keep poverty from sinking into misery. . . . But I have not come here to help anyone [trick] himself into thinking that a little charity and social work will [be enough]. . . . If we really want to get to the root of our social ills, we will have to help our country break out of the vicious circle of underdevelopment and misery. . . . It would be an unpardonable scandal if the Church were to abandon the masses in their hour of greatest need, as if [it] took no interest in helping them reach a level of human, Christian dignity compatible with real citizenship."

—Dom Hélder Câmara,
Revolution Through Peace

Skills Assessment

Primary Source On what problem does Bishop Câmara suggest that the Catholic Church focus in Brazil?

SECTION 1 Assessment

Recall
1. **Identify:** **(a)** debt slavery, **(b)** Alberto Fujimori, **(c)** Hugo Chavez, **(d)** Benedita da Silva.
2. **Define:** **(a)** import substitution, **(b)** agribusiness, **(c)** liberation theology.

Comprehension
3. How does the history of Latin America explain its cultural diversity today?
4. Describe four conditions that fed unrest in Latin America.
5. Describe how each of the following has affected Latin America: **(a)** military regimes,

(b) economic nationalism, **(c)** religion.

Critical Thinking and Writing
6. **Synthesizing Information** Review the Setting the Scene and the picture of Lima, Peru, on the first pages of the section. Use the primary source and the picture to write an editorial commenting on the condition of poor families in Latin America.
7. **Recognizing Causes and Effects** Explain the causes and effects of the debt crisis that afflicted Latin America and other parts of the world in the 1980s.

Go Online
PHSchool.com

Use the Internet to find information about urban populations in Latin America. Identify the largest cities in order of population, and plot these cities on a map. Create a database that indicates each city's population and the year the data were gathered. For help with this activity, use **Web Code mkd-3739.**

Latin America, the United States, and the World

Reading Focus

- How did communist rule affect Cuba?
- What policies has the United States followed in Latin America?
- What global issues have linked Latin America to other regions of the world?

Vocabulary

literacy rate
embargo

Taking Notes

Make an organizer like the one shown here to outline relations between the United States and nations of Latin America. Complete the chart as you read. Add as many boxes as you need.

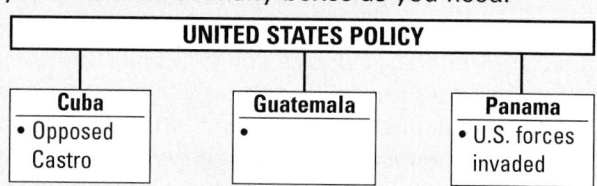

UNITED STATES POLICY		

Cuba	Guatemala	Panama
• Opposed Castro	•	• U.S. forces invaded

Main Idea Latin American nations have developed policies in response to United States influence, regional issues, and global issues.

Setting the Scene "The duty of every revolutionary is to make revolution," declared Cuban dictator Fidel Castro in 1962. After bringing about sweeping changes in his island nation, Castro vowed to export communism to other countries in the region. During the Cold War, the threat of communist revolution had a strong influence on United States policy toward Latin America. Meanwhile, Latin American nations tried to limit United States influence in the region. Today, Latin American nations are building new political and economic relations in the global arena.

Communism in Cuba

After the Spanish-American War, Cuba won independence from Spain. However, Cuba was controlled by the United States under the Platt Amendment to the Cuban Constitution until 1935. During this time, American investors bought up Cuban plantations and mills, and the United States became the chief buyer of Cuba's sugar. It continued to support military dictators.

Castro In the 1950s, a young lawyer, Fidel Castro, rallied forces opposed to the corrupt Batista regime. By 1959, Castro had led his tiny guerrilla army to victory. Cubans cheered the rebel as a hero. For many, the joy soon wore off as Castro turned Cuba into a communist state. Castro nationalized foreign-owned sugar plantations and other businesses. He put most land under government control and distributed the rest to peasant farmers.

While Castro imposed harsh authoritarian rule, he did improve conditions for the poor. During the 1960s, Cuba provided basic health care for all, promoted equality for women, and increased the nation's literacy rate, the percentage of a population that can read and write. But communist dictatorship angered middle-class Cubans. Critics were jailed or silenced, and hundreds of thousands fled to the United States.

Cold War Tensions The Cuban Revolution alarmed the United States, especially as Castro turned to the Soviet Union for aid. In 1961, the United States backed a plot by anti-Castro exiles to invade Cuba and overthrow Castro. An invasion force landed at the Bay of Pigs in Cuba but was quickly crushed. The next year, the United States imposed an embargo on Cuba. An embargo is a ban on trade. Castro sought closer ties to the Soviet Union. He let the Soviets build nuclear missile bases in Cuba, just 90 miles from Florida. The threat of nearby Soviet nuclear bases outraged the United States and touched off a dangerous crisis.

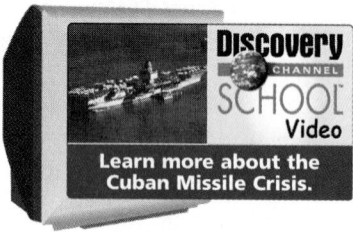

Learn more about the Cuban Missile Crisis.

Biography

Fidel Castro 1926(?) —

While studying law at the University of Havana, Castro and other students took part in a failed attempt to invade the Dominican Republic and overthrow its dictator, Rafael Trujillo. Castro earned his law degree and became a vocal opponent of dictator Fulgencio Batista. In 1953, Castro led an attack on an army barracks. The assault failed and resulted in his imprisonment. After his release, he went into exile in Mexico. In 1956, he returned to Cuba and launched the guerrilla war that eventually led to his victory.

Theme: Impact of the Individual How did Castro demonstrate an ability to overcome failure?

In October 1962, President John Kennedy declared a naval blockade of Cuba and demanded that the Soviets remove the weapons. For several days during the Cuban missile crisis, the superpowers stood on the brink of nuclear war. In the end, Soviet leader Nikita Khrushchev backed down. He agreed to remove the missiles from Cuba.

Over the next decades, Castro tried to encourage revolution in other Latin American nations. Cuba also sent troops to Africa to help the socialist government of Angola. In response, the United States continued its efforts to isolate Cuba and undermine Castro. The Soviets, meanwhile, provided massive economic and military aid to Cuba.

Recent Trends When the Soviet Union collapsed in the early 1990s, Cuba lost its chief ally and trading partner. Without Soviet financial aid, Cuba's economy fell into a shambles. In response, Castro encouraged tourism, allowed some features of a market economy, and welcomed foreign investment. At the same time, however, he vowed to preserve communism.

The United States refused to negotiate with Castro, despite the urgings of the United Nations and Latin American leaders, who argued that Cuba no longer posed a threat. Still, as American business people visited the country and baseball teams from the two nations competed, it seemed less and less likely that either Cuban communism or the American embargo would endure for long.

The United States and Latin America

Like powerful nations in many times and places, the United States developed a sphere of influence that included smaller neighboring states. The United States was the leading investor and trading partner for most nations in Latin America. Profits from United States-owned companies flowed from Latin America to the north. At the same time, cultural influences drifted both north and south.

Despite their links, the United States and its neighbors had very different views of one another. The United States saw itself as the defender of democracy and capitalism and the source of humanitarian aid. Many Latin Americans, however, resented that they lived under the shadow of the "colossus of the north."

Intervention During the Cold War, the United States intervened repeatedly in Latin America. It did so to protect its interests and to prevent the spread of communism. The United States backed anti-communist dictators and helped equip and train their soldiers to fight rebel uprisings. It even helped topple leftist leaders.

In 1954, for example, the United States helped Guatemalan soldiers overthrow a popularly elected president, Jacobo Arbenz. This action came after he had enacted land reforms that threatened United States-owned businesses. In the 1970s, after socialist Salvador Allende (ah YEHN day) was elected president of Chile, President Richard Nixon told officials to "make the [Chilean] economy scream." In 1973, the United States quietly lent its support to a military coup that overthrew Allende.

Other United States interventions in Latin America were unrelated to the threat of communism. In 1989, United States forces invaded Panama and overthrew the government of General Manuel Noriega. Noriega was removed from Panama and then tried, convicted, and imprisoned for drug trafficking. In the 1990s, the United States used economic pressure and the threat of military action to force military rulers from power in Haiti.

Many Latin Americans opposed United States economic and military intervention. Although they perhaps admired the wealth and technology of the United States, they often resented its political, economic, and cultural influence in Latin America.

Did You Know?

Escape From Cuba

To flee poverty and political repression, many Cuban *balseros* (rafters) braved 90 miles of open sea to reach the United States. Men, women, and children crossed the Straits of Florida on rickety rafts, small boats, and smugglers' speedboats. Not all survived the trip.

Sun, waves, winds, and even hurricanes imperiled those trying to escape from Cuba. "The weather was so bad that we were lost for the next two days," said one balsero. "We were pushed into the middle of the Atlantic . . . [and] were followed by sharks." The sole survivor of another voyage recalled: "When the raft fell apart, all of us grabbed whatever tire and wood we could."

Theme: Political and Social Systems Why were people willing to risk the voyage from Cuba to Florida?

Cutting Down Lives?

As loggers cut down trees in the Amazon rain forest, medical experts worry. They worry because they know that vital medicines—both discovered and undiscovered—are derived from plants found only in the Amazon and other rain forests. For example, the bark of the cinchona tree produces quinine, which is used for treating malaria. Curare, used by Indians of the Amazon as a dart poison, serves as a muscle relaxant during surgery. A wild Amazonian yam provides a drug that can be used in the treatment of autoimmune diseases and some forms of cancer. One day, the medical experts fear, the loss of plant life in the rain forests and other ecosystems might result in the loss of human life.

Theme: Global Interaction
How might destruction of rain forests lead to loss of human life?

Regional Organizations   Despite disagreements, Latin American nations and the United States did work together. The Organization of American States (OAS) was formed in 1948 to promote democracy, economic cooperation, and human rights. Members pledged not to interfere "directly or indirectly, for any reason whatever, in the internal or external affairs of any other State." Although the United States often dominated the OAS, Latin American members did at times pursue an independent line.

The Castro revolution and other Cold War tensions led President Kennedy to launch the Alliance for Progress in 1961. Under this ambitious program, the United States offered billions in loans and investments. In exchange, Latin American governments were to enact genuine reforms. The goals were to promote education and land reform, reduce inequality and poverty, weaken dictatorships, and help countries avoid revolutions.

The alliance produced little progress. Landowners and the business elite in many countries opposed basic reforms. The United States provided aid to Latin America, but never on the scale proposed by Kennedy.

Regional and Global Issues

By the end of the Cold War, many Latin American nations had reduced their dependence on the United States, although it remained their chief trading partner. Increasingly, they were tied to the global economy. Oil-rich Venezuela joined Arab nations in OPEC, while Brazil worked with coffee-exporting nations of Africa to support coffee prices.

Many Latin American nations increased trade and cultural links to European countries. Some exported food or minerals to Asian nations. Japanese investments in Latin America, especially in Brazil, rose rapidly.

Regional Ties   In Latin America, as elsewhere around the world, regional trading blocs gained importance in the 1990s. Such groups created larger markets by lowering trade barriers among neighboring countries. In 1993, Mexico linked its economy to those of the United States and Canada through NAFTA. Two years later, a new South American trading bloc, Mercosur, paved the way for increased trade among Argentina, Brazil, Paraguay, and Uruguay. The new groups operated alongside older blocs that linked Andean, Caribbean, or Central American nations. Talks were also underway to create a hemisphere-wide free-trade zone that would be even larger than the expanding European Union.

The Drug Wars   Regional cooperation was essential to efforts to control the illegal drug trade. Indians in Colombia, Peru, and Bolivia had for centuries grown coca for their own uses. However, as drug use increased in various parts of the world, criminal gangs, also known as drug cartels, began producing and exporting ever-larger quantities of cocaine and other drugs. By the 1970s, drug lords were reaping huge profits, which they used to bribe government officials. They also hired assassins to kill judges, journalists, and others who spoke out against them.

In the 1980s, the United States declared a "war on drugs." To halt the flow of drugs, the United States pressed governments in Colombia, Peru, and other countries to destroy coca crops and move against the cartels. Governments cooperated, but many Latin Americans argued that the root of the problem was not the supply of drugs but the growing demand for illegal drugs in the United States.

Development Versus the Environment   Concerns about the environment also raised some troubling issues for Latin America and the world.

Developing nations insisted that they needed to exploit their land and other resources if they wanted economic growth. "You cannot talk ecology to people who are struggling to survive," said a Brazilian delegate at an international conference on the environment. Developing nations pointed out that western powers had long since cleared many of their forests and mined their lands. What right, they asked, did industrial nations have to tell them to stop developing their resources?

The most widely publicized issue was the rapid destruction of the Amazon rain forest, which occupies more than a million square miles in the heart of Brazil. It is rich in mineral resources needed for economic growth. It also could provide land to millions of landless peasants. Since the 1930s, Brazil has opened more and more of this area to development. By the 1970s and 1980s, vast tracts of forest were being bulldozed and burned for farms, cattle ranches, highways, and even newly planned cities.

Environmentalists argued that deforestation had enormous costs. They called the Amazon rain forest "the lungs of the world" because it plays a key role in absorbing poisonous carbon dioxide from the air and releasing essential oxygen. It has been home to 15 million species of plants and animals, which have been threatened by development. Some forms of plant life might even hold undiscovered cures for diseases.

Another environmental concern was rapid development, which meant disaster for many native peoples. Isolation had protected bands of Native American forest dwellers for centuries. Land-hungry farmers, speculators, and foreign mining companies converged on the forest, threatening these ancient ways of life. Many Indians died of diseases introduced by the newcomers. Others were killed in conflicts provoked by impatient developers moving into the forest.

Migration Latin American immigration to the United States increased rapidly after the 1970s. Poverty, civil war, and repressive governments led many people to flee their homelands. Like earlier immigrants, they sought freedom and economic opportunity.

By the early 2000s, Latin Americans were the largest immigrant group in the United States. Immigrants came from all parts of Latin America and the Caribbean. Many entered the United States legally and became citizens. A large number, however, were illegal immigrants. As a result, pressure rose to halt illegal immigration. After the 2001 terrorist attacks, the United States moved to strengthen border controls.

SECTION 2 Assessment

Recall

1. **Identify:** **(a)** Fidel Castro, **(b)** Bay of Pigs, **(c)** Cuban missile crisis, **(d)** Salvador Allende, **(e)** Manuel Noriega, **(f)** OAS, **(g)** Alliance for Progress, **(h)** NAFTA, **(i)** Mercosur, **(j)** drug cartel.
2. **Define:** **(a)** literacy rate, **(b)** embargo.

Comprehension

3. What changes did communism bring to life in Cuba?
4. Describe how United States political and economic policies have affected relations with countries of Latin America.
5. How have Latin American nations addressed regional and global issues?

Critical Thinking and Writing

6. **Connecting to Geography** **(a)** What environmental issues face Latin American nations? **(b)** Which of the five themes of geography seems most closely linked to these issues? Explain.
7. **Recognizing Causes and Effects** **(a)** How did the anti-communist stance of the United States affect Cuba? **(b)** How did the collapse of the Soviet Union affect Cuba?

Go Online
PHSchool.com

Use the Internet to find recent news articles concerning one Latin American nation's involvement with one of the regional or global issues discussed in this section. Using the news articles, prepare a radio broadcast to deliver to the class. For help with this activity, use **Web Code mkd-3743.**

Mexico, Central America, and the Caribbean

Reading Focus

- What conditions have changed and what conditions have remained the same in Mexico?

- Why did Central American countries suffer civil wars?

- What were the causes of Haiti's political and economic struggles?

Vocabulary

ejido

maquiladora

contra

Taking Notes

Make a table like the one below. Add key information about Mexico, Nicaragua, and two other countries.

	MEXICO	NICARAGUA		
POLITICS				
ECONOMICS	Land redistribution			

Main Idea Although Mexico underwent change with relatively little turmoil, several Central American countries were torn by civil war.

Primary Source

Heading Toward Democracy
Octavio Paz, a Mexican poet, philosopher, and winner of a Nobel Prize for literature, comments on democracy in Latin America:

"Latin American democracy was a late arrival on the scene, and it has been disfigured and betrayed time and time again. It has been weak, hesitant, rebellious, its own worst enemy, all too eager to worship the demagogue, corrupted by money, riddled with favoritism and nepotism. And yet almost everything good that has been achieved in Latin America in the last century and a half has been accomplished under democratic rule, or, as in Mexico, a rule heading toward democracy. A great deal still remains to be done."

—Octavio Paz, *One Earth, Four or Five Worlds: Reflections on Contemporary History*

Skills Assessment

Primary Source Does Paz favor or oppose democracy? Explain.

Setting the Scene

Oscar Romero was a conservative member of El Salvador's elite until he became archbishop. Then, he began to condemn government death squads that were killing peasants and students opposed to the government. From his pulpit, he announced, "The church would betray . . . its fidelity to the gospel if it stopped being . . . a defender of . . . every legitimate struggle to achieve a more just society."

Romero's outspoken stance cost him his life. On March 24, 1980, as he said mass, shots rang out. Moments later, Romero lay dead, a victim of the death squads he had denounced. But others took his place, and the protest against injustice continued. As one Salvadoran activist commented, "If you silence a prophet, he will speak out through his people."

In the latter half of the 1900s, El Salvador and other Central American countries were battered by civil wars. To the north, their larger and richer neighbor, Mexico, weathered those decades with relatively less turmoil.

Continuity and Change in Mexico

As you have read, Mexico endured a long, violent revolution in the early 1900s. After the revolution, government officials became committed—at least in theory—to improving conditions for the poor.

The Rural Poor In the 1930s, Mexico's president, Lázaro Cárdenas, had taken steps to fulfill the promises of the Mexican Revolution—especially land reform. He distributed millions of acres of land to peasants. Most was given to *ejidos* (eh HEE dohs), or peasant cooperatives. Some families also received small plots to farm themselves.

Over the years, however, the land reform program proved unsuccessful. Much of the land given to peasants was arid. It needed to be irrigated and fertilized to be productive. As rural populations grew, the land was subdivided and exhausted from overfarming. Presidents after Cárdenas paid less attention to Mexico's rural poor. Instead, they favored agribusinesses that produced cash-earning export crops.

As conditions worsened, many peasants migrated to towns and cities, especially to the capital. The population of Mexico City mushroomed from 1.5 million in 1940 to about 20 million in 1995.

The PRI in Control Since the Mexican Revolution, a single party—the Institutional Revolutionary Party (PRI)—has dominated Mexican politics. It claimed to represent all groups—from workers and peasants to business-industrial interests and the military. There were some other small political parties, but PRI bosses moved forcefully against any serious opposition.

In part, the PRI held on to power by responding to social ills with reform programs for education, welfare, and health. As a result, the party generally kept discontent from exploding into violence. Yet, in 1968, student protests shook Mexico as they did other western countries. Riot police and the army brutally suppressed the turmoil. The riots and the government's response received worldwide attention because the summer Olympic games were held in Mexico City that year. Despite widespread criticism, the PRI remained in power.

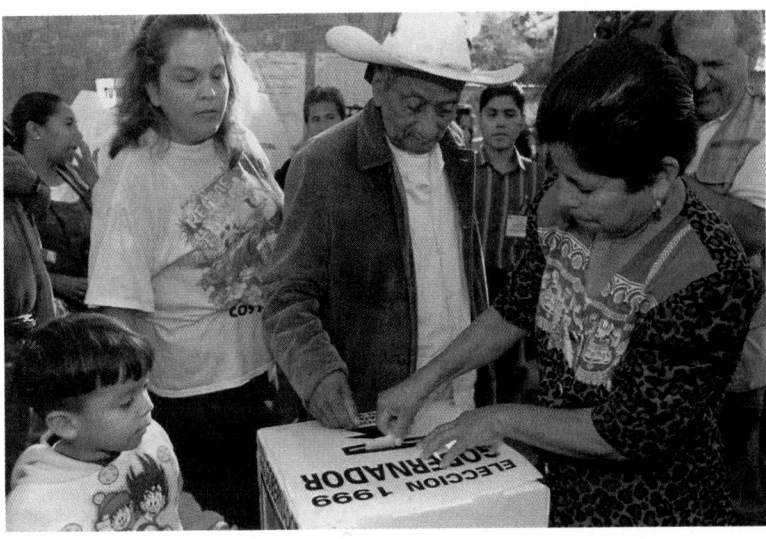

Mexican Democracy
For about 70 years, a single political party, the PRI, dominated Mexico's government. In 2000, Mexicans elected a president from an opposition party, Alliance for Change. The couple here are using a ballot box to vote.

Theme: Political and Social Systems Why is it important for a democracy to have at least two major political parties?

From time to time, the government faced rebel uprisings. One outbreak occurred in Chiapas, a state in southern Mexico which had a large Native American population. Discontent was high there because most Indians had benefited little from the nation's economic growth. In 1994, rebels took up arms and challenged the government. They demanded land reforms and rights for Native Americans. By skillfully using the media, the Chiapas rebels became international heroes. Yet they failed to achieve their goals.

Political Change Under intense pressure, the PRI had to make some election reforms. Stung by corruption and drug scandals along with internal splits, it lost its majority in the national legislature. In 2000, an opposition candidate, Vicente Fox, won election as Mexico's president, ending the PRI's long grip on power. Fox pushed to end official corruption, reduce poverty, and spur economic growth. He also tried to protect the rights of Mexico's indigenous people. Despite reforms, most Mexicans remained poor. Tens of thousands risked their lives to cross the border of the United States to find jobs.

Economic Ups and Downs After World War II, Mexico pushed ahead with efforts to foster import substitution, reduce foreign influence, and expand agriculture. To promote industry, the government worked closely with private businesses. It invested in building roads, dams, and ports. It also encouraged tourism.

From the 1940s to the early 1980s, both manufacturing and agriculture made huge gains. Mexico's economy became the second largest in Latin America after that of Brazil. This growth turned Mexico from an agricultural society into a mostly urban, industrial society. In the late 1970s, new oil discoveries and rising oil prices spurred an economic boom.

In the 1980s, however, global economic trends worked against Mexico. A worldwide recession, falling oil prices, and rising interest rates plunged the country deeply into debt. Like other debtor nations, Mexico cut spending on social and other programs so that it could make its debt payments. To spur economic recovery, the government reduced barriers to foreign businesses and privatized some industries.

Poverty and Prosperity As the 1900s came to an end, Mexico remained a disturbing mix of prosperity and poverty. *Maquiladoras* (mah kee luh DOHR uhs), or assembly plants owned by multinational corporations, flourished along Mexico's northern border. These plants used cheap Mexican labor to assemble imported parts for cars and electronic goods. Finished products were then exported to the United States, Japan, and elsewhere. The *maquiladoras* provided jobs for many Mexicans—most of them women.

The China-Panama Connection

In the 1970s, the United States hoped for the best when it agreed to give up control of the Panama Canal at the end of the century. But in 1999, some United States leaders were not so optimistic. Senator Trent Lott sounded the alarm that "U.S. naval ships will be at the mercy of Chinese-controlled pilots."

The root of his fear was that the Panamanian government had made a deal with a company based in Hong Kong to run two ports near the canal entrances. Most observers felt that Senator Lott's fears were groundless. After all, the Hong Kong company had an impressive record in managing 19 other ports around the world.

Of more concern, thought some observers, was the fragile Panamanian government. In 1999, Mireya Moscoso took office as president. Her late husband had been elected president three times. He was also deposed by the Panamanian army three times.

Theme: Continuity and Change Why did the change in canal ownership cause some to worry?

Still, environmental problems in the plants, plus the government's refusal to let workers organize, led to labor protests.

Despite economic growth, most Mexicans remained poor. The economy could not produce enough jobs to keep up with rapid population growth. Wealth continued to be unequally distributed. The top 10 percent of the people controlled over 40 percent of the wealth, while the poorest 20 percent earned less than 2 percent of national income.

Links to the United States Mexico has felt the powerful influence of its northern neighbor. In the 1930s, Mexico set out to reduce economic influence through import substitution. Yet the nation continued to rely on investment capital from the United States. In 1995, a $20 billion loan from the United States bailed Mexico out of an economic crisis.

In 1993, Mexico, the United States, and Canada signed NAFTA. Supporters claimed that the free-trade association would boost prosperity by lowering trade barriers, thus opening up a huge regional market. NAFTA did bring some new business and investments to Mexico. At the same time, however, it hurt Mexican manufacturers, who could not compete with a flood of goods from the United States.

Issues such as illegal immigration and drug smuggling created tension between Mexico and the United States. Some employers in the United States, especially commercial farmers, relied on Mexican migrant workers to harvest crops for low wages. But as growing numbers of Mexicans crossed the border illegally, many people in the United States came to resent the newcomers. Despite their differences, both nations cooperated on solving issues of international concern such as environmental problems.

War and Peace in Central America

In Central America, unrest threatened the ruling elite of military, business, and landowning interests. Discontent grew in the cities and among rural Indian communities that had long suffered from poverty and oppression. Fearing the spread of communism, the United States intervened repeatedly in the region.

Nicaragua Along with Mexico and Cuba, Nicaragua was one of three Latin American countries to have a genuine revolution in the twentieth century. From 1936 to 1979, the Somoza family ruled—and looted—Nicaragua. Due to their strong anti-communist stand, they enjoyed United States backing. In the 1970s, various groups opposed to Anastasio Somoza joined forces. They called themselves Sandinistas after Augusto Sandino, a revolutionary of the 1930s. Like Sandino, they were reform-minded nationalists. The Sandinistas included a large number of women and leftist students.

In 1979, the revolutionaries ousted Somoza and set out to reshape Nicaragua. Under Sandinista president Daniel Ortega, they introduced land reform and other socialist policies. Fearing that Nicaragua would become "another Cuba," President Ronald Reagan secretly backed the contras— guerrillas who fought against the Sandinistas.

A long civil war weakened the economy but did not unseat the Sandinistas. Other Central American countries finally helped both sides to reach a compromise and stop the fighting. In 1990, Violeta Chamorro, a moderate, won election as president. The Sandinistas peacefully handed over power but kept control of the army.

Over the next decade, rival political parties, including the Sandinistas, competed for power in Nicaragua. Although the economy has grown as exports have dramatically risen, many people remained poor, unemployment was still high, and the country had a heavy debt burden. In 1998,

Hurricane Strikes!

In October 1998, Hurricane Mitch hovered just off the coast of Honduras for two days, dumping a torrent of rain. Then, Mitch swept across much of Central America. Widespread flooding and mud-slides killed thousands, making this hurricane the deadliest Atlantic storm in 200 years.

Fast Facts

- Some regions received up to two feet of rain a day during Hurricane Mitch.

- It has been estimated that it will take more than 15 years for the economies of Central America to recover.

- Earlier deforestation contributed to the devastating mudslides.

The Impact of Hurricane Mitch

Nation	Deaths	Property Loss (estimated)
Honduras	5,657	$3,705 million
Nicaragua	3,045	$969 million
Guatemala	268	$698 million
El Salvador	240	$334 million

Source: Inter-American Development Bank

Hurricane Mitch dealt a devastating social and economic blow to Central America, whose nations were just recovering from decades of civil war.

Firefighters and volunteers dig victims from the mud in Guatemala City, Guatemala. Roaring flood waters and fast-flowing rivers of mud carried away entire villages.

A resident of Mango Bay, Honduras, salvages what he can from his home. Almost 130,000 homes across Central America were destroyed or damaged, leaving an estimated 460,000 people homeless.

Portfolio Assessment

Conduct research to find out more about a recent hurricane. Then, prepare a class presentation on its impact. If possible, include first-person accounts or photographs of the hurricane you have selected.

Go Online
PHSchool.com

For: Culture and current events in Central America
Visit: PHSchool.com
Web Code: mkd-3748

Central American Street Scene

In this colorful folk art painting by Jorge Ferman, one can learn much about the culture of the Central American country of Honduras. Note especially the architecture, clothing, landscape, and plant life in the painting.

Theme: Geography and History What does the painting suggest about the climate and landscape of Central America?

Hurricane Mitch, one of the most destructive storms of the century, added to the nation's woes by devastating much of the country. As the new century began, both developed democracy and real prosperity still lay in the future.

Guatemala Fearing growing communist influence and threats to American interests, the United States helped oust Guatemala's reformist government in 1954. Although the military and landowners regained power, they faced constant challenges from leftist guerrilla movements. During decades of civil war, the government routinely tortured and murdered critics, including student and labor leaders.

The chief victims were the Native American majority, some of whom had taken part in antigovernment actions. An estimated 30,000 died during the 1980s alone. Some were killed fighting for the land they tilled but did not own. Others were shot as military forces exterminated whole villages.

Although a civilian government took power in the mid-1980s, the military remained a powerful force behind the scenes. The United States pressured the government to halt the fighting. In 1996, the 30-year civil war finally ended when the government and guerrillas signed a peace agreement that recognized the rights of the Guatemalan people.

El Salvador The ruling class of military officials and wealthy landowners was also challenged in El Salvador. Here, as elsewhere in Latin America, reformers and revolutionaries found new support in the Catholic Church. In the 1970s, some Church leaders in Latin America abandoned traditional ties to the elite and instead pressed for reform. Inspired by the ideas of liberation theology, Salvadoran priests preached that God was "a God of justice and love who acts on the side of the poor and oppressed." Archbishop Oscar Romero even proclaimed: "When all peaceful means have been exhausted, the church considers insurrection moral and justified."

During a vicious 12-year civil war, right-wing death squads slaughtered church workers, student and labor leaders, and anyone else thought to sympathize with leftists. In 1980, Archbishop Romero fell victim to the fighting, gunned down as he celebrated mass in a chapel. Meanwhile, the United States pressed the government to make some reforms. However, it also provided weapons and other aid to help the military battle rebel guerrillas.

Finally, in 1991, both sides agreed to a UN-brokered peace. After elections were held, former enemies met in the congress, not in battle. However, problems remained. The civil war had ravaged the economy, which still depended on a single export—coffee. Despite large-scale aid from the International Monetary Fund, El Salvador remained a developing nation with a fragile democracy.

Struggle in Haiti

Like other Latin American countries, the Caribbean nation of Haiti has endured a history of dictatorial rule and rebellion. Since independence in 1804, a small upper class controlled the economy and ruled the rural poor majority.

From Dictatorship to Democracy From 1957 to 1971, Dr. François Duvalier (doo vahl YAY) ruled Haiti. "Papa Doc," as he was called, used his brutal secret police, the *Tontons Macoutes,* to crush opposition and terrorize the people. His son, "Baby Doc," was driven into exile in 1986, but a succession of military leaders then ruled the island nation.

In 1990 and again in 2000, voters chose Jean-Bertrand Aristide as president. A former Catholic priest and supporter of liberation theology, Aristide pledged to advance Haiti at least "from misery to dignified poverty." During his first term, he was ousted by the military. He was later returned to office by the threat of United States military action.

An Uncertain Future Despite his pledge, Aristide was unable to make meaningful reforms. Haiti remained the poorest nation in the Western Hemisphere. Eighty percent of Haitians lived in the worst poverty. The country lacked roads, electricity, and other basic services. Political violence and high crime rates discouraged foreign investment.

Haiti was just one example of the many Central American and Caribbean countries that faced a tangled set of political, social, and economic problems. Natural disasters such as hurricanes or earthquakes further added to their ills. Most of these nations also faced rapid population growth while their economies grew slowly, if at all. In many countries, the gap between the rich and the poor was huge, with the best land held by one or two percent of the people. Official corruption was widespread, and governments failed to address the root causes of poverty. As a result, social and political unrest remained.

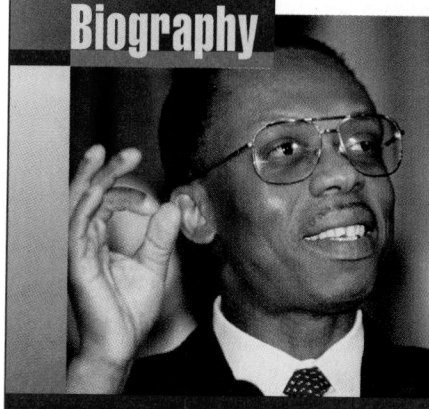

Biography

Jean-Bertrand Aristide
1953—

"Can we continue to find this situation of violence that is imposed on the poor normal?" asked Jean-Bertrand Aristide in a 1982 sermon. "No. We must end this regime," the young priest concluded.

In September 1988, an armed group of Haitian security forces, known as the *Tontons Macoutes,* attacked Aristide and his followers in church. They set fire to the church and killed a number of Aristide's supporters. Aristide escaped, but he was soon forced to resign as a priest. Two years later, Aristide became a presidential candidate—in part, to bring the killers to justice.

Theme: Impact of the Individual Why did Aristide become involved in politics?

SECTION 3 Assessment

Recall

1. **Identify:** (a) Lázaro Cárdenas, (b) PRI, (c) Chiapas, (d) Vicente Fox, (e) Sandinistas, (f) Violeta Chamorro, (g) Oscar Romero, (h) Jean-Bertrand Aristide.
2. **Define:** (a) *ejido,* (b) *maquiladora,* (c) contra.

Comprehension

3. (a) How has Mexican politics changed in recent years? (b) Identify recent developments in the Mexican economy.
4. (a) Who were the opposing sides in El Salvador's civil war? (b) How did the civil war end?

5. What problems have hindered the development of democracy in Haiti?

Critical Thinking and Writing

6. **Predicting Consequences** How might the collapse of the Soviet Union and the end of the Cold War affect relations between the United States and the nations of Central America?
7. **Identifying Main Ideas** Reread the subsection Struggle in Haiti. Then, write the main idea of each paragraph in the subsection.

Activity

Analyzing a Newspaper Article Find a newspaper article on a recent election in Central America. Read it to find out the "Five W's": *who, what, where, when,* and *why.* Write down questions about the article and answers to those questions using information you learn from the article.

Focus on Argentina and Brazil

Reading Focus

- What challenges has democracy faced in Argentina?
- How did Brazil's government change in recent times?
- Why did Brazil's "economic miracle" have limited success?

Vocabulary

favela

plebiscite

squatter

Taking Notes

Make a Venn diagram like the one below. Use it to record important facts about recent developments in Argentina and Brazil. In the middle section, list things that are true of both nations.

ARGENTINA
- Facts revealed about the "dirty war"

- Democratic elections restored in 1980s

BRAZIL
- People voted against a monarchy

Main Idea Both Argentina and Brazil have overcome serious political and economic challenges as they became modernized.

Setting the Scene One year at Rio de Janeiro's annual carnival parade, a float was based on the story of *Alice's Adventures in Wonderland.* After Alice shrank to tiny size and then grew very tall, a caterpillar on the float asked her, "Who are you?"

Alice replied: "I no longer know who I am. First, I was small like Brazil, underdeveloped, with many problems. Suddenly I grew, became a giant, a great power, but with many problems."

The caterpillar reassured Alice: "I am a caterpillar, but I turn myself into a butterfly. This could happen to you." The float expressed optimism for Brazil, a nation that has experienced many changes over recent decades.

Brazil is one of a dozen independent nations of South America. Here we will look at the two largest South American republics—Argentina and Brazil. History, geography, and other forces have shaped each country's efforts to develop a stable government and a strong, modern economy.

Dictatorship and Democracy in Argentina

In the early 1900s, Argentina was the largest Spanish-speaking nation in the world and the richest nation in Latin America. It had a fairly stable government dominated by the wealthy elite. Its economy was fed by exports of beef and wheat, mostly to Britain. Argentina attracted millions of immigrants, many of whom worked in the factories of Buenos Aires. Then the Great Depression struck. For the next 50 years, Argentina was plagued by economic crises, social unrest, and military rule.

Perón in Power In 1946, Juan Perón was elected president. He appealed to Argentine nationalism by limiting foreign-owned businesses and promoting import substitution. By boosting wages, strengthening labor unions, and enacting social reforms, Perón won the loyalty of the working classes.

Perón was helped by his glamorous wife Eva Duarte Perón, who had risen from poverty to fame as an actress. As Perón's chief aide, she had clinics built and gave money to the sick and

Juan and Eva Perón
Despite their authoritarian rule, the charismatic Peróns captured the imagination of working-class Argentinians. Years later, audiences around the world were captivated by *Evita,* a musical play based on the life of Mrs. Perón.

Theme: Impact of the Individual How did the Peróns win popular support?

unemployed. To secure more votes for her husband, she helped women gain the right to vote. Meanwhile, she used public funds to enjoy an extravagant lifestyle. "You, too, will have clothes as rich as mine," she promised the poor women of Argentina.

While Juan Perón wooed the urban poor, his authoritarian government stifled opposition. Many educated people fled Argentina. Perón's policies led to a huge debt and soaring inflation. In 1955, Perón was ousted by a military coup and forced into exile.

Military Rule For two decades, the military was in and out of power, and supporters of Perón urged a return to his policies. In 1973, an aging Perón did return, and he was again elected president. His new wife, Isabel, was chosen vice president. When he died the next year, Isabel Perón became president—the first woman head of state in the Western Hemisphere. As she faced economic and political crises, terrorists on the left and on the right disrupted the country. In 1976, the military took power.

To combat leftist guerrillas, the army waged a "dirty war," terrorizing people that they claimed were enemies of the state. They tortured and murdered thousands of citizens. As many as 20,000 people disappeared after being taken from their homes. Week after week, in the Plaza de Mayo in Buenos Aires, mothers marched silently, holding pictures of their children who had disappeared. The "Mothers of the Plaza de Mayo" gained worldwide attention.

In 1982, the military hoped to mask economic troubles by seizing the British-ruled Falkland Islands. Argentina had long claimed these islands, which it called the Malvinas. In a brief war, the British retook the Falklands. Defeat undermined the power of Argentina's military, and it was forced to hold free elections.

Democracy Restored In 1983, elected officials restored democracy to Argentina. Despite economic setbacks and corruption scandals, democratic rule survived. In time, facts emerged about the military's "dirty war" against the people. However, few of those accused of torture and murder were brought to trial.

Argentina, like many Latin American nations, experienced economic swings. The economy grew in the 1990s, aided by the country's rich natural resources and well-educated workforce. Inflation eased. The government imposed financial reforms required by the IMF to receive loans and aid. Critics of the reforms, though, objected to the privatization of state-run industries and protested the high jobless rate. Another ongoing problem was the concentration of wealth in the hands of a few.

By 2000, Argentina faced a desperate new crisis. Recession hit. The nation's debt mushroomed, and its currency lost value. As the economy neared collapse, strikes and unrest spread. The government seemed unable to solve the crisis. By 2003, the difficulties had eased somewhat. Still, Argentineans would feel the effects of the crash for years to come.

Economic Activity in Argentina

- Meatpacking and food processing
- Textiles
- Metals
- Chemicals
- Car assembly
- Wheat
- Corn

Azimuthal Equal Area Projection
0   250   500 Miles
0   250   500 Kilometers

Skills Assessment

Geography Argentina's wide variety of resources and industries has contributed to the nation's economic growth.

1. **Location** On the map, locate **(a)** Buenos Aires, **(b)** Falkland Islands, **(c)** Brazil.
2. **Region** Using latitude and longitude, identify the major agricultural region of Argentina.
3. **Critical Thinking Drawing Conclusions** Based on the map, identify one geographic characteristic that is common to most of the major cities in Argentina.

Urbanization in Brazil

1994

22.4% rural

77.6% urban

2025 (estimate)

11.1% rural

88.9% urban

Source: UN Population Division

Skills Assessment

Graph The cityscape above is of São Paulo. Unlike other Latin American countries that have only one major city, Brazil has more than a dozen. **Over the years, have more Brazilians migrated *to* cities or *from* cities? How do you think this pattern affects the Brazilian economy? Explain.**

Brazil's People and Government

Brazil occupies almost half of South America. Its varied landscapes include the mighty Amazon River and the world's largest tropical forest. Northeastern Brazil, however, is an arid plain. Brazil's rich resources include minerals, timber, and rich farmlands that yield cash crops such as coffee and sugar. Geographic conditions have contributed to uneven settlement patterns. About 90 percent of Brazilians live within 200 miles of the Atlantic coast. To draw settlers inland, the government has encouraged development of the interior.

Population Unlike its South American neighbors, Brazil was settled by people from Portugal, not Spain. With a population over 173 million, the nation has more people than any of its Spanish-speaking neighbors. Brazil has a diverse society. Afonso Celso, a noted Brazilian patriot, considered this diversity to be a source of national strength. In his words, "Three elements contributed to the formation of the Brazilian people: the American Indian, the African, and the Portuguese." In the 1900s, many Japanese and Germans settled in Brazil, adding to its cultural mix.

Most Brazilians are Roman Catholic, but a growing number of people embrace evangelical Protestant faiths. Others practice Candomblè, a form of worship that blends African and Christian beliefs.

Rapid population growth and class divisions have contributed to poverty in Brazil. In the cities, where more than 75 percent of Brazilians live, the sharp contrast between rich and poor is seen everywhere. Teeming, garbage-strewn *favelas,* or slums, ring the major cities, which boast luxurious high-rise apartment buildings and wealthy shopping areas. In the *favelas* around São Paulo and Rio de Janeiro, thousands of homeless children survive on the streets without families or education.

Political Instability Like its neighbors, Brazil has had its share of dictators and military rulers. They pursued modernization under the motto "order and progress."

Between 1930 and 1945, dictator Getúlio Vargas allied himself with the working poor. Like Perón in Argentina, he improved wages and workers' benefits, favored labor unions, and gave women the right to vote. The military eventually toppled Vargas, but they allowed elected presidents to rule Brazil for 20 years thereafter.

By 1964, economic problems and fear of communism led the military to take over again. The seizure of power was quietly supported by the United States, which was even willing to provide some aid to the military. The assistance was not needed. Backed by the middle and upper classes, the generals wielded enormous power. They tortured and jailed critics, censored the press, and ignored calls for social reform.

In the mid-1980s, though, the military gradually eased their grip on power. In 1989, Brazilians were finally able to vote directly for a president for the first time in 29 years. To determine if Brazil should remain a republic or return to being a monarchy, a plebiscite was held in 1993. A plebiscite is a vote in which people approve or reject a proposal. The people of Brazil voted to keep their republic.

Brazil's "Economic Miracle"

"Brazil is a country of the future, and always will be." This Brazilian saying suggests both the nation's potential and its many setbacks. For more than a century, Brazil has weathered many boom-and-bust cycles.

Early Development In the early 1900s, the huge demand for Brazilian rubber suddenly fell off, causing economic hardships. Coffee then replaced rubber as the major export. But again and again, declining prices for coffee or natural disasters wreaked havoc on the economy.

In the 1930s, Brazil moved away from dependence on a single export by diversifying its economy. Vargas encouraged industry. He built highways, hydroelectric plants, and schools. During and after World War II, industry continued to expand. In the 1950s, President Juscelino Kubitschek (zhooh suh LEE nuh KOO bih chehk) promised "fifty years of progress in five." He opened up the Amazon forest region to settlers by carving out a new capital, Brasília, hundreds of miles from the Atlantic coast.

Brazil's Economic Miracle
Diversification, modernization, and foreign investments have helped Brazil's economy grow. In the picture, robots assemble cars in a Ford automotive plant in Brazil.

Theme: Economics and Technology Why did Brazil's economy suffer when it relied too much on a single export?

Helping the Street Children of Brazil

Poverty is a widespread problem in Brazil. Of the poor who wander the streets in search of work, food, or shelter, thousands are children. Journalist James Brooke describes Projecto Axé (Project Force), which helps Brazilian street children.

"Salvador, Brazil 1993

'Street children face two choices: death or jail,' said Cesare de Florio La Rocca, director of the program and an immigrant from Italy. 'These youths are beings in development. If we don't act here and now, it will be too late.' . . .

To compete with the lure of street life, which can be fascinating as well as deadly, Mr. La Rocca's social workers offer their own lure, Afro-Brazilian culture. . . .

When Salvador's children show interest, Axé workers offer drumming lessons in the youth corps of the city's internationally known Afro dance and drum groups . . . and culture classes at one of the city's most important Afro-Brazilian religious centers. . . .

Using activities that appeal to children, Axé builds bridges for them to leave a short-term world of the street to a world of plans for the future. 'They are assimilating life habits of discipline and punctuality,' Mr. La Rocca said. 'If a youth goes straight from the street to a job, he will fail.'

Moving beyond cultural activities, Axé offers literacy classes and apprenticeships in a recycled paper workshop and in a silk-screen T-shirt design studio. Each child taking part in activities gets three meals every weekday, bus fare, new clothes, and a spending allowance of $8 a week. In existence for three years, Axé says that last year it helped 768 Axé children reestablish family links and return home. In a measure of growing business interest in the program . . . a local construction company has started taking older Axé boys as apprentice laborers."

—James Brooke, *The New York Times*

Street children wash their clothes in a public fountain in São Paulo, Brazil.

Skills Assessment

1. La Rocca believes that street youths who learn discipline are more likely to
   A hold down a job.
   B survive on the streets.
   C get along with others.
   D commit crimes.

2. Projecto Axé tries to help street children by offering
   E shelter.
   F apprenticeships.
   G family counseling.
   H medical care.

3. **Critical Thinking Analyzing Primary Sources (a)** What point is the photographer trying to make? **(b)** Based on both the primary source and the photograph, what assumptions can you make about the street children and how society views them?

Skills Tip

Photographers sometimes combine two contrasting images in a single frame to convey a message. This technique is called juxtaposition.

Impressive Growth "Power in the world," said one Brazilian leader, "is a great nation that has territory, population, wealth, financial resources, technology, material goods, minerals." Brazil had almost all of these. Under the military, experts ran the economy, which for a time chalked up impressive growth. Brazil began producing everything from steel and cars to shoes. People talked of Brazil's "economic miracle," like those in postwar Germany or Japan. The miracle enriched a few. To most Brazilians, however, it brought little or no benefit.

Economic Challenges In the 1980s, Brazil, like other developing nations, faced a host of economic problems—from inflation fed by higher oil prices to a staggering debt. Population growth and migration strained the government's ability to provide services as millions of people flooded Brazil's major cities. Conditions for the poor worsened when the government cut spending in response to the debt crisis. Despite environmental concerns, economic development of the Amazon region continued.

One of Brazil's enduring problems was the unequal distribution of land. A handful of wealthy families owned more than 50 percent of the land, much of which was unused. A protest group, the Movement of Landless Rural Workers, urged peasants to become squatters, or people who settle on land that they do not own. As a result, clashes often erupted between squatters and landowners.

In the 1990s, President Fernando Henrique Cardosa pushed through reforms to spur economic growth and ease inflation. In response to the Landless Movement, he distributed some land to peasants. He also privatized some state-run industries. In 2002, voters elected Luiz Inacia Lula da Silva as president, Lula, as he was called, was Brazil's first leftist president in more than 40 years. He pledged to end hunger and corruption and ease economic woes. Like previous presidents, Lula also had to tackle deep-rooted social problems. As Lula warned, solving Brazil's problem could take more than one term.

Looking Ahead

In recent years, Brazil's economy accounted for two fifths of Latin America's output. It also ranked among the world's economic giants. With vast human and natural resources, Brazil was eager to become an economic superpower and overcome a history of economic boom and bust.

SECTION 4 Assessment

Recall
1. **Identify: (a)** Juan Perón, **(b)** Eva Perón, **(c)** Isabel Perón, **(d)** "dirty war," **(e)** Falklands, **(f)** Getúlio Vargas, **(g)** Brasília.
2. **Define: (a)** *favela,* **(b)** plebiscite, **(c)** squatter.

Comprehension
3. **(a)** How have dictatorships affected Argentina? **(b)** What steps did the nation take toward democracy?
4. Why did military rulers seize power in Brazil?

5. **(a)** Describe the Brazilian economic miracle. **(b)** What problems have threatened Brazil's economy since the 1980s?

Critical Thinking and Writing
6. **Analyzing Information** What benefits and drawbacks might result from building a "cult of personality" around figures like Juan and Eva Perón?
7. **Comparing** Review the political developments that occurred in Brazil and Argentina between 1945 and the 1980s. Were the political conditions generally similar or different? Explain.

Activity

Staging a Skit
Present a three-act skit that portrays major events in Argentina from the 1940s to today. The first act should present the Peróns. The second act should show Argentina under military rule. The final act should highlight the restoration of democracy.

CHAPTER 24 Review and Assessment

Creating a Chapter Summary

Make a concept web like the partially completed model below. Fill in the blank circles. Add branches and circles as needed.

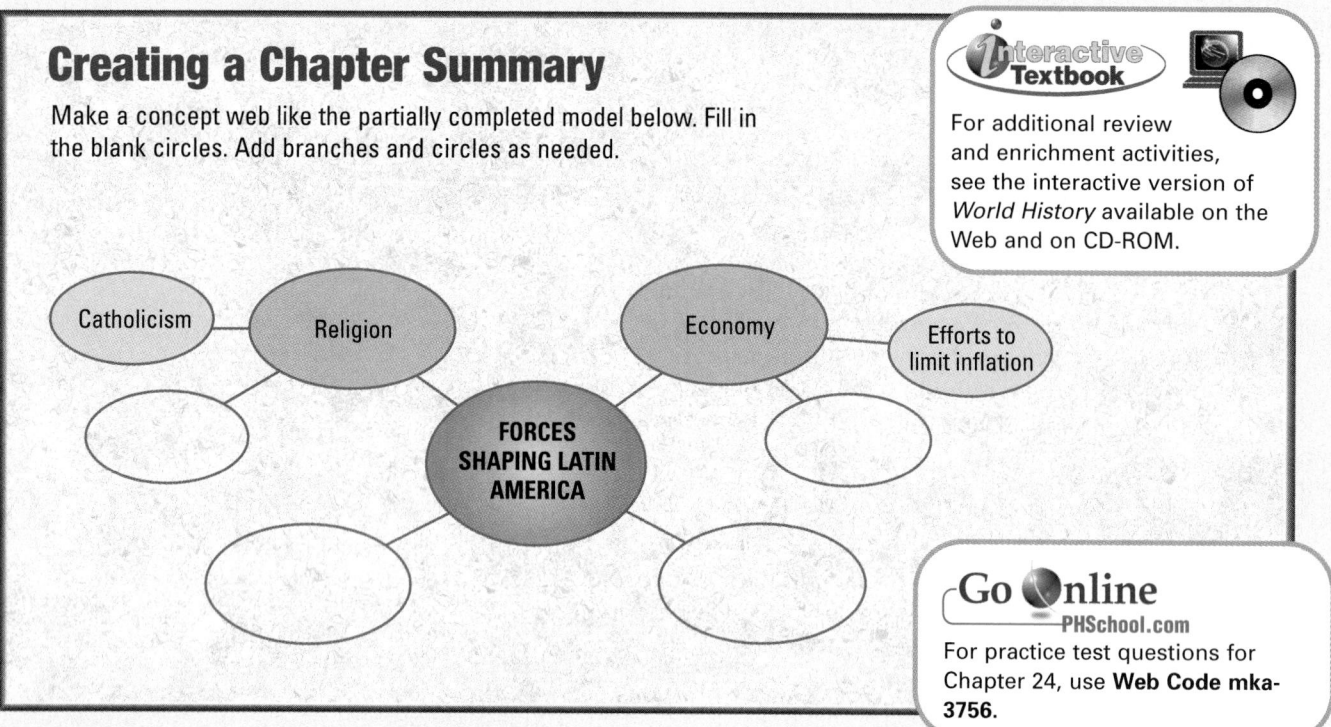

Catholicism — Religion

Economy — Efforts to limit inflation

FORCES SHAPING LATIN AMERICA

Interactive Textbook

For additional review and enrichment activities, see the interactive version of *World History* available on the Web and on CD-ROM.

Go Online
PHSchool.com
For practice test questions for Chapter 24, use **Web Code mka-3756.**

Building Vocabulary

Review the meanings of the terms below. For each term, write a sentence that includes the term.

1. import substitution
2. liberation theology
3. literacy rate
4. embargo
5. squatter

Recalling Key Facts

6. How did the distribution of wealth in Latin America cause problems after World War II?

7. How did military regimes affect nations such as Argentina and Chile?

8. Why did relations between the United States and Cuba worsen after 1959?

9. Describe the *maquiladoras* and their effect on Mexico.

10. (a) Who forced Jean-Bertrand Aristide from power in Haiti? (b) Who returned him to power?

11. What steps did Argentina take toward democratic rule in the 1980s?

12. Has economic growth benefited all Brazilians? Explain.

Critical Thinking and Writing

13. **Drawing Conclusions** How can a wide gap between rich and poor make it difficult for democracy to flourish?

14. **Recognizing Points of View** Environmentalists have called on Brazil to halt destruction of the Amazon rain forest. **(a)** Why do environmentalists take this view? **(b)** Why do some people think that it is unfair for developed nations to urge developing nations to protect the environment?

15. **Linking Past and Present** How does Latin America's colonial past help to explain the uneven distribution of land that is common in much of the region today?

16. **Connecting to Geography** (a) How do geography and climate benefit economic growth in Latin America? (b) How do they hinder economic growth?

17. **Making Generalizations** Do you think the general trend in Latin America in the 1980s and 1990s was toward democracy or toward dictatorship? Explain.

Read the news article below about the 1996 visit of Pope John Paul II to Nicaragua. Then, answer the questions that follow.

"MANAGUA, Nicaragua (Feb. 7, 1996)— Pope John Paul on Wednesday hailed Central America's transformation from superpower battleground to peaceful democracy, saying the change showed the hand of God in human history. In impromptu remarks at the end of a joyful open-air Mass celebrated before more than 150,000 cheering supporters in a lakeside plaza, John Paul . . . said, 'Today we can see that you are the master of your own human, Christian, Nicaraguan destiny.' The crowd gathered beneath the tropical blue sky roared 'Pope, Pope, Pope' in approval and thundered its applause. . . . During his 1983 visit, the Pope was forced to shout for silence as Sandinista protesters heckled him during Mass. . . . The Pope said on arriving on Wednesday that his message remained the same as in 1983—one of peace and reconciliation. . . . Analysts say the Sandinistas, now in opposition, have no option but to play the Catholic card if they want to have a chance of winning the presidential election this year in a country where enthusiasm for the Pope has reached fever pitch."

—Reuters Information Service

18. Why do you think the pope called Central America a superpower battleground?
19. **(a)** How did the response to the pope in 1996 differ from the response to him in 1983? **(b)** How can you explain the change?
20. Based on the article, what type of government did Nicaragua have in 1996? Explain.
21. What information in the article is opinion rather than fact?

Skills Tip

Note that a news article can contain both factual reporting and author commentary.

This photograph shows Cuban refugees. Use the photograph and information from the chapter to answer the following questions:

22. What land are the people probably trying to reach?
23. What means of propulsion does the raft rely on?
24. How seaworthy does the raft appear to be? Explain.
25. Why were these people willing to make this voyage?
26. What risks might they face during the voyage from Cuba?

Go Online

PHSchool.com

Search the Internet to learn more about the Organization of American States. Design a brochure that includes a brief description of the group's history, a list of its current goals, and a diagram of its organizational structure. For help with this activity, use **Web Code mkd-3757.**

TEST PREPARATION

Use the table and your knowledge of social studies to answer the following question.

Programs of Mao Zedong

Program	The Great Leap Forward	The Cultural Revolution
Goals	• Increase farm and factory output	• Renew communist loyalties
Methods	• Communes • Production quotas	• Red Guards attack professors and other officials
Results	• Program fails • Two years of hunger and low production	• Economy slows • China closes to outside world • People fear arrest • Civil war threatened

1. This table supports the conclusion that Mao Zedong

   A had the loyalty and support of most of the Chinese people.

   B achieved his goals at a great cost to the Chinese people.

   C used strong, authoritarian methods to govern China.

   D was determined to turn China into a world power.

2. The major goal of the Green Revolution has been to

   A increase agricultural output.

   B slow population growth.

   C preserve the world's rain forests.

   D reduce the use of pesticides and farm machinery.

3. The major goal of the European Union has been to

   A create a single government for all of Europe.

   B reduce trade barriers among European nations.

   C encourage the growth of the welfare state in Europe.

   D provide economic aid to developing nations.

4. In the decades following World War II, Ghana and Vietnam were similar in that both

   A fought wars of independence.

   B became Cold War hot spots.

   C shook off colonial rule.

   D experienced a decrease in nationalism.

Use the quotation and your knowledge of social studies to answer the following question.

"The tradition of absolute power that began with pre-Columbian empires, and the tradition that might makes right that the Spanish and Portuguese explorers practiced, were perpetuated in the nineteenth century by our caudillos and our oligarchies. . . ."

5. In this excerpt, the author is primarily discussing the

   A history and principles of liberation theology.

   B need to fight the spread of communism in Latin America.

   C reasons many people migrate from Latin America to the United States.

   D obstacles to creating stable democratic governments in Latin America.

6. Which statement best explains why India was partitioned in 1947?

A The British feared a united India.

B One region of India wanted to remain under British rule.

C Religious conflicts led to a political division.

D Communist supporters wanted a separate state.

7. After the collapse of the Soviet Union, Russia

A moved from a command economy to a free market economy.

B became a single-party military dictatorship.

C banned former Communists from running for office.

D broke all ties with Eastern Europe.

8. Which events are listed in correct chronological order?

A Nelson Mandela is imprisoned; apartheid is established; free elections are held in South Africa.

B Nelson Mandela becomes president of South Africa; apartheid ends; South African blacks are sent to homelands.

C Free elections are held in South Africa; Nelson Mandela is released from prison; African National Congress is formed.

D African National Congress is formed; apartheid ends; Nelson Mandela becomes president of South Africa.

Use the maps and your knowledge of social studies to answer the following question.

9. What happened to the area southwest of Israel shown in gray on the map?

A It was lost by Israel in a later war.

B It was returned to Egypt as the result of a treaty.

C It was granted limited self-rule by Israel.

D It became a permanent part of Israel.

Writing Practice

10. Write a definition of the phrase "economic interdependence." Then, list and describe three examples of interdependence in the modern world.

11. Describe two benefits of technology in today's world and two challenges created by technology. Then, explain whether you think the effects of rapid technological growth have been mostly positive or mostly negative.

During your study of world history, you may have worked on many projects and activities. In this unit, you have an opportunity to work on a final project. This final project is a case study on a contemporary issue. In this project you can apply the knowledge and the skills you have developed while studying world history to a topic of current interest. Then you can demonstrate what you know in a presentation to the class.

CASE STUDY **1** Russia and Germany: After Communism

CASE STUDY **2** Ukraine and Yugoslavia: The Resurgence of Nationalism

CASE STUDY **3** Japan and Mexico: The Path to Prosperity

CASE STUDY **4** Argentina and South Africa: The Road to Democracy

CASE STUDY **5** The Czech Republic and South Korea: Democracy and Economic Development

CASE STUDY **6** Women in National Development: Bangladesh and Norway

CASE STUDY **7** Civic Participation: Australia and the United States

The Case Study Project Overview tells how to analyze and research a case study topic. It also provides ways to present your case study as a project. Refer to the Project Overview as you work on your case study project.

The Case Study Project

What is a case study? A case study is an in-depth analysis of an issue or topic carried out by looking carefully at specific cases, or examples. In this unit, the topics range from the fall of communism in Europe to the future of democracy in the world. The specific examples are countries that illustrate the topic.

Choosing a Topic

In this unit you will find seven case study topics. Your teacher may assign one or more of the case study topics to you. Or your teacher may want you to choose one or more topics.

Because these projects deal with large topics, your teacher might want you to share the work with other students. You may, however, develop your case study as an individual project if your teacher approves.

Analyzing Your Topic

How will you begin to work on your case study project? The first step is to analyze your topic. This means breaking it down into smaller pieces or subtopics. Later, you will put these pieces back together to create a presentation based on your research.

General Categories of Human Activity You might begin by looking at your topic in terms of five general categories of human activity. They are shown in the diagram below. If you are part of a team, one member might be responsible for gathering information on each of these categories then sharing the information with the rest of the group.

Geographic Factors As you get deeper into your subject, focus on some of the geographic factors that underlie the five categories of human activity. These include

● natural and political boundaries

● scarcity or abundance of natural resources

● problems with bordering states

● industrial development

● transportation and communication systems

General Categories of Human Activity

The first step in working on your case study project is to analyze your topic. To do this, look at the topic in terms of the five general categories. Depending on the topic, not all factors may apply.

Historical Factors Also try to look at the historical factors that relate to your subject. What events that happened in the past still have an impact on the world of today? What recent changes or developments are important to your case study? Have they created new problems? Have they made old problems better or worse?

Finally, think about how these long-range historical factors and recent developments interact. Can you spot any trends or patterns that are likely to have an impact on the future?

Putting Your Project Together

Your case study project will have the following three parts:

- a **presentation** of your topic based on your research
- an **interview** or question and answer period following the presentation
- a **project journal** that can be added to your world history portfolio

The Presentation

In your presentation, you will present what you learned from your case study to an audience. This presentation should

- introduce the topic of your case study.
- show the impact of this topic in the countries you studied.
- draw some conclusions as to the importance of this topic to those countries and the rest of the world.

On page 663 you will find a list of different methods of presentation. Read the list and choose one presentation method. Be sure to get your teacher's approval. You may want to illustrate your presentation with visuals such as maps, time lines, graphs, pictures, and videos.

The Interview

After your presentation, be prepared to answer questions from your audience. Your audience will probably be made up mainly of students and your teacher. It might also include parents, school staff, and representatives from your community.

The purpose of the interview is twofold. First, it provides audience members with an opportunity to learn more about issues of special interest to them. Second, it gives you and your team members a chance to demonstrate your knowledge. During the interview you will be able to share stories, facts, reactions, or conclusions that were not part of your original presentation.

The Project

The project journal will be a record of your own research and reflections on your case study. It should include the following:

- **A brief overview of your case study.** The overview should define your topic and briefly describe the countries in your case study.

- **A research record.** Your research record should list all of the resources you used for your case study.

- **A short essay.** In this essay, describe what you think is important about your case study from the following two points of view:

A local citizen's perspective. First, look at your case study from the point of view of a citizen who lives in one of the nations you are studying. Ask yourself: "If I were a citizen of this country, what would my greatest concerns about this topic be? My greatest hopes?"

An American perspective. Second, look at your case study from an American perspective. Ask yourself: "Why should Americans be interested in this topic or in the countries I studied? How might developments in these countries affect the United States? What have I learned that might make me a better citizen?"

Methods of Presentation

Your case study can be presented in any one of the following ways:

- **POSTER DISPLAY:** A large visual display of the sort you might find in a museum, library, or information kiosk. Your intended audience would be the general public.

- **EXPERT BRIEFING:** A live presentation of your case study to a group with a professional interest in your topic. Your audience might be the president of the United States and his cabinet, a government agency, or a group of business leaders.

- **NEWSPAPER OR NEWSMAGAZINE REPORT:** A special feature or section in a newspaper or newsmagazine devoted to an in-depth report on your topic. Your intended audience would be readers of that periodical.

- **VIDEO DOCUMENTARY:** A film or video based on your case study. Your audience might be moviegoers or television viewers.

- **TELEVISION NEWS FEATURE:** An in-depth television news feature based on your case study. It might appear on the nightly news or one of the television news programs. You can present your story live or prerecord it on video. Your audience would be the general television-viewing public.

- **WEB SITE OR MULTIMEDIA PROJECT:** A computer-based multimedia presentation that could be published on a computer disk or the World Wide Web. Your audience would be computer users and Web browsers around the globe.

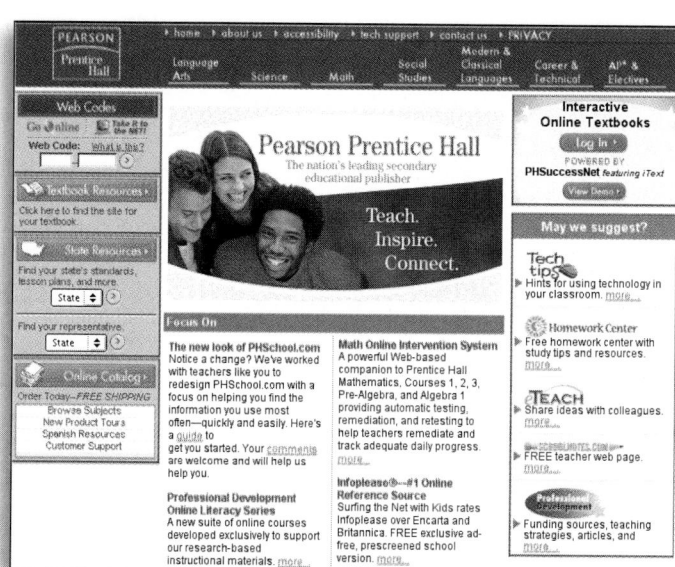

CASE STUDY PROJECT OVERVIEW

Researching Your Topic

Each case study includes a list of resources to use while researching your topic. Your research, however, should go beyond the list. You will also want to study recent news stories, interview experts, talk with foreign students, and locate people who have visited the countries in your case study. You can find these resources by using the library, the Internet, and the organizations listed on the next page.

IN YOUR LIBRARY

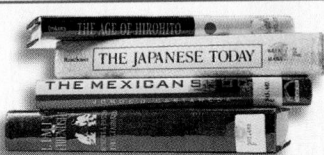

Your library is a good starting point for research. You may want to begin by consulting print or electronic encyclopedias, atlases, almanacs, and factbooks such as the *Central Intelligence Agency World Fact Book.*

Look for recent magazine and newspaper stories on your subject. You can find more in-depth articles in such journals as *Foreign Affairs, The National Interest, Journal of Democracy,* and *World Politics.* To locate such articles, use *The Reader's Guide to Periodical Literature,* newspaper indexes, and electronic indexes to periodicals such as Infotrac. Your reference librarian will show you how to use these guides.

ON THE INTERNET

The Internet will connect you to a treasure trove of information, experts, and illustrations such as maps, pictures, and film clips. You can launch your search using one of the standard search engines such as Yahoo, Alta Vista, Lycos, or Infoseek. From there you can link to Web sites created by government agencies, scholars, trade groups, and students from around the world.

The Internet can also link you to a vast array of electronic news sources including online newspapers, radio and television news providers, and online magazines.

Project Scoring Guide

Your case study project will be evaluated according to how well you demonstrated the following:

1. **Knowledge of history, geography, and your research data**
   In your presentation and interview did you
   - demonstrate a thorough knowledge and understanding of your topic?
   - use quotations and statistics to support your main points?
   - present information that is clear, well-organized, and factually accurate?
   - answer questions accurately?

2. **Ability to communicate ideas**
   In your presentation and interview did you
   - combine information from many sources into an interesting and informative story?
   - take clear positions and support them in an organized and persuasive manner?
   - use visuals effectively to enhance your key points?

3. **Research, writing, and thinking skills**
   In your project journal did you
   - clearly define your case study?
   - provide a written record of your research?
   - analyze information on your topic from multiple perspectives?
   - pay attention to grammar and spelling rules?

4. **Teamwork skills**
   In your group did you
   - stay on task?
   - divide up the work fairly?
   - listen to and express ideas and views?
   - allow for and accept differing opinions?
   - resolve conflicts satisfactorily to all members?

Organizations to Help You Research

The following world affairs organizations may help you locate information and experts to interview as part of your research. Like any organization, each of these groups has its own purpose, perspective on the world, and political point of view. You will want to pay attention to any possible biases as you evaluate any materials these organizations provide.

Asia Foundation, P.O. Box 193223, San Francisco, CA 94119-3223. The Asia Foundation assists economic, political, and social development in Asia and supports exchange programs between Asia and the United States.

Foreign Policy Association, 470 Park Avenue South, New York, NY 10016-6819. This organization provides educational materials on foreign policy issues, including its magazine *Headline.*

Foreign Policy Research Institute, 1528 Walnut Street, Suite 610, Philadelphia, PA 19102-3604. The institute produces educational materials on international affairs, including its magazine *Orbis* and newsletter *Footnotes.*

Goethe Institute, German Cultural Center, 1014 5th Avenue, New York, NY 10028. This institute provides information on cultural life in Germany and German language instruction.

Hoover Institution on War, Revolution and Peace, Stanford University, Stanford, CA 94305-6010. The Hoover Institution is an international research center for the study of political, economic, and social change in the twentieth century.

Institute for Contemporary Studies, 720 Market Street, 4th Floor, San Francisco, CA 94102. This research center prepares studies on domestic and foreign policy issues.

Institute of the Americas, 10111 North Torrey Pines Road, La Jolla, CA 92037. This institution encourages economic, political, and social reform in the Americas by strengthening relations between Latin America, the United States, and Canada, as well as through the publication of its periodical *Hemisfile.*

Japan Society, 333 E. 47th Street, New York, NY 10017. The Japan Society is dedicated to furthering understanding and cultural exchange between the peoples of Japan and the United States.

Korea Society, 950 3rd Avenue, 8th Floor, New York, NY 10022. The Korea Society works to increase understanding and cultural exchange between the peoples of Korea and the United States.

Pan-American Society of California, 312 Sutter Street, Suite 506, San Francisco, CA 94108. This organization promotes mutual understanding among peoples of the Americas.

Population Reference Bureau (PRB), 1875 Connecticut Avenue NW, Suite 520, Washington, DC 20009. PRB gathers and publishes information about United States and international population trends.

Society for International Development (SID), San Francisco Bay Area Chapter, c/o Asia Foundation, P.O. Box 3223, San Francisco, CA 94119-3223. SID is an international organization of people who are interested in international economic, political, and social development.

World Resources Institute (WRI), 1709 New York Avenue NW, Washington, DC 20006. WRI provides research and technical assistance on global environmental and economic development issues.

Russia and Germany: After Communism

Case Study Topic

The fall of communism in Europe led to the breakup of the Soviet Union and also to the reunification of Germany. In this case study, you will report on the changes brought to Russia and Germany by the fall of communism.

How to Complete Case Study 1

● Be sure to read or review the **Project Overview** on pages 660–665. It describes how to complete a case study.

● Then, read the **background information** on this page and on page 667. It will provide a starting point for your research.

● Next, study the **map and charts** on the next page for additional data.

● Finally, on page 668, you will find **Voices and Views**, a collection of quotations. Analyze them and add them to your research.

● On page 669 is a list of **what you need to include** in your case study presentation. Also provided is a list of **resources** for your research.

Background Information

If you looked at a map of Europe before 1987 and compared it with one created in 1992, you would notice some big differences. The 1987 map would show the Soviet Union, East Germany, and West Germany. The 1992 map would show Russia, a united Germany, and a number of new nations that formerly were Soviet republics.

What brought about these changes? First, communism came to an abrupt end in Europe. Second, the Cold War between East and West ended. These two developments caused the Soviet Union to break apart and Germany to reunite.

The Collapse of Communism in Europe

Few people expected communism in Europe to collapse when it did. Fewer still would have predicted that the end would begin in Poland. In the early 1980s, however, Polish workers, students, and dissidents came together with one goal: to destroy the communist system Poland had lived under since World War II.

From Poland across Eastern Europe, communist leaders tried to cling to power by promising reforms. However, people did not want a new and improved totalitarian system. In one country after another, they poured into the streets demanding democracy. One by one, communist governments fell.

The Federal Republic of Germany

On October 3, 1990, East and West Germany were united for the first time since the end of World War II. Most Germans supported reunification, but feelings soured as the true costs became clear. Prosperous West Germans had to pay higher taxes to finance the rebuilding of the former East Germany. As old government-run factories closed in the east, unemployment rose.

Unemployment and resentment of "foreigners" led to new support for far-right parties. Some neo-Nazis blamed immigrants for the hard times and viciously attacked foreign workers. Most Germans condemned such actions. However, the problem of racism is particularly sensitive in Germany because of the nation's history in the twentieth century.

Germans sought solutions to their economic problems. The government reduced the costs of welfare programs and tried to balance the budget through tax reform. But a global economic slowdown led to even higher unemployment. The recession of the early 2000s came as a shock to Germany, a country that had experienced almost constant economic growth since the 1950s.

Data for Your Case Study

Use the map and the chart below as you research your case study project. You may also use the data in your case study presentation.

Russia: Political

ARCTIC OCEAN

Anadyr
Tiksi
Magadan
Archangel
Moscow
RUSSIA
Ufa
Rostov-na-Donu
Novosibirsk
Irkutsk
Vladivostok

⊛ National capital
● Other city

Azimuthal Equal Area Projection
0   500   1000 Miles
0   500   1000 Kilometers

RUSSIA AND GERMANY AT A GLANCE	Russia	Germany
Total land area	6,592,735 mi² (17,075,200 km²)	137,846 mi² (357,021 km²)
Population	145 million	82 million
Number of people per square mile	22 (8 per km²)	608 (235 per km²)
Urban population	76%	87%
Per capita GDP (in U.S. dollars)	$7,700	$23,400

Sources: *DK World Desk Reference*, 2003; Infoplease.com, 2003

Russia

In August 1991, supporters of democracy led by Boris Yeltsin seized power in Moscow. One of Yeltsin's first acts was to outlaw the Communist party. After 74 years, the communist era had come to an end. Just weeks later, 9 of the 15 republics that made up the Soviet Union had declared their independence. Russia faced many challenges as it moved from communism toward democracy. Some of these follow:

Many Russians were disappointed by the failure of politicians to greatly improve their living standards. The fall of communism swept away the securities of communism—long-term employment, guaranteed housing, and a basic diet—hitting the elderly particularly hard.

Crime levels rose alarmingly. Organized crime and corruption among business and government officials have been especially troublesome.

Minority groups pursuing separatism have been brutally suppressed. This was especially evident in the ferocious military campaign in Chechnya.

There have been power struggles between the central government and regional governments. Recently, President Vladimir Putin concentrated greater power in the presidency.

Voices and Views

On the Transformation of Russia

Data for Your Case Study

Analyze these quotations as you research your case study. You may also use the quotations in your case study presentation.

"The Russian Federation—Russia shall be a democratic, federative, law-based state with a republican form of government."

—Article I, Russian Constitution

"In the place of a totalitarian state which terrorized the world for 45 years, a civilized Commonwealth of Independent States has been formed."

—Russian Foreign Minister Andrei Kozyrev

"We have given you freedom of enterprise. You can determine your own wages. We are setting prices free. We are forming a free market. . . . Now it is up to you to show us what you are worth."

—Boris Yeltsin to the Russian people, 1991

"It will be a healthy society with healthy youth. . . . We'll have hippies and Yuppies, just like the rest of the world."

—Ilya Reznikov, Moscow university student

"For many years we couldn't speak about anything. Now we can suddenly talk. It's all very strange, but great. Things are getting better."

—Ann Goodenko, teenager in the city of Stavrobol

"Maybe things will be better for our children. But not for us. It's chaos here. It will take 10 or 20 years for my country to improve."

—Sergei Kalina, St. Petersburg student

"Once you've tasted this freedom, it's impossible to go back."

—Moscow high-school student

On German Reunification

"Wir sind wieder wer."
("We are somebody again.")

—Slogan seen across Germany in 1990

"We Jews cannot contemplate a united Germany without feelings of inner resistance."

—Elie Wiesel, Holocaust survivor, author, and activist

"I fear the superpatriotism of nationalism again. We still haven't worked out our history yet. We haven't come to terms with Nazism. East Germans have thought even less about it."

—Thorsten Laute, West Berlin student

"We Germans got married in a hurry and enjoyed it. Now we must get to know each other. Normally it is the other way around, but, then, what is normal in Germany?"

—Egon Bohn, West German politician

"This is not unification, it's an annexation."

—Margit Venner, East German psychologist

"An *Ossi* meets a *Wessi* and says, 'We are one people!' To which the *Wessi* replies, 'So are we!'"

—Joke told by German Foreign Minister Hans-Dietrich Genscher to illustrate the difficulty of uniting East and West Germans

"The Germans are being given a second chance. That is the rarest of gifts, and one can only hope that they will do justice to it. The Germans deserve friends who feel the burden of the past, as so many of them do, but who have compassion for a people who have had so rich and terrifying a history."

—Fritz Stern, professor of history, Columbia University

The Reichstag, shown above, became the seat of the German Parliament in 1999.

Researching and Presenting Case Study 1

RESEARCHING

As you research "Russia and Germany: After Communism," remember that your case study project will have the following three parts:

- a **presentation** based on your research and reflection on the topic
- an **oral interview** to follow your presentation
- a **project journal** that will include a case study overview, research log, and an essay on the significance of your topic

See pages 660–665 for a detailed description of these elements.

PRESENTING

Your presentation on this topic should include the following:

- a **brief overview or time line** of key events leading up to the fall of communism in Europe
- a **description** of the immediate impact of the fall of communism on Germany and Russia
- an **examination** of the problems Russians face as they make the transition from dictatorship to democracy and from a command economy to a free enterprise system
- a **concluding statement** on the significance of these historic changes for the peoples of Germany and Russia and for the United States

Go Online
PHSchool.com

To learn about Russia and Germany, use **Web Code mme-1001.**

Resources

In Your World History Textbook

To locate useful background information on this topic in your textbook, check the index under the following headings: *communism, Marxism, socialism, Germany, East Germany, West Germany, Russia, Soviet Union*

In Your Library

✔Daniels, Robert V. *A Documentary History of Communism from Lenin to Gorbachev.* Hanover, NH: University Press of New England, 1993. Also, *Soviet Communism from Reform to Collapse.* Lexington, MA: D.C. Heath., 1995.

✔Darnton, Robert. *Berlin Journal* New York: W.W. Norton, 1993.

✔Fischer, Marc. *After the Wall: Germany, the Germans, and the Burdens of History.* New York: Simon & Schuster, 1995.

✔Fulbrook, Mary. *The Divided Nation: A History of Germany , 1918–1990.* Oxford: Oxford University Press, 1992.

✔Lapidus, Gail W., ed. *The New Russia: Troubled Transformation.* Boulder, CO: Westview Press, 1994.

✔Remick, David. *Lenin's Tomb: The Last Days of the Soviet Empire.* New York: Random House, 1994.

✔Shlaes, Amity. *Germany: The Empire Within.* New York: Farrar, Strauss, & Giroux, 1991.

Ukraine and Yugoslavia: The Resurgence of Nationalism

Background Information

As communism collapsed in Eastern Europe, nationalism resurfaced across the region. Two countries, Ukraine and Yugoslavia, have had very different experiences in the post-communist era.

An Independent Ukraine

Ukrainians trace their history back to the 700s and the founding of Kiev, the first Russian state. Much later, Ukraine was ruled by Lithuania and Poland.

In the early 1600s, Ukraine sought Russian aid to throw off foreign rule. As a result, however, Ukraine became part of the growing Russian empire. Ukraine remained under Russian, and later Soviet, domination until the late 1980s. During this time, though, Ukrainians preserved their national identity.

Soviet rule left a bitter legacy in Ukraine. Joseph Stalin's brutal policy of collectivization brought immense suffering and famine to this rich agricultural land. Stalin also launched a campaign of terror against Ukrainians in an effort to suppress their language and culture.

As the Soviet Union collapsed, Ukrainians were quick to break away and revive their ancient nation. In 1991, Ukrainians voted overwhelmingly in favor of independence. Since then, the government has struggled to bring about economic and political reforms. Ukraine still maintains close economic and political ties to Russia, even as Ukrainian nationalism remains strong.

The Rise and Fall of Yugoslavia

In contrast to Ukraine's long history, Yugoslavia is a new country. It was created in 1919 after World War I. Nationalism among the many peoples of the Balkans had helped trigger that war. The creation of Yugoslavia brought much of the Balkan region under one government, but the new country faced deep divisions. It had two alphabets, three main religions, four languages, and many rival ethnic groups. Its territory was divided into six republics and two provinces.

This patchwork nation was ruled by a monarch until the Nazis invaded during World War II. After the war, resistance hero and communist leader Josip Broz Tito seized power. Tito's strong-arm rule kept ethnic rivalries under control. After he died in 1980, however, nationalist tensions resurfaced as rival ethnic groups competed for power. Croats, Slovenes, and other ethnic groups resented the more numerous and politically powerful Serbs.

As communism collapsed in Eastern Europe, nationalist tensions led to the breakup of Yugoslavia. Slovenia, Croatia, Macedonia, and Bosnia-Herzegovina declared independence. Only Serbia along with tiny Montenegro remained united under the name of the Federal Republic of Yugoslavia.

Data for Your Case Study

Use the map and chart as you research your case study project. You may also use the data in your case study presentation.

Ethnic Groups in the Former Yugoslavia

Legend:
- Slovenes
- Croats
- Serbs
- Bosnians (Muslims)
- Montenegrins
- Macedonians
- Hungarians
- Albanians
- Ethnic mixture

SLOVENIA
CROATIA
BOSNIA & HERZEGOVINA
Serbia
SERBIA & MONTENEGRO
Montenegro
Kosovo
MACEDONIA
ADRIATIC SEA

Azimuthal Equal-Area Projection
0 50 100 Miles
0 50 100 Kilometers

	Ukraine	Serbia and Montenegro
Total land area	233,089 mi² (603,700 km²)	39,517 mi² (102,350 km²)
Population	48 million	10.7 million
Number of people per square mile	208 (80 per km²)	266 (103 per km²)
Urban population	68%	52%
Per capita GDP (in U.S. dollars)	$4,200	$2,250
Ethnic divisions	Ukrainian, 78%; Russian, 17%; Jewish, 1%; other, 5%	Serb, 63%; Albanian, 17%; Montenegrin, 5%; Hungarian, 3%; other, 13%
Religions	Ukrainian Orthodox, 76%; Ukrainian Catholic, 13.5%; Jewish, 2.3%; Other, 8.2%	Orthodox, 65%; Muslim, 19%; Roman Catholic, 4%; Protestant, 1%; other, 11%

UKRAINE AND SERBIA AND MONTENEGRO

Sources: *DK World Desk Reference*, 2003; Infoplease.com, 2003

However, Serbia tried to keep the other republics from breaking away. In the early 1990s, Serb forces resorted to "ethnic cleansing." They tried to kill or drive away rival ethnic groups. Massacres occurred in Bosnia and Herzegovina. United States and NATO intervention brought an uneasy peace under the 1995 Dayton Accords. But in 1998, fighting erupted in the province of Kosovo, where Muslim Albanians battled for independence. Once again, NATO launched air strikes against Serb forces and restored a fragile peace. American and NATO forces remained in the region in order to prevent new fighting.

In 2003, Yugoslavia became the confederation of Serbia and Montenegro. But ethnic and religious divisions remained, and the country's new constitution guaranteed both republics the option to secede from the country in 2006.

Voices and Views

On Ukrainian Independence

Data for Your Case Study

Analyze these quotations as you research your case study. You may also use the quotations in your case study presentation.

"Ukraine is as big as France, and this year we produced as much grain—50 million tons, or one ton for everyone living in the republic. But France does not have food shortages and we do."

—Ivan Plusch, Ukrainian official, before independence vote

"All our people really want is to speak their own language, worship in their own churches, have something to buy in the shops, and live at peace—without having to ask for these rights."

—Vasili Shpitser, Ukrainian mayor, before independence vote

"To lose Ukraine would be like cutting off a limb for many Russians. It is very difficult for them to accept."

—Oles Donji, Ukrainian student leader, before independence vote

"A great historic event has occurred, which I am confident will change not only the life of the Ukrainian people but the face of the world. . . . The Soviet Union has disintegrated. . . . An independent Ukraine is born."

—Leonid Kuchma, first president of Ukraine, after independence vote

"The Ukrainians have in their hands the fate of the nation, that of the other republics of the former Soviet Union and our neighbors in Europe. . . . They have enjoyed their nationalism, but let them think hard about what they say and do. Much depends on it."

—Russian official, after 1991 independence vote

On the Breakup of Yugoslavia

"By their oppression the Communists created this longing among the people to express their religious and national identity. Perhaps in four or five years we shall have passed through the mine field to the horizon of a civil society."

—Alija Izetbegovic, Bosnian Muslim leader, 1990

"What we want is to preserve our people's unity. . . . The Serbs do not want to accept being broken apart. Enough of breaking the Serbs apart! . . . We cannot accept that."

—Radovan Karadzic, Bosnian Serb leader and indicted war criminal, 1992

"Yugoslavia did not deteriorate suddenly, but gradually and methodically, step by step through the 1980s, becoming poorer and meaner and more hate-filled by the year. That's why every conversation I had was so sad. We were shouting to the outside world about a coming catastrophe, but no one wanted to hear our awful secret. No one was interested."

—Robert D. Kaplan, American journalist

"I want to see my parents again. . . . I love everyone: Serbs, Muslims, Croats, they are all my brothers. This is what my parents taught me. Why were they killed?"

—Nerimina Guso, 13-year-old Bosnian Muslim

"My imagination does not go far enough to see Serbs, Moslems, Croats co-existing again for as long as the children and the people who can remember this terrible Bosnian war are alive."

—Dobrica Cosic, former president of Yugoslavia

"Searching for the one who started it is a waste of time. Once it had started, the massacres were unstoppable."

—Macedonian officer fighting in Croatia

Ukrainians at a pro-independence rally in 1991

Researching and Presenting Case Study 2

RESEARCHING

As you research "Ukraine and Yugoslavia: The Resurgence of Nationalism," remember that your case study project will have the following three parts:
- a **presentation** based on your research and reflection on the topic
- an **oral interview** to follow your presentation
- a **project journal** that will include a case study overview, research log, and an essay on the significance of your topic

See pages 660–665 for a detailed description of these elements.

PRESENTING

Your presentation on this topic should include the following:
- a **brief overview or time line** of the key events that led to independence for Ukraine and the breakup of Yugoslavia
- a **description** of how nation-building has proceeded in Ukraine since independence
- a **summary** of the ethnic conflicts that erupted during the breakup of Yugoslavia
- a **comparison** of the effects of nationalism on Ukraine and Yugoslavia
- a **concluding statement** on the significance of these historic changes for the peoples of Ukraine, Yugoslavia, and the United States

To learn about Ukraine and Serbia and Montenegro, use **Web Code mmk-1002**.

Resources

In Your World History Textbook

To locate useful background information on this topic in your textbook, check the index under the following headings: **nationalism, Ukraine, Russia, Soviet Union, Yugoslavia, Balkans, Bosnia, Serbia**

In Your Library

✔Conquest, Robert. ***Harvest of Sorrow: Soviet Collectivism and the Terror-Famine.*** New York: Oxford University Press, 1986.

✔Dink, Nadia, & Adrian Karatnychy. ***The Hidden Nations: The People Challenge the Soviet Union.*** New York: Morrow, 1991.

✔Glenny, Misha. ***The Fall of Yugoslavia: The Third Balkan War.*** New York: Penguin Books, 1993.

✔Kaplan, Robert D. ***Balkan Ghosts: A Journey Through History.*** New York: St. Martin's Press, 1993.

✔Kuzio, Taras, & Andrew Wilson. ***Ukraine from Perestroika to Independence.*** New York: St. Martin's Press, 1994.

✔Malcolm, Noel. ***Bosnia: A Short History.*** New York: New York University Press, 1994.

✔Moynihan, Patrick. ***Pandaemonium: Ethnicity in International Politics.*** New York: Oxford University Press, 1993.

✔Ramet, Sabrina P. ***Nationalism and Federalism in Yugoslavia, 1962–1991.*** Bloomington: Indiana University Press, 1992.

✔Sjelten, Tom. ***Sarajevo Daily: A City and Its Newspaper Under Siege.*** New York: HarperCollins, 1995.

Japan and Mexico: The Path to Prosperity

Case Study Topic

In this case study, you will compare and contrast the means by which Japan and Mexico have worked to achieve economic prosperity.

How to Complete Case Study 3

● Be sure to read or review the **Project Overview** on pages 660–665. It describes how to complete a case study.

● Then, read the **background information** on this page and on page 675. It will provide a starting point for your research.

● Next, study the **graphs and chart** on the next page for additional data.

● Finally, on page 676, you will find **Voices and Views**, a collection of quotations. Analyze them and add them to your research.

● On page 677 is a list of **what you need to include** in your case study presentation. Also provided is a list of **resources** for your research.

Background Information

Over the last 150 years, nations have taken different paths toward modernization, building strong industrial economies. One path is capitalism, under which most economic decisions are made by the free market and private enterprise is encouraged. A second path is socialism, under which economic decisions are made by the government, which also controls industry and agriculture.

A third path taken by many nations is a mixed economy with elements of capitalism and socialism. A mixed economy often includes three features: the government (1) takes a large role in planning and regulating the economy, (2) it may nationalize key resources and industries, and (3) it may pass tough laws to protect domestic industries from foreign competition. Both Japan and Mexico have adopted their own forms of a mixed economy with varying results.

Japan

Japan's big push toward modernization began during the Meiji Restoration in 1868. Reformers took control of the government and set out to make Japan a strong modern nation and the equal of western industrial nations. By the early 1900s, Japan was on its way to achieving this goal.

The Great Depression hit the Japanese economy hard. Partly in response to economic setbacks, Japanese nationalists and militarists promoted a policy of territorial expansion as a way to improve the economy. As a result, Japan's push to build a vast empire led to decades of war with its neighbors. When World War II ended in 1945, the nation lay in ruins.

After the war, with a new government in place, the Japanese set about to rebuild their economy. Led by the dominant Liberal Democratic Party (LDP) and greatly aided by the government, Japanese businesses built new factories and invested in new technologies. With a well-educated, skilled work force, Japan moved ahead quickly.

In 1952, when American occupation forces withdrew from Japan, the nation's gross domestic product (GDP) was only about one third that of France or Britain. By the late 1970s, however, its GDP equaled that of both those countries combined. Japan's rapid economic recovery is often called an "economic miracle."

Today, Japan has the world's second-most-powerful economy after that of the United States. Since the late 1990s, however, its economy has suffered severe setbacks. Its banking system almost collapsed. Corruption scandals revealed problems with the close ties between the government and businesses. Recovery was slow, causing many Japanese to question their nation's political and economic leadership.

Mexico

Although Mexico, like Japan, took the approach of a mixed economy, its history and conditions were very different from Japan's. Mexico set out to modernize after a long and turbulent revolution that raged from 1910 to 1920. During the

Data for Your Case Study

Use the graphs and chart as you research your case study project. You may also use the data in your case study presentation.

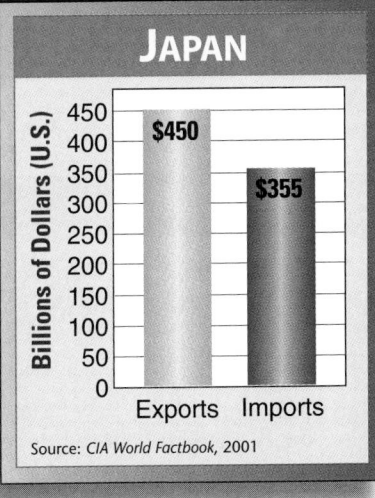

JAPAN

Source: *CIA World Factbook*, 2001

Japan's chief trading partners: Southeast Asia, United States, China, Australia

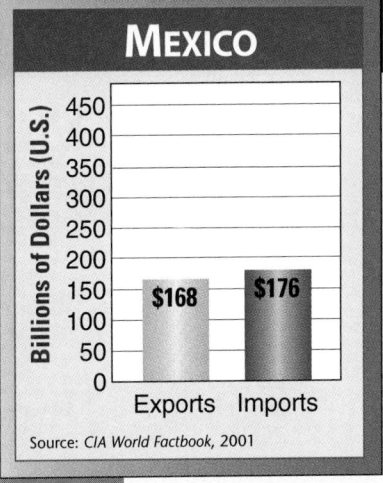

MEXICO

Source: *CIA World Factbook*, 2001

Mexico's chief trading partners: United States, Japan, Western Europe

JAPAN AND MEXICO AT A GLANCE

	Japan	Mexico
Total land area	145,882 mi^2 (377,835 km^2)	761,602 mi^2 (1,972,550 km^2)
Population	127.2 million	104.9 million
Number of people per square mile	876 (338 per km^2)	136 (53 per km^2)
Urban population	79%	74%
Per capita GDP (in U.S. dollars)	$27,200	$9,000
Natural resources	Negligible mineral resources, fish	Petroleum, silver, copper, gold, lead, zinc, natural gas, timber
Percentage of arable land	12%	13%
Adult literacy (age 15 and over can read and write)	99%	90%

Sources: *DK World Desk Reference*, 2003; Infoplease.com, 2003

revolution, poverty-stricken peasants and workers battled powerful landowners and business interests.

Mexico's constitution gives the government much power over economic resources, such as land, minerals, and oil. During the 1920s and 1930s, Mexico struggled to recover from the revolution and the Great Depression.

For decades, the Institutional Revolutionary Party (PRI) controlled the government. To achieve its goals, the PRI pursued a policy of economic nationalism. It limited foreign investment and ownership of key industries and passed laws affecting landownership.

By the 1990s, the PRI was facing challenges to its political monopoly. It also suffered economic reversals and a severe banking crisis. In response, the PRI supported major economic and political reforms. By approving the North American Free Trade Agreement (NAFTA), it opened Mexico to foreign investment and allowed more outside competition. Exports rose and the economy improved, although poverty remained widespread. More recently, the PRI lost the presidency for the first time since the 1930s.

Voices and Views

On Japan's Economic Miracle

Data for Your Case Study

Analyze these quotations as you research your case study. You may also use the quotations in your case study presentation.

"Workers will find true happiness through work, for work will always be the basis of society."

—Slogan on Toyota factory wall

"We're no longer satisfied simply with working hard. . . . We need to keep a good balance between work and something else, like families."

—Norio Gomi, 1989

"We're more interested today in consuming than working. And you know what we're most interested in consuming? Leisure."

—Japanese Finance Ministry worker, 1989

"Japan may be the world's richest nation, but something is terribly wrong when white collar workers in top firms cannot afford to buy a house, or even pay for their children's education."

—Hidezo Inaba, Chairman, Industrial Policy Research Institute, 1987

"Despite the recession, people are still happy with continued job security. . . . Job security is so sacred."

—Shijuro Ogata, 1997

"As Japan searches for a path to take into the next century, the challenges of building a modern market economy—and the resulting anxiety—are disconcertingly similar to those in the former communist world. In Japan almost as much as in Russia, there is a consensus that the old economic and political system was ill-suited for the future, and that society must move several steps in the direction of American-style capitalism, but that this will be as painful as it is inevitable."

—*New York Times,* 1997

"They'll have to work harder and harder just to stay in place. I wonder what it will be like in 20 or 30 years."

—Japanese employee Toshi-yuki Hozawa, on his sons' future, 1997

On Political Ferment in Mexico

"Our elections are so sophisticated that we can tell who won hours before the polls close," boasts an American. "So what?" replies his Mexican friend. "Here we can tell months before."

—Old Mexican joke

"We will never know if Mexico is a democracy until the presidency falls to the opposition."

—Sergio Sarmento, television news director

"Those who bleed the country are those who have the most: the governors, deputies, senators, and presidents. . . . The majority of our people are poor. Of the 70 million people in our country I think only 100 or 500 are millionaires. If our country is a democracy, this isn't right—*ricos* [rich people] with castles on the coasts, while in some pueblos the

parents don't have food to put in their children's mouths."

—Augustin Peréz, Mexican worker

"It simply was no longer logical for a Mexican to vote for the PRI, a party that has a dark complicity [involvement] with corruption."

—Cuauhtemoc Cardenas, opposition party leader, elected mayor of Mexico City, 1997

"I would ask that we must have a renewed attitude, that we must have a long-term view, that we must have the capacity to change problems into opportunities, that we must work together to make out of our nations, great nations. We have gone through an in-depth change in Mexico. . . . We are a democratic government with great legitimacy and moral authority."

—Vicente Fox, opposition party candidate, elected president of Mexico in 2000

A worker inspects a car at a Japanese automobile factory.

Researching and Presenting Case Study 3

RESEARCHING

As you research "Japan and Mexico: The Path to Prosperity," remember that your case study project will have three parts:
- a **presentation** based on your research and reflection on the topic
- an **oral interview** to follow your presentation
- a **project journal** that will include a case study overview, research log, and an essay on the significance of your topic

See pages 660–665 for a detailed description of these elements.

PRESENTING

Your presentation on this topic should include the following:
- a **brief overview or time line** of key events in the economic and political development of Japan since the Meiji Restoration and of Mexico since the Mexican Revolution
- an **examination** of Japan's post-war economic miracle and the challenges Japan faces today
- an **analysis** of Mexico's path toward modernization under the PRI and recent efforts to open Mexico's economy to foreign investment and trade
- a **comparison** of one-party rule in Japan and in Mexico as well as efforts to open each nation's political system to more competition
- a **concluding statement** on the importance to the United States of a prosperous and peaceful Japan and Mexico

 Go Online PHSchool.com — To learn about Japan and Mexico, use **Web Code mmk-1003.**

Resources

In Your World History Textbook

To locate useful background information on this topic in your textbook, check the index under the following headings: *economy, economic nationalism, debt crisis, trade, North American Free Trade Association (NAFTA), Association of Southeast Asian Nations (ASEAN), Japan, Mexico*

In Your Library

✔Castaneda, Jorge. *The Mexican Shock: Its Meaning for the United States.* New York: New Press, 1995.

✔Irokawa, Daikichi. *The Age of Hirohito: In Search of Modern Japan.* New York: Free Press, 1995.

✔Krauze, Enrique. *Mexico, Biography of Power: A History of Modern Mexico.* New York: HarperCollins, 1997.

✔Lincoln, Edward. *Japan's New Global Role.* Washington, DC: Brookings Institution, 1995.

✔Pastor, Robert A., and Jorge Castaneda. *Limits to Friendship: The United States and Mexico.* New York: Random House, 1989.

✔Ross, John. *Rebellion at the Roots: Indian Uprising in Chiapas.* Monroe, ME: Common Courage Press, 1994.

✔Sato, Ryuzo. *The Chrysanthemum and the Eagle: The Future of U.S.–Japan Relations.* New York: New York University Press, 1995.

✔Schlesinger, Jacob M. *Shadow Shoguns: The Rise and Fall of Japan's Postwar Political Machine.* New York: Simon & Schuster, 1997.

Argentina and South Africa: The Road to Democracy

Case Study Topic

In this case study, you will examine how Argentina and South Africa moved from authoritarian rule toward democratic government.

How to Complete Case Study 4

● Be sure to read or review the **Project Overview** on pages 660–665. It describes how to complete a case study.

● Then, read the **background information** on this page and on page 679. It will provide a starting point for your research.

● Next, study the **chart** on the next page for additional data.

● Finally, on page 680, you will find **Voices and Views,** a collection of quotations. Analyze them and add them to your research.

● On page 681 is a list of **what you need to include** in your case study presentation. Also provided is a list of **resources** for your research.

Background Information

Not long ago, it was hard to find a country in Latin America or Africa that was not ruled by an authoritarian government or by the military. Today, in contrast, most Latin American countries and a growing number of African nations have elected governments. In some of these nations, the road to democracy was relatively peaceful. More often, however, that transition has been marked by violence and bloodshed. Such was the case in both Argentina and South Africa.

Argentina

In the 1920s, Argentina ranked among the world's ten richest nations and was ruled by a democratically elected government. The Great Depression, however, shattered Argentina's prosperity and its leaders' commitment to democracy. Since 1930, some 25 governments have come to power in that country, more than half of them following military coups.

After the last military coup in 1976, the ruling generals declared war on "enemies of the state." Over the next few years, tens of thousands of people disappeared in what Argentines called their "dirty war." Public outrage forced the generals to turn over power to an elected government in 1983. Since then, Argentina's fragile democracy has survived coup attempts, runaway inflation, corruption scandals, and widespread social unrest.

Many Argentine citizens have demanded justice for the victims of the "dirty war." Of some 7,000 possible defendants in cases involving the disappeared, however, only 60 or so people were charged with crimes. Fewer still were brought to trial, convicted, and jailed.

In 1991, saying that he wanted to "close a black chapter" in Argentina's history, newly elected President Carlos Saul Menem pardoned even those few. Still, for many that "black chapter" could not be closed so easily. Nearly 50,000 people filled the streets of Buenos Aires to protest the pardons.

South Africa

South Africa is the richest nation in Africa. Until recently, it was also the most racially divided as well. Under the system of apartheid, South Africans were rigidly segregated on the basis of race, with whites dominating all other racial groups.

The harshness of the apartheid regime brought South Africa worldwide condemnation backed by economic sanctions. It also led to ever-increasing unrest and violence at home. In 1990, newly elected President F. W. de Klerk called for an end to apartheid. Four years later, South Africans of all races went to the

Data for Your Case Study

Use this chart as you research your case study project. You may also use this data in your case study presentation.

ARGENTINA AND SOUTH AFRICA AT A GLANCE		
	Argentina	**South Africa**
Total land area	1,068,296 mi^2 (2,766,890 km^2)	471,008 mi^2 (1,219,912 km^2)
Population	38.7 million	42.7 million
Number of people per square mile	35 (14 per km^2)	93 (36 per km^2)
Urban population	90%	55%
Per capita GDP (in U.S. dollars)	$12,000	$9,400
Adult literacy (age 15 and over can read and write)	97%	85%
Life expectancy at birth	73 years	52 years
Ethnic divisions	Europeans (mostly of Spanish and Italian descent), 97%; other (mostly Indian or mestizo), 3%	Black, 75.2%; white, 13.6%; colored, 8.6%; Indian, 2.6%
Natural resources	Fertile plains of the Pampas, lead, zinc, tin, copper, iron ore, manganese, petroleum, uranium	Gold, chromium, antimony, coal, iron ore, manganese, nickel, phosphates, tin, uranium, gem diamonds, platinum, copper, vanadium, salt, natural gas

Sources: *DK World Desk Reference*, 2003; Infoplease.com, 2003

polls and elected Nelson Mandela as their country's first black president. Since that historic election, South Africa's government has worked hard to heal the wounds of apartheid by exposing them to the light of truth.

In 1996, a Truth and Reconciliation Commission was created in South Africa to investigate murders and other human rights abuses committed during the apartheid era. Those who agreed to tell the truth were promised amnesty, or pardons, in exchange for their confessions.

In all, about 8,000 people applied for amnesty. As they and their victims testified before the commission, South Africans learned of the horrible deeds done to defend—and fight—apartheid. Police told of assassinations. Politicians confessed to bombings. Anti-apartheid activists admitted to murders.

Confronting the past has not been easy for South Africans. Many agree, however, that it is necessary. "If you look at history," said one white apartheid opponent who was severely injured in a terrorist bomb attack, "some countries try to bury the past. No nation has ever succeeded. If we try to ignore or bury the past, it will haunt us, even destroy us."

Voices and Views

On Argentina's Fragile Democracy

Data for Your Case Study

Analyze these quotations as you research your case study. You may also use the quotations in your case study presentation.

"There is no democracy without voting, but voting in and of itself is not sufficient. Democracy is a form of governing and of organizing a society [based on] respect for the dignity of man. It is inconceivable without justice."

—Raúl Alfonsín, former president of Argentina

"Twenty years later, more than nine thousand Argentine families still do not know exactly what happened to the person who was once yanked away from his or her home by agents of the state, never to be seen again. At the time, the military authorities told them they could not know and would never know. . . . Now democratically elected leaders . . . tell them that they should not want to know."

—Juan Méndez, Human Rights Watch

"One of the things that I simply will not do now is shut up. The women of my generation in Latin America have been taught that the man is always in charge and the woman is silent even in the face of injustice. . . . Now I know that we have to speak about the injustices publicly. If not, we are accomplices."

—Maria del Rosario de Cerruti, Mother of the Plaza de Mayo

"I've often gone to the Plaza de Mayo, like an idiot, like a coward, hiding behind the trees, to watch the mothers walking around the plaza on behalf of the disappeared, knowing that I had thirty disappeared persons on my conscience."

—Francisco Sciligo, first to break the military's pact of silence on crimes of the "dirty war"

On South Africa After Apartheid

"The people who structured apartheid and put it on the law books were not evil people. . . . Apartheid was, in its idealist form, a plan to make all the people of South Africa free."

—F. W. de Klerk, last white president of South Africa

"While we were desperately holding on to our mad little system, we never dared participate in the intellectual life of the 20th century. Now all those debates are opening up to us. We have rejoined the human race."

—Ken Owen, white newspaper editor

"My school used to be all-white. Now, it's open to all races. The school is two-thirds white and one-third other races. . . . Now I have friends from all races. Three years ago, you were never around them; you didn't even know about them."

—Marianneke Zondstra, 15, white student

"We're able to go to far better schools now that apartheid has been abolished. . . . Everything is better, and it happened because for the first time we are able to choose the schools we want to attend."

—Carmen Fernandis, 14, Colored student

"The images of South Africans going to the polls that day are burned in my memory. Great lines of patient people snaking through the dirt roads and streets of towns and cities; old women who have waited half a century to cast their first vote saying they felt like human beings for the first time in their lives; white men and women saying they were proud to live in a free country at last. . . . It was as if we were a nation reborn."

—Nelson Mandela on first all-race elections

Two women vote in South Africa's first all-race elections in 1994.

Researching and Presenting Case Study 4

RESEARCHING

As you research "Argentina and South Africa: The Road to Democracy," remember that your case study project will have the following three parts:
- a **presentation** based on your research and reflection on the topic
- an **oral interview** to follow your presentation
- a **project journal** that will include a case study overview, research log, and an essay on the significance of your topic

See pages 660–665 for a detailed description of these elements.

PRESENTING

Your presentation on this topic should include the following:
- a **brief overview or time line** of key events leading up to the transition to democracy in Argentina and South Africa
- an **examination** of the social and economic challenges confronting Argentina's government
- an **analysis** of challenges facing South Africa's majority government as it seeks to overcome the legacy of apartheid
- a **comparison** of efforts by both countries to seek justice for victims of the former regime
- a **concluding statement** on the importance of these transitions to democracy for Argentines, South Africans, and Americans

 Go Online PHSchool.com   To learn about Argentina and South Africa, use **Web Code mme-1004.**

Resources

In Your World History Textbook

To locate useful background information on this subject in your textbook, check the index under the following headings: *democracy, apartheid, Argentina, Latin America, South Africa*

In Your Library

✔Bouvard, Marguerite Guzman. *Revolutionizing Motherhood: The Mothers of the Plaza de Mayo.* Wilmington, DE: Scholarly Resources, 1994.

✔Crassweller, Robert D. *Perón and the Enigmas of Argentina.* New York: W.W. Norton, 1987.

✔Mandela, Nelson. *Long Walk to Freedom: The Autobiography of Nelson Mandela.* Boston: Little, Brown, 1994.

✔Poneman, Daniel. *Argentina: Democracy on Trial.* New York: Paragon House Publishers, 1987.

✔Sparks, Allister. *Tomorrow Is Another Country: The Inside Story of South Africa's Road to Change.* Chicago: University of Chicago Press, 1995.

✔Suzman, Helen. *In No Uncertain Terms: A South African Memoir.* New York: Alfred A. Knopf, 1993.

✔Timmerman, Jacobo. *Prisoner Without a Name, Cell Without a Number.* New York: Random House, 1988.

✔Thompson, Leonard. *A History of South Africa.* Princeton: Yale University Press, 1996.

✔Waldmeir, Patti. *Anatomy of a Miracle: The End of Apartheid and the Birth of the New South Africa.* New York: W.W. Norton, 1997.

The Czech Republic and South Korea: Democracy and Economic Development

Case Study Topic

The Czech Republic has a democratic government that is determined to foster economic development. South Korea became an economic powerhouse under an authoritarian government. In this case study, you will report on the state of democracy and economic development in these two countries.

How to Complete Case Study 5

- Be sure to read or review the **Project Overview** on pages 660–665. It describes how to complete a case study.

- Then, read the **background information** on this page and on page 683. It will provide a starting point for your research.

- Next, study the **maps and chart** on the next page for additional data.

- Finally, on page 684, you will find **Voices and Views**, a collection of quotations. Analyze them and add them to your research.

- On page 685 is a list of **what you need to include** in your case study presentation. Also provided is a list of **resources** for your research.

Background Information

Is political freedom essential to economic development? Not necessarily, or at least not at first, say some economists and historians. Apart from the United States and Great Britain, few of the world's wealthiest democracies developed their modern economies entirely under democratic rule.

Still, many economists agree that there is a strong link between economic development and democracy. Once people get used to some measure of economic freedom, they often begin to work for political rights and freedoms as well. Some economists believe that as a nation becomes more prosperous, it also becomes more democratic.

The Czech Republic

After World War I, Czechoslovakia was one of the most prosperous and democratic nations in Europe. It might still be so had it not been taken over by communists after World War II. Under communist rule, the freedoms that had once been part of Czech life became distant memories.

Following the example of the USSR, Czechoslovakia's communist rulers stressed the building of heavy industry in their economic development plans. Agriculture and the production of consumer goods were neglected. Rather than create prosperity, this lopsided approach to development produced food shortages, scarce housing, and poor-quality consumer goods.

In 1989, Czechoslovakians staged mass protests to oust their communist rulers in what human rights activist Vaclav Havel has called the "velvet revolution." Less than three years later, Czechs and Slovaks agreed to a "velvet divorce." In 1993, the country was divided to form two new nations, the Czech Republic and Slovakia.

The Czech Republic rapidly privatized its economy by the mid-1990s. Privatization is the selling of state-owned industries to private investors. Today, the Czech economy benefits from a skilled labor force and German investment funds. The city of Prague attracts tourists from around the world.

South Korea

Fifty years ago, South Korea was one of the world's poorest nations with a per capita GDP of $100. Today, the Republic of Korea is a major industrial power with a GDP of about $12,600 per person. In that period, South Korea transformed itself from an agrarian society that could not even produce a bicycle to the world's seventh largest automobile maker and a leading producer of semiconductors and high-tech electronics.

For most of those years, South Koreans lived under a dictatorship dominated by the military. Under military rule, the government launched an ambitious

Data for Your Case Study

Use the maps and the chart below as you research your case study project. You may also use this data in your case study presentation.

Czechoslovakia, Before 1993

Azimuthal Equal Area Projection

0   100   200 Miles
0   100   200 Kilometers

Prague
CZECHOSLOVAKIA
Bratislava
Danube R.
Elbe R.

N W E S

⊛ National capital
• Other city

Czech Republic and Slovakia

Azimuthal Equal Area Projection

0   100   200 Miles
0   100   200 Kilometers

Prague
CZECH REPUBLIC
SLOVAKIA
Bratislava
Danube R.
Elbe R.

N W E S

⊛ National capital

CZECH REPUBLIC AND SOUTH KOREA AT A GLANCE

	Czech Republic	South Korea
Total land area	30,450 mi² (78,866 km²)	38,023 mi² (98,480 km²)
Population	10.2 million	48.2 million
Number of people per square mile	338 (131 per km²)	1,236 (477 per km²)
Urban population	75%	82%
Per capita GDP (in U.S. dollars)	$14,400	$18,000
Adult literacy (age 15 and over can read and write)	99.9%	98%
Natural resources	Hard coal, soft coal, kaolin, clay, graphite, timber	Coal, tungsten, graphite, molybdenum, lead, hydropower potential
Industries	Metallurgy, machinery and equipment, motor vehicles, glass, armaments	Electronics, automobile production, chemicals, shipbuilding, steel, textiles, clothing, footwear, food processing
Trading partners	Germany, Slovakia, Austria, Italy, Poland, France	United States, Japan, China, Hong Kong, Taiwan, Saudi Arabia, Australia

Sources: *DK World Desk Reference*, 2003; Infoplease.com, 2003

program of industrial and economic development. Economic planners used loans and favors to promote the growth of one industry after another. These industries were dominated by huge, octopuslike corporations known as *chaebol.*

In 1987, a wave of pro-democracy protests and riots rocked South Korea. Unable to quell the unrest, the government finally agreed to democratic reforms.

In 1995, South Korea's government was hit by scandal when it was charged with taking $307 million in bribes from businessmen. In early 1996, former presidents Roh Tae Woo and Chun Doo Hwan were both charged with treason in connection with the deaths of about 200 pro-democracy demonstrators. Some Korea watchers pointed out that, although shocking, the former presidents' downfall was evidence of the development of democratic principles and the rule of law.

Voices and Views

On the Czechs' Transition from Totalitarianism

Data for Your Case Study

Analyze these quotations as you research your case study. You may also use the quotations in your case study presentation.

"The behavior of people during this transition from totalitarianism is quite similar to that of someone who had just been released from prison. . . . We were used to being in prison. There were only a few rules, but they were very strong rules. And now we have freedom. But what to do with it?"

—Dana Nemcova, sociologist

"It wasn't so bad under communism, and now it's much worse."

—Complaint of older Czechs

"The majority of people is willing to sell freedom for social security. There is a real danger that they will be tempted to follow any leader who will promise them this security."

—Juraj Mesik, environmentalist

"If we want a democracy, we need an economy that works. And in order to have an economy that works, we need a democracy."

—Ivan Havel, computer scientist

"Communists, we forgive you. Please come back!"

—Half-serious Czech joke

"I am convinced that we will never build a democratic state based on the rule of law if we do not at the same time build a state that is . . . humane, moral, intellectual and spiritual, and cultural. The best laws . . . will not in themselves guarantee legality or freedom or human rights."

—President Vaclav Havel

On Democracy in South Korea

"Democracy is the founding principle of our country. . . . Democracy alone is the road to freedom, the road to economic equality, and the road to social welfare. Democracy alone is the road for the people of the Republic of Korea to feel purposeful and proud."

—President Kim Dae Jung

"Politics that is controlled by money is not democracy. Democracy gives an equal vote to all people, and everyone—the learned and the unlearned, the rich and poor—has the right to exercise his or her vote. . . . In reality, however, this basic principle of democracy is being greatly undermined in Korea. Money sways politics."

—Lee Young-hee, Korean law professor

"I was active in politics for a long time, and I have always believed that the way politics was conducted in this country was wrong. I firmly believe that politics should be free of the yoke of money."

—Kim Young Sam, former president of South Korea

"The two groups that had wielded the most power in Korea over the last 30 years are the military and the *chaebol*. The military may be said to have gone back to their barracks, but the *chaebol* have become even more powerful."

—Chung Un-chan, Korean economist

"After ten years of democratization, many people increasingly feel a sense of crisis that Korean democracy is adrift, if not on the verge of running aground."

—Jaung Hoon, Korean political scientist

The business district of Seoul, South Korea's capital

Researching and Presenting Case Study 5

RESEARCHING

As you research "The Czech Republic and South Korea: Democracy and Economic Development," remember that your case study project will have the following three parts:

- a **presentation** based on your research and reflection on the topic
- an **oral interview** to follow your presentation
- a **project journal** that will include a case study overview, research log, and an essay on the significance of your topic

See pages 660–665 for a detailed description of these elements.

PRESENTING

Your presentation on this topic should include the following:

- a **brief overview or time line** of key events leading up to the transition to democracy in the Czech Republic and South Korea
- an **examination** of the challenges facing the Czech Republic as it tries to establish a democratic government and a market economy at the same time
- an **analysis** of the strengths and weaknesses of South Korea's democratic government
- a **comparison** of the impact of corruption in both nations
- a **concluding statement** on what we can learn from the experiences of the Czech Republic and South Korea about the prospects of the world's newest democracies

To learn about the Czech Republic and South Korea, use **Web Code mme-1005.**

Resources

In Your World History Textbook

To locate useful background information on this subject in your textbook, check the index under the following headings: *democracy, developing nations, economy, Czechoslovakia, Czech Republic, Eastern Europe, Korea, South Korea*

In Your Library

✔Cummings, Bruce. *Korea's Place in the Sun: A Modern History.* New York: W.W. Norton, 1997.

✔Lee, Kenneth B. *Korea and East Asia: The Story of Phoenix.* New York: Praeger, 1997.

✔MacDonald, Donald Stone, & Donald N. Clark, Eds. *The Koreans: Contemporary Politics and Society.* Boulder: Westview Press, 1996.

✔ *Mini Dragons: South Korea.* PBS Video, 1995.

✔Nagorski, Andrew. *The Birth of Freedom: Shaping Lives and Societies in the New Eastern Europe.* New York: Simon & Schuster, 1993.

✔Pridham, Geoffrey, & Paul Lewis, Eds. *Stabilizing Fragile Democracies: New Party Systems in Southern and Eastern Europe.* New York: Routledge, 1995.

✔Sommer, Mark. *Living in Freedom: The Exhilaration and Anguish of Prague's Second Spring.* San Francisco: Mercury House, 1992.

✔Wheaton, Bernard, & Zdenek Kavan. *The Velvet Revolution: Czechoslovakia, 1988–1991.* Boulder: Westview Press, 1992.

Women in National Development: Bangladesh and Norway

NORWAY

BANGLADESH

Case Study Topic

Women worldwide have challenged and begun to change their political and economic roles as citizens. In this case study, you will report on how women in two countries—Bangladesh and Norway—have taken an active role in government and economic development.

How to Complete Case Study 6

- Be sure to read or review the **Project Overview** on pages 660–665. It describes how to complete a case study.

- Then, read the **background information** on this page and on page 687. It will provide a starting point for your research.

- Next, study the **chart** on the next page for additional data.

- Finally, on page 688, you will find **Voices and Views**, a collection of quotations. Analyze them and add them to your research.

- On page 689 is a list of **what you need to include** in your case study presentation. Also provided is a list of **resources** for your research.

Background Information

Women today play increasingly important roles in the economic development of their nations. Worldwide, women are the sole breadwinners in one in three households. Seventy percent of all small businesses are run by women. In Asia and Africa, women farmers raise from 60 to 80 percent of the food grown in their countries.

Women are also increasing their participation in political life. In the world's newest democracies, such as South Africa, women have gained the right to vote and run for public office at the same time as men. In the older democracies, women are running for office—and winning—in greater numbers than ever before. Another measure of women's progress in political life is the growing number of women who have served as prime ministers or presidents—in countries as different as Bangladesh and Norway.

Bangladesh

Bangladesh is one of the world's poorest and most densely populated nations. Since gaining its independence from Pakistan in 1971, the people of Bangladesh have endured famines, devastating storms, and political turmoil.

Traditionally, the status of women has been low in this country. Today, however, Bangladeshi women are gaining new respect and economic independence thanks to the work of Muhammad Yunus, founder of the Grameen ("Village") Bank. The Grameen Bank lends small amounts of money to the poorest of the poor—landless women—on the basis of trust. The women then use this money to start businesses and earn enough not only to repay the loans, but to improve their lives.

Women in Bangladesh have also become more active politically. In 1991, Begum Khalida Zia became Bangladesh's first female prime minister.

Yunus's idea of "microcredit"—lending small amounts to poor people so that they can help themselves out of poverty—has spread from Bangladesh to more than 50 nations, including the United States. "These millions of small people with their millions of small pursuits," says Yunus, "can add up to create the biggest development wonder."

Data for Your Case Study

Use this chart as you research your case study project. You may also use the data in your case study presentation.

BANGLADESH AND NORWAY AT A GLANCE		
	Bangladesh	**Norway**
Total land area	55,598 mi^2 (144,000 km^2)	125,181 mi^2 (324,220 km^2)
Population	138.4 million	4.5 million
Number of people per square mile	2,716 (1,048 per km^2)	38 (15 per km^2)
Urban population	25%	76%
Per capita GDP (in U.S. dollars)	$1,750	$30,800
Natural resources	Natural gas, arable land, timber, coal	Petroleum, copper, natural gas, pyrites, nickel, iron ore, zinc, lead, fish, timber, hydropower
Arable land	61%	3%
Life expectancy	60.5 years	78.8 years
Men	60.7 years	75.9 years
Women	60.3 years	81.9 years
Adult literacy	56%	100%
Men	63%	100%
Women	49%	100%
Women as a percentage of total labor force	38%	46%
Parliamentary seats held by women	10%	36%
Women in administrative and management jobs	5%	31%
Salaries of women as a percentage of men's incomes	23%	41%

Sources: *DK World Desk Reference*, 2003, Infoplease.com, 2003

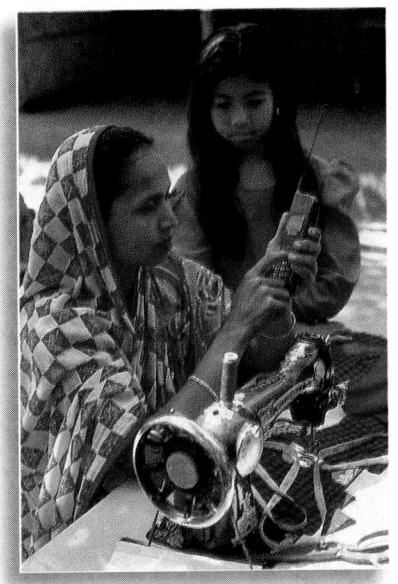

A Grameen Bank borrower in Bangladesh uses a cellular telephone to run her business. Under a program set up by the Grameen Bank, the telephones were provided exclusively to bank borrowers in villages without telephone service.

Norway

In contrast to Bangladesh, Norway is one of the world's richest and least densely populated nations. After World War II, Norway discovered large deposits of oil and natural gas off its coast. Today, it is the world's second-largest oil exporter.

Norway is also among the leading nations in the percentage of women in top government and political positions. Norwegian women won the right to vote in 1907. By 1990, not only were its prime minister, Dr. Gro Harlem Bruntland, and half her cabinet women, but three of the country's major political parties were headed by women. In the early 2000s, women generally held about 40 percent of the seats in Norway's parliament.

Voices and Views

On Women and Economic Development

Data for Your Case Study

Analyze these quotations and the chart on the next page as you research your case study. You may also use the quotations and the chart in your case study presentation.

"Everyone, without discrimination, has the right to equal pay for equal work."
—United Nations Universal Declaration of Human Rights, 1948

"Women make up half the world, are responsible for nearly two thirds of all working hours, yet they earn one tenth of the world's income and own less than one percent of the world's property."
—United Nations Report on the Status of Women, 1985

"I can assure you that if the right environment and incentives were created for women farmers, and the problems facing them now were addressed, the sustainable end of hunger would be a reality."
—Dr. Ester Afua Ocloo, entrepreneur, Ghana

"We found that many positive things could be achieved by lending to women. Because when a woman's income increases, the immediate beneficiaries are the children. A woman looks to the future with a planned strategy to improve the family situation. Men don't pay attention to such things."
—Muhammad Yunus, founder of Bangladesh's Grameen Bank

"These women have become a lot braver because of the Grameen Bank. Previously, if any strange man came, they would go into their houses. . . . Now they come out and talk."
—Oirashibala Dhor, Grameen Bank borrower in Bangladesh

On Women in Politics

"In no country do women have political status, access, or influence equal to men."
—Barbara Nelson, American professor of public affairs and Najma Chowdhury, Bangladeshi political scientist

"To be successful, a woman has to be much better at her job than a man."
—Golda Meir, Prime Minister of Israel from 1969 to 1974

"The biggest asset for a woman candidate is being a woman, and the biggest liability is not being a man."
—Barbara Curran, former New Jersey Assemblywoman

"Democracy minus women is not democracy."
—Slogan of Russia's First Independent Women's Forum

"The feminists have become far too strident [harsh-sounding] and have done damage to the cause of women by making us out to be something we're not. You get on because you have the right talents."
—Margaret Thatcher, Prime Minister of Britain from 1979 to 1990

"I was elected by the women of Ireland, who instead of rocking the cradle, rocked the system."
—Mary Robinson, elected president of Ireland in 1990 and Ireland's first woman president

"You no longer think: these are three women talking. Where are the men?"
—Bernt Aardal, Norwegian researcher, after a televised debate by three female party leaders

WOMEN HEADS OF STATE SINCE 1960

Corazon Aquino, president of the Philippines, 1986–1992

Sirimavo Bandaranaike, prime minister of Sri Lanka, 1960–1965, 1970–1977, and 1994–2000

Benazir Bhutto, prime minister of Pakistan, 1988–1990 and 1993–1996

Violeta Barrios de Chamorro, president of Nicaragua, 1990–1997

Helen Clark, became prime minister of New Zealand in 1999

Indira Gandhi, prime minister of India, 1966–1977 and 1980–1984

Tarja Halonen, became president of Finland in 2000

Chandrika Kumaratunge, became prime minister of Sri Lanka in 1994

Gloria Macapagal-Arroyo, became president of the Philippines in 2001

Mary McAleese, became president of Ireland in 1997

Golda Meir, prime minister of Israel, 1969–1974

Mireya Moscoso, became president of Panama in 1999

Isabel Perón, president of Argentina, 1974–1976

Mary Robinson, president of Ireland, 1990–1997

Suzanne Romer, became prime minister of the Netherlands Antilles in 1998

Jennifer Smith, became premier of Bermuda in 1998

Megawati Sukarnoputri, became president of Indonesia in 2001

Margaret Thatcher, prime minister of the United Kingdom, 1979–1990

Varia Vike-Freiberga, became president of Latvia in 1999

Khaleda Zia, reelected prime minister of Bangladesh in 2001

Resources

In Your World History Textbook

To locate useful background information on this topic in your textbook, check the index under the following headings: *women, economy, welfare state, Bangladesh, South Asia, Norway*

In Your Library

✔Baxter, Craig. *Bangladesh: From a Nation to a State.* Boulder: Westview, 1997.

✔Bornstein, David. *The Price of a Dream: The Story of the Grameen Bank.* New York: Simon & Schuster, 1996.

✔Langley, Winston E., Ed. *Women's Rights in International Documents: A Sourcebook with Commentary.* Jefferson, NC: McFarland, 1991.

✔Liswood, Laura. *Women World Leaders: Fifteen Great Politicians Tell Their Stories.* New York: HarperCollins, 1997.

✔Nelson, Barbara J., & Najma Chowdhury. *Women and Politics Worldwide.* New Haven: Yale University Press, 1994.

✔Todd, Helen. *Women at the Center: Grameen Bank Borrowers After One Decade.* Boulder: Westview, 1997.

✔Wahid, Abu N. M., Ed. *The Grameen Bank: Poverty Relief in Bangladesh.* Boulder: Westview, 1993.

✔Wahid, Abu N. M., & Charles E. Weis, Eds. *The Economy of Bangladesh: Problems and Prospects.* New York: Praeger, 1996.

Researching and Presenting Case Study 6

RESEARCHING

As you research "Women in National Development: Bangladesh and Norway," remember that your case study project will have the following three parts:
- a **presentation** based on your research and reflection on the topic
- an **oral interview** to follow your presentation
- a **project journal** that will include a case study overview, research log, and an essay on the significance of your topic

See pages 660–665 for a detailed description of these elements.

PRESENTING

Your presentation on this topic should include the following:
- a **brief overview** of the economies of Bangladesh and Norway
- a **description** of how the Grameen Bank has improved women's lives in Bangladesh
- a **survey** of the political gains women have made in Norway
- a **comparison** of the barriers to political and economic equality faced by women in each country
- a **concluding statement** on the significance of women's changing political and economic roles to the peoples of Bangladesh, Norway, and the United States

Civic Participation: Australia and the United States

Case Study Topic

A key component in a representative democrary is the electorate—the body of voters who elect those who govern. Although voter turnout is critical to the future of democratic governments, voter participation is declining in some countries. In this case study, you will investigate the decline in civic participation in two democracies—the United States and Australia. You will also report on what must be done to revitalize civic life in the United States.

How to Complete Case Study 7

● Be sure to read or review the **Project Overview** on pages 660–665. It describes how to complete a case study.

● Then, read the **background information** on this page and on page 691. It will provide a starting point for your research.

● Next, study the **map and chart** on the next page for additional data.

● Finally, on page 692, you will find **Voices and Views,** a collection of quotations. Analyze them and add them to your research.

● On page 693 is a list of **what you need to include** in your case study presentation. Also provided is a list of **resources** for your research.

Background Information

From El Salvador in Central America to Poland in Eastern Europe to the Philippines in East Asia, democracy is on the rise. The number of people living under governments they have chosen themselves has increased dramatically in the past two decades. Worldwide, the future of democracy has never looked brighter.

In many older democracies, however, some people are worried. From Switzerland in Western Europe to Australia in the Western Pacific to the United States in North America, more and more people are choosing not to participate in politics and government, sometimes not even bothering to vote. Growing public apathy has caused concerned citizens to ask two questions: Why are people "dropping out" of politics and civic life? What can be done to reverse this disturbing trend?

Australia

Australia has been a democracy since it gained its independence from Great Britain in 1901. In 1924, its parliament adopted a system of compulsory voting for national elections. Under Australia's election law, individuals over the age of 18 are required by law to register to vote and to cast ballots at every federal election. Failure to register or to vote can be punished by fines and even imprisonment.

As a result of this system, Australia has one of the highest voter turnout rates in the world, usually well above 90 percent. However, while Australians vote in large numbers, there are signs of growing political apathy. A recent study by a parliamentary committee revealed "a remarkable level of ignorance in the Australian population about even quite elementary aspects of politics and government."

Concern about the health of Australian democracy has led to a renewed debate over compulsory voting. Supporters of the system argue that democratic government means rule by the people. Therefore, elections should be decided by all of the people. In their view, voting is a civic duty—the same as jury service or paying taxes.

Critics of compulsory voting make two main arguments. The first is that in a democracy, the right to vote should also include the right not to vote. The second is that compulsory voting allows politicians to take voters for granted. Because politicians do not have to convince voters to vote, the critics argue, they are not as sensitive to the interests and needs of the people as they should be.

Data for Your Case Study

Use this map and the chart below as you research your case study project. You may also use the data in your case study presentation.

Free

Not free

Partly free

Not applicable

N
W E
S

Robinson Projection

AUSTRALIA AND THE UNITED STATES AT A GLANCE		
	Australia	**United States**
Total land area	2,967,893 mi² (7,686,850 km²)	3,717,792 mi² (9,629,091 km²)
Population	19.7 million	290.3 million
Number of people per square mile	7 (3 per km²)	80 (31 per km²)
Urban population	85%	77%
Per capita GDP (in U.S. dollars)	$24,000	$36,300
Adult literacy (age 15 and over can read and write)	100%	99%
Life expectancy at birth	79 years	77 years
Ethnic divisions	Caucasian, 92%; Asian, 7%; aboriginal and other, 1%	White, 80.7%; Hispanic, 13.4%; Black, 12.7%; American Indian, 0.9%
Religion	Anglican, 26.1%; Roman Catholic, 26%; other Christian, 24.3%; no religion, 13%; non-Christian, 11%	Protestant, 56%; Roman Catholic, 28%; Jewish, 2%; other, 4%; none, 10%

Sources: *DK World Desk Reference*, 2003; Infoplease.com, 2003

The United States

In the United States, voting is voluntary. For many years, though, some citizens were denied the right to vote. Change came slowly. The Fifteenth Amendment allowed African American men the right to vote. In 1920, the Nineteenth Amendment gave women suffrage. More recently, the Twenty-sixth Amendment lowered the voting age to 18, and the Voting Rights Act eliminated barriers that had kept minorities from voting. Today, any qualified citizen over the age of 18 can register to vote.

While the number of people eligible to vote has increased, voter participation in national elections has been steadily decreasing—from 63 percent in the early 1960s to 51 percent in 2000. Although the turnout in 2000 was up from 49 percent in 1996, the slight increase did not reverse a long-term trend in declining voter participation.

Voices and Views

On Compulsory Voting in Australia

Data for Your Case Study

Analyze these quotations and the graph on the next page as you research your case study. You may also use the quotations and the graph in your case study presentation.

"It shall be the duty of every elector to record a vote at each election."

—Commonwealth Electoral Act

"I am one who believes a system where 95 percent of adults vote is more democratic than one in which 50 percent vote. That voting is analogous to [like] other citizen's duties: paying taxes, jury and military service, and sending children to school."

—Laurie Oakes

"Surely it is a fundamental human right to be left alone, to be allowed to live one's own life within the law but otherwise unmolested, and to take no interest in politics at all except by choice."

—Padraic McGuinness, newspaper columnist

"Insisting that citizens vote encourages everyone to think about the issues."

—*The Courier Mail,* an Australian newspaper

"Compulsory voting keeps down the cost of campaigns. The most expensive part of a campaign where there is not compulsory voting is having to 'turn out the vote.'"

—Chris Puplick, Australian politician

"Recent figures show that many did not vote in the last State election and were not fined. This shows what an unenforceable, wasteful use of taxpayer's money compulsory voting is."

—Letter to the editor of the *Adelaide Advertiser,* Adelaide, Australia

On Voluntary Voting in the United States

"No right is more precious in a free country than that of having a voice in the election of those who make the laws under which . . . we must live. Other rights . . . are illusionary . . . if the right to vote is undermined."

—United States Supreme Court in *Wesberry* v. *Sanders*

"Nobody will ever deprive the American people of the right to vote but the American people themselves—and the only way they could is by not voting."

—President Franklin Delano Roosevelt

"Americans hate politics as it is now practiced because we have lost all sense of the public good. . . . They understand instinctively that politics these days is not about finding solutions. It is about discovering postures that offer short-term political benefits."

—E. J. Dionne, Jr., journalist

"Democracy is not a thing, it is a process. Self-government cannot be put on automatic pilot."

—League of Women Voters

"The probability that a lone vote will actually affect an election outcome is minuscule. . . . Quite simply, for many Americans voting just doesn't seem worth the effort."

—Ruy A. Teixeira, Economic Policy Institute

"People often say, with pride, 'I'm not interested in politics.' They might as well say, 'I'm not interested in my standard of living, my health, my job, my rights, my freedoms, my future or any future.' . . . If we mean to keep any control over our world and lives, we must be interested in politics."

—Martha Gellhorn, journalist

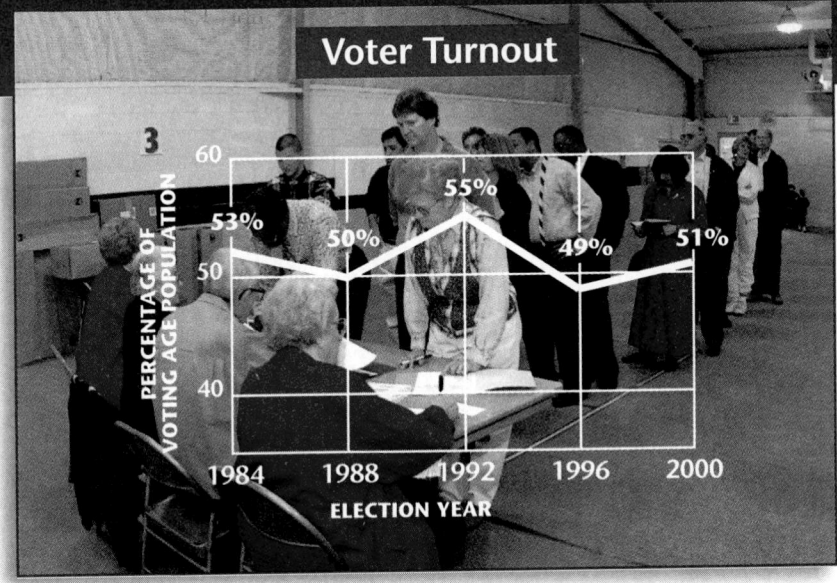

Voter Turnout

55%
53%
50%
49%
51%

PERCENTAGE OF VOTING AGE POPULATION

60
50
40

1984   1988   1992   1996   2000
ELECTION YEAR

Voter turnout in presidential elections dropped from 55 percent in 1992 to 49 percent in 1996 but picked up again in 2000.

Researching and Presenting Case Study 7

RESEARCHING

For this case study, your focus should be on voter participation in your community. To learn more about what can be done to increase voter participation where you live, you will want to interview the following:

- elected officials and local political party leaders
- local chapter of the League of Women Voters

As you research "Civic Participation: Australia and the United States," remember that your case study project will have the following three parts:

- a **presentation** based on your research and reflection on the topic
- an **oral interview** to follow your presentation
- a **project journal** that will include a case study overview, a research log, and an essay on the significance of your topic

See pages 660–665 for a detailed description of these elements.

PRESENTING

Your presentation on this topic should include the following:

- a **brief review** of voter participation rates in Australia and the United States since World War II
- a **summary** of Australia's compulsory voting laws and the main arguments for and against this system
- an **opinion** of why you think voter turnout has dropped in the United States since the 1960s
- **recommendations** on reversing this trend
- a **concluding statement** on the importance of informed and involved citizens to the future of democracy, both in the United States and worldwide

Go Online
PHSchool.com

To learn about Australia and the United States, use **Web Code mme-1007.**

Resources

In Your World History Textbook

To locate useful background information on this topic in your textbook, check the index under the following headings: *demo-cracy, social contract, suffrage, Australia, United States*

In Your Library

✔Dionne, E. J., Jr.
Why Americans Hate Politics. New York: Simon & Schuster, 1992.

✔Ravitch, Diane, & Abigail Thernstrom, Eds.
The Democracy Reader: Classic and Modern Speeches, Essays, Poems, Declarations, and Documents on Freedom and Human Rights Worldwide. New York: HarperCollins, 1993.

✔Smith, Sam.
Sam Smith's Great American Political Repair Manual: How to Rebuild Our Country So the Politics Aren't Broken and Politicians Aren't Fixed. New York: W.W. Norton, 1997.

✔Tipp, Stacey L., & Carol Wekesser, Eds.
Politics in America: Opposing Viewpoints. San Diego: Greenhaven Press, 1992.

On the World Wide Web

For information on U.S. voting trends, you might begin by going to the League of Women Voters' Web site and reading its 1997 report entitled *Charting the Health of American Democracy.*

For information on Australia's election laws and voter turnout, look for the Web sites of the Australian Electoral Commission and Australia's Parliamentary Education Office.

Reference Section

CONTENTS

Primary Sources and Literature 695

World Atlas 722

Glossary 734

Spanish Glossary 742

Index 751

Credits 774

PRIMARY SOURCES AND LITERATURE

Niccolò Machiavelli: *Discourses* 696

Bernal Díaz: *The True History of the Conquest of New Spain* 697

King Affonso I: *Letter to King John of Portugal* 698

Miguel de Cervantes: *Don Quixote* 699

The English Bill of Rights 700

John Locke: *Two Treatises on Government* 701

Jean-Jacques Rousseau: *The Social Contract* 702

Declaration of the Rights of Man and the Citizen 703

Miguel Hidalgo: *Decree of Hidalgo* 704

Simón Bolívar: *Address to the Congress of Venezuela* 705

Charles Dickens: *Hard Times* 706

Fukuzawa Yukichi: *Autobiography* 707

Erich Maria Remarque: *All Quiet on the Western Front* 708

Mohandas Gandhi: *Hind Swaraj* 709

Franklin D. Roosevelt: *The Four Freedoms* 710

The Universal Declaration of Human Rights 711

Mao Zedong: *The People's Democratic Dictatorship* 712

Chinua Achebe: *Things Fall Apart* 713

Kwame Nkrumah: *Autobiography* 714

Lech Walesa: *Nobel Peace Prize Lecture* 715

Mikhail Gorbachev: *Perestroika* 716

Vaclav Havel: *New Year's Address* 717

Mario Vargas Llosa: *Latin America, the Democratic Option* 718

Aung San Suu Kyi: *Freedom From Fear* 719

Nelson Mandela: *Glory and Hope* 720

Harry Wu: *The Outlook for China, Human Rights* 721

Niccolò Machiavelli: *Discourses*

The Florentine writer Niccolò Machiavelli (1469–1527) is best known for his book *The Prince*, in which he describes how a ruler can get and keep power. However, in his book *Discourses on the First Ten Books of Titus Livy,* Machiavelli concludes that the best-governed state is ruled by the people rather than by a ruthless prince.

Vocabulary Before you read the selection, look up the following words in a dictionary: **populace, subservient, licentious, trepidation.**

Main Idea In his *Discourses,* Machiavelli describes methods for establishing and preserving republics.

In short, to bring this topic to conclusion, I say that, just as princely forms of government have endured for a very long time, so, too, have republican forms of government; and that in both cases it has been essential for them to be regulated by laws. For a prince who does what he likes is a lunatic; and a populace which does what it likes is unwise. If, therefore, it be a question of a prince subservient to the laws and of a populace chained up by laws, more virtue will be found in the populace than in the prince; and if it be a question of either of them loosed from control by the law, there will be found fewer errors in the populace than in the prince, and these of less moment and much easier to put right. For a licentious and turbulent populace, when a good man can obtain a hearing, can easily be brought to behave itself; but there is no one to talk to a bad prince, nor is there any remedy except the sword. . . .

When the populace has thrown off all restraint, it is not the mad things it does that are terrifying, nor is it of present evils that one is afraid, but of what may come of them, for amidst such confusion there may come to be a tyrant. In the case of bad princes it is just the opposite: it is present evils that are terrifying, but for the future there is hope, since men are convinced that the evil ways of a bad prince may make for freedom in the end. . . . The reason why people are prejudiced against the populace is because of the populace anyone may speak ill without fear and openly, even when the populace is ruling. But of princes people speak with the utmost trepidation and the utmost reserve.

Analyzing Primary Sources

1. Machiavelli states that the only way to bring an unruly prince under the law is to
   A obtain a hearing.
   B use physical combat.
   C discuss the people's legal rights.
   D choose a tyrant.

2. Machiavelli concludes that the greatest threat posed by an unlawful populace is the
   E rise of a dictator.
   F violence of the mob.
   G loss of a prince.
   H destruction of property.

3. **Critical Thinking Making Inferences (a)** According to Machiavelli, what do princely and republican forms of government have in common? **(b)** Why do you think Machiavelli believes that the populace loosed from control is more subject to criticism than a prince loosed from control?

Bernal Díaz: *The True History of the Conquest of New Spain*

Bernal Díaz del Castillo (c. 1492–1581) accompanied Hernan Cortés on his conquest of the Aztecs in present-day Mexico. Díaz wrote his history many years later to refute what he viewed as inaccurate accounts of the conquest. The following excerpt describes a meeting between Cortés and Moctezuma, the Aztec king, in the Aztec city of Tenochtitlán.

Vocabulary Before you read the selection, look up the following words in a dictionary: **oratory, league.**

Main Idea This memoir provides an account of the Aztec capital of Tenochtitlán at the time of the Spanish conquest.

When we climbed to the top of the great [temple] there was a kind of platform, with huge stones where they put the poor Indians to be sacrificed, and an image like a dragon and other evil figures, with a great deal of blood that had been shed that day. Moctezuma, accompanied by two priests, came out from an oratory dedicated to the worship of his cursed idols. . . .

Then Moctezuma took him [Cortés] by the hand and bade him look at his great city and at all the other cities rising from the water, and the many towns around the lake. . . .

There we stood looking, for that large and evil temple was so high that it towered over everything. From there we could see all three of the causeways that led into Mexico. . . .

We saw the fresh water that came from Chapultepec, which supplied the city, and the bridges on the three causeways, built at certain intervals so the water could go from one part of the lake to another, and a multitude of canoes, some arriving with provisions and others leaving with merchandise. We saw that every house in this great city and in the others built on the water could be reached only by wooden drawbridges or by canoe. We saw temples built like towers and fortresses in these cities, all white-washed; it was a sight to see. . . .

After taking a good look and considering all that we had seen, we looked again at the great square and the throngs of people, some buying and others selling. The buzzing of their voices could be heard more than a league away. There were soldiers among us who had been in many parts of the world, in Constantinople and Rome and all over Italy, who said that they had never before seen a market place so large and so well laid out, and so filled with people.

Aztec gold ornament

Analyzing Primary Sources

1. What scene is Bernal Díaz describing in this excerpt?

   A a view of Tenochtitlán's market and surroundings from the top of a tall temple

   B an indoor temple with many religious statues

   C a view of Tenochtitlán's temple from the market place

   D a view of the markets in Constantinople and Rome

2. Which of the following best describes the author's view of the Aztecs?

   E generous and busy

   F evil and prosperous

   G loving and kind

   H athletic and loud

3. **Critical Thinking Recognizing Points of View** Which words and phrases in the excerpt above reveal the author's opinion of the Aztec's religion?

King Affonso I:
Letter to King John of Portugal

In 1490, the Portuguese converted the son of a Kongo king to Christianity and then helped him to assume his father's throne. The king, born Nzinga Mbemba, was renamed Affonso. King Affonso soon realized that his relationship with Portugal had extremely negative consequences, as can be seen from his letter in 1526 to King John of Portugal.

Vocabulary Before you read the selection, look up the following words in a dictionary: **comply, jurisdiction, depopulated.**

Main Idea In this letter, the king of Kongo asks the king of Portugal to end the slave trade.

African carving of Portuguese soldiers

Sir, Your Highness of Portugal should know how our Kingdom is being lost in so many ways. This is caused by the excessive freedom given by your officials to the men and merchants who are allowed to come to this Kingdom to set up shops with goods and many things which have been prohibited by us. Many of our vassals, whom we had in obedience, do not comply because they have the things in greater abundance than we ourselves. It was with these things that we had them content and subjected under our jurisdiction, so it is doing a great harm not only to the service of God, but to the security and peace of our Kingdoms and State as well.

And we cannot reckon how great the damage is, since the mentioned merchants are taking every day our natives, sons of the land and the sons of our noblemen and vassals and our relatives. The thieves and men of bad conscience grab them wishing to have the things and wares of this Kingdom which they are ambitious of; they grab them and get them to be sold. And so great, Sir, is the corruption and licentiousness that our country is being completely depopulated, and your Highness should not agree with this nor accept it as in your service. And to avoid it we need from those your Kingdoms no more than some priests and a few people to teach in schools, and no other goods except wine and flour for the holy sacrament.

That is why we beg of Your Highness to help and assist us in this matter, commanding your factors that they should not send here either merchants or wares, because *it is our will that in these kingdoms there should not be any trade of slaves nor outlet for them.* Concerning what is referred to above, again we beg of Your Highness to agree with it. . . .

Analyzing Primary Sources

1. Which of the following best describes the author's purpose in writing this letter?

   A to ask the king for money to help in ending the slave trade

   B to inform the king of the abuses taking place and to ask for his help in ending them

   C to inform the king about the extent of trade taking place in the kingdom

   D to ask the king for an explanation for why people are being enslaved

2. What does Affonso request of King John in the last paragraph?

   E that he not send any merchants or wares

   F that he send teachers

   G that he send priests

   H that he pray for Affonso

3. **Critical Thinking Recognizing Causes and Effects** According to King Affonso, how have the Portuguese affected his kingdom and state?

Miguel de Cervantes: *Don Quixote*

In his novel *Don Quixote,* Spanish writer Miguel de Cervantes tells the story of a madman who thinks he is a medieval knight. While Don Quixote's exploits often seem ridiculous, his devotion to the virtues underlying chivalry give his actions dignity. In this famous excerpt, Don Quixote does battle with a group of windmills against the advice of his down-to-earth companion, Sancho Panza.

Vocabulary Before you read the selection, look up the following words in a dictionary: **nigh, leagues, millstone, caitiffs.**

Main Idea In this excerpt, Don Quixote's devotion to knighthood leads him to attack a windmill, which he sees as a menacing giant.

Just then they came in sight of thirty or forty windmills that rise from that plain, and no sooner did Don Quixote see them than he said to his squire: "Fortune is guiding our affairs better than we ourselves could have wished. Do you see over yonder, friend Sancho, thirty or forty hulking giants? I intend to do battle with them and slay them. With the spoils we shall begin to be rich, for this is a righteous war. . . ."

"What giants?" asked Sancho Panza.

"Those you see over there," replied his master, "with the long arms; some of them have them well-nigh two leagues in length."

"Take care, sir," cried Sancho. "Those over there are not giants but windmills, and those things that seem to be armed are their sails, which when they are whirled around by the wind turn the millstone."

"It is clear," replied Don Quixote, "that you are not experienced in adventures. Those are giants, and if you are afraid, turn aside and pray whilst I enter into fierce and unequal battle with them."

Uttering these words, he clapped spurs to Rozinante, his steed, without heeding the cries of his squire, Sancho, who warned him that he was not going to attack giants, but windmills. But so convinced was he that they were giants that he neither heard his squire's shouts nor did he notice what they were, though he was very near them. Instead, he rushed on, shouting in a loud voice: "Fly not, cowards and vile caitiffs; one knight alone attacks you!" At that moment a slight breeze arose and the great sails began to move. . . .

He ran his lance into the sail, but the wind twisted it with such violence that it shivered the lance in pieces and dragged both rider and horse after it, rolling them over and over on the ground, sorely damaged.

Analyzing Literature

1. When Don Quixote attacks the giants, he expects
   A to gain great wealth.
   B to fail because he fights alone.
   C Sancho to join him.
   D to be tossed in the air.

2. Don Quixote believes a knight should
   E attack only after being attacked.
   F act boldly when he finds an enemy.
   G seek help before fighting an unequal battle.
   H enter a battle only to gain material wealth.

3. **Critical Thinking Drawing Conclusions**
   (a) What values of chivalry motivate Don Quixote's attack on the windmills? **(b)** How do you think Cervantes feels about Don Quixote and his ideals? Explain.

The English Bill of Rights

When the Catholic king, James II, was forced from the English throne in 1688, Parliament offered the crown to his Protestant daughter Mary and her husband William of Orange. But Parliament insisted that William and Mary submit to a Bill of Rights. This document, a continuation of the struggle between the crown and Parliament, sums up the powers that Parliament had been seeking since the Petition of Right in 1628.

Vocabulary Before you read the selection, look up the following words in a dictionary: **subvert, extirpate, abdicated, prerogative, redress.**

Main Idea This document ensured the superiority of Parliament over the monarchy and spelled out basic rights.

Whereas, the late King James II . . . did endeavor to subvert and extirpate the Protestant religion and the laws and liberties of this kingdom . . . and whereas the said late King James II having abdicated the government, and the throne being vacant. . . .

The said lords [Parliament] . . . being now assembled in a full and free representative [body] of this nation . . . do in the first place . . . declare:

1. That the pretended power of suspending of laws or the execution of laws by regal authority without consent of Parliament is illegal. . . .
4. That levying money for or to the use of the crown by pretense of prerogative without grant of Parliament . . . is illegal;
5. That it is the right of the subjects to petition the king, and all commitments and prosecutions for such petitioning are illegal.
6. That . . . raising or keeping a standing army within the kingdom in time of peace, unless it be with consent of Parliament, is against law. . . .
8. That election of members of Parliament ought to be free. . . .
9. That the freedom of speech and debates or proceedings in Parliament ought not to be challenged or questioned in any court or place out of Parliament. . . .
10. That excessive bail ought not to be required, nor excessive fines imposed, nor cruel and unusual punishments inflicted. . . .
13. And that, for redress of all grievances and for the amending, strengthening, and preserving of the laws, Parliaments ought to be held frequently. . . .

English Houses of Parliament (1800s)

Analyzing Primary Sources

1. Which of the following statements best summarizes these excerpts from the Bill of Rights?

   A The king's powers are limited by the Parliament.

   B The Parliament's powers are limited by the monarch.

   C The Parliament's duty is to amend and preserve laws.

   D The king's powers to raise an army are unlimited.

2. This Bill of Rights required the monarch to

   E raise money for paying the members of Parliament.

   F summon Parliament regularly.

   G cancel laws he or she considered unjust.

   H keep a standing army to defend the country.

3. **Critical Thinking Making Inferences** Why do you think the members of Parliament included item 9? Why do you think this item was important?

John Locke: *Two Treatises on Government*

English philosopher John Locke (1632–1704) published *Two Treatises on Government* in 1690. In the writings, Locke holds that all people possess natural rights, including property and personal freedom. Locke also states that governments hold their power only with the consent of the people. Locke's ideas heavily influenced revolutions in America and France.

Vocabulary Before you read the selection, look up the following words in a dictionary: **promulgated, extemporary, inroads, transgress, endeavor, forfeit, devolves.**

Main Idea In this essay, Locke states that the primary purpose of government is to protect the natural rights of the people.

But though men, when they enter into society give up the equality, liberty, and executive power they had in the state of Nature into the hands of society . . . the power of the society or legislative constituted by them can never be supposed to extend farther than the common good. . . . Whoever has the legislative or supreme power of any commonwealth, is bound to govern by established standing laws, promulgated and known to the people, and not by extemporary decrees, by [unbiased] and upright judges, who are to decide controversies by those laws; and to employ the force of the community at home only in the execution of such laws, or abroad to prevent or redress foreign injuries and secure the community from inroads and invasion. And all this to be directed to no other end but the peace, safety, and public good of the people. . . .

The reason why men enter into society is the preservation of their property; and the end while they choose and authorize a legislative is that there may be laws made, and rules set, as guards and fences to the properties of all the society, . . .

Whensoever, therefore, the legislative [power] shall transgress this fundamental rule of society, and either by ambition, fear, folly, or corruption, endeavor to grasp themselves, or put into the hands of any other, an absolute power over the lives, liberties, and estates of the people, by this breach of trust they forfeit the power the people had put into their hands for quite contrary ends, and it devolves to the people; who have a right to resume their original liberty, and by the establishment of a new legislative (such as they shall think fit), provide for their own safety and security. . . .

Analyzing Primary Sources

1. Which of the following statements best summarizes the excerpt above?

   A People should give up their fundamental rights in order to establish absolute monarchies.

   B People establish governments in order to set and enforce laws. If a government does not do this, the people may abolish it.

   C Most legislative powers are corrupt.

   D Judges may need to act outside the law.

2. Which of the following groups has the final authority of government in Locke's opinion?

   E the legislature

   F the prince

   G the people

   H the judges

3. **Critical Thinking Making Inferences** According to Locke, what do people give up when they enter into a society? Why do you think people do this?

Jean-Jacques Rousseau:
The Social Contract

In *The Social Contract*, Rousseau (1712–1778) proposes an ideal society formed through a "social contract," and based on the natural will of the people. Rousseau believed that people in their natural state were basically good but were corrupted by the evils of society. The first lines of *The Social Contract*, "Man is born free, but is everywhere in chains," reflect this idea.

Vocabulary Before you read the selection, look up the following words in a dictionary: **indivisible, sovereign.**

Main Idea **In consenting to form a government, Rousseau says, individuals choose to give up their self-interest in favor of the common good.**

Find a form of association that defends and protects the person and goods of each associate with all the common force, and by means of which each one, uniting with all, nevertheless obeys only himself and remains as free as before. This is the fundamental problem which is solved by the social contract. . . .

[F]irst of all, since each one gives his entire self, the condition is equal for everyone, and since the condition is equal for everyone, no one has an interest in making it burdensome for the others. . . .

If, then, everything that is not the essence of the social compact is set aside, one will find that it can be reduced to the following terms: Each of us puts his person and all his power in common under the supreme direction of the general will; and in a body we receive each member as an indivisible part of the whole.

Instantly, in place of the private person of each contracting party, this act of association produces a moral and collective body, composed of as many members as there are voices in the assembly, which receives from this same act its unity, its common self, its life, and its will. This public person, formed thus by the union of all the others, formerly took the name City, and now takes that of Republic or body politic, which its members call State when it is passive, Sovereign when active, Power when comparing it to similar bodies. As for the associates, they collectively take the name People; and individually are called Citizens as participants in the sovereign authority, and Subjects as subjects to the laws of the State. . . .

Analyzing Primary Sources

1. According to Rousseau, "social contract" provides a solution to the fundamental problem of finding a form of government in which

   A people's differences can be solved peacefully.

   B people remain as free as they were without government.

   C people are not subject to unjust or immoral laws.

   D minorities are protected.

2. The Republic or body politic is defined by Rousseau as the

   E assembly.

   F collective body formed when the social contract is dissolved.

   G collective body formed when private persons enter into the social contract.

   H collective body appointed by the king.

3. **Critical Thinking Drawing Conclusions** Why does Rousseau believe that people are safe putting themselves under the direction of the "general will"?

Declaration of the Rights of Man and the Citizen

The French National Assembly issued this document in 1789 after having overthrown the established government in the early stages of the French Revolution. The document was modeled in part on the English Bill of Rights and on the American Declaration of Independence.

Vocabulary Before you read the selection, look up the following words in a dictionary: **auspices, imprescriptible, indispensable.**

Main Idea This declaration states the natural rights of French citizens and establishes the equality of all citizens before the law.

Therefore the National Assembly recognizes and proclaims, in the presence and under the auspices of the Supreme Being, the following rights of man and of the citizen:

1. Men are born and remain free and equal in rights. Social distinctions may be founded only upon the general good.
2. The aim of all political association is the preservation of the natural and imprescriptible rights of man. These rights are liberty, property, security, and resistance to oppression. . . .
4. Liberty consists in the freedom to do everything which injures no one else. . . .
5. Law can only prohibit such actions as are hurtful to society. . . .
6. Law is the expression of the general will. Every citizen has a right to participate personally, or through his representative, in its formation. It must be the same for all, whether it protects or punishes. All citizens, being equal in the eyes of the law, are equally eligible to all dignities and to all public positions and occupations, according to their abilities, and without distinction except that of their virtues and talents.
7. No person shall be accused, arrested, or imprisoned except in the cases and according to the forms prescribed by law. . . .
9. As all persons are held innocent until they shall have been declared guilty, if arrest shall be deemed indispensable, all harshness not essential to the securing of the prisoner's person shall be severely repressed by law. . . .
11. The free communication of ideas and opinions is one of the most precious of the rights of man. Every citizen may, accordingly, speak, write, and print with freedom. . . .
13. A common contribution is essential for the maintenance of the public [military] forces and for the cost of administration. This should be equitably distributed among all the citizens in proportion to their means.

Paris protesters during the French Revolution

Analyzing Primary Sources

1. Which of the following describes the tax policy set forth in this document?

   A All citizens must pay the same amount of tax.

   B Only citizens in the military must pay taxes.

   C All citizens pay taxes in proportion to their wealth.

   D There should be no taxes imposed on citizens.

2. Which article above specifically protects citizens from police brutality and torture?

   E 5

   F 6

   G 9

   H 11

3. **Critical Thinking Applying Information** Give one real-life example of each of the four natural rights listed under article 2.

Miguel Hidalgo:
Decree of Hidalgo

Father Miguel Hidalgo of Mexico called for freedom from Spanish rule in 1810. The following decree, also issued in 1810 from Guadalajara, Jalisco, was an attempt to gain additional support for the uprising from Native Americans, blacks, and mestizos. In the end, Hidalgo's rebellion failed because creoles feared that more rights for Native Americans and an end to slavery would cost them power. Less than one year after the start of the uprising, Hidalgo was captured and executed, and his followers scattered.

Vocabulary Before you read the selection, look up the following words in a dictionary: **yoke, exactions**.

Main Idea In this decree, Hidalgo calls for an end to slavery and to the heavy taxes imposed on the poor in Mexico.

Miguel Hidalgo

From the happy moment that the valiant American nation took up arms to shake off the heavy yoke that has oppressed it for three centuries, one of the principal objectives has been to extinguish such duties that cannot advance its fortune, especially those which in these critical circumstances do not well serve that end or provide for the real need of the kingdom in meeting the costs of the struggle, so therefore there is now put forward here the most urgent remedy in the following declarations:

1. That all owners of slaves shall give them their freedom before the end of ten days, under penalty of death, which shall be applied to those who violate this article.
2. That from now on the collection of tributes according to [race] shall cease, as shall exactions that are demanded of the Indians.
3. That all legal business, documents, letters and actions can be on common paper, with the requirement of the seal totally abolished.

Analyzing Primary Sources

1. Item 2 of the Decree of Hidalgo calls for an end to
   A slavery.
   B collection of any taxes.
   C collection of taxes based on race.
   D all business transactions with mestizos and Indians.

2. What does "the seal" probably symbolize in item 3 above?
   E approval from Spanish authorities
   F a postage stamp
   G a special type of paper used for legal documents
   H respect for Native American traditions

3. **Critical Thinking Defending a Position**
   Latin American liberation movements were often based on Enlightenment ideas about natural rights. Describe some of the natural rights Hidalgo could have listed in his decree as explanations for why he wished to abolish slavery, taxes based on race, and the requirement of the seal.

Simón Bolívar: *Address to the Congress of Venezuela*

Encouraged by the revolutions in British North America and France, colonists in Spanish South America soon began to create a force for independence. Simón Bolívar was one of the leaders of this movement. The excerpt below, from Bolívar's Address to the Second National Congress of Venezuela, was given in 1819.

Vocabulary Before you read the selection, look up the following words in a dictionary: **pernicious, inflexible, arduous, erroneous, incentives, succulent.**

Main Idea In this speech, Bolívar offers advice on what type of government to set up in Venezuela.

Subject to the threefold yoke of ignorance, tyranny, and vice, the American people have been unable to acquire knowledge, power, or [civic] virtue. The lessons we received and the models we studied, as pupils of such pernicious teachers, were most destructive. . . .

If a people, perverted by their training, succeed in achieving their liberty, they will soon lose it, for it would be of no avail to endeavor to explain to them that happiness consists in the practice of virtue; that the rule of law is more powerful than the rule of tyrants, because, as the laws are more inflexible, everyone should submit to their beneficent austerity; that proper morals, and not force, are the bases of law; and that to practice justice is to practice liberty. Therefore, Legislators, your work is so much the more arduous, inasmuch as you have to reeducate men who have been corrupted by erroneous illusions and false incentives. Liberty, says Rousseau, is a succulent morsel, but one difficult to digest. . . .

Simón Bolívar

Legislators, meditate well before you choose. Forget not that you are to lay the political foundation for a newly born nation which can rise to the heights of greatness that Nature has marked out for it if you but proportion this foundation in keeping with the high plane that it aspires to attain. Unless your choice is based upon the peculiar . . . experience of Venezuelan people—a factor that should guide you in determining the nature and form of government you are about to adopt for the well-being of the people . . . the result of our reforms will again be slavery.

Analyzing Primary Sources

1. Which statement best summarizes Bolívar's view of the people of Latin America?

   A They have not been well prepared for self-government by their former Spanish rulers.

   B They have been well prepared for self-government by the Spanish.

   C They had been ruled fairly by the Spanish.

   D They have very little desire for self-government.

2. Bolívar states that a government will be most effective if it

   E adheres closely to theories of good government.

   F imitates other successful governments.

   G is molded to fit the character of the nation for which it is built.

   H is based on the rule of law.

3. **Critical Thinking Defending a Position** Would you describe Bolívar as practical or idealistic? Use examples from the excerpt to defend your opinion.

Charles Dickens: *Hard Times*

In *Hard Times,* Charles Dickens protests the dehumanizing conditions of factory life in nineteenth-century England. In this excerpt from the novel, Dickens describes early morning in a fictional factory town named Coketown. (Coke is a form of coal.)

Vocabulary Before you read the selection, look up the following words in a dictionary: **clogs, melancholy, monotony, consign, decomposition, unfathomable, shrouded.**

Main Idea — In this excerpt from the novel, Dickens depicts the labor conditions of the early Industrial Revolution.

The Fairy palaces burst into illumination, before pale morning showed the monstrous serpents of smoke trailing themselves over Coketown. A clattering of clogs upon the pavement; a rapid ringing of bells; and all the melancholy mad elephants, polished and oiled up for the day's monotony, were at their heavy exercise again.

Stephen bent over his loom, quiet, watchful, and steady. A special contrast, as every man was in the forest of looms where Stephen worked, to the crashing, smashing, tearing piece of mechanism at which he laboured. Never fear, good people of an anxious turn of mind, that Art will consign Nature to Oblivion. Set anywhere, side by side, the work of God and the work of man; and the former, even though it be a troop of Hands of very small account, will gain in dignity from the comparison.

So many hundred Hands in this Mill; so many hundred horse Steam Power. It is known, to the force of a single pound weight, what the engine will do; but, not all the calculators of the National Debt can tell me the capacity for good or evil, for love or hatred, for patriotism or discontent, for the decomposition of virtue into vice, or the reverse, at any single moment in the soul of one of these its quiet servants, with the composed faces and the regulated actions. There is no mystery in it; there is an unfathomable mystery in the meanest of them, for ever. . . .

The day grew strong, and showed itself outside, even against the flaming lights within. The lights were turned out, and the work went on. The rain fell, and the Smoke-serpents, submissive to the curse of all that tribe, trailed themselves upon the earth. In the waste-yard outside, the steam from the escape pipe, the litter of barrels and old iron, the shining heaps of coals, the ashes everywhere, were shrouded in a veil of mist and rain.

The work went on, until the noon-bell rang. More clattering upon the pavements. The looms, and wheels, and Hands all out of gear for an hour.

A spinning mule

Analyzing Primary Sources

1. What are the "melancholy mad elephants" to which Dickens refers in the excerpt above?

   A factory workers

   B factory owners

   C power looms

   D steam locomotives

2. According to this passage, facts cannot predict

   E the national debt.

   F the potential output of a factory.

   G the amount of work an individual can complete in a day.

   H the capacity of any individual for good or evil.

3. **Critical Thinking Making Inferences**
   (a) Why does Dickens refer to the factory workers as "Hands"? **(b)** What seems to be his attitude toward the workers?
   (c) What seems to be his general attitude toward the Industrial Revolution?

Fukuzawa Yukichi: *Autobiography*

In 1860, Fukuzawa Yukichi joined the first Japanese mission to the United States. When he returned home, he wrote articles and books explaining western customs and practices to the Japanese. This selection from his *Auto-biography* recalls his impressions of his first days in San Francisco.

Vocabulary Before you read the selection, look up the following words in a dictionary: **inexplicable, revered.**

Main Idea   In this autobiography, Fukuzawa Yukichi shows some of the differences between American and Japanese cultures and attitudes.

All of us wore the usual pair of swords at our sides and the [rope] sandals. So attired, we were taken to the modern hotel. There we noticed, covering the interior, the valuable carpets which in Japan only the more wealthy could buy from importers' shops at so much a square inch to make purses and tobacco pouches with. Here the carpet was laid over an entire room—something quite astounding—upon this costly fabric walked our hosts wearing the shoes with which they had come in from the streets!

One evening our hosts said that some ladies and gentlemen were having a dancing party and that they would be glad to have us attend it. We went. To our dismay we could not make out what they were doing. The ladies and gentlemen seemed to be hopping about the room together. As funny as it was, we knew it would be rude to laugh, and we controlled our expressions with difficulty as the dancing went on. These were but a few of the instances of our bewilderment at the strange customs of American society.

When we were taking leave, our host and hostess kindly offered us horses to ride home on. This pleased us, for a chance to ride horseback again was a relief. . . . We touched whip to the horses and rode back to our quarters at a trot. The Americans watched us and exclaimed at the Japanese ability in riding. So neither of us really knew much about the other after all. . . .

Things social, political, and economic proved most inexplicable. One day, on a sudden thought, I asked a gentleman where the descendants of George Washington might be. He replied, "I think there is a woman who is directly descended from Washington. I don't know where she is now, but I think I have heard she is married." His answer was so very casual that it shocked me.

Of course, I knew that America was a republic with a new president every four years, but I could not help feeling that the family of Washington would be revered above all other families. My reasoning was based on the reverence in Japan for the founders of the great line of rulers. . . .

Japanese textile workers

Analyzing Primary Sources

1. Fukuzawa views the dance with

   A fear.

   B horror.

   C reverence.

   D amusement.

2. What conclusion does Fukuzawa come to after the incident with the horses?

   E Americans do not understand the Japanese.

   F Americans do not respect the Japanese.

   G Americans are not as skilled riders as the Japanese.

   H Americans are more skillful riders than the Japanese.

3. **Critical Thinking Recognizing Points of View (a)** Why did Fukuzawa Yukichi expect Americans to treat the descendants of George Washington with respect? **(b)** What does this incident suggest about the differing cultural values of Japan and the United States?

Erich Maria Remarque:
All Quiet on the Western Front

Erich Maria Remarque was wounded five times while serving in the German army during World War I. In 1928, he published *All Quiet on the Western Front*, which is often considered the greatest novel about the war. It follows the narrator, Paul Baumer, from eager recruit to disillusioned veteran. In this passage, Paul is trapped for hours in a foxhole with a French soldier he has just killed.

Vocabulary Before you read the selection, look up the following word in a dictionary: **abstraction**.

Main Idea **In this excerpt from a novel, a young German soldier expresses his horror at killing a man hand-to-hand.**

In the afternoon, about three, he is dead.

I breathe freely again. But only for a short time. Soon the silence is more unbearable than the groans. I wish the gurgling were there again, gasping hoarse, now whistling softly and again hoarse and loud.

It is mad, what I do. But I must do something. I prop the dead man up again so that he lies comfortably, although he feels nothing any more. I close his eyes. They are brown, his hair is black and a bit curly at the sides. . . .

The silence spreads. I talk and must talk. So I speak to him and say to him: "Comrade, I did not want to kill you. If you jumped in here again, I would not do it, if you would be sensible too. But you were only an idea to me before, an abstraction that lived in my mind and called forth its appropriate response. It was that abstraction I stabbed. But now, for the first time, I see you are a man like me. I thought of your hand-grenades, of your bayonet, of your rifle; now I see your wife and your face and our fellowship. Forgive me, comrade. We always see it too late. Why do they never tell us that you are poor devils like us, that your mothers are just as anxious as ours, and that we have the same fear of death, and the same dying and the same agony—Forgive me, comrade; how could you be my enemy? If we threw away these rifles and this uniform you could be my brother just like Kat and Albert. Take twenty years of my life, comrade, and stand up—take more, for I do not know what I can even attempt to do with it now."

German soldiers on their way to the front

Analyzing Literature

1. Why does Paul finally speak to the French soldier?

   A He does not know that the French soldier is dead.

   B He hopes to nurse the French soldier back to life.

   C He wants to brag about his victory over his enemy.

   D He can no longer stand the silence in the foxhole.

2. According to Paul, he can no longer see the French soldier as

   E an abstraction.

   F a human being.

   G a "poor devil."

   H a dead body.

3. **Critical Thinking Recognizing Points of View** **(a)** What does Paul mean by "We always see it too late"? **(b)** How does this passage reflect what you know about the morale of soldiers late in the war?

Mohandas Gandhi: *Hind Swaraj*

Mohandas Gandhi led a successful, peaceful revolution in India against British rule. In the following excerpt from his book *Hind Swaraj* (*Indian Home Rule*), published in 1938, Gandhi explains the ideas behind his non-violent method of passive resistance in the form of an imaginary conversation between an editor and a reader.

Vocabulary Before you read the selection, look up the following words in a dictionary: **repugnant, breach**.

Main Idea In this imaginary interview, Gandhi explains the ideas behind his nonviolent method of passive resistance.

Editor: Passive resistance is a method of securing rights by personal suffering; it is the reverse of resistance by arms. When I refuse to do a thing that is repugnant to my conscience, I use soul-force. For instance, the Government of the day has passed a law which is applicable to me. I do not like it. If by using violence I force the Government to repeal the law, I am employing what may be termed body-force. If I do not obey the law and accept the penalty for its breach, I use soul-force. It involves sacrifice of self.

Everybody admits that sacrifice of self is infinitely superior to sacrifice of others. Moreover, if this kind of force is used in a cause that is unjust, only the person using it suffers. He does not make others suffer for his mistakes. . . . No man can claim that he is absolutely in the right or that a particular thing is wrong because he thinks so, but it is wrong for him so long as that is his deliberate judgment. It is therefore meet [proper] that he should not do that which he knows to be wrong, and suffer the consequence whatever it may be. This is the key to the use of soul-force.

Reader: You would then disregard laws—this is rank disloyalty. We have always been considered a law-abiding nation. You seem to be going even beyond the extremists. They say that we must obey the laws that have been passed, but that if the laws be bad, we must drive out the lawgivers even by force.

Editor: Whether I go beyond them or whether I do not is a matter of no consequence to either of us. We simply want to find out what is right and to act accordingly. The real meaning of the statement that we are a law-abiding nation is that we are passive resisters. When we do not like certain laws, we do not break the heads of law-givers but we suffer and do not submit to the laws.

Mohandas Gandhi

Analyzing Primary Sources

1. What is the goal of passive resistance?

   A to bring about peaceful change

   B to gain support for violence

   C to discover truth

   D to injure wrongdoers

2. The author defines soul-force as

   E weapons used for peaceful purposes.

   F refusal to obey a law that is unjust and accepting the penalty.

   G trying to determine what is right.

   H obeying all laws while working to overthrow the lawmakers.

3. **Critical Thinking Understanding Sequence (a)** According to Gandhi, could soul-force ever be used to support an unjust cause? **(b)** What does Gandhi mean when he says that a person using soul-force "does not make others suffer for his mistakes"?

Franklin D. Roosevelt:
The Four Freedoms

Franklin D. Roosevelt delivered the following address to Congress in January 1941, after having been elected to a third term as president of the United States. In the speech, he described the "four freedoms" that he hoped would be secured throughout the world. As he spoke, most of Europe had already fallen to Hitler's tyranny and Great Britain was struggling against the threat of German invasion.

Vocabulary Before you read the selection, look up the following words in a dictionary: **perpetual, quick-lime**.

Main Idea In this speech, Roosevelt vows to protect what he describes as the four "essential human freedoms."

In the future days, which we seek to make secure, we look forward to a world founded upon four essential human freedoms.

The first is freedom of speech and expression—everywhere in the world.

The second is freedom of every person to worship God in his own way—everywhere in the world.

The third is freedom from want—which translated into world terms, means economic understandings which will secure to every nation a healthy peace time life for its inhabitants—everywhere in the world.

The fourth is freedom from fear—which translated into world terms, means a worldwide reduction of armaments to such a point and in such a thorough fashion that no nation will be in a position to commit an act of physical aggression against any neighbor—anywhere in the world. . . .

Since the beginning of our American history we have been engaged in change—in a perpetual peaceful revolution—a revolution which goes on steadily, quietly adjusting itself to changing conditions—without the concentration camp or the quick-lime in the ditch. The world order which we seek is the cooperation of free countries, working together in a friendly civilized society.

This nation has placed its destiny in the hands and heads and hearts of its millions of free men and women; and its faith in freedom under the guidance of God. Freedom means the supremacy of human rights everywhere. Our support goes to those who struggle to gain those rights or keep them. Our strength is in our unity of purpose.

To that high concept there can be no end save victory.

Honolulu Star-Bulletin 1st EXTRA

WAR!

(Associated Press by Transpacific Telephone)
SAN FRANCISCO, Dec. 7.—President Roosevelt announced this morning that Japanese planes had attacked Manila and Pearl Harbor.

OAHU BOMBED BY JAPANESE PLANES

Newspaper headline, December 7, 1941

Analyzing Primary Sources

1. Being able to make a living and support one's family is an example of

   A freedom of speech.

   B freedom of worship.

   C freedom from want.

   D freedom from fear.

2. Roosevelt thinks the nation's strength comes from

   E citizens worshipping together.

   F its support for other nations.

   G citizens working together for a common purpose.

   H carrying out change in a peaceful manner.

3. **Critical Thinking** Applying Information
   (a) Describe some of the specific actions that might be necessary to secure "freedom from fear," as Roosevelt describes it.
   (b) How does American foreign policy in the years before the United States entered World War II reflect Roosevelt's views?

The Universal Declaration of Human Rights

The General Assembly of the United Nations adopted this declaration on December 10, 1948. They hoped that it would become a standard by which liberty and freedom could be judged throughout the world.

Vocabulary Before you read the selection, look up the following words in a dictionary: **servitude, arbitrary**.

Main Idea This UN declaration sets forth the basic liberties and freedoms to which all people are entitled.

Article 1 All human beings are born free and equal in dignity and rights. They are endowed with reason and conscience and should act towards one another in a spirit of brotherhood.

Article 2 Everyone is entitled to all the rights and freedoms set forth in this Declaration, without distinction of any kind, such as race, color, sex, language, religion, political or other opinion, national or social origin, property, birth or other status. . . .

Article 3 Everyone has the right to life, liberty and security of person.

Article 4 No one shall be held in slavery or servitude. . . .

Article 5 No one shall be subjected to torture or to cruel, inhuman or degrading treatment or punishment. . . .

Article 9 No one shall be subjected to arbitrary arrest, detention or exile. . . .

Article 13 Everyone has the right to freedom of movement. . . .

Article 18 Everyone has the right to freedom of thought, conscience and religion. . . .

Article 19 Everyone has the right to freedom of opinion and expression. . . .

Article 20 Everyone has the right to freedom of peaceful assembly and association. . . .

Article 23 Everyone has the right to work, to free choice of employment, to just and favorable conditions of work and to protection against unemployment. . . .

Article 25 Everyone has the right to a standard of living adequate for the health and well-being of himself and of his family, including food, clothing, housing and medical care and necessary social services, and the right to security in the event of unemployment, sickness, disability, widowhood, old age or other lack of livelihood. . . .

Article 26 Everyone has the right to education. Education shall be free, at least in the elementary and fundamental stages.

United Nations building in New York City

Analyzing Primary Sources

1. Which of the following statements would best be supported by Article 5?

   A The United Nations will take action to punish a nation that uses torture.

   B Trial by jury should be considered a basic human right.

   C Punishments that inflict pain on prisoners are a violation of basic human rights.

   D Long prison sentences are a form of cruel and inhuman punishment.

2. Which of the following articles states that a person has the right to live free from hunger?

   E Article 1

   F Article 9

   G Article 23

   H Article 25

3. **Critical Thinking Drawing Conclusions** In what ways might the existence of this declaration benefit people living under an oppressive government?

Mao Zedong: *The People's Democratic Dictatorship*

In this speech, given in 1949 on the anniversary of the founding of the Communist Party, Mao Zedong explains the philosophy that guides China under his leadership. Mao's ideas were heavily influenced by the communist philosopher Karl Marx.

Vocabulary Before you read the selection, look up the following words in a dictionary: **henchmen, reactionaries, apparatus.**

Main Idea In this speech, Mao explains what groups of people will be denied basic rights in his government and why.

Who are the "people"? At the present stage in China, they are the working class, the peasantry, the petit bourgeoisie and the national bourgeoisie.

Under the leadership of the working class and the Communist Party, these classes unite to create their own state and elect their own government so as to enforce their dictatorship over the henchmen of imperialism—the landlord class and bureaucratic capitalist class. . . . The people's government will suppress such persons. It will only permit them to behave themselves properly. It will not allow them to speak or act wildly. Should they do so, they will be instantly curbed and punished. The democratic system is to be carried out within the ranks of the people, giving them freedom of speech, assembly and association. The right to vote is given only to the people, not to the reactionaries.

These two things, democracy for the people and dictatorship for the reactionaries, when combined, constitute the people's democratic dictatorship.

Why must things be done in this way? Everyone is very clear on this point. If things were not done like this, the revolution would fail, the people would suffer and the state would perish. . . .

Our present task is to strengthen the people's state apparatus—meaning principally the people's army, the people's police and the people's courts—thereby safeguarding national defense and protecting the people's interests. Given these conditions, China, under the leadership of the working class and the Communist Party, can develop steadily from an agricultural into an industrial country and from a New Democratic into a Socialist and, eventually, Communist society, eliminating classes and realizing universal harmony.

Mao Zedong

Analyzing Primary Sources

1. According to Mao, what class of people are the "reactionaries"?

   A the peasants

   B the bourgeoisie

   C the landlords and capitalists

   D the working class

2. Mao claims that the Communist Party in China represents the interests of

   E landlords.

   F capitalists.

   G imperialists.

   H working class.

3. **Critical Thinking Recognizing Points of View** (a) Why does Mao Zedong claim that the "people's government" is justified in denying some groups of people the right to freedom of speech? (b) How does Mao's view of democracy differ from that generally accepted by most Americans?

Chinua Achebe: *Things Fall Apart*

In his famous 1959 novel *Things Fall Apart*, Nigerian writer Chinua Achebe described the effects imperialism had on traditional Ibo society. In this excerpt, Okonkwo returns to his village to discover that the traditional laws have been supplanted by European religion and government.

Main Idea In this excerpt from a novel, two characters discuss the ways in which Europeans were able to gain power in an African village.

"Perhaps I have been away too long," Okonkwo said almost to himself. "But I cannot understand these things you tell me. What is it that has happened to our people? Why have they lost the power to fight?"

"Have you not heard how the white man wiped out Abame?" asked Obierika.

"I have heard," said Okonkwo. "But I have also heard that Abame people were weak and foolish. Why did they not fight back? . . . We would be cowards to compare ourselves with the men of Abame. Their fathers had never dared to stand before our ancestors. We must fight these men and drive them from the land."

"It is already too late," said Obierika sadly. "Our own men and our sons have joined the ranks of the stranger. They have joined his religion and they help to uphold his government. If we should try to drive out the white men in Umuofia we should find it easy. There are only two of them. But what of our own people who are following their way and have been given power? They would go to Umuru and bring the soldiers, and we would be like Abame." He paused for a long time and then said: "I told you on my last visit to Mbanta how they hanged Aneto."

"What has happened to that piece of land in dispute?" asked Okonkwo.

"The white man's court has decided that it should belong to Nnama's family, who had given much money to the white man's messengers and interpreter."

"Does the white man understand our custom about land?"

"How can he when he does not even speak our tongue? But he says that our customs are bad; and our own brothers who have taken up his religion also say that our customs are bad. How do you think we can fight when our own brothers have turned against us? The white man is very clever. He came quietly and peaceably with his religion. We were amused at his foolishness and allowed him to stay. Now he has won our brothers, and our clan can no longer act like one. He has put a knife on the things that held us together and we have fallen apart."

Analyzing Primary Sources

1. In this passage, Okonkwo says that he wants to
   A drive the Europeans away.
   B learn European customs.
   C teach African customs to the Europeans.
   D go to war against Abame.

2. In this passage, Obierika feels helpless because
   E Okonkwo stayed away too long.
   F he fears the Abame tribe.
   G the tribe has divided into opposing factions.
   H he has lost his family's land in a court dispute.

3. **Critical Thinking** **Recognizing Points of View** **(a)** According to Obierika, how have Europeans "put a knife on the things that held us together"? **(b)** Why do you think a contemporary Nigerian author would choose to write a novel about the early days of imperialism?

Kwame Nkrumah: *Autobiography*

Kwame Nkrumah led the people of Gold Coast in their quest for independence from Britain. After succeeding in 1957, Nkrumah became the first prime minister and renamed the country Ghana. In this excerpt from his *Autobiography*, Nkrumah speaks of the need to establish economic independence as a means of maintaining political independence.

Main Idea In this excerpt, Nkrumah describes his goals of political freedom and the difficult work of building an independent economy.

Independence for the Gold Coast was my aim. It was a colony, and I have always regarded colonialism as the policy by which a foreign power binds territories to herself by political ties, with the primary object of promoting her own economic advantage. No one need be surprised if this system has led to disturbances and political tension in many territories. There are few people who would not rid themselves of such domination if they could. . . .

I saw that the whole solution to [our] problem lay in political freedom for our people, for it is only when a people are politically free that other races can give them the respect that is due them. It is impossible to talk of equality of races in any other terms. No people without a government of their own can expect to be treated on the same level as people of independent sovereign states. It is far better to be

Kwame Nkrumah (second from right) at an independence celebration

free to govern or misgovern yourself than to be governed by anybody else. . . .

Once freedom is gained, a greater task comes into view. All dependent territories are backward in education, in science, in agriculture, and in industry. The economic independence that should follow and maintain political independence demands every effort from the people, a total mobilization of brain and manpower resources. What other countries have taken three hundred years or more to achieve, a once dependent territory must try to accomplish in a generation if it is to survive.

Analyzing Primary Sources

1. In this passage, how does the author define colonialism?

   A a balanced political alliance between a foreign power and a territory

   B a balanced economic alliance between a foreign power and a territory

   C a system in which a ruling country helps residents of a colony develop their economy

   D a system in which a ruling country administers a colony in order to promote its own economic gain

2. Nkrumah viewed political independence as a means of gaining

   E respect from other sovereign states.

   F great personal wealth.

   G a better system of education.

   H better resources.

3. **Critical Thinking** **Defending a Position** Nkrumah states that newly independent countries must establish economic independence quickly in order to survive. Give reasons to support this statement.

Lech Walesa:
Nobel Peace Prize Lecture

Lech Walesa organized an independent trade union in Poland known as Solidarity. After a successful strike by Solidarity members in 1980, the Polish Communist government granted the workers many new rights and higher wages. A year later, however, the gains were withdrawn and Solidarity was outlawed. Lech Walesa was awarded the Nobel Peace Prize in 1983 for his work promoting freedom in Poland. This lecture was delivered at a time when Solidarity was still illegal.

Main Idea In this speech, Walesa declares his solidarity with all people in the world who work to secure peace, justice, and human rights.

May I repeat that the fundamental necessity in Poland is now understanding and dialogue. I think that the same applies to the whole world: we should go on talking, we must not close any doors or do anything that would block the road to an understanding. And we must remember that only peace built on the foundations of justice and moral order can be a lasting one.

In many parts of the world the people are searching for a solution which would link the two basic values: peace and justice. The two are like bread and salt for mankind. Every nation and every community have the inalienable right to these values. No conflicts can be resolved without doing everything possible to follow that road. Our times require that these aspirations which exist the world over must be recognized.

Our efforts and harsh experiences have revealed to the world the value of human solidarity. Accepting this honorable distinction I am thinking of those with whom I am linked by the spirit of solidarity.

—first of all, of those who in the struggle for the workers' and civic rights in my country paid the highest price—the price of life;
—of my friends who paid for the defense of "Solidarity" with the loss of freedom, who were sentenced to prison terms or are awaiting trial;
—of my countrymen who saw in the "Solidarity" movement the fulfillment of their aspirations as workers and citizens, who are subjected to humiliations and ready for sacrifices, who have learn[ed] to link courage with wisdom and who persist in loyalty to the cause we have embarked upon;
—of all those who are struggling throughout the world for workers' and union rights, for the dignity of a working man, for human rights.

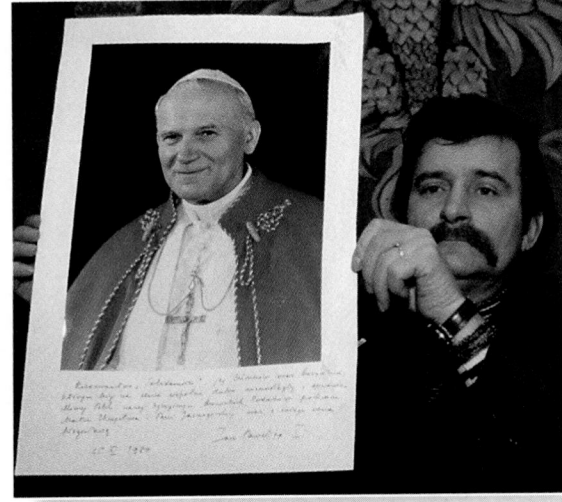

Lech Walesa holding up a picture of Pope John Paul II

Analyzing Primary Sources

1. What does Walesa claim has been the result of the struggles of the Polish workers?

   A They have succeeded in bringing peace and justice to Poland.

   B They have failed to encourage the growth of understanding and dialogue.

   C They have taught the world the value of human solidarity.

   D They have taught the world the value of freedom.

2. What were the members of Solidarity struggling for?

   E government loyalty

   F shorter prison terms

   G workers' and civic rights

   H bread and salt

3. **Critical Thinking Defending a Position** Do you agree with Walesa's idea that the only way to build a lasting peace is to establish justice?

Mikhail Gorbachev: *Perestroika*

Mikhail Gorbachev's economic and political reforms paved the way for the independence of Eastern Europe, the breakup of the Soviet Union, and the end of the Cold War. In the following speech delivered in 1989, Gorbachev asks the people of the Soviet Union to maintain confidence in the changes brought about by perestroika despite the difficulties and criticisms of the program.

Main Idea In this speech, Gorbachev restates the benefits of his program of political and economic reform.

Good evening, comrades, I am here to talk to you about our current affairs. The situation in the country is not simple. We all know and feel this. Everything has become entangled in a tight knot: Scarcity on the consumer goods market, conflicts in ethnic relations, and difficult and sometimes painful processes in the public consciousness, resulting from the overcoming of distortions and from the renewal of socialism. People are trying to understand where we have found ourselves at the moment, evaluating the pluses and minuses of the path we have covered during the last four-plus years, the development of democracy and the pace of the economic and political reforms. . . .

Some are ready to give up perestroika and return to the past. Others, who consider themselves "active reformers," want to head perestroika onto the path of rash decisions and hasty projects, prompted by ambition rather than concern for real progress. . . .

True, perestroika is meeting with many difficulties. But it is radical change, a revolution in the economy and in policy, in the ways of thinking and in people's consciousness, in the entire pattern of our life. Besides, we have not been able to avoid mistakes in our practical actions in the course of perestroika. But perestroika has opened up realistic opportunities for society's renewal, for giving society a new quality and for creating truly humane and democratic socialism. It has returned to the great nation a sense of dignity and given the Soviet people a sense of freedom. It is a powerful source of social, spiritual, and, I should say, patriotic energy for decades to come.

That is why we must do everything to continue perestroika on the basis of the ideas and principles proclaimed by the party. And we must not allow those who are using the difficulties we have met to impose on society doubts about the correctness of the path we have chosen.

Mikhail Gorbachev

Analyzing Primary Sources

1. Which of the following statements best summarizes this excerpt?

   A Perestroika imposes too many reforms on society.

   B Perestroika is a great source of human dignity.

   C Perestroika must continue despite mistakes and criticism.

   D Perestroika does not allow for enough freedom.

2. Gorbachev states that the "active reformers" want to

   E return to the past.

   F end the policy of perestroika.

   G speed up the pace of reforms under perestroika.

   H further debate the policy of perestroika.

3. **Critical Thinking Recognizing Bias (a)** How does Gorbachev discredit the ideas of "active reformers" in this excerpt? **(b)** Why would Gorbachev be anxious to defend perestroika?

Vaclav Havel: *New Year's Address*

Vaclav Havel was a leading dissident and human rights activist in communist Czechoslovakia. When the "democracy movement" swept through Eastern Europe in 1989, Havel was elected president. In the following speech delivered on January 1, 1990, Havel asks the citizens of Czechoslovakia to accept responsibility for their past and to move forward in building a democracy.

Vocabulary Before you read the selection, look up the following words in a dictionary: **immutable, perpetuate**.

Main Idea In this speech, Havel calls upon Czech citizens to be active participants in their new democracy.

Our country is not flourishing. The enormous creative and spiritual potential of our nations is being wasted. Entire branches of industry produce goods that are of no interest to anyone, while we lack the things we need. . . . We now have the most contaminated environment in all of Europe. . . .

But all this is not even the main problem. The worst thing is that we live in a contaminated moral environment. We have fallen morally ill because we became used to saying one thing and thinking another. We have learned not to believe in anything, to ignore each other, to care only about ourselves. Notions such as love, friendship, compassion, humility, or forgiveness have lost their depth and dimensions. . . . Only a few of us managed to cry out loud that the powers-that-be should not be all-powerful. . . .

We have all become used to the totalitarian system and accepted it as an immutable fact, thus helping to perpetuate it. In other words, we are all . . . responsible for the creation of the totalitarian machinery. . . .

Why do I say this? It would be very unwise to think of the sad legacy of the last forty years as something alien or something inherited from a distant relative. On the contrary, we have to accept this legacy as something we have inflicted on ourselves. If we accept it as such, we will understand that it is up to all of us, and only us, to do something about it. We cannot blame the previous rulers for everything—not only because it would be untrue, but also because it could weaken our sense of duty, our obligation to act independently, freely, sensibly, and quickly. Let us not be mistaken: even the best government in the world, the best parliament, and the best president cannot do much on their own. And in any case, it would be wrong to expect a cure-all from them alone. Freedom and democracy, after all, require everyone to participate and thus to share responsibility.

Analyzing Primary Sources

1. What does Havel mean when he says that the people of Czechoslovakia "have the most contaminated environment in all of Europe"?

   A The people have become dishonest and uninterested.

   B The people have been disrespectful of the environment.

   C The people are by nature unwise and unruly.

   D The people have lost their respect for the law.

2. According to Havel, why must everyone participate in the new democracy?

   E to correct the wrongs of the past

   F to share responsibility

   G to prevent totalitarianism

   H to prevent environmental pollution

3. **Critical Thinking Recognizing Causes and Effects** Why does Havel ask that the people of Czechoslovakia accept their responsibility for the totalitarian machinery of the past?

Mario Vargas Llosa: *Latin America, The Democratic Option*

In this speech delivered in 1990, Peruvian writer Mario Vargas Llosa describes the changes that are needed to maintain and extend democracy in Latin America.

Vocabulary Before you read the selection, look up the following words in a dictionary: **unprecedented, superficial, oligarchies.**

Main Idea In this speech, Vargas Llosa describes what is needed to sustain democracy in Latin America.

The democratization of Latin America, even though it has today an unprecedented popular base, is very fragile. To maintain and extend this popular base, governments will have to prove to their citizens that democracy means not only the end of political brutality but progress—concrete benefits in areas such as labor, health, and education, where so much remains to be done. But, given Latin America's current economic crisis, when the prices of its exports are hitting record lows and the weight of its foreign debt is crushing, those governments have virtually no alternative but to demand that their citizens—especially the poor—make even greater sacrifices than they've already made. . . . A realistic and ethically sound approach that our creditors could take would be to demand that each debtor nation pay what it can without placing its stability in jeopardy. . . .

If we want democracy to take hold in our countries, our most urgent task is to broaden it, give it substance and truth. Democracy is fragile in so many countries because it is superficial, a mere framework within which institutions and political parties go about their business in their traditionally arbitrary, bullying way. . . .

Perhaps the hardest struggle we Latin Americans will have will be against ourselves. Centuries of intolerance, of absolute truths, of despotic governments, weigh us down—and it won't be easy to shake that burden off. The tradition of absolute power that began with our pre-Columbian empires, and the tradition that might makes right that the Spanish and Portuguese explorers practiced, were perpetuated in the nineteenth century, after our independence, by our caudillos and our oligarchies, often with the blessing or direct intervention of foreign powers.

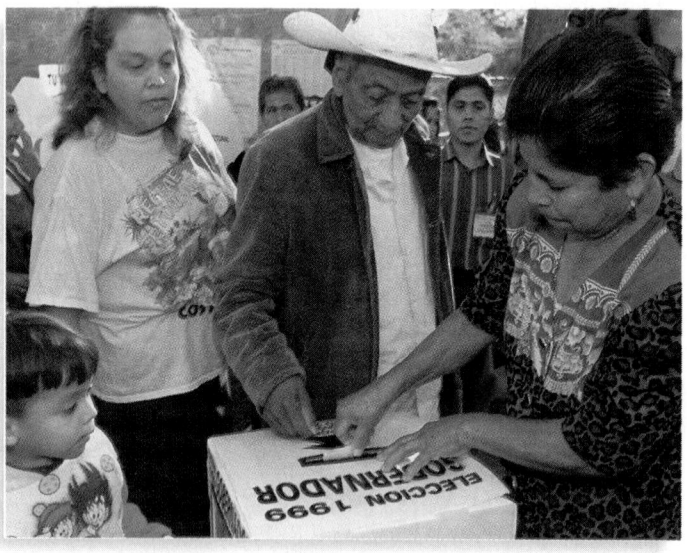

Mexicans voting

Analyzing Primary Sources

1. The author states that democratic governments in Latin American countries have to provide

   A real improvements in labor, health, and education.

   B higher incomes.

   C a stronger, more authoritative government.

   D greater understanding of their history.

2. The author states that many democratic governments are fragile because they

   E lack authority.

   F do not always act democratically.

   G lack international support.

   H lack strong political parties.

3. **Critical Thinking Identifying Main Ideas** In the last paragraph, the author describes obstacles to democracy in Latin America. Restate the main idea in your own words.

Aung San Suu Kyi:
Freedom From Fear

Aung San Suu Kyi, leader of Myanmar's National League for Democracy and winner of the Nobel Peace Prize, has worked courageously for human rights and democracy in her country. Because of her opposition to Myanmar's ruling military junta, she was held under house arrest from 1989 to 1995 and severely restricted thereafter.

Vocabulary Before you read the selection, look up the following words in a dictionary: **unremitting, insidious, inherent, enervating, miasma, wellspring, trite, bulwarks.**

Main Idea In this essay, Aung San Suu Kyi describes the need for courage when living under an oppressive government.

Fearlessness may be a gift but perhaps more precious is the courage acquired through endeavor, courage that comes from cultivating the habit of refusing to let fear dictate one's actions, courage that could be described as 'grace under pressure'—grace which is renewed repeatedly in the face of harsh, unremitting pressure.

Within a system which denies the existence of basic human rights, fear tends to be the order of the day. Fear of imprisonment, fear of torture, fear of death, fear of losing friends, family, property or means of livelihood, fear of poverty, fear of isolation, fear of failure. A most insidious form of fear is that which masquerades as common sense or even wisdom, condemning as foolish, reckless, insignificant or futile the small, daily acts of courage which help to preserve man's self-respect and inherent human dignity. It is not easy for a people conditioned by fear under the iron rule of the principle that might is right to free themselves from the enervating miasma of fear. Yet even under the most crushing state machinery courage rises up again and again, for fear is not the natural state of civilized man.

The wellspring of courage and endurance in the face of unbridled power is generally a firm belief in the sanctity of ethical principles combined with a historical sense that despite all setbacks the condition of man is set on an ultimate course for both spiritual and material advancement. . . . It is man's vision of a world fit for rational, civilized humanity which leads him to dare and to suffer to build societies free from want and fear. Concepts such as truth, justice and compassion cannot be dismissed as trite when these are often the only bulwarks which stand against ruthless power.

Aung San Suu Kyi

Analyzing Primary Sources

1. According to the author, why do people work against all odds to build societies free from want and fear?

   A because they have a dream of a just world

   B because they dismiss truth and justice as trite

   C because they are powerless against injustice

   D because they want to learn how to gain courage

2. What are the sources of courage according to the author?

   E power and history

   F belief in ethical principles and a sense that progress is inevitable

   G belief in truth and compassion

   H power and endurance

3. **Critical Thinking Applying Information** Give one example of a person refusing to let fear dictate his or her actions.

Nelson Mandela: *Glory and Hope*

Nelson Mandela delivered this speech after having been elected president in South Africa's first multiracial elections in 1994. Knowing that the injustices of apartheid would not be easily erased, Mandela asked the people to work together for peace and justice.

Vocabulary Before you read the selection, look up the following words in a dictionary: **emancipation, covenant, reconciliation**.

Main Idea In this speech, Mandela calls upon black and white South Africans to work together to build a new nation based on justice.

Today, all of us do, by our presence here, and by our celebrations . . . confer glory and hope to newborn liberty.

Out of the experience of an extraordinary human disaster that lasted too long must be born a society of which all humanity will be proud.

Our daily deeds as ordinary South Africans must produce an actual South African reality that will reinforce humanity's belief in justice, strengthen its confidence in the nobility of the human soul and sustain all our hopes for a glorious life for all. . . .

Nelson Mandela (right) with F. W. de Klerk

The time for the healing of the wounds has come. . . .

The time to build is upon us.

We have, at last, achieved our political emancipation. We pledge ourselves to liberate all our people from the continuing bondage of poverty, deprivation, suffering, gender and other discrimination.

We have triumphed in the effort to implant hope in the breasts of the millions of our people. We enter into a covenant that we shall build the society in which all South Africans, both black and white, will be able to walk tall, without any fear in their hearts, assured of the inalienable right to human dignity—a rainbow nation at peace with itself and the world. . . .

We understand it still that there is no easy road to freedom.

We know it well that none of us acting alone can achieve success.

We must therefore act together as a united people, for national reconciliation, for nation building, for the birth of a new world.

Let there be justice for all. Let there be peace for all. Let there be work, bread, water, and salt for all. . . . The sun shall never set on so glorious a human achievement!

Analyzing Primary Sources

1. In this speech, Mandela is celebrating
   A the birth of a new, free nation.
   B decades of peace and justice.
   C the easy road to freedom.
   D the end of violence.

2. Which of the following best summarizes the excerpt?
   E We must find work for all.
   F We must not take the path of violence.
   G We must now finish the work of freedom that we have started.
   H We must correct the injustices of South Africa's past through severe punishments.

3. **Critical Thinking Making Inferences (a)** In addition to political freedom, what further "freedoms" does Mandela call for in his speech? **(b)** What does Mandela mean by "reconciliation"?

Harry Wu: *The Outlook for China, Human Rights*

Author and human rights activist Harry Wu was imprisoned in China for 19 years because of his criticisms of the communist regime. The excerpt below is from a speech Wu delivered in 1996.

Vocabulary Before you read the selection, look up the following words in a dictionary: **specter, superstructure, vulcanizing.**

Main Idea In this speech, Wu describes the system of forced labor camps run by China's communist government.

Sometimes people ask me, "What are you fighting for?" And my answer is quite simple. I want to see the word *laogai* in every dictionary in every language in the world; I want to see the laogai ended. . . .

The economic boom made possible by capitalism makes profits for both the West and China. But despite the huge profits earned by China's external trade, ordinary people enjoy only a tiny part. The communist government puts most of the profits into upgrading its weapons systems, into internal and external political activities, and into maintaining the nation's political stability. . . .

Today, a specter is hovering over Mainland China—capitalism. Communism is dead; it is no longer believed in by the Chinese in general nor even by the majority of Communist Party members. The "capitalistic" economic boom has made the superstructure of the communist regime appear pretty on the outside, but its pillars are heavily damaged. Looming in front of China are some huge crises.

At the core of the human rights question in China today is China's fundamental machinery for crushing human beings physically, psychologically and spiritually: the laogai camp system, of which we have identified 1,100 camps. It is also an integral part of the national economy. Its importance is illustrated by some basic facts: one third of China's tea is produced in laogai camps; 60 percent of China's rubber vulcanizing chemicals are produced in a single laogai camp in Shanghai; the first and second chain hoist works in the country to receive direct export authority are laogai camps in Zhejiang Province; one of the largest and earliest exporters of hand tools is a camp in Shanghai; an unknown but significant amount of China's cotton crop is grown by prisoners. I could go on and on and on. . . . The laogai is not simply a prison system, it is a political tool for maintaining the Communist Party's totalitarian rule.

Chinese human rights protester

Analyzing Primary Sources

1. What is a laogai?

   A a labor camp for prisoners

   B a warehouse for exports

   C a chemical plant

   D a tea or cotton plantation

2. The damaged "pillars" described by Wu in the third paragraph of this excerpt are a symbol of the

   E non-communist leadership.

   F economy of the country.

   G communist regime's lack of true support by the people.

   H Chinese prison system under the communist government.

3. **Critical Thinking Synthesizing Information**
   (a) Why do you think the author describes the laogai as "a political tool for maintaining the Communist Party's totalitarian rule"? **(b)** What is the economic role of the labor camps?

The World: Political

ARCTIC OCEAN

80°N 160°W 140°W 120°W 100°W 80°W 60

Gr
(D

ALASKA
(U.S.)

60°N

CANADA

NORTH

AMERICA

40°N

UNITED STATES

Bermuda (Br.)

ATLANTIC OCEA

See inset below

Tropic of Cancer

MEXICO

20°N

HAWAII (U.S.)

Caribbean Sea

GUYANA

VENEZUELA

PACIFIC OCEAN

COLOMBIA

FR. GUIANA

0° Equator

Galápagos Is.
(Ecuador)

SURINAME

ECUADOR

SOUTH

KIRIBATI

AMERICA

BRAZIL

SAMOA

American
Samoa (U.S.)

PERU

FIJI
IS.

Cook
Islands
(N.Z.)

French
Polynesia
(Fr.)

BOLIVIA

20°S

TONGA

PARAGUAY

Tropic of Capricorn

Pitcairn I.
(Br.)

CHILE

Easter I.
(Chile)

URUGUAY

ARGENTINA

40°S

Robinson Projection

0   1000   2000 Miles

0   1000   2000 Kilometers

Falkland Is.
(Br.)

Central America and the Caribbean

60°S

Antarctic Circle

UNITED
STATES

B
A
H
A
M
A
S

80°S

Tropic of Cancer

Gulf of Mexico

ATLANTIC
OCEAN

20°N

CUBA

Puerto
Rico
(U.S.)

Virgin Is. (Br.)

MEXICO

HAITI

DOMINICAN
REPUBLIC

Virgin Islands (U.S.)

ANTIGUA AND
BARBUDA

JAMAICA

ST. KITTS
AND NEVIS

Guadeloupe (Fr.)

BELIZE

DOMINICA

GUATEMALA

Caribbean Sea

Martinique (Fr.)

HONDURAS

ST. LUCIA

EL SALVADOR

NICARAGUA

ST. VINCENT AND
THE GRENADINES

Aruba
(Neth.)

Netherlands
Antilles
(Neth.)

BARBADOS

GRENADA

10°N

COSTA
RICA

TRINIDAD
AND
TOBAGO

Azimuthal Equal Area Projection

0   200   400 Miles

0   200   400 Kilometers

PANAMA

VENEZUELA

90°W

80°W

COLOMBIA

SOUTH AMERICA

70

GUYANA

SURINAME

Svalbard (Nor.)

ICELAND

EUROPE

See inset below

RUSSIA

ASIA

KAZAKHSTAN

MONGOLIA

UZBEKISTAN
GEORGIA
ARMENIA
TURKMENISTAN
KYRGYZSTAN
TAJIKISTAN

TURKEY
AZERBAIJAN

N. KOREA
JAPAN
S. KOREA

Madeira Is.
(Port.)

TUNISIA

ISRAEL
IRAQ
IRAN
AFGHAN-
ISTAN

CHINA

Canary Is.
(Sp.)
MOROCCO

JORDAN
KUWAIT
BAHRAIN
QATAR
PAKISTAN

NEPAL
BHUTAN

WESTERN SAHARA
(Mor.)

ALGERIA
LIBYA
EGYPT

SAUDI
ARABIA
U.A.E.
OMAN

INDIA
BANGLADESH

MYANMAR
(BURMA)
LAOS

TAIWAN

PACIFIC OCEAN

AFRICA
NIGER
CHAD
SUDAN

ERITREA
YEMEN

DJIBOUTI

THAILAND
VIETNAM

Northern
Mariana
Is.
(U.S.)

Guam
(U.S.)

MARSHALL IS.

NIGERIA

CENTRAL
AFRICAN REP.
ETHIOPIA
SOMALIA

SRI
LANKA
CAMBODIA

BRUNEI

PALAU

**FEDERATED STATES
OF MICRONESIA**

CAMEROON
UGANDA
KENYA

MALDIVES

MALAYSIA

EQUATORIAL
GUINEA
GABON
CONGO
DEM. REP.
CONGO
RWANDA
BURUNDI

SEYCHELLES

SINGAPORE

INDONESIA

NAURU
KIRIBATI

See inset below

Cabinda
(Angola)

TANZANIA

PAPUA
NEW GUINEA
SOLOMON
IS.
TUVALU

**ATLANTIC
OCEAN**

ANGOLA
MALAWI
ZAMBIA

COMOROS

EAST
TIMOR

VANUATU
New
Caledonia
(Fr.)

FIJI
IS.

NAMIBIA
ZIMBABWE
BOTSWANA

MOZAMBIQUE
MADAGASCAR
Réunion
(Fr.)
MAURITIUS

INDIAN OCEAN

AUSTRALIA

SOUTH
AFRICA
SWAZILAND
LESOTHO

N
W   E
S

NEW ZEALAND

ANTARCTICA

West Africa

ALGERIA

MAURITANIA

MALI

N
W   E
S

NIGER

SENEGAL

GAMBIA

BURKINA FASO

GUINEA

BENIN

GUINEA-
BISSAU

CÔTE
D'IVOIRE
GHANA
TOGO
NIGERIA

SIERRA LEONE
LIBERIA

Mercator Projection

0   250   500 Miles

0   250   500 Kilometers

0°   Equator

**ATLANTIC
OCEAN**

Gulf of Guinea

SÃO TOMÉ AND
PRÍNCIPE

Europe

Azimuthal Equal Area Projection

0   300   600 Miles

0   300   600 Kilometers

Arctic Circle
60°N

FINLAND

NORWAY

NORTH Sea
SWEDEN
ESTONIA
LATVIA

UNITED
KINGDOM

RUSSIA

10°W

IRELAND

DENMARK

Baltic Sea
LITHUANIA
RUSSIA

N
W   E
S

BELARUS

NETH.
BELG.
GERMANY
POLAND

**ATLANTIC
OCEAN**

50°N

LUX.
LIECH.
CZECH
REP.
SLOVAKIA

UKRAINE

FRANCE

SWITZ.
AUSTRIA HUNGARY

MOLDOVA

SLOVENIA

MONACO

ROMANIA

PORTUGAL

ANDORRA
SAN
MARINO
CROATIA
BOSNIA &
HERZ.
ITALY
SERBIA &
MONT.

Black Sea

SPAIN

BULGARIA
MACEDONIA

40°N

ALBANIA
GREECE

TURKEY

40°E

Gibraltar (Br.)

CYPRUS

SYRIA

MOROCCO
ALGERIA

TUNISIA   MALTA

Mediterranean Sea

LEBANON

10°E
20°E
30°E

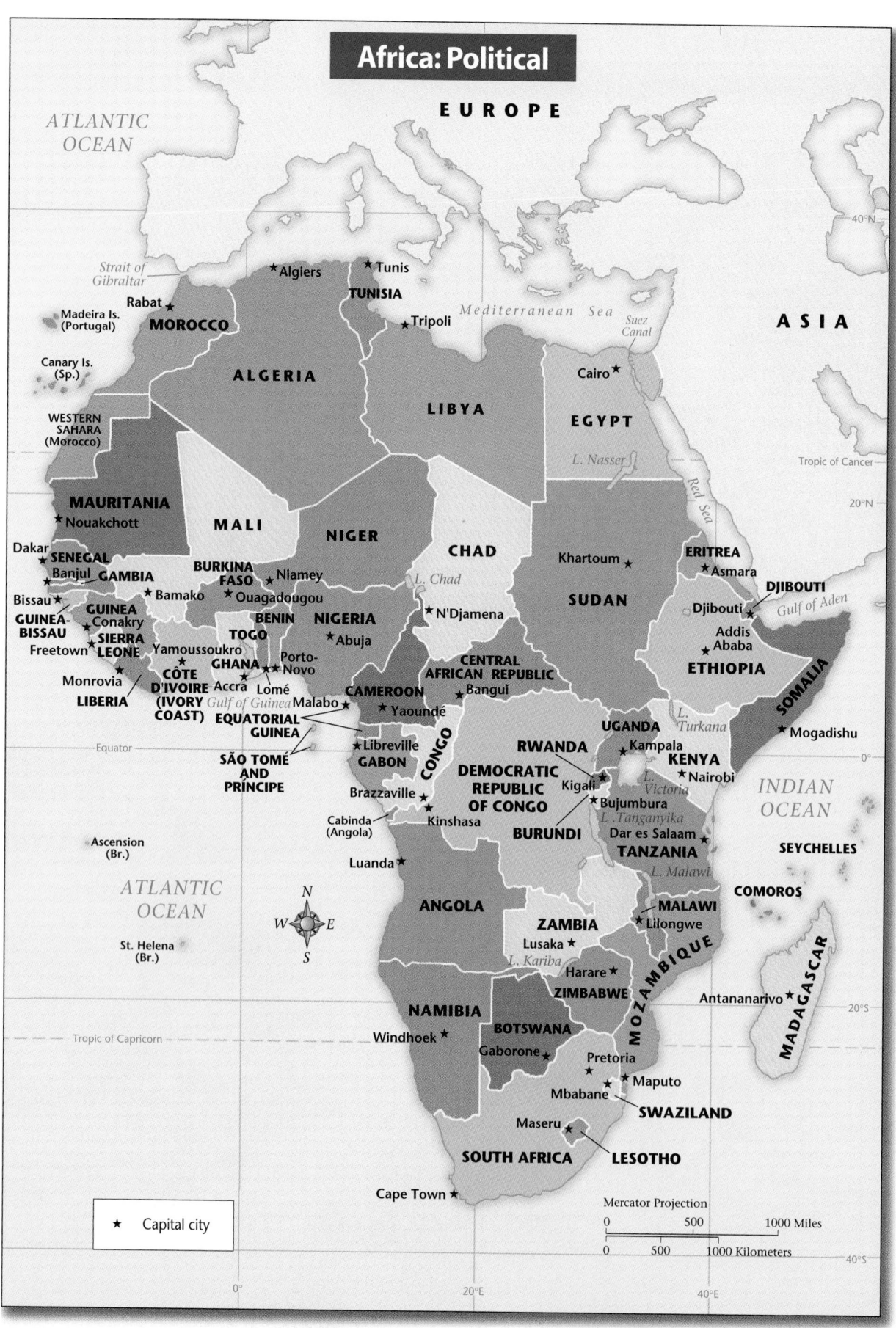

Africa: Political

EUROPE

ATLANTIC OCEAN

Strait of Gibraltar

★Algiers   ★Tunis

TUNISIA

★Tripoli

Mediterranean Sea   *Suez Canal*

Madeira Is. (Portugal)   Rabat ★

MOROCCO

ASIA

Canary Is. (Sp.)

ALGERIA   LIBYA   ★Cairo

EGYPT

Tropic of Cancer

WESTERN SAHARA (Morocco)

L. Nasser

20°N

MAURITANIA   ★Nouakchott

MALI   NIGER   CHAD   Khartoum★   ERITREA   ★Asmara

DJIBOUTI

Dakar   SENEGAL   BURKINA FASO   ★Niamey   *L. Chad*   SUDAN   Djibouti★   *Gulf of Aden*

Banjul★ GAMBIA   Bamako★   Ouagadougou   ★N'Djamena   Addis Ababa★

Bissau★   GUINEA   Conakry★   NIGERIA   CENTRAL AFRICAN REPUBLIC   ETHIOPIA

GUINEA-BISSAU   BENIN   ★Abuja

SIERRA LEONE   TOGO

Freetown★   Yamoussoukro★   GHANA   Porto-Novo   ★Bangui   SOMALIA

Monrovia★   CÔTE D'IVOIRE (IVORY COAST)   Accra★   Lomé   Malabo★   ★Yaoundé   L. Turkana   ★Mogadishu

LIBERIA   *Gulf of Guinea*   CAMEROON   UGANDA   KENYA

EQUATORIAL GUINEA   Libreville★   RWANDA   Kampala★   0°

Equator

SÃO TOMÉ AND PRÍNCIPE   GABON   CONGO   DEMOCRATIC REPUBLIC OF CONGO   Kigali★   ★Nairobi

Brazzaville★   Bujumbura★   *L. Victoria*   INDIAN OCEAN

Ascension (Br.)   Cabinda (Angola)   Kinshasa   BURUNDI   *L. Tanganyika*   Dar es Salaam★   SEYCHELLES

ATLANTIC OCEAN   Luanda★   TANZANIA

St. Helena (Br.)   ANGOLA   COMOROS

N   *L. Malawi*

W   E   MALAWI   ★Lilongwe

S   ZAMBIA   MOZAMBIQUE   MADAGASCAR

Lusaka★   *L. Kariba*   Harare★   Antananarivo★

NAMIBIA   ZIMBABWE   20°S

Tropic of Capricorn   BOTSWANA

Windhoek★   Gaborone★   Pretoria★   Maputo

Mbabane★   SWAZILAND

Maseru★

SOUTH AFRICA   LESOTHO

★ Capital city

Cape Town★

Mercator Projection

0   500   1000 Miles
0   500   1000 Kilometers

0°   20°E   40°E   40°S

Africa: Physical

ATLANTIC OCEAN

EUROPE

ASIA

Strait of Gibraltar

Madeira Is.

Canary Is.

ATLAS MOUNTAINS

Mediterranean Sea

Suez Canal

LIBYAN DESERT

S A H A R A

Nile R.

L. Nasser

NUBIAN DESERT

Tropic of Cancer

20°N

TIBESTI MTS.

Red Sea

Senegal R.

Niger R.

L. Chad

Blue Nile R.

White Nile R.

Gulf of Aden

ETHIOPIAN HIGHLANDS

HORN OF AFRICA

Gulf of Guinea

Congo R.

CONGO BASIN

GREAT RIFT VALLEY

Turkana

Equator

0°

L. Victoria

L.Tanganyika

INDIAN OCEAN

KATANGA PLATEAU

L. Malawi

ATLANTIC OCEAN

N
W E
S

Zambezi R.

L. Kariba

Madagascar

20°S

NAMIB DESERT

Tropic of Capricorn

KALAHARI DESERT

Orange R.

DRAKENSBERG RANGE

Land Elevation

Feet	Meters
14,000	4,000
7,000	2,000
1,500	500
700	200
0	0
Below sea level	Below sea level

Mercator Projection

0   500   1000 Miles

0   500   1000 Kilometers

40°S

0°

20°E

40°E

40°N

World Atlas

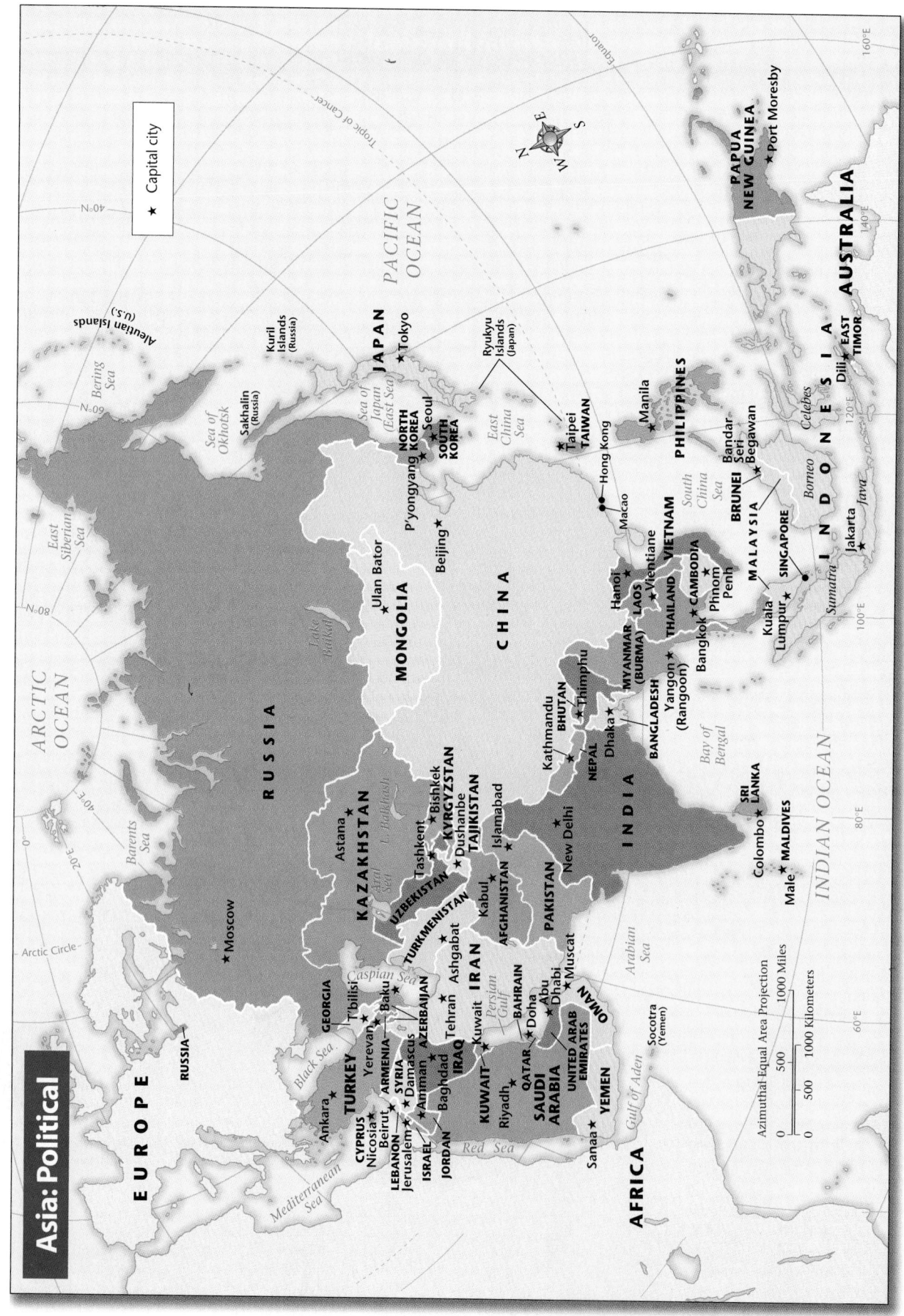

Asia: Political

World Atlas

Capital city ★

EUROPE

RUSSIA

ARCTIC OCEAN

Arctic Circle

Barents Sea

East Siberian Sea

Bering Sea

Aleutian Islands (U.S.)

Sea of Okhotsk

Sakhalin (Russia)

Kuril Islands (Russia)

PACIFIC OCEAN

Tropic of Cancer

Equator

Moscow ★

RUSSIA

Lake Baikal

MONGOLIA
Ulan Bator ★

JAPAN
Tokyo ★

Sea of Japan (East Sea)

NORTH KOREA
P'yongyang ★

SOUTH KOREA
Seoul ★

East China Sea

Ryukyu Islands (Japan)

CHINA

Beijing ★

KAZAKHSTAN
Astana ★

Aral Sea

L. Balkhash

Bishkek ★
KYRGYZSTAN

Tashkent ★

UZBEKISTAN

Dushanbe ★
TAJIKISTAN

Taipei ★
TAIWAN

Hong Kong ★
Macao ●

Manila ★

PHILIPPINES

South China Sea

Bandar Seri Begawan ★

BRUNEI

Borneo

Celebes

INDONESIA

AUSTRALIA

PAPUA NEW GUINEA
★ Port Moresby

GEORGIA
Tbilisi ★

TURKEY
Ankara ★

CYPRUS
Nicosia ★
Beirut ★
LEBANON
Jerusalem ★
ISRAEL

Yerevan ★
ARMENIA
Damascus ★
SYRIA
Amman ★
JORDAN

Black Sea

Caspian Sea

Baku ★
AZERBAIJAN

Tehran ★

Baghdad ★
IRAQ

Kuwait ★
KUWAIT

Riyadh ★
SAUDI ARABIA

Persian Gulf

TURKMENISTAN
Ashgabat ★

IRAN

BAHRAIN
QATAR
Doha ★
Abu Dhabi ★
UNITED ARAB EMIRATES

Kabul ★
AFGHANISTAN

Islamabad ★

PAKISTAN

New Delhi ★

Muscat ★
OMAN

Arabian Sea

YEMEN
Sanaa ★

Gulf of Aden

Socotra (Yemen)

Red Sea

AFRICA

Mediterranean Sea

Kathmandu ★
NEPAL

Thimphu ★
BHUTAN

INDIA

MYANMAR (BURMA)
Yangon (Rangoon) ★

BANGLADESH
Dhaka ★

Bay of Bengal

SRI LANKA
Colombo ★

Male ★
MALDIVES

INDIAN OCEAN

Hanoi ★
LAOS
Vientiane ★
VIETNAM
Phnom Penh ★
CAMBODIA
THAILAND
Bangkok ★

MALAYSIA
Kuala Lumpur ★
SINGAPORE ★

Sumatra

Jakarta ★

Java

Dili ★
EAST TIMOR

Azimuthal Equal Area Projection

1000 Miles
1000 Kilometers
500
0

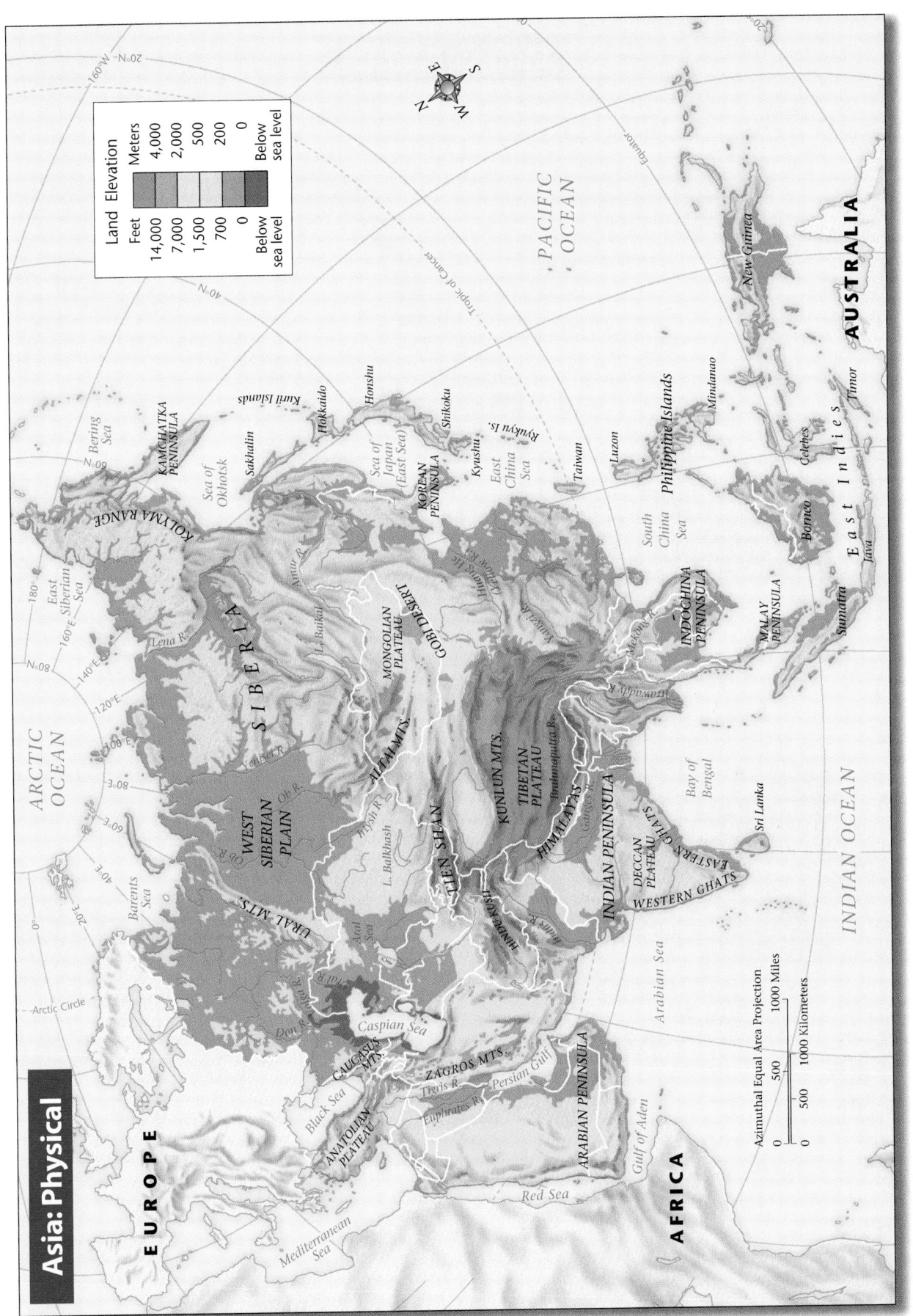

Asia: Physical

Land Elevation

Feet	Meters
14,000	4,000
7,000	2,000
1,500	500
700	200
0	0
Below sea level	Below sea level

ARCTIC OCEAN

EUROPE

Barents Sea

East Siberian Sea

Bering Sea

KOLYMA RANGE

KAMCHATKA PENINSULA

Sea of Okhotsk

Sakhalin

Kuril Islands

Hokkaido

Honshu

Sea of Japan (East Sea)

Shikoku

Kyushu

KOREAN PENINSULA

East China Sea

Ryukyu Is.

Taiwan

PACIFIC OCEAN

Tropic of Cancer

Equator

New Guinea

AUSTRALIA

Timor

East Indies

Java

Sumatra

Celebes

Borneo

Mindanao

Luzon

Philippine Islands

South China Sea

MALAY PENINSULA

INDOCHINA PENINSULA

Mekong R.

Irrawaddy R.

Bay of Bengal

Sri Lanka

INDIAN OCEAN

Arabian Sea

EASTERN GHATS

WESTERN GHATS

DECCAN PLATEAU

INDIAN PENINSULA

HIMALAYAS

Brahmaputra R.

Ganges R.

Indus R.

HINDU KUSH

TIBETAN PLATEAU

KUNLUN MTS.

TIEN SHAN

ALTAI MTS.

GOBI DESERT

MONGOLIAN PLATEAU

Yangtze R.

Huang He (Yellow R.)

SIBERIA

Amur R.

L. Baikal

Lena R.

Yenisey R.

Ob R.

Irtysh R.

L. Balkhash

WEST SIBERIAN PLAIN

URAL MTS.

Aral Sea

Amu Darya

Syr Darya

Caspian Sea

CAUCASUS MTS.

Black Sea

ANATOLIAN PLATEAU

Mediterranean Sea

ZAGROS MTS.

Tigris R.

Euphrates R.

Persian Gulf

ARABIAN PENINSULA

Red Sea

Gulf of Aden

AFRICA

Azimuthal Equal Area Projection

1000 Miles

1000 Kilometers

500

500

0

0

World Atlas

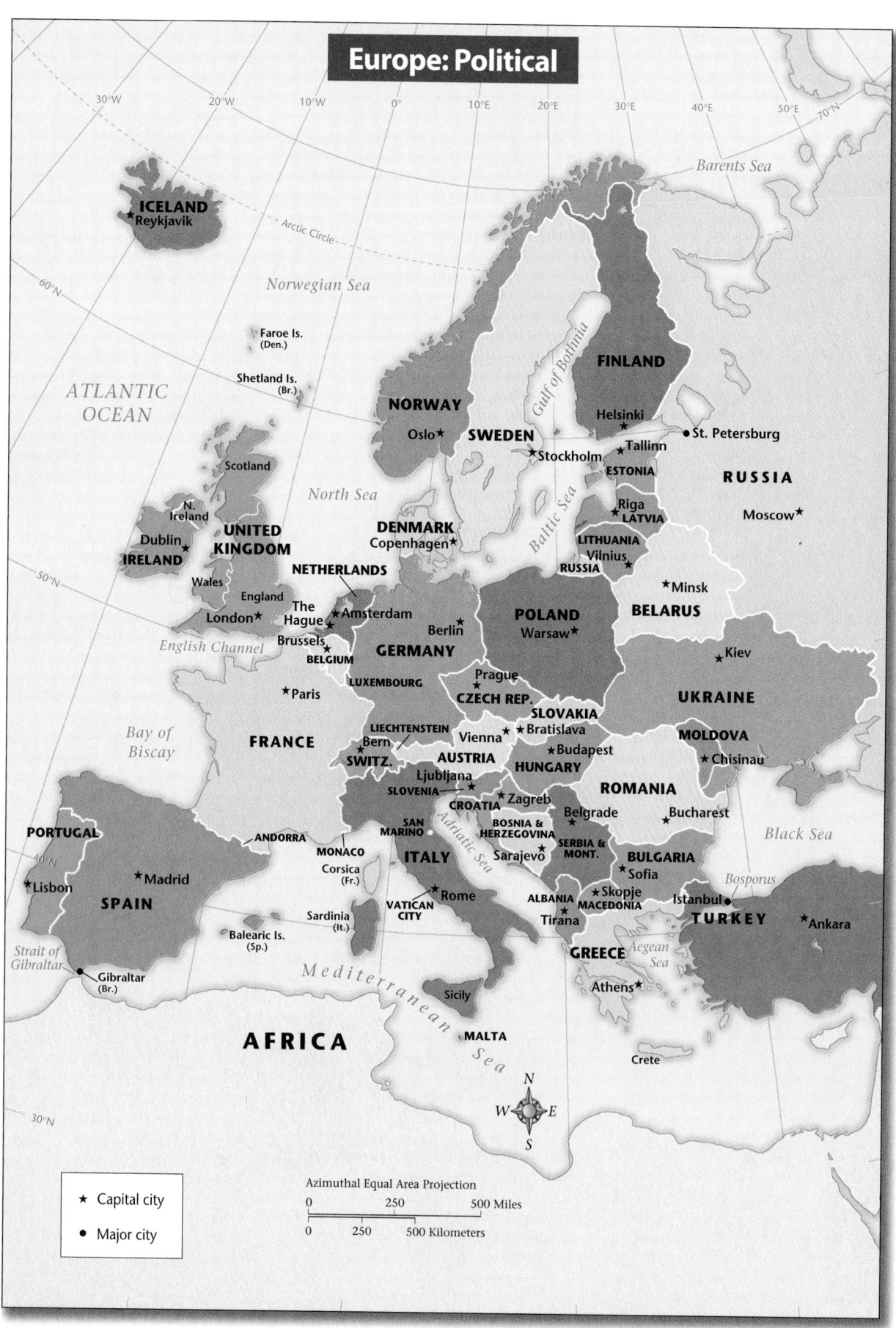

Europe: Political

- 30°W 20°W 10°W 0° 10°E 20°E 30°E 40°E 50°E 70°N

Barents Sea

ICELAND
★ Reykjavik

- - Arctic Circle - -

Norwegian Sea

60°N

Faroe Is.
(Den.)

Shetland Is.
(Br.)

FINLAND

**ATLANTIC
OCEAN**

Helsinki
★

Scotland

Gulf of Bothnia

NORWAY

Oslo ★

SWEDEN

• St. Petersburg

Tallinn ★

★ Stockholm

ESTONIA

RUSSIA

North Sea

Baltic Sea

Riga ★
LATVIA

N.
Ireland

Moscow ★

**UNITED
KINGDOM**

Dublin ★

DENMARK
Copenhagen ★

LITHUANIA
Vilnius

IRELAND

Wales

NETHERLANDS

★

RUSSIA

50°N

England

★ Minsk

The
Hague ★

★ Amsterdam

London ★

Berlin

BELARUS

Brussels
★

GERMANY

★

POLAND
Warsaw ★

BELGIUM

English Channel

★ Kiev

LUXEMBOURG

Prague
★

★ Paris

CZECH REP.

UKRAINE

SLOVAKIA

LIECHTENSTEIN

★ Bratislava

*Bay of
Biscay*

Vienna
★

MOLDOVA

Bern

FRANCE

★

SWITZ.

★ Budapest

AUSTRIA

★ Chisinau

Ljubljana

HUNGARY

SLOVENIA

★ Zagreb

ROMANIA

CROATIA

**SAN
MARINO**

Belgrade ★

★ Bucharest

PORTUGAL

ANDORRA

Adriatic Sea

**BOSNIA &
HERZEGOVINA**

Black Sea

MONACO

40°N

ITALY

**SERBIA &
MONT.**

BULGARIA

Corsica
(Fr.)

Sarajevo ★

★ Lisbon

★ Madrid

Rome ★

★ Sofia

Bosporus

SPAIN

**VATICAN
CITY**

ALBANIA

★ Skopje
MACEDONIA

Istanbul •

Sardinia
(It.)

Tirana ★

TURKEY

★ Ankara

Balearic Is.
(Sp.)

*Aegean
Sea*

*Strait of
Gibraltar*

• Gibraltar
(Br.)

M e d i t e r r a n e a n   S e a

Sicily

GREECE

Athens ★

AFRICA

• **MALTA**

Crete

30°N

N
W ✦ E
S

Azimuthal Equal Area Projection

0   250   500 Miles

0   250   500 Kilometers

★ Capital city

• Major city

Europe: Physical

Iceland

Arctic Circle

ATLANTIC
OCEAN

Norwegian Sea

Faroe Is.

Shetland Is.

Barents Sea

KJØLEN MTS.
SCANDINAVIAN PENINSULA

Gulf of Bothnia

Volga R.

North Sea

JUTLAND
PENINSULA

British Isles

Baltic Sea

Thames R.

Ruhr
Valley

Elbe R.

NORTHERN EUROPEAN PLAIN

Oder R.

Vistula R.

Dnieper R.

English Channel

Seine R.

Rhine R.

CARPATHIAN MTS.

Dniester R.

Don

Bay of
Biscay

Loire R.

Rhône R.

A L P S

Po R.

IBERIAN
PENINSULA

PYRENEES

Garonne R.

Ebro R.

Tagus R.

Guadiana R.

APENNINES
ITALIAN PENINSULA

Corsica

Sardinia

Balearic
Islands

Adriatic Sea

DINARIC ALPS

Danube R.

BALKAN MTS.

BALKAN
PENINSULA

Black Sea

Bosporus

PINDUS MTS.

Aegean
Sea

Dardanelles

Strait of
Gibraltar

Sicily

Crete

Mediterranean Sea

AFRICA

Land Elevation

Feet		Meters
14,000		4,000
7,000		2,000
1,500		500
700		200
0		0
Below sea level		Below sea level
	Icecaps	

N
W E
S

Azimuthal Equal Area Projection

0   250   500 Miles

0   250   500 Kilometers

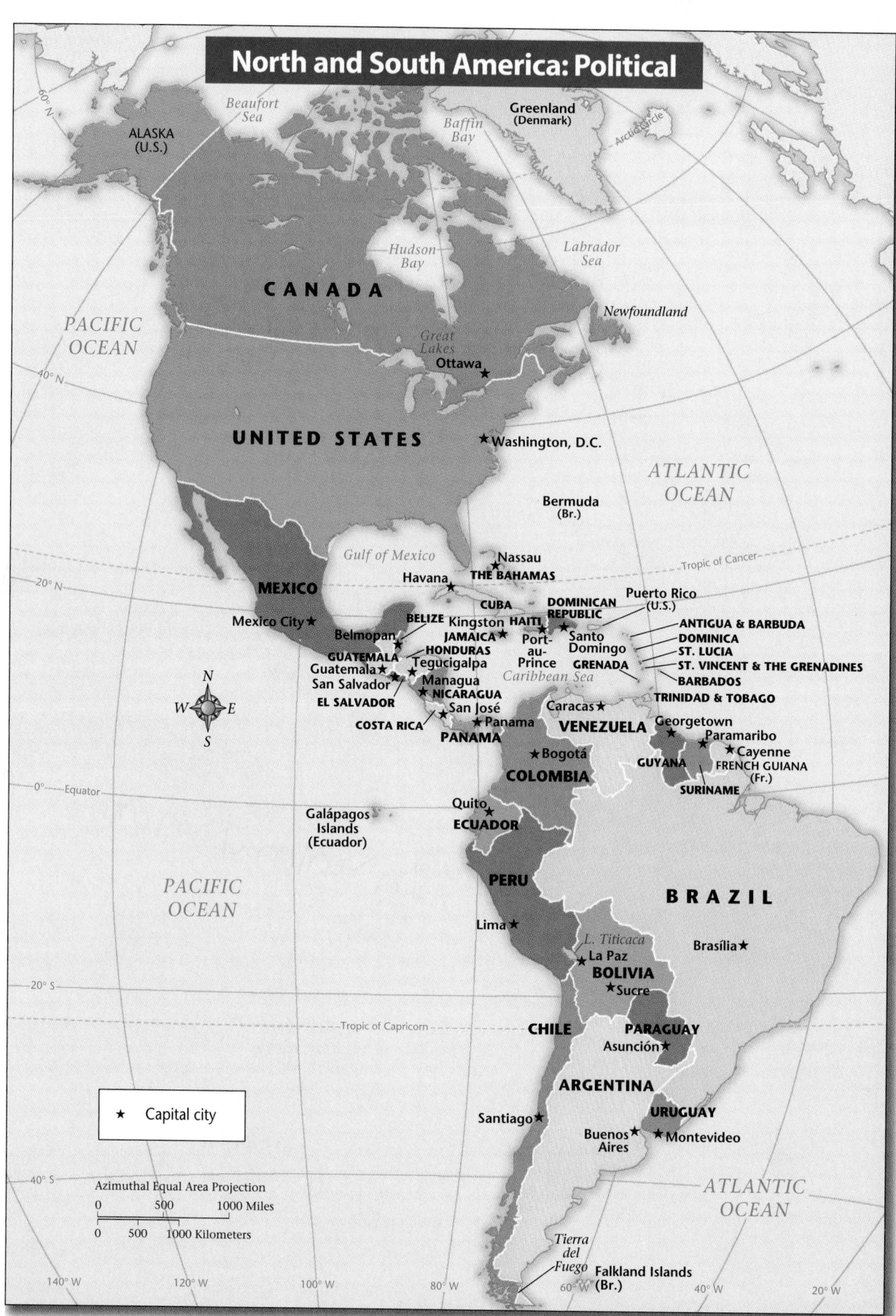

North and South America: Political

ALASKA
(U.S.)

Beaufort Sea

Greenland
(Denmark)

Baffin Bay

Arctic Circle

PACIFIC
OCEAN

Hudson Bay

Labrador Sea

CANADA

Great Lakes

Newfoundland

Ottawa ★

40° N

UNITED STATES

★Washington, D.C.

ATLANTIC
OCEAN

Bermuda
(Br.)

Gulf of Mexico

Nassau

Tropic of Cancer

20° N

MEXICO

Havana ★

Nassau
THE BAHAMAS

Puerto Rico
(U.S.)

Mexico City ★

BELIZE
Belmopan

CUBA

DOMINICAN
REPUBLIC

ANTIGUA & BARBUDA

HAITI

DOMINICA

Kingston

JAMAICA ★

Santo
Domingo

ST. LUCIA

GUATEMALA

HONDURAS

Port-
au-
Prince

GRENADA

ST. VINCENT & THE GRENADINES

Guatemala ★
San Salvador ★

Tegucigalpa ★

BARBADOS

Managua ★

Caribbean Sea

TRINIDAD & TOBAGO

EL SALVADOR

NICARAGUA

N

San José ★

Caracas ★

Georgetown

Paramaribo

W   E

COSTA RICA

★ Panama

VENEZUELA

★Cayenne

PANAMA

★ Bogotá

GUYANA

FRENCH GUIANA
(Fr.)

S

COLOMBIA

SURINAME

0° — Equator

Galápagos
Islands
(Ecuador)

Quito ★

ECUADOR

PACIFIC
OCEAN

PERU

B R A Z I L

Lima ★

L. Titicaca

Brasília ★

★ La Paz

20° S

BOLIVIA

★ Sucre

Tropic of Capricorn

CHILE

PARAGUAY

Asunción ★

★ Capital city

ARGENTINA

URUGUAY

Santiago ★

Buenos
Aires ★

★ Montevideo

40° S

Azimuthal Equal Area Projection

0   500   1000 Miles

0   500   1000 Kilometers

Tierra del Fuego

Falkland Islands
(Br.)

140° W   120° W   100° W   80° W   60° W   40° W   20° W

North and South America: Physical

Bering Strait

Bering Sea

Beaufort Sea

Yukon R.

GREENLAND

Baffin Bay

Arctic Circle

60°N

Mackenzie R.

CANADIAN SHIELD

Hudson Bay

Labrador Sea

NORTH AMERICA

Lake Winnipeg

40°N

ROCKY MOUNTAINS

GREAT PLAINS

Great Lakes

St. Lawrence R.

CASCADES

Missouri R.

Mississippi R.

Ohio R.

APPALACHIAN MTS.

PACIFIC OCEAN

SIERRA NEVADA

Great Salt Lake

Colorado R.

ATLANTIC OCEAN

BAJA CALIFORNIA

SIERRA MADRE OCCIDENTAL

Rio Grande

SIERRA MADRE ORIENTAL

Gulf of Mexico

Tropic of Cancer

20°N

YUCATÁN PENINSULA

Cuba

Hispaniola

Caribbean Sea

N
W · E
S

CENTRAL AMERICA

ISTHMUS OF PANAMA

LLANOS

Orinoco R.

GUIANA HIGHLANDS

São Francisco R.

Galápagos Islands

Equator

AMAZON

BASIN

Amazon R.

0°

ANDES

SOUTH AMERICA

BRAZILIAN HIGHLANDS

PACIFIC OCEAN

L. Titicaca

MOUNTAINS

ATACAMA DESERT

20°S

Land Elevation

Feet		Meters
14,000		4,000
7,000		2,000
1,500		500
700		200
0		0
Below sea level		Below sea level
	Icecaps	

Paraná R.

Tropic of Capricorn

ATLANTIC OCEAN

PAMPAS

Azimuthal Equal Area Projection

0   500   1000 Miles

0   500   1000 Kilometers

PATAGONIA

Tierra Del Fuego

Falkland Islands

40°S

140°W   120°W   100°W   80°W   60°W   40°W   20°W

Australia, New Zealand, and Oceania: Political–Physical

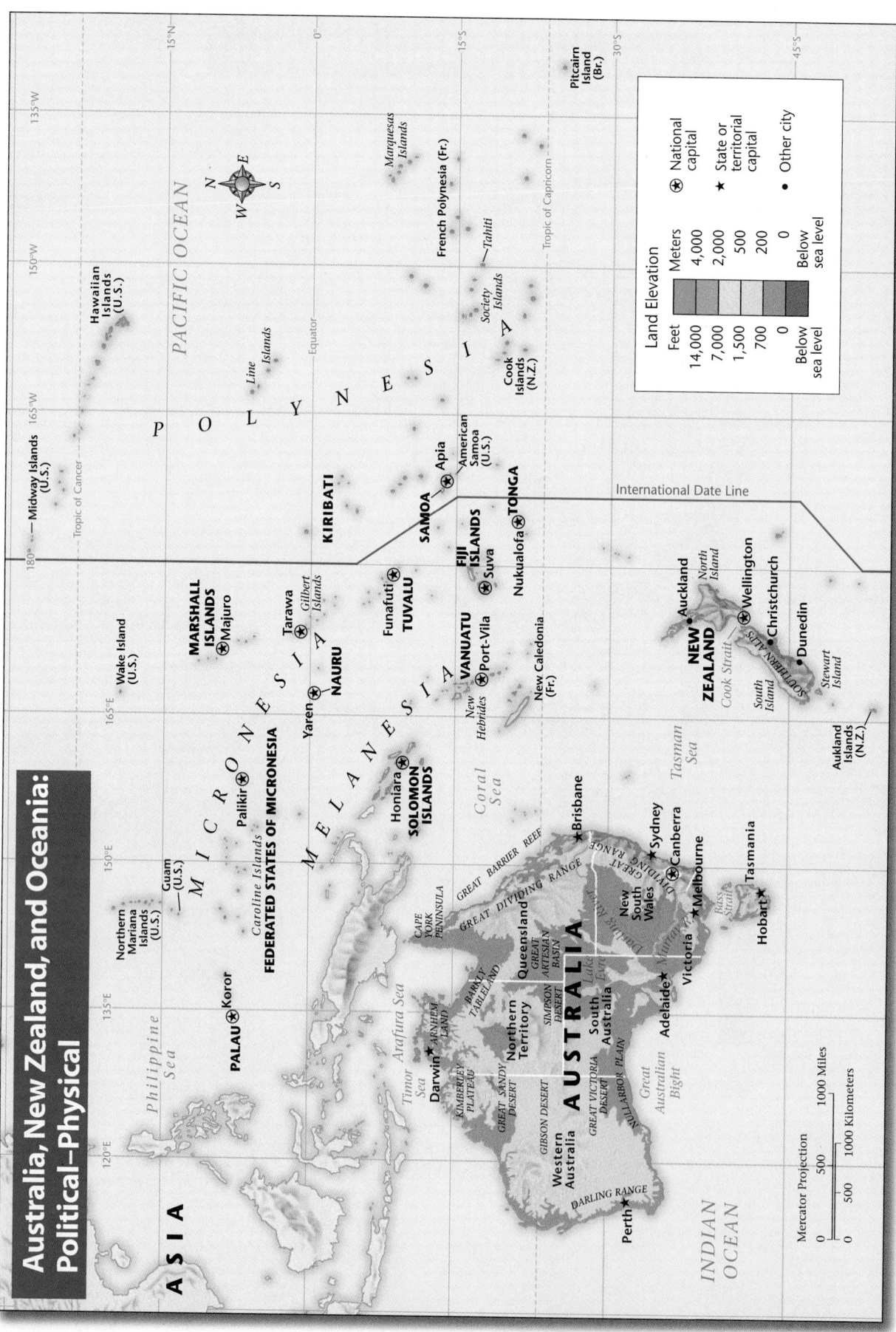

ASIA

PACIFIC OCEAN

Hawaiian Islands (U.S.)

Midway Islands (U.S.)

Line Islands

Marquesas Islands

French Polynesia (Fr.)

Tahiti

Society Islands

Cook Islands (N.Z.)

P O L Y N E S I A

Equator

Tropic of Cancer

Tropic of Capricorn

KIRIBATI

SAMOA
Apia

American Samoa (U.S.)

TONGA

International Date Line

Funafuti
TUVALU

FIJI ISLANDS
Suva

Nukualofa

Tarawa
Gilbert Islands

M I C R O N E S I A

MARSHALL ISLANDS
Majuro

Wake Island (U.S.)

NAURU
Yaren

VANUATU
Port-Vila

New Hebrides

New Caledonia (Fr.)

Auckland
North Island
NEW ZEALAND

Wellington
Christchurch
Dunedin
SOUTHERN ALPS
South Island
Cook Strait

Stewart Island

Aukland Islands (N.Z.)

Palikir
FEDERATED STATES OF MICRONESIA

Caroline Islands

Honiara
SOLOMON ISLANDS

M E L A N E S I A

Coral Sea

Tasman Sea

Guam (U.S.)

Northern Mariana Islands (U.S.)

PALAU
Koror

Philippine Sea

Timor Sea

Arafura Sea

Brisbane

GREAT BARRIER REEF

CAPE YORK PENINSULA

GREAT DIVIDING RANGE

Queensland

GREAT ARTESIAN BASIN

BARKLY TABLELAND

ARNHEM LAND

Darwin

KIMBERLEY PLATEAU

Northern Territory

SIMPSON DESERT

GREAT SANDY DESERT

GIBSON DESERT

Western Australia

GREAT VICTORIA DESERT

South Australia

A U S T R A L I A

Lake Eyre

Murray River

Darling River

New South Wales

Sydney
Canberra
Melbourne
Victoria

GREAT DIVIDING RANGE

Tasmania
Hobart

Bass Strait

Adelaide

NULLARBOR PLAIN

Great Australian Bight

DARLING RANGE

Perth

INDIAN OCEAN

Pitcairn Island (Br.)

Legend

Land Elevation

Feet	Meters
14,000	4,000
7,000	2,000
1,500	500
700	200
0	0
Below sea level	Below sea level

⊛ National capital
★ State or territorial capital
• Other city

Mercator Projection

0   500   1000 Miles
0   500   1000 Kilometers

Understanding Map Projections

Geographers and historians use globes and maps to represent the Earth. A globe is like a small model of the Earth. It shows major geographic features, representing the landmasses and bodies of water accurately. However, a globe is not always convenient to use. A map, on the other hand, which can be printed on a piece of paper or in a book, is a more convenient way to show the Earth. Unfortunately, no map can be an exact picture of the Earth because all maps are flat and the Earth's surface is curved.

Mapmakers have developed many ways of showing the curved Earth on a flat surface. Each of these ways is called a map projection. The three maps on this page show different types of map projections—each with its advantages and disadvantages.

Robinson Projection The Robinson projection shows correct shapes and sizes of landmasses for most parts of the world. They are commonly used today by geographers. You will find numerous Robinson projections in this book. The locator maps that appear with most of the maps in the book are Robinson projections.

Mercator Projection The Mercator projection, one of the earliest projections developed, accurately shows the directions north, south, east, and west. As you can see, the parallels and meridians are straight lines intersecting each other at right angles. This makes it easy to plot distances on the map. As a result, Mercator projections are useful for showing sailors' routes and ocean currents. Sizes become distorted, however, as you move farther away from the equator.

Interrupted Projection The Interrupted projection shows the sizes and shapes of landmasses accurately. However, the interruptions in the oceans make it difficult to measure distances and judge directions across water.

Map Projections

Robinson Projection

Mercator Projection

Interrupted Projection

World Atlas

Skills Assessment

Geography Map projections enable mapmakers to show the curved Earth on a flat page. Each of the projections shown here has its advantages and disadvantages.

1. **Location** *On the maps, locate (a) North America, (b) Africa, (c) Australia.*
2. **Region** *(a) On an Interrupted projection, which continent is divided into sections? Why is it divided? (b) List three pages in this textbook on which you can find a Robinson projection.*
3. **Critical Thinking** **Comparing** *Locate Antarctica on the Robinson and Mercator projections. On which map is its size shown more accurately? Explain why this is so.*

Glossary

This Glossary defines many important terms and phrases. Some terms are phonetically respelled to aid in pronunciation. See the Pronunciation Key below for an explanation of the respellings. The page number following each definition is the page on which the term or phrase is first discussed in a chapter. All terms that appear in blue type in the text are included in this Glossary.

PRONUNCIATION KEY When difficult terms or names first appear in the text, they are respelled to aid in pronunciation. A syllable in small capital letters receives the most stress. The key below lists the letters used for respelling. It includes examples of words using each sound and shows how they are respelled.

Symbol	Example	Respelling
a	hat	(hat)
ay	pay, late	(pay), (layt)
ah	star, hot	(stahr), (haht)
ai	air, dare	(air), (dair)
aw	law, all	(law), (awl)
eh	met	(meht)
ee	bee, eat	(bee), (eet)
er	learn, sir, fur	(lern), (ser), (fer)
ih	fit	(fiht)
ī	mile	(mīle)
ir	ear	(ir)
oh	no	(noh)
oi	soil, boy	(soil), (boi)
oo	root, rule	(root), (rool)
or	born, door	(born), (dor)
ow	plow, out	(plow), (owt)
u	put, book	(put), (buk)
uh	fun	(fuhn)
yoo	few, use	(fyoo), (yooz)
ch	chill, reach	(chihl), (reech)
g	go, dig	(goh), (dihg)
j	jet, gently, bridge	(jeht), (JEHNT lee), (brihj)
k	kite, cup	(kīt), (kuhp)
ks	mix	(mihks)
kw	quick	(kwihk)
ng	bring	(brihng)
s	say, cent	(say), (sehnt)
sh	she, crash	(shee), (krash)
th	three	(three)
y	yet, onion	(yeht), (UHN yuhn)
z	zip, always	(zihp), (AWL wayz)
zh	treasure	(TREH zher)

A

abdicate give up a high office (p. 188)

abolitionist one who fought for the end of slavery in the United States (p. 307)

absentee landlord one who owns a large estate but does not live there (p. 298)

absolute monarch ruler with complete authority over the government and lives of the people he or she governs (p. 111)

abstract style of art composed of lines, colors, and shapes, usually having no recognizable subject matter (p. 451)

acid rain form of pollution in which toxic chemicals in the air come back to the Earth as rain, snow, or hail (p. 515)

acropolis (uh KRAHP uh lihs) highest and most fortified point within a Greek city-state (p. 11)

agribusiness large commercial farm owned by a multinational corporation (p. 636)

ahimsa (uh HIM sah) Hindu belief in nonviolence and a reverence for all life (p. 430)

alliance formal agreement between two or more nations or powers to cooperate and come to one another's defense (p. 85)

anarchist someone who wants to abolish all government (p. 278)

anesthetic drug that prevents pain during surgery (p. 196)

annex add a territory onto an existing state or country (pp. 184, 271)

annul cancel or invalidate (p. 50)

Anschluss union of Austria and Germany (p. 470)

apartheid policy of strict racial separation in South Africa; abolished in 1989 (p. 425)

appeasement policy of giving in to an aggressor's demands in order to keep the peace (p. 469)

aristocracy government headed by a privileged minority or upper class (p. 11)

armada fleet of ships (p. 112)

armistice mutual agreement to end fighting in a war (p. 391)

artisan skilled craftworker (p. 3)

assembly line industrial production method that breaks down a complex job into a series of smaller tasks (p. 244)

astrolabe instrument used to determine latitude by measuring the position of the stars (p. 63)

atheism belief that there is no god (p. 412)

atrocity brutal act committed against innocent people (p. 389)

autonomy self-rule (p. 218)

ayatollah title given to a learned Shiite Muslim legal expert (p. 596)

B

balance of power distribution of military and economic power that prevents any one nation from becoming too strong (p. 118)

baroque ornate style of art and architecture popular in the 1600s and 1700s (p. 151)

blitzkrieg lightning war (p. 473)

blockade shutting off of a port to keep people or supplies from moving in or out (p. 185)

bourgeoisie (boor zhwah ZEE) the middle class (p. 167)

boyar landowning noble in Russia under the czars (p. 130)

brahman according to Aryan belief, the single spiritual power that resides in all things (p. 7)

bureaucracy system of managing government through departments run by appointed officials (p. 3)

C

cabinet parliamentary advisors to the king who originally met in a small room, or "cabinet" (p. 156)

caliph successor to Muhammad as political and religious leader of the Muslims (p. 22)

canonize recognize one as a saint (p. 50)

capital money or wealth (p. 199)

capital offense crime punishable by death (p. 296)

capitalism economic system in which the means of production are privately owned and operated for profit (p. 102)

caravel improved type of sailing ship in the 1400s (p. 63)

cartel association of large corporations formed to fix prices, set production quotas, or divide up markets (p. 247)

cartographer mapmaker (p. 63)

caste in traditional Indian society, unchangeable social group into which a person is born (p. 7)

caudillo military dictator in Latin America (p. 357)

cease-fire halt in fighting (p. 572)

censorship restriction on access to ideas and information (p. 149)

chancellor prime minister (pp. 269, 459, 534)

chivalry code of conduct for knights during the Middle Ages (p. 17)

circumnavigate travel all the way around the Earth (p. 66)

city-state political unit made up of a city and the surrounding lands (p. 4)

civil disobedience refusal to obey unjust laws (p. 430)

civil rights movement effort in the 1950s and 1960s to end discrimination and ensure equal rights for all Americans (p. 539)

civil war war fought between two groups of people in the same nation (p. 85)

client state nation dependent on the support of a stronger power (p. 597)

coalition temporary alliance of various political parties (pp. 303, 536)

collaborator person who cooperates with an enemy (p. 480)

collective large farm owned and operated by peasants as a group (p. 407)

collective security system in which a group of nations acts as one to preserve the peace of all (p. 393)

collectivization pooling of land and labor in an attempt to increase efficiency (p. 560)

colossus giant (p. 282)

command economy system in which government officials make all basic economic decisions (p. 406)

Glossary

commissar Communist party official assigned to the army to teach party principles and ensure party loyalty (p. 404)

common law system of law that is the same for all people, based on court decisions that have become accepted legal principles (p. 18)

commune community in which property is held in common, living quarters are shared, and physical needs are provided in exchange for work at assigned jobs (p. 561)

communism form of socialism advocated by Karl Marx; according to Marx, class struggle was inevitable and would lead to the creation of a classless society in which all wealth and property would be owned by the community as a whole (p. 210)

compact agreement (p. 93)

compromise acceptable middle ground (p. 50)

concentration camp detention center for civilians who are considered enemies of a state (p. 463)

concession special economic rights given to a foreign power (p. 328)

confederation unification (p. 352)

conquistador (kahn KEES tuh dor) name for the Spanish explorers who claimed lands in the Americas for Spain in the 1500s and 1600s (p. 84)

conscription "the draft," which required all young men to be ready for military or other service (p. 690)

constitutional government government whose power is defined and limited by law (p. 155)

containment Cold War policy of limiting communism to areas already under Soviet control (p. 491)

contra guerrilla who fought against the Sandinistas in Nicaragua (p. 644)

convoy group of merchant ships protected by warships (p. 386)

corporation business owned by many investors who buy shares of stock and risk only the amount of their investment (p. 247)

creole person in Spain's colonies in the Americas who was an American-born descendant of Spanish settlers (pp. 89, 225)

crusade holy war (p. 19)

cult of domesticity idealization of women and the home (p. 254)

cultural diffusion spread of ideas, customs, and technologies from one people to another (p. 4)

cuneiform (kyoo NEE uh form) wedge-shaped writing of the ancient Sumerians (p. 5)

cyclone fierce circular windstorm (p. 584)

czar title of the ruler of the Russian empire (p. 21)

D

daimyo (DĪ myoh) warrior lord directly below the shogun in feudal Japan (p. 27)

debt service paying interest on loans (p. 584)

default fail to make payments (p. 544)

deficit gap between what a government spends and what it takes in through taxes and other sources (p. 538)

deficit spending situation in which a government spends more money than it takes in (p. 168)

deforestation the destruction of forest land (pp. 331, 584)

delta triangular area of marshland formed by deposits of silt at the mouth of some rivers (p. 594)

democracy government in which the people hold ruling power (p. 11)

depopulation reduction in population (p. 126)

desalinization process of converting salty sea water into fresh water (p. 588)

desertification process by which fertile or semidesert land becomes desert (p. 614)

détente easing of tensions between the United States and the Soviet Union in the 1970s (p. 527)

diaspora (di AS puhr uh) the scattering of people (p. 5)

diet assembly or legislature (p. 345)

direct democracy system of government in which citizens participate directly in the day-to-day affairs of government rather than through elected representatives (p. 11)

disarmament reduction of armed forces and weapons (p. 445)

dissenter Protestant whose views and opinions differed with those of the Church of England (p. 120)

dissident someone who speaks out against the government (p. 542)

divine right belief that a ruler's authority comes directly from God (p. 111)

dominion self-governing nation (p. 352)

domino theory belief that if one nation fell to communism, neighboring nations would also fall, like a row of falling dominoes (p. 571)

Duma elected national legislature in Russia (p. 287)

dynamo machine used to generate electricity (p. 244)

dynastic cycle rise and fall of Chinese dynasties according to the Mandate of Heaven (p. 7)

dynasty ruling family (p. 7)

E

e-commerce business and trade conducted over the Internet (p. 518)

economic dependence economic relationship, controlled by a developed nation, in which a less-developed nation exports raw materials to the developed nation and imports manufactured goods, capital, and technological know-how (p. 357)

ejido (eh HEE doh) Mexican peasant cooperative (p. 642)

elector one of seven German princes who would choose the Holy Roman emperor (p. 125)

electorate body of people allowed to vote (p. 293)

elite upper class (p. 324)

emancipation granting of freedom to serfs or slaves (p. 284)

embargo ban on trade (pp. 572, 638)

emigration movement away from one's homeland (p. 278)

émigré (EHM ih gray) person who flees his or her country for political reasons (p. 174)

empire group of states or territories controlled by one ruler (p. 3)

enclosure in England in the 1700s, the process of taking over and fencing off public lands (p. 197)

encomienda right the Spanish government granted to its American colonists to demand labor or tribute from Native Americans (p. 88)

engraving art form in which an artist etches a design on a metal plate with acid and then uses the plate to make multiple prints (p. 40)

enlightened despot absolute ruler who uses power to bring about political and social change (p. 150)

entente nonbinding agreement to follow common policies (p. 379)

entrepreneur person who assumes financial risks in the hope of making a profit (p. 102)

environmentalist one who raises an alarm about threats to the planet's fragile environment (p. 515)

ethics moral standards of behavior (p. 5)

ethnic cleansing policy of killing or forcibly removing people of certain ethnic groups (p. 550)

ethnic group large group of people who share the same language and cultural heritage (p. 21)

euro common currency used by member nations of the European Union (p. 530)

excommunication exclusion from the Roman Catholic Church as a penalty for refusing to obey Church laws (p. 19)

expansionism policy of increasing the amount of territory a government holds (p. 306)

extraterritoriality right of foreigners to be protected by the laws of their own nation (p. 334)

F

faction small group (p. 171)

factory place in which workers and machines are brought together to produce large quantities of goods (p. 200)

favela Brazilian slum (p. 650)

federal republic government in which power is divided between the national, or federal, government and the states (p. 161)

federal system system in which powers are divided between a strong central government and local governments (p. 581)

feminist movement sought equal access for women to jobs and promotions, equal pay for equal work, and an end to sexual harassment on the job (p. 517)

feudalism (FYOO duhl ihz uhm) loosely organized system of government in which local lords governed their own lands but owed military service and other support to a greater lord (p. 16)

fief (FEEF) in the Middle Ages, an estate granted by a lord to a vassal in exchange for service and loyalty (p. 16)

filial piety respect for parents (p. 9)

flapper in the United States and Europe in the 1920s, a rebellious young woman (p. 454)

free trade trade between countries without quotas, tariffs, or other restrictions (p. 295)

fundamentalist one who stresses the fundamental, or basic, values of his or her faith (p. 517)

G

general strike strike by workers in many different industries at the same time (p. 446)

genetic engineering altering of the chemical code carried by all living things (p. 518)

genocide deliberate attempt to destroy an entire religious or ethnic group (pp. 327, 479)

germ theory idea that certain microbes might cause specific infectious diseases (p. 249)

ghetto separate section of a city where members of a minority group are forced to live (p. 53)

glasnost policy of openness instituted by Soviet leader Mikhail Gorbachev in the 1980s (p. 544)

global warming worldwide temperature increase (p. 515)

gravity force that tends to pull one mass or object to another (p. 56)

griot (GREE oh) professional storyteller in early West Africa (p. 25)

gross domestic product total value of all goods and services produced by a nation (p. 557)

guerrilla warfare fighting carried on through hit-and-run raids (p. 186)

guild in the Middle Ages, association of merchants or artisans who cooperated to protect their economic interests (p. 17)

H

habeas corpus principle that a person cannot be held in prison without first being charged with a specific crime (p. 124)

hajj one of the Five Pillars of Islam, the pilgrimage to Mecca that all Muslims are expected to make at least once in their lifetime (p. 22)

harijan "child of God," Gandhi's term for an untouchable in the caste system (p. 583)

hejab traditional form of dress worn by Muslim women (p. 591)

heliocentric based on the belief that the sun is the center of the universe (p. 54)

hierarchy (HĪ uhr ahr kee) system of ranking people within a society (p. 4)

home rule local self-government (p. 300)

homogeneous society society that has a common culture and language (p. 346)

humanism intellectual movement at the heart of the Italian Renaissance that focused on worldly subjects rather than on religious issues (p. 35)

humanities study of subjects taught in ancient Greece and Rome, such as grammar, rhetoric, poetry, and history (p. 36)

human rights basic rights and freedoms (p. 508)

hypothesis possible explanation (p. 55)

I

ideology system of thought and belief (pp. 216, 505)

immunity natural protection (p. 84)

imperialism domination by one country of the political, economic, or cultural life of another country or region (p. 316)

import substitution government policy of encouraging local manufacturers to produce goods that would replace imports (p. 635)

impressionism school of painting of the late 1800s and early 1900s that tried to capture fleeting visual impressions (p. 263)

indemnity payment for losses in war (p. 334)

indigenous original or native to a country or region (p. 351)

Glossary

indulgence in the Roman Catholic Church, pardon for sins committed during a person's lifetime (p. 44)

inflation economic cycle that involves a rapid rise in prices linked to a sharp increase in the amount of money available (p. 102)

intendant official appointed by French King Louis XIV to govern the provinces, collect taxes, and recruit soldiers (p. 116)

interchangeable parts identical components that can be used in place of one another in manufacturing (p. 244)

interdependence mutual dependence of countries on goods, resources, and knowledge from other parts of the world (p. 507)

intifada mass uprising mounted by Palestinians in territory held by Israel (p. 598)

island-hopping method used by Allied forces to recapture some Japanese-held islands in the Pacific while bypassing others (p. 486)

isolationism policy of limited involvement in world affairs (p. 311)

J

joint stock company private trading company in which shares are sold to investors to finance business ventures (p. 102)

joint venture business organized by two parties, with profits shared by both participants (p. 563)

jury group of people sworn to make a decision in a legal case (p. 18)

K

kaiser (KĪ zer) emperor of Germany (p. 271)

kamikaze (kah mih KAH zee) Japanese pilot who undertook a suicide mission (p. 487)

kibbutz collective farm in Israel (p. 588)

kiva large underground chamber used by the Anasazi for religious ceremonies (p. 15)

knight noble in Europe who served as a mounted warrior for a lord in the Middle Ages (p. 16)

kulak wealthy peasant in the Soviet Union in the 1930s (p. 408)

Kulturkampf Bismarck's "battle for civilization," in which his goal was to make Catholics put loyalty to the state above their allegiance to the Church (p. 273)

L

labor union workers' organization (p. 207)

laissez faire policy allowing business to operate with little or no government interference (p. 148)

legitimacy principle by which monarchies that had been unseated by the French Revolution or Napoleon were restored (p. 191)

levée morning ritual during which nobles would wait upon King Louis XIV (p. 116)

libel knowing publication of false and damaging statements (p. 304)

liberation theology movement in the 1960s and 1970s urging the Roman Catholic Church to take a more active role in changing the social conditions that contributed to poverty and oppression in Latin America (pp. 517, 637)

limited monarchy government in which a constitution or legislative body limits the monarch's powers (p. 124)

literacy rate percentage of people who can read and write (p. 638)

Loyalist colonist who supported Britain during the American Revolution (p. 160)

M

mandate after World War I, a territory that was administered by a western power (p. 394)

manor during the Middle Ages in Europe, a lord's estate, which included one or more villages and the surrounding lands (p. 17)

maquiladora (mah kee luh DOHR uh) foreign-owned industrial plant in Mexico in which local workers assemble imported parts into finished goods (p. 643)

margin buying paying part of the cost of stocks while borrowing the rest from brokers (p. 446)

matrilineal term for a family organization in which kinship ties are traced through the mother (p. 68)

means of production farms, factories, railways, and other large businesses that produce and distribute goods (p. 210)

mercantilism policy by which a nation sought to export more than it imported in order to build its supply of gold and silver (p. 104)

mercenary soldier serving in a foreign army for pay (p. 126)

messiah savior sent by God (p. 13)

mestizo person in Spain's colonies in the Americas who was of Native American and European descent (pp. 89, 225)

militarism glorification of the military (p. 379)

militia band of citizen soldiers (p. 600)

missionary someone sent on a religious mission (p. 319)

mixed economy economic system with both private and state-run enterprises (p. 614)

mobilize prepare military forces for war (p. 381)

modernization building a stable government while developing a country economically (p. 505)

monarchy government in which a king or queen exercises central power (p. 11)

monopoly complete control of a product or business by one person or group (p. 99)

monotheistic believing in one God (p. 5)

mosque Muslim house of worship (p. 23)

mulatto in Spain's colonies in the Americas, person of African and European descent (pp. 89, 225)

multinational corporation enterprise with branches in many countries (p. 511)

mutual-aid society self-help group set up to aid sick or injured workers (p. 251)

mystic person who devotes his or her life to seeking spiritual truths (p. 7)

N

nationalism a strong feeling of pride in and devotion to one's country (p. 181)

nationalization takeover of property or resources by the government (p. 422)

natural law rule or law that governs human nature (p. 144)

natural right right that belongs to all humans from birth (p. 145)

neutrality policy of supporting neither side in a war (p. 381)

nirvana in Buddhism, union with the universe and release from the cycle of rebirth (p. 8)

no-fly zone area over which Iraqi aircraft were not permitted to fly after the Persian Gulf War (p. 601)

nomad person who moves from place to place in search of food (p. 2)

no man's land empty tract of land where everything has been destroyed by war (p. 385)

nonaligned not allied with either side in a conflict (p. 505)

nuclear family family unit consisting of parents and children (p. 25)

O

oligarchy government in which ruling power belongs to a few people (p. 11)

one-party system country that has a single political party (p. 613)

outpost distant military station (p. 71)

overproduction condition in which production of goods exceeds the demand for them (p. 445)

P

pacifism opposition to all war (pp. 376, 469)

padi field (p. 70)

pandemic spread of a disease across a large area, country, continent, or the entire world (p. 392)

partition divide (pp. 133, 580)

pasha provincial ruler in the Ottoman empire (p. 326)

patrician member of the landholding upper class in ancient Rome (p. 12)

patron person who provides financial support for the arts (p. 35)

penal colony place where people convicted of crimes are sent (p. 296)

peninsular member of the highest class in Spain's colonies in the Americas (pp. 88, 225)

peon worker forced to labor for a landlord in order to pay off a debt (p. 88)

peonage system by which workers owe labor to pay their debts (p. 359)

perestroika restructuring of the Soviet government and economy in the 1980s (p. 544)

perspective artistic technique used to give drawings and paintings a three-dimensional effect (p. 37)

pharaoh (FAIR oh) title of the rulers of ancient Egypt (p. 4)

philosophe member of a group of Enlightenment thinkers who tried to apply the methods of science to the improvement of society (p. 145)

physiocrat Enlightenment thinker who searched for natural laws to explain economics (p. 148)

pictogram drawing used to represent a word (p. 3)

plantation large estate run by an owner or overseer and worked by laborers who live there (p. 88)

plebeian (plih BEE uhn) member of the lower class in ancient Rome, including farmers, merchants, artisans, and traders (p. 12)

plebiscite ballot in which voters have a direct say on an issue (pp. 182, 651)

pogrom violent mob attack on a Jewish community (p. 286)

polis city-state in ancient Greece (p. 11)

polygamy custom that allows men to have more than one wife (p. 426)

polytheistic believing in many gods (p. 7)

predestination idea that God long ago determined who will gain salvation (p. 48)

premier prime minister (p. 303)

prime minister head of the cabinet in a parliamentary government; usually the leader of the largest party in the legislature (p. 156)

privateer pirate (p. 91)

privatization selling off of state-owned industries to private investors (p. 512)

proletariat working class (pp. 211, 400)

propaganda spreading of ideas and information to promote a certain cause or to damage an opposing cause (p. 388)

prophet spiritual leader believed to be interpreting God's will (p. 5)

protectorate country with its own government but under the control of an outside power (p. 318)

provisional temporary (p. 303)

psychoanalysis method of studying how the mind works and treating mental disorders (p. 451)

R

racism belief that one racial group is superior to another (p. 259)

radar device used to detect the flight of airplanes (p. 474)

realism artistic movement whose aim was to represent the world as it is (p. 261)

Realpolitik realistic politics based on the needs of the state (p. 269)

recant give up one's views or beliefs (p. 45)

recession period of reduced economic activity (pp. 220, 528)

recognize formally agree to treat a country as a legitimate state with a legitimate government (p. 587)

regionalism loyalty to a local area (p. 357)

Reich German empire (p. 271)

reincarnation in Hinduism, belief in the rebirth of the soul in another bodily form (p. 8)

reparation payment for war damages or damages caused by imprisonment (pp. 392, 482)

repeal cancel (pp. 98, 296)

republic system of government in which officials are chosen by the people (p. 12)

repudiate reject (p. 461)

revenue money taken in through taxes (p. 93)

rococo personal, elegant style of art and architecture made popular during the mid-1700s and featuring fancy design in the shape of leaves, shells, and scrolls (p. 151)

Glossary

romanticism nineteenth-century artistic movement that appealed to emotion rather than reason (p. 260)

rotten borough rural town in England that sent members to Parliament despite having few or no voters (p. 293)

S

sacrament sacred ritual of the Roman Catholic Church (p. 19)

salon informal social gathering at which writers, artists, and philosophers exchanged ideas; originated in France in the 1600s (p. 149)

samurai member of the warrior class in Japanese feudal society (p. 27)

sanction penalty (p. 468)

satellite dependent state (p. 492)

sati Hindu custom that called for a wife to join her husband in death by throwing herself on his funeral pyre (p. 329)

scapegoat person, group, or thing forced to take the blame for the crimes or mistakes of others (p. 52)

schism permanent division in a church (p. 20)

scientific method painstaking method used to confirm findings and to prove or disprove a hypothesis (p. 55)

scribe in ancient civilizations, specially trained person who knew how to read, write and keep records (p. 5)

scurvy disease caused by the lack of vitamin C in someone's diet (p. 63)

secede withdraw (p. 309)

secret ballot votes cast without announcing them publicly (p. 293)

sect small religious group (p. 13)

secular having to do with worldly, rather than religious, matters (p. 17)

segregation separation of the races (p. 539)

self-determination right of people to choose their own form of government (p. 391)

separatism movement advocating that Quebec separate from Canada and become an independent nation (p. 540)

sepoy Indian soldier in an army set up by the French or English East India company (pp. 74, 329)

serf in medieval Europe, peasant bound to the lord's land (p. 17)

service industry industry that provides a service rather than a product (p. 528)

shantytown slum on the outskirts of a city that lacks basic services, such as running water (p. 516)

shogun in Japanese feudal society, supreme military commander who held more power than the emperor (p. 27)

smelt melt in order to get the pure metal away from its waste matter (p. 198)

social contract agreement by which people give up their freedom to a powerful government in order to avoid chaos (p. 145)

social gospel movement of the 1800s that urged Christians to do social service (p. 259)

socialism system in which the people as a whole rather than private individuals own all property and operate all businesses (p. 210)

socialist realism artistic style whose goal was to promote socialism by showing Soviet life in a positive light (p. 413)

social welfare programs to help people in need (p. 274)

sonar device used to detect the path of submarines (p. 474)

soviet council of workers and soldiers set up by Russian revolutionaries in 1917 (p. 401)

special enterprise zone area in China where foreigners can own and operate industries (p. 563)

sphere of influence area in which an outside power claims exclusive investment or trading privileges (p. 318)

squatter person who settles on land he or she does not own (p. 653)

stalemate deadlock in which neither side is able to defeat the other (p. 383)

standard of living measures the quality and availability of necessities and comforts in a society (p. 252)

stock shares in a company (p. 247)

stream of consciousness literary technique that probes a character's random thoughts and feelings (p. 452)

stupa large domelike Buddhist shrine (p. 69)

suffrage right to vote (p. 176)

sultan Muslim ruler (p. 23)

summit conference of leaders and experts from around the world (p. 507)

superpower nation strong enough to influence the acts and policies of other nations (p. 505)

surplus extra or excess (p. 539)

surrealism artistic movement that attempts to portray the workings of the unconscious mind (p. 451)

T

tariff tax on imported goods (p. 104)

temperance movement campaign to limit or ban the use of alcoholic beverages (p. 256)

tenement building multistory building divided into crowded apartments (p. 203)

terrorism deliberate use of random violence, especially against civilians, to achieve political goals (p. 509)

theocracy government run by religious leaders (pp. 48, 596)

total war channeling of a nation's entire resources into a war effort (p. 388)

totalitarian state government in which a one-party dictatorship regulates every aspect of citizens' lives (p. 411)

trade deficit situation in which a country imports more than it exports (pp. 333, 557)

trade surplus situation in which a country exports more than it imports (p. 333)

triangular trade colonial trade route among Europe and its colonies, the West Indies, and Africa in which goods were exchanged for slaves (p. 98)

tributary state independent state that has to acknowledge the supremacy of another state and pay tribute to its ruler (p. 26)

tribute payment that conquered peoples were forced to make to their conquerors (p. 14)

Glossary

truce temporary peace (p. 226)

turnpike privately built road that charges a fee to travelers who use it (p. 202)

U

U-boat submarine (p. 386)

ultimatum final set of demands (p. 381)

ultranationalist extreme nationalist (p. 437)

ultraroyalist émigré noble or member of the clergy in France who opposed constitutional government and favored the restoration of the old regime (p. 219)

universal manhood suffrage right of all adult men to vote (p. 217)

urbanization movement of people from rural areas to cities (p. 203)

urban renewal rebuilding of the poor areas of a city (p. 250)

utilitarianism idea that the goal of society should be to bring about the greatest happiness for the greatest number of people (p. 209)

utopia ideal society (p. 41)

V

vassal in medieval Europe, a lord who was granted land in exchange for service and loyalty to a greater lord (p. 16)

vernacular everyday language of ordinary people (p. 19)

viceroy representative who ruled one of Spain's provinces in the Americas in the king's name; one who governed in India in the name of the British monarch (pp. 87, 330)

W

war crime act that violates international rules of war (p. 551)

warm-water port port that is free of ice all year (p. 131)

welfare state system in which the government takes responsibility for its citizens' social and economic needs (p. 527)

westernization adoption of western ideas, technology, and culture (p. 129)

women's suffrage right of women to vote (p. 256)

Z

zaibatsu (ZĪ BAHT soo) since the late 1800s, powerful banking and industrial families in Japan (pp. 345, 557)

zemstvo local elected assembly set up in Russia under Alexander II (p. 284)

zeppelin large, gas-filled balloon (p. 386)

ziggurat (ZIHG oo rat) pyramid-temple dedicated to the chief god or goddess of an ancient Sumerian city-state (p. 4)

Glossary

A

abdicate/abdicar renunciar a un alto puesto oficial (pág. 188)

abolitionist/abolicionista persona que luchó para poner fin a la esclavitud en Estados Unidos (pág. 307)

absentee landlord/dueño ausente dueño de una gran propiedad que no vive en ella (pág. 298)

absolute monarch/monarca absoluto gobernante que tiene autoridad absoluta sobre la administración y la vida de los que están bajo su mando (pág. 111)

abstract/abstracto estilo artístico caracterizado por líneas, colores y formas que generalmente no tienen un tema reconocible (pág. 451)

acid rain/lluvia ácida forma de polución en la que los productos químicos tóxicos que se encuentran en el aire vuelven a la tierra en la lluvia, nieve o granizo (pág. 515)

acropolis/acrópolis el punto más alto y fortificado de una ciudad estado griega (pág. 11)

agribusiness/agroindustria gran granja comercial que pertenece a una corporación multinacional (pág. 636)

ahimsa/ahimsa creencia hindú en la no violencia y en el respeto a todas las formas de vida (pág. 430)

alliance/alianza acuerdo formal de cooperación y defensa mutua entre dos o más naciones o poderes (pág. 85)

anarchist/anarquista persona que quiere abolir toda forma de gobierno (pág. 278)

anesthetic/anestesia droga que suprime el dolor durante la cirugía (pág. 196)

annex/anexar agregar un territorio a un estado o país existente (págs. 184, 271)

annul/anular cancelar o invalidar (pág. 50)

Anschluss/Anschluss unión de Austria y Alemania (pág. 470)

apartheid/apartheid política de estricta separación racial en Sudáfrica que fue abolida en 1989 (pág. 425)

appeasement/contemporización política de aceptación de las exigencias de un agresor para mantener la paz (pág. 469)

aristocracy/aristocracia gobierno encabezado por una minoría privilegiada o de clase alta (pág. 11)

armada/armada flota de barcos (pág. 112)

armistice/armisticio acuerdo para dejar de luchar en una guerra (pág. 391)

artisan/artesano trabajador cualificado que hace objetos a mano (pág. 3)

assembly line/cadena de montaje método de producción que divide un trabajo complejo en una serie de tareas menores (pág. 244)

astrolabe/astrolabio instrumento que mide la posición de las estrellas para determinar la latitud (pág. 63)

atheism/ateísmo creencia de que Dios no existe (pág. 412)

atrocity/atrocidad acto brutal cometido en contra de inocentes (pág. 389)

autonomy/autonomía autogobierno (pág. 218)

ayatollah/ayatolá título que le se da al líder religioso musulmán chiíta que interpreta las leyes del corán (pág. 596)

B

balance of power/equilibrio de poder distribución del poder militar y económico que evita que una nación se vuelva demasiado fuerte (pág. 118)

baroque/barroco estilo artístico y arquitectónico elaborado que se dio en los siglos XVII y XVIII (pág. 151)

blitzkrieg/guerra relámpago guerra intensa y muy breve (pág. 473)

blockade/bloqueo cierre de un puerto para evitar que las personas o provisiones puedan entrar o salir (pág. 185)

bourgeoisie/burguesía clase media (pág. 167)

boyar/boyar noble ruso que poseía tierras en la época de los zares (pág. 130)

brahman/brahmán de acuerdo con la creencia aria, el poder espiritual que reside en todas las cosas (pág. 7)

C

cabinet/gabinete miembros del parlamento consejeros del rey que originalmente se reunían en un pequeño cuarto o "gabinete" (pág. 156)

caliph/califa sucesor de Mahoma como líder religioso y político de los musulmanes (pág. 22)

canonize/canonizar reconocer a alguien como santo (pág. 50)

capital/capital dinero o riqueza (pág. 199)

capital offense/ofensa capital crimen que puede castigarse con la muerte (pág. 296)

capitalism/capitalismo sistema económico por el que los medios de producción son propiedad privada y se administran para obtener beneficios (pág. 102)

caravel/carabela embarcación rápida y ligera a vela del siglo XV (pág. 63)

cartel/cartel asociación de grandes corporaciones formada para fijar precios, establecer cuotas de producción o repartirse los mercados (pág. 247)

cartographer/cartógrafo persona que hace mapas (pág. 63)

caste/casta grupo social en la sociedad tradicional de India, en el que una persona nace y del que no se puede cambiar (pág. 7)

cataract/catarata cascada, caída de agua (pág. 25)

caudillo/caudillo térmiono que se refiere a un dictador militar en América Latina (pág. 357)

cease-fire/tregua alto en la lucha (pág. 572)

censorship/censura restricción en el acceso a ideas o información (pág. 149)

Spanish Glossary

chancelor/canciller primer ministro (págs. 269, 459, 534)

chivalry/caballerosidad código de conducta de los caballeros durante la Edad Media (pág. 17)

circumnavigate/circunnavegar navegar alrededor de la Tierra (pág. 66)

city-state/ciudad estado unidad política compuesta por una ciudad y las tierras que la rodean (pág. 4)

civil disobedience/desobediencia civil negarse a obedecer leyes injustas (pág. 430)

civil rights movement/movimiento por los derechos civiles esfuerzo en las décadas de los 1950s y 1960s para acabar con la discriminación y asegurar los mismos derechos para todos los estadounidenses (pág. 539)

civil war/guerra civil guerra en la que luchan dos grupos de personas de una misma nación (pág. 85)

client state/estado dependiente nación que depende del apoyo de una potencia mayor (pág. 597)

coalition/coalición alianza temporal de varios partidos políticos (págs. 303, 536)

collaborator/colaborador persona que coopera con el enemigo (pág. 480)

collective/granja colectiva granja grande que pertenece a campesinos que la administran en grupo (pág. 407)

collective security/seguridad colectiva sistema por el que un grupo de naciones actúa como una para preservar la paz común (pág. 393)

collectivization/colectivización unión de tierras y del trabajo de varias personas o entidades para lograr una mayor eficacia (pág. 560)

colossus/coloso gigante (pág. 282)

command economy/economía de control sistema en el que los funcionarios del gobierno toman todas las decisiones económicas básicas (pág. 406)

commissar/comisario funcionario del partido comunista asignado al ejército para enseñar los principios del partido y asegurar la lealtad al mismo (pág. 404)

common law/ley común sistema legal igual para todos, basado en las decisiones de las cortes que se han vuelto principios legales aceptados (pág. 18)

commune/comuna comunidad en la que la propiedad es común, se comparte la vivienda y se cubren las necesidades físicas a cambio de trabajar en ocupaciones asignadas (pág. 561)

communism/comunismo forma de socialismo defendida por Karl Marx; según él la lucha de clases era inevitable, y llevaría a la creación de una sociedad sin clases en la que todas las propiedades pasarían a ser propiedad de la comunidad (pág. 210)

compact/pacto acuerdo (pág. 93)

compromise/acuerdo aceptación de una posición intermedia (pág. 50)

concentration camp/campo de concentración centro de detención para civiles a los que se considera enemigos del estado (pág. 463)

concession/concesión derechos económicos especiales que se dan a un poder extranjero (pág. 328)

confederation/confederación unificación (pág. 352)

conquistador/conquistador término que se refiere a los exploradores españoles que apropiaron tierras en América para España en los siglos XVI y XVII (pág. 84)

conscription/conscripción llamado a filas que exigía que todos los hombres jóvenes estuvieran listos para el servicio militar u otro servicio (pág. 388)

constitutional government/gobierno constitucional gobierno cuyo poder está definido y limitado por la ley (pág. 155)

containment/contención política de la Guerra Fría para limitar el comunismo a las áreas bajo control soviético (pág. 491)

contra/contra guerrilla que luchaba contra los sandinistas en Nicaragua (pág. 644)

convoy/convoy grupo de barcos mercantes protegidos por barcos de guerra (pág. 386)

corporation/corporación negocio propiedad de muchos inversores que compran acciones, y sólo arriesgan el monto de su inversión (pág. 247)

creole/criollo descendiente de colonos españoles nacido en las colonias españolas de América (págs. 89, 225)

crusade/cruzada guerra santa (pág. 19)

cult of domesticity/culto a lo doméstico idealización de las mujeres y del hogar (pág. 254)

cultural diffusion/difusión cultural divulgación de ideas, costumbres y tecnología a distintos pueblos o culturas (pág. 4)

cuneiform/cuneiforme tipo de escritura de los antiguos sumerios cuyos caracteres tenían forma de cuña (pág. 5)

cyclone/ciclón fuerte tormenta de viento de forma circular (pág. 584)

czar/zar título del regente del imperio ruso (pág. 21)

D

daimyo/daimio señor de la guerra que en el Japón feudal estaba directamente abajo del shogún (pág. 27)

debt service/obligación de deuda pago de interés sobre préstamos (pág. 584)

default/cese de pagos imposibilidad de realizar pagos (pág. 544)

deficit/déficit lapso entre los gastos de un gobierno y las recaudaciones por impuestos y otras fuentes de ingresos (pág. 538)

deficit spending/gasto deficitario situación en la que un gobierno gasta más de lo que recauda (pág. 168)

deforestation/deforestación destrucción de tierras forestales (págs. 331, 584)

delta/delta área triangular de tierra pantanosa que se forma en la boca de algunos ríos con los depósitos de limo (pág. 594)

democracy/democracia gobierno en el que es el pueblo quien tiene el poder de gobernar (pág. 11)

depopulation/despoblación reducción del número de la población (pág. 126)

desalination/desalinización proceso para convertir el agua salada del mar en agua dulce (pág. 588)

desertification/desertización proceso por el que la tierra fértil o semifértil se convierte en desierto (pág. 614)

détente/distensión relajamiento de las tensiones entre Estados Unidos y la Unión Soviética de los 1970s (pág. 527)

diaspora/diáspora diseminación de un pueblo (pág. 5)

diet/asamblea legislatura o asamblea legislativa (pág. 345)

direct democracy/democracia directa sistema de gobierno en el que los ciudadanos participan directamente en lugar de a través de representantes electos en los asuntos del día a día del gobierno (pág. 11)

disarmament/desarme reducción de las fuerzas armadas y del armamento (pág. 445)

dissenter/disidente protestante cuyos puntos de vista y opiniones diferían de los de la Iglesia de Inglaterra (pág. 120)

dissident/disidente alguien que habla en contra del gobierno (pág. 542)

divine right/derecho divino creencia de que la autoridad de un gobernante proviene directamente de Dios (pág. 111)

dominion/dominio nación que se gobierna a sí misma (pág. 352)

domino theory/teoría del dominó creencia de que si una nación caía ante el comunismo, las naciones vecinas también caerían, como una hilera de piezas de dominó (pág. 571)

Duma/Duma en Rusia, asamblea legislativa nacional electa (pág. 287)

dynamo/dinamo máquina que se usa para generar electricidad (pág. 244)

dynastic cycle/ciclo dinástico florecimiento y caída de las dinastías chinas de acuerdo con el Mandato del Cielo (pág. 7)

dynasty/dinastía familia gobernante (pág. 7)

E

e-commerce/comercio electrónico comercio y negocios que se realizan en Internet (pág. 518)

economic dependence/dependencia económica relación económica controlada por una nación desarrollada, en la que una nación menos desarrollada exporta materias primas e importa objetos manufacturados, capital y conocimiento tecnológico (pág. 357)

ejido/**ejido** cooperativa de campesinos mexicanos (pág. 642)

elector/elector uno de los siete príncipes germanos que elegían al emperador sagrado de Roma (pág. 125)

electorate/electorado conjunto de personas a quienes se permite votar (pág. 293)

elite/élite clase alta (pág. 324)

emancipation/emancipación concesión de libertad a esclavos o siervos (pág. 284)

embargo/embargo prohibición de comerciar (págs. 572, 638)

emigration/emigración trasladarse de su propio país a otro (pág. 278)

émigré/exiliado persona que deja su país por razones políticas (pág. 174)

empire/imperio grupo de estados o territorios controlados por un gobernante (pág. 3)

enclosure/cercamiento en Inglaterra en el siglo XVIII, el proceso de apropiación y cercado de tierras públicas (pág. 197)

encomienda/encomienda derecho a exigir tributo o trabajo a los nativos americanos, que el gobierno español otorgó a sus colonos en América (pág. 88)

engraving/grabado forma de arte en la que un artista graba un diseño con ácido en una placa de metal y después la usa para producir múltiples impresiones (pág. 40)

enlightened despot/déspota ilustrado gobernante absoluto que usa su poder para precipitar cambios políticos y sociales (pág. 150)

entente/pacto acuerdo no obligatorio de seguir una política en común (pág. 379)

entrepreneur/empresario persona que asume riesgos financieros con la esperanza de obtener beneficios (pág. 102)

environmentalist/ecologista quien saca a la luz las amenazas contra el frágil medio ambiente del planeta (pág. 515)

ethics/ética estándar moral de conducta (pág. 5)

ethnic cleansing/limpieza étnica política de matar o expulsar a las personas de ciertos grupos étnicos (pág. 550)

ethnic group/grupo étnico grupo grande de personas que comparten el idioma y la herencia cultural (pág. 21)

euro/euro moneda usada por las naciones que pertenecen a la Unión Europea (pág. 530)

excommunication/excomunión exclusión de la Iglesia Católica Romana como castigo por negarse a obedecer las leyes de la iglesia (pág. 19)

expansionism/expansionismo política de aumentar el territorio que posee un gobierno (pág. 306)

extraterritoriality/extraterritorialidad derecho de los extranjeros a recibir protección de las leyes de su propio país (pág. 334)

Spanish Glossary

F

faction/facción grupo pequeño (pág. 171)

factory/fábrica lugar donde los trabajadores y las máquinas producen grandes cantidades de mercaderías (pág. 200)

favela/*favela* en Brasil, barriada de casas muy pobres (pág. 650)

federal republic/república federal gobierno en el que el poder se divide entre el gobierno nacional o federal y los estados (pág. 161)

federal system/sistema federal sistema en el que el poder se divide entre un gobierno central fuerte y los gobiernos locales (pág. 581)

feminist movement/movimiento feminista movimiento que procura el acceso igualitario de las mujeres al trabajo y las promociones, igualdad de salario por un igual trabajo y el fin del acoso sexual (pág. 517)

feudalism/feudalismo vago sistema de gobierno en el que los señores gobernaban sus propias tierras pero debían servicio militar y otras formas de apoyo a un superior (pág. 16)

fief/feudo en la Edad Media, propiedad que el señor daba a un vasallo a cambio de servicios y lealtad (pág. 16)

filial piety/piedad filial respeto hacia los padres (pág. 9)

flapper/*flapper* mujer joven y rebelde de los 1920s en Estados Unidos y Europa (pág. 454)

free trade/libre comercio comercio entre países, sin cuotas, tasas u otras restricciones (pág. 295)

fundamentalist/fundamentalista persona que pone énfasis en los valores fundamentales o básicos de su fe (pág. 517)

G

general strike/huelga general huelga de trabajadores de muchas industrias diferentes al mismo tiempo (pág. 446)

genetic engineering/ingeniería genética alteración del código genético que portan todas las formas de vida (pág. 518)

genocide/genocidio intento deliberado de destruir la totalidad de un grupo religioso o étnico (págs. 327, 479)

germ theory/teoría de los gérmenes idea de que ciertos microbios podrían causar enfermedades infecciosas específicas (pág. 249)

ghetto/ghetto área separada de una ciudad donde se fuerza a vivir a los miembros de una minoría (pág. 53)

glasnost/*glasnost* política de apertura instituida por el líder soviético Mikhail Gorbachev de los 1980s (pág. 544)

global warming/calentamiento global aumento de la temperatura del planeta (pág. 515)

gravity/gravedad fuerza que atrae una masa u objeto hacia otro (pág. 56)

griot/*griot* antiguo narrador de historias profesional en África Occidental (pág. 25)

gross domestic product/producto interior bruto valor de todos los productos y servicios producidos por una nación (pág. 557)

guerrilla warfare/guerra de guerrillas lucha que se caracteriza por rápidos ataques y retiradas (pág. 186)

guild/gremio en la Edad Media, asociación de comerciantes o artesanos que cooperaban para proteger sus intereses económicos (pág. 17)

H

habeas corpus/habeas corpus principio por el que no puede encarcelarse a una persona sin haber sido antes condenada formalmente por un crimen específico (pág. 124)

hajj/hayyi uno de los Cinco Pilares del Islam, la peregrinación a la Meca que se espera hagan todos los musulmanes por lo menos una vez en la vida (pág. 22)

harijan/*harijan* "niño de Dios", término usado por Gandhi para designar a un intocable de la sistema de castas (pág. 583)

hejab/*hejab* vestido tradicional usado por las mujeres musulmanas (pág. 591)

heliocentric/heliocéntrico sistema basado en la creencia de que el sol es el centro del universo (pág. 54)

hierarchy/jerarquía sistema que clasifica a las personas de una sociedad (pág. 4)

home rule/autogobierno autogobierno local (pág. 300)

homogeneous society/sociedad homogénea sociedad que tiene un lenguaje y una cultura común (pág. 346)

humanism/humanismo movimiento intelectual en el apogeo del Renacimiento italiano centrado en temas de este mundo en lugar de en temas religiosos (pág. 35)

humanities/humanidades estudio de materias que se enseñaban en la antigua Grecia y Roma, tales como gramática, retórica, poesía e historia (pág. 36)

human rights/derechos humanos básico derechos y libertades (pág. 508)

hypothesis/hipótesis explicación posible (pág. 55)

I

ideology/ideología sistema de pensamiento y creencias (págs. 216, 505)

immunity/inmunidad protección natural (pág. 84)

imperialism/imperialismo dominio por parte de un país de la vida política, económica o cultural de otro país o región (pág. 316)

import substitution/substitución de importaciones política del gobierno de alentar a los fabricantes locales para que produzcan mercaderías que reemplacen importaciones (pág. 635)

impressionism/impresionismo escuela de pintura de finales del siglo XIX y principios del siglo XX que trataba de captar impresiones visuales fugaces (pág. 263)

indemnity/indemnización compensación como pago por pérdidas de guerra (pág. 334)

indigenous/indígena original o nativo de un país o región (pág. 351)

indulgence/indulgencia perdón por los pecados cometidos en vida concedido por la Iglesia Católica Romana (pág. 44)

inflation/inflación ciclo económico caracterizado por un rápida subida de los precios ligada a un aumento rápido del dinero disponible (pág. 102)

intendant/intendente oficial nombrado por el rey francés Luis XIV para gobernar las provincias, recaudar impuestos y reclutar soldados (pág. 116)

interchangeable parts/repuestos intercambiables componentes idénticos que pueden usarse unos en lugar de los otros en el proceso de producción (pág. 244)

interdependence/interdependencia dependencia mutua de los países con los de otras partes del mundo en cuanto a productos, recursos y conocimiento (pág. 507)

intifada/intifada rebelión masiva de los palestinos en territorios ocupados por Israel (pág. 598)

island-hopping/salteo de islas método usado por las fuerzas aliadas para recapturar ciertas islas del Pacífico en poder de los japoneses, mientras salteaban otras (pág. 486)

isolationism/aislamiento política de intervención limitada en asuntos de orden mundial (pág. 311)

J

jihad/yihad en el Islam, un esfuerzo al servicio de Dios (pág. 319)

joint stock company/compañía de capital social compañía comercial privada cuyas acciones se venden a inversores para financiar aventuras empresariales (pág. 102)

joint venture/empresa en común negocio organizado por dos partes, que comparten las ganancias (pág. 563)

jury/jurado grupo de personas que bajo juramento deben tomar una decisión en un caso legal (pág. 18)

K

kaiser/kaiser emperador de Alemania (pág. 271)

kamikaze/kamikaze piloto japonés que emprendía una misión suicida (pág. 487)

kibbutz/kibbutz granja colectiva en Israel (pág. 588)

kiva/kiva gran cámara subterránea usada por los anazasi para realizar ceremonias religiosas (pág. 15)

knight/caballero en Europa medieval, noble que servía como guerrero a caballo para un señor (pág. 16)

kulak/kulak campesino adinerado de la Unión Soviética de los 1930s (pág. 408)

Kulturkampf/Kulturkampf "batalla por la civilización" de Bismarck, cuyo objetivo era que los católicos pusieran la lealtad al estado por encima de la lealtad a la Iglesia (pág. 273)

L

labor union/sindicato organización de trabajadores (pág. 207)

laissez faire/*laissez faire* política que permite que los negocios operen con poca o ninguna intervención del estado (pág. 148)

legitimacy/legitimidad principio por el que las monarquías que habían sido derrocadas por la Revolución Francesa o por Napoleón debían restituirse (pág. 191)

levée/recepción matutina ritual de la mañana en el que los nobles atendían al rey Luis XIV (pág. 116)

libel/libelo publicación intencional de declaraciones falsas que perjudican a alguien (pág. 304)

liberation theology/teología de la liberación movimiento de los 1960s y 1970s que urgía a la Iglesia Católica Romana a adoptar un rol más activo para cambiar las condiciones sociales que contribuían a la pobreza y la opresión en Latinoamérica (págs. 517, 637)

limited monarchy/monarquía limitada gobierno en el que la constitución o el cuerpo legislativo limitan los poderes de la monarquía (pág. 124)

literacy rate/tasa de alfabetización porcentaje de personas que pueden leer y escribir (pág. 638)

Loyalist/*Loyalist* colono leal a Gran Bretaña durante la Revolución Norteamericana (pág. 160)

M

mandate/mandato territorio administrado por un poder occidental después de la Primera Guerra Mundial (pág. 394)

manor/feudo propiedad de un Señor que incluía uno o más pueblos y las tierras que los rodeaban en la Edad Media en Europa (pág. 17)

*maquiladora/***maquiladora** planta industrial mexicana de dueños extranjeros en la que los trabajadores locales ensamblan partes importadas para obtener productos acabados (pág. 643)

margin buying/transacción a crédito operación en la que se paga parte del costo total de unas acciones, y se pide prestado el resto a los corredores de bolsa (pág. 446)

matrilineal/matrilineal organización familiar en la que los lazos de parentesco se siguen a través de la madre (pág. 68)

means of production/medios de producción granjas, fábricas, ferrocarriles y otros grandes negocios que producen y distribuyen mercancías (pág. 210)

mercantilism/mercantilismo política por la que una nación trataba de exportar más de lo que importaba para aumentar sus reservas de oro y plata (pág. 104)

mercenary/mercenario soldado que sirve en un ejército extranjero a cambio de dinero (pág. 126)

messiah/mesías salvador enviado por Dios (pág. 13)

mestizo/mestizo persona de las colonias españolas de América descendiente de nativos y europeos (págs. 89, 225)

militarism/militarismo glorificación de los militares (pág. 379)

militia/milicia tropas de soldados civiles (pág. 600)

missionary/misionero persona a quien se envía en una misión religiosa (pág. 319)

mixed economy/economía mixta sistema económico que combina empresas estatales y privadas (pág. 614)

mobilize/mobilizar preparar las fuerzas militares para la guerra (pág. 381)

modernization/modernización construir un gobierno estable mientras se desarrolla económicamente un país (pág. 505)

monarchy/monarquía gobierno en el que el poder reside en el rey o la reina (pág. 11)

monopoly/monopolio control total de un producto o negocio por una persona o grupo (pág. 99)

monotheistic/monoteísta creencia en un solo Dios (pág. 5)

mosque/mezquita templo musulmán (pág. 23)

mulatto/mulato en las colonias españolas de América, descendiente de africanos y europeos (págs. 89, 225)

multinational corporation/corporación multinacional empresa con sucursales en muchos países (pág. 511)

mutual-aid society/sociedad de socorro mutuo grupo de auto apoyo establecido para ayudar a los trabajadores enfermos o heridos en accidente laboral (pág. 251)

mystic/místico persona que dedica su vida a buscar verdades espirituales (pág. 7)

N

nationalism/nacionalismo fuerte sentimiento de orgullo y devoción hacia el propio país (pág. 181)

nationalization/nacionalización apropiación de propiedades o recursos por parte del gobierno (pág. 422)

natural law/ley natural reglas o leyes que gobiernan la naturaleza humana (pág. 144)

natural right/derecho natural derechos que todas las personas tienen desde el momento en que nacen (pág. 145)

neutrality/neutralidad política de no apoyar en una guerra a ninguno de los bandos (pág. 381)

nirvana/nirvana en el budismo, unión con el universo y liberación del ciclo de la reencarnación (pág. 8)

no-fly zone/zona de vuelo prohibido área sobre la que no se permitía volar a los aviones iraquíes después de la Guerra del Golfo Persa (pág. 601)

nomad/nómada persona que se traslada de un lugar a otro en busca de alimentos (pág. 2)

no man's land/tierra de nadie área de tierra vacía donde la guerra lo ha destruido todo (pág. 385)

nonaligned/no alineado que no se alía con ninguno de los bandos en un conflicto (pág. 505)

nuclear family/familia nuclear unidad familiar que consiste en los padres y sus hijos (pág. 25)

O

oligarchy/oligarquía gobierno en el que el poder de gobernar está en manos de unas pocas personas (pág. 11)

one-party system/sistema de partido único país que tiene un solo partido político (pág. 613)

outpost/puesto de avanzada estacionamiento militar distante (pág. 71)

overproduction/superproducción condición en la que la producción de mercancías excede la demanda (pág. 445)

P

pacifism/pacifismo oposición a las guerras (págs. 376, 469)

padi/arrozal campo de arroz (pág. 70)

pandemic/pandemia propagación de una enfermedad a una gran área, país, continente o al mundo entero (pág. 392)

partition/partición parte, división (págs. 133, 580)

pasha/bajá gobernante provincial del imperio otomano (pág. 326)

patrician/patricio miembro de la clase alta terrateniente en la antigua Roma (pág. 12)

patron/mecenas persona que proporciona apoyo financiero a la cultura y las artes (pág. 35)

penal colony/colonia penal lugar al que se manda a los condenados por crímenes (pág. 296)

peninsular/peninsular miembro de la clase más alta en las colonias españolas de América (págs. 88, 225)

peon/peón trabajador forzado a trabajar para un terrateniente para pagar una deuda (pág. 88)

peonage/peonaje sistema en el que los trabajadores deben trabajo como pago por sus deudas (pág. 359)

perestroika/perestroika reestructuración del gobierno y la economía soviética de los 1980s(pág. 544)

perspective/perspectiva técnica artística usada para lograr el efecto de tercera dimensión en dibujos y pinturas (pág. 37)

pharaoh/faraón título de los gobernantes del antiguo Egipto (pág. 4)

philosophe/philosophe miembro de un grupo de pensadores de la Ilustración que trataron de aplicar métodos científicos para mejorar la sociedad (pág. 145)

physiocrat/fisiócrata pensador de la Ilustración que buscaba leyes naturales para explicar la economía (pág. 148)

pictogram/pictograma dibujo utilizado para representar una palabra (pág. 3)

plantation/plantación gran propiedad administrada por un dueño o capataz y cultivada por trabajadores que viven en ella (pág. 88)

plebeian/plebeyo en la antigua Roma, miembro de clase baja, que incluía granjeros, mercaderes, artesanos y comerciantes (pág. 12)

plebiscite/plebiscito votación en la que los votantes expresan su opinión sobre un tema en particular (págs. 182, 651)

pogrom/pogrom ataque violento de una multitud hacia una comunidad judía (pág. 286)

polis/ciudad estado ciudad de la antigua Grecia que tenía su propio gobierno (pág. 11)

polygamy/poligamia costumbre que permite a los hombres tener más que una esposa (pág. 426)

polytheistic/politeísta creencia en muchos dioses (pág. 7)

predestination/predestinación idea de que Dios determinó hace mucho tiempo quién alcanzaría la salvación (pág. 48)

premier/*premier* primer ministro (pág. 303)

prime minister/primer ministro jefe del gabinete en un gobierno parlamentario; generalmente el líder del partido mayoritario de la legislatura (pág. 156)

privateer/bucanero pirata (pág. 91)

privatization/privatización venta de industrias del estado a inversores privados (pág. 512)

proletariat/proletariado clase trabajadora (págs. 211, 400)

propaganda/propaganda divulgación de ideas para promover cierta causa o para perjudicar una causa opuesta (pág. 388)

prophet/profeta líder espiritual a quien se le atribuye la interpretación de la voluntad de Dios (pág. 5)

protectorate/protectorado país con su propio gobierno pero que está bajo el control de una potencia exterior (pág. 318)

provisional/provisional temporal (pág. 303)

psychoanalysis/psicoanálisis método que estudia el funcionamiento de la mente y trata los desórdenes mentales (pág. 451)

R

racism/racismo creencia de que un grupo racial es superior a otro (pág. 259)

radar/radar mecanismo usado para detectar el vuelo de aviones (pág. 474)

realism/realismo movimiento artístico cuyo objetivo era representar el mundo tal como es (pág. 261)

Realpolitik/Realpolitik política realista basada en las necesidades del estado (pág. 269)

recant/retractarse abandonar las propias creencias o puntos de vista (pág. 45)

recession/recesión período de reducción de la actividad económica (págs. 220, 528)

recognize/reconocer aceptar formalmente tratar a un país como un estado legítimo con un gobierno legítimo (pág. 587)

regionalism/regionalismo lealtad a un área local (pág. 357)

Reich/Reich imperio alemán (pág. 271)

reincarnation/reencarnación en el hinduismo, creencia del renacimiento del alma en otra forma corporal (pág. 8)

reparation/indemnización pago por daños de guerra o daños causados por encarcelamiento (págs. 392, 482)

repeal/revocar cancelar (págs. 98, 296)

republic/república sistema de gobierno en el que los gobernantes son elegidos por el pueblo (pág. 12)

repudiate/repudiar rechazar (pág. 461)

revenue/rentas públicas dinero que se recauda por impuestos (pág. 93)

rococo/rococó estilo artístico y arquitectónico elegante y personal que se dio a mediados del siglo XVIII y que presentaba sofisticados diseños en forma de hojas, conchas marinas y volutas (pág. 151)

romanticism/romanticismo movimiento artístico del siglo XIX que apelaba a la emoción más que a la razón (pág. 260)

rotten borough/"distrito podrido" en Inglaterra, ciudad rural que enviaba miembros al parlamento a pesar de no tener o tener pocos votantes (pág. 293)

S

sacrament/sacramento ritual sagrado de la Iglesia Católica Romana (pág. 19)

salon/salón reunión social informal en la que escritores, artistas y filósofos intercambian ideas; comenzó en Francia en el siglo XVII (pág. 149)

samurai/samurai miembro de la clase guerrera en la sociedad japonesa feudal (pág. 27)

sanction/sanción pena (pág. 468)

satellite/satélite término que se refiere a un estado dependiente (pág. 492)

sati/sati costumbre hindú que requería que la esposa se uniera a su marido en la muerte por arrojándose a su pira funeraria (pág. 329)

scapegoat/chivo expiatorio persona, grupo o cosa a quien se culpa por los crímenes o faltas de otros (pág. 52)

schism/cisma división permanente de una iglesia (pág. 20)

Spanish Glossary

scientific method/método científico método concienzudo que se usa para confirmar hallazgos y poner a prueba hipótesis (pág. 55)

scribe/escriba en las civilizaciones antiguas, persona especialmente entrenada que sabía leer, escribir y mantener registros (pág. 5)

scurvy/escorbuto enfermedad causada por la falta de vitamina C en la dieta (pág. 63)

secede/separar retirarse (pág. 309)

secret ballot/voto secreto votos que se dan sin hacerlos públicos (pág. 293)

sect/secta pequeño grupo religioso (pág. 13)

secular/secular que tiene que ver más con asuntos mundanos que religiosos (pág. 17)

segregation/segregación separación de las razas (pág. 539)

self-determination/autodeterminación derecho de los pueblos a elegir su propia forma de gobierno (pág. 391)

separatism/separatismo movimiento que apoyaba la separación de Quebec de Canadá y buscaba el hacer de Quebec una nación independiente (pág. 540)

sepoy/cipayo soldado de India que servía en un ejército inglés o francés de la East India Company (págs. 74, 329)

serf/siervo en la Europa medieval, campesino ligado a la tierra del Señor (pág. 17)

service industry/industria de servicios industria que ofrece servicios en vez de productos (pág. 528)

shantytown/ciudad perdida viviendas precarias en las afueras de una ciudad que carecen de servicios básicos como agua corriente (pág. 516)

shogun/shogún en la sociedad feudal japonesa, jefe militar supremo con más poder que el emperador (pág. 27)

smelt/fundir fundir mineral para separar el mineral puro del desperdicio (pág. 198)

social contract/contrato social acuerdo por el que las personas entregan su libertad a un gobierno poderoso para evitar el caos (pág. 145)

social gospel/evangelio social movimiento del siglo XIX que urgía a los cristianos a que hicieran el servicio social (pág. 259)

socialism/socialismo sistema en el que el pueblo como un todo, más que los individuos, son dueños de todas la propiedades y manejan todos los negocios (pág. 210)

socialist realism/realismo socialista estilo artístico cuyo objetivo era promover el socialismo mostrando la vida en la Unión Soviética desde una perspectiva positiva (pág. 413)

social welfare/bienestar social programas de ayuda a las personas necesitadas (pág. 274)

sonar/sonar aparato que se usa para detectar la ruta de los submarinos (pág. 474)

soviet/soviet consejo de trabajadores y soldados establecido por los revolucionarios rusos en 1917 (pág. 401)

special enterprise zone/zona especial de empresas área en China donde los extranjeros pueden dirigir y ser dueños de industrias (pág. 563)

sphere of influence/esfera de influencia área en la que un poder exterior se reserva privilegios comerciales o la exclusividad de realizar inversiones exclusivas (pág. 318)

squatter/ocupante ilegal persona que se establece en tierras que no le pertenecen (pág. 653)

stalemate/punto muerto estancamiento en una confrontación, en el que ninguna de las partes puede vencer a la otra (pág. 383)

standard of living/estándar de vida medida de la calidad y disponibilidad de las necesidades básicas y de los lujos en una sociedad (pág. 252)

stock/acciones títulos o valores de una compañía (pág. 247)

stream of consciousness/flujo de conciencia técnica literaria que investiga pensamientos y sentimientos de un personaje, al azar (pág. 452)

stupa/*stupa* gran altar budista en forma de cúpula (pág. 69)

suffrage/sufragio derecho al voto (pág. 176)

sultan/sultán gobernante musulmán (pág. 23)

summit/cumbre reunión de líderes y expertos de distintas partes del mundo (pág. 507)

superpower/superpotencia nación lo suficientemente poderosa como para influir en los actos y políticas de otras naciones (pág. 505)

surplus/excedente exceso, extra (pág. 539)

surrealism/surrealismo movimiento artístico que trata de mostrar el funcionamiento del inconciente (pág. 451)

T

tariff/tasa impuesto a mercancías importadas (pág. 104)

temperance movement/campaña de moderación campaña para limitar o prohibir el uso de bebidas alcohólicas (pág. 256)

tenement building/inquilinato edificio de varios pisos dividido en apartamentos llenos de gente (pág. 203)

terrorism/terrorismo uso deliberado de la violencia al azar, especialmente en contra de civiles, para lograr fines políticos (pág. 509)

theocracy/teocracia gobierno administrado por líderes religiosos (págs. 48, 596)

total war/estado de guerra canalización de todos los recursos de una nación hacia la guerra (pág. 388)

totalitarian state/estado totalitario gobierno en el que una dictadura de partido único regula todos los aspectos de la vida de los ciudadanos (pág. 411)

trade deficit/déficit comercial situación en la que un país importa más de lo que exporta (págs. 333, 557)

trade surplus/excedente comercial situación en la que un país exporta más de lo que importa (pág. 333)

Spanish Glossary

triangular trade/comercio triangular ruta colonial de comercio entre Europa y sus colonias en las Indias Occidentales y África, en donde las mercancías se cambiaban por esclavos (pág. 98)

tributary state/estado tributario estado independiente que debe reconocer la supremacía de otro estado y pagar tributo a su gobernante (pág. 26)

tribute/tributo pago obligatorio de los pueblos conquistados a los conquistadores (pág. 14)

truce/tregua paz temporaria (pág. 226)

turnpike/carretera de peaje camino construido por intereses privados que cobran un peaje a los viajeros que lo usan (pág. 202)

U

U-boat/submarino nave que puede viajar bajo el agua (pág. 386)

ultimatum/ultimatum conjunto final de exigencias (pág. 381)

ultranationalist/ultranacionalista nacionalista extremo (pág. 437)

ultraroyalist/ultrarealista en Francia, noble exiliado o miembro de la iglesia que se oponía al régimen constitucional y apoyaba la reinstauración del antiguo régimen (pág. 219)

universal manhood suffrage/sufragio universal masculino derecho de todos los hombres adultos a votar (pág. 217)

urbanization/urbanización movimiento de personas de las áreas rurales a las ciudades (pág. 203)

urban renewal/renovación urbana reconstrucción de las áreas pobres de una ciudad (pág. 250)

utilitarianism/utilitarismo idea de que el objetivo de la sociedad debería ser lograr la mayor felicidad posible para el mayor número posible de personas (pág. 209)

utopia/utopía sociedad ideal (pág. 41)

V

vassal/vasallo en la Europa Medieval, señor a quien se le otorgaron tierras a cambio de servicios y lealtad a un señor más poderoso (pág. 16)

vernacular/vernacular lenguaje diario de las personas comunes (pág. 19)

viceroy/virrey representante que regía una de las provincias de España en las Américas en nombre del rey; quien gobernaba en India en nombre del monarca británico (págs. 87, 330)

W

war crime/crimen de guerra acto que viola las leyes internacionales de guerra (pág. 551)

warm-water port/puerto de aguas templadas puerto que carece de hielo en todo el año (pág. 131)

welfare state/estado de bienestar social sistema en el que el gobierno acepta la responsabilidad de las necesidades sociales y económicas de sus ciudadanos (pág. 527)

westernization/occidentalización adopción de las ideas, tecnología y cultura occidentales (pág. 129)

women's suffrage/sufragio femenino derecho de las mujeres a votar (pág. 256)

Z

zaibatsu/*zaibatsu* familias japonesas de banqueros e industriales poderosos desde finales del siglo XIX (págs. 345, 557)

zemstvo/*zemstvo* asamblea local electa que se estableció en Rusia en la época de Alejandro II (pág. 284)

zeppelin/zepelín dirigible, gran globo lleno de gas (pág. 386)

ziggurat/zigurat templo piramidal dedicado al dios o diosa principal de una antigua ciudad estado sumeria (pág. 4)

Spanish Glossary

Index

Italicized letters after page numbers refer to the following: *c* = chart; *g* = graph; *m* = map; *n* = footnote; *p* = picture; *ps* = primary source.

A

Abaid Amaan Karume, 620
Abbassid dynasty, 22
abolitionists, 307
Aborigine
　definition of, 353
absolute monarchies, 111, 115–116, 119, 120, 145, 283
Academy Awards, 452
Achebe, Chinua, 713*ps*
acid rain, 515, 540
Acosta, Joseph, 101*ps*
Acropolis, 11
Act of Supremacy, 50, 119
Act of Union, 142
activities
　Internet, 59, 86, 107, 135, 163, 193, 213, 233, 265, 289, 313, 339, 367, 397, 417, 441, 465, 495, 523, 553, 577, 603, 629, 655
　Portfolio, 31, 141, 239, 373, 501
　Unit Theme, 138, 236, 370, 498
Adams, John, 159
adaptation, 2
Address to the Congress of Venezuela (Bolívar), 705*ps*
Adenauer, Konrad, 534
Adowa, battle of, 324
Adventures in the Rifle Brigade (Kincaid), 193*ps*
Aegean Sea, 10
Affonso, king of Kongo, 98, 98*p*, 698*ps*
Afghanistan, 542, 585, 601
Africa
　in 1800s, 319–320
　"African diaspora," 627
　African Union, 611
　AIDS in, 615
　and apartheid, 508
　Bantu migrations, 24
　and Berlin Conference, 241, 315, 322
　and Christianity, 24, 25, 616–617, 619
　cities first developed in, 2–3
　civil wars in, 613, 619
　and coffee prices, 640
　and Cold War, 610–611, 626
　colonial legacy in, 606
　debt crisis in, 614–615
　deforestation in, 615
　desertification in, 615*m*
　drought in, 615
　European colonization of, 96
　famines in, 424, 615
　Greenbelt movement, 615
　health care in, 607, 617*p*
　imperialism in 1914, 321*m*
　Islam in, 24, 25, 617
　kingdoms and trading states

of, 24–25, 24*m*
　land claims in 1675, 83*m*
　military rule in, 613, 619
　mixed economic policies in, 614
　National Liberation Front (FLN), 610
　nationalism in, 607, 609
　nations emerging in, 605*m*
　and *négritude* movement, 425
　and oil industry, 618*p*
　Organization of African Unity (OAU), 611
　Pan-African Congress, 425, 441
　parliamentary systems in, 612
　reforms in, 613
　religion in, 24, 25
　resistance to colonial rule, 324, 424–425
　resistance to slave trade, 98
　rise of new states in, 99–100
　slave trade, 88, 96–98, 320
　time line for, 2–3, 8–9, 16–17
　and trade, 315*m*
　and United Nations, 611
　urbanization in, 616
　wildlife preservation, 614
　and World War I, 387
　and World War II, 474, 482–483, 607*p*.
　See also specific countries
African Americans
　and *Brown* v. *Board of Education of Topeka,* 539
　emancipation of, 309
　and Fifteenth Amendment, 308, 309
　and Liberia, 195
　and music, 452–453
　and segregation, 309, 539
　and voting, 161, 307, 308, 309, 539.
　See also slavery
"African diaspora," 627
African National Congress (ANC), 425, 623
Afrikaners, 623, 624
Age of Exploration, 60–66
Age of Reason, 144–150.
　See also Enlightenment
agriculture
　agribusinesses, 636
　collective farming, 407–409, 542, 560, 670
　and Columbian Exchange, 101
　corn, 76, 101
　and enclosure, 197
　farming in Old Stone Age, 2
　Green Revolution, 502, 520
　Industrial Revolution and agricultural revolution, 197
　of Native Americans, 76, 95
　and population growth, 2
　potatoes, 76, 101, 150, 223, 298–300, 340
Aguinaldo, Emilio, 350

Agustín I, emperor of Mexico, 229
ahimsa, 430
AIDS, 512, 518, 615
airplanes, 241, 246, 267, 386
Akbar the Great, 74, 108
Akhmatova, Anna, 415
Akira Kurosawa, 521
Akkad, 5
Alaska, 306
Albanians, 509, 551
Albert, prince of England, 293
Albuquerque, Afonso de, 71
alcoholism, 250
Alexander I, czar of Russia, 187, 190, 283
Alexander II, czar of Russia, 241, 283–284
Alexander III, czar of Russia, 284, 286
Alexander VI, Pope, 64
Alexander the Great, 11
Alexandra, czarina of Russia, 400, 401
Alexandria, 11
Algeria, 314, 322, 324, 326, 482, 533, 610
Algonquins, 95
Alighieri, Dante, 19
All Quiet on the Western Front (Remarque), 444*ps*, 452, 462, 708*ps*
Allende, Salvador, 639
Alliance for Progress, 640
alphabets, 5, 27
al-Qaida, 509, 585, 590, 601
Alsace, 376, 393, 448
Alvarado, Pedro de, 85*p*
Amado, Gilbert, 357
Amazon rain forest, 640, 641
Amazon River, 650
American Federation of Labor, 311
American Revolution, 160, 160*m*, 168, 171
Americas
　colonial power struggles in, 94
　conquest in, 84–86
　cultural blending in, 89, 89*p*
　early civilizations in, 14–15
　horses introduced in, 89
　land claims in 1675, 83*m*
　land claims about 1750, 94*m*
　Spanish empire in, 85–86
　time line for, 2–3, 8–9, 16–17
　See also Middle America; North America; South America; *see also* specific countries
Amin, Idi, 613
Amish, 49
Amritsar massacre, 429
Anabaptists, 49
Analyzing Cartoons
　See skills
Analyzing Cause and Effect
　See skills
Analyzing Charts and Graphs
　See skills

Analyzing Paintings and Drawings
　See skills
Analyzing Photographs
　See skills
Analyzing Primary Sources
　See skills
Analyzing Propaganda
　See skills
anarchists, definition of, 278
Anasazis, 15, 16
Anawrata, king of Burma, 67, 69
ANC
　See African National Congress (ANC)
And Quiet Flows the Don (Sholokhov), 415
And They Are Like Wild Beasts (Goya), 187*p*
Andes mountains, 15, 230
anesthetic, 196, 250
Angkor Wat, 68, 69
Anglican Church, 50, 156
Angola, 322, 513, 626, 627, 639
Anguissola, Sofonisba, 37
annulment, 49
　See also divorce
Antarctica, 505
Anthony, Susan B., 256
antisemitism, 304, 428, 459, 460
apartheid, 425, 508, 678–679
apartments, 90
appeasement, definition of, 469
Aquino, Benigno, 573
Aquino, Corazon, 573, 573*p*, 689
Arab, Egypt as Arab leader, 593–594
Arabia, 22
Arab League, 587
Arafat, Yasir, 598
Arbenz, Jacobo, 639
architecture
　acropolis, 11
　apartment buildings of Native Americans, 90
　Bauhaus school, 452
　and civilization, 2
　and Industrial Revolution, 196
　mosques, 23
　Native American architecture, 90
　of the Renaissance, 37
　skyscrapers, 196, 250
　ziggurats, 5
Argentina
　case study of, 678–681
　democracy in, 631, 678–681
　demographics on, 679
　"dirty war" in, 649, 678
　economic activity in, 649*m*
　economic growth in 19th century, 357
　gross domestic product (GDP), 679
　independence from Spain, 230
　inflation in, 678
　and Mercosur, 636, 640

Index

military rule in, 634, 649
and Perón, 648–649
political corruption scandals, 678
privatization of industry in, 649
quotations on democracy in, 680
woman president in, 637
Argonne Forest, battle of, 390
Arias, Arnulfo, 636
Aristide, Jean-Bertrand, 647, 647*p*
aristocracy, definition of, 11
Aristotle
ideas of, 11
on relationships in natural world, 514*ps*
and Renaissance, 35, 55–56
Arkwright, Richard, 200
Armenia, 546
Armenian massacre, 326–327
arms race, 526
Armstrong, Louis, 452–453
Arp, Hans, 451
art
abstract art, 451
baroque art, 151
calligraphy, 26
censorship of, 413–415
and civilization, 2
and computers, 519
cubism, 451
dadaism, 451
engravings, 40
folk art, xxxv*p*, 646*p*
and global culture, 521
impressionism, 262
mosaics, 22
murals, 422, 423
oil paint developed, 40
perspective in, 36*p*
postimpressionism, 263
and realism, 262–263
of Renaissance, 32–33, 36–38
and revolution, 221
rococo style, 151
and romanticism, 261
and socialist realism, 413, 413*p*
of Spain's Golden Age, 112–113
surrealism, 451
wood block printing, 27
"Art and Practice of Japanese Management, The" (Mickel-thwaite), 557*ps*
Art of War, The (Sun Tzu), 377*ps*
Articles of Confederation, 160
Aryans, 6–7
As You Like It (Shakespeare), 42*ps*
Asante kingdom, 99, 109, 319, 324
Asia
cities first developed in, 2–3
financial crisis, 512, 574
independence in, 579*m*
time line for, 2–3, 8–9, 16–17
and trade, 315*m*
and World War I, 387

See also Southeast Asia; specific countries
Asia Foundation, 665
"Asian tigers," 566
Asking Questions
See skills
assassination
of British governor of Bermuda, 504
of Ferdinand, archduke of Austria-Hungary, 374
of Henry IV, king of France, 115
of Peter III, czar of Russia, 132
of Peter Stolypin, 287
assembly lines, 244, 246*p*
assessments
Chapter: 58, 80, 106, 134, 162, 192, 212, 232, 264, 288, 312, 338, 366, 396, 416, 440, 464, 494, 522, 552, 576, 602, 628, 654
Portfolio: 42, 73, 90, 117, 152, 189, 205, 221, 255, 285, 299, 335, 364, 384, 414, 438, 453, 475, 519, 543, 564, 595, 625, 645
Assignment in Utopia (Lyons), 417*ps*
Association of Southeast Asian Nations, 507, 574
Astor, Nancy, 454
astrolabe, 63, 65*p*
Aswan High Dam, 593–594
Atahualpa, 85
Atatürk, Kemal, 418, 426–427, 426*p*, 592, 593
Atatürk Dam, 588
Athens, 11
Atlantic Charter, 477
atomic bombs, 488
atomic theory, 257–258
Auden, W. H., 472
Augsburg, Peace of, 46
Augustus Caesar, 12, 456
Aung San Suu Kyi, 574*p*, 719*ps*
Auschwitz, 479–480, 489
Austerlitz, Battle of, 187
Australia
and Aborigines, 353, 354
case study on, 690–693
civic participation in, 690, 693
compulsory voting in, 690, 692
and democracy, 690
geography of, 354*m*
gross domestic product (GDP), 691
and Industrial Revolution, 243
Outback, 354
as penal colony, 296–297, 353–354
and self-government, 354–355
2000 Olympic games in, 508*p*
and World War I, 387
Austria
Austro-Prussian War, 271
Germany united with, 470

Hapsburg Austria, 127
and partition of Poland, 109, 133
and Quadruple Alliance, 191
religious tolerance in, 150
as republic, 394
serfdom abolished in, 150
War of Austrian Succession, 127, 128
and World War I, 381
Austria-Hungary
assassination of Archduke Francis Ferdinand, 374
Dual Monarchy, 267
and Triple Alliance, 379
Austro-Prussian War, 271, 277
Autobiography (Franklin), 149*ps*
Autobiography (Fukuzawa Yukichi), 707*ps*
Autobiography (Nkrumah), 714*ps*
automobiles, 246, 315, 557
Axis Powers, 439, 469
Axum kingdom, 9, 24, 25
Azerbaijan, 546
Aztec empire
and Cortés, 60, 82
government of, 14
height of, 17
and murals, 423
religion of, 14–15
and Spain, 60, 82, 84–85
and Tenochtitlán, 84–85, 86
See also Mexico
Azuela, Mariano, 420

B
Babangida, Ibrahim, 619
Babur, 23, 74
Babylon, 5
Bach, Johann Sebastian, 142, 151
Bacon, Francis, 55–56
Baghdad, 22, 23, 387
balance of power, definition of, 118
Balbo, Italo, 455
Balboa, Vasco Núñez de, 65
Balfour Declaration, 428, 587
Balkans
and nationalism, 281, 378, 380
revolution in, 217
"Ballad of East and West, The" (Kipling), 361*ps*
ballet, 151, 285
See also dance
Bamum, 322
bananas, 101, 104, 365
Bandaranaike, Sirimavo, 689
Bangladesh, 583, 686–689
Bantu migrations, 24
Baptists, 49, 122
Barbados, 94
Barrios de Chamorro, Violeta, 689
barter economies, 362
Bastille, 143, 164, 170
Bataan Death March, 485–486
Battle of Adowa, 324

Battle of Argonne Forest, 390
Battle of Austerlitz, 187
Battle of Britain, 474, 476
Battle of the Bulge, 486
Battle of El Alamein, 482
Battle of Gallipoli, 387
Battle of Lepanto, 111
Battle of the Marne, 383
Battle of Marston Moor, 121*p*
Battle of Midway, 486
Battle of the Nations, 188
Battle of Saratoga, 160
Battle of Somme, 374
Battle of Stalingrad, 484
Battle of Tannenburg, 386
Battle of Trafalgar, 185
Battle of Waterloo, 165, 188
Battle of Yorktown, 143
Battleship Potemkin (Eisenstein), 414
Bay of Pigs, 638
Beagle, 258
"Beard tax," 129
Bedford College, 257
Beeton, Isabella, 207
Beeton's Book of Household Management (Beeton), 207*ps*
Beijing, 337, 434, 435, 563
Belarus, 546
Belgian Congo, 321–322, 620
See also Zaire
Belgium
African colonies, 321–322, 620
and Battle of the Bulge, 486
and European unity, 528
and Industrial Revolution, 242
and Locarno treaties, 445
as part of Holland, 191
revolution of, 222
and World War II, 381
Bell, Alexander Graham, 246
Bell, Doctor, 393
Ben-Gurion, David, 597
Bentham, Jeremy, 209
Benz, Karl, 246
Bergen Belsen, 479–480
Bering Strait, 131
Bering, Vitus, 131
Berlin, 492, 535
Berlin airlift, 492, 493
Berlin Conference, 241, 315, 322
Berlin Wall, 526, 535, 535*p*, 555, 605
Bermuda, 504
Bertini, Catherine, 629*ps*
Bessemer, Henry, 244
Bhutto, Benazir, 689
Bhutto, Zulfikar Ali, 583
Biafra, 611, 619
Bible, 21, 44, 50, 125
Bill of Rights, 161
bin Laden, Osama, 509, 585, 601
biography
See list of, xvi
Birmingham, 293
Bishopsgate Street (Doré), 209*p*
Bismarck, Otto von
biography of, 273*p*

Index

"blood and iron" speech of, 268*ps*
as chancellor of Prussia, 269, 272
and German wars, 269, 271
and Great War, 376
as Iron Chancellor, 273–274
and *Kulturkampf,* 273
and *Realpolitik,* 269, 273, 276
and social reform, 273
and Triple Alliance, 379
Black Death, 19, 40, 62
Black Sea, 131, 133
Black Jacobins (James), 227*ps*
"Black Woman" (Senghor), 425
Blair, Tony, 532
blockade, definition of, 185
Bloody Sunday, 267*p,* 286–287, 289
Blücher, General, 188
Blum, Leon, 448
B'nai B'rith, 259
"boat people," 572
Boer War, 315, 322
Boers, 100, 320
Bohemia, 125, 127
Boleyn, Anne, 50
Bolívar, Simón, 214, 226, 231, 233, 240, 356, 564*ps,* 705*ps*
Bolsheviks
    as elite leadership group, 402
    and November Revolution, 402–403
    Old Bolsheviks, 408
    and Russian government takeover, 401, 418
    Winter Palace overrun by, 398, 403
    See also communism
Bolshoi Theater, 285
Bonaparte, Caroline, queen of Naples, 186
Bonaparte, Elisa, Grand Duchess of Tuscany, 186
Bonaparte, Jerome, king of Westphalia, 186
Bonaparte, Joseph, as king of Spain, 184–185
Bonaparte, Louis, king of Holland, 186
Bonaparte, Louis Napoleon
    See also Napoleon III, emperor of France
Bonaparte, Napoleon
    abdication of, 165, 188
    Age of Napoleon, 182–190
    annexation of European countries, 184
    and Battle of Trafalgar, 185
    birth of, 182
    and Continental System, 185, 186
    death of, 188
    and Directory, 180
    Directory overthrown by, 182–183
    divorce of, 187
    as emperor of France, 165, 183, 194
    exile of, 188
    Egyptian invasion by, 325

as First Consul, 183
Grand Army, 187, 189, 476
and Haiti, 226, 228
Holy Roman Empire abolished by, 184, 190, 268
legacy of, 188, 190
and Louisiana Purchase, 190
Napoleonic Code, 184, 186
rise to power, 182–185
Russian invasion by, 165, 186, 187–188, 189
Book of Common Prayer (Cranmer), 50
Book of the Courtier (Castiglione), 38–39
bookkeeping, 102
Boolean language, xlvii–xlix
Booth, Catherine, 259
Booth, Evangeline, 259*p*
Booth, William, 259
Bornu, 99
Bosnia, 380, 511, 538
Bosporus strait, 326
Boston, 158, 159
Boulton, Matthew, 198
Bounty, 355
bourgeoisie, 167, 210–211
Boxer Uprising, 336–337
boyars, 130, 132–133
Boyle, Robert, 57
Bradford, William, 93*ps*
Brady, Mathew B., 263
Brahe, Tycho, 54–55
brahman, 7, 8
Brandenburg Concertos, 142
Brandt, Willy, 535
Braque, Georges, 451
Brasília, 651
Brazil
    and agribusinesses, 636
    Amazon rain forest, 640, 641
    and Candomblé, 650
    and coffee, 357, 365, 640, 650
    deforestation in, 636
    economic crisis in, 512
    "economic miracle" of 651, 651*p,* 653
    ethnic diversity in, 632*g*
    and *favelas,* 650
    independence from Portugal, 231
    and inflation, 653
    Landless Movement, 653
    major cities of, 650*p*
    and Mercosur, 636, 640
    military government in, 634
    plantation economies in, 91
    as Portuguese colony, 89, 91, 650
    poverty in, 633, 652
    and privatization of industry, 653
    as republic, 291
    and rubber, 357
    and squatters, 653
    street children in, 652
    and sugar, 650
brazilwood, 89
Brest-Litovsk, Treaty of, 389
Brezhnev Doctrine, 542, 544, 548
Brezhnev, Leonid, 541–542

Bridge, J. H., 242
Britain, Battle of, 474, 476
British Commonwealth of Nations, 447
British East India Company
    See East India Company
Brittain, Vera, 389
Brontë, Charlotte, 260
Bronze Age, 2
Bronze Horseman, The (Pushkin), 131
Brooke, James, 652
Brooke, W. B., 277
Brown v. Board of Education of Topeka, 539
Browning, O., 168
Bruegel, Pieter, 40
Brunei, 67
Brunelleschi, Filippo, 37
Bruntland, Gro Harlem, 686–687
Bryan, William Jennings, 308
bubonic plague, 19
Budapest, 267, 549*p*
Buddha, 8, 69
Buddhism
    development of, 8
    Falun Gong sect, 565
    in Japan, 16
    Mahayana Buddhism, 70
    and nirvana, 8
    in Southeast Asia, 67, 68, 69
    Theravada Buddhism, 70
Buenos Aires, 649
Bulgaria, 386, 480, 544
Bulge, Battle of the, 486
Bundesrat, 271
bureaucracy, 3, 26
Burke, Edmund, 174
Burma, 67, 348, 349, 478, 574
Burton, Richard, 320
Burundi, 620
Bush, George, 600
Bush, George W., 538
Byron, Lord, 218, 260
Byzantine empire, 16, 19, 20–21
Byzantium, 13

C
cabinet system, 156
Cabot, John, 66
Cabral, Pedro Alvarez, 65
cahiers, 169
Cahokia, 15
calendars, 14
calligraphy, 26
Calvin, John, 46, 48*ps*
Calvinists, 120
Cambodia, 67, 69, 349, 507, 513, 571, 572–573
Cambodian Odyssey, A (Haing Ngor), 573*ps*
Cambridge University, 257
camels, 24–25
Câmera, Dom Hélder, 637
Canaan, 5
Canada
    and British Commonwealth of Nations, 447
    British North American Act of 1867, 352
    British takeover of, 94, 351

Canada Act of 1791, 351
Canadian Pacific Railway, 341, 352–353
and Commonwealth of Nations, 540
as dominion, 352
Durham Report, 352
and freedom of speech, 146
and Group of Eight, 507
and Industrial Revolution, 243
immigration to, 353, 540
Japanese internment camps in, 482
Lower Canada, 351
map 1867–1914, 352*m*
métis revolt, 353
and NATO, 493
as New France, 92–93
and North American Free Trade Association (NAFTA), 540, 640, 644
and Quebec separatism, 540
and self-rule, 351–353
and Seven Years' War, 154
Upper Canada, 351
and World War I, 387
cancer, 518, 640
Candide (Voltaire), 149
Candomblé, 650
cannon, 272*p*
Canons and Decrees of the Holy Council of Trent, 59*ps*
Cape Colony, 320, 322
Cape of Good Hope, 63
Cape Town, 72, 100
capital, 199
capitalism, 102, 211
"captains of industry," 248
caravels, 63, 65*p*
Cardenas, Cuauhtemoc, 676
Cárdenas, Lázaro, 642
Cardoso, Fernando Henrique, 653
Caribbean islands, 65, 84, 94–95, 425
Carlyle, Thomas, 207
Carnegie, Andrew, 311
Carranza, Venustiano, 422
cartels, 248
Carter, Jimmy, 537
Carthage, 8
Cartier, George Étienne, 352
Cartier, Jacques, 66
cartographers, 63
case studies
    definition of, 660
    evaluation scoring guide for, 664
    interviews for, 661, 662
    presentation of, 661, 663
    project journal for, 661, 662
    research for, 664–665
    topic analysis for, 660–661
    topics choice for, 660
    See also specific country case studies
cash crops, 331*p,* 614
caste system, 7, 9, 430, 583
Castiglione, Baldassare, 38–39
Castlereagh, Robert, 190
castles, 16

Index

Castro, Fidel, 524, 630, 635, 638
"Casualties, The" (Clark), 618ps
Catherine of Aragon, 50
Catherine the Great, 131,
132–133, 132p, 174, 194, 282
Catholic Church
See Roman Catholic Church
Catholic Reformation, 51–52
caudillos, 357, 634
Cavaliers, 120–121
Cavell, Edith, 389, 389p
Cavour, Count Camillo, 275,
276, 277
Ceausescu, Nicolae, 548
Celso, Afonso, 650
censorship, 149
Central Powers, 379
Cervantes, Don Tomas Mateo,
225p
Cervantes, Miguel de, 43, 113,
699ps
Ceuta, 63
Cha Ruizhen, 435
Chamberlain, Neville, 471, 474
Chamorro, Violeta, 644
Champlain, Samuel de, 92p
Chao Phraya River, 67
Chaplin, Charlie, 452
Charlemagne, 16
Charles I, king of England, 120
Charles II, king of England,
121–123, 123p
Charles V, 45, 53, 110–111
Charles VI, Holy Roman
emperor, 127
Charles X, king of France,
219–220, 222
Charles the Great
See Charlemagne
Charter of French Liberties,
219
Charts and Graphs
See skills
Chavez, Hugo, 635
Chavín culture, 3
Chavín gold carvings, 8
Chechnya, 545
Chekhov, Anton, 514
chemistry, 57, 244
Chernobyl nuclear plant, 515,
543
Chiang Kai–shek
See Jiang Jieshi
Chiapas, 643
Child of the Dark (de Jesus),
632ps
children
and AIDS, 615
child labor, 204, 206, 210,
252, 297
day care, 210, 412
female infanticide, 565
and poverty, 510, 513
as slaves in Bangladesh, 584
and starvation, 513
"Children of the First Fleet"
(*National Geographic*), 354ps
Chile, 85, 230, 634, 636, 639
China
agriculture, 76
and arranged marriage, 433
Boxer Uprising, 336–337

bureaucracy of, 26
China-Panama connection,
644
Christian missionaries in, 72,
75–76
civil service in, 70, 336
civil war, 434m, 441m, 572
and Cold War, 562
collective farming in, 560
communes in, 561
and communism, 433–434,
505, 560–561
Confucianism in, 433
and cotton, 76
Cultural Revolution,
561–562, 577, 578, 604
economic disasters in, 561
and education, 47
Emperor Qianlong, 61,
76–77, 83, 142
England's trade rejected,
76–77, 109
and footbinding, 433
and freedom of speech, 146
geography of, 7
golden ages of, 25
Great Leap Forward, 561
Great Wall of, 27
Guomindang party, 433–434,
435, 466
Han dynasty, 9, 26, 70
and Hong Kong, 566
and human rights, 508–509
human rights issues, 565
Hundred Days of Reform,
336
and Japan, 336, 346, 374, 387,
395, 432–433, 435, 439, 468,
477, 558
and Korea, 27, 346–347
and Legalism, 9
Long March, 399, 419,
434–435, 466
and Mandate of Heaven, 7
May Fourth Movement, 433,
433p
as Middle Kingdom, 7
Ming dynasty, 17, 27, 32,
75–76
Mongol invasion of, 27
nationalists in, 560
nationalized businesses, 560
and North Korea, 568
Open Door Policy, 336
Opium War, 215, 333–334,
343
and papermaking, 9
paper money used in, 26
as People's Republic of, 467,
554, 560, 630
population control, 513, 563,
565
porcelain of, 76
Portugal trading with, 75–76
printing in, 27, 43
prison labor, 565
Qin dynasty, 9
Qing dynasty, 76–77, 334,
336, 432
and "rape of Nanjing," 435
Red Guards, 562
reform in, 334, 336, 562–563

as republic, 337, 432–433
Revolutionary Alliance, 337
"self-strengthening move-
ment," 336
and Shang dynasty, 3, 7
and silk, 9, 27, 76
Song dynasty, 16, 26, 27
and space age, 520
special enterprise zones, 563
student protests in, 433
Sui dynasty, 26
Taiping Rebellion, 215, 334
and Taiwan, 566–567
Tang dynasty, 70
Three Principles of the
People, 337, 432
Tiananmen Square Mas-
sacre, 563–564
and trade, 67, 76–77, 164
and Treaty of Nanjing, 240,
334
tributary states of, 25
and United Nations, 490
and United States of America, 435
and Vietnam, 70
western imperialism, 1914,
336m
westernization of, 334
women rulers of, 335p, 336,
337
writing development in, 2
and yin and yang, 7
and Zhou dynasty, 7, 9
Chirac, Jacques, 534
chivalry, 16
chocolate, 101
Choctaw people, 300
cholera, 203, 250
Chopin, Frederic, 261
Chorbachi, Wasma'a K., 590
Choson dynasty, 78
Christ, 13, 36, 37
Christianity
and Africa, 24, 25, 616–617,
619
beliefs of, 17
forced conversion to, 84,
87–88
missionaries of, 72, 79,
87–88, 92, 320
persecution of Christians, 79
Protestant Reformation,
44–46
and slave trade, 98
spread of, 13, 16, 21, 24, 63,
72
and taxation by Muslims, 22
See also Protestants; religion;
Roman Catholic Church;
specific denominations
Chulalongkorn, king of Siam,
349
church
See Protestants; Roman
Catholic Church; specific
denominations
Church of England, 50, 93n,
120, 122, 124, 298, 300
Churchill, Winston
on appeasement, 471
and communism, 491

and Roosevelt, 477
speeches of, 474ps, 491ps
and Stalin, 477
Ci Xi, empress of China, 334,
335p, 336, 337
Cinchona tree, 640
cinnamon, 62
circle graphs, xxxii
city-states, in Italy, 34–35
civil disobedience, 430, 539
civil rights movement, 539
civil service
in China, 90, 336
civilization
beginnings of, 2–3
and cultural diffusion, 4
features of, 2
spread of, 3
Clark, John Pepper, 618
Clemenceau, Georges, 301
*Clemenceau and the Third
Republic* (Jackson), 301ps
Clermont, 194, 202
Clinton, Bill, 539, 599
Clive, Robert, 74
cloning, 518
cloves, 62, 72, 103
coal, 198, 345
cocaine, 640
Cockerill, William, 242
Code of Hammurabi, 5
coffee, 357, 361p, 640, 650
Colbert, Jean Baptiste, 116,
118
Cold War
and Africa, 610–611, 626
arms race, 493
beginning of, 490–491
and China, 562
end of, 506, 527, 544
in Europe, 492m
and Germany's division, 534
as global, 505
and Great Liberation, 506m
and imperialism, 504
and India, 584
and Middle East, 597
nonaligned countries in, 505
and North Korea, 568, 569
and nuclear threat, 526–527,
526p
propaganda war, 493
and "shooting wars," 505
and South Korea, 568, 569
collaborators, 480
collective farming, 670
Colombia, 230, 360, 640
Columbian Exchange, 101–104
Columbus, Christopher, 35,
63–65, 66, 82, 84
Comintern, 410
*Commentaries of the Great
Afonso de Albuquerque, The*,
71ps
Common Market, 533
Common Sense (Paine), 158ps,
292ps
Commonwealth of Nations,
533
communes, 561
communications, 43, 244,
246–247

communism
  in China, 433–434
  collapse of in Europe, 666
  and containment, 491, 537
  definition of, 210
  and domino theory, 571
  fascism compared with, 456,
    458
  and Great Depression, 446
  outlawed in Russia, 667
  and "Reds," 403, 410, 448
  and Russian Revolution of
    1917, 211
  "war communism," 404, 405
  See also Bolsheviks; Marxism
Communist Manifesto, The
  (Marx and Engels), 195, 210,
  211*ps*
compact, definition of, 93
Comparing and Contrasting
  See skills
Complete Poetical Works
  (Wordsworth), 260*ps*
Composition No. 4 (Leger), 442
comprehension questions, xliv
computers, 503, 518, 519
concentration camps, 463,
  479–480, 489
concessions
  definition of, 328
confession, 46
Confucianism, 9, 27, 47*ps*, 70
Confucius, 8, 9
Congo
  See Kongo
Congo Free State, 322
Congress of Vienna, 190–191,
  190*m*, 216, 219, 222, 266, 268,
  275, 279, 296
conquistadors, 84–85, 85*p*
conscription, 388
Conservatives, 216
Constantine, 13, 20, 21
Constantinople, 20, 23, 32, 326*p*
containment, 491
Continental Army, 159
Continental Congress, 159, 160
Continental System, 185
contras, 644
Cook, James, 353
Coolidge, Calvin, 449
Copernicus, Nicolaus, 35,
  54–55
corn, 76, 101
Corn, Charles, 103
Corn Laws, 295–296
corporations, 247
Corregidor, 485
Corsica, 182
Cortés, Hernán, 60, 82, 84
Costa Rica, xl, 229
cotton
  in Americas, 2
  British cotton trade 1850,
    200*m*
  as cash crop, 331*p*
  Chinese cotton, 76
  Indian cotton, 74, 330–331
  See also textiles
Council of the Indies, 87
Council of Trent, 51, 59
Courbet, Gustave, 261, 262–263

Cousteau, Jacques, 515*p*
Cranmer, Thomas, 50
Creation of Adam (Michelangelo), 38
creoles, 88–89, 225, 226
Crete, 10
crime
  punishment of, 296, 296*p*
  and tenements, 250
  war crimes, 489, 551
Crimean War, 276, 283, 303
criminal law, 296, 596
Crises in English History
  (Henning), 251
Cromwell, Oliver, 121–122
crusades, 19, 44
Crystal Palace, 195, 199
Cuba
  and Angola, 626, 627
  Bay of Pigs, 638
  and Castro, 524, 630
  communism in, 638–639
  embargo on, 638
  and Good Neighbor Policy,
    423
  missile crisis, 542, 554
  poverty in, 639
  ruling class in, 225*p*
  and Spain, 84, 350, 360
  and Spanish-American War,
    350, 360
cubism, 451
cultural diffusion
  in Americas, 89, 89*p*
  Columbian Exchange,
    101–102
  and trade, 4
Cultural Revolution, 561–562
culture
  and China, 334
  and Columbian Exchange,
    101–102
  global culture, 520–521
  and imperialism, 363, 516
  and Japan, 437
  nomadic cultures, 2
  popular culture, 452–453,
    520–521
  and Russia, 129, 282
  urbanization, 516
cuneiform writing, 5
curare, 640
Curie, Marie, 450, 450*p*
Curran, Barbara, 688
Cuzco, 15
cyclones, 73
Cyprus, 536, 593
Czech Republic, 527, 547, 549
  democracy in, 682–685
  demographics on, 683
  economic development in,
    682–685
  gross domestic product
    (GDP), 683
  quotations on transition
    from totalitarianism, 684
  unemployment statistics,
    682
  "velvet divorce," 682
  "velvet revolution," 682
Czechoslovakia, 394, 445, 458
  German invasion of, 471

  pro-Soviet communist
    government in, 491, 548
  and Sudetenland, 470

D

D-Day, 484
Da Gama, Vasco, 60, 63, 71, 82
Da Messina, Antonello, 36
Da Silva, Benedita, 637
Da Silva, Luiz Inacia Lula, 653
Da Vinci, Leonardo, 33, 33*p*, 37,
  56*p*
Dadaism, 451
Daguerre, Louis, 240, 263
Dahomey, 99
Daimler, Gottlieb, 246
daimyo, 29, 342, 343
Daladier, Edouard, 471
Dali, Salvador, 451
Dalai Lama, 565
Dalton, John, 257
dance, 151, 285, 454
Dante, 19
Daoism, 9, 70
Darby, Abraham, 198
Dardanelles, 326, 387, 491
Darwin, Charles, 241, 258–259
Daumier, Honoré, 221
David, Jacques Louis, 169, 181
Davies, Emily, 257
day care, 210, 412
"Days With Lenin" (Gorky),
  404*ps*
Dayton Accords, 550
De Beauvoir, Simone, 531
De Gaulle, Charles, 474, 534,
  610
De Gouges, Olympe, 180*ps*
De Jesus, Carolina Maria, 632
De Klerk, F. W., 605, 624, 678
De la Cruz, Sor Juana Inés, 89
De las Casas, Bartolomé, xli,
  88, 88*ps*
De Lesseps, Ferdinand, 302,
  327–328
De Ségur, Philippe Paul, 188
De Staël, Germaine, 147, 148*p*
death
  Industrial Revolution and
    death rates, 198
"death camps," 479–480, 489
Death of Old Yokohama
  (Poole), 438
debt service, 584
Decembrist Revolt, 283
Declaration of Independence,
  159, 159*ps*, 226
Declaration of Pilnitz, 175
Declaration of the Rights of
  Man and the Citizen, 172,
  703*ps*
Declaration of the Rights of
  Woman (de Gouges), 180
Declarations of the Ayatollah
  Khomeini, 592*ps*
decolonization, 507
Decree of Hidalgo (Hidalgo),
  704*ps*
Defoe, Daniel, 153
deforestation, 331, 584, 615,
  636, 640, 641
Degas, Edgar, 263

Delacroix, Eugène, 261
Delhi, 23
Delhi Sultanate, 17
demilitarized zone (DMZ), 568
democracy
  definition of, 11
Democratic Republic of Congo
  See Belgian Congo; Zaire
Demoiselles d'Avignon, Les
  (Picasso), 364
Deng Xiaoping, 562, 565
Denmark, 210, 473, 480, 530, 536
Descartes, René, 55–56
desertification, 615*m*
D'Este, Isabella, 36
Destination of Enslaved
  Africans, 1500–1870, xxxiiig
détente, 526–527, 542
developing world, 505,
  511–513, 538
diamonds, 623*p*
Dias, Bartholomeu, 63
diaspora, 5
Díaz, Bernal, 697*ps*
Díaz, Porfirio, 359
Dickens, Charles, 262, 706*ps*
Diderot, Denis, 147, 147*ps*, 150
Diet at Worms, 45, 46
direct democracy, 11
direct rule, 318
Directory, 171, 179–180
disarmament, 445
disasters
  at Chernobyl nuclear plant,
    515, 543
  earthquakes in Turkey,
    592–593, 593*p*
  hurricanes, 645, 646
  Tokyo earthquake of 1923,
    438
Discourse on Method
  (Descartes), 56
Discourses (Machiavelli), 595*ps*
disease
  AIDS, 518, 615
  Black Death, 62
  bubonic plague, 19
  cancer, 518, 640
  cholera, 203, 250
  and germ theory, 249
  malaria, 249, 640
  smallpox, 144*p*, 518, 607
  tuberculosis, 249, 250
  yellow fever, 226, 228, 249,
    607
  See also medicine
Dispatches From Paris (Browning), 168*ps*
Disraeli, Benjamin, 292*ps*, 294,
  294*p*, 297
Distinguishing Fact and
  Opinion
  See skills
diversity
  and Columbian Exchange,
    101–104
  in Europe, 531
  in Middle East, 586–588
Divine Comedy (Dante), 19
divine right, 111, 120
divorce, 180
  See also annulment

Index

Djojohadikusumo, Sumitro, 514
Djugashvili, Joseph
  See Stalin, Joseph
Doctor Zhivago (Pasternak), 415
Doctors Without Borders, 611
dodo bird, 72*p*
Doll's House, A (Ibsen), 262
Dom Pedro, king of Brazil, 231
Dominican Republic, 84, 360
dominion
  definition of, 352
domino theory, 571
Don Quixote (Cervantes), 43, 113, 699*ps*
Donatello, 37
donkeys, 101
Doré, Gustave, 209
Douglass, Frederick, 307
draft, 388
Drake, Francis, 91, 112
drama
  French drama, 116
  and realism, 262
  of Shakespeare, 42
  See also literature
Dresden, 486
Dreyfus, Alfred, 304–305, 304*p*
drought, 615
drug wars, 640
Dual Monarchy, 267
Dubček, Alexander, 548
DuBois, W.E.B., 425
Duma, 287
Dumas, Alexandre, 260
Dunkirk, miracle of, 473–474
"Dunkirk: May 28–June 4, 1940" (Williams), 495*ps*
Dürer, Albrecht, 40, 41*p*
Dutch
  African outposts, 96
  Cape Town settlement, 72
  colonies seized by England, 94
  and dikes, 197
  explorations of, 66
  Malacca's seizure from Portugal, 61, 72
  sea power of, 72
  See also Netherlands
Dutch East India Company, 72, 103, 348
Dutch East Indies, 477
Dutch Reformed Church, 48
Duvalier, François ("Papa Doc"), 647
Duvalier, Jean-Claude ("Baby Doc"), 647
Dyer, Reginald, 429
dynamite, 244
dynamos, 244
dynasty
  definition of, 7
  See also specific dynasties

E
Eakins, Thomas, 263
East Germany, 492–493, 534, 535, 544
  demographics on, 667
  Stasi, 666

  West Germany united with, 666
  See also Germany; West Germany
East India Company, 73–74, 154, 329–330
East Pakistan, 583
East Timor, 506, 574
Eastern Europe
  antisemitism in, 428
  inflation in, 549
  Jews in, 428
  resistance to communism in, 547–548
  self-determination in, 394
  Soviet control over, 542
  See also specific countries
Eastern Orthodox Church, 20, 21
Economic Development of Europe (Ogg and Sharp), 273
economics
  barter economies, 362
  capital, 199
  capitalism, 102, 211, 362
  cartels, 248
  command economies, 406–407, 542
  commercial revolution, 102–104
  corporations, 247
  deficit spending, 168, 539
  as "dismal science," 209
  economic nationalism, 675
  economics of dependence, 357, 362, 513
  entrepreneurs, 102
  feudalism, 16–17, 27, 342
  free market, 148
  free trade, 295–296
  global economy, 361–362
  Great Depression, 446, 449
  gross domestic product (GDP), 557
  and import substitution, 635
  inflation, 102, 113, 459–460, 459*p*, 549, 653, 678
  and interdependence, 507, 511
  joint stock companies, 102
  laissez-faire economics, 148, 208–209
  margin buying, 446
  mercantilism, 104, 148
  mixed economies, 614
  money economies, 362
  monopolies, 247–248
  nationalization, 422, 528, 532, 560
  New Deal, 449
  New York Stock Exchange crash, 419
  overproduction, 445
  peons, 88
  plantation economies, 88, 91, 93, 97, 226, 362, 424
  post-World War I economic issues, 444–445
  and privatization of industry, 512, 528, 544, 649, 653
  putting out system, 102, 104, 200

  recession, 220, 528
  stock market crash of 1929, 399
  and tariffs, 104, 296, 423, 446, 528, 530
  trade deficits, 333, 557
  trade surplus, 333
  utilitarianism, 209
  See also global economy
Ecuador, 85, 230
Edict of Nantes, 115, 118
Edison, Thomas, 244
Edo, 342, 343
education
  colonial education, 89
  in East Africa, 323
  and French Revolution, 181
  growth of public education, 256–257
  and missionaries, 363
  and women, 89, 257
Edward VI, king of England, 50
Edward VII, king of England, 316, 318*p*
Egypt
  as Arab leader, 593–594
  Bonaparte's invasion of, 325
  early civilization, 4
  and independence, 442
  and Israel, 593, 598
  Middle Kingdom, 4
  modernization of, 327–328
  Muslim Brotherhood, 426
  New Kingdom, 4
  and oil industry, 588
  Old Kingdom, 4
  religion of early civilization, 4
  and Suez Canal, 291, 327–328, 593
  United Kingdom control of, 322, 426
Eiffel Tower, 250, 251*p*
Einstein, Albert, 450, 463
Eire, 447*n*
Eisenhower, Dwight D., 482, 484, 489, 538
Eisenstein, Sergei, 414
El Alamein, Battle of, 482
El Greco, 112–113
El Grito de Dolores, 228–229
El Salvador, 229, 513, 642, 646–647
Elba, 188
Election II—Canvassing for Votes, The (Hogarth), 156*p*
electorate, 293
electricity, 244
Eliot, T. S., 452
Elizabeth I, queen of England, 50, 50*p*, 111–112, 119
Ellington, Duke, 453
Ellis Island, 310
Emancipation Proclamation, 284
embargo, 572, 638
emigration, definition of, 278
empire, 3
enclosure, 197
encomiendas, 88
Encyclopedia or Classified Dictionary of the Sciences,

Arts, and Occupations (Diderot), 147, 147*ps*, 149
Enemy of the People, An (Ibsen), 262
Engels, Friedrich, 210, 211
England
  and Act of Union, 142
  African colonization, 96
  American colonies of, 89, 93–94
  Bill of Rights, 123, 124
  Caribbean colonies of, 94
  and Cavaliers, 120–121
  China's refusal to trade with, 76–77, 109
  Civil War, 61, 108, 120–121, 144
  as Commonwealth, 121–122
  constitutional government of, 155–156
  Dutch colonies seized by, 94
  English common law, 18
  explorations of, 66
  and freedom of speech, 146
  French defeat at Quebec, 83
  Glorious Revolution, 124, 155, 156, 169
  Great Council of, 18
  growth of royal power in, 18
  and Jews, 122
  Petition of Right, 124
  and piracy, 91
  plantation economies of, 93
  and Protestant Reformation, 49–51
  and Roman Catholic Church, 50, 119, 124
  and Roundheads, 120–121
  slave trade, 97
  Spanish conflicts, 111–112
  Stuart dynasty, 119–120
  tobacco industry, 92
  Toleration Act of 1689, 124
  Tudor dynasty, 119
  unification of, 18
  See also parliament; United Kingdom of Great Britain
"English Bill of Rights, The," 124, 700*ps*
English Channel, 473–474
English Channel tunnel, 532
English East India Company
  See East India Company
enlightened despots, 150
Enlightenment
  and censorship, 149
  and *philosophes*, 145, 147
  and Scientific Revolution, 144
  and socialism, 210
  and women, 147–148
entente, definition of, 379
entrepreneurs, 102
environment, 514, 515, 640–641
Epitaphs (Pope), 56*ps*
Equiano, Olaudah, 96*ps*, 98*ps*, 107*ps*
Erasmus, Desiderius, 40*ps*, 41, 44
Ernst, Max, 451
Escobar, Vincente, 225
Escorial, 111

Esquivel, Arcadio, xxxvi
Essay on Man (Pope), 144*ps*
"Essay on the Principle of
   Population" (Malthus), 208
Estates General, 115, 168–169
Esterhazy, Ferdinand, 304
Estonia, 394, 403, 473, 544
ethics
   medical, 518
Ethiopia, 324, 419, 466, 468
ethnic conflicts, 548, 582, 593,
   619
   ethnic cleansing, 550, 551, 617
   See also genocide
ethnic groups, definition of, 21
Etruscans, 12
Euclid, 35
Euphrates River, 5, 588
euro currency, 525, 530, 533
Europe
   aggression in 1939, 471*m*
   and Congress of Vienna
      1815, 190*m*
   country boundaries, 1914
      and 1920, 394*m*
   dictatorship, 1917–1939,
      443*m*
   in early Middle Ages, 16–17
   ethnic diversity in, 531
   and expansion, 105
   exploration voyages,
      1487–1609, 64*m*
   migration to Western Eu-
      rope, 530*m*
   Europe and nationalism,
      279–281
   post-World War I economic
      issues, 444–445
   revolutions, 1815–1829, 215*m*
   revolutions, 1830 and 1848,
      222*m*
   time line for, 2–3, 8–9, 16–17
   unification of countries in,
      267*m*
   and World War II, 483*m*
   See also specific countries
Europe Since 1815 (Hazen), 274
European Common Market,
   636
European Community (EC),
   528, 604
European Parliament, 530
European Union, 507, 525,
   529–530, 549
evaluation questions, xliv
Evelyn, John, 122*ps*
Everingham, Matthew,
   353–354, 354*ps*
evolution, theory of, 241, 258
excommunication
   and banned books, 147
   definition of, 18
   of Martin Luther, 45
expansionism, 306

F

Fabergé eggs, 400
Fabian Society, 297
factories
   and assembly lines, 244, 246*p*
   and child labor, 204, 206, 210,
      252, 297

factory system, 243, 244
   first factories, 200, 205
   and labor laws, 297
Faerie Queene (Spenser), 50
Falkland Islands, 649
Falun Gong Buddhism, 565
   See also Buddhism
family
   single-parent families, 531
famine, 290, 298–300, 340, 424,
   615
Faraday, Michael, 244
fascism
   communism compared with,
      456, 458
   description of, 456, 458
   in Italy, 455–456
   and Social Darwinism, 456
*Fascist Dictatorship in Italy,
   The* (Salvemini), 465*ps*
Fatal Shore, The (Hughes), 353*ps*
Faud, king of Egypt, 426
Faust (Goethe), 260
favelas, 650
federal system of government,
   581
female infanticide, 565
feminist movement, 517
Fénelon, Archbishop François
   de, 135
Fenian Brotherhood, 300
Ferdinand, archduke of
   Austria-Hungary, 374, 380
Ferdinand, Holy Roman
   emperor, 125
Ferdinand, king of Bohemia,
   125
Ferdinand, king of Spain, 64,
   110, 113
Ferguson, Miriam, 454
Ferman, Jorge, 646
Ferreira, Zeferino Diego, 421
Ferris wheel, 251*p*
feudalism
   and crusades, 19
   in Europe, 16–17
   in Japan, 27, 342
Ficino, Marsilio, 34*ps*
fiefs, 16
Fifteenth Amendment, 308
filial piety, 9
filmmaking, 414, 452
"final solution," 463
Finnegans Wake (Joyce), 452
Firebird, 285
Firmont, Henry Essex Edge-
   worth de, 177
First Book of Maccabees, 597*ps*
First Estate, 166
First Universal Peace Confer-
   ence, 376
First World, 505*n*
First Zionist Congress, 291, 305
Five Pillars of Islam, 22
Flanders, 40
flappers, 454, 454*p*
flooding
   of Nile River, 594
Florence, 34–35, 275
Fodio, Usman dan, 99–100
folk art, xxxv*p*, 646
Food and Agricultural

Organization, 490
footbinding, 433
For Whom the Bell Tolls
   (Hemingway), 470
Forbes, Archibald, 303
Ford, Henry, 246
Foreign Policy Association, 665
Foreign Policy Research Insti-
   tute, 665
Forging the Anchor (Muler),
   204*p*
Four Freedoms, The (Roosevelt,
   F.), 710*ps*
Fourteen Points, 391, 393
Fox, Vicente, 631, 643
France
   African colonization by, 96
   and Algeria, 314, 322, 324,
      326, 533, 534
   Allied invasion of, 484
   and Alsace and Lorraine,
      376, 393, 448
   and American Revolution,
      160, 168, 171
   and appeasement of Ger-
      many, 469, 470
   Austria at war with, 175,
      180, 187
   Britain at war with, 175, 178,
      180
   British defeat at Quebec, 83
   and Canada, 94, 351
   Caribbean colonies of, 94
   Charter of French Liberties,
      219
   citizens, 180, 679
   civil war in, 303
   colonial imperialism of, 318
   Committee of Public Safety,
      178
   as constitutional monarchy,
      171, 219
   corvée, 168
   and Crimean War, 303
   and Dawes Plan, 460
   and Dreyfus Affair, 304–305
   and Enlightenment, 145, 149
   Estates General, 115, 168–169
   and European unity, 528
   "February Days," 220
   Fifth Republic, 534
   First Estate, 166
   First Republic, 220
   Fourth Republic, 533
   Franco-Prussian War, 271,
      272, 376, 379, 381
   French Indochina, 349, 477,
      478, 505
   French Union for Women's
      Suffrage, 305
   Fronde, 115, 120
   and Germany's reparations
      for World War I, 393–394
   Grand Army, 187, 189
   and Group of Eight, 507
   and Haiti, 226, 228, 266, 340
   Huguenots, 48
   and Indochina, 336
   and Industrial Revolution,
      242
   Italy's war declaration on,
      474

"June Days," 220
   and Lebanon, 428
   and Locarno treaties, 445
   Maginot Line, 448
   mercantilism, 116
   and Munich Conference,
      470, 471
   and Napoleon III, 301–303
   and Napoleonic Code, 184,
      186, 188
   National Assembly, 170, 171,
      172, 173, 220, 303
   National Guard, 171
   and nationalized industry,
      528, 534
   navy reduction, 445
   Netherlands at war with, 178
   Paris Commune, 303
   population and land owner-
      ship statistics 1789, 167
   Protestant Reformation in, 48
   Prussia at war with, 175, 178
   revolutionary France at war
      1793, 165*m*
   and salons, 149–150
   Second Empire, 301–302
   Second Estate, 166, 166–167
   Second Republic, 220
   and separation of church
      and state, 305
   Seven Years' War, 154, 168
   and slavery, 97, 226
   and socialism, 534
   and Southeast Asia, 348
   and Soviet Union, 448
   Spain at war with, 178,
      186–187
   storming Bastille, 143, 164,
      170
   and Suez Canal, 291
   and Syria, 428
   Tennis Court Oath, 169, 170
   Third Estate, 166, 169–170
   Third Republic, 301, 448
   and Thirty Years' War, 126
   tobacco industry, 92
   and Tunisia, 322
   and United Nations, 490
   Versailles, 116–117
   Vichy government, 474, 480
   and Vietnam, 533, 610
   voting rights in, 169, 176,
      220, 302, 305
   war declared on Germany,
      472
   and World War I, 379, 381,
      382, 383, 385, 387, 389, 392
   and World War II, 474
   See also French Revolution
Francis I, emperor of Austria,
   279, 280
Francis I, king of France, 91
Francis Joseph, emperor of
   Austria-Hungary, 280, 381
Franciscan friars, 87–88
Franco, Francisco, 470, 536
Franco-Prussian War, 271, 272,
   277, 291, 301, 376, 379, 381
Frankfurt Assembly, 224, 269
Franklin, Benjamin, 149*p*, 158,
   244

Index

Frederick II, king of Prussia, 127, 128, 133, 142, 150
Frederick William I, king of Prussia, 127–128
Frederick William IV, king of Prussia, 223–224, 269
Freedom from Fear (Aung San Suu Kyi), 719*ps*
"Free French", 474
Freeman, Cathy, 508*p*
free market, 148
free trade, 295
Freedom and Development (Nyerere), 504*ps*
freedom of speech, 146
French East India Company, 74
French and Indian War, 109, 154, 159
French Indochina, 349, 477, 478, 505, 571
French pope, 18
French Revolution
  and Age of Napoleon, 171, 182–190
  Constitution of 1791, 173
  and declaration of war with European countries, 175
  Directory, 171, 179–180
  and émigrés, 174
  and French Republic, 176
  and Jacobins, 175, 176
  and National Assembly, 170
  and National Assembly, 171, 172, 173
  reaction of other countries to, 174–175
  Reign of Terror, 164, 171, 177, 178–179, 179*p*
  Revolution of 1830, 219–220
  Revolution of 1848, 220, 222–223
  sans-culottes, 175
  social change created by, 180–181
  state of control of Catholic Church in France, 173
  and storming Bastille, 143, 164, 170
  and violence, 176
  and voting rights, 176
  and women, 172–173, 173*p*, 180
  See also France
French Union for Women's Suffrage, 305
Freud, Sigmund, 450–451
From Absolutism to Revolution (Rowen), 115
Fronde, 115, 120
Fujimori, Alberto, 635
Fukuzawa Yukichi, 707*ps*
Fulani people, 619
Fulton, Robert, 194, 202, 243, 314
fundamentalism, 517
fur trapping, 92
Futa Toro, 98

G
Gachet, Paul-Ferdinand, 263
Galileo Galilei, 33, 54, 54*p*, 55
Gallipoli, battle of, 387

Gandhi, Indira, 581, 582, 583, 583*p*, 689
Gandhi, Mohandas, 419, 429–431, 466, 516, 539, 581, 609, 709*ps*
Gandhi, Rajiv, 509, 581, 582
Gandhi, Sonia, 581
Ganges River, 6
Gao Xingzu, 435
Gapon, Father George, 286–287, 289
Gargantua and Pantagruel (Rabelais), 41, 43
Garibaldi: Great Lives Observed (Smith), 277
Garibaldi, Giuseppe, 276*p*, 277
Garrison, William Lloyd, 307
Garvey, Marcus, 425, 609
Gaza Strip, 598, 599*m*
Gauguin, Paul, 263
GDP
  See gross domestic product (GDP)
General Agreement on Tariffs and Trade (GATT), 507
genetic engineering, 518
genocide, 327, 479–480
Geoffrin, Madame, 150
geography
  of ancient Greece, 10*m*
  of Australia, 354*m*
  of China, 7
  and developing nations, 512
  of New Zealand, 354*m*
  of Siberia, 131
  of United Kingdom of Great Britain, 154
geology, 258
George, David Lloyd, 393
George I, king of England, 151
George II, king of England, 156
George III, king of England, 76–77, 157, 159, 197
George V, king of England, 379
Georgia, 546
germ theory, 249
Germany
  Allied occupation of, 490
  antisemitism in, 428, 459, 462–463, 479–480
  and "Aryan race," 470
  Austria united with, 470
  and Axis Powers, 439
  Bundesrat, 271
  and communism, 459
  Czechoslovakia invaded by, 471
  and D-Day, 484
  and Dawes Plan, 460
  "death camps," 479–480, 489
  division after World War II, 492–493, 534
  empire of, 271, 272–273
  and Franco-Prussian War, 376, 379
  Frankfurt Assembly, 224, 269
  and genocide, 479–480
  German Confederation, 191, 271
  Gestapo, 461
  and Great Depression, 460, 461

and Group of Eight, 507
and Holocaust, 480, 489
industrial progress in, 272–273
and Industrial Revolution, 242
and inflation, 459–460, 459*p*
and *Kristallnacht*, 443, 463
labor unions legalized in, 241, 252
and *Lebensraum*, 460
Lenin assisted by, 402
and Locarno treaties, 445
Luftwaffe, 474, 476
nonaggression pact with Stalin, 471
and occupation of Rhineland, 469
Peasant's Revolt in, 46
Poland invaded by, 399, 419, 466, 472, 473, 473*p*
and propaganda, 462
and Protestant Reformation, 33, 44–46
purge of culture in, 462
quotations on reunification of, 668
and racism, 462
Reichstag, 271, 461
reparations for World War I, 393–395, 448, 459
reunification of, 535, 548
revolution in, 223–224
and Rome-Berlin-Tokyo Axis, 469
and Russian invasion, 476
and Schlieffen Plan, 381, 383
Second Reich, 271, 341, 461
Social Democratic party, 273, 274
and social reform, 273–274
SS troops, 461
and Sudetenland, 470
and swastika, 461*p*
Third Reich, 461–462, 470
as totalitarian state, 461
and Treaty of Versailles, 393–394, 469
unification of, 268–269, 269*m*, 271
voting rights in, 459
and war crimes, 489
and war with Denmark, 271
Weimar Republic, 459–460
as welfare state, 528
witch hunts in, 52
and World War I, 379, 381, 382, 383, 385, 386–387, 390
and World War II, 399, 472, 474–477, 478, 479–480, 482–484, 486
Zollverein, 268–269
See also East Germany; Hitler
Germany, Federal Republic of:
  case study on, 666–669
  and communist collapse, 666–669
  quotations on reunification of Germany, 668
Germinal (Zola), 247*ps*, 262
Gestapo, 461
Getman, Nikolai, 411

Ghana, 17, 25, 516, 554, 578, 604, 608, 609
ghettos, 53, 479
Gladstone, William, 294, 294*p*, 297, 300
glasnost, 544
"glass ceiling," 531
Glass Palace Chronicle of the Kings of Burma, The, 67*ps*
global economy
  and Age of Imperialism, 361–362
  debt crisis, 511–512
  and economic dependence, 513
  and imperialism, 361–362
  and interdependence, 507, 511
  and migration, 511
  multinational corporations, 511
  in 1990s, 503*m*
  poor nations, 510,
  and privatization, 512
  rich nations, 510,
  slowdown in, 525, 631
  trends in, 510–515
  and United States, 538
  See also economics
global interaction
  Columbian Exchange, 101–104
  global culture, 520–521
  global summits, 507
  trade between Europe, Africa, and Asia around 1700, 61*m*
  westernization, 129, 282, 334, 363, 437, 516, 520–521
  See also global economics; trade; World War I; World War II
global warming, 515
Glorious Revolution, 124, 155, 156, 169
Glory and Hope (Mandela), 720*ps*
Godwin, William, 210
Goethe Institute, 665
Goethe, Johann Wolfgang von, 260
Golan Heights, 598, 599
gold
  African gold, 25, 63
  and inflation, 102, 113
  and mercantilism, 104
  monopolies over, 99
  and Spain, 110
Gold Coast, 609
  See also Ghana
Golden Hind, 91
Golden Temple at Amritsar, 579, 581–582
Goldin, Claudia, 531*ps*
gondolas, 34
González, Beatriz, 634
Gorbachev, Mikhail, 527, 544, 544p, 548, 716*ps*
Gordon, George, 218, 260
Gorky, Maxim, 404
government deficit spending, 168

governments
absolute monarchies, 111,
115–116, 119, 120, 145, 283
of ancient Greece, 11
autocratic rule, 130
and bureaucracy, 3
cabinet system, 156
and censorship, 149
and civilization, 2
coalition governments, 536
communism, 210
constitutional governments,
155–156, 219
constitutional monarchies,
171, 292
democracy, 11
dictatorships, 456
direct democracy, 11
and divine right, 111, 120
enlightened despots, 150
federal republics, 161, 581
and freedom of speech, 146
and hierarchies, 5
and legitimacy, 191
limited monarchies, 173
mandates, 394–395
military governments, 634
monarchies, 11, 111, 119, 120,
145, 171, 173
and monopolies, 99, 154, 430
and natural rights, 145
oligarchies, 11, 156
organized government
development, 3
and patricians, 12
and plebeians, 12
popular sovereignty, 159
protectorates, 318
republics, 12
self-determination, 391
and shoguns, 27
socialism, 209–210
spheres of influence, 318
theocracy, 48, 596
totalitarian governments,
411–415, 457
and tribute, 14, 26
utilitarianism, 209
welfare states, 527–528
Goya, Francisco, 187
Grain of Wheat, A (Ngugi wa
Thiong'o), 606
Grameen ("Village") Bank, 686
Grand Duchy of Warsaw, 184
Grant, Ulysses S., 309
Great Britain
See United Kingdom of
Great Britain
Great Depression
and appeasement policies
toward Germany, 469
and Argentina, 648
and Germany, 460, 461
and Japan, 437
Japan affected by, 674
and Latin America, 422
Mexico affected by, 675
and United States, 443
Great Hunger in Ireland, 290,
298–300, 340
Great Leap Forward, 561
Great Liberation, 506*m*

Great Purge of Stalin, 399, 408,
410, 443
Great Pyramid, 2
Great Reform Act, 290
Great Wall of China, 27
Great Zimbabwe, 622
Greater East Asia Co-Prosperity
Sphere, 480
Greece
ancient Greece, 8, 10–11, 10*m*
democratic government in,
536
and independence, 218
Italian invasion of, 474
and Truman Doctrine, 491
and World War II, 474
Green Revolution, 502, 520,
566, 582
Greenbelt movement, 615
Grimm, Jacob, 266
Grimm, William, 266
Grimmelshausen, Jacob von,
126
griots, 25
Gross Clinic, The (Eakins), 263
gross domestic product (GDP),
557
Grossman, David, 598
Group of Eight, 507
Guadalcanal, 486
Guadeloupe, 94
Guam, 311, 360
Guang Xu, emperor of China,
335*p*, 336
Guangzhou, 75, 76, 435
Guatemala, 229, 513, 639, 646
guerrilla warfare, 187, 218, 480,
551, 573, 598
guilds, 17
guillotine, 164*p*, 177, 179
Guillotin, Joseph, 179
Guns of August, The (Tuch-
man), 382*ps*
Guomindang party, 433–434,
435, 466
Gupta dynasty, 8–9
Gutenberg Bible, 32, 43, 60
Gutenberg, Johann, 43
gypsies, 479

H
Hague Tribunal, 376
Haiti
Bolívar in, 230
dictatorship in, 647
as French colony, 84
and Good Neighbor Policy,
423
as Hispaniola, 84
and independence, 214,
226–228, 266, 340
slave revolt in, 226
hajj, 22, 25
Hamas, 599, 601
Hamburg, 486
Hammurabi, king of Babylon, 5
Han dynasty, 9, 26, 70
Handel, George Frederick, 151
Hanfeizi, 9
Hapsburg empire
decline of, 279–280, 391
Dual Monarchy, 280–281

end of, 391
and Holy Roman Empire,
110–111
and Thirty Years' War,
125–126
Harappa, 6
Hard Times (Dickens), 706*ps*
Hargreaves, James, 200
harijans, 583
Harvard University, 89, 122
Harvey, William, 57
Hatshepsut, queen of Egypt, 4
Hausa people, 619
Haussmann, Georges, 250
Havel, Vaclav, 547, 548, 682,
684, 717*ps*
Hawaii, 349, 365
Hebrews, 5
hejab, 591, 591*p*
heliocentric solar system, 54
Hellenistic Age, 8, 11
Helsinki Accords, 508
Hemingway, Ernest, 452, 470
hemophilia, 401
Henry III, king of France, 49
Henry IV, king of France, 115
Henry VII, king of England, 66
Henry VIII, king of England,
49, 49*p*, 119
Henry the Navigator, 63
*Heritage of World Civiliza-
tions, The* (Craig), 128
Herzl, Theodor, 291, 304–305,
428
Hidalgo, Father Miguel, 214,
228–229, 704*ps*
hierarchy
definition of, 5
hieroglyphic writing of Mayas,
14
High Middle Ages, 18–19
See also Middle Ages
Himalayas, 584
Hind Swaraj, 709*ps*
Hinduism
and ahimsa, 430
and brahman, 8
and caste system, 430
development of, 8
and Muslims, 74, 332, 431,
506, 580, 581,
and reincarnation, 8
and Sikhs, 582
in Southeast Asia, 68, 69, 70
Hirohito, emperor of Japan,
436, 436*p*, 488, 556
Hiroshima, 487–488, 488*p*
Hispaniola, 84
historiography, 382
Histórís da Minha Infância
(Amado), 357*ps*
History of the African People, A
(Kenyatta) 424*ps*
*History of the Carnegie Steel
Company* (Bridge), 242*ps*
Hitler, Adolph
arrest of, 459
assassination attempts on,
486
blitzkriegs, 473
and communism, 476
Franco supported by, 470

and Jews, 462–463
and *Lebensraum*, 460
and Mussolini, 469*p*
Nazi party leader, 460
nonaggression pact with
Stalin, 471
and occupation of
Rhineland, 469
and peace as weakness, 468
rise to power, 443, 459,
460–461
and Russian invasion, 476,
483–484
suicide of, 486
and Third Reich, 461–462
and Volkswagen Beetle, 534
writings of, 460, 462*ps*, 472
Hizbullah, 599, 601
Ho Chi Minh, 571, 572
Hobbes, Thomas, 120, 144–145
Hoess, Rudolf, 489
Hogarth, William, 156
Hohenzollern family, 127, 269
Holland, kingdom of, 222
Holocaust, 479–480, 481,
489–490, 578, 587
See also Hitler; *Kristallnacht*;
Nazi party
Holy Roman Empire
abolishment of, 184, 190, 268
established by pope, 18
as First Reich of Germany,
461
Holy wars, 19
*Home Was the Land of Morning
Calm* (Kang), 569
Homer, 10, 36
Honduras, 229, 365, 646
Hong Kong, 478, 555, 558*g*, 566,
567, 644
Hong Xiuquan, 334
Honshu, 27
Hoover, Herbert, 449
Hoover Institution on War,
Revolution and Peace, 665
Hopewell culture, 9, 15
Hopi Indians, 15
horses, 89, 95, 101
Houston, P., 518
Howells, William Dean, 245*ps*
Hu Yungong, 435
Huang He, 334
Huang He valley, 7
Hudson, Henry, 66
Hugo, Victor, 221, 262
Huguenots, 48, 114, 118
Hu Jintao, 565
*Human Record: Sources of
Global History, volume 2*,
439
human rights, 508–509
See also Bill of Rights; chil-
dren; civil rights move-
ment; crime; criminal law;
Declaration of the Rights
of Man and the Citizen;
English Bill of Rights;
ethnic cleansing; feedom
of speech; genocide; labor
unions; natural laws;
natural rights; segrega-
tion; slavery; suffrage;

Index

Universal Declaration of Human Rights; voting; women

humanism, 35–36, 41

Humanities Link
See list of, xiv

Hungary
and Dual Monarchy, 267
and "freedom fighters," 547
and Hapsburgs, 127
Hungarian uprising, 549*p*
and NATO, 527, 549
and Ottoman empire, 110
as republic, 394
resistance to communism in, 547–548
revolution in, 223
and World War II, 474

hunter-gatherers, 2

Hurricane Mitch, 645, 646

Hussein, Sadam, 588, 598, 600

Hutus, 509

"Hymn of Hate" (Lissauer), 389*ps*

hypothetical questions, xlv

I

Ibn Ali, Husayn, 387

Ibo people, 425, 619

Ibsen, Henrik, 262

Identifying Main Ideas and Summarizing
See skills

Identifying Points of View and Frame of Reference
See skills

ideology
definition of, 505

Ignatius of Loyola, 51–52

Ii Naosuke, 342

Ikeda Daisaku, 245*ps*

Iliad (Homer), 10

immigration, 531, 539, 574, 641

imperialism
and Asia, 348–350
and Cold War, 504
definition of, 316
and economic dependence, 357, 362
and global economy, 361–362
impact on western culture, 365
in India to 1858, 330*m*
and Industrial Revolution, 316–318
and political tensions, 365
and religion, 363
and Social Darwinism, 317
western imperialism, 317–318, 325–326
and westernization, 363
and World War I, 365, 378

import substitution, 635

Impressionists, 262, 263

"In Memory of W. B. Yeats" (Auden), 472*ps*

Incan empire, 15, 17;
and Spanish conquest, 33

Index of Forbidden Books, 51

India
agricultural transformation

in, 330–331
and Akbar the Great, 74, 108
Amritsar massacre, 429, 442
Bharatiya Janata party (BJP), 581
Buddhism developed in, 8
caste system in, 7, 9, 430, 583
and Cold War, 584
and cyclones, 73
as democracy, 581–582
economic reform in, 582
ethnic conflict in, 506
and Gandhi, 419, 429–431
and Golden Temple at Amritsar, 579, 581–582
and Green Revolution, 582
harijans, 583
Hinduism developed in, 8
impact on Southeast Asia, 68–69
and independence, 467, 504, 578, 604
Indian National Congress, 332
Indian National Constitution, 580*ps*
and Indus Valley civilization, 6–7
industrial accidents in, 515
Maurya dynasty, 8
and Mother Teresa, 582
Mughal India, 74
Muslim League, 332, 431, 580
Muslims in, 23
nationalism movement in, 332
nonaligned in Cold War, 505
and nuclear weapons, 508
obstacles to development of, 512–513
partition of, 580
population growth in, 582
railroads in, 330, 331, 332, 582
Salt March, 419, 430–431, 431*p*
and sati, 329, 331
and Self-Employed Women's Association (SEWA), 583
and self-rule, 429–431
Sepoy Rebellion, 314, 329
textile industry, 74, 330
and trade, 8, 63, 67
and United Kingdom, 154, 290, 329–332
and World War I, 387, 429*p*
and World War II, 431

Indian National Congress, 332

Indian Ocean, 71

Indies, Council of the, 87

indigenous people
definition of, 351

indirect rule, 318

individualism, 35–36, 145, 146, 147–148, 160–163, 208–211
See also humanism; natural rights

Indochina, 336, 480

Indonesia, 62, 67, 348, 477, 573, 575

indulgences, sale of, 44–46

Indus Valley civilization, 2, 6–7

Industrial Revolution
and agricultural revolution, 197
and canal building, 202
effects on society, 253–259
and electricity, 244
and factory system, 243, 244
and imperialism, 316–318
industrial growth 1800–1900, 241*m*
industry centers 1871, 243*m*
and population explosion, 198
and standard of living, 252
and steel industry, 242
and technological development, 198
and tenements, 203
and transportation, 202
in United Kingdom, 196, 199–200
and urbanization, 203, 310

inflation
in Argentina, 678
in Brazil, 653
in Eastern Europe, 549
in Germany, 459–460, 459*p*
and gold from Americas, 102, 113

influenza, 392

Inquisition, 51, 55, 72, 111

Inside Iran (Simpson), 603*ps*

Institute of American Indian Arts Museum, 90*p*

Institute of the Americas, 665

Institute for Contemporary Studies, 665

Institutes of the Christian Religion (Calvin), 48

Institutional Revolutionary Party (PRI), 642–643

interdependence, 507, 511

International Monetary Fund (IMF), 507–508, 512, 546, 590

International Olympic Committee, 508

International Red Cross, 508, 611

International Space Station, 520

Internet, 150
advanced search on, xlix
Boolean language, xlviii–xlix
exploration on, xlix
keywords, xlviii
Prentice Hall world history Web site, xxviii
researching on, 664
searching on, xlviii
site evaluations, xlix
Virtual Field Trips, xxviii
Web site self-tests, xxviii

intifada, 598

Iran, 23, 328, 427, 578, 594, 596

Iraq, 428, 509, 538, 588, 598, 600–601
war in, 601

Ireland, 121–122
British oppression in, 155
and Catholic Emancipation

Act, 298
Easter Rising, 447, 447*p*
and European Union, 530
Great Hunger, 290, 298–300, 340
and home rule, 300, 447
and Irish Republican Army (IRA), 447, 533
nationalist movement in, 298
reunification of, 533
and terrorism, 509

Irish Free State, 447

Irish Republican Army (IRA), 533

Iron Curtain speech, 491*ps*

ironworking, 5, 6, 24

Irrawaddy River, 67, 67*p*

Isabella, queen of Spain, 64, 113

Islam
in Africa, 24, 25, 83, 617
emergence of, 22
Five Pillars of Islam, 22
fundamentalism, 590
and hajj, 22, 25
Islamic crusades, 99–100
Islamic revival in Middle East, 590
as monotheistic, 22
revolution in, 596
and Sharia, 590, 591, 596
Shiite Muslims, 601
in Southeast Asia, 69, 70
spread of, 16, 22
and women, 591
See also Muslims

Israel
Arab-Israeli conflict, 588, 598–599, 599*m*
birth of, 587–588
citizen's army of, 597
and Egypt, 593
and kibbutzim, 588
kingdom of, 5
Oslo accords, 598–599
water resources, 588

Istanbul, 20, 23, 281

Italy
anarchists in, 278
and and Rome-Berlin-Tokyo Axis, 469
and Axis Powers, 439
"Black Shirts," 455
city-states of, 34–35
coalition governments in, 536
"corporate state" of, 456
and emigration, 278
and Ethiopia, 324, 419, 466, 468
and European unity, 528
fascism in, 455–456
Greece invaded by, 474
and Group of Eight, 507
hostility with Roman Catholic Church, 278
and Libya, 322
and Mafia, 536
and Mussolini, 455–456
and nationalism, 275–278
North Africa invasion, 474
and Paris Peace Conference,

Index

395, 455
Renaissance in, 32, 34–39, 35*m*
revolution in, 223
and totalitarianism, 457, 458
and trade, 62
and Triple Alliance, 379
unification of, 266, 275–277, 277*m*, 302–303
and war crimes, 489
war declared on France, 474
and World War I, 386–387
and World War II, 474, 478, 483
Iturbide, Augustín, 229
Ivan (III) the Great, czar of Russia, 17
Ivan (IV) the Terrible, czar of Russia, 21
Ivory, 319, 319*p*
Iwo Jima, 485*p,*487

J

J'Accuse (Zola), 304
Jacobins, 175, 176
Jacobs, Aletta, 376
Jamaica, 94, 233
James I, king of England, 119, 120, 123
James II, king of England, 124
Jamestown, 82, 93, 108
Jane Eyre (Brontë), 260
Japan
   Allied occupation of, 490
   and Rome-Berlin-Tokyo Axis, 469
   atomic bombings on, 487–488
   and Axis Powers, 439
   bars trade with West, 61
   case study on, 674–677
   and children, 344
   and China, 27, 336, 346, 374, 387, 395, 432–433, 435, 439, 468, 477, 558
   Christian missionaries in, 72, 79
   clothing, manufacturing, 344
   and Commodore Perry, 340, 343
   daimyo, 29, 342, 343
   Diet, 345, 436, 556
   earthquakes, 438, 559
   economic growth of, 674–677
   "economic miracle" of, 556–558
   electronic goods, 557
   empire expansion 1934, 437*m*
   feudalism in, 27, 342
   and Great Depression, 674
   and Greater East Asia Co-Prosperity Sphere, 480
   gross domestic product (GDP), 674
   and Group of Eight, 507
   health statistics 1999, 513
   as homogeneous society, 346
   and Industrial Revolution, 243
   international politics, 558
   and investments, 344

Japanese screens, 78
kamikaze pilots, 487
and Kawasaki family, 345
and Korea, 78, 346–347
and League of Nations, 437, 468
Liberal Democratic Party (LDP), 559, 674
Manchurian Incident, 437, 443, 445, 468
Meiji empire, 344–346
Meiji Restoration, 674
military expansion, 346–347
and Nanjing, 419, 435
nationalism in, 437
navy reductions, 436
occupation by U.S., 556–557, 568
and OPEC, 558
overcrowding in, 559, 559*p*
and Paris Peace Conference, 433
Pearl Harbor, bombing of, 435, 467, 477–478, 478*p*
political corruption scandals in, 674
and POWs, 480
quotations on prosperity of, 676
railroads of, 346
"rape of Nanjing," 435
and Russian civil war, 403
Russo-Japanese War, 286, 346, 347
samurai, 29, 342, 343
seclusion policy, 342
shipbuilding industry, 557
shoguns, 27, 79
and socialism, 437
and space age, 520
steel industry of, 345
tea ceremony, 329, 343*p*
Tokugawa shogunate, 79, 342–343, 346
Tokyo earthquake of 1923, 438
trade policies of, 83, 557
and Treaty of Kanagawa, 343
and Treaty of Portsmouth, 346
and urban living, 559
and war crimes, 489
westernization of, 437
women in Japanese society, 344, 345, 436, 556, 559
and World War I, 387
and World War II, 439, 477–478, 480, 486–488
zaibatsu, 345, 436, 437, 557
Japan Society, 665
Japanese Imperialism and the Massacre in Nanjing (Gao Xingzu, Wu Shimin, Hu Yungong, Cha Ruizhen), 435*ps*
Java, 70, 361
jazz, 452–453
Jefferson, Thomas, 159, 306
Jenner, Edward, 144
Jerusalem, 5, 587, 598, 599, 599*m*
Jesuits, 51–52, 87

Jesus, 13, 36
Jews
   and antisemitism, 304, 428, 459, 460, 479–480
   and concentration camps, 463
   and "death camps," 479–480
   and Dreyfus Affair, 304–305
   and England, 122
   and "final solution," 463
   First Zionist Congress, 291
   as Germany's scapegoats, 459, 460
   ghettos, 53
   and Holocaust, 480, 481, 578, 587
   and Irish Great Hunger, 300
   and *Kristallnacht,* 443
   and Martin Luther, 53
   and Palestine, 428
   pogroms in Russia, 286, 287, 304
   in Poland, 53
   and Protestant Reformation, 52–53
   and Soviet Union, 412
   and Spain, 113, 118
   taxation by Muslims, 22
   and Zionism, 291, 304–305, 428
Jiang Jieshi, 434–435, 560, 562, 566
Jiang Zemin, 565
Jinnah, Muhammad Ali, 431, 580
job specialization, 2
Johannesburg, 425
John I, king of Portugal, 63
John Paul II, Pope, 548, 548*p,* 655
Johnson, Lyndon, 538
joint stock companies, 102
Joint United Nations Programme on HIV/AIDS, 615
joint ventures, definition of, 563
Jordan, 513, 588, 598
Joseph II, emperor of Austria, 133, 150
Journal of Antonio Pigafetta, 66*ps*
Joyce, James, 452
Juárez, Benito, 358, 367
Judaism, 5, 13
   See also Jews
Junkers, 127–128, 269
jury system, 18
Justin, Byzantine emperor, 20
Justinian's Code, 20
Juvenal, xxxvi

K

Kaiser, Robert G., 542
kamikaze pilots, 487
Kanagawa, Treaty of, 343
Kandinsky, Vasily, 451
Kang, K. Connie, 569
Karageorge, 217*p,* 218
Kashmir, 506, 584 ,
Kaunda, Kenneth, 613*ps*
Kawasaki family, 345
Kay, J. P., 203

Kay, John, 200
Kazakhstan, 546
Kellogg-Brand Pact of 1928, 445
Kennan, George, 491
Kennedy, John F., 537*ps,* 538, 640
Kenya, 424–425, 518, 606, 609–610, 615
Kenyatta, Jomo, 424*ps,* 609–610, 609*ps*
Kepler, Johannes, 54–55
Khmer empire, 69
Khmer Rouge, 572–573
Khmer Temple, 68*p*
Khomeini, Ayatollah Ruholla, 592, 596*p*
Khrushchev, Nikita, 541, 541*p,* 548, 639
kibbutzim, 428, 588
Kiev, 21
Kikuyu people, 424–425, 609
Kilwa, 319
Kim Il Sung, 568, 570
Kim Jong Il, 570
Kim Young Sam, 684
Kincaid, J., 193
King, Martin Luther, 539, 539*p,* 624
Kipling, Rudyard, 317, 361
Kitty Hawk, 246
kiva, 15
Klaus, Vaclav, 682
Klee, Paul, 451
knights, 16
Knox, John, 48
Koch, Robert, 249
Kohl, Helmut, 535
Kollontai, Alexandra, 413
Kollwitz, Käthe, 444
Kongo, 16, 60, 98
Koori people, 353
Korea
   and China, 27, 346–347
   Choson dynasty, 78
   demilitarized zone (DMZ), 568
   and March First Movement, 347
   as Hermit Kingdom, 78, 347
   isolation of, 78
   Japan's invasion of, 78
   Korean War, 505, 524, 537, 568*m*
   and Treaty of Portsmouth, 346
   See also North Korea; South Korea
Korea Society, 665
Korean War, 505, 524, 537, 568*m*
Kosovo, 380, 509, 538, 551
Kosovo Liberation Army, 551
Kossuth, Louis, 223, 223*p*
Kostunica, Vojislav, 551
kowtow, 76
Kremlin, 403
Kristallnacht, 443, 463
Krupp, Alfred, 247
Krupp works, 272
Krupskaya, Nadezhda, 402, 405, 412
Kubitschek, Juscelino, 651

Index

Kulturkampf, 273
Kumaratunge, Chandrika, 689
Kurds, 506, 509, 586, 588, 601
Kurnakov, Sergyei N., 397
Kush, 24
 See also Nubia
Kuwait, 538, 588, 588*g*, 600–601

L

"La Marseillaise," 181*ps*
labor unions, 207, 210, 241, 251, 252, 311
Lafayette, Marquis de, 171
laissez faire, 148, 208–209, 295
Landless Movement in Brazil, 653
language
 Boolean language, xlvii–xlix
 and Columbian Exchange, 102
 development of, 2
 endangered languages, 516
 Quechua, 15
 Singhalese, 585
 Swahili, 319, 621
 Tamil, 585
Laos, 67, 349, 363, 571
La Rocca, Cesare de Florio, 652
Last Supper, The (Leonardo), 37
Latin America: A Concise Interpretive History (Burns), 91
Latin America, the Democratic Option (Llosa), 718*ps*
Latin America
 and Alliance for Progress, 640
 and *caudillos,* 357, 634
 colonial legacy, 356
 and creoles, 225
 description of, 225*n*
 development versus environment, 640–641
 and drug wars, 640
 economic imperialism in, 356–360
 economics of dependence, 357
 Good Neighbor Policy, 423
 and Great Depression, 422
 ideologies in, 634
 and immigration to U.S., 641
 and import substitution, 635
 independence revolution in, 225–231
 independent nations in 1844, 228*m*
 and liberation theology, 517
 and mestizos, 225
 military regimes in, 634, 634*p*
 Organization of American States (OAS), 630, 640
 and peninsulares, 88, 225
 population density in, 631*m*
 racial prejudice in, 356
 and regionalism, 357
 and slavery, 225
 social structure in, 633
 and United States, 639–640
 urbanization, 633–634
 women in government,

636–637, 636*p*
 See also Americas; specific countries
latitude, xxxiv
Latvia, 394, 403, 473, 544
Laud, William, Archbishop of Canterbury, 120
Lavoisier, Antoine, 144
law
 and civil disobedience, 430, 539
 Code of Hammurabi, 5
 criminal law, 596
 English Bill of Rights, 123, 124
 English common law, 18
 and jury system, 18
 Justinian's Code, 20
 labor laws, 297
 Laws of the Indies, 88
 Napoleonic Code, 184, 186, 188, 305
 natural laws, 144
 Sharia, 590, 591, 596
Lawrence, T. E. (Lawrence of Arabia), 387
lawyers, 104
Lazarus, Emma, 306
League of Nations, 395, 410, 437, 445, 448, 468
 and Italian sanctions, 468
 and Japanese sanctions, 468
Learning From Maps
 See skills
Lebanon, 428, 513, 599–600
Lebensraum, 460
LeBrun, Elisabeth Vigée, 151
Lee Kwan Yew, 567, 567*ps*
Lee, Robert E., 309
Lee Teng-hui, 566
Leeuwenhoek, Anthony van, 57
Legalism, 9
Leger, Fernand, 442
legitimacy,
 definition of, 191
Lend-Lease Act, 477
Lenin, Vladimir Ilyich Ulyanov
 assassination attempts on, 404
 as Bolshevik leader, 402
 and Comintern, 410
 death of, 405
 exile of, 402
 marriage of, 402
 NEP (New Economic Policy), 398, 405–406
 as radical activist, 286
 speeches of, 402
 and Treaty of Brest-Litovsk, 389
 and "war communism," 405
Leningrad, 476
Leopold II, king of Belgium, 321
Lepanto, battle of, 111
Les Misérables (Hugo), 221, 262
"Letter From Jamaica" (Bolívar), 233*ps*
Letter to King John of Portugal (Affonso), 698*ps*

Levellers, 122
Leviathan (Hobbes), 120*ps*
liberalism, 217
liberation theology, 517, 637
Liberator (Garrison), 307
Liberia, 195, 320, 324
Liberty Leading the People (Delacroix), 261
libraries, 5
Libya, 322, 474
Life and Writings (Mazzini), 275*ps*
life expectancy
 in industrial areas, 1850–1910, 249*g*
Life of Benito Mussolini (Sarfatti), 457
Life of Gustavus Vassa, The (Equiano), 400*ps*, 107*ps*
"Life Story of a Villista, The" (Ferreira), 421*ps*
Liliuokalani, queen of Hawaii, 349
Lincoln, Abraham, 113*ps*, 284, 309, 309*p*
Line of Demarcation, 64–65
Lissauer, Ernst, 389
literature
 of ancient Greece, 10
 of Egyptian life, 595
 of Enlightenment, 153
 griots, 25
 Renaissance literature, 38–39, 42
 and revolution, 221
 and romanticism, 260
 of Spain's Golden Age, 113
 stream-of-consciousness writing, 452
 See also Bible; drama
Lithuania, 394, 403, 473, 480, 544, 670
"Little Red Book," 562
Litvak, Lily, 482
Liverpool-Manchester Railroad, 195
Lives of the Most Eminent Italian Painters, Sculptors, and Architects (Vasari), 37*ps*
Livingstone, David, 320, 321
Llosa, Mario Vargas, 718*ps*
Lloyd George, David, 297
Locarno treaties, 442, 445
Locke, John, 144–145, 159, 160–161, 172, 701*ps*
Log of Christopher Columbus, The (Fuson), 81
London Daily News, 303*ps*
"London Poor" (Hollingshead), 265*ps*
longitude, xxx
Long March of Mao Zedong, 399, 419, 434–435, 466
Long Parliament, 120
Lorraine, 376, 393, 448, 533
Lott, Trent, 644
Louis Philippe, king of France, 220
Louis XIII, king of France, 115
Louis XIV, king of France, 114–118
 correspondence of, 135

 death of, 109
 and French Academies, 116
 and French debt, 168
 and French domination of Europe, 301
 and New France, 92–93
 nobles' rights restricted by, 166–167
 parties of, 114
 portrait of, 118*p*
 and royal absolutism, 115–116, 119
 and Versailles, 116–118, 272
Louis XV, king of France, 118, 168
Louis XVI, king of France
 acceptance of National Assembly, 170
 as Citizen Capet, 181
 and Estates General, 169
 execution of, 176–178
 and French Revolution, 173
 and reform failures, 168–169
 and Robespierre, 178
Louis XVIII, king of France, 188, 191, 219
Louisiana Purchase, 190, 214, 306
L'Ouverture, Toussaint, 226, 227, 227*p*, 228
Luddites, 206
Luftwaffe, 474, 476
Lugard, Frederick, 316
Luks, George, 375
Lusitania, 374, 390
Luther, Martin, 33, 44–46, 45*ps*, 46*p*, 47*ps*
Luxembourg, 191, 528
Lyons, Eugene, 417
Lytton, Constance, 295

M

Maathi, Wangari, 615
Macao, 75
MacArthur, Douglas, 485, 556, 568
Macartney, Lord, 76, 77*p*
Macaulay, Catharine, 147
Macaulay, Thomas, 331, 332
McCarthy, Joseph, 537
Macdonald, John, 352
Macedonia, 11
Machiavelli, Niccolò, 39, 696*ps*
Mackenzie, William Lyon, 351
McLuhan, Marshall, 43
Madero, Francisco, 420
Mafia, 536
Magellan, Ferdinand, 60, 65–66
magic,
 and witch hunts, 52
Magic Flute, The (Mozart), 152
Maginot Line, 448
Magna Carta, 17, 155, 204, 207, 208, 209*ps*
Magyars, 16
Mahan, Alfred T., 311
Mahayana Buddhism, 70
Mahfouz, Naguib, 595
Making Inferences and Drawing Conclusions
 See skills
Making Valid Generalizations
 See skills

Malacca, 60, 61, 71
Malacca strait, 67
malaria, 249, 640
Malaya, 348, 478
Mali kingdom, 17, 25
Malinche, 85
Malindi, 96
Malthus, Thomas, 208–209, 258
Malvinas, 649
Manchester, 206, 293
Manchuria, 346, 435, 443, 468
Mandate of Heaven, 7
mandates, 394–395
Mandela, Nelson, 605, 622, 623, 678, 720ps
Mandelstam, Osip, 413, 415
Manifest Destiny, 306
Manucci, Niccolò, 75
Mao Zedong, 146, 467, 505, 554, 604, 712ps
  death of, 562
  establishment of People's Republic of China, 560
  "Little Red Book," 562
  Long March of, 399, 419, 434–435, 466
  and North Korea, 568
  and one-party totalitarian state, 561
  picture of, 561p
Maori people, 340, 355
maps
  land claims in Americas, 1675, 83m
  land claims in Americas about 1750, 94m
  of ancient Greece, 10m
  Arab lands, 427m
  Arab-Israeli conflicts, 599m
  Argentina's economic activity, 649m
  Asia independence, 579m
  Asia's trade, 315m
  Australia, 354m
  bodies of water, xxx
  Canadian map, 1867–1914, 352m
  China's civil war, 1925–1935, 434m, 441m
  Cold War in Europe, 492m
  compass of, xxx
  Congress of Vienna 1815, 190m
  desertification, 615m
  dictatorships in Europe 1917–1939, 394m
  Europe during World War II, 483m
  European aggression, 1939, 471m
  European revolutions, 1815–1829, 215m
  European unification, 267m
  explorations voyages 1487–1609, 64m
  German unification, 269m
  Greece, 10m
  imperialism in India, 330m
  Industrial Revolution, 195m, 241m, 243m
  Japan, 437m
  Korean War, 568m

Latin America, 228m, 631m
latitude and longitude, xxx
learning from, xxx–xxxi
locator maps, xxx
map of ancient Middle East, 4m
Middle East, 4m, 427m, 599m
nationalism movements 1910–1939, 491m
New Zealand, 354m
North America 1783, 143m
North American map in 1783, 143m
political areas on, xxx
railroads of Great Britain, 201m
religions of Western Europe, 51m
Renaissance, 35m
revolutionary France at war, 1793, 165m
Russia, 20m, 130m, 399m, 667m
scale use, xxx
Serbia, 671m
Southeast Asia, 69m, 81m, 349m
Thirty Years' War, 126m
titles of, xxx
trade, 99m, 200m
United States, 200m
western imperialism in China, 1914, 336m
World War I, 1914–1918, 375m, 378m
World War II, 467m, 483m, 487m
See also list of, xx; skills
maquiladoras, 643–644
Marconi, Guglielmo, 246–247
Marcos, Ferdinand, 555, 573
Marcus Aurelius, 12, 13
margarine, 474
margin buying, 446
Maria Theresa, Holy Roman empress, 127, 127p, 150
Marie Antoinette, queen of France, 127, 172, 173, 178
Marina, Doña, 85
Marne, battle of the, 383
Marquise de Rouget With Her Two Children (LeBrun), 151
marriage
  arranged marriage, 433
  child marriage, 331
  and Industrial Revolution, 254
  polygamy, 426
"Marseillaise, La," 181
Marseille, 103
Marshall Plan, 492, 527
Martinique, 94
Martson Moor, Battle of, 121p
Marx, Karl, 146, 195, 210, 286, 402
Marxism, 210–211, 273
  See also Communism
Mary, queen of England, 50
Massachusetts Bay Colony, 122
Mathematical Principles of Natural Philosophy (Newton), 56

mathematics, 22, 35
Matisse, Henri, 451
matrilineal descent, 68
Mau Mau, 609
Mauritius, 72
Maurya, Asoka, 8
Maurya, Chandragupta, 8
Maurya dynasty, 8
Maxim, Hiram, 318p
Maxim machine guns, 317, 318p
Maximilian, Archduke of Austria, 302, 359
May Fourth Movement, 433, 433p
Mayan civilization, 9, 14, 16
Mazarin, Cardinal Jules, 115
Mazzini, Giuseppe, 266p, 275, 277
Mazzoni, Anna, 253
Mbeki, Thabo, 624
Mecca, 22, 25
Medicare, 538
Medici family, 32, 34–35
medicine
  genetic engineering, 518
  germ theory, 249
  and Industrial Revolution, 196
  organ transplants, 518
  and population growth, 249–250
  and Renaissance, 57
  vaccines, 249
  See also disease
Meiji, emperor of Japan, 344, 345
Mein Kampf (Hitler), 460, 472
Meir, Golda, 688, 689
Mekong River, 67
Melanesia, 349
Méliès, Georges, 452
Memoirs (Catherine the Great), 133ps
Mendeleyev, Dmitri, 257–258
Menelik II, king of Ethiopia, 324
Menem, Carlos Saul, president of Argentina, 678
Menes, king, ancient Egypt, 2, 4
Mennonites, 49
mercantilism, 104, 148, 154
mercenaries, 126
merchant guilds, 17
Mercosur, 636, 640
Meroë, 8, 24
Mesopotamia, 5
Messiah, 13
Messiah (Handel), 151
mestizos, 89, 225
Methodist Church, 206
métis, 353
Metternich, Clemens von, 190, 191p, 216, 218, 222, 224, 279
Mexico
  Alliance for Change, 643
  case study on, 674–677
  and Chiapas, 643
  and conquistadors, 84–85
  Constitution of 1917, 422
  and Cortés, 60

early civilizations in, 2
economic growth of, 674–677
economic nationalism in, 675
and French rule, 302
and Great Depression, 675
independence from Spain, 228–229, 290
Institutional Revolutionary Party (PRI), 642–643, 675
invasion of United States, 423
and Benito Juárez, 358
and maquiladoras, 643–644
Mayan civilization in, 9, 14
Mexican Independence Day, 229
Mexican Revolution, 418, 420–422
and Monroe Doctrine, 359
and nationalism, 422–423
nationalization of industry in, 422, 443
and North American Free Trade Association (NAFTA), 507, 540, 636, 640, 644, 675
oil industry, 422, 443
and Olympic games, 643
peasants in, 420
peonage in, 359
political scandals in, 674
poverty in, 633, 642
PRI (Institutional Revolutionary Party), 422
quotations on prosperity of, 676
reforms in, 422
Republic of, 229
revolution in, 398, 674–675
and Santa Anna, 358
stability struggles of, 358–359
and Texas, 358
trading partners of, 675
U.S. at war with, 358, 359–360
and Zapatistas, 420
See also Aztec empire
Mexico City, 84, 85, 89, 643
Michelangelo, 37–38
Micronesia, 349
microscope, 57
Middle Ages, 16–17
  See also High Middle Ages
Middle America, 14–15, 228
  See also specific countries
Middle East
  in 1920s, 427m
  and African slavery, 97
  Arab-Israeli conflicts, 588, 598–599, 599m
  diversity in, 586–588
  economic policies, 590
  governments in, 588
  Islamic revival in, 590
  map of ancient Middle East, 4m
  map of water resources, xxxim
  and nuclear weapons, 597–598
  and Organization of

Index

Petroleum Exporting
  Countries (OPEC), 511,
  528, 538, 558, 588
Oslo accords, 598–599
Palestinian intifada, 598
Persian Gulf Wars, 579,
  600–601
superpower rivalries in, 597
water resources, 588–589,
  589m
Middle Kingdom, China as, 7
Middle Kingdom of Egypt, 2
Middle Passage, 97–98
Midsummer Night's Dream, A
  (Shakespeare), 42
Midway, Battle of, 486
militarism
  definition of, 379
  and disarmament, 445
  in Germany, 461p
  in Japan, 439
Mill, John Stuart, 209
Mill Life at Styal (Kay), 203ps
Millennium Dome, 503p
Milosevic, Slobodan, 550, 551
Milton, John, 146
Ming dynasty, 17, 27, 32, 75–76
minimum wage, 422
Minoan civilization, 3, 10
Miracle of Dunkirk, 473–474
missionaries
  in Africa, 320
  of Christianity, 21, 72, 75–76,
    79, 87–88
  in New France, 92
  and westernization, 363
Mississippian civilization, 15,
  16
Missouri, 488
Mitterrand, François, 529ps,
  533, 534
Mobuto Sese Seko, 620
Mochican civilization, 9
Moctezuma, 85
Modern and Contemporary
  European History, 1815–1940
  (Schapiro), 268
Mohanti, Prafulla, 516
Mohenjo-Daro, 6
Molière, 116
Moluccas, 62, 348
Mombasa, 96, 319
Mona Lisa (Leonardo), 33
monarchies
  absolute monarchies, 111,
    119, 120, 145
  constitutional monarchies,
    171
  definition of, 11
  limited monarchies, 173
Monet, Claude, 262, 263
money, 26, 525, 530, 533
Mongkut, king of Siam, 349
Mongols, 21, 27
monopolies, 247–248, 430
monotheism, 5, 22
Monroe Doctrine, 340, 359, 360
Monroe, James, 359
monsoons, 67–68
montage, 414
Montenegro, 551, 670
Montesquieu, Baron de, 145,

145p, 147, 149, 160–161
Montgomery, Bernard, 482
More, Thomas, 41, 50, 210
Morelos, Father José, 229
Mormons, 307
Morocco, 482
Morse, Samuel F.B., 246–247
Mosaddiq, Muhammad, 594
mosaics, 22
Moscosco, Mireya, 636, 644
Moscow, 403, 476
mosquitoes, 226
"most favored nation," 343
Mother Teresa, 582
Mothers Against War, 377
"Mothers of the Plaza de
  Mayo," 649
Mott, Lucretia, 309
Mount Holyoke, 257
Mozambique, 322, 626
Mozart, Wolfgang Amadeus,
  150, 152, 153
Mrs. Dalloway (Woolf), 452
Mt. Everest, 584
Mubarak, Hosni, 594
Mugabe, Robert, 622
Mughal dynasty, 23
Mughal India, 74
Muhammad, prophet of Islam,
  16, 22
Muhammad Ahmad, 325
Muhammad Ali, 314, 327
mulattoes, 89, 225, 226
Muler, William James, 204
Müller, Doctor, 393
Munich Conference, 470, 471
Musa, Mansa, 25, 32
Musharraf, Pervez, 579, 583
music, 151, 221, 261, 452–453,
  519, 521
Muslim empire, 19, 22–23
Muslim League, 332, 431, 580
Muslims
  and Charlemagne's empire,
    16
  and Hindus, 74, 332, 431,
    580, 581
  in India, 23, 506
  National Liberation Front
    (FLN), 610
  in the Philippines, 573
  reform movements, 325–326
  Shiite Muslims, 601
  and Southeast Asia, 71
  and Spain, 110, 113, 118
  sultans, 23
  Taliban, 585
  and trade, 62
  and western culture, 517
  and western imperialism,
    325–326
  See also Islam
Mussolini, Benito
  execution of, 486
  fascist dictatorship of, 442
  Franco supported by, 470
  and Hitler, 469p
  as Il Duce, 456
  imperialist ambitions of, 468
  overthrow of, 483
  and peace as weakness, 468
  rise of, 455–456

troops in North Africa, 474
mutual-aid societies, 251
Muzorewa, Bishop Abel, 377
Mwinyi, Ali Hassan, 621
Myanmar, 67, 69, 348, 513, 573
Mycenaean people, 10
mystics, 7

N
NAFTA
  See North American Free
    Trade Association (NAF-
    TA)
Nagako, empress of Japan, 436
Nagasaki, 488
Nagy, Imre, 547–548
Namibia, 624, 626, 626p
Nanjing, 435
Nanjing, Treaty of, 240, 334
Naples, 275
Napoleon III, emperor of
  France, 222, 250, 271, 272,
  276, 291, 301–303, 301p, 359
Napoleonic Code, 186, 188, 305
Nasser, Gamal Abdal, 578, 586,
  593–594
National Liberation Front
  (FLN), 610
National Socialist German
  Workers Party
  See Nazi party
National Union for the Total
  Independence of Angola
  (UNITA), 627
nationalism
  cultural nationalism, 423
  definition of, 181, 217
  economic nationalism, 423
  impact of, 186
  major movements,
    1910–1939, 419m, 504
nationalization of industry,
  422, 528, 532
Native American Population of
  Central Mexico, xlig
Native Americans
  and American Revolution,
    160
  early civilizations of, 15, 16
  and European diseases, 95
  forced conversion to Chris-
    tianity, 84, 87–88
  pueblos, 15
  and reservations, 307
  slavery of, 88
NATO
  See North Atlantic Treaty
    Organization (NATO)
natural laws, 144
natural rights, 145
natural selection, 258–259
navigation, 63, 65
Navigation Acts, 158
Nazi party
  and education, 462
  and genocide, 479–480
  Hitler as leader of, 460
  and Holocaust, 480, 481
  ideology revival, 535–536
  nonaggression pact with
    Soviet Union, 471
  and racism, 462

and religion, 462
  and swastika, 461p
  See also Germany; Hitler,
    Adolph
Neanderthal, 258
Necker, Jacques, 168
N'Dour, Youssou, 521p
Nefertiti, queen of Egypt, 5p
négritude movement, 425
Nehanda, Shona leader, 324
Nehru, Jawaharlal, 547ps,
  580ps, 581, 582, 584
Nelson, Horatio, 185
Neolithic age, 2, 14
Netherlands, 48, 53, 111, 126,
  160, 191, 513, 528
  See also Dutch; Holland,
    kingdom of
neutrality, 381
New Deal, 449, 538
New France, 92–93
New Netherland, 94
New Stone Age, 2
New Testament, 41
New Year's Address (Havel),
  717ps
New York, 158
New York Stock Exchange, 419,
  446, 449
New York Times, The, 531ps, 652
New Zealand
  annexed by U.K., 340
  and British Commonwealth
    of Nations, 447
  geography of, 354m
  and Industrial Revolution,
    243
  Maori struggles in, 355
  as penal colony, 296–297
  and self-government, 355
  and women's suffrage, 291
  and World War I, 387
Newcomen, Thomas, 198
Newfoundland, 66, 154
Newton, Isaac, 56–57
Ney, Michel, 188
Ngo Dinh Diem, 571, 572
NGOs
  See nongovernmental organ-
    izations (NGOs)
Ngugi wa Thiong'o, 606
Nguyen Sa, 523ps
Nicaragua, 229, 423, 637,
  644–646
Nicholas I, czar of Russia, 283
Nicholas II, czar of Russia,
  286–287, 289, 379, 400
Nicolson, Harold, 393
Niemoller, Martin, 764, 764ps
Nigeria, 25, 425, 506, 512, 513,
  611, 618, 619
Nightingale, Florence, 250, 250p
Nijinsky, Vaslav, 285p
Nile River, 4, 594
Niña, 64
95 Theses, 33, 45
nirvana, 8
Nixon, Richard, 538, 572, 608
Njoya, king of Bamum, 322
Nkomo, Joshua, 622
"Nkosi Sikelel' iAfrika" (God
  Bless Africa), 622

Index

Nkrumah, Kwame, 608, 608*p*, 609, 714*ps*
"No Time" (Nguyen Sa), 523
Nobel, Alfred, 244, 376
Nobel Peace Prize, 624
Nobel Peace Prize Lecture (Walesa), 715*ps*
nomadic cultures, 2
nongovernmental organizations (NGOs), 508
nonviolent resistance, 430
Norgay, Tenzing, 584
Noriega, Manuel, 639
Normandy, 484
Normans, 17
North America
French and Indian War, 109
penal colonies in, 353
plantation economies in, 93
North American Free Trade Agreement (NAFTA), 507, 540, 636, 640, 644, 675
North Atlantic Treaty Organization (NATO), 493, 526, 527, 534, 536, 545, 549, 550–551
North Korea, 542, 568, 569, 570
See also Korea; South Korea
North Vietnam, 542
See also Vietnam
Northern Ireland, 509, 533
See also Ireland
Norway, 473, 536
demographics on, 687
gross domestic product (GDP), 687
women in national development, 686–689
Nothing Less Than Victory (Pluskat), 484*ps*
Nova Scotia, 154
Nubia, 3, 24
nuclear family, 25
Nuclear Non-Proliferation Treaty (NPT), 508
Nuclear Test Ban Treaty, 526–527
nuclear weapons, 302
atomic bombs, 488
and Iran, 596
and North Korea, 570
and Pakistan, 584–585
Nuremberg trials, 489
Nyerere, Julius, 504, 610, 613, 620–621
nylon, 474

O

OAS
See Organization of American States (OAS)
OAU
See Organization of African Unity (OAU)
Obasanjo, Olusegun, 619
Obrenovic, Milos, 218
Ocalan, Abdullah, 586
Oceania, 349*n*
O'Connell, Daniel, 298
October Manifesto, 287
Odyssey (Homer), 10
Of Plymouth Plantation: 1620–1647 (Bradford), 93*ps*

O'Higgins, Bernardo, 230
oil industry
and Africa, 618*p*
and global economy, 510
in Iran, 427
in Mexico, 357, 393, 422
offshore oil rigs, 528*p*
oil crisis in 1970s, 511, 524, 528
power of, 328
in Venezuela, 357
See also Organization of Petroleum Exporting Countries (OPEC)
Okinawa, 487
Old Stone Age, 2
oligarchy, 11, 156
Olmec civilization, 3, 8, 13
Olympic games, 376, 508*p*, 624, 643
On the Christian Life (Calvin), 48*ps*
On the Origin of Species (Darwin), 241, 258–259
On the Revolutions of the Heavenly Spheres (Copernicus), 54–55
On the Structure of the Human Body (Vesalius), 57
"On This Day I Complete My Thirty–Sixth Year" (Gordon, Byron), 218*ps*
One Earth, Four or Five Worlds: Reflections on Contemporary History (Paz), 642*ps*
Ontario, 351
OPEC
See Organization of Petroleum Exporting Countries (OPEC)
opera, 151
Operation Barbarossa, 476–477
Operation Desert Storm, 482
Operation Sea Lion, 476
Opium War, 215, 333–334, 333*p*, 343, 567
organ transplants, 518
Organization of African Unity (OAU), 610
Organization of American States (OAS), 630, 640
Organization of Petroleum Exporting Countries (OPEC), 328, 511, 528, 538, 558, 588, 640
See also oil industry
Orozco, José Clemente, 423
Ortega, Daniel, 644
Orwell, George, 446
Oslo accords, 598–599
Otto, Nikolaus, 246
Ottoman empire
Armenian massacre, 326–327
collapse of, 426
Constantinople conquered by, 20
diversity of peoples, 281
Hungary occupied by, 110
revolts in, 217, 218
rise of, 23
Serbs defeated by, 17
and World War I, 387

and Young Turks, 326
Outlook for China, Human Rights, The (Wu), 721*ps*
overproduction, 445
Owen, Robert, 194, 210
Oxfam, 611
Oyo, 99

P

Pacific Ocean, discovery of, 65–66
Pacific Rim, 574–575
pacifism
definition of, 376, 469
Pagan, kingdom of, 69
Pageant of Europe (Stearns), 179
Pahlavi dynasty, 427
Paine, Thomas, 158, 292
Pak Chi-won, 78
Pakistan
creation of, 431, 467, 580
economy of, 584
government of, 583–584
and nuclear weapons, 508, 584–585
Palestine, 428, 587, 588, 599
Palestine Liberation Organization (PLO), 598
Pamela (Richardson), 153
Pan American Society of California, 665
Pan-African Congress, 425, 441
Pan-Africanism, 425
Pan-Arabism, 427, 587
Panama, 65, 360, 636, 637, 639, 644
Panama Canal, 241, 341, 360, 374
pandemic, 392
Pankhurst, Emmeline, 298, 298*p*
papermaking, 9
Paraguay, 640
Paré, Ambroise, 57
Parents, The (Kollwitz), 444*p*
Paris
Eiffel Tower, 250, 251*p*
and Enlightenment, 149
French Revolution, 143, 164, 170, 176
Paris Commune, 172, 303
as revolutionary center, 171
sewer system, 250
siege in 1870, 302, 302*m*
storming Bastille in, 143, 164, 170
and urban renewal, 250
and World War II, 484
Paris Peace Conference, 375, 393, 394, 395, 427–428
Park, Mungo, 320
parliament
Act of Supremacy, 50, 119
and Act of Union, 142
cabinet system, 156
and Great Council, 18
House of Commons, 156, 157
House of Lords, 156–157, 294
Long Parliament, 120
Navigation Acts, 158
and reform, 292

"power of the purse," 124
See also England; United Kingdom of Great Britain
Parnell, Charles Stewart, 300
Parrots, The (González), 634
Passy, Frédéric, 376
Pasternak, Boris, 415
Pasteur, Louis, 249
pasteurization, 249
patricians, 12
patrons, 35, 44
Paul, apostle, 13
Paul III, Pope, 59
Paul IV, Pope, 53
Paul VI, Pope, 510
Pax Romana (Roman Peace), 8, 12, 13
Paz, Octavio, 642
Peace of Augsburg, 46
Peacemaking, 1919 (Nicholson), 393*ps*
Peace of Westphalia, 126, 127
Pearl Harbor, 435, 467, 477–478, 478*p*
pearls, 110
penal colonies, 296–297, 353–354
peninsulares, 88, 225
peons, 88, 359
People's Democratic Dictatorship, The (Mao Zedong), 712*ps*
People's Republic of China, 467, 554, 560, 562–565, 566, 630
See also China
pepper, 62, 72
perestroika, 544
Perestroika (Gorbachev), 716*ps*
Pericles, 8, 11
Perón, Eva, 648–649, 648*p*
Perón, Isabel, 649, 689
Perón, Juan, 648–649, 648*p*
Perry, Matthew, 340, 343
Persian empire, 3
Persian Gulf Wars, 579, 600–601
Persian Letters (Montesquieu), 145, 149
Persistence of Memory, The (Dali), 451*p*
Peru
civil war in, 85
ethnic diversity in, 632*g*, 633
Inca civilization in, 15
poverty in, 633*p*
and Spain, 85
temple platforms in, 2
Peter the Great, 109, 129–132, 282
Peter III, czar of Russia, 132
Peterloo Massacre, 206
Petition of Right, 120
Petrarch, Francesco, 36
Petrograd, 401, 402
See also St. Petersburg
Phan Thanh Gian, 348
pharaohs, 3, 4
Philadelphia, 158, 159, 160
Philip, king of Macedonia, 11
Philip II, king of Spain, 37, 72, 108, 111–112, 111*p*, 112*m*, 113, 115

Index

Philip V, king of Spain, 118
Philippa, queen of Portugal, 63
Philippines
  Bataan Death March,
    485–486
  geography of, 67
  independence from Spain,
    267, 341
  independence from U.S., 573
  Islam in, 573
  and Magellan's exploration,
    66
  nationalist struggles in, 350
  "people power," 555
  Spain's conquest of, 72, 79
  and Spanish-American War,
    311, 350, 360
  urbanization of, 573
  as U.S. territory, 311, 350
  and World War II, 478, 485
philosophes, 145, 147, 149, 150,
  172
philosophy, 144, 145
  See also specific philosophers
Phoenicians, 5
"phony war," 473
photography, 240, 263, 274*p*
physiocrats, 148
Picasso, Pablo, 364, 451
Pietà (Michelangelo), 37
pilgrimages, 46
Pilgrims, 33, 93, 93*n*
Pilsudski, Joseph, 458
pineapples, 365
Pinochet, Augusto, 634
Pinta, 64
Pinzón, Martin Alonso, 81
piracy, 91, 112
Pitcairn Island, 355
Pizarro, Francisco, 85
plantations, 88, 91, 93, 97, 226,
  362, 424
Plato, 11
Platt Amendment, 360, 423
plebeians, 12
plebiscite, 183, 651
PLO
  See Palestine Liberation
    Organization (PLO)
Pluskcat, Werner, 484
Plymouth Colony, 33
Poem of the Cid, 19
Poems (Michelangelo), 38
poetry
  of Rudyard Kipling, 317, 361
  of World War I, 388, 389
pogroms, 286, 287, 304
poison gas, 384, 385–386
Pol Pot, 573
Poland
  communist collapse in, 666
  and democracy, 548
  German invasion of, 399,
    419, 466, 472, 473, 473*p*
  health statistics 1999, 513
  independence regained, 394,
    403, 544
  Jewish settlements in, 53
  and Locarno treaties, 445
  and NATO, 527, 549
  partition of, 109, 133
  pro-Soviet communist

  government in, 491
  revolution for independence
    in, 223
  and Solidarity, 548
  Ukraine ruled by, 670
polis, 11
"Political Justice" (Godwin),
  210
political parties, 155–156
Polk, Samuel, 359
polygamy, 426
Polynesia, 349
Poole, Otis Manchester, 438
poor nations, 510
Pope, Alexander, 56, 144
Popes: John Paul II, 548, 655
**Popular Liberation Movement
  of Angola (MPLA),** 627
population
  in Bangladesh, 584
  China's control of, 513, 563,
    565
  and developing nations, 512
  and development of farm-
    ing, 2
  in India, 583
  and Industrial Revolution,
    198, 208
  and landownership in
    France, 1789, 167
  Latin American population
    density, 631*m*
  and medicine, 249–250
  Native American population
    decline, 388*g,* 397
**Population Reference Bureau
  (PRB),** 665
porcelain, 76
Portrait of Dr. Gachet (Van
  Gogh), 263*p*
Portsmouth, Treaty of, 346
Portugal
  African colonization, 96, 626
  and Angola, 322
  Brazilian colony of, 89, 91,
    231, 650
  democratic government in,
    536
  empire in East, 71–72
  and European Union, 536
  explorations of, 63
  Goa seized by, 71
  and Inquisition, 72
  Japan's trade with, 78–79
  and Line of Demarcation,
    64–65
  and Malacca, 60, 72
  and Mozambique, 322
  and NATO, 536
  plantation economies of, 91
  Prince Henry, 30, 63
  religious intolerance of
    missionaries from, 72
  shipbuilding by, 63
  trade with China, 75–76
postimpressionists, 263
potatoes, 76, 101, 150, 298–300,
  340
  and famine, 223
poverty, 510, 513, 633–634,
  633*p,* 639, 642, 650, 652
Prague, 223

Praise of Folly, The (Erasmus),
  41
Pravda, 409, 411
PRB
  See Population Reference
    Bureau (PRB)
predestination, 48
**Prentice Hall World History
  Web site,** xxviii
Presbyterians, 122
**PRI (Institutional Revolution-
  ary Party),** 422
Priestley, Joseph, 144
primary sources
  analysis of, xxxvi–xxxvii
  bias identification, xxxvi
  captions of, xxxvi
  definition of, xxxvi
  fact and opinion identifica-
    tion, xxxvi–xxxvii
  political cartoons as, xxxvii
  reliability of, xxxvii
  source lines, xxxvii
  See also list of, xvii–xviii;
    skills
prime minister, 156
Prince Henry, 30, 63
Princip, Gavrilo, 380
Principles of Geology (Lyell),
  258
printing, 27, 32, 43, 60
prison labor, 565
Prisons and Prisoners (Lytton),
  295*p*
privateers, 91
privatization of industry, 512,
  528, 544, 649, 653
**Problem Solving and Decision
  Making**
  See skills
*Proclamation of the National
  Convention,* 178
proletariat, 210–211
propaganda, 388–389, 411, 457,
  462, 482, 493
prophets, 5
protectorates, 318
**Protestant and Catholic land-
  ownership in Ireland,** xxxiig
**Protestant Reformation, and
  Renaissance,** 44–46, 48
Protestants
  and American colonies, 93*n*
  and Church of England, 120
  and Edict of Nantes, 115, 118
  and Inquisition, 111
  naming of, 46
  persecution of, 114, 118
  and Thirty Years' War, 108
  See also Christianity; Luther,
    Martin; religion; specific
    denominations
Prussia
  Austro-Prussian War, 271
  Franco-Prussian War, 271,
    272, 376, 379
  and Junkers, 127–128, 269
  and partition of Poland, 109,
    133
  and Quadruple Alliance, 191
  revolution in, 223–224
  rise of, 127–128

Zollverein, 268–269
  See also Germany
psychoanalysis, 451
Ptolemy, 35, 54
Pueblo Indians, 90
pueblos, 15
Puerto Rico, 84, 311, 360
purdah, 331
purgatory, 45
Puritans, 93*n,* 120, 122, 124
Pushkin, Alexander, 131
Putin, Vladimir, 545
"putting-out" system, 102, 104,
  200
pyramids, 3, 4, 5

Q

Qajars, 23, 328
Qianlong, emperor of China,
  61*p,* 76–77, 83, 142
Qin dynasty, 9
Qing dynasty, 76–77, 78, 334,
  336, 432
Quadruple Alliance, 191
Quakers, 49, 122, 124, 300
Quebec, 83, 92, 94, 351, 540
Quechua language, 15
questions
  analytical questions, xliv
  asking questions, xliv–xlv
  comprehension questions,
    xliv
  evaluation questions, xlv
  four categories of, xliv
  hypothetical questions, xlv
quinine, 317, 640
quipus, 15
Quran, 22

R

Rabelais, Francois, 41, 43
Rabin, Yitzhak, 598–599
Racine, Jean, 116
racism, 259, 356, 462, 479–480
radar, 474
radio, 246–247, 452
radioactivity, 450
Raffles, Stamford, 567
railroads
  Canadian Pacific Railway,
    352–353
  and colonial rule, 362
  in France, 302
  in Great Britain, 1840 and
    1850, 201*m*
  impact of, 201
  in India, 330, 331, 332, 582
  in Japan, 346
  Liverpool-Manchester
    Railroad, 195
  POWs building of, 480
  transcontinental railroad in
    U.S., 310
rain forests, 640, 641
Ram Mohun Roy, 331
Ramses II, pharaoh, 3, 4
"Rape of Nanjing," 435
Raphael, 38
Rasputin, Gregory, 401, 401*p*
Ray, Satyajit, 521
Readings in European History
  (Robinson), 271*ps*

Index

Reagan, Ronald, 538, 644
Realpolitik, 269, 273, 276
recession, 220, 528
Recognizing Bias and Propaganda
   See skills
Red Guards, 562
Red River, 67
refugees, 511*p*
regionalism, 357
Reichstag, 271, 461
Reign of Terror, 164, 171, 177, 178–179, 179*p*
reincarnation, 8
religion
   in Africa, 24, 25
   of ancient Egypt, 4
   atheism, 412
   of Aztec civilization, 14–15
   of Aztecs, 13–14
   and baptism, 49
   Candomblè, 650
   and civilization, 2
   daoism, 9, 70
   fundamentalism, 517, 590
   of Indus Valley civilizations, 7
   and Industrial Revolution, 259
   liberation theology, 517
   and liberation theology, 637
   Methodist Church, 206
   and modern society, 517
   and monotheism, 5, 22
   Mormons, 307
   95 Theses, 33
   and Peace of Augsburg, 46
   persecution of religious groups, 79, 93, 412
   and polytheism, 7
   and predestination, 48
   and sects, 13
   and social gospel, 259
   and war, 108, 114–115
   Western Europe's major religions 1600, 51*m*
   See also Buddhism; Hinduism; Huguenots; Islam; Jews; Judaism; Muslims; Protestants; Roman Catholic Church; other specific religions and denominations
Remarque, Erich Maria, 444, 452, 462, 708*ps*
Rembrandt, 72, 151
Renaissance
   and artists, 33, 36–38, 40
   description of, 36–37
   humanism, 35–36, 41
   in Italy, 32, 34–39, 35*m*
   Northern Renaissance, 40–43
   and scientific revolution, 54–57
   in Spain, 43
reparations, 392, 393–395, 448, 459, 482
republic, definition of, 12
restoration, 122–124, 123*p*
Revolution Through Peace (Cámara), 637*ps*
Reza Khan, 427

Reza Pahlavi, Muhammad, 594
Rhodes, Cecil, 362, 362*p*, 622
Rhodesia, 362, 424
Ricardo, David, 209, 217
Ricci, Matteo, 75–76
rice production, 70, 93
rich nations, 510
Richard III (Shakespeare), 43
Richardson, Samuel, 153
Richelieu, Cardinal Armand, 115, 115*p*
Riel, Louis, 353
Rivera, Diego, 422, 423
Rizal, José, 350, 350*p*
Road to Wigan Pier, The (Orwell), 446*ps*
"robber barons," 248
Robespierre, Maximilien, 178–179, 178*p*
Robinson Crusoe (Defoe), 153
Robinson, Mary, 688, 689
Robota, Rosa, 480
Rockefeller, John D., 247, 311
Roland, Jeanne, 180
Roman Catholic Church
   and annulment, 49–50
   Catholic Reformation, 51–52
   and censorship, 149
   Concordat of 1801, 183
   and confession, 46
   and England, 50, 119, 124
   and Enlightenment, 147
   and excommunication, 18, 45, 147
   and forced conversion to Christianity, 72, 87–88
   and French pope, 18
   and Holy Roman Empire, 18
   hostility with unified Italy, 278
   and Huguenots, 114–115
   Index of Forbidden Books, 51
   and indulgences, 44, 46
   and Ireland, 298
   and Justinian's Code, 20
   and liberation theology, 637
   missionaries of, 21
   Native Americans' forced conversion to, 84, 87–88
   and Philippines, 350
   and pilgrimages, 46
   and prayers to saints, 46
   and Protestant Reformation, 44–46
   and purgatory, 45
   schism in, 20
   Second Vatican Council, 517
   secular power of, 17
   and Thirty Years' War, 108
   and Vatican, 278
Roman empire, 12–13
Roman Peace (Pax Romana), 12, 13
Roman republic, 8, 12
Romania, 544, 548
Romanov dynasty, 129–132, 400
romanticism, 240, 260
Rome, 455–456
   See also Roman empire;

Roman republic
Rome-Berlin-Tokyo Axis, 469
Romeo and Juliet (Shakespeare), 43
Romero, Archbishop Oscar, 642, 646
Rommel, Erwin, 474, 482, 486, 486*p*
Roosevelt Corollary, 360
Roosevelt, Franklin D., 359, 423, 449, 458, 477, 487, 538, 692, 710*ps*
Roosevelt, Theodore, 311, 359
rotten boroughs, 293
Rouen Cathedral, 262*p*, 263
Roundheads, 120–121
Rousseau, Jean–Jacques, 147, 160–161, 702*ps*
rubber, 357, 474, 575
Rubens, Peter Paul, 40
Ruhr Valley, 459–460
Russia
   and absolutism, 283
   and Alaska sale, 306
   as autocracy, 400
   ballet, 285
   "beard tax," 129
   Bloody Sunday, 267*p*, 286–287, 289
   and Bolsheviks, 398, 401, 402
   and Bosporus Strait, 326
   and boyars, 130, 132–133
   calendar of, 401*n*
   case study on, 666–669
   Chechnya revolt, 545–546
   Cheka, 404
   civil war in, 399*m*, 403–404
   commissars, 404
   communist collapse in, 666–669
   and Crimean War, 276
   and Dardenelles, 326
   Decembrist Revolt, 283
   demographics on, 667
   Duma, 287, 400–401
   economic crisis in, 512
   expansion, 1689–1796, 130*m*
   foreign debt, 544–545
   free-market economy of, 545*p*
   gross domestic product (GDP), 667
   and Group of Eight, 507
   growth, 1330–1584, 20*m*
   and Industrial Revolution, 243
   industry growth, 286
   and Iran, 328
   Japan at war with, 286
   and Korea, 346–347
   map of, 667*m*
   March Revolution, 400–401
   Mongol conquest of, 21
   November Revolution, 402–403
   and nuclear weapons, 527
   October Manifesto, 287
   and Pan-Slavism, 378
   and partition of Poland, 109, 133
   pogroms, 286, 287, 304
   population demographics in

1897, 400
   privatized industry in, 544
   and Quadruple Alliance, 191
   quotations on transformation of, 668
   Red Guards, 402–403
   and Reds, 403
   republic of, 544–546
   revolution in, 211, 287, 375, 389, 398, 399*m*, 400, 402–403, 418
   Revolution of 1917, 301, 398–403
   rise of, 21
   and Romanov dynasty, 129–132, 400
   Russification, 284, 286
   Russo-Japanese War, 346, 347
   Serbia supported by, 218, 378, 381
   and serfdom, 130, 283–284, 283*p*
   and soviets, 401
   and Treaty of Brest-Litovsk, 389, 403
   and United Nations, 490
   "war communism" in, 404
   war with Sweden, 131
   and warm water port, 131, 133
   westernization of, 129, 282
   and Whites, 403
   Winter Palace, 287, 289
   and World War I, 379, 381, 382, 383, 386, 389, 401
   zemstvos, 284
   See also Soviet Union; Stalin, Joseph
Russian Orthodox Church, 130, 284, 412, 412*p*
Russia From the Inside (Kaiser), 542*ps*
Russia Under the Bolshevik Regime, 404
Russo-Japanese War, 346, 347
Rwanda, 506, 509, 511, 611*p*, 617, 619

S

Sadat, Anwar, 594, 598
Safavid empire, 23, 328
Sahara, 24–25
St. Bartholomew's Day Massacre, 114
St. Helena, 188
St. Lawrence River, 92
St. Lawrence Seaway, 540
St. Paul's Cathedral, 475*p*
St. Petersburg, 131, 389, 401
   See also Petrograd
Salazar, Antonio de Oliveira, 536, 626
salons, 149–150
salt, 25
   See also spices
Salt March, 419, 430–431, 431*p*, 466
Salvation Army, 259
Salvemini, Gaetano, 465
Samoa, 349
samurai, 27, 342, 343

Index

San Martín, José de, 230, 230p
San Xavier del Bac, 90p
sanctions
    definition of, 468
Sandinistas, 644
Sandino, Augusto César, 423,
    644
sans-culottes, 175
Santa Anna, Antonio López de,
    358
Santa Maria, 64
São Paulo, 650p
Saratoga, Battle of, 160
Sardinia, 276, 276n
Saro-Wiwa, Ken, 619
SARS, 518, 555
sati, 329, 331
Satires (Juvenal), xxxvi
Saudi Arabia, 558g, 588, 588g,
    589, 601
Scents of Eden, The (Corn), 103
Schlieffen, Alfred von, 381
Schlieffen Plan, 381, 383
Schmahl, Jeanne-Elizabeth,
    305
Schönbrunn Palace, 280p
School of Athens (Raphael), 38
science
    and chemistry, 57
    and hypothesis, 55
    and Industrial Revolution,
        257–258
    natural selection, 258–259
    and radioactivity, 450
    and relativity, 450
    and Renaissance, 54–57
    scientific method, 55p
    Scientific Revolution, 144
    theory of evolution, 241, 258
Scotland, 120, 153, 208
Scott, Sir Walter, 260
Scottish Presbyterian Church,
    48
Scrapbook, 1900–1914 (Bailey),
    247ps
scribes, 5
sea dogs, 112
Second Continental Congress,
    159
Second Estate, 166–167
Second Pan-African Congress,
    441
Second Sex, The (de Beauvoir),
    531
Second World, 505n
sects, 13
secularism, 180–181
segregation, 309, 539
Selassie, Haile, 468, 468p
self-determination
    definition of, 391
Self-Employed Women's
    Association (SEWA), 583
Selkirk, Alexander, 153
Senegal, 25, 98, 425, 503, 612p
Senghor, Léopold, 425
Sepoy Rebellion, 314, 329–330
Sequencing
    See skills
Serbia, 218, 378, 380, 381, 394,
    551, 670, 671m
Serbia and Montenegro, 551

serfs, 17, 150, 283, 283p, 284
service industries, 528
Seurat, Georges, 263
Seven Years' War, 154, 157, 159,
    168
Shah Abbas, 23
Shaka, 100, 320, 340
Shakespeare, William, 42, 43
Shang dynasty, 3, 7
Shanghai, 434
shantytowns, 516, 634
Sharia, 517, 590, 591, 596
Sharon, Ariel, 599
Sheep Well, The (de Vega), 113
Shi Huangdi, 8, 9
Shiite Muslims, 601
shipbuilding, 63, 557
Shiva, 69
shoguns, 27, 79
Short Description of the De-
    struction of the Indies (De las
    Casas), xlips , 88ps
Siam, 349
Siberia, 131, 283, 408, 476
SID
    See Society for International
        Development (SID)
Siddhartha Gautama, 8
    See also Buddha
Sierra Leone, 320
Sikhs, 329, 580, 581–582
Silesia, 127
silk industry, 9, 23, 27, 74, 76
silver, 87, 104, 110, 113
Simplicissimus (Grimmels-
    hausen), 126
Sinai Peninsula, 598
Singapore, 67, 348, 512, 566,
    567–568
Singh, Ranjit, 329
Siqueiros, David Alfaro, 423
Sistine Chapel, 38
Skara Brae settlement, 2
skills
    Analyzing Cartoons, 146,
        233, 313, 339, 381, 495, 523
    Analyzing Cause and Effect,
        xlii–xliii, 10, 53, 105, 185,
        252, 367, 449, 546, 585
    Analyzing Charts and
        Graphs, xxxii–xxxiii, 53,
        55, 86, 105, 107, 163, 174,
        182, 185, 213, 231, 249, 252,
        265, 367, 392, 395, 403, 408,
        449, 465, 490, 513, 527,546,
        547, 553, 558, 585, 629, 632
    Analyzing Paintings and
        Drawings, 38, 41, 45, 59,
        74, 85, 111, 118, 144, 157,
        173, 187, 204, 261, 270, 279,
        288, 293, 296, 304, 346, 411,
        413, 422, 444, 634
    Analyzing Photographs, 246,
        274, 323, 363, 382, 390, 409,
        454, 457, 459, 462, 481, 562,
        589, 603, 655
    Analyzing Primary Sources,
        xxxvi–xxxvii, 37, 48, 59,
        66, 71, 77, 81, 88, 93, 107,
        120, 133, 135, 147, 159, 163,
        168, 177, 181, 193, 207, 211,
        213, 218, 227, 233, 247, 256,

265, 270, 271, 275, 289, 292,
303, 315, 317, 323, 334, 339,
353, 357, 367, 387, 393, 397,
404, 417, 421,425, 435, 441,
446, 463, 465, 481, 484, 491,
495, 507, 518, 523, 531, 542,
553, 557, 569, 571, 577, 581,
698, 603, 608, 613, 619, 629,
637, 642, 652, 655,
    Asking Questions, xliv–xlv
    Comparing and Contrasting,
        xxxviii–xxxix, 58, 70, 86,
        118, 133, 175, 192, 207, 278,
        350, 366, 410, 415, 416, 540,
        550, 576, 602, 653
    Distinguishing Fact and
        Opinion, 294, 521, 522,
        629, 655
    Identifying Main Ideas and
        Summarizing, 86, 277, 287,
        294, 303, 312, 360, 437, 445,
        464, 536, 552, 595, 621, 627,
        647, 660, 663, 665, 676, 677,
        682, 692, 694, 696
    Identifying Points of View,
        47, 53, 77, 106, 113, 146,
        245, 264, 377, 464, 514, 654,
        673
    Learning From Maps,
        xxx–xxi, 35, 51, 64–65, 69,
        81, 94, 99, 112, 126, 130,
        135, 155, 160, 184, 190, 300,
        222, 228, 243, 229, 277, 281,
        289, 302, 307, 321, 327, 330,
        336, 349, 352, 354, 358, 378,
        385, 394, 407, 427, 434, 437,
        441, 471, 483, 487, 492, 506,
        530, 550, 568, 572, 577, 581,
        599, 600, 615, 649
    Making Inferences and
        Drawing Conclusions, 10,
        24, 39, 57, 64, 74, 103, 126,
        128, 177, 201, 264, 287,294,
        308, 312, 321, 385, 394, 395,
        440, 649, 654, 660
    Making Valid Generaliza-
        tions, 79, 279, 337, 409,
        488, 654, 662
    Problem Solving and Deci-
        sion Making, xlvi–xlvii,
        47, 66, 91, 100, 185, 224,
        245, 281, 305, 328, 337, 377,
        488, 515, 546, 552, 601
    Recognizing Bias and Propa-
        ganda, 177, 318, 388, 397,
        409, 417, 457, 569, 577
    Sequencing, 58, 69, 113, 158,
        170, 176, 192, 268, 275, 301,
        329, 350, 429, 439, 473, 494,
        495, 552, 571, 597, 606, 627,
        685
    Synthesizing Information,
        xl–xli, 42, 103, 107, 123,
        155, 201, 227, 287, 308, 344,
        409, 457, 529, 589
    Transferring Information
        From One Medium to
        Another, 11, 13, 14, 55, 57,
        58, 62, 71, 73, 75, 80, 84, 86,
        87, 92, 99, 101, 105, 107,
        114, 119, 196, 199, 203, 213,
        216, 219, 225, 279, 289, 295,

306, 311, 312, 316, 318, 319,
327, 329, 333, 397, 400, 405,
468, 485, 489, 494, 510, 513,
588, 618, 622, 628, 629, 632
    Using the Internet,
        xlviii–xlix, 59, 81, 107, 135,
        163, 193, 213, 233, 265, 289,
        313, 339, 367, 397, 417, 441,
        465, 495, 523, 553, 577, 603,
        629, 655
    Using Special-Purpose
        Maps, 349, 351, 354, 358,
        437, 589, 615, 649, 680, 690,
        691
skyscrapers, 196, 250
slavery
    of Africans, 83, 96–98, 320
    and American Revolution,
        160
    and Caribbean islands, 94,
        225
    and Christian missionaries,
        98
    destination of enslaved
        Africans, 1500–1870, xxxiii
    and French Revolution, 181
    impact of Atlantic slave
        trade, 98
    and Middle Passage, 97–98
    of Native Americans, 88
    and plantation economies,
        88, 97, 101, 226
    and Siam, 349
    slave revolt in Haiti, 226–228
    and tobacco, 97
    and triangular trade, 97–98
    and United Kingdom of
        Great Britain, 296
    in United States, 284, 290,
        309
    and voting, 161
    women as abolitionists, 256
    World Antislavery Conven-
        tion, 309
Slavs, 21
Slovakia, 682
Slovenia, 550
smallpox, 144p, 518, 607
smelting, 198
Smith, Adam, 148, 208p, 211,
    217, 295
smuggling, 158
social classes
    caste system, 7, 9, 430, 583
    and civilization, 2
    colonial society, 88–89
    and Industrial Revolution,
        253–254
    middle class, 206–207
    working class, 206, 251–252
social contract, 145
Social Contract, The
    (Rousseau), 147, 702ps
Social Darwinism, 259, 317,
    379, 456
social gospel, 259
Social Security system, 449, 538
socialism, 209–210, 218, 513
socialist realism, 413, 413p
Society for International
    Development (SID), 665
Socrates, 11

solidarity, 548
"Solitude of Self, The" (Stanton), 256*ps*
Solomon, king of Israel, 5, 468
solution implementation, xlvii
Somme, battle of, 374
Somme River, 385
Somoza, Anastasio, 644
sonar, 474
Song dynasty, 16, 26, 27
Songhai kingdom, 25
Soninke people, 25
Sonnets to Laura (Petrarch), 36
Sources of Indian Tradition (de Bary), 332
South Africa
  and African National Congress (ANC), 425, 623
  Afrikaner Nationalism, 623
  all-race elections in, 605
  and apartheid, 425, 508, 623, 678–679
  Boer War, 315
  British settlement in, 214
  case study on, 678–681
  democracy in, 678–681
  demographics on, 679
  and diamonds, 623
  elections in, 625
  gross domestic product (GDP), 679
  and Mohandas Gandhi, 429–430
  quotations on apartheid, 680
  reform in, 624
  Truth and Reconciliation Commission in, 679
  See also Union of South Africa
South America
  civil wars in, 231
  and independence from Spain, 226–231
  Spanish empire in, 85
South Korea, 512, 555, 566, 568, 569, 570
  democracy in, 682–685
  demographics on, 683
  economic development in, 682–685
  gross domestic product (GDP), 682, 683
  quotations on democracy, 684
  See also Korea; North Korea
Southeast Asia
  and Buddhism, 67, 68, 69
  empires and kingdoms of, 69*m*, 81*m*
  geography of, 67
  and Hinduism, 68, 69
  India's impact on, 68–69
  and Islam, 70, 71
  Khmer empire, 69
  Pagan kingdom, 69
  Srivijaya empire, 69–70
  and trade, 68
  western imperialism and, 348–349, 349*m*
  and World War II, 478, 485
  See also specific countries

Southern Common Market, 636
Southern Rhodesia, 622
Southwest African People's Organization (SWAPO), 626
Soviet Union
  Afghanistan invaded by, 542
  agricultural revolution in, 407–408
  and atheism, 412
  Brezhnev Doctrine, 542, 544
  and censorship, 413–415
  and Chernobyl nuclear plant, 515, 543
  and Cold War, 490–491
  collapse of, 506, 525, 527, 544, 579, 598
  and collective farming, 407–409, 542
  and Comintern, 410
  command economy of, 406–407, 542
  communist control of, 412, 527
  constitution of, 405
  de-Stalinization of, 541
  and education, 412
  establishment of, 405
  and filmmaking, 414
  foreign policy, 410
  and France, 448
  glasnost, 544
  Great Purge, 399, 408, 410, 443
  Israel recognized by, 587
  and kulaks, 408, 411
  and labor camps, 408, 411*p*
  land area of 1917–1938, 407*m*
  and League of Nations, 410
  Manchuria invaded by, 488
  and Marshall Plan, 492
  and medical care, 412
  and Middle East, 597
  NEP (New Economic Policy), 406
  nonaggression pact with Hitler, 471
  Old Bolsheviks, 408
  and People's Republic of China, 562
  perestroika, 544
  and propaganda, 411
  and religion, 412
  society of, 412–413
  and space age, 518, 520
  and Spanish Civil War, 470
  and *Sputnik,* 518, 524
  standard of living in, 407, 412
  steel industry in, 408
  as superpower, 505
  symbols of, 405*p*
  as totalitarian state, 411–415, 458
  and United Nations, 490
  and Warsaw Pact, 467, 493, 526, 542
  and women, 412
  and World War II, 483–484
  See also Russia; Stalin
Soweto, 425
space age, 502, 518, 520

Spain
  and Abraham Lincoln Brigade, 470
  and American Revolution, 160
  audiencia, 87
  Civil War in, 466, 469–470
  conquistadors, 84–85
  Council of the Indies, 87
  democratic government in, 536
  empire in Americas, 87–88
  English conflicts, 111–112
  and European Union, 536
  explorations of, 63–65
  as fascist dictatorship, 470
  France at war with, 178, 186–187
  Golden Age of, 112–113
  and guerrilla warfare, 187
  and Guernica air raid, 470
  and Incan empire, 33
  and International Brigades, 470
  Jews expelled from, 113, 118
  Laws of the Indies, 88
  and Line of Demarcation, 64–65
  Loyalists, 470
  Muslims in, 110, 113, 118
  Nationalists, 470
  and NATO, 536
  and Peru, 15, 33
  and Philippines, 72, 79, 267, 341
  plantation economies of, 88, 97
  as republic, 469
  and revolution in Latin America, 225–231
  silver riches in Americas, 87, 110
  Spanish Armada, 112
  Spanish-American War, 311, 350, 360
  and trade, 88
  viceroys, 87
  War of Spanish Succession, 118
Spanish Armada, 112
Spanish-American War, 311, 350, 360
Sparta, 11
special enterprise zones, 563
speech, freedom of, 146
Spenser, Edmund, 50
spheres of influence, 318
Sphinx, 2
Spice Islands, 66, 72, 348
spices
  clove market, 103
  search for, 62–66
  value of, 62, 72
  See also salt
Spirit of the Laws, The (Montesquieu), 145
Sputnik, 518, 524
Sri Lanka, 365, 582
Srivijaya empire, 69–70
SS troops, 461
stalemate, definition of, 383

Stalin, Joseph
  biography of, 406, 406*p*
  and Churchill, 477
  and collective farming, 670
  "cult of personality" of, 411
  five-year plans of, 399, 406–408
  goals in Eastern Europe, 491
  Great Purge, 399, 408, 410, 443
  and kulaks, 408
  and Lenin's death, 405
  and Marshall Plan, 492
  nonaggression pact with Hitler, 471
  Poland invaded by, 473
  See also Russia; Soviet Union
Stalingrad, Battle of, 484
standard of living
  definition of, 252
Standard Oil Company, 247, 311
Standfield, John, 353
Stanley, Henry, 321
Stanton, Elizabeth Cady, 256, 265, 309
statement of surrender (Kwangsi Bandit Group), 334*ps*
status quo, definition of, 190
steam power, 194, 202, 314
steel industry, 242, 244, 345
steel production, 1880–1910, xxxiiig, 265*g*
Stein, Gertrude, 454
Stephenson, George, 202
stock, 247
Stolypin, Peter, 287, 287*p*
Stone Age, 2
Stone Breakers (Courbet), 261, 262–263
Stowe, Harriet Beecher, 309
Strait of Hormuz, 600
Strait of Magellan, 66
Strait of Malacca, 567
strikes, 446
Stuart dynasty, 119–120
stupas, 69
submarines, 386
Sudan, 322, 325, 604, 613
Sudetenland, 470
Suez Canal, 291, 327–328, 327*p*, 330, 426, 578, 593
suffrage, 176
  See also voting
sugar, 88, 97, 101, 226, 357, 650
Sugihara Chiune, 480
Suharto, President, 574
Sui dynasty, 26
"Suicide in the Trenches" (Sassoon), 388
Suleiman, Ottoman sultan, 17, 23, 110
Sullivan, Louis, 250
sultans, 23
Sumatra, 70
Sumer, 5
Sun Also Rises, The (Hemingway), 452
sun god, 86
Sun King, Louis XIV, 115–116
Sun Tzu, 377

Index

Sun Yixian, 315, 337, 337*p*, 432, 433–434
Sunda strait, 67
superpowers, 505, 537–538, 546, 597
surrealism, 451
Suryavaraman II, king of Khmer empire, 69
Suttner, Bertha von, 380
Swahili, 319, 621
swastika, 461
Sweden, 131, 536
Swiss Federation, 126
Switzerland, 48, 52, 445
Sybil (Disraeli), 292*ps*
Sydney, Australia, 508*p*
Syngman Rhee, 568
Synthesizing Information
    See skills
Syria
    as French mandate, 428
    government of, 588
    and Israel, 598

T
Taharqa, king of Nubia, 8
Tahiti, 263
Taíno people, 84
Taiping Rebellion, 215, 334
Taiwan, 336, 346, 560, 562, 566–567
Talbot, William Fox, 263
Talleyrand, Charles Maurice de, 190–191
Taliban, 585
Tang dynasty, 70
Tang Taizong, 26
Tanganyika, 620
tanks, 386
Tannenberg, battle of, 386
Tanzania, 504, 604, 610, 613, 620–621
tariffs, 104, 296, 423, 446, 528, 530
taxation
    "beard tax," 129
    and Magna Carta, 18
    and Petition of Right, 120
    of religious groups, 22
tea, 329, 343*p*
technology
    computers, 503, 518, 519
    effects of, 245
    and Green Revolution, 502, 520
    in medicine, 518
    and Industrial Revolution, 198,
    printing press, 43, 244, 246–247
    radar, 474
    sonar, 474
    and transportation, 202, 244
Tehran, 596
Teherani, Zade, 603
telegraph, 246–247
telephone, 246
temperance movement, 256
Ten Commandments, 5, 13
tenements, 203, 250
Tennis Court Oath, 169*p*, 181
Tenochtitlán, 84–85, 86

Teresa of Avila, 52
terrorism, 509, 538, 539, 585, 601
    9/11, 509, 585
    al-Qaida, 509, 585, 590, 601
    bin Laden, Osama, 509, 585, 601
    Hamas, 600
    Hizbullah, 600
    Irish Republican Army (IRA), 533
    Mau Mau, 609
    Taliban, 585
    urban terrorism, 635
Tet Offensive, 554, 572
Tetzel, Johann, 45, 45*p*
textiles, 200*m*, 205
    See also cotton
Thailand, 67, 68, 69, 349
Thatcher, Margaret, 529*ps*, 532, 532*p*, 538
    as prime minister of U.K., 689
theocracy, 48, 596
Theodora, Byzantine empress, 20
Thera Arahanta, 67
Theravada Buddhism, 70
    See also Buddhism
Things Fall Apart (Achebe), 713*ps*
Third Estate, 166, 167, 169–170
Third of May, 1808, The (Goya), 187*p*
Third World, 505*n*, 538
Third World Women Speak Out (Houston), 518*ps*
Thirteenth Amendment, 284
Thirty Years' War, 108, 125–127, 126*m*
Thoreau, Henry David, 430
Three Musketeers, The (Dumas), 260
Thyssen, August, 272
Tiananmen Square Massacre, 563–564
Tiber River, 12
Tibet, 565
Tigris River, 5, 588
Timbuktu, 25
time lines, 2–3, 8–9, 16–17, 32–33, 60–61, 82–83, 108–109, 123, 136–137, 142–143, 164–165, 194–195, 214–215, 234–235, 240–241, 266–267, 290–291, 314–315, 340–341, 368–369, 374–375, 398–399, 418–419, 442–443, 466–467, 496–497, 502–503, 524–525, 554–555, 578–579, 604–605, 630–631
Tito, Josip, 548
Tito, Josip-Broz, 670
tobacco industry, 92, 93, 97
Tocqueville, Alexis de, 219
Tohono O'odham Indians, 90
Tojo Hideki, 477
Tokugawa Ieyasu, 29
Tokugawa shogunate, 29, 79, 342–343, 346
Tokyo, 343
Toleration Act of 1689, 124
Toles, Tom, 514*ps*

Tontons Macoutes, 647
tools
    and ironworking, 5, 6, 24
Torah, 5
Tordesillas, Treaty of, 89
Tory party, 293*n*
To Save a Life: Stories of Jewish Rescue (Yaari), 463*ps*
total war, 388, 482
totalitarianism, 411, 457, 459, 561
Tour de France, 532
Touré, Samori, 324
Townshend, Charles, 197
trade
    Americas and, 88
    between Europe, Africa, and Asia around 1700, 61*m*
    and Black Death, 62
    caravans, 25
    Columbian Exchange, 101–102
    and crusades, 19
    East Africa trade routes, 25
    and embargos, 572
    free trade, 295
    Japan's trade policies of, 78
    Korea's trade policies, 78
    in Middle Ages, 17
    Open Door Policy, 336
    routes in the Southern Seas, 67–68
    slave trade, 83, 96–98
    trade deficts, 557
trade deficit
    definition of, 333
trade surplus
    definition of, 333
Trafalgar, Battle of, 185
Transferring Information From One Medium to Another
    See skills
transportation
    automobiles, 246, 315, 557
    bicycles, 563*p*
    and shipbuilding, 63, 557
    steamboat, 194, 202, 244
Treaties at Locarno, 442, 445
Treaty of Brest-Litovsk, 389, 403
Treaty of Kanagawa, 343
Treaty of Nanjing, 240, 334
Treaty of Paris, 94, 154, 160
Treaty of Portsmouth, 346
Treaty of Tordesillas, 89
Treaty of Utrecht, 118, 154
Treaty of Versailles, 375, 393–394, 433, 472
trench rats, 384
Trent, Council of, 51, 59
triangular trade, 97–98, 99*m*
tributary states, 25
tribute, 14, 26
Trip to the Moon, A (Méliès), 452
Triple Alliance, 379
Trojan War, 10
Trotsky, Leon, 402–403, 404, 406
True History of the Conquest of New Spain, The (Díaz), 697*ps*
Truman Doctrine, 491

Truman, Harry S., 487, 491, 492, 538, 539
Trung Nhi, 70
Trung Trac, 70
Truth, Sojourner, 256
tuberculosis, 249, 250
Tuchman, Barbara, 382
Tudor dynasty, 119
Tull, Jethro, 197
Tullius, 36
Turkey
    and Cyprus, 536
    and democracy, 592–593
    earthquakes in, 592–593, 593*p*
    and Kurds, 586, 588, 593
    modernization of, 418, 426–427
    and Truman Doctrine, 491
    water resources, 588
Turner, J.M.W., 240, 261
Tuscans, 275
Tussaud, Marie, 176
Tutsis, 509
Tutu, Bishop Desmond, 624, 624*p*
Tutu, Osei, 99
Twelfth Night (Shakespeare), 43
Two Treatises of Government (Locke), 145, 701*ps*

U
U-boats, 386, 390, 391
Uganda, 613, 615, 617
Ukraine, 21, 403, 408, 546
    case study on, 670–673
    demographics on, 671
    quotations on breakup of, 672
    resurgence of nationalism in, 670–673
ultimatum
    definition of, 381
Uncle Tom's Cabin (Stowe), 309
Underdogs, The (Azuela), 420
Union of South Africa, 291, 322, 425
    See also British Commonwealth of Nations; South Africa
United Kingdom of Great Britain
    and Act of Union, 142, 155
    African colonies of, 424–425
    American colonies of, 158–160
    and appeasement of Germany, 469, 470
    and Asante kingdom, 324
    Balfour Declaration, 428, 587
    and Battle of Britain, 474, 476
    and Battle of Trafalgar, 185
    blitz, 475, 476
    and Boer War, 315, 322
    and British Commonwealth of Nations, 447
    British North America Act of 1867, 352
    Burma annexed by, 348
    and Canada, 352

Canada Act of 1791, 351
Chartist Movement, 293
colonial imperialism of, 318
and Common Market, 533
and Commonwealth of
    Nations, 533
and communism, 446
as constitutional monarchy,
    292
Corn Laws, 295–296
cotton trade 1850, 200m
crime and punishment,
    598–599
and Crimean War, 276, 303
Durham Report, 352
Education Act, 297
and Egypt, 322, 426, 442
and European Union, 530
Fabian Society, 297
factories in, 200
and Falkland Islands, 649
foreign policies, 447
free trade, 295–296
geography of, 154
and Germany's reparations
    after World War I, 392–394
global power of, 154–155
Great Reform Act, 290
and Group of Eight, 507
and Hong Kong, 555, 567
and India, 290, 429–431, 467,
    504, 578
in Industrial Revolution,
    196, 199–200
industry centers, 1825, 195m
and Iran, 328
and Iraq, 428
and Ireland, 298–300, 447
mercantilist policies of, 158
and Munich Conference,
    470, 471
and nationalized industry,
    528, 532
naval power of, 154
Navigation Acts, 158
navy reduction, 445
New Zealand annexed by,
    340
as oligarchy, 156
Operation Sea Lion, 476
Opium War, 215, 333–334,
    343, 567
and Palestine, 428
political parties of, 293–294
post–World War I era,
    446–447
"putting-out" system, 102,
    104, 200
and Quadruple Alliance, 191
railroad development in,
    195, 201m
Reform Act of 1832, 293
Reform Bill of 1867, 294
and religion, 292
Royal Air Force, 476
and Russian civil war, 403
and Sepoy Rebellion, 314,
    329
Seven Years' War, 157, 159
and slavery, 296
social classes, 156–157
and socialism, 446

and South Africa, 214
and Spanish Civil War, 472
and Sudan, 322
and Suez Canal, 328, 426
slave trade monopoly in
    Spanish America, 154
and Treaty of Nanjing, 240,
    334
and United Nations, 490
U.S. at war with, 165
Victorian Era, 254, 255
voting rights in, 292, 293,
    297–298
and War of 1812, 185
war declared on Germany,
    472
as welfare state, 532
and World War I, 379, 381,
    382, 386, 387, 389, 390–391,
    392
and World War II, 472,
    473–476
and Zulus, 324
See also England; parliament
United Nations
    and Afghanistan, 585
    and African nations, 611
    and AIDS, 615
    in Belgian Congo, 620
    Charter of, 507ps
    creation of, 490, 502
    and Cyprus, 593
    and decolonization, 507
    and human rights, 509
    and Iraq, 601
    and Korean War, 568
    in Kosovo, 551
    and People's Republic of
        China, 562
    and Soviet bloc, 546
    and women's rights, 517
United Nations Report on the
    Status of Women, 688
United Nations Universal
    Declaration of Human
    Rights, 688
United States of America
    American hostages in Iran,
        596
    American Revolution, 160,
        160m
    Articles of Confederation,
        160
    budget deficit, 539
    budget surplus, 539
    case study on, 690–693
    and China, 435, 562
    civic participation in,
        690–693
    civil rights movement in, 539
    Civil War, 290, 309
    Constitution of, 160–161,
        164, 226
    Continental Congress, 159,
        160
    Dawes Plan, 460
    Declaration of Indepen-
        dence, 159
    and democracy, 691
    as federal republic, 161
    and freedom of speech, 146
    and global economy, 538

and "Good Neighbor
    Policy," 423
and Great Depression, 443
gross domestic product
    (GDP), 691
and Group of Eight, 507
and Guam, 311
Hawaii annexed by, 350
health statistics, 1999, 513
and immigration, 306, 310
immigration policies, 437,
    448, 539, 641
and Industrial Revolution,
    242–243
Israel recognized by, 587
Japan occupied by, 556–557,
    568
Japanese internment camps
    in, 482
and labor unions, 311
and Latin America, 639–640
and League of Nations, 395,
    448
Lend-Lease Act, 477
Louisiana Purchase, 190,
    214, 306
and Marshall Plan, 492
and Medicare, 538
Mexico at war with, 358,
    359–360
Mexico's invasion, 423
and Middle East, 597
Monroe Doctrine, 359, 360
and NATO, 493, 526
navy reduction, 445
Neutrality Acts, 469, 477
and New Deal, 449
and North American Free
    Trade Association
    (NAFTA), 540, 640, 644
Pancho Villa's invasion of,
    418
and Pearl Harbor bombing,
    435, 467, 477–478, 478p
and People's Republic of
    China, 562
and Philippines, 311
Platt Amendment, 360, 423
and Puerto Rico, 311
"Red Scare," 410, 448
Roosevelt Corollary, 360
and Russian civil war, 403
and slavery, 284, 290, 307,
    309
Social Security system, 449,
    538
space program, 502
Spanish-American War, 311,
    350, 360
as superpower, 505, 537–538
and Taiwan, 566
territorial expansion of,
    306–307, 307m
Texas annexed by, 358
thirteen original colonies of,
    158–159
and Treaty of Kanagawa, 343
Truman Doctrine, 491
and United Nations, 490
Vietnam War, 524, 554,
    571–572
voting rights in, 161, 307,

308, 539, 691, 692
and War of 1812, 185
war with United Kingdom,
    165
women's rights movement,
    309
and World War I, 375,
    390–391
and World War II, 477–478
Universal Declaration of Hu-
    man Rights, The, 508, 711ps
University of Mexico, 89
Uprising, The (Daumier), 221p
Ural Mountains, 131, 476
urban renewal, 250
urbanization, 203, 516, 573,
    616, 633–634
Uruguay, 512, 640
Using Special-Purpose Maps
    See skills
Using the Internet
    See skills
Usman dan Fodio, 319, 325
utilitarianism, 209
Utopia (More), 41
Utopians, 210
Utrecht, Treaty of, 118, 154

V
V-E Day, 486
vaccines, 249
Valley Forge, 160
Van Eyck, Hubert, 40
Van Eyck, Jan, 40
Van Gogh, Vincent, 263
Van Leeuwenhoek, Anthony,
    57
Vargas, Getúlio, 651
Vasari, Giorgio, 37
vassals, 16
Vatican, 278
Vedas, 7
Vega, Lope de, 113
Velázquez, Diego, 113
Venezuela, 532, 535, 588g, 635,
    640, 659
Venice
    islands and, 34
    Jewish ghetto in, 53
Vera Cruz, 423
Verdun, 385
vernacular writing, 19
Verne, Jules, 244
Versailles, 116–117, 167, 169,
    270, 272
Versailles, Treaty of, 375,
    393–394, 433
Vesalius, Andreas, 57
Vespucci, Amerigo, 65
Vichy government, 474, 480
Victor Emmanuel II, king of
    Sardinia and Italy, 276, 277,
    278
Victor Emmanuel III, king of
    Italy, 456
Victoria Falls, 320p
Victorian Age, 254, 255,
    293–294
Victoria, queen of England,
    292, 293–294, 293p, 297–298,
    379

Vienna, Congress of, 190–191, 190*m*, 222, 266, 268, 275, 279
Vietnam, 67, 70, 505
  "boat people," 572
  colonial war in, 533
  and France, 610
  U.S. involvement in, 537–538
  western imperialism and, 348–349
  See also North Vietnam; Vietnam War
Vietnam War, 524, 554, 571–572, 572*m*
Vietnamese Declaration of Independence, 571*ps*
Vikings, 16, 21
Villa, Francisco "Pancho," 418, 420, 421
Vindication of the Rights of Woman, A (Wollstonecraft), 148
Virgil, 36
Virtual Field Trips, xxviii
Vishnu, 69
Voices and Views, 668, 672, 676, 680, 684, 688, 692
Volkswagen Beetle, 534*p*
Volta, Alessandro, 244
Voltaire, 125, 145, 147, 149, 150, 163
Von Moltke, Helmuth, 271, 377
voting
  compulsory voting in Australia, 690
  electorate, 293, 294
  in France, 169, 176, 220, 302, 305
  in Germany, 459
  in United States, 161, 307, 308, 539, 691, 692
  universal manhood suffrage, 217, 251, 293, 302
  women's voting rights, 161, 256, 291, 297–298, 305, 308, 389, 436, 459, 469
  and working-class men, 207, 294

W
Wagner, Richard, 221, 462
Wajed, Sheikh Hasina, 689
Walesa, Lech, 548, 715*ps*
Walpole, Robert, 156
war
  Cold War, 490–491, 492*m*, 504–506
  and conscription, 388
  "dirty war" in Argentina, 649, 678
  drug wars, 640
  holy wars, 19
  justification for, 377
  and neutrality, 381
  propaganda war, 388–389
  and reparations, 392, 393–394
  and scarcity, 2
  and stalemate, 383
  total war, 388, 482
  trench warfare, 383
  Trojan War, 10
  war crimes, 489, 551

  See also specific wars
War of Austrian Succession, 127, 128
War of 1812, 185
War of Spanish Succession, 118
war on terrorism, 509, 533, 544
Warsaw Pact, 467, 493, 542, 548
Washington, George, 159, 161*p*, 171, 311
Waste Land, The (Eliot), 452
Water Music (Handel), 151
Water Resources in the Middle East, xxxi*m*, 589*m*
Waterloo, Battle of, 165, 188
Watt, James, 194, 198, 198*p*, 243
Way of Subjects, The, 439
Wealth of Nations, The (Smith), 148, 208
weapons
  cannon, 272*p*
  iron weapons, 24
  machine guns, 317, 318*p*, 386
  of Old Stone Age, 2
  poison gas, 384, 385–386
  weapons of mass destruction (WMD), 508, 509, 601
Web site self-tests, xxvii
welfare states, 527–528
Wellington, Duke of, 165, 187, 188
Wesley, John, 206
West Bank, 598, 599*m*
West Germany, 492–493, 528, 534
  demographics on, 667
  East Germany united with, 666
  See also East Germany; Germany
West Indies, 65, 84, 425
West Pakistan, 583
  See also Pakistan
westernization, 129, 282, 334, 363, 437, 516, 520–521
Westphalia, Peace of, 126, 127
whaling, 349
What-Not or Ladies' Handbook, The, 253
Whig party, 293, 293*n*
"White Man's Burden, The" (Kipling), 317*ps*
WHO
  See World Health Organization (WHO)
Wiesel, Elie, 668
wildlife preservation, 614
William the Conqueror, 18
William I, kaiser of Germany, 269–271, 272
William II, kaiser of Germany, 274, 322, 323*p*, 379, 381, 391
William III, king of England, 124
Wilson, Woodrow, 390–395
Winter Palace, 287, 289, 403
witchcraft, 52
witch hunts, 52
Witte, Serge, 286
Wojtyla, Karol, 548
women
  as abolitionists, 256
  in Africa, 616

  as artists, 37
  in Chinese society, 337
  and developing nations, 517–518
  and education, 89, 257, 284
  and employment, 297
  and Enlightenment, 147
  in Europe, 105, 454
  feminist movement, 517
  and French Revolution, 172–173, 173*p*, 180
  and "glass ceiling," 531
  in government in Latin America, 636, 636*p*
  and hejab, 591, 591*p*
  and Industrial Revolution, 204
  and Islam, 591
  in Japanese society, 344, 345–346, 436, 556, 559
  and matrilineal descent, 68
  in Mexico, 422
  in national politics, 686–689
  political activism in 19th century, 254, 256
  and polygamy, 426
  and purdah, 331
  and Puritans, 122
  in Russia, 401
  and sati, 329, 331
  Self-Employed Women's Association (SEWA), 583
  in Southeast Asia, 68, 349
  in Soviet Union, 412–413
  in Sparta, 11
  United Nations Report on the Status of Women, 688
  and voting, 161, 256, 291, 295, 297–298, 305, 308, 389, 436, 459, 469
  and witch hunts, 52
  Women's Land Army, 389
  women's rights movement in U.S., 309
  "Women's War" in Nigeria, 425
  and World War I, 389
  and World War II, 482
Women's Auxiliary Air Force (WAAF), 482*p*
Women's International League for Peace and Freedom, 376
Women's Land Army, 389
wood block printing, 27
Woolf, Virginia, 452
Wordsworth, William, 260
working class, 206, 251–252
World Antislavery Convention, 309
World Bank, 507–508, 512, 546, 584
World Food Programme, 629
World Health Organization (WHO), 490, 507
World Resources Institute (WRI), 665
World Trade Organization (WTO), 507
World War I
  Allies, 379, 386–387
  armistice, 375, 391
  assassination of Archduke

  Francis Ferdinand of Austria-Hungary, 374, 380
  beginning of, 267, 315, 381
  casualty statistics, 392*c*
  Central Powers, 379, 386, 387
  Christmas Truce, 383
  conditions leading to, 376–379, 382
  desertions during, 389
  Eastern Front, 386
  economic impact of, 388
  European alliances, 1914, 378*m*
  map, 1914–1918, 375*m*
  and Paris Peace Conference, 375, 393, 394, 395
  and poison gas, 384, 385–386
  postwar economic issues, 444–445
  and Schlieffen Plan, 381, 383
  technology used in, 385–386
  trench warfare, 383, 385
  Western Front, 383, 385, 389
  and women, 389
  and Zimmermann note, 390
World War II
  in Africa, 474, 482–483, 483*m*, 607*p*
  and atomic bombs, 487–488
  Bataan Death March, 485–486
  beginning of, 399, 466, 472
  and blitzkriegs, 473
  casualty statistics, 490*c*
  D-Day, 484
  Eastern Front, 477*p*
  ending of, 467
  in Europe, 483*m*
  and German use of genocide, 479–480
  and Greater East Asia Co-Prosperity Sphere, 480
  and Holocaust, 480, 481, 587
  Japan defeat, 486–488
  major battles of, 467*m*, 474, 476, 482, 484, 486
  miracle of Dunkirk, 473–474
  Nazis defeat, 486
  and North Africa, 474
  Nuremberg trials, 489
  Operation Barbarossa, 476–477
  Operation Sea Lion, 476
  in Pacific, 485–486, 487*m*
  "phony war," 473
  prison camps, 485
  and propaganda, 482
  total war, 482
  V-E Day, 486
  Western Front, 480
  and women, 482
Worms, Diet of, 45, 46
WRI
  See World Resources Institute (WRI)
Wright, Frank Lloyd, 452
Wright, Orville, 241, 246, 267
Wright, Wilbur, 241, 246, 267
writing
  Chinese writing, 2, 26
  and civilization, 2
  cuneiform writing, 5

development of, 3
hieroglyphic writing of
Mayas, 14
Phoenician alphabet, 5
and scribes, 5
vernacular writing, 19
WTO
See World Trade Organization (WTO)
Wu Shimin, 435
Wu, Harry, 721*ps*
Wycliffe, John, 49

X

Xu Wenxing, 566

Y

Yaa Asantewaa, queen of
Asante, 324
Yamato dynasty, 27
Yang, 7
See also Yin
Yao people, 319, 324
Yaari, Sophie, 463*ps*
Yeats, William Butler, 450
Yellow fever, 226, 228, 249, 607
Yellow Wind, The (Grossman),
598*ps*
Yeltsin, Boris, 544, 545, 667, 668
Yin, 7
See also Yang

Yorktown, Battle of, 143
Yoruba people, 619
Young Italy, 266
Yuan Shikai, 432
Yugoslavia, 394, 474, 527, 548,
549–551, 670–673
case study on, 670–673
Yunus, Muhammad, 686, 688
Yussoupov, Felix, 401

Z

zaibatsu, 345, 436, 437, 557
Zaire, 611, 617, 620
Zambia, 613
Zanzibar, 620

Zapata, Emiliano, 420
Zapatistas, 420
Zapotec Indians, 358
zeppelins, 386
Zheng He, 27
Zhou dynasty, 7, 9
Zia, Begum Khalida, 686
Ziggurats, 5
Zimbabwe, 362, 605, 614, 622
Zimmermann note, 390
Zionism, 291, 304–305, 428, 593
Zola, Émile, 247, 262, 304
Zollverein, 268–269
Zulus, 100, 320, 324, 340

Index

Credits

troit Institute of Arts, 1995. Palacio Nacional stairway, Mexico City. © Dirk Bakker, photographer 373 left: *The Persistence of Memory,* Salvador Dali, The Museum of Modern Art, New York © 1996 Demart Pro Arte, Geneva/Artists Rights Society (ARS), New York; right: Archive Photos 374 top: National Archives; left: Culver Pictures, Inc.; right: Imperial War Museum/ Archive Photos 375 left: Library of Congress; right: Collection of Whitney Museum of American Art 377 Courtesy of the Library of Congress 378 L'Illustration Paris 379 Christel Gerstenberg/Corbis 381 John McCutchon/The Chicago Tribune, 1914 Photo: Ken Karp 382 Bildarchiv Preussischer Kulturhesitz, Berlin 383 Courtesy National Archives 384 background: CORBIS; bottom, left: Culver Pictures, Inc.; bottom, right: René Dazy Collection, Paris 386 top: Smithsonian Institution; middle: Bilderdrenst Suddeutscher Verlag, Munich; bottom: © James A. Bryant 388 The Granger Collection, New York 389 CORBIS 390 National Archives 397 The Imperial War Museum, London 398 top, left: Sovfoto/Novosti; left: *The Storming of the Winter Palace, 7th November 1917,* 1939, Central Museum of the Revolution, Moscow, Russia/The Bridgeman Art Library, London/New York; right: Sovfoto/Eastfoto 399 left: The Granger Collection, New York; right: David King Collection 401 Archiv für Kunst und Geschichte, London 402 *Lenin and a Manifestation,* 1919 (detail), Private Collection/Novosti/ The Bridgeman Art Library, London/New York 403 Hulton Getty/Liaison Agency 405 top: Courtesy of the Library of Congress; bottom: Sovfoto/Novosti 406 AP/Wide World Photos 408 CORBIS/Scheufler Collection 409 The Bettmann Archive/ CORBIS 411 Gulag Prisoners, Getman/The Jamestown Foundation, Washington, D.C. 412 Sovfoto/ Novosti 413 Scala/Art Resource, NY 414 top: Sovfoto/Eastfoto; middle: Archiv für Kunst und Geschichte, London; bottom: Itar-Tass/Sovfoto 418 top, left: Photograph © The Detroit Institute of Arts, 1995. Palacio Nacional stairway, Mexico City. © Dirk Bakker, photographer, detail; left: The Central Zionist Archives; right: Irene Hubbell/Root Resources 419 CORBIS Sygma 421 The Granger Collection, New York 422 Photograph © The Detroit Institute of Arts, 1995. Palacio Nacional stairway, Mexico City. © Dirk Bakker, photographer, detail 425 Julio Donoso/Contact Press Images/PNI 426 Turkish Culture and Information Office, NYC 429 Culver Pictures, Inc. 430 By permission of The British Library (F839) 431 Popperfoto/Archive Photos 433 Roger Viollet/Liaison Agency 436 AP/Wide World Photos 438 inset: CORBIS/Bettmann 442 top, left: © Topham/The Image Works; middle: *Composition No. 4,* 1920, Fernand Leger, Musée Leger, Biot, France/The Bridgeman Art Library, London/New York; right:

CORBIS 443 left: Private Collection/ The Bridgeman Art Library, London/ New York; right: The Granger Collection, New York 444 top: Courtesy of the Library of Congress; bottom: © Elke Walford/Hamburger Kunsthalle, Hamburg 445 The Granger Collection, New York 446 The Granger Collection, New York 447 The Granger Collection, New York 450 Private Collection/The Bridgeman Art Library, London/New York 451 *The Persistence of Memory,* Salvador Dali, The Museum of Modern Art, New York © 1996 Demart Pro Arte, Geneva/Artists Rights Society (ARS), New York 453 top, right: CORBIS/Bettmann; bottom, right: Frank Driggs/Archive Photos; middle: CORBIS/Frank Driggs 454 top: CORBIS 457 right: © by Giancarlo Costa/Ferrovie Dello Stato, 1940 457 left: Italian Government Tourist Board 459 CORBIS 460 Bildarchiv Preussischer Kulturbesitz 461 © Keystone/The Image Works 462 © Topham/The Image Works 466 top, left: Brown Brothers; left: The Granger Collection, New York; right: Movietone News/CORBIS/ Bettmann-UPI 467 left: The Granger Collection, New York; right: CORBIS/Bettmann 468 CORBIS/ Bettmann 469 CORBIS/ Bettmann-UPI 473 The Granger Collection, New York 475 background: Brown Brothers; right: Hulton Gehy/Liaison Agency 477 CORBIS 478 Archive Pictures, Inc. 479 Courtesy National Archives 481 top: CORBIS/ Ira Nowinski; bottom, right: CORBIS/Bettmann-UPI 482 top: The Imperial War Museum, London; bottom: © Michael Patrick/Folio, Inc. 485 AP/Wide World Photos 486 CORBIS/Bettmann 488 left: Archive Photos; right: AP/Wide World Photos 490 CORBIS/Bettmann 495 The Granger Collection, New York 498–499 Earth Imaging/Tony Stone Images 500 left: NASA/Science Photo Library/Photo Researchers, Inc.; middle: © Regis Bossu/CORBIS Sygma; right: SuperStock 501 left: Marlene Nelson, Copyright Wasma'a K. Chorbachi; middle: Nik Wheeler/CORBIS; right: Mireille Vautier/Woodfin Camp & Associates 502 top, left: Bob Martin/Sports Illustrated; left: Rudi Von Briel/PhotoEdit; right: NASA/Science Photo Library/Photo Researchers, Inc. 503 left: Marc & Evelyne Bernheim/ Woodfin Camp & Associates; right: AP/Wide World Photos 505 CORBIS 508 right: Reuters NewMedia, Inc./CORBIS; left: Mario Tama/Getty Images Inc. 509 Cartoon by John Spencer reprinted with permission, Philadelphia Business Journal 511 top: AP/Wide World Photos; bottom: Betty Press/ Woodfin Camp & Associates 513 United Nations 514 TOLES © 1992 The Buffalo News. Reprinted with permission of UNIVERSAL PRESS SYNDICATE. All rights reserved. 515 Yousuf Karsh/Woodfin Camp & Associates 516 NASA/Johnson Space Center 517 top: Betty Press/ Woodfin Camp & Associates; bottom: Steve Vidler/SuperStock 519 top: Yagi Stu-

dio/SuperStock; middle: CORBIS Sygma; bottom: Michael Newman/ PhotoEdit 520 NASA 521 AP/Wide World Photos 523 ABU-The Sunday Observer, Bombay/Rothco Cartoons 524 top, left: © Regis Bossu/CORBIS Sygma; left: Sovfoto/Tass; right: Halstead/Liaison Agency 525 left: CORBIS/Reuters; top, right: 0851 Gamma/Liaison Agency; middle, right: Tony Stone Images; bottom, right: 0851 Gamma/Liaison Agency 526 © Hulton Getty/Liaison Agency © Hulton Getty/Liaison Agency 528 Georg Gerster/Photo Researchers, Inc. 532 Courtesy of German Information Center 533 CORBIS Sygma 534 © Thomas Del Braise/The Stock Market 535 left: Lionel Cironneau/ AP/Wide World Photos; right: © Regis Bossu/CORBIS Sygma 537 J. Baylor Roberts/National Geographic Society 539 Dan Budnik/Woodfin Camp & Associates 540 top: © La Presse/CORBIS Sygma; bottom: © J. P. Laffont/CORBIS Sygma 541 Carl Mydans/Life Magazine © Time Inc. 543 Gerd Ludwig/National Geographic Society 544 Vladimir Shone/Liaison Agency 545 AP/Wide World Photos 547 Dean Conger/ CORBIS 548 © Chuck Fishman/Contact Press Images 549 left: Darolle/ CORBIS Sygma; right: Vittoriano Rastelli/CORBIS 554 left: (detail) China Stock/Liu Ligun, artist; right: CORBIS/Paul Lowel; top, left: © Fallender/Sipa Press 555 left: Alberto Garcia/SABA/CORBIS; right: AP/Wide World Photos 556 © Hulton Getty/Liaison Agency 559 Ken Straiton/The Stock Market 561 Jack Novak/SuperStock 562 Camera Press/Retna, LTD 563 Greg Baker/AP/Wide World Photos 564 left: © 1989 Stuart Franklin/Magnum Photos, Inc.; background: © Fallender/Sipa Press 566 Courtesy National Archives, photo no. (ARC 542281) 567 © Naomi Duguid/Asia Access 569 © Hulton-Deutsch Collection/CORBIS 570 AP/Wide World Photos 573 © AFP/CORBIS 574 © Stuart Isett/CORBIS Sygma 575 © Robert Fried/www.robertfriedphotography.com 578 top, left: Raghu Rai/Magnum Photos, Inc.; middle, top: Amrit P. Singh; middle, bottom: Alain Evrard/Photo Researchers, Inc.; right: AP/Wide World Photos 579 left: S. Compoint/CORBIS Sygma; right: ©Mirrorpix/Getty Images 580 Corel Professional Photos CD-ROM™ 582 Raghu Rai/Magnum Photos, Inc. 583 Eddie Adams/Liaison Agency 584 AP/Wide World Photos 587 © 1997 Richard T. Nowitz 589 Ray Ellis/Photo Researchers, Inc. 590 Marlene Nelson, Copyright Wasma'a K. Chorbachi 591 © Peter Turnley/CORBIS 593 Reuters/Kai Pfaffenbach/Archive Photos 514 Howard Sochurek/Life Magazine © Time Inc. 595 left: David Turnley/CORBIS; top: Caputo/Stock Boston; top, right: Jean-Claude Aunos/Liaison Agency; bottom, right: Nacerdine Zebar/Liaison Agency 596 © 1999 Michael Coyne/Black Star 597 D. Wells/Image Works 603 Jagdish Agarwa/Dinodia Picture Agency 604 top, left:

Peter Turnley/CORBIS; middle: AP/Wide World Photos; right: Robert Frerck/Odyssey Productions/Chicago 605 AP/Wide World Photos 607 Courtesy of the Director, National Army Museum 608 CORBIS/Bettmann-UPI 609 Hulton Getty/Liaison Agency 610 Bas/Rothco Cartoons 611 Reza/ImaxCORBIS 612 AP/Wide World Photos 616 Nik Wheeler/CORBIS 617 © Marc & Evelyne Bernheim/Woodfin Camp & Associates 618 Bruno Barbey/Magnum 621 AP/Wide World Photos 622 Corel Professional Photos CD-ROM™ 623 left: Gamma Presse Images/Liaison Agency; right: Shahn Kermani/Liaison Agency 624 Joe Traver/Liaison Agency 625 background: Peter Turnley/CORBIS; inset: Noel Quidu/Liaison Agency 626 © T. Hegenbart/Black Star 630 top, left: Ary Diesendruck/Tony Stone Images; left: Americas Magazine OAS; right: AP/Wide World Photos 631 left: Alain Mingam/Liaison Agency; middle: Enrique Shore/Woodfin Camp & Associates; right: Marco Ugarte/AP/Wide World Photos 633 Vera Lentz/Black Star 635–636 Courtesy of the artist. 636 Reuters/Eliana Aponte/Archive Photos 638 U.S. Naval Photographic Center 639 CORBIS/Reuters 640 Mireille Vautier/Woodfin Camp & Associates 643 AP/Wide World Photos 644 Don Goode/Photo Researchers, Inc. 645 middle: AP/Wide World Photos; background: © Ilkka Ulimonen/CORBIS Sygma 646 Mireille Vautier/Woodfin Camp & Associates 647 AP/Wide World Photos 648 AP/Wide World Photos 650 Ary Diesendruck/Tony Stone Images 651 © Les Stone/CORBIS Sygma 652 Ben Gibson/Katz/Woodfin Camp & Associates 655 AP/Wide World Photos 661–664 Mark Thayer Photography 669 Francisco Conde/Impact Visuals 673 Lee Malis/Liaison Agency 677 Abril/Liaison Agency 681 Kuninori Takahashi/Impact Visuals 685 Wolfgang Kaehler Photography 687 Gilles Saussler/ Liaison Agency 693 AP/Photo/ Northeast Miss. Daily Press, Karl Floyd/Wide World 697 Lee Boltin Picture Library 698 Nationalmuseet, Copenhagen, Denmark/The Bridgeman Art Library, London 700 British Information Service 703 Private Collection/Ken Welsh/The Bridgeman Art Library, London/NY 704 Schalkwijk/Art Resource, NY 705 Dannielle Hayes/Omni-Photo Communications, Inc. 706 The Science Museum/Science & Society Picture Library 707 (detail), Museum of Fine Arts, Boston/Laurie Platt Winfrey, Inc. 708 Bildarchiv Preussischer Kulturhesitz, Berlin 709 By permission of The British Library (F839) 710 The Granger Collection, New York 711 Rudi Von Briel/PhotoEdit 712 SuperStock 714 CORBIS 715 © Chuck Fishman/Contact Press Images 716 Vlastimir Shone/Liaison Agency 718 AP/Wide World Photos 719 © Stuart Isett/CORBIS Sygma 720 Reuters/CORBIS 721 © Fallender/Sipa Press

Acknowledgments

227 Excerpt from *The Black Jacobins: Toussaint L'Ouverture and the San Domingo Revolution* by C.L.R. James. Used by permission of Secker & Warburg publishers. **277** From "A Foreign Volunteer at the Battle of the Volturno, April 2, 1860" from *Garibaldi: Great Lives Observed,* edited by Denis Mack Smith. Copyright © 1969 by Prentice-Hall, Inc. **415** Excerpt from "Requiem," translated by Robin Kemball, Copyright © 1974 by Robin Kemball, from *Selected Poems* by Anna Akhmatova, edited and translated by Walter Arndt. Reprinted by permission of Robin Kemball. **417** From *Assignment in Utopia* by Eugene Lyons. Copyright © 1937, by Harcourt, Brace & World, Inc. Published in Great Britain by George G. Harrap & Co. Ltd. **421** Excerpt from "Zeferino Diego Ferreira: The Life Story of a Villista," by Laura Cummings. Copyright © 1999 by University of Arizona J*ournal of the Southwest.* **435** Excerpt from *Japanese Imperialism and the Massacre in Nanjing,* translated by Robert P. Gray. Copyright © 1996. **463** "To Save a Life: Stories of Holocaust Rescue," by Ellen Land-Weber. Used by permission of Illinois Press: Champaign, IL © 2000. **472** Four lines of "In Memory of W. B. Yeats," from *W. H. Auden: Collected Poems* by W. H. Auden. Copyright © 1940 and renewed 1968 by W. H. Auden. **484** From "Major Werner Pluskat, aged 32, 352ⁿᵈ Artillery Regiment, 352ⁿᵈ Division" from *Nothing Less Than Victory: An Oral History of D-Day* by Russell Miller. Copyright © 1993 by Russell Miller. Reprinted by permission of Peters, Fraser & Dunlop

Group, Ltd. **523** Excerpt from "No Time" by Nguyen Sa from *A Thousand Years of Vietnamese Poetry* (ed. Nguyen Ngoc Bich). Copyright „ 1962, 1967, 1968, 1969, 1970, 1971, 1972, 1974, by Asia Society, Inc. Reprinted by permission of the translator, Nguyen Ngoc Bich. **531** "A Man's Place" from *The New York Times Magazine,* May 16, 1999, by Claudia Goldin in a conversation moderated by Michael Weinstein. Copyright © 1999, The New York Times Company. **545** Quoted by Alexander Solzhenitsyn in the *New York Times,* January 4, 1997. Copyright © 1997, The New York Times Company. **553** From "Liberal Leaders Warn Yeltsin to Protect His People,". Copyright © Reuters Limited, 1999. **557** "The Art and Practice of Japanese Management," adapted from THE WITCH DOCTORS by John Micklethwait and Adrian Wooldridge. Times Books-US; Lillian Heinemann-UK; 1996. **569** HOME WAS THE LAND OF THE MORNING CALM. Copyright © 1995 by K. Connie Kang. Reprinted by permission of Perseus Books Publishers, a member of Perseus Books, L.L.C. **577** From VOICES FROM THE WHIRLWIND by Feng Jicai, translated by Deborah Cao and Lawrence Tedes. Copyright © 1991 by Random House, Inc. Copyright © 1990 by Foreign Language Press. Reprinted by permission of Pantheon Books, a division of Random House, Inc. **599** Excerpt from "A Man is Like a Stalk of Wheat" from *The Yellow Wind* by David Grossman. Translation copyright © 1988 by Haim Watzman. Reprinted by permission of Farrar, Straus and Giroux, LLC. **608** Excerpt from "Negro Nation of

Ghana is Born in Africa" by Thomas F. Brady. Copyright © 1957, The New York Times Company. Reprinted by permission. **637** Excerpt from *Revolution Through Peace (World Perspectives Series)* by Dom Hélder Câmara. English translation copyright © 1971 by Harper & Row Publishers, Inc. Reprinted by permission of HarperCollins Publishers, Inc. Translated from the Portuguese by Amparo McLean. First published in Brazil as REVOLUCAO DENTRO DA PAZ. World Perspectives—Volume Forty-five, planned and edited by Ruth Nanda Anshen. **652** Excerpt from "For Brazil's Street Children, a Happy Path to Take" by James Brooke. Copyright © 1993, The New York Times Company. Reprinted by permission. **697** "The True History of the Conquest of New Spain" from *The Bernal Díaz Chronicles,* translated by Albert Idell. Translation copyright © 1956 by Albert Idell. Used by permission of Doubleday, a division of Bantam Doubleday Dell Publishing Group, Inc. **699** Excerpt from *Don Quixote of La Mancha* by Miguel de Cervantes; translated by Walter Starkie. Copyright © 1957 by Macmillan & Co., Ltd., London. Translation copyright © 1964 by Walter Starkie and published by The New American Library. **707** Excerpt from *The Autobiography of Fukuzawa Yukichi,* translated by Eiichi Kiyooka. Copyright © 1966 by Columbia University Press. Reprinted by permission of the publisher. **708** Excerpt from *All Quiet on the Western Front* by Erich Maria Remarque. "Im Western Nichts Neues," copyright 1928 by Ullstein A. G.; Copyright renewed © 1956 by Erich Maria Remarque.

Copyright © 1929, 1930 by Little, Brown and Company; copyright © renewed 1957, 1958 by Erich Maria Remarque. All Rights Reserved. **713** Excerpt from *Things Fall Apart* by Chinua Achebe. Copyright © 1959 by Chinua Achebe. Reprinted by permission of Heinemann Educational Publishers, a division of Reed Educational & Professional Publishing Ltd. **716** "Perestroika" by Mikhail Gorbachev from *Vital Speeches Of the Day,* from The City News. **717** "New Years Address" from *Uncaptive Minds* by Vaclav Havel. Reprinted by permission of Uncaptive Minds, a publication of the Institute for Democracy in Eastern Europe. **718** "Latin America: the Democracy Option" by Mario Vargas Llosa from *Harper's Magazine.* Copyright © 1987 by Harper's Magazine. **719** From *Freedom From Fear and Other Writings* by Aung San Suu Kyi, forwarded by Vaclav Havel, translated by Michael Aris. Translation copyright © 1991 by Aung San Suu Kyi and Michael Aris. Used by permission of Penguin, a division of Penguin Books USA, Inc. **720** "Glory and Hope" by Nelson Mandela from *Vital Speeches Of the Day, from* The City News. **721** "The Outlook for China: Human Rights" by Harry Wu from *Vital Speeches Of the Day,* from The City News.

Note: Every effort has been made to locate the copyright owner of material reprinted in this book. Omissions brought to our attention will be corrected in subsequent editions.